HALSBURY'S
Laws of England

FIFTH EDITION
2014

Volume 79

This is volume 79 of the Fifth Edition of Halsbury's Laws of England, containing the titles PARTNERSHIP, PATENTS AND REGISTERED DESIGNS and PEERAGES AND DIGNITIES.

The title PARTNERSHIP replaces the title PARTNERSHIP, contained in volume 79 (2008); the title PATENTS AND REGISTERED DESIGNS replaces the title PATENTS AND REGISTERED DESIGNS, contained in volume 79 (2008); and the title PEERAGES AND DIGNITIES replaces the title PEERAGES AND DIGNITIES, contained in volume 79 (2008). Upon receipt of volume 79 (2014), volume 79 (2008) may be archived.

For a full list of volumes comprised in a current set of Halsbury's Laws of England please see overleaf.

Fifth Edition volumes:

1 (2008), 2 (2008), 3 (2011), 4 (2011), 5 (2013), 6 (2011), 7 (2008), 8 (2010), 9 (2012), 10 (2012), 11 (2009), 12 (2009), 13 (2009), 14 (2009), 15 (2009), 16 (2011), 17 (2011), 18 (2009), 19 (2011), 20 (2014), 21 (2011), 22 (2012), 23 (2013), 24 (2010), 25 (2010), 26 (2010), 27 (2010), 28 (2010), 30 (2012), 31 (2012), 32 (2012), 33 (2013), 34 (2011), 35 (2011), 36 (2011), 37 (2013), 38 (2013), 38A (2013), 39 (2009), 40 (2009), 41 (2009), 42 (2011), 43 (2011), 44 (2011), 45 (2010), 46 (2010), 47 (2014), 47A (2014), 48 (2008), 49 (2008), 50 (2008), 51 (2013), 52 (2014), 53 (2014), 54 (2008), 55 (2012), 56 (2011), 57 (2012), 58 (2014), 58A (2014), 59 (2014), 59A (2014), 60 (2011), 61 (2010), 62 (2012), 63 (2012), 64 (2012), 65 (2008), 66 (2009), 67 (2008), 68 (2008), 69 (2009), 70 (2012), 71 (2013), 72 (2009), 73 (2009), 74 (2011), 75 (2013), 76 (2013), 77 (2010), 78 (2010), 79 (2014), 80 (2013), 81 (2010), 82 (2010), 83 (2010), 84 (2013), 84A (2013), 85 (2012), 86 (2013), 87 (2012), 88 (2012), 88A (2013), 89 (2011), 90 (2011), 91 (2012), 92 (2010), 93 (2008), 94 (2008), 95 (2013), 96 (2012), 97 (2010), 97A (2014), 98 (2013), 99 (2012), 100 (2009), 101 (2009), 102 (2010), 103 (2010), 104 (2014)

Fourth Edition volumes (bold figures represent reissues):

12(1)

Additional Materials:

Sentencing and Disposition of Offenders (Release and Recall of Prisoners) containing vol **92** (2010) paras 761–820; *Tort (Conversion and Wrongful Interference with Goods)* containing vol **45(2)** (Reissue) paras 542–686

Fourth and Fifth Edition volumes:

2014 Consolidated Index (A–E), 2014 Consolidated Index (F–O), 2014 Consolidated Index (P–Z), 2015 Consolidated Table of Statutes, 2015 Consolidated Table of Statutory Instruments, etc, 2014 Consolidated Table of Cases (A–G), 2014 Consolidated Table of Cases (H–Q), 2014 Consolidated Table of Cases (R–Z, ECJ Cases)

Updating and ancillary materials:

2014 Annual Cumulative Supplement; Monthly Current Service; Annual Abridgments 1974–2013

October 2014

HALSBURY'S
Laws of England

Volume 79

2014

 LexisNexis®

Members of the LexisNexis Group worldwide

United Kingdom	LexisNexis, a Division of Reed Elsevier (UK) Ltd, Lexis House, 30 Farringdon Street, LONDON, EC4A 4HH, and 9–10, St Andrew Square, EDINBURGH, EH2 2AF
Australia	LexisNexis Butterworths, Chatswood, New South Wales
Austria	LexisNexis Verlag ARD Orac GmbH & Co KG, Vienna
Benelux	LexisNexis Benelux, Amsterdam
Canada	LexisNexis Canada, Markham, Ontario
China	LexisNexis China, Beijing and Shanghai
France	LexisNexis SA, Paris
Germany	LexisNexis GmbH, Dusseldorf
Hong Kong	LexisNexis Hong Kong, Hong Kong
India	LexisNexis India, New Delhi
Italy	Giuffrè Editore, Milan
Japan	LexisNexis Japan, Tokyo
Malaysia	Malayan Law Journal Sdn Bhd, Kuala Lumpur
New Zealand	LexisNexis NZ Ltd, Wellington
Singapore	LexisNexis Singapore, Singapore
South Africa	LexisNexis Butterworths, Durban
USA	LexisNexis, Dayton, Ohio

FIRST EDITION	*Published in 31 volumes between 1907 and 1917*
SECOND EDITION	*Published in 37 volumes between 1931 and 1942*
THIRD EDITION	*Published in 43 volumes between 1952 and 1964*
FOURTH EDITION	*Published in 56 volumes between 1973 and 1987, with reissues between 1988 and 2008*
FIFTH EDITION	*Published between 2008 and 2014, with reissues from 2014*

A CIP Catalogue record for this book is available from the British Library.

ISBN 13 (complete set, standard binding): 9781405734394

ISBN 13: 9781405790338

ISBN 978-1-4057-9033-8

9 781405 790338

Typeset by Letterpart Limited, Caterham on the Hill, Surrey CR3 5XL
Printed and bound by CPI Group (UK) Ltd, Croydon, CR0 4YY
Visit LexisNexis at www.lexisnexis.co.uk

PARTNERSHIP

Consultant Editor
JOHN MACHELL QC, LLB,
of Serle Court, Lincoln's Inn

PATENTS AND REGISTERED DESIGNS

Content Advisor
LAURA THOMPSON, MA (Cantab),
Diploma in Intellectual Property Law and Practice;
Solicitor, LexisNexis (Intellectual Property and IT, Lexis®PSL);
member of CIPA, AIPPI

PEERAGES AND DIGNITIES

Title Advisor
BRENDAN KEITH
Registrar of Lords' Interests, House of Lords;
Clerk to the Committee for Privileges and Conduct (Peerage Claims)

The law stated in this volume is in general that in force on 1 September 2014, although subsequent changes have been included wherever possible.

Any future updating material will be found in the Current Service and annual Cumulative Supplement to Halsbury's Laws of England.

TABLE OF CONTENTS

Volume 79

PARTNERSHIP

PATENTS AND REGISTERED DESIGNS

PEERAGES AND DIGNITIES

HOW TO USE HALSBURY'S LAWS OF ENGLAND

Volumes

Each text volume of Halsbury's Laws of England contains the law on the titles contained in it as at a date stated at the front of the volume (the operative date).

Information contained in Halsbury's Laws of England may be accessed in several ways.

First, by using the tables of contents.

Each volume contains both a general Table of Contents, and a specific Table of Contents for each title contained in it. From these tables you will be directed to the relevant part of the work.

Readers should note that the current arrangement of titles can be found in the Current Service.

Secondly, by using tables of statutes, statutory instruments, cases or other materials.

If you know the name of the Act, statutory instrument or case with which your research is concerned, you should consult the Consolidated Tables of statutes, cases and so on (published as separate volumes) which will direct you to the relevant volume and paragraph. The Consolidated Tables will indicate if the volume referred to is a Fifth Edition volume.

(Each individual text volume also includes tables of those materials used as authority in that volume.)

Thirdly, by using the indexes.

If you are uncertain of the general subject area of your research, you should go to the Consolidated Index (published as separate volumes) for reference to the relevant volume(s) and paragraph(s). The Consolidated Index will indicate if the volume referred to is a Fifth Edition volume.

(Each individual text volume also includes an index to the material contained therein.)

Additional Materials

The reorganisation of the title scheme of Halsbury's Laws for the Fifth Edition means that from time to time Fourth Edition volumes will be *partially* replaced by Fifth Edition volumes.

In certain instances an Additional Materials softbound book will be issued, in which will be reproduced material which has not yet been replaced by a Fifth Edition title. This will enable users to remove specific Fourth Edition volumes from the shelf and save valuable space pending the replacement of that material in the Fifth Edition. These softbound books are supplied to volumes subscribers free of charge. They continue to form part of the set of Halsbury's Laws Fourth Edition Reissue, and will be updated by the annual Cumulative Supplement and monthly Noter-Up in the usual way.

Updating publications

The text volumes of Halsbury's Laws should be used in conjunction with the annual Cumulative Supplement and the monthly Noter-Up.

The annual Cumulative Supplement

The Supplement gives details of all changes between the operative date of the text volume and the operative date of the Supplement. It is arranged in the same volume, title and paragraph order as the text volumes. Developments affecting particular points of law are noted to the relevant paragraph(s) of the text volumes. As from the commencement of the Fifth Edition, the Supplement will clearly distinguish between Fourth and Fifth Edition titles.

For narrative treatment of material noted in the Cumulative Supplement, go to the Annual Abridgment volume for the relevant year.

Destination Tables

In certain titles in the annual *Cumulative Supplement*, reference is made to Destination Tables showing the destination of consolidated legislation. Those Destination Tables are to be found either at the end of the titles within the annual *Cumulative Supplement*, or in a separate *Destination Tables* booklet provided from time to time with the *Cumulative Supplement*.

The Noter-Up

The Noter-Up is contained in the Current Service Noter-Up booklet, issued monthly and noting changes since the publication of the annual Cumulative Supplement. Also arranged in the same volume, title and paragraph order as the text volumes, the Noter-Up follows the style of the Cumulative Supplement. As from the commencement of the Fifth Edition, the Noter-Up will clearly distinguish between Fourth and Fifth Edition titles.

For narrative treatment of material noted in the Noter-Up, go to the relevant Monthly Review.

REFERENCES AND ABBREVIATIONS

ACT	Australian Capital Territory
A-G	Attorney General
Admin	Administrative Court
Admlty	Admiralty Court
Adv-Gen	Advocate General
affd	affirmed
affg	affirming
Alta	Alberta
App	Appendix
art	article
Aust	Australia
B	Baron
BC	British Columbia
C	Command Paper (of a series published before 1900)
c	chapter number of an Act
CA	Court of Appeal
CAC	Central Arbitration Committee
CA in Ch	Court of Appeal in Chancery
CB	Chief Baron
CCA	Court of Criminal Appeal
CCR	County Court Rules 1981 (as subsequently amended)
CCR	Court for Crown Cases Reserved
C-MAC	Courts-Martial Appeal Court
CO	Crown Office
COD	Crown Office Digest
CPR	Civil Procedure Rules
Can	Canada
Cd	Command Paper (of the series published 1900–18)
Cf	compare
Ch	Chancery Division
ch	chapter
cl	clause
Cm	Command Paper (of the series published 1986 to date)

Cmd	Command Paper (of the series published 1919–56)
Cmnd	Command Paper (of the series published 1956–86)
Comm	Commercial Court
Comr	Commissioner
Court Forms (2nd Edn)	Atkin's Encyclopaedia of Court Forms in Civil Proceedings, 2nd Edn. See note 2 post.
CrimPR	Criminal Procedure Rules
DC...	Divisional Court
DPP	Director of Public Prosecutions
EAT	Employment Appeal Tribunal
EC..	European Community
ECJ..	Court of Justice of the European Community
EComHR...............................	European Commission of Human Rights
ECSC......................................	European Coal and Steel Community
ECtHR Rules of Court...........	Rules of Court of the European Court of Human Rights
EEC..	European Economic Community
EFTA	European Free Trade Association
EWCA Civ	Official neutral citation for judgments of the Court of Appeal (Civil Division)
EWCA Crim...........................	Official neutral citation for judgments of the Court of Appeal (Criminal Division)
EWHC....................................	Official neutral citation for judgments of the High Court
Edn..	Edition
Euratom	European Atomic Energy Community
Ex Ch....................................	Court of Exchequer Chamber
ex p	ex parte
Fam	Family Division
Fed	Federal
Forms & Precedents (5th Edn).....................................	Encyclopaedia of Forms and Precedents other than Court Forms, 5th Edn. See note 2 post.
GLC	Greater London Council
HC	High Court
HC	House of Commons
HK	Hong Kong
HL...	House of Lords
IAT..	Immigration Appeal Tribunal
ILM	International Legal Materials
INLR	Immigration and Nationality Law Reports
IRC..	Inland Revenue Commissioners
Ind..	India

Int Rels	International Relations
Ir	Ireland
J	Justice
JA	Judge of Appeal
Kan	Kansas
LA	Lord Advocate
LC	Lord Chancellor
LCC	London County Council
LCJ	Lord Chief Justice
LJ	Lord Justice of Appeal
LoN	League of Nations
MR	Master of the Rolls
Man	Manitoba
n	note
NB	New Brunswick
NI	Northern Ireland
NS	Nova Scotia
NSW	New South Wales
NY	New York
NZ	New Zealand
OHIM	Office for Harmonisation in the Internal Market
OJ	The Official Journal of the European Community published by the Office for Official Publications of the European Community
Ont	Ontario
P	President
PC	Judicial Committee of the Privy Council
PEI	Prince Edward Island
Pat	Patents Court
q	question
QB	Queen's Bench Division
QBD	Queen's Bench Division of the High Court
Qld	Queensland
Que	Quebec
r	rule
RDC	Rural District Council
RPC	Restrictive Practices Court
RSC	Rules of the Supreme Court 1965 (as subsequently amended)
reg	regulation
Res	Resolution
revsd	reversed

Rly......................................	Railway
s.......................................	section
SA.....................................	South Africa
S Aust................................	South Australia
SC.....................................	Supreme Court
SI......................................	Statutory Instruments published by authority
SR & O...............................	Statutory Rules and Orders published by authority
SR & O Rev 1904	Revised Edition comprising all Public and General Statutory Rules and Orders in force on 31 December 1903
SR & O Rev 1948	Revised Edition comprising all Public and General Statutory Rules and Orders and Statutory Instruments in force on 31 December 1948
SRNI	Statutory Rules of Northern Ireland
STI.....................................	Simon's Tax Intelligence (1973–1995); Simon's Weekly Tax Intelligence (1996-current)
Sask	Saskatchewan
Sch.....................................	Schedule
Sess....................................	Session
Sing	Singapore
TCC	Technology and Construction Court
TS......................................	Treaty Series
Tanz...................................	Tanzania
Tas.....................................	Tasmania
UDC...................................	Urban District Council
UKHL..................................	Official neutral citation for judgments of the House of Lords
UKPC	Official neutral citation for judgments of the Privy Council
UN	United Nations
V-C.....................................	Vice-Chancellor
Vict....................................	Victoria
W Aust................................	Western Australia
Zimb	Zimbabwe

NOTE 1. A general list of the abbreviations of law reports and other sources used in this work can be found at the beginning of the Consolidated Table of Cases.

NOTE 2. Where references are made to other publications, the volume number precedes and the page number follows the name of the publication; eg the reference '12 Forms & Precedents (5th Edn) 44' refers to volume 12 of the Encyclopaedia of Forms and Precedents, page 44.

NOTE 3. An English statute is cited by short title or, where there is no short title, by regnal year and chapter number together with the name by which it is commonly known or a description of its subject matter and date. In the case of a foreign statute, the mode of citation generally follows the style of citation in use in the country concerned with the addition, where necessary, of the name of the country in parentheses.

NOTE 4. A statutory instrument is cited by short title, if any, followed by the year and number, or, if unnumbered, the date.

TABLE OF STATUTES

TABLE OF STATUTORY INSTRUMENTS

TABLE OF CIVIL PROCEDURE

Civil Procedure Rules 1998, SI 1998/3132 (CPR)

Practice Directions supplementing the Civil Procedure Rules 1998, SI 1998/3132 (CPR)

Other Practice Directions

TABLE OF EUROPEAN UNION LEGISLATION

TABLE OF CONVENTIONS ETC

TABLE OF
NON-STATUTORY MATERIAL

TABLE OF CASES

PARA

PARA

M

PARA

R

PARA

V

Decisions of the European Court of Justice are listed below numerically. These decisions
are also included in the preceding alphabetical list.

PARTNERSHIP

1. CREATION AND DURATION OF PARTNERSHIPS

(1) NATURE OF PARTNERSHIP

1. Meaning of 'partnership' and 'firm'. Partnership[1] is the relation which subsists between persons carrying on a business in common with a view of profit[2]. The persons who have entered into partnership with one another are called collectively a 'firm'[3]. The parties who make up a partnership may be individuals, companies (as in corporate partnerships)[4] or may be other partnerships (as in group partnerships)[5].

The relation between members of any company or association which is a company registered under the Companies Act 2006[6], or formed or incorporated by or in pursuance of any other Act of Parliament, letters patent or royal charter, is not a partnership[7], although some of the latter may be partners with one another[8]. The relation between promoters associated only to form a company is not a partnership[9]; nor is the relation between executors carrying on under the powers of the will and in the same firm name a business owned solely by their testator in itself a partnership[10]. It is also unlikely that a purely domestic arrangement will constitute a partnership[11].

1   An ordinary partnership is a partnership composed of definite individuals, bound together by contract between themselves to continue combined for some joint object either during pleasure or during a limited time, and is essentially composed of the persons originally entering into the contract with one another: *Smith v Anderson* (1880) 15 ChD 247 at 273, CA, per James LJ. It would appear that, in some circumstances, what is registered as a partnership for VAT purposes (see PARA 102; and VALUE ADDED TAX) can also make supplies as an unincorporated association: *Alberni String Quartet v Customs and Excise Comrs* [1990] VATTR 166 (an unusual case). The basis of the relationship between partners is contractual, and there is no reason why the doctrine of termination by acceptance of a repudiatory breach should not apply to an agreement to enter into partnership or to the contractual obligations which the partners mutually undertake to observe after the partnership has come to an end, although it now appears doubtful that a contract governing a continuing partnership can be terminated, or that a partnership can be dissolved, by the acceptance of a repudiatory breach: see the dicta of Lord Millett in *Hurst v Bryk* [2002] 1 AC 185 at 193–196, [2000] 2 All ER 193 at 198–202, HL; *Mullins v Laughton* [2002] EWHC 2761 (Ch) at [86]–[93], [2003] Ch 250 at [86]–[93], [2003] 4 All ER 94 at [86]–[93], per Neuberger J; and *Golstein v Bishop* [2014] EWCA Civ 10, [2014] 3 All ER 397. See also *Hitchman v Crouch Butler Savage Associates* (1983) 127 Sol Jo 441, CA; *Fulwell v Bragg* (1982) 127 Sol Jo 171; *Redgrave v Hurd* (1881) 20 ChD 1, CA; *Adam v Newbigging* (1888) 13 App Cas 308, HL. It may also be set aside for undue influence (see *Goldsworthy v Brickell* [1987] Ch 378, [1987] 1 All ER 853 (tenancy agreement giving the defendant partner an option to purchase a farm upon terms which were very favourable to the latter)): see further CONTRACT vol 22 (2012) PARA 294 et seq. Partnership differs from a company or association which continues even if the members are constantly changing (*Smith v Anderson*). On any change of partner, the old partnership ends and a new one begins: see COMPANIES vol 14 (2009) PARA 1 et seq. For a review of the old authorities which define a partnership see *Pooley v Driver* (1876) 5 ChD 458 at 471 et seq per Jessel MR.

2   Partnership Act 1890 s 1(1). As to the sharing of profits as evidence that a partnership exists see PARA 14. The Partnership Act 1890 is merely declaratory (*British Homes Assurance Corpn Ltd v Paterson* [1902] 2 Ch 404 at 410 per Farwell J) and, except so far as they are inconsistent with the express provisions of the Partnership Act 1890, the rules of equity and of common law applicable to partnership are still in force (s 46). Where persons intend to become partners together, they do not become such unless and until they commence trading as such. For the purpose of determining whether a partnership has commenced, persons who have agreed to carry on a business as a joint venture are not partners until they embark on the activity in question: see *Khan v Miah* [2001] 1 All ER 20, [2000] 1 WLR 2123, HL; *Ilott v Williams* [2013] EWCA Civ 645, [2013] All ER (D) 55 (Jun); and PARAS 4, 6. It may be that persons as yet merely intending to enter into partnership together owe each other a duty of good faith; sed quaere. As to prospective joint venturers see *Lac Minerals Ltd v International Corona*

Resources Ltd [1990] FSR 441, Can SC. As to partners' duty of good faith generally see PARA 105; and as to the duration of partnerships see PARAS 37–38.

3   Partnership Act 1890 s 4(1). The name under which their business is carried on is called the 'firm name': s 4(1).

4   For examples of corporate partnerships see *Re Rudd & Son Ltd* [1984] Ch 237, [1984] 3 All ER 225; *Newstead v Frost* [1980] 1 All ER 363, [1980] 1 WLR 135, HL (individual and company in partnership together). As to difficulties which may be encountered where one or more members of a firm are companies see e g *Scher v Policyholders Protection Board* [1993] 3 All ER 384, [1993] 2 WLR 479, CA; varied sub nom *Scher v Policyholders Protection Board (No 2)* [1993] 4 All ER 840, [1993] 3 WLR 1030, sub nom *Scher v Policyholders Protection Board (Nos 1 and 2)* [1994] 2 AC 57, [1994] 2 All ER 37n, HL.

5   For an example of a group partnership (and the problems that can arise in the management of such partnerships) see *Nixon v Wood* [1987] 2 EGLR 26, CA.

6   See COMPANIES vol 14 (2009) PARA 16 et seq.

7   Partnership Act 1890 s 1(2) (amended by the Statute Law (Repeals) Act 1998; and by SI 2009/1941). It has been held that a family company, ie a company owned and run by and for the benefit of members of a family, may fall into the category of 'quasi partnership' involving similar relations of mutual trust and understanding as are symptomatic of a partnership proper: see e g *Jesner v Jarrad Properties Ltd* [1993] BCLC 1032, [1992] BCC 807, Ct of Sess; *O'Neill v Phillips* [1999] 2 All ER 961, [1999] 2 BCLC 1, HL.

8   See PARA 32.

9   *Wood v Duke of Argyll* (1844) 6 Man & G 928; *Keith Spicer Ltd v Mansell* [1970] 1 All ER 462, [1970] 1 WLR 333, CA. Promoters may be partners if they carry on in common with a view of profit the business of buying property in order to sell it to a company or companies which they form to purchase it. See further COMPANIES vol 14 (2009) PARA 67.

10   *Re Fisher & Sons* [1912] 2 KB 491. Representatives of a deceased partner who are entitled to profits, but who never interfere in the business, are not liable as partners in the firm: *Holme v Hammond* (1872) LR 7 Exch 218.

11   *Britton v Customs and Excise Comrs* [1986] VATTR 209 (husband and wife). Where a partnership does not exist, but an individual has allowed himself to be represented as being a partner, the court has no jurisdiction to wind up the insolvent 'partnership': see *Re C & M Ashberg* (1990) Times, 17 July. As to the dissolution of partnerships generally see PARA 173 et seq; and as to insolvent partnerships generally see PARAS 8, 232; and BANKRUPTCY AND INDIVIDUAL INSOLVENCY vol 5 (2013) PARA 851 et seq; COMPANY AND PARTNERSHIP INSOLVENCY vol 17 (2011) PARAS 1209–1361.

2.   Lack of legal personality.   Under English law it has long been established that a partnership or firm is not a 'person' or legal entity[1], although the firm may sue and be sued in the firm name[2]. However, some legislation does render partnerships criminally liable as independent entities[3]. Under the Corporate Manslaughter and Corporate Homicide Act 2007, a partnership is guilty of corporate manslaughter if the way in which its activities are managed or organised causes a person's death and amounts to a gross breach of a relevant duty of care owed by the partnership to the deceased[4]; and for these purposes a partnership is to be treated as owing whatever duties of care it would owe if it were a body corporate[5]. A firm or partnership also enjoys some degree of recognition as a separate entity for the purposes of taxation legislation[6].

In contrast, the legal entity known as a limited liability partnership is clearly a body corporate with legal personality separate from that of its members[7].

1   *Sadler v Whiteman* [1910] 1 KB 868 at 889, CA, per Farwell J ('In English law a firm as such has no existence'); *Re Vagliano Anthracite Collieries Ltd* (1910) 79 LJ Ch 769; *R v Holden* [1912] 1 KB 483 at 487, CCA; *Meyer & Co v Faber (No 2)* [1923] 2 Ch 421, CA. As to the separate legal personality of companies see COMPANIES vol 14 (2009) PARA 2.

For examples of how the courts have approached the issue of legal personality see *Sheppard & Cooper Ltd v TSB Bank plc* [1997] 2 BCLC 222, [1996] 12 LS Gaz R 30, CA ('When you have a big firm of accountants, or solicitors …, a reference in a contract of this nature to 'the firm' must be taken to mean the partners for the time being of the firm, whenever the time arises': per Sir John Balcombe LJ at 227); *Kelly v Northern Ireland Housing Executive, Loughran v Northern Ireland Housing Executive* [1999] 1 AC 428, [1998] 3 WLR 735, HL (a firm, as a service provider, could be engaged in a contract 'personally to execute any work or labour' through an individual partner); *Dave v Robinska* [2003] ICR 1248, [2003] NLJR 921, [2003] All ER (D) 35 (Jun), EAT (a claim could be brought by an expelled partner against the sole remaining partner, in the remaining partner's own name on the basis that he represented the firm; if a complaint was made by an expelled partner in a larger partnership, proceedings would be brought against the remaining partners).

2   See PARA 78 et seq. As to the firm name see PARA 7.

3   See e g the Sea Fishing (Enforcement of Community Control Measures) Order 2000, SI 2000/51, art 11(2), which provides that where any offence under art 3 committed by a partnership is proved to have been committed with the consent or connivance of, or to be attributable to any neglect on the part of, a partner, he as well as the partnership is guilty of the offence and is liable to be proceeded against and punished accordingly. It was held in *R v W Stevenson & Sons (a partnership)* [2008] EWCA Crim 273, (2008) Times, 5 March, [2008] All ER (D) 351 (Feb) that it is possible for this provision to render a partnership criminally liable as a separate entity from the individual partners. In as much as business activities were conducted in the name of a partnership and the partnership had identifiable assets that were distinct from the personal assets of each partner, there was no reason why a partnership should not be treated, for the purposes of the criminal law, as a separate entity from the partners who were members of it: *R v W Stevenson & Sons (a partnership)*.

4   Corporate Manslaughter and Corporate Homicide Act 2007 s 1(1), (2)(d).

5   Corporate Manslaughter and Corporate Homicide Act 2007 s 14(1). Proceedings for an offence under the Act alleged to have been committed by a partnership are to be brought in the name of the partnership (and not in that of any of its members): s 14(2). A fine imposed on a partnership on its conviction of an offence under the Act is to be paid out of the funds of the partnership: s 14(3). Section 14 does not apply to a partnership that is a legal person under the law by which it is governed: s 14(4).

6   See e g the Value Added Tax Act 1994 s 45; and PARA 102.

7   See the Limited Liability Partnerships Act 2000 s 1(1), (2); and PARA 233.

3.   Partnerships and limited liability.   One significant difference between a partnership and a company is that, in general, a partnership does not confer limited liability on the partners. However, a partnership formed under the Limited Partnerships Act 1907 provides for a limited partner's liability to creditors of the firm to be limited[1]. In addition, the members of a limited liability partnership are not, ordinarily, liable for the debts and obligations of the limited liability partnership, although such an entity is a body corporate and not, in fact, a form of partnership[2].

1   See PARA 217 et seq.

2   A limited liability partnership is a body corporate, with legal personality separate from that of its members, which is governed by the Limited Liability Partnerships Act 2000, the Limited Liability Partnerships Regulations 2001, SI 2001/1090, the Limited Liability Partnerships (Accounts and Audit) (Application of Companies Act 2006) Regulations 2008, SI 2008/1911, and the Limited Liability Partnerships (Application of Companies Act 2006) Regulations 2009, SI 2009/1804: see PARA 233 et seq.

4.   Essentials of partnership.   Partnership involves a contract between the partners to engage in a business with a view to profit[1]. For the purpose of determining whether a partnership has commenced, persons who have agreed to carry on a business as a joint venture are not partners until they embark on the activity in question[2].

Each partner may contribute either property, skill or labour. A person who contributes property without labour, and has the rights of a partner, is usually termed a 'sleeping' or 'dormant partner', but a sleeping partner may, however, contribute nothing at all[3].

The question whether or not there is a partnership is one of mixed law and fact[4].

1 'I have always understood the definition of partnership to be a mutual participation in profit and loss' (*Green v Beesley* (1835) 2 Bing NC 108 at 112 per Tindal CJ); but this cannot now be regarded as an exhaustive definition. Cf *Jeffrey v Bamford* [1921] 2 KB 351 at 358–359 per McCardie J ('community or participation in loss' is not 'essential to the legal notion of partnership').

2 *Khan v Miah* [2001] 1 All ER 20, [2000] 1 WLR 2123, HL. 'The question is not whether the [business] had commenced trading, but whether the parties had done enough to be found to have commenced the joint enterprise in which they had agreed to engage': *Khan v Miah* at 25 and 2128, per Lord Millett. See also *Ilott v Williams* [2013] EWCA Civ 645, [2013] All ER (D) 55 (Jun).

3 *Pooley v Driver* (1876) 5 ChD 458 at 472–473.

4 *Keith Spicer Ltd v Mansell* [1970] 1 All ER 462 at 463, [1970] 1 WLR 333 at 335, CA, per Harman LJ. See also *Saywell v Pope (Inspector of Taxes)* [1979] STC 824.

5. Relation between partners. The relation between partners is not that of debtor and creditor, unless and until the partnership accounts have been finally taken after dissolution and a balance has been ascertained to be owing from one to another[1].

1 *Richardson v Bank of England* (1838) 4 My & Cr 165 at 171–172; *De Tastet v Shaw* (1818) 1 B & Ald 664; and *Hurst v Bryk* [2002] 1 AC 185 at 193–196, [2000] 2 All ER 193 at 198–202, HL. An order for the taking of an account will not be ordered where to do so would serve no useful purpose: *Brown v Rivlin* [1983] CA Transcript 56 (retired partner whose share had passed to the continuing partner under the terms of the partnership agreement held not to have a continuing interest in the firm's assets, so that the continuing partner was able to pursue the retired partner in respect of a specific sum of money wrongfully extracted from the firm without having to take a partnership account first); applying *Gopala Chetty v Vijayaraghavachariar* [1922] 1 AC 488, PC. Cf *Prole v Masterman* (1855) 21 Beav 61 (where, in relation to a debt owed to a director of a company, the ordinary rule was defeated simply because the other directors had not pursued an action for an account themselves); and see PARA 157. As to the acknowledgment or part payment of a debt by one partner to another see PARA 198. As to dissolution see PARA 173 et seq.

6. Business. The existence of a business is essential to a partnership, and for this purpose 'business' includes every trade, occupation or profession[1]. The idea involved is that of joint operation for the sake of gain[2]. Therefore, voluntary associations for the purpose of carrying out temporary functions of a social character are not partnerships[3]. Instances of other associations for a common object which are not partnerships, properly so called, are clubs[4], trade protection societies[5] and building and other benefit societies[6].

A partnership did not formerly exist[7] between the trustees of a deed for the benefit of creditors and the debtor or between the inspector and committee under a deed of inspectorship and the debtor when the debtor was employed to carry on the business under the supervision of the trustees or inspector and committee[8], especially if the object of the arrangement was to wind up the business and not to continue it with a view to future profits[9].

1 Partnership Act 1890 s 45. It also includes a separate commercial adventure: *Re Abenheim, ex p Abenheim* (1913) 109 LT 219. 'To constitute a partnership the parties must have agreed to carry on business, or to share profits in some way in common': *Mollwo, March & Co v Court of Wards* (1872) LR 4 PC 419 at 436 per Sir Montagu Smith. As to the phrase 'carrying on business' see *Pathirana v Pathirana* [1967] 1 AC 233 at 239, [1966] 3 WLR 666 at 670–671, PC, per Lord Upjohn. See also *Khan v Miah* [2001] 1 All ER 20, [2000] 1 WLR 2123, HL; and *Ilott v Williams* [2013] EWCA Civ 645, [2013] All ER (D) 55 (Jun).

A trading partnership has been defined as one which consists of buying and selling goods: *Higgins v Beauchamp* [1914] 3 KB 1192 at 1195, DC, per Lush J (business of cinematograph theatre proprietors not trading partnership); and see *Wheatley v Smithers* [1906] 2 KB 321, CA (auctioneers not trading partnership). In order to ascertain whether or not a particular concern amounts to a 'trade', that concern's transactions as a whole must be construed, and such a construction should not be altered by referring to the parties' paramount intentions: *Ensign Tankers (Leasing) Ltd v Stokes (Inspector of Taxes)* [1992] 1 AC 655, [1992] 2 All ER 275, HL (although authorities on the point can be fairly narrowly decided one way or the other; and see *Overseas Containers (Finance) Ltd v Stoker (Inspector of Taxes)* [1989] 1 WLR 606, [1989] STC 364, CA (non-partnership case)); and see *Barclays Mercantile Industrial Finance Ltd v Melluish (Inspector of Taxes)* [1990] STC 314; *Stirling v Dietsmann Management Systems Ltd* [1991] IRLR 368, EAT; *Beautiland Co Ltd v IRC* [1991] STC 467, PC (non-partnership cases); and note 2. A partnership is a single 'trade' notwithstanding that it is carried on from several offices around the country, individual partners being assigned to a particular office: *C Connelly & Co v Wilbey (Inspector of Taxes)* [1992] STC 783. Professional league football is a 'trade': *Hall v Victoria Football League and Clarke* [1982] VR 64, Vict SC; and see *Kirkham v Williams (Inspector of Taxes)* [1991] 1 WLR 863, CA; and the guidance in *Marson (Inspector of Taxes) v Morton* [1986] 1 WLR 1343 (where the court held that, although each case depended upon its own facts, decided cases were nevertheless useful in determining whether a particular type of concern amounted to 'trade'). As to the type of considerations that apply when considering whether or not a particular venture is commercial or simply carried on for pleasure see *GB Turnbull Ltd v Customs and Excise Comrs* [1984] VATTR 247; and COMPANIES vol 14 (2009) PARA 1. Where an excise licence trade is carried on at any set of premises by two or more persons in partnership, then, subject to the provisions of any enactment relating to the licence or trade in question, not more than one licence is required to be held by those persons in respect of those premises at any one time: Customs and Excise Management Act 1979 s 101(3) (amended by the Finance Act 1986 s 8(6), Sch 5 para 1); see CUSTOMS AND EXCISE vol 31 (2012) PARA 609.

The expression 'business' would not appear to include an activity carried out solely for pleasure and without a motive for profit, even though 'guests' did make some financial contribution: *Customs and Excise Comrs v Lord Fisher* [1981] 2 All ER 147 (annual pheasant shoots held not subject to VAT); and see *Neuvale Ltd v Customs and Excise Comrs* [1989] STC 395, CA (both non-partnership cases).

2   *R v Robson* (1885) 16 QBD 137 at 140, CCR, per Lord Coleridge CJ. Where the building activities, plant and equipment of a firm of builders and decorators were transferred to a limited company, and only the firm's land remained as a partnership asset but the firm continued to trade, it was decided that the land in question was held by the firm as trading stock, not (as the taxpayer argued) as merely a non-trading investment: *Watts (t/a AA Watts) v Hart (Inspector of Taxes)* [1984] STC 548; but see *Sugarwhite v Budd (Inspector of Taxes)* [1988] STC 533, CA (non-partnership case). As to joint adventures see PARA 11. Thus a so-called partnership for running the Old Berkeley and other coaches was held not to be a partnership (*Goddard v Mills* (1929) Times, 16 February); and it is conceived that a shooting syndicate would not ordinarily be a partnership (see note 1).

3   See CONTRACT vol 22 (2012) PARA 350.

4   *Flemyng v Hector* (1836) 2 M & W 172 at 178–187; *Wise v Perpetual Trustee Co Ltd* [1903] AC 139 at 149, PC. See also CLUBS vol 13 (2009) PARAS 205, 213.

5   *Todd v Emly* (1841) 8 M & W 505; *Caldicott v Griffiths* (1853) 8 Exch 898.

6   *Brownlie v Russell* (1883) 8 App Cas 235, HL. As to building societies see FINANCIAL SERVICES AND INSTITUTIONS vol 50 (2008) PARA 1856 et seq. As to friendly societies see FINANCIAL SERVICES AND INSTITUTIONS vol 50 (2008) PARA 2081 et seq. Friendly societies are not partnerships within either the Partnership Act 1890 or the general acceptation of the term: see *Re Lead Co's Workmen's Fund Society, Lowes v Governor & Co for Smelting Down Lead with Pit and Sea Coal* [1904] 2 Ch 196, where the court disapproved the misuse of the term 'partnership' in *Lloyd v Loaring* (1802) 6 Ves 773; *Beaumont v Meredith* (1814) 3 Ves & B 180; and *Silver v Barnes* (1839) 6 Bing NC 180. A non-profit-making organisation was held to be carrying on a business within the meaning and for the purposes of its leasehold covenant against business user: *Florent v Horez* (1983) 48 P & CR 166, CA; and see LANDLORD AND TENANT vol 62 (2012) PARA 650.

7   Ie under the old bankruptcy law.

8   *Price v Groom* (1848) 2 Exch 542 (trustees of deed for benefit of creditors); *Marconi's Wireless Telegraph Co Ltd v Newman* [1930] 2 KB 292 (inspector and committee under deed of inspectorship), following *Cox v Hickman* (1860) 8 HL Cas 268; *Redpath v Wigg* (1866) LR 1 Exch 335; and *Easterbrook v Barker* (1870) LR 6 CP 1. As to insolvent partnerships generally see PARAS 98, 232; BANKRUPTCY AND INDIVIDUAL INSOLVENCY vol 5 (2013) PARA 851 et seq; COMPANY AND PARTNERSHIP INSOLVENCY vol 17 (2011) PARAS 1209–1361.

9   *Coates v Williams* (1852) 7 Exch 205, following *Janes v Whitbread* (1851) 11 CB 406.

7. Firm name. The name under which partners carry on business is their firm name[1]. The firm name is not the name of a corporation but simply the name under which the partners carry on the joint business[2].

1 See the Partnership Act 1890 s 4(1); and PARA 1. The name of a newspaper is not a firm name (*De Bernales v New York Herald* [1893] 2 QB 97n), but a club name may be a firm name (*Firmin & Sons Ltd v International Club* (1889) 5 TLR 694, CA).

2 *Re Smith, Fleming & Co, ex p Harding* (1879) 12 ChD 557 at 567, CA. See also *Sadler v Whiteman* [1910] 1 KB 868 at 889, CA (on appeal [1910] AC 514, HL); and *R v Holden* [1912] 1 KB 483, CCA. A partner who has sold his share of goodwill to the other partner cannot restrain the continued use of his own name in connection with the business: *Tottey v Kemp* (1970) 215 Estates Gazette 1021.

8. Disclosure requirements under the Companies Act 2006. The Companies Act 2006 makes the following provision[1] where a partnership[2] is carrying on business[3] in the United Kingdom under a business name[4] (that is a name other than: (1) the surnames[5] of all partners who are individuals; and (2) the corporate names of all partners who are bodies corporate, in either case without any addition other than a permitted addition)[6].

Such a partnership must state the name of each member of the partnership (and in relation to each person so named, an address at which service of any document relating in any way to the business will be effective[7]) in legible characters, on all business letters, written orders for goods or services to be supplied to the business, invoices and receipts issued in the course of the business, and written demands for payment of debts arising in the course of the business[8]. However, there is an exemption from this requirement in respect of large partnerships so that this does not apply in relation to a document issued by a partnership of more than 20 persons if: (a) the partnership maintains at its principal place of business a list of the names of all the partners; (b) no partner's name appears in the document, except in the text or as a signatory; and (c) the document states in legible characters the address of the partnership's principal place of business and that the list of the partners' names is open to inspection there[9].

In any premises where the business is carried on, and to which customers of the business or suppliers of goods or services to the business have access, the partnership must display in a prominent position, so that it may easily be read by such customers or suppliers, a notice containing the required information[10].

A person who without reasonable excuse fails to comply with the disclosure requirements in respect of business documents[11] and business premises[12] commits an offence[13], and if it is committed by a body corporate, an offence is also committed by every officer of the body who is in default[14].

Where any legal proceedings are brought by a partnership to enforce a right arising out of a contract made in the course of a business in respect of which the partners were, at the time the contract was made, in breach of the disclosure provisions[15], the proceedings must be dismissed if the defendant shows: (i) that he has a claim against the claimant arising out of the contract that he has been unable to pursue by reason of the latter's breach of the disclosure requirements[16]; or (ii) that he has suffered some financial loss in connection with the contract by reason of the claimant's breach of those requirements, unless the court is satisfied that it is just and equitable to permit the proceedings to continue[17]. However, this does not affect the right of any person to enforce such rights as he may have against another person in any proceedings brought by that person[18].

1   The Companies Act 2006 ss 1200–1208 were brought fully into force on 1 October 2009: see the Companies Act 2006 (Commencement No 8, Transitional Provisions and Savings) Order 2008, SI 2008/2860, art 3(x). They replace provisions previously in force under the Business Names Act 1985 (repealed).

2   'Partnership' means:
     (1)   a partnership within the Partnership Act 1890; or
     (2)   a limited partnership registered under the Limited Partnerships Act 1907,
     or a firm or entity of a similar character formed under the law of a country or territory outside the United Kingdom: Companies Act 2006 s 1208. 'United Kingdom' means Great Britain and Northern Ireland: Interpretation Act 1978 s 5, Sch 1. 'Great Britain' means England, Scotland and Wales: Union with Scotland Act 1706 preamble art I; Interpretation Act 1978 s 22(1), Sch 2 para 5(a). Neither the Isle of Man nor the Channel Islands are within the United Kingdom. See further CONSTITUTIONAL AND ADMINISTRATIVE LAW vol 20 (2014) PARA 3.

3   'Business' includes a profession: Companies Act 2006 s 1208.

4   Companies Act 2006 s 1200(1).

5   'Surname', in relation to a peer or person usually known by a British title different from his surname, means the title by which he is known: Companies Act 2006 s 1208.

6   Companies Act 2006 s 1200(2). The following are the permitted additions for a partnership: (1) the forenames of individual partners or the initials of those forenames, or where two or more individual partners have the same surname, the addition of 's' at the end of that surname; (2) an addition merely indicating that the business is carried on in succession to a former owner of the business: s 1200(3). 'Initial' includes any recognised abbreviation of a name: s 1208.

7   If the partnership has a place of business in the United Kingdom, the address must be in the United Kingdom; if individual partnership does not have a place of business in the United Kingdom, the address must be an address at which service of documents can be effected by physical delivery and the delivery of documents is capable of being recorded by the obtaining of an acknowledgment of delivery: Companies Act 2006 ss 1201(2), (3) (s 1201 substituted by SI 2009/3182).

8   Companies Act 2006 ss 1201(1), 1202(1) (s 1201 as substituted: see note 7). The partnership must secure that this information is immediately given, by written notice, to any person with whom anything is done or discussed in the course of the business and who asks for that information: s 1202(2). The Secretary of State may by regulations (which are subject to negative resolution procedure) require that such notices be given in a specified form: s 1202(3), (4). At the date at which this volume states the law no such regulations had been made. In any enactment, 'Secretary of State' means one of Her Majesty's principal Secretaries of State: see the Interpretation Act 1978 Sch 1. The office of Secretary of State is a unified office, and in law each Secretary of State is capable of performing the functions of all or any of them: see CONSTITUTIONAL AND ADMINISTRATIVE LAW vol 20 (2014) PARA 153. For the purposes of the Companies Act 2006, the powers of the Secretary of State are exercised in practice by the Secretary of State for Business, Innovation and Skills: see COMPANIES vol 14 (2009) PARA 6.

9   Companies Act 2006 ss 1202(1), 1203(1), (2). Where a partnership maintains a list of the partners' names for the purposes of s 1203 any person may inspect the list during office hours: s 1203(3). Where an inspection required by a person in accordance with s 1203 is refused, an offence is committed by any member of the partnership concerned who without reasonable excuse refused the inspection or permitted it to be refused: s 1203(4). A person guilty of this offence is liable on summary conviction to a fine not exceeding level 3 on the standard scale and, for continued contravention, a daily default fine not exceeding one-tenth of level 3 on the standard scale: s 1203(5). As to the standard scale see SENTENCING AND DISPOSITION OF OFFENDERS vol 92 (2010) PARA 142.

10   Companies Act 2006 s 1204(1). The required information is the name of each member of the partnership (and in relation to each person so named, an address in the United Kingdom at which service of any document relating in any way to the business will be effective): see s 1201; and the text and note 7. The Secretary of State may by regulations (which are subject to negative resolution procedure) require that such notices be displayed in a specified form: s 1204(2), (3).

11   Ie the Companies Act 2006 s 1202 and regulations made under it (see the text and notes 7–8): s 1205(4).

12   Ie the Companies Act 2006 s 1204 and regulations made under it (see the text and note 10): s 1205(4).

13   Companies Act 2006 s 1205(1). A person guilty of the offence is liable on summary conviction to a fine not exceeding level 3 on the standard scale and, for continued contravention, a daily default fine not exceeding one-tenth of level 3 on the standard scale: s 1205(3).

14   Companies Act 2006 s 1205(2).

15   Ie the Companies Act 2006 s 1202(1), (2) or s 1204(1).

16 Ie the requirements of the Companies Act 2006 Pt 41 Ch 2 (ss 1200–1206) and the requirements
of regulations made under it: s 1206(3).

17 Companies Act 2006 s 1206(1), (2).

18 Companies Act 2006 s 1206(4).

(2) THE QUESTION WHETHER A PARTNERSHIP EXISTS

(i) Co-ownership of Property

9. Co-ownership and partnership distinguished. Joint tenancy, tenancy in
common, joint property, common property or part ownership does not, of itself,
create a partnership between the co-owners as to anything so held or owned,
whether or not they share any profits made by the use of it[1]. Whether co-owners
are also partners is a question of fact and law. The mode in which the property
has been dealt with and divided and the way in which it and any consequent
proceeds and income have been treated in the books may well prove important,
because persons who are only co-owners keep books on a different footing from
those who are also partners[2].

1 Partnership Act 1890 s 2(1). Thus co-owners of a racehorse who share equally the expenses of
keeping, training and running the horse are not necessarily partners as regards the horse,
although there may be a partnership between them in the business of running the horse for
profit: *French v Styring* (1857) 2 CBNS 357 at 366; cf *Green v Briggs* (1848) 6 Hare 395.

2 See *Re Hulton, Hulton v Lister* (1890) 62 LT 200, CA. As to the partners' right to full accounts
and information concerning the firm's affairs see PARA 134. As to the manner in which
partnership accounts are framed see PARA 154.

10. Co-owners of land. Co-owners of land who merely share the expenses of
management and divide the income arising from their land in specified shares are
not thereby constituted partners[1]. Nor is it a partnership if two co-owners agree
that one is to manage and provide funds for the repair of a house, and that the
net rent is to be divided between them equally[2].

If, however, co-owners use their land or other property for the purpose of
carrying on any business, they are partners as regards the business[3], and prima
facie, although not necessarily[4], also as regards the property employed[5]. Thus, if
land is bought by two persons with the object of improving and selling it in
building lots, there may be a partnership between them as regards the land[6]; and
a third person (for example a surveyor) who contributes skill and labour, but
neither land nor money, may, if he is entitled to share in the profits, be a partner
with them, especially if he shares losses as well as profits[7]. To constitute a
partnership, the property of the co-owners must be employed in a business with
the object of producing a return in the shape of profits or of adding to its value[8].

1 See the Partnership Act 1890 s 2(1); and PARA 9.

2 *French v Styring* (1857) 2 CBNS 357 at 366 per Willes J. As to partnership land see PARA 117.
As to trusts of land see the Trusts of Land and Appointment of Trustees Act 1996; and TRUSTS
AND POWERS. As to the rule that partnership land is sold on dissolution see PARA 207.

3 Thus the working of a colliery of which the owners were tenants in common constituted a
partnership between them as regards the business of the colliery: *Jefferys v Smith* (1820) 1
Jac & W 298; *Fereday v Wightwick* (1829) 1 Russ & M 45; *County of Gloucester Bank v
Rudry Merthyr Steam and House Coal Colliery Co* [1895] 1 Ch 629 at 637, CA. As to the
respective rights enjoyed by co-owners of mines see MINES, MINERALS AND QUARRIES vol 76
(2013) PARA 366 et seq.

4 *Meyer v Sharpe* (1813) 5 Taunt 74; *Crawshay v Maule* (1818) 1 Swan 495 at 518; *French v
Styring* (1857) 2 CBNS 357; *Davis v Davis* [1894] 1 Ch 393. The fact that the firm pays the rent
of a lease which is in one partner's name, or that it has paid the stamp duty on the grant of the
lease, is not conclusive evidence that the lease is partnership property: *Hodson v Cashmore*

(1972) 226 Estates Gazette 1203. As to which assets may or may not constitute partnership property generally see PARA 115 et seq. If a firm becomes incorporated, then, by transferring its assets to the newly incorporated company, it may be in breach of a covenant in its lease against parting with possession of the leasehold property which it occupies: *Lam Kee Ying Sdn Bhd v Lam Shes Tong (t/a Lian Joo Co)* [1975] AC 247, [1974] 3 All ER 137, PC; but see *Harrison v Povey, London County Freehold and Leasehold Properties Ltd v Harrison and Povey* (1956) 168 Estates Gazette 613, CA (where it was held that the tenant partner who had left the premises from which the firm traded and had set up his own business elsewhere leaving his co-partner in possession had not parted with possession of the leased premises and was not therefore in breach of the terms of the lease). See also *Bristol Corpn v Westcott* (1879) 12 ChD 461, CA; *Gian Singh & Co v Devraj Nahar* [1965] 1 All ER 768, [1965] 1 WLR 412, PC; and see *Varley v Coppard* (1872) LR 7 CP 505; *Langton v Henson* (1905) 92 LT 805; and LANDLORD AND TENANT vol 62 (2012) PARA 631.

5   *Forster v Hale* (1798) 3 Ves 696; affd (1800) 5 Ves 308 at 309. If a partnership in a colliery was found to exist, the property necessary for the purposes of that partnership was, by operation of law, held for the purposes of the partnership: *Waterer v Waterer* (1873) LR 15 Eq 402; *Syers v Syers* (1876) 1 App Cas 174, HL; *Davies v Games* (1879) 12 ChD 813; and see *Jardine-Paterson v Fraser* 1974 SLT 93.

6   *Dale v Hamilton* (1846) 5 Hare 369 at 393 (on appeal (1847) 2 Ph 266); *Darby v Darby* (1856) 3 Drew 495; *Re Hulton, Hulton v Lister* (1890) 62 LT 200, CA.

7   *Moore v Davis* (1879) 11 ChD 261 at 265.

8   *Kay v Johnston* (1856) 21 Beav 536 at 537; cf *Re Leslie, Leslie v French* (1883) 23 ChD 552; *Leigh v Dickeson* (1883) 12 QBD 194 (affd (1884) 15 QBD 60, CA); *Robinson v Ashton, Ashton v Robinson* (1875) LR 20 Eq 25; and see PARA 6.

11.   Joint adventure. If two persons jointly export their individual goods for sale as a joint adventure, dividing the profits of the transaction in specified shares, there is no partnership as regards the separate parcel of goods provided by each until they are brought into the common stock[1]. Conversely, if they are jointly concerned in the purchase, they are not partners unless they are also jointly concerned in the future sale[2]. Where, however, they agree to embark in a joint adventure for the purchase and sale of goods, there is a partnership as regards all the goods bought in pursuance of the agreement, and each is liable for the price of the goods bought by the other[3]; and, if goods bought for a joint adventure by two persons are wholly paid for by one of them, while the other contributes skill and labour in return for a share of the profits, there may be a partnership between them of such a nature that the goods are partnership property[4]. Similarly, if a sole patentee and a financier who supplies the necessary funds work a patent in partnership for four years and are advertised as joint patentees, the patent may become partnership property[5]. A wife who actively helps her husband in a business but receives no wages can be a partner in a joint enterprise[6].

1   *Reid v Hollinshed* (1825) 7 Dow & Ry KB 444; *Alexander v Long* (1884) 1 TLR 145.

2   *Coope v Eyre* (1788) 1 Hy Bl 37 at 49 per Lord Loughborough CJ (where the property purchased was to be divided); cf *Hoare v Dawes* (1780) 1 Doug KB 371; *Gibson v Lupton* (1832) 9 Bing 297.

3   *Gouthwaite v Duckworth* (1810) 12 East 421, followed and applied in *Karmali Abdulla Allarakhia v Vora Karimji Jiwanji* (1914) LR 42 Ind App 48, PC, where *Saville v Robertson* (1792) 4 Term Rep 720 was distinguished.

4   *Reid v Hollinshed* (1825) 7 Dow & Ry KB 444; *Alexander v Long* (1884) 1 TLR 145.

5   *Kenny's Patent Button-Holeing Co Ltd v Somervell and Lutwyche* (1878) 38 LT 878.

6   *Nixon v Nixon* [1969] 3 All ER 1133, [1969] 1 WLR 1676, CA.

12.   Partnership without joint ownership. Persons may be partners, either generally or in some particular business or isolated transaction, even though all or part of the property used for the purposes of that business transaction may not be the subject of joint ownership but may belong to some or one of them individually[1].

1 Thus, where two persons carried on the business of running a stage coach or a stage wagon, each supplying his own horses for part of the journey and dividing the profits according to the mileage worked by their teams, they were held to be partners: *Fromont v Coupland* (1824) 2 Bing 170 (all the fares received by one partner, who accounted to the other); *Russell v Austwick* (1826) 1 Sim 52 (each received the fares earned in his district and accounted to the other, but there was no partnership as regards the horses, and therefore one partner was not liable for goods supplied to the other for the use of the horses which were his separate property). See also *Barton v Hanson* (1809) 2 Taunt 49; cf *Wilson v Whitehead* (1842) 10 M & W 503; *Osborne v Jullion* (1856) 3 Drew 596; *Moore v Davis* (1879) 11 ChD 261 at 265; and the cases cited in PARA 118.

(ii) Sharing Gross Returns

13. Sharing of gross returns not prima facie evidence of partnership. The sharing of gross returns does not of itself create a partnership, whether the persons sharing such returns have or have not a joint or common right or interest in any property from which or from the use of which the returns are derived[1]. The receipt of a share of gross returns, as distinguished from the receipt of a share of profits, is not even prima facie evidence of partnership[2]. Even where the expenses are jointly borne, the same rules seem to apply[3].

1 Partnership Act 1890 s 2(2); and see *Lyon v Knowles* (1863) 3 B & S 556 at 564; affd (1864) 5 B & S 751, Ex Ch.
2 Cf the Partnership Act 1890 s 2(3); and see PARA 14 et seq. As to the effect of association of promoters of a company see PARA 1. If one of two joint owners of a ship takes the exclusive management of it, bearing all the expenses, and pays one-third of the gross earnings to the other joint owner, the joint owners are not partners: *Burnard v Aaron and Sharpley* (1862) 31 LJCP 334; distinguished on another point in *Associated Portland Cement Manufacturers (1910) Ltd v Ashton* [1915] 2 KB 1, CA (owner and master). If a ship belongs to one person and is worked by another who receives one-half of the gross earnings, these persons are not partners: *Dry v Boswell* (1808) 1 Camp 329. Cf *Wish v Small* (1808) 1 Camp 331n (share of profits held to represent rent for pasturage of cattle). In both cases, if the net profits had been shared, the parties would have been partners: see PARA 14.
3 *French v Styring* (1857) 2 CBNS 357 (two joint owners of a racehorse shared the gross winnings, the horse being kept, trained and run by one only, but the expenses of keeping, training and running it were borne by them jointly). See also PARA 9. The owner of a theatre who pays certain outgoings and receives one-half of the gross receipts of public performances given by the occupier is not a partner, at any rate if the management is in the hands of the occupier: *Lyon v Knowles* (1863) 3 B & S 556; affd (1864) 5 B & S 751, Ex Ch. For an example of how persons trading together as partners may agree between themselves the manner in which unusual expenses should be borne and shown in their annual accounts see *MacKinlay (Inspector of Taxes) v Arthur Young McClelland Moores & Co (a firm)* [1990] 2 AC 239, [1990] 1 All ER 45, HL (decided under the Income and Corporation Taxes Act 1970 s 130(a) (repealed): see now the Income Tax (Trading and Other Income) Act 2005 s 34; the Corporation Tax Act 2009 s 54; and INCOME TAXATION vol 58 (2014) PARA 177 et seq), although, as that case shows, whether unusual expenses are deductible against profits depends on the 'wholly and exclusively' test. As to taxation generally see PARA 99 et seq. As to the partners' right to see the accounts and books of their firm see PARA 134; and as to the basis upon which accounts are framed see PARA 154.

(iii) Sharing Profits

14. Sharing profits as evidence of partnership. The receipt by a person of a share of the profits of a business is prima facie evidence that he is a partner in the business[1]. If the matter stops there, it is evidence upon which the court must act[2], but the receipt of such a share, or of a payment contingent on or varying with the profits of a business, does not of itself make him a partner in the business[3]. The question is whether the business is conducted so as to constitute the relationship of principal and agent between the person taking the profits and those actually carrying on the business[4]. The terms of the arrangement between the parties must be fairly considered as a whole; and, if the receipt of profits is only one of such terms, it is not conclusive, and the court will give effect to the entire arrangement[5]. What has to be considered is what rights the contract has given to one of the parties as against the other[6]. The division of profits need not, however, reflect the actual contribution that each partner makes to the business[7].

Whilst share of profits constitutes prima facie evidence of partnership, it is not definitive in itself; it is possible, for example, for a person to be a partner in a firm if he and the other partners agreed that, rather than being entitled to participate in the firm's profits, he should be paid a specified sum by the firm, irrespective of profits, for work to be done by him on its behalf[8].

1   Partnership Act 1890 s 2(3). See *Parker v Walker* 1961 SLT 252, SC (share-fishing); *Rush and Tomkins Construction Ltd v Vieweger Construction Co Ltd* (1964) 45 DLR (2d) 122, Alta SC; revsd on another point [1965] SCR 195, 48 DLR (2d) 509, Can SC (contractors and engineers together constructing highway and sharing profits). See also *Geary v Rankine* [2012] EWCA Civ 555, [2012] 2 FCR 461 (couple ran guest house together; no evidence of shared profits and no partnership).
    In this context, the term 'business' relates not merely to a life-long or a universal business or a long undertaking, but to any separate commercial adventure in which people may embark: *Re Abenheim, ex p Abenheim* (1913) 109 LT 219.
2   *Davis v Davis* [1894] 1 Ch 393 at 399 per North J; *Walker West Developments Ltd v F J Emmett Ltd* (1978) 252 Estates Gazette 1171, CA (developers and builders sharing profits but not losses held to be partners).
3   Partnership Act 1890 s 2(3). The Partnership Act 1890, which repeals but substantially re-enacts 28 & 29 Vict c 86 (Partnership) ('Bovill's Act') (1865) declares and settles the law according pre-existing rules of equity and common law: Partnership Act 1890 s 46; and see *Strathearn Gordon Associates Ltd v Customs and Excise Comrs* [1985] VATTR 79 (the fact that a company participating in property developments provided property management services in exchange for a share of profit, did not convert what was prima facie remuneration for the supply of services into a partnership).
4   *Bullen v Sharp* (1865) LR 1 CP 86 at 112, Ex Ch, per Blackburn J. See also *Cox v Hickman* (1860) 8 HL Cas 268 at 304, 312; *Re English and Irish Church and University Assurance Society (No 2)* (1863) 1 Hem & M 85; *Kilshaw v Jukes* (1863) 3 B & S 847; *Shaw v Galt* (1864) 16 ICLR 357 at 375; *Holme v Hammond* (1872) LR 7 Exch 218.
5   *Davis v Davis* [1894] 1 Ch 393.
6   *Walker v Hirsch* (1884) 27 ChD 460 at 468, CA, per Cotton LJ; and at 470–471, doubting *Pawsey v Armstrong* (1881) 18 ChD 698. 'The question is, what is the true construction of the document and what are the rights arising from it': *Walker v Hirsch* (1884) 27 ChD 460 at 472, CA, per Lindley LJ. See also *Ross v Parkyns* (1875) LR 20 Eq 331; *London Financial Association v Kelk* (1884) 26 ChD 107 at 143; *White & Co v Churchyard* (1887) 3 TLR 428; *Badeley v Consolidated Bank* (1888) 38 ChD 238 at 258, 263, CA; *Re Young, ex p Jones* [1896] 2 QB 484; *Re Jane, ex p Trustee* (1914) 110 LT 556, CA; *Re Beard & Co, ex p Trustee* [1915] HBR 191 at 200, CA, per Cozens Hardy MR.
7   *Ward v Newalls Insulation Co Ltd* [1998] 2 All ER 690, [1998] 1 WLR 1722, CA.
8   *M Young Legal Associates Ltd v Zahid Solicitors (a firm)* [2006] EWCA Civ 613, [2006] 1 WLR 2562, [2006] All ER (D) 227 (May).

15.   Sharing profits and losses.   If losses as well as profits are shared, the presumption of partnership is stronger[1]. This is so even if the agreement stipulates that each party is to bear only an aliquot share of loss[2]. The fact that losses are shared is not, however, conclusive as to the existence of a partnership[3].

There is no joint ownership, and no partnership, where each of several joint adventurers supplies separate parcels of goods which are to be sold, and the profits are divided rateably among them[4], or where one person buys and pays for the goods and the profit or loss is to be shared by himself and another[5]. For a partnership to be constituted the parties must be jointly interested in the purchase and also jointly interested in the future sale[6].

1   *Green v Beesley* (1835) 2 Bing NC 108; *Brett v Beckwith* (1856) 26 LJ Ch 130; *Noakes v Barlow* (1872) 26 LT 136, Ex Ch.

2   *Brown v Tapscott* (1840) 6 M & W 119; *McInroy v Hargrove* (1867) 15 WR 777.

3   *Walker v Hirsch* (1884) 27 ChD 460, CA. See also *Sutton & Co v Grey* [1894] 1 QB 285, CA; and see PARA 4 note 1.

4   *Heap v Dobson* (1863) 15 CBNS 460. See PARA 11.

5   *Alfaro v De la Torre* (1876) 24 WR 510; cf *Reid v Hollinshead* (1825) 4 B & C 867 (both parties interested in both the purchase and sale, although one found all the money and the other gave his time and skill).

6   *Hoare v Dawes* (1780) 1 Doug KB 371; cf *Coope v Eyre* (1788) 1 Hy Bl 37; *Gibson v Lupton* (1832) 9 Bing 297. As to whether a fisherman who shares profits is a partner see *Parker v Walker* 1961 SLT 252, SC.

16.   Persons having too indirect an interest in profits to be partners.   A person receiving by way of annuity or otherwise a portion of the profits of a business in consideration of the sale by him of the goodwill of the business is not by reason only of such receipt a partner in the business or liable as such[1]. The true test of whether a partnership was intended is whether there was a joint business or whether the parties were intending to carry on the business as the agents of each other[2]. Similarly, the widow, widower, surviving civil partner or child of a deceased partner, receiving by way of annuity a portion of the profits made in the business in which the deceased person was a partner, is not by reason only of such receipt a partner in the business or liable as such[3].

1   Partnership Act 1890 s 2(3)(e) (re-enacting 28 & 29 Vict c 86 (Partnership) ('Bovill's Act') (1865) s 4).

2   *Hawksley v Outram* [1892] 3 Ch 359 at 377, CA, per Lopes LJ (vendors were entitled to receive a share of profits in respect of purchase money left in the business, but the agreement as a whole was inconsistent with the inference that the purchasers were carrying on the business on behalf of themselves and the vendors); cf *Chitty v Boorman* (1890) 7 TLR 43; *Pratt v Strick* (1932) 17 TC 459 (vendor of a medical practice covenanted to introduce the purchaser to his patients and to assist him in the practice for a period during which the earnings and expenses should belong to, and be borne by, them equally; there was held to be no partnership between them during that period); cf *Rawlinson v Clarke* (1846) 15 M & W 292, Ex Ch.

3   Partnership Act 1890 s 2(3)(c) (amended by the Civil Partnership Act 2004 s 261(1), Sch 27 para 2) (re-enacting 28 & 29 Vict c 86 (Partnership) ('Bovill's Act') (1865) s 3: see further PARA 14 note 3); *Re Jones, ex p Harper* (1857) 1 De G & J 180.

17.   Salaried partners and employees.   A contract for the remuneration of a servant or agent of a person engaged in a business by a share of the profits of the business does not of itself make the servant or agent a partner in the business or liable as such[1]. A person cannot be both a partner in, and an employee of, a partnership[2]. The expression 'salaried partner' is not a term of art, but is generally used to mean a person who receives a fixed remuneration irrespective of profits and who is in fact an employee but is held out to the world to be a partner[3]. The partnership will then be bound by his acts whether or not he is actually a partner. His salary may be a charge on the profits[4]. Where a person receives both salary and a share of the profits, it may be evidence that he is an employee rather than a partner[5]. However, an agreement for a person to be paid a specified sum for work to be done by him on behalf of a firm does not necessarily preclude his thereby becoming a partner of it[6].

A former partner may be employed by the partnership business as an employee rather than as a partner[7]. An employee[8] of a firm may be entitled to sue for wrongful dismissal if the firm is dissolved[9].

If an employee or agent also bears losses, he may be a partner[10]. If his agreement gives him rights usually given to a partner or contains provisions applicable to a partner, for example that he is not to pledge the other's credit, the inference of partnership is conclusive[11].

1   Partnership Act 1890 s 2(3)(b). See *Benjamin v Porteus* (1796) 2 Hy Bl 590 (explained in *Re Nevill, ex p White* (1871) 6 Ch App 397 at 404–405 per Mellish LJ); *R v Holmes* (1811) 2 Lew CC 256; *Meyer v Sharpe* (1813) 5 Taunt 74; *Burnell v Hunt* (1841) 5 Jur 650; *Re Closson, ex p Harris* (1845) De G 165; *Pott v Eyton and Jones* (1846) 3 CB 32; *Rawlinson v Clarke* (1846) 15 M & W 292 at 302, Ex Ch (followed and applied in *Pratt v Strick* (1932) 17 TC 459); *Re Ellins, ex p Hickin* (1850) 3 De G & Sm 662; *Stocker v Brockelbank* (1851) 3 Mac & G 250; *Andrews v Pugh* (1854) 24 LJ Ch 58; *Edmundson v Thompson and Blakey* (1861) 31 LJ Ex 207; *Walker v Hirsch* (1884) 27 ChD 460, CA (disapproving *Pawsey v Armstrong* (1881) 18 ChD 698). Nor, on the application by a creditor to wind up the partnership, will the fact that a person allows himself to be held out as a partner confer jurisdiction by estoppel on a court where no partnership in fact exists: *Re C & M Ashberg* (1990) Times, 17 July. A salaried partner may be liable to account to the partners of the firm for profits that he received from his appointment as liquidator or receiver carried out whilst employed by the firm: *Casson Beckman & Partners v Papi* [1991] BCLC 299, [1991] BCC 68, CA (although this case does not concern a salaried partner's liability to third parties qua partner but only his duties qua employee, it does show that such an employee's liability may actually mirror that owing as between partners); and see *Clarke v Newland* [1991] 1 All ER 397, CA.

2   See *Ellis v Joseph Ellis & Co* [1905] 1 KB 324; *Cowell v Quilter Goodison & Co Ltd* [1989] IRLR 392; and *Tiffin v Lester Aldridge LLP* [2012] EWCA Civ 35, [2012] 2 All ER 1113; although query the effect of the Law of Property Act 1925 s 82 (see *Bates van Winkelhof v Clyde & Co LLP* [2014] UKSC 32 at [29], [52], [56]–[59], [2014] 3 All ER 225 at [29], [52], [56]–[59], per Lady Hale DP and Lord Carnwath SCJ; and CONTRACT vol 22 (2012) PARA 644).

3   *Stekel v Ellice* [1973] 1 All ER 465, [1973] 1 WLR 191; and see *Turnock v Taylor* (1961) 180 Estates Gazette 773, CA. See also *Tiffin v Lester Aldridge LLP* [2012] EWCA Civ 35, [2012] 2 All ER 1113 ('fixed share partner' was partner not employee).

4   *Marsh v Stacey* (1963) 107 Sol Jo 512, CA.

5   *Ross v Parkyns* (1875) LR 20 Eq 331 at 336.

6   *M Young Legal Associates Ltd v Zahid Solicitors (a firm)* [2006] EWCA Civ 613, [2006] 1 WLR 2562, [2006] All ER (D) 227 (May).

7   *Easdown v Cobb* [1940] 1 All ER 49, HL. See further EMPLOYMENT vol 39 (2014) PARA 13.

8   But not a partner: *Cowell v Quilter Goodison & Co Ltd and QG Management Services Ltd* [1989] IRLR 392, CA.

9   *Tunstall v Condon* [1980] ICR 786, EAT; cf *Burgess v O'Brien* (1966) 1 KIR 99, ITR 164. In each case, however, the precise terms of the contract of employment in question must be examined: see *Brace v Calder* [1895] 2 QB 253, CA; *Phillips v Alhambra Palace Co* [1901] 1 KB 59. It is, however, submitted that, where upon the dissolution of the firm a full-scale winding up and sale of the partnership assets takes effect (see PARA 205 et seq), such termination of employees' contracts of employment will not occur in practice until the winding up has been completed, sed quaere; in *Tunstall v Condon* [1980] ICR 786, EAT, it had been agreed that after dissolution each of the two partners should simply keep his office from which to carry on in business on his own account. Further, if the dissolution is merely a technical one (ie caused solely by a change in the identity of the partners without a consequent winding up) it is unlikely that such a dissolution would entitle employees to sue for wrongful dismissal: see the Employment Rights Act 1996; the Transfer of Undertakings (Protection of Employment) Regulations 2006, SI 2006/246; *Tunstall v Condon* [1980] ICR 786 at 791, EAT; *Allen & Son v Coventry* [1980] ICR 9, EAT (where one of two partners in a firm of solicitors had transferred his 70% interest in the firm to the continuing partner); and EMPLOYMENT vol 41 (2014) PARA 726 et seq. See also *Secretary of State for Employment v Spence* [1987] QB 179, [1986] 3 All ER 616, CA. Furthermore, if a partnership is dissolved and the business is subsequently transferred as a going concern, it is doubtful whether the Employment Rights Act 1996 and the Transfer of Undertakings (Protection of Employment) Regulations 2006, SI 2006/246 (see EMPLOYMENT vol 39 (2014) PARA 111 et seq; EMPLOYMENT vol 41A (2014) PARA 1162 et seq) will apply to its

employees since their contracts of employment would already have been terminated by the prior dissolution; sed quaere. Where a partner subsequently becomes an employee, he may have difficulty in proving the requisite continuity of employment (see *Cowell v Quilter Goodison & Co Ltd and QG Management Services Ltd* [1989] IRLR 392, CA); and, where an employee's contract of employment has been terminated by the dissolution of the partnership, he may be entitled to practise in what would prima facie have been contravention of a covenant in restraint of trade contained in his contract of employment (*Briggs v Oates* [1991] 1 All ER 407).

10 *Smith v Watson* (1824) 2 B & C 401; *Reid v Hollinshead* (1825) 4 B & C 867. Cf *Walker v Hirsch* (1884) 27 ChD 460, CA. It does not follow that he cannot be a partner without sharing losses: see PARA 4 note 1; and PARA 15.

11 *Pole v Leask* (1863) 9 Jur NS 829, HL; *Moore v Davis* (1879) 11 ChD 261.

18. Receipt of debt out of profits. The receipt by a person of a debt or other liquidated amount, by instalments or otherwise, out of the accruing profits of a business does not of itself make him a partner in the business or liable as such[1].

1 Partnership Act 1890 s 2(3)(a) (which extended the law to agreements not touched by 28 & 29 Vict c 86 (Partnership) ('Bovill's Act') (1865): see PARA 14 note 3).

19. Share of profits as interest on loan. The advance of money by way of loan to a person engaged or about to engage in any business on a contract with that person that the lender is to receive a rate of interest varying with the profits, or is to receive a share of the profits arising from carrying on the business, does not of itself make the lender a partner with the person or persons carrying on the business or liable as such, provided that the contract is in writing and signed by or on behalf of all the parties to it[1]. It is immaterial whether the amount payable as interest increases or decreases, or whether a maximum rate is fixed which is liable only to decrease in proportion to the profits, if the agreement to that effect is clear[2].

If the lender leaves the debt on deposit at interest and upon the further term that he is to be credited with a share of profits, he is not a partner and may prove as an ordinary creditor[3].

The fact that the lender has an option to become a partner[4] or to require his nominee to be taken into partnership within a specified period does not make him a partner[5].

1 Partnership Act 1890 s 2(3)(d). See *Re Whittaker, ex p Macmillan* (1871) 24 LT 143; *Re Howard, ex p Tennant* (1877) 6 ChD 303, CA; *Re Young, ex p Jones* [1896] 2 QB 484. Thus, a person who agrees to pay to a business firm money to be used in buying goods for the business in consideration of a fixed rate of interest and a share of the profits of a specified branch of the business may not be a partner (*Meyer v Schacher* (1878) 38 LT 97), but such an agreement may constitute a breach of a covenant by the lender with his partners not to engage directly or indirectly in any other business (*Cooper v Page* (1876) 34 LT 90). It has been suggested that, if there is no agreement in writing, the intending lender must be regarded as a partner (*Re Fort, ex p Schofield* [1897] 2 QB 495 at 501, CA, per A L Smith LJ); but this dictum has not yet received authoritative confirmation, and the question would appear to depend upon the real intention of the parties. As to the necessity for the agreement to be in writing see DEEDS AND OTHER INSTRUMENTS vol 32 (2012) PARA 355 et seq.

2 *Re Vince, ex p Trustee in Bankruptcy* [1892] 1 QB 587.

3 *Re Pinto Leite & Nephews, ex p Visconde des Olivaes* [1929] 1 Ch 221. As to the position of the lender in the bankruptcy of the borrower see BANKRUPTCY AND INDIVIDUAL INSOLVENCY vol 5 (2013) PARA 598.

4 *Re Vanderplank, ex p Turquand* (1841) 2 Mont D & De G 339.

5 *Re Harris, ex p Davis* (1863) 4 De GJ & Sm 523. See PARA 20.

20. When a lender is a partner. The effect of an advance in consideration of a share of profits may easily be to place the intending lender in the position of a partner with all its consequences and liabilities[1], even though this may not be the intention of the parties and though the agreement may contain an express declaration to the contrary[2]. If the agreement gives the supposed lender the rights and privileges of a partner[3], no device or contrivance will enable him to escape the liabilities of a partner[4]. If he is not a partner, he is merely a creditor whose rights are limited by statute[5]. A lender may, however, stipulate for large powers, some of which might be consistent with the position either of a creditor or a sleeping partner, and, if such powers are reasonably necessary for the protection of his interest as a lender, they will not be held to make him a partner[6].

1   *Syers v Syers* (1876) 1 App Cas 174, HL.
2   *Re Megevand, ex p Delhasse* (1878) 7 ChD 511, CA.
3   *Debenham v Phillips* (1887) 3 TLR 512; *Badeley v Consolidated Bank* (1888) 38 ChD 238, CA.
4   'If a partnership in fact exists, a community of interest in the adventure being carried on in fact, no concealment of name, no verbal equivalent for the ordinary phrases of profit and loss, no indirect expedient for enforcing control over the adventure will prevent the substance and reality of the transaction from being adjudged to be a partnership': *Adam v Newbigging* (1888) 13 App Cas 308 at 315, HL, per Lord Halsbury LC. See also *Pooley v Driver* (1876) 5 ChD 458; cf *Courtenay v Wagstaff* (1864) 16 CBNS 110; *Re Megevand, ex p Delhasse* (1878) 7 ChD 511, CA; *Frowde v Williams* (1886) 56 LJQB 62, DC; *Stewart v Buchanan* (1903) 6 F (Ct of Sess) 15; *Fenston v Johnstone* (1940) 23 TC 29.
5   *Re Howard, ex p Tennant* (1877) 6 ChD 303, CA; *Kelly v Scotto* (1880) 49 LJ Ch 383; *Iggesunds Bruk Akt v Von Dadelszen* (1887) 3 TLR 517, CA. See also BANKRUPTCY AND INDIVIDUAL INSOLVENCY vol 5 (2013) PARA 598.
6   *Hollom v Whichelow* (1895) 64 LJQB 170.

21.   Lender is postponed to ordinary creditors.   A lender who receives a rate of interest varying with the profits of a business, or a share of the profits of a business carried on by the borrower[1], cannot prove in competition with creditors for value in the bankruptcy or insolvency of the borrower[2], whether the agreement is written or oral[3]. However, if the agreement is vague and unintelligible, it may be void for uncertainty, in which case the lender may prove as an ordinary creditor[4].

1   See PARA 20.
2   See the Partnership Act 1890 s 3; *Re Mason, ex p Bing* [1899] 1 QB 810 (where the loan to a firm was continued to the surviving partner); and BANKRUPTCY AND INDIVIDUAL INSOLVENCY vol 5 (2013) PARA 598.
3   *Re Fort, ex p Schofield* [1897] 2 QB 495, CA.
4   *Re Vince, ex p Baxter* [1892] 2 QB 478, CA; cf *Re Fort, ex p Schofield* [1897] 2 QB 495, CA.

22.   Vendor of goodwill who takes a share of profits.   A vendor of the goodwill of a business in consideration of a share of profits cannot prove in the bankruptcy or insolvency of the buyer in competition with the creditors for value[1].

1   See the Partnership Act 1890 s 3; and BANKRUPTCY AND INDIVIDUAL INSOLVENCY vol 5 (2013) PARA 598. As to the disposal of goodwill on the dissolution of a partnership see PARA 212.

(3) FORMATION AND DURATION

(i) Evidence of Formation; Partnership Agreements

23.   Evidence in writing.   The formation and terms of a partnership[1] may be evidenced by a partnership deed[2], by an agreement signed by the partners, by an unsigned document drafted by one partner and adopted and acted on by the others[3], and even by an informal document initialled by the partners and intended only to form instructions for a formal document[4].

A document signed by one person only, which would otherwise have been invalid for want of mutuality, may become evidence of the terms of a partnership if acted upon[5].

1 As to the contractual basis on which the relationship is founded see PARA 1 note 1.
2 For the usual provisions in a partnership agreement see PARA 26.
3 *Worts v Pern* (1707) 3 Bro Parl Cas 548, HL; *Baxter v West* (1860) 1 Drew & Sm 173.
4 *England v Curling* (1844) 8 Beav 129. Each member of a firm has a property in his own copy of a partnership deed executed in multiple: *Forbes v Samuel* [1913] 3 KB 706 at 722–724.
5 *Heyhoe v Burge* (1850) 9 CB 431.

24. Oral evidence. The existence of a partnership may be established by oral evidence even when a written partnership agreement is in existence[1]. Admissions made by a person in a former claim[2], or in an income tax return[3], that he is a partner, or a verdict on an issue directed to try whether a person is a partner[4], or even the advertisement of a dissolution[5] may be used as evidence to establish a partnership. A partnership agreement may probably be proved by oral evidence, even if the partnership is to deal with land[6], but such an agreement, for example an alleged agreement of partnership in the profits of land alone, when the parties have not acted as partners so that the existence of a partnership is in doubt, is probably subject to the general statutory provisions relating to contracts for the sale or other disposition of an interest in land[7], namely that, unless the agreement in question is in writing, incorporating all the expressly agreed terms of the contract in one document or, where contracts are exchanged, in each and signed by or on behalf of each party to the contract, the agreement will be void[8].

As to whether there is or is not a partnership, the court will look at the statements of the parties as one factor in order to consider the substance of the agreement[9], but the use by the parties of the word 'partner' is not conclusive evidence of partnership[10].

1 *Alderson v Clay* (1816) 1 Stark 405. As to evidence in writing see PARA 23.
2 *Studdy v Sanders* (1823) 2 Dow & Ry KB 347.
3 *Fogg v Gaulter and Blane* (1960) 110 L Jo 718.
4 *Whately v Menheim* (1797) 2 Esp 607.
5 *Ex p Matthews* (1814) 3 Ves & B 125.
6 As to the position under the old law, i e the Statute of Frauds (1677) s 4 (the predecessor to the Law of Property Act 1925 s 40), where proof by oral evidence was permissible see *Gray v Smith* (1889) 43 ChD 208 at 211, CA, per Kekewich J; *Forster v Hale* (1800) 5 Ves 308; *Dale v Hamilton* (1846) 5 Hare 369 (on appeal (1847) 2 Ph 266) (cf *Essex v Essex* (1855) 20 Beav 442); *Re De Nicols, De Nicols v Curlier* [1900] 2 Ch 410. The Law of Property Act 1925 s 40 (contracts for the sale or other disposition of land to be evidenced in writing; doctrine of part performance) was repealed with effect from 27 September 1989: see the Law of Property (Miscellaneous Provisions) Act 1989 ss 2(8), 4, 5(3), (4), Sch 2. An agreement for the sale or other disposition of land made on or after 27 September 1989 must comply with the provisions of the Law of Property (Miscellaneous Provisions) Act 1989 s 2 (see CONVEYANCING vol 23 (2013) PARA 151); sed quaere whether the same principles relating to partnership agreements involving land will still apply under the Law of Property (Miscellaneous Provisions) Act 1989.
7 See *Caddick v Skidmore* (1857) 3 Jur NS 1185; *Isaacs v Evans* [1899] WN 261; *Toogood v Farrell* [1988] 2 EGLR 233, CA (agreement by a retiring partner to grant the continuing partners a sublease of the premises which the firm used for its business) (decided under the Law of Property Act 1925 s 40 (repealed)). It is uncertain whether the same principles will be applied under the Law of Property (Miscellaneous Provisions) Act 1989 s 2: see note 6.
8 See the Law of Property (Miscellaneous Provisions) Act 1989 s 2 (amended by the Trusts of Land and Appointment of Trustees Act 1996 s 25(2), Sch 4; and by SI 2001/3649, SI 2006/2383 and SI 2009/1342); and *Spiro v Glencrown Properties Ltd* [1991] Ch 537, [1991] 1 All ER 600 (option to purchase).
9 See *Greville v Venables* [2007] EWCA Civ 878, [2008] All ER (D) 132 (Jan) (no express agreement to form partnership).

10 *Thames Cruises Ltd v George Wheeler Launches Ltd* [2003] EWHC 3093 (Ch), [2003] All ER (D) 285 (Dec) (lay people use the word 'partner' in a colloquial sense meaning people who go into business in some way without being true partners in law). See also *Weiner v Harris* [1910] 1 KB 285 at 290, CA, per Cozens-Hardy MR (not a partnership case): 'Two parties enter into a transaction and say "It is hereby declared there is no partnership between us". The court pays no regard to that. The court looks at the transaction and says "Is this, in point of law, really a partnership?" It is not in the least conclusive that the parties have used a term or language intended to indicate the transaction is not that which in law it is'.

25.   Mode of dealing. The mode of dealing adopted by partners is evidence of the formation and original terms of a partnership if those terms are not set out in any document. Partners are bound by the duties and obligations which are implied in every partnership contract if and so far as the express contract does not deal with them[1] and subject to the provisions of any statute[2].

The mutual rights and duties of partners, whether ascertained by agreement or defined by the Partnership Act 1890, may be varied by the consent of all the partners, and such consent may be either express or inferred from a course of dealing[3]. This is so even if the agreement is evidenced by writing[4]. An alteration in a partnership deed appearing on the face of the deed (where it is not made or presumed to have been made before execution[5]) cannot be taken into consideration[6], and, if an oral agreement is alleged to vary the partnership agreement so as to affect the partners' financial interests, the intention to produce this effect must clearly appear by the evidence[7].

Under the court's general jurisdiction over the property of minors, the court may vary a partnership agreement which is unduly onerous to a surviving partner where the new arrangement will be more beneficial for minors interested in the estate of a deceased partner[8].

1 *Smith v Jeyes* (1841) 4 Beav 503.
2 See eg the Scrap Metal Dealers Act 2013 s 3, Sch 1 para 2; and TRADE AND INDUSTRY.
3 Partnership Act 1890 s 19. See also *Const v Harris* (1824) Turn & R 496; *England v Curling* (1844) 8 Beav 129; *Vale of Neath and South Wales Brewery Co, Keene's Executors' Case* (1853) 3 De GM & G 272; *Austen v Boys* (1858) 2 De G & J 626 (following *Geddes v Wallace* (1820) 2 Bli 270, HL); *Coventry v Barclay* (1863) 33 Beav 1 (on appeal (1864) 3 De GJ & Sm 320); *Pilling v Pilling* (1865) 3 De GJ & Sm 162 (where the books were kept, and certain expenses were paid, otherwise than in accordance with the partnership agreement); *Peat v Smith* (1889) 5 TLR 306. Where a firm governed by a deed was joined by a new partner who never executed the deed because he did not agree all its terms, it was held that a new partnership at will had come into effect between all the parties, irrespective of the terms of the deed: *Firth v Amslake* (1964) 108 Sol Jo 198; but see *Austen v Boys* (1857) 24 Beav 598 (affd (1858) 2 De G & J 626); *Zamikoff v Lundy* [1970] 2 OR 8, 9 DLR (3d) 637 (affd sub nom *Whisper Holdings Ltd v Zamikoff* [1971] SCR 933, 19 DLR (3d) 114); and PARAS 38, 204. See also *Hudgell Yeates & Co v Watson* [1978] QB 451, [1978] 2 All ER 363, CA.
4 See PARA 23.
5 As to alterations in deeds and their effect see DEEDS AND OTHER INSTRUMENTS vol 32 (2012) PARA 284.
6 *Re Duncan and Pryce* [1913] WN 117, DC.
7 *Lawes v Lawes* (1878) 9 ChD 98.
8 *Martindale v Martindale* (1855) 1 Jur NS 932. As to the approval of compromises in claims to which a minor is a party see CHILDREN AND YOUNG PERSONS vol 10 (2012) PARA 1326.

26.   Partnership agreements. The relations between partners are usually regulated by partnership agreements. Many provisions of the Partnership Act 1890 apply only in the absence of any agreement to the contrary, and so the agreement may supersede numerous provisions of the statute.

Partnership agreements are governed by the law of contract[1] and will be construed according to normal canons of construction[2], so that a court will construe a partnership agreement in the light of partners' objectives[3], and terms may be implied by the court to give the agreement business efficacy[4].

Partnership agreements are usually in writing, but, even so, may be varied orally[5]. The principal matters[6] which are commonly governed[7] by partnership agreements are: the firm name[8]; the duration of the partnership[9]; the capital needed, and its provision in cash or other assets; the firm's banking account and the drawing of cheques; and terms to be observed during the continuance of the partnership, for example the banking of receipts, the payment of outgoings, the sharing of profits and losses, weekly or monthly drawings on account, loans by a partner to the firm, holidays and illness, duties and attention to business, management, misconduct and expulsion[10], and arbitration[11]. Finally, provision may be made for the dissolution of the partnership by effluxion of time or the death, bankruptcy or retirement of a partner[12]; or for ex-partners to be restrained from competing with the firm[13]. The continuing partners may be required or given an option to purchase the share of a deceased or retiring partner[14], in which case the partnership agreement may provide for an indemnity against partnership liabilities including income tax[15].

1   As to the contractual basis of the relationship of partnership see PARA 1 note 1.
2   See *A-G of Belize v Belize Telecom Ltd* [2009] UKPC 10, [2009] 2 All ER 1127, [2009] 2 All ER (Comm) 1, where Nicholls LJ emphasised that courts now generally prefer a modern, purposive approach to questions of construction, with regard to statutes, as opposed to the older mechanical rules of construction.
3   *Hitchman v Crouch Butler Savage Associates* (1983) 127 Sol Jo 441, CA (clause in the partnership agreement requiring a particular partner to sign all expulsion notices held not to apply where it was that partner who was being expelled by his co-partners). If a partner expels his co-partner, giving a wrong or inadequate reason for such expulsion, the former may yet justify the expulsion if there were at the time facts in existence which would have provided a good reason, even if he did not know of them at the time: *Boston Deep Sea Fishing and Ice Co v Ansell* (1888) 39 ChD 339 at 352, 364, CA.
4   *Miles v Clarke* [1953] 1 All ER 779, [1953] 1 WLR 537, where Harman J applied the 'implied term' test in order to ascertain which assets were partnership assets. In that case the two-man partnership of photographers had been in existence for only a short time, one of the partners having previously been the sole owner of the majority of the tangible assets, the other of the business's goodwill.
5   See PARAS 24–25.
6   Partnership agreements contain other provisions: eg in a partnership between solicitors, provision may be made concerning partnership appointments, trainee solicitors and legacies from clients, and specially valued employees may need consideration. In a medical partnership, provision may be made for appointments, cars, instruments, drugs and visits. As to the inclusion of an express power to dissolve the firm on notice see PARA 190.
7   It is sometimes found convenient to set out in partnership agreements the substance of some of the provisions of the Partnership Act 1890 eg s 5 (see PARA 39), s 24 (see PARA 109 et seq), s 28 (see PARA 134), s 30 (see PARA 107) and s 31 (see PARA 125).
8   As to the firm name see PARA 7.
9   As to the duration of partnerships see PARA 37 et seq.
10   As to expulsion see PARA 178.
11   As to the effect of an arbitration clause on the right to claim dissolution by the court see PARA 182. As to arbitration generally see **ARBITRATION**.
12   As to dissolution see PARA 173 et seq; and as to the rectification of an agreement embodying the terms of a firm's dissolution see *Rehman v Ahmad* [1993] CLY 679, Ct of Sess. See *Tann v Herrington* [2009] EWHC 445 (Ch), [2009] Bus LR 1051, [2009] All ER (D) 135 (Mar) (two-partner firm; fact that retirement caused dissolution did not prevent operation of retirement provisions in partnership agreement).
13   See PARA 27; and **COMPETITION** vol 18 (2009) PARA 377 et seq.
14   As to such provisions see PARA 200.
15   As to a partner's implied right to an indemnity in such a case see PARA 199. As to a partner's liability to income tax see PARA 99. As to the liability for inheritance tax on a partner's estate see PARA 101.

27.   Covenants in restraint of trade. Partnership agreements often contain provisions prohibiting an outgoing partner from carrying on a similar trade or profession within specified limits of time and distance[1]. Such provisions are not enforceable unless the restrictions are reasonable[2]. In order to uphold a covenant in restraint of trade, the claimant must establish that: (1) he has a legitimate interest capable of being protected; (2) the restrictive covenants are no more than adequate to protect the interest (meaning not excessive as regards area, duration or prohibited activities); and (3) without the enforcement of such covenants, the interest or goodwill could be injured or damaged[3].

It will usually be easier to prove that a covenant in restraint of trade is reasonable if it applies equally as between all members of the firm[4], but the court is less willing to avoid such provisions than it is to avoid similar provisions in contracts of employment[5].

Where some part of an otherwise void covenant in restraint of trade is reasonable, it may, where it satisfies the 'blue pencil' test, be severed by the court and thus remain enforceable[6].

1   *Shackle v Baker* (1808) 14 Ves 468; *Morris v Colman* (1812) 18 Ves 437. See also *Cooper v Watlington* (1784) 2 Chit 451; *Cooper v Page* (1876) 34 LT 90 (where one partner agreed to advance money to a third person on terms that he should receive, by way of interest, a share of the profits of the business carried on by that person, and it was held that this was a breach of covenant 'not to engage directly or indirectly in any other business'); *Prescott v Dunwoody Sports Marketing* [2007] EWCA Civ 461, [2007] 1 WLR 2343. Such covenants will normally be strictly construed; but see *Clarke v Newland* [1991] 1 All ER 397, CA. Covenants in restraint of trade in the National Health Service are governed by normal principles, notwithstanding that the goodwill which the covenants are designed to protect is unsaleable (see the National Health Service Act 2006 s 259, Sch 21; and HEALTH SERVICES vol 54 (2008) PARAS 273–276) and notwithstanding previous authority to the opposite effect (*Kerr v Morris* [1987] Ch 90, [1986] 3 All ER 217, overruling *Hensman v Traill* (1980) 124 Sol Jo 776; and see *Peyton v Mindham* [1971] 3 All ER 1215, [1972] 1 WLR 8, not following *Macfarlane v Kent* [1965] 2 All ER 376, [1965] 1 WLR 1019). An injunction may be granted to prevent breach: see PARA 171. The courts have, in the past, struck down restraints that were aimed at restricting a client's freedom to choose the legal adviser of his choice (see *Oswald Hickson Collier & Co v Carter-Ruck* [1984] AC 720n, [1984] 2 All ER 15, CA; cf *Edwards v Worboys* [1984] AC 724n, [1984] 2 WLR 850n, CA) but have also upheld such covenants as well (see *Bridge v Deacons (a firm)* [1984] AC 705, sub nom *Deacons (a firm) v Bridge* [1984] 2 All ER 19, PC). Where, however, there is a general dissolution of the partnership (see PARA 173 et seq), the partners will not (unless the right to do so has been expressly provided for: see *Peyton v Mindham* [1971] 3 All ER 1215, [1972] 1 WLR 8) be able to enforce such covenants against their co-partners: *Brace v Calder* [1895] 2 QB 253; *Briggs v Oates* [1991] 1 All ER 407, [1990] ICR 473 (applying the principle to a salaried partner); and see PARA 171 (injunctions after dissolution) and PARAS 214–215 (injunctions protecting the value of a firm's goodwill whilst being wound up). As to whether the consideration received in return for the imposition upon it of a covenant in restraint of trade arises from the disposal of an asset for capital gains tax purposes and is therefore taxable see *Kirby (Inspector of Taxes) v Thorn EMI plc* [1988] 2 All ER 947, [1988] 1 WLR 445, CA (company case). As to covenants in restraint of trade generally see COMPETITION vol 18 (2009) PARA 377 et seq.

2   *Rayner v Pegler* (1964) 189 Estates Gazette 967; *Bridge v Deacons (a firm)* [1984] AC 705, sub nom *Deacons (a firm) v Bridge* [1984] 2 All ER 19, PC (where the fact that inadequate consideration was given for the retiring partner's share of goodwill did not of itself lead to the covenant in restraint of trade being held to be unreasonable); but, where the court is considering whether or not the covenant in restraint of trade is severable, the severability of the consideration given for the restraint will be scrutinised (*Sadler v Imperial Life Assurance Co of Canada Ltd* [1988] IRLR 388). The true test of enforceability lies in whether or not the enforcing party is seeking merely to protect his legitimate interests (*Bridge v Deacons (a firm)* [1984] AC 705, sub nom *Deacons (a firm) v Bridge* [1984] 2 All ER 19, PC); and the concept of proportionality as regards the interests to be protected of the covenantor and covenantee respectively has no place in deciding whether a particular covenant is valid or not (*Allied Dunbar (Frank Weisinger) Ltd v Weisinger* [1988] IRLR 60). What is 'reasonable' will be viewed in light of the factual matrix existing at the time the covenant was entered into and of

the object which the covenant was intended to achieve: *Clarke v Newland* [1991] 1 All ER 397, CA (salaried partner's covenant in restraint of trade). It does not matter that, in any event, clients do not wish to continue dealing with the party entitled to protection: *John Michael Design plc v Cooke* [1987] 2 All ER 332, CA (case involving an employee). Even where the court regards a particular covenant as probably void for being unreasonable, the court may enforce it in proceedings for an interim injunction: *Curson & Poole (a firm) v Rash* (1982) 263 Estates Gazette 518, CA (balance of convenience); and see PARA 171.

3 *Espley v Williams* [1997] 08 EG 137, CA (covenant preventing estate agent, for a period of two years, from acting as estate agent in residential property within two miles of former firm upheld).

4 *Bridge v Deacons (a firm)* [1984] AC 705, sub nom *Deacons (a firm) v Bridge* [1984] 2 All ER 19, PC; but see *Clarke v Newland* [1991] 1 All ER 397, CA.

5 *Whitehill v Bradford* [1952] Ch 236 at 245–246, [1952] 1 All ER 115 at 17, CA, per Sir Raymond Evershed MR; but see *Geraghty v Minter* (1979) 26 ALR 141, Aust HC. For an employee's covenant in restraint of trade that was held to be too wide to be enforceable see *Marley Tile Co Ltd v Johnson* [1982] IRLR 75, CA.

6 *Sadler v Imperial Life Assurance Co of Canada Ltd* [1988] IRLR 388; *Business Seating (Renovations) Ltd v Broad* [1989] ICR 729 (both cases involving employees).

(ii) Personal Capacity

28. Minors. There is nothing to prevent a person who has not attained the age of 18[1] from becoming a partner; and, until his contract of partnership is disaffirmed, he is a member of the firm[2]. He will not, however, during his minority incur liability to his co-partners or to third parties for the debts of the firm or for the acts of his co-partners[3]; but, if on behalf of the partnership he enters into contracts with third persons, those contracts bind his adult partners[4]. When the minor reaches the age of 18, or in some cases a younger age, he may choose to repudiate the partnership agreement, in which event his adult co-partners may either seek a restitution order under the Minors' Contracts Act 1987 or insist that the partnership assets are to be applied in payment of the partnership liabilities before he receives anything[5]. A partner who is a minor who commits a wrong, as, for example, by falsely representing his firm to be connected with a stranger's business, may be restrained by injunction and ordered to pay costs[6]; likewise, a minor is liable in equity for fraudulent misrepresentation[7], as by holding himself out as a person of full age[8].

In a claim against partners, a partner who is a minor ought not to be joined as a defendant[9]; and, if the claim is brought against them in the name of the firm and judgment is given against them, it should be entered against the firm exclusive of the minor[10].

On attaining the age of 18, the minor may repudiate the partnership contract[11], but on such repudiation he cannot recover a premium paid by him under a partnership contract on which he has acted[12], if he has derived any real benefit from the contract. It is otherwise if there has been an entire failure of consideration[13]. If he adopts the contract and continues the partnership after attaining his majority, he is liable for the firm's debts contracted during his minority[14], and he cannot claim as against his co-partners to share the profits without also sharing the losses of the concern[15].

1 A person attains full age on attaining the age of 18: see the Family Law Reform Act 1969 s 1(1); and CHILDREN AND YOUNG PERSONS vol 9 (2012) PARA 1.

2 *Lovell and Christmas v Beauchamp* [1894] AC 607 at 611, HL, per Lord Herschell LC.

3 *Harris v Beauchamp Bros* [1893] 2 QB 534, CA; *Lovell and Christmas v Beauchamp* [1894] AC 607 at 611, HL, per Lord Herschell LC.

4 See CHILDREN AND YOUNG PERSONS vol 9 (2012) PARA 16.

5   *Burgess v Merrill* (1812) 4 Taunt 468. See also CHILDREN AND YOUNG PERSONS vol 9 (2012) PARAS 4, 12. As to the effect of the minority of a partner on proceedings for dissolution or winding up see PARA 189.

6   *Chubb v Griffiths* (1865) 35 Beav 127; *Lemprière v Lange* (1879) 12 ChD 675; *Woolf v Woolf* [1899] 1 Ch 343; and see CHILDREN AND YOUNG PERSONS vol 9 (2012) PARA 26.

7   *Re Jones, ex p Jones* (1881) 18 ChD 109 at 120, CA; and see CHILDREN AND YOUNG PERSONS vol 9 (2012) PARA 20.

8   *Re Lees and Smith, ex p Lees, ex p Heatherly* (1836) 1 Deac 705; cf *Ex p Watson* (1809) 16 Ves 264; *Re Bates, ex p Bates* (1841) 2 Mont D & De G 337. No representation that the minor who so trades is of full age arises, however, out of the mere fact of his carrying on the trade: *Re King, ex p Unity Joint Stock Mutual Banking Association* (1858) 3 De G & J 63.

9   *Chandler v Parkes* (1800) 3 Esp 76; *Jaffray v Frebain* (1803) 5 Esp 47; *Gibbs v Merrill* (1810) 3 Taunt 307; *Burgess v Merrill* (1812) 4 Taunt 468.

10   *Lovell and Christmas v Beauchamp* [1894] AC 607 at 613, HL.

11   *Goode v Harrison* (1821) 5 B & Ald 147; see CHILDREN AND YOUNG PERSONS vol 9 (2012) PARA 25.

12   *Holmes v Blogg* (1817) 8 Taunt 35; *Re Burrows, ex p Taylor* (1856) 8 De GM & G 254; *Wilson v Kearse* (1800) Peake Add Cas 196.

13   *Hamilton v Vaughan-Sherrin Electrical Engineering Co* [1894] 3 Ch 589; cf *Corpe v Overton* (1833) 10 Bing 252.

14   *Goode v Harrison* (1821) 5 B & Ald 147. 'A trading of a sort is deposed to, but that was during infancy; if, however, that trading was carried on after the trader became adult, though in a much less degree, the quantity of trading would not make him the less a trader': *Ex p Moule* (1808) 14 Ves 602 at 603 per Lord Eldon LC.

15   *North Western Rly Co v M'Michael, Birkenhead, Lancashire and Cheshire Junction Rly Co v Pilcher* (1850) 5 Exch 114 at 123, 126; *Cork and Bandon Rly Co v Cazenove* (1847) 10 QB 935; *Constantinople and Alexandria Hotel Co, Ebbett's Case* (1870) 5 Ch App 302.

29. Aliens. An alien[1] who is not an enemy may enter into and carry out a contract of partnership in England and Wales with another such alien or with a British national[2]. An alien enemy[3] is incapable of entering into a contract of partnership[4]. If an alien is a partner when he becomes an alien enemy, the partnership is forthwith dissolved[5]. He does not, however, forfeit his rights after dissolution either to his partner or partners or to the Crown, but his ability to enforce these rights is suspended as long as he remains an alien enemy[6]. The partnership which has been dissolved is not reconstituted when he ceases to be an enemy[7]. The incapacity of an alien enemy can be wholly or partially removed by a licence from the Crown[8].

1   As to who are aliens see BRITISH NATIONALITY vol 4 (2011) PARA 411.

2   *Wells v Williams* (1697) 1 Salk 46; *Porter v Freudenberg* [1915] 1 KB 857 at 869, CA; *Johnstone v Pedlar* [1921] 2 AC 262 at 273, 276, 296, HL.

3   As to alien enemies see ARMED CONFLICT AND EMERGENCY vol 3 (2011) PARA 194 et seq.

4   'There can be no partnership between alien enemies and a subject of this country when war has once been declared. Commercial intercourse is prohibited, and immediately that prohibition comes into force it is impossible for the relationship of partners to subsist, at any rate during the war': *R v Kupfer* [1915] 2 KB 321 at 338, CCA, per Lord Reading CJ. See also *Hugh Stevenson & Sons Ltd v AG für Cartonnagen-Industrie* [1918] AC 239, HL; and ARMED CONFLICT AND EMERGENCY vol 3 (2011) PARA 194 et seq. The view expressed by Shearman J in *Feldt v Chamberlain* (1914) 58 Sol Jo 788 that 'the partnership is only dissolved as regards the alien enemy partner and that English partners are not affected', is of doubtful authority. As to the appointment of a receiver and manager where some of the partners have become alien enemies see PARA 162.

5   See note 4.

6   *Hugh Stevenson & Sons Ltd v AG für Cartonnagen-Industrie* [1918] AC 239 at 245, 247, HL.

7   Cf *Porter v Freudenberg* [1915] 1 KB 857 at 873–874, CA.

8   *Princess Thurn and Taxis v Moffitt* [1915] 1 Ch 58; and see *Porter v Freudenberg* [1915] 1 KB 857 at 874, CA.

30. No incapacity on grounds of gender, race etc. It is unlawful for a firm, in relation to a position as partner in the firm, to discriminate against any person because of a protected characteristic[1], namely on the grounds of age, disability, gender reassignment, marriage[2] or civil partnership, pregnancy or maternity, race, religion or belief, sex or sexual orientation[3].

1   See the Equality Act 2010 s 4; and DISCRIMINATION vol 33 (2013) PARA 48 et seq.
2   Marriage of same sex couples is also now lawful in the law of England and Wales, and such marriages have the same effect as marriages of opposite sex couples: see the Marriage (Same Sex Couples) Act 2013 s 1(1), 11(1); and MATRIMONIAL AND CIVIL PARTNERSHIP LAW. It is provided that the law of England and Wales, including all England and Wales legislation whenever passed or made, is to have effect accordingly and that references to marriage and related terms in existing legislation (ie primary legislation passed before 14 May 2014 or subordinate legislation made on or before 17 July 2013) are to be read as including references to marriage of same sex couples, so that, in existing legislation, a reference to 'husband' can mean a man married to a man, or a woman married to a woman, and so on: see s 11(2), (7), Sch 3 para 1; and MATRIMONIAL AND CIVIL PARTNERSHIP LAW. This does not however alter the effect of any private legal instrument (as defined) made before 13 March 2014 and is subject to any contrary provision made by or under the Marriage (Same Sex Couples) Act 2013 or by any new England and Wales legislation (ie primary legislation passed after 14 May 2014 or subordinate legislation made after 17 July 2013): see s 11(7), Sch 4 paras 1(1), (2), 27; and MATRIMONIAL AND CIVIL PARTNERSHIP LAW.
3   See the Equality Act 2010 Pt 2 Ch 2 (ss 13–27), Pt 5 (ss 39–83); DISCRIMINATION vol 33 (2013) PARA 65 et seq; and as to discrimination see further PARA 112.

31. Persons suffering from mental disorder. A partnership agreement entered into by a person apparently sane, where that person is not known by the other parties to be otherwise[1] and where there are no proceedings under the Mental Capacity Act 2005[2] in progress, is binding on him even if in fact he was suffering from a mental disorder at the time[3]. If, however, the other parties knew him to be suffering from a mental disorder, the agreement will be set aside[4].

1   See *Hart v O'Connor* [1985] AC 1000, [1985] 2 All ER 880, PC (contract case); and note 3.
2   Ie under the Mental Capacity Act 2005 s 16, under which the Court of Protection may, by making an order, make decisions or appoint a deputy to make decisions on a person's behalf in relation to matters concerning his personal welfare, or property and affairs where he lacks capacity to do so himself: see MENTAL HEALTH AND CAPACITY vol 75 (2013) PARA 734. See also *Re Marshall, Marshall v Whateley* [1920] 1 Ch 284.
3   *Hart v O'Connor* [1985] AC 1000, [1985] 2 All ER 880, PC (the validity of the contract was to be judged by the same standards as a contract made by a person of sound mind; the fact that there was inequality of bargaining power did not give the person of unsound mind the right to end the contract unless such unfairness amounted to equitable fraud which would have permitted him to avoid the contract if he had been sane).
4   *Molton v Camroux* (1848) 2 Exch 487 (affd (1849) 4 Exch 17); *Imperial Loan Co v Stone* [1892] 1 QB 599, CA; and see MENTAL HEALTH AND CAPACITY vol 75 (2013) PARA 614. As to dissolution on the grounds of mental disorder see PARA 183.

32. Companies and other corporations. A corporation can enter into partnership with an individual person[1], or with another corporation whatever may be its nationality and wherever it may be situate[2]. A local authority may also be a partner[3].

Such partnerships may, however, be illegal if they fail to fulfil statutory requirements. For example, a partnership of professional persons, all of whom are required to be qualified, might be illegal if it included a corporation[4].

Many of the provisions of the Partnership Act 1890 are difficult to apply to corporate bodies[5], especially those dealing with death and bankruptcy[6].

Partnerships with a corporate member are specifically recognised by income tax legislation[7].

1   *Newstead (Inspector of Taxes) v Frost* [1980] 1 All ER 363, [1980] 1 WLR 135, HL. Note that a company's capacity is no longer limited by its constitution and the power of the board of directors to bind the company, or authorise others to do so, is deemed to be free of any limitation under the company's constitution: see the Companies Act 2006 ss 39, 40; and COMPANIES vol 14 (2009) PARAS 263, 265. As to corporate partnerships generally see PARA 1 note 4.

2   See *Hugh Stevenson & Sons Ltd v AG für Cartonnagen-Industrie* [1918] AC 239, HL (partnership between English and German companies); *Hogar Estates Ltd in Trust v Shebron Holdings Ltd* (1979) 25 OR (2d) 543, 101 DLR (3d) 509 (Ont). As to enemy aliens see PARA 29.

3   *Jones v Secretary of State for Wales* (1974) 28 P & CR 280, CA.

4   See PARA 33.

5   See especially the Partnership Act 1890 s 29(2) (see PARA 106), s 30 (see PARA 107), s 33 (see PARAS 175–176), s 36(3) (see PARA 77) and s 39 (see PARA 205).

6   Provisions as to death and bankruptcy can hardly apply to corporations notwithstanding the definition of 'person' in the Interpretation Act 1978 s 5, Sch 1, as including a body of persons corporate or unincorporate.

7   See the Corporation Tax Act 2009 ss 1259–1273; the Corporation Tax Act 2010 Pt 22 Ch 3 (ss 958–962); and INCOME TAXATION vol 59 (2014) PARAS 1941–1943.

(iii) Legality of Partnership

33. Illegality. A partnership may be illegal under statute or at common law. A partnership in the profits of a crime[1] or formed for making profits out of a business which is contrary to public policy or which cannot be carried on except illegally[2] is itself illegal[3]. It may be illegal if one of its partners is an unlicensed or unqualified person[4]. If a partnership has as its object or effect the prevention, restriction or distortion of competition, it will not per se be illegal, although it may be rendered null and void[5] or result in the partnership being referred to the Competition and Markets Authority[6]. Although it may adopt any style or title and may describe itself as a company, and may transfer its shares by delivery of certificates, it must not assume to be nor usurp the rights or powers of a corporation[7].

It is no longer illegal for a solicitor to take into partnership an unadmitted person[8]; nor is it illegal for a solicitor who holds public office to agree that his emoluments are to form part of the profits of his firm[9]; nor for a solicitor to agree to pay part of the profits of his business to an unqualified person[10]; nor for a retired solicitor to permit the use of his name by his former partners[11].

The partnership is dissolved when it becomes an illegal partnership[12]. The knowledge of any partners of the event making it illegal is irrelevant[13].

1   *Everet v Williams* (1725) 2 Pothier on Obligations by Evans 3n, cited in Lindley & Banks on Partnership (19th Edn) para 8–08.

2   See CONTRACT vol 22 (2012) PARA 424 et seq.

3   *Foster v Driscoll, Lindsay v Attfield, Lindsay v Driscoll* [1929] 1 KB 470 at 500–501, CA (agreement held to be void on the ground that it was a breach of international comity). This decision was approved in *Regazzoni v KC Sethia* (1944) Ltd [1958] AC 301, [1957] 3 All ER 286, HL; but see *Re Grazebrook, ex p Chavasse* (1865) 4 De GJ & Sm 655 (blockade running). See also *Biggs v Lawrence* (1789) 3 Term Rep 454; *Clugas v Penaluna* (1791) 4 Term Rep 466 (sale of smuggled goods). A partnership formed for the carrying on of a bookmaking or betting business is illegal if it is intended or contemplated that such a partnership business should be carried on in a manner prohibited by statute: *Thwaites v Coulthwaite* [1896] 1 Ch 496 at 499 per Chitty J; *Jeffrey v Bamford* [1921] 2 KB 351 at 355, 360 per McCardie J (disapproving dictum of Fletcher Moulton LJ in *Hyams v Stuart King* [1908] 2 KB 696 at 718, CA, and opinion of Darling J in *O'Connor and Ould v Ralston* [1920] 3 KB 451); and see also LICENSING AND GAMBLING. As to the effect of a potentially illegal contract upon an arbitration clause contained in the contract see *Harbour Assurance Co (UK) Ltd v Kansa General International Insurance Co Ltd* [1993] QB 701, [1993] 3 All ER 897, CA.

4   The possible statutory restrictions are numerous. See e g the following:

(1) The Gambling Act 2005 s 33 (operating licence required for providing facilities for gambling: see LICENSING AND GAMBLING vol 68 (2008) PARA 615). Provided that a partner in a bookmaking partnership who does not have a bookmaker's licence does not himself secure or negotiate bets, the partnership is not illegal: see *Dungate v Lee* [1969] 1 Ch 545, [1967] 1 All ER 241.

(2) The Solicitors Act 1974 ss 1, 20 (unqualified person not to act as solicitor: see LEGAL PROFESSIONS vol 65 (2008) PARAS 589, 635).

(3) The Estate Agents Act 1979 s 1 (restrictions on the carrying on of estate agency work: see AGENCY vol 1 (2008) PARA 240 et seq).

(4) The Financial Services and Markets Act 2000 s 19 (prohibition on carrying on regulated activities except by authorised or exempt persons: see FINANCIAL SERVICES AND INSTITUTIONS vol 48 (2008) PARA 80).

(5) The Medical Act 1983 s 46 (prohibition on any person not fully registered under the Act from suing for any fee for any medical services rendered: see MEDICAL PROFESSIONS vol 74 (2011) PARA 207).

(6) The Dentists Act 1984 s 38 (prohibition on any persons other than registered dentists and registered dental care professionals from carrying on the practice of dentistry: see MEDICAL PROFESSIONS vol 74 (2011) PARA 425).

(7) The Copyright, Designs and Patents Act 1988 s 276 (prohibition on carrying on business under any name or description which contains the words 'patent agent' or 'patent attorney' unless all the partners are registered patent agents or the partnership satisfies the prescribed conditions: see PATENTS AND REGISTERED DESIGNS vol 79 (2014) PARA 613).

Functions of local authorities under the Estate Agents Act 1979 and the Gambling Act 2005 are 'relevant functions' for the purposes of the Regulatory Enforcement and Sanctions Act 2008 s 4, Sch 3: see LOCAL GOVERNMENT vol 69 (2009) PARA 733. In relation to an offence created under the Estate Agents Act 1979 and the Gambling Act 2005, the Office of Fair Trading, local weights and measures authorities and the Gambling Commission are regulators, and an offence is a relevant offence, for the purposes of the Regulatory Enforcement and Sanctions Act 2008 Pt 3 (ss 36–71) (civil sanctions): ss 37(1), (2), 38(1), (2), Sch 5, Sch 6; and see CONSTITUTIONAL AND ADMINISTRATIVE LAW vol 20 (2014) PARA 331 et seq.

5 See Case IV/30.261 *Re Application of Ideal-Standard GmbH* [1988] FSR 574, EC Commission; and COMPETITION vol 18 (2009) PARA 65 et seq.

6 The Competition and Markets Authority was established under the Enterprise and Regulatory Reform Act 2013, and took over the functions of the former Competition Commission and Office of Fair Trading as from 1 April 2014: see ss 25, 26, Schs 5, 6; the Enterprise and Regulatory Reform Act 2013 (Commencement No 6, Transitional Provisions and Savings) Order 2014, SI 2014/416; and COMPETITION vol 18 (2009) PARA 9 et seq.

7 *Re Mexican and South American Co, Grisewood and Smith's Case, De Pass's Case* (1859) 4 De G & J 544; *Re Mexican and South American Co, Aston's Case* (1859) 4 De G & J 320; *Maugham v Sharpe* (1864) 17 CBNS 443. Cf *Re General Co for Promotion of Land Credit* (1870) 5 Ch App 363; affd sub nom *Princess of Reuss v Bos* (1871) LR 5 HL 176.

8 See the Courts and Legal Services Act 1990 s 66(1) (repealing the Solicitors Act 1974 s 39); and LEGAL PROFESSIONS. See also *Williams v Jones* (1826) 5 B & C 108 (where oral evidence that the written agreement was not intended to take effect until such person was admitted was rejected). See also *Hudgell Yeates & Co v Watson* [1978] QB 451, [1978] 2 All ER 363, CA, where a solicitor allowed his practising certificate to lapse and it was held (following *Martin v Sherry* [1905] 2 IR 62, Ir CA) that the Partnership Act 1890 s 34 and the Solicitors Act 1957 s 18 (repealed: see now the Solicitors Act 1974 s 20), caused dissolution of his partnership, immediately, but that his co-partners instantly comprised among themselves a new partnership by operation of law. See also *Hill v Clifford* [1907] 2 Ch 236, CA (affd [1908] AC 12, HL (dentists struck off register)); *R v Kupfer* [1915] 2 KB 321, CCA.

9 *Clarke v Richards* (1835) 1 Y & C Ex 351; *Sterry v Clifton* (1850) 9 CB 110.

10 *Bunn v Guy* (1803) 4 East 190; *Candler v Candler* (1821) Jac 225 at 231.

11 *Aubin v Holt* (1855) 2 K & J 66.

12 As to dissolution see PARA 173 et seq.

13 *Hudgell Yeates & Co v Watson* [1978] QB 451, [1978] 2 All ER 363, CA.

34. General effect of illegality.

An agreement for an illegal partnership will not be specifically enforced, even though partly performed[1], nor can damages be recovered for breach of it[2]; and, if the whole purpose of the partnership is illegal, the court will not recognise it, or enforce any rights which the supposed partners would otherwise have[3], especially where the parties have agreed to enter, as partners, into a transaction which they know to be illegal[4]. Therefore, an action will not lie for an account of profits of illegal underwriting[5], even though the defendant does not plead the illegality, if it is brought to the notice of the court[6]; and, if the claimant's case discloses the illegality of the transaction, the court will not help him[7]. Where partners are engaged in illegal contracts and one of them pays the whole of the partnership debt in respect of the illegal transaction, he cannot enforce contribution against his partners[8]. It is no part of the duty of the court to aid either in carrying out an illegal contract or in dividing the proceeds arising from an illegal contract between the parties to that illegal contract; and no claim can be maintained either for the one purpose or for the other[9]; but, if a partnership is not illegal in itself, the fact that the partners have evaded a statute is not a bar to a claim by one of them against the others for an account[10].

1   *Ewing v Osbaldiston* (1837) 2 My & Cr 53. As to illegal contracts generally see CONTRACT vol 22 (2012) PARA 424 et seq. As to specific performance generally see SPECIFIC PERFORMANCE vol 95 (2013) PARA 301 et seq.

2   *Duvergier v Fellows* (1828) 5 Bing 248; affd (1832) 1 Cl & Fin 39, HL.

3   *Higginson v Simpson* (1877) 2 CPD 76; but see *Howard v Shirlstar Container Transport Ltd* [1990] 3 All ER 366, [1990] 1 WLR 1292, CA (non-partnership case), where the plaintiff was entitled to enforce a contract and thus benefit from his own fraud, notwithstanding that the purpose of the contract was to perform an illegal act, since (in the exceptional circumstances) to do so was not an affront to the public conscience. See also *Rowan v Dann* (1991) 64 P & CR 202, CA (where the plaintiff who had been negotiating with the defendant in relation to a proposed joint business venture agreement for an illegal purpose was entitled, upon failure of the venture so that the illegal purpose common to both parties had not yet been effected, to resign therefrom and be restored to his original position); and see PARA 33 note 3.

4   *Holman v Johnson* (1775) 1 Cowp 341; *Lees v Smith* (1797) 7 Term Rep 338; *Cousins v Smith* (1807) 13 Ves 542; *De Begnis v Armistead* (1833) 10 Bing 107; *Saffery v Mayer* [1901] 1 KB 11, CA.

5   *Booth v Hodgson* (1795) 6 Term Rep 405; *Aubert v Maze* (1801) 2 Bos & P 371; *Knowles v Haughton* (1805) 11 Ves 168; *Re Scott, ex p Bell* (1813) 1 M & S 751. Partnerships for underwriting were formerly illegal (6 Geo 1 c 18 (Royal Exchange and London Assurance Corporation) (1719)), but this statute was repealed on this point by 5 Geo 4 c 114 (Marine Assurance) (1824) (repealed).

6   *Scott v Brown, Doering, McNab & Co, Slaughter and May v Brown, Doering, McNab & Co* [1892] 2 QB 724, CA; *North Western Salt Co Ltd v Electrolytic Alkali Co Ltd* [1914] AC 461, HL (where a contract is on the face of it illegal, the court will decline to enforce it, whether illegality is pleaded or not; but, where the question of illegality depends upon the surrounding circumstances, then, as a general rule, the court will not entertain the question unless it is raised by the statement of case).

7   *Gedge v Royal Exchange Assurance Corpn* [1900] 2 QB 214; cf *Thomson v Thomson* (1802) 7 Ves 470; and see generally CONTRACT vol 22 (2012) PARA 424 et seq.

8   *Cannan v Bryce* (1819) 3 B & Ald 179, overruling *Faikney v Reynous* (1767) 4 Burr 2069, and *Petrie v Hannay* (1789) 3 Term Rep 418.

9   *Sykes v Beadon* (1879) 11 ChD 170 at 193, 196 per Jessel MR; cf *Foster v Driscoll, Lindsay v Attfield, Lindsay v Driscoll* [1929] 1 KB 470, CA.

10   *Sharp v Taylor* (1849) 2 Ph 801; cf *Tenant v Elliott* (1797) 1 Bos & P 3; *Farmer v Russell* (1798) 1 Bos & P 296; *Thomson v Thomson* (1802) 7 Ves 470; but see *Re South Wales Atlantic Steam Ship Co* (1876) 2 ChD 763, CA. See also PARAS 33, 152.

35.   Enforcement of rights of innocent parties.   A person who has obtained money from his partners for an illegal transaction which he has represented as being legal will not be allowed to keep the money[1]. The members of an illegal association do not lose their legal rights as owners of property[2]. Furthermore, before the illegal purpose is carried out, the court can assist the persons who have contributed money for such a purpose to recover it from the persons who have collected it, and may order those who collected it to render an account[3].

1   *Sykes v Beadon* (1879) 11 ChD 170 at 193, 196 per Jessel MR; cf *Foster v Driscoll, Lindsay v Attfield, Lindsay v Driscoll* [1929] 1 KB 470, CA; and see *Hale v Hale* (1841) 4 Beav 369.
2   *R v Frankland* (1863) Le & Ca 276, CCR.
3   *Greenberg v Cooperstein* [1926] Ch 657; and see *Rowan v Dann* (1991) 64 P & CR 202, CA (joint venturers); and PARAS 33 note 3, 34 note 3.

36. Partial illegality. If the fundamental objects of a partnership are legal, the fact that the partnership agreement or rules contain illegal provisions does not invalidate the whole[1]; and, if the objects of the partnership can, and are intended to, be carried out without any breach of the common law or statute, the fact that one partner has been guilty of illegal acts[2] in the conduct of the business does not make the partnership illegal or prevent an innocent partner from enforcing the partnership obligations[3].

1   *Collins v Locke* (1879) 4 App Cas 674, PC; *Swaine v Wilson* (1889) 24 QBD 252, CA. See also *R v Whitmarsh, Re National Land Co* (1850) 15 QB 600; *Re One And All Sickness and Accident Assurance Association* (1909) 25 TLR 674 (valid trust not illegal association); cf *Greenberg v Cooperstein* [1926] Ch 657 (gain by members, if not by association, enough to make it illegal).
2   Or has failed to comply with the relevant licensing regulations: see *Dodge v Eisenman* (1985) 23 DLR (4th) 711, 68 BCLR 327, BC CA (compromise agreement in a non-partnership business venture). The position may, however, be different with respect to solicitors, barristers and members of other recognised professional bodies: see *Hudgell Yeates & Co v Watson* [1978] QB 451, [1978] 2 All ER 363, CA. As to illegal partnerships generally see PARA 33 et seq.
3   *Harvey v Hart* [1894] WN 72 (following *De Mattos v Benjamin* (1894) 63 LJQB 248, and distinguishing *Higginson v Simpson* (1877) 2 CPD 76); *Thwaites v Coulthwaite* [1896] 1 Ch 496; *Dungate v Lee* [1969] 1 Ch 545 at 550, [1967] 1 All ER 241 at 250. Where the case depends upon the construction of the illegal contract and the defendant's construction is preferred by the court, the defendant may be able to rely on that construction, and he cannot be held to be relying on his own wrong thereby: *Thornton v Abbey National plc* (1993) Times, 4 March, CA (non-partnership case); and see PARAS 33–34.

(iv) Duration of Partnership

37. Duration of partnership. A partnership may be entered into for: (1) a fixed term; (2) a single adventure or undertaking; or (3) an undefined time[1].

Unless otherwise agreed, where the partnership is for a fixed term, it terminates on the expiration of that term[2]. A partnership entered into for a single undertaking is dissolved by the expiry of that undertaking[3]. Where no fixed term has been agreed upon for the duration of the partnership, it is a partnership at will[4] and any partner may determine it at any time on giving notice of his intention to do so to all the other partners[5]. Where a specified term, albeit one of indefinite duration, has been agreed upon, there is no power to dissolve by notice[6].

Where there is no express agreement to continue a partnership for a definite period, there may be an implied agreement to do so[7]. The fact that the partners have bought a lease for a fixed term is not in itself sufficient evidence of such an implied agreement[8], nor is the incurring of debts[9]. The burden of proving such an implied agreement is upon the person who alleges its existence[10], and the provisions relied on must be clearly inconsistent with the general right to dissolve[11]. There is no presumption that a sub-partnership is to be for the same term as the principal partnership[12].

1   See the Partnership Act 1890 s 32.
2   Partnership Act 1890 s 32(a). If a fixed term partnership is continued after the expiry of that term without express new agreement, a partnership at will arises: s 27(1); and see the text and notes 4–5; and PARA 38.

3   Partnership Act 1890 s 32(b). See *Reade v Bentley* (1858) 4 K & J 656; *McClean v Kennard* (1874) 9 Ch App 336. The principle is similar to that where a company is incorporated for the purpose of undertaking a single venture: see *Virdi v Abbey Leisure Ltd* [1990] BCLC 342, [1990] BCC 60, CA. As to the relationship and duties which may exist between persons who are as yet merely negotiating to enter into partnership together see PARA 1 note 2.

4   *Moss v Elphick* [1910] 1 KB 846, CA; *Abbott v Abbott* [1936] 3 All ER 823; *Walters v Bingham, Bingham v Walters* [1988] 1 FTLR 260.

5   Partnership Act 1890 ss 26(1), 32(c). Where the partnership has originally been constituted by deed, a notice in writing, signed by the partner giving it, is sufficient for this purpose: s 26(2); and see *Doe d Waithman v Miles* (1816) 4 Camp 373. The issue and service of a writ (*Unsworth v Jordan* [1896] WN 2, overruling *Shepherd v Allen* (1864) 33 Beav 577) and the service of a defence (*Syers v Syers* (1876) 1 App Cas 174, HL) have also been held to be a sufficient notice. As to the date from which dissolution will be ordered see *Lyon v Tweddell* (1881) 17 ChD 529, CA. 'There is no technicality, no magic as to the mode of expression': *Syers v Syers* (1876) 1 App Cas 174 at 183, HL, per Lord Cairns LC.

 The Court of Protection has power to dissolve a partnership by service of a dissolution notice where a partner lacks capacity because he is unable to make a decision for himself because of an impairment of, or a disturbance in the functioning of, the mind or brain: see the Mental Capacity Act 2005 ss 2, 16, 18(1)(e); and MENTAL HEALTH AND CAPACITY vol 75 (2013) PARAS 603, 727, 734.

 As to dissolution on notice see further PARA 173. As to the notice of dissolution see PARAS 193–195.

6   *Moss v Elphick* [1910] 1 KB 465 (affd [1910] 1 KB 846, CA); *Abbott v Abbott* [1936] 3 All ER 823; *Walters v Bingham, Bingham v Walters* [1988] 1 FTLR 260.

7   *Crawshay v Maule* (1818) 1 Swan 495.

8   *Syers v Syers* (1876) 1 App Cas 174, HL; *Featherstonhaugh v Fenwick* (1810) 17 Ves 298; *Crawshay v Maule* (1818) 1 Swan 495; *Jefferys v Smith* (1820) 1 Jac & W 298 at 301; *Alcock v Taylor* (1830) Taml 506; *Burdon v Barkus* (1862) 4 De GF & J 42. However, a lease by one partner to his firm expires at the end of the term fixed for the partnership, even if expressed to be for a longer period: see *Pocock v Carter* [1912] 1 Ch 663; and LANDLORD AND TENANT vol 62 (2012) PARA 239.

9   *King v Accumulative Life Fund and General Assurance Co* (1857) 3 CBNS 151.

10   *Burdon v Barkus* (1862) 4 De GF & J 42.

11   *Baxter v Plenderleath* (1824) 2 LJOS Ch 119.

12   *Frost v Moulton* (1856) 21 Beav 596. As to sub-partnerships see PARA 111.

38.   Continuation of business.   Where there is a continuation of the business by the partners, or such of them as habitually acted in it during the term, without any settlement or liquidation of the partnership affairs, there is a statutory presumption that the partnership will continue in existence as between those partners[1]. However, the terms upon which the partnership will continue will depend upon whether the continuation stems simply from a dissolution caused by the expiry of a fixed term[2] where the partners (or such of them as habitually acted in it during the term) carry on as before, or whether the reason for the continuation stems not from the expiry of a fixed term but from the admission or departure of a partner[3].

In the former case, where a partnership entered into for a fixed term is continued after the term has expired, and without any express new agreement[4], the rights and duties of the partners remain the same as they were at the expiration of the term, so far as is consistent with the incidents of a partnership at will[5]. Among provisions which are consistent with these incidents are an arbitration clause[6], a power to nominate a successor[7] and, as a general rule, a right of pre-emption[8]. Provisions suitable to an agreement for a term of years are not so consistent, such as clauses in the nature of penalties[9] and, in some cases, rights of pre-emption[10]. The mode of realisation of assets prescribed by an agreement for a term of years may not apply to a dissolution at the end of a subsequent partnership at will[11]; and a surety for one of the partners is discharged by the new agreement for partnership at will which is implied by the continuation of the firm after the term has expired[12]. Clauses providing for the expulsion of a partner may be regarded as consistent with the incidents of a partnership at will so as to survive the expiry of a fixed term, but the position is not clear[13].

In the latter case, where there has been a dissolution caused by the admission or departure of a new partner, there is no such presumption, and the terms of the new partnership, unless contrary agreement is reached between the partners[14], will be those applicable under the Partnership Act 1890[15].

1 Partnership Act 1890 s 27(2); and see PARA 204. See also *Stekel v Ellice* [1973] 1 All ER 465, [1973] 1 WLR 191. In *Hudgell Yeates & Co v Watson* [1978] QB 451, [1978] 2 All ER 363, CA, a partnership was dissolved by operation of law when one partner became unqualified, and it was held that a new partnership among the others commenced immediately. As to the position on dissolution see PARA 204. Once it has been found that a partner leaving a partnership has effectively agreed to retire, this will ex hypothesi imply the continuation of the partnership, albeit as newly constituted; and such retiring partner will not be entitled to a claim for an account and winding up of the firm: *Sobell v Boston* [1975] 2 All ER 282, [1975] 1 WLR 1587; and see *Brown v Rivlin* [1983] CA Transcript 56.

2 See PARA 37.

3 As to admission of partners see PARA 111 et seq.

4 As to what may constitute an express new agreement see *Walters v Bingham, Bingham v Walters* [1988] 1 FTLR 260 (where it was held that a resolution at a partners' meeting, pending the adoption of a new partnership agreement, to continue upon the terms of a draft deed of partnership, which was, like the original term of the partnership, expressed to continue for a fixed term (a term which had already expired as at the date of the partners' meeting), was sufficient to constitute an express new agreement, thus negativing the implication that the partnership continued as a partnership at will).

5 Partnership Act 1890 s 27(1). See *King v Chuck* (1853) 17 Beav 325; *Essex v Essex* (1855) 20 Beav 442; *Cox v Willoughby* (1880) 13 ChD 863; *Neilson v Mossend Iron Co* (1886) 11 App Cas 298, HL; *Daw v Herring* [1892] 1 Ch 284; *Campbell v Campbell* (1893) 6 R 137, HL; *Murphy v Power* [1923] 1 IR 68, Ir CA (where alternative rights were given, one of which was obviously inapplicable to a partnership at will, and it was held that the benefit of the other alternative could not be claimed). As to partnerships at will see PARAS 37–38.

6 *Cope v Cope* (1885) 52 LT 607; *Gillett v Thornton* (1875) LR 19 Eq 599.

7 *Cuffe v Murtagh* (1881) 7 LR Ir 411.

8 *Brooks v Brooks* (1901) 85 LT 453; *M'Gown v Henderson* 1914 SC 839, Ct of Sess.

9 *Hogg v Hogg* (1876) 35 LT 792.

10 *Yates v Finn* (1880) 13 ChD 839, explained in *Daw v Herring* [1892] 1 Ch 284 at 289–290 per Stirling J; *Murphy v Power* [1923] 1 IR 68, Ir CA.

11 *Woods v Lamb* (1866) 35 LJ Ch 309.

12 *Small v Currie* (1854) 18 Jur 731.

13 *Clark v Leach* (1862) 32 Beav 14; affd (1863) 1 De GJ & Sm 409, not followed in *Walters v Bingham, Bingham v Walters* [1988] 1 FTLR 260.

14 See *Hensman v Traill* (1980) 124 Sol Jo 776 (overruled on other grounds by *Kerr v Morris* [1987] Ch 90, [1986] 3 All ER 217, CA), where it was held that, following the retirement of one of the partners, and in light of the continuing two doctors' conduct thereafter, the two continued in partnership together upon all the old terms save as to the unilateral covenant in restraint of trade which one of the partners had expressly objected to, following the third partner's retirement. See also *Walters v Bingham, Bingham v Walters* [1988] 1 FTLR 260 and *Watts (t/a A A Watts) v Hart (Inspector of Taxes)* [1984] STC 548 (where, with the exception of its land, the assets of a partnership were transferred to a limited company and then, on the company's liquidation, back to the partnership; it was held that, since the partnership had continued to trade during these transfers, the land remained an asset of the partnership and continued throughout to be held on the original basis, namely, as trading stock, not merely as an investment).

15 *Firth v Amslake* (1964) 108 Sol Jo 198 (where, following the entry of a third partner into the practice, one of the two original partners refused to agree to various terms of the new draft partnership deed that was subsequently drawn up; it was held (and despite the fact that all three partners had agreed in principle to sign the draft when it had subsequently been drawn up by the firm's solicitors) that the new three-partner firm had superseded the old two-partner firm so that, since there was no express agreement as to the terms upon which this new partnership

would be operated, a partnership at will, governed by the provisions of the Partnership Act 1890, arose); cf *Austen v Boys* (1857) 24 Beav 598 (affd (1858) 2 De G & J 626); *Zamikoff v Lundy* [1970] 2 OR 8, 9 DLR (3d) 637 (affd sub nom *Whisper Holdings Ltd v Zamikoff* [1971] SCR 933, 19 DLR (3d) 114) (new partner's conduct explicable only on the basis that they had accepted that the partnership was governed by the original partnership agreement).

2. RELATIONS BETWEEN PARTNERS AND THIRD PERSONS

(1) POWER OF ONE PARTNER TO BIND THE FIRM AND LIABILITY OF PARTNERS TO THIRD PERSONS

(i) Contractual Liability

A. GENERAL PRINCIPLES

39. Authority of partners founded on agency. Every partner is an agent of the firm and his other partners for the purpose of the business of the partnership[1]. The acts of every partner who does any act for carrying on, in the usual way, business of the kind carried on by the firm of which he is a member bind the firm and his partners[2], unless the partner so acting has no authority to act for the firm in a particular matter, and the person with whom he is dealing knows that he has no authority, or does not know or believe him to be a partner[3]. An act done by any partner within the scope of his actual or implied authority renders the other partners liable to persons dealing with him as representing the firm[4].

Notice to any partner who habitually acts in the partnership business of any matter relating to partnership affairs operates as notice to the firm, except in the case of a fraud on the firm committed by or with the consent of that partner[5].

A sleeping partner is bound by contracts made by the ostensible partners in the ordinary course of the partnership business[6]. A partner cannot escape liability by merely giving notice that he has sold his share in the business when he has not in fact done so[7]. The death of a partner does not preclude the surviving partner or partners from drawing on the partnership account[8].

1 Partnership Act 1890 s 5; *British Homes Assurance Corpn Ltd v Paterson* [1902] 2 Ch 404. Because of this basic principle it was held in *Re Scientific Investment Pension Plan, Clark v Hicks* (1992) Times, 10 December that, where a solicitor procured the services of partners in his own firm in order to assist him in carrying out his duties as a trustee of a pension plan, he was not an independent trustee as required by the Social Security Pensions Act 1975 and the regulations thereunder. In *Central Motors (Birmingham) v PA & SNP Wadsworth (t/a Pensagain)* [1982] CA Transcript 231, it was held that by reason of the agency which exists between partners, a cheque signed by one partner, below the printed name of the firm, was sufficient to bind the firm, notwithstanding that the firm's bank mandate required both partners to sign each cheque; (obiter) but that, where such agency does not exist, the bank must honour the mandate that it has with its customer. As to the principles of agency see further AGENCY.

2 Partnership Act 1890 s 5; *Mercantile Credit Co Ltd v Garrod* [1962] 3 All ER 1103. The substance and detail of a transaction must be examined to see whether it is the kind of transaction forming part of the ordinary business of a partner: *JJ Coughlan v Ruparelia* [2003] EWCA Civ 1057, 147 Sol Jo LB 905, [2003] All ER (D) 344 (Jul). Once a partnership had treated a particular transaction as part of its business then, whether or not that transaction was part of the regular business of the partnership, the transaction became part of the partnership business, with the consequence that the partnership was bound not merely by the transaction but also by any other liabilities connected with the transaction: *Governor and Co of the Bank of Scotland v Henry Butcher & Co* [2003] EWCA Civ 67, [2003] 2 All ER (Comm) 557.

The Partnership Act 1890 s 5 does not override the statutory provisions (see CONTRACT vol 22 (2012) PARA 222 et seq) requiring a contract to be evidenced by a note or memorandum in writing signed by the party to be charged or by some person lawfully authorised by him to sign: *Brettel v Williams* (1849) 4 Exch 623; *Keen v Mear* [1920] 2 Ch 574.

3 Partnership Act 1890 s 5. As to limitations on authority see PARAS 40, 53. As to the liability of the firm for wrongs committed by a partner acting in the ordinary course of business of the firm or with the authority of his co-partners see s 10; and PARA 69.

4   *Bottomley v Nuttall* (1858) 5 CBNS 122. Cf the Partnership Act 1890 s 6 (see PARA 52) and
    Land v Burton (1935) 79 Sol Jo 180, where it was held that the receipt by a partner of a deposit
    from a person seeking employment in the firm was not within the ordinary course of the
    partnership business of estate agents, surveyors and valuers, and accordingly did not render
    another partner who had attempted to dissolve the partnership liable. See also *United Bank of
    Kuwait v Hammoud, City Trust Ltd v Levy* [1988] 3 All ER 418, [1988] 1 WLR 1051, CA
    (salaried partner in a firm of solicitors gave undertakings to provide security for various loans;
    the lenders, having been led to believe that the requests of the firm's clients arose out of
    exchange control and property transactions, which were matters upon which a solicitor's advice
    might be sought, were held entitled to enforce the undertakings against the firm; the solicitor
    had ostensible authority to act for the firm in the manner in which he had in giving the
    undertakings). In that case, however, since the partner concerned appeared only to be a salaried
    partner, the Partnership Act 1890 s 5 should not have applied to him in any event (see PARA 75
    note 5), although the point does not appear to have been raised in argument on either side.
5   Partnership Act 1890 s 16; and see *Mercantile Credit Co Ltd v Garrod* [1962] 3 All ER 1103. It
    appears that service on a partner of a copy of the memorandum formerly required by the
    Moneylenders Act 1927 s 6(1) (repealed) was not service on another partner: see *John W
    Grahame (English Financiers) Ltd v Ingram* [1955] 2 All ER 320 at 322, [1955] 1 WLR 563 at
    565–566, CA. The reason for the exception of fraud is that a fraudulent partner is unlikely to
    fulfil the duty of passing on the notice to the other partners: see *Re Hampshire Land Co* [1896]
    2 Ch 743 at 749, approved in *Houghton & Co v Nothard Lowe and Wills Ltd* [1928] AC 1 at
    15, HL, and applied in *Kwei Tek Chao (t/a Zung Fu Co) v British Traders and Shippers Ltd*
    [1954] 2 QB 459 at 471, [1954] 1 All ER 779 at 784–785. See COMPANIES vol 14 (2009) PARA
    127.
6   *Beckham v Drake* (1841) 9 M & W 79 (affd on this point sub nom *Drake v Beckham* (1843)
    11 M & W 315, Ex Ch); *Mercantile Credit Co Ltd v Garrod* [1962] 3 All ER 1103. As to the
    meaning of 'sleeping partner' see PARA 4.
7   *Vice v Fleming* (1827) 1 Y & J 227. It would be otherwise if the notice were held to amount to
    an unqualified restriction of future liability: *Vice v Fleming* (1827) 1 Y & J 227.
8   *Backhouse v Charlton* (1878) 8 ChD 444.

40.   Limitations on authority of partners.   If it has been agreed between the
partners that any restriction is to be placed on the power of any one or more of
them to bind the firm, no act done in contravention of the agreement is binding
on the firm with respect to persons having notice of the agreement[1]. The express
or implied authority of a partner cannot, however, be limited by a private
arrangement between the partners of which the person dealing with the partner
has no notice[2], except where the limitation is imposed upon a partner who is not
known or believed by that person to be a partner[3].

An agreement by one partner to transact business in an unusual way does not
bind his partners who have not authorised and have no notice of that
agreement[4].

A partner cannot delegate his authority without the consent, whether express
or implied, of his partners[5]. Acts prima facie within his implied authority do not
bind him or his firm if the person he deals with knows he has no such authority[6].

1   Partnership Act 1890 s 8. See also *Lord Gallway v Mathew and Smithson* (1808) 10 East 264;
    Alderson v Pope (1808) 1 Camp 404n; and PARA 58 text and note 1.
2   *Edmunds v Bushell and Jones* (1865) LR 1 QB 97; cf *Hambro v Burnand* [1904] 2 KB 10, CA;
    Mercantile Credit Co Ltd v Garrod [1962] 3 All ER 1103.
3   See the Partnership Act 1890 s 5; cf *Lloyds Bank Ltd v Swiss Bankverein, Union of London and
    Smiths Bank Ltd v Swiss Bankverein* (1912) 107 LT 309 at 313 per Hamilton J (affd (1913) 108
    LT 143, CA). It was said in *Watteau v Fenwick* [1893] 1 QB 346 (a case of agency) that an
    undisclosed principal was liable for the acts of his agent, even though the agent was neither held
    out as such, nor expressly authorised, but the dictum must be regarded as of doubtful authority:
    see *Kinahan & Co Ltd v Parry* [1910] 2 KB 389 (revsd [1911] 1 KB 459, CA); *Lloyds Bank Ltd
    v Swiss Bankverein, Union of London and Smiths Bank Ltd v Swiss Bankverein* (1912) 107 LT
    309; affd (1913) 108 LT 143, CA. As to the circumstances in which a person dealing with
    someone in a firm is entitled to treat that person as a partner of the firm see *United Bank of
    Kuwait v Hammoud, City Trust Ltd v Levy* [1988] 3 All ER 418, [1988] 1 WLR 1051, CA.

4   *Bignold v Waterhouse* (1813) 1 M & S 255 (agreement to carry parcels free of charge); cf *Land
    v Burton* (1935) 79 Sol Jo 180; *Mercantile Credit Co Ltd v Garrod* [1962] 3 All ER 1103.

5   *Re Robinson, ex p Holdsworth* (1841) 1 Mont D & De G 475.
6   See PARA 58.

B. INSTANCES OF IMPLIED AUTHORITY

41.   Extent of implied authority.   The implied authority of partners will be
affected by any special course of dealing, but apart from this it will not extend to
anything done otherwise than in the usual course of the partnership business[1]
and in the way in which it would usually be done in businesses of that kind[2].
Thus, a bill given by a partner in respect of transactions not relating to the
partnership does not render his partners liable[3].

Where the nature of the partnership has been defined or agreed upon, no
partner has implied authority to compel the others to embark in a different
business[4]. Nor can a change be made in the nature of the partnership business
without either an express agreement or the consent of all existing partners[5]. A
partner has no implied authority to make his co-partners partners with another
person in another business, but may bind them to a partnership with another
person for a single venture[6].

A managing partner has authority to defend a claim brought against the firm
which relates to its usual business[7].

1   *Hasleham v Young* (1844) 5 QB 833. A partner who enters into any contract, eg a bond, which
    is outside the scope of his authority, does not bind his firm but renders himself liable: *Fortune v
    Young* 1918 SC 1, Ct of Sess. What is 'usual' in the type of business in question may vary from
    time to time: see eg *United Bank of Kuwait v Hammoud, City Trust Ltd v Levy* [1988] 3 All ER
    418, [1988] 1 WLR 1051, CA (implied authority of solicitors to give an undertaking); *National
    Commercial Banking Corpn of Australia Ltd v Batty* (1986) 65 ALR 385, Aust HC; and PARA
    69. An assurance by a solicitor that his undertaking is given in the usual course of business is not
    sufficient to bind his partner where, on an objective view, the undertaking had not been given in
    relation to an underlying transaction of a kind which was part of the usual business of a
    solicitor: *Hirst v Etherington* [1999] 31 LS Gaz R 42, [1999] All ER (D) 797, CA. See also
    Customs and Excise Comrs v Evans (t/a The Grape Escape Wine Bar) [1982] STC 342 at 349
    (where Glidewell J said obiter that an appeal against a VAT assessment entered into and
    prosecuted by one partner alone would bind the firm); *Sutherland v Gustar (Inspector of Taxes)*
    [1994] Ch 304, [1994] STC 387, CA (one of six partners entitled to appeal against the
    Commissioners of Inland Revenue notwithstanding the fact that the partner's five co-partners
    objected to the appeal); *Mephistopheles Debt Collection Service (a firm) v Lotay* [1994] 1 WLR
    1064, [1995] 1 BCLC 41, CA (where partners sue in the firm's name, an appeal is an application
    'brought by' all the partners). As to a firm's capacity to sue see PARA 78 et seq. As to the
    authority of a partner in a firm of solicitors to sign a bill of costs due to that firm see the
    Solicitors Act 1974 s 69(1), (2)(a); *Bartletts De Reya v Byrne* (1983) 127 Sol Jo 69; and LEGAL
    PROFESSIONS vol 66 (2009) PARA 956.

2   *Kirk v Blurton* (1841) 9 M & W 284, referred to in *Forbes v Marshall* (1855) 11 Exch 166, and
    in *Stephens v Reynolds* (1860) 5 H & N 513 at 517 per Martin B; *Nicholson v Ricketts* (1860)
    2 E & E 497. See *Re Land Credit Co of Ireland, Weikersheim's Case* (1873) 8 Ch App 831;
    Niemann v Niemann (1889) 43 ChD 198, CA (acceptance of shares); *Mercantile Credit Co Ltd
    v Garrod* [1962] 3 All ER 1103. As to the implied authority of a partner to insure see
    INSURANCE vol 60 (2011) PARA 76.

3   *Re Prothero, ex p Agace* (1792) 2 Cox Eq Cas 312.

4   *Natusch v Irving* (1824) 2 Coop temp Cott 358. An example is adding marine insurance to life
    and fire insurances: *Singleton v Knight* (1888) 13 App Cas 788, PC.

5   See the Partnership Act 1890 s 24(8); and PARA 109.

6   *Mann v D'Arcy* [1968] 2 All ER 172, [1968] 1 WLR 893.

7   *Tomlinson v Broadsmith* [1896] 1 QB 386, CA. As to claims against partners and firms
    generally see PARA 83 et seq.

42.   Acts beyond implied authority.   A partner has no implied authority to execute deeds on behalf of his firm[1]. Nor does the implied authority of a partner extend to acts not usually incidental to the scope of the partnership business, for example the giving of guarantees by a member of a trading firm[2]. A partner has authority to lend the firm's money upon mortgage when such a transaction is part of the ordinary business of the firm[3], but a partner has, as a rule, no authority to take as security any property to which a liability is attached[4]. Although a partner may bind his co-partners to a partnership with a third person for a single venture, he has no authority to bind them to a partnership carrying on another business[5]. A solicitor has no implied authority to accept an appointment as a trustee[6].

1   *Harrison v Jackson* (1797) 7 Term Rep 207; *Marchant v Morton, Down & Co* [1901] 2 KB 829. Although a deed executed by one partner who has implied authority to borrow money may not be valid as a legal mortgage, it may, however, create a good equitable security: *Re Boyd, Re Wilson and Vause, ex p Bosanquet* (1847) De G 432; *Re Briggs & Co, ex p Wright* [1906] 2 KB 209. See also the Partnership Act 1890 s 6; and PARA 52. Even if a partner does have express authority to execute deeds on behalf of his firm, it may yet be very difficult to render his co-partners liable under any deed executed by him; the form of the deed will ultimately determine whether the firm as a whole is bound: see *Marchant v Morton, Down & Co* [1901] 2 KB 829. See also *Combes' Case* (1613) 9 Co Rep 75a; *Wilks v Back* (1802) 2 East 142; *Appleton v Binks* (1804) 5 East 148; *Hall v Bainbridge* (1840) 1 Man & G 42; *Re International Contract Co, Pickering's Claim* (1871) 6 Ch App 525.
2   See PARA 43. For other examples of what may come within a partner's implied authority see the cases cited in PARA 41 notes 1–7.
3   *Re Land Credit Co of Ireland, Weikersheim's Case* (1873) 8 Ch App 831.
4   See *Niemann v Niemann* (1889) 43 ChD 198, CA (where it was held that, in the absence of special authority, there was no power for one partner to accept shares in a company, even if fully paid up, in satisfaction of a debt owed to the firm). See, however, *Re Land Credit Co of Ireland, Weikersheim's Case* (1873) 8 Ch App 831 (shares accepted by a partner in a firm of bankers).
5   *Re European Society Arbitration Acts, ex p British Nation Life Assurance Association Liquidators* (1878) 8 ChD 679; *Mann v D'Arcy* [1968] 2 All ER 172, [1968] 1 WLR 893.
6   *Re Bell's Indenture, Bell v Hickley* [1980] 3 All ER 425 at 437, [1980] 1 WLR 1217 at 1230 per Vinelott J, citing *Re Fryer, Martindale v Picquot* (1857) 3 K & J 317.

43.   Guarantees.   A partner in a trading firm does not have implied authority to give guarantees where such acts are not incidental to the scope of the partnership business[1]. A guarantee signed by one partner in the firm name does not bind the other partners unless it is in the regular line of business of the firm, or unless he has their express authority to give the guarantee[2]. However, in the absence of express authority, it may be sufficient that the partners were subsequently informed of the guarantee[3]. A continuing guarantee or cautionary obligation given either to a firm or to a third person in respect of the transactions of a firm is, in the absence of agreement to the contrary, revoked as to future transactions by any change in the constitution of the firm to which, or of the firm in respect of the transactions of which, the guarantee or obligation was given[4].

1   *Duncan v Lowndes and Bateman* (1813) 3 Camp 478; *Hasleham v Young* (1844) 5 QB 833; *Brettel v Williams* (1849) 4 Exch 623. See also PARA 42.
2   *Crawford v Stirling* (1802) 4 Esp 207; *Sandilands v Marsh* (1819) 2 B & Ald 673; *Brettel v Williams* (1849) 4 Exch 623; *Re Smith, Fleming & Co, ex p Harding* (1879) 12 ChD 557, CA.
3   *Governor and Co of the Bank of Scotland v Henry Butcher & Co* [2003] EWCA Civ 67, [2003] 2 All ER (Comm) 557.
4   Partnership Act 1890 s 18; but see *Universal Co v Yip* [1986] CA Transcript 581 (where it was held that the guarantee that had been given by the defendant to a firm was not revoked by reason of the firm's having been sold and its assets transferred to a limited company). As to guarantee and indemnity see generally FINANCIAL SERVICES AND INSTITUTIONS vol 49 (2008) PARA 1013 et seq.

44.   Bills of exchange.   A partner in a trading firm has implied authority to draw, accept and indorse bills of exchange and other negotiable instruments on behalf of his firm in the ordinary course of its business[1], but not otherwise[2]; and the firm is liable even if the transaction is fraudulent and unauthorised, if the holder has no notice of such fraud[3]. Save in relation to cheques[4] this implied authority does not, however, extend to firms which are not trading partnerships, such as solicitors[5] or commission agents[6]. The fact that a bill is given for a partner's private debt raises a presumption that he had no authority to sign the name of the firm for that purpose and throws the burden of proving such authority on the holder of the bill[7]; and the holder of a bill purporting to bind a firm will be restrained from negotiating it if he knows that it is in fact unauthorised or fraudulent[8]. If, however, a bill is taken in good faith without such knowledge at the time, subsequent knowledge of the misconduct of the partner in giving the security is immaterial[9].

1   *Harrison v Jackson* (1797) 7 Term Rep 207 at 210; *Williamson v Johnson* (1823) 1 B & C 146. The inference to be drawn from a partner signing a printed firm cheque is that he is drawing a cheque on the firm: *Ringham v Hackett* (1980) 124 Sol Jo 201, CA, applied in *Central Motors (Birmingham) v PA & SNP Wadsworth (t/a Pensagain)* [1982] CA Transcript 231 (signature on a cheque below the printed name of the firm by one partner alone bound the firm notwithstanding that, by the firm's mandate, the signature of both partners was required). As to bills of exchange and other negotiable instruments see FINANCIAL SERVICES AND INSTITUTIONS vol 49 (2008) PARA 1400 et seq.
2   *Re Cunningham & Co Ltd, Simpson's Claim* (1887) 36 ChD 532.
3   *Lane v Williams* (1692) 2 Vern 277; *Sutton v Gregory* (1797) Peake Add Cas 150; *Arden v Sharpe and Gilson* (1797) 2 Esp 524; *Wells v Masterman* (1799) 2 Esp 731; *Musgrave v Drake* (1843) 5 QB 185, (1843) 1 Dav & Mer 347; *Wiseman v Easton* (1863) 8 LT 637; *Hogg v Skeen* (1865) 18 CBNS 426; *Bunarsee Dass v Gholam Hossein* (1870) 13 Moo Ind App 358 at 363, PC; *Garland v Jacomb* (1873) LR 8 Exch 216. See PARA 54.
4   See *Laws v Rand* (1857) 3 CBNS 442; *Backhouse v Charlton* (1878) 8 ChD 444; and see *Ringham v Hackett* (1980) 124 Sol Jo 201, CA (no distinction between trading and non-trading partnerships made).
5   *Hedley v Bainbridge* (1842) 3 QB 316; *Garland v Jacomb* (1873) LR 8 Exch 216. Nor has a partner in a firm of solicitors implied authority to give a post-dated cheque: *Forster v Mackreth* (1867) LR 2 Exch 163. As to solicitors generally see LEGAL PROFESSIONS. As to what may constitute a trading partnership see PARA 6 note 1.
6   *Yates v Dalton* (1858) 28 LJ Ex 69; and see AUCTION vol 4 (2011) PARA 6.
7   *Ridley v Taylor* (1810) 13 East 175; *Frankland v M'Gusty* (1830) 1 Knapp 274, PC; *Leverson v Lane* (1862) 13 CBNS 278.
8   *Hood v Aston* (1826) 1 Russ 412.
9   *Swan v Steele* (1806) 7 East 210.

45.   Borrowing money.   The implied power of a partner extends to the borrowing of money for the purposes of the business, where the business is of a kind that cannot be carried on in the usual way without such a power[1], but not for the purpose of providing the capital to be contributed by any individual partner[2]. Where the limit of contribution is fixed by express agreement among the partners, a partner cannot, at all events as between himself and his partners, bind them by borrowing beyond the stipulated sum[3].

1   See e g *Fisher v Tayler* (1843) 2 Hare 218 (on appeal (1843) 2 LTOS 205); *Bank of Australasia v Breillat* (1847) 6 Moo PCC 152 at 194 (ordinary trading partnerships). As to what may constitute a trading partnership see PARA 6 note 1. As to mining partnerships see *Dickinson v Valpy* (1829) 10 B & C 128; *Ricketts v Bennett and Field* (1847) 4 CB 686 and the cases there cited. As to borrowing, for the purposes of the firm, by a partner in his own name see PARA 55. See also MORTGAGE vol 77 (2010) PARA 165 et seq.
2   *Greenslade v Dower* (1828) 1 Man & Ry KB 640.
3   *Re Worcester Corn Exchange Co* (1853) 3 De GM & G 180 at 187.

46.   Pledging assets for partnership debt. A surviving partner can give a valid security on the partnership assets for a partnership debt incurred before the death of his partner[1]. Moreover, this is a general power which a partner continues to possess after the dissolution of the partnership of which he is member in so far as the exercise of such power may be necessary to wind up the affairs of the partnership and to complete transactions begun but unfinished at the time of the dissolution, but not otherwise[2]. In such a case the firm is, however, not bound by the acts of a partner who has become bankrupt[3]; nor after the appointment of a receiver by the court may a partner deal with the partnership assets so as to create a valid security[4].

1   *Re Clough, Bradford Commercial Banking Co v Cure* (1885) 31 ChD 324.
2   Partnership Act 1890 s 38; *Re Litherland, ex p Howden* (1842) 2 Mont D & De G 574; *Butchart v Dresser* (1853) 4 De GM & G 542; *Brown v Kidger* (1858) 3 H & N 853; *Re Bourne, Bourne v Bourne* [1906] 2 Ch 427, CA. This power also applies in relation to any prosecution of the partnership by virtue of the Partnerships (Prosecution) (Scotland) Act 2013 s 1: Partnership Act 1890 s 38 (amended by the Partnerships (Prosecution) (Scotland) Act 2013 s 6(1), (2)). The authority of a partner in these circumstances to pledge the partnership property does not enable him to bind his partners personally (*Blaine v Holland* (1889) 60 LT 285, PC); nor are the other partners liable if the advances have been made solely on the credit of the borrowing partner and not on that of the partnership, and the application of the money to the purposes of the partnership does not in itself make it liable (*Emly v Lye* (1812) 15 East 7; *Smith v Craven* (1831) 1 Cr & J 500).
3   Partnership Act 1890 s 38 proviso. This proviso does not, however, affect the liability of any person who has after the bankruptcy represented himself or knowingly suffered himself to be represented as a partner of the bankrupt: s 38 proviso.
4   *Hills v Reeves* (1882) 30 WR 439; affd 31 WR 209, CA. As to the appointment of a receiver see PARA 161.

47.   Pledging partnership credit or assets for private debt. Where one partner pledges the firm's credit for a purpose apparently not connected with its ordinary course of business[1], the firm is not bound unless he is in fact specially authorised by the other partners[2]. Therefore, a partner who holds shares as trustee for his firm cannot give a valid charge upon them for his private debt to a lender who knows that they belong to the firm[3]; but, if he has power to borrow money, he can give a charge on partnership property for his own debt to a person who has no notice that the property is not his own[4]; and, prima facie, a person who in good faith lends to such a partner on the credit of the partnership is entitled to assume that the transaction is for partnership purposes and authorised, unless he has notice of suspicious circumstances which ought to put him on inquiry[5]. A partner who has pledged the firm's assets for his private debt may not sue, as a member of the firm, to set aside the transaction[6].

1   Note that the Partnership Act 1890 s 7 refers to a purpose 'connected with' the firm's ordinary course of business. As to what may be held to be in the ordinary course of business see PARAS 39, 69.
2   Partnership Act 1890 s 7. Section 7 does not, however, affect any personal liability incurred by an individual partner: s 7. See also MORTGAGE vol 77 (2010) PARA 162 et seq.
3   *Wilkinson v Eykyn* (1866) 14 WR 470.
4   *Tupper v Haythorne* (1815) Gow 135n; *Raba v Ryland* (1819) Gow 132. Such assignment is, however, subject to the partnership debts: *Young v Keighley* (1808) 15 Ves 557.
5   *Reid v Hollinshed* (1825) 7 Dow & Ry KB 444; *Loyd v Freshfield* (1826) 2 C & P 325; *Okell v Eaton and Okell* (1874) 31 LT 330.
6   *Brownrigg v Rae* (1850) 5 Exch 489. An innocent partner may, however, obtain equitable relief: *Midland Rly Co v Taylor* (1862) 8 HL Cas 751; *Piercy v Fynney* (1871) LR 12 Eq 69.

48.   Receipt of debts owing to the firm. A partner has implied authority to receive and give a good discharge for debts due to his firm, but not for a debt owing to one of his partners in his personal capacity[1]. If the partners appoint a person to receive partnership debts, their own implied authority is not revoked[2].

A payment by a debtor of the partnership to one of the partners is prima facie a payment to the partnership[3].

1   *Powell v Brodhurst* [1901] 2 Ch 160.
2   *Bristow and Porter v Taylor* (1817) 2 Stark 50.
3   *Moore v Smith* (1851) 14 Beav 393.

49.   Release of debts and compromise of claims.   Where payment of a debt owing to a firm has been made, a partner in that firm has implied authority to release that debt[1], even where it is released by deed executed by him 'for self and partner'[2]; but under normal principles a mere covenant not to sue by one partner only does not release a partnership debt[3], and a partner has no implied authority to discharge a separate debt of his own by agreeing that it should be set off against a debt due to his firm[4]. A release, not by deed, of one partner by a creditor of the firm does not necessarily release the other partners[5], but a release, by receipt, of one debtor on a joint and several judgment debt has been held to release his co-debtor, where there was no ground for importing into the document an intention to reserve rights against the co-debtor[6]. In the absence of fraud, one partner may release a cause of action in which he and his partners are claimants[7], but he must have express authority to consent to judgment[8], or to refer a dispute to arbitration[9] or to compromise a claim[10]. A managing partner has implied authority to defend a claim against the firm in relation to the partnership business[11].

1   *Hawkshaw v Parkins* (1819) 2 Swan 539; and see CONTRACT vol 22 (2012) PARA 649.
2   *Wilkinson v Lindo* (1840) 7 M & W 81.
3   *Hutton v Eyre* (1815) 6 Taunt 289; *Walmesley v Cooper* (1839) 11 Ad & El 216.
4   *Kendal v Wood* (1870) LR 6 Exch 243; *Piercy v Fynney* (1871) LR 12 Eq 69.
5   *Re Armitage, ex p Good* (1877) 5 ChD 46, CA. An example is where the surrounding circumstances show that the release was limited: see *Re EWA* [1901] 2 KB 642 at 652, CA, per Collins LJ.
6   *Re EWA* [1901] 2 KB 642, CA. As to guarantee and indemnity see generally FINANCIAL SERVICES AND INSTITUTIONS vol 49 (2008) PARA 1013 et seq.
7   *Arton v Booth* (1820) 4 Moore CP 192; *Furnival v Weston* (1822) 7 Moore CP 356; *Barker v Richardson* (1827) 1 Y & J 362. As to claims by partners and firms see PARA 78 et seq.
8   *Hambidge v De la Crouée* (1846) 3 CB 742; cf *Munster v Cox* (1885) 10 App Cas 680, HL.
9   *Stead v Salt* (1825) 3 Bing 101; *Re Crowder, ex p Nolte* (1826) 2 Gl & J 295; *Adams v Bankart* (1835) 1 Cr M & R 681; *Hatton v Royle* (1858) 3 H & N 500. In *Thomas v Atherton* (1878) 10 ChD 185, CA, the co-partners were bound by acquiescence. A reference to arbitration may perhaps be described as being a usual way of carrying on a particular partnership business so as to bring the matter within the scope of the authority of a partner.
10 *Crane v Lewis* (1887) 36 WR 480. A release in compromise of a claim against one partner for damages for a joint tort may release all the members of the firm: *Howe v Oliver* (1908) 24 TLR 781; *Brinsmead v Harrison* (1872) LR 7 CP 547.
11 *Tomlinson v Broadsmith* [1896] 1 QB 386, CA.

50.   Payment of firm's debts.   Each partner has implied authority to pay debts owing by the firm[1]. Part payment of a debt by a partner may be presumed to have been made by him as agent of the firm, and may, therefore, prevent a limitation period from running in favour of his partners[2].

1   The authority of partners is founded on agency: see PARA 39.
2   *Goodwin v Parton and Page* (1880) 42 LT 568, CA. As to the effect which part payment of debts, or payment of interest on debts, by a continuing partner has on the position of a retired partner, see LIMITATION PERIODS vol 68 (2008) PARA 1209.

51.   Powers of attorney.   A general power of attorney[1] in favour of one member of a firm does not confer any authority on his partners[2]. Nor does it generally impose any liability on the firm for his wrongful acts in the exercise of the power[3]. A power of attorney by one partner to another, authorising him to sell all or any of the donor's property, enables him to sell the partnership property[4]. A power of attorney for the purpose of exercising the powers and privileges under a specified deed of partnership has been held not to authorise a notice of dissolution and an assignment of the partnership assets[5].

1   As to powers of attorney generally see AGENCY vol 1 (2008) PARA 16.
2   *Edmiston v Wright* (1807) 1 Camp 88. Where a donor who carried on business on his own account and also in partnership executed two powers of attorney in favour of his wife authorising her to indorse and to accept bills, she was held not to be authorised to accept bills for the purpose of the partnership: *Attwood v Munnings* (1827) 7 B & C 278. Cf *Jacobs v Morris* [1902] 1 Ch 816, CA.
3   *Chilton v Cooke & Sons* (1877) 37 LT 607.
4   *Hawksley v Outram* [1892] 3 Ch 359, CA.
5   *Harper v Godsell* (1870) LR 5 QB 422.

C. ACTS DONE BY AUTHORISED PERSON IN THE FIRM NAME

52.   Acts done and documents executed in the firm name.   An act or instrument relating to the business of the firm done or executed in the firm name[1], or in any other manner showing an intention to bind the firm, by any person thereto authorised, whether a partner or not, is binding on the firm and all the partners[2]. A deed executed by one partner for himself and his partner in the presence of the latter binds both[3].

Where, however, goods ordered by two partners in the joint partnership name are delivered to one only and accepted by him on behalf of another business of his own, the other partner is not liable for their price[4]. Similarly, where a partner, acting on behalf of the firm, makes a contract of a personal character for a term of years with a person who does not know of the partnership, that person can put an end to the contract on the death of the partner[5].

1   Statute may make provision for a firm's signature on instruments executed on behalf of the firm: see e g the Solicitors Act 1974 s 69(1), (2)(a), (2A), (2B); *Bartletts De Reya v Byrne* (1983) 127 Sol Jo 69; and LEGAL PROFESSIONS vol 66 (2009) PARA 956. As to the firm name see PARA 7.
2   Partnership Act 1890 s 6; and see the cases cited in PARA 54 note 3. The general rules of law relating to the execution of deeds and negotiable instruments are not affected by this provision: s 6 proviso. As to bills of exchange and other negotiable instruments see FINANCIAL SERVICES AND INSTITUTIONS vol 49 (2008) PARA 1400 et seq. As to deeds generally see DEEDS AND OTHER INSTRUMENTS. As to what acts are within a partner's implied authority for the purposes of s 5 (and, therefore, what actions by a partner will bind his firm) see generally PARAS 41–51.
3   *Ball v Dunsterville* (1791) 4 Term Rep 313; *Burn v Burn* (1798) 3 Ves 573 at 578. As to the execution of deeds generally see DEEDS AND OTHER INSTRUMENTS vol 32 (2012) PARA 227 et seq. As to whether a partner has implied authority to execute a deed on behalf of his firm see PARA 42.
4   *Re Christopher, ex p Harris* (1816) 1 Madd 583 (where, as the deliverers of goods knew, there had been a dissolution of the firm in the interval between the order for and the delivery of the goods in question). As to the liability of a retired partner generally see PARA 76.
5   *Robson v Drummond* (1831) 2 B & Ad 303; c f *Stevens v Benning* (1854) 1 K & J 168 (affd (1855) 6 De GM & G 223).

D. ACTS DONE IN NAME OF INDIVIDUAL PARTNER

53.   Contracts and execution of documents.   A partner cannot bind the others by a guarantee apparently unconnected with the partnership[1], but he may do so where a mutual authority is proved by a previous course of practice of, or by adoption of, the partners, or by the usage of similar partnerships[2]. An approval of a draft agreement signed by one member of a firm may bind the other partners[3], and a contract for a lease signed by one partner has been held to bind the others where an analogous oral contract had been entered into and possession taken by all[4].

1   *Duncan v Lowndes and Bateman* (1813) 3 Camp 478; *Hasleham v Young* (1844) 5 QB 833. As to the execution of deeds by a partner on behalf of the firm as a whole, and as to the extent to which such a deed will bind his co-partners, see PARA 42 note 1.

2   *Brettel v Williams* (1849) 4 Exch 623 at 629, 630, commenting on *Ex p Gardom* (1808) 15 Ves 286.

3   *Brogden v Metropolitan Rly Co* (1877) 2 App Cas 666, HL.

4   *Sharp v Milligan* (1856) 22 Beav 606; and see *City of London Gas Light and Coke Co v Nicholls* (1826) 2 C & P 365 (all partners liable for the gas supplied to the firm's place of business although leased to one of them only). A deed signed by one partner only, not as an escrow, may bind him, even though it is not binding on the others: *Bowker v Burdekin* (1843) 11 M & W 128; and see *Cumberlege v Lawson* (1857) 1 CBNS 709; *Lascaridi v Gurney* (1863) 9 Jur NS 302; *Fortune v Young* 1918 SC 1; *Harrison v Povey, London County Freehold and Leasehold Properties Ltd v Harrison and Povey* (1956) 168 Estates Gazette 613.

54.   Bills of exchange.   A bill drawn on a firm, and accepted by a partner in the firm's name and in his own, may bind the firm, but, if it does so, it does not bind him separately[1]. A bill given for partnership purposes by a partner in his own name, and not in the firm's name, does not bind the other partners[2]; but, if given in a name which the court finds to be intended for and substantially identical with, or habitually used as, that of the firm, although not strictly accurate, it binds the other partners[3].

1   *Re Barnard, Edwards v Barnard* (1886) 32 ChD 447, CA. Nor is the partner severally liable if the bill is accepted by the partner 'for the partnership and self': *Malcomson v Malcomson* (1878) 1 LR Ir 228. See also the Bills of Exchange Act 1882 s 23 proviso (2). As to bills of exchange and other negotiable instruments see FINANCIAL SERVICES AND INSTITUTIONS vol 49 (2008) PARA 1400 et seq.

2   *Re Adansonia Fibre Co, Miles' Claim* (1874) 9 Ch App 635. As to the effect of a cheque given in the firm's name and signed by only one partner where the firm's bank mandate required both partners to sign all such cheques see PARA 44.

3   *Williamson v Johnson* (1823) 1 B & C 146 (where bill was given in the name of 'H & F' instead of 'H & Co'); *South Carolina Bank v Case* (1828) 8 B & C 427, explained in *Nicholson v Ricketts* (1860) 2 E & E 497, and in *Re Adansonia Fibre Co, Miles' Claim* (1874) 9 Ch App 635; *Faith v Richmond* (1840) 11 Ad & El 339, where those members of the firm who used the name were held liable but not the firm itself.

55.   Money used by the firm.   The mere fact that money borrowed by a partner in his own name on security belonging to him personally has been used for the purposes of his firm with the knowledge of his partners does not render them liable[1]. There is no implication of law, from the mere existence of a trading partnership, that a partner has authority to bind the firm by opening a bank account on its behalf in his own name[2].

1   *Bevan v Lewis* (1827) 1 Sim 376. He may, however, be entitled to be indemnified by them: *Browne v Gibbins* (1725) 5 Bro Parl Cas 491, HL; *Re Oundle Union Brewery Co, Croxton's Case* (1852) 5 De G & Sm 432.

2   *Alliance Bank Ltd v Kearsley* (1871) LR 6 CP 433. As to a partner's implied authority to borrow on behalf of the firm see PARA 45 et seq. As to the meaning of 'trading partnership' see PARA 6 note 1.

56.   Promises to pay the firm's debt. If a partner promises in his own name to pay a debt of his firm, he alone is liable on the promise, and he cannot raise the defence that the debt was a joint liability[1].

1   *Murray v Somerville* (1809) 2 Camp 98n.

57.   Admissions and representations. An admission or representation made by any partner concerning the partnership affairs, and in the ordinary course of its business[1], is evidence against the firm[2].

1   As to what may be held to be in the ordinary course of business see PARAS 39, 69.
2   Partnership Act 1890 s 15; and see CIVIL PROCEDURE vol 11 (2009) PARA 819.

E.   RATIFICATION, REPUDIATION AND ACQUIESCENCE

58.   Ratification, repudiation and acquiescence in unauthorised acts by co-partners. Transactions which would prima facie be within the implied authority of a partner do not bind his firm if he has, in fact, to the knowledge of the person dealing with him, no authority to carry out these transactions[1].

When a partner exceeds his authority, the other partners may, however, adopt the transaction, and are then bound by it[2]; and they may be bound if they have notice of the transaction and raise no objection. Notice to that partner is not notice to the others[3]; nor is notice to a clerk employed by a partnership of unauthorised transactions by a partner constructive notice to an individual partner who has no actual knowledge of those transactions[4].

If a partner's unauthorised acts become known to his co-partner, who merely complains of them without taking any further step, and allows a record of them to remain in the firm books, the co-partner may be bound by the doctrine of acquiescence[5].

A firm may be permitted to ratify a partner's unauthorised acts only if it also ratifies other acts connected with them[6].

1   See the Partnership Act 1890 ss 5, 8; *Lord Galway v Matthew and Smithson* (1808) 1 Camp 403; *Heilbut v Nevill* (1869) LR 4 CP 354 (affd (1870) LR 5 CP 478). The holder of a bill indorsed or accepted by one partner cannot sue the other partners if he knew, when he took the bill, that that partner had no authority to indorse or accept it: *Arden v Sharpe and Gilson* (1797) 2 Esp 524; *Lord Galway v Matthew and Smithson* (1808) 1 Camp 403; *Heilbut v Nevill* (1869) LR 4 CP 354 (affd (1870) LR 5 CP 478); *Hogarth v Latham & Co* (1878) 3 QBD 643, CA. Cf *Greenslade v Dower* (1828) 7 B & C 635. Where the name of the firm is that of one of the partners who does not carry on a separate business, a bill drawn or accepted in such name is presumed to be a partnership bill, unless it is proved to have been given as the bill of the individual partner and not of the firm: *Yorkshire Banking Co v Beatson (1), Leeds and County Banking Co v Beatson* (1879) 4 CPD 204; affd on different grounds (1880) 5 CPD 109, CA. Cf *Re Blackburn, ex p Bolitho* (1817) Buck 100; *Lloyd v Ashby* (1831) 2 B & Ad 23; but see *Wintle v Crowther* (1831) 1 Cr & J 316.
2   *Willis v Dyson* (1816) 1 Stark 164. As to the conditions which must exist to constitute a binding adoption of acts a priori unauthorised see *Marsh v Joseph* [1897] 1 Ch 213 at 246, CA, per Lord Russell of Killowen CJ; and see AGENCY vol 1 (2008) PARAS 66–67. In case of the repudiation of a contract entered into by one partner within the scope of his authority, the partnership is liable for everything done under the contract before receipt of notice of repudiation by the party contracting with the partner, or subsequently in respect of liabilities already incurred: *Smith v Ure* (1833) 2 Knapp 188, PC.
3   *Williamson v Barbour* (1877) 9 ChD 529 at 536.
4   *Lacey v Hill, Leney v Hill* (1876) 4 ChD 537 at 549, CA; affd sub nom *Read v Bailey* (1877) 3 App Cas 94, HL.
5   *Cragg v Ford* (1842) 1 Y & C Ch Cas 280 at 285. As to acquiescence see EQUITABLE JURISDICTION vol 47 (2014) PARA 252 et seq.

6   The unauthorised obtaining of bank drafts by a partner could not be ratified unless the subsequent misdealing with them was also ratified: *Commercial Banking Co of Sydney Ltd v Mann* [1961] AC 1, [1960] 3 All ER 482, PC; and see *Lipkin Gorman (a firm) v Karpnale Ltd* [1991] 2 AC 548, [1992] 4 All ER 512, HL.

(ii) Non-contractual Liability

59.   Civil and criminal liability of the firm.   Where, by any wrongful act or omission of any partner acting in the ordinary course of the business of the firm[1], or with the authority of his co-partners, loss or injury is caused to any person not being a partner in the firm, or any penalty is incurred, the firm is liable to the same extent as the partner so acting or omitting to act[2]. This provision of the Partnership Act 1890[3] is not confined to torts[4] or other common law wrongs; it applies whenever injury is caused to a non-partner, or any penalty is incurred by any wrongful act or omission of any partner[5]. The section is concerned only with fault-based liability[6]. It therefore applies to the misapplication of money (despite this being specifically covered by another provision of the Act)[7] and extends also to crimes[8].

Every partner is liable jointly with his co-partners and also severally for everything which the firm becomes liable in this way while he is a partner[9]. The firm is therefore liable for torts[10], equitable wrongs[11] and crimes[12] committed by partners in the ordinary course of the partnership business.

1   As to what may be held to be in the ordinary course of business see PARAS 39, 69.
2   See the Partnership Act 1890 s 10; and PARA 69.
3   Ie the Partnership Act 1890 s 10: see the text and notes 1–3.
4   See PARAS 60–64. As to liability for torts generally see TORT vol 97 (2010) PARA 401 et seq.
5   *Dubai Aluminium Co Ltd v Salaam* [2002] UKHL 48, [2003] 2 AC 366 at [103] per Lord Millett.
6   *Dubai Aluminium Co Ltd v Salaam* [2002] UKHL 48, [2003] 2 AC 366 at [103] per Lord Millett.
7   Ie the Partnership Act 1890 s 11, which deals specifically with the misapplication of money or property received: see PARA 66. See also s 13 (improper employment of trust property); and PARA 67. The following distinction was drawn between these provisions by Lord Millett in *Dubai Aluminium Co Ltd v Salaam* [2002] UKHL 48 at [110]–[111], [2003] 2 AC 366 at [110]–[111]: 'The Partnership Act 1890 ss 11, 13 are not concerned with wrongdoing or with vicarious liability but with the original liability of the firm to account for receipts ... The innocent partners are not vicariously liable for the misappropriation, which will have occurred outside the ordinary course of the firm's business. But they are liable to restore the money if the requirements of the general law of knowing receipt are satisfied. ... The critical distinction between s 10 on the one hand and ss 11 and 13 on the other is not between liability at common law and liability in equity, but between vicarious liability for wrongdoing and original liability for receipts. The firm (s 10) and its innocent partners (s 9) are vicariously liable for a partner's conduct provided that three conditions are satisfied: (1) his conduct must be wrongful, that is to say it must give rise to fault-based liability and not, for example, merely receipt-based liability in unjust enrichment; (2) it must cause damage to the claimant; and (3) it must be carried out in the ordinary course of the firm's business'.
8   See PARA 65; and CRIMINAL LAW vol 25 (2010) PARA 108.
9   See the Partnership Act 1890 s 12; and PARA 69.
10 See PARAS 60 et seq, 69.
11 As to equitable wrongs see PARA 67.
12 As to criminal liability see PARA 65.

60.   Liability for negligence.   Partners are jointly and severally liable[1] for the negligence[2] of one partner in the ordinary course of the partnership business[3].

1   As to joint and several liability for torts under the Partnership Act 1890 s 10 see PARA 69.
2   *Ashworth v Stanwix* (1861) 3 E & E 701 (injury to employee caused by partner's negligence); *Mellors v Shaw and Unwin* (1861) 1 B & S 437; *Kirkintilloch Equitable Co-operative*

Society Ltd v Livingstone 1972 SLT 154 (negligence of a single partner in his work as an auditor). As to the principles of liability for negligence generally see NEGLIGENCE.

3   As to what may be held to be in the ordinary course of business see PARAS 39, 69.

61.   Liability for misrepresentation.   Innocent partners are liable for the misrepresentations of one of their partners in matters connected with the ordinary business of the firm[1].

1   *Rapp v Latham* (1819) 2 B & Ald 795. As to joint and several liability for torts under the Partnership Act 1890 s 10 see PARA 69. As to misrepresentation generally see MISREPRESENTATION. As to what may be held to be in the ordinary course of business see PARAS 39, 69.

62.   Liability for trespass.   One partner is not liable for the trespass of another unless committed with his knowledge or ratified by him[1].

1   *Petrie v Lamont* (1841) Car & M 93; and see *Thomas v Atherton* (1878) 10 ChD 185 at 196, CA. As to trespass generally see TORT vol 97 (2010) PARA 562 et seq. As to joint and several liability for torts under the Partnership Act 1890 s 10 see PARA 69.

63.   Liability for malicious prosecution.   If a partner maliciously prosecutes a person for stealing the partnership property, it would seem that neither the firm nor the other partners are liable to a claim for malicious prosecution and wrongful imprisonment merely because the property was partnership property[1].

1   *Arbuckle v Taylor* (1815) 3 Dow 160, HL. As to malicious prosecution generally see TORT vol 97 (2010) PARA 627 et seq. As to joint and several liability for torts under the Partnership Act 1890 s 10 see PARA 69.

64.   Liability for defamation.   In a defamation claim against a firm where all the partners had published the libel but each could claim qualified privilege, only the partner against whom malice was shown was held liable[1].

1   *Meekins v Henson* [1964] 1 QB 472, [1962] 1 All ER 899. As to defamation generally see DEFAMATION vol 32 (2012) PARA 501 et seq. As to joint and several liability for torts under the Partnership Act 1890 s 10 see PARA 69.

65.   Criminal liability.   The provision of the Partnership Act 1890 which renders the firm liable to the same extent as the wrong-doing partner where he acts in the ordinary course of the business of the firm, or with the authority of his co-partners[1] applies to crimes[2] as well as torts[3], and the other partners themselves may therefore face prosecution[4].

A person may be criminally liable if false descriptions are made recklessly by his partner and he does not actively disassociate himself from them[5].

A firm may be liable for the fraud of a partner in certain circumstances[6]. A firm cannot acquire property in goods obtained by the fraud of one partner to which the rest are not privy if they are obtained by the partner with a preconceived design of raising money upon them and then absconding without payment[7].

1   Ie the Partnership Act 1890 s 10: see PARA 69.
2   See the references in the Partnership Act 1890 s 10 to 'any wrongful act or omission' and to 'any penalty incurred': see PARA 69.
3   See PARAS 60 et seq, 69.
4   See *Clode v Barnes* [1974] 1 All ER 1166, [1974] 1 WLR 544 (partner convicted of offence under the Trade Descriptions Act 1968 as he was deemed to be a joint supplier of car to which the false description had been applied by the other partner). As to lack of separate legal personality for partnerships see PARA 2.

5 *Parsons v Barnes* [1973] Crim LR 537, DC. As to a partner's liability for his co-partner's driving offence see *Bennett v Richardson* [1980] RTR 358, DC.

6 *Cleather v Twisden* (1884) 28 ChD 340, CA (other partners not liable for fraud); *Hughes v Twisden* (1886) 55 LJ Ch 481 (solicitors); and see *National Commercial Banking Corpn of Australia v Batty* (1986) 65 ALR 385, Aust HC (accountants); *United Bank of Kuwait v Hammoud, City Trust Ltd v Levy* [1988] 3 All ER 418, [1988] 1 WLR 1051, CA (solicitor gave undertaking to firm's clients' prospective lenders knowing that the firm did not have sufficient funds to justify the undertaking; firm held liable). See also *Dubai Aluminium Co Ltd v Salaam* [2002] UKHL 48, [2003] 2 AC 366 (co-partners held liable for A's dishonest assistance in a fraudulent scheme in drafting bogus agreements because these acts were so closely connected with the acts A was authorised to do that they might fairly and properly be regarded as done by him while acting in the ordinary course of the firms' business); and PARA 69.

7 *Kilby v Wilson* (1825) Ry & M 178 at 181 per Abbott CJ.

66. Misapplication of money. Where one partner acting within the scope of his apparent authority receives the money or property of a third person and misapplies it[1], or where a firm in the course of its business[2] receives money or property of a third person, and the money or property so received is misapplied by one or more of the partners while it is in the custody of the firm[3], the firm is liable to make good the loss[4]. Every partner is liable jointly with his co-partners and also severally for everything for which the firm becomes liable, while he is a partner, under this provision[5]. Liability may similarly be incurred under the provision which renders the firm liable to the same extent as the wrong-doing partner where, in acting in the ordinary course of the business of the firm, or with the authority of his co-partners, loss or injury is caused to any person not being a partner in the firm, or any penalty is incurred[6].

1 Partnership Act 1890 s 11(a).
2 As to what may be held to be in the ordinary course of business see PARAS 39, 69.
3 Partnership Act 1890 s 11(b).
4 Partnership Act 1890 s 11; *Marquise de Ribeyre v Barclay* (1857) 23 Beav 107; *Re Collie, ex p Adamson* (1878) 8 ChD 807, CA. The firm will not be liable where the money misapplied was not received by it in the course of its business, but as a result of a contract entered into with the defaulting partner individually and not as a member of the firm: *New Mining and Exploring Syndicate Ltd v Chalmers and Hunter* 1912 SC 126. The partners will be jointly and severally liable for misappropriation of money where an undertaking, within the scope of the partnership business, had been given by one partner to apply money, paid to him by a client of the firm, for a specific purpose: *Atkinson v Mackreth* (1866) LR 2 Eq 570.

'[The Partnership Act 1890] s 11 and s 13 are both concerned with third party money received by the firm. Section 11 deals with money which is properly received by the firm (or by one of the partners acting within the scope of his apparent authority) for and on behalf of the third party but which is subsequently misapplied. The firm is liable to make good the loss. Section 13 is concerned with money held by a partner in some other capacity, such as trustee, which is misapplied by him and then improperly and in breach of trust employed by him in the partnership business. His partners can be made liable only in accordance with the ordinary principles of knowing receipt': *Bass Brewers Ltd v Appleby* [1997] 2 BCLC 700 at 711, CA, per Millett LJ. As to the Partnership Act 1890 s 13 see PARA 67.

5 Partnership Act 1890 s 12. The provision referred to is s 11: see the text and notes 1–4.
6 See the Partnership Act 1890 s 10; and PARA 75.

67. Breach of trust. If a partner who is acting individually as a trustee improperly employs trust property in the business or on the account of the partnership, no other partner is liable for the trust property to the beneficiaries[1]. However, this does not affect any liability incurred by any partner by reason of his having notice of a breach of trust[2]. Nor does it prevent trust money from being followed and recovered from the firm if still in its possession or under its control[3]. Where the other partners are implicated in the breach of trust, the liability arising out of it is joint and several[4].

Where a trustee improperly lends trust money to a firm, and the partners know or ought to be treated as knowing the facts, they themselves are implicated in the breach of trust, and are jointly and severally liable for it[5].

1   Partnership Act 1890 s 13. See *Coomer v Bromley* (1852) 5 De G & Sm 532.
    As to the distinction between the spheres of operation of the Partnership Act 1890 s 11 and s 13 see *Bass Brewers Ltd v Appleby* [1997] 2 BCLC 700 at 711, CA, per Millett LJ; and PARA 72 note 4.
    Whilst the Partnership Act 1890 s 10 (liability of the firm for wrongs committed in the course of business: see PARA 69) can apply to instances of knowing assistance (see *Dubai Aluminium Co Ltd v Salaam* [2002] UKHL 48, [2003] 2 AC 366; *Liggins v Lumsden* [1999–2001] MLRep 601), the Partnership Act 1890 s 13 has been distinguished from s 10 on the basis that breaches of trust do not generally occur in the ordinary course of the business: see *Walker v Stones* [2001] QB 902, [2000] 4 All ER 412, CA; *Dubai Aluminium Co Ltd v Salaam* [2002] UKHL 48 at [134], [2003] 2 AC 366 at [134] per Lord Millett.
2   Partnership Act 1890 s 13 proviso (1); *Re Moxon, ex p Heaton* (1819) Buck 386; *Re Harford, ex p Poulson* (1844) De G 79. See also *Twyford v Trial* (1834) 7 Sim 92, where in special circumstances incoming partners were held not liable although they knew of the breach of trust.
3   Partnership Act 1890 s 13 proviso (2).
4   *Re Acraman, ex p Woodin* (1843) 3 Mont D & De G 399; *Blyth v Fladgate, Morgan v Blyth, Smith v Blyth* [1891] 1 Ch 337 at 353. As to the joint and several liability of partners see PARA 69.
5   *Re Acraman, ex p Woodin* (1843) 3 Mont D & De G 399. As to the circumstances in which liability as constructive trustee may be imposed upon a person see EQUITABLE JURISDICTION vol 47 (2014) PARA 229; TRUSTS AND POWERS vol 98 (2013) PARA 25. It was held in *Re Biddulph, ex p Burton* (1843) 3 Mont D & De G 364 that, where one partner in a firm of bankers who was not a trustee invests trust money in improper securities with the knowledge of his partners, they are jointly liable as bankers but not jointly and severally liable as trustees. In *Re Kent County Gas Light & Coke Co Ltd* [1913] 1 Ch 92 it was held that, in order to give a creditor a right of double proof, there must be distinct contracts made with the firm and the partners.

(iii) Nature of Liability to Third Persons

68.   Joint liability on contracts. A partnership is not a 'person' or legal entity in its own right, but it may sue and be sued in the firm name[1]. A reference in a contract to 'the firm' must be taken to mean the partners themselves[2]. Every partner in a firm is liable jointly with the other partners for all debts and obligations of the firm incurred while he is a partner[3]. A promissory note signed by one partner for himself and his named partners may create only a joint liability even if it begins 'I promise to pay'[4]; and a promissory note given by a firm (and a stranger as surety) has been held only to impose a joint liability on the members of the firm[5]. An undertaking to pay the debts of a third person signed in the firm name and by each partner in his own name, so as to amount to a joint and several guarantee, creates a joint and several liability[6].

1   See PARA 2.
2   See *Sheppard & Cooper Ltd v TSB Bank plc* [1997] 2 BCLC 222, [1996] 12 LS Gaz R 30, CA; *Kelly v Northern Ireland Housing Executive, Loughran v Northern Ireland Housing Executive* [1999] 1 AC 428, [1998] 3 WLR 735, HL; *Dave v Robinska* [2003] ICR 1248, [2003] NLJR 921, [2003] All ER (D) 35 (Jun), EAT; and PARA 2.
3   Partnership Act 1890 s 9. This provision is declaratory of the former law. It is founded on the principle that every partner is an agent of the firm and his other partners for the purpose of the business of the partnership: see s 5; and PARA 39. As to the effect of a joint covenant entered into by partners see DEEDS AND OTHER INSTRUMENTS vol 32 (2012) PARA 462. See also the Civil Liability (Contribution) Act 1978; and PARA 85. As to the liability of the separate estate of a deceased partner see WILLS AND INTESTACY vol 103 (2010) PARA 1235. As to the determination of a partnership contract on the death of a partner see PARA 52 text and note 5.
4   *Re Clarke, ex p Buckley* (1845) 14 M & W 469.

5 *Re Manley, ex p Wilson* (1842) 3 Mont D & De G 57.
6 *Re Smith, Fleming & Co, ex p Harding* (1879) 12 ChD 557, CA.

69. Joint and several liability for wrongs. Where, by any wrongful act[1] or omission of any partner acting in the ordinary course of the business of the firm[2], or with the authority of his co-partners, loss or injury is caused to any person not being a partner in the firm, or any penalty is incurred, the firm is liable to the same extent as the partner so acting or omitting to act[3]. Every partner is liable jointly with his co-partners and also severally for everything for which the firm becomes liable, while he is a partner, under this provision[4]. All the members of a firm are liable for the wrongful acts of a partner which are committed in the ordinary course of business as carried on by that particular firm (even if the transaction in question is not within the usual scope of similar businesses[5]) or to secure an object which would be within the ordinary scope of the partnership business, if attained by legitimate means[6].

1 See note 2.
2 One partner's wrongful act, although not authorised by his co-partners, could nevertheless be said to have been done 'in the ordinary course of the business of the firm' if it could fairly and properly be regarded as done by the partner while acting in the ordinary course of the firm's business; and whether it could be so regarded was for the court to evaluate as a question of law: *Dubai Aluminium Co Ltd v Salaam* [2002] UKHL 48, [2003] 2 AC 366. See also *Flynn v Robin Thompson & Partners (a firm)* (2000) Times, 14 March, CA (assault alleged to have been carried out in court precincts by solicitor could not be said to amount to a wrongful act of a partner acting in the course of the business of the firm); *JJ Coughlan Ltd v Ruparelia* [2003] EWCA Civ 1057, 147 Sol Jo LB 905, [2003] All ER (D) 344 (Jul) (fraudulent investment scheme was so far removed from what a solicitor partner had been authorised to do, his actions could not be regarded as done in the course of the firm's business); cf *McHugh v Kerr* [2003] EWHC 2985 (Ch), [2003] All ER (D) 156 (Dec) (buying and selling of shares is part of the ordinary course of business for a firm of accountants; partnership held liable for partner's fraudulent dealings). As to what may be held to be in the ordinary course of business see also PARA 45.
3 Partnership Act 1890 s 10; and see *Meekins v Henson* [1964] 1 QB 472, [1962] 1 All ER 899. This provision equates the position of a partner with that of an employer or a principal: *Meekins v Henson* [1964] 1 QB 472 at 477, [1962] 1 All ER 899 at 902 per Winn J. Where a partner acts fraudulently and without the scope of his implied authority, his firm is not liable therefor: *National Commercial Banking Corpn of Australia Ltd v Batty* (1986) 65 ALR 385, Aust HC; but see *United Bank of Kuwait v Hammoud, City Trust Ltd v Levy* [1988] 3 All ER 418, [1988] 1 WLR 1051, CA; and PARA 47. As to the power of a partner to bind the firm see the Partnership Act 1890 s 5; and PARA 39.
4 Partnership Act 1890 s 12. The provision referred to is s 10: see the text and notes 1–3.
5 *Rhodes v Moules* [1895] 1 Ch 236, CA.
6 *Hamlyn v Houston & Co* [1903] 1 KB 81 at 85, CA.

(iv) Holding Out as Partners

70. Liability arising from holding out or representation. Anyone who represents himself, or knowingly[1] allows himself to be represented, as a partner may be liable as a partner to third persons[2] and for partnership taxation[3]. He is liable to anyone who on the faith of any such representation has given credit to the firm, whether the representation has or has not been made or communicated to the person so giving credit by or with the knowledge of the apparent partner making the representation or suffering it to be made[4]. Each partner is the agent of the others to make contracts on behalf of the firm[5]. Therefore, the members of the firm are liable as though they were actually partners with, and therefore the agents of, a person who holds himself out as a partner[6]. The liability depends upon the inducement by the representation of a dealing with the firm, so that it will not extend to negligent driving or similar torts[7]. He is estopped from denying the truth of such representation, and is therefore subject to the same liabilities as if he were, in fact, a partner[8], even though he contributes neither capital nor labour, and has no interest in the profits of the business, or is indemnified against all possibility of loss[9], and even if he is employed in it merely as a clerk or servant[10], or, having been a partner, has retired without giving proper notice of that fact[11].

A representation that a person is willing or intends to become a partner is not enough; and persons to whom it is made ought to inquire whether he subsequently became a partner[12].

1   Negligence or carelessness in suffering the representation to be made is not enough to found liability: see *Tower Cabinet Co Ltd v Ingram* [1949] 2 KB 397, [1949] 1 All ER 1033, DC.

2   Partnership Act 1890 s 14(1). See *Nationwide Building Society v Lewis* [1998] Ch 482, [1998] 3 All ER 143, CA (a salaried partner in firm of solicitors who had been held out as a partner cannot be held liable for the firm's negligence in the absence of direct evidence of reliance on that holding out); and *UCB Home Loans Corpn Ltd v Soni* [2013] EWCA Civ 62, [2013] NLJR 208, [2013] All ER (D) 133 (Feb) (solicitor not liable for mortgage fraud committed by former partner: unaware of misrepresentations made by him). As to salaried partners see further PARA 17.

3   *Peter v Customs and Excise Comrs* Man/76/88 (unreported) (person estopped from denying that he was a partner for the purpose of assessment to VAT). The fact that a person allows himself to be held out as a partner cannot, however, confer jurisdiction on the court by estoppel so as to enable it to order that a non-partnership business be wound up as though it were a partnership: *Re C & M Ashberg* (1990) Times, 17 July.

4   Partnership Act 1890 s 14(1); and see PARA 72. 'There can be no doubt that persons may be partners towards the world and yet not be partners as between themselves': *Re Stanton Iron Co* (1855) 21 Beav 164 at 169 per Romilly MR. See also *Jacobsen v Hennekenius* (1714) 5 Bro Parl Cas 482, HL; *Waugh v Carver* (1793) 2 Hy Bl 235 at 246; *Mulford v Griffin* (1858) 1 F & F 145. As to estoppel by representation see ESTOPPEL vol 47 (2014) PARA 355 et seq.

5   See PARA 39 et seq. As to agency generally see AGENCY.

6   *Reynell v Lewis, Wyld v Hopkins* (1846) 15 M & W 517 at 527. The juridical basis for this liability is, however, unclear: see *Hudgell Yeates & Co v Watson* [1978] QB 451 at 467, [1978] 2 All ER 363 at 372, 373, CA, per Waller LJ.

7   *Smith v Bailey* [1891] 2 QB 403, CA, disapproving *Stables v Eley* (1825) 1 C & P 614; and see TORT vol 97 (2010) PARA 401 et seq. As to the ordinary liability of partners for torts see PARAS 59 et seq, 69.

8   The doctrine of holding out is a branch of the doctrine of estoppel: see *Re Fraser, ex p Central Bank of London* [1892] 2 QB 633 at 637, CA, per Lord Esher MR. See also *Mollwo, March & Co v Court of Wards* (1872) LR 4 PC 419 at 435 per Sir Montagu Smith; and ESTOPPEL vol 47 (2014) PARA 361 et seq. Cf *Glossop v Colman* (1815) 1 Stark 25.

9   *Waugh v Carver* (1793) 2 Hy Bl 235 at 246; *Bond v Pittard* (1838) 3 M & W 357.

10 *Peacock v Peacock* (1809) 2 Camp 45; *Ex p Watson* (1815) 19 Ves 459 at 461; *Kirkwood v Cheetham* (1862) 2 F & F 798; cf *Cornelius v Harrison* (1862) 2 F & F 758; *Hardman v Booth* (1863) 1 H & C 803.

11 See PARAS 73, 76 et seq.

12 *Bourne v Freeth* (1829) 9 B & C 632; cf *Reynell v Lewis, Wyld v Hopkins* (1846) 15 M & W 517 at 529; and see MISREPRESENTATION vol 76 (2013) PARA 704.

71.   Who may enforce liability arising from representation. The estoppel[1] can only be relied upon, and the liability be enforced, by persons to whom the representation of partnership has been made and who have acted upon the faith of it[2]. A representation subsequent to the transaction sued upon is not enough to fix liability on the quasi-partner[3]; and a representation limited to a particular concern or class of business may not constitute a general representation so as to create liability in matters not connected with that particular concern or class of business[4]. A general representation to the public is not sufficient unless the person giving credit heard of it and acted upon it[5].

1   Ie the estoppel from denying the truth of a representation of partnership: see PARA 70; and ESTOPPEL.

2 *Re Fraser, ex p Central Bank of London* [1892] 2 QB 633 at 637, CA. See also *M'Iver v Humble* (1812) 16 East 169 at 174; *Lloyd v Ashby* (1825) 2 C & P 138; *Carter v Whalley* (1830) 1 B & Ad 11 at 14.

3 *Baird v Planque* (1858) 1 F & F 344.

4 *De Berkom v Smith and Lewis* (1793) 1 Esp 29.

5 *Ford v Whitmarsh* (1840) H & W 53. 'Each case of this nature must depend on its own circumstances with reference to the effect of the defendant's language and conduct on the plaintiff 's mind': *Lake v Duke of Argyll* (1844) 6 QB 477 at 480. See also *Wood v Duke of Argyll* (1844) 6 Man & G 928.

72. Modes of holding out.

The representation of partnership may be made or communicated either by words, spoken or written, or by conduct[1]; and may be so made or communicated either by the quasi-partner or by a third person[2]. In the latter case, the supposed partner is not bound unless the representation has been made with his knowledge and assent[3]; but, if he has himself made, or expressly or impliedly authorised, such a representation, he is liable even though he may not know that it has been communicated to the person who has acted upon it[4]. In the case of a representation by a third person, it is sufficient if the quasi-partner has been so described as to be clearly identified, even if his name has not been mentioned and may even have been refused[5].

To constitute representation by conduct the acts relied upon must not be ambiguous[6]. A former partner is not held out as a partner merely by the continued use by the firm from which he has retired of a firm name consisting of his surname with the addition of the words '& Co'[7].

1 Partnership Act 1890 s 14(1).

2 *Dickinson v Valpy* (1829) 10 B & C 128 at 140–141; *Martyn v Gray* (1863) 14 CBNS 824 at 839. See also *Walter v Ashton* [1902] 2 Ch 282 (cycles advertised as 'Times cycles'). As to the general distinction between statements of intention and representations of fact see MISREPRESENTATION vol 76 (2013) PARAS 704–705.

3 *Fox v Clifton* (1830) 6 Bing 776 at 794. Assent will bind him, even though it was obtained by promises of irresponsibility or by misrepresentation, if the person to whom he was held out was not a party to such promises or misrepresentation: *Ellis v Schmoeck* (1829) 5 Bing 521; *Collingwood v Berkeley* (1863) 15 CBNS 145; *Maddick v Marshall* (1863) 16 CBNS 387 (affd (1864) 17 CBNS 829, Ex Ch). In *Vice v Lady Anson* (1827) 7 B & C 409 a person who erroneously believed herself to be a partner, and held herself out as such, but not to the plaintiff, was held not to be liable as a partner.

4 Partnership Act 1890 s 14(1).

5 *Martyn v Gray* (1863) 14 CBNS 824.

6 *Edmundson v Thompson and Blakey* (1861) 2 F & F 564. See also *Elite Business Systems UK Ltd v Price* [2005] EWCA Civ 920, [2005] All ER (D) 342 (Jul) (defendant could not reasonably have foreseen that by opening a bank account to assist his son with his business, it would lead third parties to form the view that he was in partnership with his son).

7 *Burchell v Wilde* [1900] 1 Ch 551, CA; *Townsend v Jarman* [1900] 2 Ch 698 at 705; cf *Rosher v Young* (1901) 17 TLR 347. As to the firm name see further PARA 7.

73. Retired and deceased partners.

The rule of estoppel by representation[1] applies to a former partner who has retired without giving proper notice of dissolution[2]. The representation is a continuing one as regards persons who have dealt with the old firm unless and until such notice is given, but not as regards new customers or creditors who never knew that he was a partner[3]. Where, however, on the death of a partner the business is continued by the surviving partners under the old name, the rule does not apply so as to impose liability upon the personal representatives of the late partner for transactions of the surviving partners after his death[4], even as regards old customers or creditors who have no notice of his death; and on this ground the court has refused to restrain the surviving partners from using his name[5].

1   See PARA 70.
2   Cf the Partnership Act 1890 s 36; and PARA 194. See also *Brown v Leonard* (1816) 2 Chit 120.
    The liability would arise in the case of a person ceasing to be a partner if he 'had done business
    with the plaintiff before as a member of a firm or had so publicly appeared as to satisfy a jury
    that the plaintiff must have believed him to be such partner, or if he had suffered the plaintiff to
    continue in and act upon that belief by omitting to give notice that he had ceased to be a
    partner': *Carter v Whalley* (1830) 1 B & Ad 11 at 14 per Parke J. See also ESTOPPEL vol 47
    (2014) PARA 355 et seq.
3   *Waugh v Carver* (1793) 2 Hy Bl 235; *Newsome v Coles* (1811) 2 Camp 617, followed by
    Kay LJ in *Re Fraser, ex p Central Bank of London* [1892] 2 QB 633, CA; *Ex p Watson* (1815)
    19 Ves 459 at 461; *Williams v Keats* (1817) 2 Stark 290; *Scarf v Jardine* (1882) 7 App Cas 345
    at 349, 356, HL.
4   Partnership Act 1890 s 14(2); *Devaynes v Noble, Houlton's Case* (1816) 1 Mer 529 at 616;
    Vulliamy v Noble (1817) 3 Mer 593 at 614.
5   *Webster v Webster* (1791) 3 Swan 490n.

74.   Enforcement of liability of persons held out.   Where judgment has been
obtained against a firm, execution may issue, with the permission of the court,
against a person whose liability arose from holding out[1].

1   See *Davis v Hyman & Co* [1903] 1 KB 854, CA.

(v) Duration of Liability

75.   Commencement of liability.   A person who is admitted as a partner into
an existing firm does not thereby become liable to the firm's creditors for
anything done before he became a partner[1], unless there is some agreement to the
contrary[2].

Where prospective partners have agreed to enter into partnership with effect
from a certain date on terms to be embodied in a formal partnership agreement
to be executed on that date, a partner is nevertheless liable for the debts incurred
by his firm from the date on which the partnership commences trading, even if
the partnership deed is executed at a later date[3], notwithstanding an
arrangement to the contrary between himself and his partners[4].

An agreement for a partnership in certain events does not render the parties
liable for the acts or defaults of each other as partners until the events happen,
unless there has been 'holding out'[5]; and abortive negotiations for a partnership
on the terms of a certain draft agreement are not sufficient to render the parties
liable as partners[6].

1   Partnership Act 1890 s 17(1); *Shirreff v Wilks* (1800) 1 East 48; *Lucas v Beach* (1840) 1
    Man & G 417; *Beale v Mouls* (1847) 10 QB 976; *Newton v Belcher* (1848) 12 QB 921; *Dyke
    v Brewer* (1849) 2 Car & Kir 828; and see *Craufurd v Cocks* (1851) 6 Exch 287. Knowledge by
    a creditor of the old firm that the new partner had joined the firm is not a necessary ingredient
    in determining his liability to that creditor: *Scott v Beale and Bishop* (1859) 6 Jur NS 559.
    Promoters of a bill for a railway are liable from the date of association and not merely from the
    passing of the bill (*Holmes v Higgins* (1822) 1 B & C 74); but it may be questioned whether
    Holmes v Higgins (1822) 1 B & C 74 and *Lucas v Beach* (1840) 1 Man & G 417 were really
    cases of partnership. As to the nature of the relationship between persons who are intending to
    enter into partnership together, where no partnership yet exists, and as to their duties to each
    other, see PARA 1.
2   Thus the fact that a purchaser of goods later agrees to share his profits with another does not
    permit the vendor to sue that other for the price: *Young v Hunter* (1812) 4 Taunt 582. Cf
    Mawman v Gillett (1809) 2 Taunt 325n. Even if a new partner agrees with the firm that he will
    enjoy back-dated rights as a partner, his liability for goods supplied to the firm is not
    back-dated: *Wilsford v Wood* (1794) 1 Esp 181. As to the joint liability of various individuals
    who contribute to one cargo of goods see *Saville v Robertson* (1792) 4 Term Rep 720;
    cf *Gouthwaite v Duckworth* (1810) 12 East 421, followed and applied in *Karmali Abdulla
    Allarakhia v Vora Karimji Jiwanji* (1914) LR 42 Ind App 48, PC, where Lord Dunedin

distinguished *Saville v Robertson* (1792) 4 Term Rep 720. See also PARA 11; cf *Barton v Hanson* (1809) 2 Taunt 49; *Young v Hunter* (1812) 4 Taunt 582.

Novation operates so that a retiring partner may be discharged from existing liabilities by an express or implied agreement to the effect between himself, the members of the firm as newly constituted and the creditor: see the Partnership Act 1890 s 17(3); and PARA 76. An incoming partner may accept pre-existing liabilities of the firm in the same way, but it will be easier to infer novation with respect to future liabilities on a continuing contract than it will be to infer novation as regards existing liabilities incurred prior to the change in the partnership: see *Re Burton Marsden Douglas (a firm); Marsden v Guide Dogs for the Blind Association* [2004] EWHC 593 (Ch) at [28]–[33], [2004] 3 All ER 222 at [28]–[33], per Lloyd J. As to the effect of novation upon contractual liability see CONTRACT vol 22 (2012) PARA 598 et seq.

3   *Battley v Lewis* (1840) 1 Man & G 155 (where the partners began trading on the agreed date); cf *Vere v Ashby* (1829) 10 B & C 288.

4   *Wilson v Lewis* (1840) 2 Man & G 197. If, however, the agreement is executed on the correct date but the business is not in fact commenced for some time thereafter, there can be no implied agency nor, therefore, liability in the intervening period. Equally, if the facts are equivocal or there is nothing to suggest that the partnership agreement commenced on a date earlier or later than that on which the partnership agreement was executed, each partner's agency will be treated as commencing on the date on which the agreement was so executed, and evidence of an oral agreement that it was to commence on a future (ie different) date is inadmissible: *Williams v Jones* (1826) 5 B & C 108. As to the creation of partnerships by written agreement see PARA 23; and as to proving the existence of a partnership by oral evidence see PARA 24.

5   *Dickinson v Valpy* (1829) 10 B & C 128 at 141–142 per Parke J. Quaere whether such liability by 'holding out' can exist where in fact no partnership exists: see *Hudgell Yeates & Co v Watson* [1978] QB 451 at 467, [1978] 2 All ER 363 at 372–373, CA, per Waller LJ. As to 'holding out' as a partner see PARA 70 et seq. A person with an option to become a partner within a certain time is not liable for goods supplied to the firm during that time before he exercises the option (*Gabriel v Evill* (1842) 9 M & W 297), nor in respect of bills drawn during that time (*Gabriel v Evill* and *Dickinson v Valpy* (1829) 10 B & C 128).

6   *Ex p Peele* (1802) 6 Ves 602; *Re Vanderplank, ex p Turquand* (1841) 2 Mont D & De G 339.

76. Liability for debts incurred before a partner's retirement.

A partner who retires from a firm does not thereby cease to be liable for partnership debts or obligations incurred before his retirement[1]; but he may be discharged from any existing liabilities by an agreement to that effect between himself and the members of the firm as newly constituted and the creditors, and this agreement may be either express or inferred as a fact from the course of dealing between the creditors and the firm as newly constituted[2]. The same principles apply when the retiring partner has been only a sleeping partner[3]. Legal costs relating to a claim which is pending when the partner retires are treated as a liability incurred when the solicitor was retained[4].

No agreement between partners with regard to the incidence of a partnership liability can in itself affect the rights of creditors[5]. Therefore, an agreement by continuing partners to indemnify a retiring partner against the partnership debts[6] does not extinguish the joint liability of the partners to creditors, although, as between the partners, the retiring partner is in the position of a surety[7].

1   Partnership Act 1890 s 17(2). See *Roughead v White* 1913 SC 162 (retired partner unsuccessfully claimed to be relieved of his liabilities in respect of bonds entered into during the partnership). In *Welsh v Knarston* 1972 SLT 96 a firm of solicitors negligently failed to begin proceedings before the relevant limitation period expired, and it was held that a partner who had retired after the firm was instructed but before the expiration of the limitation period was jointly liable. The meaning of 'retire' was considered in *Earle v Cow* (1920) 36 TLR 713, where Sargant J held that partners retired when the firm was turned into a limited company. See also *Friends Provident Life and Pensions Ltd v Evans* [2006] EWCA Civ 581, [2006] All ER (D) 388 (Mar).

2   Partnership Act 1890 s 17(3). See *Daniel v Cross* (1796) 3 Ves 277; *Newmarch v Clay* (1811) 14 East 239; *Hobson v Cowley* (1858) 27 LJ Ex 205; *Hooper v Keay* (1875) 1 QBD 178; *Bilborough v Holmes* (1876) 5 ChD 255; *Cripps v Tappin & Co* (1882) Cab & El 13; *Re Head, Head v Head* [1893] 3 Ch 426. Mere knowledge by the creditor of the change of firm is not

sufficient, however, to discharge the retiring partner: *Blew v Wyatt* (1832) 5 C & P 397; and see *Thompson v Percival* (1834) 5 B & Ad 925; *Re Family Endowment Society* (1870) 5 Ch App 118. As to the circumstances which determine whether or not a retiring partner is discharged from liability see *Heath v Percival* (1720) 1 P Wms 682; *Dickenson v Lockyer* (1798) 4 Ves 36; *Bedford v Deakin* (1818) 2 B & Ald 210; *Re Robertson, ex p Gould* (1834) 4 Deac & Ch 547; *Kirwan v Kirwan* (1834) 2 Cr & M 617; *Thompson v Percival* (1834) 5 B & Ad 925; *Hart v Alexander* (1837) 2 M & W 484; *Benson v Hadfield* (1844) 4 Hare 32; *Cummins v Cummins* (1845) 3 Jo & Lat 64 at 87; *Harris v Farwell* (1851) 15 Beav 31; *Spenceley v Greenwood* (1858) 1 F & F 297; *Brinsmead & Son v Locke & Son* (1889) 5 TLR 542; cf *Re Worters, ex p Oakes* (1841) 2 Mont D & De G 234; *Re Smith, Knight & Co, ex p Gibson* (1869) 4 Ch App 662. It is doubtful whether *Lodge v Dicas* (1820) 3 B & Ald 611 and *David v Ellice* (1826) 5 B & C 196 could now be supported. As to implied novation for incoming partners see PARA 75 note 2.

3 *Court v Berlin* [1897] 2 QB 396, CA, followed in *Welsh v Knarston* 1972 SLT 96. Executors of a deceased partner who are entitled to a share of profits but do not take any part in conducting the business are not liable as partners: see *Holme v Hammond* (1872) LR 7 Exch 218. See also WILLS AND INTESTACY vol 103 (2010) PARA 1241. As to the meaning of 'sleeping partner' see PARA 4.

4 *Court v Berlin* [1897] 2 QB 396, CA. It is questionable, however, whether the retiring partner might escape liability for the costs incurred, after he retires, by withdrawing his retainer or by giving notice of dissolution to the solicitor: *Court v Berlin* [1897] 2 QB 396 at 399, CA, per Lord Esher MR and at 401 per A L Smith LJ. See also on this point *Welsh v Knarston* 1972 SLT 96.

5 *Gough v Davies and Gibbons* (1817) 4 Price 200.

6 Even if not expressly agreed, such indemnity will, however, normally be implied when a partner retires: *Gray v Smith* (1889) 43 ChD 208, CA; and see PARA 199.

7 *Rodgers v Maw* (1846) 4 Dow & L 66; and see *Oakeley v Pasheller* (1836) 4 Cl & Fin 207, HL (distinguished in *Swire v Redman* (1876) 1 QBD 536 and in *Oakford v European and American Steam Shipping Co Ltd* (1863) 1 Hem & M 182; followed in *Rouse v Bradford Banking Co Ltd* [1894] AC 586, HL); *Goldfarb v Bartlett and Kremer* [1920] 1 KB 639 (where it was held (following *Rouse v Bradford Banking Co Ltd* [1894] AC 586, HL) that a retiring partner who was liable only as a surety on a bill of exchange under an agreement known to the creditor was released owing to time being given to the principal debtors). Cf *Re Douglas, ex p The Executors of James Douglas* [1930] 1 Ch 342. As to sureties, guarantee and indemnity see generally FINANCIAL SERVICES AND INSTITUTIONS vol 49 (2008) PARA 1013 et seq. An exceptional case in relation to the continuation of a firm's guarantee (and which may have ramifications in relation to a retiring partner's continuing liability under a guarantee given by his firm whilst he was a partner) is *Universal Co v Yip* [1986] CA Transcript 581, where it was held that a guarantee continued to bind the guarantor for the benefit of a firm, notwithstanding that the firm had subsequently been taken over by a limited company; and see PARA 42. The rule in *Devaynes v Noble, Clayton's Case* (1816) 1 Mer 572 also has clear ramifications for a retired partner's continuing liability. However, there has been a trend away from applying the rule where to do so would be impractical or would result in an injustice: see *Barlow Clowes International Ltd (in liquidation) v Vaughan* [1992] 4 All ER 22, CA (company case); and EQUITABLE JURISDICTION vol 47 (2014) PARA 241. Where there is an express covenant to indemnify, the retiring partner or the personal representative of a deceased partner may not insist upon the immediate discharge by the continuing partners of debts for which no demand for payment has been made. The right to enforce the covenant arises when the demand has been made, and not before: *Bradford v Gammon* [1925] Ch 132 at 139.

77. Liability for debts incurred after a partner's retirement. A retiring partner may be liable for subsequent debts if no proper notice of dissolution has been given to the creditors[1], or even if such notice has been given but he has left his name in the firm style[2]; but the estate of a partner who dies, or who becomes bankrupt, or of a partner who, not having been known to a creditor dealing with the firm to be a partner, retires from the firm, is not liable for partnership debts contracted after the date of the death, bankruptcy or retirement respectively[3]. Liability for costs, incurred after the date of retirement, of an action begun before and pending at such date is not for this purpose a subsequent debt[4].

1   See the Partnership Act 1890 s 36(1), (2); and PARAS 194–195; *Parkin v Carruthers* (1800) 3 Esp 248; *Osborne v Harper* (1804) 5 East 225; *Farrar v Deflinne* (1843) 1 Car & Kir 580; *Slack v Parker* (1886) 54 LT 212. As to estoppel by representation of retired partners see PARA 73. As to notices of dissolution see PARAS 193–195.

2   *Williams v Keats* (1817) 2 Stark 290. The rule as to holding out (see PARA 70 et seq) does not apply so as to impose liability on the personal representatives of a deceased partner, where the business is continued by the surviving partners: see PARA 73.

3   Partnership Act 1890 s 36(3); and see *Tower Cabinet Co Ltd v Ingram* [1949] 2 KB 397, [1949] 1 All ER 1033, DC (claimant company did not know the defendant as a partner before the dissolution of the partnership and, therefore, he was not liable for debts contracted with the company after that date). A dormant partner may retire from a firm without giving notice to the world: *Heath v Sansom* (1832) 4 B & Ad 172 at 177 per Patteson J. See also *Evans v Drummond* (1801) 4 Esp 89; *Robinson v Wilkinson* (1817) 3 Price 538; *Crawshay v Maule* (1818) 1 Swan 495; *Dolman v Orchard* (1825) 2 C & P 104; *Western Bank of Scotland v Needell* (1859) 1 F & F 461; *Powles v Page* (1846) 3 CB 16. As to a firm's obligation to state each existing partner's name on all business letters, written orders, invoices, receipts and written demands for payment of business debts see PARAS 7–8.

4   *Court v Berlin* [1897] 2 QB 396, CA; and see PARA 76 note 4.

(2) LEGAL PROCEEDINGS

(i) Claims by Partners and Firms

78.   Firm's capacity to sue. Although a firm is not a legal entity[1], all the members of a firm may sue on a contract made in the firm name[2], or on a contract made by one of them as agent for the firm[3], and, when there is joint damage, all may bring a claim in tort, founded upon such damage[4]. Alternatively, and if the contract upon which the claim is founded was made by only one partner for the benefit of the firm, that partner may sue in his own name without joining his partners as parties[5].

As a matter of procedure[6], partners carrying on business within the jurisdiction must sue or be sued[7] in the name of the firm of which they were partners at the time when the cause of action accrued, unless it is inappropriate to do so[8].

1   See PARAS 1–2.
2   As to the firm name see PARA 7.

3   *Skinner v Stocks* (1821) 4 B & Ald 437; *Cothay v Fennell* (1830) 10 B & C 671; *Alexander v Barker* (1831) 2 Cr & J 133. A continuing partner may be entitled to sue alone on a contract made with him and a retired partner jointly (*Atkinson v Laing* (1822) Dow & Ry NP 16), or made on his behalf, even after dissolution, by a retired partner (*Cox v Hubbard* (1847) 4 CB 317). An active partner might sue without joining his sleeping partner as a claimant (*Leveck v Shaftoe* (1796) 2 Esp 468), but an ostensible partner whose name appeared in the firm was held to be a necessary claimant, even though he was in fact only in receipt of a salary (*Guidon v Robson* (1809) 2 Camp 302). As to a single partner's power to sue alone upon a contract made in his own name but for the benefit of the continuing (not dissolved) firm see note 5. As to a partner's power to prosecute proceedings in relation to matters regarding his firm's taxation see *Customs and Excise Comrs v Evans (t/a The Grape Escape Wine Bar)* [1982] STC 342 obiter per Glidewell J; but see *Re Sutherland & Partners' Appeal* [1994] STC 387, CA; and PARA 41.

4   *Longman v Pole* (1828) Mood & M 223; and see DEFAMATION vol 32 (2012) PARA 527. As to injunctions by firms against third persons see PARA 169.

5   See *Roberts v J W Ward and Son (a firm)* [1985] CA Transcript 71 (where the fact that a partner was seeking to recover an unliquidated sum in respect of losses which he and his co-partners had suffered, so that, to some extent, he was seeking to recover damages for loss that he had not suffered himself, was held to be no bar to his recovering for the full amount of such loss). See also *Hudson v Robinson* (1816) 4 M & S 475; *Driver v Burton* (1852) 17 QB 989. As to a partner's right to sue in his own name alone in relation to the firm's tax liabilities see note 3; and PARA 41 note 1.

6   See CPR 7.2A; *Practice Direction—How to Start Proceedings* PD 7A paras 5A–5C; PARA 79 et seq; and CIVIL PROCEDURE vol 11 (2009) PARA 224. Cases decided under RSC Ord 81 (now repealed), which governed actions by and against partnerships before the advent of CPR 7.2A, are included for illustration. See eg *Roberts v J W Ward and Son (a firm)* [1985] CA Transcript 71; *Meyer & Co v Faber (No 2)* [1923] 2 Ch 421 at 435, 439, CA; *Mephistopheles Debt Collection Service (a firm) v Lotay* [1994] 26 LS Gaz R 36, CA. As to High Court and county court procedure generally see CIVIL PROCEDURE. As to the substitution of a claimant where there has been a mistake as to the existence of a firm, see CPR 19(2); and *Noble Lowndes & Partners v Hadfields Ltd* [1939] Ch 569; *W Hill & Son v Tannerhill* [1944] 1 KB 472, CA.

7   For an exceptional case where it was held that the service of a writ on a partnership was valid, notwithstanding that the partnership had already, and by the date of such service, become a limited company see *Willmott v Berry Bros (a firm)* (1981) 126 Sol Jo 209, CA (newly formed company had taken no steps to inform the public of its incorporation and had continued to trade at its old place of business without apparent change; it was held that, in those circumstances, service upon the partnership could be identified as service upon the same business as that which actually comprised the limited company); and see PARA 83 note 4.

8   See CPR 7.2A; *Practice Direction—How to Start Proceedings* PD 7A paras 5A.1, 5A.3.

79.   Requirement for partnership to be carrying on business in the jurisdiction. Partners[1] may only sue or be sued in the name of the firm[2] if they carry on business within the jurisdiction at the time when the cause of action accrued[3]. If the firm has an office of its own in England and Wales at which a partner or manager is in control carrying on the business, that is sufficient[4]. The fact that a partner resides in, or comes regularly to, England or Wales for the purpose of transacting business for the firm is not sufficient[5]. If the firm has only an office in England and Wales where business for the firm is done by an agent, the question whether it is carrying on business within the jurisdiction depends on the agent's powers and authority[6]. These rules apply to Scottish, Irish or colonial firms in the same manner as they do to foreign firms, for the question does not depend on allegiance but on jurisdiction[7].

1   'Partners' includes persons claiming to be entitled as partners and persons alleged to be partners: CPR 7.2A; *Practice Direction—How to Start Proceedings* PD 7A para 5A.2.

2   As to the firm name see PARA 7.

3   *Practice Direction—How to Start Proceedings* PD 7A para 5A.1. See further CIVIL PROCEDURE.

4   *Shepherd v Hirsch, Pritchard & Co* (1890) 45 ChD 231; *Lysaght v Clark & Co* [1891] 1 QB 552, DC; *Worcester City and County Banking Co v Firbank, Pauling & Co* [1894] 1 QB 784, CA.

5   *Western National Bank of City of New York v Perez, Triana & Co* [1891] 1 QB 304, CA; *Indigo Co v Ogilvy* [1891] 2 Ch 31, CA; *Heinemann & Co v Hale & Co* [1891] 2 QB 83, CA; *Singleton v Roberts, Stocks & Co* (1894) 70 LT 687, DC. A stand taken for nine days at a show may be a fixed place of business sufficient to bring a firm within the jurisdiction: *Dunlop Pneumatic Tyre Co Ltd v AG für Motor und Motorfahrzeugbau vorm Cudell & Co* [1902] 1 KB 342, CA. See further the cases cited in PARA 83 et seq (proceedings against a firm).

6   Thus, it is not sufficient if the agent merely has authority to take orders or to show samples: *Baillie v Goodwin* (1886) 33 ChD 604; *Grant v Anderson & Co* [1892] 1 QB 108, CA, followed and applied in *Okura & Co Ltd v Forsbacka Jernverks Aktiebolag* [1914] 1 KB 715, CA (foreign corporation employed an agent in England); and see *The Lalandia* [1933] P 56. If, however, the agent has power to contract on behalf of the firm, it is otherwise: *Compagnie Générale Trans-Atlantique v Thomas Law & Co, La Bourgogne* [1899] AC 431, HL; *Dunlop Pneumatic Tyre Co Ltd v AG für Motor und Motorfahrzeugbau vorm Cudell & Co* [1902] 1 KB 342, CA; *Thames and Mersey Marine Insurance Co v Societa di Navigazione a Vapore del Lloyd Austriaco* (1914) 111 LT 97, CA.

7   *Worcester City and County Banking Co v Firbank, Pauling & Co* [1894] 1 QB 784 at 787, CA, per Lord Esher MR. A foreign firm may, however, agree to accept service within the jurisdiction: *Tharsis Sulphur and Copper Co Ltd v Société des Métaux* (1889) 58 LJQB 435, DC.

80.   Individual partners suing in firm name. Where the partnership has a name, unless it is inappropriate to do so, claims must be brought in the name under which that partnership carried on business at the time the cause of action accrued[1]. If partners object to one of their number suing a third person in the firm's name, he may be ordered to indemnify them against the costs[2]. Claims by the partnership may be made either against a stranger or against a member of the firm[3].

1 CPR 7.2A; *Practice Direction—How to Start Proceedings* PD 7A para 5A.3. There may have been a change in the personnel of the firm between the date of the cause of action and the issue of the claim form. This is of importance where the firm is the defendant: see PARA 88. See further CIVIL PROCEDURE. As to the firm name see PARA 7.
2 *Whitehead v Hughes* (1834) 2 Cr & M 318; *Seal and Edgelow v Kingston* [1908] 2 KB 579, CA.
3 As to claims by firms against their own partners see PARA 81.

81. Claims by firms against own partners or firms with a common partner. A partnership may bring a claim against its own member, but a firm claiming money due from one of its partners in connection with the firm can only obtain a partnership account[1].

Where two firms share one or more partners, either firm may sue the other in the firm name[2] if both firms carry on business within the jurisdiction[3].

1 See *Meyer & Co v Faber (No 2)* [1923] 2 Ch 421, CA (where it was held that the members of the partnership, either in the firm's name or as individuals, could not sue another member of the partnership for sums which he happened to have in his hands without taking the partnership accounts, the only relief available being in respect of money found to be owing to the other members of the partnership as the result of the taking of an account of partnership dealings); and see PARAS 5 note 1, 134, 157. The court will not require the taking of an account where to do so would serve no useful purpose: see *Brown v Rivlin* [1983] CA Transcript 56, applying *Gopala Chetty v Vijayaraghavachariar* [1922] 1 AC 488, PC; *Sobell v Boston* [1975] 2 All ER 282, [1975] 1 WLR 1587. As to claims for an account see EQUITABLE JURISDICTION vol 47 (2014) PARA 49 et seq; and PARA 149 et seq. As to the nature of the relationship between partners, and as to the remedies which a partner has against his co-partners for breach of the duty of good faith, see PARA 105.
2 As to the firm name see PARA 7.
3 See CPR 7.2A; *Practice Direction—How to Start Proceedings* PD 7A para 5A. See further CIVIL PROCEDURE.

82. Set-off of debt of individual partner. A debt owed by a partner to a third person may not be set off by that third person against a claim for a debt owed by him to the firm[1]. This rule is subject to contrary agreement, and does not apply if the indebted partner was the only apparent owner of the business of the firm when the debt to the firm was incurred[2], or has become the sole owner under an agreement which operates as a novation of the debt owing to the firm[3].

1 *Gordon v Ellis* (1846) 3 Dow & L 803; *Jebsen v East and West India Dock Co* (1875) LR 10 CP 300. Cf *Jackson v Yeats* [1912] 1 IR 267 (where it was held that there was no right of retainer in respect of a debt due by a legatee to the firm in which the testator was a partner); and conversely *Re Pennington and Owen Ltd* [1925] Ch 825, CA (where it was held that a debt due by a partnership firm cannot be set off against a separate debt due to one of the partners). Similarly, where a firm has a bank account at a bank at which a partner also has a private account, it is probably true that debts outstanding in the one account may not be set off against the other unless the partner holds his private account merely as nominee for the firm; sed quaere. For non-partnership cases see *Bhogal v Punjab National Bank, Basna v Punjab National Bank* [1988] 2 All ER 296, CA; *Uttamchandani v Central Bank of India* (1989) 133 Sol Jo 262, CA; but see *MS Fashions Ltd v Bank of Credit and Commerce International SA (in liquidation)* [1993] Ch 425, [1993] 3 All ER 769, CA (where the director of a company which owed money to the insolvent bank and who had guaranteed the company's debt was able to set off the sums he was owed by the bank in his private account against his liability under the guarantee); distinguished in *Re Bank of Credit and Commerce International SA* (1994) Times, 22 March; and see *Stein v Blake* [1994] Ch 16, [1993] 4 All ER 225, CA. As to the nature of a

bank's right of set-off see *Re K* [1990] 2 QB 298, [1990] 2 All ER 562; and CIVIL PROCEDURE vol 11 (2009) PARA 634 et seq. As to set-off in corporate insolvency see COMPANY AND PARTNERSHIP INSOLVENCY vol 17 (2011) PARA 746.

2   *Stracey and Ross v Deey* (1789) 7 Term Rep 361n; *Muggeridge's v Smith & Co* (1884) 1 TLR 166; cf *Baker v Gent* (1892) 9 TLR 159. See also *Spurr v Cass, Cass v Spurr* (1870) LR 5 QB 656.

3   *Burgess v Morton* (1894) 10 TLR 339, CA (revsd [1896] AC 136, HL, solely on the ground that the Court of Appeal was not competent to hear an appeal from a judge determining a question as arbitrator by agreement).

(ii) Claims against Partners and Firms

83.   Claims against partnerships. Two or more persons carrying on business within the jurisdiction[1] must be sued in the name of the firm[2] of which they were partners[3] at the time when the cause of action accrued, unless it is inappropriate to do so[4].

1   As to what amounts to carrying on business within the jurisdiction see PARA 79.
     A foreign firm can agree that service on an agent within the jurisdiction is to be valid (*Montgomery, Jones & Co v Liebenthal & Co* [1898] 1 QB 487, CA), but it cannot agree that the court is to have power to direct service upon it out of the jurisdiction (*British Wagon Co v Gray* [1896] 1 QB 35, CA). In the absence of any such agreement, if a firm does not carry on business within the jurisdiction, it is a foreign firm and the partners must be sued individually, and service of a claim form in the firm name has no effect: *Western National Bank of City of New York v Perez, Triana & Co* [1891] 1 QB 304, CA. See also *Indigo Co v Ogilvy* [1891] 2 Ch 31, CA; *Dobson v Festi, Rasini & Co* [1891] 2 QB 92, CA; *Von Hellfeld v Rechnitzer and Mayer Frères & Co* [1914] 1 Ch 748, CA (service out of the jurisdiction in the firm name upon a foreign partnership not carrying on business in England was set aside, in the absence of evidence that by the foreign law a partnership was a totally different legal entity from the individuals who composed it). If a foreign firm brings a claim within the jurisdiction, a counterclaim may be made against it (*Griendtoveen v Hamlyn & Co* (1892) 8 TLR 231); but cf *South African Republic v La Compagnie Franco-Belge du Chemin de Fer du Nord* [1897] 2 Ch 487, CA (inability to bring an independent claim held not to be a ground for allowing an inconvenient counterclaim). See, however, *Oxnard Financing SA v Rahn* [1998] 3 All ER 19, [1998] 1 WLR 1465, CA, where it was held possible to sue a foreign partnership which was not a corporation and did not carry on business within the jurisdiction in the English courts, either by naming as defendants the individual natural persons who were partners in it, who traded under that name and who were sued in that capacity as partners, or by reference to the partnership entity itself. See further CIVIL PROCEDURE.
2   As to the firm name see PARA 7.
3   See PARA 79 note 1.
4   CPR 7.2A; *Practice Direction—How to Start Proceedings* PD 7A paras 5A.1, 5A.3. See also *Western National Bank of City of New York v Perez, Triana & Co* [1891] 1 QB 304, CA. It is not apparent what circumstances may be deemed 'inappropriate' for these purposes. As to claims against individual partners see PARA 84.

84.   Claims against individual partners. Subject to the requirement to bring claims against the name under which the partnership carried on business at the time the cause of action accrued[1], a claimant may in certain circumstances sue all the partners individually[2]; but then they must all be made defendants. If he sues some only of the partners, the defendants can insist on the other partners being made parties if they are within the jurisdiction and can be found[3]; but an active partner who has ordered goods may be sued alone and cannot plead the joint liability of a sleeping partner as a defence[4].

1   Ie the requirement in CPR 7.2A; *Practice Direction—How to Start Proceedings* PD 7 paras 5A.1, 5A.3; see PARA 83. Prior to the enactment of the Civil Procedure Rules, suing partners in their firm name was optional: see the permissive wording in RSC Ord 81 (repealed).
2   *Practice Direction—How to Start Proceedings* PD 7 para 5A.3 applies only where the partnership has a name, and provides that the claim must be brought against the name under

which the partnership carried on business at the time when the cause of action accrued unless it is inappropriate to do so. The CPR do not define the circumstances that may be deemed 'inappropriate' for these purposes.

3   *Robinson v Geisel* [1894] 2 QB 685 at 687, CA. He need not join a sleeping partner as defendant if his contract had been made with one partner only, who concealed from him the fact of the partnership: see *Mullett v Hook* (1827) Mood & M 88, overruling *Dubois v Ludert* (1814) 5 Taunt 609; *De Mautort v Saunders* (1830) 1 B & Ad 398.

4   *Ex p Hodgkinson* (1815) 19 Ves 291; *Ex p Norfolk* (1815) 19 Ves 455; *Re Starkey and Whiteside, ex p Chuck* (1832) 8 Bing 469.

85.   Unsatisfied judgment against one partner no bar to claim against others.
In a claim to enforce the joint liability of partners, an unsatisfied judgment against one of them is no bar to a future claim against the others[1].

1   Civil Liability (Contribution) Act 1978 s 3, reversing the effect of *King v Hoare* (1844) 13 M & W 494; *Kendall v Hamilton* (1879) 4 App Cas 504, HL. See also *Liverpool Borough Bank v Walker* (1859) 4 De G & J 24; *Plumer v Gregory* (1874) LR 18 Eq 621; *Re Hodgson, Beckett v Ramsdale* (1885) 31 ChD 177, CA; *Blyth v Fladgate, Morgan v Blyth, Smith v Blyth* [1891] 1 Ch 337 at 353; *Re Outram, ex p Ashworth and Outram* (1893) 63 LJQB 308, DC.

86.   Claim against personal representatives. If all the partners are dead, the personal representatives of the last survivor may be sued in respect of a liability of the firm without making the personal representatives of the others defendants[1].

1   *Golding v Vaughan* (1782) 2 Chit 436; *Calder v Rutherford* (1822) 3 Brod & Bing 302; and see WILLS AND INTESTACY vol 103 (2010) PARA 1234 et seq.

87.   Service of claim form on a partnership. The claim form may be served personally on a partnership where partners are being sued in the name of their firm by leaving it with: (1) a partner[1]; or (2) a person who, at the time of service, has the control or management[2] of the partnership business at its principal place of business[3].

Where no solicitor is acting for the party to be served, and the individual who is being sued in the name of the firm has not given an address for service, the document must be sent or transmitted to, or left at his usual or last known residence, or the principal or last known place of business of the firm[4].

Where it appears to the court that there is a good reason to authorise service by a method not permitted by the Civil Procedure Rules, the court may make an order permitting service by an alternative method or at an alternative place[5].

1   CPR 6.5(3)(c)(i). As to service of documents see further CIVIL PROCEDURE vol 11 (2009) PARA 138 et seq.

2   This does not include an agent of the firm whose only duty is to show samples and transmit orders (*Baillie v Goodwin* (1886) 33 ChD 604); or a receiver and manager appointed by the court, since the person served must have control and management under authority from the partners, and must thus be the servant of the firm (*Re Flowers & Co* [1897] 1 QB 14, CA (a bankruptcy case)). See *Kenneth Allison Ltd v AE Limehouse & Co (a firm)* [1992] 2 AC 105, [1991] 4 All ER 500, HL (a case concerning RSC Ord 81 r 3 (now repealed); where service was effected not upon the person having control or management of the partnership business, but upon an employee who had been given express authority by a partner to accept service of proceedings, and the plaintiff relied upon this authorisation by handing the writ to that employee, such service, although not complying with rules of court, did constitute valid service). As to whether service on the person having control or management of the partnership business is good service where the firm has, by the date of service, become incorporated see *Willmott v Berry Bros (a firm)* (1981) 126 Sol Jo 209, CA (service on a defendant firm at its old place of business constituted good service, even though, unbeknown to the plaintiff, the firm had, by that date, already become a limited company; after incorporation the defendant had continued to trade and let itself be known as a partnership).

3   CPR 6.5(3)(c)(ii). Where service was effected upon a person having control and five days later upon a partner, and judgment in default was signed on the first service before the eight days had elapsed from service on the partner, the judgment was set aside: *Alden v Beckley & Co* (1890) 25 QBD 543, DC. As to what comprises a principal place of business see *Weatherley v Calder & Co* (1889) 61 LT 508, DC (partnership); cf *Davies v British Geon Ltd* [1957] 1 QB 1, [1956] 3 All ER 389, CA (company).

4   CPR 6.9(1), (2). Where a claimant has reason to believe that such address of the defendant is an address at which the defendant no longer resides or carries on business, the claimant must take reasonable steps to ascertain the address of the defendant's current residence or place of business ('current address'): CPR 6.9(3). Where, having taken the reasonable steps required by CPR 6.9(3), the claimant ascertains the defendant's current address, the claim form must be served at that address (CPR 6.9(4)(a)); or, if the claimant is unable to ascertain the defendant's current address, the claimant must consider whether there is an alternative place where, or an alternative method by which, service may be effected (CPR 6.9(4)(b)). If, under CPR 6.9(4)(b), there is such a place where or a method by which service may be effected, the claimant must make an application under CPR 6.15 (see the text and note 5): CPR 6.9(5). Where CPR 6.9(3) applies, the claimant may serve on the defendant's usual or last known address in accordance with the table in CPR 6.9(2) where the claimant cannot ascertain the defendant's current residence or place of business and cannot ascertain an alternative place or an alternative method under CPR 6.9(4)(b): CPR 6.9(6).

See *Austin Rover Group v Crouch Butler Savage Associates (a firm)* [1986] 3 All ER 50, [1986] 1 WLR 1102, CA (even where a copy of the writ had been sent to the wrong address, the service would still be treated as good service if the copy did actually come into the hands of a partner at the correct address).

5   CPR 6.15(1). Service by an alternative method (or substituted service as it was formerly called) has, for example, been ordered where there was no person in apparent control and no partner could be served: see *Shillito v Child & Co* [1883] WN 208. See also *Worcester City and County Banking Co v Firbank, Pauling & Co* [1894] 1 QB 784 at 788, CA, per Lord Esher MR (substituted service cannot be ordered upon a partner who is resident out of the jurisdiction by service upon someone in England and Wales); cf *Coles v Gurney* (1815) 1 Madd 187; *Figgins v Ward* (1834) 2 Cr & M 424; *Leese v Martin* (1871) LR 13 Eq 77. As to service out of the jurisdiction see *Practice Direction—Service Out of the Jurisdiction* PD 6B; and CIVIL PROCEDURE vol 11 (2009) PARA 156 et seq.

88.   Acknowledgment of service.   Where a claim is brought against a partnership, service must be acknowledged in the name of the partnership on behalf of all persons who were partners at the time when the cause of action accrued[1]. The acknowledgment of service may be signed by any of those partners, or by any person authorised by any of those partners to sign it[2].

1   *Practice Direction—Acknowledgment of Service* PD10 para 4.4(1). As to acknowledgment of service see further CIVIL PROCEDURE vol 11 (2009) PARAS 184–186.
2   *Practice Direction—Acknowledgment of Service* PD10 para 4.4(2).

89.   Partnership membership statements.   A partnership membership statement is a written statement of the names and last known places of residence of all the persons who were partners in the partnership at the time when the cause of action accrued[1]. If the partners are requested to provide a copy of a partnership membership statement by any party to a claim, the partners must do so within 14 days of receipt of the request[2]. In that request the party seeking a copy of a partnership membership statement must specify the date when the relevant cause of action accrued[3].

1   CPR 7.2A; *Practice Direction—How to Start Proceedings* PD 7A para 5B.1.
2   CPR 7.2A; *Practice Direction—How to Start Proceedings* PD 7A para 5B.2.
3   CPR 7.2A; *Practice Direction—How to Start Proceedings* PD 7A para 5B.3.

90.   Disclosure of partnership books.   If partnership books are produced in a claim relating to the business of the firm, the partners may seal up all entries other than those which relate to the cause of action[1].

1   *Re Pickering, Pickering v Pickering* (1883) 25 ChD 247, CA. As to disclosure of documents see CIVIL PROCEDURE vol 11 (2009) PARA 538 et seq. As to the effect on the firm of admissions or representations made by one partner concerning the partnership affairs see PARA 57. As to the production of books in partnership claims see PARA 136.

(iii) Judgments and Execution against Partners and Firms

91.   Enforcing a judgment or order against a partnership. A judgment or order made against a partnership may be enforced against any property of the partnership within the jurisdiction[1].

A judgment or order made against a partnership may be enforced against any person who is not a limited partner and who:

(1)   acknowledged service of the claim form as a partner[2];

(2)   having been served as a partner with the claim form, failed to acknowledge service of it[3];

(3)   admitted in his statement of case that he is or was a partner at a material time[4]; or

(4)   was found by the court to have been a partner at a material time[5].

However, a judgment or order made against a partnership may not be enforced against a limited partner or a member of the partnership who was ordinarily resident outside the jurisdiction when the claim form was issued unless he:

(a)   acknowledged service of the claim form as a partner[6];

(b)   was served within the jurisdiction with the claim form as a partner[7]; or

(c)   was served out of the jurisdiction with the claim form, as a partner, with the permission[8] of the court[9].

A judgment creditor wishing to enforce a judgment or order against a person in any other circumstances[10] must apply to the court for permission to enforce the judgment or order[11].

1   *Practice Direction—Enforcement of Judgments and Orders* PD 70 para 6A.1. As to execution against partnership property for the separate debt of a partner see PARA 94 et seq.

2   *Practice Direction—Enforcement of Judgments and Orders* PD 70 para 6A.2(1). As to acknowledgment of service see PARA 88.

3   *Practice Direction—Enforcement of Judgments and Orders* PD 70 para 6A.2(2).

4   *Practice Direction—Enforcement of Judgments and Orders* PD 70 para 6A.2(3).

5   *Practice Direction—Enforcement of Judgments and Orders* PD 70 para 6A.2(4). See *Clark v Cullen* (1882) 9 QBD 355, DC; *Western National Bank of City of New York v Perez, Triana & Co* [1891] 1 QB 304, CA; *Re Handford, Frances & Co, ex p Handford, Frances & Co* [1899] 1 QB 566 at 570, CA. It has been suggested that, where one partner dies before the claim is brought or between service of the claim form and judgment, judgment can only be obtained against the surviving partners and be enforced against them and the partnership assets if the legal personal representatives of the deceased partner are added as parties. Where all the partners die after service but before judgment, judgment cannot be entered at all: *Ellis v Wadeson* [1899] 1 QB 714 at 718–719, CA, per Romer LJ. Whether the claim could be continued against the personal representatives depends upon the nature of the claim: see *Kirk v Todd* (1882) 21 ChD 484, CA; *Ellis v Wadeson* [1899] 1 QB 714 at 718, CA. As to the effect of the death of parties and the survival of rights of action see WILLS AND INTESTACY vol 103 (2010) PARA 1279 et seq.

6   *Practice Direction—Enforcement of Judgments and Orders* PD 70 para 6A.3(1).

7   *Practice Direction—Enforcement of Judgments and Orders* PD 70 para 6A.3(2).

8   Ie given under CPR Pt 6 Section IV (CPR 6.30–6.47).

9   *Practice Direction—Enforcement of Judgments and Orders* PD 70 para 6A.3(3).

10 Ie in circumstances not set out in *Practice Direction—Enforcement of Judgments and Orders* PD 70 para 6A.2 or para 6A.3: see the text and notes 2–9.

11 *Practice Direction—Enforcement of Judgments and Orders* PD 70 para 6A.4.

92.   Effect of judgment against a single partner. Judgment for debt or damage recovered against one person is no bar to a claim against any other person jointly liable in respect of the same debt or damage[1]. On the application of a judgment creditor, a partner's share in the firm may be charged[2].

1   See the Civil Liability (Contribution) Act 1978 s 3; and PARA 85 note 1. As to entitlement to contribution see s 1; and TORT vol 97 (2010) PARA 450 et seq. As to a partner's right to indemnity see PARA 137 et seq.
2   See PARA 95.

93.   Attachment of debts owed by a partnership. Where debts are due or accruing due to a judgment creditor from a partnership[1], an interim third party debt order[2] relating to such debts must be served on:

(1)   a member of the partnership within the jurisdiction[3];

(2)   a person authorised by a partner[4]; or

(3)   some other person having the control or management of the partnership business[5].

Where an interim third party debt order requires a partnership to appear before the court, it will be sufficient for a partner to appear before the court[6].

1   *Practice Direction—Third Party Debt Orders* PD 72 para 3A.1.
2   Ie under CPR 72.4(2): see CIVIL PROCEDURE.
3   *Practice Direction—Third Party Debt Orders* PD 72 para 3A.2(1).
4   *Practice Direction—Third Party Debt Orders* PD 72 para 3A.2(2).
5   *Practice Direction—Third Party Debt Orders* PD 72 para 3A.2(3). As to persons having control or management of the partnership business see PARA 87 note 2.
6   *Practice Direction—Third Party Debt Orders* PD 72 para 3A.3.

94.   Enforcement of judgment for separate debts. Execution cannot be levied against partnership property for the separate debt of a partner[1], but the court[2] on the application[3] of the judgment creditor of a partner may make an order charging the share of the partner who is a judgment debtor with payment of the amount of the judgment debt and the interest on it[4].

1   Partnership Act 1890 s 23(1) (amended by the Statute Law Revision Act 1908) ('A writ of execution may not issue on any partnership property except on a judgment against the firm'). As to legal proceedings against a firm generally see PARA 83. As to judgments against firms see PARA 91. A charging order may be made against a partner's interest as such, subject to his co-partner's right to redeem the interest charged: see PARA 97.

2   For these purposes, 'court' means the High Court or the county court: Partnership Act 1890 s 23(2) (amended by the Courts Act 1971 s 56(4), Sch 11 Pt II; and the Crime and Courts Act 2013 s 17(5), Sch 9 para 118). The powers conferred on a judge by the Partnership Act 1890 s 23 may be exercised by a master, the Admiralty Registrar, or a district judge: CPR 73.22; *Practice Direction—Charging Orders, Stop Orders and Stop Notices* PD 73 para 6.3.

3   Applications for an order under the Partnership Act 1890 s 23 made by a judgment creditor of a partner, and applications for any order by a partner of the judgment debtor in consequence of any application made by the judgment creditor under s 23, must be made in accordance with CPR Pt 23: *Practice Direction—Charging Orders, Stop Orders and Stop Notices* PD 73 paras 6.1, 6.2. Every application notice filed by a judgment creditor, and every order made following such an application, must be served on the judgment debtor and on any of the other partners that are within the jurisdiction: *Practice Direction—Charging Orders, Stop Orders and Stop Notices* PD 73 para 6.4. Every application notice filed by a partner of a judgment debtor, and every order made following such an application, must be served on the judgment creditor and the judgment debtor, and on the other partners of the judgment debtor who are not joined in the application and who are within the jurisdiction: *Practice Direction—Charging Orders, Stop Orders and Stop Notices* PD 73 para 6.5. An application notice or order served on one or

more, but not all, of the partners of a partnership is deemed to have been served on all the partners of that partnership: *Practice Direction—Charging Orders, Stop Orders and Stop Notices* PD 73 para 6.6.

4   Partnership Act 1890 s 23(2).

95. Effect of charging order. The effect of a charging order[1] is the same as if the partner had executed or signed a document charging his share with the debt[2]. Such an order is valid even if the indebted partner is a person suffering from a mental disorder[3], but may not be made over a deceased partner's share held by his executors[4]. If the indebted partner becomes a bankrupt, the charging order does not take priority over the title of his trustee in bankruptcy[5].

1   As to the procedure to be followed when applying for a charging order see PARA 94.

2   *Brown, Janson & Co v A Hutchinson & Co* [1895] 2 QB 126 at 131, CA; and see the Partnership Act 1890 ss 23(2), 31(1); PARAS 94, 125; and BANKRUPTCY AND INDIVIDUAL INSOLVENCY vol 5 (2013) PARA 710. Quaere to what extent the Law of Property (Miscellaneous Provisions) Act 1989 s 2(1) (a contract for the sale or other disposition of land to be made in writing signed by or on behalf of the parties and incorporating all the terms of such sale or other disposition: see PARA 24 note 7; and CONVEYANCING vol 23 (2013) PARA 151) affects charges on land created without complying with such requirements: see REAL PROPERTY AND REGISTRATION vol 87 (2012) PARA 182. As to the nature of a partner's share see PARA 121 et seq.

3   *Re Seager Hunt* [1900] 2 Ch 54n. The rule applies to a partner in a foreign firm having a branch in England and Wales: *Brown, Janson & Co v Hutchinson & Co* [1895] 1 QB 737, CA.

4   *Stewart v Rhodes* [1900] 1 Ch 386, CA.

5   This principle stems from the fact that a charging order made under the Partnership Act 1890 s 23 was not regarded as a completed execution for the purposes of the Bankruptcy Act 1914 s 40 (repealed): see *Re Hutchinson, ex p Hutchinson* (1885) 16 QBD 515 and *Wild v Southwood* [1897] 1 QB 317, following *Re O'Shea's Settlement, Courage v O'Shea* [1895] 1 Ch 325, CA; cf *Re Gershon and Levy, ex p Coote and Richards, ex p Westcott & Sons* [1915] 2 KB 527 (where the doctrine of relation back applied to an equitable charge obtained by solicitors and the charging order was not binding on the trustee). Whilst the doctrine of relation back has no application under the Insolvency Act 1986, it is apprehended that the same rule would apply (both to corporate and individual partners) where the indebted partner is adjudged bankrupt or where the partnership is wound up as an insolvent company, as the case may be, under the Insolvency Act 1986; sed quaere. As to partnership insolvency proceedings generally see PARA 98; and COMPANY AND PARTNERSHIP INSOLVENCY vol 17 (2011) PARAS 1209–1361.

96. Ancillary relief; receivers, accounts and inquiries. When a charging order is made[1], the court[2] may appoint, by the same or a subsequent order, a receiver[3] of the partner's share of profits, whether already declared or accruing, and of any other money coming to him from the partnership[4]. It may also direct such accounts and inquiries and give such orders and directions as it might have done if the charge had been made by the partner in favour of the judgment creditor, or as the case may require[5]; but this jurisdiction is discretionary and will be exercised only in special circumstances, for example with a view to a dissolution[6].

1   As to the procedure to be followed when applying for a charging order see PARA 94.

2   As to the meaning of 'court' see PARA 94 note 2.

3   See CIVIL PROCEDURE vol 12 (2009) PARA 1501 et seq. As to the right of a partner generally to apply for the appointment of a receiver see PARA 161.

4   Partnership Act 1890 s 23(2). As to the effect of the appointment of a receiver by the court see *Brown, Janson & Co v A Hutchinson & Co* [1895] 1 QB 737 at 740, CA; and RECEIVERS vol 88 (2012) PARA 73 et seq.

5   Partnership Act 1890 s 23(2). As to the rights of a chargee see PARA 125.

6   *Brown, Janson & Co v Hutchinson & Co* [1895] 2 QB 126 at 130–131, CA. An account will not, as a rule, be ordered during the continuance of a partnership: *Brown, Janson & Co v Hutchinson & Co* at 132. As to accounts between partners see PARA 149 et seq.

97. Rights of other partners when one partner's interest is charged. The partners or partner of a member of a firm whose interest has been charged[1] are at liberty at any time to redeem it[2], or, in the case of a sale being directed by the court, to purchase it[3], or they may dissolve the partnership[4].

1   Ie under the Partnership Act 1890 s 23: see PARA 94 et seq.
2   Partnership Act 1890 s 23(3).
3   Partnership Act 1890 s 23(3): see *Perens v Johnson, Johnson v Perens* (1857) 3 Sm & G 419.
4   Partnership Act 1890 s 33(2); and see PARA 176.

(iv) Insolvency Proceedings

98. Insolvency proceedings. The Lord Chancellor may, by order[1], provide that such provisions of the Insolvency Act 1986 as may be specified in the order are to apply in relation to insolvent partnerships with such modifications as may be specified[2]. Such an order may make different provision for different cases and may contain such incidental, supplemental and transitional provisions as may appear to the Lord Chancellor and the Lord Chief Justice necessary or expedient[3].

The current order is the Insolvent Partnerships Order 1994[4] which contains provisions relating to the following:

(1)   voluntary arrangements for insolvent partnerships[5];
(2)   administrations for insolvent partnerships[6];
(3)   winding up of an insolvent partnership as an unregistered company on the petition of a creditor where no concurrent petition is presented against a member[7];
(4)   winding up of an insolvent partnership as an unregistered company on the petition of a creditor where concurrent petitions are presented against one or more members[8];
(5)   winding up of an insolvent partnership as an unregistered company on a member's petition where no concurrent petition is presented against a member[9];
(6)   winding up of an insolvent partnership as an unregistered company on a member's petition where concurrent petitions are presented against all members[10];
(7)   insolvency proceedings not involving the winding up of an insolvent partnership as an unregistered company where individual members present a joint bankruptcy petition[11]; and
(8)   winding up of an unregistered company which is a member of an insolvent partnership being wound up by virtue of the Insolvent Partnerships Order 1994[12].

Where an insolvent partnership is wound up as an unregistered company under Part V of the Insolvency Act 1986[13], certain provisions of the Company Directors Disqualification Act 1986[14] apply with modifications[15].

The above provisions do not affect the position where executors carry on a testator's business; if the executors are acting purely in their capacity as such and are not partners with each other, they cannot be adjudicated bankrupt as partners[16].

1   Ie by order made by statutory instrument subject to annulment in pursuance of a resolution of either House of Parliament, with the concurrence of the Secretary of State and the Lord Chief Justice: Insolvency Act 1986 s 420(1), (3) (s 420(1) amended by the Constitutional Reform Act 2005 s 15(1), Sch 4 paras 185, 191(1), (2)). The Lord Chief Justice may nominate a judicial office holder (see the Constitutional Reform Act 2005 s 109(4)) to exercise his functions under

the Insolvency Act 1986 s 420: s 420(4) (added by the Constitutional Reform Act 2005 Sch 4 paras 185, 191(1), (4)). See also the Insolvency Act 1986 s 420(1A), (1B) (added by SI 2002/1037); and BANKRUPTCY AND INDIVIDUAL INSOLVENCY vol 5 (2013) PARAS 830, 851; COMPANY AND PARTNERSHIP INSOLVENCY vol 17 (2011) PARA 1209.

2 Insolvency Act 1986 s 420(1). Partnership insolvency is covered in detail elsewhere in this work: see COMPANY AND PARTNERSHIP INSOLVENCY vol 17 (2011) PARAS 1209–1361.

3 Insolvency Act 1986 s 420(2).

4 Ie the Insolvent Partnerships Order 1994, SI 1994/2421.

5 See the Insolvent Partnerships Order 1994, SI 1994/2421, arts 4, 5; and COMPANY AND PARTNERSHIP INSOLVENCY vol 17 (2011) PARAS 1212–1234.

6 See the Insolvent Partnerships Order 1994, SI 1994/2421, art 6; and COMPANY AND PARTNERSHIP INSOLVENCY vol 17 (2011) PARAS 1235–1258.

7 See the Insolvent Partnerships Order 1994, SI 1994/2421, art 7; and COMPANY AND PARTNERSHIP INSOLVENCY vol 17 (2011) PARAS 1259–1272.

8 See the Insolvent Partnerships Order 1994, SI 1994/2421, art 8 (amended by SI 2002/1308; SI 2006/622); and COMPANY AND PARTNERSHIP INSOLVENCY vol 17 (2011) PARAS 1273–1310.

9 See the Insolvent Partnerships Order 1994, SI 1994/2421, art 9; and COMPANY AND PARTNERSHIP INSOLVENCY vol 17 (2011) PARAS 1311–1316.

10 See the Insolvent Partnerships Order 1994, SI 1994/2421, art 10; and COMPANY AND PARTNERSHIP INSOLVENCY vol 17 (2011) PARAS 1317–1322.

11 See the Insolvent Partnerships Order 1994, SI 1994/2421, art 11; and COMPANY AND PARTNERSHIP INSOLVENCY vol 17 (2011) PARAS 1323–1349.

12 See the Insolvent Partnerships Order 1994, SI 1994/2421, art 12; and COMPANY AND PARTNERSHIP INSOLVENCY vol 17 (2011) PARA 1350.

13 Ie the Insolvency Act 1986 Pt V (ss 220–229): see COMPANY AND PARTNERSHIP INSOLVENCY vol 17 (2011) PARA 1109 et seq.

14 Ie the Company Directors Disqualification Act 1986 ss 1, 1A, 6–10, 13–15, 17, 19(c), 20, Sch 1: see COMPANIES vol 15 (2009) PARA 1575 et seq; COMPANY AND PARTNERSHIP INSOLVENCY vol 17 (2011) PARA 1070 et seq.

15 See the Insolvent Partnerships Order 1994, SI 1994/2421, art 16; and COMPANY AND PARTNERSHIP INSOLVENCY vol 17 (2011) PARAS 1355–1361.

16 *Re Fisher & Sons* [1912] 2 KB 491. See also *Re C & M Ashberg* (1990) Times, 17 July (where it was held that the court had jurisdiction to wind up an insolvent partnership only where a partnership in fact existed; it was not sufficient to prove that the alleged partner had merely allowed herself to be held out as a partner where otherwise no partnership existed, and neither the Partnership Act 1890 s 14 (person liable by holding out: see PARAS 70, 72) nor the doctrine of estoppel would assist the petitioner).

(3) TAXATION

99. Liability to income tax and corporation tax. Since a partnership has, in English law, no separate legal identity, but is recognised as nothing more than a useful means by which to refer to all the partners who, from time to time, make up the partnership, there would prima facie appear to be no reason for any special provisions to apply to partnerships in relation to income tax; each partner's liability therefor could simply be treated as part of his own individual taxation liability[1]. For example, where a trade or profession is carried on by persons in partnership, the partnership is not, unless the contrary intention appears, to be treated for income tax or corporation tax purposes as an entity which is separate and distinct from those persons[2].

There are, however, special statutory provisions in respect of income tax relating to partners, the principal provisions concerning: (1) partnerships involving companies[3]; (2) limited partners[4]; (3) limited liability partnerships[5]; and (4) capital allowances[6].

1 As to partnerships' lack of legal personality see PARA 2.

2 See the Income Tax (Trading and Other Income) Act 2005 s 848; the Corporation Tax Act 2009 s 1258; and INCOME TAXATION vol 59 (2014) PARAS 1806, 1939. See also INCOME TAXATION vol 59 (2014) PARAS 1938–1944.

3   See the Corporation Tax Act 2009 ss 1259–1265; the Corporation Tax Act 2010 ss 958–962; and INCOME TAXATION vol 59 (2014) PARAS 1941–1942.
4   See the Corporation Tax Act 2010 ss 56–58. As to limited partnerships see PARA 217 et seq.
5   See the Income Tax (Trading and Other Income) Act 2005 s 863; the Corporation Tax Act 2009 s 1273; the Corporation Tax Act 2010 ss 59–61; and INCOME TAXATION vol 59 (2014) PARAS 1943–1944.
6   See eg the Capital Allowances Act 2001 ss 557, 558; and INCOME TAXATION vol 58 (2014) PARA 145.

100.   Liability to capital gains tax. Where two or more persons carry on a trade or business in partnership capital gains tax in respect of chargeable gains accruing to them on the disposal of any partnership assets must be assessed and charged on them separately[1]; and any partnership dealings must be treated as dealings by the partners and not by the firm as such[2].

If a person resident in the United Kingdom (the 'resident partner') is a member of a partnership which resides outside the United Kingdom or which carries on any trade, profession or business the control and management of which is situated outside the United Kingdom, and any of the capital gains of the partnership are relieved[3] from capital gains tax or corporation tax in the United Kingdom, then the arrangements (so far as providing for that relief) do not affect any liability to capital gains tax or corporation tax in respect of the resident partner's share of any capital gains of the partnership[4].

1   See the Taxation of Chargeable Gains Act 1992 s 59(1)(a); and CAPITAL GAINS TAXATION vol 6 (2011) PARA 824. As to the liability of partners generally to capital gains tax see CAPITAL GAINS TAXATION vol 6 (2011) PARAS 824–831.
2   See the Taxation of Chargeable Gains Act 1992 s 59(1)(b); and CAPITAL GAINS TAXATION vol 6 (2011) PARA 824.

3   Ie by virtue of any arrangements that have effect under the Taxation (International and Other Provisions) Act 2010 s 2(1): see INCOME TAXATION vol 58A (2014) PARA 1370 et seq.

4   See the Taxation of Chargeable Gains Act 1992 s 59(2), (3) (added by the Income Tax (Trading and Other Income) Act 2005 s 882(1), Sch 1 paras 426, 431(1), (3); amended by the Corporation Tax Act 2009 s 1322, Sch 1 paras 358, 365; the Taxation of Chargeable Gains Act 1992 s 59(2) further amended by the Taxation (International and Other Provisions) Act 2010 s 374, Sch 8 paras 40, 43). As to the meaning of 'United Kingdom' see PARA 8 note 2.

101.   Liability to inheritance tax. Inheritance tax[1], being chargeable primarily on death, renders the majority of inter vivos transfers of value potentially exempt, so that such transfers become chargeable only if the donor dies within the next seven years following the transfer[2]. Thus, if, upon the commencement or during the continuation of the firm or upon the death or retirement of a partner, a gratuitous transfer or assignment of one or more partner's shares is effected[3], such transfer or assignment will, in the usual case, constitute a potentially exempt transfer[4].

1   As to inheritance tax generally see INHERITANCE TAXATION.
2   As to potentially exempt transfers see INHERITANCE TAXATION vol 59A (2014) PARAS 44–47.

3   Eg by the rearrangement of partners' capital-sharing ratios, by the acquisition of a share in the firm's assets by a new partner upon the basis of the written down value of the firm's capital assets, ie ignoring any capital profits, or by the provision of annuities to former partners and their dependants where, for example, although the former partner has given full consideration for the annuity, it is unenforceable or where the annuity is enforceable but was not included within the partnership agreement for full consideration. Upon the formation or dissolution of a partnership, or upon the death or retirement of a partner or upon the admission of a new partner, care should be taken to ensure that all the relevant reliefs, such as business property relief under the Inheritance Tax Act 1984 Pt V Ch I (ss 103–114) (see INHERITANCE TAXATION

vol 59A (2014) PARA 170 et seq) and agricultural property relief under Pt V Ch II (ss 115–124C) (see INHERITANCE TAXATION vol 59A (2014) PARA 180 et seq) are utilised.

4   See note 2.

102.   Liability to VAT. The registration under the Value Added Tax Act 1994 of persons carrying on a business in partnership, or carrying on in partnership any other activities in the course or furtherance of which they acquire goods from other member states, may be in the name of the firm; and no account is to be taken, in determining for any purpose of that Act whether goods or services are supplied to or by such persons or are acquired by such persons from another member state, of any change in the partnership[1].

Until the date on which a change in the partnership is notified to the Commissioners for Her Majesty's Revenue and Customs a person who has ceased to be a member of a partnership is to be regarded as continuing to be a partner for the purposes of the Value Added Tax Act 1994 and, in particular, for the purpose of any liability for VAT on the supply of goods or services by the partnership or on the acquisition of goods by the partnership from another member state[2].

Where a person ceases to be a member of a partnership during a prescribed accounting period any notice which is served on the partnership and relates to, or to any matter arising in, that period or any earlier period during the whole or part of which he was a member of the partnership is to be treated as served also on him[3].

These provisions[4] do not affect the extent to which a partner is liable[5] for VAT owed by the firm; but where a person is a partner in a firm during part only of a prescribed accounting period, his liability for VAT on the supply by the firm of goods or services during that accounting period or on the acquisition during that period by the firm of any goods from another member state is to be such proportion of the firm's liability as may be just[6].

1   See the Value Added Tax Act 1994 s 45(1); and VALUE ADDED TAX vol 99 (2012) PARA 23.
2   See the Value Added Tax Act 1994 s 45(2); and VALUE ADDED TAX vol 99 (2012) PARA 23. Note that this provision is expressly without prejudice to the Partnership Act 1890 s 36 (rights of persons dealing with firm against apparent members of firm): see PARA 194.
3   See the Value Added Tax Act 1994 s 45(3); and VALUE ADDED TAX vol 99 (2012) PARA 23. Any notice, whether of assessment or otherwise, which is addressed to a partnership by the name in which it is registered by virtue of s 45(1) and is served in accordance with the Value Added Tax Act 1994 is to be treated as served on the partnership and, accordingly, where s 45(3) applies, as served also on the former partner: see s 45(4); and VALUE ADDED TAX vol 99 (2012) PARA 23. Note that this is expressly without prejudice to the Partnership Act 1890 s 16 (notice to acting partner to be notice to the firm): see PARA 39.
4   Ie the Value Added Tax Act 1995 s 45(1), (3): see the text and notes 1, 3.
5   Ie under the Partnership Act 1890 s 9: see PARA 68.
6   See the Value Added Tax Act 1994 s 45(5); and VALUE ADDED TAX vol 99 (2012) PARA 23.

103.   National insurance contributions. Class 4 national insurance contributions in respect of partnership profits and gains may be charged on a partner separately or may be the subject of a joint assessment[1].

1   See the Social Security Contributions and Benefits Act 1992 s 16(3), Sch 2 para 4(1), (2); and WELFARE BENEFITS AND STATE PENSIONS vol 104 (2014) PARA 396.

104.   Liability to stamp duty and stamp duty land tax. On normal principles, ad valorem stamp duty will be chargeable upon partners where they execute a deed or other document in order to effect a conveyance or transfer of any partnership asset, whether during the currency of the partnership or on its dissolution[1]. For the purposes of stamp duty land tax, a chargeable interest held on behalf of a partnership is treated as held by or on behalf of the partners and a land transaction entered into for the purposes of a partnership is treated as entered into by or on behalf of all of the partners[2].

1   As to stamp duty on particular instruments see STAMP TAXES vol 96 (2012) PARA 329 et seq.
2   Finance Act 2003 s 104, Sch 15 para 2. As to stamp duty land tax see the Finance Act 2003 Pt 4 (ss 42–124); and STAMP TAXES vol 96 (2012) PARA 425 et seq.

3. RELATIONS BETWEEN PARTNERS

(1) NECESSITY FOR GOOD FAITH

105. Basis of the relationship. Ordinary partnerships are presumed by law to be based on the mutual trust and confidence of each partner in the integrity of every other partner; and as a result partners owe each other a duty of good faith[1]. While a breach of this duty[2] may sound in damages[3], it is not a universal rule[4].

1   This principle is firmly established in equity: see eg *Floydd v Cheney, Cheney v Floydd* [1970] Ch 602, [1970] 1 All ER 446; *Thompson's Trustee in Bankruptcy v Heaton* [1974] 1 All ER 1239, [1974] 1 WLR 605. 'In all partnerships, whether it is expressed in the deed or not, the partners are bound to be true and faithful to each other': *Const v Harris* (1824) Turn & R 496 per Lord Eldon LC. The principle is not expressly enunciated by the Partnership Act 1890, but it is recognised and embodied in the provisions contained in s 29 (see PARA 106) and s 30 (see PARA 107). As to the good faith required when serving a dissolution notice see *Walters v Bingham, Bingham v Walters* [1988] 1 FTLR 260 at 267–268 obiter per Browne-Wilkinson V-C; and see *Peyton v Mindham* [1971] 3 All ER 1215 at 1221, [1972] 1 WLR 8 at 14. As to a solicitor's duty to disclose information to his partners, notwithstanding the duty of confidentiality which he owes to his clients, see *Moser v Cotton* [1990] NLJR 1313, CA. A partner owes his fellow partners a duty of care not to cause loss to the firm by rendering it liable in damages to third parties: *Ross Harper & Murphy v Banks* 2000 SC 500, Ct of Sess. Prospective partners have a duty to disclose all material matters in negotiating partnership agreements; although breach of the duty of disclosure would generally give rise merely to a right of rescission, where the breach of the duty of disclosure was fraudulent, a party to whom the duty was owed who suffered loss by reason of the breach might recover damages for that loss in the tort of deceit: see *Conlon v Simms* [2006] EWCA Civ 1749, [2007] 3 All ER 802, [2008] 1 WLR 484.

It is now generally accepted that the relationship between partners is fiduciary and that therefore they also owe each other a fiduciary duty. Strong authority for the proposition that partners do owe each other such a duty may be found in *Helmore v Smith (1)* (1887) 35 ChD 436 at 444, CA (where Bacon V-C stated that 'if fiduciary relation means anything, I cannot conceive a clearer case of fiduciary relation than that which exists between partners. Their mutual trust and confidence is the life blood of the concern. It is because they trust each other that they are partners in the first instance; it is because they continue to trust each other that the business goes on'); and in *Cassells v Stewart* (1881) 6 App Cas 64 at 79, HL (where Lord Blackburn said of a partner that it is 'because he is the agent that the fiduciary relation arises'); and see *Thompson's Trustee in Bankruptcy v Heaton* [1974] 1 All ER 1239 at 1249, [1974] 1 WLR 605 at 612–613 per Pennycuick V-C. However, in *Hogar Estates Ltd in Trust v Shebron Holdings Ltd* (1979) 25 OR (2d) 543, 101 DLR (3d) 509 (Ont) the High Court of Ontario warned against categorising the duty of a partner in this context; and see *Kingscroft Insurance Co Ltd v HS Weavers (Underwriting) Agencies Ltd* [1993] 1 Lloyd's Rep 187. As to the position where a partner holds money or other assets belonging to the firm see *Piddocke v Burt* [1894] 1 Ch 343 (where it was held that a partner who, as agent for the firm, received money from a third party, did not hold that money as trustee for his co-partners); but, in relation to the position where a firm has already been dissolved, see *Gordon v Gonda* [1955] 2 All ER 762 at 766, [1955] 1 WLR 885 at 893–894, CA; *Roxburgh Dinardo & Partners' Judicial Factor v Dinardo* 1992 GWD 6–322, Ct of Sess (where one partner held all the assets of the dissolved firm, the other all the liabilities and it was held that the former partner held the assets upon a constructive trust for the benefit of the latter).

As to fiduciary relationships generally see EQUITABLE JURISDICTION vol 47 (2014) PARA 228 et seq.

2   As to whether specific acts (or perhaps omissions) will be held to be in breach of the duty of good faith is a question of fact and will depend upon the circumstances of the case: see (in relation to employees) *Bliss v South East Thames Regional Health Authority* [1987] ICR 700, [1985] IRLR 308, CA (where it was held that the defendant's request that the plaintiff undergo a psychiatric examination, the plaintiff having written offensive letters to members of staff, constituted a repudiatory breach of the implied term of the contract between them); *United Bank Ltd v Akhtar* [1989] IRLR 507, EAT (exercise of a mobility clause).

3 See *Trimble v Goldberg* [1906] AC 494 at 500, PC, obiter per Lord Macnaghten; *Ferguson v Mackay* 1985 SLT 95. The principle that a breach of the duty of good faith may sound in damages may also be imported by analogy from non-partnership cases (sed quaere): see *Sanders v Parry* [1967] 2 All ER 803, [1967] 1 WLR 753 (duty owed by employee); *Imperial Group Pension Trust Ltd v Imperial Tobacco Ltd* [1991] 2 All ER 597 at 605–606, [1991] 1 WLR 589 at 597 per Browne-Wilkinson V-C (a pension fund case); *Downsview Nominees Ltd v First City Corpn Ltd* [1993] AC 295, [1993] 3 All ER 626, PC (duty owed by mortgagee/receiver).

4 See eg *Uphoff v International Energy Trading Ltd* (1989) Times, 4 February, CA (where it was held that no claim for damages lay, even though the breach in question, namely non-disclosure between co-venturers, constituted a breach of a fiduciary nature). Where the duty is not fiduciary, a breach will not sound in damages: see *Banque Keyser Ullman SA v Skandia Life (UK) Insurance Co Ltd* [1990] 1 QB 665, [1990] 2 All ER 923; *Bank of Nova Scotia v Hellenic Mutual War Risks Association (Bermuda) Ltd* [1990] 1 QB 818, [1989] 3 All ER 628, CA.

106. General duty to account for profit received. Every partner must account to the firm for any benefit derived by him without the consent of the other partners from any transaction concerning the partnership, or from any use by him of the partnership property, name or business connection[1]. This also applies to transactions undertaken after a partnership has been dissolved by the death of a partner, and before its affairs have been completely wound up, either by any surviving partner or by the personal representatives of the deceased partner[2].

It follows that in the conduct of the firm's business a partner must not make any exclusive profit or private advantage for himself[3]. A new agreement which he makes after the partnership is dissolved but before it is wound up is a partnership asset[4]. A partner may, however, derive private benefit in matters entirely outside the scope of, and not in competition with, the partnership business by the use of information acquired in the partnership[5]. He may also, without his partners' knowledge, buy another partner's share in the firm or make a purchase which is not within the scope of, or in rivalry with or injurious to, the firm[6]. If he is the firm's landlord, he may forfeit the firm's lease[7].

A partner must not place himself in a position which gives him a bias against the fair discharge of his duty to the firm[8]. A managing partner should enter in the partnership books all money which he withdraws for his separate use, and omission to do so or concealment of any such transaction may amount to fraud[9].

1 Partnership Act 1890 s 29(1). See *Lindsley v Woodfull* [2004] EWCA Civ 165, [2004] 2 BCLC 131 (the duty to account may operate only for a limited and defined time if the partners expressly so agree). See also *John Taylors (a firm) v Masons (a firm)* [2001] EWCA Civ 2106, [2001] All ER (D) 381 (Nov).

2 Partnership Act 1890 s 29(2). See *Thompson's Trustee in Bankruptcy v Heaton* [1974] 1 All ER 1239, [1974] 1 WLR 605. A duty to account may also arise even before parties have become partners (see *Van Gestel v Cann* (1987) Times, 7 August, CA); but whether such a duty arises would appear to depend upon whether a special relationship is found to exist between intending partners (see PARAS 1 note 2, 105 note 1).

3 Cf *Hichens v Congreve* (1828) cited in 1 Russ & M 150; *Fawcett v Whitehouse* (1829) 1 Russ & M 132; *Gordon v Holland, Holland v Gordon* (1913) 108 LT 385, PC (where a partner improperly sold partnership assets to a purchaser for value without notice and repurchased them for himself, and was held liable to account for all profits made by him); *Blundon v Storm* [1972] SCR 135, 20 DLR (3d) 413, Can SC; *Hogar Estates Ltd in Trust v Shebron Holdings Ltd* (1979) 25 OR (2d) 543, 101 DLR (3d) 509 (Ont). For Warren J's analysis of the fiduciary duty of loyalty in partnership law see *Wilkinson v West Coast Capital* [2005] EWHC 3009 (Ch), [2007] BCC 717, [2005] All ER (D) 346 (Dec).

4 *Pathirana v Pathirana* [1967] 1 AC 233, [1966] 3 WLR 666, PC. As to the continuation of the partnership business after dissolution see PARA 197 et seq.

5 *Aas v Benham* [1891] 2 Ch 244, CA. Cf the position of those in a true fiduciary position: see EQUITABLE JURISDICTION vol 47 (2014) PARAS 231–232. Quaere whether partners are or may be in a fiduciary position vis-à-vis their co-partners: see PARA 105.

6 *Cassels v Stewart* (1881) 6 App Cas 64, HL; *Trimble v Goldberg* [1906] AC 494, PC; *Hogar Estates Ltd in Trust v Shebron Holdings Ltd* (1979) 25 OR (2d) 543, 101 DLR (3d) 509 (Ont).

7   *Brenner v Rose* [1973] 2 All ER 535 at 539, [1973] 1 WLR 443 at 447 per Brightman J, referring to *Bevan v Webb* [1905] 1 Ch 620. Such forfeiture may, however, constitute a breach of trust as between himself and his co-partners: see *Sykes v Land* [1984] 2 EGLR 8, 271 Estates Gazette 1264, CA.

8   *Burton v Wookey* (1822) 6 Madd 367 (defendant obtained goods for the firm by bartering his own shop goods in exchange); *Bentley v Craven* (1853) 18 Beav 75; *Dunne v English* (1874) LR 18 Eq 524. A mere exposure to a temptation to be dishonest was not sufficient to justify the court's interference (*Glassington v Thwaites* (1823) 1 Sim & St 124); but this may no longer be good law (see *Hogar Estates Ltd in Trust v Shebron Holdings Ltd* (1979) 25 OR (2d) 543, 101 DLR (3d) 509 (Ont); and EQUITABLE JURISDICTION vol 47 (2014) PARA 233).

9   *Re Hay, ex p Smith* (1821) 6 Madd 2.

107. Duty not to compete with the firm. If a partner, without the consent of his co-partners, carries on any business of the same nature as, and competing with that of, the firm, he must account for and pay over to the firm all profits made by him in that business[1].

A covenant in a partnership agreement restraining competition between the partners may be enforced by the court[2].

1   Partnership Act 1890 s 30. See *Dean v MacDowell* (1878) 8 ChD 345, CA. Cf *Somerville v MacKay* (1810) 16 Ves 382; *Burton v Wookey* (1822) 6 Madd 367; *Russell v Austwick* (1826) 1 Sim 52; *Gardner v M'Cutcheon* (1842) 4 Beav 534; *Lock v Lynam* (1854) 4 I Ch R 188; *Miller v Mackay (No 2)* (1865) 34 Beav 295. See also *Carlyon-Britton v Lumb* (1922) 38 TLR 298 ('the salary from any office' held to include the pay received by a solicitor while an army officer during the 1914–18 war; decided not under the Partnership Act 1890 s 30 but upon the construction of the parties' partnership agreement).

2   As to covenants in restraint of competition see PARA 27; and COMPETITION vol 18 (2009) PARA 377 et seq. As to injunctions enforcing such covenants see PARA 165 et seq; and CIVIL PROCEDURE vol 11 (2009) PARA 457.

108. Renewal of partnership lease. The renewal of a lease of the partnership property by one or more of the partners without the privity of the others enures for the benefit of all[1]. The rule is the same when the intention to renew is communicated to the others if they are prompt to assert their rights[2]; and it is immaterial whether the term of the partnership is definite or indefinite, or whether the landlord would have refused to renew to the partners who are not privy to the renewal[3]. The personal representatives of a deceased partner may have a right to share in the profits derived from a renewal of the lease by the surviving partner[4]. If one partner declines to concur in taking a renewed lease of property where a branch of the firm's business is carried on, and the partnership agreement provides that the business is to be carried on at such place as the partners agree, no other partner can take a renewed lease in his own name and insist upon continuing the branch on account of the firm[5].

1   'The old lease was the foundation of the new lease; ... the tenant-right of renewal arising out of the old lease giving the partners the benefit of this new lease': *Clegg v Fishwick* (1849) 1 Mac & G 294 at 298 per Lord Cottenham LC; and see *Chan v Zacharia* (1983) 154 CLR 178, 53 ALR 417, Aust HC. See also EQUITABLE JURISDICTION vol 47 (2014) PARAS 229–230.

2   *Clegg v Edmondson* (1857) 8 De GM & G 787; *Re Biss, Biss v Biss* [1903] 2 Ch 40 at 61, CA. See also MINES, MINERALS AND QUARRIES vol 76 (2013) PARA 368 et seq (considerations specially affecting mining property).

3   *Featherstonhaugh v Fenwick* (1810) 17 Ves 298.

4   *Clements v Hall* (1858) 2 De G & J 173.

5   *Clements v Norris* (1878) 8 ChD 129, CA.

(2) MANAGEMENT OF PARTNERSHIP AFFAIRS

109.   Powers of individual partners and of majority.   Subject to any agreement express or implied between the partners, every partner may inspect the partnership books[1] and may take part in the management of the partnership business[2], and, subject to any such agreement, any difference arising as to ordinary matters connected with the partnership business may be decided by a majority of the partners[3]; but the majority must act in good faith and every partner must have the opportunity of being heard[4].

A majority of partners cannot, however, change the nature of the partnership business; for this purpose, the consent of all the existing partners is required[5]. Nor, it seems, can a majority, when selling their own shares in the partnership, sell the shares of the dissentient partners[6]. A majority of partners cannot expel any partner, unless the power to do so has been conferred by express agreement between the partners[7].

The diligence required of a partner may be limited by the partnership agreement to that part of the business which is conducted by him[8].

The management and control of a group partnership present special difficulties[9].

1   See the Partnership Act 1890 s 24(9); *Inversiones Frieira SL v Colyzeo Investors II LLP* [2011] EWHC 1762 (Ch), [2012] 1 BCLC 469; *Inversiones Frieira SL v Colyzeo Investors II LLP* [2012] EWHC 1450 (Ch), [2012] Bus LR 1136; and PARA 135.

2   Partnership Act 1890 s 24(5). In *Donaldson v Williams* (1833) 1 Cr & M 345, it was held that one of two partners, joint tenants of a house where their joint business was carried on, had a right to authorise a joint weekly servant to remain in the house although the other partner had regularly given him a week's notice to leave. The exclusion of a partner from the management of the partnership business may be restrained by injunction: see PARA 166.

3   Partnership Act 1890 s 24(8). The admission of a pupil or apprentice with a view to training him in the knowledge of the business falls within 'ordinary matters connected with the partnership business': *Highley v Walker* (1910) 26 TLR 685.

4   'I call that the act of all, which is the act of the majority, provided all are consulted and the majority are acting bona fide, meeting, not for the purpose of negativing what any one may have to offer, but for the purpose of negativing what, when they are met together, they may, after due consideration, think proper to negative': *Const v Harris* (1824) Turn & R 496 at 525 per Lord Eldon LC. If there is any agreement by the majority, before hearing the minority, to override in any event the views of the minority, such conduct is not consistent with good faith: *Great Western Rly Co v Rushout* (1852) 5 De G & Sm 290 at 310. The minority must not, however, be merely obstructive, and may, after reasonable discussion, be overruled: see *Wall v London and Northern Assets Corpn* [1898] 2 Ch 469, CA.

5   Partnership Act 1890 s 24(8); *Natusch v Irving* (1824) 2 Coop temp Cott 358; *A-G v Great Northern Rly Co* (1860) 1 Drew & Sm 154; and see PARA 41. What are the limits of deviation which will justify the court's interference on behalf of a dissentient minority depends upon the circumstances of each case, and the right to relief may be lost through laches or acquiescence: *Gregory v Patchett* (1864) 33 Beav 595.

6   *Chapple v Cadell* (1822) Jac 537.

7   Partnership Act 1890 s 25. As to expulsion see PARA 178.

8   *Smith v Mules* (1852) 9 Hare 556.

9   See *Nixon v Wood* [1987] 2 EGLR 26, CA.

110.   Remuneration for management.   A managing partner, like any other partner, is not entitled to remuneration for acting in the partnership business unless there is an express or implied agreement to that effect[1]. An exception to this rule is where an express (or perhaps an implied) obligation is, by virtue of a firm's partnership agreement, imposed upon partners to devote their whole time and attention to the firm's affairs and one or more partners in breach of this obligation wilfully leaves his or their co-partners to carry on the business unaided[2].

After dissolution, however, a partner carrying on the firm's business in its winding up may be entitled to remuneration notwithstanding the absence of any express or implied agreement therefor[3]. Thus, a surviving partner who carries on the business profitably, retaining the capital of his deceased partner, is entitled to just allowances for management[4] unless he is himself the executor of the deceased partner[5]; and, where one partner is suffering from a mental disorder, his co-partners may be entitled to remuneration for managing the firm's business in its winding up[6].

1   Partnership Act 1890 s 24(6); *Thornton v Proctor* (1792) 1 Anst 94; *Holmes v Higgins* (1822) 1 B & C 74 (partner did work as a surveyor); *Hutcheson v Smith* (1842) 5 I Eq R 117; *Robinson v Anderson* (1855) 20 Beav 98 at 103–104 (affd 7 De GM & G 239). Cf *Whittle v M'Farlane* (1830) 1 Knapp 311 (remuneration for the collection of book debts due to a preceding partnership not allowed); *Turnock v Taylor* (1961) 180 Estates Gazette 773, CA. As to the meaning of 'salaried partner' see PARA 17. Where, however, the person managing the partnership business is not a partner but a creditor of the partnership to whom the partners may have assigned the partnership assets as security for the partnership debt due to him, that person may not claim remuneration for his (largely unsuccessful) management notwithstanding the fact that the partners have acquiesced in and agreed to his being paid remuneration, where the partners' agreement and acquiescence have been made under pressure: *Barrett v Hartley* (1866) 14 WR 684. Even where there is express agreement that a particular partner will be allowed remuneration for acting in the partnership business, such agreement may not survive the firm's dissolution: *Tibbits v Phillips* (1853) 10 Hare 355 (managing partner held not to be entitled to such remuneration whilst acting in the winding up of the partnership after its dissolution).

2   *Airey v Borham* (1861) 29 Beav 620 (partner complying with his obligation held entitled to just allowances for his efforts); cf *Webster v Bray* (1849) 7 Hare 159 (inequality of labour contemplated from the beginning so that there was no express or implied obligation to devote full-time attention to the firm's affairs). As to the rule that profits must be shared equally unless agreed otherwise see, however, PARA 128.

3   See *Harris v Sleep* [1897] 2 Ch 80, CA (one partner who was appointed receiver and manager without remuneration of the firm's affairs after its dissolution held entitled to wages for work done by him which proved beneficial to the business, even though such work formed no part of his duties qua receiver and manager); cf *Tibbits v Phillips* (1853) 10 Hare 355. As to the continuation of partners' authority after dissolution see PARA 197.

4   *Brown v De Tastet* (1819) Jac 284; *Re Aldridge, Aldridge v Aldridge* [1894] 2 Ch 97; *Featherstonhaugh v Turner* (1858) 25 Beav 382; *Crawshay v Collins* (1826) 2 Russ 325; and see PARA 200 note 5.

5   *Burden v Burden* (1813) 1 Ves & B 170; *Stocken v Dawson* (1843) 6 Beav 371.

6   *Mellersh v Keen* (1859) 27 Beav 236.

(3) ADMISSION OF OTHER PARTNERS

111. New partner admitted only by consent of all. Subject to any agreement express or implied between the partners, no person may be introduced as a partner without the consent of all existing partners[1]. The terms on which he is admitted are, therefore, usually determined by express agreement. An attempt by one partner to introduce a new partner without consent amounts only to an assignment of part of his share in the partnership[2]. It may create a sub-partnership between the newcomer and the person who introduced him, but it does not confer upon the newcomer the rights of a partner as against the original firm[3] unless the person who introduced him has implied authority to make his partners co-partners with another person[4].

1   Partnership Act 1890 s 24(7). This is a fundamental principle of partnership law: see *Crawshay v Maule* (1818) 1 Swan 495 at 509n et seq; cf *Lovegrove v Nelson* (1834) 3 My & K 1 at 20.

According to the fundamental principles of partnership law the admission (or retirement) of a partner will technically cause the dissolution of the old firm and the constitution of a new firm: see PARAS 38, 178, 204.

2   *Re Slyth, ex p Barrow* (1815) 2 Rose 252 at 255; *Bray v Fromont* (1821) 6 Madd 5.
3   As to the rights of an assignee see PARA 125. As to those of the assignee of a limited partner see PARA 228. As to the duration of a sub-partnership see PARA 37.
4   *Mann v D'Arcy* [1968] 2 All ER 172, [1968] 1 WLR 893; and see PARA 41.

112.   Discrimination. A firm[1] or proposed firm[2] must not discriminate[3] against or victimise[4] a person:

(1)   in the arrangements it makes for deciding to whom to offer a position as a partner[5];

(2)   as to the terms on which it offers the person a position as a partner[6];

(3)   by not offering the person a position as a partner[7].

A firm must not, in relation to a position as a partner, harass[8] a partner[9] or a person who has applied for the position[10]. A proposed firm must not, in relation to a position as a partner, harass a person who has applied for the position[11].

1   For these purposes persons who have entered into partnership with one another are called collectively a 'firm': Partnership Act 1890 s 4(1) (applied by the Equality Act 2010 s 46(1), (2)). As to the meaning of 'partnership' see PARA 1.
2   'Proposed firm' means persons proposing to form themselves into a partnership: Equality Act 2010 s 46(1), (3).
3   As to direct discrimination see DISCRIMINATION vol 33 (2013) PARA 65; and as to indirect discrimination see DISCRIMINATION vol 33 (2013) PARA 72.
4   As to victimisation see DISCRIMINATION vol 33 (2013) PARA 75.
5   Equality Act 2010 s 44(1)(a), (5)(a). In the application of s 44 to a limited partnership within the meaning of the Limited Partnership Act 1907, 'partner' means a general partner within the meaning of that Act: Equality Act 2010 s 44(8); and see PARA 218. As to the meaning of 'arrangements' see DISCRIMINATION vol 33 (2013) PARA 111. For a partial exception to these provisions in connection with occupational requirements (including religious requirements) see Sch 9 paras 1–3; and DISCRIMINATION vol 33 (2013) PARAS 153–155.
6   Equality Act 2010 s 44(1)(b), (5)(b).
7   Equality Act 2010 s 44(1)(c), (5)(c). See DISCRIMINATION vol 33 (2013) PARA 116. For a partial exception to these provisions in connection with occupational requirements (including religious requirements) see Sch 9 paras 1–3; and DISCRIMINATION vol 33 (2013) PARAS 153–155.
     In addition, A firm (A) must not discriminate against or victimise a partner: (1) as to the terms on which B is a partner; (2) in the way A affords B access, or by not affording B access, to opportunities for promotion, transfer or training or for receiving any other benefit, facility or service; (3) by expelling B; (4) by subjecting B to any other detriment: s 44(2)(a)–(d), (6)(a)–(d). As to the meaning of 'benefit, facility or service' see DISCRIMINATION vol 33 (2013) PARA 111. A reference to expelling a partner of a firm or a member of an LLP includes a reference to the termination of the person's position as such: (a) by the expiry of a period (including a period expiring by reference to an event or circumstance); (b) by an act of the person (including giving notice) in circumstances such that the person is entitled, because of the conduct of other partners or members, to terminate the position without notice; (c) (in the case of a partner of a firm) as a result of the dissolution of the partnership: s 46(1), (6). Heads (a) and (c) do not apply if, immediately after the termination, the position is renewed on the same terms: s 46(1), (7). As to the meaning of 'detriment' see DISCRIMINATION vol 33 (2013) PARA 75. As to the meaning of 'LLP' see PARA 242 note 1. For exceptions to these provisions see Sch 9 paras 1–3, 15, 19; and DISCRIMINATION vol 33 (2013) PARAS 153–155, 161, 164.
8   As to harassment see DISCRIMINATION vol 33 (2013) PARA 73.
9   Equality Act 2010 s 44(3)(a).
10   Equality Act 2010 s 44(3)(b).
11   Equality Act 2010 s 44(4).

113.   Power to nominate a partner. If a partnership agreement permits a partner to nominate his successor on his death or retirement[1], the firm comes under an obligation to admit the nominee as a partner[2], but cannot compel him to become a partner[3]. Even if one partner has covenanted with another that his nominee is to become a partner with the other, the court will not specifically enforce the covenant against the nominee; and, if no provision has been made for the event of his refusal to become a partner, the partnership will be declared dissolved, but without prejudice to any right of action which the covenantee may have against the covenantor or his estate for breach of the covenant[4].

1   The inclusion in a partnership agreement of such a power is now rare.

2   *Byrne v Reid* [1902] 2 Ch 735, CA. As to the remedies of a rejected nominee see *M'Neill v Reid* (1832) 9 Bing 68 (damages); *Byrne v Reid* (rejected nominee held to be entitled to such relief as the courts of equity were in the habit of granting as between partners), distinguished in *Re Franklin and Swathling's Arbitration* [1929] 1 Ch 238 (rejected nominee held to have no right to require a reference, as he was no party to the submission to arbitration under the partnership agreement). Executors having a duty to nominate certain persons as partners, with power to exclude one of them, have the right to exclude him if, without fraud, they unite in doing so: *Wainwright v Waterman* (1791) 1 Ves 311. Where, however, a partnership agreement gave a partner the power, by will or otherwise, to nominate a successor, the bequest to his widow of his entire estate did not constitute such a nomination: *Thomson v Thomson* 1962 SLT 109, HL.

3   *Madgwick v Wimble* (1843) 6 Beav 495.

4   *Downs v Collins* (1848) 6 Hare 418; *Lancaster v Allsup* (1887) 57 LT 53; and see *Kershaw v Matthews* (1826) 2 Russ 62.

114. Conditions of entry must be complied with. A person who has an option to enter a partnership must comply strictly with the conditions of the option[1]. He must make his election within the time fixed[2], and, if no time is fixed, the option is lost unless it is exercised within a reasonable time[3]. Before making his election, he is entitled to have a reasonable time for inspecting the affairs of the partnership, but not to have the accounts formally taken[4]. Before his option is exercisable, he cannot prevent the partnership being dissolved by the mutual consent of the partners[5]. Although the effect of the agreement between the partners may be to create a trust of the share in favour of the nominee[6], it is not an immediate trust, but one to arise at a future time, at any rate when the nominee's right is contingent, and will attach only upon the then existing assets[7].

An incoming partner is subject to the terms of the partnership, except as varied by express agreement, although he may not be bound by a special term of which he had no notice[8].

1   See *Brooke v Garrod* (1857) 3 K & J 608; *Watney v Trist* (1876) 45 LJ Ch 412. A power to introduce two sons as pupils or clerks, with the option of their becoming partners, does not extend to the introduction of a third son as pupil or clerk to succeed a son who has died without becoming a partner: *Watney v Trist* (1876) 45 LJ Ch 412 (where there was a provision restricting the employment of clerks and servants).

2   *Holland v King* (1848) 6 CB 727. During that period surviving partners must not do any act prejudicial to the value of the business, which, in the event of the option being declined, may be directed to be sold: *Evans v Hughes* (1854) 18 Jur 691 (changing the firm style).

3   *Vansittart v Osborne* (1871) 20 WR 195.

4   *Pigott v Bagley* (1825) M'Cle & Yo 569, Ex Ch.

5   *Ehrmann v Ehrmann* (1894) 72 LT 17. When, however, a person assigns his business to three persons as partners, on the terms that there shall be reserved a share of the profits for his nominee, who is to have the option of being admitted a partner on attaining his majority, the partnership cannot be prematurely dissolved without that person's consent: *Allhusen v Borries* (1867) 15 WR 739.

6   *Page v Cox* (1852) 10 Hare 163.

7   *Ehrmann v Ehrmann* (1894) 72 LT 17, questioning the observations in *Re Flavell, Murray v Flavell* (1883) 25 ChD 89 at 102, CA, per Cotton LJ.

8   *Austen v Boys* (1857) 24 Beav 598 at 606; affd (1858) 2 De G & J 626.

(4) PARTNERSHIP PROPERTY AND SEPARATE PROPERTY OF PARTNERS

115. Partnership property. All property and rights and interests in property originally brought into the partnership stock or acquired, whether by purchase or otherwise[1], on account of the firm, or for the purposes and in the course of the partnership business, must be held and applied by the partners exclusively for the purposes of the partnership and in accordance with the partnership agreement[2]. Bank drafts obtained by a partner in excess of his authority do not, however, become partnership property[3].

A partner may be guilty of theft of partnership property[4], and, if he treats it in a manner which can only be justified by the right to exclusive possession, he may be liable in tort for conversion[5].

1   See *Waterer v Waterer* (1873) LR 15 Eq 402. Property given to some only of the partners to replace lost partnership property is not included: *Campbell v Mullett* (1819) 2 Swan 551. As to trust money used by the firm in breach of trust see PARA 203.
     As to the difficulty which may be encountered in trying to ascertain which assets are partnership property see *Barton v Morris* [1985] 2 All ER 1032, [1985] 1 WLR 1257, where it was held that the asset in question (a guest house) was not a partnership asset, but was held by the partners as joint tenants, notwithstanding that the guest house was shown in the partnership accounts as a partnership asset. The crucial question was what was intended by the partners. In that case, the fact that the guest house was shown in the accounts was explicable for another reason, namely, the plaintiff's desire to put everything in the accounts 'for the sake of completeness'. Similarly, where an asset is held on a sham lease by one of the parties to a joint venture agreement, that lease will be held to belong to the joint venture and not to the 'tenant' personally, where this is the true intention of the parties: *Rowan v Dann* (1991) 64 P & CR 202, CA. In *Miles v Clarke* [1953] 1 All ER 779, [1953] 1 WLR 537 (a photographers' partnership), Harman J was prepared to conclude that no terms as to which assets constituted partnership property (as opposed to partners' separate property) were to be implied save those required to give business efficacy to the arrangement. As a result, only those consumable items which constituted stock-in-trade (photographic film) were held to be partnership assets; the lease of the premises from which the firm carried on in business (which was in the defendant's name only) and the goodwill which the plaintiff had brought into the business remained each partner's respective separate property. As to which assets will not constitute property for the purposes of a partner's lien under the Partnership Act 1890 s 39 (see PARA 205) see *Faulks v Faulks* [1992] 1 EGLR 9 (milk quota which had been registered in the name of the partnership). See also *Browell v Goodyear* (2000) Times, 24 October (the way to estimate the value of work undertaken on a 'no win, no fee' basis in progress at the dissolution date of a firm of solicitors was to establish what proportion of a particular class of work was likely to be completed successfully in due course, then to establish what percentage of that work had already been completed by the firm at the date of dissolution); not following *Robertson v Brent and Haggitt* [1972] NZLR 406, NZ SC (work in progress in a solicitors' firm held not to be an asset).
2   Partnership Act 1890 s 20(1). See *Don King Productions Inc v Warren* [2000] Ch 291, [1999] 2 All ER 218, CA (partnership property within the Partnership Act 1890 s 20 included that to which a partner was entitled and which all the partners expressly or by implication agreed should, as between themselves, be treated as partnership property. It was immaterial, as between the partners, whether it could be assigned by the partner in whose name it stood to the partners jointly). See also *Strover v Strover* [2005] EWHC 860 (Ch), (2005) Times, 30 May, [2005] All ER (D) 115 (May) (life assurance policy moneys which continued to be paid by partner after retirement were held to be assets of the original partnership). Furthermore, it would appear that, once an asset is bought for a firm and forms part of its assets, any extras which are subsequently purchased for that asset may also constitute partnership assets: *Broadhead Peel & Co v Customs and Excise Comrs* [1984] VATTR 195 (Land Rover and sun-roof).
3   *Commercial Banking Co of Sydney Ltd v Mann* [1961] AC 1, [1960] 3 All ER 482, PC.
4   *R v Bonner* [1970] 2 All ER 97n, [1970] 1 WLR 838, CA; and see CRIMINAL LAW vol 25 (2010) PARA 285. For remarks on the earlier law see *R v Jesse Smith* (1870) LR 1 CCR 266 at 269 per Bovill CJ.
5   *Baker v Barclays Bank Ltd* [1955] 2 All ER 571 at 576, [1955] 1 WLR 822 at 827 per Devlin J; and see *Farrar v Beswick* (1836) 1 Mood & R 527; *Wilkinson v Haygarth* (1846) 12 QB 837

(on appeal sub nom *Haggarth v Wilkinson* (1848) 12 QB 851, Ex Ch); *Morgan v Marquis* (1853) 9 Exch 145; *Commercial Banking Co of Sydney Ltd v Mann* [1961] AC 1, [1960] 3 All ER 482, PC.

116. Presumption as to property purchased with partnership funds. Unless the contrary intention appears, property bought with money belonging to the firm is deemed to have been bought on account of the firm[1]. The mere fact that the business is conducted on property belonging to one partner does not necessarily make it partnership property[2]. If, however, the property has been purchased out of partnership assets and held as part of the partnership stock, it is immaterial that it has not actually been used for carrying on the partnership business upon it or by means of it[3]. Thus, where the transaction is in substance the purchase of a mixed property, for example a farm and the stock as a going concern[4], or a nursery-ground and the business carried on upon it[5], the property so acquired is partnership property[6].

1 Partnership Act 1890 s 21; *Tibbets v Phillips* (1853) 10 Hare 355; *Helmore v Smith (1)* (1887) 35 ChD 436, CA; *Wray v Wray* [1905] 2 Ch 349. It is immaterial that the purchase is made in the name of one partner only, if it is clear that he is not to hold it for himself alone: *Morris v Barrett* (1829) 3 Y & J 384. See *Broadhead Peel & Co v Customs and Excise Comrs* [1984] VATTR 195; and PARA 115. If property was partnership property, then there is a strong presumption that the right of survivorship is not intended to apply; but partners might nevertheless agree to vary the normal rule of partnership property in favour of their own autonomous consent to their being beneficial joint tenants with the standard consequences of that arrangement: *Bathurst v Scarborow* [2004] EWCA Civ 411, 148 Sol Jo LB 420, [2004] All ER (D) 19 (Apr) (clear evidence that house was purchased by partners as joint tenants in full knowledge of the consequences; one partner subsequently died; right of survivorship applied).
2 *Davis v Davis* [1894] 1 Ch 393 at 401. Where the property upon which the business is carried on is, and is declared by the partnership agreement to be, the property of one partner, and the agreement contains no provision as to the tenancy of the partnership, but only a general direction that 'all rent' is to be paid out of yearly profits, the court infers that the partnership was intended to hold the property on a tenancy during the continuance of the partnership, and not on a tenancy from year to year or at will: *Pocock v Carter* [1912] 1 Ch 663. Cf *Lee v Crawford* (1912) 46 ILT 81; and see PARAS 173 note 2, 175 note 1.
3 *Murtagh v Costello* (1881) 7 LR Ir 428. 'If the property purchased is substantially involved in the partnership business, it is to be held as purchased for partnership purposes': *Murtagh v Costello* (1881) 7 LR Ir 428 at 436.
4 *Davies v Games* (1879) 12 ChD 813.
5 *Waterer v Waterer* (1873) LR 15 Eq 402.
6 See further PARA 117 note 5.

117. Partnership land and tenancies. Partners cannot grant a lease to themselves alone in circumstances where to do so would create a complete identity between the landlord and the tenants of the land in question[1]; but, where some partners are and some are not the owners of the land in question, the owning partners may grant a lease to themselves and the other, non-owning, partners[2], provided that the lease is in writing and complies with all the relevant statutory requirements. Where no such lease has been effected, merely a non-exclusive licence to occupy the premises from which the firm effects business will be inferred in favour of the non-owning partners[3].

If partners own land as co-owners, it may be partnership property or not[4]; and they may be partners in the profits derived from its use, even though the land itself or their estate or interest in it is not partnership property[5]. Where such partners purchase out of their profits other land to be used in like manner, the land purchased belongs to them, in the absence of an agreement to the contrary, not as partners but as co-owners for the same respective estates and interests as are held by them in the original land at the date of the purchase[6].

A firm will not obtain relief from forfeiture of its lease merely because one of its partners is the landlord[7].

Where a business tenancy is held jointly by business and non-business tenants, the business tenants alone may apply to the court for a new tenancy under the Landlord and Tenant Act 1954[8].

1   *Rye v Rye* [1962] AC 496, [1962] 1 All ER 146, HL; *Lie v Mohile* [2014] EWCA Civ 728, [2014] All ER (D) 16 (Jun).

2   See eg *Parsons v Parsons* (1983) 127 Sol Jo 823; *Goldsworthy v Brickell* [1987] Ch 378, [1987] 1 All ER 853, CA (parties had entered into a lease of a farm and subsequently became partners); *IRC v Gray (surviving executor of Lady Fox deceased)* [1994] STC 360, CA; *Dickson v MacGregor* 1992 SLT 83. The purchase of a business and its goodwill does not of itself confer on the purchaser any right of occupation of the premises from which the business was previously effected: *Vandersteen v Agius* (1992) 65 P & CR 266, [1992] NPC 108, CA.

3   *Harrison-Broadley v Smith* [1964] 1 All ER 867, [1964] 1 WLR 456, CA (decided under the Agricultural Holdings Act 1948 s 2(1) (repealed): see now the Agricultural Holdings Act 1986 s 2(1); and AGRICULTURAL LAND vol 1 (2008) PARA 327).

4   See PARAS 115–116. As to co-owners of partnership property see PARA 10. As to the conveyancing considerations on a sale to a firm see PARA 118 note 3.

5   See *Crawshay v Maule* (1818) 1 Swan 495 at 518, 523 per Lord Eldon LC. When land is bought by partners in trade for partnership purposes and paid for out of partnership assets, the presumption that it is partnership land becomes practically conclusive: *Re Laurence, ex p M'Kenna, Bank of England Case* (1861) 3 De GF & J 645 at 659 per Turner LJ. See also *Smith v Smith* (1800) 5 Ves 189; cf *Jardine-Paterson v Fraser* 1974 SLT 93. Payment of the rent by a firm is not conclusive that the lease is the firm's: *Hodson v Cashmore* (1972) 226 Estates Gazette 1203. As to co-owners of land who are not partners see PARA 10. As to the rule that partnership land is to be sold on dissolution see PARA 207.

6   Partnership Act 1890 s 20(3); *Steward v Blakeway* (1869) 4 Ch App 603 (affg (1868) LR 6 Eq 479); *Davies v Games* (1879) 12 ChD 813. See also *Christie v Christie* [1917] 1 IR 17 (land bought out of profits derived in part only from partnership property). 'It is not the law that partners in business who are owners of the property by means of which the business is carried on are necessarily partners as regards that property': *Davis v Davis* [1894] 1 Ch 393 at 401 per North J. However, in *Morris v Barrett* (1829) 3 Y & J 384, although the original land was not partnership property, land afterwards bought and paid for out of profits was, in the circumstances, held to be partnership property. If co-owners of business property agree that the property is to be partnership assets, and the trade is carried on there, the mortgagee of the interest of one of the partners is put upon inquiry with regard to the agreement between them when he is aware that the property is used for partnership purposes: *Cavander v Bulteel* (1873) 9 Ch App 79 (mortgagee postponed to the lien of the other partner for the excess share of debts discharged by the other partner although incurred after the date of the mortgage).

7   *Brenner v Rose* [1973] 2 All ER 535, [1973] 1 WLR 443; and see RECEIVERS vol 88 (2012) PARA 90. Where, however, a partner serves a notice to quit in his capacity as landlord, he is not entitled to refuse to consent to service of a counter-notice where he is under a duty as trustee to preserve partnership property: *Sykes v Land* [1984] 2 EGLR 8, 271 Estates Gazette 1264, CA.

8   See the Landlord and Tenant Act 1954 s 41A(5); and LANDLORD AND TENANT vol 63 (2012) PARA 882. As to applications for new tenancies see s 24(1); and LANDLORD AND TENANT vol 63 (2012) PARA 829.

118.   Effect of co-ownership. Equity recognises no right of survivorship as regards partnership property[1]. Where a legal estate in land is vested in partners as part of their partnership property[2], it is held by them as joint tenants[3]. The legal estate in the land is accordingly subject to the rights of survivorship which are incident to a joint tenancy[4], but the beneficial interest in the partnership property is held exclusively for the purpose of the partnership and in accordance with the partnership agreement[5]. The estate of a deceased partner is entitled, not specifically, but in value, to a share of the chattels used for the purposes of the business[6], and, on his death, the value of his share is regarded as the price to be paid by the continuing firm[7].

To effect a sale of land held by the partnership, the partners must observe trustees' duties of consultation[8].

1   This has been expressed by the maxim *jus accrescendi inter mercatores locum non habet* (the right of survivorship does not apply among businessmen): see Co Litt 182a; 2 Bl Com (14th Edn) 185. See, however, *Reilly v Walsh* (1848) 11 I Eq R 22; and *Buckley v Barber* (1851) 6 Exch 164, although this case has been disapproved. In *Bathurst v Scarborow* [2004] EWCA Civ 411, 148 Sol Jo LB 420, [2004] All ER (D) 19 (Apr) there was clear evidence that a house was purchased by partners as joint tenants in full knowledge of the consequences, and when one partner subsequently died the right of survivorship applied.

2   Land may be vested at law in one partner only and also be partnership property: see *Re Rayleigh Weir Stadium* [1954] 2 All ER 283, [1954] 1 WLR 786. In such a case, the other partner has, it seems, an equitable right to his share and thus a right to have a share of the proceeds of sale of the land: see *Re Rayleigh Weir Stadium* [1954] 2 All ER 283 at 286, [1954] 1 WLR 786 at 791.

3   *Re Fuller's Contract* [1933] Ch 652 (where it was decided that the transitional provisions contained in the Law of Property Act 1925 s 39(4), Sch 1 Pt IV applied to land conveyed to partners as joint tenants 'as part of their co-partnership estate'); followed in *Canny Gabriel Castle Jackson Advertising Pty Ltd v Volume Sales (Finance) Pty Ltd* (1974) 131 CLR 321, Aust HC; but see *IRC v Gray (surviving executor of Lady Fox deceased)* [1994] STC 360, CA (notwithstanding the equitable doctrine of conversion, Lady Fox's freehold estate in a farm could be valued, together with her interest in the partnership which held a tenancy of the farm, as a 'single unit' of property for capital gains tax purposes); and INHERITANCE TAXATION vol 59A (2014) PARA 233 et seq. See further the Law of Property Act 1925 ss 34(1), 36; and REAL PROPERTY AND REGISTRATION vol 87 (2012) PARAS 198, 214 et seq. Before 1 January 1926 a surviving partner with the legal estate vested in him (see the Partnership Act 1890 s 20(2)) could sell and convey the partnership property alone: *Re Bourne, Bourne v Bourne* [1906] 2 Ch 427, CA. Today, any trust of property which consists of or includes land is held as a trust of land: see the Trusts of Land and Appointment of Trustees Act 1996 s 1; and REAL PROPERTY AND REGISTRATION vol 87 (2012) PARA 105. In the case of every trust for sale of land created by a disposition there is to be implied (despite any provision to the contrary made by the disposition) a power for the trustees to postpone sale of the land; and the trustees are not liable in any way for postponing sale of the land, in the exercise of their discretion, for an indefinite period: see s 4; and SETTLEMENTS vol 91 (2012) PARA 804.

4   Partnership Act 1890 s 20(2); and see REAL PROPERTY AND REGISTRATION vol 87 (2012) PARA 203.

5   Partnership Act 1890 s 20(1). Accordingly the undivided property of a deceased or retiring partner must not be continued in the business without an express or implied agreement: *Crawshay v Collins* (1808) 15 Ves 218.

6   *Stuart v Marquis of Bute* (1806) 11 Ves 657 at 665; *Bligh v Brent* (1837) 2 Y & C Ex 268; *Ashworth v Munn* (1880) 15 ChD 363 at 369, CA.

7   *Ewing v Ewing* (1882) 8 App Cas 822, HL.

8   If a disposition creating a trust of land requires the consent of more than two persons to the exercise by the trustees of any function relating to the land, the consent of any two of them to the exercise of the function is sufficient in favour of a purchaser: see the Trusts of Land and Appointment of Trustees Act 1996 s 10. As to consultation with beneficiaries see s 11. See further TRUSTS AND POWERS vol 98 (2013) PARA 477.

119. Partnership property transferred to partner. Partners may transfer partnership property to one of themselves or to a limited company of which the partners are shareholders[1], and such a transfer is valid against the firm's creditors[2], if it is done in good faith[3] and if it has been completed; but, if the agreement remains executory, the property remains joint[4].

Similarly, if the personal representatives of a deceased partner sell his share to the surviving partner or partners, relying simply on a covenant of indemnity against the partnership debts, or if, on the true construction of the partnership agreement, they lose their right against the surviving partner or partners to have the partnership assets applied to the payment of the partnership liabilities, the joint property becomes the separate property of the surviving partner or partners[5].

1   See *Gordon v IRC* 1991 SLT 730, Ct of Sess.

2   *Bolton v Puller* (1796) 1 Bos & P 539; *Ex p Ruffin* (1801) 6 Ves 119; *Re Henderson and
    Morley, ex p Freeman* (1819) Buck 471. As to the effect of the assignment of a lease see
    LANDLORD AND TENANT vol 62 (2012) PARA 631. As to partnership leases see PARA 117. As to
    the distinction between the joint and the separate estate see further COMPANY AND PARTNERSHIP
    INSOLVENCY vol 17 (2011) PARA 1297.

3   See *Re Lightoller, ex p Peake* (1816) 1 Madd 346; *Re Walker, Re Hardy, ex p Walker* (1862) 4
    De GF & J 509; cf *Re Edwards-Wood, ex p Mayou* (1865) 4 De GJ & Sm 664. As to
    transactions at an undervalue and preferences where an individual is adjudged bankrupt see
    BANKRUPTCY AND INDIVIDUAL INSOLVENCY vol 5 (2013) PARA 678 et seq. As to transactions at
    an undervalue and preferences where a partnership is wound up as an unregistered company see
    COMPANY AND PARTNERSHIP INSOLVENCY vol 17 (2011) PARA 801 et seq. As to insolvent
    partnerships generally see PARAS 98, 232; and BANKRUPTCY AND INDIVIDUAL INSOLVENCY vol 5
    (2013) PARA 851 et seq; COMPANY AND PARTNERSHIP INSOLVENCY vol 17 (2011) PARAS
    1209–1361.

4   'The agreement need not be entirely completed, but nothing must remain to be done to make it
    operative' (*Pearce v Bulteel* [1916] 2 Ch 544 at 556 per Neville J), eg if payment is to be
    guaranteed by a surety and he refuses to join in the transfer (*Re Mallam, ex p Wheeler* (1817)
    Buck 25). In such circumstances notice of the partner's retirement in the London, Edinburgh or
    Belfast Gazette and in circulars to customers does not suffice to complete the transfer: *Re
    Mallam, ex p Wheeler* (1817) Buck 25. See also *Re Johnston and Danson, ex p Cooper* (1840)
    1 Mont D & De G 358; *Re Kemptner* (1869) LR 8 Eq 286; *Re Wright, ex p Wood* (1879) 10
    ChD 554, CA; *Re Head, ex p Kemp* (1893) 10 Morr 76, DC. As to Gazette advertisements see
    PARA 195.

5   *Re Simpson* (1874) 9 Ch App 572; cf *Re Fox, Brunker v Fox* (1915) 49 ILT 224 (where it was
    held that the partnership assets retained their character as such, in a case where a provision in
    the partnership agreement that the assets should be purchased by the surviving partner was
    never effected owing to his death). If, however, the partnership agreement is merely intended to
    vest the partnership assets in the surviving partner subject to payment of the partnership debts,
    the assets which were joint assets at the death remain joint assets, available to the joint creditors
    (*Re White, ex p Morley* (1873) 8 Ch App 1026; followed in *Re White, ex p Dear* (1876) 1 ChD
    514, CA; and *Re Mellor, ex p Manchester Bank* (1879) 12 ChD 917 (affd sub nom *Re Mellor,
    ex p Butcher* (1880) 13 ChD 465, CA)), and the executors having paid, or become liable for, the
    partnership debts are entitled to be indemnified out of such assets (*Re Daniel, ex p Powell*
    (1896) 75 LT 143). Cf *Re Head, ex p Kemp* (1893) 10 Morr 76, DC.

120.   Partner's property transferred to firm.
The separate property of one or
more partners may be converted into the joint property of the firm[1]; but the mere
fact that the partnership profits are made by means of the separate property of
one partner does not convert that property into joint property[2].

1   *Re Bowers, ex p Owen* (1851) 4 De G & Sm 351 (where one partner, B, was separate owner of
    stock-in-trade and furniture, and it was inferred and held by the court that the stock-in-trade
    had become joint property, subject to an account in which the firm would be debited in favour
    of B with the value of articles which belonged to him or for which he had paid; a different
    inference was drawn as to the furniture which was held to have remained the separate property
    of B); *Miles v Clarke* [1953] 1 All ER 779, [1953] 1 WLR 537; cf *Re Fear and Coward,
    ex p Hare* (1835) 2 Mont & A 478 (where the furniture had been treated by the partners as joint
    property). As to the principle of these cases see *Re Ashley, ex p Murton* (1840) 1 Mont D
    & De G 252 at 261 per Sir George Rose. Where the owner of a mill and its machinery admitted
    two partners, and the value of the property was entered in the partnership books as the amount
    of his capital, and all additions and improvements during the partnership were made at the
    expense of the firm, the property was held to have become joint property: *Robinson v Ashton,
    Ashton v Robinson* (1875) LR 20 Eq 25. Cf *Hills v Parker* (1861) 7 Jur NS 833, HL, and *Pilling
    v Pilling* (1865) 3 De GJ & Sm 162. Thus, if a patent belonging solely to one partner is
    'dedicated to the purposes of the partnership', it becomes joint property: *Kenny's Patent
    Button-Holeing Co Ltd v Somervell and Lutwyche* (1878) 38 LT 878. Even where an asset
    which is owned by the partners as their separate property is shown in the partnership accounts
    as being a partnership asset, this will not necessarily constitute evidence of an implied agreement
    to transfer the asset into the joint property of the firm: *Barton v Morris* [1985] 2 All ER 1032,
    [1985] 1 WLR 1257; and see PARA 115.

2　*Burdon v Barkus* (1862) 4 De GF & J 42, distinguishing *Jackson v Jackson* (1804) 9 Ves 591; *Fromont v Coupland* (1824) 2 Bing 170; *Smith v Watson* (1824) 2 B & C 401; and see *Pocock v Carter* [1912] 1 Ch 663. See also *Miles v Clarke* [1953] 1 All ER 779, [1953] 1 WLR 537; and PARAS 115–116.

　　Formerly, if the owner of a business held out to the world as a partner, a person who had in fact no interest in that business, and permitted him to act as such, and the two were jointly adjudicated bankrupts, the owner was estopped from saying that the assets of the business were not joint property (*Re Rowland and Crankshaw* (1866) 1 Ch App 421; *Re Pulsford, ex p Hayman* (1878) 8 ChD 11, CA); but, where the holding out was only to a very few creditors, and there was no holding out to the world, it might be that there was no partnership and consequently no joint property (*Re Wright, ex p Sheen* (1877) 6 ChD 235, CA; cf *Re Reay, ex p Arbouin and Allnutt, Re Reay, ex p Gonne* (1846) De G 359). The doctrine of reputed ownership has no application, however, under the Insolvency Act 1986. As to insolvent partnerships generally see PARAS 98, 232; and BANKRUPTCY AND INDIVIDUAL INSOLVENCY vol 5 (2013) PARA 851 et seq; COMPANY AND PARTNERSHIP INSOLVENCY vol 17 (2011) PARAS 1209–1361.

(5) SHARES IN PARTNERSHIPS

(i) Nature and Amount of Shares

121. Partner's share in net assets only. A partner's share is his proportion of the joint assets after their realisation and conversion into money and after payment and discharge of the joint debts and liabilities[1]. It follows that during the currency of a partnership each partner's share comprises a bundle of the different types of property right included within the assets of the firm, whether of land, personalty or choses (or things) in action, and is unascertained in value[2]. The share includes sums advanced by any partner beyond his due proportion[3], and, therefore, separate creditors of a partner may not be paid out of partnership assets until the claims of the other partners upon the partnership are satisfied[4]. After the death of one partner in a firm of two, the surviving partner may give a valid charge over partnership property by way of security for a debt incurred during the lifetime of the other[5]. A share of the assets, bequeathed to a surviving partner, is not thereby relieved from its liability for the joint debts[6]; but this principle cannot be taken so far as to invalidate a bequest of a partnership share if the partnership is solvent and the testator desires to bequeath partnership freeholds free of partnership debts[7].

1　*Garbett v Veale* (1843) 5 QB 408. See also *Marshall v Maclure* (1885) 10 App Cas 325 at 334, PC. Joint debts are payable primarily out of joint assets if sufficient, even though secured by a charge on the separate property of one partner (*Re Ritson, Ritson v Ritson* [1898] 1 Ch 667; affd [1899] 1 Ch 128, CA), although one of the persons entitled to share in the assets, eg a partner who is a minor, may not be personally liable for the joint debts (*Lovell and Christmas v Beauchamp* [1894] AC 607, HL). See PARA 28; and CHILDREN AND YOUNG PERSONS vol 9 (2012) PARAS 88–89; WILLS AND INTESTACY vol 103 (2010) PARAS 1005–1007.

2　See *Hadlee v IRC* [1993] AC 524, [1993] 2 WLR 696, PC; *Re Ritson, Ritson v Ritson* [1899] 1 Ch 128; *Rodriguez v Speyer Bros* [1919] AC 59 at 68, HL, per Lord Finlay LC; *Burdett-Coutts v IRC* [1960] 3 All ER 153, [1960] 1 WLR 1027. A partner's beneficial share has been described as an equitable interest as opposed to a 'mere equity': *Canny Gabriel Jackson Advertising Pty Ltd v Volume Sales (Finance) Pty Ltd* (1974) 131 CLR 321, Aust HC. As to the nature of a partner's share for inheritance tax purposes see *Gray (surviving executor of Lady Fox deceased) v IRC* [1994] STC 360, CA. As to the formalities required for the sale or other disposition of an interest in land, and as to whether such formalities are required in the case of a partnership comprising land as one of its assets, see PARA 24.

3　*West v Skip* (1749) 1 Ves Sen 239. See also the Partnership Act 1890 s 39; and PARAS 141, 205, 211. As to a partner's right to an indemnity and lien see PARA 137 et seq.

4　*Croft v Pyke* (1733) 3 P Wms 180; *West v Skip* (1749) 1 Ves Sen 239; *Holderness v Shackels* (1828) 8 B & C 612. Nor can money lent by a partner to his firm be recovered at common law without an action for an account: see PARAS 5, 10, 134, 157.

5   *Re Clough, Bradford Commercial Banking Co v Cure* (1885) 31 ChD 324; *Re Bourne, Bourne v Bourne* [1906] 2 Ch 427 at 434, CA; and see PARAS 46, 198.
6   *Farquhar v Hadden* (1871) 7 Ch App 1.
7   *Re Holland, Brettell v Holland* [1907] 2 Ch 88.

122.   Separate property.   Partners may convert their joint property into the separate property of one or more of their number[1], but, to render an agreement for such partition complete, possession of the property must be delivered to the acquiring partner[2].

A partner may have the right to work a patent, even though he may not be entitled to a share in the patent itself[3]. Land or other assets which produce partnership profit may be separately owned[4].

1   *Bolton v Puller* (1796) 1 Bos & P 539; and see PARA 119.
2   *Re Christopher, ex p Harris* (1816) 1 Madd 583.
3   *Kenny's Patent Button-Holeing Co Ltd v Somervell and Lutwyche* (1878) 38 LT 878.
4   As to partnership property see PARA 115; and as to land see PARA 117.

123.   Partners' shares prima facie equal.   Subject to any agreement express or implied between the partners, all the partners are entitled to share equally in the capital and profits of the business, and must contribute equally towards the losses, whether of capital or otherwise, sustained by the firm[1]. The rule of equality may be negatived by the terms of the contract or by the course of dealing[2].

1   See the Partnership Act 1890 s 24(1); and PARA 128.
2   See PARA 128. See also the Partnership Act 1890 s 19; and PARA 25.

(ii) Dealings by a Partner with his Share

124.   Effect of assignment of partner's share.   An assignment by a partner of his partnership share entitles the assignee to limited rights only[1]. Recognition by the other partners may, however, confer the rights of a partner on an assignee[2], and the terms of the partnership agreement may be such as to place the assignee in the position of the assignor[3]. A partner who has an unconditional right to transfer his share is relieved from liability by an actual assignment of which notice is given to the other partners, even if the assignee is insolvent[4].

1   See the Partnership Act 1890 s 31(1); *Bray v Fromont* (1821) 6 Madd 5; and PARA 125. As to the effect of a partner's attempt to assign part of his profit share to his family in order to reduce his income tax liability where the partner continued to act for the firm see *Hadlee v IRC* [1993] AC 524, [1993] 2 WLR 696, PC (where the unrealisable nature of a partner's share during the currency of the partnership was emphasised). As to attempts to reduce liability to value added tax see *Fengate Developments (a partnership) v Customs and Excise Comrs* [2004] EWCA Civ 1591, [2005] STC 191.
2   *Jefferys v Smith* (1827) 3 Russ 158.
3   *Fox v Clifton* (1832) 9 Bing 115; *Pinkett v Wright* (1842) 2 Hare 120 (affd sub nom *Murray v Pinkett* (1846) 12 Cl & Fin 764, HL); *Re Pennant and Craigwen Consolidated Lead Mining Co, Mayhew's Case* (1854) 5 De GM & G 837. As to the case of a limited partnership see PARA 228.
4   *Jefferys v Smith* (1827) 3 Russ 158. The right of an equitable mortgagee of partnership property is not varied by a subsequent dissolution of partnership between the mortgagors and the bankruptcy of the continuing partner, even though there has been a substitution of a separate collateral security for a joint collateral security given before the dissolution: *Re Draper, ex p Booth* (1832) 1 LJ Bcy 81.

125.   Limited rights of assignee.   An assignment by any partner of his share in the partnership, whether absolute or by way of mortgage or redeemable charge, does not, as against the other partners, entitle the assignee, during the continuance of the partnership, to interfere in the management or administration of the partnership business or affairs[1], or to require any accounts of the partnership transactions, or to inspect the partnership books[2], but entitles the assignee only to receive the share of profits to which the assigning partner would otherwise be entitled[3], and the assignee must accept the account of profits agreed to by the partners[4]. He may not be a necessary party to a partnership claim[5]. He takes subject to the rights of the other partners, and is affected by equities arising between the assignor and his partners after the date of the assignment[6]. A purchaser of a share must indemnify his vendor against the partnership liabilities[7].

An assignee or mortgagee is, however, entitled on dissolution of the partnership, whether as respects all the partners or as respects his assignor, to receive the share of the partnership assets to which his assignor is entitled as between himself and the other partners and to call for an account as from the date of the dissolution for the purpose of ascertaining that share[8], and, where the assignor's co-partners have notice of the assignment, the assignee is not affected by any agreement or dealing between the partners with regard to the assigned share subsequent to such assignment[9]; and a mortgagee of shares in a mining partnership is entitled to foreclosure[10].

1 An agreement in good faith for payment of salaries to partners has been held to be binding on assignees as part of 'management and administration': *Re Garwood's Trusts, Garwood v Paynter* [1903] 1 Ch 236.
2 Partnership Act 1890 s 31(1); *Bergmann v Macmillan* (1881) 17 ChD 423. As to the partnership books see PARAS 109, 135.
3 Partnership Act 1890 s 31(1); *Glyn v Hood* (1859) 1 Giff 328 (affd (1860) 1 De GF & J 334); *Cavander v Bulteel* (1873) 9 Ch App 79.
4 Partnership Act 1890 s 31(1).
5 See PARA 145.
6 *Smith v Parkes* (1852) 16 Beav 115; *Kelly v Hutton* (1868) 3 Ch App 703; *Cavander v Bulteel* (1873) 9 Ch App 79; *Dodson v Downey* [1901] 2 Ch 620.
7 *Dodson v Downey* [1901] 2 Ch 620; and see *Mills v United Counties Bank Ltd* [1912] 1 Ch 231, CA.
8 Partnership Act 1890 s 31(2); *Watts v Driscoll* [1901] 1 Ch 294, CA. If, however, there has been no dissolution, the account will be taken from the date of issue of the writ in an action by the mortgagee to realise his security: see *Whetham v Davey* (1885) 30 ChD 574. In a claim by an assignee for an account after dissolution, the assigning partner is a necessary party, since his obligation to account to his co-partners is not one which can be assigned: *Public Trustee v Elder* [1926] Ch 266; affd [1926] Ch 776, CA.
9 *Watts v Driscoll* [1901] 1 Ch 294, CA; and see *Re Garwood's Trusts, Garwood v Paynter* [1903] 1 Ch 236.
10 *Redmayne v Forster* (1866) LR 2 Eq 467.

126. Partner's right of pre-emption. A continuing partner's right of pre-emption given by the partnership contract is recognised by the court as a right of great value and importance, and is enforceable, in proper cases, by injunction or specific performance[1]. The right may lapse if not exercised with due diligence on notice[2].

1 *Homfray v Fothergill* (1866) LR 1 Eq 567; and see *Stewart v Stuart* (1823) 1 LJOS Ch 61. As to enforcement by way of injunction and specific performance generally see CIVIL PROCEDURE vol 11 (2009) PARA 331 et seq; SPECIFIC PERFORMANCE vol 95 (2013) PARA 301 et seq.
2 *Rowlands v Evans, Williams v Rowlands* (1861) 30 Beav 302. The same applies if the offer cannot be made as provided by the partnership agreement: *Chapple v Cadell* (1822) Jac 537.

127. Assignment of share to a partner. An assignment of his interest by one partner to another, where there are only two partners, operates as a dissolution[1], but probably not where there are more than two[2]. Known insolvency of the concern does not vitiate the sale of his share by one partner to the other if no fraud is intended[3].

One of several partners may purchase the share of another for his own benefit, and not for the benefit of the firm[4]. Where, at the instance of a partner's judgment creditor, that partner's share is ordered to be sold, the purchase of the share by the judgment debtor's co-partners will be set aside if there is any unfairness in their conduct in respect of the sale[5].

1   *Heath v Sansom* (1832) 4 B & Ad 172. As to dissolution of the partnership see further PARA 173 et seq.

2   Ie having regard to the Partnership Act 1890 s 31 (see PARA 125): see *Emanuel v Symon* [1907] 1 KB 235 at 241–242 per Channell J; *Sturgeon Bros v Salmon* (1906) 22 TLR 584. Such an assignment is at all events a circumstance which the court may consider in determining whether to decree a dissolution.

3   *Re Lightoller, ex p Peake* (1816) 1 Madd 346. As to the rights of a partner whose share has been seized by a sheriff and sold see PARA 134 note 1. As to transactions at an undervalue and preferences where an individual is adjudged bankrupt see BANKRUPTCY AND INDIVIDUAL INSOLVENCY vol 5 (2013) PARA 678 et seq; as to transactions at an undervalue and preferences where a partnership is wound up as an unregistered company see COMPANY AND PARTNERSHIP INSOLVENCY vol 17 (2011) PARA 801 et seq. As to insolvent partnerships generally see PARAS 98, 232; and BANKRUPTCY AND INDIVIDUAL INSOLVENCY vol 5 (2013) PARA 851 et seq; COMPANY AND PARTNERSHIP INSOLVENCY vol 17 (2011) PARAS 1209–1361.

4   *Cassels v Stewart* (1881) 6 App Cas 64, HL.

5   *Perens v Johnson, Johnson v Perens* (1857) 3 Sm & G 419.

(6) DIVISION OF PROFITS AND INCIDENCE OF LOSSES

128. Partners' rights to equal shares. Subject to any agreement express or implied between the partners, all the partners are entitled to share equally in the capital and profits[1] of the business[2]. This presumption may be negatived either by express agreement[3] or by implication, which may arise from the course of dealing by the partners[4], although the burden of proof is on the partner who alleges inequality[5]. In order to rebut the presumption of equality, a partner seeking to alter the distribution of profits must detail the changes to the other partners, who must contractually accept the unequal distribution[6]. Even where one partner does much more work than another, the rule of equality applies in the absence of any previous arrangement between the partners[7].

All the partners are entitled to share in the profits made by any one or more of them from transactions arising out of the business[8], but the salary received by a partner in respect of an official position held by him is not prima facie to be treated as profits so as to be shared by the others[9].

1   There is no single definition of the word 'profits' which will fit all cases: *Bond v Barrow Haematite Steel Co* [1902] 1 Ch 353 at 366 per Farwell J. Cf, however, the definition given by Fletcher Moulton LJ in *Re Spanish Prospecting Co Ltd* [1911] 1 Ch 92 at 98, CA. The rise in value of fixed plant or real estate belonging to a partnership is profit: *Robinson v Ashton, Ashton v Robinson* (1875) LR 20 Eq 25 at 28 per Jessel MR. Upon the construction of a particular partnership agreement 'profits' has been held to mean profits actually realised: *Croker v Kreeft, Kreeft v Croker* (1865) 13 LT 136. See also *Badham v Williams* (1902) 86 LT 191. In the case of a limited liability company, profits have been held to consist of the credit balance in the profit and loss account of each year: *Evling v Israel and Oppenheimer Ltd* [1918] 1 Ch 101. In *Bishop v Nicol's Trustees* 1921 SC 229, 'profits' was held to mean profits available for division after deduction of excess profits duty. The Partnership Act 1890 s 24(1) applies to post-dissolution profits: see *Popat v Shonchhatra* [1997] 3 All ER 800, [1997] 1 WLR 1367, CA; *Emerson v Estate of Thomas Emerson (deceased)* [2004] EWCA Civ 170, [2004] 1 BCLC 575.

2 Partnership Act 1890 s 24(1); and see PARA 123. See *Peacock v Peacock* (1809) 16 Ves 49; *Farrar v Beswick* (1836) 1 Mood & R 527; *Robinson v Anderson* (1855) 20 Beav 98 (affd 7 De GM & G 239). Cf *Sharpe v Cummings* (1844) 2 Dow & L 504. Where partners contribute to the capital of the partnership by funding the cost of acquiring partnership assets, those contributions are not determinative of the size of the partners' respective shares of the assets, since subject to any agreement to the contrary, the partners are entitled to share equally in the partnership property: *Popat v Shonchhatra* [1997] 3 All ER 800, [1997] 1 WLR 1367, CA.

3 See the Partnership Act 1890 s 24; and see *Robley v Brooke* (1833) 7 Bli NS 90, HL; *Warner v Smith* (1863) 1 De GJ & Sm 337; *Bell v Barnett* (1872) 21 WR 119.

4 *Stewart v Forbes* (1849) 1 Mac & G 137. See further PARA 110. See also the Partnership Act 1890 s 19; and PARA 25.

5 *Robinson v Anderson* (1855) 20 Beav 98; affd 7 De GM & G 239.

6 *Joyce v Morrissey* [1999] EMLR 233, [1998] 47 LS Gaz R 29, CA (failure of the partners to object to accounts drawn up on the basis of unequal distribution was not sufficient to rebut the presumption of equality).

7 *Webster v Bray* (1849) 7 Hare 159 at 178–179; *Robinson v Anderson* (1855) 20 Beav 98 (affd 7 De GM & G 239); *Joyce v Morrissey* [1999] EMLR 233, [1998] 47 LS Gaz R 29, CA. As to management remuneration, however, see PARA 110.

8 *Hancock v Heaton* (1874) 30 LT 592 (affd 22 WR 784); and see *Bentley v Craven* (1853) 18 Beav 75; the Partnership Act 1890 s 29; and PARA 106.

9 *Alston v Sims* (1855) 1 Jur NS 438. It is otherwise when so treated by the partners themselves: *Collins v Jackson, Jackson v Collins* (1862) 31 Beav 645. Cf *Carlyon-Britton v Lumb* (1922) 38 TLR 298, where 'the salary from any office' was treated under the partnership deed as profits, and was held to include the pay received by a solicitor while an officer in the army during the 1914–18 war.

129. Partner's delay in claiming profits. The right to claim a share of profits may be lost to a partner by laches[1], but only if his interest in the business is merely executory and not a present legal interest which is executed[2]. In the former case, laches is sufficient to preclude him from obtaining equitable relief[3]; in the latter case, mere laches will not disentitle him from his legal rights unless it amounts to a waiver[4] or abandonment[5] of them.

Laches or acquiescence will not bar a firm's claim for profits against a partner or former partner who has secretly obtained the renewal of a partnership licence for himself[6].

1 As to the doctrine of laches see EQUITABLE JURISDICTION vol 47 (2014) PARA 253 et seq. As to limitation periods see the Limitation Act 1980; and LIMITATION PERIODS.

2 The distinction is discussed in *Rule v Jewell* (1881) 18 ChD 660 at 662 et seq per Kay J.

3 *Prendergast v Turton* (1841) 1 Y & C Ch Cas 98 (affd (1843) 13 LJ Ch 268); *Jones v North Vancouver Land and Improvement Co* [1910] AC 317 at 328, PC. Where there has been laches, the mere assertion of rights, unaccompanied by any act to give effect to it, is not sufficient to preserve them (*Clegg v Edmondson* (1857) 8 De GM & G 787), especially where there has been expenditure in a speculative undertaking (*Norway v Rowe* (1812) 19 Ves 144; *M'Lure v Ripley* (1850) 2 Mac & G 274). Recognition may, however, counterbalance laches: *Penny v Pickwick* (1852) 16 Beav 246; *Clements v Hall* (1858) 2 De G & J 173.

4 *Clarke and Chapman v Hart* (1858) 6 HL Cas 633 at 655; *Rule v Jewell* (1881) 18 ChD 660, distinguishing *Clarke and Chapman v Hart* (1858) 6 HL Cas 633 and *Prendergast v Turton* (1841) 1 Y & C Ch Cas 98 (affd (1843) 13 LJ Ch 268).

5 *Palmer v Moore* [1900] AC 293, PC. See also *Lake v Craddock* (1733) 3 P Wms 158.

6 *Blundon v Storm* [1972] SCR 135, 20 DLR (3d) 413, Can SC; and see PARA 106.

130. Profits made after dissolution. A partner continuing the business with partnership assets after dissolution must account for profits[1] up to the final winding up of the concern[2]; and surviving partners who carry on the business must account for the profits of the share of a deceased partner up to the time of the liquidation of the assets[3].

In the absence of any agreement to the contrary, the outgoing partner[4], or his personal representative if he is dead, has a statutory right to elect to charge the continuing or surviving partner either with the share of profits since the dissolution which the court may find to be attributable to the use of his share of the assets, or, at his option, to interest at 5 per cent per annum from the date of dissolution on the amount of that share[5]. This right exists even where, under the partnership agreement, the continuing or surviving partner has an option to buy the share of the outgoing or deceased partner, unless the terms of the option have been duly exercised[6]. If, however, the option is exercised, the outgoing partner or the representative of the partner is not entitled to any further share of profits[7]; his rights are governed by the partnership agreement[8]. Profits left in the business are not necessarily regarded as capital, for example for the purpose of bearing interest, unless there is an agreement to this effect, or unless they are treated as capital in the partnership books[9].

1   *Crawshay v Collins* (1826) 2 Russ 325. He may, however, have a claim for 'just allowances': *Crawshay v Collins* (1826) 2 Russ 325 at 347; and see PARAS 110, 128. As to the distribution of profits after dissolution see PARA 200 et seq. See also *John Taylors (a firm) v Masons (a firm)* [2001] EWCA Civ 2106, [2001] All ER (D) 381 (Nov) (goodwill and business connections could amount to a partnership asset which might exist following the dissolution of a partnership).

2   This is not necessarily in the same proportions as those in which the shares were held: *Willett v Blanford* (1842) 1 Hare 253; *Yates v Finn* (1880) 13 ChD 839. As to liability to account for profits after retirement where the outgoing partner had not fully declared his interest in a competing company see *Lindsley v Woodfull* [2004] EWCA Civ 165, [2004] 2 BCLC 131.

3   *Vyse v Foster* (1874) LR 7 HL 318; *Hordern v Hordern* [1910] AC 465, PC; cf *Croft v Pyke* (1733) 3 P Wms 180 (bankrupt partner). See also the Partnership Act 1890 s 29; and PARA 106. Where a partnership has been dissolved on the outbreak of war by reason of one of the partners becoming an alien enemy, he will be entitled to his share together with the profits made by it: *Hugh Stevenson & Sons Ltd v AG für Cartonnagen-Industrie* [1918] AC 239 at 244, 246, HL. As to the capacity of aliens see PARA 29. Where one of the assets of a dissolved partnership is the lease of a farm occupied by one partner, and that partner's executors purchase the freehold reversion on the lease, any profit they make from the purchase is partnership profit: *Thompson's Trustee in Bankruptcy v Heaton* [1974] 1 All ER 1239, [1974] 1 WLR 605; and see PARAS 106–107.

4   For a consideration of the construction of this term in the Partnership Act 1890 s 42 see *Hopper v Hopper* [2008] EWHC 228 (Ch), [2008] 1 FCR 557, [2008] All ER (D) 275 (Feb), where Briggs J at [154] said: 'Where ... a partnership is dissolved by the death of one of its members, the question whether any other partner is to be treated, on the one hand as a "surviving or continuing partner" or on the other hand as an "outgoing partner" depends in relation to each such partner whether he or she was party to the carrying on of the business of the firm with its capital or assets without any final settlement of accounts. In a two partner firm dissolved by the death by one of them, no problem arises. In a firm of more than two partners, the business of the firm may be carried on by one or more of the survivors. If all of them carry it on, then the Partnership Act 1890 s 42 applies to regulate the mutual rights of the deceased partner's estate against all the surviving partners. On the other hand, if following the dissolution caused by a death of one of the partners, only some of the others carry on the business, then the partner or partners who do not may qualify, alongside the estate of the deceased, as outgoing partners for the purposes of claims under s 42(1)'.

5   Partnership Act 1890 s 42(1). Cf *Watson v Haggitt* [1928] AC 127, PC (partner's salary not deducted before ascertaining the share of net annual profits after dissolution, notwithstanding a contrary provision concerning net profits during the partnership). See also *Sobell v Boston* [1975] 2 All ER 282, [1975] 1 WLR 1587. Where there has been a general dissolution (as opposed to a technical dissolution caused by the retirement (as in *Sobell v Boston* [1975] 2 All ER 282, [1975] 1 WLR 1587) or the expulsion or the death of a partner where, by virtue of the partnership agreement, the continuing or surviving partners acquire the outgoing partner's share at a valuation) so that the firm must be wound up and its assets sold, the option under the Partnership Act 1890 s 42(1) does not extend to capital profits or losses ie to the increase or decrease in value of the partnership property between dissolution and the conclusion of winding up: see *Popat v Shonchhatra* [1997] 3 All ER 800, [1997] 1 WLR 1367, CA; *Emerson v Estate of Thomas Emerson (deceased)* [2004] EWCA Civ 170, [2004] 1 BCLC 575 (the outgoing partner's share would be ascertained by reference to the Partnership Act 1890 s 24(1): see PARA

128). A partner is entitled to such capital profits in any event since the amount of the share is valued as at the date it is realised, not the date of death: *Meagher v Meagher* [1961] IR 96; and see *Barclays Bank Trust Co Ltd v Bluff* [1982] Ch 172, [1981] 3 All ER 232, approved and followed in *Chandroutie v Gajadhar* [1987] AC 147, [1987] 2 WLR 1, PC (where the plaintiff surviving partner had been ousted from the partnership business and the other partner, the plaintiff 's son, had subsequently died, so dissolving the partnership; the surviving partner sought an account and winding up three years after her son had died; it was held that, notwithstanding the delay, the plaintiff was entitled to the relief sought, and the fact that she had brought the action against the non-partner, the son's widow, who had carried on the business after her husband's death rather than her son's personal representatives, was no bar to recovery).

Where, after a general dissolution of the firm, one partner holds all the assets of the firm and the other partner all the liabilities, a constructive trust may be imposed on the former, who may, additionally, have to pay compound interest (at the commercial rate) to his former partner in respect of the value of those assets which he holds: *Roxburgh Dinardo & Partners' Judicial Factor v Dinardo* 1992 GWD 6–322, Ct of Sess (the facts of which are, however, extreme).

The reference in the Partnership Act 1890 s 42(1) to 'the partnership assets' is to the net partnership assets; and the 'share' for the purposes of s 42(1) is to be assessed by reference to the share which the partner in question was entitled to receive at the conclusion of the winding up process: *Sandhu v Gill* [2005] EWCA Civ 1297, [2006] Ch 456, [2006] 2 All ER 22.

6   Partnership Act 1890 s 42(2). As to the position of an outgoing partner whose share is purchased see PARA 200.

7   Partnership Act 1890 s 42(2). If any partner assuming to act in exercise of the option does not comply strictly with it, he is liable to account: s 42(2).

8   See PARA 26.

9   *Dinham v Bradford* (1869) 5 Ch App 519 at 524; cf *Pilsworth v Mosse* (1862) 14 I Ch R 163; *Ibbotson v Elam* (1865) LR 1 Eq 188; *Wood v Scoles* (1866) 1 Ch App 369; *Binney v Mutrie* (1886) 12 App Cas 160, PC; *Straker v Wilson* (1871) 6 Ch App 503 at 510; *Garwood v Garwood* (1911) 105 LT 231, CA. Since annuities, ie payments made out of partnership profits by a continuing partner or partners to a retired partner or his estate, constitute a deductible expense of the partnership business, such annuities will affect the income tax liability of the continuing partner or partners to pay tax: see *IRC v Hogarth* 1941 SC 1; *IRC v Hunter* 1955 SC 248; *IRC v H* 1955 SLT (Notes) 60; and INCOME TAXATION vol 58 (2014) PARA 555.

131.   Partners bear losses equally.   In the absence of express or implied agreement, partners must contribute equally towards losses, whether of capital or otherwise, sustained by the firm[1]. When the profits are not shared equally, the losses are, in the absence of agreement, to be borne in the same proportions as the profits are shared[2], regardless of whether one partner has put up more capital than the other[3].

The liability of a partner to contribute to losses may be limited or excluded as between the partners by express or implied agreement[4], and will not necessarily be extended by the fact that the loss is mainly attributable to his acts[5].

1   Partnership Act 1890 s 24(1).

2   *Re Albion Life Assurance Society* (1880) 15 ChD 79; affd 16 ChD 83, CA.

3   *Nowell v Nowell* (1869) LR 7 Eq 538. In such a case, however, the losses are borne by the partners before their capital is repaid to them: *Garner v Murray* [1904] 1 Ch 57; and see PARA 210.

4   Partnership Act 1890 s 24(1); *Geddes v Wallace* (1820) 2 Bli 270, HL. As to the sharing of losses being evidence of the existence of a partnership see PARA 15.

5   *Cragg v Ford* (1842) 1 Y & C Ch Cas 280. As to the right of a partner to indemnity see PARAS 137–138. Where a partner is injured by a negligent act and his incapacity causes a reduction in the profits of the partnership, he can recover his share of the loss in a claim for damages for personal injuries: see *Lee v Sheard* [1956] 1 QB 192, [1955] 3 All ER 777, CA.

132.   Rights of personal representatives of deceased partner.   Where a partnership has been formed for the purpose of effecting a specific undertaking or object and a partner in that firm dies, the surviving partners cannot compel the executor of a deceased partner to accept a valuation; he is entitled to a share of the profits found due on completion of the undertaking[1]. The principles adopted during a partnership with regard to ascertaining what is capital and what is income have been held, upon the construction of the will of a deceased partner, to govern the interest of a deceased partner during the continuance of the business by his trustees or executors[2]. Undrawn profits in an accounting period prior to the death of a partner are, however, capital of the estate of the deceased partner unless his will otherwise provides[3].

1   *McClean v Kennard* (1874) 9 Ch App 336; and see *Reade v Bentley* (1858) 4 K & J 656; cf *Ambler v Bolton* (1872) LR 14 Eq 427.

2   *Gow v Forster* (1884) 26 ChD 672. For example, in the absence of agreement, the conventional periods of accounting should be observed: *Browne v Collins* (1871) LR 12 Eq 586.

3   *Re Robbins, Midland Bank Executor and Trustee Co Ltd v Melville* [1941] Ch 434, [1941] 2 All ER 601.

133.   When interest is payable on a partner's capital. Except when he has made actual payment or advance beyond the amount of capital which he has agreed to subscribe[1], a partner is not entitled, before the ascertainment of profits, to interest on the capital subscribed by him[2], unless there is an express or implied agreement, or a particular course of dealing between the partners as shown by the partnership books, or a trade custom to the contrary[3]; but the court allows interest on the restitution of money of the firm which has been expended or withheld by a partner, and of secret profits made by a partner in breach of good faith towards his partners[4].

1   See the Partnership Act 1890 s 24(3); and PARA 137.

2   Partnership Act 1890 s 24(4).

3   Further, the ordinary rule is that a partner is not charged with interest in respect of overdrawings: *Suleman v Abdul Latif* (1930) LR 57 Ind App 245 at 249, PC, per Lord Russell of Killowen (where it was held that, in a decree for dissolution and taking of the partnership accounts, interest should be allowed only from the date of the final decree by which the amount, if any, was found due, and not from the date of the plaint). Cf *Boddam v Ryley* (1783) 1 Bro CC 239, (1785) 2 Bro CC 2 (on appeal (1787) 4 Bro Parl Cas 561, HL); *Millar v Craig* (1843) 6 Beav 433; *Stevens v Cook* (1859) 5 Jur NS 1415; *Rhodes v Rhodes* (1860) 6 Jur NS 600; *Hill v King* (1863) 3 De GJ & Sm 418; *Cooke v Benbow* (1865) 3 De GJ & Sm 1; *Rishton v Grissell* (1868) LR 5 Eq 326. In *Boddam v Ryley* (1783) 1 Bro CC 239, (1785) 2 Bro CC 2 (on appeal (1787) 4 Bro Parl Cas 561, HL) no interest was allowed to the estate of a surviving partner who had kept the accounts so badly that a considerable interval elapsed before the balances could be ascertained. Even if the terms of a partnership agreement provide for the payment of interest on capital, such interest will not be payable after the date of the dissolution unless so agreed: *Watney v Wells* (1867) 2 Ch App 250; *Barfield v Loughborough* (1872) 8 Ch App 1. Nor is a partner under the terms of a partnership agreement entitled to be credited with the amount of undivided profits as additional capital, and accordingly to receive interest on them, unless they have been so treated in the partnership books or otherwise left in the business as capital by agreement: *Dinham v Bradford* (1869) 5 Ch App 519. Under the terms of a partnership agreement which provides for payment of interest on capital and also for payment of interest (instead of profits) on the value of the share of a deceased or retiring partner as it stands on the last account, the estate of a deceased partner has been held to be entitled to interest on his capital, and also interest on the value of his share instead of profits: *Browning v Browning* (1862) 31 Beav 316.

4   *Fawcett v Whitehouse* (1829) 1 Russ & M 132; *York and North Midland Rly Co v Hudson* (1853) 16 Beav 485 at 505; *Hart v Clarke* (1854) 6 De GM & G 232 at 254 (affd on other grounds sub nom *Clarke and Chapman v Hart* (1858) 6 HL Cas 633); *Evans v Coventry* (1857) 8 De GM & G 835. See also *Stainton v Carron Co* (1857) 24 Beav 346 at 362. Where, however, accounts have not been asked for, or only demanded at irregular intervals, the accounting party will not be charged with interest on balances retained in his hands in the absence of any wilful withholding, or falsification of the accounts, or other fraudulent dealing with the money: *Turner v Burkinshaw* (1867) 2 Ch App 488.

(7) ACCOUNTS

134. Partners' rights to accounts. Each partner, or his legal personal representative, is entitled as against the other partners to true accounts and to full information of all things affecting the partnership[1]. He may insist that the firm's capital assets are properly valued in the accounts notwithstanding past practice[2]. An auditor's certificate as to an amount of undrawn profits is not binding if founded on a mistaken interpretation of a written agreement[3]. If on retiring a partner has left his capital in the business, reserving a right of access to the books, and liberty to call in his capital upon breach of provisions which are intended to satisfy him as to the continued solvency of the firm, his personal representatives are entitled to accounts at their discretion[4].

Where a partner retires, by express or implied agreement, either ad hoc or in accordance with the partnership agreement, and leaves his share in the firm, he no longer has any continuing interest or share in the assets, but is merely a creditor of the firm so that the retiring partner may sue the continuing partners for the value of his share in the assets of the firm or for any sum that the continuing partners agreed to pay the former upon his retirement without the necessity, first of all, of taking a general account[5].

1 Partnership Act 1890 s 28. See *Habershon v Blurton* (1847) 1 De G & Sm 121 (plaintiff's share and interest in the partnership were seized under a fieri facias and sold by the sheriff to a person who sold to the plaintiff's partner; plaintiff was held to be entitled to an account, as there might be something coming to him which was not seizable by the sheriff); and *Hammonds (a firm) v Jones* [2009] EWCA Civ 1400, [2009] All ER (D) 208 (Dec) (partner in legal firm bound by accounts in year in which he left partnership). An order for accounts may be obtained even though the claimant has misconducted himself in relation to the partnership business: *Ram Singh v Ram Chand* (1923) LR 51 Ind App 154, PC. A partner's duty to his co-partner under the Partnership Act 1890 s 28 may override that partner's duty of confidentiality which as a solicitor he owes to his client: see *Moser v Cotton* [1990] NLJR 1313, CA (on the facts a somewhat unusual case). See also PARA 149 et seq.

  Where a partnership is formed under the law of any part of the United Kingdom and each of its members is either: (1) a limited company; or (2) an unlimited company, or a Scottish partnership, each of whose members is a limited company, then the Partnerships (Accounts) Regulations 2008, SI 2008/569 (amended by SI 2013/2005), govern the form in which the accounts are to be drawn up. As to the requirements of accounts generally see COMPANIES vol 15 (2009) PARA 708 et seq.

2 See *Noble v Noble* 1965 SLT 415. However, where the right is to a payment in respect of a partner's share on retirement or death and the right is based on an agreement between the partners, there is no presumption that the value of assets is to be determined by their current market value rather than their historical costs as shown in the partnership books: *Re White, White v Minnis* [2001] Ch 393, [2000] 3 All ER 618, CA (considering *Cruikshank v Sutherland* (1922) 92 LJ Ch 136, HL); *Drake v Harvey* [2011] EWCA Civ 838, [2012] 1 All ER (Comm) 617; and *Ham v Ham* [2013] EWCA Civ 1301, [2013] All ER (D) 356 (Oct). As to when goodwill should be treated as an asset see PARA 215. As to when certain assets generally will be held to be partnership assets, whether or not they are included within the partnership accounts as assets of the firm, see PARAS 115–116.

3 *Smith v Gale* [1974] 1 All ER 401, [1974] 1 WLR 9 (where Goulding J held that he had jurisdiction to order payment of the correct sum due).

4 *Re Bennett, Jones v Bennett* [1896] 1 Ch 778, CA.

5 *Sobell v Boston* [1975] 2 All ER 282, [1975] 1 WLR 1587; and see *Brown v Rivlin* [1983] CA Transcript 56, applying *Gopala Chetty v Vijayaraghavachariar* [1922] 1 AC 488, PC. As to the normal rule that partners are not creditors of each other see PARAS 5, 81, 157.

135. Right to inspect books and documents. Subject to express or implied agreement to the contrary, the partnership books are to be kept at the place of business of the partnership, or the principal place, if there is more than one, and every partner may, when he thinks fit, have access to and inspect and copy any of them[1]. Subject to reasonable limitations, an agent may inspect them for him[2]. They may become his exclusive property on dissolution, by agreement[3], but the court will not order the books to be taken from solvent partners, if one partner is bankrupt[4].

A partner or his agent may not make improper use of information so obtained[5]. A partner may not remove copies of partnership documents from the partnership premises to make use of them when he has dissolved the partnership[6]. Items not connected with the partnership business may be sealed up[7].

The partnership books are evidence for and against any of the partners in the absence of proof of any fraudulent or erroneous omission or insertion of items[8].

1   Partnership Act 1890 s 24(9). Partners are bound to render to any partner or his legal representatives true accounts and full information of all things affecting the partnership: see s 28; and PARA 135. See *Inversiones Frieira SL v Colyzeo Investors II LLP* [2012] EWHC 1450 (Ch), [2012] Bus LR 1136; *Re Martindale, ex p Trueman* (1832) 1 Deac & Ch 464 (assignees of a bankrupt partner obtained inspection of books which remained the property of both partners after dissolution, although a release in respect of some of the partnership's dealings had been executed and notwithstanding an interval of some 12 years between dissolution and bankruptcy); *Taylor v Rundell* (1841) 1 Y & C Ch Cas 128; *Walmsley v Walmsley* (1846) 3 Jo & Lat 556 (books withheld; the courts allowed 10% as profits). See also *Re Burnand, ex p Baker, Sutton & Co* [1904] 2 KB 68, CA.

2   *Bevan v Webb* [1901] 2 Ch 59, CA.

3   *Lingen v Simpson* (1824) 1 Sim & St 600.

4   *Re Coverdale, ex p Finch* (1832) 1 Deac & Ch 274. See also *Dacie v John* (1824) 13 Price 446 (books in custody of the former managing partner, who offered free access to them; no order made).

5   *Trego v Hunt* [1896] AC 7 at 26, HL; cf *Mutter v Eastern and Midlands Rly Co* (1888) 38 ChD 92, CA; and *Duché v Duché* (1920) 149 LT Jo 338, CA. As to production by partners who have allowed an executor to place his accounts in the general books see *Freeman v Fairlie* (1817) 3 Mer 24 at 43. The best account possible, without undue labour and expense, must be furnished. As to the sufficiency of answers to interrogatories (now termed 'requests for information') with reference to books of account see *Drake v Symes* (1859) John 647; and as to sufficiency of description of numerous documents for the purpose of production in a claim for account see *Christian v Taylor* (1841) 11 Sim 401 at 405. Where it has been referred to a special referee to take the accounts, any order for discovery required for working out the account should be made by him: *Korkis v Andrew Weir & Co* (1914) 110 LT 794, CA.

6   *Floydd v Cheney, Cheney v Floydd* [1970] Ch 602, [1970] 1 All ER 446.

7   *Re Pickering, Pickering v Pickering* (1883) 25 ChD 247, CA.

8   *Lodge v Prichard* (1853) 3 De GM & G 906. Partnership books are evidence for and against all the partners on the principle that they are the acts and declarations of such partners, being kept by themselves or by their authority by their employees and under their direction and superintendence: see *Hill v Manchester and Salford Waterworks Co* (1833) 2 Nev & MKB 573 at 582 per Denman CJ. Where, however, the issue is as to what is partnership property, the way in which the assets have been treated in the partnership accounts is not necessarily conclusive upon the issue, especially where there is another explanation for the asset's treatment vis-à-vis the accounts: see *Barton v Morris* [1985] 2 All ER 1032, [1985] 1 WLR 1257; *Noble v Noble* 1965 SLT 415; and see PARAS 115–116; and CIVIL PROCEDURE vol 11 (2009) PARA 951.

136.   Order for production of books.   Where a partnership claim is pending, books in daily use are usually ordered to be produced at the place of business, but production may be ordered in court where a party cannot be trusted with the custody of the books[1]. A defendant partner may obtain production and inspection of the partnership books and documents before service of his defence if they are in the claimant's hands and he cannot prepare his defence without such inspection[2].

A solicitor cannot, as against his former partner, claim client privilege when ordered to produce bills paid to him by clients[3].

1 *Mertens v Haigh* (1860) John 735; affd (1863) 3 De GJ & Sm 528.

2 *Pickering v Rigby* (1812) 18 Ves 484. As to the method of obtaining inspection see CIVIL PROCEDURE. See *Turney v Bayley* (1864) 4 De GJ & Sm 332 (on an interlocutory application by a party whose status as a partner was disputed, production of books was refused); and see *Turner v Bayley* (1864) 34 Beav 105. As to accounts and their production in a claim see PARA 149 et seq. As to claims against partners and firms and disclosure in such claims see PARAS 83, 90.

3 *Lewthwaite v Stimson* (1966) 110 Sol Jo 188; and see *Moser v Cotton* [1990] NLJR 1313, CA. See also LEGAL PROFESSIONS vol 66 (2009) PARA 956.

(8) RIGHT TO INDEMNITY

137. Extent of right to indemnity. Subject to any express or implied agreement, each partner is entitled to be indemnified by his firm out of its assets, or by way of contribution by his partners, in respect of payments made and personal liabilities incurred by him in the ordinary and proper conduct of the partnership business[1], or in or about anything necessarily done for the preservation of the firm's business or property[2]. The right extends to expenditure for partnership purposes made with the express or implied consent of the other partners[3]; and it is immaterial that the expenditure proves to be useless or unprofitable if it has been approved of or ratified by the firm[4].

A partner who pays more than his share of a partnership debt, whether voluntarily or not[5], is entitled to contribution from his co-partners[6]. Where one of two partners who are jointly liable has paid a judgment debt, he is entitled, in order to enforce his right to contribution, to an assignment of the judgment and of all securities for the debt[7], subject to the equities subsisting between the debtors as partners[8].

Payments or advances made by a partner for partnership purposes beyond the capital he has agreed to subscribe carry interest, subject to any express or implied agreement, at 5 per cent per annum from the date of the payment or advance[9].

1 Partnership Act 1890 s 24(2)(a). See also note 2.

2 Partnership Act 1890 s 24(2)(b). See *Browne v Gibbins* (1725) 5 Bro Parl Cas 491, HL; *Wright v Hunter* (1801) 5 Ves 792; *Denton v Rodie* (1813) 3 Camp 493; *Evans v Yeatherd* (1824) 2 Bing 133; *McOwen v Hunter* (1838) 1 Dr & Wal 347; *Prole v Masterman* (1855) 21 Beav 61; *Re Royal Bank of Australia, Robinson's Executor's Case* (1856) 6 De GM & G 572; *Re Norwich Yarn Co, ex p Bignold* (1856) 22 Beav 143. Income tax assessed on the profits of a partnership is a partnership liability: see PARA 99; and INCOME TAXATION. Accordingly, a partner who paid all the firm's income tax would in the normal course of events have the right of indemnity. Equally, where a retiring partner was given an indemnity by the continuing partner against 'all debts and liabilities of the partnership', such an indemnity was held to encompass the firm's entire income tax liability assessed against it: *Stevens v Britten* [1954] 3 All ER 385, [1954] 1 WLR 1340, CA. As to the effect of express agreements to discharge tax liabilities at dissolution see PARA 199.

3 *Gleadow v Hull Glass Co* (1849) 13 Jur 1020; *Hamilton v Smith* (1859) 28 LJ Ch 404; *Matthews v Ruggles-Brise* [1911] 1 Ch 194 (estate of a deceased partner who had taken an onerous lease as trustee for his firm held entitled to be indemnified by his partners against money paid under the covenants in the lease, although the lease (with the other partnership assets) had been assigned to a limited company which covenanted to indemnify the partners, including the trustee of the deceased, against the partnership liabilities).

4 *Burden v Burden* (1813) 1 Ves & B 170 (allowance made to a surviving partner for expenses of carrying on the business for himself and the children of the deceased partner, but not for his management or time and labour); *Cragg v Ford* (1842) 1 Y & C Ch Cas 280 (loss occurred through delay by one partner in selling); *Re Oundle Union Brewery Co, Croxton's Case* (1852) 5 De G & Sm 432; *Re Court Grange Silver-Lead Mining Co, ex p Sedgwick* (1856) 2 Jur NS 949 (acquiescence in liabilities incurred by a managing director); *Re Protestant Assurance Association, ex p Letts and Steer* (1857) 26 LJ Ch 455; *Burdon v Barkus* (1861) 3 Giff 412 (affd

(1862) 4 De GF & J 42) (outlay by the firm on property belonging exclusively to one partner); *Pawsey v Armstrong* (1881) 18 ChD 698 at 707.

5   *Sadler v Nixon* (1834) 5 B & Ad 936; *Wilson v Cutting* (1834) 10 Bing 436.

6   *Boulter v Peplow* (1850) 9 CB 493; *Batard v Hawes* (1853) 2 E & B 287; *Sedgwick v Daniell* (1857) 2 H & N 319. In the absence of special circumstances, a partner could not formerly sue for contribution at law; his remedy was in equity: *Sadler v Nixon* (1834) 5 B & Ad 936.

7   Ie under the Mercantile Law Amendment Act 1856 s 5: see FINANCIAL SERVICES AND INSTITUTIONS vol 49 (2008) PARA 1138 et seq.

8   *Dale v Powell* (1911) 105 LT 291.

9   Partnership Act 1890 s 24(3); *Spartali v Constantinidi* (1872) 20 WR 823 (interest allowed to two partners on sums advanced by them in excess of their due proportion of capital, such sums being treated as a debt wrongfully withheld).

138.   Limit on right to indemnity. The right of indemnity does not extend to joint transactions where no partnership subsists[1]. Nor does it extend to sums paid by a partner for which the partnership is not liable[2], or to losses due to his own fraud or culpable negligence in the conduct of the partnership affairs[3]. On the contrary, he must compensate or indemnify the partnership against such losses[4]. The principle of indemnity does not extend to private loans from one partner to another, but is confined to partnership transactions[5].

Partners are not entitled to be credited, as against the trustee of a bankrupt partner, with sums which he had paid as agent for the partnership before he became a partner[6].

1   *Sedgwick v Daniell* (1857) 2 H & N 319; and see RESTITUTION vol 88 (2012) PARA 486. As to the extent of the right to indemnity see PARA 137.

2   *M'Ilreath v Margetson* (1785) 4 Doug KB 278; *Re Webb* (1818) 2 Moore CP 500.

3   *Thomas v Atherton* (1878) 10 ChD 185, CA.

4   *Bury v Allen* (1845) 1 Coll 589; *Robertson v Southgate* (1848) 6 Hare 536.

5   *Ryall v Rowles* (1749) 1 Atk 165. 'The partnership stock is no further subject to debts from one partner to another than is the money which has been applied to the partnership': *Ryall v Rowles* (1749) 1 Atk 165 at 181 per Lee CJ.

6   *Smith v De Silva* (1776) 2 Cowp 469, as explained in *Holderness v Shackels* (1828) 8 B & C 612 at 618 per Lord Tenterden CJ.

139.   No indemnity because of agreement. A partner's liability to indemnify his firm may be expressly limited[1]; and a person, although liable as a partner to persons dealing with the firm, may be relieved from liability to contribute to partnership debts as between himself and his partners by the method of dealing adopted by the firm[2].

The right to indemnity will be lost if the partners agree to convert the firm property into their separate property[3].

1   *Gillan v Morrison* (1847) 1 De G & Sm 421; *Re Worcester Corn Exchange Co* (1853) 3 De GM & G 180. See also PARAS 137–138. As to the principles of contribution generally see RESTITUTION vol 88 (2012) PARA 480 et seq; FINANCIAL SERVICES AND INSTITUTIONS vol 49 (2008) PARA 1013 et seq.

2   *Geddes v Wallace* (1820) 2 Bli 270, HL. See also *Dale v Powell* (1911) 105 LT 291. See now, however, the Civil Liability (Contribution) Act 1978 s 7(3), whereby the right to recover contribution supersedes any right other than an express contractual right to recover such contribution; sed quaere whether a course of dealing between partners such as to constitute a variation of their partnership agreement under the Partnership Act 1890 s 19 (see PARA 25) constitutes such an express contractual right.

3   *Lingen v Simpson* (1824) 1 Sim & St 600; *Holroyd v Griffiths* (1856) 3 Drew 428. See also *Ex p Ruffin* (1801) 6 Ves 119; *Re Hayward, ex p Burdekin* (1842) 2 Mont D & De G 704; *Re Langmead's Trusts* (1855) 20 Beav 20 (affd 7 De GM & G 353). The right may be expressly preserved: *Holderness v Shackels* (1828) 8 B & C 612.

140. No right to indemnity where partnership illegal or there is delay. The right of contribution[1] does not exist if the partnership is itself illegal[2]; but, if the partnership is not illegal, the fact that the act for which the firm is liable is unlawful does not prevent an innocent partner from obtaining contribution from the guilty partners[3].

The right to indemnity may be lost by delay[4].

1 See PARA 137.
2 See PARAS 33–34; and *Foster v Driscoll, Lindsay v Attfield, Lindsay v Driscoll* [1929] 1 KB 470, CA.
3 *Campbell v Campbell* (1840) 7 Cl & Fin 166, HL. See also the cases cited in PARA 34. There is no lien for contributed money between co-owners who are not partners: *Kay v Johnston* (1856) 21 Beav 536; *Re Coulson's Trusts, Prichard v Coulson* (1907) 97 LT 754; cf *Leigh v Dickeson* (1884) 15 QBD 60, CA; and see *Re Leslie, Leslie v French* (1883) 23 ChD 552 at 564.
4 *West v Skip* (1749) 1 Ves Sen 239.

(9) PARTNER'S LIEN

141. Nature of partner's lien. On the dissolution of a partnership[1], each partner has a general lien on the firm's surplus assets[2], which arises out of his statutory right to have the surplus assets, after payment of the firm's debts and liabilities, applied in payment of what may be due to the partners respectively[3] after deducting what may be due from them as partners to the firm[4].

The lien is not one which affects each particular piece of property belonging to the partnership. It is in the nature of a general lien upon the surplus assets, and does not affect each particular asset so as to interfere with the right of a surviving partner to deal with the separate assets belonging to the partnership for the purposes of realisation and to give a good title to persons dealing in good faith with him in respect of those assets[5].

A partner also has a specific statutory lien on the surplus of the partnership assets, after satisfying the partnership liabilities, for any sum of money paid by him for the purchase of a share in the partnership and for any capital contributed by him, where a partnership agreement is rescinded on the ground of the fraud or misrepresentation of a co-partner[6].

1 Ie upon the general dissolution of the firm, not a technical dissolution caused by the admission or departure of a partner: see generally PARAS 33 note 8, 38, 111 note 1, 178, 204.
2 Not all a firm's assets can, however, be regarded as property which can constitute the subject of a partner's lien: *Faulks v Faulks* [1992] 1 EGLR 9 (milk quota registered in the name of a farming partnership); and see *Robertson v Brent and Haggitt* [1972] NZLR 406, NZ SC (work in progress in a solicitors' firm held not to be an asset). As to lien generally see LIEN.
3 As to the application of assets on dissolution see PARA 211.
4 See the Partnership Act 1890 s 39; and PARA 205. See also *Skipp v Harwood* (1747) 2 Swan 586; *West v Skip* (1749) 1 Ves Sen 239; *Ex p Williams* (1805) 11 Ves 3; *Ex p King* (1810) 17 Ves 115; *Harvey v Crickett* (1816) 5 M & S 336; *Hague v Dandeson* (1848) 2 Exch 741 at 745 per Parke B; *Kelly v Hutton* (1868) 3 Ch App 703 at 708–709; *Aberdare and Plymouth Co Ltd v Hankey* (1887) 3 TLR 493; *Hadlee v IRC* [1993] AC 524, [1993] 2 WLR 696, PC. It may be that in exceptional circumstances the court will go further and impose a constructive trust: see *Gordon v Gonda* [1955] 2 All ER 762, [1955] 1 WLR 885, CA; and see PARA 105. It seems that there is no lien as between persons who are merely part owners (*Re Leslie, Leslie v French* (1883) 23 ChD 552 at 563) or co-adventurers (*Re Boggs, ex p Gemmel* (1843) 3 Mont D & De G 198).
5 *Re Bourne, Bourne v Bourne* [1906] 2 Ch 427 at 432, CA, per Romer LJ. For this purpose, no distinction can be drawn between real estate held for partnership purposes and personal estate: *Re Bourne, Bourne v Bourne* [1906] 2 Ch 427 at 433, CA. As to equitable lien generally see LIEN vol 68 (2008) PARA 855 et seq.
6 See the Partnership Act 1890 s 41(a); and PARA 147. See also *Mycock v Beatson* (1879) 13 ChD 384; *Binney v Mutrie* (1886) 12 App Cas 160 at 165, PC. This lien appears wider than the

general lien because it embraces the firm's assets before deduction has been made from them of what is due to the partners. As to the contractual nature of the relationship between partners see PARA 1 note 1.

142. Extent of partner's lien. The lien of a partner may be enforced, not only against the partnership assets and the other partners, but also against all persons claiming through them in respect of their interests as partners[1], for example assignees[2], mortgagees[3], personal representatives[4], trustees in bankruptcy[5] or judgment creditors[6]. It is not enforceable against purchasers, chargees or pledgees of specific assets of the partnership who might reasonably suppose that all the partnership debts had been paid or barred by lapse of time, or who otherwise deal with the surviving or continuing partner in good faith[7]. The right extends to the satisfaction of allowances or payments agreed to be made on the dissolution[8].

During the continuance of the partnership, the right to indemnity constitutes a lien which attaches to all the property of the partnership for the time being, whatever may be its variations and changes[9]; but after dissolution it is limited to the partnership property existing as such at the date of the dissolution, and does not extend to property added to or substituted for the old stock by those who continue the business after that date[10].

1   See the Partnership Act 1890 s 39; and PARA 205. As to the lien see PARA 141; and LIEN.
2   *West v Skip* (1749) 1 Ves Sen 239; *Holderness v Shackels* (1828) 8 B & C 612 at 618.
3   *Cavander v Bulteel* (1873) 9 Ch App 79.
4   *Stocken v Dawson* (1845) 9 Beav 239; affd (1848) 17 LJ Ch 282.
5   *Re Butterworth, ex p Plant* (1835) 4 Deac & Ch 160.
6   *Skipp v Harwood* (1747) 2 Swan 586.
7   *Re Langmead's Trusts* (1855) 20 Beav 20; on appeal 7 De GM & G 353. The purchaser of the share of a partner in the partnership takes subject to the lien: *Cavander v Bulteel* (1873) 9 Ch App 79.
8   *Re Ancell, ex p Rowlandson* (1813) 2 Ves & B 172. The lien does not, however, cover liabilities not arising out of the partnership, such as private loans by one partner to another (*Ryall v Rowles* (1749) 1 Ves Sen 348), but it extends to partnership money borrowed by one of the firm (*Meliorucchi v Royal Exchange Assurance Co* (1728) 1 Eq Cas Abr 8; *Croft v Pyke* (1733) 3 P Wms 180).
9   *Skipp v Harwood* (1747) 2 Swan 586; *West v Skip* (1749) 1 Ves Sen 239; *Hadlee v IRC* [1993] AC 524, [1993] 2 WLR 696, PC.
10 *Payne v Hornby* (1858) 25 Beav 280. This view is, however, contrary to that held by Lord Hardwicke, who, in two cases arising out of the same transaction, decided that the lien of a partner on dissolution was not limited to the stock brought in, but extended to everything coming in lieu during the continuance or after the determination of the partnership: *Skipp v Harwood* (1747) 2 Swan 586; *West v Skip* (1749) 1 Ves Sen 239 at 244, 456. See also *Pennell v Deffell* (1853) 4 De GM & G 372 at 388 per Turner LJ. In *Stocken v Dawson* (1848) 17 LJ Ch 282 at 286 the parties agreed that the property should be considered to have remained unchanged. As to the loss of partnership lien by distribution by agreement of the partnership assets see PARA 139 text and note 3; and LIEN vol 68 (2008) PARA 886.

(10) ENFORCEMENT OF PARTNERS' RIGHTS BETWEEN THEMSELVES

(i) Parties to Partnership Actions

143. All partners must generally be parties or represented. The rights and liabilities of partners between themselves have been established in accordance with equitable principles[1]. In a claim for dissolution of partnership it is a general rule that all the partners who are within the jurisdiction must be before the court[2], especially where questions affecting the rights of the partners between themselves[3], or the construction of the partnership agreement[4], are raised. The personal representative of a deceased partner should be a party even if the estate of the deceased partner is reputed to be insolvent[5]; and, generally, where there is a diversity of interest, all the partners should be parties to[6] or represented in[7] the claim.

1   See EQUITABLE JURISDICTION vol 47 (2014) PARA 64.
2   *Ireton v Lewes* (1673) Cas temp Finch 96; *Hills v Nash* (1845) 1 Ph 594; *Simpson v Chapman* (1853) 4 De GM & G 154 at 167.
3   *Long v Yonge* (1830) 2 Sim 369. As to injunctions against breaches of the agreement between the partners eg against competitive trading see PARA 171.
4   *Cockburn v Thompson* (1809) 16 Ves 321; *Baldwin v Lawrence* (1824) 2 Sim & St 18; *Seddon v Connell* (1840) 10 Sim 58.
5   *Cox v Stephens* (1863) 11 WR 929; cf *Madox v Jackson* (1746) 3 Atk 405; *Seddon v Connell* (1840) 10 Sim 58.
6   *Van Sandau v Moore* (1826) 1 Russ 441; *Evans v Stokes* (1836) 1 Keen 24; *Harvey v Bignold* (1845) 8 Beav 343.
7   *Attwood v Small* (1838) 6 Cl & Fin 232, HL; *Cramer v Bird* (1868) LR 6 Eq 143.

144.   Representative parties.   Where more than one partner has the same interest in a claim, the claim may be begun, or the court may order that the claim be continued, by or against one or more of the partners who have the same interest as representatives of any other partners who have that interest[1]. Where a claim is for the benefit of all the partners, that is, where there is a community of interest, all those having similar interests may be represented, either as claimants or defendants, by one or more of their number[2]. If the common interest seems open to doubt, the court may give liberty to amend[3].

Where two persons engage in the purchase of a joint cargo, but keep separate accounts with respect to each moiety, one of them is not a necessary party to a claim for an account concerning the moiety of the other[4]; and persons who have merely a contingent right to become partners should not be joined in a claim for dissolution and accounts[5].

1   CPR 19.6(1); and see CIVIL PROCEDURE vol 11 (2009) PARA 229 et seq. See *Wood v McCarthy* [1893] 1 QB 775, DC (president and secretary of a labour protection league consisting of about 4,000 members were sued, and authorised, against their will, to defend on behalf of all the members).
2   *Cockburn v Thompson* (1809) 16 Ves 321; *Small v Attwood* (1832) You 507 (varied (1838) 6 Cl & Fin 232, HL).
3   *Bainbridge v Burton* (1840) 2 Beav 539. The cases under the old practice are not altogether uniform. A distinction was drawn between an action for an account after the partnership had come to an end (*Richardson v Hastings* (1844) 7 Beav 301; further proceedings 7 Beav 323), and an action for dissolution (*Deeks v Stanhope* (1844) 14 Sim 57), or such an action for an account as was, in effect, an action for dissolution (*Abraham v Hannay* (1843) 13 Sim 581; cf *Seddon v Connell* (1840) 10 Sim 58; *Sibley v Minton* (1857) 27 LJ Ch 53). In the former type of case it was held that an action might be maintained by some partners on behalf of themselves and others; in the latter it was held that all the partners, however numerous, were necessary parties. In *Beaumont v Meredith* (1814) 3 Ves & B 180, it was held that all the members of a benevolent society had to be parties to an action by some members against the trustees for an account. See also *Moffat v Farquharson* (1788) 2 Bro CC 338; *Chancey v May* (1722) Prec Ch 592; *Taylor v Salmon* (1838) 4 My & Cr 134.
4   *Weymouth v Boyer* (1792) 1 Ves 416. See also *Brown v De Tastet* (1819) Jac 284 (account ordered between a partner and a sub-partner without making the other two principal partners parties to the action, one of them being ignorant of the sub-partnership, and the other out of the jurisdiction).
5   *Ehrmann v Ehrmann* (1894) 72 LT 17.

145.   Necessary parties.   The assignee of a share in a partnership is not, during the continuance of the partnership, a necessary party to a claim against the other partners for an account, but after the dissolution of the partnership he may become so[1]. The personal representative of a deceased partner may sue for accounts even though he has assigned all the intestate's beneficial interest[2].

Where the share of a deceased partner is purchased by the surviving partners under a provision in the partnership agreement and the purchase money is allowed to remain in the business, contrary to the trusts of his will, all the partners who have notice of the trusts must be made defendants to a claim by the beneficiaries claiming profits made by the employment of that money in trade, and not merely such of them as are trustees[3].

Where a partner creates an equitable mortgage upon the real estate of himself and a third person in favour of his firm and dies intestate, the firm cannot enforce the security without making his personal representative a party to the claim[4].

A claim for a debt due to the partnership may, as a general rule, be brought by a surviving partner[5], and a surviving partner must be brought before the court in a claim to enforce a partnership debt against the estate of his deceased partner[6].

1   As to his rights see the Partnership Act 1890 s 31; and PARA 125. See also *Public Trustee v Elder* [1926] Ch 776, CA. In *Williams v Poole* (1873) 21 WR 252, an assignee, after dissolution, was held not to be a necessary party, being merely a 'dry trustee' for a satisfied mortgagee. A sub-partner has no right to an account from the principal partnership, but only from the partner with whom he is a sub-partner; therefore, the other partners are not necessary parties to a claim against that partner: see *Re Slyth, ex p Barrow* (1815) 2 Rose 252 at 255; *Brown v De Tastet* (1819) Jac 284. A partner who admits that another partner has no interest in the accounts may thereby lose the right to have that other partner before the court: see *Bodin v Farquhar* (1822) 1 LJOS Ch 21 (rehearing sought on the ground that that other partner ought to have been a party).

2   *Clegg v Fishwick* (1849) 1 Mac & G 294 (the effect of an assignment by an administratrix held to constitute her a trustee for the assignee).

3   *Vyse v Foster* (1874) LR 7 HL 318 at 335; cf *Pointon v Pointon* (1871) LR 12 Eq 547; and see PARA 130.

4   *Scholefield v Heafield* (1836) 7 Sim 667. As to the extent to which the Law of Property (Miscellaneous Provisions) Act 1989 s 2(1) (a contract for the sale or other disposition of land to be made in writing: see PARA 24 notes 6–7; and CONVEYANCING vol 23 (2013) PARA 151) affects equitable mortgages see REAL PROPERTY AND REGISTRATION vol 87 (2012) PARA 182.

5   *Haig v Gray* (1850) 3 De G & Sm 741; cf *Sales v Crispi* (1913) 29 TLR 491 (surviving partner of a firm which acted as business agents and managers to a variety artiste held not entitled to commission on engagements obtained by the client after the partnership was dissolved). As to the implied authority of a partner to bring and defend claims on behalf of his firm during its currency see PARAS 41, 78 et seq.

6   *Hills v M'Rae* (1851) 9 Hare 297 (surviving partner ordered to attend before the master); and see *Re Hodgson, Beckett v Ramsdale* (1885) 31 ChD 177 at 192, CA.

(ii) Fraud or Misrepresentation

A. FRAUD OR MISREPRESENTATION INDUCING PARTNERSHIP

146. Fraud invalidates an agreement, although discoverable. Fraud in inducing a person to enter into a partnership agreement is a ground for the rescission of the agreement[1], and the fact that the claimant could have discovered the truth, for example by examination of the books, is not a bar to relief[2]; nor is the fact that there cannot be restitutio in integrum after the firm in which the interest has been acquired has become insolvent[3]. In a question of rescission of his contract by a partner on the ground of fraud or misrepresentation, there is no analogy, in the case of such insolvency, between the case of an ordinary partnership and that of an incorporated company[4]. The claim by a defrauded partner against his fraudulent partner may be framed alternatively for rescission or dissolution[5], and he may in any event sue for the damages which he has sustained by reason of the fraud[6].

Misrepresentation without fraud is a sufficient ground for rescission and the repayment of capital advanced[7] and premium paid[8].

1 *Beck v Kantorowicz, Kantorowicz v Carter, Kalb v Kantorowicz* (1857) 3 K & J 230 (one partner made a secret profit on the purchase of property for the partnership). It is no defence to a claim for damages for breach of an agreement to become a partner that the claimant has been guilty of fraud in another partnership: *Andrewes v Garstin* (1861) 10 CBNS 444. As to claims for breach of an agreement to enter into partnership generally see *Walker v Harris* (1793) 1 Anst 245; *Figes v Cutler* (1822) 3 Stark 139.

2 *Rawlins v Wickham, Wickham v Rawlins* (1858) 1 Giff 355 (affd 3 De G & J 304); cf *Riddel v Smith* (1864) 12 WR 899 (plaintiff continued the partnership after discovery of misrepresentation); *Redgrave v Hurd* (1881) 20 ChD 1, CA (contract of sale rescinded and the deposit returned, but no damages awarded). See also MISREPRESENTATION vol 76 (2013) PARA 801.

3 *Adam v Newbigging* (1888) 13 App Cas 308 at 330, HL, per Lord Herschell.

4 *Adam v Newbigging* (1888) 13 App Cas 308 at 322, HL, per Lord Watson; cf MISREPRESENTATION vol 76 (2013) PARA 831.

5 *Bagot v Easton* (1877) 7 ChD 1, CA.

6 *Cruikshank v M'Vicar* (1844) 8 Beav 106; *Beck v Kantorowicz* (1857) 3 K & J 230. As to the principle that a person may not approbate and reprobate see ESTOPPEL vol 47 (2014) PARA 312.

7 *Adam v Newbigging* (1888) 13 App Cas 308, HL.

8 *Jauncey v Knowles* (1859) 29 LJ Ch 95.

147. Rights and liabilities of defrauded partner. Where a partnership agreement is rescinded on the ground of the fraud or misrepresentation of one of the parties to it, the partner entitled to rescind is entitled[1]:

(1) to a lien[2] on, or right of retention of, the surplus of the partnership assets, after satisfying the partnership liabilities, for any sum of money paid by him for the purchase of his share in the partnership and for any capital contributed by him[3];

(2) to a right of subrogation to the rights of the partnership creditors for any payments made by him to them in respect of the partnership liabilities[4]; and

(3) to be indemnified by the guilty partner against all partnership debts and liabilities[5].

A person who is induced by fraud or misrepresentation to become a partner is liable to the partnership creditors in respect of all dealings taking place while he remains a partner and, in the event of bankruptcy of the partner by whom he was defrauded, will be allowed to prove for a premium paid on entering the partnership in competition with the separate creditors of the bankrupt partner, but not in competition with the joint creditors of the firm[6].

1 These rights are without prejudice to any other right of the innocent partner: Partnership Act 1890 s 41. This provision merely declares the previous law: see *Mycock v Beatson* (1879) 13 ChD 384; *Newbigging v Adam* (1886) 34 ChD 582, CA (affd (1888) 13 App Cas 308, HL).

2 As to a partner's lien generally see PARA 141.

3 Partnership Act 1890 s 41(a).

4 Partnership Act 1890 s 41(b).

5 Partnership Act 1890 s 41(c).

6 *Re Hooper, ex p Broome* (1811) 1 Rose 69, as explained in *Bury v Allen* (1845) 1 Coll 589 at 598n, 607. Although, as against the guilty partner, he may have an equity to say that he never was a partner, it will be difficult to say so as against third persons: *Re Hooper, ex p Broome* (1811) 1 Rose 69 at 71 per Lord Eldon LC.

B. FRAUD OR MISREPRESENTATION ON PURCHASE OF PARTNERSHIP SHARE

148. Instances of fraud or misrepresentation giving rise to rescission. The sale of the share of one partner to another on the footing of a balance sheet prepared by the vendor's accountant and believed by both parties to be substantially correct may be set aside on proof that the balance sheet was grossly inaccurate and placed too high a value on the assets[1]. A purchase of a partner's share at an undervalue by a partner who kept the books and knew and concealed from his partner the inadequacy of consideration may be declared void and set aside[2]. This relief will not, however, be given when there has been no fraud or oppression, especially after long delay[3].

A sale by the executors of a deceased partner to the surviving partners will be closely scrutinised by the court, but will be supported if no unfair advantage has been taken of the executors[4]. The sale will be set aside, however, if it is at an undervalue so gross as to be deemed fraudulent[5]. A sale by the executors of a deceased partner to a surviving partner for the purpose of resale to one of the executors has been set aside[6].

1 *Charlesworth v Jennings* (1864) 34 Beav 96; and see *Smith v Gale* [1974] 1 All ER 401, [1974] 1 WLR 9.
2 *Maddeford v Austwick, Austwick v Maddeford* (1826) 1 Sim 89; affd (1833) 2 My & K 279. Nevertheless, a vendor who, after discovering that there has been concealment, elects to waive his right to full disclosure is bound by that election and neither he nor his personal representatives can repudiate the sale: *Law v Law* [1905] 1 Ch 140, CA.
3 *Knight v Marjoribanks* (1848) 11 Beav 322 (affd (1849) 2 Mac & G 10); approved in *Melbourne Banking Corpn v Brougham* (1882) 7 App Cas 307, PC. See also *Re Lightoller, ex p Peake* (1816) 1 Madd 346.
4 *Chambers v Howell* (1847) 11 Beav 6; *Hordern v Hordern* [1910] AC 465, PC. See WILLS AND INTESTACY vol 103 (2010) PARA 1028.
5 *Rice v Gordon* (1848) 11 Beav 265.
6 *Cook v Collingridge* (1823) Jac 607.

(iii) Order for Accounts

149. Time at which accounts may be ordered. In a claim by a partner, or a person claiming through him for dissolution and winding up of the affairs of the partnership, the accounts[1] are usually directed at the trial[2].

1 As to the right to an account see PARAS 134, 155.
2 As to orders for accounts see CPR 24 (summary judgment); CIVIL PROCEDURE vol 11 (2009) PARA 524 et seq; CIVIL PROCEDURE vol 12 (2009) PARA 1524. Orders for accounts have been made at other stages of the claim: see *Turquand v Wilson* (1875) 1 ChD 85. See also *Kupfer v Kupfer* (1915) 60 Sol Jo 221 (where some of the partners were British subjects interned in Germany during the 1914–18 war, the partnership was declared dissolved and the usual partnership accounts were directed, but the accounts were not to be proceeded with until three months after the declaration of peace).
　　As to the remedy of account generally see EQUITABLE JURISDICTION vol 47 (2014) PARA 49 et seq. As to the time limit in a claim for an account see LIMITATION PERIODS vol 68 (2008) PARAS 953, 1008–1009.

150. Accounts ordered where dissolution not specifically claimed. As a general rule, the court will not order an account of partnership dealings unless the claimant also claims dissolution[1]. An account may, however, be ordered without a claim for dissolution in a proper case, where a sufficient reason is shown for departing from the usual rule, as, for example, where a partner is trying to exclude his partner from some secret benefit or from the partnership, or to force him to a dissolution, or where there is a refusal to account, or where a limited account will meet the necessity or justice of the case[2].

In a claim for the administration of the estate of a deceased partner, the ordinary direction for an account of debts includes equitable debts, and therefore includes a debt due by the estate of the deceased partner on his separate account with the partnership, and a surviving partner can claim such a debt as a creditor of the deceased and have it ascertained by the taking of a partnership account[3].

1   *Forman v Homfray* (1813) 2 Ves & B 329; *Loscombe v Russell* (1830) 4 Sim 8; *Richards v Davies* (1831) 2 Russ & M 347; *Knebell v White* (1836) 2 Y & C Ex 15 at 21; cf *Waters v Taylor* (1808) 15 Ves 10. As to claims for dissolution generally and the circumstances in which such claims will be stayed see PARAS 181–182.

2   *Harrison v Armitage* (1819) 4 Madd 143 (distinguishing *Forman v Homfray* (1813) 2 Ves & B 329); *Chapple v Cadell* (1822) Jac 537; *Bentley v Bates* (1840) 4 Y & C Ex 182 (where Lord Abinger CB said that the joint owners of a colliery are in the position of mercantile partners for some purposes only, and that the rule requiring a dissolution to be claimed was meant to apply only to mercantile partnerships); *Wallworth v Holt* (1841) 4 My & Cr 619; *Richardson v Hastings* (1844) 7 Beav 301; further proceedings 7 Beav 323 (action brought to recover money and assets of the partnership, of which two members had possessed themselves); *Fairthorne v Weston* (1844) 3 Hare 387. An account may be ordered against a defendant who asserts the illegality of the partnership: see PARA 151.

3   *Paynter v Houston* (1817) 3 Mer 297; *Woolley v Gordon* (1829) Taml 11.

151.   Circumstances insufficient to bar relief.   It is no objection to a claim for an account that the defendant partner has stolen partnership assets and has not been first prosecuted[1], or that taking the accounts involves the settlement of claims in the nature of unliquidated damages[2].

The court will direct an account in England of the transactions of a partnership business carried on abroad as to which settled accounts have been established in the foreign court to the jurisdiction of which it is subject, if it is shown that the English partner has not been a party to the foreign proceedings, so that they are, as to him, res inter alios acta[3].

Although the court will not, as a rule, give its assistance to persons who carry on an illegal business, an account may be ordered against a defendant who asserts the illegality of the partnership[4].

1   *Roope v D'Avigdor* (1883) 10 QBD 412, DC.

2   *Bury v Allen* (1845) 1 Coll 589.

3   *Maunder v Lloyd* (1862) 2 John & H 718 (where it appeared that all the assets of the English partner were in England, so that no payment out of them could have been enforced except by proceedings upon the foreign judgment).

4   *Sheppard v Oxenford* (1855) 1 K & J 491, CA. No claim will lie for an account of a partnership in the profits of a crime: see *Everet v Williams* (1725) (the Highwaymen's Case). As to illegal partnerships generally see PARA 33 et seq.

152.   Defences to claim for an account.   The following may be good defences to a partner's claim for an account:

(1)   denial of partnership[1];

(2)   illegality or fraud, or forfeiture under a power contained in the partnership agreement[2];

(3)   laches[3];

(4)   expiration of the limitation period[4], although time does not run until the partnership is determined[5];

(5)   account stated or settled account[6];

(6)   award, release by deed[7], or payment and acceptance of money under an agreement to an accord and satisfaction[8].

1   As to the existence of a partnership see PARAS 4, 9 et seq.

2   *Hart v Clarke* (1854) 6 De GM & G 232; affd sub nom *Clarke and Chapman v Hart* (1858) 6 HL Cas 633.

3   As to the effect of laches see PARA 129; and EQUITABLE JURISDICTION vol 47 (2014) PARA 253 et seq; LIMITATION PERIODS vol 68 (2008) PARA 1009.

4   See the Limitation Act 1980 s 23; and LIMITATION PERIODS vol 68 (2008) PARAS 1008–1009. See also *Bridges v Mitchell* (1726) Gilb Ch 224; *Tatam v Williams* (1844) 3 Hare 347; *Noyes v Crawley* (1878) 10 ChD 31. An executor of a deceased partner may be barred by lapse of time (*Knox v Gye* (1872) LR 5 HL 656; *Taylor v Taylor* (1873) 28 LT 189), but, if a partnership is determined by death and the surviving partners carry on the new partnership without taking the accounts of the old and without interruption or settlement, the statutory time limit has no application as between the surviving partners and the representatives of the deceased partner (*Betjemann v Betjemann* [1895] 2 Ch 474, CA). Where the surviving partners, being the executors of their deceased partner, kept his share in the business and did not supply full information and accounts to the persons beneficially interested under his will, an account was directed against them at the suit of the beneficiaries after the lapse of 30 years (*Wedderburn v Wedderburn* (1836) 2 Keen 722; affd (1838) 4 My & Cr 41); and time will not run against the executors of a deceased partner so long as there are outstanding assets to be got in and the parties have dealt with one another upon the footing of the account being still open (*Millington v Holland* (1869) 18 WR 184). If one partner unlawfully excludes another from the management or control of the partnership property, time begins to run against a claim based on such exclusion from the act of exclusion: *Barton v North Staffordshire Rly Co* (1888) 38 ChD 458 at 463; *Clegg v Edmondson* (1857) 8 De GM & G 787.

5   See LIMITATION PERIODS vol 68 (2008) PARA 1009; and see also *Patel v Patel* [2007] EWCA Civ 1520, [2007] All ER (D) 276 (Dec).

6   As to account stated see CONTRACT vol 22 (2012) PARA 611 et seq; EQUITABLE JURISDICTION vol 47 (2014) PARA 52. As to settled accounts see PARA 153.

7   As to what may constitute a sufficient release see *Loretto School Ltd v Macandrew and Jenkins* 1992 SLT 615, Ct of Sess (non-partnership case); and see CONTRACT vol 22 (2012) PARAS 614–616.

8   *Brown v Perkins* (1842) 1 Hare 564. As to accord and satisfaction generally see CONTRACT vol 22 (2012) PARA 605.

153.   Reopening settled accounts.   Although a settled account[1] between the partners is a good ground of defence to a claim for an account[2], in special circumstances the court may reopen the accounts or give liberty to surcharge and falsify[3]. Settled accounts are not usually reopened in toto except upon the ground of fraud, or numerous and important errors, or mistakes affecting the whole account[4]; otherwise, the court will not usually do more than give liberty to surcharge and falsify[5]. In the absence of fraud, accounts are not reopened in favour of a party who has stood by and acquiesced in them[6]; but acquiescence in the principle of keeping an account does not amount to acquiescence in the accuracy of the items[7].

1   A settled account is one that is agreed between the parties: see EQUITABLE JURISDICTION vol 47 (2014) PARA 52. The fact that it has been stated that a certain sum is due and that that sum has then been paid does not necessarily constitute a settled account: *Phillips-Higgins v Harper* [1954] 1 QB 411, [1954] 1 All ER 116; affd [1954] 1 QB 411 at 420, [1954] 2 All ER 51, CA.

2   See *Davies v Davies* (1837) 2 Keen 534.

3   A single important error is sufficient, if fraudulent, to justify an order to open the whole account. If it is not fraudulent, the proper order is to give liberty to surcharge and falsify: *Gething v Keighley* (1878) 9 ChD 547 at 550; and see EQUITABLE JURISDICTION vol 47 (2014) PARA 54. Accounts will be reopened on the ground of fraud in spite of the existence of a stringent agreement against reopening: *Oldaker v Lavender* (1833) 6 Sim 239; *Sim v Sim* (1861) 11 I Ch R 310 at 321. In *Barrow v Barrow* (1872) 27 LT 431 goodwill had not been accounted for, and the account was in that respect and otherwise not in accordance with the terms of the partnership agreement. The mere fact that the claimant has already had an account rendered to him will not preclude him, in the absence of acquiescence, from having an account taken by the court: *Irvine v Young* (1823) 1 Sim & St 333; *Clements v Bowes* (1853) 1 Drew 684; *Hunter v*

Belcher (1863) 9 LT 501 (on appeal (1864) 2 De GJ & Sm 194). As to reopening settled accounts see further AGENCY vol 1 (2008) PARA 87; EQUITABLE JURISDICTION vol 47 (2014) PARA 53; MISTAKE vol 77 (2010) PARA 78.

4 *Pritt v Clay* (1843) 6 Beav 503; *M'Kellar v Wallace* (1853) 8 Moo PCC 378; *Williamson v Barbour* (1877) 9 ChD 529; *Gething v Keighley* (1878) 9 ChD 547 at 550; and see *Re Webb, Lambert v Still* [1894] 1 Ch 73 at 84, CA; cf *Maund v Allies* (1840) 5 Jur 860; *Laing v Campbell* (1865) 36 Beav 3.

5 *Gething v Keighley* (1878) 9 ChD 547. Where a valuation was held to be merely incidental to the carrying out of the purchase of a deceased partner's share by a surviving partner, as provided for in the partnership agreement, the court allowed the account to stand, subject to correction on proof of error of a clear and convincing character: *Hordern v Hordern* [1910] AC 465, PC.

6 *Scott v Milne* (1841) 5 Beav 215 (affd (1843) 7 Jur 709); *Millar v Craig* (1843) 6 Beav 433; *Cuthbert v Edinborough* (1872) 21 WR 98.

7 *Mosse v Salt* (1863) 32 Beav 269. See also *Phillips-Higgins v Harper* [1954] 1 QB 411, [1954] 1 All ER 116; affd [1954] 1 QB 411 at 420, [1954] 2 All ER 51, CA.

154. Basis on which accounts are framed. Accounts during the currency of a partnership must be taken according to the uniform practice of the firm[1], unless manifestly misleading[2], and even if contrary to the method prescribed by the partnership agreement[3]. Accounts framed in accordance with the firm's uniform practice but contrary to the method prescribed by the partnership agreement may well not be binding, however, upon an outgoing partner or his estate[4]. In the absence of agreement, the burden of establishing a system different from the firm's usual practice lies on the party who would gain by the varied system[5]. The executors of a deceased partner are entitled to have his share ascertained on the basis of a balance sheet as prescribed by the partnership agreement even though a balance sheet was not in fact made out at the time of his death[6].

A partner is bound by the debit items of accounts furnished by him, although the court need not accept his items on the credit side[7]. The whole partnership assets must be included in the accounts[8].

1 *Pettyt v Janeson* (1819) 6 Madd 146; *Simmons v Leonard* (1844) 3 Hare 581; *Coventry v Barclay* (1863) 33 Beav 1 (affd (1864) 3 De GJ & Sm 320); *Binney v Mutrie* (1886) 12 App Cas 160, PC. See also *Crosskill v Bower, Bower v Turner* (1863) 32 Beav 86; *Re Barber, ex p Barber* (1870) 5 Ch App 687; *Garwood v Garwood* (1911) 105 LT 231, CA. As to the form in which accounts are to be drawn up in relation to corporate partners see the Partnerships (Accounts) Regulations 2008, SI 2008/569 (amended by SI 2013/2005); and as to the requirements of accounts generally see COMPANIES vol 15 (2009) PARA 708 et seq.

2 *Noble v Noble* 1965 SLT 415, Ct of Sess. Similarly, for the purposes of income tax, the profits of a firm must be accurately stated in its accounts (see *Odeon Associated Theatres Ltd v Jones* [1971] 2 All ER 407, [1971] 1 WLR 442; affd [1973] Ch 288, [1972] 1 All ER 681, CA). See also PARA 99. A firm's accounts may not, however, be decisive upon the question as to which assets are partnership assets: *Barton v Morris* [1985] 2 All ER 1032, [1985] 1 WLR 1257; and see PARAS 115–116, 135.

3 *Jackson v Sedgwick* (1818) 1 Swan 460; but see *Lawes v Lawes* (1878) 9 ChD 98 (oral agreement to vary the time fixed by the partnership agreement for settling accounts held not to have been intended to affect the financial interests of the partners). In the absence of special agreement, the practice of making annual rests, so as to allow interest on the balances credited to the partners, will not be continued after dissolution: *Barfield v Loughborough* (1872) 8 Ch App 1 at 7; and see MORTGAGE vol 77 (2010) PARA 217.

4 *Cruickshank v Sutherland* (1922) 92 LJ Ch 136, HL (where it was held that the executors of a deceased partner were entitled to have the firm's assets revalued, notwithstanding that it had been the firm's practice, contrary to the terms of the partnership agreement, to show them at book value). See *Gadd v Gadd* [2002] EWHC 107 (Ch), [2002] All ER (D) 105 (Feb) (executors of the deceased partner had the right to insist that the accounts show the current value of the asset at the date of the account as there was no evidence to indicate that the agreement had been varied by a course of dealing on the part of the partners). There is no presumption that, on a partner's death, the value of assets is to be determined by their current market value, rather than their historical costs as shown in the partnership books: *White v Minnis* [2001] Ch 393, [2000] 3 All ER 618, CA.

5   This principle was recognised where a surviving partner, who carried on the business, claimed compound interest: *Bate v Robins* (1863) 32 Beav 73. See, however, *Noble v Noble* 1965 SLT 415, Ct of Sess.

6   *Hunter v Dowling* [1893] 1 Ch 391; affd [1893] 3 Ch 212, CA.

7   *Morehouse v Newton* (1849) 3 De G & Sm 307.

8   An unsaleable asset should be valued. For example, in accounts taken upon dissolution an unassignable contract held by one partner on behalf of the firm must be retained by him and valued as an asset: *Ambler v Bolton* (1872) LR 14 Eq 427. In some cases, however, an asset of the firm cannot be accounted for or valued upon that firm's dissolution: see *Faulks v Faulks* [1992] 1 EGLR 9 (milk quota registered in the name of the farming partnership); and see *Robertson v Brent and Haggitt* [1972] NZLR 406, NZ SC (work in progress in a solicitors' firm held not to be an asset). As to the realisation of assets on dissolution see PARA 205 et seq.

155.   Persons entitled to an account.   Either a partner himself, or his personal representative or trustee in bankruptcy, may have an account against the other partner or his personal representative; but an assignee or mortgagee of a partner's share has no right to an account from the other partners during the continuance of the partnership, although on dissolution he becomes entitled to an account from the date of the dissolution[1]. In special circumstances, strangers to the partnership are entitled to an account[2]; and the persons beneficially interested in the estate of a deceased partner, whose executor, being also a partner, uses the testator's assets in the business, are entitled to accounts from the executor, but not from the other partners unless they have notice of a breach of trust by the executor[3]. Where, however, surviving partners deal with the property of their deceased partner, knowing it to belong to his estate, they are fixed with notice of the trusts on which it is held[4].

1   See the Partnership Act 1890 s 31; and PARA 125. As to the weak position of the assignee of a partner's share see PARA 125; and as to the position of a sub-partner see PARA 145 note 1.

2   This right was recognised in *Newland v Champion* (1748) 2 Coll 46 (separate creditor of a deceased partner was plaintiff); *Cropper v Knapman* (1836) 2 Y & C Ex 338; *Millar v Craig* (1843) 6 Beav 433; *Law v Law* (1845) 2 Coll 41 (residuary legatees obtained an account, the executors of a deceased partner having agreed to purchase the shares of the other partners); *Maunder v Lloyd* (1862) 2 John & H 718; *Pointon v Pointon* (1871) LR 12 Eq 547; cf *Taylor v Taylor* (1873) 28 LT 189.

3   In order to ascertain what profits were made from a breach of trust of this kind, Lord Eldon LC ordered the executor to produce attested copies of books in the custody of the executor's partners or agents, who were not parties to the action: *Freeman v Fairlie* (1817) 3 Mer 24, as explained in *MacDonald v Richardson, Richardson v Marten* (1858) 1 Giff 81 at 87. See also *Hue v Richards* (1839) 2 Beav 305; *Vyse v Foster* (1872) LR 13 Eq 602 (on appeal 8 Ch App 309, (1874) LR 7 HL 318).

4   *Travis v Milne, Milne v Milne* (1851) 9 Hare 141. In *Hue v Richards* (1839) 2 Beav 305 the widow of a deceased partner who was beneficially interested under his will was held entitled to production of accounts from the testator's executors, one of whom was the surviving partner; and, generally, such an action may be maintained, whether the executor is a partner or not, 'in all cases where the relation between the executors and the surviving partner is such as to present a substantial impediment to the prosecution by the executors of the rights of the parties interested in the estate against the surviving partners': *Travis v Milne, Milne v Milne* (1851) 9 Hare 141 at 151 per Turner V-C. Cf *Beningfield v Baxter* (1886) 12 App Cas 167, PC; *Yeatman v Yeatman* (1877) 7 ChD 210, commenting on *Bowsher v Watkins* (1830) 1 Russ & M 277. See also *Davies v Davies* (1837) 2 Keen 534 at 539; the Partnership Act 1890 s 42(1); and PARA 130.

156.   Payment on an account.   In a series of monthly accounts in which the balances are not carried forward from one account to another, payment of the balance on the last account does not, it seems, bar a claim for the payment of balances on preceding accounts[1]; and, when the partners, on dissolution, agree to divide the partnership property in specie, and one partner takes the whole according to a valuation, a claim by the other partner for the amount payable to him may be maintained notwithstanding that the partnership accounts remain otherwise unadjusted[2].

A partner may have a right of action at any time against another for a debt which is independent of the partnership accounts[3].

1   *Brierly v Cripps* (1836) 7 C & P 709. One account is in the circumstances as final as any other; it is otherwise if they have been intended to form part of one general account: see *Fromont v Coupland* (1824) 2 Bing 170. As regards the Court's power to order an interim payment in a partnership action see *Mukerjee (Nee Sen) v Sen* [2012] EWCA Civ 1895.

2   *Jackson v Stopherd* (1834) 2 Cr & M 361. 'There may be special bargains by which particular transactions are insulated and separated from the winding up of the concern and are taken out of the general law of partnership': *Jackson v Stopherd* (1834) 2 Cr & M 361 at 366 per Bayley B. See also *Roxburgh Dinardo & Partners' Judicial Factor v Dinardo* 1992 GWD 6–322, Ct of Sess; cf *Coffee v Brian* (1825) 3 Bing 54; *Lomas v Bradshaw* (1850) 9 CB 620.

3   *Simpson v Rackham* (1831) 5 Moo & P 612; *Worrall v Grayson* (1836) 1 M & W 166.

157.   No indebtedness between partners.   Partners are not, as regards partnership dealings, considered as debtor and creditor between themselves until the concern is wound up or until there is a binding settlement of the accounts[1]; but, where exceptionally a partner has repeatedly requested the taking of an account and this has been refused, that partner may be entitled to sue his co-partners in respect of a specific debt owed to him qua partner without such an account having been taken[2]. Subject to this, it follows that one partner has no right of action against another for the balance owing to him until after final settlement of the accounts[3]; and money lent to a partnership by a partner cannot be recovered in a common law claim for money lent[4]. This rule applies only in relation to persons who are currently partners; and, once a partner has left the partnership leaving the other partners to continue the firm's business on their own account, as, for example, where the outgoing partner has retired or has been expelled, his former partners are creditors to him in respect of any part of his partnership share or other agreed entitlement as has not been paid out to him[5].

1   *Clark v Glennie* (1820) 3 Stark 10; *Bovill v Hammond* (1827) 6 B & C 149; *Richardson v Bank of England* (1838) 4 My & Cr 165; *Carr v Smith* (1843) 5 QB 128; *Meyer and Co v Faber (No 2)* [1923] 2 Ch 421, CA; and *Hurst v Bryk* [2002] 1 AC 185, [2000] 2 All ER 193, HL. The authority of a partner who is appointed to wind up the partnership affairs extends to settlement of the necessary accounts: see *Luckie v Forsyth* (1846) 3 Jo & Lat 388.

2   *Prole v Masterman* (1855) 21 Beav 61 (where, although the principles enunciated in the case mirror the arguments applicable as between partners (i e until an account has been taken, the true position between the partners cannot be seen), this case actually concerned directors of an old-style railway company).

3   *Smith v Barrow* (1788) 2 Term Rep 476; *Fromont v Coupland* (1824) 2 Bing 170; *Prole v Masterman* (1855) 21 Beav 61; *Weston v Abrahams* (1869) 20 LT 586. The situs of such cause of action when the business has been carried on by partners resident in different jurisdictions is at the principal place of business: see *Luchmeechund v Mull* (1860) 3 LT 603.

4   *Green v Hertzog* [1954] 1 WLR 1309, CA. Money so lent can only be recovered in proceedings for taking accounts under the Partnership Act 1890 s 44: see PARA 211.

5   See the Partnership Act 1890 s 43; and PARAS 5, 81, 134. See also *Sobell v Boston* [1975] 2 All ER 282, [1975] 1 WLR 1587; *Gopala Chetty v Vijayaraghavachariar* [1922] 1 AC 488, PC; *Brown v Rivlin* [1983] CA Transcript 56.

158.   Effect of dissolution and settlement of accounts.   Dissolution and mutual settlement of accounts are sufficient consideration for an implied promise to pay the balance found to be due on the taking of the account and no express promise is necessary to support a claim for payment[1].

1   *Rackstraw v Imber* (1816) Holt NP 368 (continuing partner sought unsuccessfully to attach conditions to his payment); *Moravia v Levy* (1786) 2 Term Rep 483n (where, however, there

was an express promise to pay); *Foster v Allanson* (1788) 2 Term Rep 479 at 483; cf *Wray v Milestone* (1839) 5 M & W 21; and see generally CONTRACT vol 22 (2012) PARA 611.

159. Payment into court of sums due. When it can be shown that a certain sum will be found due upon the taking of a partnership account, that sum may be ordered to be paid into court[1]. Money shown to have been received by a partner improperly, or in breach of agreement or good faith, will be ordered to be paid into court[2].

1   *Richardson v Bank of England* (1838) 4 My & Cr 165 (motion refused on the ground that the defendant not only did not admit the accuracy of the account but disputed numerous items in it); *Gaskell v Chambers* (1858) 26 Beav 360; *London Syndicate v Lord* (1878) 8 ChD 84 at 87, CA, per Jessel MR; *Freeman v Cox* (1878) 8 ChD 148 (defendant admitted that he had the firm's money in his hands); *Wanklyn v Wilson* (1887) 35 ChD 180; *Hollis v Burton* [1892] 3 Ch 226, CA (admission made in error allowed to be withdrawn, but upon the terms that money be paid into court); *Re Beeny, Ffrench v Sproston* [1894] 1 Ch 499 (the admission may be oral); *Neville v Matthewman* [1894] 3 Ch 345, CA; *Nutter v Holland* [1894] 3 Ch 408, CA. Cf *Creak v Capell* (1821) 6 Madd 114 (motion for payment in refused pending the hearing of objections); *Toulmin v Copland* (1837) 3 Y & C Ex 625; *Gretzer v Heimann* [1929] WN 244 (order refused where, although the money was admittedly partnership assets, the court was not satisfied that it belonged to the plaintiff).

2   *Jervis v White* (1802) 6 Ves 738; *Foster v Donald* (1820) 1 Jac & W 252, followed in *Birley v Kennedy* (1865) 6 New Rep 395; *Costeker v Horrox* (1839) 3 Y & C Ex 530; *Re Benson, Elletson v Pillers* [1899] 1 Ch 39. Money received by a partner on account of, and during the currency of, the partnership is not money received in a fiduciary capacity, and a partner is not liable to attachment under the Debtors Act 1869 s 4(3) (see CONTEMPT OF COURT vol 22 (2012) PARA 88) for disobeying an order to pay into court money in his hands belonging to the partnership: *Piddocke v Burt* [1894] 1 Ch 343; and see PARA 105 note 1; and EQUITABLE JURISDICTION vol 47 (2014) PARA 231.

160. Costs of partnership accounts. As a general rule, the costs of taking accounts are payable out of the partnership assets[1]. Negligence or other misconduct by a partner may render him liable for the costs of a claim as far as it has been occasioned by such misconduct[2]. If the partnership assets are not sufficient to pay the costs, the partners must contribute in proportion to their shares after adjusting their rights in other respects[3]. Thus, partnership debts and liabilities, including debts and balances due to partners by the firm in respect of advances, take priority over the costs[4].

1   *Butcher v Pooler* (1883) 24 ChD 273, CA. An order for payment of costs out of the assets is a discretionary order and is not appealable: *Butcher v Pooler* (1883) 24 ChD 273 at 280, CA, per Bowen LJ; *Jones v Welch* (1855) 1 K & J 765; *Bonville v Bonville* (1865) 35 Beav 129; *Newton v Taylor* (1874) LR 19 Eq 14 (accounts settled under an award, in pursuance of an arbitration clause contained in the partnership agreement, and the costs made payable out of the assets and in the same proportions as if the accounts had been taken by the court); *Hamer v Giles, Giles v Hamer* (1879) 11 ChD 942; *Austin v Jackson* (1879) 11 ChD 942n.

2   *Norton v Russell* (1875) LR 19 Eq 343 (defendant who had admitted default in rendering accounts, although there was no allegation or denial that anything was due from him, ordered to pay costs up to the hearing); *Hamer v Giles, Giles v Hamer* (1879) 11 ChD 942. In *Dean v MacDowell* (1878) 8 ChD 345, CA, the plaintiffs obtained an account of alleged secret profits by a partner in another business, and by a supplemental claim sought not only those profits but the partner's whole interest in the business. The first claim was dismissed but without costs as the defendant's conduct had been blameworthy; the second claim was dismissed with costs as wholly unfounded. See also PARA 171 note 9.

3   *Ross v White* [1894] 3 Ch 326, CA.

4   *Potter v Jackson* (1880) 13 ChD 845 (balance owing to a partner for rent of property occupied by the firm and for capital advanced by him); *Rosher v Crannis* (1890) 63 LT 272 (funds had been voluntarily brought in, after dissolution by a partner); cf *Davy v Scarth* [1906] 1 Ch 55 (partner who had been appointed receiver held to be entitled to payment of his remuneration

and costs in that capacity, although he was unable to pay a sum which he owed to his firm). As to the order of application of assets on a dissolution see the Partnership Act 1890 s 44(b); and PARA 211.

(iv) Receivers

161. Jurisdiction to appoint a receiver or manager. The court may by order, whether interim or final, appoint a receiver[1] in all cases in which it appears to the court to be just and convenient to do so[2], on the application of any partner, whether claimant or defendant[3], or of other persons interested in the preservation of the partnership assets, such as the personal representatives of a deceased partner[4], especially where the surviving partner fails to get in the assets[5]. The court also has jurisdiction to appoint a manager[6]. The function of a manager is to carry on the partnership business under the direction of the court; a receiver does not have this power unless he is also appointed manager[7]. The jurisdiction may be exercised even where there is an agreement for reference to arbitration[8].

1 Where the only substantial asset of a partnership is a freehold property which is already subject to a charge (the amount secured exceeding the value of the property itself), the court has no power to impose another charge upon that property in priority to the existing charge in order to secure the receiver's expenses and remuneration: *Choudhri v Palta* [1994] 1 BCLC 184, [1992] BCC 787, CA. As to a receiver's power to sell the assets of the partnership over which he has been appointed see *Murray v King* [1986] FSR 116, Aust Fed Ct (firm's copyright in the magazine which it published). As to receivers generally see RECEIVERS vol 88 (2012) PARA 1 et seq. Cf COMPANIES vol 15 (2009) PARAS 1340 et seq, 1361 et seq; MORTGAGE vol 77 (2010) PARA 560 et seq.
2 Senior Courts Act 1981 s 37(1). Any such order may be made either unconditionally or on such terms and conditions as the court thinks just: s 37(2). See further RECEIVERS vol 88 (2012) PARA 13.
3 *Katsch v Schenck* (1849) 18 LJ Ch 386.
4 *Davis v Amer* (1854) 3 Drew 64.
5 *Estwick v Conningsby* (1682) 1 Vern 118.
6 See e g *Lees v Jones* (1857) 3 Jur NS 954; *Sargant v Read* (1876) 1 ChD 600.
7 See *Re Manchester and Milford Rly Co, ex p Cambrian Rly Co* (1880) 14 ChD 645 at 653, CA; *Taylor v Neate* (1888) 39 ChD 538 at 543; and RECEIVERS vol 88 (2012) PARA 184 et seq.
8 *Machin v Bennett* [1900] WN 146; and see *Plews v Baker* (1873) LR 16 Eq 564; *Law v Garrett* (1878) 8 ChD 26, CA; *Pini v Roncoroni* [1892] 1 Ch 633; PARA 182; and ARBITRATION.

162. Circumstances justifying appointment of receiver before dissolution. Unless proceedings have been instituted for the dissolution[1] and winding up of the partnership, or for relief which will necessarily involve such dissolution and winding up[2], the courts are generally reluctant to order the appointment of a receiver and manager in respect of a subsisting partnership[3]. Even where a partnership has not been dissolved and there are no such proceedings on foot, an application for the appointment of a receiver simpliciter, as opposed to that for a receiver and manager, may, however, be more sympathetically viewed by the courts[4].

Further, and notwithstanding such general reluctance of the courts, it would appear that, where special grounds exist for the appointment of a receiver or receiver and manager, such appointment may be ordered. Misconduct by one or more partners plus jeopardy to partnership assets is, therefore, a ground for the appointment of a receiver before dissolution[5]. Where a partner is guilty of stealing the partnership assets[6] or where a surviving partner insists on continuing the business with the assets of a deceased partner[7], or fails to get in the outstanding debts, or otherwise acts to the prejudice of the assets[8], or where an acting partner denies the other partner's right to relief on the ground that the partnership is illegal and claims the whole property for himself[9], or where a new firm extends the credit of the debtors of the old firm and declines to press them for payment[10], the courts may be more willing to order the appointment of a receiver or receiver and manager in respect of a subsisting partnership. Likewise, where a partner wrongfully seeks to exclude his co-partner[11] or where he acts in breach of the terms of an agreement under which the partners agreed that a third party is to act in the winding up of the firm, the partners having divested themselves of this right[12], or has acted fraudulently towards his co-partners[13], the courts may be more willing to appoint a receiver or receiver and manager in respect of a subsisting partnership.

Where the existence or the prior dissolution of the partnership is disputed and the appointment of a receiver or receiver and manager is sought in interim proceedings before the court has had an opportunity to ascertain whether a partnership exists or whether its dissolution has been effected, as the case may be, although the court will have jurisdiction to make such appointment, it will be reluctant to do so if such appointment would cause irreparable damage to the firm[14]. Likewise, where it is contended that the partnership is illegal[15], the court is generally reluctant in interim proceedings to order the appointment of a receiver or receiver and manager. Where, however, the prospects of such a contention succeeding are small, the court may be more willing to grant such an order[16].

The nature of the partnership business and the size of the partnership will also be factors which the court will take into consideration in deciding how to exercise its discretion. Thus, in relation to professional firms, the court will be especially sensitive to the damage which may be caused by the publicity which the appointment of a receiver or receiver and manager usually entails[17]. Conversely, it will be easier to obtain such an appointment in relation to a small firm since such an appointment will affect fewer persons than it will in the case of a large firm[18].

Where some of the partners have become alien enemies, a receiver and manager will generally be appointed[19].

The court will not appoint a receiver for a purpose, neither authorised nor assented to by the partners, which it could not authorise one partner to carry out against the will of the others[20].

1   As to the position after dissolution, where the courts will generally appoint a receiver or receiver and manager and almost as a matter of course, see PARA 208 note 7. Dissolution alone was not formerly considered sufficient ground for the appointment of a receiver without some breach of duty (*Harding v Glover* (1810) 18 Ves 281) but this view is not consistent with later cases which seem to show that, in the case of a dissolved partnership, the appointment of a receiver is almost a matter of course: see *Sobell v Boston* [1975] 2 All ER 282 at 286, [1975] 1 WLR 1587 at 1590 per Goff J. As to dissolution see PARA 173 et seq.

2   See *Sheppard v Oxenford* (1855) 1 K & J 491 (where various forms of relief usually associated with dissolution were sought, although dissolution itself was not expressly claimed); *Evans v Coventry* (1854) 5 De GM & G 911 (revsg 3 Drew 75).

3   *Hall v Hall* (1850) 12 Beav 414; *Roberts v Eberhardt* (1853) Kay 148; and see *Oliver v Hamilton* (1794) 2 Anst 453; *Waters v Taylor* (1808) 15 Ves 10; *Carlen v Drury* (1812) 1 Ves & B 154; *Lawson v Morgan* (1815) 1 Price 303; *Harrison v Armitage* (1819) 4 Madd 143; *Goodman v Whitcomb* (1820) 1 Jac & W 589; *Marshall v Colman* (1820) 2 Jac & W 266; *Richards v Davies* (1831) 2 Russ & M 347; *Smith v Jeyes* (1841) 4 Beav 503; *Rowlands v Evans* (1861) 30 Beav 302. Where there has been a dissolution of the partnership caused by the death of the partners but the partners' personal representatives have carried on the partnership business, a receiver or receiver and manager will more readily be appointed, since there is not the same mutual confidence between partners' personal representatives as between partners

themselves: *Phillips v Atkinson* (1787) 2 Bro CC 272. In a mining partnership a receiver has been refused against a tenant in common, where the plaintiff had stood by and the mine proved profitable, and the defendant had incurred expenditure (*Norway v Rowe* (1812) 19 Ves 144; and see MINES, MINERALS AND QUARRIES vol 76 (2013) PARAS 368–369); and an application for the appointment of a receiver has been refused against a partner who was also an unsatisfied mortgagee (*Rowe v Wood* (1822) 2 Jac & W 553). Nor will mere disagreement and want of co-operation between the partners constitute sufficient ground for the appointment of a receiver: *Roberts v Eberhardt* (1853) Kay 148. Cf *Jefferys v Smith* (1820) 1 Jac & W 298.

4   *Const v Harris* (1824) Turn & R 496. However, in *Hall v Hall* (1850) 3 Mac & G 79 at 90, Lord Truro LC said of *Const v Harris* (1824) Turn & R 496 that it was a peculiar case since the receiver had simply a duty to perform, which might be considered purely ministerial, namely to receive the entrance money of a theatre and to apply it according to the previous arrangement between the parties until the hearing of the cause.

5   *Evans v Coventry* (1854) 5 De GM & G 911 (revsg 3 Drew 75); *Sheppard v Oxenford* (1855) 1 K & J 491; *Carlen v Drury* (1812) 1 Ves & B 154.

6   *Oliver v Hamilton* (1794) 2 Anst 453; *Medwin v Ditcham* (1882) 47 LT 250 (where, in an action for an injunction to restrain the defendant from drawing out of partnership funds more than the stipulated amount, and for a receiver, a receiver was appointed pending a reference to arbitration, even though there was no claim for dissolution of partnership); and see *Smith v Jeyes* (1841) 4 Beav 503 (where a partner was accused of diverting partnership funds).

7   *Madgwick v Wimble* (1843) 6 Beav 495.

8   *Estwick v Conningsby* (1682) 1 Vern 118. See also *Young v Buckett* (1882) 30 WR 511 (where it was held that the fact that the surviving partner was endeavouring to divert the goodwill of the business to himself was sufficient ground for the appointment of a receiver and manager at the instance of the representative of the deceased partner).

9   *Hale v Hale* (1841) 4 Beav 369 (where a receiver was appointed notwithstanding the fact that no misconduct was alleged as against the defendant partner).

10   *Collenridge v Cook* (1837) 1 Jur 771.

11   *Wilson v Greenwood* (1818) 1 Swan 471; *Blakeney v Dufaur* (1851) 15 Beav 40; and see the judgment of Long Innes J in *Tate v Barry* (1928) 28 SRNSW 380 at 387 with which Megarry J concurred in *Floydd v Cheney, Cheney v Floydd* [1970] Ch 602 at 610, [1970] 1 All ER 446 at 451–452. See also *Tibbits v Phillips* (1853) 1 WR 163 (where a manager was appointed).

12   *Davis v Amer* (1854) 3 Drew 64; and see *Turner v Major* (1862) 3 Giff 442 (where an injunction was held to be a sufficient remedy). Such grounds will exist only where the partners have already agreed to dissolve and wind up the firm, so that the courts will in any event be more willing to appoint a receiver and manager: see note 1; and PARA 208. As to the partners' personal right to wind up the firm see PARA 163.

13   See *Re Hooper, ex p Broome* (1811) 1 Rose 69.

14   For cases where the existence of a partnership was disputed see *Floydd v Cheney, Cheney v Floydd* [1970] Ch 602, [1970] 1 All ER 446; *Peacock v Peacock* (1809) 16 Ves 49; *Chapman v Beach* (1820) 1 Jac & W 594; *Hardy v Hardy* (1917) 62 Sol Jo 142; *Bowker v Henry* (1862) 6 LT 43 (where the defendant did not admit the partnership and claimed to own the whole business and the court refused to appoint a receiver upon the defendant's interlocutory motion for the appointment until that question had been determined). For cases where it was disputed that the partnership had yet been dissolved see *Fairburn v Pearson* (1850) 2 Mac & G 144 (where the motion for the appointment of a receiver was refused and an issue was directed for trial whether the partnership had been dissolved); *Wilson v Greenwood* (1818) 1 Swan 471; *Blakeney v Dufaur* (1851) 15 Beav 40 (where both partners were alleging that the partnership had been dissolved, albeit on different grounds, and a receiver was appointed until sale); *Madgwick v Wimble* (1843) 6 Beav 495 (where the court declined to decide whether a receiver should be appointed, opportunity being given to the parties to negotiate, although the Master of the Rolls did indicate that, should the parties be unable to agree, he would be minded to appoint a receiver); *Lawson v Morgan* (1815) 1 Price 303; *Baxter v West* (1858) 28 LJ Ch 169.

15   As to illegal partnerships generally see PARA 33 et seq.

16   *Hale v Hale* (1841) 4 Beav 369; and see *Sheppard v Oxenford* (1855) 1 K & J 491.

17   *Floydd v Cheney, Cheney v Floydd* [1970] Ch 602, [1970] 1 All ER 446; *Sobell v Boston* [1975] 2 All ER 282, [1975] 1 WLR 1587.

18   *Hall v Hall* (1850) 3 Mac & G 79.

19   *Feldt v Chamberlain* (1914) 58 Sol Jo 788; *Re Bechstein's Business Trusts, Berridge v Bechstein, London County and Westminster Bank v Bechstein* (1914) 58 Sol Jo 864; *Rombach v Rombach* (1914) 59 Sol Jo 90; *Armitage v Borgmann* (1914) 84 LJ Ch 784; *Kupfer v Kupfer* (1915) 60 Sol Jo 221; but see *Maxwell v Grunhut* (1914) 31 TLR 79, CA, followed in *Re Gaudig and Blum, Spalding v Lodde* (1915) 31 TLR 153 (where it was held that there is no jurisdiction to appoint

a receiver and manager to protect the property of an alien enemy on the application of his local agent and an application for the appointment of a receiver was refused).

20 *Niemann v Niemann* (1889) 43 ChD 198 at 202, CA.

163. Appointment of partner as receiver. Since the right of a solvent partner to wind up the affairs of the partnership is a personal right belonging to him qua partner[1], an order for the appointment of a receiver[2] often gives liberty to each partner to propose himself as receiver[3]; and a solvent partner will ordinarily be appointed receiver for the purposes of winding up the affairs of the firm where the other partners are bankrupt and there is no reason for distrusting him[4]. In such a case the court will direct him to give security, furnish accounts and allow access to and inspection of the partnership books by the trustee in bankruptcy, and may order him to pay balances in excess of a stated amount into court or into a joint bank account of himself and the trustee. Similarly, the court will appoint a receiver on the application of the trustee of a bankrupt partner as against the purchaser of the share of a solvent partner[5]. A retired partner who is liable for the debts of the firm may be appointed receiver[6].

1 See the Partnership Act 1890 s 38; and PARA 46.
2 Reference is made here to a partner being appointed as a receiver, but a partner may also be appointed as a manager of the partnership business; and such reference is to be construed accordingly: see PARA 161.
3 *Blakeney v Dufaur* (1851) 15 Beav 40; cf *Sargant v Read* (1876) 1 ChD 600; *Pini v Roncoroni* [1892] 1 Ch 633 at 637; 1 Seton's Judgments and Orders (7th Edn) 729. See also *Bloomer v Currie* (1907) 51 Sol Jo 277.
4 *Re Upperton, ex p Stoveld* (1823) 1 Gl & J 303; *Collins v Barker* [1893] 1 Ch 578. Where some of the partners are alien enemies, a claim by one of them to get in the debts of the firm is prima facie not maintainable; but, if the claim is in substance that of the receiver appointed by the court for this purpose, then it is not prohibited by the trading with the enemy legislation (see ARMED CONFLICT AND EMERGENCY vol 3 (2011) PARA 197), and is maintainable: *Rombach Baden Clock Co v Gent & Son* (1915) 84 LJKB 1558, following *Mercedes Daimler Motor Co Ltd v Maudslay Motor Co Ltd* (1915) 31 TLR 178.
5 *Fraser v Kershaw* (1856) 2 K & J 496.
6 *Hoffman v Duncan* (1853) 18 Jur 69.

164. Powers, liability and remuneration of receiver and manager. A receiver and manager carrying on the partnership business pending sale[1] may enter into such new contracts as are necessary for carrying on the business in the mode usual in the particular trade[2]. A receiver is not the agent of the partnership, but acts on his own responsibility, and incurs personal liability for orders given and contracts made by him, subject to a right of indemnity out of the assets in respect of all proper transactions[3]. However, a receiver appointed by the court has no right of indemnity against the partners personally[4].

Interference with a receiver is a contempt of court[5], and may be restrained by injunction[6] or punished by committal[7].

A receiver may only charge for his services if the court so directs and specifies the basis on which the receiver is to be remunerated[8]. There is no fixed rule with regard to the amount of remuneration of a receiver and manager; and each case depends upon its own circumstances[9]. A partner appointed receiver with remuneration is entitled to be paid even though he is indebted to the firm[10].

In the absence of an express covenant, a receiver and manager who is functus officio will not be restrained from carrying on a similar business on his own account[11].

1 As to a receiver's power to sell to one of the partners of the firm an asset that had been vested in both partners as partnership property see *Murray v King* [1986] FSR 116, Aust Fed Ct (firm's copyright).

2 *Taylor v Neate* (1888) 39 ChD 538 at 543, where, however, a limit for the amount of such contracts was fixed which the receiver might not exceed without the consent of the partners or the court. It is not unusual to limit a period during which a receiver and manager may act as manager, with liberty to apply to the court on the expiration of that period: see RECEIVERS vol 88 (2012) PARA 184.

3 *Burt, Boulton and Hayward v Bull* [1895] 1 QB 276, CA; *Boehm v Goodall* [1911] 1 Ch 155; c f COMPANIES vol 15 (2009) PARA 1370.

4 *Boehm v Goodall* [1911] 1 Ch 155. As to the effect of payments by a receiver on the running of time under the Limitation Act 1980 see LIMITATION PERIODS vol 68 (2008) PARA 1198.

5 *Freeland v Stansfeld* (1854) 2 Sm & G 479; *Helmore v Smith (2)* (1886) 35 ChD 449, CA (former clerk sent a circular soliciting business to customers of the firm); *King v Dopson* (1911) 56 Sol Jo 51 (circulars were issued to the effect that the original undertaking was no longer carried on); *Re Bechstein's Business Trusts, Berridge v Bechstein, London County and Westminster Bank v Bechstein* (1914) 58 Sol Jo 864 (letters sent stating that it was unpatriotic to do business with the firm). Judgment creditors who levy execution against property of which a receiver has been appointed without the permission of the court are guilty of contempt: *Lane v Sterne* (1862) 3 Giff 629; *Defries v Creed* (1865) 13 WR 632. In a proper case the court will give liberty to the receiver to pay the judgment debt (*Mitchell v Weise, ex p Friedheim* [1892] WN 139) or give the applicants a charging order on the assets (*Armstrong v Paris* (1888) 4 TLR 247), or make an order in the form settled in *Kewney v Attrill* (1886) 34 ChD 345, the effect of which is to give the applicants priority over the general body of creditors (see *Newport v Pougher* [1937] Ch 214, [1937] 1 All ER 276, CA).

6 *Dixon v Dixon* [1904] 1 Ch 161; c f *Kitcat v Sharp* (1882) 31 WR 227.

7 *King v Dopson* (1911) 56 Sol Jo 51. As to the procedure for committal see CONTEMPT OF COURT vol 22 (2012) PARA 95.

8 See CPR 69.7; *Practice Direction—Court's Power to Appoint a Receiver* PD 69 para 9; *Capewell v Revenue and Customs Comrs* [2007] UKHL 2, [2007] 2 All ER 370, [2007] 1 WLR 386; and CIVIL PROCEDURE vol 12 (2009) PARA 1506.

9 *Day v Croft* (1840) 2 Beav 488; *Prior v Bagster* (1887) 57 LT 760; *Harris v Sleep* [1897] 2 Ch 80, CA; and see PARA 110. See also RECEIVERS vol 88 (2012) PARA 141.

10 *Davy v Scarth* [1906] 1 Ch 55.

11 *Re Irish, Irish v Irish* (1888) 40 ChD 49.

(v) Injunctions

A. INJUNCTIONS IN A GOING CONCERN

165. Jurisdiction to grant an injunction. The court may by order, whether interim or final, grant an injunction in all cases in which it appears to the court to be just and convenient to do so[1]; and the court will grant an injunction, at the instance of a partner, to restrain any other partner from acting contrary to the obligations imposed upon him by the partnership relationship, whether such acts are an actual breach of express stipulations or a breach of that good faith which is the implied duty of every partner[2].

1 See the Senior Courts Act 1981 s 37(1). Any such order may be made either unconditionally or on such terms and conditions as the court thinks just: s 37(2). As to the jurisdiction of county courts see CIVIL PROCEDURE vol 11 (2009) PARA 345. It must be just as well as convenient: *Beddow v Beddow* (1878) 9 ChD 89 at 93 per Jessel MR; *Day v Brownrigg* (1878) 10 ChD 294 at 307, CA, per Jessel MR; and see CIVIL PROCEDURE vol 11 (2009) PARA 349.

2 As to the duty of good faith see PARA 105.

166. Position of partner claiming injunction. A person claiming an injunction against partners who have excluded him from the management of the firm[1] must naturally show that he is a partner and not an employee of the firm[2], and must be in a position to perform his own part of the partnership agreement[3]. Thus, an application for an injunction to restrain another partner from receiving or dealing with partnership property, founded on charges of misconduct, will be refused if the claimant has himself acted improperly[4]; and the acquiescence of one partner in acts similar to that complained of may also disentitle him to relief against his co-partners[5].

1   As to the right of each partner to participate in the firm see PARA 109.
2   *Walker v Hirsch* (1884) 27 ChD 460, CA.
3   *Smith v Fromont* (1818) 2 Swan 330; *Const v Harris* (1824) Turn & R 496 at 524.
4   *Littlewood v Caldwell* (1822) 11 Price 97 (plaintiff had improperly taken away the partnership books).
5   *Glassington v Thwaites* (1823) 1 Sim & St 124 at 131; and see *Powell v Allarton* (1835) 4 LJ Ch 91; CIVIL PROCEDURE vol 11 (2009) PARAS 467, 468; EQUITABLE JURISDICTION vol 47 (2014) PARA 252.

167.   When a claim for dissolution is necessary.   In the case of a partnership for a fixed term, it is not necessary that a partner who claims an injunction should also claim a dissolution[1]; but, as a general rule, an interim injunction is not granted unless the claimant can show facts of such gravity as would, if proved at the trial, entitle him to a dissolution[2]. Mere squabbles and improprieties arising from incompatibility of temper are insufficient; there must be some definite act amounting to breach of faith, breach of the partnership agreement, illegality or insolvency, or such gross misconduct as to imperil the business or prevent it from being properly conducted[3].

The exclusion of one partner by the others from the management of the business will be restrained by injunction, even if dissolution is not claimed[4]; but, if the partnership is one at will[5], the court may be more reluctant to interfere unless dissolution is also sought, for the defendant might immediately put an end to the partnership[6]. If, however, the act is one which tends towards the destruction of the partnership property, an injunction will be granted notwithstanding that dissolution is not sought[7].

1   *Fairthorne v Weston* (1844) 3 Hare 387; *Richardson v Hastings* (1844) 7 Beav 301 (further proceedings 7 Beav 323); *Watney v Trist* (1876) 45 LJ Ch 412. As to fixed term partnerships see PARA 37.
2   *Smith v Jeyes* (1841) 4 Beav 503.
3   *Waters v Taylor* (1808) 15 Ves 10; *Goodman v Whitcomb* (1820) 1 Jac & W 589; *Marshall v Colman* (1820) 2 Jac & W 266; *Anderson v Anderson* (1857) 25 Beav 190; *Lemann v Berger* (1876) 34 LT 235.
4   *Hall v Hall* (1850) 12 Beav 414. In *Anon* (1856) 2 K & J 441 a dissolution was claimed.
5   As to the meaning of 'partnership at will' see PARA 37.
6   *Peacock v Peacock* (1809) 16 Ves 49; *Miles v Thomas* (1839) 9 Sim 606 at 609; but see *Floydd v Cheney, Cheney v Floydd* [1970] Ch 602, [1970] 1 All ER 446 (where Megarry J held that there was no evidence of a partnership at will as the defendant contended but that, even if the partnership had been one at will, he would still have granted the injunction sought, namely against making improper use of partnership papers).
7   *Miles v Thomas* (1839) 9 Sim 606 (injunction refused, there being no danger of the subject matter in dispute being lost).

168.   Grounds for injunction.   A partner may be restrained by injunction from a breach of the partnership agreement[1]. He may also be restrained from entering into a new partnership with others for carrying on a business of the same nature and character as the old partnership before the expiration of the term of the old partnership, from publishing notices of dissolution, and from using the firm name of the old partnership in his new business[2]. Injunctions will be granted to restrain him from carrying on a business on his own account in the firm name[3], or with partnership assets[4], or against the wishes of his partners[5], or from using the assets of the firm in a separate business carried on for his own benefit[6], or from altering the partnership property without the consent of his partners[7], or from drawing, accepting or negotiating bills of exchange for his own purposes in the name of the firm[8]. He will be restrained from such conduct in the management of the business as would render it impossible for the business to be carried on in a proper manner, or would cause irreparable injury to it[9]. An injunction will not, however, be granted in respect of matters not falling within the express or implied obligations of the partnership agreement[10]; nor in respect of a possible breach of the partnership agreement which may never happen at all and cannot happen until a future period[11].

1   *Morris v Colman* (1812) 18 Ves 437.
2   *England v Curling* (1844) 8 Beav 129.
3   *Aas v Benham* [1891] 2 Ch 244, CA.
4   *Turner v Major* (1862) 3 Giff 442; *Clements v Norris* (1878) 8 ChD 129, CA.
5   *Blachford v Hawkins* (1823) 1 LJOS Ch 141.
6   *Gardner v M'Cutcheon* (1842) 4 Beav 534. See also *Glassington v Thwaites* (1823) 1 Sim & St 124, where all the partners were proprietors of a morning newspaper and had agreed not to be concerned in any other morning newspaper, and some of them afterwards became proprietors of an evening newspaper, and a general injunction to restrain competition, applied for by a partner interested in the morning newspaper only, was refused, the mere temptation of his partners to betray their duty to the morning newspaper not being sufficient ground for interference to such extent by the court; but a limited injunction was granted to restrain his partners from publishing in the evening newspaper news obtained at the expense of the firm before such news had appeared in the morning newspaper. See also *Turner v Major* (1862) 3 Giff 442.
7   *Elmslie v Beresford* [1873] WN 152.
8   Holders with notice may also be restrained from negotiating such bills: *Hood v Aston* (1826) 1 Russ 412. See also *Jervis v White* (1802) 7 Ves 413.
9   *Anderson v Wallace* (1826) 2 Mol 540; *Francis v Spittle* (1840) 9 LJ Ch 230.
10 *Glassington v Thwaites* (1823) 1 Sim & St 124.
11 *Coates v Coates* (1821) 6 Madd 287.

169.   Injunction against third person. Partners may obtain an injunction to restrain a trader from carrying on business so as to suggest, contrary to the fact, that he is their partner or agent and so expose them to a risk of litigation or liability[1].

1   *Routh v Webster* (1847) 10 Beav 561; *Walter v Ashton* [1902] 2 Ch 282. Apart from some express stipulation, a person has no right to hold out his late partner, or indeed anyone else, as his partner in business; and, if it could be shown that the defendants were holding out the claimants as their partners, the claimants would be entitled to an injunction: see *Burchell v Wilde* [1900] 1 Ch 551 at 563, CA, per Lindley MR. As to the legal capacity of a firm to sue see PARA 78. As to the partners' right to use the firm name after dissolution see PARA 212 et seq.

B.   INJUNCTIONS IN RELATION TO DISSOLUTION

170.   Injunctions ancillary to dissolution. During a claim for dissolution[1], the court will interfere by injunction, if necessary or desirable, to preserve the assets[2], or to restrain any act by a partner which would interfere with the rights of the other partners, or with the systematic and equitable winding up of the business, by causing loss or depreciation of the assets or otherwise, as, for example, where a partner is suffering from a mental disorder[3].

A partner will be restrained from carrying on the business except for the purpose of winding it up[4]; from carrying on a branch of the partnership business with partnership assets for his own benefit[5]; from getting in debts owing to the firm[6], or other assets, if he has dealt, or is likely to deal, improperly with them[7]; or from selling his share to a stranger if his partners are entitled, by contract, to an option to buy it[8].

A partner will be restrained from taking undue advantage of his legal title to eject a partner, or the personal representatives of a deceased partner, from property held by him in trust for the firm[9], or from applying the firm's assets for his own purposes, for example from dealing with a partnership lease as his own property[10]. Thus, the executors of a deceased partner may be restrained from dealing with a renewed lease otherwise than as partnership property[11].

An injunction will be granted to restrain a partner from removing the partnership books from the place of business and keeping them elsewhere, even though it amounts to an order to bring them back[12].

The court will restrain the publication of a trade secret where the information has been obtained through a partner's breach of contract or duty[13].

1   As to claims for dissolution see PARA 181.
2   See *Investment and Pensions Advisory Service Ltd v Gray* [1990] BCLC 38 (where a firm's provisional liquidator obtained an injunction (subsequently varied) against a partner of the insolvent firm in order to preserve sums that had allegedly been wrongly paid to the partner during the currency of the partnership).
3   *Anon* (1856) 2 K & J 441; *J v S* [1894] 3 Ch 72. See also *Jones v Lloyd* (1874) LR 18 Eq 265; and MENTAL HEALTH AND CAPACITY vol 75 (2013) PARA 616.
4   *De Tastet v Bordenave* (1822) Jac 516.
5   *Turner v Major* (1862) 3 Giff 442; and see *Re David and Matthews* [1899] 1 Ch 378 at 382.
6   *Read v Bowers* (1793) 4 Bro CC 441.
7   *Hartz v Schrader* (1803) 8 Ves 317; *O'Brien v Cooke* (1871) 5 IR Eq 51.
8   *Homfray v Fothergill* (1866) LR 1 Eq 567.
9   *Hawkins v Hawkins* (1858) 4 Jur NS 1044; and see *Sykes v Land* [1984] 2 EGLR 8, 271 Estates Gazette 1264, CA; cf *Brenner v Rose* [1973] 2 All ER 535, [1973] 1 WLR 443.
10   *Elliot v Brown* (1791) 3 Swan 489n; *Keech v Sandford* (1726) Sel Cas Ch 61; *Thompson's Trustee in Bankruptcy v Heaton* [1974] 1 All ER 1239, [1974] 1 WLR 605; *Chan v Zacharia* (1983) 154 CLR 178, 53 ALR 417, Aust HC (new lease of the partnership premises which had been acquired by a partner whilst the firm was being wound up held by him upon a constructive trust on behalf of his co-partners); and see PARA 106.
11   *Alder v Fouracre* (1818) 3 Swan 489; and see *Re Biss, Biss v Biss* [1903] 2 Ch 40 at 57, 61, CA. The landlord will not, however, be restrained from granting the renewed lease.
12   *Greatrex v Greatrex* (1847) 1 De G & Sm 692. As to the right of a partner to the partnership books see the Partnership Act 1890 s 24(9); and PARA 135.
13   *Morison v Moat* (1851) 9 Hare 241; affd (1852) 21 LJ Ch 248 (defendant was a volunteer). *Morrison v Moat* (1851) 9 Hare 241; affd (1852) 21 LJ Ch 248 was followed and applied in the following cases of employer and employee or principal and agent: *Tuck & Sons v Priester* (1887) 19 QBD 629, CA; *Lamb v Evans* [1893] 1 Ch 218, CA; *Robb v Green* [1895] 2 QB 315, CA. In relation to non-partnership cases see also *Faccenda Chicken Ltd v Fowler* [1987] Ch 117, [1986] 1 All ER 617, CA (and the cases there cited); *Terrapin Ltd v Builders' Supply Co (Hayes) Ltd* [1960] RPC 128, CA; *Seager v Copydex Ltd* [1967] 2 All ER 415, [1967] 1 WLR 923, CA; *Coco v AN Clark (Engineers) Ltd* [1969] RPC 41; *Schering Chemicals Ltd v Falkman Ltd* [1982] QB 1, [1982] 2 All ER 321, CA; *Fraser v Thames Television Ltd* [1984] QB 44, [1983] 2 All ER 101; *CR Smith Glaziers (Dunfermline) Ltd v Jamieson* 1992 GWD 14–789; and see EQUITABLE JURISDICTION vol 47 (2014) PARA 232. Different considerations would arise if the defendant were a purchaser for value of the secret without notice of any obligations affecting it: *Morison v Moat* (1851) 9 Hare 241 at 263; and see CIVIL PROCEDURE vol 11 (2009) PARA 436; EMPLOYMENT vol 39 (2014) PARAS 67–72. An injunction to restrain publication, by a partner, of a book explaining a patent which belonged to the partnership was, however, refused, as publication was not likely to injure or endanger the patent: *Blachford v Hawkins* (1823) 1 LJOS Ch 141.

171. Injunctions after dissolution. An injunction will not generally be granted restraining a partner from using the old firm's name after dissolution if the firm's assets are divided between the partners, because each of them is entitled to use the firm name[1]. This rule only applies subject to contrary agreement, and unless it exposes the other partners to risk of liability[2]. Whether this danger exists depends upon the circumstances of the case[3]. A surviving partner must not carry on a rival business so as to lead to the belief that it is the partnership business, and so appropriate the goodwill of the business, but the court has refused to restrain a surviving partner who was also executor and trustee of a deceased partner from carrying on a similar business[4].

Where, on dissolution, the goodwill of the business becomes the property of one of the partners, another partner will not be restrained from stating that he was formerly a partner in the old firm, but he will be restrained from using the name of the firm so as to suggest that he is carrying on the old business[5]; and a continuing partner who has purchased the assets but not the goodwill may be restrained from using, in the style of the firm, the name of his former partner[6].

If two partners have agreed that, on dissolution of the partnership, the goodwill is to belong solely to one of them, the other will be restrained from doing anything calculated to depreciate its value[7].

If a partner who has sold his share of the business to his partners has undertaken not to compete with them, he will, unless the undertaking is void as being in restraint of trade[8], be restrained by injunction from acting contrary to his undertaking[9]. Where, however, a vendor has aided his wife in subsequently commencing a similar business with her own property, the court may refuse to restrain the vendor from breach of an agreement not to carry on or be interested in any similar business[10].

1   *Banks v Gibson* (1865) 34 Beav 566; and see PARA 212 et seq. As to the firm name see PARA 7. It would appear, however, that before the winding up of the firm has been completed (ie the assets have been sold or distributed amongst the partners and a final account has been taken and agreed between the partners) partners will not be permitted to use the old firm's name on their own account, unless authorised by their co-partners, since to do so would prima facie constitute a breach of the duty of good faith and/or the duty not to make secret profits and/or the duty not to compete with the firm (see PARAS 105–108), obligations which continue by virtue of the Partnership Act 1890 s 38 (see PARA 46), notwithstanding the firm's dissolution. See also PARA 197.

2   *Webster v Webster* (1791) 3 Swan 490n; and see PARA 212 et seq.

3   *Burchell v Wilde* [1900] 1 Ch 551 at 564, CA (held that the risk was not substantial in any business sense); *Townsend v Jarman* [1900] 2 Ch 698; and see *Chappell v Griffith* (1885) 53 LT 459; *Gray v Smith* (1889) 43 ChD 208, CA. Cf *Lewis v Langdon* (1835) 7 Sim 421 (injunction granted against the executor of a deceased partner); *Hill v Fearis* [1905] 1 Ch 466. See also *Levy v Walker* (1879) 10 ChD 436, CA.

4   *Davies v Hodgson* (1858) 25 Beav 177 at 182–183; *Re David and Matthews* [1899] 1 Ch 378 at 383. Where a surviving partner bought his deceased partner's share of the trade property from his executors, a legatee of a share of the deceased partner's goodwill was held not entitled to enforce a sale of the goodwill: *Robertson v Quiddington* (1860) 28 Beav 529.

5   *Hookham v Pottage* (1872) 8 Ch App 91; cf *Matthews v Hodson* (1886) 2 TLR 899, CA. He may advertise his disassociation from a part of the firm's business, but not that that part will close: *Bradbury v Dickens* (1859) 27 Beav 53. As to the use of the firm name after dissolution see PARA 212 et seq.

6   *Scott v Rowland* (1872) 20 WR 508.

7   As to a partner's right to goodwill after dissolution and restrictions on his co-partner's right to solicit old customers see *Trego v Hunt* [1896] AC 7, HL; *Darby v Meehan* (1998) Times, 25 November; and PARA 212 note 9.

8   As to the enforceability of covenants in restraint of trade see PARA 27; and COMPETITION vol 18 (2009) PARA 377 et seq.

9   *Turner v Evans* (1852) 2 De GM & G 740; *Williams v Williams* (1818) 2 Swan 253; *Ronbar Enterprises Ltd v Green* [1954] 2 All ER 266, [1954] 1 WLR 815, CA; cf *Clifford v Phillips* (1907) 51 Sol Jo 748; *Way v Bishop* [1928] Ch 647, CA (covenant not to practise as a solicitor within a limited area held not to have been broken by acting as managing clerk at a fixed salary to a solicitor within the area). In *Dayer-Smith v Hadsley* (1913) 108 LT 897, CA (affd sub nom *Hadsley v Dayer-Smith* [1914] AC 979, HL) an injunction was granted to restrain the defendant who had opened an office just outside the prohibited area but carried on business within such area. Likewise, a breach of a mere undertaking not to compete, upon which an arbitrator has acted in fixing the price of the goodwill, has been restrained upon the ground of fraud and bad

faith, although the award was silent with regard to the restriction: *Harrison v Gardner* (1817) 2 Madd 198. In *Dean v MacDowell* (1878) 8 ChD 345, CA, it was held that, there having been no loss suffered by the covenantee, no action for damages could be maintained (see at 352 per James LJ) and that the remedy for breach of a covenant not to engage in business except for the benefit of the partnership is by claim for an injunction or dissolution; and that a claim for an account of profits made in the business which is not a competing business cannot be maintained, nor can the business itself be claimed as part of the partnership assets. See also PARA 160 note 2. As to a partner's obligation to account for secret profits see PARA 106.

10   *Smith v Hancock* [1894] 2 Ch 377, CA.

172. Injunctions against partners who purchase shares. Where a partner has agreed to buy his partner's share of the business, the court may refuse, pending a claim for specific performance of the agreement, to restrain him from publishing the accounts of the business with a view to its resale to a company[1]. If a partner who has agreed to buy his partner's share carries on the business with the whole assets without paying the purchase money, the vendor's remedy is not by an injunction to prevent the other from demolishing the property sold, nor by way of declaration that the vendor retains a lien on the property, but by a claim for an account, unless the purchaser commits acts of waste[2].

1   *Marshall v Watson* (1858) 25 Beav 501.
2   *Cofton v Horner* (1818) 5 Price 537. As to orders for account see PARA 149 et seq.

4. DISSOLUTION OF PARTNERSHIPS

(1) DISSOLUTION OTHERWISE THAN BY THE COURT

173. Dissolution on notice. Subject to any agreement between the partners[1], a partnership entered into for an undefined time and for no fixed adventure or undertaking may be dissolved by any partner by giving notice to the others of his intention to dissolve the partnership[2]. The Partnership Act 1890 does not require the notice to be in writing[3]. The partnership is then dissolved as from the date mentioned in the notice as the date of dissolution[4] or, if no date is so mentioned, as from the date of the communication of the notice[5]. The notice must amount to an unambiguous intimation of a final intention to dissolve the partnership[6], and must be given to all the partners unless the partnership agreement otherwise provides[7].

A notice duly given cannot be withdrawn without the consent of the partner receiving it[8]. If, however, the partner receiving the notice is suffering from a mental disorder[9], the notice, although it remains valid, may be withdrawn[10]. If the partnership deed requires dissolution by deed only, a submission to arbitration by deed of all matters in dispute, followed by an arbitration award by deed vesting the partnership assets in one partner as trustee for the purpose of winding up the business, is a sufficient compliance with the partnership deed[11]. In some cases, dissolution of the partnership may be effected without any notice[12].

1 See *Moss v Elphick* [1910] 1 KB 465; affd [1910] 1 KB 846, CA (agreement that the partnership was to be terminated by mutual arrangement only held to be an agreement within the meaning of the Partnership Act 1890 s 32 so that the partnership could not be dissolved by the service of a notice of dissolution by one partner where the other partner had not assented to such notice); *Abbott v Abbott* [1936] 3 All ER 823; and see *Walters v Bingham, Bingham v Walters* [1988] 1 FTLR 260, following *Moss v Elphick* [1910] 1 KB 846, CA (where a resolution was passed at a partners' meeting whereby it was agreed between the partners that the partnership would continue upon the terms of a draft partnership agreement, notwithstanding that the draft was expressed to continue only for a fixed period, pending the execution of a new deed of partnership; the partnership was held not to be for an undefined term within the meaning of the Partnership Act 1890 s 32, so that it could not be dissolved by notice). See also *Chahal v Mahal* [2005] EWCA Civ 898, [2005] 2 BCLC 655 (dissolution of a partnership at will by parties agreeing to transfer assets to a limited company).

2 Partnership Act 1890 ss 26(1), 32(c). As to partnerships of fixed duration and partnerships for fixed adventures or undertakings see PARAS 37 et seq, 174. See also *Peacock v Peacock* (1809) 16 Ves 49; *Crawshay v Maule* (1818) 1 Swan 495 at 508; *Heath v Sansom* (1832) 4 B & Ad 172 at 175; *Miles v Thomas* (1839) 9 Sim 606 at 609. The Partnership Act 1890 s 32 does not apply to a partnership at will arising after a fixed term contract has expired: see *Maillie v Swanney* 2000 SLT 464, OH.

If the business has been carried on upon property belonging to one partner and there has been no lease of that property to the firm, any right of occupation which the partner had ceases upon the dissolution; but it is apprehended that the owning partner will not be able to terminate the other partners' licences to occupy where this would prevent the orderly winding up of the firm: see the Partnership Act 1890 s 38; *Harrison-Broadley v Smith* [1964] 1 All ER 867 at 872, [1964] 1 WLR 456 at 465, CA, per Harman LJ; *IRC v Graham's Trustees* 1971 SLT 46 at 48, HL, per Lord Reid; cf *Doe d Colnaghi v Bluck* (1838) 8 C & P 464; *Benham v Gray* (1847) 5 CB 138. As to partnership property and the property of partners see PARA 115 et seq.

Since the basis of the relationship between partners is contractual (see PARA 1 note 1), a partnership agreement may, on normal principles, also be brought to an end by virtue of an agreed dissolution or by rescission of the partnership agreement on the ground of fraud or misrepresentation (see the Partnership Act 1890 s 41; and PARA 147). However, it is now doubted whether a partnership can be dissolved by one or more partners accepting a repudiatory breach on the part of other partners: see the dicta of Lord Millett in *Hurst v Bryk* [2002] 1 AC 185 at 193–196, [2000] 2 All ER 193 at 198–202, HL; cited with approval in

Mullins v Laughton [2002] EWHC 2761 (Ch), [2003] Ch 250, [2003] 4 All ER 94 (accepted repudiatory breach did not operate to dissolve the partnership). See also *Golstein v Bishop* [2014] EWCA Civ 10, [2014] 3 All ER 397. [2014] 2 WLR 1448 (the Partnership Act 1890 s 35(d) establishes, in plain language, a straightforward and unambiguous threshold test for the exercise of the court's discretionary power to dissolve a partnership, which is not expressed to depend upon repudiation; nor, where the language of the test fits the facts, is it expressed to be undermined by what, in purely contractual terms, might amount to affirmation).

3   Since the Partnership Act 1890 does not require the notice to be in writing, the expressions 'the giving of notice' and 'the receipt of notice' are to be preferred to the more limited expression 'service of notice'.

4   This presupposes that the date mentioned in the notice is later than the date upon which the notice is given to the other partners, since the Partnership Act 1890 s 26(1) refers to the partnership being dissolved '*on* giving notice ... to all the other partners' (emphasis supplied). A retrospective notice of dissolution is thus not possible, at least without the other partners' agreement.

5   Partnership Act 1890 s 32. A partnership at will is dissolved, in the absence of previous notice, from the date of service, not from the date of issue, of the writ in a claim for dissolution: *Unsworth v Jordan* [1896] WN 2. Since after dissolution accounts are taken between the partners, no partner may reap an unfair advantage by giving what was termed 'unseasonable' notice of dissolution: *Featherstonhaugh v Fenwick* (1810) 17 Ves 298 at 309; cf *Chavany v Van Sommer* (1770) 1 Swan 512n.

6   Cf *Parsons v Hayward* (1862) 4 De GF & J 474; *Steuart v Gladstone* (1878) 10 ChD 626 at 650, CA.

7   *Van Sandau v Moore* (1826) 1 Russ 441; *Wheeler v Van Wart* (1838) 9 Sim 193. It takes effect on the giving of notice: see *McLeod v Dowling* (1927) 43 TLR 655 (partnership dissolved by death before notice received by surviving partner).

8   *Jones v Lloyd* (1874) LR 18 Eq 265. A fortiori if there accrues to the recipient of the notice an option to purchase the share of the retiring partner (*Warder v Stilwell* (1856) 3 Jur NS 9); nor will a valid notice become inoperative owing to an irregularity in the mode of taking the accounts consequent upon it (*Steuart v Gladstone* (1878) 10 ChD 626 at 654, CA). The parties may, however, waive a valid notice by a subsequent agreement: *Laycock v Bulmer* (1844) 13 LJ Ex 156.

9   As to dissolution where a partner is suffering from mental disorder see PARA 183; and MENTAL HEALTH AND CAPACITY vol 75 (2013) PARAS 616, 727. As to a partner becoming incapable of managing partnership affairs see the Partnership Act 1890 s 35(b); and PARAS 183–184.

10   *Robertson v Lockie* (1846) 15 Sim 285; *Mellersh v Keen* (1859) 27 Beav 236.

11   *Hutchinson v Whitfield* (1830) Hayes 78.

12   *Bagshaw v Parker* (1847) 10 Beav 532 (partnership determinable on a specified event which happened); *Pearce v Lindsay* (1860) 3 De GJ & Sm 139 (after disputes and attempted settlement of accounts, a long correspondence as to items of account ensued, without any reference to new business or continuing connection).

174. Dissolution at fixed time or on completion of an adventure. A partnership for a fixed term, or for a single adventure or undertaking, is dissolved by the expiration of the term[1] or by the termination of the adventure or undertaking[2], as the case may be, except so far as it is deemed to continue for the purpose of winding up its affairs[3]. Agreement may be made to the contrary[4]. Alternatively, dissolution may take place prematurely, for example on death[5].

1   See the Partnership Act 1890 s 32(a); and PARA 37.

2   Partnership Act 1890 s 32(b). As to partnerships for a single adventure or undertaking see PARA 37. See also *Re Abbey Leisure Ltd* [1990] BCC 60, CA (company formed to undertake single venture).

3   See the Partnership Act 1890 s 38; and PARAS 46, 197. As to the continuation of a partnership beyond the fixed term without any express new agreement see s 27; and PARA 38.

4   Partnership Act 1890 s 32.

5   See PARA 175.

175. Dissolution on death. Subject to any agreement between the partners, a partnership is dissolved as regards all the partners by the death of any partner[1].

If a partner gives a valid notice of a dissolution but dies before the receipt or the expiration of the notice, the partnership is dissolved by the death and not by the notice[2].

Unless the partnership agreement otherwise provides, neither the surviving partners nor the personal representatives of a deceased partner are entitled or bound to continue a partnership, even if the partnership term is unexpired at the time of the death[3].

The estate of a partner who dies is not liable for partnership debts contracted after the date of the death[4], and no notice of the death is necessary[5] in order to determine the deceased's liability. Where goods are ordered before, but delivered after, the death of a partner, the debt accrues on the delivery of the goods, and the vendor, although he had no notice of the death, cannot, therefore, make the estate of the deceased partner liable for the price[6].

1 Partnership Act 1890 s 33(1); *Crawshay v Collins* (1808) 15 Ves 218 at 227; *Vulliamy v Noble* (1817) 3 Mer 593 at 614; *Crawshay v Maule* (1818) 1 Swan 495 at 508. Note, however, the case of a partnership formed for the purpose of effecting a specific undertaking or object, where it is often possible to infer an agreement that the partnership is not to dissolve upon the death of a partner but is to continue until the completion of that undertaking or object: see PARA 132. As to the devolution of partnership property on death and the rights incidental to it see PARA 121; and WILLS AND INTESTACY vol 103 (2010) PARA 919. If a partner lives until his death in a house forming part of the partnership property, being debited yearly with a sum of money in the firm books as rent, there is no tenancy in his personal representative, since any tenancy which existed determined on the dissolution of the partnership by his death: *Lee v Crawford* (1912) 46 ILT 81. As to the position where, following a firm's dissolution, the immediate termination of a partner's licence to occupy will prevent the orderly winding up of the firm see PARA 173 note 2.

2 *Bell v Nevin* (1866) 15 WR 85; *McLeod v Dowling* (1927) 43 TLR 655 (death took place before the receipt of the notice by the other partner).

3 *Pearce v Chamberlain* (1750) 2 Ves Sen 33; *Gillespie v Hamilton* (1818) 3 Madd 251; and see *Lancaster v Allsup* (1887) 57 LT 53; *Emberson v Fisher* [1944] OR 241, [1944] 2 DLR 572, Ont CA.

4 Partnership Act 1890 s 36(3). As to the liability of personal representatives for existing debts of a deceased partner see *Patel v Patel* [2007] EWCA Civ 1520, [2007] All ER (D) 276 (Dec) (where debt was found to be not a partnership debt but a simple debt and was statute barred because it accrued more than six years before the proceedings were begun).

5 *Devaynes v Noble, Houlton's Case* (1816) 1 Mer 529 at 616; *Vulliamy v Noble* (1817) 3 Mer 593 at 614; *Crawshay v Maule* (1818) 1 Swan 495 at 508. As to the effect of dissolution, by death or otherwise, on contracts with persons employed by the firm see PARAS 17, 197; and CONTRACT vol 22 (2012) PARA 474; EMPLOYMENT vol 41 (2014) PARA 732.

6 *Friend v Young* [1897] 2 Ch 421 at 429 (contract of agency held to be determined by the death of a partner in the agent's firm); *Bagel v Miller* [1903] 2 KB 212, DC. See also the Partnership Act 1890 s 9; PARA 68; and WILLS AND INTESTACY vol 103 (2010) PARA 1234. As to the effect of the death of the principal on a contract of agency see AGENCY vol 1 (2008) PARA 188.

176. Dissolution on bankruptcy or making of charging order. Subject to any agreement between the partners, a partnership is dissolved as regards all the partners by the bankruptcy of any partner[1], and the estate of the bankrupt thereupon ceases to be liable for the partnership debts incurred after the bankruptcy[2].

If a charging order is made[3] upon a partner's share in respect of his separate debt, the other partners may at their option dissolve the partnership[4].

1 Partnership Act 1890 s 33(1). As to insolvent partnerships generally see PARAS 98, 232; and BANKRUPTCY AND INDIVIDUAL INSOLVENCY vol 5 (2013) PARA 851 et seq; COMPANY AND PARTNERSHIP INSOLVENCY vol 17 (2011) PARAS 1209–1361. See further *Re Houghton and Watts, ex p Robinson* (1833) 3 Deac & Ch 376. It is the adjudication and not the presentation of the petition which dissolves the partnership: *Ex p Smith* (1800) 5 Ves 295. The rule that, on the bankruptcy of one partner, the firm is dissolved was, before the Partnership Act 1890, held not to apply to mining partnerships: *Re Borron, ex p Broadbent* (1834) 1 Mont & A 635 at

638; *Bentley v Bates* (1840) 4 Y & C Ex 182. These cases were, however, criticised in *Dodds v Preston* (1888) 59 LT 718, CA, and such cases seem now to be covered by the Partnership Act 1890 s 33(1). As to the effect of bankruptcy on the authority of a partner see s 38; and PARA 46.

2　Partnership Act 1890 s 36(3). A proviso forfeiting a partner's share on his bankruptcy is void: *Whitmore v Mason* (1861) 2 John & H 204; and see BANKRUPTCY AND INDIVIDUAL INSOLVENCY vol 5 (2013) PARA 436.

3　Ie under the Partnership Act 1890 s 23(2): see PARA 94 et seq.

4　Partnership Act 1890 s 33(2); and see *Brown, Janson & Co v Hutchinson & Co* [1895] 1 QB 737 at 738, CA, per Lindley LJ. See also PARA 97; and BANKRUPTCY AND INDIVIDUAL INSOLVENCY vol 5 (2013) PARA 710; COMPANY AND PARTNERSHIP INSOLVENCY vol 17 (2011) PARA 1209.

177.　Dissolution on illegality.

A partnership is in every case dissolved by the happening of any event which makes it unlawful for the business of the firm to be carried on or for members of the firm to carry it on in partnership[1].

1　Partnership Act 1890 s 34; *Griswold v Waddington* 15 Johns 57 (1818) (affd 16 Johns 438 (1819)); *Esposito v Bowden* (1857) 7 E & B 763, Ex Ch; *Hudgell Yeates & Co v Watson* [1978] QB 451, [1978] 2 All ER 363, CA. As to illegal partnerships generally see PARA 33 et seq.

178.　Dissolution on expulsion.

A power of expulsion conferred by a partnership agreement[1] is strictly construed and must be exercised by all the partners whose concurrence may be necessary under the partnership agreement[2]. The power of expulsion must also be exercised in the utmost good faith[3]. It is questionable to what extent a partner whom it is proposed to expel is entitled to an opportunity to meet the case against him or to explain his conduct[4].

An expulsion clause may survive the expiry of a fixed-term partnership where the partners continue the partnership as partners at will[5].

Where, by the terms of the partnership agreement, a partner may be expelled only for cause, that is to say, if one or more of the grounds which, as specified in the partnership agreement, entitle the other partners to exercise a power of expulsion, can be shown to exist, the court will scrutinise the expelled partner's behaviour so as to ascertain whether such cause existed[6].

Whether the court will require the expelling partners to specify the grounds for expulsion if, by the terms of the partnership agreement, no reasons for such expulsion are required to be given or shown, and whether the court will scrutinise the expelled partner's behaviour in order to ascertain whether such specified grounds are made out, is less clear[7].

1　Such a power is created only by express agreement, since it is not implied by law: see the Partnership Act 1890 s 25; and PARA 109.

2　*Smith v Mules* (1852) 9 Hare 556 at 570; *Re A Solicitors' Arbitration* [1962] 1 All ER 772, [1962] 1 WLR 353 (single partner unable to expel others), followed in *Bond v Hale* (1969) 72 SRNSW 201, CA; and see *Blisset v Daniel* (1853) 10 Hare 493; *Clark and Chapman v Hart* (1858) 6 HL Cas 633; *Russell v Russell* (1880) 14 ChD 471; *Fisher v Jackson* [1891] 2 Ch 84 at 93–94. This will not, however, be taken to absurd limits: *Hitchman v Crouch Butler Savage Associates* (1983) 127 Sol Jo 441, CA (clause in a partnership deed that required the senior partner to sign all expulsion notices held not to apply when it was the senior partner himself whom it was sought to expel).

3　*Barnes v Youngs* [1898] 1 Ch 414; *Carmichael v Evans* [1904] 1 Ch 486. It must not be exercised for the exclusive benefit of one or more partners individually, but for the benefit of the whole partnership: *Blisset v Daniel* (1853) 10 Hare 493 at 522; and see *Steuart v Gladstone* (1878) 10 ChD 626 at 650. As to the necessity for good faith between partners see PARA 105 et seq.

4　Although it was held in *Blisset v Daniel* (1853) 10 Hare 493 at 530–531 per Page Wood V-C that the partners should not have gone behind the plaintiff expelled partner's back, it is clear that this finding was prompted by the actions of one of the partners (Vaughan) who, in breach of his duty of good faith, sought to have the plaintiff expelled for his (Vaughan's) own ulterior motives and had coerced the other two partners into concurring in the plaintiff's expulsion, and that, had it not been for this element of bad faith, the expelling partners would not have been held to be under an obligation to give the plaintiff a hearing before expelling him. See, however, *Steuart v Gladstone* (1878) 10 ChD 626 (where Fry J appeared to elide the duty of good faith which must be exercised in expelling a partner with a duty to give the expelled partner an opportunity to be heard); *Wood v Woad* (1874) LR 9 Exch 190 (mutual insurance society); but see *Russell v Russell* (1880) 14 ChD 471 (where it was held, distinguishing *Blisset v Daniel* (1853) 10 Hare 493 and *Wood v Woad* (1874) LR 9 Exch 190, that, in the case of a two-partner firm where one partner is given an express and exclusive power to dissolve the partnership, there is no obligation, before exercising such power, to give the other partner an opportunity to be heard, sed quaere to what extent this is authority for the proposition in the case of a true expulsion). *Blisset v Daniel* (1853) 10 Hare 493 and *Wood v Woad* (1874) LR 9 Exch 190 have also been distinguished from a case in which the power of expulsion arose not by reason of 'misconduct or suspicion under some general provision' but by reason of the breach of a specific provision, namely that no partner should directly or indirectly enter into any other business: *Cooper v Page* (1876) 34 LT 90 at 92–93 per Hall V-C.

Whatever uncertainties may have previously existed in relation to the partners' duty or otherwise to give a partner whom it is proposed to expel a hearing, these were removed in *Green v Howell* [1910] 1 Ch 495, CA (albeit concerning merely a two-partner firm so that the expulsion in question actually caused its general dissolution), overruling Romer J in *Barnes v Youngs* [1898] 1 Ch 414, who had held that such an obligation did exist, and distinguishing the cases of *Wood v Woad* (1874) LR 9 Exch 190, *Steuart v Gladstone* (1878) 10 ChD 626 and *Blisset v Daniel* (1853) 10 Hare 493.

Notwithstanding *Green v Howell* [1910] 1 Ch 495, CA, the view that a partner whom it is proposed to expel should be given a hearing seems to be finding favour in New Zealand: see *Wilkie v Wilkie (No 2)* (1900) 18 NZLR 734; *Jackson v Moss* [1978] NZ Recent Law 28; *Re Northwestern Autoservices Ltd* [1980] 2 NZLR 302, NZ CA (company case). Whether this trend is reflected in England has yet to be determined; in *Kerr v Morris* [1987] Ch 90, [1986] 3 All ER 217, CA, the question was left open.

5 Ie under the Partnership Act 1890 s 27: see PARA 38. See *Walters v Bingham, Bingham v Walters* [1988] 1 FTLR 260 (where Sir Nicolas Browne-Wilkinson V-C declined to follow *Clark v Leach* (1863) 1 De GJ & Sm 409, holding that in modern partnerships with many partners, a power of expulsion is not necessarily inconsistent with a partnership at will arising after the expiry of a fixed-term partnership). As to fixed term partnerships and partnerships at will see PARA 37.

6 See *Carmichael v Evans* [1904] 1 Ch 486 at 492; *Green v Howell* [1910] 1 Ch 495, CA; *Peyton v Mindham* [1971] 3 All ER 1215 at 1220, [1972] 1 WLR 8 at 13; *Fulwell v Bragg* (1983) 127 Sol Jo 171 (decision at an interlocutory hearing). It is unclear whether, if by the terms of the partnership agreement reasons must be given for expelling a partner and no or no satisfactory or accurate grounds are given at the time of a partner's expulsion, but such grounds are discovered subsequently, these latter grounds may be relied upon by the expelling partners: see *Boston Deep Sea Fishing and Ice Co v Ansell* (1888) 39 ChD 339, CA.

7 See *Kerr v Morris* [1987] Ch 90 at 110–111, [1986] 3 All ER 217 at 228, CA, obiter per Dillon LJ (expelling partners must specify a reason for expelling a partner and prima facie such reason must be a reasonable one, even though in the partnership agreement under consideration no reason had to be given). It is submitted that this view is inconsistent with authority: see *Price v Bouch* (1986) 53 P & CR 257; *Re Gresham Life Assurance Society, ex p Penney* (1872) 8 Ch App 446; *Berry and Stewart v Tottenham Hotspur Football and Athletic Co Ltd* [1935] Ch 718; sed quaere.

179. Implied agreement to dissolve partnership. Whilst partners are clearly free to expressly agree to dissolve a partnership, there may also be circumstances which indicate that there has been an implied agreement between the partners to bring the partnership to an end[1]. For example, where the partners agree to transfer the assets of the partnership to a limited company, it will be inferred, in the absence of other evidence, that they intended to dissolve the partnership[2]. Such an agreement will not, however, be inferred if the transaction was merely intended as a tax avoidance scheme[3].

It is doubted whether an implied agreement to dissolve the partnership will be inferred where one or more partners accepts a repudiatory breach on the part of other partners[4].

1   See the Partnership Act 1890 s 32 (which is expressed to be 'subject to any agreement between the partners'); and PARA 173. 'A partnership may ... be dissolved by mutual agreement, and it may be objected that this is not mentioned [in the Partnership Act 1890] either; but in fact it is catered for by s 19 taken in conjunction with s 32(2)(a)': *Hurst v Bryk* [2002] 1 AC 185 at 195, [2000] 2 All ER 193 at 201, HL, per Lord Millett. The Partnership Act 1890 s 19 provides that the 'mutual rights and duties of partners ... may be varied by the consent of all the partners' and adds that 'such consent may be either expressed or inferred from a course of dealing': see s 19; and *Chahal v Mahal* [2005] EWCA Civ 898 at [20], [2005] 2 βCLC 655 at [20] per Neuberger LJ.

2   *Chahal v Mahal* [2005] EWCA Civ 898, [2005] 2 BCLC 655 (where, on the facts, there was no implied agreement to dissolve the firm). 'The law ... would presume, in the absence of any reason to the contrary, that the transfer of all the business and assets of a partnership to a limited company, in which all the partners are given shares pro rata to their interests in the partnership, raises the presumption that the partnership is thereby determined': *Chahal v Mahal* [2005] EWCA Civ 898 at [29], [2005] 2 BCLC 655 at [29] per Neuberger LJ.

3   *National Westminster Bank plc v Jones* [2001] 1 BCLC 98, [2000] NPC 73.

4   See the dicta of Lord Millett in *Hurst v Bryk* [2002] 1 AC 185 at 193–196, [2000] 2 All ER 193 at 198–202, HL; cited with approval in *Mullins v Laughton* [2002] EWHC 2761 (Ch), [2003] Ch 250, [2003] 4 All ER 94 (accepted repudiatory breach did not operate to dissolve the partnership). See also PARA 173.

(2) DISSOLUTION BY THE COURT

(i) Proceedings for Dissolution

180.   Jurisdiction.   The courts[1] which have jurisdiction to dissolve a partnership[2] in England and Wales are:

(1)   the High Court of Justice, to the Chancery Division of which all causes and matters for the dissolution of partnerships or the taking of partnership accounts are specially assigned[3];

(2)   the county court where either the whole assets of the partnership do not exceed £350,000 in amount or value[4], or where the parties by memorandum agree that the court is to have jurisdiction[5];

(3)   the Court of Protection under the Mental Capacity Act 2005[6], although generally applications to dissolve partnerships ought not to be made to the Court of Protection unless a receiver has been appointed and there is no substantial issue to be tried.

1   'Court' in the Partnership Act 1890 includes every court and judge having jurisdiction in the case: s 45.

2   Such a jurisdiction clearly exists only if what it is sought to be wound up is really a partnership, and parties cannot confer jurisdiction upon the court by estoppel: *Re C & M Ashberg* (1990) Times, 17 July (where the individual in question merely allowed himself to be held out as a partner). As to holding out see PARA 70 et seq; and see *Walker v Hirsch* (1884) 27 ChD 460, CA (where it was held that the plaintiff who received both a salary and a share of profits (as well as being liable for a share of the losses of the firm) was not a partner and was not therefore entitled to wind up the firm). Even where it is found that the litigants are partners in the true sense of the word, however, so that the court does have jurisdiction, at the request of one of them, to wind up the firm, the court will not necessarily be obliged to accede to such a request and may refuse to do so where the partner seeking the firm's winding up has, by the terms of the partnership agreement (and somewhat unusually), no proprietary interest in the capital and assets of the firm: see *Stekel v Ellice* [1973] 1 All ER 465, [1973] 1 WLR 191. As to the issue whether a partnership exists and, if so, who are the partners of it see PARA 9 et seq; and see *Sobell v Boston* [1975] 2 All ER 282, [1975] 1 WLR 1587; and PARA 166.

3   Senior Courts Act 1981 s 61(1), Sch 1 para 1(f); and see COURTS AND TRIBUNALS vol 24 (2010) PARA 704. As to the origin of the growth of the exclusive jurisdiction of equity see EQUITABLE JURISDICTION vol 47 (2014) PARA 63.

4   County Courts Act 1984 s 23(f) (s 23 amended by the Crime and Courts Act 2013 s 17(5), Sch 9 para 10(1)); County Court Jurisdiction Order 2014, SI 2014/503, art 3, Table; and see COURTS

AND TRIBUNALS vol 24 (2010) PARA 710 et seq. The 'whole assets' would appear to refer to the gross and not net assets of a firm, since these are the assets with which the court will have to deal when winding up a firm. The court has jurisdiction whether or not the existence of the partnership is in dispute: County Courts Act 1984 s 23(f); and see *R v Judge Lailey, ex p Koffman* [1932] 1 KB 568, CA (where it was held that the jurisdiction extended to an action where the existence of the partnership was denied). As to transfers between the Chancery Division and a county court see COURTS AND TRIBUNALS vol 24 (2010) PARA 703; CIVIL PROCEDURE vol 11 (2009) PARA 69.

5   See the County Courts Act 1984 s 24(1), (2); and COURTS AND TRIBUNALS vol 24 (2010) PARA 776.

6   See the Mental Capacity Act 2005 ss 16, 18(1)(e); PARA 183; and MENTAL HEALTH AND CAPACITY vol 75 (2013) PARA 727.

181.   Commencement of proceedings.   Proceedings for the dissolution of a partnership are started in the usual way by the court[1] issuing a claim form at the request of the claimant[2].

1   As to the courts with jurisdiction see PARA 180.
2   See CPR Pt 7; and CIVIL PROCEDURE vol 11 (2009) PARA 116 et seq. As to the alternative procedure for claims see CPR Pt 8; and CIVIL PROCEDURE vol 11 (2009) PARA 127 et seq.

182.   Reference to arbitration.   The right of a partner to claim a dissolution by the court may be controlled by an arbitration clause contained in the partnership agreement[1]. Whether the matters in dispute fall within the clause is a question for the court to decide[2] unless the parties have expressly agreed to leave it to the arbitrator[3]. If such a clause applies to all matters in dispute between the parties, the arbitrators have power to award a dissolution[4].

Upon the application of the defendant to the court[5], the court must grant a stay of proceedings unless satisfied that the arbitration agreement is null and void, inoperative, or incapable of being performed[6].

1   As to the inclusion of arbitration clauses in partnership agreements generally see PARA 26. As to the courts with jurisdiction see PARA 180. An arbitration clause will normally be a term that will, under the Partnership Act 1890 s 27 (see PARA 38), survive the expiry of a fixed-term partnership: *Gillett v Thornton* (1875) LR 19 Eq 599; and see *Morgan v William Harrison Ltd* [1907] 2 Ch 137; and PARA 38.
2   *Piercy v Young* (1879) 14 ChD 200, CA; *Vawdrey v Simpson* [1896] 1 Ch 166; *Renshaw v Queen Anne Residential Mansions Co Ltd* [1897] 1 QB 662; *Barnes v Youngs* [1898] 1 Ch 414; *Parry v Liverpool Malt Co* [1900] 1 QB 339, CA; *Olver v Hillier* [1959] 2 All ER 220, [1959] 1 WLR 551; *Nova (Jersey) Knit Ltd v Kammgarn Spinnerei GmbH* [1977] 2 All ER 463, [1977] 1 WLR 713, HL (German partnership agreement).
3   *Willesford v Watson* (1873) 8 Ch App 473; *Gillett v Thornton* (1875) LR 19 Eq 599 at 605. See also *Hackston v Hackston* 1956 SLT (Notes) 38.
4   *Russell v Russell* (1880) 14 ChD 471, approved in *Walmsley v White* (1892) 40 WR 675, CA; *Vawdrey v Simpson* [1896] 1 Ch 166; *Phoenix v Pope* [1974] 1 All ER 512, [1974] 1 WLR 719 (both following *Walmsley v White* (1892) 40 WR 675, CA). See also *Plews v Baker* (1873) LR 16 Eq 564; *Law v Garrett* (1878) 8 ChD 26, CA (forum selected by the partners was a foreign commercial court); *Belfield v Bourne* [1894] 1 Ch 521 at 523; *Vawdrey v Simpson* [1896] 1 Ch 166 at 168; *Machin v Bennett* [1900] WN 146. See further *Green v Waring* (1764) 1 Wm Bl 475; *Simmonds v Swaine* (1809) 1 Taunt 549.
5   Ie under the Arbitration Act 1996 s 9: see ARBITRATION vol 2 (2008) PARA 1222.
6   See the Arbitration Act 1996 s 9(4); and ARBITRATION vol 2 (2008) PARA 1222.

(ii) Grounds of Dissolution

A. MENTAL INCAPACITY

183.   Dissolution when partner suffering from mental incapacity.   The mental incapacity of a partner does not of itself dissolve the partnership[1]. However, if a person lacks capacity[2] in relation to a matter or matters concerning his personal welfare or his property and affairs, the Court of Protection may, by making an order, make decisions on his behalf in relation to those matters, or may appoint a deputy to make decisions on his behalf[3]. This may include the taking of a decision which will have the effect of dissolving a partnership of which the person is a member[4].

1   *Wrexham v Hudleston* (1734) 1 Swan 514n; *Waters v Taylor* (1813) 2 Ves & B 299 at 303; *Anon* (1856) 2 K & J 441 at 447; and see PARA 31; and MENTAL HEALTH AND CAPACITY vol 75 (2013) PARA 616. Until dissolution, the power of a mentally disordered person to bind his firm seems to continue, notwithstanding the rule that the insanity of the principal revokes the authority of an agent: *Yonge v Toynbee* [1910] 1 KB 215, CA. If, however, a claim for dissolution is pending, the mentally disordered person may be restrained from interfering: *J v S* [1894] 3 Ch 72.

2   A person lacks capacity in relation to a matter if at the material time he is unable to make a decision for himself in relation to the matter because of an impairment of, or a disturbance in the functioning of, the mind or brain: see the Mental Capacity Act 2005 ss 2, 3; and MENTAL HEALTH AND CAPACITY vol 75 (2013) PARA 603. It does not matter whether the impairment or disturbance is permanent or temporary: s 2(2).

3   Mental Capacity Act 2005 s 16(1), (2). The powers of the court are subject to the principles that: (1) a person must be assumed to have capacity unless it is established that he lacks capacity; (2) a person is not to be treated as unable to make a decision unless all practicable steps to help him to do so have been taken without success; (3) a person is not to be treated as unable to make a decision merely because he makes an unwise decision; (4) an act done, or decision made, under the Mental Capacity Act 2005 for or on behalf of a person who lacks capacity must be done, or made, in his best interests: see ss 1, 4, 16(3); and MENTAL HEALTH AND CAPACITY vol 75 (2013) PARAS 601, 606, 734.

4   Mental Capacity Act 2005 s 18(1)(e).

184. Special provision for dissolution in partnership agreement. Where a partnership agreement provides for dissolution in certain events, the mental incapacity of one of the partners does not prevent the partnership being dissolved in accordance with the provisions of the partnership agreement[1]. Where, however, notice of dissolution has been served on a partner who is mentally incapable, the partner serving the notice may withdraw it[2].

1   *Robertson v Lockie* (1846) 15 Sim 285; *Mellersh v Keen* (1859) 27 Beav 236. Dissolution is then effective from the date envisaged in the partnership agreement: see PARA 190.

2   *Jones v Lloyd* (1874) LR 18 Eq 265. As to the general rule that notice of dissolution cannot be withdrawn see PARA 173.

B. GROUNDS OTHER THAN MENTAL INCAPACITY

185. Permanent incapacity. On application by a partner, the court may decree a dissolution of the partnership when any partner, other than the partner suing, becomes permanently incapable in any way, otherwise than by reason of mental disorder[1], of performing his part of the partnership agreement[2].

1   The Partnership Act 1890 s 35(b) expressly excludes mental disorder from this case of dissolution; sed quaere whether this is right since s 35(a) (power of the court to order dissolution of a partnership on the grounds of the insanity of one of the partners) was repealed by the Mental Health Act 1959 s 149(2), Sch 8 Pt I. In any event the judge having jurisdiction under the Mental Capacity Act 2005 retains the power to make an order for the dissolution of any partnership of which the partner suffering from mental incapacity is a member: see ss 16, 18; PARA 183; and MENTAL HEALTH AND CAPACITY vol 75 (2013) PARA 727.

2   Partnership Act 1890 s 35(b); *Whitwell v Arthur* (1865) 35 Beav 140 (incapacity due to paralysis but, since the partner's health improved before the trial, further proceedings were stayed, although liberty to apply was reserved). As to the courts with jurisdiction see PARA 180.

186.   Conduct prejudicial to the partnership business.   On application by a partner, the court may decree a dissolution when any partner, other than the partner suing, has been guilty of such conduct as, in the opinion of the court, regard being had to the nature of the business, is calculated to affect prejudicially the carrying on of the business[1]. Thus, it has been held that the adultery of a partner is no reason for dissolving a mercantile partnership; but the immoral conduct of one of two medical partners may be a sufficient ground[2]; and embezzlement of trust funds of clients by a solicitor entitles his partner to an immediate dissolution[3].

1   Partnership Act 1890 s 35(c). As to the courts with jurisdiction see PARA 180. As to what is infamous conduct in a professional respect see eg *Clifford v Timms* [1908] AC 12, HL (professional misconduct by dentist); *Clifford v Phillips* [1908] AC 15, HL; *Re A Solicitor, ex p Law Society* [1912] 1 KB 302, DC. See also MEDICAL PROFESSIONS vol 74 (2011) PARA 497.
2   See *Anon* (1856) 2 K & J 441 at 445 per Page Wood V-C; *Snow v Milford* (1868) 18 LT 142 at 143 per Lord Romilly MR.
3   *Essell v Hayward* (1860) 30 Beav 158. Cf *Pearce v Foster* (1886) 17 QBD 536, CA, which shows that conduct by an employee may be prejudicial to the business, even though not directly connected with it; eg gambling on the Stock Exchange by a clerk justifies his dismissal from a business which has nothing to do with stock and share dealings. As to the expulsion of a partner who is guilty of conduct held to be detrimental to the firm, even though the conduct in question, namely travelling on the railway without a ticket and with intent to avoid payment of the fare for which the partner had been convicted, had no connection with the firm's business, see *Carmichael v Evans* [1904] 1 Ch 486. As to expulsion generally see PARA 178.

187.   Breach of partnership agreement or unreasonable conduct.   On application by a partner, the court may decree a dissolution when a partner, other than the partner suing, wilfully or persistently commits a breach of the partnership agreement[1], or otherwise so conducts himself in matters relating to the partnership business that it is not reasonably practicable for the other partner or partners to carry on the business in partnership with him[2].

Thus, whereas mere partnership squabbles are not sufficient to induce the court to order a dissolution[3], if a state of complete and permanent animosity exists, so that the breach between the partners is irreparable and mutual confidence is destroyed, the court will grant relief[4]. Similarly, neglect to account for money received, especially if so frequent as to be almost systematic[5], or the application of sums received to the payment of private debts[6], or refusal to account and the taking away of the partnership books[7], being acts inconsistent with the duty of a partner and destructive of the mutual confidence which ought to subsist between partners[8], afford good grounds for relief.

The court will not order dissolution on the application of the partner guilty of misconduct[9]. The court has discretion as to whether it will order him to pay the costs of an application for dissolution by his co-partner[10].

1   Partnership Act 1890 s 35(d); *Goodman v Whitcomb* (1820) 1 Jac & W 589 at 592; *Loscombe v Russell* (1830) 4 Sim 8 at 11; *Anderson v Anderson* (1857) 25 Beav 190 (one instance of breach of the partnership contract in eight years held to be insufficient ground for the interference of the court; although, as both parties admitted that it was useless to continue the partnership, a dissolution was ordered). 'It must be a studied, prolonged and continued inattention to the application of one party calling upon the other to observe that contract' (ie the partnership contract): *Marshall v Colman* (1820) 2 Jac & W 266 at 268 per Lord Eldon LC. See also *Mullins v Laughton* [2002] EWHC 2761 (Ch), [2003] Ch 250, [2003] 4 All ER 94.
2   Partnership Act 1890 s 35(d); *Waters v Taylor* (1813) 2 Ves & B 299; *Smith v Jeyes* (1841) 4 Beav 503 at 505; *Harrison v Tennant* (1856) 21 Beav 482; *Watney v Wells* (1861) 30 Beav 56 at 60. As to the courts with jurisdiction see PARA 180. There will often be an overlap between this ground for dissolution and the 'just and equitable' grounds under the Partnership Act 1890 s 35(f): see PARA 189. As to the duty of good faith see PARA 105.

3   *Wray v Hutchinson* (1834) 2 My & K 235.
4   *Baxter v West* (1860) 1 Drew & Sm 173; *Harrison v Tennant* (1856) 21 Beav 482; *Leary v Shout* (1864) 33 Beav 582; *Atwood v Maude* (1868) 3 Ch App 369 at 373; cf *Pearce v Lindsay* (1860) 3 De GJ & Sm 139. Where the court is satisfied that it is impossible for the partners to place that confidence in each other which each has a right to expect, and that such impossibility has not been caused by the person seeking to take advantage of it, it will order a dissolution: *Re Yenidje Tobacco Co Ltd* [1916] 2 Ch 426 at 430, CA, per Cozens-Hardy MR, followed in *Re Davis and Collett Ltd* [1935] Ch 693 at 701–702.
5   *Cheesman v Price* (1865) 35 Beav 142.
6   *Smith v Jeyes* (1841) 4 Beav 503.
7   *Charlton v Poulter* (1753) cited in 19 Ves at 148n (the Brewers' Case).
8   *Smith v Jeyes* (1841) 4 Beav 503 at 506.
9   See the Partnership Act 1890 s 35(d). No party is entitled to act improperly and then to say that the conduct of the partners and their feelings towards each other are such that the partnership can no longer be continued; and certainly the court would not allow any person so to act and thus to take advantage of his own wrong: *Harrison v Tennant* (1856) 21 Beav 482 at 493 per Romilly MR; and see *Re Yenidje Tobacco Co Ltd* [1916] 2 Ch 426, CA. The dictum of Lord Cairns to the contrary effect in *Atwood v Maude* (1868) 3 Ch App 369 at 373 is clearly displaced by the Partnership Act 1890 s 35(d).
10   As to the court's discretion in making orders as to costs see CPR 44.2; and CIVIL PROCEDURE vol 12 (2009) PARA 1738 et seq. See also *Hawkins v Parsons* (1862) 31 LJ Ch 479.

188. Business carried on at a loss. On application by a partner, the court may decree a dissolution when the business of the partnership can only be carried on at a loss[1]. Every partnership is entered into with a view to profit[2], and, if the business can only be carried on at a loss, the whole purpose of the partnership fails, and it may be dissolved even though the original term for which it was formed has not expired[3].

1   Partnership Act 1890 s 35(e). As to the courts with jurisdiction see PARA 180.
2   See PARA 4.
3   *Bailey v Ford* (1843) 13 Sim 495 (court, on motion before the hearing, appointed a person to sell the business and wind up the partnership); *Jennings v Baddeley* (1856) 3 K & J 78. See also *Re Suburban Hotel Co* (1867) 2 Ch App 737 at 744 per Lord Cairns LJ. If the errors can be attributed to special circumstances and cannot clearly be traced to any inherent defect in the business, the court will refuse the relief: *Handyside v Campbell* (1901) 17 TLR 623. See also *Baring v Dix* (1786) 1 Cox Eq Cas 213. If, however, the purposes of the partnership cannot be carried into effect with any reasonable prospect of profit, the court will dissolve the partnership: *Wilson v Church* (1879) 13 ChD 1 at 65, CA, per Cotton LJ (affd sub nom *National Bolivian Navigation Co v Wilson* (1880) 5 App Cas 176, HL).

     As to insolvent partnerships see PARAS 98, 232; and BANKRUPTCY AND INDIVIDUAL INSOLVENCY vol 5 (2013) PARA 851 et seq; COMPANY AND PARTNERSHIP INSOLVENCY vol 17 (2011) PARAS 1209–1361.

189. Dissolution just and equitable. On the application of a partner, the court may decree a dissolution whenever, in any case, circumstances have arisen which, in the court's opinion, render it just and equitable that the partnership be dissolved[1]. If the winding up or dissolution of a partnership is justified on other grounds, the incapacity of one partner will not prevent a sale of the partnership concern and assets[2], and the sale of the whole or of one or more of the partnership assets to the other partners will be sanctioned if it appears to be for the benefit of the partner suffering from the incapacity[3].

1   Partnership Act 1890 s 35(f). As to the courts with jurisdiction see PARA 180. The question as to what is just and equitable within the meaning of the similar provision in what is now the Insolvency Act 1986 s 122(1)(g), enabling the court to wind up a limited company when it is just and equitable to do so, has been considered in *Re Yenidje Tobacco Co Ltd* [1916] 2 Ch 426, CA (where the company was in substance a partnership): see COMPANY AND PARTNERSHIP INSOLVENCY vol 16 (2011) PARA 397. See also *Jesner v Jarrad Properties Ltd* [1992] BCC 807 (a quasi partnership where, because of a general breakdown in the mutual trust and understanding

between the family members, it was found that constant resort to legal advisers would have been likely were the quasi partner relationship to continue). In *Re JE Cade & Son Ltd* [1991] BCC 360, where two brothers had been partners in a family farming partnership which had subsequently been dissolved and the farm (previously an asset of the partnership) had then been licensed to the company of which the brothers were shareholders, it was held that, although in normal circumstances it may have been appropriate to order the winding up of the company concerned where the understanding between the members was no longer respected, an order for winding up was refused since the plaintiff sought the order not in order to protect his interests as member of the company, but as landlord of the farm. Quaere whether a partner who sought winding up under the Partnership Act 1890 s 35(f) for similar motives would be similarly precluded. Furthermore, the words 'just and equitable' in the Insolvency Act 1986 s 122(1)(g) are not to be construed as relating only to matters ejusdem generis with the grounds for winding up set out in s 122(1)(a)–(f): *Re Amalgamated Syndicate* [1897] 2 Ch 600. See generally COMPANY AND PARTNERSHIP INSOLVENCY vol 16 (2011) PARA 397.

2   It was so decided in the case of a mentally disordered partner in *Rowlands v Evans, Williams v Rowlands* (1861) 30 Beav 302. As to partnerships where one or more partners is or are suffering from mental incapacity see PARA 183 et seq.

3   *Crawshay v Maule* (1818) 1 Swan 495 at 540 (firm where one of the partners was a minor). As to minors as partners see PARA 28.

(iii) Date of Dissolution

190. Date of dissolution.   Where an application is made to the court for the dissolution of a firm[1], the firm is dissolved as from the date of judgment for such dissolution and not from some earlier date such as the issue or service of the claim form in the proceedings or the commencement of a partner's incapacity[2].

Alternatively, where a firm is dissolved by a notice of dissolution given by a partner empowered by virtue of the partnership agreement to give such notice, the firm is dissolved as from the date specified in the notice[3]. If, however, provision has been made in the partnership agreement for automatic dissolution upon the happening of some event, such as a partner becoming mentally disordered, the dissolution takes effect from the date contemplated in the partnership agreement[4].

1   Ie under the Partnership Act 1890 s 35 (see PARAS 185–189) or the Mental Capacity Act 2005 ss 16, 18 (see PARA 183). As to the dissolution of a partnership at will by notice in a normal case see PARA 173.

2   *Besch v Frolich* (1842) 1 Ph 172; *Sander v Sander* (1845) 2 Coll 276; *Re Coles, Leaf v Coles* (1852) 1 De GM & G 171; *Jones v Welch* (1855) 1 K & J 765. However, in *Phillips v Melville* [1921] NZLR 571 it was held (apparently on the ground that a partnership at will is determinable on notice: see PARA 173) that the firm was dissolved as from the date of the service of the writ; and in *Kirby v Carr* (1838) 3 Y & C Ex 184 and *Shepherd v Allen* (1864) 33 Beav 577 (overruled in *Unsworth v Jordan* [1896] WN 2) that the firm was dissolved as from the date of filing of the bill. Since in *Phillips v Melville* [1921] NZLR 571, *Kirby v Carr* (1838) 3 Y & C Ex 184 and *Shepherd v Allen* (1864) 33 Beav 577, although the firms concerned were partnerships at will, no notice of dissolution was ever given (either by way of a notice given out of court or by way of the service of a writ claiming a declaration that the firm was dissolved by reason of such service) but rather the court's jurisdiction to dissolve was being sought, the decisions would appear to be anomalous.

3   *Robertson v Lockie* (1846) 15 Sim 285; *Mellersh v Keen* (1859) 27 Beav 236; but see *Hunter v Wylie* 1993 SLT 1091n, Ct of Sess (where it was held that partners who had acted in material breach of the partnership agreement, namely by withdrawing capital without the other partners' consent, were not then entitled to exercise their contractual right to dissolve the firm).

4   *Bagshaw v Parker* (1847) 10 Beav 532. As to dissolution on the grounds of mental incapacity see PARAS 183–184.

(3) RETURN OF PREMIUMS

191. Court's discretion to order return of premiums. Where one partner has paid a premium[1] to another on entering into a partnership for a fixed term, and the partnership is dissolved before the expiration of that term, otherwise than by the death of a partner, the court may order the repayment of the premium or such part of it as it thinks just[2]. In determining the amount of premium to be returned, the court must have regard to the terms of the partnership agreement and to the length of time during which the partnership has continued[3]. The premium, being treated as paid for the whole term, is apportioned between the time which the partnership lasted and the unexpired residue[4]. The question of a return of premium should be dealt with at the trial of the claim for dissolution; afterwards the permission of the court is necessary, and this is given only if the circumstances are such that the court would give permission to bring a supplemental claim[5].

If arbitrators have power under the partnership agreement to award a dissolution, they also have power to consider the terms of the dissolution, including the question of the amount, if any, of premium to be returned[6].

1   The obligation upon an incoming partner to pay a premium as the price of his entry into the partnership is becoming increasingly rare, although it is still occasionally encountered in trading partnerships.

2   Partnership Act 1890 s 40. The principle upon which the court interferes is that the consideration in respect of which the money is paid fails (and is not obtained by the person who pays the money) in consequence of an unforeseen interruption: *Freeland v Stansfeld* (1854) 2 Sm & G 479 at 484 per Stuart V-C. See similar statements of the principle in *Tattersall v Groote* (1800) 2 Bos & P 131 at 134 per Lord Eldon LC; in *Bullock v Crockett* (1862) 3 Giff 507 at 512 per Stuart V-C; and in *Edmonds v Robinson* (1885) 29 ChD 170 at 175 per Kay J. As to premiums paid under misrepresentations see *Jauncey v Knowles* (1859) 29 LJ Ch 95; and PARAS 146–147.

3   Partnership Act 1890 s 40.

4   'The court has always treated it, I believe, as a mere arithmetical question': *Wilson v Johnstone* (1873) LR 16 Eq 606 at 609 per Wickens V-C. See also *Bury v Allen* (1845) 1 Coll 589; *Pease v Hewitt* (1862) 31 Beav 22; *Brewer v Yorke* (1882) 46 LT 289, CA. It is difficult, however, to apply the principle of extension of the premium over the whole term of the partnership where part of the consideration is not referable to the whole of the agreed period (*Bullock v Crockett* (1862) 3 Giff 507); and before the Partnership Act 1890 it was said that the court would consider all the circumstances (see e g *Lyon v Tweddell* (1881) 17 ChD 529, CA).

5   Eg if the facts were first discovered after the judgment: see *Edmonds v Robinson* (1885) 29 ChD 170.

6   *Belfield v Bourne* [1894] 1 Ch 521, distinguishing *Tattersall v Groote* (1800) 2 Bos & P 131.

192. When premiums will not be returned. The Partnership Act 1890 gives the court no jurisdiction to order the return of premiums either on the death of a partner[1], or if the dissolution is, in the judgment of the court, wholly or chiefly due to the misconduct of the partner who paid the premium[2], or when the partnership has been dissolved by an agreement containing no provision for a return of any part of the premium[3].

Neither will the court grant the relief if the partner seeking the return of his premium has expressly or impliedly waived this right[4], nor if he has become bankrupt, unless his bankruptcy is attributable to a breach of partnership duty by the partner to whom he paid the premium[5]. Where, however, the partnership has been dissolved without any fault of either party[6], or if there are faults on both sides[7], or if the recipient of the premium has himself caused the dissolution[8], or had always known of his partner's incompetence[9], the equity will be enforced by the court.

Generally, in the absence of fraud or contrary agreement, premiums are not repayable in the case of a partnership at will[10].

1   Partnership Act 1890 s 40; *Whincup v Hughes* (1871) LR 6 CP 78; *Ferns v Carr* (1885) 28 ChD 409. As to the courts with jurisdiction see PARA 180. If, however, the partner taking the premium knows at the time that he is suffering from a fatal disease and this is not known to the partner paying the premium, on the death of the former during the term an apportionment may be ordered on the ground of the failure of the consideration: see *Mackenna v Parkes* (1866) 36 LJ Ch 366; and CONTRACT vol 22 (2012) PARA 468 et seq (frustration); RESTITUTION vol 88 (2012) PARA 487 et seq (failure of consideration).

2   Partnership Act 1890 s 40(a); *Bullock v Crockett* (1862) 3 Giff 507; *Atwood v Maude* (1868) 3 Ch App 369; *Bluck v Capstick* (1879) 12 ChD 863 (unpaid premium ordered to be paid by the guilty partner); *Yates v Cousins* (1889) 60 LT 535. Conduct, although objectionable and such as would entitle his partner to a dissolution, is not sufficient to deprive the partner paying the premium of his right to return of premium (*Wilson v Johnstone* (1873) LR 16 Eq 606); nor is it material that the partner paying the premium is the party who seeks the dissolution (*Atwood v Maude* (1868) 3 Ch App 369).

3   Partnership Act 1890 s 40(b); *Lee v Page* (1861) 30 LJ Ch 857; *Belfield v Bourne* [1894] 1 Ch 521 at 527; cf *Handyside v Campbell* (1901) 17 TLR 623.

4   See *Bond v Milbourn* (1871) 20 WR 197, explained in *Rooke v Nisbet* (1881) 50 LJ Ch 588. Cf *Andrewes v Jones* (1865) 12 LT 229; *Brewer v Yorke* (1882) 46 LT 289, CA.

5   *Akhurst v Jackson* (1818) 1 Wils Ch 47. The court ordered a return of part of the premium where the partner who paid the premium was made bankrupt by the recipient (*Hamil v Stokes* (1817) 4 Price 161, Ex Ch); and where the recipient became bankrupt, having been in embarrassed circumstances at the commencement of the partnership, and the partner who paid the premium had no notice of the fact (*Freeland v Stanfeld* (1854) 2 Sm & G 479); but a return was not ordered where he had notice (*Akhurst v Jackson* (1818) 1 Wils Ch 47).

6   *Atwood v Maude* (1868) 3 Ch App 369; cf *Airey v Borham* (1861) 29 Beav 620.

7   *Astle v Wright* (1856) 23 Beav 77; *Pease v Hewitt* (1862) 31 Beav 22.

8   *Atwood v Maude* (1868) 3 Ch App 369; *Airey v Borham* (1861) 29 Beav 620; *Hamil v Stokes* (1817) 4 Price 161, Ex Ch; *Bury v Allen* (1845) 1 Coll 589 (misconduct principally that of the partner receiving the premium); *Bullock v Crockett* (1862) 3 Giff 507.

9   Incompetence is not misconduct and does not, in itself, form a bar to this equity if the incompetence was known to the partner receiving the premium at, or almost at, the commencement of the partnership and was the ground of his demanding an increased premium: *Atwood v Maude* (1868) 3 Ch App 369 at 375; *Brewer v Yorke* (1882) 46 LT 289 at 293, CA, where Brett LJ said that mere incompetence, however great, without proof of damage caused by it, ought not to be a ground for declining, upon a dissolution of partnership, to return the proportionate amount of premium; but Holker LJ dissented from this statement of the law (*Brewer v Yorke* (1882) 46 LT 289 at 295, CA).

10 See *Tattersall v Groote* (1800) 2 Bos & P 131 at 134. In the case of a partnership for no definite time, however, the recipient may not dissolve the partnership immediately and retain the premium: see *Featherstonhaugh v Turner* (1858) 25 Beav 382 at 391.

(4) NOTICE OF DISSOLUTION

193.   Advertisement of dissolution.   On the dissolution of a partnership or retirement of a partner, any partner may give public notice of the fact, and may require the other partner or partners to concur for that purpose in all necessary or proper acts, if any, which cannot be done without his or their concurrence[1].

1   Partnership Act 1890 s 37; *Troughton v Hunter* (1854) 18 Beav 470; *Hendry v Turner* (1886) 32 ChD 355. A partner may advertise that he is no longer connected with a periodical that the firm publishes, but he must not advertise that the periodical is being discontinued, if it is a firm asset which might be sold: *Bradbury v Dickens* (1859) 27 Beav 53; and see PARA 212. As to dissolution by notice see PARA 173; and as to the death of a partner see PARA 175.

194.   Old customers.   Where a person deals with a firm after a change in its constitution, he is entitled to treat all apparent members[1] of the old firm as still being members of the firm until he has notice of the change[2]. As regards those who previously had dealings with the firm, notice of the dissolution published in the appropriate Gazette[3] is not in itself sufficient[4], but evidence of facts showing that it is probable that an old customer had seen the Gazette is admissible[5].

Notice to old customers is usually given by circular letter[6], but any mode by which actual knowledge is given suffices[7]. The execution by a customer of a power of attorney to the new firm has been held to establish evidence of knowledge of the retirement of a partner[8], and proof of the preparation and transmission by a solicitor of the draft of a deed of dissolution may throw upon the solicitor the burden of showing the abandonment by the partners of intention to dissolve[9].

1   'Apparent members' means members apparent to the person dealing with the firm: *Tower Cabinet Co Ltd v Ingram* [1949] 2 KB 397, [1949] 1 All ER 1033, DC.
2   Partnership Act 1890 s 36(1).
3   As to advertisements in the appropriate Gazette see PARA 195.
4   Partnership Act 1890 s 36(2); *Graham v Hope* (1792) Peake 154; *Gorham v Thompson* (1791) Peake 42; *Re Hodgson, Beckett v Ramsdale* (1885) 31 ChD 177 at 184, CA.
5   *Godfrey v Macauley* (1795) Peake 209n.
6   The categories of client who should be notified by circular may vary according to whether there has been a general dissolution of the firm or merely a technical dissolution brought about e g by the expulsion of one of its partners: see *Fulwell v Bragg* (1983) 127 Sol Jo 171.
7   *Barfoot v Goodall* (1811) 3 Camp 147 at 149 (change by a banking partnership in its forms of cheque held to be sufficient notice to an old customer who had drawn cheques in the new form). See also *JL Smallman Ltd v O'Moore* [1959] IR 220. One insertion of an advertisement of dissolution in a newspaper proved to be taken by the customer and to have been left at his house has been admitted as evidence of notice, although not proved to have reached his hands (*Jenkins v Blizard* (1816) 1 Stark 418), but evidence of such an insertion was excluded where it was not proved that he was in the habit of taking the newspaper, although it circulated in the town where he resided (*Norwich and Lowestoft Navigation Co v Theobald* (1828) Mood & M 151).
8   *Hart v Alexander* (1837) 2 M & W 484.
9   *Paterson v Zachariah and Arnold* (1815) 1 Stark 71.

195.   Advertisement is sufficient notice to new customers. An advertisement in the London Gazette as to a firm whose principal place of business[1] is in England and Wales, in the Edinburgh Gazette as to a firm whose principal place of business is in Scotland, and in the Belfast Gazette as to a firm whose principal place of business is in Northern Ireland[2] is notice as to persons who had not had dealings with the firm before the date of the dissolution or change so advertised[3]. It is immaterial whether they have seen the advertisement in the Gazette or not; but an advertisement in any other newspaper may not be given in evidence without preliminary proof that the customer was in the habit of taking that newspaper[4]. A public advertisement in newspapers, taken at a reading room where a creditor was in the habit of reading the newspapers, has been received as evidence of knowledge, in a case in which there was no notice in the Gazette[5].

1   As to the principal place of business see PARA 87 note 3.
2   Government of Ireland (Miscellaneous Adaptations) (Northern Ireland) Order 1923, SR & O 1923/803, art 3.
3   Partnership Act 1890 s 36(2) (amended by virtue of SR & O 1921/1804); *Godfrey v Turnbull and Macauley* (1795) 1 Esp 371, sub nom *Godfrey v Macauley* Peake 209n; *Wrightson v Pullan* (1816) 1 Stark 375. As to the liability of a retired partner see PARAS 76–77.
4   *Leeson v Holt* (1816) 1 Stark 186.
5   *Rooth v Quin and Janney* (1819) 7 Price 193. As to the weight of such evidence see, however, *Hart v Alexander* (1837) 2 M & W 484 at 491, 494. See also *M'Iver v Humble* (1812) 16 East 169.

(5) ENFORCEMENT OF PARTNERS' RIGHTS ON DISSOLUTION

196. Determination of partners' rights on dissolution. On dissolution it may be necessary for the court to determine partners' rights[1] between themselves, especially where questions as to the construction of the partnership agreement are raised[2]. As a general rule, the court will not order an account of partnership dealings unless the claimant also claims dissolution[3].

1   As to the enforcement of partners' rights see PARA 143 et seq. As to the courts with jurisdiction see PARA 180.
2   See PARA 143.
3   See PARA 150. As to orders for account see PARAS 149–160.

(6) WINDING UP THE PARTNERSHIP BUSINESS

(i) Continuation of Partner's Authority

197. Partnership continues after dissolution only for winding up. After dissolution, the partnership subsists merely for the purpose of completing pending transactions, winding up the business, and adjusting the rights of the partners[1]. For these purposes, and these only, the authority, rights and obligations of the partners continue[2], including the partners' duty of good faith[3].

Dissolution of the partnership necessitates the termination of its employees' contracts of employment, which may amount to wrongful dismissal[4]. Upon dissolution partnership land, like a firm's other assets, will fall to be sold or assigned in the ordinary way[5]. Where the partnership land in question is leasehold, such a sale or assignment without the landlord's consent may result in the breach by the tenant partners of a covenant contained in the lease against parting with possession[6].

1   *Beak v Beak* (1675) 3 Swan 627; *Crawshay v Maule* (1818) 1 Swan 495 at 507. Where the business of a partnership, the term of which had expired, was continued by both partners merely for the purpose of realisation and winding up, it was held that their conduct showed an intention not to continue the former business, and that a clause in the partnership agreement providing for purchase by the survivor of the share of the other on his death had ceased to be applicable: *Myers v Myers* (1891) 60 LJ Ch 311. See also *Boghani v Nathoo* [2011] EWHC 2101 (Ch), [2011] 2 All ER (Comm) 743 (affairs of firm could not be finally wound up unless and until obligations were satisfied). As to the tax consequences of dissolution see *C Connelly & Co v Wilbey (Inspector of Taxes)* [1992] STC 783; and CAPITAL GAINS TAXATION vol 6 (2011) PARA 824 et seq.
2   See the Partnership Act 1890 s 38; and PARA 46. See also *Crawshay v Collins* (1808) 15 Ves 218 at 226 per Lord Eldon LC; *Cruikshank v M'Vicar* (1844) 8 Beav 106 at 116 per Lord Langdale MR; cf *Wood v Braddick* (1808) 1 Taunt 104 at 105; *Booth v Parks* (1828) 1 Mol 465; *Lewis v Reilly* (1841) 4 Per & Dav 629. However the Partnership Act 1890 s 38 does not extend to technical dissolution: *HLB Kidsons (formerly Kidsons Impey) v Lloyd's Underwriters Subscribing Policy No 621/PK1D00101* [2008] EWHC 2415 (Comm), [2009] 1 All ER (Comm) 760 (merger of two firms did not dissolve partnership within meaning of Partnership Act 1890 s 38). As to the difference between a continuing partnership and one in course of winding up as affecting the liability of a retired partner for acts of the continuing partner see *Smith v Winter* (1838) 4 M & W 454; and PARAS 39–40, 76–77. As to the right or otherwise of a partner to claim remuneration for managing the business of a firm during its winding up see PARA 110.
3   See *Hogar Estates Ltd in Trust v Shebron Holdings Ltd* (1979) 25 OR (2d) 543, 101 DLR (3d) 509 (Ont). As to the partners' duty of good faith see PARA 105.
4   *Tunstall v Condon* [1980] ICR 786, EAT; and see PARA 17 note 8.
5   As to which assets constitute partnership assets see PARA 115 et seq. As to the partners' right to have the firm's assets sold see PARA 205.

6   See PARA 10. For covenants as to alienation generally see LANDLORD AND TENANT vol 62 (2012) PARA 630 et seq.

198. Third party debts and liabilities. After dissolution, each partner has authority to give a valid security on partnership property for money required for the completion of a pending contract[1]; and any partner may withdraw money on deposit with a bank[2], or receive a debt and give a release or take a bill for it, even though the terms of dissolution provide that, as between the partners, the debts should be received by only one of them[3].

A recognition of a debt in a letter from one ex-partner of a dissolved firm to another is not an acknowledgment of the debt[4] so as to take it out of the Limitation Act 1980[5], and part payment of a debt by a continuing partner after dissolution does not prevent time from running under that Act in favour of a retiring partner[6].

No third person, even with notice, is concerned with the partners' own arrangements to discharge their debts[7]. Where two partners enter into a joint speculation with a third person, and afterwards dissolve their partnership, the dissolution of the partnership does not prevent the third person who continues to rely upon their joint responsibility from holding them jointly liable[8].

1   *Butchart v Dresser* (1853) 10 Hare 453; affd 4 De GM & G 542. As to the power of a surviving partner after dissolution to give security for a past partnership debt see PARA 46.

2   *Dickson v National Bank of Scotland Ltd* 1917 SC (HL) 50.

3   *King v Smith* (1829) 4 C & P 108. As between the partners, however, the benefit of such a withdrawal or receipt would have to be accounted for: see PARA 106. Under the old bankruptcy law the continuing partners were entitled to issue a bankruptcy notice in the name of the partnership in respect of a judgment obtained by the firm before dissolution: see *Re Hill, ex p Holt & Co* [1921] 2 KB 831. Whether the same principle applies under the Insolvency Act 1986 is unclear. As to insolvent partnerships generally see PARAS 98, 232; and BANKRUPTCY AND INDIVIDUAL INSOLVENCY vol 5 (2013) PARA 851 et seq; COMPANY AND PARTNERSHIP INSOLVENCY vol 17 (2011) PARAS 1209–1361.

4   See the Limitation Act 1980 s 29(5); and LIMITATION PERIODS vol 68 (2008) PARAS 1184, 1209.

5   *Re Hindmarsh* (1860) 1 Drew & Sm 129.

6   *Watson v Woodman* (1875) LR 20 Eq 721. The rule is different where the retirement is secret: see *Re Tucker, Tucker v Tucker* [1894] 3 Ch 429, CA; PARA 5; and LIMITATION PERIODS vol 68 (2008) PARA 1209.

7   See PARAS 76, 199.

8   *Ault v Goodrich* (1828) 4 Russ 430. As to the giving of notice of dissolution to clients and others see PARA 193 et seq.

199. Arrangements between partners for discharge of debts. An arrangement between the members of a dissolved partnership that the debts of the firm are to be paid and the affairs wound up by a particular partner does not bind creditors of the firm even if they have notice of such arrangement[1]; but a charge by a partner on his private property to secure his firm's banking account[2] is not available as a security for debts to the bank which are incurred after his death by the surviving partners who continue the business[3].

Provisions in partnership or retirement agreements often provide that the partner or partners continuing the firm's activities are to indemnify the outgoing partner against existing partnership liabilities[4]. Even where such an express indemnity is not given, one will normally be implied[5].

1   *Smith v Jameson* (1794) 5 Term Rep 601; and see PARA 76.

2   See FINANCIAL SERVICES AND INSTITUTIONS vol 49 (2008) PARA 815 et seq.

3   *Royal Bank of Scotland v Christie* (1841) 8 Cl & Fin 214, HL.

4   In relation to the types of liability which will be covered by an indemnity, income tax is a
     partnership debt or liability in respect of which a retiring partner may be indemnified: *Stevens v
     Britten* [1954] 3 All ER 385, [1954] 1 WLR 1340, CA. As to liability to income taxation see
     further PARA 99; and INCOME TAXATION.
5   *Gray v Smith* (1889) 43 ChD 208, CA.

(ii) Distribution of Profits Made After Dissolution

200.   Profits after purchase of share of outgoing partner. Where, by the
partnership agreement, an option is given to surviving or continuing partners to
purchase the interest of a deceased or outgoing partner[1], and that option is duly
exercised and its terms complied with in all material respects, the estate of the
deceased partner, or the outgoing partner or his estate, as the case may be, is not
entitled to any further or other share of profits[2].

The valuation of the share of a deceased partner should take place as at the
date of realisation, and not at the date of death[3]; but, where a surviving partner
exercises an option to buy the share of a deceased partner at a valuation, and the
valuation is not completed until some months after the death, the dissolution
takes effect as at the date of the death, and the executors of the deceased partner
are entitled to a share of profits up to the date of the valuation and to interest on
the amount of the valuation after that date[4]. Compensation for his work will,
however, as a rule, be allowed to the surviving partner before ascertaining the
amount of profit divisible[5].

1   If the interest of the deceased or outgoing partner includes an interest in land (which, prima
     facie, as long as the firm owns any land or proprietary interest over land, it will do), such
     purchase should be effected by means of a contract complying with the provisions of the Law of
     Property (Miscellaneous Provisions) Act 1989 s 2: see PARAS 24, 118; and CONVEYANCING
     vol 23 (2013) PARA 151. As to the nature of a partner's share in the firm generally see PARA 121.
2   Partnership Act 1890 s 42(2). Cf *Vyse v Foster* (1874) LR 7 HL 318, with *Willett v Blanford*
     (1842) 1 Hare 253. As to profits made after dissolution see PARA 130.
3   *Meagher v Meagher* [1961] IR 96 (although the court, whilst holding that the deceased partner's
     share should be valued as at the date of realisation and not the earlier date of the firm's technical
     dissolution caused by his death, held that what the deceased partner's estate was actually
     entitled to was the value of the deceased partner's share as at the date of death plus interest at
     5%). This unsatisfactory decision was distinguished in *Barclays Bank Trust Co Ltd v Bluff*
     [1982] Ch 172, [1981] 3 All ER 232 (where it was held that the outgoing partner was entitled to
     the full value of his share in the firm's assets as at the date of realisation), approved in
     Chandroutie v Gajadhar [1987] AC 147, [1987] 2 WLR 1, PC; and see PARA 202. Cf the
     position of a retiring partner: see *Sobell v Boston* [1975] 2 All ER 282, [1975] 1 WLR 1587. As
     to the valuation of partnership capital assets during the continuation of the partnership see
     Noble v Noble 1965 SLT 415, Ct of Sess; and see PARAS 115 note 1, 135 note 8, 155, 215.
     Where the share of a deceased partner was to be ascertained by reference to a general account
     made up after his death, it was held, in the absence of usage to the contrary, that the assets were
     to be taken at their fair value, and not at the value appearing in the partnership books:
     Cruikshank v Sutherland (1922) 92 LJ Ch 136, HL. However, there is no presumption that, on
     a partner's death, the value of assets is to be determined by their current market value rather
     than their historical costs as shown in the partnership books: *Re White, White v Minnis* [2001]
     Ch 393, [2000] 3 All ER 618, CA (considering *Cruikshank v Sutherland* (1922) 92 LJ
     Ch 136, HL); *Drake v Harvey* [2011] EWCA Civ 838, [2012] 1 All ER (Comm) 617; *Ham v
     Ham* [2013] EWCA Civ 1301, [2013] All ER (D) 356 (Oct). An option to purchase the share of
     a deceased partner on giving to his personal representatives notice within a limited time was
     held to be validly exercised by a notice given to his executors within the time but before probate
     had been obtained: *Kelsey v Kelsey* (1922) 91 LJ Ch 382.
4   As to the rate of interest and the time from which it is payable see *Wadsworth v Lydall* [1981]
     2 All ER 401, [1981] 1 WLR 598, CA (10% ordered under the Law Reform (Miscellaneous
     Provisions) Act 1934 s 3). As to the court's general power to award interest on debts and
     damages see the Senior Courts Act 1981 s 35A; and DAMAGES vol 12(1) (Reissue) PARA 848.

5   *Yates v Finn* (1880) 13 ChD 839 at 841; *Brown v De Tastet* (1819) Jac 284 at 298–299. Such compensation was refused where the surviving partner was the executor of the deceased, and carried on the trade for himself and the children of the deceased: *Burden v Burden* (1813) 1 Ves & B 170; *Stocken v Dawson* (1843) 6 Beav 371 at 376; *Stocken v Dawson* (1848) 17 LJ Ch 282 at 285. Cf *Cook v Collingridge* (1823) Jac 607 at 621, 623; and see PARA 110. As to the general rule that no partner is allowed more than his equal share see PARA 128.

201. Profits where share of outgoing partner not purchased. If there is no agreement that the interest of an outgoing partner may be purchased, or if the terms of such an option are not complied with[1], and the remaining partners carry on the business of the firm[2] with its capital or assets without any final settlement of accounts as between the outgoing partner or his estate, the outgoing partner or his estate has the option of taking either interest at 5 per cent per annum on the value of his share of the assets[3], or such share of the profits made after dissolution as the court may find to be attributable to the use of such share[4]. Where executors of a deceased partner accept interest on the value of the testator's share from dissolution to the date of payment, they may not subsequently elect to take a share of profits instead[5].

1   See the Partnership Act 1890 s 42(2); and PARAS 130, 200.
2   A partner may be carrying on the business even though his 'right to trade hang at all times by the most tenuous thread': *Pathirana v Pathirana* [1967] 1 AC 233 at 239, [1966] 3 WLR 666 at 670–671, PC, per Lord Upjohn.
3   The interest is calculated on the value of the share at the date it is realised, not the date of death: *Meagher v Meagher* [1961] IR 96. The reference in the Partnership Act 1890 s 42(1) to 'the partnership assets' is to the net partnership assets (ie the surplus or what remained out of the gross assets for distribution between the partners after all debts and liabilities of the partnership have been met); and the 'share' is the actual share of those assets assessed by reference to what the partner in question was entitled to receive as apportioned at the conclusion of the winding up process: *Sandhu v Gill* [2005] EWCA Civ 1297, [2006] Ch 456, [2006] 2 All ER 22. As to the determination of the proportion of profits attributable to the assets of the outgoing partner see PARA 202.
4   Partnership Act 1890 s 42(1). As to the meaning of 'profits' in s 42(1) see PARA 202 note 1. The entitlement arises even if the share of the outgoing partner is of little or no monetary value: *Pathirana v Pathirana* [1967] 1 AC 233, [1966] 3 WLR 666, PC. As to the profits made after dissolution see PARA 130. See also *Ahmed Musaji Saleji v Hashim Ebrahim Saleji* (1915) LR 42 Ind App 91, PC. For the principle on which the court acted before the Partnership Act 1890 see *Wedderburn v Wedderburn (No 4)* (1856) 22 Beav 84 at 99 per Romilly MR. See also *Vyse v Foster* (1874) LR 7 HL 318. It was well established that the use of the assets after dissolution, by partners who continued the business, entitled the outgoing partner to share in the profits produced by their use until a final settlement of accounts: *Featherstonhaugh v Fenwick* (1810) 17 Ves 298 at 309; *Turner v Major* (1862) 3 Giff 442. These provisions apply to a partnership with an alien enemy dissolved as a result of the outbreak of war, the alien enemy being entitled after the war to the profits and interest attributable to the use of his share during the war: *Hugh Stevenson & Sons Ltd v AG für Cartonnagen-Industrie* [1917] 1 KB 842, CA; affd [1918] AC 239, HL. Likewise, where a partnership had been dissolved in wartime by the trading with the enemy legislation, an active partner in England who exchanged partnership assets for other assets in his name was accountable as a constructive trustee and, as such, chargeable with interest on money representing the assets, such interest being at the rate of 5% per annum: *Gordon v Gonda* [1955] 2 All ER 762, [1955] 1 WLR 885.
5   *Smith v Everett* (1859) 27 Beav 446.

202. Determination of proportion of profits attributable to assets of outgoing partner. The court determines what proportion of the profits made after dissolution are, in the special circumstances, properly attributable to the assets of a retiring, bankrupt or deceased partner[1]. Thus, a retiring partner may be entitled to an inquiry into what assets have been so used and what use has been made of them, and an account of the profits made in the business since the dissolution[2]. In ascertaining the amount of the share of an outgoing partner, the value of the goodwill of the business, if any, must be taken into account, but it depends upon circumstances whether or not it has any appreciable value[3]. The share of profits payable after dissolution in respect of the assets of a retiring, bankrupt or deceased partner is not necessarily the share to which he was entitled before dissolution[4].

1   See the Partnership Act 1890 s 42(1) (see PARAS 130, 201); and *Simpson v Chapman* (1853) 4 De GM & G 154 at 171–172 per Turner LJ, following and approving *Willett v Blanford* (1842) 1 Hare 253. By 'profits' in the Partnership Act 1890 s 42(1) is meant income, not capital profits, so that a deceased or other outgoing partner retains his interest in the latter whichever option under s 42(1) he chooses: *Barclays Bank Trust Co Ltd v Bluff* [1982] Ch 172, [1981] 3 All ER 232; approved in *Chandroutie v Gajadhar* [1987] AC 147, [1987] 2 WLR 1, PC (partnership dissolved by the death of one of the two partners, the surviving partner carrying on the business, with the assistance of an unrelated third party, without winding up the business; the deceased partner's estate held entitled to his half-share of the proceeds of sale of the partnership assets and to his half-share of the profits made in the three years between death and final winding up); and applied in *Popat v Shonchhatra* [1997] 3 All ER 800, [1997] 1 WLR 1367, CA (the Partnership Act 1890 s 42(1) does not apply to profit made on the sale of a business when partners have made unequal contributions to partnership profits); and *Emerson (executrix of the estate of James Emerson (deceased)) v Estate of Thomas Matthew Emerson (deceased)* [2004] EWCA Civ 170, [2004] 1 BCLC 575 (the Partnership Act 1890 s 42(1) does not apply to compensation payable to farmers for livestock forced to be culled in response to an outbreak of foot and mouth disease). See also *Sandhu v Gill* [2005] EWCA Civ 1297, [2006] Ch 456, [2006] 2 All ER 22; and PARA 201. See further note 4.

2   *Featherstonhaugh v Fenwick* (1810) 17 Ves 298 at 309; *Mellersh v Keen* (1859) 27 Beav 236. For the form of inquiry see *Manley v Sartori* [1927] 1 Ch 157 at 166–167. If the defendant partner refuses to produce the books of account, the court may make an assessment: *Pathirana v Pathirana* [1967] 1 AC 233, [1966] 3 WLR 666, PC.

3   *Smith v Everett* (1859) 27 Beav 446 at 455–456. It is not necessary for the claimant to show that the goodwill has a monetary value: *Pathirana v Pathirana* [1967] 1 AC 233 at 239, [1966] 3 WLR 666 at 670–671, PC. As to disposal of goodwill see PARA 212.

4   The nature of the trade, the manner of carrying it on, the capital employed, the state of the account between the partnership and the deceased partner at the time of his death, and the conduct of parties after his death may materially affect the rights of the parties: *Willett v Blanford* (1842) 1 Hare 253 at 272 per Wigram V-C. The inquiry should be whether the profits were made by any and what application of the fund constituting the capital at the date of dissolution, or by the application of any other and what funds: *Crawshay v Collins* (1808) 15 Ves 218; and see Lord Eldon's subsequent observations as to his decree in *Crawshay v Collins* (1808) 15 Ves 218, in *Crawshay v Collins* (1826) 2 Russ 325 at 330, in *Brown v De Tastet* (1819) Jac 284 at 297, and in *Cook v Collingridge* (1823) Jac 607 at 622–623. Where trade was carried on by a surviving partner, with the larger capital of a deceased partner, wrongfully claiming to do so on his own account, the court apportioned the profits to capital, after making all proper allowances including compensation for management to the surviving partner: *Yates v Finn* (1880) 13 ChD 839.

203.   Trust money used by partnership.   When partners who are also trustees of a deceased partner lend trust money to the firm, they are personally liable as trustees to make up any money lost and account for profit or interest on it, even though it may be secured by mortgage of firm property[1]. An inquiry may be directed as to whether the beneficiaries will receive more by way of interest or profits[2]. If the partners of such trustees have notice of the breach of trust, they are under the same liability[3]. Thus, where the executor of a deceased partner improperly uses his testator's assets in the business carried on by him as surviving partner, he is the person liable to account; but persons subsequently taken into partnership by him are not liable unless they have notice of the breach of trust[4].

The appropriate rate of interest was formerly 5 per cent[5], but now it is probably the court's short-term investment rate[6]. In certain circumstances, compound interest will be ordered to be paid by the trustee, as, for example, when he was under a duty to call in and accumulate the money, but his partners may only be liable to make good the principal sum with simple interest[7].

1   *Townend v Townend* (1859) 1 Giff 201; and see *Flockton v Bunning* (1868) 8 Ch App 323n.
2   *Flockton v Bunning* (1868) 8 Ch App 323n.
3   *Flockton v Bunning* (1868) 8 Ch App 323n. As to liability for breach of trust see PARA 67.
4   *MacDonald v Richardson, Richardson v Marten* (1858) 1 Giff 81 at 89.
5   *Flockton v Bunning* (1868) 8 Ch App 323n; and see the cases cited in note 7.
6   *Bartlett v Barclays Bank Trust Co Ltd (No 2)* [1980] Ch 515 at 547, [1980] 2 All ER 92 at 98 per Brightman LJ.
7   *Jones v Foxall* (1852) 15 Beav 388 at 395–396; *Williams v Powell* (1852) 15 Beav 461 at 470. For the principles on which the court acts in cases of this kind see also *Docker v Somes* (1834) 2 My & K 655 at 665 per Lord Brougham; *Stroud v Gwyer* (1860) 28 Beav 130; *Burdick v Carrick* (1870) 5 Ch App 233; *Vyse v Foster* (1874) LR 7 HL 318 at 344 per Lord Selborne; *Re Emmet's Estate, Emmet v Emmet* (1881) 17 ChD 142; *Re Barclay, Barclay v Andrew* [1899] 1 Ch 674; *Re Davis, Davis v Davis* [1902] 2 Ch 314; *Re Davy, Hollingworth v Davy* [1908] 1 Ch 61, CA; *Gordon v Gonda* [1955] 2 All ER 762, [1955] 1 WLR 885, CA; *Wallersteiner v Moir (No 2)* [1975] QB 373, 508n, [1975] 1 All ER 849, CA.

204. Rights where new partnership arises by implication. The circumstances in which the assets are employed after the expiration of the partnership term by one partner may be such as to imply a new partnership at will, but governed otherwise, namely save as to its duration, by the provisions applicable to the previous partnership[1]. Alternatively, a new partnership at will governed only by the provisions of the Partnership Act 1890 may be created[2].

1   *Parsons v Hayward* (1862) 4 De GF & J 474; *Hudgell Yeates & Co v Watson* [1978] QB 451, [1978] 2 All ER 363, CA. As to partnerships at will see PARA 37. See also PARA 38.
2   *Firth v Amslake* (1964) 108 Sol Jo 198; cf *Austen v Boys* (1857) 24 Beav 598 (affd (1858) 2 De G & J 626); *Zamikoff v Lundy* [1970] 2 OR 8, 9 DLR (3d) 637 (affd sub nom *Whisper Holdings Ltd v Zamikoff* [1971] SCR 933, 19 DLR (3d) 114); and see PARA 38.

(iii) Realisation and Disposal of Assets

A. IN GENERAL

205. Right of application and sale of assets. Upon a general dissolution[1], each partner is entitled, as against the other partners in the firm and all persons claiming through them in respect of their interests as partners, to have the partnership property applied in payment of the firm's debts and liabilities, and after such payment to have the surplus assets applied in payment of what may be due to the partners[2] after deducting what may be due from them to the firm[3]. For this purpose, any partner or his representatives may bring a claim to have the business and affairs of the partnership wound up by the court with all proper accounts and inquiries[4]. Subject to any contrary agreement, this implies a right to have the assets sold[5] to provide a fund for discharge of liabilities, and for the adjustment of the rights of the partners among themselves.

1   As to the distinction between a general and technical dissolution and the different consequences that arise in each case see PARAS 33 note 12, 38, 111, 130 note 4, 178, 180.
2   As to the order of application of assets see PARA 211. As to the extent of the liabilities of an innocent partner who accepts the repudiation of the partnership agreement by the other partners see *Hurst v Bryk* [2002] 1 AC 185, [2000] 2 All ER 193, HL.
3   Partnership Act 1890 s 39.
4   See the Partnership Act 1890 s 39. This provision gives express statutory recognition and effect to the equitable lien which a partner has on the property of the firm and on the shares of his co-partners: see further PARA 141 et seq. Where, after a dissolution, a credit item has not been taken into account, it ought to be divided between the ex-partners in proportion to their shares

in the former partnership. If no accounts have been taken, the proper remedy is to have the accounts taken. If this right is barred by limitation, then it is too late to claim a share in such credit item: *Gopala Chetty v Vijayaraghavachariar* [1922] 1 AC 488, PC. A partner's right under the Partnership Act 1890 s 39 applies only in relation to partnership assets: see PARA 115 et seq. Where certain assets constitute the separate estate of one or more of the partners, no such lien can be claimed by the non-owning partner or partners. Equally, where the assets do constitute partnership property but by the terms of the partnership agreement one or more of the partners has or have no interest therein, the court may refuse an application by those non-owning partners for the sale of the assets under s 39: see *Stekel v Ellice* [1973] 1 All ER 465, [1973] 1 WLR 191; and see *Miles v Clarke* [1953] 1 All ER 779, [1953] 1 WLR 537 (where the ownership of assets was considered, there being no express partnership agreement except as to the division of profits). Note that a transfer of the business assets to a limited company would, in the absence of other evidence, bring about the dissolution of the partnership: *Chahal v Mahal* [2005] EWCA Civ 898, [2005] 2 BCLC 655 (on the facts, the partnership had not dissolved).

5   *Featherstonhaugh v Fenwick* (1810) 17 Ves 298; *Wild v Milne* (1859) 26 Beav 504; *Burdon v Barkus* (1861) 3 Giff 412 (on appeal (1862) 4 De GF & J 42); *Steward v Blakeway* (1869) 4 Ch App 603 at 609; cf *Rigden v Pierce* (1822) 6 Madd 353; *Re Bourne, Bourne v Bourne* [1906] 2 Ch 427 at 430–431, CA. however, the court does not have to order a sale of the partnership assets: instead, the court may think it preferable to require one or more of the partners to buy out the others: see *Syers v Syers* (1876) 1 App Cas 174, HL (partners who together owned seven-eighths of the main partnership asset (a music hall) permitted simply to buy out the interest of their co-partner at an agreed price); and see *Latchan v Martin* (1984) 134 NLJ 745, PC; *Hammond v Brearley* (unreported) 10 December 1992; and *Mullins v Laughton* [2002] EWHC 2761 (Ch) at [108]–[111], [2003] Ch 250 at [108]–[111], [2003] 4 All ER 94 at [108]–[111]. Where the partnership is not dissolved as such, but fails in limine, a sale of what would have been the partnership assets will not generally be ordered, especially where one of the parties had originally been the sole owner of the assets (*Rowan v Dann* (1991) 64 P & CR 202, CA (joint venture)); the assets in question will be held upon a constructive trust for the 'owning' party instead.

206. Provisions in partnership agreement to obviate sale. Partnership agreements often contain provisions intended to obviate a sale, especially in the event of a partial dissolution, and such provisions bind the partners[1]. If, however, such provisions cannot be carried out, a sale may be necessary, although the partnership agreement may provide for the distribution of the assets among the partners in kind, and in this event any partner or his personal representatives may apply to the court to wind up the affairs of the firm[2].

1   Whether such provisions will apply in the event of a general dissolution is a matter of construction: *Rigden v Pierce* (1822) 6 Madd 353. It appears, however, that the court will be more willing to construe such provisions in favour of a distribution rather than a sale where the asset concerned is not real property: see *Bradbury v Dickens* (1859) 27 Beav 53 (goodwill). As to partnership agreements see PARA 26.

2   See the Partnership Act 1890 s 39; and *Taylor v Neate* (1888) 39 ChD 538; cf *Cook v Collingridge* (1823) Jac 607. As to the principles upon which the court acts in ordering a sale see PARA 207. The same principles should, so far as practicable, guide the partners in disposing of the assets out of court. As to the valuation of and mode of dealing with unsaleable assets see PARA 209.

B. SALE BY ORDER OF THE COURT

207. When a sale may be ordered. In general, the court will order a sale[1] of partnership assets[2] on dissolution, unless there is agreement to the contrary[3]. It may even order a sale before dissolution[4]. A sale may be ordered where an option for a surviving or continuing partner to purchase at a valuation is not exercised[5]. Where there is an agreement that at the expiry of a fixed-term partnership[6] one partner's share in the firm is to be purchased by the other partner at a valuation, but such valuation cannot be carried out in the precise manner stipulated, in consequence of the omission to provide for an umpire, the court may decline to order a sale and may itself carry out the valuation[7].

The court will order partnership land[8] to be sold, even though there are no outstanding partnership debts[9].

1   See PARA 205 note 5.
2   As to what constitutes partnership assets see PARA 115 et seq.
3   See the Partnership Act 1890 s 39; and the cases cited in PARA 205 notes 4–5.
4   *Heath v Fisher* (1868) 38 LJ Ch 14 (where the firm's financial situation was deteriorating rapidly); and see PARA 208.
5   *Downs v Collins* (1848) 6 Hare 418. Under the old bankruptcy law a sale could also be ordered where an option for a surviving partner to purchase at a valuation was a fraud upon the bankruptcy law: see *Wilson v Greenwood* (1818) 1 Swan 471; *Whitmore v Mason* (1861) 2 John & H 204; *Collins v Barker* [1893] 1 Ch 578. Quaere whether the same principle would be applied under the Insolvency Act 1986.
6   As to fixed term partnerships see PARA 37.
7   *Dinham v Bradford* (1869) 5 Ch App 519; and see *Smith v Gale* [1974] 1 All ER 401, [1974] 1 WLR 9; *Greenbank v Pickles* [2001] 1 EGLR 1, (2000) Times, 7 November, CA. It is not the very essence and substance of the contract, so that no contract can be made out except through the medium of the arbitrators (*Dinham v Bradford* (1869) 5 Ch App 519 at 523 per Lord Hatherley LC; approved in *Hordern v Hordern* [1910] AC 465 at 474, PC); but in *Collins v Collins* (1858) 26 Beav 306, the court declined to appoint an umpire on the refusal of the parties' valuers to do so.
8   As to what is partnership land see PARAS 10, 117. Where an asset is not a partnership asset but the separate property of one or more partners, the non-owning partners can claim no lien over such an asset and a sale of that asset at the non-owning partners' instance will not be ordered: see PARA 205 note 4.
9   *Wild v Milne* (1859) 26 Beav 504; and see *Re Bourne, Bourne v Bourne* [1906] 2 Ch 427, CA. In the absence of contrary intention, the proceeds of sale of partnership land are deemed to be personal estate: see PARA 118. It is only in rare circumstances that a sale will not be ordered: see PARA 205 note 5; but see *Stekel v Ellice* [1973] 1 All ER 465, [1973] 1 WLR 191 (where the plaintiff partner had by the terms of the partnership agreement no interest in the capital and assets of the firm).

208.   Order for sale and appointment of receiver. A sale under an order of the court will be carried out in the manner most beneficial to the common interest[1]. Such an order may be made on motion before trial, where the partnership is clearly dissolved[2], or even where it is not dissolved but the position of the business is daily growing worse[3].

The matter is often referred to a master in order that he may consider the best course to pursue, and the best way of selling[4]. When one partner has a greatly preponderant interest in the concern, liberty may be given to him to submit proposals for the purchase of the shares of the other partners[5].

The court may give liberty to all or any of the partners to bid, but in that event the conduct of the sale is not given to those who have such liberty; nor may they interfere in any way with the sale[6].

If necessary, a receiver and manager may be appointed until sale[7]. If the receiver conducts the sale, he is subject to the court's directions[8] and is not invariably bound to accept the highest price for the property[9].

1   *Re Coles, Leaf v Coles* (1851) 1 De GM & G 171; *Taylor v Neate* (1888) 39 ChD 538.
2   *Crawshay v Maule* (1818) 1 Swan 495; cf *Broadwood v Goding* (1835) 5 LJ Ch 96.
3   *Bailey v Ford* (1843) 13 Sim 495. See PARA 207 text and note 4.
4   *Wilson v Greenwood* (1818) 1 Swan 471; *Crawshay v Maule* (1818) 1 Swan 495 at 529; *Madgwick v Wimble* (1843) 6 Beav 495 at 502; *Re Coles, Leaf v Coles* (1851) 1 De GM & G 171; cf *Blyth v Blyth* (1861) 4 LT 536. To avoid publicity and expense, the master has sometimes by consent held a private auction in chambers, the parties being the sole bidders.
5   *Syers v Syers* (1876) 1 App Cas 174 at 183, HL (inquiry directed as to what was the value of the interest of the other partners); and see *Latchan v Martin* (1984) 134 NLJ 745, PC; and PARA

205. Note that the exercise of this power not to order a genuine sale (as opposed merely to authorising the buying out a partner's share) conflicts with a partner's fundamental right, upon a dissolution, to have the assets of the partnership sold: see the Partnership Act 1890 s 39; and PARAS 141, 205.

6   *Wild v Milne* (1859) 26 Beav 504; *Dean v Wilson* (1878) 10 ChD 136; and see *Rowlands v Evans* (1861) 30 Beav 302.

7   *Waters v Taylor* (1813) 2 Ves & B 299 (court allowed the parties to submit proposals for the interim management of an opera house); and see *Rowlands v Evans* (1861) 30 Beav 302. Despite earlier authority to the contrary (see *Harding v Glover* (1810) 18 Ves 281), it now appears that the appointment of a receiver where it is clear that the firm must be dissolved or has been dissolved is almost a matter of course: *Sobell v Boston* [1975] 2 All ER 282 at 286, [1975] 1 WLR 1587 at 1591 per Goff J; but see *Pini v Roncoroni* [1892] 1 Ch 633 (where, notwithstanding the headnote to the report, a receiver was appointed and the other matters in dispute were referred to arbitration). Cf *Tottey v Kemp* (1970) 215 Estates Gazette 1021, where Megarry J, although acknowledging the principle, refused to appoint a receiver because the respondent partner was exercising an option to purchase the whole undertaking. As to the appointment of a receiver before dissolution see PARA 162; and RECEIVERS vol 88 (2012) PARA 38.

8   See *McGowan v Chadwick* [2002] EWCA Civ 1758, [2003] BPIR 647, [2002] All ER (D) 45 (Dec) (where the receiver was accused of breach of duty it was held that the court has discretion whether to grant permission to commence a separate claim against a receiver appointed in a partnership action, rather than to try a claim against him in the partnership action itself). As to the receiver's position generally see PARA 164.

9   He is not obliged to accept the higher offer of a tardy and vacillating bidder: *Procopi v Moschakis* (1969) 211 Estates Gazette 31.

209. Liability for loss on sale; book debts; unsaleable assets. In the absence of fraud, a partner who is entrusted with the winding up of the partnership affairs is not solely liable for loss resulting from an injudicious sale of the assets[1].

Book debts should be sold with the business when it is sold as a going concern[2]. Assets which are unsaleable must be charged in the accounts at a valuation[3].

1   *Cragg v Ford* (1842) 1 Y & C Ch Cas 280.

2   *Johnson v Helleley* (1864) 34 Beav 63; affd on another point 2 De GJ & Sm 446. The title of a periodical published by a partnership has been held to form part of the assets which ought to be realised, for what it may be worth, on dissolution: see *Bradbury v Dickens* (1859) 27 Beav 53. As to the disposal of goodwill generally see PARA 212.

3   This rule has been applied to emoluments from personal appointments (*Smith v Mules* (1852) 9 Hare 556), and to an unassignable mail contract held by a partner (*Ambler v Bolton* (1872) LR 14 Eq 427); but a specific undertaking which is the object of the partnership may be ordered to be carried out, and the ultimate account postponed until its completion (*McClean v Kennard* (1874) 9 Ch App 336); and see PARAS 132 note 1, 175 note 1.

C. PAYMENT OF LOSSES AND APPLICATION OF ASSETS REALISED

210. Liability for losses. In the absence of contrary agreement, losses, including losses and deficiencies of capital, must be paid first out of profits, next out of capital, and lastly, if necessary, by the partners individually in the proportions in which they would be entitled to share profits[1].

Where partners agree to contribute capital in unequal shares but to divide the profits equally, and the assets prove insufficient to make good the capital, each partner is treated, unless otherwise provided, as liable to contribute an equal share of the deficiency, and then the assets are applied in paying to each partner rateably what is due to him from the firm in respect of capital[2].

1   Partnership Act 1890 s 44(a). As to how losses are borne see PARA 131 et seq. Section 44 applies to the winding up of every partnership after a dissolution whatever the ground of dissolution and regardless of the conduct of the parties: *Hurst v Bryk* [2002] 1 AC 185, [2000] 2 All ER 193, HL.

2   This is the logical result of the operation of the Partnership Act 1890 s 44. This was also the rule
     before 1890: *Wood v Scoles* (1866) 1 Ch App 369; *Binney v Mutrie* (1886) 12 App Cas 160,
     PC. As to the rather more complex position where one of the partners is insolvent and thus
     unable to contribute his share see *Garner v Murray* [1904] 1 Ch 57. As to the rule that a
     partnership share is a share in the net assets only see PARA 121.

211. Application of assets after dissolution. In settling accounts between the
partners after a dissolution of partnership, the firm's assets, including the sums, if
any, contributed by the partners to make up losses or deficiencies of capital, are
applicable in the following manner and order[1]:

(1)   in payment of the firm's debts and liabilities to persons who are not
       partners[2];

(2)   in repaying to each partner rateably what is due from the firm to him
       for advances as distinct from capital[3];

(3)   in repaying to each partner rateably what is due from the firm to him in
       respect of capital[4]; and

(4)   in dividing any residue among the partners in the proportion in which
       profits are divisible[5].

In the absence of contrary agreement, the amount payable by the other
partners in respect of the share of a deceased or outgoing partner is a debt from
the other partners accruing at the date of death or dissolution, as the case may
be[6].

1   As to the priority of debts in bankruptcy see BANKRUPTCY AND INDIVIDUAL INSOLVENCY vol 5
     (2013) PARA 587 et seq. As to the postponement to other liabilities of the costs of taking a
     partnership account see PARA 160.
2   Partnership Act 1890 s 44(b)1.
3   Partnership Act 1890 s 44(b)2. No common law action for money lent lies in respect of money
     advanced by a partner to the partnership: *Green v Hertzog* [1954] 1 WLR 1309, CA. See also
     PARAS 5 note 1, 135, 157.
4   Partnership Act 1890 s 44(b)3.
5   Partnership Act 1890 s 44(b)4; *Binney v Mutrie* (1886) 12 App Cas 160, PC.
6   Partnership Act 1890 s 43.

D. DISPOSAL OF GOODWILL

212. Goodwill generally; right to use name; sale to a partner. The goodwill of
the business carried on by a partnership forms part of the assets to be realised on
dissolution[1]. If the goodwill is not sold, each partner may use the name of the
firm, if by doing so he does not hold out the other partners as still being partners
with him[2]. If a partner agrees to retire, and if on the construction of the
agreement under which he retires, although his partners buy his share, they do
not take any express assignment of the goodwill, they are not entitled to continue
the use of his name as part of the firm name[3]; and, where a business is carried on
under the name, solely or with any addition, of an outgoing partner who is still
living and not bankrupt, a purchaser of the business including the goodwill is not
entitled to use the name of the outgoing partner in such a way as to suggest that
he is still connected with the business[4], unless the right to use the firm name is
expressly assigned[5]. On dissolution, a partner may advertise that he is no longer
connected with a periodical that the firm publishes[6].

Where the goodwill becomes on dissolution the property of one of the
partners, either by purchase in the ordinary way or pursuant to a provision in the
partnership agreement[7], the outgoing partner or partners may not carry on a
similar business in the name of the old firm[8], and may not solicit old customers[9].

1   *Re David and Matthews* [1899] 1 Ch 378 at 382; *Hall v Barrows* (1863) 4 De GJ & Sm 150 at 159; *Johnson v Helleley* (1864) 34 Beav 63 (affd 2 De GJ & Sm 446) (book debts ordered to be sold with the business, so that the purchaser might secure the customers of the old firm); *Page v Ratcliffe* (1896) 74 LT 343 (affd (1897) 76 LT 63, CA); *Jennings v Jennings* [1898] 1 Ch 378 at 384; *Hill v Fearis* [1905] 1 Ch 466. Whether there is any goodwill or not seems to be a pure question of fact, and not of mixed law and fact: *A-G v Boden* [1912] 1 KB 539 at 559. Goodwill may exist even though it cannot be valued in money terms: see *Manley v Sartori* [1927] 1 Ch 157 at 166 per Romer J, approved in this context in *Pathirana v Pathirana* [1967] 1 AC 233 at 240, [1966] 3 WLR 666 at 671, PC; and see PARAS 202, 215. As to the position of a purchaser who takes a share in the firm see PARA 22. The grounds upon which goodwill ought to be treated and valued as a partnership asset are laid down in *Wedderburn v Wedderburn (No 4)* (1856) 22 Beav 84 at 104 per Romilly MR. In *Trego v Hunt* [1896] AC 7 at 17–18, HL, Lord Herschell stated that it was the connection formed (by attracting customers to the business) together with the circumstances, whether of habit or otherwise, which tended to make it permanent, that constituted the goodwill of a business; and see *Churton v Douglas* (1859) John 174 at 188; and *Darby v Meehan* (1998) Times, 25 November. See also *Byford v Oliver* [2003] EWHC 295 (Ch), [2003] EMLR 416, [2003] All ER (D) 345 (Feb), where it was held all the partners had an interest in the name 'SAXON', the goodwill and all the other assets of the partnership, but that did not mean that they owned the assets themselves. In the absence of a special provision in the partnership agreement, the partners had an interest in the realised value of the partnership assets.

As to the nature of goodwill generally see PERSONAL PROPERTY vol 80 (2013) PARA 807 et seq. As to injunctions restraining an ex-partner from harming the goodwill after dissolution see PARA 171. As to covenants in restraint of trade contained in partnership agreements see PARA 27.

2   *Burchell v Wilde* [1900] 1 Ch 551, CA; and see *Tottey v Kemp* (1970) 215 Estates Gazette 1021. As to the firm name see PARA 7. It is, however, questionable to what extent a partner may use the firm name before the firm's winding up has been completed at least where the firm name is used in order to carry on a competing business, since such competition would prima facie constitute a breach of the Partnership Act 1890 ss 29, 30 (see PARAS 106–107), as applied to partners in the period between dissolution and winding up by s 38 (see PARA 46); but see *Re David and Matthews* [1899] 1 Ch 378.

3   *Gray v Smith* (1889) 43 ChD 208, CA; and see *Jennings v Jennings* [1898] 1 Ch 378 at 384–385; *Rosher v Young* (1901) 17 TLR 347.

4   *Scott v Rowland* (1872) 26 LT 391; but see *Tottey v Kemp* (1970) 215 Estates Gazette 1021.

5   *Townsend v Jarman* [1900] 2 Ch 698 at 705.

6   *Bradbury v Dickens* (1859) 27 Beav 53.

7   It would not appear to matter for this purpose whether or not any adequate consideration is given to the retiring partner for his share of goodwill: *Bridge v Deacons (a firm)* [1984] AC 705, sub nom *Deacons (a firm) v Bridge* [1984] 2 All ER 19, PC.

8   *Jennings v Jennings* [1898] 1 Ch 378; *Trego v Hunt* [1896] AC 7, HL (overruling *Pearson v Pearson* (1884) 27 ChD 145, CA); *Re David and Matthews* [1899] 1 Ch 378; *Churston v Douglas* (1859) John 174; cf *Gillingham v Beddow* [1900] 2 Ch 242 (provision in a partnership agreement that an outgoing partner might set up a similar business in the neighbourhood held to be merely declaratory, and not to authorise the solicitation of old customers). A partner may be restrained from advertising that the firm's publication will be discontinued, if it ought to be sold as an asset: *Bradbury v Dickens* (1859) 27 Beav 53. As to the rights and restrictions affecting a vendor of goodwill generally see COMPETITION vol 18 (2009) PARA 373 et seq.

9   *Trego v Hunt* [1896] AC 7, HL, approving *Labouchere v Dawson* (1872) LR 13 Eq 322, and *Leggott v Barrett* (1880) 15 ChD 306, CA; *Re David and Matthews* [1899] 1 Ch 378; and see further the cases cited in PARA 171. In *Boorne v Wicker* [1927] 1 Ch 667, the rule was extended to a vendor's executors. The partner may carry on business with the firm's old customers, provided that he does not canvass them: see the cases cited in note 8; and *Curl Bros Ltd v Webster* [1904] 1 Ch 685. The rule against canvassing does not extend to a partner expelled under the firm's partnership agreement (*Dawson v Beeson* (1882) 22 ChD 504, CA; although, where the expelled partner has been paid the value of his share in the firm's goodwill, quaere whether there is any reason in principle why he should be treated more leniently than any other outgoing partner); or to a purchaser from the trustee in bankruptcy of an expelled partner (*Walker v Mottram* (1881) 19 ChD 355, CA; and see *Mogford v Courtenay* (1881) 45 LT 303); or to a partner whose property has been sold for the benefit of his creditors (*Green & Sons (Northampton) Ltd v Morris* [1914] 1 Ch 562; *Farey v Cooper* [1927] 2 KB 384, CA).

213.   Valuation of goodwill.   An agreement that on dissolution the partnership assets are to be taken by one partner includes goodwill[1]; and, where the outgoing partner will not be the subject of any covenant in restraint of trade[2], it must be valued on the footing that the outgoing partner is entitled to carry on a similar business[3].

1   Cf *Chapman v Heyman* (1885) 1 TLR 397 (where, upon the construction of the partnership agreement in question, it was held that the expelled partner was not entitled to his share of the firm's goodwill, although he was entitled to the full value of his share of the other partnership assets). Where after a general dissolution one partner retained the firm's assets without the other partner's agreement, it has been held (in the exceptional circumstances of the case) that the former holds those assets upon a constructive trust: *Roxburgh Dinardo & Partners' Judicial Factor v Dinardo* 1992 GWD 6–322, Ct of Sess.
2   As to covenants in restraint of trade see PARAS 27, 171; and COMPETITION vol 18 (2009) PARA 377 et seq.
3   *Hall v Barrows* (1863) 4 De GJ & Sm 150; *Reynolds v Bullock* (1878) 47 LJ Ch 773; *Re David and Matthews* [1899] 1 Ch 378; and see *Mellersh v Keen* (1859) 27 Beav 236 at 241; *Kirby (Inspector of Taxes) v Thorn EMI plc* [1988] 2 All ER 947, [1988] 1 WLR 445, CA; and PARA 212.
       As to the limits to the right of an outgoing partner to use the firm name and solicit customers of the firm where the continuing partners have acquired the outgoing partner's share of goodwill see PARA 212.

214.   Partners restrained from competing with business of old firm.   On a sale by the court, otherwise than to a partner[1], it is usual and proper to state in the particulars of conditions of sale that the vendors are to be at liberty to carry on a similar business[2]. It follows that the value of the goodwill, as an asset to be disposed of, is enhanced if the outgoing partners are bound by contract not to carry on a similar business. It is a question of construction, usually of the vendor partner's partnership agreement, whether or not they are so bound[3]. A vendor of the goodwill, whether a partner or not, may preclude himself by contract from using the name of the firm[4].

1   As to sale of goodwill to a partner see PARA 212.
2   *Johnson v Helleley* (1864) 34 Beav 63; affd 2 De GJ & Sm 446. For the decree in *Cook v Collingridge* (1823) Jac 607, in which the principles applicable to the valuation of goodwill as an asset on the sale of a partnership were laid down by Lord Eldon LC, see 27 Beav 456.
3   *Cooper v Watson* (1784) 3 Doug KB 413 (sub nom *Cooper v Watlington* 2 Chit 451); *Kennedy v Lee* (1817) 3 Mer 441 at 455.
4   *Mrs Pomeroy Ltd v Scalé* (1906) 23 TLR 170. Whether a person selling a share in a business under a power of attorney is authorised to bind his principal not to carry on a competing business was discussed, but not decided, in *Hawksley v Outram* [1892] 3 Ch 359 at 375, 378, 381, CA. A covenant, unlimited as regards space, not to carry on business in a specified name is not void as being in restraint of trade: *Vernon v Hallam* (1886) 34 ChD 748 at 751. As to covenants in restraint of trade and their enforcement by the court generally see PARAS 27, 171; and COMPETITION vol 18 (2009) PARA 377 et seq.

215.   When goodwill is to be treated as an asset.   Generally, the firm's goodwill is treated as one of its assets[1] and the fact that it is not included in the annual balance sheet drawn up for the firm does not mean that it does not exist as such a partnership asset[2]. Where, however, the value of the share of a deceased partner is by agreement governed by the firm's annual balance sheet, and such balance sheet in accordance with the partnership agreement does not include the firm's goodwill as an asset, his estate is not entitled to treat the goodwill as an asset[3].

Where a surviving partner sells the partnership business, the estate of his deceased partner is entitled to a share of the purchase money representing the value, if any, of the goodwill; but, having regard to the rights of the surviving partners to carry on a similar business, this value may be infinitesimal[4].

There are statutory restrictions on the sale of the goodwill of medical practices[5], but these do not affect the enforceability of a covenant in restraint of trade[6].

1 As to partnership property generally see PARA 115 et seq. As to the method in which such assets may be treated in the firm's annual accounts see PARAS 115 note 1, 135 note 8, 154.
2 *Wade v Jenkins* (1860) 2 Giff 509. See also the statement of Romilly MR in *Wedderburn v Wedderburn (No 4)* (1856) 22 Beav 84 at 104; and PARA 212.
3 *Hunter v Dowling* [1895] 2 Ch 223; *Scott v Scott* (1903) 89 LT 582, following *Steuart v Gladstone* (1878) 10 ChD 626, CA; cf *Cruickshank v Sutherland* (1922) 92 LJ Ch 136, HL (where the annual accounts, being framed according to the firm's usual practice but contrary to the method prescribed by the partnership agreement, were held not binding upon a deceased partner's executors); and see PARA 154.
4 *Smith v Everett* (1859) 27 Beav 446; cf *Mellersh v Keen* (1859) 27 Beav 236. It was at one time considered that, on the death of a partner, the goodwill belonged exclusively to the surviving partners (*Hammond v Douglas* (1800) 5 Ves 539; *Lewis v Langdon* (1835) 7 Sim 421), but it is now settled that it forms part of the assets of the firm in which the estate of the deceased partner is entitled to share, and, in the absence of contrary agreement, the executors of the deceased partner are entitled to have it sold with the other assets (*Re David and Matthews* [1899] 1 Ch 378 at 382; and see PARA 212).
5 See the National Health Service Act 2006 s 259, Sch 21; and HEALTH SERVICES vol 54 (2008) PARA 273.
6 *Kerr v Morris* [1987] Ch 90, [1986] 3 All ER 217, CA, overruling *Hensman v Traill* (1980) 124 Sol Jo 776. An injunction may be granted to prevent breach: see PARA 171.

216. Agreement for retention of goodwill. A partnership agreement may contain provisions which entitle surviving partners to retain the benefit of the goodwill upon terms as, for example, the payment of a share of profits to the estate of the deceased partner. It is, however, a question of construction in each case whether the provisions in the partnership agreement have that effect or not[1]; and the court will give effect to a provision in the partnership agreement that goodwill is not to be valued on the assets being taken over by a surviving partner[2]. In any event, the partnership agreement may restrain an ex-partner from competing with the firm[3].

1 *Smith v Nelson* (1905) 92 LT 313.
2 *Hordern v Hordern* [1910] AC 465, PC. See also PARA 215.
3 See PARAS 27, 214.

5. LIMITED PARTNERSHIPS

(1) CONSTITUTION

217. Statutory creation. The Limited Partnerships Act 1907 authorised the formation of limited partnerships[1], and thus rendered it possible for the first time for a person to become a partner upon the terms that his liability to the creditors of the firm should be strictly limited, like that of a shareholder in a limited company[2]. A limited partner is in the position of a sleeping partner with limited liability[3].

1 Limited Partnerships Act 1907 ss 1, 4(1). The Limited Partnerships Act 1907 as it formerly had effect in Northern Ireland is repealed in relation to Northern Ireland (see the Companies Act 2006 s 1286(2)(b)), and the enactments in force in Great Britain relating to limited partnerships are extended to Northern Ireland (see s 1286(1)). As to the meaning of 'Great Britain' see PARA 8 note 2.
2 See PARA 3. As to limited liability of shareholders see COMPANIES vol 14 (2009) PARAS 78, 102.
3 As to the meaning of 'limited partner' see PARA 218. As to the meaning of 'sleeping partner' see PARA 4.

218. Limited partners and general partners. A limited partnership must consist of one or more persons called 'general partners', who are liable for all debts and obligations of the firm[1], and one or more persons called 'limited partners', who must at the time of entering into such partnership contribute to it a sum or sums as capital or property valued at a stated amount, and who are not liable[2] for the debts or obligations of the firm beyond that amount[3]. A body corporate may be a limited partner[4].

The terms 'firm'[5], 'firm name'[6] and 'business'[7] have the same meanings as in the Partnership Act 1890[8].

A limited partnership, like an ordinary partnership, is not a legal entity[9].

1 A general partner is defined by the Limited Partnerships Act 1907 as any partner other than a limited partner: s 3. General partners are, in effect, managing partners.
2 Ie unless they act in such a way as to deprive themselves of the privileges of a limited partner: see the Limited Partnerships Act 1907 ss 4(3), 6(1); and PARA 225.
3 Limited Partnerships Act 1907 s 4(2) (amended by the Banking Act 1979 ss 46(b), 51(2), Sch 7; and by SI 2002/3203). This limited liability applies only vis-à-vis third party creditors of the firm; as between members of a firm a limited partner's liability may not be thus limited: *Reed (Inspector of Taxes) v Young* [1986] 1 WLR 649, HL.
4 Limited Partnerships Act 1907 s 4(4).
5 As to the meaning of 'firm' see the Partnership Act 1890 s 4(1); and PARA 1.
6 As to the meaning of 'firm name' see the Limited Partnerships Act 1907 s 4(1); and PARA 1 note 3.
7 As to the meaning of 'business' see the Limited Partnerships Act 1907 s 45; and PARA 6.
8 Limited Partnerships Act 1907 s 3.
9 See *Re Barnard, Martins Bank v Trustee* [1932] 1 Ch 269 at 272; and PARA 2.

219. The statutory rules and regulations. The Secretary of State[1] may make rules concerning any of the following matters:

(1)   the duties or additional duties to be performed by the registrar of companies for the purposes of the Limited Partnerships Act 1907[2];

(2)   the performance by assistant registrars and other officers of acts by the Act required to be done by the registrar[3];

(3)   the forms to be used for the purposes of the Act[4];

(4)   generally, the conduct and regulation of registrations under the Act and any matters incidental thereto[5].

The Limited Partnerships (Forms) Rules 2009 were made under this power[6].

1   Under the Limited Partnerships Act 1907 s 17 this power is exercisable by the Board of Trade. In practice this power is now exercised by the Secretary of State for Business, Innovation and Skills: see the Secretary of State for Trade and Industry Order 1970, SI 1970/1537, arts 2(1), 7(4) (lapsed); the Secretary of State (New Departments) Order 1974, SI 1974/692, art 2(3) (lapsed); the Transfer of Functions (Trade and Industry) Order 1983, SI 1983/1127; the Secretaries of State for Children, Schools and Families, for Innovation, Universities and Skills and for Business, Enterprise and Regulatory Reform Order 2007, SI 2007/3224; the Secretary of State for Business, Innovation and Skills Order 2009, SI 2009/2748; and CONSTITUTIONAL AND ADMINISTRATIVE LAW vol 20 (2014) PARA 153.

2   Limited Partnerships Act 1907 s 17(b). As to the registrar of companies see PARA 220 note 1; and COMPANIES vol 14 (2009) PARA 131 et seq.

3   Limited Partnerships Act 1907 s 17(c).

4   Limited Partnerships Act 1907 s 17(d).

5   Limited Partnerships Act 1907 s 17(e).

6   Ie the Limited Partnerships (Forms) Rules 2009, SI 2009/2160.

(2) REGISTRATION OF LIMITED PARTNERSHIPS

220. The register. The registrar of companies[1] must keep a register and index of all registered limited partnerships and of all the statements registered in relation to them[2]. On receiving any such statement, the registrar must file it and must post a certificate of registration to the firm from whom it was received[3]. The certificate of registration, or a copy of or extract from any registered statement, if duly certified to be a true copy under the hand of the registrar, must be received in evidence in all civil or criminal proceedings[4].

Any person may inspect the filed statements and may require a certificate of the registration of any limited partnership or a certified copy of or extract from any registered statement[5].

1   The registrar of companies, as successor to the registrar of joint stock companies, is the registrar of limited partnerships: Limited Partnerships Act 1907 s 15(1) (s 15 substituted by SI 2009/1941). See also the Companies Act 2006 s 1060. In the Limited Partnerships Act 1907: (1) references to the registrar in relation to the registration of a limited partnership are to the registrar to whom the application for registration is to be made (see s 8A(1)(d); and PARA 221 head (4)); (2) references to registration in a particular part of the United Kingdom are to registration by the registrar for that part of the United Kingdom; (3) references to the registrar in relation to any other matter relating to a limited partnership are to the registrar for the part of the United Kingdom in which the partnership is registered: s 15(2) (as so substituted). As to the registrar of companies see COMPANIES vol 14 (2009) PARA 131 et seq. As to the Secretary of State see PARA 219 note 1. As to the meaning of 'United Kingdom' see PARA 8 note 2.

2   Limited Partnerships Act 1907 s 14 (amended by SI 2009/1941). As to the statements see PARAS 221–222.

3   Limited Partnerships Act 1907 s 13.

4   Limited Partnerships Act 1907 s 16(2) (amended by SI 2009/1941). As to the fees payable, see the Registrar of Companies (Fees) (Limited Partnerships and Newspaper Proprietors) Regulations 2009, SI 2009/2392, reg 4, Sch 2 paras 4–6 (amended by SI 2011/319).

5   Limited Partnerships Act 1907 s 16(1) (amended by the Companies Act 2006 ss 1063(7)(a), 1295, Sch 16; and SI 2009/1941). As to the fees payable, see the Registrar of Companies (Fees) (Limited Partnerships and Newspaper Proprietors) Regulations 2009, SI 2009/2392, Sch 2 paras 4–6 (as amended: see note 4).

221. First registration. Every limited partnership must be registered as such in accordance with the provisions of the Limited Partnerships Act 1907[1]. The registrar[2] must register a limited partnership if an application is made to the registrar in accordance with the following provisions[3].

An application[4] for registration must:

(1)   specify the firm name[5] under which the limited partnership is to be registered;

(2)   contain the following details:

    (a)   the general nature of the partnership business;

    (b)   the name of each general partner[6];

    (c)   the name of each limited partner[7];

    (d)   the amount of the capital contribution of each limited partner (and whether the contribution is paid in cash or in another specified form);

    (e)   the address of the proposed principal place of business[8] of the limited partnership; and

    (f)   the term (if any) for which the limited partnership is to be entered into (beginning with the date of registration)[9];

(3)   be signed or otherwise authenticated by or on behalf of each partner; and

(4)   be made to the registrar for the part of the United Kingdom in which the principal place of business of the limited partnership is to be situated[10].

On registering a limited partnership the registrar must issue a certificate of registration[11]. The certificate must state:

(i)   the firm name of the limited partnership given in the application for registration;

(ii)   the limited partnership's registration number;

(iii)   the date of registration; and

(iv)   that the limited partnership is registered as a limited partnership under the 1907 Act[12].

The certificate is conclusive evidence that a limited partnership came into existence on the date of registration[13].

A person who knowingly and wilfully makes a statement for registration false in a material particular is guilty of an offence[14].

1   Limited Partnerships Act 1907 s 5 (amended by SI 2009/1940).

2   As to the registrar see PARA 220 note 1.

3   Limited Partnerships Act 1907 s 8 (substituted by SI 2009/1940).

4   As to the prescribed form for application see the Limited Partnerships (Forms) Rules 2009, SI 2009/2160, r 3(1), Schedule Pt 1 Form LP5.

5   Ie a name complying with the Limited Partnerships Act 1907 s 8B, which sets out conditions which must be satisfied by the firm name of a limited partnership as specified in the application for registration: s 8B(1) (ss 8A–8C added by SI 2009/1940). The name must end with: (1) the words 'limited partnership' (upper or lower case, or any combination); or (2) the abbreviation 'LP' (upper or lower case, or any combination, with or without punctuation): Limited Partnerships Act 1907 s 8B(2) (as so added). If, however, the principal place of business of a limited partnership is to be in Wales, its firm name may end with: (a) the words 'partneriaeth cyfyngedig' (upper or lower case, or any combination); or (b) the abbreviation 'PC' (upper or lower case, or any combination, with or without punctuation): s 8B(3) (as so added).

6   As to the meaning of 'general partner' see PARA 218.

7   As to the meaning of 'limited partner' see PARA 218.

8   As to the firm's principal place of business see PARA 87 note 3.

9   As to the duration of partnerships see PARAS 37–38.

10   Limited Partnerships Act 1907 s 8A (as added: see note 5). As to references to the registrar for a particular part of the United Kingdom see PARA 220 note 1. As to the meaning of 'United Kingdom' see PARA 8 note 2. As to the fee payable for the registration of a limited partnership see the Registration of Companies (Fees) (Limited Partnerships and Newspaper Proprietors) Regulations 2009, SI 2009/2392, reg 3, Sch 1 para 5 (Sch 1 para 5 amended by SI 2011/319).

11   Limited Partnerships Act 1907 s 8C(1) (as added: see note 5). The certificate must be signed by the registrar or authenticated with the registrar's seal: s 8C(2) (as so added).

12   Limited Partnerships Act 1907 s 8C(3) (as added: see note 5).

13 Limited Partnerships Act 1907 s 8C(4) (as added: see note 5).

14 See the Perjury Act 1911 s 5(b). The offence is punishable on conviction on indictment by imprisonment for a term not exceeding two years, or a fine or both: s 5; and see CRIMINAL LAW vol 26 (2010) PARA 673.

222. Notice of changes in limited partnership. If, during the continuance of a limited partnership, any change is made or occurs in the firm name[1], the general nature[2] or principal place[3] of the business, the partners or the name of any partner[4], the term or character of the partnership[5], the sum contributed by any limited partner[6], or the liability of any partner by reason of his becoming a limited partner instead of a general partner or vice versa[7], a statement[8] signed by the general partners of the firm[9], specifying the nature of the change, must be sent by post or delivered to the registrar[10] within seven days for registration[11]. If default is made in complying with the above requirements, each of the general partners is liable on summary conviction to a fine not exceeding £1 for each day during which the default continues[12].

1 Limited Partnerships Act 1907 s 9(1)(a). As to the firm name see PARA 1 note 3; definition applied by s 3. See also PARA 221 note 5. Both the previous name and the new name must be stated in the notice of change. See also PARA 7.

2 Limited Partnerships Act 1907 s 9(1)(b). Both the business previously carried on and that now carried on must be notified.

3 Limited Partnerships Act 1907 s 9(1)(c). Both the previous and the new place of business must be notified. As to the principal place of business see PARA 87 note 3.

4 Limited Partnerships Act 1907 s 9(1)(d). Changes brought about by death, transfer of interests, increase in the number of partners or change of name of any partner must be notified.

5 Limited Partnerships Act 1907 s 9(1)(e). Both the previous and the new terms must be notified. If there is or was no definite term, the previous and new conditions under which the partnership was and is now constituted must be notified.

6 Limited Partnerships Act 1907 s 9(1)(f). Any variation in the sum contributed by any limited partner must be notified. As to the meaning of 'limited partner' see PARA 218.

7 Limited Partnerships Act 1907 s 9(1)(g). As to the meaning of 'general partner' see PARA 218.

8 As to the prescribed form of statement see the Limited Partnerships (Forms) Rules 2009, SI 2009/2160, r 3(2), Schedule Pt 2 Form LP6 (substituted by SI 2013/1388).

9 It would appear that limited partners have no authority to sign such a statement: see the Limited Partnerships Act 1907 s 6(1); and PARA 225.

10 As to the registrar see PARA 220 note 1.

11 Limited Partnerships Act 1907 s 9(1) (amended by SI 2009/1941). No fee is payable.

12 Limited Partnerships Act 1907 s 9(2). It is unclear whether failure to register a change invalidates the status of the limited partnership.

223. Advertisement of changes. Notice of any arrangement or transaction by which a general partner becomes a limited partner[1], or of the assignment of the share of a limited partner to any person, must be advertised in the London, Edinburgh or Belfast Gazette, according to whether the limited partnership is registered in England, Scotland or Northern Ireland[2]. Until so advertised, the arrangement or transaction is deemed to be of no effect for the purposes of the Limited Partnerships Act 1907[3].

1 As to the meanings of 'limited partner' and 'general partner' see PARA 218.

2 Limited Partnerships Act 1907 s 10(1), (2) (s 10(2) amended by SI 2009/1941). See PARA 217 note 1.

3 Limited Partnerships Act 1907 s 10(1).

(3) MODIFICATIONS OF THE GENERAL LAW OF PARTNERSHIP

224. Application of the general law of partnership. Subject to the provisions of the Limited Partnerships Act 1907, the Partnership Act 1890[1] and the rules of equity and of common law applicable to partnerships, except so far as they are inconsistent with the express provisions of the Partnership Act 1890, apply to limited partnerships[2].

1   See PARA 1 et seq.

2   Limited Partnerships Act 1907 s 7; and see eg *Mephistopheles Debt Collection Service (a firm) v Lotay* [1994] 1 WLR 1064, [1995] 1 BCLC 41, CA. As to the necessity for registration see PARA 221.

225. Powers and liabilities of limited partner. A limited partner[1], personally or by his agent, may at any time inspect the firm's books and examine into the state and prospects of the partnership business, and may advise with the other partners thereon[2], but he must not take any other part in the management of the business[3], and he has no power to bind the firm[4]; nor may he draw out or receive back any part of his capital either directly or indirectly[5].

So long as he complies with these provisions, a limited partner is liable for the firm's debts and obligations only to the extent of his capital[6]. However, if he does draw out or receive back any part of his capital either directly or indirectly, he is liable for the firm's debts and obligations to the extent of the amount so drawn out or received back[7]. If he takes part in the management for any period, he is liable as though he were a general partner for all the firm's debts and obligations incurred during that period[8].

1   As to the meaning of 'limited partner' see PARA 218.

2   Limited Partnerships Act 1907 s 6(1) proviso. See *Inversiones Frieira SL v Colyzeo Investors II LLP* [2012] EWHC 1450 (Ch), [2012] Bus LR 1136.

3   Limited Partnerships Act 1907 s 6(1). Pursuit of a claim on behalf of a limited partnership by a limited partner on a derivative basis would be acting in the management of the partnership business: *Certain Limited Partners in Henderson PFI Secondary Fund II LLP (a firm) v Henderson PFI Secondary Fund II LP (a firm)* [2012] EWHC 3259 (Comm), [2013] QB 934, [2013] 3 All ER 887.

4   Limited Partnerships Act 1907 s 6(1). Cf PARAS 109–110.

5   Limited Partnerships Act 1907 s 4(3).
6   See the Limited Partnerships Act 1907 s 4(2); and PARA 218. As to a limited partner's liability on the firm's insolvency see PARA 232.

7   Limited Partnerships Act 1907 s 4(3).
8   Limited Partnerships Act 1907 s 6(1). As to the meaning of 'general partner' see PARA 218. See *Certain Ltd Partners in Henderson PFI Secondary Fund II LLP (a firm) v Henderson PFI Secondary Fund II LP (a firm)* [2012] EWHC 3259 (Comm), [2013] QB 934, [2013] 3 All ER 887. This is the principal practical disadvantage of a limited partnership as compared with a limited company: see COMPANIES vol 14 (2009) PARA 102. As to the enforcement of judgments against the firm see *Practice Direction—Enforcement of Judgments and Orders* PD70 para 6A; and PARA 91.

226. Insolvency, death or mental disorder of limited partner. A limited partnership is not dissolved by the bankruptcy or death of an individual limited partner[1], or by the insolvency of a corporate limited partner[2]. The limited partner's capital vests in his trustee in bankruptcy, his personal representative or the liquidator, as the case may be, who has, apparently, rights similar to those of an assignee of a share in an ordinary partnership[3].

If a limited partner becomes mentally disordered, that event is not of itself a ground for dissolution of the partnership by the court unless his share cannot otherwise be ascertained and realised[4].

1   Limited Partnerships Act 1907 s 6(2). Cf PARAS 173, 180 et seq. As to the meaning of 'limited partner' see PARA 218.
2   See BANKRUPTCY AND INDIVIDUAL INSOLVENCY vol 5 (2013) PARA 436; WILLS AND INTESTACY vol 103 (2010) PARA 919.
3   These rights are limited: see PARA 124 et seq.
4   Limited Partnerships Act 1907 s 6(2). The Partnership Act 1890 s 35(a), which provided that the court could dissolve a partnership if a partner became permanently of unsound mind, was repealed by the Mental Health Act 1959 s 149(2), Sch 8 Pt I. As to the power of the Court of Protection to dissolve a partnership of which a person suffering from mental incapacity is a member see PARA 183.

227.   Special powers of a majority of general partners.   Subject to any express or implied agreement between the partners, any difference arising as to ordinary matters connected with the partnership business may be decided by a majority of the general partners[1] instead of a majority of all the partners, as in the case of an ordinary partnership[2]. Subject to any such agreement, the general partners may admit new partners without the consent of the existing limited partners[3], whereas, in the case of an ordinary partnership, the consent of all the partners is required[4].

1   Limited Partnerships Act 1907 s 6(5)(a). As to the meaning of 'general partner' see PARA 218.
2   See the Partnership Act 1890 s 24(8); and PARA 109.
3   Limited Partnerships Act 1907 s 6(5)(d). As to the meaning of 'limited partner' see PARA 218.
4   See the Partnership Act 1890 s 24(7); and PARA 111.

228.   Assignment of or charge on share of limited partner.   A person to whom a limited partner[1] assigns his share with the consent of the general partners[2] stands, in one important respect, in a different position from the assignee of a share in an ordinary partnership[3]. Subject to any express or implied agreement between the partners, he becomes a limited partner, and has all the rights previously belonging to the assignor[4].

Subject to any such agreement, if the share of a limited partner becomes charged to secure his separate debt, this does not, as in the case of an ordinary partnership[5], entitle the other partners to dissolve the partnership[6].

1   As to the meaning of 'limited partner' see PARA 218.
2   As to the meaning of 'general partner' see PARA 218.
3   See the Partnership Act 1890 s 31; and PARAS 124–125.
4   Limited Partnerships Act 1907 s 6(5)(b).
5   See the Partnership Act 1890 s 33(2); and PARA 97. Cf s 23(2); and PARA 94.
6   Limited Partnerships Act 1907 s 6(5)(c).

229.   No right to dissolve by notice.   Subject to any express or implied agreement between the partners, a limited partner[1] is precluded from exercising the usual right of a partner in an ordinary partnership at will[2] to dissolve the partnership by notice[3].

1   As to the meaning of 'limited partner' see PARA 218.
2   As to the power of a general partner to dissolve a partnership at will by notice see the Partnership Act 1890 ss 26, 32(c); and PARA 173 et seq. As to partnerships at will see PARA 37.
3   Limited Partnerships Act 1907 s 6(5)(e).

230.   Winding up limited partnership on dissolution.   Unless the court otherwise orders, the affairs of a limited partnership are, on dissolution, to be wound up by the general partners[1]. In so doing, they must, subject to the provisions of the Limited Partnerships Act 1907, be guided by the rules applicable to the winding up of an ordinary partnership, treating the limited partners as sleeping partners[2].

1 Limited Partnerships Act 1907 s 6(3). As to the winding up of an insolvent limited partnership see PARA 232. As to the meaning of 'general partner' see PARA 218.
2 This follows from the Limited Partnerships Act 1907 s 7 (see PARA 224), which, in effect, renders the provisions governing an ordinary partnership applicable to a limited partnership in cases not specially provided for by the Act. As to the meaning of 'limited partner' see PARA 218. As to the winding up of ordinary partnerships see PARA 197 et seq.

231. Dissolution by the court. Like an ordinary partnership, a limited partnership may be dissolved by the court in the exercise of its ordinary jurisdiction[1].

1 See PARA 180. As to costs see *Re Beer, Brewer and Bowman* (1915) 113 LT 990.

232. Insolvent partnerships. Limited partnerships are governed by the ordinary law of insolvency as applied to insolvent partnerships[1]. However, the following specific provision is also made in relation to limited partnerships. Where there is a creditor's petition for the winding up of an insolvent partnership as an unregistered company and there are concurrent petitions presented against one or more members, then the court may dismiss the petition against an insolvent member who is a limited partner, if the member lodges in court for the benefit of the creditors of the partnership sufficient money or security to the court's satisfaction to meet his liability for the debts and obligations of the partnership, or the member satisfies the court that he is no longer under any liability in respect of the debts and obligations of the partnership[2]. The same provision is made in the case of a member's petition for winding up where there are concurrent petitions presented against all members[3]. A joint bankruptcy petition may be presented to the court by all the members of an insolvent partnership in their capacity as such provided that all the members are individuals and none of them is a limited partner[4].

The liability of a limited partner as contributory will be limited to the extent of his contribution[5].

1 Save as mentioned in the text to notes 2–4, the Insolvent Partnerships Order 1994, SI 1994/2421, does not distinguish between limited and ordinary partnerships. As to insolvent partnerships see PARA 98; and COMPANY AND PARTNERSHIP INSOLVENCY vol 17 (2011) PARAS 1209–1361.
2 See the Insolvency Act 1986 s 125A(7) (added as a modification by the Insolvent Partnerships Order 1994, SI 1994/2421, Sch 4 para 9); and COMPANY AND PARTNERSHIP INSOLVENCY vol 17 (2011) PARA 1283.
3 See the Insolvency Act 1986 s 125A(7) (added as a modification by the Insolvent Partnerships Order 1994, SI 1994/2421, Sch 6 para 3); and COMPANY AND PARTNERSHIP INSOLVENCY vol 17 (2011) PARA 1320.
4 See the Insolvency Act 1986 s 264 (modified by the Insolvent Partnerships Order 1994, SI 1994/2421, Sch 7 para 2); and COMPANY AND PARTNERSHIP INSOLVENCY vol 17 (2011) PARA 1324. This provision is subject to the Insolvency Act 1986 s 266(1) (modified by the Insolvent Partnerships Order 1994, SI 1994/2421, Sch 7 para 4): see the Insolvency Act 1986 s 264(1) (as so modified); and COMPANY AND PARTNERSHIP INSOLVENCY vol 17 (2011) PARA 1326.
5 See the Limited Partnerships Act 1907 s 4(2); and PARA 218.

6. LIMITED LIABILITY PARTNERSHIPS

(1) INCORPORATION AND MEMBERSHIP

233. Definition of the term 'limited liability partnership'. A limited liability partnership[1] is a body corporate, with legal personality separate from that of its members[2], which is formed by being incorporated under the Limited Liability Partnerships Act 2000[3]. A limited liability partnership has unlimited capacity[4].

1 The legal entity known as the limited liability partnership was created by the Limited Liability Partnerships Act 2000 ss 1(1), 19; Limited Liability Partnerships Act 2000 (Commencement) Order 2000, SI 2000/3316. These enactments apply to Northern Ireland and the Limited Liability Partnerships Act (Northern Ireland) 2002 is repealed: see the Companies Act 2006 s 1286(1), (2)(a).
2 Cf ordinary partnerships; and PARA 2. As to membership of limited liability partnerships see PARA 238 et seq.
3 Limited Liability Partnerships Act 2000 ss 1(2), 18. As to incorporation generally see PARA 234.
4 Limited Liability Partnerships Act 2000 s 1(3). A limited liability partnership is a 'company' for the purposes of the definition of 'associated employer' in the Equal Pay Act 1970 s 1(6)(c): *Glasgow City Council v Unison claimant* [2014] CSIH 27, [2014] IRLR 532, Ct of Sess.

234. Incorporation. For a limited liability partnership[1] to be incorporated:
(1)   two or more persons who are associated for the carrying on of a lawful business[2] with a view to profit must have subscribed their names[3] to an incorporation document[4];
(2)   the incorporation document or a copy of it must have been delivered to the registrar[5]; and
(3)   a statement made, either by a solicitor engaged in the formation of the limited liability partnership or by anyone who subscribed his name to the incorporation document, must also be delivered to the registrar confirming that there has been compliance with head (1)[6].
A fee must be paid to the registrar on incorporation[7].

The incorporation document of a limited liability partnership must (a) state the name of the limited liability partnership[8]; (b) state whether the registered office of the limited liability partnership is to be situated in England and Wales, in Wales, in Scotland or in Northern Ireland[9]; (c) state the address of that registered office[10]; (d) give the required particulars of each of the persons who are to be members of the limited liability partnership on incorporation[11]; and (e) either specify which of those persons are to be designated members[12] or state that every person who from time to time is a member of the limited liability partnership is a designated member[13].

The registrar, if satisfied that the requirements above[14] are complied with, must register the documents delivered in accordance with those requirements and give a certificate that the limited liability partnership is incorporated[15]. The certificate must state the name and registered number of the limited liability partnership, the date of its incorporation and whether the limited liability partnership's registered office is situated in England and Wales (or in Wales), in Scotland or in Northern Ireland[16]. The certificate must either be signed by the registrar or be authenticated by his official seal[17], and is conclusive evidence that the statutory requirements[18] are complied with and that the limited liability partnership is incorporated by the name specified in the incorporation document[19].

1 As to the meaning of 'limited liability partnership' see PARA 233.

2 'Business' includes every trade, profession and occupation: Limited Liability Partnerships Act 2000 s 18.

3 'Name' in relation to a member of a limited liability partnership means, if an individual, his forename and surname, or in the case of a peer or other person usually known by a title, his title instead of or in addition to either or both his forename and surname, and if a corporation, its corporate name: Limited Liability Partnerships Act 2000 s 18.

4 Limited Liability Partnerships Act 2000 s 2(1)(a). As to the incorporation document see the text and notes 8–13.

5 Limited Liability Partnerships Act 2000 s 2(1)(b) (substituted by SI 2009/1804). 'The registrar' means: (1) if the registered office of the limited liability partnership is, or is to be, situated in England and Wales or in Wales, the registrar of companies for England and Wales; (2) if the registered office of the limited liability partnership is, or is to be, in Scotland, the registrar of companies for Scotland; and (3) if the registered office of the limited liability partnership is, or is to be, in Northern Ireland, the registrar of companies for Northern Ireland: Limited Liability Partnerships Act 2000 s 18 (definition substituted by SI 2009/1804). As to the registrar of companies see PARA 220 note 1; and COMPANIES vol 14 (2009) PARA 131 et seq.

In any enactment relating to limited liability partnerships: (a) 'the registrar' has the meaning given by the Limited Liability Partnerships Act 2000 s 18; (b) 'the register' means the records kept by the registrar relating to limited liability partnerships; and (c) references to registration in a particular part of the United Kingdom are to registration by the registrar for that part of the United Kingdom: Limited Liability Partnerships (Application of Companies Act 2006) Regulations 2009, SI 2009/1804, Sch 3 para 12(1). 'Enactment' includes: (i) an enactment contained in subordinate legislation within the meaning of the Interpretation Act 1978; and (ii) an enactment contained in, or in an instrument made under, a Measure or Act of the National Assembly for Wales: Limited Liability Partnerships (Application of Companies Act 2006) Regulations 2009, SI 2009/1804, Sch 3 para 12(2).

6 Limited Liability Partnerships Act 2000 s 2(1)(c) (amended by SI 2009/1804). A person who makes such a statement knowing that it is false or not believing it to be true is guilty of an offence: Limited Liability Partnerships Act 2000 s 2(3). A person guilty of such an offence is liable, on summary conviction, to imprisonment for a period not exceeding six months or a fine not exceeding the statutory maximum, or to both, or on conviction on indictment, to imprisonment for a period not exceeding two years or a fine, or to both: s 2(4). As to the statutory maximum and the prescribed sum see SENTENCING AND DISPOSITION OF OFFENDERS vol 92 (2010) PARAS 140, 141.

7 See the Registrar of Companies (Fees) (Companies, Overseas Companies and Limited Liability Partnerships) Regulations 2012, SI 2012/1907, reg 3, Sch 1 para 10, Table item (a).

8 Limited Liability Partnerships Act 2000 s 2(2)(b). As to the name of a limited liability partnership see PARA 236.

9 Limited Liability Partnerships Act 2000 s 2(2)(c) (amended by SI 2009/1804). As to the registered office of a limited liability partnership see PARA 237.

10 Limited Liability Partnerships Act 2000 s 2(2)(d).

11 Limited Liability Partnerships Act 2000 s 2(2)(e) (substituted by SI 2009/1804). The required particulars are the particulars required to be stated in the LLP's register of members and register of members' residential addresses: Limited Liability Partnerships Act 2000 s 2(2ZA) (added by SI 2009/1804).

12 As to designated members see PARA 239.

13 Limited Liability Partnerships Act 2000 s 2(2)(f).

14 Ie the requirements of the Limited Liability Partnerships Act 2000 s 2.

15 Limited Liability Partnerships Act 2000 s 3(1) (substituted by SI 2009/1804). The registrar is under a duty to register the incorporation document and issue the certificate unless the persons associated for carrying on lawful business with a view to profit have not subscribed their names to the incorporation document (ie the requirement imposed by the Limited Liability Partnerships Act 2000 s 2(1)(a) has not been complied with): see s 3(1) (as so substituted). The registrar may accept the statement delivered under s 2(1)(c) as sufficient evidence that this requirement has been complied with: s 3(2).

16 Limited Liability Partnerships Act 2000 s 3(1A) (added by SI 2009/1804).

17 Limited Liability Partnerships Act 2000 s 3(3).

18 Ie the requirements of the Limited Liability Partnerships Act 2000 s 2.

19 Limited Liability Partnerships Act 2000 s 3(4).

235. Property transferred to a limited liability partnership in connection with its incorporation. Stamp duty is not chargeable on an instrument[1] by which property is conveyed or transferred by a person to a limited liability partnership[2] in connection with its incorporation[3] within the period of one year beginning with the date of incorporation if the following two conditions are satisfied[4]. The first condition is that at the relevant time[5] the person: (1) is a partner in a partnership comprised of all the persons who are or are to be members of the limited liability partnership (and no-one else)[6]; or (2) holds the property conveyed or transferred as nominee or bare trustee for one or more of the partners in such a partnership[7]. The second condition is that: (a) the proportions of the property conveyed or transferred to which the persons mentioned in head (1) are entitled immediately after the conveyance or transfer are the same as those to which they were entitled at the relevant time[8]; or (b) none of the differences in those proportions has arisen as part of a scheme or arrangement of which the main purpose, or one of the main purposes, is avoidance of liability to any duty or tax[9].

1 An instrument in respect of which stamp duty is not chargeable by virtue of the Limited Liability Partnerships Act 2000 s 12(1) is not to be taken to be duly stamped unless: (1) it has, in accordance with the Stamp Act 1891 s 12 (see STAMP TAXES vol 96 (2012) PARA 384), been stamped with a particular stamp denoting that it is not chargeable with any duty or that it is duly stamped; or (2) it is stamped with the duty to which it would be liable apart from the Limited Liability Partnerships Act 2000 s 12(1): s 12(6). As to stamp duty see further STAMP TAXES.
2 As to the meaning of 'limited liability partnership' see PARA 233.
3 As to incorporation see PARA 234.
4 Limited Liability Partnerships Act 2000 s 12(1).
5 'Relevant time' means: (1) if the person who conveyed or transferred the property to the limited liability partnership acquired the property after its incorporation, immediately after he acquired the property; and (2) in any other case, immediately before its incorporation: Limited Liability Partnerships Act 2000 s 12(5).
6 Limited Liability Partnerships Act 2000 s 12(2)(a).
7 Limited Liability Partnerships Act 2000 s 12(2)(b). For these purposes a person holds property as bare trustee for a partner if the partner has the exclusive right (subject only to satisfying any outstanding charge, lien or other right of the trustee to resort to the property for payment of duty, taxes, costs or other outgoings) to direct how the property is to be dealt with: s 12(4).
8 Limited Liability Partnerships Act 2000 s 12(3)(a).
9 Limited Liability Partnerships Act 2000 s 12(3)(b).

236. Name. The name of a limited liability partnership[1] must end with the expression 'limited liability partnership', or the abbreviation 'llp' or 'LLP' (or the Welsh equivalents)[2]. It is an offence for a person to carry on a business under a name or title which includes as the last words these expressions or any contraction or imitation of them, unless that person is a limited liability partnership or oversea limited liability partnership[3]. The statutory restrictions and prohibitions on company names are applied to limited liability partnerships[4].

A limited liability partnership may change its name at any time[5] and notice of the change of name must be delivered to the registrar[6]. The name of a limited liability partnership may also be changed: (1) on the determination of a new name by a company names adjudicator[7]; (2) on the determination of a new name by the court[8]; (3) on the restoration of its name[9] to the register[10].

A change of name by a limited liability partnership does not affect any of its rights or duties, or render defective any legal proceedings against it, and any legal proceedings that might have been commenced or continued against it by its former name may be commenced or continued against it by its new name[11].

1   As to the meaning of 'limited liability partnership' see PARA 233.

2   Limited Liability Partnerships Act 2000 s 1(6), Schedule para 2(1). If the incorporation document states that the registered office is to be situated in Wales, its name must end with one of the expressions 'limited liability partnership' and 'partneriaeth atebolrwydd cyfyngedig' or one of the abbreviations 'llp', LLP', 'pac' and 'PAC': Schedule para 2(2).

3   Limited Liability Partnerships Act 2000 Schedule para 7(1). A person who is guilty of such an offence is liable on summary conviction to a fine not exceeding level 3 on the standard scale: Schedule para 7(2). As to the standard scale see SENTENCING AND DISPOSITION OF OFFENDERS vol 92 (2010) PARA 142. As to the meaning of 'oversea limited liability partnership' see PARA 243 note 3.

4   Ie the Companies Act 2006 ss 53–56 (see COMPANIES vol 14 (2009) PARA 196), which are applied with modifications by the Limited Liability Partnerships (Application of Companies Act 2006) Regulations 2009, SI 2009/1804, reg 8 (amended by SI 2009/2995). In the Limited Liability Partnerships (Application of Companies Act 2006) Regulations 2009, SI 2009/1804, 'LLP' means a limited liability partnership registered under the Limited Liability Partnerships Act 2000: Limited Liability Partnerships (Application of Companies Act 2006) Regulations 2009, SI 2009/1804, reg 3(1).

An LLP must not be registered under the Limited Liability Partnerships Act 2000 by a name if, in the opinion of the Secretary of State, its use by the LLP would constitute an offence, or if it is offensive: Companies Act 2006 s 53 (as so applied). The approval of the Secretary of State is required for an LLP to be registered under the Limited Liability Partnerships Act 2000 by a name that would be likely to give the impression that the LLP is connected with: (1) Her Majesty's Government, any part of the Scottish Administration, the Welsh Assembly Government or Her Majesty's Government in Northern Ireland; (2) a local authority; or (3) any public authority specified for these purposes by regulations made by the Secretary of State: Companies Act 2006 s 54(1) (as so applied). At the date at which this volume states the law no such regulations had been made. For the purposes of s 54, 'local authority' means: (a) a local authority within the meaning of the Local Government Act 1972, the Common Council of the City of London or the Council of the Isles of Scilly; (b) a council constituted under the Local Government etc (Scotland) Act 1994 s 2; or (c) a district council in Northern Ireland; and 'public authority' includes any person or body having functions of a public nature: Companies Act 2006 s 54(2) (as so applied). Regulations under s 54 are subject to affirmative resolution procedure: s 54(3) (as so applied). As to the Secretary of State see PARA 8 note 8.

The approval of the Secretary of State is required for an LLP to be registered under the Limited Liability Partnerships Act 2000 by a name that includes a word or expression for the time being specified in regulations made by the Secretary of State under this provision: see the Companies Act 2006 s 55(1) (as so applied); and the Company, Limited Liability Partnership and Business Names (Sensitive Words and Expressions) Regulations 2009, SI 2009/2615. Regulations under the Companies Act 2006 s 55 are subject to approval after being made: s 55(2) (as so applied).

The Secretary of State may by regulations under s 54 or s 55 require that, in connection with an application for the approval of the Secretary of State under the relevant section, the applicant must seek the view of a specified Government department or other body: s 56(1) (as so applied). As to the procedure see s 56(2)–(5) (as so applied).

In addition, the provisions of the Company and Business Names (Miscellaneous Provisions) Regulations 2009, SI 2009/1085, relating to the characters, signs or symbols and punctuation that may be used in a registered name apply to LLPs: Companies Act 2006 s 57(1) (s 57 applied by the Limited Liability Partnerships (Application of Companies Act 2006) Regulations 2009, SI 2009/1804, reg 9). Those provisions are the Company and Business Names (Miscellaneous Provisions) Regulations 2009, SI 2009/1085, reg 2 and Sch 1, and any other provisions of those Regulations having effect for the purpose of those provisions: Companies Act 2006 s 57(2) (as so applied). In those provisions as they apply to LLPs: (i) for 'company' substitute 'LLP; and (ii) for 'the Act' substitute 'the Limited Liability Partnerships Act 2000': s 57(3) (as so applied). An LLP may not be registered under the Limited Liability Partnerships Act 2000 by a name that consists of or includes anything that is not permitted in accordance with the provisions applied by the Companies Act 2006 s 57: s 57(4) (as so applied).

An LLP must not be registered under the Limited Liability Partnerships Act 2000 by a name that is the same as another name appearing in the registrar's index of company names: see the Companies Act 2006 s 66 (ss 66–68 applied by the Limited Liability Partnerships (Application of Companies Act 2006) Regulations 2009, SI 2009/1804, reg 12). Also, the Secretary of State may direct an LLP to change its name if it has been registered in a name that is the same as or, in the opinion of the Secretary of State, too like a name appearing at the time of the registration in the registrar's index of company names or a name that should have appeared in that index at that time: Companies Act 2006 s 67 (as so applied); see further s 68 (as so applied).

5 Limited Liability Partnerships Act 2000 Schedule para 4(1).

6 Limited Liability Partnerships Act 2000 Schedule para 5(1). As to the registrar see PARA 234 note 5. Where the registrar receives notice of a change of name he must, unless the new name is one by which a limited liability partnership may not be registered, enter the new name on the register in place of the former name, and issue a certificate of the change of name: Schedule para 5(3) (amended by SI 2009/1804). The change of name has effect from the date on which the certificate is issued: Limited Liability Partnerships Act 2000 Schedule para 5(4).

For the fee for registration of a change of the name of a limited liability partnership, other than a change made in response to a direction of the Secretary of State under the Companies Act 2006 s 67, a determination by a company names adjudicator or a court under s 73(5) or 74(5) or on the restoration of the limited liability partnership to the register under s 1033(2)(a)(i) (as applied to limited liability partnerships) see the Registrar of Companies (Fees) (Companies, Overseas Companies and Limited Liability Partnerships) Regulations 2012, SI 2012/1907, reg 3, Sch 1 para 10, Table item (c).

7 Ie under the Companies Act 2006 s 73 (powers of adjudicator on upholding objection to name), on an application under s 69 where similarity to another name in which a person has goodwill is alleged (ss 69–74 as applied to limited liability partnerships by the Limited Liability Partnerships (Application of Companies Act 2006) Regulations 2009, SI 2009/1804, reg 12).

8 Ie under the Companies Act 2006 s 74 (appeal against decision of company names adjudicator) (as applied to limited liability partnerships: see note 7).

9 Ie under the Companies Act 2006 s 1033 (name on restoration to the register) (as applied to limited liability partnerships by the Limited Liability Partnerships (Application of Companies Act 2006) Regulations 2009, SI 2009/1804, reg 58).

10 Limited Liability Partnerships Act 2000 Schedule para 4(2) (substituted by SI 2009/1804). As to the meaning of 'register' see PARA 234 note 5.

11 Limited Liability Partnerships Act 2000 Schedule para 6.

237. Registered office. A limited liability partnership[1] must at all times have a registered office situated in England and Wales (or in Wales), in Scotland or in Northern Ireland to which all communications and notices may be addressed[2]. A limited liability partnership may change the address of its registered office by giving notice to the registrar[3].

1 As to the meaning of 'limited liability partnership' see PARA 233.

2 Companies Act 2006 s 86(1) (ss 86, 87 applied to limited liability partnerships by the Limited Liability Partnerships (Application of Companies Act 2006) Regulations 2009, SI 2009/1804, reg 16). On the incorporation of a limited liability partnership, the situation of its registered office is that stated in the incorporation document: Companies Act 2006 s 86(2) (as so applied). As to the incorporation document see PARA 234.

An LLP whose registered office is in Wales and as to which it is stated in the register that its registered office is to be situated in England and Wales, may determine that the register be amended so that it states that the LLP's registered office is to be situated in Wales: Companies Act 2006 s 88(2) (s 88 applied to limited liability partnerships by the Limited Liability Partnerships (Application of Companies Act 2006) Regulations 2009, SI 2009/1804, reg 17). An LLP whose registered office is in Wales and as to which it is stated in the register that its registered office is to be situated in Wales, may determine that the register be amended so that it states that the LLP's registered office is to be situated in England and Wales: Companies Act 2006 s 88(3) (as so applied). Where an LLP makes a determination under s 88 it must give notice to the registrar, who must amend the register accordingly and issue a new certificate of incorporation altered to meet the circumstances of the case: s 88(4) (as so applied). In the Companies Act 2006, a 'Welsh LLP' means an LLP as to which it is stated in the register that its registered office is to be situated in Wales: s 88(1) (as so applied). As to the meaning of 'LLP' see PARA 236 note 4. As to the registrar and as to the meaning of 'register' see PARA 234 note 5.

3 Companies Act 2006 s 87(1) (as applied to limited liability partnerships: see note 2). The change takes effect upon the notice being registered by the registrar, but until the end of the period of 14 days beginning with the date on which it is registered a person may validly serve any document on the LLP at the address previously registered: s 87(2) (as so applied). For the purposes of any duty of an LLP: (1) to keep available for inspection at its registered office any register, index or other document; or (2) to mention the address of its registered office in any document, an LLP that has given notice to the registrar of a change in the address of its registered office may act on

the change as from such date, not more than 14 days after the notice is given, as it may determine: s 87(3) (as so applied). Where an LLP unavoidably ceases to perform at its registered office any such duty as is mentioned in head (1) in circumstances in which it was not practicable to give prior notice to the registrar of a change in the address of its registered office, but resumes performance of that duty at other premises as soon as practicable and gives notice accordingly to the registrar of a change in the situation of its registered office within 14 days of doing so, it is not to be treated as having failed to comply with that duty: s 87(4) (as so applied).

238. Members. On the incorporation of a limited liability partnership[1] its members are the persons who subscribed their names to the incorporation document[2], other than any who have died or have been dissolved[3]. Any other person may become a member by and in accordance with an agreement with the existing members[4]. A person may cease to be a member, as well as by death or dissolution, in accordance with an agreement with the other members or, in the absence of agreement with the other members as to cessation of membership, by giving reasonable notice to the other members[5]. A member is not to be regarded for any purpose as employed by the limited liability partnership unless, if he and the other members were partners in a partnership, he would be regarded for that purpose as employed by the partnership[6].

Where a limited liability partnership carries on business without having at least two members, and does so for more than six months, a person who, for the whole or any part of the period that it so carries on business after those six months, is a member of the limited liability partnership, and knows that it is carrying on business with only one member, is liable, jointly and severally with the limited liability partnership, for the payment of the limited liability partnership's debts contracted during the period or, as the case may be, that part of it[7].

The mutual rights and duties of the members of a limited liability partnership, and the mutual rights and duties of a limited liability partnership and its members, are governed by agreement between the members, or between the limited liability partnership and its members[8]. In the absence of any such agreement, the above rights are determined, subject to the provisions of the general law and to the terms of any limited liability partnership agreement[9], by the following rules[10]:

(1) all the members of a limited liability partnership are entitled to share equally in the capital and profits of the limited liability partnership[11];

(2) the limited liability partnership must indemnify each member in respect of payments made and personal liabilities incurred by him in the ordinary and proper conduct of the business[12] of the limited liability partnership, or in or about anything necessarily done for the preservation of the business or property of the limited liability partnership[13];

(3) every member may take part in the management of the limited liability partnership[14];

(4) no member is entitled to remuneration for acting in the business or management of the limited liability partnership[15];

(5) no person may be introduced as a member or voluntarily assign an interest in a limited liability partnership without the consent of all existing members[16];

(6) any difference arising as to ordinary matters connected with the business of the limited liability partnership may be decided by a

majority of the members, but no change may be made in the nature of the business of the limited liability partnership without the consent of all the members[17];

(7) the books and records of the limited liability partnership are to be made available for inspection at the registered office[18] of the limited liability partnership or at such other place as the members think fit and every member of the limited liability partnership may, when he thinks fit, have access to and inspect and copy any of them[19];

(8) each member must render true accounts and full information of all things affecting the limited liability partnership to any member or his legal representatives[20];

(9) if a member, without the consent of the limited liability partnership, carries on any business of the same nature as and competing with the limited liability partnership, he must account for and pay over to the limited liability partnership all profits made by him in that business[21];

(10) every member must account to the limited liability partnership for any benefit derived by him without the consent of the limited liability partnership from any transaction concerning the limited liability partnership, or from any use by him of the property of the limited liability partnership, name[22] or business connection[23].

No majority of the members can expel any member unless a power to do so has been conferred by express agreement between the members[24].

A limited liability partnership does not, ordinarily at least, owe fiduciary duties to its members, and members do not owe fiduciary duties to each other, but a member may owe fiduciary duties to the limited liability partnership if the member acts as its agent[25].

Where a member of a limited liability partnership has either ceased to be a member or has died, has become bankrupt or had his estate sequestrated or has been wound up, has granted a trust deed for the benefit of his creditors, or has assigned the whole or any part of his share in the limited liability partnership, absolutely or by way of charge or security[26], then the former member or his personal representative, his trustee in bankruptcy or liquidator, his trustee under the trust deed for the benefit of his creditors, or his assignee, may not interfere in the management or administration of any business or affairs of the limited liability partnership[27].

1   As to the meaning of 'limited liability partnership' see PARA 233.
2   As to the incorporation document see PARA 234.
3   Limited Liability Partnerships Act 2000 s 4(1).
4   Limited Liability Partnerships Act 2000 s 4(2).
5   Limited Liability Partnerships Act 2000 s 4(3).
6   Limited Liability Partnerships Act 2000 s 4(4). Whilst the words 'employed by' in s 4(4) cover a person employed under a contract of service, they do not also cover those who undertake to do or perform personally any work or services for another party to the contract. Consequently, a member of an limited liability partnership may be a 'worker' within the meaning of the Employment Rights Act 1996 s 230 (see EMPLOYMENT vol 39 (2014) PARA 5): see *Bates van Winkelhof v Clyde & Co LLP* [2014] UKSC 32, [2014] 3 All ER 225, [2014] IRLR 641. In determining whether a member of a limited liability partnership is also an employee, the Limited Liability Partnerships Act 2000 s 4(4) has to be construed on the assumption that the business of the limited liability partnership has been carried on in partnership by two or more of its members as partners; and, upon that assumption, an inquiry is made as to whether or not the person whose status is in question would have been one of such partners (*Tiffin v Lester Aldridge LLP* [2012] EWCA Civ 35, [2012] 2 All ER 1113), although query whether this remains good law in the light of the dicta of Lady Hale in *Bates van Winkelhof* at [20], [21]. As to members as agents of the limited liability partnership see PARA 240.

7 Limited Liability Partnerships Act 2000 s 4A (added by SI 2009/1804).
8 Limited Liability Partnerships Act 2000 s 5(1)(a). Section 5(1) applies except as far as otherwise provided by the Limited Liability Partnerships Act 2000 or any other enactment (including subordinate legislation): ss 5(1), 18. An agreement made before the incorporation of a limited liability partnership between the persons who subscribe their names to the incorporation document may impose obligations on the limited liability partnership, to take effect at any time after its incorporation: s 5(2). As to incorporation see PARA 234.
9 'Limited liability partnership agreement' in relation to a limited liability partnership, means any agreement, express or implied, between the members of the limited liability partnership or between the limited liability partnership and the members of the limited liability partnership, which determines the mutual rights and duties of the members, and their rights and duties in relation to the limited liability partnership: Limited Liability Partnerships Regulations 2001, SI 2001/1090, reg 2.
10 Limited Liability Partnerships Regulations 2001, SI 2001/1090, reg 7.
11 Limited Liability Partnerships Regulations 2001, SI 2001/1090, reg 7(1).
12 As to the meaning of 'business' see PARA 234 note 2.
13 Limited Liability Partnerships Regulations 2001, SI 2001/1090, reg 7(2).
14 Limited Liability Partnerships Regulations 2001, SI 2001/1090, reg 7(3).
15 Limited Liability Partnerships Regulations 2001, SI 2001/1090, reg 7(4).
16 Limited Liability Partnerships Regulations 2001, SI 2001/1090, reg 7(5).
17 Limited Liability Partnerships Regulations 2001, SI 2001/1090, reg 7(6).
18 As to the registered office of a limited liability partnership see PARA 237.
19 Limited Liability Partnerships Regulations 2001, SI 2001/1090, reg 7(7).
20 Limited Liability Partnerships Regulations 2001, SI 2001/1090, reg 7(8).
21 Limited Liability Partnerships Regulations 2001, SI 2001/1090, reg 7(9).
22 As to the name of a limited liability partnership see PARA 236.
23 Limited Liability Partnerships Regulations 2001, SI 2001/1090, reg 7(10).
24 Limited Liability Partnerships Regulations 2001, SI 2001/1090, reg 8.
25 *F&C Alternative Investments (Holdings) Ltd v Barthelemy* [2011] EWHC 1731 (Ch), [2012] Ch 613, [2012] 3 WLR 10; and *Brown v InnovatorOne plc* [2012] EWHC 1321 (Comm), [2012] All ER (D) 273 (May).
26 Limited Liability Partnerships Act 2000 s 7(1).
27 Limited Liability Partnerships Act 2000 s 7(2). Section 7(2) does not affect any right to receive an amount from the limited liability partnership in that event: s 7(3).

239. Designated members. If the incorporation document[1] of a limited liability partnership[2] specifies who are to be designated members they are designated members on incorporation, and any member may become a designated member by and in accordance with an agreement with the other members, and a member may cease to be a designated member in accordance with an agreement with the other members[3]. If there would otherwise be no designated members, or only one, every member is a designated member[4]. If the incorporation document states that every person who from time to time is a member of the limited liability partnership is a designated member, every member is a designated member[5]. A limited liability partnership may at any time deliver to the registrar[6] notice that specified members are to be designated members, or notice that every person who from time to time is a member of the limited liability partnership is a designated member, and, once it is delivered, the provisions described above have effect as if that were stated in the incorporation document[7]. A person ceases to be a designated member if he ceases to be a member[8].

1 As to the incorporation document see PARA 234.
2 As to the meaning of 'limited liability partnership' see PARA 233.
3 Limited Liability Partnerships Act 2000 s 8(1). As to members see PARA 238.
4 Limited Liability Partnerships Act 2000 s 8(2).
5 Limited Liability Partnerships Act 2000 s 8(3).
6 As to the registrar see PARA 234 note 5.

7 Limited Liability Partnerships Act 2000 s 8(4).
8 Limited Liability Partnerships Act 2000 s 8(6). As to the cessation of membership see PARA 238.

240. Members as agents. Every member of a limited liability partnership[1] is the agent of the limited liability partnership[2]. However, a limited liability partnership is not bound by anything done by a member in dealing with a person if the member in fact has no authority to act for the limited liability partnership by doing that thing, and the person knows that he has no authority or does not know or believe him to be a member of the limited liability partnership[3]. Where a person has ceased to be a member of a limited liability partnership[4], the former member is to be regarded, in relation to any person dealing with the limited liability partnership, as still being a member of the limited liability partnership unless the person has notice that the former member has ceased to be a member of the limited liability partnership, or notice that the former member has ceased to be a member of the limited liability partnership has been delivered to the registrar[5]. Where a member of a limited liability partnership is liable to any person, other than another member of the limited liability partnership, as a result of a wrongful act or omission of his in the course of the business of the limited liability partnership or with its authority, the limited liability partnership is liable to the same extent as the member[6].

1 As to the meaning of 'limited liability partnership' see PARA 233. As to members see PARAS 238–239.
2 Limited Liability Partnerships Act 2000 s 6(1). As to the principles of agency applicable to partners see further PARA 39 et seq; and AGENCY.
3 Limited Liability Partnerships Act 2000 s 6(2).
4 As to ex-members of limited liability partnerships see PARA 238.
5 Limited Liability Partnerships Act 2000 s 6(3). As to the registrar see PARA 234 note 5.
6 Limited Liability Partnerships Act 2000 s 6(4). As to the liability of partners generally see PARA 39 et seq.

241. Registration of membership changes. A limited liability partnership[1] must ensure that where a person becomes or ceases to be a member[2] or designated member[3], notice is delivered to the registrar[4] within 14 days[5]. A limited liability partnership must also ensure that where there is any change in the particulars contained in its register of members or its register of members' residential addresses, notice is delivered to the registrar within 14 days[6].

Such a notice that relates to a person becoming a member or designated member must contain: (1) a statement that the member or designated member consents to acting in that capacity; and (2) in the case of a person becoming a member, a statement of the particulars of the new member that are required to be included in the limited liability partnership's register of members and its register of residential addresses[7]. Where: (a) a limited liability partnership gives notice of a change of a member's service address as stated in its register of members; and (b) the notice is not accompanied by notice of any resulting change in the particulars contained in its register of members' residential addresses, the notice must be accompanied by a statement that no such change is required[8].

If a limited liability partnership fails to comply with these requirements, the partnership and every designated member commits an offence[9].

1 As to the meaning of 'limited liability partnership' see PARA 233.
2 As to ex-members of limited liability partnerships see PARA 238.
3 As to designated members see PARA 239.
4 As to the registrar see PARA 234 note 5.

5   Limited Liability Partnerships Act 2000 s 9(1)(a). Where all the members from time to time of a limited liability partnership are designated members s 9(1)(a) does not require notice that a person has become or ceased to be a designated member as well as a member: s 9(2).

6   Limited Liability Partnerships Act 2000 s 9(1)(b) (amended by SI 2009/1804).

7   Limited Liability Partnerships Act 2000 s 9(3) (substituted by SI 2009/1804).

8   Limited Liability Partnerships Act 2000 s 9(3ZA) (added by SI 2009/1804).

9   Limited Liability Partnerships Act 2000 s 9(4) (amended by SI 2009/1804). It is a defence for a designated member charged with such an offence to prove that he took all reasonable steps for securing that the requirements of the Limited Liability Partnerships Act 2000 s 9 were complied with: s 9(5) (amended by SI 2009/1804). A person guilty of such an offence is liable on summary conviction to a fine not exceeding level 5 on the standard scale: Limited Liability Partnerships Act 2000 s 9(6). As to the standard scale see SENTENCING AND DISPOSITION OF OFFENDERS vol 92 (2010) PARA 142.

242. Discrimination. An LLP[1] or proposed LLP[2] must not discriminate[3] against or victimise[4] a person:

(1)   in the arrangements it makes for deciding to whom to offer a position as a member[5];

(2)   as to the terms on which it offers the person a position as a member[6];

(3)   by not offering the person a position as a member[7].

An LLP ('A') must not discriminate against or victimise a member ('B'):

(a)   as to the terms on which B is a member[8];

(b)   in the way A affords B access, or by not affording B access, to opportunities for promotion, transfer or training or for receiving any other benefit, facility or service[9];

(c)   by expelling B[10];

(d)   by subjecting B to any other detriment[11].

An LLP must not, in relation to a position as a member, harass[12] a member[13] or a person who has applied for the position[14]. A proposed LLP must not, in relation to a position as a member, harass a person who has applied for the position[15].

1   For these purposes, 'LLP' means a limited liability partnership within the meaning of the Limited Liability Partnerships Act 2000 (see PARA 233): Equality Act 2010 s 46(1), (4).

2   'Proposed LLP' means persons proposing to incorporate an LLP with themselves as members: Equality Act 2010 s 46(1), (5).

3   As to direct discrimination see DISCRIMINATION vol 33 (2013) PARA 65; and as to indirect discrimination see DISCRIMINATION vol 33 (2013) PARA 72.

4   As to victimisation see DISCRIMINATION vol 33 (2013) PARA 75.

5   Equality Act 2010 s 45(1)(a), (5)(a). As to the meaning of 'arrangements' see DISCRIMINATION vol 33 (2013) PARA 111. For a partial exception to these provisions in connection with occupational requirements (including religious requirements) see Sch 9 paras 1–3; and DISCRIMINATION vol 33 (2013) PARAS 153–155.

6   Equality Act 2010 s 45(1)(b), (5)(b).

7   Equality Act 2010 s 45(1)(c), (5)(c). For a partial exception to these provisions in connection with occupational requirements (including religious requirements) see Sch 9 paras 1–3; and DISCRIMINATION vol 33 (2013) PARAS 153–155.

8   Equality Act 2010 s 45(2)(a), (6)(a). For an exception relating to the provision of public services see Sch 9 para 19; and DISCRIMINATION vol 33 (2013) PARA 164.

9   Equality Act 2010 s 45(2)(b), (6)(b). As to the meaning of 'benefit, facility or service' see DISCRIMINATION vol 33 (2013) PARA 111. For a partial exception to these provisions in connection with occupational requirements (including religious requirements) see Sch 9 paras 1–3; and DISCRIMINATION vol 33 (2013) PARAS 153–155; for applicable modifications in relation to these exceptions see Sch 9 para 6(5). There are also exceptions to this provision in connection with the provision of childcare: see Sch 9 para 15; and DISCRIMINATION vol 33 (2013) PARA 161. See also note 8.

10 Equality Act 2010 s 45(2)(c), (6)(c). For a partial exception to these provisions in connection
   with occupational requirements (including religious requirements) see Sch 9 paras 1 3; and
   DISCRIMINATION vol 33 (2013) PARAS 153–155; for applicable modifications in relation to this
   exception see Sch 9 para 6(6). See also note 8.
11 Equality Act 2010 s 45(2)(d), (6)(d). As to the meaning of 'detriment' see DISCRIMINATION
   vol 33 (2013) PARA 75. See also note 8.
12 As to harassment see DISCRIMINATION vol 33 (2013) PARA 73.
13 Equality Act 2010 s 45(3)(a).
14 Equality Act 2010 s 45(3)(b).
15 Equality Act 2010 s 45(4).

(2) MODIFICATION OF EXISTING LEGISLATION

243. Application of existing law to limited liability partnerships. Partnership
law does not, in general, apply to a limited liability partnership[1], although
regulations[2] may make provision about limited liability partnerships and oversea
limited liability partnerships[3] (not being provision about insolvency or winding
up[4]) by applying or incorporating, with such modifications as appear
appropriate, any law relating to partnerships[5]. Regulations may similarly make
provision: (1) applying or incorporating, with such modifications as appear
appropriate, any law relating to companies or other corporations which would
not otherwise have effect in relation to them[6]; or (2) providing for any law
relating to companies or other corporations which would otherwise have effect
in relation to them not to apply to them or to apply to them with such
modifications as appear appropriate[7].

Provision is made by regulations about the insolvency and winding up of
limited liability partnerships by applying or incorporating, with such
modifications as appear appropriate, certain provisions of the Insolvency
Act 1986[8]. Regulations may also apply or incorporate, with such modifications
as appear appropriate, any law relating to the insolvency or winding up of
companies or other corporations which would not otherwise have effect in
relation to them, and may provide for any law relating to the insolvency or
winding up of companies or other corporations which would otherwise have
effect in relation to them not to apply to them or to apply to them with such
modifications as appear appropriate[9].

1 Limited Liability Partnerships Act 2000 s 1(5). But see ss 5, 6; and PARAS 238, 240.
2 Ie regulations made by the Secretary of State by statutory instrument: see the Limited Liability
  Partnerships Act 2000 ss 17(1), (4), (5), (6), 18 (s 17(5) amended by SI 2009/1804). Regulations
  may, in particular: (1) make provisions for dealing with non-compliance with any of the
  regulations (including the creation of criminal offences); (2) impose fees; and (3) provide for the
  exercise of functions by persons prescribed by the regulations: Limited Liability Partnerships
  Act 2000 s 17(2). They may also contain any appropriate consequential, incidental,
  supplementary or transitional provisions or savings, and make different provision for different
  purposes: s 17(3). Regulations may make in any enactment such amendments or repeals as
  appear appropriate in consequence of the Limited Liability Partnerships Act 2000 or regulations
  made under it: s 16(1). The regulations may, in particular, make amendments and repeals
  affecting companies or other corporations or partnerships: s 16(2). 'Enactment' includes
  subordinate legislation (within the meaning of the Interpretation Act 1978): Limited Liability
  Partnerships Act 2000 s 18. For the consequential amendments made by the Limited Liability
  Partnerships Regulations 2001, SI 2001/1090, see reg 9, Sch 5. As to the Secretary of State see
  PARA 8 note 8.
3 'Oversea limited liability partnership' means a body incorporated or otherwise established
  outside the United Kingdom and having such connection with the United Kingdom, and such
  other features, as regulations may prescribe: Limited Liability Partnerships Act 2000 ss 14(3), 18
  (s 14(3) amended by SI 2009/1804). As to the meaning of 'United Kingdom' see PARA 8 note 2.
4 See the text and notes 8–9.

5 Limited Liability Partnerships Act 2000 s 15(c). 'Modifications' includes additions and omissions: s 18.
6 Limited Liability Partnerships Act 2000 s 15(a). As to the application of company law to limited liability partnerships see the Limited Liability Partnerships Regulations 2001, SI 2001/1090 (amended by SI 2004/355, SI 2005/1989, SI 2007/2073, SI 2008/1911, SI 2009/1804 and SI 2009/1941; and, as from a day to be appointed, by the Third Parties (Rights against Insurers) Act 2010 s 20(3), Sch 4; at the date at which this volume states the law, no such day had been appointed); the Limited Liability Partnerships (Accounts and Audit) (Application of Companies Act 2006) Regulations 2008, SI 2008/1911 (amended by SI 2009/1342, SI 2009/1804, SI 2011/99, SI 2012/1741, SI 2012/2301, SI 2013/472 and SI 2013/2005); the Small Limited Liability Partnerships (Accounts) Regulations 2008, SI 2008/1912; the Large and Medium-sized Limited Liability Partnerships (Accounts) Regulations 2008, SI 2008/1913, which apply provisions of the Companies Act 2006 Pts 15, 16 (ss 380–539) (accounts and audit) to limited liability partnerships; the Limited Liability Partnerships (Application of Companies Act 2006) Regulations 2009, SI 2009/1804; and PARA 245.
7 Limited Liability Partnerships Act 2000 s 15(b). As to the regulations made under s 15(a), (b) see note 6.
8 See the Limited Liability Partnerships Act 2000 s 14(1); the Limited Liability Partnerships Regulations 2001, SI 2001/1090 (making provision for the application of insolvency legislation to limited liability partnerships); and PARA 244.
9 Limited Liability Partnerships Act 2000 s 14(2). See the Limited Liability Partnerships Regulations 2001, SI 2001/1090; and PARA 244.

244. Insolvency legislation. Certain provisions of the Insolvency Act 1986[1] concerning insolvency and winding up apply[2] to limited liability partnerships[3] with the following modifications to terminology:

(1) references to a company include references to a limited liability partnership[4];

(2) references to a director or to an officer of a company include references to a member[5] of a limited liability partnership[6];

(3) references to a shadow director include references to a shadow member[7];

(4) references to the Companies Acts, the Company Directors Disqualification Act 1986, the Companies Act 1989 or to any provisions of those Acts or to any provisions of the Insolvency Act 1986 include references to those Acts or provisions as they apply to limited liability partnerships by virtue of the Limited Liability Partnerships Act 2000[8];

(5) references to the articles of association of a company include references to the limited liability partnership agreement[9] of a limited liability partnership[10].

Specified modifications[11] are also made to the statutory wording of certain provisions of the Insolvency Act 1986[12], and those provisions may apply to limited liability partnerships with such further modification as the context requires[13].

Specified statutory instruments also apply (as from time to time in force) to limited liability partnerships with such modifications as the context requires for the purpose of giving effect to the relevant provisions of the Insolvency Act 1986[14].

1 Ie the Insolvency Act 1986 Pts I–IV (ss 1–219), Pts VI–VII (ss 230–251) and Pts XII–XIX (ss 386–444). These provisions are dealt with elsewhere in this work: see COMPANIES; and COMPANY AND PARTNERSHIP INSOLVENCY vol 17 (2011) PARAS 1362–1369.
2 Ie by virtue of the Limited Liability Partnerships Regulations 2001, SI 2001/1090, reg 5(1) (made under the Limited Liability Partnerships Act 2000 s 14: see PARA 243).
3 As to the meaning of 'limited liability partnership' see PARA 233. The provisions of the Limited Liability Partnerships Regulations 2001, SI 2001/1090, applying provisions of the Insolvency

Act 1986 have effect only in relation to limited liability partnerships registered in Great Britain: Limited Liability Partnerships Regulations 2001, SI 2001/1090, reg 2A(1) (reg 2A added by SI 2009/1804). As to the meaning of 'Great Britain' see PARA 8 note 2.

4   Limited Liability Partnerships Regulations 2001, SI 2001/1090, reg 5(2)(a).

5   As to members see PARAS 238–239.

6   Limited Liability Partnerships Regulations 2001, SI 2001/1090, reg 5(2)(b).

7   Limited Liability Partnerships Regulations 2001, SI 2001/1090, reg 5(2)(c). 'Shadow member', in relation to limited liability partnerships, means a person in accordance with whose directions or instructions the members of the limited liability partnership are accustomed to act, but so that a person is not deemed a shadow member by reason only that the members of the limited partnership act on advice given by him in a professional capacity: reg 2.

8   Limited Liability Partnerships Regulations 2001, SI 2001/1090, reg 5(2)(d) (amended by SI 2009/1941).

9   As to the meaning of 'limited liability partnership agreement' see PARA 238 note 9.

10   Limited Liability Partnerships Regulations 2001, SI 2001/1090, reg 5(2)(e) (amended by SI 2009/1941).

11   The detailed modifications are set out in the Limited Liability Partnerships Regulations 2001, SI 2001/1090, Sch 3 (amended by SI 2004/355, SI 2005/1989 and SI 2005/2114): see COMPANY AND PARTNERSHIP INSOLVENCY.

12   Limited Liability Partnerships Regulations 2001, SI 2001/1090, reg 5(2)(f). See note 1.

13   Limited Liability Partnerships Regulations 2001, SI 2001/1090, reg 5(2)(g).

14   Limited Liability Partnerships Regulations 2001, SI 2001/1090, reg 10(1)(b). The following subordinate legislation is specified in Sch 6 Pt II as applying with necessary modification to limited liability partnerships: the Insolvency Practitioners Regulations 1990, SI 1990/439 (revoked: see now the Insolvency Practitioners Regulations 2005, SI 2005/524); the Insolvency Practitioners (Recognised Professional Bodies) Order 1986, SI 1986/1764; the Insolvency Rules 1986, SI 1986/1925; the Insolvency Fees Order 1986, SI 1986/2030 (revoked: see now the Insolvency Proceedings (Fees) Order 2004, SI 2004/593); the Co-operation of Insolvency Courts (Designation of Relevant Countries and Territories) Order 1986, SI 1986/2123; the Co-operation of Insolvency Courts (Designation of Relevant Countries) Order 1996, SI 1996/253; the Co-operation of Insolvency Courts (Designation of Relevant Country) Order 1998, SI 1998/2766; the Insolvency Proceedings (Monetary Limits) Order 1986, SI 1986/1996; the Insolvency Practitioners Tribunal (Conduct of Investigations) Rules 1986, SI 1986/952; the Insolvency Regulations 1994, SI 1994/2507; the Insolvency (Amendment) Regulations 2000, SI 2000/485 (see BANKRUPTCY AND INDIVIDUAL INSOLVENCY; COMPANY AND PARTNERSHIP INSOLVENCY).

In the case of any conflict between any provision of the subordinate legislation listed above and any provision of the Limited Liability Partnerships Regulations 2001, SI 2001/1090, the latter must prevail: reg 10(2).

245.   Companies legislation. Specified provisions of the Companies Act 1985 relating to the investigation of companies and their affairs[1] apply to limited liability partnerships[2], except where the context otherwise requires, with the following modifications as to terminology[3]:

(1)   references to a company include references to a limited liability partnership[4];

(2)   references to the Insolvency Act 1986 include references to that Act as it applies to limited liability partnerships[5];

(3)   references in a provision of the Companies Act 1985 to other provisions of that Act or provisions of the Companies Act 2006 include references to those other provisions as they apply to limited liability partnerships[6];

(4)   references to a director of a company or to an officer of a company include references to a member of a limited liability partnership[7].

Specified modifications[8] are also made to the statutory wording of those provisions of the Companies Act 1985 along with such further modifications as the context requires for the purpose of giving effect to them[9].

The provisions of the Company Directors Disqualification Act 1986[10] apply to limited liability partnerships, except where the context otherwise requires, with the following modifications as to terminology[11]:

(a) references to a company include references to a limited liability partnership[12];

(b) references to the Companies Acts include references to the Limited Liability Partnerships Act 2000, and regulations made thereunder, and references to the companies legislation include references to the Limited Liability Partnerships Act 2000, regulations made thereunder and to any enactment applied by regulations to limited liability partnerships[13];

(c) references to the Insolvency Act 1986 include references to that Act as it applies to limited liability partnerships[14];

(d) references to a shadow director include references to a shadow member[15];

(e) references to a director of a company or to an officer of a company include references to a member of a limited liability partnership[16].

Specified modifications[17] are also made to the statutory wording of the provisions of the Company Directors Disqualification Act 1986 along with such further modifications as the context requires for the purpose of giving effect to them[18].

Specified statutory instruments also apply (as from time to time in force) to limited liability partnerships with such modifications as the context requires for the purpose of giving effect to the relevant provisions of the Companies Act 1985 and the Company Directors Disqualification Act 1986[19].

The provisions of the Companies Act 2006 which relate to accounts and audit[20] apply with modifications to limited liability partnerships[21], as do other provisions of the Companies Act 2006 relating to the formalities of doing business, name, registered office and members (including the register of members), debentures, annual returns, charges, arrangements and reconstructions, fraudulent trading, protection of members against unfair prejudice, dissolution and restoration to the register, the registrar, offences and miscellaneous matters[22] and regulations on cross-border mergers[23] and trading disclosures[24] made under that Act[25].

1 Ie those provisions of the Companies Act 1985 specified in the Limited Liability Partnerships Regulations 2001, SI 2001/1090, reg 4, Sch 2 Pt 1 col 1 (amended by SI 2004/355, SI 2007/2073, SI 2008/1911 and SI 2009/1804), namely the Companies Act 1985 ss 431–434, 436, 437, 439(5), 441, 446A–446E, 447, 447A, 448, 448A, 449–451, 451A, 452, 453A–453C, 487, Sch 15C, Sch 15D.

2 As to the meaning of 'limited liability partnership' see PARA 233.

3 Limited Liability Partnerships Regulations 2001, SI 2001/1090, reg 4(1). The provisions of the Limited Liability Partnerships Regulations 2001, SI 2001/1090, applying the Company Directors Disqualification Act 1986 have effect only in relation to limited liability partnerships registered in Great Britain: Limited Liability Partnerships Regulations 2001, SI 2001/1090, reg 2A(1) (reg 2A added by SI 2009/1804). The other provisions of the Limited Liability Partnerships Regulations 2001, SI 2001/1090, have effect in relation to limited liability partnerships registered in any part of the United Kingdom: reg 2A(2) (as so added). As to the meaning of 'Great Britain' and 'the United Kingdom' see PARA 8 note 2.

4 Limited Liability Partnerships Regulations 2001, SI 2001/1090, reg 4(1)(a).

5 Limited Liability Partnerships Regulations 2001, SI 2001/1090, reg 4(1)(c).

6 Limited Liability Partnerships Regulations 2001, SI 2001/1090, reg 4(1)(d) (substituted by SI 2009/1804).

7 Limited Liability Partnerships Regulations 2001, SI 2001/1090, reg 4(1)(g).

8 Limited Liability Partnerships Regulations 2001, SI 2001/1090, reg 4(1)(h). The detailed modifications are specified in Sch 2 Pt I col 2 (amended by SI 2007/2073) opposite the provision specified in col 1.

9   Limited Liability Partnerships Regulations 2001, SI 2001/1090, reg 4(1)(i).
10 See COMPANIES vol 15 (2009) PARA 1575 et seq; COMPANY AND PARTNERSHIP INSOLVENCY vol 17 (2011) PARA 1070 et seq.
11 Limited Liability Partnerships Regulations 2001, SI 2001/1090, reg 4(2).
12 Limited Liability Partnerships Regulations 2001, SI 2001/1090, reg 4(2)(a).
13 Limited Liability Partnerships Regulations 2001, SI 2001/1090, reg 4(2)(b).
14 Limited Liability Partnerships Regulations 2001, SI 2001/1090, reg 4(2)(d). As to the application of the Insolvency Act 1986 to limited liability partnerships see PARA 244.
15 Limited Liability Partnerships Regulations 2001, SI 2001/1090, reg 4(2)(f).
16 Limited Liability Partnerships Regulations 2001, SI 2001/1090, reg 4(2)(g).
17 Limited Liability Partnerships Regulations 2001, SI 2001/1090, reg 4(2)(h). The detailed modifications are specified in Sch 2 Pt II col 2 opposite the provision specified in col 1.
18 Limited Liability Partnerships Regulations 2001, SI 2001/1090, reg 4(2)(i).
19 Limited Liability Partnerships Regulations 2001, SI 2001/1090, reg 10(1)(a), (c) (reg 10(1)(c) amended by SI 2009/1804). The following subordinate legislation is specified in the Limited Liability Partnerships Regulations 2001, SI 2001/1090, Sch 6 Pts I, III (amended by SI 2007/2073, SI 2008/1911 and SI 2009/1804) as applying with necessary modification to limited liability partnerships: the Companies Act 1985 (Power to Enter and Remain on Premises: Procedural) Regulations 2005, SI 2005/684; the Companies (Disqualification Orders) Regulations 1986, SI 1986/2067 (revoked: see now the Companies (Disqualification Orders) Regulations 2009, SI 2009/2471); the Insolvent Companies (Disqualification of Unfit Directors) Proceedings Rules 1987, SI 1987/2023; the Contracting Out (Functions of the Official Receiver) Order 1995, SI 1995/1386; the Uncertificated Securities Regulations 1995, SI 1995/3272 (revoked: see now the Uncertificated Securities Regulations 2001, SI 2001/3755); and the Insolvent Companies (Reports on Conduct of Directors) Rules 1996, SI 1996/1909: see COMPANIES; COMPANY AND PARTNERSHIP INSOLVENCY.
    In the case of any conflict between any provision of the subordinate legislation listed above and any provision of the Limited Liability Partnerships Regulations 2001, SI 2001/1090, the latter must prevail: reg 10(2).
20 Ie the Companies Act 2006 Pt 15 (ss 380–474) and Pt 16 (ss 475–539), and also ss 1210(1)(h), 1121, 1122, 1125–1132, 1157, 1161, 1162, 1169, 1172, 1173, 1288–1290, 1292, Sch 7: see COMPANIES vol 15 (2009) PARA 708 et seq.
21 Ie by virtue of the Limited Liability Partnership (Accounts and Audit) (Application of Companies Act 2006) Regulations 2008, SI 2008/1911 (amended by SI 2009/1342, SI 2009/1804, SI 2011/99, SI 2011/1043, SI 2012/1439, SI 2012/1741, SI 2012/2301, SI 2013/472, SI 2013/618 and SI 2013/2005) (made under the Limited Liability Partnerships Act 2000 s 15: see PARA 243). As to the form and contents of accounts see the Large and Medium-sized Limited Liability Partnerships (Accounts) Regulations 2008, SI 2008/1913, and the Small Limited Liability Partnerships (Accounts) Regulations 2008, SI 2008/1912, which apply certain provisions of the Large and Medium-sized Companies and Groups (Accounts and Reports) Regulations 2008, SI 2008/410 (amended by SI 2013/472), and the Small Companies and Groups (Accounts and Director's Report) Regulations 2008, SI 2008/409 (see COMPANIES vol 15 (2009) PARA 871 et seq), with modifications to limited liability partnerships.
    For the relevant fees payable to the registrar of companies see the Registrar of Companies (Fees) (Companies, Overseas Companies and Limited Liability Partnerships) Regulations 2012, SI 2012/1907.
22 Ie the Companies Act 2006 ss 43–49, 51–57, 65–76, 82, 83, 85–88, 162–165, 240–246, 738–750, 752–754, 769–771, 774–776, 778, 782, 854–855A, 858, 859A–859Q, 895–900, 993–997, 1000–1034, 1051, 1064–1066, 1077–1079, 1081, 1082, 1084–1091, 1093–1098, 1103–1107, 1112–1113, 1121, 1122, 1125–1142, 1154–1157, 1172, 1173, 1288–1290, 1292, 1297. See COMPANIES. The application to limited liability partnerships of certain provisions of Pt 35 (ss 1059A–1119) is without prejudice to the application in relation to limited liability partnerships of the provisions of Pt 35 that are of general application, ie ss 1060(1), (2), 1061–1063, 1068–1071, 1072–1076, 1080(1), (4), (5), 1083, 1092, 1108–1111 and 1114–1119: Limited Liability Partnerships (Application of Companies Act 2006) Regulations 2009, SI 2009/1804, reg 60. As to the Companies Act 2006 Pt 35 see COMPANIES vol 14 (2009) PARA 131 et seq.
23 Ie the Companies (Cross-Border Mergers) Regulations 2007, SI 2007/2974, Pts 1–3 (regs 1–21), 5 (regs 65, 66). See COMPANIES vol 15 (2009) PARA 1451.
24 Ie the Overseas Companies Regulations 2009, SI 2009/1801, regs 58(2), 59, 61, 62, 66, 67(1), (2). See COMPANIES vol 15 (2009) PARA 1832.

25 See the Limited Liability Partnerships (Application of Companies Act 2006) Regulations 2009, SI 2009/1804 (amended by SI 2009/1833, SI 2009/2476, SI 2009/2995, SI 2012/2301, SI 2013/472 and SI 2013/628); and COMPANIES.

246.   Financial services legislation.   Certain provisions of the Financial Services and Markets Act 2000[1] apply to limited liability partnerships, except where the context requires[2], with the following modifications:

(1)   references to a company include references to a limited liability partnership[3];

(2)   references to a body include references to a limited liability partnership[4];

(3)   references to the Companies Act 1985, the Insolvency Act 1986 or to any of the provisions of those Acts include references to those Acts or provisions as they apply to limited liability partnerships by virtue of the Limited Liability Partnerships Act 2000[5].

1   Ie the Financial Services and Markets Act 2000 ss 215(3), (4), (6), 356, 359(1)–(4), 361–365, 367, 370, 371 (see FINANCIAL SERVICES AND INSTITUTIONS).
2   Limited Liability Partnerships Regulations 2001, SI 2001/1090, reg 6(1), (2) (made under the Limited Liability Partnerships Act 2000 s 15: see PARA 243). As to the meaning of 'limited liability partnership' see PARA 233.
3   Limited Liability Partnerships Regulations 2001, SI 2001/1090, reg 6(2)(a).
4   Limited Liability Partnerships Regulations 2001, SI 2001/1090, reg 6(2)(b).
5   Limited Liability Partnerships Regulations 2001, SI 2001/1090, reg 6(2)(c). As to the application of the Companies Act 1985 to limited liability partnerships see PARA 245. As to the application of the Insolvency Act 1986 to limited liability partnerships see PARA 244.

247–300.   Taxation of limited liability partnerships.   The application of the tax legislation to limited liability partnerships is dealt with elsewhere in this work[1].

1   See CAPITAL GAINS TAXATION vol 6 (2011) PARA 831; INCOME TAXATION vol 59 (2014) PARA 1943 et seq; INHERITANCE TAXATION.

PATENTS AND REGISTERED DESIGNS

1. THE PATENT SYSTEM

(1) INTRODUCTION

301. Rationale of the patent system. The purpose of the patent system is to encourage innovation and the improvement of industrial techniques[1]. In return for the disclosure of his invention[2] the inventor[3] is given a monopoly in the use of it for a period of 20 years[4] after which time it passes into the public domain.

It is not mandatory to obtain a patent[5] in order to protect a new invention; the inventor may instead choose to keep the details secret. Indeed, not all technical developments are patentable[6]. Tricks of the trade, detailed process specifications and modes of operation which do not involve an inventive step[7] may, therefore, be unpatentable, although they are capable of protection as trade secrets or know-how[8]. As a matter of public policy, discoveries, scientific theories and mathematical methods are not patentable[9]. Products whose novelty resides in the design and not in the function are not patentable[10] but may be protected either as a registered design[11] or by means of copyright[12] or by means of unregistered design right[13].

1 See the Report of the Banks Committee on the British Patent System 1970 (Cmnd 4407) para 1; White Paper on Patent Law Reform 1975 (Cmnd 6000) paras 1–4; Gowers Review of Intellectual Property (December 2006) paras 1.4–1.8.

2 The Patents Act 1977 does not define 'invention' but instead prescribes the criteria to be satisfied by a 'patentable invention': see s 1(1); and PARA 429. For the purposes of the Patents Act 1977, however, an invention for a patent for which an application has been made or for which a patent has been granted is, unless the context otherwise requires, taken to be that specified in a claim of the specification of the application or patent, as the case may be, as interpreted by the description and any drawings contained in that specification; and the extent of the protection conferred by a patent or application for a patent is to be determined accordingly: s 125(1).

3 For these purposes, 'inventor' means, in relation to an invention, the actual deviser of the invention; and 'joint inventor' is to be construed accordingly: Patents Act 1977 s 7(3). Where a person comes up with and communicates an idea consisting of all the elements in a claim, even though it is just an idea at that stage, he is normally an inventor: *Stanelco Fibre Optics Ltd's Applications* [2004] EWHC 2263 (Pat), [2005] RPC 319. To be regarded as an inventor a person must have been responsible for the inventive concept and have contributed to that invention: *Henry Bros (Magherafelt) Ltd v Ministry of Defence and Northern Ireland Office* [1997] RPC 693 (affd [1999] RPC 442, [1998] All ER (D) 545, CA); *Markem Corpn v Zipher Ltd* [2005] EWCA Civ 267, [2005] RPC 761; *University of Southampton's Applications* [2006] EWCA Civ 145, [2006] RPC 567; *Yeda Research and Development Co Ltd v Rhone-Poulenc Rorer International Holdings Inc* [2007] UKHL 43, [2008] 1 All ER 425, [2008] RPC 1.

4 As to the term of patents see PARA 338 et seq.

5 As to the meaning of 'patent' see PARA 303.

6 As to the criteria of patentability in respect of inventions see the Patents Act 1977 s 1(1); and PARA 429.

7 It is a criterion of patentability that the invention involves an inventive step: see the Patents Act 1977 s 1(1)(b); and PARA 429.

8 Trade secrets, know-how and non-patented inventions may be protected by means of a claim for breach of confidence: see EQUITABLE JURISDICTION vol 47 (2014) PARA 232. Information of a confidential nature, supplied for one purpose, may not be used by the recipient for other purposes to the detriment of the owner of the information: *Cranleigh Precision Engineering Ltd v Bryant* [1964] 3 All ER 289, [1965] 1 WLR 1293, [1966] RPC 81.

9 See the Patents Act 1977 s 1(2)(a); and PARA 430.

10 See the Patents Act 1977 s 1(2)(b); and PARA 430.

11 Ie as a design registered under the Registered Designs Act 1949: see PARA 657 et seq. The effect of registration is to give to the registered proprietor the exclusive right of commercial exploitation of the registered design: see s 7(1); and PARA 738.

12 See COPYRIGHT vol 23 (2013) PARA 603.
13 See COPYRIGHT vol 23 (2013) PARA 610.

302. Historical development of the patent system. Patents giving monopolies for new inventions were first granted by Elizabeth I to encourage the establishment of new industries within the realm. The power to grant such monopolies was abused by the Stuarts and in 1623 Parliament secured the passing of the Statute of Monopolies[1], which restricted monopolies already granted[2] and prohibited the granting of new monopolies, except to the true and first inventors of a manner of new manufacture, which others at the time of the grant were not using[3]. Modern patent legislation[4] dates from the establishment of the Patent Office in 1853[5] and the Patents, Designs and Trade Marks Act 1883[6], which established the practice of examination by the Patent Office of the patent specification before grant[7]. The official search through prior specifications to establish novelty[8] dates from the Patents and Designs Act 1907[9]. A major recasting of the statutory provisions took place in 1949 in the Patents Act 1949[10]. In respect of patents granted on applications filed on or after 1 June 1978[11] the Patents Act 1949 was replaced by the Patents Act 1977, which continues to be the principal statute in this area.

To obtain protection of patent rights outside the United Kingdom, an application must normally be made to the national offices in the individual countries. Protection can be obtained throughout Europe by application to the European Patent Office under the European Patent Convention[12], and provision is made in connection with the issuing of unitary patents in the EU, which will ultimately replace the European Patent Convention and the existing national systems within the EU[13]. Patent protection may be facilitated in many other countries through the Patent Co-operation Treaty[14].

1 Ie the Statute of Monopolies (1623), now largely superseded, but see s 6; and note 3.
2 Statute of Monopolies (1623) s 1.
3 Statute of Monopolies (1623) s 6. The grant was for a term not exceeding 14 years: s 6. As to the term of modern patents see PARA 338 et seq.
4 As to current legislation generally see PARA 304.
5 Ie under the Patent Law Amendment Act 1852 (repealed). As to the Patent Office see now PARA 577.
6 This Act has been repealed.
7 For the modern procedure see PARA 327–328.
8 See PARA 328.
9 Much of this Act has been repealed: see PARA 304.
10 A patent under the Patents Act 1949 was a grant from the Crown of a monopoly and was a matter of the Sovereign's grace. The patent was granted in a form authorised by rules made under statutory power, and was sealed with the seal of the Patent Office, which had the same effect as if the patent were sealed, as patents used to be, with the Great Seal of the United Kingdom: see the Patents Act 1949 s 21 (repealed). A patent under the Patents Act 1949 had effect throughout the United Kingdom and the Isle of Man.
11 Ie the date on which the Patents Act 1977 largely came into force: see PARA 304.
12 Ie the Convention on the Grant of European Patents (Munich, 5 October 1973; TS 20 (1978); Cmnd 7090): see PARA 644 et seq.
13 See PARA 645.
14 Ie the Patent Co-operation Treaty (Washington, 19 June 1970; TS 78 (1978); Cmnd 7340): see PARA 629 et seq.

303. Meaning of 'patent'. The word 'patent'[1] as used in this title denotes a monopoly right in respect of an invention. A patent is a collection of rights conferred by the Patents Act 1977 in respect of a patentable invention[2]. A certificate that a patent has been granted is in a form authorised by rules made pursuant to the Act[3] and must include the name of the proprietor, the date of filing of the application and the number of the patent[4]. A patent has effect throughout the United Kingdom[5] and the Isle of Man[6].

Patents and applications for them are personal property but without being things in action[7].

1   The term 'patent' (short for 'letters patent') is derived from the fact that the forms of grant were literae patentes, or open letters, being addressed to all to whom they may come. The term now bears none of its original meaning and the 'grant' is purely notional: see PARA 337. As to current legislation generally see PARA 304.
    In the Patents Act 1977 'patent' means a patent under that Act (s 130(1)). As to the meaning of 'invention' see PARA 301 note 3. The term 'patent' also includes, unless the context otherwise requires, a patent granted on an international application for a patent (UK) (ie an application filed under the Patent Co-operation Treaty (Washington, 19 June to 31 December 1970; TS 78 (1978); Cmnd 7340)), which is treated as an application under the Patents Act 1977: see s 89; and PARA 640. Similarly, a European patent (UK) (ie a patent granted under the Convention on the Grant of European Patents (Munich, 5 October 1973; TS 20 (1978); Cmnd 7090) (the European Patent Convention) designating the United Kingdom: see PARA 644 et seq) is treated as a patent granted under the Patents Act 1977: see s 77; and PARA 652.
2   See the Patents Act 1977 s 60 (acts which, if done without the consent of the proprietor of the patent, infringe the patent: see PARA 511). As to the meaning of 'patentable invention' see PARA 429.
3   See the Patents Act 1977 s 24(2); and PARA 337.
4   See the Patents Rules 2007, SI 2007/3291, r 34; and PARA 337.
5   'United Kingdom' means Great Britain and Northern Ireland: Interpretation Act 1978 s 5, Sch 1. 'Great Britain' means England, Scotland and Wales: Union with Scotland Act 1706 preamble art 1; Interpretation Act 1978 s 22(1), Sch 2 para 5(a). Neither the Isle of Man nor the Channel Islands are within the United Kingdom. The Patents Act 1977 does, however, extend to the Isle of Man, subject to any modifications contained in an Order made by Her Majesty in Council and accordingly, subject to any such order, references in the Patents Act 1977 to the United Kingdom are to be construed as including references to the Isle of Man: s 132(2). In exercise of the power so conferred the Patents (Isle of Man) Order 2013, SI 2013/2602, has been made. As to the territorial scope of the legislation generally see PARA 305.
6   See the Patents Act 1977 s 132(2).
7   Patents Act 1977 s 30(1). This reverses the position at common law, where a patent was held to be in the nature of a chose in action: see CHOSES IN ACTION vol 13 (2009) PARA 9. As to patents as personal property see PERSONAL PROPERTY vol 80 (2013) PARA 805.

(2) LEGISLATION

304.   Legislation in force. The legislation relating to patents consists primarily of the Patents Act 1977 and subordinate legislation made thereunder, which applies in respect of patents granted on applications filed on or after 1 June 1978[1]. The Act established a new code of domestic patent law and gives effect in the United Kingdom[2] to certain international conventions and treaties[3]. It fulfils two principal functions:

(1)   to harmonise internal United Kingdom patent law with European law[4] and to enable international applications filed through the Patent Co-operation Treaty[5] to enter the United Kingdom patent system[6]; and

(2)   to modernise United Kingdom patent law[7].

The Patents Act 1977 does not, however, form a complete code[8]. Many of the expressions in it are only intelligible by reference to decisions under earlier Acts[9], and many matters are covered by rules of practice[10]. Details of the UK Intellectual Property Office procedure are in large part laid down by the Patents Rules 2007[11]. In addition, certain agreements relating to patents are covered by European and international law[12].

1   See the Patents Act 1977 (Commencement No 2) Order 1978, SI 1978/586, which brought the operative provisions of the Patents Act 1977 into force on 1 June 1978. No application for a patent could be made under the legislation replaced by the Patents Act 1977, ie the Patents Act 1949, on or after that date: see the Patents Act 1977 s 127(1). Existing patents granted under the Patents Act 1949 expired after a 20-year period (see the Patents Act 1977 Sch 1 para 4) and so the provisions of the Patents Act 1949 which were preserved by the Patents Act 1977 to govern such patents have lapsed, all such patents having expired. The remainder of the Patents Act 1949 was repealed: see the Patents Act 1977 ss 127(5), 132(7), Schs 3, 6. As to the historical development of the patent system see PARA 302.

2   As to the meaning of 'United Kingdom' see PARA 303 note 5.

3   Ie the Patent Co-operation Treaty (Washington, 19 June to 31 December 1970; TS 78 (1978); Cmnd 7340) (see PARAS 629–639); the Convention on the Grant of European Patents (Munich, 5 October 1973; TS 20 (1978); Cmnd 7090) (see PARA 644 et seq); and the Patent Law Treaty (Geneva, 1 June 2000; TS 6 (2006); Cm 6779) (see PARA 656).

4   See PARA 644 et seq.

5   See note 3.

6   See the Patents Act 1977 ss 89–89B; and PARAS 640–643.

7   See generally the White Paper on Patent Law Reform 1975 (Cmnd 6000).

8   Certain other enactments directly relate to patent law: eg the Patents and Designs Act 1907 ss 62–64 (see PARA 577); the Patents, Designs, Copyright and Trade Marks (Emergency) Act 1939 (see PARAS 390, 400, 704; and ARMED CONFLICT AND EMERGENCY vol 3 (2011) PARA 208); the Crown Proceedings Act 1947 s 3 (see PARAS 403, 524; and CROWN PROCEEDINGS AND CROWN PRACTICE vol 12(1) (Reissue) PARA 113); and the Corporation Tax Act 2009 Pt 9 (ss 907–931) (see INCOME TAXATION vol 59 (2014) PARAS 2031–2035).

9   This is notably so in the provisions concerned with invalidity (see PARA 429 et seq).

10 Some such matters are reported, as official rulings or as decisions upon individual cases, in the Reports of Patent Cases (RPC) (see PARA 578); some are unpublished.

11 Ie the Patents Rules 2007, SI 2007/3291. See also the Manual of Patent Practice; and PARA 578.

12 See PARA 628 et seq.

305.   Territorial scope of legislation.   The patents legislation[1] has effect throughout the United Kingdom[2] and the Isle of Man, subject to relevant geographical modifications[3]. For the purposes of the Patents Act 1977, the territorial waters of the United Kingdom are treated as part of the United Kingdom[4]; and the Patents Act 1977 applies to acts done in an area designated by order under the Continental Shelf Act 1964[5] or specified by Order under the Petroleum Act 1998[6] as they apply to acts done in the United Kingdom[7].

It would seem that a United Kingdom patent is property situated in the United Kingdom[8].

1   As to current legislation generally see PARA 304.

2   As to the meaning of 'United Kingdom' see PARA 303 note 5.

3   See the Patents Act 1977 s 131 (amended by the Companies Consolidation (Consequential Provisions) Act 1985 Sch 2; the Arbitration Act 1996 Sch 4; and the Patents Act 2004 Sch 2 paras 1, 28); the Patents Act 1977 s 131A (added by SI 1999/1820); the Patents Act 1977 s 132(2); and the Patents (Isle of Man) Order 2013, SI 2013/2602.

4   Patents Act 1977 s 132(3). As to territorial waters generally see INTERNATIONAL RELATIONS LAW vol 61 (2010) PARA 121 et seq.

5   Ie an area designated by Order in Council under the Continental Shelf Act 1964 s 1(7): see ENERGY AND CLIMATE CHANGE vol 44 (2011) PARA 1040.

6   Ie an area specified by Order in Council under the Petroleum Act 1998 s 10(8) in connection with any activity falling within s 11(2): see ENERGY AND CLIMATE CHANGE vol 44 (2011) PARAS 1079–1080.

7   Patents Act 1977 s 132(4) (amended by the Oil and Gas (Enterprise) Act 1982 Sch 3 para 39; and the Petroleum Act 1998 Sch 4 para 14).

8   Cf *English, Scottish and Australian Bank Ltd v IRC* [1932] AC 238 at 249, HL. This case, which concerned the locality of simple contract debts, overruled *Smelting Co of Australia Ltd v IRC* [1897] 1 QB 175, CA, where it had been held that patent rights are not capable of having a local situation.

2. GRANT AND DURATION OF PATENT

(1) APPLICANTS AND APPLICATIONS

(i) The Applicant

306. Right to apply for and obtain a patent. Any person[1] may make an application for a patent[2] either alone or jointly with another[3]. A patent for an invention[4] may, however, be granted:

(1)   primarily to the inventor[5] or joint inventors[6];

(2)   in preference to the inventor or joint inventors, to any person or persons who, by virtue of any enactment or rule of law, or any foreign law or treaty or international convention, or by virtue of an enforceable term of any agreement entered into with the inventor before the making of the invention, was or were at the time of the making of the invention entitled to the whole of the property in it, other than equitable interests, in the United Kingdom[7];

(3)   in any event, to the successor or successors in title of any person or persons mentioned in head (1) or head (2) above or any person so mentioned and the successor or successors in title of another person so mentioned[8],

and to no other person[9].

Except so far as the contrary is established, a person who makes an application for a patent is taken to be the person who is entitled to be so granted a patent and two or more persons who make such an application jointly are to be taken to be the persons so entitled[10].

1   'Person' includes a body of persons corporate or unincorporate: Interpretation Act 1978 ss 5, 22(1), Sch 1, Sch 2 para 4(1)(a).
2   Ie under the Patents Act 1977: see PARA 303. As to the application see PARA 314.
3   Patents Act 1977 s 7(1). As to co-ownership of patents see PARA 371.
4   As to the meaning of 'invention' see PARA 301 note 2.
5   As to the meaning of 'inventor' see PARA 301 note 3.
6   Patents Act 1977 s 7(2)(a). As to the right of the inventor or joint inventors to be mentioned in the patent or the application for it see PARA 307. As to the meaning of 'joint inventor' see PARA 301 note 3.
7   Patents Act 1977 s 7(2)(b). For an example of an enactment giving such entitlement see s 39 (employer's right to employee's invention); and PARA 368; and in connection with the operation of s 7(2)(b) by virtue of a confidentiality agreement see *KCI Licensing Inc v Smith and Nephew plc* [2010] EWHC 1487 (Pat), [2010] FSR 740, [2010] All ER (D) 207 (Jun) (revsd on other grounds [2010] EWCA Civ 1260, [2011] FSR 226, 117 BMLR 81). As to the meaning of 'United Kingdom' see PARA 303 note 5.
8   Patents Act 1977 s 7(2)(c).
9   Patents Act 1977 s 7(2). The provisions of the Patents Act 1977 s 7 form an exhaustive code in determining who is entitled to the grant of a patent: *Yeda Research and Development Co Ltd v Rhone-Poulenc Rorer International Holdings Inc* [2007] UKHL 43, [2008] 1 All ER 425, [2008] RPC 1.
10   Patents Act 1977 s 7(4). As to the determination of questions relating to entitlement see PARA 360 et seq.

307. Mention of the inventor. The inventor or joint inventors[1] of an invention[2] have a right to be mentioned as such in any patent granted for the invention[3]. They also have a right to be so mentioned, if possible, in any published application[4] for a patent for the invention[5] and, if not so mentioned, a right to be so mentioned in an addendum or erratum slip[6].

Unless he has already given the UK Intellectual Property Office[7] the following information, an applicant for a patent must, within the prescribed period[8], file with the UK Intellectual Property Office a statement in the prescribed form[9] identifying the person or persons whom he believes to be the inventor or inventors[10] and, where the applicant is not the sole inventor or the applicants are not the joint inventors, indicating the derivation of his or their right to be granted the patent[11]. Where he fails to do so, the application is taken to be withdrawn[12]. Where a person has been so mentioned as sole or joint inventor, any other person who alleges that the former ought not to have been so mentioned may at any time apply to the Comptroller General of Patents, Designs and Trade Marks for a certificate to that effect and the Comptroller may issue a certificate[13]. If the comptroller does so issue a certificate, he must rectify accordingly any undistributed copies of the patent and of any addendum or erratum slips[14].

The inventor[15] may, before preparations for the application's publication have been completed by the UK Intellectual Property Office, apply to the comptroller[16] in writing to waive his right: (1) to have his name and address mentioned as those of the inventor[17]; or (2) to have his address mentioned as that of the inventor[18]. Where the comptroller has accepted an inventor's application to make a waiver, the inventor may apply to the comptroller to end that waiver[19]. The comptroller may, if he thinks fit, accept an application to end a waiver, and his acceptance may be made subject to such conditions as he may direct[20].

1 　As to the meanings of 'inventor' and 'joint inventor' see PARA 301 note 3.

2 　As to the meaning of 'invention' see PARA 301 note 2.

3 　Patents Act 1977 s 13(1). A person who alleges that any person ought to have been mentioned as the inventor or joint inventor of an invention may apply to the comptroller for that person to be so mentioned: (1) in any patent granted for the invention; and (2) if possible in any published application for a patent for the invention, and, if not so mentioned, in the manner prescribed by the Patents Rules 2007, SI 2007/3291, r 10(1) (see the text to note 6): r 10(2). As to the comptroller see PARA 575; and as to applications to the comptroller see PARA 347 et seq.

4 　As to the publication of applications see the Patents Act 1977 s 16; and PARA 326.

5 　Patents Act 1977 s 13(1).

6 　Patents Act 1977 s 13(1); Patents Rules 2007, SI 2007/3291, r 10(1).

7 　As to the UK Intellectual Property Office: see PARA 577.

8 　Subject to the provisions of the Patents Rules 2007, SI 2007/3291, r 21 (extensions for new applications), r 58(4) (see PARA 655), r 59(3) (see PARA 655) and r 68(2), the period prescribed for the purposes of the Patents Act 1977 s 13(2) is 16 months beginning immediately after: (1) where there is no declared priority date, the date of filing of the application; or (2) where there is a declared priority date, that date: Patents Rules 2007, SI 2007/3291, r 10(3) (amended by SI 2011/2052). As to the extension of time limits see PARA 597. As to the meaning of 'declared priority date' see PARA 310 note 9; and as to the meaning of 'date of filing' see PARA 315.

　　Where a new application is filed under the Patents Act 1977 s 8(3) (see PARA 361), s 12(6) (see PARA 363) or s 37(4) (see PARA 365) or as mentioned in s 15(9) (see PARA 316), the period prescribed for the purposes of s 13(2) is two months beginning immediately after its initiation date, or if it expires later, the period prescribed by the Patents Rules 2007, SI 2007/3291, r 10(3), and the reference in r 10(3) to the date of filing of the application is a reference to the date of filing of the earlier application: r 21(1)(a) (amended by SI 2011/2052). But where the new application is filed less than six months before the compliance date the period prescribed for the purposes of the Patents Act 1977 s 13(2) is the period ending with its initiation date: Patents Rules 2007, SI 2007/3291, r 21(2)(a). The second requirement in Sch 1 (see PARA 321) must be complied with on the initiation date or, if it expires later, before the end of the relevant period specified in Sch 1 para 3(3) (see PARA 321): r 21(3). 'Initiation date' means the date on which a new application was initiated by documents, mentioned in the Patents Act 1977 s 15(1) (see PARA 315), being filed at the UK Intellectual Property Office (see note 7): Patents Rules 2007, SI 2007/3291, r 2(1).

Where an international application for a patent (UK) has begun the national phase of the application (see PARA 641), the period prescribed for the purposes of the Patents Act 1977 s 13(2) is the period prescribed by the Patents Rules 2007, SI 2007/3291, r 10(3) or, if it expires later, the period of two months beginning immediately after the date on which the national phase begins: r 68(1), (2) (amended by SI 2011/2052).

9   A statement filed under the Patents Act 1977 s 13(2) must be made on Patents Form 7: Patents Rules 2007, SI 2007/3291, r 10(4).

10   Patents Act 1977 s 13(2)(a).

11   Patents Act 1977 s 13(2)(b). As to the consequence of failure to file a statement where required see *Nippon Piston Ring Co Ltd's Applications* [1987] RPC 120; and PARA 331.

12   Patents Act 1977 s 13(2).

13   Patents Act 1977 s 13(3).

14   Patents Act 1977 s 13(3); Patents Rules 2007, SI 2007/3291, r 10(1).

15   An application to waive the right to be mentioned may also be made by a person who is not the inventor, but who has been identified as such for the purposes of the Patents Act 1977 s 13(2): Patents Rules 2007, SI 2007/3291, r 11(6). Where a person makes an application in reliance on r 11(6), the reference to an application to waive his right to have his name and address (or his address) mentioned is to be construed as a reference to an application not to have his name and address (or his address) mentioned; and the provisions of r 11(4), (5) are to be construed accordingly: r 11(7).

16   As to the comptroller see PARA 575.

17   Patents Rules 2007, SI 2007/3291, r 11(1)(a). An application by an inventor under head (1) in the text must include his reasons for making the application, and be accepted by the comptroller where the comptroller is satisfied by those reasons: r 11(2).

18   Patents Rules 2007, SI 2007/3291, r 11(1)(b). An application by an inventor under head (2) in the text must be accepted by the comptroller: r 11(3).

19   Patents Rules 2007, SI 2007/3291, r 11(4).

20   Patents Rules 2007, SI 2007/3291, r 11(5).

(ii) Priority Dates

308. The priority date. For the purpose of ascertaining whether an invention[1] which is the subject of a patent or an application for a patent is new[2] or lacks an inventive step[3] or has been anticipated by some other applicant for a patent, it is necessary to assign to the invention a date at which these questions are to be judged. That date is known as the 'priority date'[4]. Where more than one invention is specified in an application, each invention may have a different priority date, whether or not it is the subject of a separate claim[5]. Further, in view of the provisions relating to novelty[6], it is necessary to assign a priority date not only to the claims, but also to the matter disclosed[7] by patent specifications.

1   As to the meaning of 'invention' see PARA 301 note 2.

2   As to novelty see PARA 434 et seq.

3   As to lack of inventive step see PARA 451 et seq.

4   As to the meaning of 'priority date' see PARA 310 note 6.

5   Patents Act 1977 s 125(2).

6   See the Patents Act 1977 s 2(3); and PARA 434.

7   As to what constitutes disclosure of matter see PARA 310 note 8.

309. Priority date in case of obtaining. Where a patent has been applied for by or is granted to a wrongful applicant[1], provision is made for allowing the true owner of the invention[2] to be accorded for his own application the date of filing[3] of the application which would result or has resulted in the wrongful grant[4]. To secure for the rightful owner of the invention the wrongful applicant's priority date[5] where that is earlier than the wrongful applicant's date of filing, although possible, is, however, a matter of some complexity[6].

1   As to persons who may apply for and obtain a patent see PARA 306.

2   As to the meaning of 'invention' see PARA 301 note 2.

3 As to the meaning of 'date of filing' see PARA 315.
4 See the Patents Act 1977 s 8(3) (pending applications: see PARA 361) and s 37(4) (wrongful grant: see PARA 365).
5 As to the meaning of 'priority date' see PARA 310 note 6.
6 It would seem necessary in general to apply under the Patents Act 1977 s 8 (see PARA 360), as soon as the wrongful application is published both in respect of the wrongful application itself and for authority to make an application, back-dated, corresponding to each application from which priority is sought.

310. Ascertainment of priority date. If in, or in connection with, an application for a patent[1] (the 'application in suit'), a declaration of priority is made[2], whether by the applicant or any predecessor in title of his, specifying one or more relevant applications[3] made by the applicant or any predecessor in title of his and each having a date of filing[4] during the period allowed[5], then:

(1) the priority date[6] of the invention[7] to which the application in suit relates is the date of filing of the relevant application or, if there are more than one, of the earliest of them, provided that the invention is supported by matter disclosed[8] in the earlier relevant application or applications[9];

(2) the priority date of any matter contained in the application in suit is the date of filing the relevant application, or the earliest relevant application if there is more than one, provided that the matter was disclosed in the earlier relevant application or applications[10].

Where there is no declaration of priority, the priority date of an invention to which an application for a patent relates and also of any matter, whether or not the same as the invention, contained in the application is the date of filing the application[11].

The above provisions also apply for determining the priority date of an invention for which a patent has been granted as they apply for determining the priority date of an invention to which an application for that patent relates[12].

1 Ie under the Patents Act 1977: see PARA 303.
2 Ie under the Patents Act 1977 s 5(2). A declaration for the purposes of s 5(2) must be made at the time of filing the application for a patent: Patents Rules 2007, SI 2007/3291, r 6(1). Subject to r 7(9) (see note 5), a declaration for the purposes of the Patents Act 1977 s 5(2) may be made after the date of filing provided that it is made on Patents Form 3, it is made before the end of the period of 16 months beginning immediately following the date of filing of the earlier relevant application (or if there is more than one, the earliest of them) specified in that, or any earlier, declaration and the applicant has not made a request under the Patents Act 1977 s 16(1) for publication of the application during the prescribed period (see PARA 326) or any request made was withdrawn before preparations for the application's publication have been completed by the UK Intellectual Property Office: Patents Rules 2007, SI 2007/3291, r 6(2), (3). The prescribed time limit may not be extended: see PARA 597. As to the UK Intellectual Property Office see PARA 577.

In respect of every priority application, except where the application in suit is an international application for a patent (UK) and the application number of the priority application was indicated in compliance with the Patent Co-operation Treaty (ie the Patent Co-operation Treaty (Washington, 19 June 1970; TS 78 (1978); Cmnd 7340): see PARA 629 et seq), the applicant must, before the end of the period of 16 months beginning immediately after the declared priority date (subject to the Patents Rules 2007, SI 2007/3291, r 21), furnish to the comptroller the application number of that application; otherwise the comptroller must disregard the declaration made for the purposes of the Patents Act 1977 s 5(2), in so far as it relates to the priority application: Patents Rules 2007, SI 2007/3291, r 8(1), (3), (5) (amended by SI 2011/2052). Where a new application is filed under the Patents Act 1977 s 8(3) (see PARA 361), s 12(6) (see PARA 363) or s 37(4) (see PARA 365) or as mentioned in s 15(9) (see PARA 316), the relevant period for the purposes of the Patents Rules 2007, SI 2007/3291, r 8 is two months beginning immediately after its initiation date or, if it expires later, the 16 month period specified in r 8(5): r 21(1)(b) (amended by SI 2011/2052). But where the new application is filed less than six months before the compliance date the relevant period for the purposes of the Patents Rules 2007, SI 2007/3291, r 8 is the period ending with its initiation date: r 21(2)(b). As to the meaning of 'initiation date' see PARA 307 note 8. As to the comptroller see PARA 575.

In respect of every priority application, except where the application in suit is an international application for a patent (UK) and a certified copy of the priority application was filed in compliance with the Patent Co-operation Treaty, or the priority application or a copy of the priority application is available to the comptroller, the applicant must, before the end of the period of 16 months beginning with the declared priority date (subject to the Patents Rules 2007, SI 2007/3291, r 21), furnish to the comptroller a copy of that application duly certified by the authority with which it was filed, or otherwise verified to the satisfaction of the comptroller, otherwise the comptroller must disregard the declaration made for the purposes of the Patents Act 1977 s 5(2), in so far as it relates to the priority application: Patents Rules 2007, SI 2007/3291, r 8(2), (4), (5) (amended by SI 2011/2052). As to the meaning of 'international application for a patent (UK)' see PARA 640 note 1. As to the translation of priority documents see the Patents Rules 2007, SI 2007/3291, r 9.

For the purposes of the Patents Rules 2007, SI 2007/3291, a document is available to the comptroller where: (1) it is in electronic storage (whether in the UK Intellectual Property Office or elsewhere) and he can access it by using electronic communications; or (2) it is kept at the UK Intellectual Property Office, and he has been furnished with sufficient information to obtain a copy of the document: r 2(3). But a document may be treated as unavailable to the comptroller where: (a) its accuracy cannot be verified to his satisfaction; or (b) he has to pay to access it: r 2(4).

3   As to the meaning of 'relevant application' see PARA 311.
4   As to the meaning of 'date of filing' see PARA 315. The declaration under the Patents Act 1977 s 5(2) (see the text and note 2) must specify the date of filing of each earlier relevant application and the country it was filed in or in respect of: Patents Rules 2007, SI 2007/3291, r 6(4).

The comptroller may extend any period of time specified in the Patents Act 1977 or the Patents Rules 2007, SI 2007/3291, where he is satisfied that the failure to do something under the Act or the Rules was wholly or mainly attributable to a delay in, or failure of, a communication service: r 111(1). Any such extension must be made after giving the parties such notice and subject to such conditions as the comptroller may direct: r 111(2). 'Communication service' means a service by which documents may be sent and delivered and includes post, electronic communications, and courier: r 111(3).

5   Ie the period allowed under the Patents Act 1977 s 5(2A)(a) or (b): s 5(2) (s 5(2) amended, s 5(2A)–(2C) added, by SI 2004/2357). The periods are: (1) the period of 12 months immediately following the date of filing of the earlier specified relevant application, or if there is more than one, of the earliest of them; and (2) where the comptroller has given permission under the Patents Act 1977 s 5(2B) for a late declaration to be made under s 5(2), the period commencing immediately after the end of the period allowed under head (1) above and ending at the end of the prescribed period: s 5(2A) (as so added). The applicant may make a request to the comptroller for permission to make a late declaration under s 5(2): s 5(2B) (as so added). The comptroller must grant a request made under s 5(2B) if, and only if the request complies with the relevant requirements of rules and the comptroller is satisfied that the applicant's failure to file the application in suit within the period allowed under head (1) above was unintentional: s 5(2C) (as so added). For a discussion of unintentional failure see *Sirna Therapeutics Inc's Application* [2006] RPC 351; *Re Abaco Machines (Australasia) Pty Ltd* [2007] EWHC 347 (Pat), [2007] Bus LR 897.

The period prescribed for the purposes of the Patents Act 1977 s 5(2A)(b) (see head (2) above) is two months: Patents Rules 2007, SI 2007/3291, r 7(1). The prescribed time limit may not be extended: see PARA 597. A request under the Patents Act 1977 s 5(2B) must be made on Patents Form 3 and supported by evidence of why the application in suit was not filed before the end of the period allowed under the Patents Act 1977 s 5(2A)(a) (see head (1) above): Patents Rules 2007, SI 2007/3291, r 7(2). Where that evidence does not accompany the request, the comptroller must specify a period within which the evidence must be filed: r 7(3). In relation to a new application, a request under the Patents Act 1977 s 5(2B) may be made in writing, instead of on Patents Form 3, and no evidence need accompany it: Patents Rules 2007, SI 2007/3291, r 7(4). A request under the Patents Act 1977 s 5(2B) may only be made before the end of the period allowed under s 5(2A)(b) (see head (2) above): Patents Rules 2007, SI 2007/3291, r 7(5). However, where a new application is filed after the end of that period, a request under the Patents Act 1977 s 5(2B) may be made on the initiation date: Patents Rules 2007, SI 2007/3291, r 7(6).

Where an international application for a patent (UK) has begun the national phase (see PARA 640 et seq), a request for permission to make a late declaration may be made under the Patents

Act 1977 s 5(2B) before the end of the period of one month beginning immediately after the date the national phase of the application begins: Patents Rules 2007, SI 2007/3291, r 66(3) (amended by SI 2011/2052). The prescribed time limit may not be extended: see PARA 597. A request under the Patents Act 1977 s 5(2B) may only be made where the request is made in relation to an international application for a patent (UK) (see PARA 640 et seq) or where the applicant has not made a request under s 16(1) (see PARA 326) for publication of the application during the period prescribed for the purposes of that provision or any request made was withdrawn before preparations for the application's publication have been completed by the UK Intellectual Property Office: Patents Rules 2007, SI 2007/3291, r 7(8). Where an applicant makes a request under the Patents Act 1977 s 5(2B), he must make the declaration for the purposes of s 5(2) at the same time as making that request: Patents Rules 2007, SI 2007/3291, r 7(9).

6 'Priority date' means the date determined as such under the Patents Act 1977 s 5: s 130(1). In connection with the priority date see *Hospira UK v Novartis AG* [2013] EWCA Civ 1663, [2013] All ER (D) 251 (Dec).

7 As to the meaning of 'invention' see PARA 301 note 2.

8 Matter is taken to have been disclosed in any relevant application if it was either claimed or disclosed, other than by way of a disclaimer or acknowledgment of prior art, in that application: Patents Act 1977 s 130(3). As to the meaning of 'supported by' see PARA 313.

9 Patents Act 1977 s 5(2)(a). 'Declared priority date' means the date of filing of the earliest relevant application specified in a declaration made for the purposes of s 5(2) in, or in connection with, an application in suit: Patents Rules 2007, SI 2007/3291, rr 2(1), 3(1). For these purposes there is 'no declared priority date' if: (1) no declaration has been made for the purposes of the Patents Act 1977 s 5(2); or (2) every declaration made has been withdrawn or disregarded before the end of the relevant period: Patents Rules 2007, SI 2007/3291, r 3(2). The relevant period ends: (a) in the case of an application which falls to be treated as an application for a patent under the Patents Act 1977 by virtue of a direction under s 81 (see PARA 655), when that direction is given; (b) in the case of an international application for a patent (UK), when the national phase of the application begins (see PARA 640 et seq); or (c) in any other case, when preparations for the application's publication have been completed by the UK Intellectual Property Office: Patents Rules 2007, SI 2007/3291, r 3(3). References to declarations made for the purposes of the Patents Act 1977 s 5(2) include declarations treated as made for those purposes: Patents Rules 2007, SI 2007/3291, r 3(4).

10 Patents Act 1977 s 5(2)(b). See also note 9.

11 Patents Act 1977 s 5(1).

12 Patents Act 1977 s 5(4).

311. Relevant applications. For the purposes of a declaration of priority[1] 'relevant application' means:

(1) an application for a patent under the Patents Act 1977[2];

(2) an application in or for a convention country[3] for protection in respect of an invention or an application which, in accordance with the law of a convention country or a treaty or international convention to which a convention country is a party, is equivalent to such an application[4]; or

(3) an application in or for a country (other than the United Kingdom) which is a member of the World Trade Organisation for protection in respect of an invention which, in accordance with the law of that country or a treaty or international obligation to which it is a party, is equivalent to an application for a patent under the Patents Act 1977[5].

1 Ie a declaration under the Patents Act 1977 s 5(2): see PARA 310.

2 Patents Act 1977 s 5(5)(a). As to domestic applications see s 14; and PARA 314.

3 As to convention countries see PARA 628. As to the meaning of 'United Kingdom' see PARA 303 note 5. As to the World Trade Organisation see INTERNATIONAL RELATIONS LAW vol 61 (2010) PARA 461.

4 Patents Act 1977 s 5(5)(b) (s 5(5)(aa) added, s 5(5)(b) amended, by the Intellectual Property Act 2014 Schedule para 1)). A German design application which protects the aesthetic character of an article is not an application 'in respect of' an invention and priority cannot be claimed from it: *Agfa-Gevaert AG's Application* [1982] RPC 441.

5 Patents Act 1977 s 5(5)(aa) (as added: see note 4).

312. Effect of disclosure in earlier relevant application. Where an invention[1] or other matter contained in the application in suit was also disclosed[2] in two earlier relevant applications[3] filed by the same applicant as in the case of the application in suit or a predecessor in title of his and the second of those relevant applications was specified in or in connection with the application in suit[4], the second of the relevant applications must be disregarded, so far as concerns that invention or matter[5] unless:

(1)   it was filed in or in respect of the same country as the first relevant application[6]; and

(2)   not later than the date of filing[7] the second, the first, whether or not so specified, was unconditionally withdrawn, or was abandoned or refused[8], without:

       (a)   having been made available to the public, whether in the United Kingdom[9] or elsewhere[10];

       (b)   leaving any rights outstanding[11]; and

       (c)   having served to establish a priority date in relation to another application, wherever made[12].

Where a declaration of priority is made in or in connection with the application in suit specifying an earlier relevant application, the application in suit and any patent granted in pursuance of it are not invalidated by reason only of relevant intervening acts[13], namely acts done in relation to matter disclosed in an earlier relevant application between the dates of that application and the application in suit[14].

1   As to the meaning of 'invention' see PARA 301 note 2.
2   As to what constitutes disclosure of matter see PARA 310 note 8.
3   As to the meaning of 'relevant application' see PARA 311.
4   Ie in a declaration of priority under the Patents Act 1977 s 5(2): see PARA 310.
5   Patents Act 1977 s 5(3).
6   Patents Act 1977 s 5(3)(a).
7   As to the meaning of 'date of filing' see PARA 315.
8   As to the withdrawal, abandonment and refusal of applications see PARA 331.
9   As to the meaning of 'United Kingdom' see PARA 303 note 5.
10   Patents Act 1977 s 5(3)(b)(i).
11   Patents Act 1977 s 5(3)(b)(ii).
12   Patents Act 1977 s 5(3)(b)(iii). Section 5(3) thus prevents an applicant from extending the 12-month period within which he may make a declaration of priority under s 5(2) (see PARA 310) by filing an application outside that period and then filing a later application within 12 months and claiming priority from that.
13   Patents Act 1977 s 6(1).
14   Patents Act 1977 s 6(2). Any application, or the disclosure to the public of matter contained in any application, which is to be disregarded for the purposes of s 5(3) (see the text and notes 1–12) is, however, to be disregarded for the purposes of s 6: s 6(2). Examples of relevant intervening acts are filing another application for the invention for which the earlier relevant application was made and making information available to the public about that invention or that matter or working that invention: s 6(2).

313. Meaning of 'supported by'. The expression 'supported by' in the provisions for ascertaining the priority date of an invention[1] in relation to the grant of a patent is given no statutory definition. The expression does, however, occur in the Patents Act 1977[2] where a claim is required to be 'supported by' the description. This has been construed[3] to mean that the description must contain a disclosure (an 'enabling disclosure') which contains enough to enable something within the claim to be produced[4]. Accordingly an invention will be entitled to the priority date being the date of filing of an earlier application[5] only if that earlier application not only described the invention but also contained an enabling disclosure[6].

1   Ie the Patents Act 1977 s 5(2)(a): see PARA 310.
2   Ie the Patents Act 1977 s 14(5)(c): see PARA 318.
3   Ie in the case of both the Patents Act 1977 s 5(2)(a) and s 14(5)(c).
4   *Asahi Kasei Kogyo KK's Application* [1991] RPC 485 at 536, HL, per Lord Oliver of Aylmerton and at 547 per Lord Jauncey of Tullichettle. See also *Toyama Chemical Co Ltd's Application* [1990] RPC 555; *Schering Biotech Corpn's Application* [1993] RPC 249; *Prendergast's Applications* [2000] RPC 446; *Biogen Inc v Medeva plc* [1997] RPC 1, 38 BMLR 149, HL.
5   As to earlier relevant applications see PARA 310.
6   *Asahi Kasei Kogyo KK's Application* [1991] RPC 485 at 536, HL, per Lord Oliver of Aylmerton and at 547 per Lord Jauncey of Tullichettle.

(iii)   The Application

314.   Requirements of the application. Every application for a patent[1] which is to be proceeded with[2] must be made in the prescribed form and filed at the UK Intellectual Property Office[3] in the prescribed manner[4], and must be accompanied by the prescribed fee[5].

The application must contain:

(1)   a request for the grant of a patent[6];
(2)   a specification[7]; and
(3)   an abstract[8].

The contents of all documents (including annotations to drawings[9]) contained in an application for a patent must be in English or Welsh[10]. References must only be included in the drawing where they are mentioned in either the description or the claims[11]. Tables of information may only be included in the claims if the comptroller agrees[12]. The terminology and any references used must be consistent throughout the application for a patent[13]. Where units of measurement used in the application are not standard international units of measurement, the equivalent standard international units of measurement must be provided, and where no international standard exists, units must be used which are generally accepted in the field[14]. Only technical terms, signs and symbols which are generally accepted in the field may be used[15].

Except for applications delivered in electronic form or using electronic communications[16], all documents making up an application must be on A4 matt white paper free from tears, folds or similar damage and its contents must be suitable for reproduction; frames (lines surrounding matter) must not be used[17]. In relation to documents other than drawings, the pages of the description and claims must be numbered consecutively in a single series[18], except where a sequence listing is set out at the end of the application, when it must be numbered consecutively in a separate series[19]; page numbers must be located at the top or bottom of the page (but not in the margin) in the centre[20] and the minimum margins in any document must be 20mm[21]. The request for the grant of a patent, the description, the claims and the abstract must each begin on a new sheet of paper[22]. The abstract, description and claims must use at least 1.5 line spacing, except where they form part of a translation or a sequence listing[23]. The capital letters in any typeface or font used must be more than 2mm high[24].

1   Ie under the Patents Act 1977: see PARA 303.
2   As to the initiation of applications for the purpose of acquiring a date of filing see PARA 315.
3   As to the UK Intellectual Property Office see PARA 577.

4 Patents Act 1977 s 14(1)(a). For the prescribed form of request for the grant of a patent see the Patents Rules 2007, SI 2007/3291, r 12(1), Patents Form 1. Where the documents filed at the UK Intellectual Property Office to initiate an application for a patent do not include the applicant's name and address, the comptroller must notify the applicant that his name and address are required: r 12(2). Where the applicant has been so notified, he must, before the end of the period of two months beginning immediately after the date of the notification, file his name and address; otherwise the comptroller may refuse his application: r 12(3) (amended by SI 2011/2052). As to the extension of time limits see PARA 597. As to the comptroller see PARA 575. The title of the invention must be short and indicate the matter to which the invention relates: Patents Rules 2007, SI 2007/3291, r 12(6). Where the specification includes drawings, the description must include a list of drawings briefly describing each of them: r 12(7). As to drawings see PARA 319.

5 Where an application for a patent is made, the fee prescribed for these purposes (the 'application fee') must be paid not later than the end of the period prescribed for the purposes of the Patents Act 1977 s 15(10)(c) (see PARA 315): s 14(1A) (added by SI 2004/2357). As to fees see PARA 581. For the purposes of the Patents Act 1977, 'application fee' means the fee prescribed for the purposes of s 14(1A): s 130(1) (definition added by SI 2004/2357).

6 Patents Act 1977 s 14(2)(a). The provisions of s 14(2) do not, however, prevent an application being initiated by documents complying with s 15(1) (see PARA 315): s 14(2).

7 Patents Act 1977 s 14(2)(b). See also note 6. Unless the application is delivered in electronic form or using electronic communications, the specification must be preceded by the title of the invention and must be set out in the following order: (1) description; (2) the claim or claims; and (3) any drawing referred to in the description or any claim: Patents Rules 2007, SI 2007/3291, r 12(4), (5). As to the contents of specifications see PARA 318.

8 Patents Act 1977 s 14(2)(c). See also note 6. As to the abstract see PARA 325.

9 As to drawings see PARA 319.

10 Patents Rules 2007, SI 2007/3291, r 14(1). Where the documents filed at the UK Intellectual Property Office to initiate an application for a patent include something which is or appears to be a description of the invention in a language other than English or Welsh and the applicant has not filed a translation into English or Welsh of that thing, the comptroller must notify the applicant that a translation is required: r 12(8). Where the applicant has been so notified, he must, before the end of the period of two months beginning immediately after the date of the notification, file a translation; otherwise the comptroller may refuse his application: r 12(9) (amended by SI 2011/2052). As to the extension of time limits see PARA 597. See also *Rohde and Schwarz's Application* [1980] RPC 155. A priority document is not one of the documents which make up an application for a patent: *Mitsui Engineering & Shipbuilding Co Ltd's Application* [1984] RPC 471. As to translations see PARA 595.

11 Patents Rules 2007, SI 2007/3291, r 14(4), Sch 2 para 21.

12 Patents Rules 2007, SI 2007/3291, Sch 2 para 22.

13 Patents Rules 2007, SI 2007/3291, Sch 2 para 23.

14 Patents Rules 2007, SI 2007/3291, Sch 2 para 24.

15 Patents Rules 2007, SI 2007/3291, Sch 2 para 25.

16 Patents Rules 2007, SI 2007/3291, r 14(5).

17 Patents Rules 2007, SI 2007/3291, r 14(2), Sch 2 paras 1–3.

18 Patents Rules 2007, SI 2007/3291, Sch 2 para 4.

19 Patents Rules 2007, SI 2007/3291, Sch 2 para 5.

20 Patents Rules 2007, SI 2007/3291, Sch 2 para 6.

21 Patents Rules 2007, SI 2007/3291, Sch 2 para 7.

22 Patents Rules 2007, SI 2007/3291, Sch 2 para 8.

23 Patents Rules 2007, SI 2007/3291, Sch 2 para 9.

24 Patents Rules 2007, SI 2007/3291, Sch 2 para 10.

315. Initiation of application; date of filing. The date of filing an application for a patent[1] is to be taken to be the earliest date on which documents filed at the UK Intellectual Property Office[2] to initiate the application satisfy the following conditions[3]:

(1) the documents indicate that a patent is sought[4];

(2) the documents identify the person applying for a patent or contain information sufficient to enable that person to be contacted by the UK Intellectual Property Office[5]; and

(3) the documents contain either: (a) something which is or appears to be a

description of the invention for which a patent is sought[6]; or (b) a reference, complying with the relevant requirements of rules[7], to an earlier relevant application made by the applicant or a predecessor in title of his[8].

Where documents filed at the UK Intellectual Property Office to initiate an application for a patent satisfy one or more of the conditions specified in heads (1) to (3) above, but do not satisfy all those conditions, the comptroller[9] must as soon as practicable after the filing of those documents notify the applicant of what else must be filed in order for the application to have a date of filing[10].

Where documents filed at the UK Intellectual Property Office to initiate an application for a patent satisfy all the conditions specified in heads (1) to (3) above, the comptroller must as soon as practicable after the filing of the last of those documents notify the applicant of: (i) the date of filing the application; and (ii) the requirements that must be complied with, and the periods within which they are required by the Patents Act 1977 or rules to be complied with, if the application is not to be treated as having been withdrawn[11].

Where an application has a date of filing and within the prescribed period[12] the applicant files at the UK Intellectual Property Office a drawing[13], or part of the description of the invention for which a patent is sought, and that drawing or that part of the description was missing from the application at the date of filing[14] then, unless the applicant withdraws[15] the drawing or the part of the description (the 'missing part') before the end of the prescribed period[16], the missing part is treated as included in the application[17] and the date of filing the application is the date on which the missing part is filed at the UK Intellectual Property Office[18]. However, this does not affect the power of the comptroller[19] to correct an error or mistake[20].

Where an application has a date of filing by virtue of the provisions set out above, the application is to be treated as having been withdrawn if any of the following applies[21]:

(A)   the applicant fails to file at the UK Intellectual Property Office, before the end of the prescribed period, one or more claims and the abstract[22];

(B)   where a reference to an earlier relevant application has been filed[23] the applicant fails to file at the UK Intellectual Property Office, before the end of the prescribed period, a description of the invention for which the patent is sought[24]; or the applicant fails to file at the UK Intellectual Property Office, before the end of the prescribed period, a copy of the application referred to, complying with the relevant requirements of rules[25];

(C)   the applicant fails to pay the application fee before the end of the prescribed period[26];

(D)   the applicant fails, before the end of the prescribed period, to make a request for a search[27] and pay the search fee[28].

1   Ie under the Patents Act 1977: see PARA 303.

2   As to the UK Intellectual Property Office see PARA 577.

3   Patents Act 1977 s 15(1) (s 15 substituted by SI 2004/2357).

4   Patents Act 1977 s 15(1)(a) (as substituted: see note 3).

5   Patents Act 1977 s 15(1)(b) (as substituted: see note 3).

6   Patents Act 1977 s 15(1)(c)(i) (as substituted: see note 3). The date of filing will be acquired only by matter which was disclosed in the material initially filed: *Asahi Kasei Kogyo KK's Application* [1991] RPC 485 at 526, HL, per Lord Oliver of Aylmerton and at 546 per Lord Jauncey of Tullichettle. See also *Rohde and Schwarz's Application* [1980] RPC 155.

7 A reference must include: (1) the date of filing of the earlier relevant application; (2) its application number; and (3) the country it was filed in or in respect of: Patents Rules 2007, SI 2007/3291, r 17(1). As to relevant applications see PARA 311.

8 Patents Act 1977 s 15(1)(c)(ii) (as substituted: see note 3). It is immaterial for the purposes of s 15(1)(c)(i) whether the thing is in, or is accompanied by a translation into, a language accepted by the UK Intellectual Property Office in accordance with rules or whether the thing otherwise complies with the other provisions of the Patents Act 1977 and with any relevant rules: s 15(2) (as so substituted). As to the requirements for applications which are to be proceeded with see PARA 314.

9 As to the comptroller see PARA 575.

10 Patents Act 1977 s 15(3) (as substituted: see note 3).

11 Patents Act 1977 s 15(4) (as substituted: see note 3).

12 The prescribed period is the period beginning with the date of filing of the application for a patent and ending with the date of the preliminary examination: Patents Rules 2007, SI 2007/3291, r 18(1). As to the extension of time limits see PARA 597. However, where the applicant is notified under the Patents Act 1977 s 15A(9) (see PARA 317) that a drawing or part of the description of the invention has been found to be missing, the prescribed period is the period of two months beginning immediately after the date of the notification: Patents Rules 2007, SI 2007/3291, r 18(2) (amended by SI 2011/2052).

13 As to drawings see PARA 319.

14 Patents Act 1977 s 15(5) (as substituted: see note 3).

15 An applicant may only withdraw a missing part by giving written notice to the comptroller: Patents Rules 2007, SI 2007/3291, r 18(3).

16 Patents Act 1977 s 15(6) (as substituted: see note 3).

17 Patents Act 1977 s 15(6)(a) (as substituted: see note 3).

18 Patents Act 1977 s 15(6)(b) (as substituted: see note 3). Section 15(6)(b) does not apply if: (1) on or before the date which is the date of filing the application by virtue of s 15(1) (see the text and notes 1–8) a declaration is made under s 15(2) (see note 8) in or in connection with the application; (2) the applicant makes a request for s 15(6)(b) not to apply; and (3) the request complies with the relevant requirements of rules and is made within the prescribed period: s 15(7) (as so substituted). The provisions of s 15(7) do not affect the power of the comptroller to correct an error or mistake under s 117(1) (see PARA 353): s 15(8) (as so substituted).
    A request made under head (2) must: (a) be made in writing; (b) include sufficient information to identify where in the priority application the contents of the document filed under s 15(5) (see the text to note 14) were included; and (c) be made before the end of the prescribed period (see note 14): Patents Rules 2007, SI 2007/3291, r 18(4). Any such request is considered never to have been made where: (i) the priority application does not contain every missing part filed under the Patents Act 1977 s 15(5); or (ii) the applicant fails, before the end of the relevant period, to furnish to the comptroller copies of all earlier relevant applications duly certified by the authority with which they were filed, or otherwise verified to the satisfaction of the comptroller: Patents Rules 2007, SI 2007/3291, r 18(5). Head (ii) does not apply in respect of an earlier relevant application where that application or a copy of the application is available to the comptroller (see PARA 310 note 2): r 18(6). For the purposes of head (ii) the relevant period is 16 months beginning immediately after the declared priority date or, if it expires earlier, the period of four months beginning immediately after the date on which the request was made under the Patents Act 1977 s 15(7)(b) (see head (2)): Patents Rules 2007, SI 2007/3291, r 18(7) (amended by SI 2011/2052).

19 Ie under the Patents Act 1977 s 117(1): see PARA 353.

20 Patents Act 1977 s 15(8) (as substituted: see note 3). This provision may avoid the difficulties in *Antiphon AB's Application* [1984] RPC 1 and in *VEB Kombinat Walzlager und Normteile's Application* [1987] RPC 405. The comptroller has power in appropriate circumstances to 'rescind' the grant of a patent to enable a divisional application to be filed: *Re Howmet Research Corpn's Application* [2006] EWHC 725 (Pat), [2006] RPC 657, [2006] All ER (D) 78 (Apr). As to divisional applications see PARA 316.

21 Patents Act 1977 s 15(10) (as substituted: see note 3).

22 Patents Act 1977 s 15(10)(a) (as substituted: see note 3). The period prescribed for the purposes of s 15(10)(a) is the relevant period: Patents Rules 2007, SI 2007/3291, r 22(1). For the purposes of r 22 the relevant period is: (1) where there is no declared priority date, 12 months beginning immediately after the date of filing of the application; or (2) where there is a declared priority date: (a) 12 months beginning immediately after the declared priority date; or (b) if it expires later, the period of two months beginning immediately after the date of filing of the application: r 22(7) (amended by SI 2011/2052). As to the extension of time limits see PARA 597.

The provisions of the Patents Rules 2007, SI 2007/3291, r 22(1)–(3) do not apply to a new application: r 22(4). 'New application' means a new application filed under the Patents Act 1977 s 8(3) (see PARA 361), s 12(6) (see PARA 363) or s 37(4) (see PARA 365) or as mentioned in s 15(9) (see PARA 316): Patents Rules 2007, SI 2007/3291, r 2(1). In relation to a new application: (a) the period prescribed for the purposes of the Patents Act 1977 s 15(10)(a), (b)(i), (c), (d) is two months beginning immediately after its initiation date or, if it expires later, the relevant period; and (b) the period prescribed for the purposes of s 15(10)(b)(ii) is two months beginning immediately after its initiation date or, if it expires later, the period of four months beginning immediately after the date of filing of the earlier application, and the reference in the Patents Rules 2007, SI 2007/3291, r 22(7) to the date of filing of the application is a reference to the date of filing of the earlier application: r 22(5) (amended by SI 2011/2052). But where the new application is filed less than six months before the compliance date, the period prescribed for the purposes of the Patents Act 1977 s 15(10)(a)–(d) is the period ending with its initiation date: Patents Rules 2007, SI 2007/3291, r 22(6). As to the meaning of 'initiation date' see PARA 307 note 8.

23 Ie as mentioned in the Patents Act 1977 s 15(1)(c)(ii) (see head (3)(b) in the text).

24 Patents Act 1977 s 15(10)(b)(i) (as substituted: see note 3). The period prescribed for the purposes of s 15(10)(b)(i) is the relevant period: Patents Rules 2007, SI 2007/3291, r 22(1). This period does not apply to new applications: see note 22.

Where, in relation to an application for a patent: (1) a reference to an earlier relevant application has been filed as mentioned in the Patents Act 1977 s 15(1)(c)(ii) (see the text to note 8); and (2) the description filed under s 15(10)(b)(i) discloses additional matter, that is, matter extending beyond that disclosed in the earlier relevant application, the application is not allowed to proceed unless it is amended so as to exclude the additional matter: s 76(1A) (s 76 substituted by the Copyright, Designs and Patents Act 1988 Sch 5 para 20; Patents Act 1977 s 76(1A) added by SI 2004/2357). As to the meaning of 'relevant application' see PARA 311. As to extended matter see PARA 352.

25 Patents Act 1977 s 15(10)(b)(ii) (as substituted: see note 3). The period prescribed for the purpose of s 15(10)(b)(ii) is four months beginning immediately after the date of filing of the application: Patents Rules 2007, SI 2007/3291, r 22(3) (amended by SI 2011/2052). This period does not apply to new applications: see note 22.

26 Patents Act 1977 s 15(10)(c) (as substituted: see note 3). Subject to the Patents Rules 2007, SI 2007/3291, rr 58(4), 59(3), 68(3) (see PARA 655), the period prescribed for the purposes of the Patents Act 1977 s 15(10)(c) is the relevant period: Patents Rules 2007, SI 2007/3291, r 22(2). This period does not apply to new applications: see note 22.

Where an international application for a patent (UK) has begun the national phase (see PARA 640 et seq), the period prescribed for the purposes of the Patents Act 1977 s 15(10)(c), (d) is the period prescribed by the Patents Rules 2007, SI 2007/3291, r 22(2), (7) or, if it expires later, the period of two months beginning immediately after the date on which the national phase begins: r 68(1), (3) (amended by SI 2011/2052).

27 Ie under the Patents Act 1977 s 17 (see PARA 327).

28 Patents Act 1977 s 15(10)(d) (as substituted: see note 3). Subject to the Patents Rules 2007, SI 2007/3291, rr 58(4), 59(3), 68(3) (see PARA 655), the period prescribed for the purposes of the Patents Act 1977 s 15(10)(d) is the relevant period: Patents Rules 2007, SI 2007/3291, r 22(2). See notes 22, 26. This period does not apply to new applications: see note 22.

316. Divisional applications.

316. Divisional applications. Where, after an application for a patent has been filed and before the patent is granted, a new application is filed by the original applicant or his successor in title in accordance with rules in respect of any part of the matter contained in the earlier application and the conditions relating to filing date[1] are satisfied in relation to the new application[2], the new application is treated as having, as its date of filing, the date of filing the earlier application[3].

1 Ie the conditions mentioned in the Patents Act 1977 s 15(1)(a)–(c): see PARA 315.

2 An application for a patent which: (1) is made in respect of matter disclosed in an earlier application, or in the specification of a patent which has been granted; and (2) discloses additional matter, that is, matter extending beyond that disclosed in the earlier application, as filed, or the application for the patent, as filed, may be filed as mentioned in the Patents Act 1977 s 15(9), but is not allowed to proceed unless it is amended so as to exclude the additional matter: Patents Act 1977 s 76(1) (s 76 substituted by the Copyright, Designs and

Patents Act 1988 Sch 5 para 20; Patents Act 1977 s 76(1) amended by SI 2004/2357). References to an application for a patent, as filed, are references to such an application in the state it was on the date of filing: Patents Act 1977 s 130(4). As to extended matter see PARA 352. See also _Glatt's Application_ [1983] RPC 122; _Protoned BV's Application_ [1983] FSR 110; and _Van der Lely's Application_ [1987] RPC 61, excluding claims in divisional applications to inventions 'not within the contemplation of the invention as described' in the main specification.

3   Patents Act 1977 s 15(9) (s 15 substituted by SI 2004/2357). For the purposes of the Patents Act 1977 s 15(9), a new application may not be filed if the earlier application has been terminated or withdrawn: Patents Rules 2007, SI 2007/3291, r 19(1), (2) (r 19 substituted by SI 2014/578). Where there has not been a notification under the Patents Act 1977 s 18(4) that the earlier application complies with that Act and with the Patents Rules 2007, SI 2007/3291 (a 'section 18(4) notification'), a new application may be filed before the end of the period ending three months before the compliance date of the earlier application (r 19(3), (7) (as so substituted)); where there has been a section 18(4) notification, a new application may be filed if the earlier application has not, prior to the date of the section 18(4) notification, been the subject of an examiner's report under the Patents Act 1977 s 18 which states that the earlier application does not comply with the Act and the Rules (Patents Rules 2007, SI 2007/3291, r 19(4)(a) (as so substituted; amended by SI 2014/2401)) and the period of two months beginning immediately after the date of the section 18(4) notification has not expired (Patents Rules 2007, SI 2007/3291, r 19(4)(b) (as so substituted)). Where an earlier application has been the subject of more than one section 18(4) notification, a reference in r 19(4) to a section 18(4) notification is a reference to the first of those section 18(4) notifications: r 19(5) (as so substituted). A new application must include a statement that it is filed as mentioned in the Patents Act 1977 s 15(9): Patents Rules 2007, SI 2007/3291, r 19(6) (as so substituted).

317.   Preliminary examination. The comptroller[1] must refer an application for a patent to an examiner for a preliminary examination if the application has a date of filing[2], the application has not been withdrawn or treated as withdrawn[3] and the application fee[4] has been paid[5].

On a preliminary examination of an application the examiner is required to determine whether the application complies with those requirements of the Patents Act 1977 and the rules which are designated by the rules as formal requirements for the purposes of the Act[6], and determine whether any requirements[7] remain to be complied with[8]. The examiner must report to the comptroller his determinations[9].

If on the preliminary examination of an application it is found that any drawing[10] referred to in the application, or part of the description of the invention[11] for which the patent is sought, is missing from the application, then the examiner must include this finding in his report to the comptroller[12].

If a report is made to the comptroller that not all the formal requirements have been complied with[13], the comptroller must specify a period during which the applicant has the opportunity to make observations on the report, and to amend the application so as to comply with those requirements[14]. The comptroller may refuse the application if the applicant fails to amend the application before the end of the period specified by the comptroller[15].

1   As to the comptroller see PARA 575.
2   See PARA 315.
3   As to withdrawal see PARA 331.
4   As to the meaning of 'application fee' see PARA 314 note 5.
5   Patents Act 1977 s 15A(1) (s 15A added by SI 2004/2357). As to fees see PARA 581.

6   Patents Act 1977 s 15A(2)(a) (as added: see note 5). On the preliminary examination the examiner must determine whether the application complies with the requirements of the Patents Rules 2007, SI 2007/3291, rr 6–9 (see PARA 310): r 23(1). The examiner must report to the comptroller his determinations and the comptroller must notify the applicant accordingly: r 23(2). Where, on the preliminary examination under the Patents Act 1977 s 15A of an application, the examiner finds that a declaration made for the purposes of s 5(2) (see PARA 310) specifies a date of filing for an earlier relevant application: (1) more than 12 months before the

date of filing of the application in suit; or (2) where the comptroller has given permission for a late declaration to be made under s 5(2), more than 14 months before the date of filing of the application in suit, he must report this finding to the comptroller, and the comptroller must notify the applicant accordingly: Patents Rules 2007, SI 2007/3291, r 24(1). Where the comptroller has so notified the applicant, the applicant must, before the end of the period of two months beginning immediately after the date of that notification, provide the comptroller with a corrected date; otherwise the comptroller must disregard the declaration in so far as it relates to the earlier relevant application: r 24(2) (amended by SI 2011/2052). 'Corrected date' means a date that would not have been reported by the examiner under the Patents Rules 2007, SI 2007/3291, r 24(1): r 24(3).

7   Ie under the Patents Act 1977 s 13(2) (see PARA 307) or s 15(10) (see PARA 315).
8   Patents Act 1977 s 15A(2)(b) (as added: see note 5).
9   Patents Act 1977 s 15A(3) (as added: see note 5). If a report is made to the comptroller under s 15A(3): (1) that any requirement of s 13(2) (see PARA 307) or s 15(10) (see PARA 315) has not been complied with; or (2) that a drawing or part of the description of the invention has been found to be missing, then the comptroller must notify the applicant accordingly: s 15A(9) (as so added).
10 As to drawings see PARA 319.
11 See PARA 318.
12 Patents Act 1977 s 15A(4) (as added: see note 5).
13 Patents Act 1977 s 15A(5) (as added: see note 5). The requirements of the following provisions of the Patents Rules 2007, SI 2007/3291, are formal requirements: (1) r 12(1) (application for a patent on Patents Form 1) (see PARA 314); (2) r 14(1) (application in English or Welsh) (see PARA 314); (3) r 14(2), (3) (form of documents and drawings) (see PARA 314): r 25(1). Where an application is delivered in electronic form or using electronic communications, only the requirements of r 14(1) are formal requirements: r 25(2). Where an international application for a patent (UK) (see PARA 640) was filed in accordance with the provisions of the patent co-operation treaty (ie the Patent Co-operation Treaty (Washington, 19 June 1970; TS 78 (1978); Cmnd 7340): see PARA 629 et seq), the requirements mentioned in r 25(1) are to be treated as complied with to the extent that the application complies with any corresponding provision of that treaty: r 25(3).
14 Patents Act 1977 s 15A(6) (as added: see note 5). The power to amend the application is subject to s 76 (see PARA 351): s 15A(6) (as so added).
15 Patents Act 1977 s 15A(7) (as added: see note 5). Section 15A(7) does not apply if: (1) the applicant makes observations as mentioned in s 15A(6) (see the text to note 14) before the end of the period specified by the comptroller; and (2) as a result of the observations, the comptroller is satisfied that the formal requirements have been complied with: s 15A(8) (as so added).

(iv) Specification, Claims and Abstract

318.   Contents of specification.   The specification of an application for a patent[1] must contain a description of the invention[2], a claim or claims, and any drawing referred to in the description or any claim[3]. The specification must disclose the invention in a manner which is clear enough and complete enough for the invention to be performed by a person skilled in the art[4].

The description contained in the specification has to fulfil two main conditions:

(1)   to state in clear and intelligible language what the invention is, so that others may know what the monopoly is that is granted to the proprietor of the patent; and

(2)   to state in clear and intelligible language in what manner the patented invention is to be performed, so that others may learn from the specification how practically to avail themselves of the patented invention when the patent has expired[5].

The claim or claims contained in the specification must:

(a)   define the matter for which the applicant seeks protection[6];

(b)   be clear and concise[7];

(c)   be supported by the description[8]; and

(d)   relate to one invention or to a group of inventions which are so linked as to form a single inventive concept[9].

Any drawings which are contained in a specification must satisfy certain requirements in respect of their presentation and execution[10].

1   Ie under the Patents Act 1977: see PARA 303.
2   As to the meaning of 'invention' see PARA 301 note 2.
3   Patents Act 1977 s 14(2)(b). The specification must be preceded by the title of the invention and must be set out in the following order: (1) description; (2) the claim or claims; and (3) any drawing referred to in the description or any claim: Patents Rules 2007, SI 2007/3291, r 12(4). This does not apply where an application is delivered in electronic form or using electronic communications: r 12(5). The title of the invention must be short and indicate the matter to which the invention relates: r 12(6). As to the presentation and execution of documents, other than drawings, making up the specification see PARA 314. As to failure to file claims see *R (on the application of Penife International Ltd) v HM Comptroller-General of Patents, Trademarks and Designs* [2003] EWHC 3409 (Admin), [2004] RPC 737, [2004] All ER (D) 116 (Mar).
4   Patents Act 1977 s 14(3). There is no requirement to describe every possible way in which the invention may be performed: see *Quantel Ltd v Spaceward Microsystems Ltd* [1990] RPC 83 at 136; *Generics (UK) Ltd v H Lundbeck A/S* [2008] EWCA Civ 311, [2008] RPC 437, 101 BMLR 52 (affd [2009] UKHL 12, [2009] 2 All ER 955, 107 BMLR 121). As to the presumed skill of the person to whom the specification is addressed see PARA 491; and as to specifications of applications for inventions which require for their performance the use of biological material see PARA 321.
5   *Edison and Swan United Electric Co v Holland* (1889) 6 RPC 243 at 279. Where the specification includes drawings, the description must include a list of drawings briefly describing each of them: Patents Rules 2007, SI 2007/3291, r 12(7). As a matter of practice, it is generally desirable that the description should contain an opening statement setting out the essential features of the invention (the 'consistory clause'): see PARA 323.
6   Patents Act 1977 s 14(5)(a). As to reference numerals in a claim see *Philips Electronic and Associated Industries Ltd's Patent* [1987] RPC 244; *Russell Finex Ltd v Telsonic AG* [2004] EWHC 474 (Ch), [2004] RPC 744, [2004] All ER (D) 332 (Mar).
7   Patents Act 1977 s 14(5)(b).
8   Patents Act 1977 s 14(5)(c). This requirement means that the description must be such as fairly to entitle the patentee to a monopoly of the width claimed: *Schering Biotech Corpn's Application* [1993] RPC 249. See also PARA 313. In applications for inventions claiming a further medical use, the description should include reference to appropriate in vivo or in vitro tests to show that the compounds are effective against the medical conditions cited in the application: *Hoerrmann's Application* [1996] RPC 341; followed in *Consultants Suppliers Ltd's Application* [1996] RPC 348. As to the meaning of 'support' see *Biogen Inc v Medeva plc* [1997] RPC 1 at 46–47, 38 BMLR 149 at 167–168, HL, per Lord Hoffmann.
9   Patents Act 1977 s 14(5)(d). Without prejudice to the generality of s 14(5)(d), where two or more inventions are claimed, whether in a single claim or in separate claims, and there exists between or among those inventions a technical relationship which involves one or more of the same or corresponding special technical features, then those inventions are treated as being so linked as to form a single inventive concept for the purposes of the Patents Act 1977: s 14(6); Patents Rules 2007, SI 2007/3291, r 16(1). For these purposes, 'special technical features' means those technical features which define a contribution which each of the claimed inventions, considered as a whole, make over the prior art: r 16(2). No person may, however, in any proceeding object to a patent or to an amendment of the specification of a patent on the ground that the claims contained in the specification of the patent, either as they stand or as proposed to be amended, as the case may be, relate to more than one invention or to a group of inventions which are not so linked as to form a single inventive concept: Patents Act 1977 s 26.
10   See the Patents Rules 2007, SI 2007/3291, Sch 2; and PARA 319.

319.   Drawings. Drawings forming part of an application for a patent[1] must be on A4 matt white paper free from tears, folds or similar damage and its contents must be suitable for reproduction[2]. Frames (lines surrounding matter) must not be used[3]. There must be minimum margins[4].

Drawings must be executed as follows:

(1) all drawings must be numbered consecutively in a single series[5];
(2) the drawings must begin on a new sheet of paper[6];
(3) the pages containing the drawings must be numbered consecutively in a single series[7];
(4) drawings must comprise black lines and must not be shaded[8];
(5) drawings may include cross-hatching to illustrate the cross-sections of a thing[9];
(6) any scale or other reference for making measurement must be represented diagrammatically[10];
(7) any drawing must be produced in such manner that it would still be clear if it were reduced by linear reduction to two thirds of its original size[11];
(8) a drawing must not be included in the description, the claims, the abstract or the request for the grant of a patent[12];
(9) the capital letters in any typeface or font used in any drawing must be more than 3mm high[13];
(10) references must only be included in the drawing where they are mentioned in either the description or the claims[14].

1 Ie under the Patents Act 1977 s 14: see PARA 314.
2 Patents Rules 2007, SI 2007/3291, r 14(3), Sch 2 paras 1, 2. This does not apply to an application which is delivered in electronic form or using electronic communications: r 14(5).
3 Patents Rules 2007, SI 2007/3291, Sch 2 para 3.
4 Patents Rules 2007, SI 2007/3291, Sch 2 para 11. There must be a margin around any drawing which must be at least: (1) at the top and left side, 20mm; (2) at the right side, 15mm; and (3) at the bottom, 10mm: Sch 2 para 11.
5 Patents Rules 2007, SI 2007/3291, Sch 2 para 12.
6 Patents Rules 2007, SI 2007/3291, Sch 2 para 13.
7 Patents Rules 2007, SI 2007/3291, Sch 2 para 14.
8 Patents Rules 2007, SI 2007/3291, Sch 2 para 15.
9 Patents Rules 2007, SI 2007/3291, Sch 2 para 16.
10 Patents Rules 2007, SI 2007/3291, Sch 2 para 17.
11 Patents Rules 2007, SI 2007/3291, Sch 2 para 18.
12 Patents Rules 2007, SI 2007/3291, Sch 2 para 19.
13 Patents Rules 2007, SI 2007/3291, Sch 2 para 20.
14 Patents Rules 2007, SI 2007/3291, Sch 2 para 21.

320. Selection patents. A 'selection patent' is a patent for a group of members of a known class of things or processes. Such patents are of special importance in regard to chemical discoveries. In the case of selection patents, the specification may be insufficient unless it states the advantage secured by the selection[1].

1 See *Re IG Farbenindustrie AG's Patents* (1930) 47 RPC 289 at 323; *Shell Refining and Marketing Co Ltd's Patent* [1960] RPC 35 at 52, CA; *Du Pont de Nemours & Co (Witsiepe's Application)* [1982] FSR 303, HL; *Biogen Inc v Medeva plc* [1997] RPC 1, 38 BMLR 149, HL; *Generics (UK) Ltd v H Lundbeck A/S* [2009] UKHL 12, [2009] 2 All ER 955, 107 BMLR 121. The requirement also applies to non-chemical selection patents, but then attainment of the advantage ought in any event to be a limitation upon the claims. Note that the European Patent Office does not use the tests set out in *Re IG Farbenindustrie AG's Patents* since that decision dates from a time when a clear distinction between novelty and obviousness had not been drawn: see *Dr Reddy's Laboratories (UK) Ltd v Eli Lilly & Co Ltd* [2009] EWCA Civ 1362, [2010] RPC 222, [2010] IP & T 491. As to the invalidity of selection patents on the grounds of lack of novelty and obviousness see PARAS 440, 479 respectively.

321. Biological material. The specification of an application for a patent[1], or of a patent, for an invention[2] which requires for its performance the use of or concerns biological material is to be treated as disclosing the invention in a manner which is clear enough and complete enough for the invention to be performed by a person skilled in the art if the following requirements are satisfied[3].

The requirements are:

(1) that on or before the date of filing[4] of the application, the biological material has been deposited in a depositary institution[5] and that institution will be able to furnish subsequently a sample of the biological material[6];

(2) that before the end of the relevant period[7]: (a) the name of the depositary institution and the accession number[8] of the deposit are included in the specification; and (b) where the biological material was deposited by a person other than the applicant (the 'depositor'), a statement is filed which identifies the name and address of the depositor, and a statement by the depositor has been filed, which authorises the applicant to refer to the biological material in his application and irrevocably authorises the making available to the public of the biological material[9];

(3) that the specification of the application as filed contains such relevant information as is available to the applicant on the characteristics of the biological material[10].

Where an application for a patent has been published, any person may request the comptroller[11] to issue an authorisation certificate authorising a depositary institution to make available a sample of biological material[12]. Where the application has not been published, a person who has been notified that an application has been made[13] may request the comptroller to issue an authorisation certificate[14]. A request[15] must include an undertaking by the person making the request not to make the biological material, or any material derived from it, available to any other person, and not to use the biological material, or any material derived from it, except for experimental purposes relating to the subject matter of the invention[16]. Where the comptroller grants the request, he must send copies of the request and the certificate[17] to the applicant for, or the proprietor of, the patent, the depositary institution and the person making the request[18]. In certain circumstances[19], a sample may only be made available to an expert[20]. There are rules in relation to new deposits[21].

1 Ie under the Patents Act 1977: see PARA 303. 'Specification' means the specification of an application for a patent: Patents Rules 2007, SI 2007/3291, r 13(1), Sch 1 para 3(5).

2 As to the meaning of 'invention' see PARA 301 note 2.

3 Patents Act 1977 s 125A (added by the Copyright, Designs and Patents Act 1988 Sch 5 para 30); Patents Rules 2007, SI 2007/3291, Sch 1 para 2(1). As to the validity of biotechnological developments see PARA 433.

4 As to the meaning of 'date of filing' see PARA 315.

5 'Depositary institution' means an institution which: (1) carries out the functions of receiving, accepting and storing biological material and the furnishing of samples of such biological material (whether generally or of a specific type); and (2) conducts its affairs, in so far as they relate to the carrying out of those functions, in an objective and impartial manner: Patents Rules 2007, SI 2007/3291, Sch 1 para 1.

6 Patents Rules 2007, SI 2007/3291, Sch 1 paras 2(2)(a), 3(1). This is the 'first requirement': Sch 1 para 1. Where a particular strain of micro-organism has been deposited, this will support claims to that strain and to strains derived from it but not claims to the species as a whole: *Chinoin's Application* [1986] RPC 39.

7 The relevant period is the first to expire of: (1) the period of 16 months (a) where there is no declared priority date, beginning immediately after the date of filing of the application; or (b) where there is a declared priority date, beginning with that date; (2) where the applicant has made a request under the Patents Act 1977 s 16(1) (see PARA 327) to publish the application

during the period prescribed for the purposes of that provision, the period ending with the date of the request; or (3) where the applicant was notified under the Patents Rules 2007, SI 2007/3291, r 52(2) (see PARA 579), the period of one month beginning immediately after the date of the notification: Sch 1 para 3(3) (amended by SI 2011/2052).

8   'Accession number' means the number given to the deposit by a depositary institution: Patents Rules 2007, SI 2007/3291, Sch 1 para 3(5).

9   Patents Rules 2007, SI 2007/3291, Sch 1 paras 2(2)(a), 3(2). As to the extension of time limits see PARA 597. This is the 'second requirement': Sch 1 para 1. Where: (1) the application is filed with the European Patent Office (see PARA 644) and documents have been filed under the provisions of the Convention on the Grant of European Patents (Munich, 5 October 1973; TS 20 (1978); Cmnd 7090) (the European Patent Convention: see PARA 644 et seq) corresponding to the second requirement; or (2) the application in suit is an international application for a patent (UK) and documents have been filed in accordance with the Patent Co-operation Treaty (ie the Patent Co-operation Treaty (Washington, 19 June 1970; TS 78 (1978); Cmnd 7340): see PARA 629 et seq) under the provisions of the Treaty corresponding to the second requirement, the second requirement is to be treated as having been met: Patents Rules 2007, SI 2007/3291, Sch 1 para 3(4).

10   Patents Rules 2007, SI 2007/3291, Sch 1 para 2(2)(b).

11   As to the comptroller see PARA 575.

12   Patents Rules 2007, SI 2007/3291, Sch 1 paras 1, 4(2). Sch 1 para 4 applies where Sch 1 para 7 (see the text and note 20) does not apply: Sch 1 para 4(1). A request must be made on Patents Form 8: Sch 1 para 4(4). Where the biological material has been deposited at an international depositary authority, the request must be accompanied by the relevant form required by the Budapest Treaty: Patents Rules 2007, SI 2007/3291, Sch 1 para 4(5). 'Budapest Treaty' means the Treaty on the International Recognition of the Deposit of Micro-organisms for the purposes of Patent Procedure (Budapest, 28 April 1977; TS 5 (1981); Cmnd 8136), as amended on 26 September 1980, and includes references to the regulations made under that Treaty: Patents Rules 2007, SI 2007/3291, Sch 1 para 1.

13   Ie in accordance with the Patents Act 1977 s 118(4): see PARA 579.

14   Patents Rules 2007, SI 2007/3291, Sch 1 para 4(3). See note 12.

15   Ie a request under the Patents Rules 2007, SI 2007/3291, Sch 1 para 4 or 7 (see note 20).

16   Patents Rules 2007, SI 2007/3291, Sch 1 para 5(1). The applicant for, or the proprietor of, a patent may agree to limit the effect of the undertaking in a particular case: Sch 1 para 5(2). The undertaking ceases to have effect: (1) when the application for a patent is terminated or withdrawn (but it will continue to have effect if the application is reinstated or resuscitated); or (2) when the patent ceases to have effect: Sch 1 para 5(3). Where a request is made: (a) by a government department or any person authorised in writing by a government department; and (b) for the purposes of using the patented invention for the services of the Crown, no undertaking is required and any undertaking by the government department or the person so authorised does not have effect: Sch 1 para 5(4). Where a licence under the patent to which the undertaking relates is available as of right or a compulsory licence in respect of the patent to which the undertaking relates has been granted, any undertaking made has no effect to the extent necessary to give effect to any such licence: Sch 1 para 5(5). As to licensing see PARA 377 et seq.

17   The comptroller must also send any form required by the Budapest Treaty (see note 12): Patents Rules 2007, SI 2007/3291, Sch 1 para 4(5).

18   Patents Rules 2007, SI 2007/3291, Sch 1 para 4(6).

19   Ie where (except for Crown use: see note 16): (1) the applicant requests on Patents Form 8A that a sample of the biological material should only be made available to an expert, and that request is made before the preparations for the application's publication have been completed by the UK Intellectual Property Office; and (2) in relation to an international application for a patent (UK), the applicant made a reference to the deposited biological material in accordance with the Patent Co-operation Treaty (ie the Patent Co-operation Treaty (Washington, 19 June 1970; TS 78 (1978); Cmnd 7340): see PARA 629 et seq): Patents Rules 2007, SI 2007/3291, Sch 1 para 6(1)–(3). 'Expert' means independent expert: Sch 1 para 1. Where the condition in head (1) is met, the comptroller, when he publishes the application, must include a notice that the provisions of Sch 1 para 7 apply (see note 20): Sch 1 para 6(4). Nothing in Sch 1 paras 6, 7 affects the rights under the Patents Act 1977 s 55 (see PARA 404) of any government department or any person authorised in writing by a government department: Patents Rules 2007, SI 2007/3291, Sch 1 para 6(6). As to the UK Intellectual Property Office see PARA 577.

20   Patents Rules 2007, SI 2007/3291, Sch 1 paras 6, 7. Where the conditions in note 19 heads (1) and (2) are met (except in relation to Crown use: see note 16), Sch 1 para 7 applies until the following dates: (1) where the patent is granted, the period ending with the date on which the

patent was granted; and (2) where the application is terminated or withdrawn, 20 years beginning immediately after the date of filing: Sch 1 para 6(5) (amended by SI 2011/2052). A request for a sample to be made available to an expert must be made on the Patents Rules 2007, SI 2007/3291, Patents Form 8 and must include details of the expert: Sch 1 para 7(1). Where the biological material has been deposited at an international depositary authority, the request must be accompanied by any form required by the Budapest Treaty (see note 12): Patents Rules 2007, SI 2007/3291, Sch 1 para 7(2). The comptroller must send a copy of Patents Form 8 to the applicant for the patent: Sch 1 para 7(3). Before the end of the period of one month beginning immediately after the date on which a copy of Patents Form 8 is sent by the comptroller, the applicant may give notice of his objection to the particular expert, and where he objects the comptroller must determine the matter: Sch 1 para 7(4) (amended by SI 2011/2052). Where: (a) the applicant does not object to the sample being made available; or (b) following an objection, the comptroller decides that the sample should be made available to the particular expert, the comptroller must issue a certificate authorising the release of a sample to the expert: Patents Rules 2007, SI 2007/3291, Sch 1 para 7(5). A copy of Patents Form 8 (and any form required by the Budapest Treaty) and any certificate issued under the Patents Rules 2007, SI 2007/3291, Sch 1 para 7(5) must be sent to the applicant for the patent, the depository institution where the sample of the biological material is stored, the expert and the person who made the request: Sch 1 para 7(6).

21   The following rule applies where the first, second or third circumstance occurs: Patents Rules 2007, SI 2007/3291, Sch 1 para 8(1). The first circumstance is that the biological material ceases to be available at the depositary institution because it is no longer viable: Sch 1 para 8(2). The second circumstance is that: (1) the depositary institution is, for any other reason, unable to supply the biological material; or (2) the place where the biological material is deposited is no longer a depositary institution for that type of material (whether temporarily or permanently): Sch 1 para 8(3). The third circumstance is that the biological material is transferred to a different depositary institution: Sch 1 para 8(4). The first requirement and the second requirement are treated as having been complied with throughout the relevant period, if and only if: (a) where the first or second circumstance occurs (i) a new deposit of biological material is made at the relevant depositary before the end of the relevant period, and (ii) that deposit is accompanied by a statement, signed by the person making the deposit, that the biological material deposited is the same as that originally deposited; and (b) in all circumstances, the applicant or proprietor, before the end of the relevant period, applies to the comptroller to amend the specification of the application for the patent, or the patent, so that it meets the second requirement: Sch 1 para 8(5). The prescribed time limit may not be extended: see PARA 597. The 'relevant period' is the period beginning when the first, second or third circumstance occurs and ending three months after the date on which the depositor is notified by the depositary institution that the first, second or third circumstance occurred or, where it expires later, three months after the date on which that circumstance is advertised in the Official Journal (Patents) (see PARA 578): Sch 1 para 8(6). The relevant depositary is, where only the first circumstance occurs, the depositary institution where the original deposit was made or, in any other case, any depositary institution: Sch 1 para 8(7).

322. Sequence listings.

Where the specification of an application for a patent discloses a nucleotide and/or amino acid sequence, it must include a sequence listing[1]. Where an applicant has not provided a sequence listing on filing the application[2], the comptroller[3] may specify a period within which the applicant must provide the sequence listing; and if it is not provided within this period, the comptroller may refuse the application[4].

Where a sequence listing is provided after the date of filing the application[5], the listing must be accompanied by a declaration that it does not contain matter extending beyond the sequence disclosed in the application[6].

The sequence listing must comply with any requirements and standards adopted under the Patent Co-operation Treaty for the presentation of sequence listings in patent applications[7].

A sequence listing must, if it is reasonably possible, be delivered to the comptroller in electronic form or using electronic communications, even where the application for the patent is not delivered in electronic form or using electronic communications[8].

A sequence listing may be set out either in the description or at the end of the application[9].

1　Patents Rules 2007, SI 2007/3291, rr 2(1), 13(2).
2　As to the application see PARAS 314–317.
3　As to the comptroller see PARA 575.
4　Patents Rules 2007, SI 2007/3291, r 13(3).
5　As to the date of filing see PARA 315.
6　Patents Rules 2007, SI 2007/3291, r 13(4).
7　Patents Rules 2007, SI 2007/3291, r 13(5). As to the Patent Co-operation Treaty (ie the Patent Co-operation Treaty (Washington, 19 June 1970; TS 78 (1978); Cmnd 7340)) see PARA 629 et seq.
8　Patents Rules 2007, SI 2007/3291, r 13(6). As to the use of electronic communications see PARA 582.
9　Patents Rules 2007, SI 2007/3291, r 13(7). If the sequence listing is set out at the end of the application, r 12(4) (see PARA 314) does not apply: r 13(7).

323. Body and claims. A specification[1] customarily begins, after the title, with a general preamble stating, usually in more detail than in the title, the subject to which the invention relates, indicating upon what old arrangements the invention is an improvement and the respects in which they needed improvement, and otherwise stating the objects of the invention, possibly summarising other proposals for solving the same problems, and setting out the nature of the invention in general terms[2]. This statement usually includes a clause (the 'consistory clause'[3]), in substantially the same terms as the main claim. Then follows a detailed description of one or more embodiments of the invention, often with a suggestion of alternatives. The whole of this is known as the 'body of the specification'. The specification ends with the claims, delimiting the monopoly granted by the patent. There may be included in the body, usually immediately before the claims, disclaimers of part of the matter covered by the language of the claims.

The preamble to the body and the claims, on the one hand, and the remainder of the body, on the other, have quite different functions[4]. The body, apart from the preamble, is there to instruct those skilled in the art concerned in the carrying out of the invention and must be comprehensible to and not mislead a skilled reader[5]. The claims, since they define the monopoly, will in the event of legal proceedings be scrutinised with as much care as any other document defining a legal right, and require to be as carefully drawn[6]. The preamble, which may determine the manner in which a reader approaches the claims, should be drawn with almost equal care.

1　As to the statutory requirements for specifications see PARA 318.
2　The statement of subject, and the consistory clauses, are insisted upon by the UK Intellectual Property Office and the insertion of references to prior art may also be required. The remainder of the preamble is, in general, optional. As to the UK Intellectual Property Office see PARA 577.
3　Ie from the phrase 'my invention consists …'.
4　*Electric and Musical Industries Ltd v Lissen Ltd* (1937) 54 RPC 307, CA; approved [1938] 4 All ER 221, 56 RPC 23, HL.
5　As to these requirements of the description see PARA 318.
6　As to the construction of the specification and claims generally see PARA 411 et seq.

324. Arrangement of claims. The usual practice is to begin the claims[1] with one to the invention in its broadest aspect, and to follow it with narrower claims, restricted by additional limitations to particular forms of the invention[2]. There may be claims to variants upon the original claim; and claims to a process may be coupled with claims to the product, or to the apparatus used for carrying it out[3].

Where the specification includes drawings[4], or examples of a chemical or like process, it is customary to end with a claim or claims to the invention substantially as described with reference to and as shown in the drawings, or substantially according to the examples. Such claims are permissible[5].

1   As to the statutory requirements for claims see PARA 318.
2   It is usual in British specifications for these to take the form of a main or independent claim, with subordinate or subsidiary claims, ie claims referring back to the main claim (or to earlier subordinate claims) and adding a limitation to it.
3   See eg *Re L'Air Liquide SA's Application* (1932) 49 RPC 428 (where a claim for apparatus for carrying out a process also claimed was interpreted as a claim for the apparatus per se).
4   As to drawings see PARA 319.
5   *Raleigh Cycle Co Ltd v H Miller & Co Ltd* [1948] 1 All ER 308, 65 RPC 141, HL; *Daikin Kogyo Co Ltd (Shingu's) Application* [1974] RPC 559, CA.

325.   The abstract.   The abstract contained in an application for a patent[1] must commence with a title for the invention[2] and must contain a concise summary of the matter contained in the specification[3]. That summary must include:

(1)   an indication of the technical field to which the invention belongs[4];
(2)   a technical explanation of the invention[5]; and
(3)   the principal use of the invention[6].

Where the specification contains more than one drawing[7], the abstract must include an indication of the drawing which should accompany the abstract when it is published[8]. Where it appears to the comptroller[9] that a drawing included in the specification better characterises the invention he must publish it with the abstract[10]. Where a feature of the invention included in the abstract is illustrated in a drawing, the feature must be followed by the reference for that feature used in that drawing[11].

The abstract must not contain any statement on the merits or value of the invention or its speculative application[12].

The purpose of the abstract is to give technical information[13]. It is merely a summary of an application, and cannot be relied upon separately for challenging the validity of a patent[14]. The comptroller may determine whether the abstract adequately fulfils its purpose and, if it does not, may reframe it so that it does[15].

On publication of the application the abstract does not form part of the state of the art[16].

1   Ie under the Patents Act 1977: see PARA 303.
2   Patents Rules 2007, SI 2007/3291, r 15(1). As to the meaning of 'invention' see PARA 301 note 2.
3   Patents Rules 2007, SI 2007/3291, r 15(2). As to the presentation of the abstract see PARA 314; and as to the specification see PARA 318.
4   Patents Rules 2007, SI 2007/3291, r 15(3)(a).
5   Patents Rules 2007, SI 2007/3291, r 15(3)(b).
6   Patents Rules 2007, SI 2007/3291, r 15(3)(c).
7   As to drawings see PARA 319.
8   Patents Rules 2007, SI 2007/3291, r 15(4). As to publication of the application see PARA 326.
9   As to the comptroller see PARA 575.
10 Patents Rules 2007, SI 2007/3291, r 15(5).
11 Patents Rules 2007, SI 2007/3291, r 15(6).
12 Patents Rules 2007, SI 2007/3291, r 15(7).
13 Patents Act 1977 s 14(7).
14 See *Abbott Laboratories Ltd v Medinol Ltd* [2010] EWHC 2865 (Pat), [2010] All ER (D) 151 (Nov).
15 Patents Act 1977 s 14(7).
16 Patents Act 1977 s 14(7). As to the state of the art see s 2(3); and PARA 434.

(v) Publication, Examination and Search

326. Publication of the application. An application for a patent[1] which has a date of filing[2] and which has not been withdrawn or refused[3] before preparations for its publication have been completed by the UK Intellectual Property Office[4] must be published by the comptroller[5] as soon as possible after the end of the period of 18 months calculated from the declared priority date[6] or, where there is no declared priority date, from the date of filing[7]. The application is published as filed, including not only the original claims but also any amendments of those claims and any new claims subsisting immediately before the completion of the preparations for publication[8]. The comptroller may, however, omit from the specification[9] of a published application any matter which in his opinion disparages any person in a way likely to damage him[10], or the publication or exploitation of which would in his opinion be generally expected to encourage offensive, immoral or anti-social behaviour[11].

The comptroller must in any event advertise the fact and date of publication of an application in the Official Journal (Patents)[12].

The publication of the application is subject to the protection of national security[13] and to any application by the inventor to waive his right to have his name or address mentioned[14].

1 Ie under the Patents Act 1977: see PARA 303.
2 As to the meaning of 'date of filing' see PARA 315.
3 As to the withdrawal and refusal of applications see PARA 331.

4 The comptroller must determine on a case-by-case basis when the preparations for publication have been completed: see *Intera Corpn's Application* [1986] RPC 459, CA (where it was held that an earlier rule giving the comptroller power to determine when the preparations had been completed was ultra vires). Once the preparations have been completed, the UK Intellectual Property Office has no discretion but must publish the application: see *Intera Corpn's Application* [1986] RPC 459, CA. The European Patent Office (see PARA 644) does, however, have such a discretion: see Case J-05/81 *Hormann/Publication of a European patent application* [1979–1985] EPOR 83, Legal Board of Appeal.
    As to the UK Intellectual Property Office see PARA 577.
5 As to the comptroller see PARA 575.
6 As to the meaning of 'declared priority date' see PARA 310 note 9.

7 Patents Act 1977 s 16(1); Patents Rules 2007, SI 2007/3291, r 26(1) (amended by SI 2011/2052). If so requested by the applicant, the comptroller may publish the application within the appropriate period: Patents Act 1977 s 16(1). It should be noted that, if the full 12 months' priority is claimed under s 5(2) (see PARA 310), publication will be only six months after filing. As to claims for infringement in respect of published applications see PARA 546.
    References in the Patents Act 1977 to an application for a patent being published are references to its being published under s 16 (s 130(5)); and 'published' means made available to the public, whether in the United Kingdom or elsewhere, and a document is to be taken to be published under any provision of the Patents Act 1977 if it can be inspected as of right at any place in the United Kingdom by members of the public whether on payment of a fee or not; and 'republished' is to be construed accordingly (s 130(1)). As to the meaning of 'United Kingdom' see PARA 303 note 5.
8 Patents Act 1977 s 16(1). As to the meaning of 'application as filed' see PARA 316 note 2. As to amendment before grant see PARA 329; and as to inspection of published applications see PARA 579.
9 As to the contents of specifications see PARA 318.
10 Patents Act 1977 s 16(2)(a).
11 Patents Act 1977 s 16(2)(b).
12 Patents Act 1977 s 16(1). As to the Journal see PARA 578.
13 Ie subject to the Patents Act 1977 s 22 (see PARA 334): s 16(1).
14 Patents Act 1977 s 16(1) (amended by the Patents Act 2004 Sch 2 paras 1(1), 6); Patents Rules 2007, SI 2007/3291, r 26(2).

327. Search. The comptroller[1] must refer an application for a patent[2] to an examiner[3] for a search if, and only if[4]:

   (1)   the comptroller has referred the application to an examiner for a preliminary examination[5];

   (2)   the application has not been withdrawn or treated as withdrawn[6];

   (3)   before the end of the prescribed period[7]: (a) the applicant makes a request to the UK Intellectual Property Office in the prescribed form[8] for a search; and (b) the fee prescribed for the search (the 'search fee')[9] is paid[10];

   (4)   the application includes: (a) a description of the invention for which a patent is sought; and (b) one or more claims[11]; and

   (5)   the description and each of the claims comply with the requirements of rules as to language[12].

On a search, the examiner must make such investigation as in his opinion is reasonably practicable and necessary for him to identify the documents which he thinks will be needed to decide, on a substantive examination[13], whether the invention for which a patent is sought is new[14] and involves an inventive step[15].

On any such search the examiner must determine whether or not the search would serve any useful purpose on the application as for the time being constituted and: (i) if he determines that it would serve such a purpose in relation to the whole or part of the application, he must proceed to conduct the search so far as it would serve such a purpose and must report on the results of the search to the comptroller; and (ii) if he determines that the search would not serve such a purpose in relation to the whole or part of the application, he must report accordingly to the comptroller; and in either event the applicant must be informed of the examiner's report[16].

If it appears to the examiner, either before or on conducting a search, that an application relates to two or more inventions, but that they are not so linked as to form a single inventive concept[17], he must initially only conduct a search in relation to the first invention specified in the claims of the application, but may proceed to conduct a search in relation to another invention so specified if the applicant pays the search fee in respect of the application so far as it relates to that other invention[18].

After a search has been requested for an application, the comptroller may at any time refer the application to an examiner for a supplementary search, and the above provisions[19] apply in relation to a supplementary search as they apply in relation to any other search[20].

A reference for a supplementary search in consequence of an amendment of the application made by the applicant[21], or a correction of the application, or of a document filed in connection with the application[22], may be made only on payment of the prescribed fee[23], unless the comptroller directs otherwise[24].

1   As to the comptroller see PARA 575.
2   Ie under the Patents Act 1977: see PARA 303.
3   Functions of an examiner of the UK Intellectual Property Office under the Patents Act 1977 s 17 may be contracted out: see the Contracting Out (Functions in Relation to Applications for Patents) Order 2002, SI 2002/3052. As to the UK Intellectual Property Office see PARA 577.
4   Patents Act 1977 s 17(1) (substituted by SI 2004/2357).
5   Patents Act 1977 s 17(1)(a) (as substituted: see note 4). A preliminary examination is carried out under s 15A(1) (see PARA 317).
6   Patents Act 1977 s 17(1)(b) (as substituted: see note 4). As to the withdrawal of applications see PARA 331.
7   Except for new applications, and subject to the Patents Rules 2007, SI 2007/3291, r 58(4) (see PARA 655), r 59(3) (see PARA 655) and r 68(3) (see PARA 315), the period prescribed for the

purposes of the Patents Act 1977 s 17(1) is the relevant period: Patents Rules 2007, SI 2007/3291, r 22(2), (4). The relevant period is: (1) where there is no declared priority date, 12 months beginning immediately after the date of filing of the application; or (2) where there is a declared priority date (a) 12 months beginning immediately after the declared priority date; or (b) if it expires later, the period of two months beginning immediately after the date of filing of the application: r 22(7) (amended by SI 2011/2052). In relation to a new application the prescribed period is two months beginning immediately after its initiation date or, if it expires later, the relevant period: Patents Rules 2007, SI 2007/3291, r 22(5)(a) (amended by SI 2011/2052). However, where the new application is filed less than six months before the compliance date, the prescribed period is the period ending with its initiation date: Patents Rules 2007, SI 2007/3291, r 22(6). As to the extension of time limits see PARA 597. As to the meaning of 'date of filing' see PARA 315. As to the meaning of 'declared priority date' see PARA 310 note 9. As to the meaning of 'initiation date' see PARA 307 note 8. Where an international application for a patent (UK) has begun the national phase (see PARA 640 et seq), the period prescribed for the purposes of the Patents Act 1977 s 17(1) is the period prescribed by the Patents Rules 2007, SI 2007/3291, r 22(2), (7) or, if it expires later, the period of two months beginning immediately after the date on which the national phase begins: r 68(1), (3) (amended by SI 2011/2052).

8   A request for a search must be made on Patents Form 9A: Patents Rules 2007, SI 2007/3291, r 27(1).

9   On request for a search under the Patents Act 1977 s 17(1) in accordance with the Patents Rules 2007, SI 2007/3291, r 27: (1) in respect of an international application for a patent (UK), which has already been the subject of a search by the International Searching Authority the fee payable is £120; and (2) in respect of any other application the fee payable is £150: Patents (Fees) Rules 2007, SI 2007/3292, r 2, Sch 1 (amended by SI 2010/33).

10 Patents Act 1977 s 17(1)(c) (as substituted: see note 4).

11 Patents Act 1977 s 17(1)(d) (as substituted: see note 4).

12 Patents Act 1977 s 17(1)(e) (as substituted: see note 4). As to translations see PARA 595. The filing of a translation of a priority document is not a formal requirement; accordingly the comptroller is not under an obligation to inform an applicant of his failure to file such a translation: *Mitsui Engineering & Shipbuilding Co Ltd's Application* [1984] RPC 471.

13 Ie under the Patents Act 1977 s 18 (see PARA 328).

14 As to novelty see PARA 434 et seq.

15 Patents Act 1977 s 17(4). As to inventive step see PARA 451 et seq.

16 Patents Act 1977 s 17(5). The comptroller may, if he thinks fit, send to the applicant a copy of any document (or any part of it) referred to in the examiner's report: Patents Rules 2007, SI 2007/3291, r 27(2).

17 As to inventions which form a single inventive concept see PARA 318 note 9.

18 Patents Act 1977 s 17(6). Where an examiner conducts a search in relation to the first only of two or more inventions, in accordance with s 17(6), he must report this fact to the comptroller, and the comptroller must notify the applicant accordingly: Patents Rules 2007, SI 2007/3291, r 27(3). The applicant must pay any search fee in relation to those inventions (other than the first) on or before the relevant date: r 27(4). The relevant date is the first day of the three month period ending with the compliance date of the application: r 27(5). The fee for a search under the Patents Act 1977 s 17(6) must be accompanied by Patents Form 9A: Patents Rules 2007, SI 2007/3291, r 27(6). The fee payable on request of a further search under the Patents Act 1977 s 17(6) is £150: Patents (Fees) Rules 2007, SI 2007/3292, r 2, Sch 1 (amended by SI 2010/33).

19 Ie the Patents Act 1977 s 17(4), (5) (see the text and notes 13–16).

20 Patents Act 1977 s 17(7) (amended by the Copyright, Designs and Patents Act 1988 Sch 5 para 3).

21 Ie under the Patents Act 1977 s 18(3) (see PARA 328) or s 19(1) (see PARA 329).

22 Ie under the Patents Act 1977 s 117 (see PARA 353).

23 The fee payable for a supplementary search under the Patents Act 1977 s 17(8) is £150: Patents (Fees) Rules 2007, SI 2007/3292, r 2, Sch 1 (amended by SI 2010/33).

24 Patents Act 1977 s 17(8) (added by the Copyright, Designs and Patents Act 1988 Sch 5 para 3).

328. Substantive examination and grant. Where an applicant wishes to proceed with an application for a patent[1] to grant and the conditions for the application to be referred for a search[2] are satisfied, the applicant must make a request to the UK Intellectual Property Office[3] in the prescribed form for a substantive examination[4] and pay the prescribed fee[5]. The request must be made and the fee paid either at the time of the request for a preliminary examination or within six months beginning immediately after the date of publication of the application[6]. The comptroller[7] must then refer the application to an examiner for a substantive examination[8].

If the examiner forms the view that a supplementary search[9] is required for which a fee is payable[10], he must inform the comptroller, who may decide that the substantive examination should not proceed until the fee is paid; and, if he so decides, then, unless within such period as he may allow[11] the fee is paid or the application is amended so as to render the supplementary search unnecessary[12], he may refuse the application[13].

On a substantive examination the examiner must investigate, to such extent as he considers necessary in view of any preliminary examination and search which have been carried out, whether the application complies with the statutory requirements[14] and must determine that question and report his determination to the comptroller[15]. If the examiner reports that any of those requirements are not complied with, the comptroller must give the applicant an opportunity, within a specified period, to make observations on the report and to amend the application so as to comply with those requirements[16]. If the applicant fails to satisfy the comptroller that those requirements are complied with or to amend the application so that it does comply, the comptroller may refuse the application[17].

If the examiner reports that the application, whether as originally filed or as amended[18], complies with those requirements at any time before the end of the prescribed period[19], the comptroller must so notify the applicant and, on payment within the prescribed period of any fee prescribed for grant, may grant him a patent[20]. However, where two or more applications for the same invention having the same priority date have been filed by the same applicant or his successor in title, the comptroller may on that ground refuse to grant a patent in pursuance of more than one of the applications[21].

1   Ie under the Patents Act 1977: see PARA 303.
2   Ie under the Patents Act 1977 s 17(1): see PARA 327.
3   As to the UK Intellectual Property Office see PARA 577.
4   Patents Act 1977 s 18(1)(a). A request for a substantive examination of an application must be made on Patents Form 10: Patents Rules 2007, SI 2007/3291, r 28(1).
5   Patents Act 1977 s 18(1)(b). The fee payable on request for a substantive examination of an application in accordance with the Patents Rules 2007, SI 2007/3291, r 28 is £100: Patents (Fees) Rules 2007, SI 2007/3292, r 2, Sch 1 (amended by SI 2010/33).
6   Patents Act 1977 s 18(1) (amended by SI 2004/2357); Patents Rules 2007, SI 2007/3291, r 28(2) (amended by SI 2011/2052). The Patents Rules 2007, SI 2007/3291, r 28(2) is subject to the provisions of r 60 (see PARA 655) and r 68(4) (see below) and r 28(3), (4): r 28(2). As to the publication of the application see the Patents Act 1977 s 16; and PARA 326. Where an application is subject to directions under s 22(1) or (2) (non-disclosure of information on grounds of security or safety: see PARA 334), the request must be made and the fee paid within two years of the declared priority date or, when there is no declared priority date, within two years beginning immediately after the date of filing the application: Patents Rules 2007, SI 2007/3291, r 28(3), (7) (amended by SI 2011/2052). As to the extension of time limits see PARA 597. As to the meaning of 'declared priority date' see PARA 310 note 9; and as to the meaning of 'date of filing' see PARA 315.

      Where a new application is filed under the Patents Act 1977 s 8(3) (see PARA 361), s 12(6) (see PARA 363), s 15(9) (see PARA 316) or s 37(4) (see PARA 365) then the period prescribed for the purposes of s 18(1) is: (1) two months beginning immediately after its initiation date; or (2) if it expires later, two years of the declared priority date or, when there is no declared priority date, within two years beginning immediately after the date of filing the application, and the reference to the date of filing of the application is a reference to the date of filing of the earlier application: Patents Rules 2007, SI 2007/3291, r 28(5), (7) (amended by SI 2011/2052). But where the new application is filed less than six months before the compliance date, the period prescribed for the purposes of the Patents Act 1977 s 18(1) is the period ending with its initiation date: Patents Rules 2007, SI 2007/3291, r 28(6). As to the meaning of 'initiation date' see PARA 307 note 8. As to the prescribed period following a direction under the Patents Act 1977 s 81 see the Patents Rules 2007, SI 2007/3291, r 60; and PARA 655. Where an international application for a patent (UK) has begun the national phase (see PARA 640 et seq), the period prescribed for the purposes of the Patents Act 1977 s 18(1) is 33 months beginning immediately after: (a) where there is no declared priority date, the date of filing of the application or, where there is a declared priority date, that date; or (b) if it expires later, the period of two months beginning immediately after the date on which the national phase begins: Patents Rules 2007, SI 2007/3291, r 68(4) (amended by SI 2011/2052).

7   As to the comptroller see PARA 575.

8   Patents Act 1977 s 18(1).

9   Ie under the Patents Act 1977 s 17: see PARA 327.

10 As to when an additional fee is payable see PARA 327.

11 There is no prescribed period.

12 Eg by deleting all references and claims to more than one invention.

13 Patents Act 1977 s 18(1A) (added by the Copyright, Designs and Patents Act 1988 Sch 5 para 4).

14 Ie the requirements under the Patents Act 1977 and the Patents Rules 2007, SI 2007/3291. In particular, the examiner will inquire into whether the invention is new (see PARA 434), involves an inventive step (see PARA 451 et seq) and is adequately described in the specification (see PARA 318).

15 Patents Act 1977 s 18(2) (amended by SI 2004/2357).

16 Patents Act 1977 s 18(3). Whenever the examiner reports to the comptroller under either s 18(3) or s 18(4) (see the text to notes 17–20) on whether the application complies with the requirements of the Patents Act 1977 and the Patents Rules 2007, SI 2007/3291, the comptroller must send a copy of that report to the applicant: r 29(1). The comptroller may, if he thinks fit, send to the applicant a copy of any document (or any part of it) referred to in the examiner's report: r 29(2). Where the applicant fails to respond within the period specified in the examiner's report, the comptroller has the power to extend the specified period but will do so only on adequate grounds put forward by the applicant: *Jaskowski's Application* [1981] RPC 197.

17 Patents Act 1977 s 18(3). As to appeals against refusal to grant a patent see PARA 621. Where an appeal is pending, the period for compliance may be extended: see s 20(2); and PARA 331. The application may be rejected whenever it appears that the requirements of the Act have not and cannot be met: *Re Rohde and Schwarz's Application* [1980] RPC 155.

18 Ie as amended in pursuance of the Patents Act 1977 s 15A (see PARA 317), s 18 or s 19 (see PARA 329).

19 For these purposes and for the purposes of the Patents Act 1977 s 20(1) (see PARA 331), the period prescribed is the compliance period: Patents Rules 2007, SI 2007/3291, r 30(1). The compliance period is: (1) four years and six months beginning immediately after (a) where there is no declared priority date, the date of filing of the application; or (b) where there is a declared priority date, that date; or (2) if it expires later, the period of 12 months beginning immediately after the date on which the first substantive examination report is sent to the applicant: r 30(2) (amended by SI 2011/2052). Where a new application is filed the compliance period is: (i) where it is filed under the Patents Act 1977 s 8(3), s 12(6) or s 37(4), the period specified in the Patents Rules 2007, SI 2007/3291, r 30(2) in relation to the earlier application or, if it expires later, the period of 18 months beginning immediately after the initiation date; and (ii) where it is filed as mentioned in the Patents Act 1977 s 15(9) (see PARA 315), the period specified in the Patents Rules 2007, SI 2007/3291, r 30(2) in relation to the earlier application: r 30(3) (amended by SI 2011/2052). Where the first observations report (see PARA 330) is sent to the applicant during the last three months of the period specified in the Patents Rules 2007, SI 2007/3291, r 30(2) or r 30(3), the compliance period is three months beginning immediately after the date on which that report is sent: r 30(4) (amended by SI 2011/2052). As to the extension of time limits see PARA 597.

20 Patents Act 1977 s 18(4) (amended by SI 2004/2357). The grant of a patent is subject to the provisions of the Patents Act 1977 s 19 (amendment of application before grant: see PARA 329) and s 22 (directions as to non-disclosure precluding grant: see PARA 334): s 18(4).

21 Patents Act 1977 s 18(5). This provision places a mandatory requirement on the comptroller to refuse a second grant unless the situation giving rise to the objection under the Patents Act 1977 s 18(5) is overcome: *International Business Machines Corpn (Barclay & Bigar's) Application* [1983] RPC 283.

329. Amendment of applications before grant. In addition to the two occasions when an application for a patent[1] may be amended to meet an official objection[2], the applicant may amend the application of his own volition, subject to certain conditions[3], at any time before the patent is granted[4].

The conditions are:

(1)　the applicant may amend his application only within the period beginning with the date on which the applicant is informed of the examiner's report[5] and ending with the date on which the comptroller[6] sends him the first substantive examination report[7];

(2)　after the end of this period, the applicant may:

　(a)　where the first substantive examination report states that his application complies with the statutory requirements, amend his application once before the end of the period of two months beginning immediately after the date on which that report was sent[8]; or

　(b)　where the first substantive examination report states that his application does not comply with the statutory requirements, amend his application once at the same time as he makes his first observations on, or amendments to, his application[9] and, if the first substantive examination report is sent before preparations for the application's publication have been completed by the UK Intellectual Property Office, amend his application prior to any further amendment he may make to his application[10];

(3)　the conditions in heads (1) and (2) do not apply where the comptroller consents to the amendment or to an amendment of a request for the grant of a patent[11];

(4)　where the comptroller's consent is required, or the applicant wishes to amend the request for the grant of a patent, the applicant must include the reasons for the amendment[12].

Any amendment made under the above provisions is subject to the general restriction that an application may not be amended so as to include added matter[13].

In addition to amendments made by the applicant, the comptroller may, without an application being made to him for the purpose, amend the specification[14] and abstract[15] contained in an application for a patent so as to acknowledge a registered trade mark[16].

1　Ie under the Patents Act 1977: see PARA 303.
2　Ie under the Patents Act 1977 s 15A(6) (see PARA 317) and s 18(3) (see PARA 328). No fee is required for such amendments.
3　An applicant may of his own volition amend his application in accordance with the Patents Rules 2007, SI 2007/3291, r 31 (see the text and notes 4–12).
4　Patents Act 1977 s 19(1); Patents Rules 2007, SI 2007/3291, r 31(2). A request to amend an application for a patent under the Patents Act 2007 s 19(1) must be made in writing: Patents Rules 2007, SI 2007/3291, r 31(1). The claims, as amended, must comply with the requirements of the Patents Act 1977 s 14 (see PARA 314). It is important that the amended claims be supported by the description because the patent, when granted, cannot be attacked on this ground: *Genentech Inc's Patent* [1989] RPC 147, CA; *Schering Biotech Corpn's Application* [1993] RPC 249.
5　Ie under the Patents Act 1977 s 17(5): see PARA 327.
6　As to the comptroller see PARA 575.
7　Patents Rules 2007, SI 2007/3291, r 31(3).
8　Patents Rules 2007, SI 2007/3291, r 31(4)(a) (amended by SI 2011/2052).
9　Ie under the Patents Act 1977 s 18(3) (see PARA 328).

10 Patents Rules 2007, SI 2007/3291, r 31(4)(b). As to the UK Intellectual Property Office see PARA 577.
11 Patents Rules 2007, SI 2007/3291, r 31(5).
12 Patents Rules 2007, SI 2007/3291, r 31(6).
13 See the Patents Act 1977 s 76(2); and PARA 351. See also *Flexible Directional Indicators Ltd's Application* [1994] RPC 207.
14 As to the specification see PARA 318.
15 As to abstracts see PARA 325.
16 Patents Act 1977 s 19(2). As to registered trade marks see TRADE MARKS AND TRADE NAMES vol 97A (2014) PARA 111.

(vi) Third Party Observations and Withdrawal

330. Observations by third persons on patentability. Where an application for a patent[1] has been published[2] but a patent has not been granted to the applicant, any other person may make observations in writing to the comptroller[3] on the question whether the invention is a patentable invention, stating reasons for the observations; and the comptroller must duly consider the observations[4].

The comptroller must send to the applicant a copy of any observations on patentability he receives[5] except for those which, in the opinion of the comptroller, would disparage any person in a way likely to damage such person, or be generally expected to encourage offensive, immoral or anti-social behaviour[6]. The comptroller may, if he thinks fit, send to the applicant a copy of any document referred to in the observations[7]. The comptroller must send to an examiner[8] any observations on patentability[9].

A person does not become a party to any proceedings[10] before the comptroller by reason only that he has made observations under the above provisions[11].

1 Ie under the Patents Act 1977: see PARA 303.
2 Ie under the Patents Act 1977 s 16: see PARA 326.
3 As to the comptroller see PARA 575.
4 Patents Act 1977 s 21(1). As to the meaning of 'patentable invention' see PARA 429 note 2.
5 Patents Rules 2007, SI 2007/3291, r 33(1).
6 Patents Rules 2007, SI 2007/3291, r 33(2).
7 Patents Rules 2007, SI 2007/3291, r 33(3).
8 See PARA 328.
9 Patents Rules 2007, SI 2007/3291, r 33(4). This does not apply where the observations are received after the examiner has reported under the Patents Act 1977 s 18(4) (see PARA 328) that an application complies with the requirements of the Patents Act 1977 and the Patents Rules 2007, SI 2007/3291: r 33(5).
10 Ie any proceedings under the Patents Act 1977.
11 Patents Act 1977 s 21(2).

331. Withdrawal and failure of application. An application for a patent[1] may be withdrawn at any time before the patent is granted[2]; and any withdrawal of such an application may not be revoked[3].

An application is deemed to have been withdrawn in three instances:

(1)   where an initial application[4] has a date of filing[5], it is deemed to have been withdrawn unless the applicant files the necessary documents to complete the application, pays the fee and requests a preliminary examination and search within the relevant prescribed period[6];

(2)   where no request for a substantive examination[7] is made within six months of publication of the application[8], or the prescribed fee[9] for the examination is not paid within that period, the application is deemed to have been withdrawn[10];

(3)   where the applicant fails to supply the UK Intellectual Property Office[11] with the necessary information as to the identity of the inventor within the prescribed period[12], the application will be deemed to have been withdrawn[13].

If it is not determined that an application for a patent complies before the end of the prescribed period[14] with all the statutory requirements[15], the application is treated as having been refused by the comptroller at the end of that period[16]. If at the end of the prescribed period an appeal to the Patents Court[17] is pending in respect of the application or the time within which such an appeal could be brought has not expired, that period:

(a)   where such an appeal is pending, or is brought within the said time or before the expiration of any extension of that time granted, in the case of a first extension, on an application made within that time or, in the case of a subsequent extension, on an application made before the expiration of the last previous extension, is extended until such date at the court may determine[18];

(b)   where no such appeal is pending or is so brought, continues until the end of the said time or, if any extension of that time is so granted, until the expiration of the extension or last extension so granted[19].

1   Ie under the Patents Act 1977: see PARA 303.
2   As to grant see PARA 337.
3   Patents Act 1977 s 14(9). This provision does not affect the power of the comptroller under s 117(1) (see PARA 353) to correct an error or mistake in a withdrawal of an application for a patent: s 14(10) (added by SI 2004/2357). As to the comptroller see PARA 575.
4   As to the initiation of applications see PARA 315.
5   As to the meaning of 'date of filing' see PARA 315.
6   See the Patents Act 1977 s 15(10); and PARA 317.
7   Ie under the Patents Act 1977 s 18(1): see PARA 328.
8   As to publication see PARA 326.
9   As to the prescribed fee see PARA 327 note 9. As to fees generally see PARA 581.
10 See the Patents Act 1977 s 18(1); and PARA 328.
11 As to the UK Intellectual Property Office see PARA 577.
12 As to mention of the inventor see PARA 307.
13 See the Patents Act 1977 s 13(2); and PARA 307.
14 As to the meaning of 'prescribed period' see PARA 328 note 19. As to the effect on the prescribed period when a third party makes observations under the Patents Act 1977 s 21 see the Patents Rules 2007, SI 2007/3291, r 30(4); and PARA 328 note 19. As to the meaning of 'declared priority date' see PARA 310 note 9.
15 Ie the requirements of the Patents Act 1977 and the Patents Rules 2007, SI 2007/3291.
16 Patents Act 1977 s 20(1). Section 97 (appeals from the controller: see PARA 621) applies accordingly: s 20(1).
17 As to the Patents Court see PARA 619 et seq.
18 Patents Act 1977 s 20(2)(a).
19 Patents Act 1977 s 20(2)(b).

332.   Effect of resuscitating a withdrawn application.   Where the comptroller[1] is requested to correct an error or mistake in a withdrawal of an application for a patent[2] and an application has been resuscitated in accordance with that request, the effect of that resuscitation is as follows[3]:

(1)   anything done under or in relation to the application during the period between the application being withdrawn and its resuscitation is treated as valid[4];

(2)   if the comptroller has published notice of the request[5], anything done during that period which would have constituted an infringement of the rights conferred by publication of the application if the application had

not been withdrawn is treated as an infringement of those rights if it was a continuation or repetition of an earlier act infringing those rights[6];

(3)	if the comptroller has published notice of the request[7] and, after the withdrawal of the application and before publication of the notice, a person: (a) began in good faith to do an act which would have constituted an infringement of the rights conferred by publication of the application if the withdrawal had not taken place; or (b) made in good faith effective and serious preparations to do such an act, he has the right to continue to do the act or, as the case may be, to do the act, notwithstanding the resuscitation of the application and the grant of the patent; but this right does not extend to granting a licence to another person to do the act[8];

(4)	if the act was done, or the preparations were made, in the course of a business, the person entitled to the right conferred by head (3) above may: (a) authorise the doing of that act by any partners of his for the time being in that business; and (b) assign that right, or transmit it on death (or in the case of a body corporate on its dissolution), to any person who acquires that part of the business in the course of which the act was done or the preparations were made[9].

The above provisions apply in relation to the use of a patented invention for the services of the Crown[10] as they apply in relation to infringement of the rights conferred by publication of the application for a patent or, as the case may be, infringement of the patent[11].

1	As to the comptroller see PARA 575.
2	See PARA 331.
3	Patents Act 1977 s 117A(1) (s 117A added by SI 2004/2357).
4	Patents Act 1977 s 117A(2) (as added: see note 3).
5	Ie as mentioned in the Patents Act 1977 s 117(3) (see PARA 353).
6	Patents Act 1977 s 117A(3) (as added: see note 3).
7	See note 5.
8	Patents Act 1977 s 117A(4) (as added: see note 3). As to licences see PARA 377 et seq. Where a product is disposed of to another in exercise of a right conferred by s 117A(4) or s 117A(5), that other and any person claiming through him may deal with the product in the same way as if it had been disposed of by the applicant: s 117A(6) (as so added).
9	Patents Act 1977 s 117A(5) (as added: see note 3). See note 8. As to ownership and devolution see PARA 359 et seq.
10	See PARA 403 et seq.
11	Patents Act 1977 s 117A(7) (as added (see note 3); added by the Patents Act 2004 Sch 2 paras 1(1), 23).

333. Reinstatement of applications. Where an application for a patent[1] is refused, or is treated as having been refused or withdrawn[2], as a direct consequence of a failure by the applicant to comply with a statutory requirement[3] within a period which is prescribed[4] or specified by the comptroller[5], then the comptroller may reinstate the application if, and only if:

(1)	the applicant requests him to do so[6];

(2)	the request complies with the relevant requirements of rules[7]; and

(3)	he is satisfied that the failure to comply mentioned above was unintentional[8].

The comptroller must not reinstate the application if an extension remains available[9] for the period referred to above[10], or that period is set out or specified in relation to any proceedings before the comptroller[11], or for the purposes of the declaration of priority date[12] or for the purposes of a request for reinstatement[13] or extension of time limit[14].

Where the application was made by two or more persons jointly, a request for reinstatement may, with the leave of the comptroller, be made by one or more of those persons without joining the others[15].

If the application has been published[16], then the comptroller must publish notice of a request for reinstatement in the prescribed manner[17].

The reinstatement of an application must be by order[18]. If an application is reinstated the applicant must comply with the requirement he failed to comply with earlier[19] within the further period specified by the comptroller in the order reinstating the application[20]. If the applicant fails so to comply, the application is treated as having been withdrawn on the expiry of the period specified[21].

The effect of reinstatement of an application for a patent is as follows[22]:

(a)   anything done under or in relation to the application during the period between termination and reinstatement is to be treated as valid[23];

(b)   if the application has been published[24] before its termination anything done during that period which would have constituted an infringement of the rights conferred by publication of the application if the termination had not occurred is to be treated as an infringement of those rights: (i) if done at a time when it was possible for the period referred to above[25] to be extended; or (ii) if it was a continuation or repetition of an earlier act infringing those rights[26];

(c)   if the application has been published[27] before its termination and, after the termination and before publication of notice of the request for its reinstatement, a person: (i) began in good faith to do an act which would have constituted an infringement of the rights conferred by publication of the application if the termination had not taken place; or (ii) made in good faith effective and serious preparations to do such an act, he has the right to continue to do the act or, as the case may be, to do the act, notwithstanding the reinstatement of the application and the grant of the patent; but this right does not extend to granting a licence to another person to do the act[28].

1   Ie under the Patents Act 1977: see PARA 303.
2   See PARA 331.
3   Ie a requirement of the Patents Act 1977 or the Patents Rules 2007, SI 2007/3291.
4   Ie a period set out in the Patents Act 1977 or the Patents Rules 2007, SI 2007/3291.
5   Patents Act 1977 s 20A(1) (ss 20A, 20B added by SI 2004/2357). As to the comptroller see PARA 575.
6   Patents Act 1977 s 20A(2)(a) (as added: see note 5).
7   Patents Act 1977 s 20A(2)(b) (as added: see note 5). A request under s 20A for the reinstatement of an application must be made before the end of the relevant period: Patents Rules 2007, SI 2007/3291, r 32(1). The prescribed time limit may not be extended: see PARA 597. For this purpose the relevant period is: (1) two months beginning immediately after the date on which the removal of the cause of non-compliance occurred; or (2) if it expires earlier, the period of 12 months beginning immediately after the date on which the application was terminated: r 32(2) (amended by SI 2011/2052). The request must be made on Patents Form 14: Patents Rules 2007, SI 2007/3291, r 32(3). The applicant must file evidence in support of that request: r 32(5). Where that evidence does not accompany the request, the comptroller must specify a period within which the evidence must be filed: r 32(6). Where, on consideration of that evidence, the comptroller is not satisfied that a case for an order under the Patents Act 1977 s 20A has been made out, he must notify the applicant accordingly: Patents Rules 2007, SI 2007/3291, r 32(7). The applicant may, before the end of the period of one month beginning immediately after the date of that notification, request to be heard by the comptroller: r 32(8) (amended by SI 2011/2052). Where the applicant requests a hearing, the comptroller must give

him an opportunity to be heard, after which the comptroller must determine whether the request under the Patents Act 1977 s 20A is to be allowed or refused: Patents Rules 2007, SI 2007/3291, r 32(9). Where the comptroller reinstates the application after a notice was published, he must advertise in the journal the fact that he has reinstated the application: r 32(10). In determining the date on which the removal of the cause of non-compliance occurred, the comptroller must have regard to any relevant principles applicable under the Convention on the Grant of European Patents (Munich, 5 October 1973; TS 20 (1978); Cmnd 7090) (the European Patent Convention: see PARA 644 et seq): Patents Rules 2007, SI 2007/3291, r 32(11). See also *Practice Notice (Patents Act 1977: Reinstatement of Patent Applications) (No 2)* [2011] Bus LR 1408.

8 Patents Act 1977 s 20A(2)(c) (as added: see note 5). See also *Clifford v Comptroller General of Patents, Designs and Trade Marks: Practice Note* [2011] EWHC 1433 (Ch), [2012] Bus LR 475.
9 Ie under the Patents Act 1977 or the Patents Rules 2007, SI 2007/3291.
10 Patents Act 1977 s 20A(3)(a) (as added: see note 5).
11 As to proceedings before the comptroller see PARA 516 et seq.
12 Ie under the Patents Act 1977 s 5(2A)(b) (see PARA 310).
13 Ie under the Patents Act 1977 s 20A.
14 Patents Act 1977 s 20A(3)(b) (as added: see note 5). A request for extension is made under s 117B (see PARA 597).
15 Patents Act 1977 s 20A(4) (as added: see note 5).
16 Ie under the Patents Act 1977 s 16 (see PARA 326).
17 Patents Act 1977 s 20A(5) (as added: see note 5). Where the comptroller is required to publish a notice under s 20A(5), it must be published in the Official Journal (Patents) (see PARA 578): Patents Rules 2007, SI 2007/3291, r 32(4).
18 Patents Act 1977 s 20A(6) (as added: see note 5).
19 Ie the requirement referred to in the Patents Act 1977 s 20A(1) (see the text to note 3).
20 Patents Act 1977 s 20A(7) (as added: see note 5). The further period specified under s 20A(7) must not be less than two months: s 20A(8) (as so added).
21 Patents Act 1977 s 20A(9) (as added: see note 5).
22 Patents Act 1977 s 20B(1) (as added: see note 5). The provisions of s 20B(1)–(6) (see the text and notes 23–28) apply in relation to the use of a patented invention for the services of the Crown as they apply in relation to infringement of the rights conferred by publication of the application for a patent or, as the case may be, infringement of the patent: s 20B(6A) (s 20B as so added; s 20B(6A) added by the Patents Act 2004 Sch 2 paras 1(1), 7). As to Crown use see PARA 403 et seq.
23 Patents Act 1977 s 20B(2) (as added: see note 5). 'Termination', in relation to an application, means: (1) the refusal of the application; or (2) the application being treated as having been refused or withdrawn: s 20B(7) (as so added).
24 Ie under the Patents Act 1977 s 16 (see PARA 326).
25 Ie the period referred to in the Patents Act 1977 s 20A(1) (see the text to notes 1–5).
26 Patents Act 1977 s 20B(3) (as added: see note 5).
27 See note 24.
28 Patents Act 1977 s 20B(4) (as added: see note 5). As to licences see PARA 377 et seq. If the act was done, or the preparations were made, in the course of a business, the person entitled to the right conferred by s 20B(4) may: (1) authorise the doing of that act by any partners of his for the time being in that business; and (2) assign that right, or transmit it on death (or in the case of a body corporate on its dissolution), to any person who acquires that part of the business in the course of which the act was done or the preparations were made: s 20B(5) (as so added). The right conferred by s 20B(4) does not become exercisable until the end of the period during which a request may be made under the Patents Act 1977, or under the rules, for an extension of the period referred to in s 20A(1) (see the text and notes 1–5): s 20B(4A) (added by the Intellectual Property Act 2014 Schedule para 3). As to ownership, devolution and assignment see PARA 359 et seq.
   Where a product is disposed of to another in exercise of a right conferred the Patents Act 1977 s 20B(4) or s 20B(5), that other and any person claiming through him may deal with the product in the same way as if it had been disposed of by the applicant: s 20B(6) (as so added).

(vii) Secrecy Directions and Restrictions on Filing Abroad

334. Secrecy for purposes of national security and public safety. Where an application for a patent[1] is filed in the UK Intellectual Property Office[2] and it appears to the comptroller[3] that the application contains information of a description notified to him by the Secretary of State[4] as being information the publication of which might be prejudicial to the national security, the comptroller may give directions prohibiting or restricting the publication of that information or its communication to any specified person or description of persons[5].

Similarly, if it appears to the comptroller that any application so filed contains information the publication of which might be prejudicial to the safety of the public, he may give directions prohibiting or restricting the publication of that information or its communication to any specified person or description of persons until the end of a period not exceeding three months from the end of the period prescribed for the purposes of the statutory provisions[6] relating to publication of the application[7].

The comptroller must notify the Secretary of State of any application in respect of which he has given directions and of the directions[8], and the Secretary of State must then consider whether the publication of the application[9] or the publication or communication of the information in question would be prejudicial to the national security or the safety of the public[10]. If he determines that the publication of the application or the publication or communication of that information would be prejudicial to the safety of the public, he must notify the comptroller who must continue his directions[11] until they are revoked[12].

If the Secretary of State determines that the publication of the application or the publication or communication of the information in question would be prejudicial to the national security or the safety of the public, he must reconsider the question during the period of nine months from the date of filing the application and at least once in every subsequent period of 12 months[13]. For the purposes of deciding the question, he may at any time after the expiry of the prescribed period[14] inspect the application and any documents sent to the comptroller in connection with it[15]. However, where the application contains information relating to the production or use of atomic energy or research into matters connected with such production or use, he may at any time inspect the application and any documents sent to the comptroller in connection with it or authorise a government body with responsibility for the production of atomic energy or for research into matters connected with its production or use[16], or a person appointed by such a government body, to inspect the application and any documents sent to the comptroller in connection with it[17].

If on consideration of an application at any time it appears to the Secretary of State that the publication of the application or the publication or communication of the information contained in it would not, or would no longer, be prejudicial to the national security or the safety of the public, he must give notice to the comptroller to that effect[18]. On receipt of such a notice the comptroller must revoke the directions and may, subject to such conditions, if any, as he thinks fit, extend the time for doing anything required or authorised to be done in connection with the application, whether or not that time has previously expired[19].

1   Ie under the Patents Act 1977 (see PARA 303) or any treaty or international convention to which the United Kingdom is a party: see the Patents Act 1977 s 22(1). See PARA 628 et seq. As to the meaning of 'United Kingdom' see PARA 303 note 5.
2   As to the UK Intellectual Property Office see PARA 577.
3   As to the comptroller see PARA 575.
4   As to the Secretary of State see PARA 573.

5   Patents Act 1977 s 22(1) (amended by the Patents Act 2004 Sch 2 paras 1(1), 8(1), (3)). As to the effect of such directions see PARA 335.

6 Ie the period prescribed for the purposes of the Patents Act 1977 s 16: see PARA 326. As to the period so prescribed see the Patents Rules 2007, SI 2007/3291, r 26; and PARA 326.
7 Patents Act 1977 s 22(2).
8 Patents Act 1977 s 22(5).
9 As to publication of applications see PARA 326.
10 Patents Act 1977 s 22(5)(a) (amended by the Patents Act 2004 Sch 2 paras 1(1), 8(1), (3)).
11 Ie under the Patents Act 1977 s 22(2): see the text and notes 6–7.
12 Patents Act 1977 s 22(5)(b).
13 Patents Act 1977 s 22(5)(c) (amended by the Patents Act 2004 Sch 2 paras 1(1), 8(1), (3)).
14 See note 6.
15 Patents Act 1977 s 22(6)(b).
16 See ENERGY AND CLIMATE CHANGE vol 44 (2011) PARA 787 et seq.
17 Patents Act 1977 s 22(6)(a) (amended by the Patents Act 2004 Sch 2 paras 1(1), 8(1), (4)). Where a government body or person appointed by a government body carries out an inspection which it is authorised to carry out, the body or the person must report on the inspection to the Secretary of State as soon as practicable: Patents Act 1977 s 22(6) (amended by the Patents Act 2004 Sch 2 paras 1(1), 8(1), (4)).
18 Patents Act 1977 s 22(5)(d) (amended by the Patents Act 2004 Sch 2 paras 1(1), 8(1), (3)).
19 Patents Act 1977 s 22(5)(e).

335.   Effect of directions as to secrecy.   While directions as to secrecy[1] are in force in respect of an application for a patent[2], the application may proceed to the stage where it is in order for the grant of a patent[3]. However, the application must not be published, the information to which the directions apply must not be communicated contrary to the directions, and no patent will be granted pursuant to the application[4]. If the application is an application for a European patent[5], it must not be sent to the European Patent Office[6]. Similarly, if the application is an international application for a patent[7], a copy of it must not be sent to the International Bureau[8] or to any international searching authority appointed under the Patent Co-operation Treaty[9].

Where directions as to secrecy remain in force in respect of an application after the expiry of the prescribed period[10] and the application is brought in order for the grant of a patent, then:

(1)   any working of the invention by or with the written authorisation of or to the order of a government department while the directions are in force is subject to the provisions applicable to Crown use of patented inventions[11], subject to certain modifications[12]; and

(2)   if it appears to the Secretary of State[13] that the applicant for the patent has suffered hardship by reason of the continuance in force of the directions, the Secretary of State, with Treasury consent, may make such payment, if any, by way of compensation to the applicant as appears to the Secretary of State and the Treasury to be reasonable having regard to the inventive merit and utility of the invention, the purpose for which it was designed and any other relevant circumstances[14].

Where a patent is granted pursuant to an application in respect of which directions as to secrecy have been given, no renewal fees[15] are payable in respect of any period during which the directions were in force[16].

Any person who fails to comply with any directions is guilty of an offence[17].

1 Ie directions given under the Patents Act 1977 s 22(1), (2): see PARA 334.
2 Ie under the Patents Act 1977: see PARA 303.
3 Patents Act 1977 s 22(3)(a). As to application procedures see PARA 314 et seq.
4 Patents Act 1977 s 22(3)(a). As to the publication of applications see PARA 326.
5 As to the meaning of 'European patent' see PARA 644 note 5. As to applications for European patents see PARA 646.
6 Patents Act 1977 s 22(3)(b). The comptroller may nevertheless send to the European Patent Office any information which the Convention on the Grant of European Patents (Munich,

5 October 1973; TS 20 (1978); Cmnd 7090) (the European Patent Convention) requires him to send: s 22(4). As to the European Patent Convention and the European Patent Office see PARA 644 et seq.

7   As to the meaning of 'international application for a patent' see PARA 630 note 1.

8   As to the International Bureau see PARA 630.

9   Patents Act 1977 s 22(3)(c). As to the Patent Co-operation Treaty (Washington, 19 June 1970; TS 78 (1978); Cmnd 7340) see PARA 629 et seq. As to international searches under the Treaty see PARA 632.

10 Ie the period prescribed for the purposes of the Patents Act 1977 s 16: see PARA 326.

11 Ie the Patents Act 1977 ss 55–59: see PARAS 403–410.

12 Patents Act 1977 s 22(7)(a). Sections 55–59 apply as if: (1) the working were use made by virtue of s 55; (2) the application had been published within the prescribed period; and (3) a patent had been granted at the time the application was brought in order for grant on the terms of the application as it stood at that time: s 22(7)(a).

13 As to the Secretary of State see PARA 573.

14 Patents Act 1977 s 22(7)(b). As to the Treasury see CONSTITUTIONAL AND ADMINISTRATIVE LAW vol 20 (2014) PARAS 262–265.

15 As to renewal fees see PARA 339.

16 Patents Act 1977 s 22(8).

17 Patents Act 1977 s 22(9). A person guilty of such an offence is liable on conviction on indictment to imprisonment for a term not exceeding two years or a fine, or to both, or on summary conviction to a fine not exceeding the prescribed sum: s 22(9) (amended by the Magistrates' Courts Act 1980 s 32(2)). As to the prescribed sum see SENTENCING AND DISPOSITION OF OFFENDERS vol 92 (2010) PARA 141.

336.   Restrictions on making applications abroad.   If an application for a patent[1]: (1) contains information which relates to military technology or for any other reason publication of the information might be prejudicial to national security; or (2) contains information the publication of which might be prejudicial to the safety of the public, then the following restrictions apply[2].

No person resident in the United Kingdom[3] may file or cause to be filed outside the United Kingdom an application for a patent for an invention which contains such information without written authority granted by the comptroller[4] unless:

(a)   an application for a patent for the same invention has been filed in the UK Intellectual Property Office[5] not less than six weeks before the application outside the United Kingdom[6]; and

(b)   either no directions as to secrecy have been given[7] in relation to the application in the United Kingdom or all such directions have been revoked[8].

The above provisions do not, however, apply to an application for a patent for an invention for which an application for a patent has first been filed in a country outside the United Kingdom by a person resident outside the United Kingdom[9].

A person who files or causes to be filed an application for the grant of a patent in contravention of these provisions is guilty of an offence[10] if he knows that, or is reckless as to whether, filing the application, or causing it to be filed, would be a contravention[11].

1   Ie under the Patents Act 1977: see PARA 303. For these purposes, any reference to any application for a patent includes a reference to an application for other protection for an invention (s 23(4)(a)); and any reference to either kind of application is a reference to an application under the Patents Act 1977, under the law of any country other than the United Kingdom or under any treaty or international convention to which the United Kingdom is a party (s 23(4)(b)). As to treaties and conventions see PARA 628 et seq.

2   Patents Act 1977 s 23(1A) (added by the Patents Act 2004 s 7(2)).

3   As to the meaning of 'United Kingdom' see PARA 303 note 5.

4	Patents Act 1977 s 23(1) (amended by the Patents Act 2004 s 7(1)). As to the comptroller see PARA 575.
5	As to the UK Intellectual Property Office see PARA 577.
6	Patents Act 1977 s 23(1)(a).
7	Ie under the Patents Act 1977 s 22(1), (2): see PARA 334.
8	Patents Act 1977 s 23(1)(b).
9	Patents Act 1977 s 23(2).
10	Patents Act 1977 s 23(3). A person guilty of such an offence is liable on conviction on indictment to imprisonment for a term not exceeding two years or a fine, or to both, or on summary conviction to a fine not exceeding the prescribed sum: s 23(3) (amended by the Magistrates' Courts Act 1980 s 32(2)). As to the prescribed sum see SENTENCING AND DISPOSITION OF OFFENDERS vol 92 (2010) PARA 141.
11	Patents Act 1977 s 23(3A) (added by the Patents Act 2004 s 7(3)).

(2) GRANT AND TERM

337. Procedure upon grant. As soon as practicable after a patent[1] has been granted[2], the comptroller[3] must publish in the Official Journal (Patents)[4] a notice that the patent has been granted[5].

The patent is treated as having been granted on, and takes effect from, the date of publication of the notice[6]. As soon as practicable after he publishes the notice, the comptroller must send the proprietor of the patent a certificate in the prescribed form[7] that the patent has been granted to him[8]. At the same time as he publishes the notice of grant, the comptroller must publish the specification[9] of the patent, the names of the proprietor and, if different, the inventor[10], and any other matters constituting or relating to the patent which in the controller's opinion it is desirable to publish[11]. The effect of grant is to put an end to all pre-grant procedures such as dividing out[12] and pre-grant amendment[13].

1	Ie under the Patents Act 1977: see PARA 303.
2	As to grant see PARA 328.
3	As to the comptroller see PARA 575.
4	As to the Journal see PARA 578.
5	Patents Act 1977 s 24(1).
6	Patents Act 1977 s 25(1). The power to begin an action for infringement arises upon grant: see PARA 520.
7	The certificate of grant of a patent must be in a form which includes: (1) the name of the proprietor; (2) the date of filing of the application; and (3) the number of the patent: Patents Rules 2007, SI 2007/3291, r 34.
8	Patents Act 1977 s 24(2).
9	As to the specification see PARA 318.
10	This provision does not require the comptroller to identify as inventor a person who has waived his right to be mentioned as inventor in any patent granted for the invention (see PARA 307): Patents Act 1977 s 24(4) (added by the Patents Act 2004 Sch 2 paras 1(1), 9). As to the meaning of 'inventor' see PARA 301 note 3.
11	Patents Act 1977 s 24(3).
12	See *ITT Industries Inc's Application* [1984] RPC 23.
13	See *Ogawa Chemical Industries Ltd's Applications* [1986] RPC 63.

338. Term of patents. The term of a patent[1] is, subject to lapse for non-payment of renewal fees[2], 20 years beginning with the date of filing[3] the application or with such other date as may be prescribed[4]. The term may, however, be shortened by revocation[5] or surrender[6] of the patent.

1	Ie under the Patents Act 1977: see PARA 303.
2	As to renewal fees see PARA 339.
3	As to the meaning of 'date of filing' see PARA 315.

4   Patents Act 1977 s 25(1). A rule prescribing any such other date may not be made unless a draft
    of the rule has been laid before, and approved by resolution of, each House of Parliament:
    s 25(2). At the date at which this volume states the law no such rule had been made. As to the
    making of rules generally see PARA 574.
5   As to the revocation of patents see PARA 562 et seq.
6   As to the surrender of patents see PARA 358.

339.   Renewal fees.   There is a prescribed period for the payment of a renewal
fee[1] in respect of the first renewal date[2] of a patent. The first renewal date is the
fourth anniversary of the date of filing[3], and the renewal period is also
prescribed[4].

Where a patent is granted[5] during the period of three months ending with the
fourth anniversary of the date of filing, or at any time after that anniversary: (1)
the first renewal date is the last day of the period of three months beginning
immediately after the date on which the patent was granted; and (2) the renewal
period begins with the date on which the patent was granted and ends with the
last day of the month in which that renewal date falls[6].

Where the grant of a patent is mentioned in the European Patent Bulletin[7]
during the period of three months ending with the fourth anniversary of the date
of filing, or at any time after that anniversary[8]:

(a)   the first renewal date is the later of: (i) the last day of the period of three
      months beginning immediately after the date on which the grant of the
      patent was mentioned in the European Patent Bulletin ('case A'); or (ii)
      the next anniversary of the date of filing to fall after the date on which
      the grant of the patent was so mentioned ('case B')[9]; and

(b)   the renewal period is: (i) in case A, the period beginning with the date
      on which the grant of the patent was mentioned in the European Patent
      Bulletin and ending with the last day of the month in which the first
      renewal date falls; or (ii) in case B, three months ending with the last
      day of the month in which the first renewal date falls[10].

The period for the payment of a renewal fee in respect of renewal dates
subsequent to the first renewal date is three months ending with the last day of
the month in which the renewal date falls[11]. The second renewal date is the next
anniversary of the date of filing to fall after the first renewal date; and each
subsequent renewal date is the anniversary of the previous renewal date[12].

If the renewal fee is not paid before the end of the renewal period, the patent
ceases to have effect[13]. The prescribed form must be filed before the end of the
renewal period[14]. On receipt of the renewal fee the comptroller[15] must issue a
certificate of payment[16].

If, however, during the period ending with the sixth month after the month in
which the prescribed period ends the renewal fee and any prescribed additional
fee[17] are paid, the patent is treated as if it had never expired[18]. Accordingly:

(A)   anything done under or in relation to the patent during that further
      period is valid[19];

(B)   an act which would constitute an infringement of the patent if it had not
      expired constitutes such an infringement[20]; and

(C)   an act which would constitute the use of the patented invention[21] for the
      services of the Crown[22] if the patent had not expired constitutes such
      use[23].

Where the renewal fee has not been received by the end of the renewal period the comptroller must send a renewal notice to the proprietor of the patent reminding him that payment is overdue and of the consequences of non-payment[24].

No renewal fees are payable in respect of any period during which directions as to secrecy are in force in respect of a patent[25]. Renewal fees in respect of patents which are subject to licences of right[26] are half those otherwise payable[27]. Where a patent has lapsed through failure to pay any renewal fee, an application for restoration may be made[28].

1 'Renewal fee' means the fee prescribed in respect of a renewal date: Patents Rules 2007, SI 2007/3291, r 36(1). As to renewal fees see the Patents (Fees) Rules 2007, SI 2007/3292, r 4(1), Sch 2 Pt 1; and as to fees generally see PARA 581.

2 'Renewal date' has the meaning given in the Patents Rules 2007, SI 2007/3291, r 37(2)–(4) (see the text and notes 3–10) or r 38 (see the text and notes 11–12): r 36(1).

3 Patents Rules 2007, SI 2007/3291, r 37(2)(a). As to the meaning of 'date of filing' see PARA 315.

4 See the Patents Rules 2007, SI 2007/3291, rr 36(1), 37(2)(b). 'Renewal period' means the period prescribed by r 37 or r 38 (see the text and notes 5–12) for the payment of a renewal fee unless a renewal fee is payable by virtue of the Patents Act 1977 s 77(5A) (see PARA 652), in which case in the Patents Rules 2007, SI 2007/3291, r 36(1), 39, 41 'renewal period' means the period in which the fee is payable under the Patents Act 1977 s 77(5A) and the Patents Rules 2007, SI 2007/3291, r 41A: r 36(1) (amended by SI 2014/2401). The prescribed time limit may not be extended: see PARA 597.

5 Ie under the Patents Act 1977: see PARA 303.

6 Patents Rules 2007, SI 2007/3291, r 37(3) (amended by SI 2011/2052). The fee to be paid to keep a patent in force after the first renewal date is the sum of the following amounts: (1) the amount specified in relation to the relevant anniversary; and (2) the amounts specified in relation to all previous anniversaries: Patents (Fees) Rules 2007, SI 2007/3292, r 4(2). The relevant anniversary is the last anniversary to fall on or before the first renewal date: r 4(4).

7 See PARA 652 note 3.

8 Patents Rules 2007, SI 2007/3291, r 37(4). The fee to be paid to keep a patent in force after the first renewal date is the amount specified in relation to the relevant anniversary: Patents (Fees) Rules 2007, SI 2007/3292, r 4(3). As to the relevant anniversary see note 6.

9 Patents Rules 2007, SI 2007/3291, r 37(4)(a) (amended by SI 2011/2052).

10 Patents Rules 2007, SI 2007/3291, r 37(4)(b).

11 Patents Rules 2007, SI 2007/3291, r 38(1), (2). The prescribed time limit may not be extended: see PARA 597.

12 Patents Rules 2007, SI 2007/3291, r 38(3).

13 See the Patents Act 1977 s 25(3) (substituted by the Patents Act 2004 s 8(1)). If the renewal fee is not paid before the end of the renewal period, the patent ceases to have effect either: (1) where the renewal fee is payable by virtue of the Patents Act 1977 s 77(5A), at the end of the final day of the renewal period; or (2) in any other case, at the end of the renewal date: Patents Rules 2007, SI 2007/3291, r 36(2) (amended by SI 2014/2401).

14 Patents Form 12 must be filed before the end of the renewal period: Patents Rules 2007, SI 2007/3291, r 36(3). However, where payment is made under the Patents Act 1977 s 25(4) (see the text and notes 18–23) or s 28(3) (see PARA 355), Patents Form 12 must accompany the renewal fee and the prescribed additional fee: Patents Rules 2007, SI 2007/3291, r 36(4).

15 As to the comptroller see PARA 575.

16 Patents Rules 2007, SI 2007/3291, r 36(5).

17 For additional fees see the Patents (Fees) Rules 2007, SI 2007/3292, r 5, Sch 2 (substituted by SI 2010/33).

18 Patents Act 1977 s 25(4) (amended by the Patents Act 2004 s 8(2)).

19 Patents Act 1977 s 25(4)(a).

20 Patents Act 1977 s 25(4)(b). As to acts which constitute infringement see PARA 499 et seq.

21 As to the meaning of 'patented invention' see PARA 370 note 27.

22 As to the meaning of 'services of the Crown' see PARA 404 note 3.

23 Patents Act 1977 s 25(4)(c). As to Crown use see PARA 403 et seq.

24 See the Patents Act 1977 s 25(5); and the Patents Rules 2007, SI 2007/3291, r 39(1), (2), (4) (r 39(2) amended by SI 2014/2401) (providing that where the renewal fee remains unpaid, the comptroller must send a renewal notice to the proprietor of the patent: (1) where the renewal fee is payable by virtue of the Patents Act 1977 s 77(5A), before the end of the period of six weeks

beginning immediately after the later of the end of the renewal period and the date on which the comptroller receives notification of the restoration of the patent from the European Patent Office; and (2) in any other case, before the end of the period of six weeks beginning immediately after the end of the renewal period). The comptroller must send the renewal notice to the address specified by the proprietor on payment of the last renewal fee, or to another address that has since been notified to the comptroller for that purpose by the proprietor or, where such an address has not been so specified or notified, the address for service entered in the register: Patents Rules 2007, SI 2007/3291, r 39(3).

25   See the Patents Act 1977 s 22(8); and PARA 335.

26   As to licences of right see PARA 391.

27   See the Patents Act 1977 s 46(3)(d); and PARA 391.

28   See the Patents Act 1977 s 28; and PARA 354.

(3) SUPPLEMENTARY PROTECTION CERTIFICATES

340.   Supplementary protection for medicinal and plant protection products. Supplementary protection certificates may be issued in respect of medicinal products[1] and plant protection products[2] for the purpose of extending the period of patent protection for those products[3]. Any product protected by a patent in the territory of a member state and subject, prior to being placed on the market as a medicinal or plant protection product, to an administrative authorisation procedure[4] may be[5] the subject of a supplementary protection certificate[6].

A certificate must be granted if, in the member state in which the application for a supplementary protection certificate is submitted and at the date of that application:

(1)   the product is protected by a basic patent in force[7];

(2)   a valid authorisation to place the product on the market as a medicinal or plant protection product has been granted[8];

(3)   the product has not already been the subject of a supplementary protection certificate[9];

(4)   the authorisation referred to in head (2) above is the first authorisation[10] to place the product on the market as a medicinal or plant protection product[11].

Within the limits of the protection conferred by the basic patent, the protection conferred by a supplementary protection certificate extends only to the product covered by the authorisation to place the corresponding medicinal or plant protection product on the market and for any use of the product as a medicinal or plant protection product that has been authorised before the expiry of the certificate[12]. Subject thereto, the certificate confers the same rights as conferred by the basic patent and is subject to the same limitations and the same obligations[13].

The certificate must be granted to the holder of the basic patent or his successors in title[14].

Certain provisions of the Patents Act 1977 are applied with modifications to supplementary protection certificates[15].

1   'Medicinal product' means any substance or combination of substances presented for treating or preventing disease in human beings or animals and any substance or combination of substances which may be administered to human beings or animals with a view to making a medical diagnosis or to restoring, correcting or modifying physiological functions in humans or in animals; and 'product' means the active ingredient or combination of active ingredients of a medicinal product: see Parliament and Council Regulation (EC) 469/2009 (OJ L152, 16.6.2009, p 1) concerning the creation of a supplementary protection certificate for medicinal products art 1(a), (b). See Case C-431/04 *Re Massachusetts Institute of Technology* [2006] ECR I-4089, [2006] RPC 872, [2007] IP & T 44, ECJ (an excipient which allows a slow-release form of a

drug is not an active ingredient); Case C-258/99 *BASF AG v Bureau voor de Industriële Eigendom (BIE)* [2001] ECR I-3643, [2002] RPC 9, [2001] All ER (D) 138 (May) (medicinal products differing only in their impurity levels are different 'products' for the purposes of a supplementary protection certificate); *Yeda Research and Development Co Ltd v Comptroller General of Patents* [2010] EWHC 1733 (Pat), [2010] RPC 791, [2011] IP & T 671 (for the purpose of deciding what is a 'product', focus must be on what it is rather than what it does; and only the active ingredients are relevant). In connection with what amounts to an 'active ingredient' see Case C-431/04 *Re Massachusetts Institute of Technology* [2006] ECR I-4089, [2006] RPC 872, [2007] IP & T 44; *GlaxoSmithKline Biologicals SA v Comptroller General of Patents, Designs and Trademarks* [2013] EWHC 619 (Pat), [2013] RPC 635, [2013] All ER (D) 208 (Mar); Case C-210/13 *GlaxoSmithKline Biologicals SA v Comptroller General of Patents, Designs and Trademarks* [2014] RPC 505; and (finding that a case involving a plant protection product may be interpreted consistently with those involving medicinal products) Case C-11/13 *Bayer CropScience AG v Deutsches Patent-und Markenamt* [2014] All ER (D) 11 (Jul).

2 'Plant protection products' means active substances and preparations containing one or more active substances, put up in the form in which they are supplied to the user, intended to: (1) protect plants or plant products against all harmful organisms or prevent the action of such organisms, in so far as such substances or preparations are not otherwise defined; (2) influence the life processes of plants, other than as a nutrient (eg plant growth regulators); (3) preserve plant products, in so far as such substances or products are not subject to special EU Council or Commission provisions on preservatives; (4) destroy undesirable plants; or (5) destroy parts of plants, check or prevent undesirable growth of plants: see Parliament and Council Regulation (EC) 1610/1996 (OJ L198, 8.8.96, p 30) concerning the creation of a supplementary protection certificate for plant protection products art 1(1). 'Active substance', 'substance' and 'product' are defined: see art 1(2), (3), (8).

3 See Parliament and Council Regulation (EC) 469/2009 (OJ L152, 16.6.2009, p 1) concerning the creation of a supplementary protection certificate for medicinal products; Parliament and Council Regulation (EC) 1610/1996 (OJ L198, 8.8.96, p 30) concerning the creation of a supplementary protection certificate for plant protection products; the text and notes 4–15; and PARAS 341–344. The Patents Act 1977 defines a 'supplementary protection certificate' as a certificate issued under Parliament and Council Regulation (EC) 469/2009 (OJ L152, 16.6.2009, p 1) or, as the case may be, Parliament and Council Regulation (EC) 1610/1996 (OJ L198, 8.8.96, p 30): Patents Act 1977 s 128B(2) (s 128B, Sch 4A added by SI 2007/3293; amended by SI 2014/2411)).

4 Ie as defined in Parliament and Council Regulation (EC) 469/2009 (OJ L152, 16.6.2009, p 1) art 2; and Parliament and Council Regulation (EC) 1610/1996 (OJ L198, 8.8.96, p 30) art 2. Where the submission of samples of a medicinal product to the competent authority with a view to obtaining a marketing authorisation gives rise to a patent infringement, EU law does not preclude a prohibition on obtaining authorisation beyond the maximum authorised period where that period corresponds to the actual average duration of obtaining such authorisation in the member state concerned: Case C-316/95 *Generics BV v Smith Kline & French Laboratories Ltd* [1997] ECR I-3929, [1997] RPC 801, 41 BMLR 116, ECJ.

5 Ie under the terms and conditions provided for in Parliament and Council Regulation (EC) 469/2009 (OJ L152, 16.6.2009, p 1) or, as the case may be, Parliament and Council Regulation (EC) 1610/1996 (OJ L198, 8.8.96, p 30).

6 Parliament and Council Regulation (EC) 469/2009 (OJ L152, 16.6.2009, p 1) arts 1(d), 2; Parliament and Council Regulation (EC) 1610/1996 (OJ L198, 8.8.96, p 30) arts 1(10), 2. The supplementary protection scheme is not for the general protection of the fruits of research; the scheme compensates for the lost time in the exploitation of patented inventions: *Re Aktiebolaget Draco* [1996] RPC 417, 32 BMLR 37. A product placed on the market before obtaining the appropriate marketing authorisation cannot be the subject of a supplementary protection certificate: see Case C-195/09 *Synthon BV v Merz Pharma GmbH & Co KGaA* [2011] ECR I-7011, [2012] RPC 37, [2011] IP & T 767, ECJ; Case C-427/09 *Generics (UK) Ltd v Synaptech Inc* [2011] ECR I-7099, [2012] RPC 70, [2011] IP & T 801, ECJ.

7 Parliament and Council Regulation (EC) 469/2009 (OJ L152, 16.6.2009, p 1) art 3(a); Parliament and Council Regulation (EC) 1610/1996 (OJ L198, 8.8.96, p 30) art 3(1)(a). For the purposes of Parliament and Council Regulation (EC) 469/2009 (OJ L152, 16.6.2009, p 1) 'basic patent' means a patent which protects a product as such, a process to obtain a product or an application of a product, and which is designated by its holder for the purpose of the procedure for grant of a supplementary protection certificate (art 1(c), (d)); for the purposes of Parliament and Council Regulation (EC) 1610/1996 (OJ L198, 8.8.96, p 30) 'basic patent' means a patent which protects a product as such, a preparation, a process to obtain a product or an application of a product, and which is designated by its holder for the purpose of the procedure for grant of

a certificate (art 1(9)). To determine whether a product is protected by a basic patent, reference must be made to the national law governing the patent: C-392/97 *Re Farmitalia Carlo Erba Srl* [1999] ECR I-5553, [2000] 2 CMLR 253, [2000] RPC 580, ECJ; *Takeda Chemical Industries Ltd's SPC Applications* [2004] RPC 1.

The words 'protected by a basic patent' in Parliament and Council Regulation (EC) 469/2009 (OJ L152, 16.6.2009, p 1) art 3 and Parliament and Council Regulation (EC) 1610/1996 (OJ L198, 8.8.96, p 30) art 3 preclude the grant of a supplementary protection certificate relating to active ingredients which are not 'specified in the wording of the claims of the basic patent': see Case C-322/10 *Medeva BV v Comptroller General of Patents* [2011] ECR-I 12051, [2012] RPC 607 (applied in Case C-518/10 *Yeda Research and Development Co Ltd v Comptroller General of Patents, Designs and Trade Marks* (25 November 2011, unreported); Case C-414/11 *Daiichi Sankyo Co Ltd v Demo Anonimos Viomikhaniki kai Emporiki Etairia Farmakon* [2014] Bus LR 1, [2013] All ER (D) 262 (Jul) (in which the Court of Justice of the European Union referred to active ingredients 'identified' (not 'specified') in the wording of the claims of the basic patent). The ambit of 'specified' ranges from express naming through description, necessary implication and reasonable interpretation: see *Medeva BV v Comptroller General of Patents* [2012] EWCA Civ 523, [2012] 3 CMLR 191, [2012] RPC 649; in connection with 'specified in the wording', and in particular the lack of clarity as to what that expression amounts to, see further *Novartis Pharmaceuticals UK v Medimmume* [2012] EWHC 181 (Pat), [2012] FSR 667; *Actavis Group PTC EHF v Sanofi* [2012] EWHC 2290 (Pat), [2012] All ER (D) 45 (Aug); Case C-443/12 *Actavis Group PTC EHF v Sanofi* 2014] RPC 591, [2013] All ER (D) 158 (Dec); and Case C-493/12 *Eli Lilly and Co Ltd v Human Genome Sciences Inc* [2014] RPC 605, [2014] IP & T 101, [2013] All ER (D) 157 (Dec), CJEU (in order to be 'protected by a basic patent in force' it is not necessary for the active ingredient to be identified in the claims of the patent by a structural formula); *Eli Lilly and Co Ltd v Human Genome Sciences Inc* [2014] EWHC 2404 (Pat), [2014] All ER (D) 229 (Jul) (the High Court proceedings following the decision of the CJEU previously cited). See also Case C-630/10 *University of Queensland v Comptroller General of Patents, Designs and Trade Marks* [2011] ECR I-12231, [2012] All ER (D) 177 (Feb) (in which the CJEU held that the words 'protected by a basic patent' preclude the grant of a certificate for a product other than that identified in the wording of the claims of that patent as the product deriving from the process in question, and that whether it is possible to obtain the product directly as a result of that process is irrelevant for this purpose).

Where a medicinal or plant protection product is covered by several basic patents, Parliament and Council Regulation (EC) 469/2009 (OJ L152, 16.6.2009, p 1) and Parliament and Council Regulation (EC) 1610/1996 (OJ L198, 8.8.96, p 30) do not preclude the grant of a supplementary protection certificate to each holder of a basic patent, but only one supplementary protection certificate can be granted for each basic patent: see Case C-181/95 *Biogen v Smithkline Beecham Biologicals SA* [1997] RPC 833, ECJ. Where multiple products are protected by a single basic patent, the regulations preclude the granting of a certificate for each individual product: Case C-443/12 *Actavis Group PTC EHF v Sanofi* [2013] All ER (D) 158 (Dec).

8   Parliament and Council Regulation (EC) 469/2009 (OJ L152, 16.6.2009, p 1) art 3(b); Parliament and Council Regulation (EC) 1610/1996 (OJ L198, 8.8.96, p 30) art 3(1)(b). A supplementary protection certificate may be granted for a patented active ingredient where the marketing authorisation relied upon is for a medicinal product that contains not only that active ingredient but also other active ingredients: see Case C-322/10 *Medeva BV v Comptroller General of Patents* [2011] ECR I-12051, [2012] RPC 607, [2011] All ER (D) 201 (Nov); Case C-422/10 *Georgetown University v Comptroller General of Patents, Designs and Trade Marks* [2011] ECR I-12157, ECJ.

9   Parliament and Council Regulation (EC) 469/2009 (OJ L152, 16.6.2009, p 1) art 3(c); Parliament and Council Regulation (EC) 1610/1996 (OJ L198, 8.8.96, p 30) art 3(1)(c). Thus the patent holder is in general precluded from obtaining, on the basis of one and the same basic patent, more than one supplementary protection certificate in connection with any given product (see Case C-443/12 *Actavis Group PTC EHF v Sanofi* [2014] RPC 591, [2014] IP & T 189, [2013] All ER (D) 158 (Dec), ECJ); however, it is possible for a patent owner to have more than one certificate for a particular patent if that patent protects several different active ingredients or combinations of active ingredients (see Case C-484/12 *Georgetown University v Octrooicentrum Nederland* [2014] IP & T 202).

10   In connection with which authorisation is the 'first authorisation' in cases of multiple authorisations see Case C-617/12 *Astrazenica AB v Comptroller General of Patents, Designs and Trade Marks* [2014] RPC 489.

11 Parliament and Council Regulation (EC) 469/2009 (OJ L152, 16.6.2009, p 1) art 3(d); Parliament and Council Regulation (EC) 1610/1996 (OJ L198, 8.8.96, p 30) art 3(1)(d). The regulations do not prevent the granting of a certificate for a medicinal product comprising an active ingredient where there has been an earlier marketing authorisation for a different medicinal product containing the same active ingredient: see Case C-130/11 *Neurim Pharmaceuticals (1991) v Comptroller General of Patents* [2013] RPC 555, [2012] All ER (D) 369 (Jul). See also *Chiron Corpn's and Novo Nordisk A/S's Supplementary Protection Certificate Application* [2005] RPC 587 (the grant of a supplementary protection certificate for a product to one holder of a basic patent before an application is lodged in relation to the same product by a different holder of a different basic patent on the basis of a common marketing authorisation does not provide a ground for rejecting the later application under Parliament and Council Regulation (EC) 469/2009 (OJ L152, 16.6.2009, p 1) art 3 or Parliament and Council Regulation (EC) 1610/1996 (OJ L198, 8.8.96, p 30) art 3(1)); and Case C-31/03 *Pharmacia Italia SpA v Deutsches Patentamt* [2004] ECR I-10001, [2005] RPC 640, ECJ (authorisation as a veterinary product was held to be the first market authorisation for a supplementary protection certificate application made on the basis of a medicinal product for human use). See also *Takeda Chemical Industries Supplementary Protection Certificate Application (No 2)* [2004] RPC 20.

12 Parliament and Council Regulation (EC) 469/2009 (OJ L152, 16.6.2009, p 1) art 4; Parliament and Council Regulation (EC) 1610/1996 (OJ L198, 8.8.96, p 30) art 4. A supplementary protection certificate is capable of covering a medicinal or plant protection product in any of its derived forms enjoying the protection of the basic patent: see Case C-392/97 *Re Farmitalia Carlo Erba Srl's Supplementary Protection Certificate Application* [1999] ECR I-5553, [2000] 2 CMLR 253, [2000] RPC 580, ECJ. A supplementary protection certificate for a product containing an active ingredient can be enforced against third party products containing that ingredient whether or not other active ingredients are also present: see Case C-442/11 *Novartis v Actavis UK* (9 February 2012, unreported).

13 Parliament and Council Regulation (EC) 469/2009 (OJ L152, 16.6.2009, p 1) art 5; Parliament and Council Regulation (EC) 1610/1996 (OJ L198, 8.8.96, p 30) art 5. See *Research Corp's Supplementary Protection Certificate* [1994] RPC 667.

14 Parliament and Council Regulation (EC) 469/2009 (OJ L152, 16.6.2009, p 1) art 6; Parliament and Council Regulation (EC) 1610/1996 (OJ L198, 8.8.96, p 30) art 6.

15 See the Patents Act 1977 s 128B(1), Sch 4A paras 1, 2, 3, 4 (as added and amended: see note 3).

341. Application for supplementary protection certificate. The application for a supplementary protection certificate must be made in the prescribed form[1] and filed at the UK Intellectual Property Office[2] accompanied by the prescribed fee[3] within six months of the date on which the authorisation[4] to place the product[5] on the market as a medicinal or plant protection product[6] was granted[7]. Where, however, that authorisation is granted before the basic patent[8] is granted, the application for a certificate must be lodged within six months of the date on which the patent is granted[9]. Where the application for a supplementary protection certificate is concerned with a medicinal product, the application for an extension of the duration[10] may be made when lodging the application for a certificate or when the application for the certificate is pending and the appropriate requirements[11] are fulfilled[12]; and the application for an extension of the duration of a certificate already granted must be lodged not later than two years before the expiry of the certificate[13]. No corresponding provision is made for supplementary protection certificates concerned with plant protection products.

The application for a certificate must contain:

(1)   a request for the grant of a certificate, stating in particular:
   (a)   the name and address of the applicant;
   (b)   if he has appointed a representative, the name and address of the representative;
   (c)   the number of the basic patent and the title of the invention;
   (d)   the number and date of the first authorisation to place the

product on the market and, if this authorisation is not the first authorisation for placing the product on the market in the European Union, the number and date of that authorisation;

(2)   a copy of the authorisation to place the product on the market, in which the product is identified, containing in particular the number and date of the authorisation and the summary of the product characteristics;

(3)   if the authorisation referred to in head (2) above is not the first authorisation for placing the product on the market as a medicinal or plant protection product in the EU, information regarding the identity of the product thus authorised and the legal provision under which the authorisation procedure took place, together with a copy of the notice publishing the authorisation in the appropriate official publication[14].

The application for a certificate must be lodged with the competent industrial property office of the member state which granted the basic patent or on whose behalf it was granted and in which the authorisation[15] to place the product on the market was obtained, unless the member state designates another authority for the purpose[16]. Notification of the application for a certificate must be published by the appropriate authority[17]; and the notification must contain at least the following information:

(i)   the name and address of the applicant;

(ii)   the number of the basic patent;

(iii)   the title of the invention;

(iv)   the number and date of the authorisation to place the product on the market[18] and the product identified in that authorisation;

(v)   where relevant, the number and date of the first authorisation to place the product on the market in the EU; and

(vi)   (in the case of an application relating to a medicinal product only) where applicable, an indication that the application includes an application for an extension of the duration[19].

1   An application for a supplementary protection certificate must be made on Patents Form SP1: Patents Rules 2007, SI 2007/3291, r 116(1)(a).
2   As to the UK Intellectual Property Office see PARA 577. See further text and note 13.
3   Member states may provide that a fee is to be payable upon application for a certificate: Parliament and Council Regulation (EC) 469/2009 (OJ L152, 16.6.2009, p 1) concerning the creation of a supplementary protection certificate for medicinal products, art 8(4); Parliament and Council Regulation (EC) 1610/1996 (OJ L198, 8.8.96, p 30) concerning the creation of a supplementary protection certificate for plant protection products art 8(2).
     A supplementary protection certificate does not take effect unless: (1) the prescribed fee is paid before the end of the prescribed period; or (2) the prescribed fee and any prescribed additional fee are paid before the end of the period of six months beginning immediately after the prescribed period: Patents Act 1977 s 128B(1), Sch 4A para 5 (s 128B, Sch 4A added by SI 2007/3293). The prescribed period is: (a) three months ending with the start date; or (b) where the certificate is granted after the beginning of that period, three months beginning immediately after the date the supplementary protection certificate is granted: Patents Rules 2007, SI 2007/3291, r 116(2) (amended by SI 2011/2052). The prescribed time limit may not be extended: see PARA 597.
     The prescribed fee payable for a supplementary protection certificate to take effect is set in accordance with the following: Patents (Fees) Rules 2007, SI 2007/3292, r 6(1). Where the certificate expires during the period of one year beginning with: (i) the start date, the fee is £600; (ii) the first anniversary of the start date, the fee is £1,300; (iii) the second anniversary of the start date, the fee is £2,100; (iv) the third anniversary of the start date, the fee is £3,000; or (v) the fourth anniversary of the start date, the fee is £4,000: r 6(2). The additional fee prescribed for the purposes of head (2) above is half the prescribed fee: r 6(4). 'Start date' is the first day following the day on which the basic patent expires: r 6(5). As to the meaning of 'basic patent' see PARA 340 note 7. The period in r 6(2) must be calculated without reference to any extension

of the duration of a supplementary protection certificate under Parliament and Council Regulation (EC) 469/2009 (OJ L152, 16.6.2009, p 1) art 13.3: Patents (Fees) Rules 2007, SI 2007/3292, r 6(3).

4   Ie the authorisation referred to in Parliament and Council Regulation (EC) 469/2009 (OJ L152, 16.6.2009, p 1) art 3(b) or Parliament and Council Regulation (EC) 1610/1996 (OJ L198, 8.8.96, p 30) art 3(1)(b): see PARA 340.

5   As to the meaning of 'product' see PARA 340 note 2.

6   As to the meanings of 'medicinal product' and 'plant protection product' see PARA 340 notes 1, 2.

7   Parliament and Council Regulation (EC) 469/2009 (OJ L152, 16.6.2009, p 1) art 7(1); Parliament and Council Regulation (EC) 1610/1996 (OJ L198, 8.8.96, p 30) art 7(1); Patents Act 1977 ss 14(1), 128B, Sch 4A para 1(1), (2) (as added (see note 3); prospectively amended (but not so as to affect the meaning of the text) by the Intellectual Property Act 2014 s 16(3)). Parliament and Council Regulation (EC) 1610/1996 (OJ L198, 8.8.96, p 30) art 7(1) precludes an application for a supplementary protection certificate being lodged before the date on which the plant protection product has obtained the marketing authorisation referred to in art 3(1)(b) (see PARA 340): see Case C-210/12 *Sumitomo Chemical Co Ltd v Deutsches Patent-und Markenamt* (17 October 2013, unreported).

8   As to the meaning of 'basic patent' see PARA 340 note 7.

9   Parliament and Council Regulation (EC) 469/2009 (OJ L152, 16.6.2009, p 1) art 7(2); Parliament and Council Regulation (EC) 1610/1996 (OJ L198, 8.8.96, p 30) art 7(2).

10 For the purposes of Parliament and Council Regulation (EC) 469/2009 (OJ L152, 16.6.2009, p 1) 'application for an extension of the duration' means an application for an extension of the duration of the certificate pursuant to European Parliament and Council Regulation (EC) 469/2009 (OJ L152, 16.6.2009, p 1) art 13.3 and of European Parliament and Council Regulation (EC) 1901/2006 (OJ L378, 27.12.2006, p 1) on medicinal products for paediatric use, art 36: art 1(e).

11 Ie of Parliament and Council Regulation (EC) 469/2009 (OJ L152, 16.6.2009, p 1) art 8.1(d) or 8.2: see the text and note 14.

12 Parliament and Council Regulation (EC) 469/2009 (OJ L152, 16.6.2009, p 1) art 7(3).

13 Parliament and Council Regulation (EC) 469/2009 (OJ L152, 16.6.2009, p 1) art 7(4).

14 Parliament and Council Regulation (EC) 469/2009 (OJ L152, 16.6.2009, p 1) art 8(1)(a)–(c); Parliament and Council Regulation (EC) 1610/1996 (OJ L198, 8.8.96, p 30) art 8(1)(a)–(c). Where the application for a certificate concerning a medicinal product includes a request for an extension of the duration, the application must contain: (1) a copy of the statement indicating compliance with an agreed completed paediatric investigation plan as referred to in Council Regulation (EC) 1901/2006 (OJ L378, 27.12.2006, p 1) art 36(1); (2) where necessary, in addition to the copy of the authorisations to place the product on the market as referred to in head (2) in the text, proof that it has authorisations to place the product on the market of all other member states, as referred to in Council Regulation (EC) 1901/2006 (OJ L378, 27.12.2006, p 1) art 36(3): Parliament and Council Regulation (EC) 469/2009 (OJ L152, 16.6.2009, p 1) art 8(1)(d). Where an application for a certificate is pending, an application for an extended duration in accordance with art 7(3) (see the text to note 12) must include the particulars referred to in art 8(1)(d) and a reference to the application for a certificate already filed: art 8(2). The application for an extension of the duration of a certificate already granted must contain the particulars referred to in art 8(1)(d) and a copy of the certificate already granted: art 8(1)(b). An application for an extension of the duration of a supplementary protection certificate under art 8 must be made on Patents Form SP4: Patents Rules 2007, SI 2007/3291, r 116(1)(b). As to the fee payable see the Patents (Fees) Rules 2007, SI 2007/3292, r 2, Sch 1. In connection with applications under these provisions see also *EI du Pont Nemours & Co v United Kingdom Intellectual Property Office* [2009] EWCA Civ 966, [2010] RPC 158, 111 BMLR 15; and PARA 342. No corresponding provision is made for certificates concerned with plant protection products.

15 See note 4.

16 Parliament and Council Regulation (EC) 469/2009 (OJ L152, 16.6.2009, p 1) art 9(1); Parliament and Council Regulation (EC) 1610/1996 (OJ L198, 8.8.96, p 30) art 9(1). The competent industrial property office for the purposes of lodging an application for a supplementary protection certificate in the United Kingdom is the UK Intellectual Property Office: see the Patents Act 1977 s 14(1)(a), Sch 4A para 1(2) (as added: see note 3). As to the meaning of 'United Kingdom' see PARA 303 note 5.

17 Ie the authority referred to in Parliament and Council Regulation (EC) 469/2009 (OJ L152, 16.6.2009, p 1) art 9(1) or, as the case may be, Parliament and Council Regulation (EC) 1610/1996 (OJ L198, 8.8.96, p 30) art 9(1): see the text and note 16.

18 See note 4.
19 European Parliament and Council Regulation (EC) 469/2009 (OJ L152, 16.6.2009, p 1) art 9(2); Parliament and Council Regulation (EC) 1610/1996 (OJ L198, 8.8.96, p 30) art 9(2). The comptroller (see PARA 575) must send a notice to the applicant for the certificate: (1) before the beginning of the period of two months immediately preceding the start date; or (2) where the certificate is granted as mentioned in the Patents Rules 2007, SI 2007/3291, r 116(2)(b) (see note 3), on the date the certificate is granted: r 116(3). The notice must notify the applicant for the certificate of: (a) the fact that payment is required for the certificate to take effect; (b) the prescribed fee due; (c) the date before which payment must be made; and (d) the start date: r 116(4). The prescribed fee must be accompanied by Patents Form SP2; and once a certificate relating to a medicinal product has taken effect no further fee may be paid to extend the term of the certificate unless an application for an extension of the duration of the certificate is made under Parliament and Council Regulation (EC) 469/2009 (OJ L152, 16.6.2009, p 1): Patents Rules 2007, SI 2007/3291, r 16(5). Where the prescribed fee is not paid before the end of the period prescribed for the purposes of the Patents Act 1977 Sch 4A para 5 (see note 3), the comptroller, before the end of the period of six weeks beginning immediately after the end of that prescribed period, and if the fee remains unpaid, must send a notice to the applicant for the certificate: Patents Rules 2007, SI 2007/3291, r 16(6). The notice must remind the applicant for the certificate that payment is overdue and of the consequences of non-payment: r 16(7). The comptroller must send the notices to the applicant's address for service, and the address to which a renewal notice would be sent to the proprietor of the basic patent under r 39(3) (see PARA 339): r 116(8).

342.   Grant of supplementary protection certificate or rejection of application.
Where the application for a supplementary protection certificate and the product[1] to which it relates meets the prescribed conditions[2], the relevant authority[3] must grant the certificate[4]; but that authority must[5] reject the application for a certificate if the application or the product to which it relates does not meet the prescribed conditions[6]. Where the application for a certificate does not meet the conditions relating to the content of such an application[7], the relevant authority must ask the applicant to rectify the irregularity, or to settle the fee, within a stated time[8]. If the irregularity is not so rectified or the fee is not so settled within the stated time, the relevant authority must reject the application[9].

Member states may provide that the authority is to grant certificates without verifying that certain of the conditions[10] for obtaining a certificate are met[11].

Notification of the fact that a certificate has been granted must be published by the relevant authority; and the notification must contain at least the following information:

(1)   the name and address of the holder of the certificate;
(2)   the number of the basic patent[12];
(3)   the title of the invention;
(4)   the number and date of the authorisation to place the product on the market[13] and the product identified in that authorisation;
(5)   where relevant, the number and date of the first authorisation to place the product on the market in the EU; and
(6)   the duration of the certificate[14].

Notification of the fact that the application for a certificate has been rejected must be published by the relevant authority; and the notification must contain at least the like information[15] as on the notification of the application for a certificate[16].

Member states may require that the certificate be subject to the payment of annual fees[17].

1   As to the meaning of 'product' see PARA 340 note 2.

2   Ie the conditions laid down in European Parliament and Council Regulation (EC) 469/2009
    (OJ L152, 16.6.2009, p 1) concerning the creation of a supplementary protection certificate for
    medicinal products or, as the case may be, Parliament and Council Regulation (EC) 1610/1996
    (OJ L198, 8.8.96, p 30) concerning the creation of a supplementary protection certificate for
    plant protection products (see PARA 340).

3   Ie the authority referred to in Parliament and Council Regulation (EC) 469/2009 (OJ L152,
    16.6.2009, p 1) art 9(1) or, as the case may be, Parliament and Council Regulation (EC)
    1610/1996 (OJ L198, 8.8.96, p 30) art 9(1): see PARA 341.

4   Parliament and Council Regulation (EC) 469/2009 (OJ L152, 16.6.2009, p 1) art 10(1);
    Parliament and Council Regulation (EC) 1610/1996 (OJ L198, 8.8.96, p 30) art 10(1).

5   Ie subject to Parliament and Council Regulation (EC) 469/2009 (OJ L152, 16.6.2009, p 1)
    art 10(3) or, as the case may be, Parliament and Council Regulation (EC) 1610/1996 (OJ L198,
    8.8.96, p 30) art 10(3): see the text and notes 7–8.

6   Parliament and Council Regulation (EC) 469/2009 (OJ L152, 16.6.2009, p 1) art 10(2);
    Parliament and Council Regulation (EC) 1610/1996 (OJ L198, 8.8.96, p 30) art 10(2).

7   Ie the conditions laid down in Parliament and Council Regulation (EC) 469/2009 (OJ L152,
    16.6.2009, p 1) art 8 or, as the case may be, Parliament and Council Regulation (EC) 1610/1996
    (OJ L198, 8.8.96, p 30) art 8: see PARA 341.

8   Parliament and Council Regulation (EC) 469/2009 (OJ L152, 16.6.2009, p 1) art 10(3);
    Parliament and Council Regulation (EC) 1610/1996 (OJ L198, 8.8.96, p 30) art 10(3). The
    concept of 'irregularity' in art 10.3 must be given a wide interpretation and can encompass cases
    where a defect is cured after the date of the application: see *EI du Pont Nemours & Co v United
    Kingdom Intellectual Property Office* [2009] EWCA Civ 966, [2010] RPC 158, 111 BMLR 15.

9   Parliament and Council Regulation (EC) 469/2009 (OJ L152, 16.6.2009, p 1) art 10(4);
    Parliament and Council Regulation (EC) 1610/1996 (OJ L198, 8.8.96, p 30) art 10(4).

10 Ie the conditions laid down in Parliament and Council Regulation (EC) 469/2009 (OJ L152,
    16.6.2009, p 1) art 3(c), (d) or, as the case may be, Parliament and Council Regulation (EC)
    1610/1996 (OJ L198, 8.8.96, p 30) art 3(1)(c), (d): see PARA 340.

11 European Parliament and Council Regulation (EC) 469/2009 (OJ L152, 16.6.2009, p 1)
    art 10(5); Parliament and Council Regulation (EC) 1610/1996 (OJ L198, 8.8.96, p 30)
    art 10(5).

12 As to the meaning of 'basic patent' see PARA 340 note 7.

13 Ie the authorisation referred to in Parliament and Council Regulation (EC) 469/2009 (OJ L152,
    16.6.2009, p 1) art 3(b) or, as the case may be, Parliament and Council Regulation (EC)
    1610/1996 (OJ L198, 8.8.96, p 30) art 3(1)(b): see PARA 340.

14 Parliament and Council Regulation (EC) 469/2009 (OJ L152, 16.6.2009, p 1) art 11(1);
    Parliament and Council Regulation (EC) 1610/1996 (OJ L198, 8.8.96, p 30) art 11(1).

15 Ie the information listed in European Parliament and Council Regulation (EC) 469/2009
    (OJ L152, 16.6.2009, p 1) art 9(2) or, as the case may be, Parliament and Council Regulation
    (EC) 1610/1996 (OJ L198, 8.8.96, p 30) art 9(2): see PARA 341.

16 Parliament and Council Regulation (EC) 469/2009 (OJ L152, 16.6.2009, p 1) art 11(2);
    Parliament and Council Regulation (EC) 1610/1996 (OJ L198, 8.8.96, p 30) art 11(2).

17 Parliament and Council Regulation (EC) 469/2009 (OJ L152, 16.6.2009, p 1) art 12; Parliament
    and Council Regulation (EC) 1610/1996 (OJ L198, 8.8.96, p 30) art 12. As to fees see the
    Patents (Fees) Rules 2007, SI 2007/3292, rr, 2, 6, Sch 1.

343.   Validity of supplementary protection certificate.   The supplementary
protection certificate is invalid if:

(1)   it was granted contrary to the conditions for obtaining a certificate[1];

(2)   the basic patent[2] has lapsed before its lawful term expires[3];

(3)   the basic patent is revoked or limited to the extent that the product[4] for
      which the certificate was granted would no longer be protected by the
      claims of the basic patent or, after the basic patent has expired, grounds
      for revocation exist which would have justified such revocation or
      limitation[5].

Any person may submit an application or bring an action for a declaration of
invalidity of the certificate before the body responsible under national law for the
revocation of the corresponding basic patent[6].

If the certificate is so invalid, notification thereof must be published by the relevant authority[7]. The decisions of the relevant authority or of the national body are open to the same appeals as those provided for in national law against similar decisions taken in respect of national patents[8]. The procedural provisions applicable under national law to the corresponding basic patent apply to the certificate unless that law lays down special procedural provisions for certificates[9].

1   Ie contrary to the provisions of European Parliament and Council Regulation (EC) 469/2009 (OJ L152, 16.6.2009, p 1) concerning the creation of a supplementary protection certificate for medicinal products, art 3 or, as the case may be, Parliament and Council Regulation (EC) 1610/1996 (OJ L198, 8.8.96, p 30) concerning the creation of a supplementary protection certificate for plant protection products, art 3 (see PARA 340).

2   As to the meaning of 'basic patent' see PARA 340 note 7.

3   As to the term of a supplementary protection certificate see PARA 344.

4   As to the meaning of 'product' see PARA 340 note 2.

5   Parliament and Council Regulation (EC) 469/2009 (OJ L152, 16.6.2009, p 1) art 15(1); Parliament and Council Regulation (EC) 1610/1996 (OJ L198, 8.8.96, p 30) art 15(1).

6   Parliament and Council Regulation (EC) 469/2009 (OJ L152, 16.6.2009, p 1) art 15(2); Parliament and Council Regulation (EC) 1610/1996 (OJ L198, 8.8.96, p 30) art 15(2). In the case of a certificate relating to a medicinal product the revocation of an extension of the duration may also be revoked: see Parliament and Council Regulation (EC) 469/2009 (OJ L152, 16.6.2009, p 1) art 16.

7   Parliament and Council Regulation (EC) 469/2009 (OJ L152, 16.6.2009, p 1) art 17(1); Parliament and Council Regulation (EC) 1610/1996 (OJ L198, 8.8.96, p 30) art 16. As to the relevant authority see PARA 342 note 3.

8   Parliament and Council Regulation (EC) 469/2009 (OJ L152, 16.6.2009, p 1) art 18; Parliament and Council Regulation (EC) 1610/1996 (OJ L198, 8.8.96, p 30) art 17(1).

9   Parliament and Council Regulation (EC) 469/2009 (OJ L152, 16.6.2009, p 1) art 19(1); Parliament and Council Regulation (EC) 1610/1996 (OJ L198, 8.8.96, p 30) art 18(1).

344. Term of supplementary protection certificate. The supplementary protection certificate takes effect at the end of the lawful term of the basic patent[1] for a period equal to the period which elapsed between the date on which the application for a basic patent was lodged and the date of the first authorisation to place the product on the market in the EU reduced by a period of five years[2]. The duration of the certificate may not, however, exceed five years from the date on which it takes effect[3].

The certificate lapses:

(1)   at the end of the specified period[4];

(2)   if the certificate-holder surrenders it;

(3)   if the annual fee[5] is not paid in time;

(4)   if and so long as the product[6] covered by the certificate may no longer be placed on the market following the withdrawal of the appropriate authorisation or authorisations to place on the market[7].

If the certificate lapses in accordance with head (2), (3) or (4) above, notification thereof must be published by the relevant authority[8].

1   As to the meaning of 'basic patent' see PARA 340 note 7.

2   Parliament and Council Regulation (EC) 469/2009 (OJ L152, 16.6.2009, p 1) concerning the creation of a supplementary protection certificate for medicinal products, art 13(1); Parliament and Council Regulation (EC) 1610/1996 (OJ L198, 8.8.96, p 30) concerning the creation of a supplementary protection certificate for plant protection products, art 13(1). The periods under Parliament and Council Regulation (EC) 469/2009 (OJ L152, 16.6.2009, p 1) arts 13(1), 13(2) may be extended by six months where European Parliament and Council Regulation (EC) 1901/2006 (OJ L378, 27.12.2006, p 1) on medicinal products for paediatric use applies: Parliament and Council Regulation (EC) 469/2009 (OJ L152, 16.6.2009, p 1) art 13(3). As to the effect of this on the protected term see e g Case C-125/10 *Merck Sharp & Dohme Corpn v*

Deutsches Patent-und Markenamt (9 June 2011, unreported). See *Dr Reddy's Laboratories (UK) Ltd v Warner Lambert Company LLC* [2012] EWHC 3715 (Pat), [2013] RPC 819, 130 BMLR 97 (unsuccessful challenge to extension of certificate).

3   Parliament and Council Regulation (EC) 469/2009 (OJ L152, 16.6.2009, p 1) art 13(2); Parliament and Council Regulation (EC) 1610/1996 (OJ L198, 8.8.96, p 30) art 13(2). Parliament and Council Regulation (EC) 469/2009 (OJ L152, 16.6.2009, p 1) recital 9 and Parliament and Council Regulation (EC) 1610/1996 (OJ L198, 8.8.96, p 30) recital 11 refers to the holder of a patent and certificate enjoying an overall maximum of 15 years' exclusivity, and the effect of this and of Parliament and Council Regulation (EC) 469/2009 (OJ L152, 16.6.2009, p 1) art 13 and Parliament and Council Regulation (EC) 1610/1996 (OJ L198, 8.8.96, p 30) art 13 is to preclude the grant of a supplementary protection certificate for a period which extends the period of exclusivity beyond 15 years from the first EU marketing authorisation: see Case C-555/13 *Merck Canada Inc v Accord Healthcare Ltd* (13 February 2014, unreported). In connection with medicinal products only see note 2.

4   Ie the period provided for in Parliament and Council Regulation (EC) 469/2009 (OJ L152, 16.6.2009, p 1) art 13 or, as the case may be, Parliament and Council Regulation (EC) 1610/1996 (OJ L198, 8.8.96, p 30) art 13: see the text and notes 1–3.

5   Ie the annual fee laid down in accordance with Parliament and Council Regulation (EC) 469/2009 (OJ L152, 16.6.2009, p 1) art 12 or, as the case may be, Parliament and Council Regulation (EC) 1610/1996 (OJ L198, 8.8.96, p 30) art 12: see PARA 342.

6   As to the meaning of 'product' see PARA 340 note 2.

7   Parliament and Council Regulation (EC) 469/2009 (OJ L152, 16.6.2009, p 1) art 14; Parliament and Council Regulation (EC) 1610/1996 (OJ L198, 8.8.96, p 30) art 14.

8   Parliament and Council Regulation (EC) 469/2009 (OJ L152, 16.6.2009, p 1) art 17(1); Parliament and Council Regulation (EC) 1610/1996 (OJ L198, 8.8.96, p 30) art 16.

3. POST-GRANT AMENDMENT, RESTORATION AND SURRENDER

(1) AMENDMENT

345. In general. A patent[1] or an application[2] for a patent, as the case may be, may be amended at any time between the date of filing[3] of the application and the expiry of the patent[4]. Once a patent has been granted[5], the specification[6] may only be amended, with leave, either on formal application to the comptroller[7] or in proceedings before the court[8] or the comptroller in which the validity of the patent may be put in issue[9]. Any amendment allowed is subject to certain statutory restrictions[10] and to the right of members of the public to oppose[11].

The comptroller may, without any application being made to him for the purpose, amend the specification of a patent so as to acknowledge a registered trade mark[12].

1   Ie a patent under the Patents Act 1977: see PARA 303.
2   As to the application see PARA 314.
3   As to the meaning of 'date of filing' see PARA 315.
4   As to the term of a patent see PARA 338; and as to the amendment of applications before grant see PARA 329.
5   As to grant see PARA 337.
6   As to the specification see PARA 318.
7   Ie under the Patents Act 1977 s 27(1): see PARA 346. As to the comptroller see PARA 575.
8   As to the meaning of 'court' see PARA 619 note 1.
9   Ie under the Patents Act 1977 s 75(1): see PARA 346. As to proceedings in which the validity of a patent may be put in issue see s 74; and PARA 519.
10   As to these restrictions see PARA 351.
11   See the Patents Act 1977 ss 27(5), 75(2); and PARA 347. See note 12.

12   Patents Act 1977 s 27(4). For these purposes, the reference to a registered trade mark is to be construed as a reference to a registered trade mark within the meaning of the Trade Marks Act 1994 (see **TRADE MARKS AND TRADE NAMES** vol 97A (2014) PARA 111): s 106(1), Sch 4 para 1(1), (2). In considering whether or not to allow an application or amendment under the Patents Act 1977 ss 27, 75, the comptroller must have regard to any relevant principles applicable under the Convention on the Grant of European Patents (Munich, 5 October 1973; TS 20 (1978); Cmnd 7090) (the European Patent Convention: see PARA 644 et seq): Patents Act 1977 ss 27(6), 75(5) (added by the Patents Act 2004 s 2(1), (5)).

346. Applications for leave to amend. Where there are no proceedings pending[1] before the court[2] or the comptroller[3] in which the validity of the patent may be put in issue[4], the comptroller, on application made by the proprietor of the patent[5], may allow the specification[6] of the patent to be amended, subject to such conditions, if any, as he thinks fit[7]. There is no power to entertain such an application made while any such proceedings are pending[8], and an amendment allowed upon such an application would be invalid[9].

In any proceedings before the court or the comptroller in which the validity of a patent may be put in issue the court or the comptroller, as the case may be, may allow the proprietor of the patent to amend the specification in such manner, and subject to such terms as to advertising[10] the proposed amendment and as to costs, expenses or otherwise as the court or the comptroller thinks fit[11].

If, in any proceedings before the court or the comptroller for the revocation of the patent[12] the court or the comptroller determines that the patent is invalidated only to a limited extent, the court or the comptroller may allow the specification to be amended instead of revoking the patent[13].

Any amendment allowed under these provisions is subject to certain statutory restrictions[14].

1   Proceedings cease to be pending when: (1) the Court of Appeal makes a final order, even though an appeal to the House of Lords remains unheard (*Cropper v Smith (No 2)* (1884) 28 ChD 148, 1 RPC 254); (2) the Court of Appeal delivers judgment, but no final order is drawn up pending an application to the UK Intellectual Property Office for leave to amend (*Deshaw Reclamation Process Ltd's Application* (1952) 69 RPC 214); or (3) the parties have settled all differences, even though no order has been made disposing of the proceedings (*Lever Bros and Unilever Ltd's Patent* (1955) 72 RPC 198, CA); and, generally, when there is no question outstanding upon which the court is required to exercise any jurisdiction (*Lever Bros and Unilever Ltd's Patent* at 205). Proceedings are still pending, however, where the parties have settled all differences and the defendants have agreed to submit to an injunction because, irrespective of consent, the court still has to decide whether or not to grant an injunction (*Critchley Bros Ltd v Engelmann and Buckham Ltd* [1971] RPC 346); likewise proceedings are still pending where a Tomlin Order (see CIVIL PROCEDURE vol 12 (2009) PARA 1141) has not yet been made by the court (*Congoleum Industries Inc v Armstrong Cork Co Ltd* [1977] RPC 77). In such cases the court will allow amendment only where: (a) the amendments are not substantial in amount or in effect; (b) there is no apparent matter of controversy; and (c) no matter of public interest arises: *Imperial Chemical Industries plc v Ram Bathrooms plc and Rohm GmbH* [1994] FSR 181.
    As to the UK Intellectual Property Office see PARA 577.
2   As to the meaning of 'court' see PARA 619 note 1.
3   As to the comptroller see PARA 575.
4   As to such proceedings see the Patents Act 1977 s 74 (see PARA 519); and as to the validity of patents see PARA 429 et seq.
5   As to the application see PARA 347.
6   As to the specification see PARA 318.
7   Patents Act 1977 s 27(1), (2). In considering whether or not to allow an application under s 27, the comptroller must have regard to any relevant principles applicable under the Convention on the Grant of European Patents (Munich, 5 October 1973; TS 20 (1978); Cmnd 7090) (the European Patent Convention: see PARA 644 et seq): Patents Act 1977 s 27(6) (added by the Patents Act 2004 s 2(1)).
8   Patents Act 1977 s 27(2).
9   No such limitation applies to the correction of clerical errors by the comptroller: see PARA 353.
10   As to advertisements see PARAS 347–348.
11   Patents Act 1977 s 75(1) (amended by the Patents Act 2004 Sch 2 paras 1(1), 19). As to the procedure on application to the court see PARA 348. In considering whether or not to allow an amendment proposed under the Patents Act 1977 s 75, the court or the comptroller must have regard to any relevant principles applicable under the European Patent Convention: Patents Act 1977 s 75(5) (added by the Patents Act 2004 s 2(5)).
12   Ie under the Patents Act 1977 s 72: see PARAS 562–563.
13   Patents Act 1977 s 72(4) (amended by the Patents Act 2004 ss 4, 16(2), Sch 3). The patent will be revoked unless the specification is amended under the Patents Act 1977 s 75 within a specified time to the satisfaction of the court or the comptroller, as the case may be: s 72(4). See eg *Hallen Co v Brabantia (UK) Ltd* [1990] FSR 134, [1989] RPC 307. The reference in the Patents Act 1977 s 72(4) to the specification being amended is to its being amended under s 75 and also, in the case of a European patent (UK), to its being amended under any provision of the European Patent Convention under which the claims of the patent may be limited by amendment at the request of the proprietor: Patents Act 1977 s 72(4A) (added by the Patents Act 2004 s 4). As to the meaning of 'European patent (UK)' see PARA 652 note 1.
14   See the Patents Act 1977 s 76(2), (3); and PARA 351.

347.   Procedure on application to the comptroller.   An application by the proprietor of a patent[1] to the comptroller[2] for leave to amend the specification[3] of a patent must be made in writing, identify the proposed amendment and state the reason for making the amendment[4]. The application must, if it is reasonably possible, be delivered to the comptroller in electronic form or using electronic communications[5]. The comptroller may, if he thinks fit, direct the proprietor to file a copy of the specification with the amendment applied for marked on it[6]. Where the specification of a European patent (UK)[7] was published in a language other than English, the proprietor must file a translation into English of the part of the specification which he is applying to amend and a translation of the amendment[8]. The comptroller may, if he thinks fit, direct the proprietor to file a translation into English of the specification as published[9].

Where the court[10] or the comptroller allows the proprietor of a patent to amend the specification of the patent, the comptroller may direct him to file an amended specification which complies with the formal requirements[11].

A person may give notice to the comptroller of his opposition to an application to amend a specification by the proprietor of a patent, and if he does so the comptroller must notify the proprietor and consider the opposition in deciding whether to grant the application[12].

Where in any proceedings before the comptroller the validity of a patent is put in issue[13] and the proprietor of the patent applies to the comptroller for leave to amend the specification[14], any person may give notice of opposition to the proposed amendment, and if he does so the court or the comptroller must notify the proprietor and consider the opposition in deciding whether the amendment or any amendment should be allowed[15].

Where an application for amendment, whether made for that purpose or in the course of other proceedings before the comptroller, is not opposed, but the comptroller is not disposed to allow the amendment, the applicant may ask to be heard before the application is refused[16].

Any amendment allowed is subject to certain statutory restrictions[17].

An appeal lies to the Patents Court from any decision of the comptroller under these provisions[18].

1   Ie under the Patents Act 1977: see PARA 303.
2   Ie under the Patents Act 1977 s 27(1): see PARA 346. As to the comptroller see PARA 575. As to proceedings before the comptroller see PARAS 598–606.
3   As to the specification see PARA 318.
4   Patents Rules 2007, SI 2007/3291, r 35(1).
5   Patents Rules 2007, SI 2007/3291, r 35(2).
6   Patents Rules 2007, SI 2007/3291, r 35(3).
7   As to the meaning of 'European patent (UK)' see PARA 652 note 1.
8   Patents Rules 2007, SI 2007/3291, r 35(4).
9   Patents Rules 2007, SI 2007/3291, r 35(5).
10 As to the meaning of 'court' see PARA 619 note 1.
11 Patents Rules 2007, SI 2007/3291, r 35(6). The amended specification must comply with the requirements of r 14, Sch 2 (see PARA 319): r 35(6).
12 Patents Act 1977 s 27(5).
13 As to such proceedings see PARA 519.
14 Ie under the Patents Act 1977 s 75(1): see PARA 346.
15 Patents Act 1977 s 75(2).
16 See the Patents Act 1977 s 101; and PARA 591.
17 See the Patents Act 1977 s 76(3); and PARA 351. As to the effect of an amendment see PARA 349.
18 Patents Act 1977 s 97(1). As to appeals generally see PARAS 621–624.

348.   Procedure on application to the court. An application for permission to amend the specification of a patent[1] by the proprietor of the patent must be made by application notice[2]. The application notice must give particulars of the proposed amendment sought and the grounds upon which the amendment is sought[3]. The application notice must state whether the applicant will contend that the claims prior to amendment are valid and it must be served by the applicant on all parties and the comptroller[4] within seven days of its issue[5]. The application notice must, if it is reasonably possible, be served on the comptroller electronically[6].

Unless the court[7] otherwise orders, the comptroller will forthwith advertise the application to amend in the Official Journal (Patents)[8]. The advertisement will state that any person may apply to the comptroller for a copy of the application notice[9]. Within 14 days of the first appearance of the advertisement any person who wishes to oppose the application must file and serve on all parties and the comptroller a notice opposing the application which must include the grounds relied on[10]. Within 28 days of the first appearance of the advertisement the applicant must apply to the court for directions[11].

Unless the court otherwise orders, the applicant must within seven days serve on the comptroller any order of the court on the application[12].

1 Ie under the Patents Act 1977 s 75 (see PARA 346).
2 CPR 63.10(1). As to application notices see CIVIL PROCEDURE vol 11 (2009) PARA 303. Where an application for an order under the Patents Act 1977 s 75 (see PARA 346) is made to the court, the applicant must notify the comptroller, who is entitled to appear and be heard and must appear if so directed by the court: s 75(4).
3 CPR 63.10(2)(a).
4 As to the comptroller see PARA 575.
5 CPR 63.10(2)(b), (c). See *Nikken Kosakusho Works v Pioneer Trading Co* [2005] EWCA Civ 906, [2006] FSR 41, [2005] All ER (D) 350 (Jun); *Zipher Ltd v Markem Systems Ltd* [2007] EWHC 154 (Pat), [2007] FSR 481.
6 CPR 63.10(3). Where the application notice is served on the comptroller electronically, it must comply with any requirements for the sending of electronic communications to the comptroller: *Practice Direction—Intellectual Property Claims* PD 63 para 12.2.
7 As to the meaning of 'court' see PARA 619 note 1.
8 CPR 63.10(4), (9). As to the Official Journal (Patents) see PARA 578.
9 CPR 63.10(5).
10 CPR 63.10(6).
11 CPR 63.10(7). Not later than two days before the first hearing date the applicant, the comptroller if he wishes to be heard, the parties to the proceedings and any other opponent, must file and serve a document stating the directions sought: *Practice Direction—Intellectual Property Claims* PD 63 para 12.1.
12 CPR 63.10(8).

349. Effect of amendment. Any amendment of the specification of a patent[1] allowed by the comptroller[2] or the court[3] has effect and is deemed always to have had effect from the grant of the patent[4]. It is unlikely, therefore, that the right to make any lawful amendment can be challenged except on the ground of fraud[5], although there is power to revoke a patent where the matter disclosed[6] in the specification of the patent extends beyond that disclosed in the application for the patent as filed[7] or where the protection conferred by the patent has been extended by an amendment which should not have been allowed[8]. Further, it is by no means certain that an order of the comptroller allowing a forbidden amendment would not be void[9].

1 Ie under the Patents Act 1977: see PARA 303.
2 Ie under the Patents Act 1977 ss 27(1), 75(1): see PARA 346. As to the comptroller see PARA 575.
3 Ie under the Patents Act 1977 s 75(1): see PARA 346. As to the meaning of 'court' see PARA 619 note 1.
4 Patents Act 1977 ss 27(3), 75(3). As to grant see PARA 337.
5 This was explicit in the Patents Act 1949 s 31(2) (repealed) and seems to follow from the wording of the Patents Act 1977 ss 27(3), 75(3).
6 As to the disclosure of matter see PARA 351.
7 See the Patents Act 1977 s 72(1)(d); and PARA 562. As to the meaning of 'application as filed' see PARA 316 note 2.
8 See the Patents Act 1977 s 72(1)(e); and PARA 562.
9 See the Patents Act 1977 s 76(2), (3); and PARA 351.

350. Allowability of amendments. The European Patent Convention[1] makes provision for a European patent to be limited by a post-grant amendment of the claims at the request of the proprietor[2]. Any decision to limit the European patent takes effect in all the contracting states in which the patent has been granted[3]. When considering whether or not to grant the request to limit the patent, the European Patent Office[4] must first examine whether the requirements laid down in the Implementing Regulations have been met[5] and, if so, it must decide to limit the patent in accordance with the Implementing Regulations or else reject the request[6]. When the court[7] or the comptroller[8] is considering a post-grant amendment under the Patents Act 1977, it or he must have regard to any relevant principles applicable under the European Patent Convention[9]. The fact that the amendment would leave the patent still invalid was, and is likely to remain, a ground for refusing leave to amend[10].

1   Ie the Convention on the Grant of European Patents (Munich, 5 October 1973; TS 20 (1978); Cmnd 7090): see PARA 644 et seq.
2   See the European Patent Convention art 105a(1). The request for an amendment may not be filed while opposition proceedings in respect of the European patent are pending: art 105a(2).
3   European Patent Convention art 105b(3). It takes effect on the date on which mention of the decision is published in the European Patent Bulletin: art 105b(3).
4   As to the European Patent Office see PARA 644 note 2.
5   European Patent Convention art 105b(1). See the Implementing Regulations r 91.
6   European Patent Convention art 105b(2).
7   As to the meaning of 'court' see PARA 619 note 1.
8   As to the comptroller see PARA 575.
9   See the Patents Act 1977 ss 27(6), 75(5); and PARA 346.
10 See e g *Bristol-Myers Co (Johnson's) Application* [1979] RPC 450; *LG Philips LCD Co Ltd v Tatung (UK) Ltd* [2006] EWCA Civ 1774, [2007] RPC 509.

351. Restrictions on amendment. No amendment of an application for a patent[1] may be allowed[2] if it results in the application disclosing matter extending beyond that disclosed in the application as filed[3]; and no amendment of the specification[4] of a patent may be allowed[5] if it results in the specification disclosing additional matter or extends the protection conferred by the patent[6].

Matter is taken to have been disclosed in any relevant application[7] or in the specification of a patent if it was either claimed or disclosed, otherwise than by way of disclaimer or acknowledgment of prior art, in that application or specification[8]. It is a ground of revocation that the protection conferred by the patent has been extended by an amendment which should not have been allowed[9].

1   As to the application see PARA 314.
2   Ie under the Patents Act 1977 s 15A(6) (see PARA 317), s 18(3) (see PARA 328) or s 19(1) (see PARA 329).
3   Patents Act 1977 s 76(2) (substituted by the Copyright, Designs and Patents Act 1988 Sch 5 para 20; and amended by SI 2004/2357). As to the meaning of 'application as filed' see PARA 316 note 2. As to added matter see PARA 352.
4   As to the specification see PARA 318.
5   Ie under the Patents Act 1977 s 27(1) (see PARA 346), s 73 (see PARA 569) or s 75 (see PARAS 346–347).
6   Patents Act 1977 s 76(3) (substituted by the Copyright, Designs and Patents Act 1988 Sch 5 para 20). The necessary comparison must be performed with the application as filed and not with the specification prior to amendment: *Triumph Actuation Systems LLC v Aeroquip-Vickers Ltd* [2007] EWHC 1367 (Pat) at [41], [2007] All ER (D) 150 (Jun) at [41] per Pumfrey J.
7   Ie within the meaning of the Patents Act 1977 s 5: see PARA 311.
8   Patents Act 1977 s 130(3). As a source of disclosure, claims are not accorded any higher status than the description: *Asahi Kasei Kogyo KK's Application* [1991] RPC 485 at 533, HL, per

Lord Oliver of Aylmerton; *AC Edwards Ltd v Acme Signs & Displays Ltd* [1992] RPC 131, CA. A specific disclaimer does not add matter if it is inserted into a claim to avoid an 'accidental' anticipation: see *Sudarshan Chemical Industries Ltd v Clariant Produkte (Deutschland) GmbH* [2013] EWCA Civ 919, [2014] RPC 171, [2013] Bus LR 1188.

9   Patents Act 1977 s 72(1)(e). See also PARA 562.

352.   Added matter; extended protection.   The test to be applied in deciding whether an application discloses matter extending beyond that disclosed in the application as filed, or whether the specification of a granted patent discloses matter extending beyond that disclosed in the specification as filed, is whether the patentee has disclosed either by deletion or addition any inventive concept which was not disclosed before[1]. For example, deletion of an essential feature from a claim may result in the amended claim disclosing a materially different invention from that disclosed in the specification and claims of the application, with the result that the invention disclosed after amendment would extend beyond that disclosed in the application[2]; but the omission of non-essential features may not result in an extension of the disclosure if the result is that a different invention is not disclosed in the amended specification[3]. An 'intermediate generalisation', namely taking features which had been disclosed only in one particular context and having no inventive significance and introducing them into a claim deprived of that context, amounts to added matter[4]. It is necessary to ascertain first what the unamended specification as a whole, including the claims, disclosed either explicitly or implicitly to the skilled reader, secondly to do the same in respect of the patent as granted and thirdly to compare the two disclosures and decide whether the amended specification contains information which is not derived directly and unambiguously from that which the specification contained previously[5].

1   *Southco Inc v Dzus Fastener Europe Ltd* [1992] RPC 299 at 320, CA per Purchas LJ. See also *AC Edwards Ltd v Acme Signs & Displays Ltd* [1992] RPC 131, CA; *T Bonzel v Intervention Ltd (No 3)* [1991] RPC 553; *Raychem Ltd's Applications* [1986] RPC 547; *Reckitt & Colman Products Ltd v Richardson-Vicks Ltd*; *Smith Kline Beecham v Richardson-Vicks Inc* [1995] RPC 568, 25 BMLR 63; *LG Philips LCD Co Ltd v Tatung (UK) Ltd* [2006] EWCA Civ 1774, [2007] RPC 509; *G 01/93 Advanced Semiconductor Products* [1995] EPOR 97; *European Central Bank v Document Security Systems Inc* [2007] EWHC 600 (Ch), [2007] All ER (D) 420 (Mar) (affd [2008] EWCA Civ 192, [2008] All ER (D) 277 (Mar)), approved in *Vector Corpn v Glatt Air Techniques Inc* [2007] EWCA Civ 805, [2008] RPC 243, [2007] All ER (D) 297 (Oct); *Napp Pharmaceutical Holdings Ltd v Ratiopharm* [2009] EWCA Civ 252, [2009] RPC 539, [2009] All ER (D) 20 (Apr) (not everything falling within the scope of a claim will necessarily be disclosed in the patent); *Smith & Nephew plc v Convatec Technologies Inc* [2012] EWCA Civ 1638, [2013] RPC 223; *AP Racing Ltd v Alcon Components Ltd* [2013] EWPCC 3, [2013] All ER (D) 366 (Feb). For a summary of the test for added matter see *Gedeon Richter plc v Bayer Pharma AG* [2012] EWCA Civ 235 at [11]–[17], [2012] NLJR 426, [2012] All ER (D) 87 (Mar).

2   *Raychem Ltd's Applications* [1986] RPC 547; *Harding's Patent* [1988] RPC 515. Pre-grant amendments which widen claims are not prohibited by the Patents Act 1977 s 76 provided that the widening does not amount to an extension of matter. Post-grant widening amendments are expressly prohibited by s 76(3)(b): see PARA 351.

3   *Southco Inc v Dzus Fastener Europe Ltd* [1992] RPC 299, CA. See also Case T-331/87 *Houdaille/Removal of Feature* [1991] EPOR 194, Technical Board of Appeal.

4   See *Re Palmaz's European Patents (UK)* [1999] RPC 47, [2000] All ER (D) 357, [2000] IP & T 693; *LG Philips LCD Co Ltd v Tatung (UK) Ltd* [2006] EWCA Civ 1774, [2007] RPC 509; *Vector Corpn v Glatt Air Techniques Inc* [2007] EWCA Civ 805, [2008] RPC 243, [2007] All ER (D) 297 (Oct).

5   Case T-151/84 *Thomson-CSF's Application* [1988] EPOR 29, Technical Board of Appeal; Case T-467/90 *Thomson-CSF/Spooling process for optical fibre gyroscope* [1991] EPOR 115, Technical Board of Appeal, applied in *AC Edwards Ltd v Acme Signs & Displays Ltd* [1992] RPC 131, CA. See also *T Bonzel v Intervention Ltd (No 3)* [1991] RPC 553; *Mölnlycke AB v*

Procter and Gamble Ltd (No 5) [1994] RPC 49 at 135, CA; *Flexible Directional Indicators Ltd's Application* [1994] RPC 207 (pre-grant amendment); *Richardson-Vicks' Patent* [1995] RPC 568; *European Central Bank v Document Security Systems Inc* [2007] EWHC 600 (Ch), [2007] All ER (D) 420 (Mar) (affd [2008] EWCA Civ 192, [2008] All ER (D) 277 (Mar)), approved in *Vector Corpn v Glatt Air Techniques Inc* [2007] EWCA Civ 805, [2008] RPC 243, [2007] All ER (D) 297 (Oct); *Nokia OYJ (Nokia Corporation) v Ipcom GmbH & Co Kg* [2012] EWCA Civ 567, [2013] RPC 73.

353.   Correction of clerical errors.   The comptroller[1] may correct any error of translation or transcription, clerical error or mistake in any specification of a patent or application for a patent[2] or any document filed in connection with such a patent or application[3]. Where the comptroller is requested to correct such an error or mistake, any person may give the comptroller notice of opposition to the request and the comptroller must determine the matter[4].

Where the comptroller is requested to correct an error or mistake in a withdrawal of an application for a patent[5], and: (1) the application was published[6]; and (2) details of the withdrawal were published by the comptroller, the comptroller must publish notice of such a request in the Official Journal (Patents)[7]. Where the comptroller publishes such a notice, he may only correct an error or mistake by order[8].

The comptroller also has certain powers of correction in relation to international applications[9]. The comptroller's powers of correction are limited to mistakes in documents and do not extend to procedural mistakes[10].

1   As to the comptroller see PARA 575.
2   As to the specification see PARA 318; and as to the application see PARA 314. Where the request is to correct a specification of a patent or application, the request will not be granted unless the correction is obvious (meaning that it is immediately evident that nothing else could have been intended in the original specification): Patents Rules 2007, SI 2007/3291, r 105(3). However, this does not apply where the error in the specification of the patent or application is connected to the delivery of the application in electronic form or using electronic communications: r 105(4).
3   Patents Act 1977 s 117(1); and see *Dukhovoskoi's Applications* [1985] RPC 8. Where the comptroller determines that no person could reasonably object to the correction no advertisement need be published under the Patents Rules 2007, SI 2007/3291, r 75 (see PARA 598): r 105(5).
4   Patents Act 1977 s 117(2). A request to the comptroller to correct an error or mistake under s 117 must be made in writing and identify the proposed correction: Patents Rules 2007, SI 2007/3291, r 105(1). The comptroller may, if he thinks fit, require the person requesting a correction to produce a copy of the document indicating the correction: r 105(2). The correction of a name, address or address for service must be made under r 49 (see PARA 589): r 105(7).
5   As to withdrawal of applications see PARA 331.
6   Ie published under the Patents Act 1977 s 16: see PARA 326.
7   Patents Act 1977 s 117(3) (added by SI 2004/2357); Patents Rules 2007, SI 2007/3291, r 105(6). As to the Journal see PARA 578.
8   Patents Act 1977 s 117(4) (added by SI 2004/2357).
9   See the Patents Rules 2007, SI 2007/3291, rr 71, 72; and PARA 640.
10   *Klein Schanzlin & Becker AG's Application* [1985] RPC 241 (failure to file priority document in time not capable of correction under the Patents Act 1977 s 117(1)).

(2)   RESTORATION

354.   Lapsed patents.   A patent ceases to have effect on the expiration of the period provided for the payment of any renewal fee if the fee is not paid within that period or within the following six months[1]. A patent which has thus ceased to have effect may, however, be restored on application made to the comptroller[2] at any time within the prescribed period[3]. For the purposes of an application for restoration, a patent ceases to have effect on the expiry of the period allowed for payment of the renewal fee and not on the expiry of the six months' period of grace[4].

1   See the Patents Act 1977 s 25(3), (4); and PARA 339.
2   As to the comptroller see PARA 575.
3   Patents Act 1977 s 28(1) (substituted by the Copyright, Designs and Patents Act 1988 Sch 5 para 6(1), (2)). An application under the Patents Act 1977 s 28 for restoration of a patent may be made at any time before the end of the period ending with the thirteenth month after the month in which the period specified in s 25(4) ends: Patents Rules 2007, SI 2007/3291, r 40(1). Where: (1) a patent has ceased to have effect because a renewal fee has not been paid by the end of the renewal period; and (2) the renewal fee and the prescribed additional fee have not been paid by the end of the period specified in the Patents Act 1977 s 25(4) (the 'extended period'), the comptroller must, before the end of the period of six weeks beginning immediately after the end of the extended period, send a notice to the proprietor of the patent stating that the extended period has expired and referring him to the provisions of s 28 (see PARAS 355–356): Patents Rules 2007, SI 2007/3291, r 41(1), (2). The comptroller must send the notice to the address specified by r 39(3) (see PARA 339): r 41(3).
4   *Daido Kogyo KK's Patent* [1984] RPC 97, CA.

355. Restoration of lapsed patents. Where a patent has ceased to have effect by reason of a failure to pay any renewal fee[1], an application for the restoration of the patent may be made to the comptroller[2] at any time within the prescribed period[3]. Notice of the application must be published by the comptroller in the Official Journal (Patents)[4]. Such an application, which must be on the prescribed form[5], may be made by the person who was the proprietor of the patent or by any other person who would have been entitled to the patent if it had not ceased to have effect[6]. Where the patent was held by two or more persons jointly, the application may, with the leave of the comptroller, be made by one or more of them without joining the others[7]. If the comptroller is satisfied that the failure of the proprietor of the patent: (1) to pay the renewal fee within the prescribed period; or (2) to pay that fee and any prescribed additional fee within the period of six months immediately following the end of that period, was unintentional[8], the comptroller must by order restore the patent on payment of any unpaid renewal fee and any prescribed additional fee[9].

Where the comptroller grants an application he must advertise the fact in the Official Journal (Patents)[10]. If, however, upon consideration of the evidence, the comptroller is not satisfied that a case for an order has been made out, he must notify the applicant accordingly[11]. The applicant may then, before the end of the period of one month beginning immediately after the date of that notification, request to be heard by the comptroller[12] and the comptroller must then give the applicant an opportunity to be heard before he determines whether to grant or refuse the application[13].

1   Ie under the Patents Act 1977 s 25(3): see PARA 339. As to renewal fees see PARA 339.
2   As to the comptroller see PARA 575.
3   Patents Act 1977 s 28(1) (substituted by the Copyright, Designs and Patents Act 1988 Sch 5 para 6(1), (2)). An application under the Patents Act 1977 s 28 for restoration of a patent may be made at any time before the end of the period ending with the thirteenth month after the month in which the period specified in s 25(4) ends (see PARA 339): Patents Rules 2007, SI 2007/3291, r 40(1). The prescribed time limit may not be extended: see PARA 597.
4   Patents Act 1977 s 28(2A) (added by the Copyright, Designs and Patents Act 1988 Sch 5 para 6(1), (3)); Patents Rules 2007, SI 2007/3291, r 40(3). As to the Journal see PARA 578.
5   The application must be made on Patents Form 16: Patents Rules 2007, SI 2007/3291, r 40(2). The applicant must file evidence in support of the application: r 40(4). If that evidence does not accompany the application, the comptroller must specify a period within which the evidence is to be filed: r 40(5).

6   Patents Act 1977 s 28(2). As to ownership see PARA 359 et seq.

7   Patents Act 1977 s 28(2). As to the exercise of the comptroller's discretion see PARA 591.

8   See *Sirna Therapeutics Inc's Application* [2006] RPC 351; *Matsushita Electric Industrial Co Ltd v Comptroller-General of Patents* [2008] EWHC 2071 (Pat), [2008] RPC 944 (the mere assertion that the failure to pay renewal fees was unintentional was insufficient for this purpose).

9   Patents Act 1977 s 28(3) (substituted by SI 2004/2357; and amended by the Patents Act 2004 s 8(3)). As to prescribed additional fees see PARA 339.

10   Patents Rules 2007, SI 2007/3291, r 40(9).

11   Patents Rules 2007, SI 2007/3291, r 40(6).

12   Patents Rules 2007, SI 2007/3291, r 40(7) (amended by SI 2011/2052).

13   Patents Rules 2007, SI 2007/3291, r 40(8). As to appeals against a decision of the comptroller see PARA 621.

356.   Conditions of restoration. An order for the restoration of a lapsed patent[1] may be made subject to such conditions as the comptroller[2] thinks fit, including a condition requiring compliance with any provisions relating to registration[3] which have not been complied with[4]. If the proprietor of the patent fails to comply with any condition of such an order, the comptroller may revoke the order and give such directions consequential on the revocation as he thinks fit[5]. An appeal lies to the Patents Court[6] from any decision of the comptroller under these provisions[7]. A condition may be imposed that the protection given to third parties[8] be extended to cover the period until judgment[9].

1   Ie an order made under the Patents Act 1977 s 28(3): see PARA 355.

2   As to the comptroller see PARA 575.

3   As to registration see PARA 583 et seq.

4   Patents Act 1977 s 28(4).

5   Patents Act 1977 s 28(4). The comptroller must give any party to a proceeding before him an opportunity of being heard before exercising his power under this provision: see s 101; and PARA 591.

6   As to the Patents Court see PARA 619 et seq.

7   Patents Act 1977 s 97(1). As to appeals generally see PARAS 621–624.

8   See PARA 357.

9   *Daido Kogyo KK's Patent* [1984] RPC 97, CA. See also *Re Eveready Battery Co Inc's Patent* [2000] RPC 852.

357.   Effect on third persons of restoration of lapsed patents. The effect of an order for the restoration of a patent[1] is as follows[2].

Anything done under or in relation to the patent during the period between expiry and restoration is treated as valid[3]; and anything done during that period which would have constituted an infringement[4] if the patent had not expired is treated as an infringement:

(1)   if done at a time when it was possible for the patent to be renewed[5]; or

(2)   if it was a continuation or repetition of an earlier infringing act[6].

If, after it was no longer possible for the patent to be so renewed, and before publication of notice of the application for restoration, a person:

(a)   began in good faith to do an act which would have constituted an infringement of the patent if it had not expired; or

(b)   made in good faith effective and serious preparations to do such an act,

he has the right to continue to do the act or, as the case may be, to do the act, notwithstanding the restoration of the patent; but this right does not extend to granting a licence to another person to do the act[7].

If the act was done, or the preparations were made, in the course of a business, the person entitled to the right so conferred[8] may:

(i)　　authorise the doing of that act by any partners of his for the time being in that business; and

(ii)　　assign that right, or transmit it on death, or in the case of a body corporate on its dissolution, to any person who acquires that part of the business in the course of which the act was done or the preparations were made[9].

Where a product is disposed of to another person in exercise of the rights so conferred[10], that other and any person claiming through him may deal with the product in the same way as if it had been disposed of by the registered proprietor of the patent[11].

The above provisions apply in relation to the use of a patent for the services of the Crown[12] as they apply in relation to infringement of the patent[13].

1　As to restoration of a patent see PARA 355.
2　Patents Act 1977 s 28A(1) (s 28A added by the Copyright, Designs and Patents Act 1988 Sch 5 para 7).
3　Patents Act 1977 s 28A(2) (as added: see note 2).
4　As to acts which constitute an infringement see PARA 511 et seq.
5　Ie under the Patents Act 1977 s 25(4): see PARA 339.
6　Patents Act 1977 s 28A(3) (as added: see note 2).
7　Patents Act 1977 s 28A(4) (as added: see note 2). Section 28A(4) corresponds to s 28(5)(b), (6) (repealed). The decision in *Daido Kogyo KK's Patent* [1984] RPC 97, CA (restoration made conditional upon the protection given to third parties by the Patents Act 1977 s 28(6) (repealed) being extended to cover the period until judgment) may accordingly still be relevant, although the situation there obtaining is unlikely to recur as the comptroller now has a statutory obligation to publish notice of the application for restoration in the Official Journal (Patents): see s 28(2A); and PARA 355.
8　Ie the right conferred by the Patents Act 1977 s 28A(4): see the text to note 7.
9　Patents Act 1977 s 28A(5) (as added: see note 2).
10　Ie the rights conferred by the Patents Act 1977 s 28A(4) or (5): see the text to notes 7–9.
11　Patents Act 1977 s 28A(6) (as added: see note 2).
12　As to the meaning of 'services of the Crown' and 'use for the services of the Crown' see PARA 404 note 3.
13　Patents Act 1977 s 28A(7) (as added: see note 2).

(3)　SURRENDER

358.　Surrender. The proprietor of a patent may offer to surrender his patent at any time by notice[1] given to the comptroller[2]. A person may give notice to the comptroller of his opposition to the surrender of a patent, and if he does so the comptroller must notify the proprietor of the patent and determine the question[3].

If the comptroller is satisfied that the patent may properly be surrendered, he may accept the offer and, as from the date when notice of his acceptance is published in the Official Journal (Patents)[4], the patent ceases to have effect[5]. No action for infringement[6] lies, however, in respect of any act done before that date and no right to compensation accrues for any use of the patented invention[7] before that date for the services of the Crown[8].

1　The notice of an offer by a proprietor to surrender a patent must be in writing and include: (1) a declaration that no action is pending before the court for infringement or revocation of the patent; or (2) where such an action is pending, the particulars of the action: Patents Rules 2007, SI 2007/3291, r 42.
2　Patents Act 1977 s 29(1). As to the comptroller see PARA 575.
3　Patents Act 1977 s 29(2).
4　As to the Journal see PARA 580.
5　Patents Act 1977 s 29(3). See *Dyson Ltd's Patent* [2003] RPC 24; *Dyson Ltd's Patent (No 2)* [2003] RPC 848.

6   As to proceedings for infringement see PARA 520 et seq.
7   As to the meaning of 'patented invention' see PARA 370 note 27.
8   Patents Act 1977 s 29(3). As to the meaning of 'use for the services of the Crown' see PARA 404
      note 3. As to Crown use generally see PARA 403 et seq; and as to appeals against decisions of the
      comptroller see PARAS 621–624.

4. OWNERSHIP, DEVOLUTION AND ASSIGNMENT

(1) OWNERSHIP

359. In general. An invention[1] is personal property[2] and, except in certain cases of inventions made by employees[3], belongs primarily to the inventor or joint inventors[4]. A patent or an application for a patent[5] is also personal property[6], and rights in inventions, patents and applications[7] may therefore devolve or be transferred[8] at any stage from prior to the making of the invention[9] to the expiry of the patent[10] in the same way as other personal property, provided that any related agreement is not in unreasonable restraint of trade[11].

Questions and disputes as to the ownership of inventions, patents and applications for patents, and rights in them, being questions which relate to the ownership of personal property rights, are therefore within the inherent jurisdiction of the court[12], subject to a limitation period of two years after the grant of the patent in question[13]. The two-year limitation period does not apply, however, if it is shown that the proprietor of the patent knew at the time of the grant or, as the case may be, of the transfer of the patent to him, that he was not entitled to the grant[14]. In addition, there is a UK Intellectual Property Office[15] jurisdiction, subject to the same limitation[16], to deal with such questions and disputes, which may be referred to the comptroller for determination[17]. The comptroller may also determine questions about entitlement to foreign patents[18], provided that the patent in question has not been granted elsewhere, and settle disputes between joint applicants or proprietors, as the case may be, as to procedure[19] and as to the assignment or licensing of a patent[20]. In any of these cases, other than disputes between joint applicants or joint proprietors, the comptroller may, however, decline to deal with the question or dispute referred to him on the ground that it would more properly be determined by the court[21].

1 As to the meaning of 'invention' see PARA 301 note 2.
2 See PERSONAL PROPERTY vol 80 (2013) PARA 822.
3 As to rights in employees' inventions see PARA 368.
4 See the Patents Act 1977 s 7(2)(a); and PARA 306. As to the meanings of 'inventor' and 'joint inventor' see PARA 301 note 3.
5 As to the application see PARA 314.

6 Patents Act 1977 s 30(1). All patents and applications are expressly not choses in action: Patents Act 1977 s 30(1). See CHOSES IN ACTION vol 13 (2009) PARA 9.

7 For these purposes, 'right', in relation to any patent or application, includes an interest in the patent or application and, without prejudice to the foregoing, any reference to a right in a patent includes a reference to a share in the patent: Patents Act 1977 s 130(1). This may include equitable interests: *Kakkar v Szelke* [1989] FSR 225, CA.

8 See the Patents Act 1977 s 30; and PARAS 372–373.
9 See the Patents Act 1977 s 7(2)(b); and PARA 306. In the case of inventions made by employees which by virtue of s 39 (see PARA 368) belong to the employee, any contract which purports to diminish his rights in any invention made prior to the contract is unenforceable to that extent: see s 42(2); and PARA 368.

10 As to the term of patents see PARA 338.
11 As to restraint of trade see COMPETITION vol 18 (2009) PARAS 377–441.
12 As to the meaning of 'court' see PARA 619 note 1. This jurisdiction is subject to certain limitations in respect of questions relating to European patents: see the Patents Act 1977 s 82; and PARA 364.

13 See the Patents Act 1977 s 37(9); and PARA 366. As to the two-year period see *Yeda Research and Development Co Ltd v Rhone Poulenc Rorer International Holdings Inc* [2007] UKHL 43, [2008] 1 All ER 425, [2008] RPC 1. Proceedings in which this jurisdiction is invoked are

normally taken by the Patents Court or by the Intellectual Property Enterprise Court. As to the Patents Court see PARA 619 et seq; and as to the Intellectual Property Enterprise Court see PARA 626 et seq.

14	See the Patents Act 1977 s 37(9); and PARA 366.
15	As to the UK Intellectual Property Office see PARA 577.
16	See the Patents Act 1977 s 37(5); and PARA 366.
17	Ie under the Patents Act 1977 s 8(1) (reference before grant: see PARA 360) and s 37(1) (reference after grant: see PARA 365). As to the comptroller see PARA 575.
18	Ie under the Patents Act 1977 s 12: see PARA 363.
19	Ie under the Patents Act 1977 s 10 (see PARA 360) and s 12(4) (see PARA 363).
20	Ie under the Patents Act 1977 s 37(1)(c) (see PARA 365).
21	See the Patents Act 1977 s 8(7) (see PARA 360), s 12(2) (see PARA 363) and s 37(8) (see PARA 365). As to when the comptroller should decline jurisdiction in favour of the court see *Luxim Corpn v Ceravision Ltd* [2007] EWHC 1624 (Ch), [2007] RPC 797, [2007] All ER (D) 116 (Jul). Where the comptroller so declines to deal with a question, any person seeking the court's determination of that question must issue a claim form within 14 days of the comptroller's decision: CPR 63.11. The presence of allegations of improper conduct or breach of fiduciary duty may lead the comptroller to decline jurisdiction: *Reflex Modulation Ltd v Alteristic Instruments Ltd* BL O/084/08, C-G.

**360.	Determination of right to patent before grant.**	At any time before a patent has been granted[1] for an invention[2], whether or not an application[3] has been made for it, any person may refer to the comptroller[4] the question whether he is entitled to be granted a patent for that invention[5], either alone or with any other persons, or has or would have any right[6] in or under any patent so granted or any application for such a patent[7]. Similarly, at any time before a patent has been granted for an invention, any of two or more co-proprietors of an application for a patent for that invention may refer to the comptroller the question whether any right in or under the application should be transferred or granted to any other person[8]. In both these cases, the comptroller must determine the question referred and may make such order as he thinks fit to give effect to the determination[9]. If, however, it appears to him that the question referred involves matters which would more properly be determined by the court[10], he may decline to deal with it[11].

Where a reference has been made to the comptroller under these provisions but has not been determined before the time when the application is first in order for a grant of a patent, that fact does not prevent the grant of a patent[12]. However, on the grant of the patent the person who made the reference is treated as having referred to the comptroller the question whether the patent has been granted to the person entitled to it[13].

If any dispute arises between joint applicants for a patent as to whether or in what manner the application should be proceeded with, the comptroller, on a request made by any of the parties, may give such directions as he thinks fit for enabling the application to proceed in the name of one or more of the parties alone or for regulating the manner in which it is to be proceeded with, or for both those purposes, according as the case may require[14].

1	As to grant see PARA 337.
2	As to the meaning of 'invention' see PARA 301 note 2. In the context of a dispute as to entitlement the term 'invention' means that which was conceived by the applicant for the patent to be his invention, whether patentable or not: *Viziball Ltd's Application* [1988] RPC 213. The precise formulation of the claims is not important: *Norris's Patent* [1988] RPC 159.
3	As to the application see PARA 314.
4	As to the comptroller see PARA 575.
5	Ie under the Patents Act 1977 s 7(2): see PARA 306.
6	As to the meaning of 'right' see PARA 359 note 7.

7   Patents Act 1977 s 8(1)(a). As to proceedings before the comptroller see the Patents Rules 2007,
    SI 2007/3291, Pt 7 (rr 73–91); and PARAS 598–606.
8   Patents Act 1977 s 8(1)(b). As to the transfer of rights in or under an application see s 30; and
    PARAS 372–373. See *Yeda Research and Development Co Ltd v Rhone Poulenc Rorer
    International Holdings Inc* [2007] UKHL 43, [2008] 1 All ER 425, [2008] RPC 1.
9   Patents Act 1977 s 8(1). As to particular orders which the comptroller may make on a reference
    under s 8(1)(a) see PARA 361.
10 As to the meaning of 'court' see PARA 619 note 1.
11 Patents Act 1977 s 8(7). As to the procedure in this case see PARA 359 note 21.
12 Patents Act 1977 s 9.
13 Patents Act 1977 s 9. As to questions referred in this case see s 37; and PARA 365.
14 Patents Act 1977 s 10. As to the effect of such directions on any third party rights under an
    application for a patent see PARA 362.

361. Relief available from the comptroller. Where at any time before a patent
has been granted[1] for an invention[2] a person refers a question relating to his
entitlement to a patent for it[3], the comptroller[4] must determine the question and
may make such order as he thinks fit to give effect to that determination[5]. In
particular, where the reference is made between the filing of an application[6] for a
patent and the grant of a patent pursuant to the application, the comptroller
may[7]:

(1)   order that the application is to proceed in the name of the person
      making the reference, either solely or jointly with that of any other
      applicant, instead of in the name of the applicant or any specified
      applicant[8];

(2)   where the reference was made by two or more persons, order that the
      application is to proceed in all their names jointly[9];

(3)   refuse to grant a patent in pursuance of the application or order the
      application to be amended[10] so as to exclude any of the matters in
      respect of which the question was referred[11];

(4)   make an order transferring or granting any licence or other right[12] in or
      under the application[13] and give directions to any person for carrying
      out the provisions of any such order[14].

Where, however, on a reference it is alleged that, by virtue of any transaction,
instrument or event relating to an invention or an application for a patent, any
person other than the inventor[15] or the applicant for the patent has become
entitled to be granted, whether alone or with any other persons, a patent for the
invention or has or would have any right in or under any patent so granted or
any application for any such patent, an order may not be made under head
(1), (2) or (4) above on the reference unless notice of the reference is given to the
applicant and any such person, except any of them who is a party to the
reference[16].

Where a question relating to entitlement to a patent is referred to the
comptroller after an application for the patent has been made and:

(a)   the comptroller orders the application for a patent for the invention to
      which the question relates to be amended[17];

(b)   the application is refused[18] before the comptroller has disposed of the
      reference, whether the reference was made before or after the
      publication of the application[19]; or

(c)   the application is refused under any other provision of the Patents
      Act 1977 or is withdrawn[20] before the comptroller has disposed of the
      reference, whether the application is refused or withdrawn before or
      after its publication[21],

the comptroller may order that any person by whom the reference was made may make a new application for a patent, within the prescribed period[22], for the whole or part of any matter comprised in the earlier application or, as the case may be, for all or any of the matter excluded from the earlier application[23].

Where a person refers to the comptroller any question relating to rights under a joint application for a patent[24], any order made may contain directions to any person for transferring or granting any right in or under the application[25].

If any person to whom the comptroller has given directions[26] fails to do anything necessary for carrying out those directions within 14 days after the date of the directions, the comptroller, on application by any person in whose favour or on whose reference the directions were given, may authorise him to do that thing on behalf of the person to whom the directions were given[27].

No directions may be given by the comptroller under these provisions so as to affect the mutual rights or obligations of trustees or of the personal representatives of deceased persons, or their rights or obligations as such[28].

1   As to grant see PARA 337.
2   As to the meaning of 'invention' see PARA 301 note 2.
3   Ie under the Patents Act 1977 s 8(1)(a): see PARA 360.
4   As to the comptroller see PARA 575.
5   Patents Act 1977 s 8(1). As to proceedings before the comptroller see the Patents Rules 2007, SI 2007/3291, Pt 7 (rr 73–91); and PARAS 598–606. For guidance in relation to patent entitlement disputes see *University of Southampton's Applications* [2004] EWHC 2107 (Pat), [2005] RPC 11 (on appeal *IDA Ltd v University of Southampton* [2006] EWCA Civ 145, [2006] RPC 567, [2006] All ER (D) 22 (Mar)). See also *Hughes v Paxman* [2006] EWCA Civ 818, [2007] RPC 34.
6   As to the filing of an application see PARA 317.
7   The following provisions do not apply where the application is refused or withdrawn before the reference is disposed of by the comptroller: Patents Act 1977 s 8(2).
8   Patents Act 1977 s 8(2)(a).
9   Patents Act 1977 s 8(2)(b).
10   As to the amendment of applications before grant see PARA 329.
11   Patents Act 1977 s 8(2)(c).
12   As to the meaning of 'right' see PARA 359 note 7.
13   As to rights in or under an application and the transfer of them see the Patents Act 1977 s 30; and PARAS 372–373.
14   Patents Act 1977 s 8(2)(d). As to the effect of non-compliance with directions see the text to notes 26–27.
15   As to the meaning of 'inventor' see PARA 301 note 3.
16   Patents Act 1977 s 8(6).
17   Patents Act 1977 s 8(3)(a).
18   Ie under the Patents Act 1977 s 8(2)(c): see the text to notes 10–11.
19   Patents Act 1977 s 8(3)(b). As to publication of the application see PARA 326.
20   As to the refusal and withdrawal of applications see PARA 331.
21   Patents Act 1977 s 8(3)(c) (amended by the Patents Act 2004 s 6(1)).
22   The period prescribed for filing a new application under the Patents Act 1977 s 8(3) is the relevant period: Patents Rules 2007, SI 2007/3291, r 20(1). The relevant period is: (1) where the comptroller's decision to make an order under that provision is not appealed, three months beginning immediately after the date on which the order was made; or (2) where that decision is appealed, three months beginning immediately after the date on which the appeal was finally disposed of: r 20(3) (amended by SI 2011/2052). The comptroller may however, if he thinks fit, shorten the relevant period after giving the parties such notice and subject to such conditions as the comptroller may direct: Patents Rules 2007, SI 2007/3291, r 20(4).
23   Patents Act 1977 s 8(3). See *Viziball Ltd's Application* [1988] RPC 213. An application for a patent which: (1) is made in respect of matter disclosed in an earlier application, or in the specification of a patent which has been granted; and (2) discloses additional matter, that is matter extending beyond that disclosed in the earlier application, as filed, or the application for the patent, as filed, may be filed under the Patents Act 1977 s 8(3) but may not be allowed to proceed unless it is amended so as to exclude the additional matter: s 76(1) (substituted by the Copyright, Designs and Patents Act 1988 Sch 5 para 20). As to the disclosure of matter see PARA

351. Where such a new application is made, it is treated as having been filed on the date of filing the earlier application: Patents Act 1977 s 8(3). As to the meaning of 'date of filing' see PARA 315.

24 Ie under the Patents Act 1977 s 8(1)(b): see PARA 360.
25 Patents Act 1977 s 8(4).
26 Ie contained in an order made under the Patents Act 1977 s 8(2)(d), (4).
27 Patents Act 1977 s 8(5).
28 Patents Act 1977 s 8(8).

362.   Effect of transfer on rights of third persons of application for patent.
Where an order is made or directions are given[1] that an application for a patent[2] is to proceed in the name of one or some of the original applicants, whether or not it is also to proceed in the name of some other person, any licences[3] or other rights[4] in or under the application continue in force and are treated as granted by the persons in whose name the application is to proceed, subject to the provisions of the order and any directions[5].

Where, however, an order is made or directions are given[6] that an application for a patent is to proceed in the name of one or more persons none of whom was an original applicant, on the ground that the original applicant or applicants was or were not entitled to be granted the patent[7], any licences or other rights in or under the application lapse on the registration[8] of that person or those persons as the applicant or applicants or, where the application has not been published[9], on the making of the order, subject to the provisions of the order and any directions[10].

If, however, before registration of a reference[11] resulting in the making of such an order the original applicant or any of the applicants[12] or a licensee[13] of the applicant, acting in good faith, worked the invention in question in the United Kingdom[14] or made effective and serious preparations to do so, that or those original applicant or applicants or the licensee, on making a request within the prescribed period[15] to the person in whose name the application is to proceed, is or are entitled to be granted a licence other than an exclusive licence[16] to continue working or, as the case may be, to work the invention[17]. If, before registration of a reference resulting in the making of such an order, the original applicant or applicants or licensee has acted in such a way, he may, on making a request within the prescribed period to the new applicant, be entitled to be granted a licence (but not an exclusive licence) to continue working or, as the case may be, to work the invention so far as it is the subject of the new application[18]. Any such licence[19] must be granted for a reasonable period and on reasonable terms[20].

Further, where an order is made[21], the person in whose name the application is to proceed or, as the case may be, the person who makes the new application, or any person claiming that he is entitled to be granted any such licence may refer to the comptroller[22] for determination of the question whether the latter is so entitled and whether any such period is or terms are reasonable[23]. The comptroller, if he considers it appropriate, may order the grant of such a licence[24].

1 Ie under the Patents Act 1977 s 8 (see PARA 361) or s 10 (see PARA 360).
2 As to the application see PARA 314.
3 As to licences see PARA 377 et seq.
4 As to the meaning of 'right' see PARA 359 note 7.
5 Patents Act 1977 s 11(1). Without prejudice to any other method of enforcement, any order for the grant of a licence under s 11 has effect as if it were a deed, executed by the proprietor of the patent and all other necessary parties, granting a licence in accordance with the order: s 108.
6 Ie under the Patents Act 1977 s 8 (see PARA 361).

7   As to who may be granted a patent see PARA 306.
8   As to registration see PARA 583 et seq.
9   As to publication of the application see PARA 326.
10   Patents Act 1977 s 11(2).
11   Ie under the Patents Act 1977 s 8 (see PARA 361).
12   Patents Act 1977 s 11(3)(a).
13   Patents Act 1977 s 11(3)(b).
14   As to the meaning of 'United Kingdom' see PARA 303 note 5.
15   The period prescribed for the purposes of the Patents Act 1977 s 11(3), (3A) (see the text and
     note 18) is two months beginning immediately after: (1) where s 11 is applied by s 12(5) (foreign
     and convention patents: see PARA 363), the date on which the order under s 12(1) was made;
     and (2) in any other case, the date on which the order under s 8 was made (see PARA 361):
     Patents Rules 2007, SI 2007/3291, r 90(1) (amended by SI 2011/2052).
16   As to the meaning of 'exclusive licence' see PARA 379.
17   Patents Act 1977 s 11(3).
18   Patents Act 1977 s 11(3A) (added by the Patents Act 2004 s 6(2)).
19   Ie a licence under the Patents Act 1977 s 11(3) or s 11(3A) (see the text and notes 17–18).
20   Patents Act 1977 s 11(4) (amended by the Patents Act 2004 s 6(3)).
21   Ie an order under the Patents Act 1977 s 11(2) (see the text to notes 6–10) or s 11(3A) (see the
     text to note 18).
22   As to the comptroller see PARA 575.
23   Patents Act 1977 s 11(5) (amended by the Patents Act 2004 s 6(4)). As to proceedings before the
     comptroller see the Patents Rules 2007, SI 2007/3291, Pt 7 (rr 73–91); and PARAS 598–606.
24   Patents Act 1977 s 11(5).

363.   Determination of right to foreign patents.   At any time before a patent[1] is
granted for an invention in pursuance of an application made under the law of
any country other than the United Kingdom or under any treaty or international
convention, whether or not that application has been made:

(1)   any person may refer to the comptroller[2] the question whether he is
         entitled to be granted, either alone or with any other persons, any such
         patent for that invention or has or would have any right[3] in or under
         any such patent or an application for such a patent[4]; or

(2)   any of two or more co-proprietors of an application for such a patent
         for that invention may so refer the question whether any right in or
         under the application should be transferred or granted to any other
         person[5].

The comptroller must determine the question so far as he is able to and may
make such order as he thinks fit to give effect to the determination[6]. If, however,
it appears to the comptroller that the question referred involves matters which
would more properly be determined by the court[7], he may decline to deal with
it[8]. The comptroller also has jurisdiction to determine disputes between joint
applicants for any such foreign patent as to whether the application should
proceed[9]. In certain cases, namely:

(a)   where an application for a European patent (UK)[10] is refused or
         withdrawn, or the designation of the United Kingdom in the application
         is withdrawn, whether before or after publication of the application but
         before a question relating to the right to the patent has been referred to
         the comptroller[11] or before proceedings relating to that right have begun
         before the relevant convention court[12];

(b)   where an application has been made for a European patent (UK) and on
         such a reference to the comptroller under head (1) or head (2) above or
         any such proceedings as are mentioned in head (a) above the
         comptroller, the court or the relevant convention court determines by a
         final decision[13], whether before or after publication of the application,

that a person other than the applicant has the right to the patent, but that person requests the European Patent Office that the application for the patent should be refused[14]; or

(c)   where an international application for a patent (UK)[15] is withdrawn, or the designation of the United Kingdom in the application is withdrawn, whether before or after the making of any reference[16] or the publication of the application[17],

the comptroller may order:

(i)   that any person, other than the applicant, who appears to him to be entitled to be granted a patent[18] may within the prescribed period[19] apply[20] for such a patent for the whole or part of any matter comprised in the earlier application[21]; and

(ii)   that, if the later application is filed, it is to be treated as having been filed on the date of filing[22] the earlier application[23].

1   For these purposes, references to a patent and an application for a patent include respectively references to protection in respect of an invention and an application which, in accordance with the law of any country other than the United Kingdom or any treaty or international convention, is equivalent to an application for a patent or for such protection: Patents Act 1977 s 12(7)(a). As to foreign patents and applications generally see PARA 306 et seq. As to the meaning of 'United Kingdom' see PARA 303 note 5.

2   As to the comptroller see PARA 575.

3   As to the meaning of 'right' see PARA 359 note 7.

4   Patents Act 1977 s 12(1)(a). As to proceedings before the comptroller see the Patents Rules 2007, SI 2007/3291, Pt 7 (rr 73–91); and PARAS 598–606. As to rights under patents see PARA 359. See eg *Cannings' United States Application* [1992] RPC 459 (where the comptroller made a determination in relation to a United States application which was the national phase of an international application made through the Patent Co-operation Treaty); *LIFFE Administration and Management v Pinkava* [2007] EWCA Civ 217, [2007] 4 All ER 981, [2007] RPC 667 (which concerned rights in US patent applications with subject matter not patentable in the United Kingdom). As to the Patent Co-operation Treaty (ie the Patent Co-operation Treaty (Washington, 19 June 1970; TS 78 (1978); Cmnd 7340) see PARA 629 et seq. As to the national phase see PARA 641.

5   Patents Act 1977 s 12(1)(b).

6   Patents Act 1977 s 12(1). Section 11 (see PARA 362) applies to any orders made under s 12(1) and to any orders made and directions given by the relevant convention court with respect to a question corresponding to any question which may be determined under s 12(1): s 12(5). See also PARA 362 note 15. For these purposes, 'relevant convention court', in relation to any proceedings under the Convention on the Grant of European Patents (Munich, 5 October 1973; TS 20 (1978); Cmnd 7090) (the European Patent Convention) or the Patent Co-operation Treaty, means that court or other body which under that convention or treaty has jurisdiction over those proceedings, including, where it has such jurisdiction, any department of the European Patent Office (see PARA 644): Patents Act 1977 s 130(1) (amended by the Patents Act 2004 s 16(1), (2), Sch 2 paras 1(1), 27(b), Sch 3). As to those conventions see PARA 629 et seq.
    The Patents Act 1977 s 12(1), in its application to a European patent and an application for any such patent, has effect subject to s 82 (see PARA 364): s 12(3).

7   As to the meaning of 'court' see PARA 619 note 1.

8   Patents Act 1977 s 12(2).

9   The Patents Act 1977 s 10 (see PARA 360), except so much of it as enables the comptroller to regulate the manner in which an application is to proceed, applies to disputes between joint applicants for any such patent as is mentioned in s 12(1) as it applies to joint applicants for a patent under the Patents Act 1977: s 12(4).

10   As to the meaning of 'European patent (UK)' see PARA 652 note 1. As to European patents generally see PARA 644 et seq.

11   Ie under the Patents Act 1977 s 12(1): see the text to notes 1–6.

12   Patents Act 1977 s 12(6)(a) (amended by the Patents Act 2004 Sch 2 paras 1(1), 5(a)).

13   For these purposes, a decision is taken to be final when the time for appealing from it has expired without an appeal being brought or, where an appeal is brought, when it is finally disposed of: Patents Act 1977 s 12(7)(b).

14 Patents Act 1977 s 12(6)(b).
15 As to the meaning of 'international application for a patent (UK)' see PARA 640 note 1. As to international patents generally see PARA 628 et seq.
16 Ie under the Patents Act 1977 s 12(1): see the text to notes 1–6.
17 Patents Act 1977 s 12(6)(c) (amended by the Patents Act 2004 Sch 2 paras 1(1), 5(b)).
18 Ie a patent under the Patents Act 1977. As to persons entitled to be granted such a patent see PARA 306.
19 The period prescribed for filing a new application under the Patents Act 1977 s 12(6) is the relevant period: Patents Rules 2007, SI 2007/3291, r 20(1). The relevant period is: (1) where the comptroller's decision to make an order under that provision is not appealed, three months beginning immediately after the date on which the order was made; or (2) where that decision is appealed, three months beginning immediately after the date on which the appeal was finally disposed of: r 20(3) (amended by SI 2011/2052). The comptroller may however, if he thinks fit, shorten the relevant period after giving the parties such notice and subject to such conditions as the comptroller may direct: Patents Rules 2007, SI 2007/3291, r 20(4).
20 As to the application see PARA 314.
21 An application for a patent which: (1) is made in respect of matter disclosed in an earlier application, or in the specification of a patent which has been granted; and (2) discloses additional matter, that is matter extending beyond that disclosed in the earlier application, as filed, or the application for the patent, as filed, may be filed under the Patents Act 1977 s 12 but may not be allowed to proceed unless it is amended so as to exclude the additional matter: s 76(1) (substituted by the Copyright, Designs and Patents Act 1988 s 295, Sch 5 para 20). As to the disclosure of matter see PARA 351.
22 As to the meaning of 'date of filing' see PARA 315.
23 Patents Act 1977 s 12(6).

364. Jurisdiction to determine questions as to right to European patents. The jurisdiction of the court[1] and the comptroller[2] to determine questions[3] about entitlement to European patents[4] is subject to certain conditions[5] in the case of:

(1) a question arising before the grant of a European patent as to whether a person has a right to be granted a European patent or a share in any such patent[6]; or

(2) any such question (an 'employer-employee question') between an employer[7] and an employee[8], or their successors in title, arising out of an application for a European patent for an invention made by the employee[9].

The court and the comptroller have jurisdiction to determine any question under head (1) above if either of the following conditions is satisfied, namely:

(a) the applicant for the patent has his residence or principal place of business in the United Kingdom[10]; or

(b) the other party claims that the patent should be granted to him and he has his residence or principal place of business in the United Kingdom and the applicant does not have his residence or principal place of business in any of the relevant contracting states[11];

and also if, in either of those cases, there is no written evidence that the parties have agreed to submit to the jurisdiction of the competent authority of a relevant contracting state other than the United Kingdom[12].

Similarly, the court and the comptroller have jurisdiction to determine an employer-employee question if either of the following conditions is satisfied, namely:

(i) the employee is mainly employed in the United Kingdom[13]; or

(ii) the employee is not mainly employed anywhere or his place of main employment cannot be determined, but the employer has a place of business in the United Kingdom to which the employee is attached, whether or not he is also attached elsewhere[14];

and also if, in either of those cases, there is no written evidence that the parties have agreed to submit to the jurisdiction of the competent authority of a relevant contracting state other than the United Kingdom or, where there is such evidence of such an agreement, if the law applicable to the contract of employment does not recognise the validity of the agreement[15].

In addition, without prejudice to the above provisions, the court and the comptroller have jurisdiction to determine any question under head (1) or head (2) above if there is written evidence that the parties have agreed to submit to the jurisdiction of the court or the comptroller, as the case may be, and, in the case of an employer-employee question, the law applicable to the contract of employment recognises the validity of the agreement[16].

If, after proceedings to determine a question under head (1) or head (2) above have been brought before the competent authority of a relevant contracting state other than the United Kingdom, proceedings are begun before the court or a reference is made to the comptroller[17] to determine that question, the court or the comptroller, as the case may be, must stay the proceedings unless or until the competent authority of that other state either determines to decline jurisdiction and no appeal lies from the determination or the time for appealing expires[18], or makes a determination which the court or the comptroller refuses to recognise[19].

A determination of a question under head (1) or head (2) above by the competent authority of a relevant contracting state other than the United Kingdom from which no appeal lies or in respect of which the time for appealing has expired is recognised in the United Kingdom as if it had been made by the court or the comptroller unless the court or he refuses to recognise it[20]. The court or the comptroller may refuse to recognise any such determination that the applicant for a European patent had no right to be granted the patent, or any share in it, if either the applicant did not contest the proceedings in question because he was not notified of them at all or in the proper manner or was not notified of them in time for him to contest the proceedings[21], or the determination in the proceedings in question conflicts with the determination of the competent authority of any relevant contracting state in proceedings instituted earlier between the same parties as in the proceedings in question[22].

1   As to the meaning of 'court' see PARA 619 note 1.
2   As to the comptroller see PARA 575.
3   Ie under the Patents Act 1977 s 12: see PARA 363. For these purposes, references to the determination of a question include respectively references, in the case of the court, to the making of a declaration with respect to that question and, in the case of the court or the comptroller, to the making of an order under s 12 in relation to that question: s 82(8). As to the comptroller's power to award costs on a reference under s 12 see *Rizla Ltd's Application* [1993] RPC 365.
4   As to the meaning of 'European patent' see PARA 644 note 5. As to European patents generally see PARA 644 et seq.
5   Patents Act 1977 s 82(1). Section 12 (see PARA 363) does not confer jurisdiction on the comptroller to determine a question to which s 82 applies except in accordance with s 82(3)–(9) (see the text and notes 3, 6–19): s 82(2).
6   This includes whether or not the person has any equitable interest in the patent eg under a constructive trust: *Kakkar v Szelke* [1989] FSR 225, CA. As to shares in patents see PARA 359 note 7.
7   For these purposes, 'employer', in relation to an employee, means the person by whom the employee is or was employed: Patents Act 1977 s 130(1). As to the meaning of 'employee' see note 8.
8   For these purposes, 'employee' means a person who works or, where the employment has ceased, worked under a contract of employment or in employment under or for the purposes of a government department or a person who serves (or served) in the naval, military or air forces of the Crown: Patents Act 1977 s 130(1) (amended by the Armed Forces Act 1981 s 22(1), (3)).

9   Patents Act 1977 s 82(3).
10 Patents Act 1977 s 82(4)(a). As to the meaning of 'United Kingdom' see PARA 303 note 5.
11 Patents Act 1977 s 82(4)(b). For these purposes, 'relevant contracting state' means a country
    which is a party to the Convention on the Grant of European Patents (Munich, 5 October 1973;
    TS 20 (1978); Cmnd 7090) (the European Patent Convention) and has not exercised its right
    under the convention to exclude the application of the protocol to the convention known as the
    'Protocol on Recognition': Patents Act 1977 s 82(9). As to the convention see PARA 644.
12 Patents Act 1977 s 82(4).
13 Patents Act 1977 s 82(5)(a).
14 Patents Act 1977 s 82(5)(b).
15 Patents Act 1977 s 82(5) (amended by the Contracts (Applicable Law) Act 1990 Sch 4 para 3).
    As to the law applicable to the contract see CONFLICT OF LAWS vol 19 (2011) PARA 628 et seq.
16 Patents Act 1977 s 82(6) (amended by the Contracts (Applicable Law) Act 1990 Sch 4 para 3).
17 Ie under the Patents Act 1977 s 12: see PARA 363.
18 Patents Act 1977 s 82(7)(a).
19 Patents Act 1977 s 82(7)(b).
20 Patents Act 1977 s 83(1). Where in proceedings before the comptroller a person seeks
    recognition of a relevant determination, he must furnish to the comptroller a copy of the
    determination duly certified by the relevant official of the competent authority: Patents
    Rules 2007, SI 2007/3291, r 61(1). 'Relevant determination' means the determination of a
    question to which the Patents Act 1977 s 82 applies by the competent authority of a relevant
    contracting state other than the United Kingdom: Patents Rules 2007, SI 2007/3291, r 61(2).
21 Patents Act 1977 s 83(2)(a).
22 Patents Act 1977 s 83(2)(b).

365.   Determination of right to patent after grant. After a patent has been
granted[1] for an invention[2], any person having or claiming a proprietary interest
in or under the patent may refer to the comptroller[3] the question:

(1)   who is or are the true proprietor or proprietors of the patent;
(2)   whether the patent should have been granted[4] to the person or persons
        to whom it was granted; or
(3)   whether any right[5] in or under the patent should be transferred[6] or
        granted to any other person or persons[7].

The comptroller must determine the question and make such order as he
thinks fit to give effect to the determination[8].

Such an order may contain provision:

(a)   directing that the person by whom the reference is made be included,
        whether or not to the exclusion of any other person, among the persons
        registered[9] as proprietors of the patent[10];
(b)   directing the registration of a transaction, instrument or event by virtue
        of which that person has acquired any right in or under the patent[11];
(c)   granting any licence or other right in or under the patent[12];
(d)   directing the proprietor of the patent or any person having any right in
        or under the patent to do anything specified in the order as necessary to
        carry out the other provisions of the order[13].

Where the comptroller finds on such a reference that the patent was granted
to a person not entitled to be granted that patent, whether alone or with other
persons, and on an application for revocation[14] makes an order on the ground
for the conditional or unconditional revocation of the patent, the comptroller
may order that the person by whom the application was made or his successor in
title may make a new application for a patent:

(i)   in the case of unconditional revocation, for the whole of the matter
        comprised in the specification of that patent[15]; and
(ii)   in the case of conditional revocation, for the matter which in the
        comptroller's opinion should be excluded from that specification by
        amendment[16].

Where such a new application is made[17], it is treated as having been filed on the date of filing[18] the application for the patent to which the reference relates[19].

Where a question is so referred to the comptroller, an order may not be made[20] on the reference unless notice of the reference is given to all persons registered as proprietor of the patent or as having a right in or under the patent, except those who are parties to the reference[21].

If it appears to the comptroller on such a reference that the question referred to him would more properly be determined by the court[22], he may decline to deal with it and, without prejudice to the court's jurisdiction to determine any such question and make a declaration, the court has jurisdiction to do so[23], subject to certain statutory limitations[24].

1 As to grant see PARA 337.
2 As to the meaning of 'invention' see PARA 301 note 2.
3 As to the comptroller see PARA 575.
4 As to who may be granted a patent see PARA 306.
5 As to the meaning of 'right' see PARA 359 note 7.
6 As to the transfer of rights under a patent see PARA 372 et seq.
7 Patents Act 1977 s 37(1) (substituted by the Copyright, Designs and Patents Act 1988 Sch 5 para 9(1), (2)). As to proceedings before the comptroller see the Patents Rules 2007, SI 2007/3291, Pt 7 (rr 73–91); and PARAS 598–606. Where a co-proprietor of a patent applies, the comptroller has the power to order that licences under the patent be granted: *Hughes v Paxman* [2006] EWCA Civ 818, [2007] RPC 34. As to the application of the Patents Act 1977 s 37 to EU compulsory licences see PARA 401.
8 Patents Act 1977 s 37(1) (as substituted: see note 7). See *Norris's Patent* [1988] RPC 159. An order under the Patents Act 1977 s 37 must not be so made as to affect the mutual rights or obligations of trustees or of the personal representatives of a deceased person, or their rights or obligations as such: s 37(6). For the statutory limitations as to time on the comptroller's jurisdiction see PARA 366.
9 As to registration see PARA 583 et seq.
10 Patents Act 1977 s 37(2)(a). The court cannot make an order pursuant to s 37(2) to a person who has no proprietary interest in the patent; the purpose of s 37(2) is to enable the comptroller to resolve a dispute between those sharing the proprietary interest: *Cinpres Gas Injection Ltd v Melea Ltd* [2006] EWHC 2950 (Ch), [2007] Bus LR 20, [2006] All ER (D) 305 (Nov). See also *Henry Bros (Magherafelt) Ltd v Ministry of Defence and Northern Ireland Office* [1997] RPC 693; affd [1999] RPC 442, [1998] All ER (D) 545, CA.
11 Patents Act 1977 s 37(2)(b).
12 Patents Act 1977 s 37(2)(c).
13 Patents Act 1977 s 37(2)(d). If any person to whom such directions have been given fails to do anything necessary for carrying out any such directions within 14 days after the date of the order containing the directions, the comptroller may, on application made to him by any person in whose favour or on whose reference the order containing the directions was made, authorise that person to do that thing on behalf of the person to whom the directions were given: s 37(3).
14 Ie under the Patents Act 1977 s 72: see PARA 563. As to revocation generally see PARA 562 et seq.
15 Patents Act 1977 s 37(4)(a).
16 Patents Act 1977 s 37(4)(b). As to the specification see PARA 318; and as to amendment of the specification see PARA 347.
17 An application for a patent which: (1) is made in respect of matter disclosed in an earlier application, or in the specification of a patent which has been granted; and (2) discloses additional matter, that is matter extending beyond that disclosed in the earlier application, as filed, or the application for the patent, as filed, may be filed under the Patents Act 1977 s 37(4) but may not be allowed to proceed unless it is amended so as to exclude the additional matter: s 76(1) (substituted by the Copyright, Designs and Patents Act 1988 Sch 5 para 20). As to the disclosure of matter see PARA 351.
18 As to the meaning of 'date of filing' see PARA 315.
19 Patents Act 1977 s 37(4) (amended by the Copyright, Designs and Patents Act 1988 Sch 5 para 9(1), (3)(a)). A new application for a patent may be filed under the Patents Act 1977 s 37(4) before the end of the relevant period: Patents Rules 2007, SI 2007/3291, r 20(2). The relevant period is: (1) where the comptroller's decision to make an order under that provision is

not appealed, three months beginning immediately after the date on which the order was made; or (2) where that decision is appealed, three months beginning immediately after the date on which the appeal was finally disposed of: r 20(3) (amended by SI 2011/2052). However, the comptroller may, if he thinks fit, shorten the relevant period after giving the parties such notice and subject to such conditions as the comptroller may direct: Patents Rules 2007, SI 2007/3291, r 20(4). As to appeals see PARAS 621–624.

20   Ie by virtue of the Patents Act 1977 s 37(2) (see the text to notes 9–13) or under s 37(4) (see the text to notes 18–19).

21   Patents Act 1977 s 37(7) (amended by the Copyright, Designs and Patents Act 1988 Sch 5 para 9(1), (3)(a)).

22   As to the meaning of 'court' see PARA 619 note 1. As to when the comptroller should decline jurisdiction in favour of the court see *Luxim Corpn v Ceravision Ltd* [2007] EWHC 1624 (Ch), [2007] RPC 797, [2007] All ER (D) 116 (Jul). Where the comptroller so declines to deal with a question, any person seeking the court's determination of that question must issue a claim form within 14 days of the comptroller's decision: CPR 63.11. The presence of allegations of improper conduct or breach of fiduciary duty may lead the comptroller to decline jurisdiction: *Reflex Modulation Ltd v Alteristic Instruments Ltd* BL O/084/08, C-G.

23   Patents Act 1977 s 37(8) (amended by the Copyright, Designs and Patents Act 1988 Sch 5 para 9(1), (3)(b)). As to procedure see PARA 359.

24   See the Patents Act 1977 s 37(9); and PARA 366.

366. Disputes two years after grant. Where a question as to entitlement to a patent is referred to the comptroller[1] or proceedings are commenced invoking the jurisdiction of the court[2] the second anniversary of the date of the grant of the patent[3]:

(1)   the comptroller may not make an order transferring the patent in question[4] or allowing a new application to be made[5]; and

(2)   the court, in exercise of its declaratory jurisdiction[6], may not determine the question whether the patent was granted to a person not so entitled,

unless, in either case, it is shown that any person registered[7] as a proprietor of the patent knew at the time of the grant or transfer of the patent to him, as the case may be, that he was not entitled to the patent[8].

1   Ie under the Patents Act 1977 s 37(1): see PARA 365. As to the comptroller see PARA 575. As to the effect of the two-year limitation period see *Yeda Research and Development Co Ltd v Rhone-Poulenc Rorer International Holdings Inc* [2007] UKHL 43, [2008] 1 All ER 425, [2008] RPC 1.

2   Ie under the Patents Act 1977 s 37(8): see PARA 365. As to the meaning of 'court' see PARA 619 note 1.

3   As to grant see PARA 337.

4   Ie under the Patents Act 1977 s 37(2): see PARA 365.

5   Ie under the Patents Act 1977 s 37(4): see PARA 365.

6   Ie under the Patents Act 1977 s 37(8): see PARA 365.

7   As to registration see PARA 583 et seq.

8   Patents Act 1977 s 37(5), (9) (amended by the Intellectual Property Act 2014 Schedule para 3(1)(a)).

367. Effect on third persons of transfer of patent. Where an order is made[1] that a patent be transferred from any person or persons (the 'old proprietor or proprietors') to one or more persons, whether or not including an old proprietor, then, subject to the provisions of the order, any licences[2] or other rights[3] granted or created by the old proprietor or proprietors continue in force and are treated as granted by the person or persons to whom the patent is ordered to be transferred (the 'new proprietor or proprietors')[4].

Where an order is so made that a patent is to be transferred from the old proprietor or proprietors to one or more persons none of whom was an old proprietor, on the ground that the patent was granted to a person not entitled to be granted the patent[5], any licences or other rights in or under the patent lapse on the registration[6] of that person or those persons as the new proprietor or proprietors of the patent, subject to the provisions of the order[7].

Where an order is so made that a patent is to be so transferred or that a person other than an old proprietor may make a new application for a patent, and, before the reference of the question[8] resulting in the making of any such order is registered, the old proprietor or proprietors or a licensee of the patent, acting in good faith, worked the invention in question in the United Kingdom[9] or made effective and serious preparations to do so, the old proprietor or proprietors or the licensee, on making a request to the new proprietor or proprietors or, as the case may be, the new applicant, within the prescribed period[10], is or are entitled to be granted a licence, other than an exclusive licence[11], to work or to continue working the invention, as the case may be, so far as it is the subject of the new application[12]. Any such licence must be granted for a reasonable period and on reasonable terms[13]. The new proprietor or proprietors of the patent or, as the case may be, the new applicant or any person claiming that he is entitled to be granted any such licence may refer to the comptroller[14] the question whether that person is so entitled and whether any such period is or terms are reasonable[15]; and the comptroller must determine the question and may, if he considers it appropriate, order the grant of such a licence[16].

1　Ie under the Patents Act 1977 s 37: see PARA 365.
2　As to licences see PARA 377 et seq.
3　As to the meaning of 'right' see PARA 359 note 7.
4　Patents Act 1977 s 38(1). Section 38 is subject to s 33 (effect of registration on rights in patents: see PARAS 586–587): s 38(1). Without prejudice to any other method of enforcement, any order for the grant of a licence under s 38 has effect as if it were a deed, executed by the proprietor of the patent and all other necessary parties, granting a licence in accordance with the order: s 108. As to the application of s 38 to EU compulsory licences see PARA 401.
5　As to entitlement see PARA 306.
6　As to registration see PARA 583 et seq.
7　Patents Act 1977 s 38(2).
8　Ie under the Patents Act 1977 s 37: see PARA 365.
9　As to the meaning of 'United Kingdom' see PARA 303 note 5.
10　The period prescribed for the purposes of the Patents Act 1977 s 38(3) is two months beginning immediately after the date on which the order mentioned in s 38(2) was made: Patents Rules 2007, SI 2007/3291, r 90(2) (amended by SI 2011/2052).
11　As to the meaning of 'exclusive licence' see PARA 379.
12　Patents Act 1977 s 38(3) (amended by the Patents Act 2004 Sch 2 paras 1(1), 10(1), (2)).
13　Patents Act 1977 s 38(4).
14　As to the comptroller see PARA 575.
15　As to proceedings before the comptroller see the Patents Rules 2007, SI 2007/3291, Pt 7 (rr 73–91); and PARAS 598–606.
16　Patents Act 1977 s 38(5) (amended by the Patents Act 2004 Sch 2 paras 1(1), 10(1), (3)).

368. Rights in employees' inventions. Where the rights in an invention[1] made by an employee[2] have not been dealt with by agreement[3], then, subject to certain conditions as to the place of his employment[4], and notwithstanding anything in any rule of law[5], an invention made by an employee is taken, as between him and his employer[6], to belong to his employer for all purposes[7] if:

(1)　it was made in the course of the normal duties of the employee or in the course of duties falling outside his normal duties, but specifically assigned to him, and the circumstances in either case were such that an invention might reasonably be expected to result from the carrying out of his duties[8]; or

(2)　the invention was made in the course of the duties of the employee and, at the time of making the invention, because of the nature of his duties and the particular responsibilities arising from the nature of his duties he had a special obligation to further the interests of the employer's undertaking[9].

Any other invention made by an employee is taken, as between him and his employer, to belong to the employee[10].

Any term in a contract, whenever made, relating to inventions made by an employee, and entered into by him either with the employer (alone or with another)[11] or with some other person at the request of the employer or pursuant to the employee's contract of employment[12], which diminishes the employee's rights[13] in inventions of any description made by him after the date of the contract, or in or under patents[14] for those inventions or applications for such patents, is unenforceable against him to the extent that it diminishes his rights in an invention of that description so made, or in or under a patent for such an invention or an application for any such patent[15].

Where by virtue of these provisions an invention belongs, as between him and his employer, to an employee, nothing done:

(a)   by or on behalf of the employee or any person claiming under him for the purposes of pursuing an application for a patent; or

(b)   by any person for the purpose of performing or working the invention,

is to be taken to infringe any copyright[16] or design right[17] to which, as between him and his employer, his employer is entitled in any model or document relating to the invention[18].

1   As to the meaning of 'invention' see PARA 301 note 2.
2   As to the meaning of 'employee' see PARA 364 note 8. In the Patents Act 1977 ss 39–43, except so far as the context otherwise requires, references to the making of an invention by an employee are references to his making it alone or jointly with any other person, but do not include references to his merely contributing advice or other assistance in the making of an invention by another employee: s 43(3).
3   As to the enforceability of contracts relating to employees' inventions see the Patents Act 1977 s 42 (see the text and notes 11–15).
4   The Patents Act 1977 ss 39–42 do not apply to an invention made by an employee unless, at the time he made the invention, one of the following conditions was satisfied in his case, that is to say: (1) he was mainly employed in the United Kingdom; or (2) he was not mainly employed anywhere or his place of employment could not be determined, but his employer had a place of business in the United Kingdom to which the employee was attached, whether or not he was also attached elsewhere: s 43(2). As to the meaning of 'United Kingdom' see PARA 303 note 5.
5   Cases decided before the enactment of the Patents Act 1977 are of doubtful guidance: *Liffe Administration and Management v Pinkava* [2007] EWCA Civ 217 at [57], [2007] 4 All ER 981 at [57], [2007] RPC 667 at [57] per Sir Andrew Morritt C.
6   As to the meaning of 'employer' see PARA 364 note 7.
7   Ie for the purposes of the Patents Act 1977 and all other purposes. Section 39 does not allow an employee to retain a beneficial interest in his invention by way of constructive trust: *French v Mason* [1999] FSR 597, [1998] All ER (D) 486.
8   Patents Act 1977 s 39(1)(a). See *Harris' Patent* [1985] RPC 19. Extra or different duties undertaken are not to be regarded only as duties 'specifically assigned' as it is quite possible for them in the course of time to become 'normal' under the Patents Act 1977 s 39(1): *LIFFE Administration and Management v Pinkava* [2007] EWCA Civ 217, [2007] 4 All ER 981, [2007] RPC 667. See also *Greater Glasgow Health Board's Application* [1996] RPC 207.
9   Patents Act 1977 s 39(1)(b). See *Harris' Patent* [1985] RPC 19.
10   Patents Act 1977 s 39(2).
11   Patents Act 1977 s 42(1)(a).
12   Patents Act 1977 s 42(1)(b).
13   As to the meaning of 'right' see PARA 359 note 7.
14   In the Patents Act 1977 ss 39–42, references to a patent and to a patent being granted are respectively references to a patent or other protection and to its being granted whether under the law of the United Kingdom or the law in force in any other country or under any treaty or

international convention: s 43(4) (amended by the Copyright, Designs and Patents Act 1988 Sch 5 para 11(2)). As to treaties and international conventions see PARA 628 et seq.

15 Patents Act 1977 s 42(2). Section 42(2) is not, however, to be construed as derogating from any duty of confidentiality owed by an employee to his employer by virtue of any rule of law or otherwise: s 42(3). As to the duty of confidentiality in an employment context see EMPLOYMENT vol 39 (2009) PARA 58; CONFIDENCE AND INFORMATIONAL PRIVACY vol 19 (2011) PARAS 23, 24. Section 42 applies to any arrangement made with a Crown employee by or on behalf of the Crown as his employer as it applies to any contract made between an employee and an employer other than the Crown: s 42(4). For these purposes, 'Crown employee' means a person employed under or for the purposes of a government department or any officer or body exercising on behalf of the Crown functions conferred by any enactment or a person serving in the naval, military or air forces of the Crown: s 42(4) (amended by the Armed Forces Act 1981 s 22(1), (2)).

16 As to copyright see COPYRIGHT vol 23 (2013) PARAS 603, 653 et seq.

17 As to design right see COPYRIGHT vol 23 (2013) PARAS 610, 1048 et seq.

18 Patents Act 1977 s 39(3) (added by the Copyright, Designs and Patents Act 1988 Sch 5 para 11(1)).

369. Compensation of employees for certain inventions. Where it appears to the court[1] or the comptroller[2] on an application made by an employee[3] within the prescribed period[4]:

(1)   that the employee has made an invention[5] belonging to the employer[6] for which a patent has been granted[7];

(2)   that the invention or the patent for it is, having regard among other things to the size and nature of the employer's undertaking, of outstanding benefit[8] to the employer; and

(3)   that by reason of those facts it is just that the employee should be awarded compensation to be paid by the employer,

the court or the comptroller may award him compensation[9].

The court or the comptroller may also award compensation to an employee on such an application where it appears to the court or the comptroller that:

(a)   a patent has been granted for an invention made by and belonging to the employee[10];

(b)   the employee's rights in the invention, or in any patent or application for a patent[11] for the invention, have been assigned[12] to the employer or an exclusive licence[13] under the patent or application has been granted to the employer[14];

(c)   the benefit derived by the employee from the contract of assignment or grant or any ancillary contract (the 'relevant contract') is inadequate in relation to the benefit derived by the employer[15] from the invention or the patent for it or both[16]; and

(d)   by reason of those facts it is just that the employee should be awarded compensation to be paid by the employer in addition to the benefit derived from the relevant contract[17].

If it appears to the comptroller on an application under the above provisions that the application involves matters which would more properly be determined by the court, he may decline to deal with it[18].

The above provisions do not, however, apply to the invention of an employee where a relevant collective agreement[19] provides for the payment of compensation in respect of inventions of the same description as that invention to employees of the same description as that employee[20].

1   As to the meaning of 'court' see PARA 619 note 1. An application by an employee for compensation under the Patents Act 1977 s 40(1) or (2) must be made in a claim form and within the prescribed period: CPR 63.12(1). The prescribed period begins on the date of the grant of the patent and ends one year after the patent has ceased to have effect: CPR 63.12(2).

Where a patent has ceased to have effect as a result of failure to pay the renewal fees within the prescribed period (see PARA 339) and application for restoration is made to the comptroller under the Patents Act 1977 s 28 (see PARA 355), the prescribed period: (1) if restoration is ordered, continues as if the patent had remained continuously in effect; or (2) if restoration is refused, is treated as expiring one year after the patent ceased to have effect, or six months after the refusal, whichever is the later: CPR 63.12(3).

Where an employee applies for compensation under the Patents Act 1977 s 40(1) or (2), the court must at the case management conference give directions as to: (a) the manner in which the evidence, including any accounts of expenditure and receipts relating to the claim, is to be given at the hearing of the claim and if written evidence is to be given, the period within which witness statements or affidavits must be filed; and (b) the provision to the claimant by the defendant or a person deputed by him, of reasonable facilities for inspecting and taking extracts from the accounts by which the defendant proposes to verify the accounts in head (a) or from which those accounts have been derived: *Practice Direction—Intellectual Property Claims* PD 63 para 13.1.

In proceedings under the Patents Act 1977 s 40, the court, in determining whether to award costs or expenses to any party and what costs or expenses to award, must have regard to all the relevant circumstances, including the financial position of the parties: s 106(1), (1A)(a) (s 106(1) amended, and s 106(1A) added, by the Patents Act 2004 s 14). If in any such proceedings the Patents Court directs that any costs of one party are to be paid by another party, the court may settle the amount of the cost by fixing a lump sum or may direct that the costs are to be taxed on a scale specified by the court, being a scale of costs prescribed by rules of court: Patents Act 1977 s 106(2) (amended by the Constitutional Reform Act 2005 Sch 11 para 23(1), (4)).

2   As to the comptroller see PARA 575. As to proceedings before the comptroller see the Patents Rules 2007, SI 2007/3291, Pt 7 (rr 73–91); and PARAS 598–606. All relevant patents must be identified on the prescribed form: *British Steel plc's Patent* [1992] RPC 117.

3   As to the meaning of 'employee' see PARA 364 note 8.

4   The period prescribed for the purposes of the Patents Act 1977 s 40(1) and (2) is the period beginning with the date of grant of the patent and ending one year after the patent ceased to have effect: Patents Rules 2007, SI 2007/3291, r 91(1). However, if an application for restoration is made under the Patents Act 1977 s 28 (see PARA 355) and: (1) the application is granted, the prescribed period continues as if the patent had remained continuously in effect; or (2) the application is refused, the prescribed period is the period beginning immediately after the date of grant of the patent and ending one year after the patent ceased to have effect or, if it expires later, the period of six months beginning with the date on which the application was refused: Patents Rules 2007, SI 2007/3291, r 91(2) (amended by SI 2011/2052). As to the grant and term of patents see PARAS 337–338.

5   As to the making of an invention by an employee see PARA 368 note 2.

6   As to the meaning of 'employer' see PARA 364 note 7. For these purposes, references to an invention belonging to an employer or employee are references to its so belonging as between the employer and the employee: Patents Act 1977 s 40(7). As to when an invention is deemed to belong to an employer see PARA 368.

7   As to references to a patent being granted see PARA 368 note 14.

8   As to what constitutes an 'outstanding benefit' see *Kelly v GE Healthcare Ltd* [2009] EWHC 181 (Pat) at [18]–[23], [2009] RPC 363 at [18]–[23], per Floyd J, cited in *Shanks v Unilever plc* [2014] EWHC 1647 (Pat), [2014] All ER (D) 05 (Jun) (which discusses the law in this area). For these purposes, 'benefit' means benefit in money or money's worth: Patents Act 1977 s 43(7). 'Outstanding' means something out of the ordinary and not as such would normally be expected to arise from the results of the duties for which the employee was paid: *GEC Avionics Ltd's Patent* [1992] RPC 107. The onus is on the employee to prove that the patent was of outstanding benefit and that the benefit derived from the patent and not the invention: *Memco-Med Ltd's Patent* [1992] RPC 403.

9   Patents Act 1977 s 40(1) (substituted by the Patents Act 2004 s 10(1), (8)). As to the amount of compensation see PARA 370. The law on employee compensation under the Patents Act 1977 s 40(1) is comprehensively reviewed in *Kelly v GE Healthcare Ltd* [2009] EWHC 181 (Pat) at [5]–[60], [2009] RPC 363 at [5]–[60], per Floyd J. For applications for compensation in which the employee did not succeed see *GEC Avionics Ltd's Patent* [1992] RPC 107; *British Steel plc's Patent* [1992] RPC 117; *Memco-Med Ltd's Patent* [1992] RPC 403; *Shanks v Unilever plc* [2014] EWHC 1647 (Pat), [2014] All ER (D) 05 (Jun).

10 Patents Act 1977 s 40(2)(a). Section 40(2) has effect notwithstanding anything in the relevant contract or any agreement applicable to the invention, other than a relevant collective agreement: s 40(4). As to the meaning of 'relevant collective agreement' see note 19. As to when an invention is deemed to belong to an employee see PARA 368.

11 As to the meaning of 'right' see PARA 359 note 7.

12 As to assignment see PARA 373.

13 As to the meaning of 'exclusive licence' see PARA 379.

14 Patents Act 1977 s 40(2)(b). See also note 10.

15 For these purposes, the benefit derived or expected to be derived by an employer from an invention or patent includes, where he dies before any award is made under the Patents Act 1977 s 40 in respect of the patent, any benefit derived or expected to be derived from it by his personal representatives or by any person in whom it was vested by their assent: s 43(5) (amended by the Patents Act 2004 s 10(6), (8)). The benefit derived or expected to be derived by an employer from an invention does not include any benefit derived or expected to be derived from the invention after the patent for it has expired or has been surrendered or revoked: Patents Act 1977 s 43(5A) (added by the Patents Act 2004 s 10(7), (8)).

16 Patents Act 1977 s 40(2)(c) (amended by the Patents Act 2004 s 10(2), (8)). See also note 10.

17 Patents Act 1977 s 40(2)(d). See also note 10.

18 Patents Act 1977 s 40(5). Where the comptroller declines to deal with an application under s 40(5), any person seeking the court's determination of that application must issue a claim form within 14 days of the comptroller's decision: CPR 63.11(1)(b).

19 For these purposes, 'relevant collective agreement' means a collective agreement within the meaning of the Trade Union and Labour Relations (Consolidation) Act 1992, made by or on behalf of a trade union to which the employee belongs, and by the employer or an employer's association to which the employer belongs which is in force at the time of the making of the invention: Patents Act 1977 s 40(6) (amended by the Trade Union and Labour Relations (Consolidation) Act 1992 Sch 2 para 9); and see EMPLOYMENT vol 41 (2009) PARA 1042.

20 Patents Act 1977 s 40(3).

370. Award and assessment of compensation. An award of compensation[1] to an employee[2] in relation to a patent for an invention[3] must be such as will secure for the employee a fair share, having regard to all the circumstances, of the benefit which the employer has derived, or may reasonably be expected to derive[4], from any of the following: (1) the invention in question; (2) the patent for the invention; (3) the assignment or grant of the property or any right in the invention[5] or the property in, or any right under, an application for that patent, to a person connected with the employer[6].

In determining the fair share of the benefit to be secured for an employee in respect of an invention which has always belonged to an employer, the court[7] or the comptroller[8] must, among other things, take the following matters into account[9]:

(a) the nature of the employee's duties, his remuneration and the other advantages he derives or has derived from his employment or has derived[10] in relation to the invention[11];

(b) the effort and skill which the employee has devoted to making the invention[12];

(c) the effort and skill which any other person has devoted to making the invention jointly with the employee concerned, and the advice and other assistance contributed by any other employee who is not a joint inventor[13] of the invention[14]; and

(d) the contribution made by the employer to the making, developing and working of the invention by the provision of advice, facilities and other assistance, by the provision of opportunities and by his managerial and commercial skill and activities[15].

In determining the fair share of the benefit to be secured for an employee in respect of an invention which originally belonged to him, the court or the comptroller must, among other things, take the following matters into account[16]:

(i) any conditions in a licence or licences granted in respect of the invention or the patent for it[17];

(ii)   the extent to which the invention was made jointly by the employee with any other person[18]; and

(iii)   the contribution made by the employer to the making, developing and working of the invention as mentioned in head (d) above[19].

Any order for payment of compensation may be an order for payment of a lump sum or for a periodical payment, or both[20].

Without prejudice to the rule[21] that a statutory power may in general be exercised from time to time, the refusal of the court or the comptroller to make an order on an application by an employee[22] does not prevent a further application being made by him or any successor in title of his[23]. Where such an order has been made, the court or the comptroller, as the case may be, on the application of either the employer or employee[24], may vary or discharge it, or suspend any provision of it and revive any provision so suspended[25].

Where an employee dies before an award is made[26] in respect of a patented invention[27] made by him, his personal representatives or their successors in title may exercise his right to proceed with an application for compensation[28].

1   Ie an award under the Patents Act 1977 s 40(1), (2): see PARA 369.
2   As to the meaning of 'employee' see PARA 364 note 8.
3   As to the meaning of 'invention' see PARA 301 note 2.
4   As to the meaning of 'benefit derived or expected to be derived by an employer' see PARA 369 note 15; as to the meaning of 'benefit' see PARA 369 note 8; and as to the meaning of 'employer' see PARA 364 note 7.
5   As to employers' rights in an invention see PARA 368.
6   Patents Act 1977 s 41(1) (substituted by the Patents Act 2004 s 10(3), (8)). As to the meaning of 'right' see PARA 359 note 7. As to transactions in patents and applications for patents see PARAS 372–373. For the purposes of the Patents Act 1977 s 41(1), the amount of any benefit derived or expected to be derived by an employer from the assignment or grant of: (1) the property in, or any right in or under, a patent for the invention or an application for such a patent; or (2) the property or any right in the invention, to a person connected with him must be taken to be the amount which could reasonably be expected to be so derived by the employer if that person had not been connected with him: s 41(2). In s 41(2), the words 'that person' refer to the actual assignee with its actual attributes: see *Shanks v Unilever plc* [2010] EWCA Civ 1283, [2011] RPC 352, 117 BMLT 176.
    Where the Crown or a Research Council in its capacity as employer assigns or grants the property in, or any right in or under, an invention, patent or application for a patent to a body having among its functions that of developing or exploiting inventions resulting from public research and does so for no consideration or only a nominal consideration, any benefit derived from the invention, patent or application by that body is to be treated for the purposes of the Patents Act 1977 s 41(1), (2) as so derived by the Crown or, as the case may be, Research Council: s 41(3). For these purposes, 'Research Council' means a body which is a Research Council for the purposes of the Science and Technology Act 1965 or the Arts and Humanities Research Council (as defined by the Higher Education Act 2004 s 1) (see NATIONAL CULTURAL HERITAGE vol 77 (2010) PARA 967 et seq): Patents Act 1977 s 41(3) (amended by the Higher Education Act 2004 Sch 6 para 5). As to the application of the Patents Act 1977 s 41 to EU compulsory licences see PARA 401.
7   As to the meaning of 'court' see PARA 619 note 1.
8   As to the comptroller see PARA 575.
9   Patents Act 1977 s 41(4) (amended by the Patents Act 2004 ss 10(4), (8), 16(2), Sch 3).
10 Ie under the Patents Act 1977.
11 Patents Act 1977 s 41(4)(a).
12 Patents Act 1977 s 41(4)(b).
13 As to the meaning of 'joint inventor' see PARA 301 note 3.
14 Patents Act 1977 s 41(4)(c).
15 Patents Act 1977 s 41(4)(d).
16 Patents Act 1977 s 41(5) (amended by the Patents Act 2004 ss 10(4), (8), 16(2), Sch 3).
17 Patents Act 1977 s 41(5)(a) (amended by the Patents Act 2004 s 10(5), (8)). As to licences see PARA 377 et seq.
18 Patents Act 1977 s 41(5)(b).

19 Patents Act 1977 s 41(5)(c).

20 Patents Act 1977 s 41(6). Any sums awarded by the comptroller are, if a county court so orders, recoverable under the County Courts Act 1984 s 85 (see CIVIL PROCEDURE vol 12 (2009) PARA 1283) or otherwise as if they were payable under an order of that court: Patents Act 1977 s 41(9) (amended by the Tribunals, Courts and Enforcement Act 2007 s 62(3), Sch 13 paras 39, 40).

21 Ie the Interpretation Act 1978 s 12: see STATUTES AND LEGISLATIVE PROCESS vol 96 (2012) PARA 1022.

22 Ie an application under the Patents Act 1977 s 40: see PARA 369.

23 Patents Act 1977 s 41(7). As to devolution of rights in respect of patents see PARA 372.

24 As to proceedings before the comptroller see the Patents Rules 2007, SI 2007/3291, Pt 7 (rr 73–91); and PARAS 598–606.

25 Patents Act 1977 s 41(8). Section 40(5) (see PARA 369) applies to the application as it applies to an application under s 40: s 41(8).

26 Ie under the Patents Act 1977 s 40.

27 'Patented invention' means an invention for which a patent is granted; and 'patented process' is to be construed accordingly: Patents Act 1977 s 130(1).

28 Patents Act 1977 s 43(6).

371. Rights of co-owners. Where a patent is granted[1] to two or more persons, then, subject to any agreement to the contrary, each of them is entitled to an equal undivided share in the patent[2], and each of them is entitled, by himself or his agents, to do in respect of the invention[3] concerned, for his own benefit and without the consent of or the need to account to the other or others, any act which would otherwise amount to an infringement of the patent concerned[4]. However, except under a direction from the comptroller[5] and subject to any agreement for the time being in force, where two or more persons are proprietors of a patent, none of them may amend the specification of the patent[6] or apply for such an amendment to be allowed or for the patent to be revoked[7] or grant a licence under the patent[8], or assign or mortgage a share in the patent[9] without the consent of the other or others[10].

Where a patented product[11] is disposed of by any of two or more proprietors to any person, that person and any other person claiming through him are entitled to deal with the product in the same way as if it had been disposed of by a sole registered proprietor[12]. One of two or more co-proprietors may not form a company to work the patent, or otherwise allow manufacture by an independent contractor, without the consent of the others[13], but a purchaser of a patented article from one proprietor is not concerned with the arrangements for manufacture[14]. Subject to any directions by the comptroller[15], where two or more persons are proprietors of a patent, anyone else may supply one of those persons with the means, relating to an essential element of the invention, for putting the invention into effect; and such a supply of those means does not amount to an infringement of the patent[16].

The above provisions also have effect in relation to an application for a patent[17].

1 As to grant see PARA 337.

2 Patents Act 1977 s 36(1). See *Young v Wilson* (1955) 72 RPC 351 (right to exploit without accounting may be ousted by agreement).

3 As to the meaning of 'invention' see PARA 301 note 2.

4 Patents Act 1977 s 36(2)(a). Any such act does not amount to an infringement of the patent: s 36(2)(b). As to proceedings for infringement see PARA 520 et seq. However, nothing in s 36(1), (2) affects the mutual rights or obligations of trustees or personal representatives of a deceased person or their rights and obligation as such: s 36(6).

5 Ie under the Patents Act 1977 s 8 (see PARA 361), s 12 (see PARA 363) and s 37 (see PARA 365). As to the comptroller see PARA 575.

6 As to amendment see PARA 347 et seq.

7   As to revocation see PARA 562 et seq.
8   As to licences see PARA 377 et seq.
9   As to transactions in rights in patents see PARA 372 et seq.
10 Patents Act 1977 s 36(3) (amended by the Patents Act 2004 s 9).
11 For these purposes, 'patented product' means a product which is a patented invention or, in relation to a patented process, a product obtained directly by means of the process or to which the process has been applied: Patents Act 1977 s 130(1). As to the meanings of 'patented invention' and 'patented process' see PARA 370 note 27.
12 Patents Act 1977 s 36(5). As to registration see PARA 583 et seq.
13 As to the distinction between working by an agent and by an independent contractor see *Howard and Bullough Ltd v Tweedales and Smalley* (1895) 12 RPC 519; *Henry Bros (Magherafelt) Ltd v Ministry of Defence and Northern Ireland Office* [1997] RPC 693 (affd [1999] RPC 442, [1998] All ER (D) 545, CA).
14 See the Patents Act 1977 s 36(5); and PARA 505.
15 See note 5.
16 Patents Act 1977 s 36(4).
17 Patents Act 1977 s 36(7). References to a patent and a patent being granted accordingly include references respectively to any such application and to the application being filed (s 36(7)(a)); and the reference in s 36(5) (see the text to notes 11–12) to a patented product is to be construed accordingly (s 36(7)(b)). As to the application see PARA 314.

372.   Devolution.   Any patent or application for a patent[1] is personal property, without being a thing in action[2], and, subject to certain statutory provisions[3], any patent or any application for a patent vests by operation of law in the same way as any other personal property[4]. A patent cannot, however, be taken in execution or reached by a judgment creditor otherwise than by bankruptcy[5].

Where the legal owner of a patent is a corporation which ceases to exist, for example by dissolution of a company, an order vesting the patent in the beneficial owner can be obtained[6]. Where the beneficial owner dies intestate, the patent belongs, in default of any other beneficiary taking all absolute interest, to the Crown[7] as bona vacantia and does not disappear by merger[8].

A person who becomes entitled to a patent or an interest in a patent by transmission or operation of law, may, but need not, register his title in the register of patents[9].

1   As to the application see PARA 314.
2   Patents Act 1977 s 30(1). See CHOSES IN ACTION vol 13 (2009) PARA 9; PERSONAL PROPERTY vol 80 (2013) PARA 822.
3   The Patents Act 1977 s 30(2)–(4) has effect subject to the subsequent provisions of the Patents Act 1977: s 30(5).
4   Patents Act 1977 s 30(3). A patent or application for a patent or right in it may be vested by an assent of personal representatives (s 30(3)), but any such assent is void unless it is in writing and is signed by or on behalf of the personal representative (s 30(6)(b)). As to the meaning of 'right' see PARA 359 note 7. As to as to transmission on bankruptcy see *Hesse v Stevenson* (1803) 3 Bos & P 565; *M'Alpine v Mangnall* (1846) 3 CB 496, Ex Ch; and BANKRUPTCY AND INDIVIDUAL INSOLVENCY vol 5 (2013) PARA 438. Patents granted after the bankruptcy adjudication and before discharge vest in the trustee in bankruptcy: *Hesse v Stevenson*.
5   *British Mutoscope and Biograph Co Ltd v Homer* [1901] 1 Ch 671, 18 RPC 177; *Edwards & Co v Picard* [1909] 2 KB 903, CA. In *A-G v Lord Oswald* (1848) 10 Dunl (Ct of Sess) 969, the statement in Bell's Commentaries that a patent is unattachable by any diligence but adjudication was approved.
6   See *Re Dutton's Patents* (1923) 67 Sol Jo 403, 40 RPC 84.
7   Or to the Duchy of Lancaster or the Duke of Cornwall for the time being, as the case may be: Administration of Estates Act 1925 s 46(1)(vi).
8   See *Re Dutton's Patents* (1923) 67 Sol Jo 403, 40 RPC 84; the Administration of Estates Act 1925 s 46(1)(vi); and WILLS AND INTESTACY vol 102 (2010) PARA 513.
9   See the Patents Act 1977 ss 32–34; PARA 583 et seq; and *Re Casey's Patents, Stewart v Casey* [1892] 1 Ch 104, CA.

(2) ASSIGNMENT

373. In general. Any patent or application for a patent[1] or any right[2] in such a patent or application may be assigned or mortgaged[3]. An assignment[4] or mortgage[5] is, however, void unless it is in writing and signed by or on behalf of the assignor or mortgagor or, in the case of a body corporate, is so signed or is under the seal of that body[6]. An assignment of a patent or any such application or a share[7] in it may confer on the assignee the right to bring proceedings for previous infringements[8] or previous Crown use[9]. The assignee or mortgagee of a patent may, but need not, register his title or mortgage in the register of patents[10].

1 As to the application see PARA 314.
2 As to the meaning of 'right' see PARA 359 note 7.
3 Patents Act 1977 s 30(2). Where there are two or more co-proprietors of a patent, any assignment or mortgage is subject to the consent of all of them: see ss 30(2), 36(3); and PARA 371. Future rights in respect of a patent are included in an assignment of the interest in a patent: *Buchanan v Alba Diagnostics Ltd* [2004] UKHL 5, [2004] RPC 681.
4 The word 'assignment' in these provisions has to be read as referring only to those forms of assignment which can take effect by a document complying with the formalities in the Patents Act 1977 s 30(6): see *Siemens Schweiz AG v Thorn Security Ltd* [2008] EWCA Civ 1161, [2009] RPC 69, [2008] All ER (D) 211 (Oct).
5 'Mortgage', when used as a noun, includes a charge for securing money or money's worth and, when used as a verb, is to be construed accordingly: Patents Act 1977 s 130(1).
6 Patents Act 1977 s 30(6)(a), (6A) (s 30(6)(a) amended, and s 30(6A) added, by SI 2004/2357). In all cases of partial assignment it should be clearly stated who is to pay renewal fees. As to renewal fees see PARA 339. An assignment of the right to apply for a patent must also be in writing signed by the assignor (*Xtralite (Rooflights) Ltd v Hartington Conway Ltd* [2004] RPC 137, C-G) but an estoppel could bind the true owner despite the lack of writing (*Xtralite (Rooflights) Ltd v Hartington Conway Ltd* [2003] EWHC 1872 (Ch), [2004] RPC 161, [2003] All ER (D) 555 (Jul)).
7 As to shares in patents see PARA 359 note 7.
8 Ie proceedings under the Patents Act 1977 s 61 or s 69: see PARAS 522, 543, 546, 547, 553.
9 Patents Act 1977 s 30(7). As to such Crown use see s 58; and PARA 409.
10 As to registration see PARA 583 et seq.

374. Covenants. There is no implied covenant for validity[1] when a patent[2] is assigned[3], but an assignor is estopped from denying validity as against his assignee[4]. An assignor may, however, exclude liability in respect of his right to assign the patent[5].

A covenant to pay a sum out of the profits derived from the use of the invention or by way of royalty runs with the patent and is binding on a legal assignee of the patent with notice of the covenant[6]. A charge may also arise in favour of a solicitor who has successfully defended a claim for revocation[7]. Charges on patents belonging to limited companies must be registered[8].

1 As to validity of a patent see PARA 425 et seq.
2 The following principles were established in respect of assignments under previous legislation (see PARA 302) but continue to apply to assignments of patents under the Patents Act 1977. As to assignment generally see PARA 373.
3 *Hall v Conder* (1857) 26 LJCP 138, 288, Ex Ch; *Smith v Neale* (1857) 26 LJCP 143. The same rule applies to agreements to assign: *Hall v Conder*; *Smith v Buckingham* (1870) 18 WR 314; *Liardet v Hammond Electric Light and Power Co* (1883) 31 WR 710.
4 *Walton v Lavater* (1860) 8 CBNS 162. An assignor is not, however, so estopped as against the assignee of his trustee in bankruptcy: *Smith v Cropper* (1885) 10 App Cas 249, 2 RPC 17, HL. Where there is an express covenant as to validity in an agreement, or an undertaking to execute an assignment containing such a covenant, the purchaser is entitled to set up the invalidity of the patents, or some of them, as a defence to an action on the agreement: see *Hazlehurst v Rylands* (1890) 9 RPC 1, CA; *Nadel v Martin* (1903) 20 RPC 721, CA (affd (1905) 23 RPC 41, HL);

Berchem v Wren (1904) 21 RPC 683. A statement that the assignor is the original inventor does not amount to a warranty of validity: *Thompson v Jefferson* (1928) 45 RPC 309, PC. This is, however, subject to the provisions relating to anti-competitive practices: see COMPETITION vol 18 (2009) PARAS 3, 155 et seq.

5   See the Unfair Contract Terms Act 1977 ss 1(2), 3, Sch 1 para 1(c); and CONTRACT vol 22 (2012) PARA 416.

6   *Werderman v Société Générale d'Electricité* (1881) 19 ChD 246, CA, followed in *Dansk Rekylriffel Syndikat Akt v Snell* [1908] 2 Ch 127, 25 RPC 421, and explained in *Bagot Pneumatic Tyre Co v Clipper Pneumatic Tyre Co* [1902] 1 Ch 146, 19 RPC 69, CA (where it was held that equitable assignees are not so bound).

7   See *Re Brown's Patent* (1915) 32 RPC 491. As to proceedings for revocation see PARA 562 et seq. The charge extends to the interests of the parties who have not appeared: *Re Brown's Patent*. See LEGAL PROFESSIONS vol 66 (2009) PARA 996 et seq.

8   See the Companies Act 2006 ss 860(1), (7)(i), 861(4); and COMPANIES vol 15 (2009) PARAS 1279, 1281.

375.   Agreements for sale. Agreements as to the sale of a patent[1], or any interest in a patent, need not be in writing[2], and may be enforced in the ordinary way by an order for specific performance[3] or, in the case of an agreement for sale made before grant of the patent[4], by applying to the comptroller[5] for a direction that the application proceed in the name of the purchaser[6].

1   The following principles were established in respect of assignments under previous legislation (see PARA 302) but continue to apply to assignments of patents under the Patents Act 1977. As to assignment generally see PARA 373.

2   See *Smith v Neale* (1857) 26 LJCP 143, although this particular point was not dealt with in the argument. As to covenants for validity in such agreements see PARA 374.

3   See *Bewley v Hancock* (1856) 6 De GM & G 391; *Printing and Numerical Registering Co v Sampson* (1875) LR 19 Eq 462; *Liardet v Hammond Electric Light and Power Co* (1883) 31 WR 710; *Re Casey's Patent, Stewart v Casey* [1892] 1 Ch 104, 9 RPC 9, CA; *Coflexip Stena Offshore Ltd's Patent* [1997] RPC 179 at 188. Equitable rights can be enforced as to foreign patents: see *Worthington Pumping Engine Co v Moore* (1902) 20 RPC 41; *Richmond & Co Ltd v Wrightson* (1904) 22 RPC 25. See also SPECIFIC PERFORMANCE vol 95 (2013) PARA 330.

4   As to grant see PARA 337.

5   As to the comptroller see PARA 575.

6   See the Patents Act 1977 s 8; and PARAS 360–361. See also *Coflexip Stena Offshore Ltd's Patent* [1997] RPC 179.

376.   Agreements to assign future patents. In general, an agreement to assign patents[1] for future inventions either generally or for particular subjects is not necessarily contrary to public policy and may be upheld[2]. The commonest form of such agreement relates to improvements relating to named inventions, although somewhat broader terms are often used[3]. Such an agreement made between an employee[4] and his employer[5] is, however, unenforceable[6]. Further, under the EU rules relating to competition[7], an obligation of a licensee under a patent licence to assign to the licensor any patents granted for improvements made by the licensee may be void[8].

1   The following principles were established in respect of assignments under previous legislation (see PARA 302) but continue to apply to assignments of patents under the Patents Act 1977. As to assignment generally see PARA 373.

2   *Bewley v Hancock* (1856) 6 De GM & G 391; *Printing and Numerical Registering Co v Sampson* (1875) LR 19 Eq 462. In *Sadgrove v Godfrey* (1919) 37 RPC 7, one of the agreements sued on contained a provision that one of the parties should not invent machines of a named class, but the question as to whether such a provision was void was not decided.

3   The question of what is an 'improvement' has been discussed in a number of cases: see *Wilson v Barbour* (1888) 5 RPC 675, CA; *Valveless Gas Engine Syndicate Ltd v Day* (1898) 16 RPC 97, CA; *Davies v Davies Patent Boiler Ltd* (1908) 25 RPC 823; *Hopkins v Linotype and Machinery Ltd* (1910) 101 LT 898, 27 RPC 109, HL; *Osram-Robertson Lamp Works Ltd v Public Trustee* (1920) 37 RPC 189; *Vislok Ltd v Peters* (1927) 44 RPC 235. In *Davies v Curtis*

and Harvey Ltd (1903) 20 RPC 561, CA, Romer LJ suggested that an 'improvement' must be something coming within the claim of the original patent, but there are certainly cases in which a wider interpretation has been attached to the term. But 'improvement' is not a term of art and could have wider or narrower meanings according to the context: *Buchanan v Alba Diagnostics Ltd* [2004] UKHL 5, [2004] RPC 681, 2004 SLT 255. Where the covenant extends to patents 'of which the assignor may become possessed', it includes patents which he may acquire by purchase (*Printing and Numerical Registering Co v Sampson* (1875) LR 19 Eq 462), but not those in which he merely acquires an equitable interest together with other persons (*Pneumatic Tyre Co Ltd v Dunlop* (1896) 12 TLR 620, 13 RPC 553, CA).

4   As to the meaning of 'employee' see PARA 364 note 8.

5   As to the meaning of 'employer' see PARA 364 note 7.

6   See the Patents Act 1977 s 42(2); and PARA 368.

7   See the Treaty on the Functioning of the European Union (Rome, 25 March 1957; TS 1 (1973); Cmnd 5179) arts 101–118; and COMPETITION vol 18 (2009) PARA 61 et seq.

8   *Re the Agreement of A Raymond & Co* [1972] CMLR D45, EC Commission; *Re the Agreement between Kabel-und Metallwerke Neumeyer AG and Les Etablissements Luchaire SA* [1975] 2 CMLR D40, EC Commission. As to block exemptions for certain categories of patent licensing agreements see Commission Regulation (EC) 2349/84 (OJ L219, 16.8.84, p 15); Commission Regulation (EC) 240/96 (OJ L31, 9.2.96, p 2); and COMPETITION vol 18 (2009) PARA 61 et seq. But an assignment of future improvements was held not to be an unreasonable restraint of trade at common law: *Buchanan v Alba Diagnostics Ltd* [2004] UKHL 5, [2004] RPC 681, 2004 SLT 255.

5. LICENCES AND CROWN USE

(1) LICENCES BY AGREEMENT

377. Power to license. Subject to the rights of co-owners[1], a licence may be granted under any patent or application[2] for a patent for working the invention[3] which is the subject of the patent or application[4]. To the extent that the licence so provides, a sub-licence may be granted under any such licence and any such licence or sub-licence may be assigned or mortgaged[5]. Any such licence or sub-licence vests by operation of law in the same way as any other personal property[6] and may be vested by an assent of personal representatives[7]. Notice of the grant of the licence may be entered on the register of patents[8], and a licence duly granted and registered is binding on the successors in title of the proprietor of the patent who granted it. Equally, if the covenants contained in the licence agreement[9] are assignable[10], the assignee may enforce them against the licensee[11].

1   Ie subject to the Patents Act 1977 s 36(3): see PARA 371.
2   As to the application see PARA 314.
3   As to the meaning of 'invention' see PARA 301 note 2.
4   Patents Act 1977 s 30(4). A licensee may call upon the legal owner to perform all acts contracted for in the licence: *Frentzell v Dougill* (1904) 21 RPC 641. As to the effect of licences against the Crown and government departments see PARA 403.
5   Patents Act 1977 s 30(4)(a). See also PARA 381.
6   As to personal property generally see **PERSONAL PROPERTY** vol 80 (2013) PARA 801 et seq.
7   Patents Act 1977 s 30(4)(b). Any such assent is void unless it is in writing and signed by or on behalf of the personal representative: see s 30(6)(b) (amended by SI 2004/2357).
8   As to the register see PARA 583. As to the effect of registration or notice of rights in patents see the Patents Act 1977 s 33; and PARA 587.
9   As to covenants see PARA 386.
10   As to assignment see the text to note 5; and PARA 381.
11   *National Carbonising Co Ltd v British Coal Distillation Ltd* [1936] 2 All ER 1012, 54 RPC 41, CA.

378. Form of licence. No special form or words is or are required for the grant of a licence[1] under a patent, and licences under hand, parol licences[2], implied licences[3] and licences by estoppel[4] are well recognised. A licence need not be in writing for notice of it to be registered[5].

The forms of licence agreements are well established[6]. An agreement to grant a licence, if the parties act on it, is treated in equity as a licence[7]. An agreement to renew a licence on the same terms as originally applied to it is presumed where a licensee continues to manufacture and pay royalties after the expiration of his licence[8]; and an agreement for a licence is presumed where user of an invention has been permitted during negotiations for a licence[9]. A parol licence, in order to be enforceable, must be certain in its terms[10].

1   As to the power to license see PARA 377. An assignment of an existing licence is, however, void unless it is in writing and signed by or on behalf of the parties to the assignment, or, in the case of a body corporate, it is so signed or is under the seal of that body: Patents Act 1977 s 30(6)(a) (6A) (s 30(6)(a) amended, s 30(6A) added, by SI 2004/2357).
2   *Chanter v Dewhurst* (1844) 13 LJ Ex 198; *Chanter v Johnson* (1845) 14 LJ Ex 289; *Crossley v Dixon* (1863) 10 HL Cas 293.
3   Eg the implied licence given to purchasers from the patentee or from a licensee who has power to sell: see PARA 384.
4   *Kenny's Patent Button-Holeing Co Ltd v Somervell and Lutwyche* (1878) 38 LT 878; *Lawson v Macpherson & Co* (1897) 14 RPC 696; *Badische Anilin und Soda Fabrik v Isler* [1906] 1 Ch 605, 23 RPC 173 (affd [1906] 2 Ch 443, 23 RPC 633, CA).

5   Any transaction, instrument or event affecting rights in or under a patent may be registered: Patents Act 1977 s 32(2)(b) (substituted by the Patents, Designs and Marks Act 1986 Sch 1 para 4); and see PARAS 583–584. As to the overriding of unregistered licence rights see the Patents Act 1977 s 33(1); and PARA 587.

6   An agreement that, subject to certain specified matters, a licence was to be in 'the normal terms of a patent licence' was treated by the court as enforceable in *Miles-Martin Pen Co Ltd and Martin v Selsdon Fountain Pen Co Ltd* (1950) 67 RPC 64, CA.

7   Cf *Ward v Livesey* (1887) 5 RPC 102; *Postcard Automatic Supply Co v Samuel* (1889) 6 RPC 560; but see *Henderson v Shiels* (1906) 24 RPC 108.

8   *Warwick v Hooper* (1850) 3 Mac & G 60; *Goucher v Clayton* (1865) 13 LT 115. As to royalties see PARA 388.

9   *Tweedale v Howard and Bullough Ltd* (1896) 13 RPC 522. In some cases the proposed licensee may be in a position to elect whether or not he will be treated as a licensee: *Postcard Automatic Supply Co v Samuel* (1889) 6 RPC 560. Where the negotiations for a licence fell through, damages were refused for acts done with the patentee's knowledge during such negotiations: *Coslett Anti-Rust Syndicate Ltd v Lennox* (1912) 29 RPC 477. The licence may preclude the proprietor of the patent from suing for infringement prior to the licence: *Campbell v G Hopkins & Sons (Clerkenwell) Ltd* (1931) 49 RPC 38.

10   An oral agreement to grant a licence at royalties to be fixed by arbitration was upheld, and in default of arbitration royalties were fixed by the official referee: see *Fleming v JS Doig (Grimsby) Ltd* (1921) 38 RPC 57; *Mellor v William Beardmore & Co Ltd* (1926) 43 RPC 361 (varied (1927) 44 RPC 175); *Brake v Radermacher* (1903) 20 RPC 631.

379. Limits of licence. A licence granted under a patent[1] may be limited as to persons[2], time, place[3], manufacture, use or sale[4]. If the licence is limited, proceedings for infringement of the patent will lie against the licensee for acts done outside the ambit of the licence[5]. A sole licence is one by which the proprietor of the patent agrees to grant no other licence for the technical field concerned within the licensed district during the currency of the licence, and, if the proprietor also agrees that he will not himself exercise the invention in that technical field either generally or within the particular district, the licence is termed an 'exclusive licence'[6]. For the purposes of the Patents Act 1977, 'exclusive licence' means a licence from the proprietor of or applicant for a patent conferring on the licensee, or on him and persons authorised by him, to the exclusion of all other persons (including the proprietor or applicant), any right in respect of the invention to which the patent or application relates[7].

1   As to the power to license see PARA 377.

2   A licence is in general personal in the absence of express terms: *British Mutoscope and Biograph Co Ltd v Homer* [1901] 1 Ch 671, 18 RPC 177; *National Carbonising Co Ltd v British Coal Distillation Ltd* [1936] 2 All ER 1012, 54 RPC 41, CA; and see PARA 381 note 3.

3   See PARA 381. For an action for infringement outside the licensed area see *Fuel Economy Co Ltd v Murray* [1930] 2 Ch 93, 47 RPC 346, CA.

4   See PARA 381.

5   *Fuel Economy Co Ltd v Murray* [1930] 2 Ch 93, 47 RPC 346, CA. As to proceedings for infringement see PARA 520 et seq.

6   *Rapid Steel Co v Blankstone* (1907) 24 RPC 529.

7   Patents Act 1977 s 130(1). 'Exclusive licensee' and 'non-exclusive licence' are to be construed accordingly: s 130(1). A licence to be the exclusive manufacturer for the licensor is not an exclusive licence of a right 'in respect of the invention to which the patent relates' but is merely a contractual restriction: *Bondax Carpets Ltd v Advance Carpet Tiles* [1993] FSR 162. See also *Dendron GmbH v University of California (No 3)* [2004] EWHC 589 (Pat), [2005] 1 WLR 200, [2004] FSR 861 (exclusive licensee's authority to grant exclusive sub-licence challenged).

380. Distinction between licence and assignment. There is a fundamental distinction between a licence granted under a patent[1] and an assignment of the patent[2]. An assignee stands in the place of the proprietor of the patent and derives his rights from the grant of the patent, whereas a licensee, although having a proprietary interest in the patent[3], derives his title from the proprietor by a permission which permits him to do acts which would otherwise be prohibited and which confers upon him no rights as against the general public[4]. An exclusive licensee[5] is, however, in a somewhat different position from other licensees; he may sue for infringement within the field of his exclusive licence in his own name[6], and by the terms of his licence may acquire substantially the whole of the rights in the patent[7].

1   As to the power to license see PARA 377.
2   As to assignments of patents see PARA 373 et seq; and as to assignments of licences see PARA 381.
3   *British Nylon Spinners Ltd v Imperial Chemical Industries Ltd* [1953] Ch 19, [1952] 2 All ER 780, 69 RPC 288, CA.
4   See eg *Gillette Safety Razor Co Ltd v AW Gamage Ltd* (1908) 25 RPC 492; revsd 25 RPC 782, CA.
5   As to the meaning of 'exclusive licensee' see PARA 379 note 7.
6   As to proceedings for infringement see PARA 520 et seq. As to the meaning of 'exclusive licence' see PARA 379.
7   As to the meaning of 'right' see PARA 359 note 7.

381.   Assignment of licence.   A licence granted under a patent[1] may be assigned[2] to the extent that the licence so provides[3]. The licensee may exercise his powers by himself, his servants or his agents, although not by an independent contractor[4]. If a licence is assignable[5], it may be assigned to a person with a business more extensive than that of the original licensee[6].

1   As to the power to license see PARA 377.
2   An assignment of a licence probably needs to be in writing and signed by the assignor: see the Patents Act 1977 s 30(6)(a); and PARA 373.
3   Patents Act 1977 s 30(4)(a); and see PARA 377. Even where a licence is not assignable, if the proprietor of the patent accepts royalties from the assignee of the licence, he is estopped from disputing the assignment: *Lawson v Macpherson & Co* (1897) 14 RPC 696. As to royalties see PARA 388.
4   *Dixon v London Small Arms Co Ltd* (1876) 1 App Cas 632, HL; *Allen & Hanburys Ltd's (Salbutamol) Patent* [1987] RPC 327 at 380, CA, per Dillon LJ. See also *Henry Bros (Magherafelt) Ltd v Ministry of Defence and Northern Ireland Office* [1997] RPC 693. As to what is and is not manufacture by a licensee see *Dunlop Pneumatic Tyre Co Ltd v Holborn Tyre Co Ltd* (1901) 18 RPC 222; *Dunlop Pneumatic Co Ltd v Cresswell Cheshire Rubber Co* (1901) 18 RPC 473; *Dunlop Pneumatic Tyre Co Ltd v North British Rubber Co Ltd* (1904) 21 RPC 161, CA. See also PARA 371 note 13.
5   A licence to A and his assigns was held by Maule J in *Bower v Hodges* (1853) 22 LJCP 194 to imply a power to sub-license, but this decision, it is submitted, is not of general application. Cf the Patents Act 1977 s 30(4)(a); and PARA 377. As to whether the benefit of a sub-licence is assigned with the head licence see *Massman v Massman and Custodian of Enemy Property* (1944) 61 RPC 12, CA.
6   *Bown v Humber & Co Ltd* (1889) 6 RPC 9 (assignee entitled to use the licence both at premises used by assignor and at assignee's other premises).

382.   Agreements for licence.   Specific performance may be granted of agreements for the grant of licences under patents[1]. The ordinary rules as to the invalidity of an instrument obtained by fraud or executed by both parties under a mutual mistake apply to licences[2].

1   *Brake v Radermacher* (1903) 20 RPC 631; *British Nylon Spinners Ltd v Imperial Chemical Industries Ltd* [1953] Ch 19, [1952] 2 All ER 780, 69 RPC 288, CA. As to the power to license see PARA 377.
2   *McDougall Bros v Partington* (1890) 7 RPC 216; *Ashworth v Law* (1890) 7 RPC 231; *Edison-Bell Consolidated Phonograph Co Ltd v Rosenberg and Scott* (1899) 16 RPC 608; *Cambridge Antibody Technology v Abbott Biotechnology Ltd* [2004] EWHC 2974 (Pat), [2005] FSR 590, [2004] All ER (D) 323 (Dec); *QR Sciences Ltd v BTG International Ltd* [2005] EWHC 670 (Ch), [2005] FSR 909, [2005] All ER (D) 196 (Apr). This does not apply, however, to a mutual mistake as to the validity of the patent: cf *Taylor v Hare* (1805) 1 Bos & PNR 260.

383.   Construction of licence.   Generally, a licence granted under a patent[1] to manufacture implies a licence to use[2], and a licence to vend gives the right to licence purchasers to use, or sell again, the article purchased[3]. A licence merely to 'use and exercise' may also from its general terms be extended so as to authorise manufacture and sale[4], or import for subsequent sale and distribution[5]. A personal licence to use certain goods, the property of the licensor, does not, however, give the power to license others to use them[6]. If a licence only permits the making of an article of a particular kind, proceedings for infringement will lie against the licensee for making articles within the patent and not within the licence[7]. If a licence is in respect of any chemical compound 'invented' at the date of the licence, it does not cover compounds which at that date had not been made and tested, but which were known only by their chemical formulae[8].

1   As to the power to license see PARA 377.
2   See, however, *Basset v Graydon* (1897) 14 RPC 701, HL; *Huntoon Co v Kolynos (Inc)* [1930] 1 Ch 528, 47 RPC 403, CA.
3   *Thomas v Hunt* (1864) 17 CBNS 183; *National Phonograph Co of Australia Ltd v Menck* [1911] AC 336, 28 RPC 229, PC. A licence to vend does not, however, necessarily give the right to limit the licence so given to purchasers: see PARA 384.
4   *Dunlop Pneumatic Tyre Co Ltd v North British Rubber Co Ltd* (1904) 21 RPC 161, CA.
5   See *Pfizer Corpn v Ministry of Health* [1965] AC 512, [1965] 1 All ER 450, [1965] RPC 261, HL.
6   *British Mutoscope and Biograph Co Ltd v Homer* [1901] 1 Ch 671, 18 RPC 177.
7   *SA pour la Fabrication d'Appareils d'Eclairage v Midland Lighting Co* (1897) 14 RPC 419; *Dunlop Pneumatic Tyre Co Ltd v Buckingham and Adams Cycle and Motor Co Ltd* (1901) 18 RPC 423, CA. As to proceedings for infringement see PARA 520 et seq.
8   *Beecham Group Ltd v Bristol Laboratories International SA* [1978] RPC 521, HL.

384.   Implied and limited licences.   An article sold by the proprietor of a patent[1] or his licensee[2], or by one of the co-proprietors[3], is presumed to be free of patent claims, giving the purchaser the right to use it as if there were no patent[4]. Under domestic law, however, if at the time of sale[5] the purchaser has notice of some restriction[6], imposed by the proprietor or those representing him, that restriction will bind the purchaser[7], although the court will not presume that the purchaser knew of the restriction merely because notice of it was marked upon the article, if the marking was not such as to be apparent under ordinary conditions to a customer at the time of the sale[8]. Furthermore, if there is knowledge of the restriction, there need not be knowledge of the extent of the restriction[9]. Attempts to impose such a restriction will, however, contravene EU law if the restriction would affect trade between member states, as in almost every such case it would[10]. If a limitation of licence is lawful, the position is the same whether the article is purchased direct from the proprietor of the patent, from a vendor expressly licensed to sell it, or from some other person into whose hands it has later fallen[11]; and a purchaser without notice of limitations will acquire a full licence, although not even the original manufacturer of the article had power to grant a full licence[12].

In the absence of express terms to the contrary, the licence obtained by a purchaser from the proprietor of the patent in one country extends to all other countries where that proprietor owns the patent rights[13]. Under English national law the licence obtained by a purchaser from a manufacturer who is licensed to manufacture and sell only in one country does not, however, so extend[14], but, here again, once the proprietor of the patent has allowed the patented goods to reach the market in one member state, the doctrine of exhaustion of rights debars him from enforcing his patent anywhere else in the European Union[15].

1   As to ownership of a patent see PARA 359 et seq.

2   As to the power to license see PARA 377.

3   As to disposals of patented products by co-proprietors see PARA 371.

4   *Incandescent Gas Light Co Ltd v Cantelo* (1895) 11 TLR 381, 12 RPC 262; *Scottish Vacuum Cleaner Co Ltd v Provincial Cinematograph Theatres Ltd* (1915) 32 RPC 353.

5   *Gillette Industries Ltd v Bernstein* [1942] Ch 45, [1941] 3 All ER 248, 58 RPC 271, CA. See also *Incandescent Gas Light Co Ltd v Cantelo* (1895) 11 TLR 381, 12 RPC 262; *Scottish Vacuum Cleaner Co Ltd v Provincial Cinematograph Theatres Ltd* (1915) 32 RPC 353, Ct of Sess.

6   The restriction may be a limitation as to price (*Columbia Graphophone Co Ltd v Murray* (1922) 39 RPC 239) provided: (1) it is not a minimum resale price restriction (see COMPETITION vol 18 (2009) PARA 116 et seq); (2) it is not a limitation as to the class of trader (*Re Co-operative Union Ltd's Application* (1933) 50 RPC 161); or (3) it does not require the affixing of a licence plate to the article (*Hazeltine Corpn v Lissen Ltd* (1938) 56 RPC 62). A restriction as to the sale price may apply to new and second hand articles: *Columbia Graphophone Co v Thoms* (1924) 41 RPC 294. It is sufficient that the purchaser has notice that the restriction exists, without knowing that it is imposed by virtue of a limited patent licence: *Dunlop Rubber Co Ltd v Longlife Battery Depot* [1958] 3 All ER 197, [1958] 1 WLR 1033, [1958] RPC 473.

7   *National Phonograph Co of Australia Ltd v Menck* [1911] AC 336, 28 RPC 229, PC. It is doubtful, however, whether a licensee without power to sub-license can impose restrictions upon purchasers from him: see *Gillette Safety Razor Co Ltd v AW Gamage Ltd* (1908) 25 RPC 492.

8   A notice embossed on the article is ineffective if the article is usually sold wrapped up (*Alfred Dunhill Ltd v Griffith Bros* (1933) 51 RPC 93); and a notice on the wrapper is ineffective if the purchaser does not see it until after purchase (*Dunlop Rubber Co Ltd v Longlife Battery Depot* [1958] 3 All ER 197, [1958] 1 WLR 1033, [1958] RPC 473, CA). Registration of a licence does not give notice of its contents to a purchaser: *Heap v Hartley* (1889) 42 ChD 461, 6 RPC 495, CA; *Scottish Vacuum Cleaner Co Ltd v Provincial Cinematograph Theatres Ltd* (1915) 32 RPC 353, Ct of Sess.

9   *Columbia Phonograph Co, General v Regent Fittings Co* (1913) 30 RPC 484; *Columbia Graphophone Co v Vanner* (1916) 33 RPC 104; *Columbia Graphophone Co Ltd v Murray* (1922) 39 RPC 239; *Columbia Graphophone Co v Thoms* (1924) 41 RPC 294; *Sterling Drug Inc v CH Beck Ltd* [1973] RPC 915.

10   Ie under the provisions of the Treaty on the Functioning of the European Union (Rome, 25 March 1957; TS 1 (1973); Cmnd 5179) relating to the free movement of goods (arts 28–37) and competition (arts 101–118). Exclusive licensing agreements are inherently restrictive and must comply with the technology transfer block exemption under Commission Regulation (EC) 240/96 (OJ L31, 9.2.96, p 2) (see COMPETITION vol 18 (2009) PARAS 61 et seq, 67) or else be notified to the European Commission for individual exemption (see COMPETITION vol 18 (2009) PARA 66).

11   See the cases cited in notes 4–9. It is the rights of subsequent purchasers that become the subject of litigation in this connection, since relations between the proprietor of the patent and purchasers directly from him will be governed by contract.

12   *Badische Anilin und Soda Fabrik v Isler* [1906] 1 Ch 605, 23 RPC 173 per Buckley J; on appeal [1906] 2 Ch 443, 23 RPC 633, CA; *Hazeltine Corpn v Lissen Ltd* (1938) 56 RPC 62.

13   *Betts v Willmott* (1871) 6 Ch App 239, CA; *National Phonograph Co of Australia Ltd v Menck* [1911] AC 336, 28 RPC 229, PC.

14   The licensee-manufacturer himself does not by implication acquire any such licence (*SA des Manufactures de Glaces v Tilghman's Patent Sand Blast Co* (1883) 25 ChD 1, CA), so that purchasers from him can expect to be in no better position (*Coppin v Palmer* (1898) 15 RPC 373). Cf *Dunlop Pneumatic Tyre Co Ltd v Buckingham and Adams Cycle and Motor Co Ltd* (1901) 18 RPC 423, CA.

15   See note 10.

385. Implied terms.

The ordinary rules of construction of contracts apply to implying terms in a licence granted under a patent[1]. There is ordinarily no implied term that a licensee will manufacture or use his licence[2].

1   *BP Refinery (Westernport) Pty Ltd v Shire of Hastings* (1978) 52 ALJR 20 at 26, PC; *Liverpool City Council v Irwin* [1977] AC 239, [1976] 2 All ER 39, HL; *Campbell v G Hopkins & Sons (Clerkenwell) Ltd* (1931) 49 RPC 38; and see PARA 383.

2   It is therefore customary in an exclusive licence to provide for minimum royalties, or other minimum payments, to safeguard the proprietor of the patent against failure effectively to work the licence; and provisions to cover the case of failure to work so complete as to abuse the patent monopoly (see PARA 394) may be desirable. In the case of any licence, but especially an exclusive licence, it is not unusual to provide expressly that the licensee use his 'best endeavours' to work the invention. This is a very stringent term: see *Terrell v Mabie Todd & Co Ltd* (1952) 69 RPC 234 and the cases there cited; *Transfield Pty Ltd v Arlo International Ltd* [1981] RPC 141, Aust HC. As to the meaning of 'exclusive licence' see PARA 379.

386.   Covenants. Ordinary conveyancing practice assumes that there is no implied covenant by a licensor of a patent[1] that manufacture under his patent will not constitute an infringement of any other patent, but express covenants to this effect are not unusual in international agreements[2]. A covenant by the proprietor of a patent by all means in his power to protect and defend a patent from infringement implies a covenant to pay renewal fees[3]. Where there is a covenant for quiet enjoyment, an exclusive licensee[4] can call upon the proprietor to restrain infringement[5]. No covenant that the licensed patents are valid will in general be implied[6]. A covenant for quiet enjoyment probably does, however, import a limited covenant that the proprietor has not done any act invalidating the patent, for example omitted to pay renewal fees[7]. It is a breach of contract in the case of an exclusive licence[8] if the proprietor himself uses or works the patent[9]. A licensor will be restrained from using threats of infringement proceedings against the licensee[10]. In the absence of express provisions making the performance of a covenant for quiet enjoyment a condition precedent to the covenant for the payment of royalties[11], the court will not construe it as such. A breach of the former covenant is, therefore, available only by way of counterclaim and not as a defence to an action for royalties[12]. It would seem that there is not necessarily an obligation on a licensor to keep the patent in force, although in some cases this may be inferred from the general terms of the licence[13].

1   As to the power to license see PARA 377.
2   It is necessary to limit such a covenant to cases where the licensee works to particular designs or specifications, and usual to limit the damages for breach to the amount of the royalties otherwise due to the proprietor of the patent.
3   *Lines v Usher* (1897) 14 RPC 206, CA; *Cummings v Stewart (No 2)* [1913] 1 IR 95, 30 RPC 1. In both these cases *Mills v Carson* (1892) 9 RPC 338 was distinguished. As to renewal fees see PARA 339.
4   As to the meaning of 'exclusive licensee' see PARA 379 text and note 7.
5   *Mills v Carson* (1892) 10 RPC 9, CA. It is not necessary that an action should be brought in every case if the infringement is effectively kept down: *Dunlop Pneumatic Tyre Co Ltd v North British Rubber Co Ltd* (1904) 21 RPC 161, CA. There is no such obligation in the case of other licences: *Bessimer v Wright* (1858) 31 LTOS 213. An exclusive licensee may in any event sue for infringement in his own name: see PARA 520. As to proceedings for infringement see PARA 520 et seq.
6   *Bessimer v Wright* (1858) 31 LTOS 213.
7   Cf PARA 374 note 4. As to quiet enjoyment see the text and note 11.
8   As to the meaning of 'exclusive licence' see PARA 379.
9   *Rapid Steel Co v Blankstone* (1907) 24 RPC 529.
10 *Clark v Adie* (1873) 21 WR 456 (on appeal 21 WR 764); *SA des Manufactures de Glaces v Tilghman's Patent Sand Blast Co* (1883) 25 ChD 1, CA. As to such threats generally see PARA 555 et seq.
11 As to royalties see PARA 388.
12 *Mills v Carson* (1892) 10 RPC 9, CA; *Huntoon Co v Kolynos (Inc)* [1930] 1 Ch 528, 47 RPC 403, CA. If, however, there is such a condition and the patent has been allowed to lapse, royalties paid in ignorance of this may be recovered: *Lines v Usher* (1897) 14 RPC 206, CA.
13 *Mills v Carson* (1892) 10 RPC 9, CA; *Lines v Usher* (1897) 14 RPC 206, CA.

387. Challenge of validity by licensee. A covenant[1] by a licensee not to dispute validity of the patent[2] under which the licence is granted[3] is likely to be void under European law, although the licensor may reserve the right to determine the licence[4] in the event of such a challenge[5]. A plea of invalidity is not, however, a defence to an action to recover royalties[6] under the licence[7].

1 As to covenants generally see PARA 386.
2 As to the validity of patents see PARA 425 et seq.
3 As to the power to license see PARA 377.
4 As to the determination of licences generally see PARA 389.

5 A 'no-challenge' clause is usually contrary to the Treaty on the Functioning of the European Union (Rome, 25 March 1957; TS 1 (1973); Cmnd 5179) art 101 (competition rules applying to undertakings): see *Re the Agreements of the Davidson Rubber Co* [1972] CMLR D52, EC Commission; *Re the Agreement of A Raymond & Co* [1972] CMLR D45, EC Commission; *Re the Agreement of the Kabel-und Metallwerke Neumeyer AG and Les Etablissements Luchaire SA* [1975] 2 CMLR D40, EC Commission; *Association des Ouvriers en Instruments de Precision v Beyrard* [1976] 1 CMLR D14, EC Commission; *IMA AG v Windsurfing International Inc* [1984] 1 CMLR 1, [1984] FSR 146, ECJ; but see Case 65/86 *Bayer AG v Maschinenfabrik Hennocke GmbH v Süllhöfer* [1988] ECR 5249, [1990] 4 CMLR 182, [1990] FSR 300, ECJ (where a no-challenge clause in a royalty-free licence was upheld). See also Commission Regulation (EC) 240/96 (OJ L31, 9.2.96, p 2); and COMPETITION vol 18 (2009) PARA 61 et seq.
6 As to royalties see PARA 388.

7 *Fuel Economy Co Ltd v Murray* [1930] 2 Ch 93, 47 RPC 346, CA. Validity in any case may not be put in issue in proceedings in contract (see the Patents Act 1977 s 74(2); and PARA 519), although a counterclaim for revocation of the patent would seem to be permissible.

388. Royalties. Royalties may be made payable on any basis and on any articles manufactured by a licensee under a patent[1], whether within or without the patent[2], and may continue to be payable whether or not the patent is valid[3] and until such time as the licence is determined[4]. Money paid for royalties under a licence cannot be recovered on the ground that the patent was invalid, unless the licence so provides[5]. Where a licence is given under an application for a patent but no patent is granted, it would seem that money paid cannot be recovered, as the licensee has been protected from possible proceedings for infringement from the date of publication of the specification[6].

Royalties due under a licence carry interest[7]. An assignee of a share of the profits can have an account of royalties taken against the licensee, provided that the account is taken in such circumstances as will bind the assignor[8]. A covenant to render accounts is generally only auxiliary to the covenant to pay[9]. An auditor required to 'verify' the amount of the royalties payable by a licensee must check statements by the licensee as to what articles manufactured by him are, and what are not, within the licence, and a covenant to supply such an auditor with necessary information must be construed accordingly[10]. A covenant to permit the grantor to inspect accounts will ordinarily continue in force even if the agreement is determined[11]. There have been many cases as to the amount of royalty payable under licences, but, as each case depends upon the wording of the particular agreement, no general rule can be deduced[12].

There seems to be no objection to the proprietor of the patent suing for royalties, or in the alternative for infringement, in cases where the existence of a licence may be disputed[13].

1 As to the power to license see PARA 377.

2 *Baird v Neilson* (1842) 8 Cl & Fin 726, HL. Payment of royalties on non-patented goods may, however, contravene the Treaty on the Functioning of the European Union (Rome, 25 March

1957; TS 1 (1973); Cmnd 5179) art 101: see COMPETITION vol 18 (2009) PARA 61 et seq. See, however, Commission Regulation (EC) 240/96 (OJ L31, 9.2.96, p 2); and COMPETITION vol 18 (2009) PARA 61 et seq.

3   *Mills v Carson* (1892) 9 TLR 80, 10 RPC 9, CA; *African Gold Recovery Co Ltd v Sheba Gold Mining Co Ltd* (1897) 2 Com Cas 277, 14 RPC 660. As to the validity of a patent see PARA 425 et seq.

4   See Case 320/87 *Ottung v Klee & Weilbach A/S* [1989] ECR 1177, [1991] FSR 657, ECJ.

5   *Taylor v Hare* (1805) 1 Bos & PNR 260.

6   *Otto v Singer* (1889) 7 RPC 7. The same applies if the granted patent covers less than the original application: *Haddan v Smith* (1847) 10 LTOS 154. As to proceedings for infringement see PARA 520 et seq.

7   *Redges v Mulliner* (1892) 10 RPC 21. In *Gill v Stone & Co Ltd* (1911) 28 RPC 329 a notice was given that interest at 5% would be claimed, and interest was allowed from the date when royalties became payable. Nevertheless, it is correct practice to provide explicitly for this in the licence agreement.

8   *Bergmann v Macmillan* (1881) 17 ChD 423.

9   *Bower v Hodges* (1853) 22 LJCP 194. Failure to keep proper books may, however, be a material breach of the conditions and lead to forfeiture of the licence: *Ward v Livesey* (1887) 5 RPC 102.

10 *Fomento (Sterling Area) Ltd v Selsdon Fountain Pen Co Ltd* [1958] 1 All ER 11 at 20, [1958] 1 WLR 45 at 57, [1958] RPC 8 at 17, HL, per Lord Morton of Henryton and at 23, 61 and 20 per Lord Denning.

11 *Anglo-American Asphalt Co Ltd v Crowley Russell & Co Ltd* [1945] 2 All ER 324 (where the licensee was ordered to give inspection of books for six years back from the date of the writ, although royalty statements and payments had been accepted by the licensor throughout the life of the agreement).

12 See eg *Hall v Bainbridge and Enderby* (1843) 5 QB 233 (liability to pay royalties on orders taken although the patented invention was not in fact used); *Tielens v Hooper* (1850) 20 LJ Ex 78 (provision for a minimum payment per annum, with a right to terminate the licence if this was not paid, held not to amount to a covenant to pay that minimum amount); *Oxley v Holden* (1860) 30 LJCP 68 (liability to pay royalties for fixing articles for which a royalty was payable); *Edwards v Normandy* (1864) 12 WR 548 (interpretation of 'profits' for royalty purposes); *Goucher v Clayton* (1865) 13 LT 115 (whether higher or lower royalty was payable for user, after the end of the licence term, and liability to pay royalty on renewal of patented parts); *Siemans v Taylor* (1892) 9 RPC 393 (liability to pay full royalties after some of the patents had expired); *Bagott Pneumatic Tyre Co v Clipper Pneumatic Tyre Co* [1902] 1 Ch 146, 19 RPC 69, CA (interpretation of 'profits' for royalty purposes, and liability of assignees to be sued); *Fomento (Sterling Area) Ltd v Selsdon Fountain Pen Co Ltd* [1958] 1 All ER 11, [1958] 1 WLR 45, [1958] RPC 8, HL, upholding on this point [1956] RPC 344, CA (agreement to reduce royalties if licence 'at a lower royalty' granted to another); *Bristol Repetition Ltd v Fomento (Sterling Area) Ltd* [1961] RPC 222 (liability to pay full royalties after some patents had expired); *Hansen v Magnavox Electronics Co Ltd* [1977] RPC 301, CA (liability to pay royalties after some patents had expired); *Shiley Inc's Patent* [1988] RPC 97 (the rate of royalty for a surgical device is higher than that for a mechanical device (range usually 5–7%) but lower than that of a pharmaceutical invention (range usually 25–30%)); *Cambridge Display Technology Ltd v EI Dupont de Nemours & Co* [2004] EWHC 1415 (Ch), [2005] FSR 253, [2004] All ER (D) 186 (Jun) (when first payment of minimum royalty due).

13 *Haddan v Smith* (1847) 10 LTOS 154; cf *Postcard Automatic Supply Co v Samuel* (1889) 6 RPC 560.

389. Powers to determine licence. The question whether either party may terminate a licence depends upon its special terms. If the licence agreement is silent as to determination, there is no presumption that it is intended to be permanent[1]. If there is provision for termination in certain events, there may be a presumption that it cannot be determined otherwise[2]. If the licence is expressed to be for a definite time, it cannot be revoked[3] except for acts bringing about forfeiture[4], nor may the licensee disclaim it[5]. If there is a provision that a licence is determinable on a certain date, if certain provisions have not been complied with, acceptance of royalties after that date may estop the licensor from terminating it[6].

1   If there is a presumption, it is rather in favour of a power to determine upon reasonable notice (reasonable, that is, at the date of the notice): *Martin-Baker Aircraft Co Ltd v Canadian Flight Equipment Ltd* [1955] 2 QB 556 at 577, 581, [1955] 2 All ER 722 at 732, 735, 72 RPC 236 at 243, 245 per McNair J. See also *Dorling v Honnor Marine Ltd* [1965] Ch 1, [1964] 1 All ER 241, CA (copyright licence).

2   *Guyot v Thomson* [1894] 3 Ch 388, 11 RPC 541, CA; *Cutlan v Dawson* (1897) 14 RPC 249, CA.

3   *Guyot v Thomson* [1894] 3 Ch 388, 11 RPC 541, CA; *Ward v Livesey* (1887) 5 RPC 102.

4   A mere breach of covenant, eg to pay renewal fees (*Mills v Carson* (1892) 9 TLR 80, 10 RPC 9, CA), or to sue infringers (*Huntoon Co v Kolynos (Inc)* [1930] 1 Ch 528, 47 RPC 403), or to provide working instructions (*Cheetham v Nuthall* (1893) 10 RPC 321), does not give rise to forfeiture. See also the cases cited in notes 2, 3. The court has power to grant relief against forfeiture to contracts concerning the transfer of proprietary or possessory rights (*Sport International Bussum BV v Inter-Footwear Ltd* [1984] 2 All ER 321, [1984] 1 WLR 776, HL; *BICC plc v Burndy Corpn* [1985] Ch 232, [1985] 1 All ER 417, [1985] RPC 273 at 305, CA); but this does not extend to contracts creating such rights (*Sport International Bussum BV v Inter-Footwear Ltd* at 325 and at 794 per Lord Templeman).

5   *Cutlan v Dawson* (1897) 14 RPC 249, CA.

6   *Warwick v Hooper* (1850) 3 Mac & G 60.

390. Effect of war. A patent licence is not invalid by reason of the fact that the proprietor of the patent or any person otherwise interested in it is an enemy[1] if, were he not an enemy, it would have been in force in favour of a person resident in the United Kingdom[2]; nor is any contract, in so far as it relates to such a licence, invalid by reason of the fact that any party to it is an enemy[3]. This does not, however, validate grants or assignments of licences[4], or contracts, made during the existence of a state of war, and such as to be invalid apart from this provision, nor does it authorise the performance of a licence agreement in a manner unlawful by reason of war[5]. The Crown has special powers to make use of patented inventions for the efficient prosecution of any war in which it may be engaged[6].

1   For these purposes, 'enemy' has the same meaning as in the Trading with the Enemy Act 1939 (see s 2; and ARMED CONFLICT AND EMERGENCY vol 3 (2011) PARA 198): Patents, Designs, Copyright and Trade Marks (Emergency) Act 1939 s 10(1).

2   As to the meaning of 'United Kingdom' see PARA 303 note 5.

3   See the Patents, Designs, Copyright and Trade Marks (Emergency) Act 1939 s 1(1); and ARMED CONFLICT AND EMERGENCY vol 3 (2011) PARA 208.

4   As to the power to license see PARA 377; and as to assignments of licences see PARA 381.

5   Patents, Designs, Copyright and Trade Marks (Emergency) Act 1939 s 1(1) proviso; and ARMED CONFLICT AND EMERGENCY vol 3 (2011) PARA 208.

6   See the Patents Act 1977 s 59(1)(a); and PARA 410.

(2) LICENCES OF RIGHT

391. Entry of licences of right. At any time after the grant of a patent[1] its proprietor may apply to the comptroller[2] for an entry to be made in the register[3] to the effect that licences under the patent are to be available as of right[4]. Where such an application is made, the comptroller must give notice of the application to any person registered as having a right[5] in or under the patent and, if satisfied that the proprietor of the patent is not precluded by contract from granting licences under the patent, must make the entry applied for[6].

Where such an entry is made in respect of a patent:

(1)   any person is, at any time after the entry is made, entitled as of right to a licence under the patent on such terms as may be settled by agreement or, in default of agreement, by the comptroller on the application of the proprietor or the person requiring the licence[7];

(2)　the comptroller may, on the application of the holder of any licence granted[8] under the patent before the entry was made, order the licence to be exchanged for a licence of right on terms so settled[9];

(3)　if in proceedings for infringement[10] of the patent, otherwise than by the importation of any article from a country which is not an EU member state, the defendant undertakes[11] to take a licence on such terms, no injunction may be granted against him and the amount, if any, recoverable against him by way of damages must not exceed double the amount which would have been payable by him as licensee if such a licence on those terms had been granted before the earliest infringement[12];

(4)　if the expiry date in relation to a renewal fee[13] falls after the date of the entry, that fee is to be half the fee which would be payable had the entry not been made[14].

The licensee under a licence of right may, unless, in the case of a licence the terms of which are settled by agreement, the licence otherwise expressly provides, request the proprietor to take proceedings to prevent any infringement of the patent, and, if the proprietor refuses or neglects to do so within two months after being so requested, the licensee may institute proceedings for the infringement in his own name as if he were the proprietor, making the proprietor a defendant[15]. A proprietor so added as defendant is not liable for any costs or expenses unless he enters an appearance and takes part in the proceedings[16].

1　As to grant see PARA 337.
2　As to the comptroller see PARA 575.
3　As to the register see PARA 583 et seq.
4　Patents Act 1977 s 46(1). An application under s 46(1) must be made on Patents Form 28: Patents Rules 2007, SI 2007/3291, r 43(1).
5　As to the meaning of 'right' see PARA 359 note 7.
6　Patents Act 1977 s 46(2). Where an entry is made in the register to the effect that licences under a patent are to be available as of right, the comptroller must advertise the entry in the Official Journal (Patents) (see PARA 578): Patents Rules 2007, SI 2007/3291, r 43(2). As to the application of the Patents Act 1977 s 46(2) to EU compulsory licences see PARA 401.
7　Patents Act 1977 s 46(3)(a). An application by a person other than the proprietor to the comptroller under s 46(3)(a) or (b) must be made on Patents Form 2 and be accompanied by two copies of the draft of the licence he proposes should be granted: Patents Rules 2007, SI 2007/3291, r 89(1). The comptroller must notify the proprietor of the patent that an application has been made and must send a copy of the draft licence with the notification: r 89(2), (3). In the notification, the comptroller must specify a period within which the proprietor may file a statement of grounds: r 89(4). The proprietor must file a statement of grounds in accordance with r 76(4) (see PARA 599); otherwise he is treated as supporting the applicant's case: r 89(5). Proceedings are to continue under Pt 7 (rr 73–91) (see PARAS 598–606) as if they had been started under r 76(1) (see PARA 599) and for those purposes the proprietor is the 'claimant' and the applicant is the 'defendant': r 89(6).

　　See *Beecham Group plc v Gist-Brocades NV* [1986] 1 WLR 51, [1986] RPC 203, HL (procedure on extension of patent). Terms of a licence of right can include the right to grant sub-licences to subsidiary companies when appropriate: *Hilti AG's Patent* [1988] RPC 51. Where the entry has been made compulsorily (eg under the Patents Act 1977 ss 48–51 (see PARA 394 et seq)), the comptroller may settle terms of a licence notwithstanding that the applicant is challenging the validity of the patent in infringement proceedings: *EI Du Pont De Nemours & Co (Blades') Patent* [1988] RPC 479. As to settlement of terms see also *Smith Kline & French Laboratories Ltd's (Cimetidine) Patents* [1990] RPC 203, CA; *American Cyanamid Co's (Fenbufen) Patent* [1990] RPC 309; *Research Corpn's (Carboplatin) Patent* [1990] RPC 663; *Cabot Safety Corpn's Patent* [1992] RPC 39; *Smith Kline & French Laboratories Ltd v Harris Pharmaceuticals Ltd* [1992] FSR 110; *Research Corpn's Supplementary Protection Certificate (No 2)* [1996] RPC 320. An applicant for a licence of right is not precluded from challenging the validity of the patent in other proceedings: *EI Du Pont De Nemours & Co (Blades') Patent*

    [1988] RPC 479. In all the cases cited in this note, the patent had been compulsorily endorsed licences of right under the Patents Act 1977 Sch 1 (now spent).

8   As to the power to license see PARA 377.

9   Patents Act 1977 s 46(3)(b). See also note 7.

10 As to proceedings for infringement see PARA 520 et seq.

11 The undertaking may be given at the time before final order in the proceedings, without any admission of liability: Patents Act 1977 s 46(3A) (added by the Copyright, Designs and Patents Act 1988 Sch 5 para 12(1), (3)).

12 Patents Act 1977 s 46(3)(c) (amended by the Copyright, Designs and Patents Act 1988 Sch 5 para 12(1), (2)).

13 As to renewal fees see PARA 339.

14 Patents Act 1977 s 46(3)(d) (substituted by the Patents Act 2004 s 8(4)(a)). For the purposes of the Patents Act 1977 s 46(3)(d), the expiry date in relation to a renewal fee is the day at the end of which, by virtue of s 25(3) (see PARA 339), the patent in question ceases to have effect if that fee is not paid: s 46(3B) (added by the Patents Act 2004 s 8(4)(b)).

15 Patents Act 1977 s 46(4).

16 Patents Act 1977 s 46(5). As to proceedings for infringement see PARA 516 et seq.

392. Cancellation of entry as to licences of right. At any time after an entry[1] has been made on the register[2] that licences are available as of right under a patent[3], the proprietor of the patent may apply[4] to the comptroller[5] for cancellation of the entry[6]. Where such an application is made and the balance paid of all renewal fees which would have been payable if the entry had not been made, the comptroller may cancel the entry if satisfied that there is no existing licence under the patent or that all licensees under the patent consent to the application[7].

Within the period of two months beginning immediately after the making of the relevant entry, any person who claims that the proprietor is, and was at the time of the entry, precluded by a contract in which the claimant is interested from granting licences under the patent may apply to the comptroller for cancellation of the entry[8]. Where the comptroller is satisfied, on such an application, that the proprietor is and was so precluded, he must cancel the entry, and the proprietor is then liable to pay, within a period specified by the comptroller, a sum equal to the balance of all renewal fees which would have been payable if the entry had not been made, and the patent ceases to have effect at the expiration of that period[9] if that sum is not so paid[10].

Where an entry is cancelled under these provisions, the rights and liabilities of the proprietor are afterwards the same as if the entry had not been made[11].

Where an application has been made under these provisions, then, in the case of an application by the proprietor[12], any person[13], and, in the case of an application by a person claiming that the proprietor is precluded from granting licences[14], the proprietor[15], may, within four weeks beginning immediately after the advertisement of the application for cancellation in the Official Journal (Patents), give notice to the comptroller of opposition to the cancellation[16]. In considering the application, the comptroller must determine whether the opposition is justified[17].

1   Ie an entry under the Patents Act 1977 s 46: see PARA 391.

2   As to the register see PARA 583 et seq.

3   See PARA 391.

4   An application under the Patents Act 1977 s 47(1) for the cancellation of an entry made under s 46 (see PARA 391) must be made on Patents Form 30: Patents Rules 2007, SI 2007/3291, r 43(3).

5   As to the comptroller see PARA 575.

6   Patents Act 1977 s 47(1).

7   Patents Act 1977 s 47(2). As to renewal fees see PARA 339.

8   Patents Act 1977 s 47(3); Patents Rules 2007, SI 2007/3291, r 43(4) (amended by
    SI 2011/2052). The prescribed time limit may not be extended: see PARA 597. As to proceedings
    before the comptroller see the Patents Rules 2007, SI 2007/3291, Pt 7 (rr 73–91); and PARAS
    598–606.
9   As to the restoration of lapsed patents see PARA 355.
10 Patents Act 1977 s 47(4).
11 Patents Act 1977 s 47(5).
12 Ie an application under the Patents Act 1977 s 47(1): see the text and notes 1–6.
13 See the Patents Act 1977 s 47(6)(a).
14 Ie on an application under the Patents Act 1977 s 47(3): see the text and note 8.
15 See the Patents Act 1977 s 47(6)(b).
16 Patents Act 1977 s 47(6); Patents Rules 2007, SI 2007/3291, r 77(8), (10) (r 77(8) amended by
    SI 2011/2052).
17 Patents Act 1977 s 47(6). As to appeals from the comptroller's decision see PARA 571.

(3) COMPULSORY LICENCES

393. Kinds of compulsory licensing. There are two sets of provisions for the
compulsory licensing of patents:
   (1)   provisions for licensing in case of abuse of monopoly[1] which could
          apply to many patents, but have been little used; and
   (2)   a provision for the licensing of enemy patents in time of war[2].
   In addition, the Crown has certain rights to make use of patented inventions,
and technical information relating to them, without the consent of the proprietor
of the patent[3].

1   See PARA 394 et seq.
2   See PARA 400.
3   See PARA 404 et seq.

394. Grounds for compulsory licensing in case of abuse of monopoly. At any
time after the expiration of three years, or of such other period as may be
prescribed, from the date of the grant of a patent[1], any person may apply to the
comptroller[2] for compulsory licensing[3] on one or more of the following grounds:
   (1)   in the case of an application made in respect of a patent whose
          proprietor is a WTO proprietor[4], the relevant grounds are[5]:
          (a)   where the patented invention[6] is a product, that a demand for the
                 product in the United Kingdom[7] is not being met on reasonable
                 terms[8];
          (b)   that by reason of the refusal of the proprietor of the patent[9] to
                 grant a licence or licences on reasonable terms[10]: (i) the
                 exploitation in the United Kingdom of any other patented
                 invention which involves an important technical advance of
                 considerable economic significance in relation to the invention for
                 which the patent concerned was granted is prevented or hindered;
                 or (ii) the establishment or development of commercial or
                 industrial activities in the United Kingdom is unfairly
                 prejudiced[11];
          (c)   that by reason of conditions imposed by the proprietor of the
                 patent on the grant of licences under the patent, or on the disposal
                 or use of the patented product or on the use of the patented
                 process, the manufacture, use or disposal of materials not
                 protected by the patent, or the establishment or development of
                 commercial or industrial activities in the United Kingdom, is
                 unfairly prejudiced[12].

(2)   in the case of an application in respect of a patent whose proprietor is not a WTO proprietor, the relevant grounds are[13]:

     (a)   where the patented invention is capable of being commercially worked in the United Kingdom[14], that it is not being so worked[15] or is not being so worked to the fullest extent that is reasonably practicable[16];

     (b)   where the patented invention is a product, that a demand for the product in the United Kingdom is not being met on reasonable terms, or is being met to a substantial extent by importation from a country which is not a member state[17];

     (c)   where the patented invention is capable of being commercially worked in the United Kingdom, that it is being prevented or hindered from being so worked[18], where the invention is a product, by the importation of the product from a country which is not a member state[19] or, where the invention is a process, by the importation from such a country of a product obtained directly by means of the process or to which the process has been applied[20];

     (d)   that by reason of the refusal of the proprietor of the patent to grant a licence or licences on reasonable terms: (i) a market for the export of any patented product made in the United Kingdom is not being supplied[21]; (ii) the working or efficient working in the United Kingdom of any other patented invention which makes a substantial contribution to the art is prevented or hindered[22]; or (iii) the establishment or development of commercial or industrial activities in the United Kingdom is unfairly prejudiced[23];

     (e)   that by reason of conditions imposed by the proprietor of the patent on the grant of licences under the patent, or on the disposal or use of the patented product or on the use of the patented process, the manufacture, use or disposal of materials not protected by the patent, or the establishment or development of commercial or industrial activities in the United Kingdom, is unfairly prejudiced[24].

1   As to grant see PARA 337.

2   As to the comptroller see PARA 575. As to proceedings before the comptroller see the Patents Rules 2007, SI 2007/3291, Pt 7 (rr 73–91); and PARAS 598–606. The burden of proof to show that one or more of the grounds of the Patents Act 1977 s 48 is met is on the applicant for the compulsory licence: *Richco Plastic Co's Patent* [1989] RPC 722.

3   Patents Act 1977 s 48(1) (s 48 substituted, ss 48A, 48B added, by SI 1999/1899). The application may be: (1) for a licence under the patent; (2) for an entry to be made in the register to the effect that licences under the patent are to be available as of right; or (3) where the applicant is a government department, for the grant to any person specified in the application of a licence under the patent: Patents Act 1977 s 48(1)(a)–(c) (as so substituted). As to opposition, appeal and arbitration in respect of such applications see PARA 399; and as to the possible relief which may be applied for see PARA 395. The applicant for a compulsory licence does not have to admit the validity of the patent and may challenge it in other proceedings, although this may result in the application being stayed until the outcome of those proceedings is known: *Halcon SD Group Inc's Patents* [1989] RPC 1. The applicant does not have to show a definite intention to work the licence; a genuine interest is enough to found an application: *Halcon SD Group Inc's Patents*.

4   A proprietor is a WTO proprietor for the purposes of the Patents Act 1977 ss 48, 48A, 48B, 50 and 52 if: (1) he is a national of, or is domiciled in, a country which is a member of the World Trade Organisation; or (2) he has a real and effective industrial or commercial establishment in such a country: s 48(5) (as substituted: see note 3). As to the World Trade Organisation see INTERNATIONAL RELATIONS LAW vol 61 (2010) PARA 461. No order or entry may be made under s 48 in respect of a patent whose proprietor is a WTO proprietor unless: (a) the applicant has made efforts to obtain a licence from the proprietor on reasonable commercial terms and

conditions; and (b) his efforts have not been successful within a reasonable period: s 48A(2) (as so added). No order or entry may be so made if the patented invention is in the field of semi-conductor technology: Patents Act 1977 s 48A(3) (as so added).

5   Patents Act 1977 ss 48(4)(a), 48A(1) (as substituted and added: see note 3).

6   As to the meaning of 'patented invention' see PARA 370 note 27; and see *Re Lake's Patent* (1909) 26 RPC 443.

7   As to the meaning of 'United Kingdom' see PARA 303 note 5. Demand must be an existing demand, and not one which the applicant hopes to create: *Re Cathro's Application* (1934) 51 RPC 75.

8   Patents Act 1977 s 48A(1)(a) (as added: see note 3).

9   Ie as distinct from his exclusive licensee: *Re Colbourne Engineering Co Ltd's Application* (1954) 72 RPC 169. As to refusal see *Re Loewe Radio Co Ltd's Application* (1929) 46 RPC 479. As to the meaning of 'exclusive licensee' see PARA 379 note 7.

10 It may be reasonable to insist upon licensing a group of patents together, and demand a royalty regardless of whether or not use is made of the patents: *Re Brownie Wireless Co of Great Britain Ltd* (1929) 46 RPC 457. As to royalties see PARA 388.

11 Patents Act 1977 s 48A(1)(b) (as added: see note 3). No order or entry may be made under s 48 in respect of a patent on the ground mentioned in head (1)(b)(i) in the text unless the comptroller is satisfied that the proprietor of the patent for the other invention is able and willing to grant the proprietor of the patent concerned and his licensees a licence under the patent for the other invention on reasonable terms: s 48A(4) (as so added). A licence granted in pursuance of an order or entry so made must not be assigned except to a person to whom the patent for the other invention is also assigned: s 48A(5) (as so added). It may be fair for the proprietor of the patent to hold to his monopoly until he has recovered the cost of developing the invention: *Re Colbourne Engineering Co Ltd's Application* (1954) 72 RPC 169.

12 Patents Act 1977 s 48A(1)(c) (as added: see note 3).

13 Patents Act 1977 ss 48(4)(b), 48B(1) (as substituted and added: see note 3).

14 An invention is not incapable of being worked in the United Kingdom because specially skilled labour or special tools are required to be imported: *Johnson's Patent* (1909) 26 RPC 52; *Wardwell's Patent* (1913) 30 RPC 408. The only inventions likely to be held incapable of being worked in the United Kingdom are inventions dealing with activities not found there eg gold mining. Non-working in the United Kingdom of an invention which is worked abroad requires an explanation: *Re The Application of A Hamson & Son (London) Ltd* [1958] RPC 88. A licensee who is willing to work the invention in the United Kingdom should be given the opportunity to do so even though the proprietor of the patent can justify his failure on the ground that it would be uneconomical to do so: *Re Kalle & Co AG's Patent* [1966] FSR 112. There is some doubt as to the position where working is prohibited by law, in particular by another patent monopoly; cf *Re Taylor's Patent* [1912] 1 Ch 635, 29 RPC 296; and PARA 395.

    Where: (1) an application is made on the ground that the patented invention is not being commercially worked in the United Kingdom or is not being so worked to the fullest extent that is reasonably practicable; and (2) it appears to the comptroller that the time which has elapsed since the publication in the journal of a notice of the grant of the patent has for any reason been insufficient to enable the invention to be so worked, he may by order adjourn the application for such period as will in his opinion give sufficient time for the invention to be so worked: Patents Act 1977 s 48B(2) (as added: see note 3).

15 Ie by the proprietor of the patent, or licensees, or infringers: *Re Mercedes Daimler Co's Application* (1910) 27 RPC 762; *Re Wardwell's Patent* (1913) 30 RPC 408; *Hill's Patent* (1915) 32 RPC 475. Thus an applicant for compulsory licensing who has already commenced manufacture may not rely on this ground.

16 Patents Act 1977 s 48B(1)(a) (as added: see note 3). No order or entry may be made under s 48 in respect of a patent on the ground mentioned in s 48B(1)(a) if: (1) the patented invention is being commercially worked in a country which is a member state; and (2) demand in the United Kingdom is being met by importation from that country: s 48B(3) (as so added).

    Where the application is on the ground that the invention is not being worked to the fullest extent possible, the applicant may be required to establish what demand might be expected and the extent to which it is not met: *Kamborian's Patent* [1961] RPC 403.

17 Patents Act 1977 s 48B(1)(b) (as added: see note 3).

18 Importation does not necessarily hinder working in the United Kingdom; it may foster it by creating a demand for the article imported: *McKechnie Bros Ltd's Application* (1934) 51 RPC 461 at 472 per Luxmoore J. A proprietor of a patent should be careful not to build up the market in the United Kingdom solely by importation: see *Fette's Patent* [1961] RPC 396.

19 Patents Act 1977 s 48B(1)(c)(i) (as added: see note 3).

20 Patents Act 1977 s 48B(1)(c)(ii) (as added: see note 3).

21 Patents Act 1977 s 48B(1)(d)(i) (as added: see note 3). No entry may be made in the register on the ground mentioned in s 48B(1)(d)(i), and any licence granted under s 48 on that ground must contain such provisions as appear to the comptroller to be expedient for restricting the countries in which any product concerned may be disposed of or used by the licensee: s 48B(4) (as so added).

22 Patents Act 1977 s 48B(1)(d)(ii) (as added: see note 3). No order or entry may be made under s 48 in respect of a patent on the ground mentioned in s 48B(1)(d)(ii) unless the comptroller is satisfied that the proprietor of the patent for the other invention is able and willing to grant to the proprietor of the patent concerned and his licensees a licence under the patent for the other invention on reasonable terms: s 48B(5) (as so added).

23 Patents Act 1977 s 48B(1)(d)(iii) (as added: see note 3).

24 Patents Act 1977 s 48B(1)(e) (as added: see note 3).

395. Possible relief for abuse of monopoly. Where, on an application in respect of a patent for compulsory licensing in the case of abuse of monopoly[1], the comptroller[2] is satisfied that any of the grounds on which the application is made[3] are established, he may:

(1) order[4] the grant of a licence to the applicant on such terms[5] as the comptroller thinks fit[6];

(2) make an entry in the register[7] that licences under the patent are to be available as of right[8];

(3) where the applicant is a government department[9], order the grant of a licence to the person specified in the application on such terms as the comptroller thinks fit[10].

An application may be made for relief under these provisions in respect of a patent notwithstanding that the applicant is already the holder of a licence under the patent, and no person is estopped or barred from alleging any of the grounds on which such an application may be made by reason of any admission made by him, whether in such a licence or otherwise, or by reason of his having accepted such a licence[11].

Where a holder of a licence does apply for relief, the comptroller may, if he orders the grant of a licence to the applicant, order the existing licence to be cancelled[12] or, instead of ordering the grant of a licence, may order the existing licence to be amended[13].

Where the comptroller is satisfied on an application made for relief in respect of a patent that the manufacture, use or disposal of materials not protected by it is unfairly prejudiced by reason of conditions imposed by the proprietor of the patent on the grant of licences under the patent, or on the disposal or use of the patented product[14] or the use of the patented process[15], he may order the grant of licences under the patent to such customers of the applicant as he thinks fit as well as to the applicant[16].

Any licence granted pursuant to an order or by virtue of an entry under these provisions entitles the licensee to institute proceedings for infringement[17] in his own name if the proprietor fails to institute such proceedings[18].

No order or entry may be made under the above provisions which would be at variance with any treaty or international convention to which the United Kingdom[19] is a party[20], and Her Majesty may by Order in Council provide that the comptroller may not, otherwise than for purposes of the public interest, make an order or entry in respect of a patent in pursuance of an application under the above provisions if the invention concerned is being commercially worked in any relevant country[21] specified in the Order and demand in the United Kingdom for any patented product resulting from that working is being met by importation from that country[22].

In any proceedings on an application made in relation to a patent under the statutory provisions relating to compulsory licences[23] any statement with respect to any activity in relation to the patented invention, or with respect to the grant or refusal of licences under the patent, contained in a competition regulator's report[24] is prima facie evidence of the matters stated[25].

1 Ie an application under the Patents Act 1977 s 48(1): see PARA 394.

2 As to the comptroller see PARA 575.

3 Ie the grounds specified in the Patents Act 1977 s 48A(1) or s 48B(1): see PARA 394.

4 Ie on an application under the Patents Act 1977 s 48(1)(a): see PARA 394.

5 A licence granted in pursuance of an order or entry made under the Patents Act 1977 s 48 in respect of a patent whose proprietor is a WTO proprietor (see PARA 394 note 4): (1) must not be exclusive; (2) must not be assigned except to a person to whom there is also assigned the part of the enterprise that enjoys the use of the patented invention, or the part of the goodwill that belongs to that part; (3) must be predominantly for the supply of the market in the United Kingdom; (4) must include conditions entitling the proprietor of the patent concerned to remuneration adequate in the circumstances of the case, taking into account the economic value of the licence; and (5) must be limited in scope and in duration to the purpose for which the licence was granted: s 48A(6) (s 48 substituted, s 48A added, by SI 1999/1899).

6 Patents Act 1977 s 48(2)(a) (as substituted: see note 5). Without prejudice to any other method of enforcement, any order for the grant of a licence under the Patents Act 1977 s 48 or s 49 has effect as if it were a deed, executed by the proprietor of the patent and all other necessary parties, granting a licence in accordance with the order: s 108. For a form of licence see *Re Application by A Hamson & Son (London) Ltd* [1958] RPC 88, although the extremely wide powers of sub-licensing contained in that licence are possibly exceptional.

7 Ie on an application under the Patents Act 1977 s 48(1)(b): see PARA 394. As to the register see PARA 583 et seq.

8 Patents Act 1977 s 48(2)(b) (as substituted: see note 5). The comptroller may make an entry in the register notwithstanding any contract which would have precluded the entry on the application of the proprietor of the patent under s 46 (see PARA 391) (s 53(3)); and any entry made under s 48 has the same effect as an entry made under s 46 (s 53(4)).

9 Ie where the application is made under the Patents Act 1977 s 48(1)(c): see PARA 394.

10 Patents Act 1977 s 48(2)(c) (as substituted: see note 5).

11 Patents Act 1977 s 48(3) (as substituted: see note 5).

12 Patents Act 1977 s 49(2)(a).

13 Patents Act 1977 s 49(2)(b).

14 As to the meaning of 'patented product' see PARA 371 note 11.

15 As to the meaning of 'patented process' see PARA 370 note 27.

16 Patents Act 1977 s 49(1). Although this provision incorporates a ground for an application, it operates whether or not the application is made on that ground. As to the effect of such an order see note 6.

17 As to proceedings for infringement see PARA 520 et seq.

18 Patents Act 1977 s 49(4); applying s 46(4), (5) (see PARA 391).

19 As to the meaning of 'United Kingdom' see PARA 303 note 5.

20 Patents Act 1977 s 53(5). As to treaties and conventions see PARA 628 et seq.

21 For these purposes, 'relevant country' means a country other than a member state or a member of the World Trade Organisation whose law in the opinion of Her Majesty in Council incorporates or will incorporate provisions treating the working of an invention in, and importation from, the United Kingdom in a similar way to that in which the Order in Council would, if made, treat the working of an invention in, and importation from, that country: Patents Act 1977 s 54(2) (amended by SI 1999/1899).

22 Patents Act 1977 s 54(1).

23 Ie the Patents Act 1977 s 48.

24 Ie a report laid before Parliament under the Fair Trading Act 1973 Pt VII (ss 81–83) (repealed), the Competition Act 1980 s 17 or published under the Enterprise Act 2002 Pt 3 (ss 22–130) or Pt 4 (ss 131–184): see COMPETITION vol 18 (2009) PARAS 238, 281.

25 Patents Act 1977 s 53(2) (amended by the Copyright, Designs and Patents Act 1988 Sch 5 para 15(a), (b); the Enterprise Act 2002 Sch 25 para 8(1), (4); SI 1999/506; SI 2014/892).

396. Relevant considerations. The power of compulsory licensing in respect of a patent whose proprietor is not a WTO proprietor[1] on grounds of abuse of monopoly[2] must be exercised with a view to securing the following general purposes[3]:

(1) that inventions which can[4] be worked on a commercial scale in the United Kingdom[5] and which should in the public interest be so worked must be worked there without undue delay and to the fullest extent that is reasonably practicable[6];

(2) that the inventor[7] or other person beneficially entitled to a patent must receive reasonable remuneration having regard to the nature of the invention[8];

(3) that the interests of any person for the time being working or developing an invention in the United Kingdom under the protection of a patent must not be unfairly prejudiced[9].

Subject to the above considerations, the following matters must be taken into account by the comptroller in deciding whether to exercise the power[10]:

(a) the nature of the invention, the time which has elapsed since the publication in the Official Journal (Patents)[11] of a notice of the grant of the patent[12] and the measures already taken by the proprietor or any licensee to make full use of the invention[13];

(b) the ability of any person to whom a licence would be granted under the order to work the invention to the public advantage[14]; and

(c) the risks to be undertaken by that person in providing capital and working the invention if the application for an order is granted[15].

Matters subsequent to the making of the application for a compulsory licence need not, however, be taken into account[16].

It would seem that it is always an objection to an application for a compulsory licence that the acts of the proprietor of the patent himself were justified and legitimate[17].

1 As to the meaning of 'WTO proprietor' see PARA 394 note 4.
2 Ie the comptroller's powers on an application under the Patents Act 1977 s 48: see PARAS 394–395. As to the comptroller see PARA 575.
3 Patents Act 1977 s 50(1) (amended by SI 1999/1899).
4 Cf the use of the expression 'capable of being' in PARA 394.
5 As to the meaning of 'United Kingdom' see PARA 303 note 5.
6 Patents Act 1977 s 50(1)(a).
7 As to the meaning of 'inventor' see PARA 301 note 3.
8 Patents Act 1977 s 50(1)(b).
9 Patents Act 1977 s 50(1)(c).
10 Patents Act 1977 s 50(2) (amended by SI 1999/1899).
11 As to the Journal see PARA 578.
12 As to the publication of such a notice see PARA 337.
13 Patents Act 1977 s 50(2)(a).
14 Patents Act 1977 s 50(2)(b). The applicant for the licence must show that he is likely to have available various resources including the technical expertise and know-how for putting the invention into practice in a way which would benefit the public: *Enviro-Spray Systems Inc's Patents* [1986] RPC 147. Where an applicant is unable to satisfy the Patents Act 1977 s 50(2)(b), a licence should not be granted with the intention that it be worked, not by the applicant, but by a sub-licensee: *Re Therma-Tru Corpn's Patent* [1997] RPC 777.
15 Patents Act 1977 s 50(2)(c).
16 Patents Act 1977 s 50(2). See *Zanetti-Streccia's Patent* [1973] RPC 227. As to when working after the date of the application will be ignored see *Re McKechnie Bros Ltd's Application* (1934) 51 RPC 461; *Re Fabricmeter Co Ltd's Application* (1935) 53 RPC 307; *Re Boult's Patent* (1909) 26 RPC 383.
17 See the Patents Act 1977 s 53(5); and the International Convention for the Protection of Industrial Property (Lisbon, 31 October 1958; TS 38 (1962); Cmnd 1715) art 5A(4). No order

or entry may be made in pursuance of any application under the Patents Act 1977 ss 48–51 (see PARAS 394–395, 397–398) which would be at variance with any treaty or international convention to which the United Kingdom is a party: s 53(5). As to treaties and international conventions see PARA 628 et seq.

397. Powers exercisable following merger and market investigations. The Competition and Markets Authority[1] or (as the case may be) the Secretary of State[2] may apply to the comptroller[3] to take action[4] where:

(1) the provisions of the Enterprise Act 2002[5] relating to powers to take remedial action following merger or market investigations apply[6];

(2) the Competition and Markets Authority or (as the case may be) the Secretary of State considers that it would be appropriate to make an application[7] for the purpose of remedying, mitigating or preventing a matter which cannot be dealt with under the enactment concerned[8]; and

(3) the matter concerned involves: (a) conditions in licences[9] granted under a patent by its proprietor restricting the use of the invention[10] by the licensee or the right of the proprietor to grant other licences[11]; or (b) a refusal by the proprietor of a patent to grant licences on reasonable terms[12].

Before making an application the Competition and Markets Authority or (as the case may be) the Secretary of State must publish, in such manner as it or he thinks appropriate, a notice describing the nature of the proposed application and must consider any representations which may be made within 30 days of such publication by persons whose interests appear to it or him to be affected[13].

The comptroller may, if it appears to him on an application[14] that the application is made in accordance with the above provisions, by order cancel or modify any condition concerned of the kind mentioned in head (3)(a) above or may, instead or in addition, make an entry in the register[15] to the effect that licences under the patent are to be available as of right[16].

1 The Competition and Markets Authority was established under the Enterprise and Regulatory Reform Act 2013, and took over the functions of the former Competition Commission and Office of Fair Trading as from 1 April 2014: see ss 25, 26, Schs 5, 6; the Enterprise and Regulatory Reform Act 2013 (Commencement No 6, Transitional Provisions and Savings) Order 2014, SI 2014/416; and COMPETITION vol 18 (2009) PARA 9 et seq.
2 As to the Secretary of State see PARA 573.
3 As to the comptroller see PARA 575.
4 Patents Act 1977 s 50A(2) (s 50A added by the Enterprise Act 2002 Sch 25 para 8(1), (2); Patents Act 1977 s 50A(1)(a), (b), (2), (6) amended by SI 2014/892)).
5 Ie the Enterprise Act 2002 ss 41(2), 55(2), 66(6), 75(2), 83(2), 138(2), 147(2), 147A(2), 160(2), Sch 7 paras 5(2), 10(2): see COMPETITION. See also the Enterprise Act 2002 (Protection of Legitimate Interests) Order 2003, SI 2003/1592, art 16, Sch 4 para 3. References in the Enterprise Act 2002 s 35, 36, 47, 63, 134, 141 or 141A (questions to be decided by the Competition and Markets Authority in its reports) to taking action under s 41(2), 55, 66, 138, 147 or 147A include references to taking action under the Patents Act 1977 s 50A(2) (see the text to notes 1–4): s 50A(6) (as added and amended: see note 4).
6 Patents Act 1977 s 50A(1)(a) (as added and amended: see note 4).
7 Ie under the Patents Act 1977 s 50A.
8 Patents Act 1977 s 50A(1)(b) (as added and amended: see note 4).
9 As to licences generally see PARA 377 et seq.
10 As to the meaning of 'invention' see PARA 301 note 2.
11 Patents Act 1977 s 50A(1)(c)(i) (as added: see note 4).
12 Patents Act 1977 s 50A(1)(c)(ii) (as added: see note 4).
13 Patents Act 1977 s 50A(3) (as added: see note 4).
14 Ie an application under the Patents Act 1977 s 50A.
15 As to the register see PARA 583.
16 Patents Act 1977 s 50A(4) (as added: see note 4). As to licences of right see PARAS 391–392. Action taken by virtue of s 50A(4) in consequence of an application under s 50A(2) (see the text

to notes 1–4) where an enactment mentioned in s 50A(1)(a) (see note 5) applies is to be treated, for the purposes of the Enterprise Act 2002 ss 91(3), 92(1)(a), 162(1) and 166(3) (duties to register and keep under review enforcement orders etc), as if it were the making of an enforcement order (within the meaning of the Part concerned) under the relevant power in Pt 3 (ss 22–130) or (as the case may be) Pt 4 (ss 131–184) of that Act: Patents Act 1977 s 50A(7) (as so added).

398. Powers exercisable in consequence of report of Competition and Markets Authority. The appropriate minister or ministers[1] may apply to the comptroller[2] for compulsory licensing where a report of the Competition and Markets Authority has been laid before Parliament containing conclusions to the effect:

(1)   on a competition reference, that a person was engaged in an anticompetitive practice which operated or may be expected to operate against the public interest; or

(2)   on a reference of public bodies and certain other persons[3], that a person is pursuing a course of conduct which operates against the public interest[4].

Before making such an application, the appropriate minister or ministers must publish, in such manner as he or they think appropriate, a notice describing the nature of the proposed application and must consider any representations which may be made within 30 days of such publication by persons whose interests appear to him or them to be affected[5].

If on an application under the above provisions it appears to the comptroller that the matters specified in the Competition and Markets Authority's report as being those which in the Authority's opinion operate, or operated or may be expected to operate, against the public interest include: (a) conditions in licences granted under a patent by its proprietor restricting the use of the invention by the licensee or the right of the proprietor to grant other licences; or (b) a refusal by the proprietor of a patent to grant licences on reasonable terms, he may by order cancel or modify any such condition or may, instead or in addition, make an entry in the register to the effect that licences under the patent are to be available as of right[6].

1   For these purposes, 'appropriate minister or ministers' means the minister or ministers to whom the report of the Competition and Markets Authority was made: Patents Act 1977 s 51(4) (s 51 substituted by the Copyright, Designs and Patents Act 1988 Sch 5 para 14; Patents Act 1977 s 51(1), (3), (4) amended by SI 2014/892). As to the Competition and Markets Authority see PARA 397 note 1.

2   As to the comptroller see PARA 575.

3   Ie a reference under the Competition Act 1980 s 11: see COMPETITION vol 18 (2009) PARA 10.

4   Patents Act 1977 s 51(1) (as substituted and amended (see note 1); and amended by SI 1999/506). As to proceedings before the comptroller see the Patents Rules 2007, SI 2007/3291, Pt 7 (rr 73–91); and PARAS 598–606.

5   Patents Act 1977 s 51(2) (as substituted: see note 1).

6   Patents Act 1977 s 51(3) (as substituted and amended: see note 1). As to licences of right see PARAS 391–392.

399. Opposition, appeal and arbitration. The proprietor of the patent concerned or any other person wishing to oppose an application for the grant of compulsory licences[1] may give to the comptroller[2] notice of opposition in accordance with the prescribed procedure[3]. The comptroller must consider the opposition in deciding whether to grant the application[4].

Where an order or entry has been made[5] in respect of a patent whose proprietor is a WTO proprietor[6]:

(1)   the proprietor or any other person may, in accordance with rules, apply

to the comptroller to have the order revoked or the entry cancelled on the grounds that the circumstances which led to the making of the order or entry have ceased to exist and are unlikely to recur[7];

(2) any person wishing to oppose an application under head (1) above may, in accordance with rules, give to the comptroller notice of opposition[8]; and

(3) the comptroller must consider any opposition in deciding whether to grant the application[9].

If it appears to the comptroller on an application under head (1) above that the circumstances which led to the making of the order or entry have ceased to exist and are unlikely to recur, he may revoke the order or cancel the entry and terminate any licence granted to a person in pursuance of the order or entry subject to such terms and conditions as he thinks necessary for the protection of the legitimate interests of that person[10].

Where an appeal[11] is brought from an order made by the comptroller in pursuance of an application for compulsory licensing[12] or from a decision of his to make an entry in the register[13] in pursuance of such an application or from a revocation or cancellation made by him[14] or from a refusal of his to make such an order, entry, revocation or cancellation, the Attorney General, or such other person who has a right of audience as he may appoint, is entitled to appear and be heard[15].

Where an application[16] is opposed and either the parties consent[17] or the proceedings require a prolonged examination of documents or any scientific or local investigation which cannot in the comptroller's opinion conveniently be made before him[18], he may at any time order the whole of the proceedings, or any question or issue of fact arising in them, to be referred to an arbitrator agreed on by the parties or, in default of agreement, appointed by the comptroller[19].

1 Ie an application under the Patents Act 1977 ss 48–51: see PARAS 394–398.
2 As to the comptroller see PARA 575.
3 Patents Act 1977 s 52(1) (s 52 substituted by SI 1999/1899). As to proceedings before the comptroller see the Patents Rules 2007, SI 2007/3291, Pt 7 (rr 73–91); and PARAS 598–606.
4 Patents Act 1977 s 52(1) (as substituted: see note 3).
5 Ie under the Patents Act 1977 s 48: see PARAS 394–395.
6 Patents Act 1977 s 52(2) (as substituted: see note 3). As to the meaning of 'WTO proprietor' see PARA 394 note 4.
7 Patents Act 1977 s 52(2)(a) (as substituted: see note 3).
8 Patents Act 1977 s 52(2)(b) (as substituted: see note 3).
9 Patents Act 1977 s 52(2)(c) (as substituted: see note 3).
10 Patents Act 1977 s 52(3) (as substituted: see note 3).
11 As to appeals generally see PARA 570 et seq.
12 Ie an order under the Patents Act 1977 ss 48–51: see PARAS 394–398.
13 As to the register see PARA 583 et seq.
14 Ie under the Patents Act 1977 s 52(3) (see the text to note 10).
15 Patents Act 1977 s 52(4) (as substituted: see note 3); amended by the Intellectual Property Act 2014 Schedule para 4(1)). As to the Attorney General see CONSTITUTIONAL AND ADMINISTRATIVE LAW vol 20 (2014) PARA 273.
16 Ie under the Patents Act 1977 ss 48–51 (see PARAS 305–398) or s 52(2) (see the text to notes 5–9).
17 Patents Act 1977 s 52(5)(a) (as substituted: see note 3).
18 Patents Act 1977 s 52(5)(b) (as substituted: see note 3).
19 Patents Act 1977 s 52(5) (as substituted: see note 3). Where the whole of the proceedings are so referred, then, unless the parties otherwise agree before the arbitrator's award is made, an appeal lies from the award to the court: s 52(6) (as substituted: see note 3). Where a question or issue of fact is so referred, the arbitrator must report his findings to the comptroller: s 52(7) (as so substituted). As to arbitration generally see ARBITRATION vol 2 (2008) PARA 1201 et seq.

400.   Licensing enemy patents in time of war.   The comptroller[1] may grant to any person who is not an enemy or an enemy subject a licence under any patent of which the owner is an enemy or an enemy subject, or in which an enemy or enemy subject is entitled to any other interest, or in which an enemy or enemy subject[2] has previously been entitled to an interest, whenever the comptroller is satisfied:

(1)   that the proposed licensee desires to exercise the rights conferred by the patent and is in a position to do so; and

(2)   that it is in the interest of all or any of Her Majesty's subjects that those rights should be exercised[3].

Such a licence may be exclusive[4], may be made notwithstanding the existence of any other licence and so as to take away any right in relation to the patent held by any person which is inconsistent with the new licence, and may be made on any terms the comptroller thinks expedient[5]. The comptroller has a general discretion to vary and revoke such licences[6]. A wrong decision that a proprietor is an enemy or enemy subject does not invalidate the grant of a licence[7]. The licensee may sue for infringement[8], even though he is only a non-exclusive licensee[9].

There is provision for opposition to an application to the comptroller for such a licence[10], but none for appeal from his decision.

1   As to the comptroller see PARA 575.
2   Ie, it would seem, a person who at the date of the grant is an enemy or enemy subject. Thus, although these provisions are permanently in force, the powers conferred only exist in time of war: see *Re IG Farbenindustrie AG's Agreement* [1941] Ch 147, [1940] 4 All ER 486, 58 RPC 31 (revsd on appeal [1944] Ch 41, [1943] 2 All ER 525, 60 RPC 193, CA); *Novello & Co Ltd v Hinrichsen Edition Ltd* [1951] Ch 1026 at 1031, [1951] 2 All ER 457 at 460, 68 RPC 243 at 245, 250–251, CA, per Sir Raymond Evershed MR.
3   Patents, Designs, Copyright and Trade Marks (Emergency) Act 1939 s 2(1) (amended by the Statute Law (Repeals) Act 1995).
4   As to the meaning of 'exclusive licence' see PARA 379.
5   See the Patents, Designs, Copyright and Trade Marks (Emergency) Act 1939 s 2(2)–(4), (6).
6   See the Patents, Designs, Copyright and Trade Marks (Emergency) Act 1939 s 2(7), (8).
7   Patents, Designs, Copyright and Trade Marks (Emergency) Act 1939 s 7(2). Entries in the register are prima facie evidence of the nationalities and places of residence there stated: s 7(1). As to the register see PARA 583 et seq.
8   Patents, Designs, Copyright and Trade Marks (Emergency) Act 1939 s 2(5). Unless the court directs otherwise, any non-enemy patentee must be made a party to the proceedings in the usual way: s 2(5). As to the court's discretion see *Novello & Co Ltd v Ernst Eulenburg Ltd* [1950] 1 All ER 44, CA. As to proceedings for infringement see PARA 521 et seq.
9   *Novello & Co Ltd v Ernst Eulenburg Ltd* [1950] 1 All ER 44, CA.
10 See the Patents, Designs, Copyright and Trade Marks (Emergency) Act 1939 s 2(7), (8). As to procedure see s 8.

401.   EU compulsory licences.   A procedure for the grant of compulsory licences in relation to patents and supplementary protection certificates concerning the manufacture and sale of pharmaceutical products, when such products are intended for export to eligible importing countries in need of such products in order to address public health problems was established by European Regulation[1]. Member states are required to grant an EU compulsory licence to any person making an application in accordance with the Regulation[2].

In the application to EU compulsory licences of certain provisions of the Patents Act 1977[3]: (1) references to a licence under a patent[4]; (2) references to a right under a patent[5]; and (3) references to a proprietary interest under a patent, include an EU compulsory licence[6].

Any order for the grant of an EU compulsory licence, without prejudice to any other method of enforcement, has effect as if it were a deed, executed by the proprietor of the patent and all other necessary parties, granting a licence in accordance with the order[7].

1 Ie by Council Regulation (EC) 816/2006 (OJ L157, 9.6.2006, p 1) on compulsory licensing of patents relating to the manufacture of pharmaceutical products for export to countries with public health problems (the 'Compulsory Licensing Regulation').

2 Council Regulation (EC) 816/2006 (OJ L157, 9.6.1006, p 1) art 1; Patents Act 1977 s 128A(1), (6) (s 128A added by SI 2007/3293). Such an application must be in accordance with Council Regulation (EC) 816/2006 (OJ L157, 9.6.1006, p 1) art 6 and subject to the conditions set out in arts 6–10: art 1.

3 The provisions referred to are: the Patents Act 1977 ss 32, 33 (registration of patents etc) (see PARAS 583–586), s 37 (determination of right to patent after grant) (see PARA 365), s 38 (effect of transfer etc of patent under s 37) (see PARA 367), apart from s 38(2) and s 38(3)–(5) so far as relating to s 38(2) (see PARA 367), s 41 (amount of compensation) (see PARA 370), s 46(2) (notice of application for entry that licences are available as of right) (see PARA 391), s 57(1), (2) (rights of third parties in respect of Crown use) (see PARA 407): s 128A(3) (as added: see note 2).

4 As to licences generally see PARA 377 et seq.

5 As to the meaning of 'right' see PARA 359 note 7.

6 Patents Act 1977 s 128A(2) (as added: see note 2). In the following provisions references to the Patents Act 1977 include the Compulsory Licensing Regulation: the Patents Act 1977 ss 97–99B, 101–103, 105, 107 (legal proceedings) (see PARA 516 et seq), s 119 (service by post) (see PARA 581), s 120 (hours of business and excluded days) (see PARA 577), s 121 (comptroller's annual report) (see PARA 576), s 123 (rules) (see PARA 578), s 124A (use of electronic communications) (see PARA 582), s 130(8) (disapplication of the Arbitration Act 1996 Pt 1) (see PARA 575): Patents Act 1977 s 128A(4) (as added: see note 2).

7 Patents Act 1977 ss 108, 128A(5) (as added: see note 2).

(4) RESTRICTIONS ON CONTRACTS

402. Terms in restraint of trade. Conditions in a licence which are in restraint of trade must be reasonable both as between the parties and in the interest of the public[1]. A condition imposing penalties upon manufacture of more than a certain quantity of the patented article may be reasonable[2]. A condition that the licensee is not to make goods or execute works competing with those the subject of the licence may be reasonable[3], as may a condition that a licensee is only to sell the goods of the patentee[4]. A covenant to assign future patent rights may be good[5], unless given by an employee[6].

Any term in a patent licence which may affect trade between EU member states must comply with the provisions of the Treaty on the Functioning of the European Union relating to competition[7]. A block exemption is, however, granted[8] on certain licensing agreements in respect of patent[9].

1 The burden of showing that an agreement that is reasonable between the parties is unreasonable in the public interest is a heavy one. The rule stated is part of the general law, not special to patent licences: see *Tool Metal Manufacturing Co Ltd v Tungsten Electric Co Ltd* [1955] 2 All ER 657 at 662, 72 RPC 209 at 213, HL, per Viscount Simonds. As to the effect of conditions in restraint of trade generally see COMPETITION vol 18 (2009) PARA 377 et seq.

2 *Tool Metal Manufacturing Co Ltd v Tungsten Electric Co Ltd* [1955] 2 All ER 657, [1955] 1 WLR 761, 72 RPC 209, HL. Such a condition may, however, be contrary to the Treaty on the Functioning of the European Union (Rome, 25 March 1957; TS 1 (1973); Cmnd 5179) art 101 (competition rules applying to undertakings: see further COMPETITION).

3 *Jones v Lees* (1856) 1 H & N 189; *Nordenfelt v Maxim Nordenfelt Guns and Ammunition Co* [1894] AC 535, HL; *Mouchel v Cubitt & Co* (1907) 24 RPC 194. Such a condition may, however, be contrary to the Treaty on the Functioning of the European Union art 101 (see note 2): see *Association des Ouvriers en Instruments de Précision v Beyrard* [1976] 1 CMLR D14; and Commission Regulation (EC) 2349/84 (OJ 1984 L219, 16.8.84, p 15) art 3.5. See further COMPETITION vol 18 (2009) PARA 61 et seq.

4   Such a condition is probably contrary to the Treaty on the Functioning of the European Union (Rome, 25 March 1957; TS 1 (1973); Cmnd 5179) art 101 (see note 2): see Commission Regulation (EC) 2349/84 (OJ 1984 L219, 16.8.84, p 15) art 3.3; and COMPETITION vol 18 (2009) PARA 67.

5   *Printing and Numerical Registering Co v Sampson* (1875) LR 19 Eq 462; *Buchanan v Alba Diagnostics Ltd* [2004] UKHL 5, [2004] RPC 681, 2004 SLT 255 (assignment of future improvements not an unreasonable restraint of trade at common law). Such a covenant may, however, be contrary to the Treaty on the Functioning of the European Union (Rome, 25 March 1957; TS 1 (1973); Cmnd 5179) art 101 (see note 2): see Commission Regulation (EC) 2349/84 (OJ 1984 L219, 16.8.84, p 15) art 3.8.

6   See PARA 369.

7   Ie the Treaty on the Functioning of the European Union (Rome, 25 March 1957; TS 1 (1973); Cmnd 5179) arts 101–118: see COMPETITION vol 18 (2009) PARA 61 et seq.

8   Ie by Commission Regulation (EC) 2349/84 (OJ 1984 L219, 16.8.84, p 15) or Commission Regulation (EC) 240/96 (OJ L31, 9.2.96, p 2): see COMPETITION vol 18 (2009) PARA 61.

9   See COMPETITION vol 18 (2009) PARA 67 et seq.

(5) CROWN USE OF PATENTED INVENTIONS

403.   Effect of patents against the Crown; infringement and Crown use.
Subject to certain exceptions[1], a patent has the same effect against the Crown as it has against a subject[2]. The rights of any government department to make use of patented inventions for the services of the Crown[3] are not, however, affected by the statutory provisions[4] which permit, in certain circumstances, claims against the Crown for infringement of a patent[5].

Further, nothing in the Patents Act 1977 affects the right of the Crown or of any person deriving title directly or indirectly from the Crown to dispose of or use articles forfeited under the laws relating to customs and excise[6].

1   Ie the Patents Act 1977 ss 55–59: see PARAS 404–410.
2   See the Patents Act 1977 s 129.
3   Ie the rights under the Patents Act 1977 s 55: see PARA 404.
4   Ie the Crown Proceedings Act 1947 s 3(1)(a): see PARA 524.
5   See the Crown Proceedings Act 1947 s 3(1), (2); and PARA 524.
6   Patents Act 1977 s 122. As to the Crown's rights to dispose of or use articles so forfeited see the Customs and Excise Management Act 1979 s 139(4), (5), Sch 3 para 16; and CUSTOMS AND EXCISE vol 31 (2012) PARAS 1152, 1155.

404.   Use of patented inventions for services of the Crown. Notwithstanding anything in the Patents Act 1977, any government department and any person authorised in writing by a government department may do any of the following acts in the United Kingdom[1] in relation to a patented invention[2] for the services of the Crown[3], without the consent of the proprietor of the patent[4]:

(1)   where the invention is a product:

    (a)   make, use, import or keep the product, or sell or offer to sell it where to do so would be incidental or ancillary to making, using, importing or keeping it[5]; or

    (b)   in any event, sell or offer to sell it for foreign defence purposes[6] or for the production or supply of specified drugs and medicines[7], or dispose or offer to dispose of it, otherwise than by selling it, for any purpose whatever[8];

(2)   where the invention is a process, use it or do in relation to any product obtained directly by means of the process anything mentioned in head (1) above[9];

(3)   without prejudice to the foregoing, where the invention or any product

obtained directly by means of the invention is a specified drug or medicine, sell or offer to sell the drug or medicine[10];

(4)   supply or offer to supply to any person any of the means, relating to an essential element of the invention, for putting the invention into effect[11];

(5)   dispose or offer to dispose of anything which was made, used, imported or kept in the exercise of the powers conferred by these provisions and which is no longer required for the purpose for which it was made, used, imported or kept, as the case may be[12].

Anything done by virtue of these provisions does not amount to an infringement of the patent concerned[13].

The authority of a government department in respect of an invention may be given either before or after the patent is granted[14] and either before or after the use in respect of which the authority is given is made, and may be given to any person whether or not he is authorised directly or indirectly by the proprietor of the patent to do anything in relation to the invention[15].

Where any use of an invention is made by or with the authority of a government department, then, unless it appears to the department that it would be contrary to the public interest to do so, the department must notify the proprietor as soon as practicable after the second of the following events, that is to say, the use is begun and the patent is granted, and furnish him with such information as to the extent of the use as he may from time to time require[16].

A person who acquires anything disposed of in the exercise of powers conferred by these provisions, and any person claiming through him, may deal with it in the same manner as if the patent were held on behalf of the Crown[17].

1   As to the meaning of 'United Kingdom' see PARA 303 note 5.

2   As to the meaning of 'patented invention' see PARA 370 note 27. Any reference in the Patents Act 1977 s 55 to a patented invention, in relation to any time, is a reference to an invention for which a patent has before that time been, or is subsequently, granted: s 56(1).

3   Except so far as the context otherwise requires, 'services of the Crown' includes: (1) the supply of anything for foreign defence purposes; (2) the production or supply of specified drugs and medicines; and (3) such purposes relating to the production or use of atomic energy or research into matters connected with it as the Secretary of State thinks necessary or expedient: Patents Act 1977 ss 56(2), 130(1). Any reference to the services of the Crown includes, as respects any period of emergency, a reference to the purposes in s 59(1)(a)–(g) (see PARA 410): s 59(1). As to the meaning of 'period of emergency' see PARA 410 note 1. 'Use for the services of the Crown' is to be construed accordingly: ss 56(2), 130(1); and see note 13. Nothing in the National Health Service and Community Care Act 1990 s 60(1) (removal of Crown immunity from health service bodies: see HEALTH SERVICES vol 54 (2008) PARAS 94, 136) affects the extent of the expression 'services of the Crown' where it appears in the Patents Act 1977 ss 55–59; and accordingly services provided in pursuance of any power or duty of the Secretary of State under the National Health Service Act 2006 (see HEALTH SERVICES vol 54 (2008) PARA 6) continue to be regarded as included in that expression, whether the services are in fact provided by a health service body, a National Health Service Trust or any other person: National Health Service and Community Care Act 1990 s 60(4) (amended by the National Health Service (Consequential Provisions) Act 2006 s 2, Sch 1 paras 128, 131(b)). As to the Secretary of State see PARA 573. Use by a health authority exercising the functions of the Secretary of State, devolved through the provisions of the National Health Service Act 1977 and the regulations made thereunder, is Crown use: *Dory v Sheffield Health Authority* [1991] FSR 221.

4   Patents Act 1977 s 55(1). The power conferred by s 55(1) on a government department, or person authorised in writing by a government department, in relation to the use of patented inventions for the services of the Crown is exercisable for the purposes of a visiting force or headquarters to the extent that it would be exercisable if the visiting force or headquarters were a part of any of the home forces, but this does not authorise the doing of any act falling within s 55(1)(a)(ii) or (c) (see heads (1)(b), (3) in the text), or the doing of anything which is for a purpose relating to the production or use of atomic energy or research into matters connected therewith: Visiting Forces and International Headquarters (Application of Law) Order 1999, SI 1999/1736, art 6, Sch 4 para 2(1), (2). In relation to the exercise of these powers, the Patents

Act 1977 ss 55–58 (apart from s 56(2)–(4)) have effect with any reference in those provisions to the use of a patented invention for the services of the Crown being construed as a reference to the use of such an invention for the purposes of a visiting force or headquarters: Visiting Forces and International Headquarters (Application of Law) Order 1999, SI 1999/1736, art 6, Sch 4 para 2(3). As to visiting forces and headquarters see ARMED FORCES vol 3 (2011) PARA 405 et seq.

5   Patents Act 1977 s 55(1)(a)(i).

6   For these purposes, references to a sale or supply of anything for foreign defence purposes are references to a sale or supply of the thing: (1) to the government of any country outside the United Kingdom, in pursuance of an agreement or arrangement between the United Kingdom government and the government of that country, where the thing is required for the defence of that country or of any other country whose government is party to any agreement or arrangement with the United Kingdom government in respect of defence matters; or (2) to the United Nations, or to the government of any country belonging to that organisation, in pursuance of an agreement or arrangement between the United Kingdom government and that organisation or government, where the thing is required for any armed forces operating in pursuance of a resolution of that organisation or any organ of that organisation: Patents Act 1977 s 56(3).

7   For these purposes, the Patents Act 1977 s 56(4) (amended by the National Health Service (Scotland) Act 1978 s 109, Sch 16 para 45; the National Health Service (Primary Care) Act 1997 s 41(10), Sch 2 para 2; the Health and Social Care Act 2001 s 67(1), Sch 5 para 4; the Health and Social Care (Community Health and Standards) Act 2003 ss 184, 196, Sch 11 para 6, Sch 14 Pt 4; the National Health Service (Consequential Provisions) Act 2006 s 2, Sch 1 paras 57, 58; SI 2004/957; SI 2006/1056) provides that specified drugs and medicines are drugs and medicines which are both:
    (1)   required for the provision of:
        (a)   primary medical services under the National Health Service Act 2006, the National Health Service (Wales) Act 2006 (see HEALTH SERVICES), or corresponding provisions of the law in force in Scotland, Northern Ireland or the Isle of Man or primary dental services under the National Health Service Act 2006, the National Health Service (Wales) Act 2006, or any corresponding provisions of the law in force in Northern Ireland or the Isle of Man;
        (b)   pharmaceutical services, general medical services or general dental services under the National Health Service Act 2006 Pt 7 Ch 1 or the National Health Service (Wales) Act 2006 Pt 7 Ch 1 (in the case of pharmaceutical services) (see HEALTH SERVICES vol 54 (2008) PARA 339 et seq), or the corresponding provisions of the law in force in Scotland, Northern Ireland or the Isle of Man; or
        (c)   local pharmaceutical services provided under a pilot scheme established under the National Health Service Act 2006 s 134 or the National Health Service (Wales) Act 2006 s 92 (see HEALTH SERVICES vol 54 (2008) PARA 419), or an LPS scheme established under the National Health Service Act 2006 Sch 12 or the National Health Service (Wales) Act 2006 Sch 7 (see HEALTH SERVICES vol 54 (2008) PARAS 431–432), or under any corresponding provision of the law in force in the Isle of Man; and
    (2)   specified for these purposes in regulations made by the Secretary of State.
At the date at which this volume states the law no such regulations had been made.

8   Patents Act 1977 s 55(1)(a)(ii).

9   Patents Act 1977 s 55(1)(b).

10   Patents Act 1977 s 55(1)(c).

11   Patents Act 1977 s 55(1)(d).

12   Patents Act 1977 s 55(1)(e).

13   Patents Act 1977 s 55(1). Any act done in relation to an invention by virtue of these provisions is referred to as use of the invention, and 'use' is to be construed accordingly: s 55(2). See also note 3. As to compensation for such use see PARA 405; and as to infringement see PARA 499 et seq.

14   As to grant see PARA 337.

15   Patents Act 1977 s 55(6). Retrospective authority given under s 55(6) takes away any cause of action which the patentee might have had against the person before the authority was given and substitutes a right of remuneration under s 55(4) (see PARA 405): *Dory v Sheffield Health Authority* [1991] FSR 221.

16   Patents Act 1977 s 55(7).

17   Patents Act 1977 s 55(8).

405. Compensation for Crown use. Any use by a government department of a patented invention[1] made after the publication of the application for the patent for the invention[2], or in consequence of a relevant communication[3] made after the priority date[4] of the invention otherwise than in confidence[5], must be made on such terms as may be agreed, either before or after the use, by the government department and the proprietor of the patent, with Treasury approval, or, in default of such agreement, on such terms as may be determined[6] by the court[7].

Any such use of an invention which, before its priority date, has been duly recorded by or tried by or on behalf of a government department or the United Kingdom Atomic Energy Authority[8] otherwise than in consequence of a relevant communication made in confidence may, however, be made free of any royalty[9] or other payment to the proprietor[10].

Where an invention is used at any time after publication of an application for a patent for the invention but before such a patent is granted[11], and the terms for its use as agreed or determined by the court include terms as to payment for the use, then, notwithstanding anything in those terms, any such payment is recoverable only after such a patent is granted[12], and if the use would[13], if the patent had been granted on the date of the publication of the application, have infringed not only the patent but also the claims (as interpreted by the description and any drawings referred to in the description or claims)[14] in the form in which they were contained in the application immediately before the preparations for its publication were completed by the UK Intellectual Property Office[15].

1 Ie any use made by virtue of the Patents Act 1977 s 55(1): see PARA 404. As to the meaning of 'patented invention' for the purposes of s 55 see PARA 404 note 2; and as to the meaning of 'use' see PARA 404 note 13.
2 Patents Act 1977 s 55(4)(a). As to the publication of patent applications see PARA 326.
3 For these purposes, 'relevant communication' means a communication of the invention directly or indirectly by the proprietor of the patent or any person from whom he derives title: Patents Act 1977 s 55(9).
4 As to the meaning of 'priority date' see PARA 310 note 6.
5 Patents Act 1977 s 55(4)(b).
6 Ie on a reference under the Patents Act 1977 s 58: see PARA 409.
7 Patents Act 1977 s 55(4). Section 55(4) is without prejudice to any rule of law relating to the confidentiality of information: s 55(10). As to the meaning of 'court' see PARA 619 note 1.
8 As to the United Kingdom Atomic Energy Authority see ENERGY AND CLIMATE CHANGE vol 44 (2011) PARA 787 et seq.
9 As to royalties see PARA 388.
10 Patents Act 1977 s 55(3).
11 As to grant see PARA 337.
12 Patents Act 1977 s 55(5)(a).
13 Ie apart from the Patents Act 1977 s 55.
14 As to claims see PARAS 323–324; and as to proceedings for infringement see PARA 520.
15 Patents Act 1977 s 55(5)(b). As to the UK Intellectual Property Office see PARA 577.

406. Persons entitled to compensation. Compensation for use of a patented invention[1] under Crown powers[2] is payable to the proprietor of the patent[3], except in the following three cases when it is payable, wholly or in part, to a licensee or an assignor, as the case may be:

(1)   where an exclusive licence[4] granted otherwise than for royalties[5] or other benefits determined by reference to the working of the invention is in force under the patent or the application concerned, then, in relation to anything done in respect of the invention which would, but for the provisions as to Crown powers of use[6], be an infringement of the rights of the licensee, and compensation is payable to the licensee[7];

(2)　　where there is any other exclusive licence, the licensee is entitled to recover from the proprietor of the patent or application such part of any compensation as they may agree to be just having regard to any expenditure incurred by the licensee in developing the invention, or in making payments to the proprietor in consideration of the licence, other than royalties or other payments determined by reference to the use of the invention[8]; and in default of agreement the apportionment may be determined by the court[9] accordingly[10];

(3)　　subject to the entitlement under head (1) above, where the patent, or the right to the grant of the patent, has been assigned[11] to the proprietor in consideration of royalties or other benefits determined by reference to the working of the invention, the compensation must be divided between the proprietor and the assignor in such proportion as they may agree or, in default of agreement, as may be determined by the court[12].

1　Ie any use made by virtue of the Patents Act 1977 s 55(1): see PARA 404. As to the meaning of 'patented invention' for the purposes of s 55(1), see PARA 404 note 2; as to the meaning of 'use' see PARA 404 note 13. As to compensation for use of information see PARA 407.
2　Ie any use made by virtue of the Patents Act 1977 s 55(1).
3　See the Patents Act 1977 s 55(4); and PARA 405.
4　As to the meaning of 'exclusive licence' see PARA 379.
5　As to royalties see PARA 388.
6　Ie the provisions of the Patents Act 1977 ss 55, 57.
7　See the Patents Act 1977 s 57(3)(a). If, however, the licensee uses the invention under Crown authority, there is no right of compensation: s 57(3)(b).
8　See the Patents Act 1977 s 57(5)–(7). Any agreement by the proprietor of the patent or application and the department concerned under s 55(4) as to the amount of compensation payable is of no effect unless the licensee consents to it; and any determination by the court under s 55(4) is of no effect unless the licensee has been informed of the reference to the court and is given an opportunity to be heard: s 57(8). As to the meaning of 'court' see PARA 619 note 1.
9　Ie under the Patents Act 1977 s 58: see PARA 409.
10　Patents Act 1977 s 57(7). In making the apportionment the court will normally follow any agreement between the parties as to division of royalties: *Patchett's Patent* [1967] RPC 237, CA.
11　As to entitlement to a patent see PARA 306; and as to assignment see PARA 373.
12　Patents Act 1977 s 57(4)(a). Any act done in respect of the invention for the services of the Crown by the proprietor of the patent or application to the order of a government department attracts compensation as if done under Crown authority: s 57(4)(b). As to the meaning of 'services of the Crown' see PARA 404 note 3.

407.　Rights of third persons and use of information. In relation to any use made for the services of the Crown[1] of an invention by a government department or a person authorised by a government department[2] or anything done for the services of the Crown to the order of a government department by the proprietor of a patent in respect of a patented invention[3] or by the proprietor of an application in respect of an invention for which an application for a patent has been filed[4] and is still pending, the provisions of any licence[5], assignment[6] or agreement made[7] between the proprietor of the patent or applicant for a patent, or any person who derives title from him or from whom he derives title, and any person other than a government department[8] are of no effect, so far as those provisions restrict or regulate the working of the invention or the use of any model, document or information relating to the invention, or provide for the making of payments in respect of or calculated by reference to any such use[9], and in connection with such working or use of an invention, the reproduction or publication of any model or document does not infringe any copyright[10] or design right[11] subsisting in the model or document or any topography right[12]. In such a case, the rules governing compensation for Crown use[13] and procedure for determination of disputes as to Crown use[14] apply as if the person entitled to the benefit of the contractual provision or copyright concerned was the proprietor of the patent[15].

In addition, Crown contractors may be authorised to use technical information, other than that relating to a patented invention, discharged from restrictions imposed by, or obligations to make payments under, agreements with other persons[16].

1 As to the meaning of 'services of the Crown' and 'use for the services of the Crown' see PARA 404 note 3.
2 Ie anything done under the Patents Act 1977 s 55(1): see PARA 404.
3 As to the meaning of 'patented invention' see PARA 370 note 27.
4 As to the filing of an application see PARA 317.
5 As to licences see PARA 377 et seq.
6 As to assignment see PARA 373.

7 This applies to a licence, assignment or agreement whenever made: see the Patents Act 1977 s 57(2).
8 Patents Act 1977 s 57(2). As to the application of s 57 to EU compulsory licences see PARA 401.

9 This provision does not release a licensee from an obligation in normal form to pay minimum royalties: cf *No-Nail Cases Pty Ltd v No-Nail Boxes Ltd* [1944] KB 629 at 641, [1944] 1 All ER 528 at 531, 61 RPC 94 at 102, 107, CA, per Du Parcq LJ; on appeal [1946] AC 447, [1946] 1 All ER 523, 63 RPC 44, HL.
10 As to copyright see COPYRIGHT vol 23 (2013) PARAS 603, 653 et seq.
11 As to design right see COPYRIGHT vol 23 (2013) PARAS 610, 1048 et seq.

12 Patents Act 1977 s 57(1) (amended by the Copyright, Designs and Patents Act 1988 Sch 7 para 20; and SI 1987/1497). Nothing in the Patents Act 1977 s 57 is to be construed as authorising the disclosure to a government department or any other person of any model, document or information to the use of which this provision applies in contravention of any such licence, assignment or agreement: s 57(10).
13 Ie the Patents Act 1977 s 55(4): see PARA 405.
14 Ie the Patents Act 1977 s 58: see PARA 409.

15 See the Patents Act 1977 s 57(9).
16 See the Defence Contracts Act 1958 ss 2, 3, 4; and ARMED CONFLICT AND EMERGENCY vol 3 (2011) PARAS 209–210.

408. Compensation for loss of profit. Where use is made of an invention for the services of the Crown[1], the government department concerned[2] must pay:

(1)	to the proprietor of the patent; or

(2)	if there is an exclusive licence[3] in force in respect of the patent, to the exclusive licensee[4],

compensation for any loss resulting from his not being awarded a contract to supply the patented product[5] or, as the case may be, to perform the patented process[6] or supply a thing made by means of the patented process[7].

Compensation is payable only to the extent that such a contract could have been fulfilled from his existing manufacturing or other capacity but is payable notwithstanding the existence of circumstances rendering him ineligible for the award of such a contract[8].

In determining the loss, regard must be had to the profit which would have been made on such a contract and to the extent to which any manufacturing or other capacity was under-used[9].

No compensation is payable in respect of any failure to secure contracts to supply the patented product or, as the case may be, to perform the patented process or supply a thing made by means of the patented process, otherwise than for the services of the Crown[10].

The amount payable, if not agreed between the proprietor or licensee and the government department concerned with the approval of the Treasury[11], must be determined by the court[12] on a reference[13] and is in addition to any amount payable under the statutory provisions[14] relating to the use of patented inventions by the Crown and the rights of third parties in respect of Crown use[15].

1 As to the meaning of 'use for the services of the Crown' see PARA 404 note 3.
2 For these purposes, 'government department concerned', in relation to any use of an invention for the services of the Crown, means the government department by whom or on whose authority the use was made: Patents Act 1977 s 57A(6) (s 57A added by the Copyright, Designs and Patents Act 1988 Sch 5 para 16(1),(4)).
3 As to the meaning of 'exclusive licence' see PARA 379.
4 As to the meaning of 'exclusive licensee' see PARA 379 note 7.
5 As to the meaning of 'patented product' see PARA 371 note 11.
6 As to the meaning of 'patented process' see PARA 370 note 27.
7 Patents Act 1977 s 57A(1) (as added: see note 2).
8 Patents Act 1977 s 57A(2) (as added: see note 2).
9 Patents Act 1977 s 57A(3) (as added: see note 2).
10 Patents Act 1977 s 57A(4) (as added: see note 2).
11 As to the Treasury see CONSTITUTIONAL AND ADMINISTRATIVE LAW vol 20 (2014) PARAS 262–265.
12 As to the meaning of 'court' see PARA 619 note 1.
13 Ie on reference under the Patents Act 1977 s 58: see PARA 409.
14 Ie under the Patents Act 1977 s 55 (see PARAS 404–405) or s 57 (see PARAS 406–407).
15 Patents Act 1977 s 57A(5) (as added: see note 2).

409. Disputes as to Crown use. Any dispute as to:
  (1) the exercise by a government department or a person authorised by a government department of Crown powers[1];
  (2) terms for the use of an invention for the services of the Crown[2] under those powers[3];
  (3) the right of any person to receive any part of a payment[4] made or agreed to be made or determined by the court[5]; or
  (4) the right of any person to receive a payment for compensation for loss of profit[6],
may be referred to the court by either party to the dispute after a patent has been granted for the invention[7]. The court may at any time order the whole proceedings or any question or issue of fact arising in them to be referred, on such terms as it may direct, to a judge of the Technology and Construction Court appointed as an arbitrator or to an arbitrator[8].

In determining any dispute between a government department and any person as to the terms for the use of an invention for the services of the Crown, the court must have regard:
  (a) to any benefit or compensation which that person or any person from whom he derives title may have received or may be entitled to receive directly or indirectly from any government department in respect of the invention in question[9];
  (b) to whether that person or any person from whom he derives title has in the court's opinion without reasonable cause failed to comply with a request of the department to use the invention for the services of the Crown on reasonable terms[10].

If in such proceedings any question arises as to whether an invention has been recorded or tried so as to exclude any right to compensation[11], and the disclosure of any document recording the invention, or of any evidence of its trial, would in the department's opinion be prejudicial to the public interest, the disclosure may be made confidentially to the other party's legal representative or to an independent expert mutually agreed upon[12].

There are special provisions as to compensation in the case of restored lapsed patents[13]; where an amendment of the specification of a patent has been allowed[14]; where the validity of a patent[15] is put in issue in the proceedings[16]; where there is a European patent (UK)[17]; and where an application for a patent has been published[18] but the patent has not yet been granted[19].

There are restrictions on the right of a new proprietor or exclusive licensee[20] of a patent under a transaction, instrument or event which is registrable[21] to compensation in respect of Crown use of the invention before the transaction is registered[22].

1 Ie the powers conferred under the Patents Act 1977 s 55: see PARA 404.
2 As to the meaning of 'use' see PARA 404 note 13; and as to the meaning of 'services of the Crown' see PARA 404 note 3.
3 Ie as provided for under the Patents Act 1977 s 55(4): see PARA 405.
4 Ie under the Patents Act 1977 s 57(3)–(7): see PARA 406.
5 Ie in pursuance of the Patents Act 1977 s 55(4): see PARA 405. As to the meaning of 'court' see PARA 619 note 1.
6 Ie a payment under the Patents Act 1977 s 57A: see PARA 408.
7 Patents Act 1977 s 58(1) (substituted by the Copyright, Designs and Patents Act 1988 Sch 5 para 16(2)). One of two or more joint proprietors of a patent or application for a patent may refer a dispute to the court without the concurrence of the others, but must not do so unless the others are made parties to the proceedings, but any of the others made a defendant is not liable for any costs or expenses unless he enters an appearance and takes part in the proceedings: Patents Act 1977 s 58(13). As to proceedings before the court see PARA 619 et seq.
    In determining whether or not to grant any relief under the Patents Act 1977 s 58(1)(a)–(c) (see heads (1)–(3) in the text) and the nature and extent of the relief granted the court must, subject to s 58(5)–(13), apply the principles applied by the court to the granting of relief under the Patents Act 1949 s 48: Patents Act 1977 s 58(4) (amended by the Copyright, Designs and Patents Act 1988 Sch 5 para 16(2)). See *Henry Bros (Magherafelt) Ltd v Ministry of Defence and Northern Ireland Office* [1997] RPC 693 (affd [1999] RPC 442, [1998] All ER (D) 545), where the Crown successfully resisted a claim to compensation by seeking revocation on the ground that it was the true owner or co-owner of the patent.
8 Patents Act 1977 s 58(12); References to the court in these provisions are to be construed accordingly: s 58(12). As to judges of the Technology and Construction Court see ARBITRATION vol 2 (2008) PARA 1226.
9 Patents Act 1977 s 58(3)(a).
10 Patents Act 1977 s 58(3)(b).
11 Ie under the Patents Act 1977 s 55(3): see PARA 405.
12 Patents Act 1977 s 58(2) (amended by the Intellectual Property Act 2014 Schedule para 4(2)).
13 The court may refuse to grant relief by way of compensation in respect of the use of an invention for Crown services during any further period specified under the Patents Act 1977 s 25(4) (see PARA 339), but before the payment of the renewal fee and any prescribed additional fee: s 58(5). As to the restoration of lapsed patents see PARA 355.
14 Where an amendment of the specification of a patent has been allowed under any of the provisions of the Patents Act 1977, the court may not grant relief by way of compensation under s 58 in respect of any such use before the decision to allow the amendment unless the court is satisfied that: (1) the specification of the patent as published was framed in good faith and with reasonable skill and knowledge; and (2) the relief is sought in good faith: s 58(6) (amended by the Patents Act 2004 s 2(2)(a)). As to such amendments see PARA 346.
15 As to the validity of a patent see PARA 425 et seq.
16 If it is found that the patent is only partially valid, the court may grant relief to the proprietor of the patent in respect of that part which is found to be valid and to have been used for Crown services: Patents Act 1977 s 58(7).
    Where in any such proceedings it is found that a patent is only partially valid, the court may not grant relief by way of compensation, costs or expenses except where the proprietor of the patent proves that: (1) the specification of the patent was framed in good faith and with reasonable skill and knowledge; and (2) the relief is sought in good faith, and in that event the

court may grant relief in respect of that part of the patent which is valid and has been so used, subject to the discretion of the court as to costs and expenses and as to the date from which compensation should be awarded: s 58(8) (amended by the Patents Act 2004 s 2(2)(b)). As a condition of any such relief the court may direct that the specification of the patent must be amended to its satisfaction upon an application made for that purpose under the Patents Act 1977 s 75 (see PARA 347), and an application may be so made accordingly, whether or not all other issues in the proceedings have been determined: s 58(9).

17 The court may grant such relief in the case of a European patent (UK) on condition that the claims of the patent are limited to its satisfaction by the European Patent Office (see PARA 644) at the request of the proprietor: Patents Act 1977 s 58(9A) (added by the Patents Act 2004 s 3(2)). See also the Patents Act 1977 s 77(3); and PARA 652. As to the meaning of 'European patent (UK)' see PARA 652 note 1. As to European patents generally see PARA 644 et seq.

18 As to publication of the application see PARA 326.

19 In considering the amount of any compensation for the use of an invention for the services of the Crown after publication of an application for a patent for the invention and before such a patent is granted, the court must consider whether or not it would have been reasonable to expect, from a consideration of the application as published under the Patents Act 1977 s 16 (see PARA 326), that a patent would be granted conferring on the proprietor of the patent protection for an act of the same description as that found to constitute that use; and, if the court finds that it would not have been reasonable, it must reduce the compensation to such amount as it thinks just: s 58(10).

20 As to the meaning of 'exclusive licensee' see PARA 379 note 7.

21 Ie a transaction, instrument or event to which the Patents Act 1977 s 33 applies: see PARAS 586–587.

22 No compensation is payable unless: (1) the transaction, instrument or event is registered within the period of six months beginning with its date; or (2) the court is satisfied that it was not practicable to register the transaction, instrument or event before the end of that period and that it was registered as soon as practicable thereafter: Patents Act 1977 s 58(11) (amended by the Copyright, Designs and Patents Act 1988 Sch 5 para 16(3)).

410. Special provisions as to Crown use during emergency. During any period of emergency[1] the powers exercisable in relation to an invention by a government department or a person authorised by a government department[2] include power to use the invention[3] for any purpose which appears to the department necessary or expedient:

(1)   for the efficient prosecution of any war in which Her Majesty may be engaged;

(2)   for the maintenance of supplies and services essential to the life of the community;

(3)   for securing a sufficiency of supplies and services essential to the well-being of the community;

(4)   for promoting the productivity of industry, commerce and agriculture;

(5)   for fostering and directing exports and reducing imports, or imports of any classes, from all or any countries and for redressing the balance of trade;

(6)   generally for ensuring that the whole resources of the community are available for use, and are used, in a manner best calculated to serve the interests of the community; or

(7)   for assisting the relief of suffering and the restoration and distribution of essential supplies and services in any country or territory outside the United Kingdom[4] which is in grave distress as the result of war[5].

1   For these purposes, 'period of emergency' means any period beginning with such date as may be declared by Order in Council to be the commencement, and ending with such date as may be so declared to be the termination, of a period of emergency for the purposes of these provisions: Patents Act 1977 s 59(3).

2   Ie under the Patents Act 1977 s 55: see PARA 404.

3   For these purposes, the use of an invention includes, in addition to any act constituting such use
     by virtue of the Patents Act 1977 s 55 (see PARAS 404–405), any act which would, apart from
     s 55 and s 59, amount to an infringement of the patent concerned (see PARA 499 et seq) or, as the
     case may be, give rise to a right under s 69 to bring proceedings in respect of the application
     concerned (see PARAS 546–547); and any reference in the Patents Act 1977 to 'use for the
     services of the Crown' is, as respects any period of emergency, to be construed accordingly:
     s 59(2).

4   As to the meaning of 'United Kingdom' see PARA 303 note 5.

5   Patents Act 1977 s 59(1).

6. CONSTRUCTION OF SPECIFICATION AND CLAIMS

(1) THE SPECIFICATION

411. General rule. No special rules are applicable to the construction of the specification[1] of a patent[2]. As the specification is addressed to the person skilled in the art[3], the court must be instructed as to the meaning of technical terms and the background of the art, so as to read the specification with the understanding of the person skilled in the art[4]. The question of construction is necessarily antecedent to the determination of the issue of infringement[5] and of all issues of validity[6] depending upon the scope of the claims[7].

1   As to the specification see PARA 318.
2   *Kirin-Amgen Inc v Hoechst Marion Roussel Ltd* [2004] UKHL 46, [2005] 1 All ER 667, [2005] RPC 169 at 185. As to the general rules for construction of documents see DEEDS AND OTHER INSTRUMENTS vol 32 (2012) PARA 364 et seq.
3   *Kirin-Amgen Inc v Hoechst Marion Roussel Ltd* [2004] UKHL 46, [2005] 1 All ER 667, [2005] RPC 169 at 185. As to an addressee of a specification see PARA 491.
4   See *American Cyanamid Co v Ethicon Ltd* [1979] RPC 215; *Kirin-Amgen Inc v Hoechst Marion Roussel Ltd* [2004] UKHL 46, [2005] 1 All ER 667, [2005] RPC 169 at 185. When determining the meaning to be given to technical words in a patent specification, there is no rebuttable presumption that the words be given a technical meaning: *Hoechst Celanese Corpn v BP Chemicals Ltd* [1999] FSR 319, CA.
5   As to proceedings for infringement see PARA 520 et seq.
6   As to the validity of patents see PARA 425 et seq.
7   In consequence, substantially all patent actions exemplify the practice of the courts in construing specifications. It has been stated that it is unnecessary and usually undesirable to refer to decisions prior to *Catnic Components Ltd v Hill & Smith Ltd* [1982] RPC 183 at 237, HL: see *Codex Corpn v Racal-Milgo Ltd* [1983] RPC 369, CA; *C Van der Lely NV v Ruston's Engineering Co Ltd* [1985] RPC 461, CA. The modern approach is to regard *Kirin-Amgen Inc v Hoechst Marion Roussel Ltd* [2004] UKHL 46, [2005] 1 All ER 667, [2005] RPC 169 as setting out the proper approach: see *Research in Motion UK Ltd v Inpro Licensing SARL* [2006] EWHC 70 (Pat), [2006] RPC 517, [2006] All ER (D) 150 (Feb); *Ranbaxy UK Ltd v Warner-Lambert Co* [2005] EWHC 2142 (Pat), [2006] FSR 209, [2006] IP & T 336, [2005] All ER (D) 124 (Oct) (affd [2006] EWCA Civ 876, [2007] RPC 65, [2006] All ER (D) 322 (Jun)). As to the construction of claims see PARA 414; and as to claims generally see PARAS 323–324.

412. Construction. A specification[1] is construed neither in favour of nor against the proprietor of the patent[2]. It should be so construed as not to lead to a foolish result or one which the proprietor could not have contemplated[3]; for example, the court will tend to avoid constructions which would make the claim[4] cover what the specification admits to be old[5] or is the negation of the whole point of the invention[6].

1   As to the specification see PARA 318.
2   *Assidoman Multipack Ltd v Mead Corpn* [1995] RPC 321 at 332, CA; *BASF v Smithkline Beecham plc* [2003] EWCA Civ 872, [2003] RPC 855.
3   *Electric and Musical Industries Ltd v Lissen Ltd* [1938] 4 All ER 221 at 224, 56 RPC 23 at 39, HL, per Lord Russell of Killowen; *Minnesota Mining & Manufacturing Co v Rennicks (UK) Ltd* [1992] RPC 331 at 342; *Rediffusion Simulation Ltd v Link-Miles Ltd* [1993] FSR 369; *Wesley Jessen Corpn v Coopervision Ltd* [2003] RPC 355, Patents County Court.
4   As to claims generally see PARAS 323–324.
5   See *Tubes Ltd v Perfecta Seamless Steel Tube Co Ltd* (1902) 20 RPC 77 at 95, HL; *Generics (UK) Ltd v H Lundbeck A/S* [2009] UKHL 12, [2009] 2 All ER 955, [2009] IP & T 496; but cf note 6. It must also be construed so as to avoid prior art: *Molins v Industrial Machinery Co Ltd* [1937] 4 All ER 295, 55 RPC 31 at 39; *Glaverbel SA v British Coal Corpn* [1995] RPC 255 at 270, CA.
6   See *Ranbaxy UK Ltd v Warner-Lambert Co* [2006] EWCA Civ 876 at [49], [2007] RPC 65 at [49], [2006] All ER (D) 322 (Jun) at [49]. If, however, such a construction is the correct one,

it must be adopted: *Cleveland Graphite Bronze Co and Vandervell Products Ltd v Glacier Metal Co Ltd* (1949) 66 RPC 157 at 161, CA, per Greene MR; approved (1950) 67 RPC 149 at 153, HL.

413. Reading of specification as a whole. The specification[1] is to be read as a whole, including any drawings[2]; the claims are only a part of the specification (although a part having a special function[3]), and in no sense comprise a separate document[4]. The body of the specification should be read first[5]. The title is part of the specification for the purposes of construction[6]. In reading a specification, a distinction must be drawn between introductory statements as to the purpose of the invention or the class of apparatus to which it relates and the description of the invention itself[7].

1   As to the specification see PARA 318.
2   See the Patents Act 1977 s 125(1); and PARA 301 note 2. As to drawings see PARA 319.
3   Ie to delineate the patentee's monopoly: *Rockwater v Technip France SA* [2004] EWCA Civ 381, [2004] RPC 919 at 951, [2005] IP & T 304; *Kirin-Amgen Inc v Hoechst Marion Roussel Ltd* [2004] UKHL 46, [2005] 1 All ER 667, [2005] RPC 169 at 182; *Assidoman Multipack Ltd v Mead Corpn* [1995] RPC 321 at 332; *BASF v Smithkline Beecham plc* [2003] EWCA Civ 872, [2003] RPC 855 at 881; *Electric and Musical Industries Ltd v Lissen Ltd* (1937) 54 RPC 307 at 322, CA (on appeal [1938] 4 All ER 221, 56 RPC 23, HL).
4   *Electric and Musical Industries Ltd v Lissen Ltd* [1938] 4 All ER 221 at 224–225, 56 RPC 23 at 39, HL, per Lord Russell of Killowen.
5   *Arnold v Bradbury* (1871) 6 Ch App 706; *Tubes Ltd v Perfecta Seamless Steel Tube Co Ltd* (1900) 17 RPC 569.
6   See *Newton v Vaucher* (1852) 21 LJ Ex 305; *Oxley v Holden* (1860) 30 LJCP 68; *Mullard Radio Valve Co Ltd v Philco Radio and Television Corpn* [1936] 2 All ER 920, 53 RPC 323, HL. As to the title generally see PARA 318 note 3.
7   *Dudgeon v Thomson* (1877) 3 App Cas 34 at 40, HL.

(2) THE CLAIMS

414. Construction of claims. The scope of protection conferred by a patent is, unless the context otherwise requires, that specified in a claim[1] of the specification of the patent[2]. The specification must, however, be read as a whole, through the eyes of the person skilled in the art[3], because thereby the necessary background of the words used in the claims may be affected or defined by what is said in the body of the specification[4]. The specification should be given a purposive construction rather than a purely literal one derived from the application of meticulous verbal analysis[5]. The specification is concerned with what the skilled person would have understood the patentee to mean. What the patentee would have been understood to mean depends not only on the words he has chosen but also on the identity of the audience he is taken to have been addressing and the knowledge and assumptions attributed to that audience. The skilled person comes to a reading of the specification with the common general knowledge of the art and reads the specification on the assumption that its purpose is both to describe and to demarcate an invention. Purposive construction does not mean that there is an extension of or a going beyond the definition of the technical matter for which the patentee sought protection in the claims. The question is always what the person skilled in the art would have understood the patentee to mean[6].

The aim of purposive construction is to determine which features were put forward by the patentee, by the language of the claims, as the essential features of the invention and, in particular, whether persons with practical knowledge and experience of the kind of work in which the invention was intended to be used would understand that strict compliance with particular words or phrases of the claim was intended by the proprietor of the patent to be essential; only where this is the intention will the patent be avoided by variants having no material effect on the way the invention works[7].

A guideline as to interpretation is provided by the Protocol on the Interpretation of Article 69 of the European Patent Convention[8]. The Protocol declares, in its English text[9], that the corresponding provision of the Convention[10] is not to be interpreted in the sense that the extent of protection conferred by the patent is that defined by the strict, literal meaning of the wording used in the claims, the description and drawings being employed only for the purpose of resolving an ambiguity found in the claims. Nor should it be interpreted in the sense that the claims serve only as a guideline and that the actual protection conferred may extend to what, from a consideration of the description and drawings by a person skilled in the art, the proprietor of the patent has contemplated. On the contrary, it is to be interpreted as defining a position between these extremes which combines a fair protection for the proprietor with a reasonable degree of certainty for third parties. The purposive construction now applied by the court[11] is the same approach to construction as set out in the Protocol[12]. The Protocol, in its English text, also states that for the purpose of determining the protection conferred by a European patent, due account must be taken of any element which is equivalent to an element specified in the claims[13].

Where there is a statement in the specification of the advantages of an invention[14], or of the difficulties which it overcomes[15], a claim may be read as limited to forms having these advantages or adapted to meet these difficulties[16].

1   As to claims generally see PARAS 323–324.

2   See the Patents Act 1977 s 125(1); and PARA 301 note 2. The principles of claims construction are summarised in *Virgin Atlantic Airways Ltd v Premium Aircraft Interiors UK Ltd* [2009] EWCA Civ 1062 at [5]–[22], [201] RPC 192 at [5]–[22], [2009] All ER (D) 235 (Oct), per Jacob LJ (citing *Kirin-Amgen Inc v Hoechst Marion Roussel Ltd* [2004] UKHL 46, [2005] 1 All ER 667, [2005] RPC 169).

3   As to persons skilled in the art see PARA 491.

4   See eg *Insituform Technical Services Ltd v Inliner UK plc* [1992] RPC 83 at 90; *Rediffusion Simulation Ltd v Link-Miles Ltd* [1993] FSR 369 at 385; *M-Systems Flash Disk Pioneers Ltd v Trek 2000 International Ltd* [2008] EWHC 102 (Pat), [2008] RPC 405, [2008] All ER (D) 201 (Jan).

5   *Catnic Components Ltd v Hill & Smith Ltd* [1982] RPC 183 at 243, HL.

6   *Kirin-Amgen Inc v Hoechst Marion Roussel Ltd* [2004] UKHL 46 at [32]–[34], [2005] 1 All ER 667 at [32]–[34], [2005] RPC 169 at 185–186 per Lord Hoffmann. See also *Virgin Atlantic Airways Ltd v Premium Aircraft Interiors UK Ltd* [2009] EWCA Civ 1062, [2010] RPC 192, [2009] All ER (D) 235 (Oct); *Virgin Atlantic Airways Ltd v Premium Aircraft Interiors UK Ltd* [2011] EWCA Civ 163, [2013] RPC 659, [2012] IP & T 344; *Ranbaxy (UK) Ltd v AstraZeneca AB* [2011] EWHC 1831 (Pat), [2011] FSR 1011, [2011] All ER (D) 166 (Jul); *Sandvik Intellectual Property AB v Kennametal UK Ltd* [2011] EWHC 3311 (Pat), [2012] RPC 501, [2011] All ER (D) 137 (Dec); *MedImmune Ltd v Novartis Pharmaceuticals UK Ltd* [2012] EWCA Civ 1234, [2013] RPC 659, [2013] IP & T 536.

7   *Catnic Components Ltd v Hill & Smith Ltd* [1982] RPC 183 at 237, HL. It has been stated, however, that it is unnecessary and usually undesirable to refer to decisions prior to *Catnic Components Ltd v Hill & Smith Ltd*: see *Codex Corpn v Racal-Milgo Ltd* [1983] RPC 369, CA; *C Van der Lely NV v Ruston's Engineering Co Ltd* [1985] RPC 461, CA. The modern view is to regard *Kirin-Amgen Inc v Hoechst Marion Roussel Ltd* [2004] UKHL 46, [2005] 1 All ER 667, [2005] RPC 169 as setting out the proper approach: see PARA 411 note 7.

8   Patents Act 1977 s 125(3), which applies the Convention on the Grant of European Patents (Munich, 5 October 1973; TS 20 (1978); Cmnd 7090) (the European Patent Convention) Protocol for the purposes of the Patents Act 1977 s 125. See the European Patent Convention Protocol art 1. As to the European Patent Convention see PARA 644 et seq.

9   See the European Patent Convention Protocol art 1; and note 8.

10   Ie the European Patent Convention art 69, with which the Patents Act 1977 s 125(1) largely corresponds.

11   Ie that in *Catnic Components Ltd v Hill & Smith Ltd* [1982] RPC 183 at 237, HL; *Kirin-Amgen Inc v Hoechst Marion Roussel Ltd* [2004] UKHL 46, [2005] 1 All ER 667, [2005] RPC 169; *Ancon Ltd v ACS Stainless Steel Fixings Ltd* [2009] EWCA Civ 498, [2009] All ER (D) 148 (Jun).

12   See the European Patent Convention Protocol art 1; and note 8. *Improver Corpn v Remington Consumer Products Ltd* [1989] RPC 69 at 76, CA; *Southco Inc v Dzus Fastener Europe Ltd* [1992] RPC 299 at 312, CA, per Purchas LJ; *Horne Engineering Co Ltd v Reliance Water Controls Ltd* [2000] RPC 90, [2000] FSR 90; *Assidoman Multipack Ltd v Mead Corpn* [1995] RPC 321, CA; *Kirin-Amgen Inc v Hoechst Marion Roussel Ltd* [2004] UKHL 46, [2005] 1 All ER 667, [2005] RPC 169.

13   See the European Patent Convention Protocol art 2; and note 8. It is not clear to what extent the Protocol art 2 will result in an alteration of the approach of the English courts to infringement but *Rockwater v Technip France SA* [2004] EWCA Civ 381, [2004] RPC 919, [2005] IP & T 304, is no longer good law on this point. See also *Kirin-Amgen Inc v Hoechst Marion Roussel Ltd* [2004] UKHL 46, [2005] 1 All ER 667, [2005] RPC 169 at 190, where it was held that equivalence might be an important part of the background of facts known to the skilled addressee which would affect what he understood the claims to mean.

14   See *M-Systems Flash Disk Pioneers Ltd v Trek 2000 International Ltd* [2008] EWHC 102 (Pat), [2008] RPC 405, [2008] All ER (D) 201 (Jan). These advantages must, however, be distinctly set out: see *British Celanese Ltd v Courtaulds Ltd* (1933) 50 RPC 259 at 291, CA; on appeal (1935) 52 RPC 171 at 193, HL.

15   *Jackson v Wolstenhulmes* (1884) 1 RPC 105, CA; *Clay v Allcock & Co Ltd* (1906) 23 RPC 745 at 750, CA.

16   Cf *Raleigh Cycle Co Ltd v H Miller & Co Ltd* (1946) 63 RPC 113 at 133–138, CA; affd [1948] 1 All ER 308, 65 RPC 141, HL.

415.   Unworkable embodiments.   It is uncertain to what extent a claim which is clear in its terms may be read as excluding forms of the invention which the addressee would know to be unworkable[1]. A claim should be read so as to avoid if possible an absurd result[2].

1   See eg *Minnesota Mining & Manufacturing Co v Rennicks (UK) Ltd* [1992] RPC 331. Cf the cases cited to PARA 414.

2   *Henriksen v Tallon Ltd* [1965] RPC 434, HL; *Wesley Jessen Corpn v Coopervision Ltd* [2003] RPC 355, Patents County Court.

416.   Specification its own dictionary.   To a large extent the specification[1] is treated as supplying its own dictionary[2], that is to say, where it is clear from the body of the specification that the proprietor of a patent has used a term in his claims in a particular sense, it will be interpreted in that sense, even if it is not the ordinary sense of the term[3]. The question is always what the person skilled in the art would have understood the patentee to be using the language of the claim to mean[4].

1   As to the specification see PARA 318.

2   *Electric and Musical Industries Ltd v Lissen Ltd* (1937) 54 RPC 307 at 322, CA; on appeal [1938] 4 All ER 221 at 227, 56 RPC 23 at 41, CA, per Lord Russell of Killowen.

3   *Catnic Components Ltd v Hill & Smith Ltd* [1982] RPC 183, HL (meaning of 'vertical'); *Rockwater v Technip France SA* [2004] EWCA Civ 381, [2004] RPC 919, [2005] IP & T 304.

4   *Kirin-Amgen Inc v Hoechst Marion Roussel Ltd* [2004] UKHL 46 at [34], [2005] 1 All ER 667 at [34], [2005] RPC 169 at 186 per Lord Hoffmann. As to persons skilled in the art see PARA 491.

417.   Admissions in specification.   It is uncertain to what extent the proprietor of a patent is bound by erroneous admissions in his specification[1] as to what is old[2]. It is also uncertain whether the description of an invention as 'relating to' devices of a certain sort amounts to an admission that such devices are old[3]. To claim an invention as consisting in the presence of certain additional features in articles of a certain 'type' does not debar the proprietor from asserting that the invention is a combination of all the features together, including those of the 'type'[4]. Reference to an integer of a combination as being 'of the kind known per se in which ...' admits that things of that kind are well known[5].

1 As to the specification see PARA 318.
2 *Sonotone Corpn v Multitone Electric Co Ltd* (1955) 72 RPC 131 at 140, CA, discussing *Chapman and Cook and Lectro Linx Ltd v Deltavis Ltd* (1930) 47 RPC 163 at 173. A patentee is not estopped from contradicting an erroneous statement in a specification on which another party has not relied: *Gerber Garment Technology Inc v Lectra Systems Ltd* [1995] FSR 492, CA.
3 *Sonotone Corpn v Multitone Electric Co Ltd* (1955) 72 RPC 131 at 139–140, CA.
4 *Martin and Biro Swan Ltd v H Millwood Ltd* [1956] RPC 125 at 140, HL.
5 *Allmänna Svenska Elektriska AB v Burntisland Shipbuilding Co Ltd* (1952) 69 RPC 63 at 71, CA.

418. Reference to original specification.

The full history of the specification[1] from the version originally filed is available for inspection[2]. Statements made to the UK Intellectual Property Office[3] during prosecution may amount to admissions against interest[4].

1 As to the specification see PARA 318.
2 See the Patents Act 1977 s 118; and PARA 579.
3 As to the UK Intellectual Property Office see PARA 577.
4 *Furr v CD Truline (Building Products) Ltd* [1985] FSR 553 at 563; *Wesley Jessen Corpn v Coopervision Ltd* [2003] RPC 355 at 382, Patents County Court. However, it is not permissible to have regard to arguments before the European Patent Office (see PARA 644) in opposition proceedings: *Kirin-Amgen Inc v Hoechst Marion Roussel Ltd* [2004] UKHL 46, [2005] 1 All ER 667, [2005] RPC 169. As to the relevance of file history see *Bristol-Myers Squibb Co v Baker Norton Pharmaceuticals Inc* [2000] IP & T 908, [1999] RPC 253 at 274, CA.

419. Effect of claims 'for' a particular use or purpose.

Claims[1] to an article 'for' a particular use or purpose may give rise to considerable difficulty. Such a claim cannot have novelty over a disclosure of the same article 'for' another purpose[2] except where the article is invented for use in a method of treatment of the human or animal body by surgery or therapy or of diagnosis practised on the human or animal body[3]. It is, however, uncertain to what extent such a claim covers articles intended to be used for a different purpose or in a different way[4]. 'For' may mean 'suitable for'[5]. A claim 'for use in' is a mere statement of intent and does not clearly define the invention as required[6].

1 As to claims generally see PARAS 323–324.
2 *Adhesive Dry Mounting Co Ltd v Trapp & Co* (1910) 27 RPC 341; *Furr v CD Truline (Building Products) Ltd* [1985] FSR 553.
3 See the Patents Act 1977 s 4A; and PARA 432.
4 See *Vickers, Sons & Co Ltd v Siddell* (1890) 15 App Cas 496 at 505, 7 RPC 292 at 306, HL; *Lyon v Goddard* (1894) 11 RPC 113; *Re l'Air Liquide SA's Application* (1932) 49 RPC 428; *Berkeley and Young Ltd and Goodman Ltd v Stillwell, Darby & Co Ltd and Konig* (1940) 57 RPC 291. Cf *Mullard Radio Valve Co Ltd v Philco Radio and Television Corpn* [1936] 2 All ER 920, 53 RPC 323, HL (claim to process to be carried out with certain apparatus).
5 *Raleigh Cycle Co Ltd v H Miller & Co Ltd* (1946) 63 RPC 113 at 137, CA (on appeal [1948] 1 All ER 308, 65 RPC 141, HL); *Insituform Technical Services Ltd v Inliner UK plc* [1992] RPC 83.
6 Ie under the Patents Act 1977 s 14(5)(a), (b) (see PARA 318): *EI du Pont de Nemours & Co (Buege's) Application* [1984] RPC 17.

420. Claims in different language.

The ordinary rule is to construe claims[1] couched in different language as not being co-extensive[2]. This is, however, by no means an absolute rule[3], and there have been cases in which, by reason of the wording of the specification or the subject matter of the patent, each of a series of claims has been construed as being practically identical[4].

1 As to claims see PARAS 323–324.
2 *Multiform Displays Ltd v Whitmarley Displays Ltd* [1956] RPC 143 at 161, CA (per Romer LJ dissenting; upheld [1957] RPC 260, HL), citing *Parkinson v Simon* (1894) 11 RPC 493, CA (affd (1895) 12 RPC 403 at 407, HL).
3 It is not a ground for invalidating a specification that it claims the same thing over again in different language: *Van Berkel v RD Simpson Ltd* (1906) 24 RPC 117 at 137. See also *Wenham Gas Co Ltd v Champion Gas Lamp Co* (1891) 9 RPC 49 at 55, CA; *Edison-Bell Phonograph Corpn Ltd v Smith* (1894) 10 TLR 522, 11 RPC 389, CA; *New Vacuum Heating Co Ltd v Steel and Wilson* (1915) 32 RPC 162 at 171, Ct of Sess; *S Parkes & Co Ltd v Cocker Bros Ltd* (1929) 46 RPC 241 at 247, CA.
4 See eg *Thompson & Co v American Braided Wire Co* (1888) 5 TLR 537, 6 RPC 518, HL; *Duckett Ltd v Whitehead* (1895) 12 RPC 187 (affd 12 RPC 376, CA, where the whole of the claims were interpreted as for the special combination); *Brown v Sperry Gyroscope Co Ltd* (1925) 42 RPC 111 (affd 43 RPC 1, CA); *Mergenthaler Linotype Co v Intertype Co Ltd* (1926) 42 TLR 682, 43 RPC 239, CA; *Submarine Signal Co v Henry Hughes & Son Ltd* (1931) 49 RPC 149; *British Hartford-Fairmont Syndicate Ltd v Jackson Bros (Knottingley) Ltd* (1932) 49 RPC 495 at 525, CA (affd (1934) 51 RPC 254 at 261–262, HL); *Cowper v Paper Sacks Pty Ltd* [1932] AC 709, 49 RPC 601, PC. As to the competing languages of the patent and its translation see *Siemens Schweiz AG v Thorn Security Ltd* [2007] EWHC 2242 (Ch) at [10]–[12], [2008] RPC 58 at [10]–[12], [2007] All ER (D) 61 (Oct), per Mann J.

421. Effect of the expression 'substantially as described'. It was formerly customary to end claims[1] with such phrases as 'substantially as described' or 'substantially as and for the purpose described'. In such a case, these words will be read as importing into the claims the limitation, upon the features listed in the claim, that they should have those characteristics set out as essential for them in the body of the specification[2]. The modern practice is, however, to include only one or at most a few such claims, following upon broad claims without such words; and to include in them express references to the drawings or examples in the specification, if any. In such cases, the presumption is that the claim to the invention 'substantially as described' is meant to be a narrow claim, limited to things possessing all the features set out in the specification as essential or important to the invention[3]. Not every limitation found in earlier claims is necessarily to be imported into a claim to the drawings[4], and a feature only to be found in the drawings[5], or said in the body of the specification to be preferable only[6], will seldom be so imported.

1 As to claims see PARAS 323–324.
2 See *Parkinson v Simon* (1894) 11 RPC 493, CA; affd (1895) 12 RPC 403, HL.
3 *Raleigh Cycle Co Ltd v H Miller & Co Ltd* [1948] 1 All ER 308 at 320–321, 65 RPC 141 at 157–158, HL, per Lord Moreton of Henryton; cf *Daikin Kogyo Co Ltd (Shingu's) Application* [1974] RPC 559, CA (where a claim to a process 'substantially as hereinbefore described, with particular reference to examples 2 and 3' was construed as a claim to a single process capable of being carried out within certain limits of variation and not as a claim to a number of alternate processes). See also *Rotocrop International Ltd v Genbourne Ltd* [1982] FSR 241.
4 *Raleigh Cycle Co Ltd v H Miller & Co Ltd* [1948] 1 All ER 308 at 323, 65 RPC 141 at 160, HL, per Lord Moreton of Henryton.
5 *Clark v Adie* (1877) 2 App Cas 315 at 342, HL; *Hinks & Son v Safety Lighting Co* (1876) 4 ChD 607; *Crosthwaite v Moorwood, Sons & Co* (1894) 11 RPC 555 at 561; *Tolson and Tolson v John Speight & Sons* (1896) 13 RPC 718; *Palmer Tyre Ltd v Pneumatic Tyre Co Ltd* (1899) 16 RPC 451 at 480; *British Motor Traction Co Ltd v Friswell* (1901) 18 RPC 497; *Re Scott's Patent* (1903) 20 RPC 257, CA; *Rhodes and Edmondson v British Cotton and Wool Dyers Association Ltd* (1910) 28 RPC 67. In *George Hattersley & Sons Ltd v George Hodgson Ltd* (1906) 23 RPC 192, HL, it was held that the invention should be confined to the exact form shown in the drawings in order to meet the objection of non-utility.

6   *Gammons v Battersby* (1904) 21 RPC 322, CA; *Clay v Allcock & Co Ltd* (1906) 23 RPC 745, CA; *Walsh v Albert Baker & Co (1898) Ltd* (1930) 47 RPC 458, CA.

422. Single claims. Generally a single claim[1] is construed as comprising a single invention, unless it is clear from the specification that the contrary is intended[2]. In chemical cases a claim to a generic class of compounds may be construed as a claim to a number of sub-classes or indeed as a set of claims to specific individual compounds falling within the class[3].

1   As to claims see PARAS 323–324.
2   Eg it is a matter of construction whether a claim is directed to a racemate, one or more enantiomers, or both: *Ranbaxy UK Ltd v Warner-Lambert Co* [2006] EWCA Civ 876, [2007] RPC 65, [2006] All ER (D) 322 (Jun); *Generics (UK) Ltd v H Lundbeck A/S* [2009] UKHL 12, [2009] 2 All ER 955, [2009] IP & T 496. A patent may relate to a group of inventions which are linked to form a single inventive concept: see the Patents Act 1977 s 14(5)(d); and PARA 318. Where more than one invention is specified in a claim, each invention may have a different priority date: see the Patents Act 1977 s 125(2); and PARA 308.
3   See *Merck & Co (Macek's) Patent* [1967] RPC 157; *Ethyl Corpn (Cook's) Patent* [1970] RPC 227; *Imperial Chemical Industries Ltd (Howe's) Application* [1977] RPC 121; *Allen and Hanburys (Hayes') Application* [1977] RPC 113.

423. Interpretation of 'or'. The word 'or' is generally interpreted as disjunctive[1]. In a number of cases the word has, however, been interpreted as merely introducing another definition of a technical term[2].

1   *Elliott v Turner* (1845) 15 LJCP 49; *Simpson v Holliday* (1866) LR 1 HL 315. In *British United Shoe Machinery Co Ltd v Standard Rotary Machine Co Ltd* (1916) 33 RPC 373, CA (on appeal (1917) 35 RPC 33, HL), a claim for certain integers 'with or without' another integer was held bad, although it was admittedly obvious that the apparatus could not act without this integer or its equivalent. Cf *Higginson and Arundel v Pyman* (1926) 43 RPC 291 at 298, CA.
2   *Hills v London Gas Light Co* (1860) 29 LJ Ex 409; *Hills v Liverpool United Gaslight Co* (1862) 32 LJ Ch 28 ('hydrated or precipitated oxides of iron'); *Kaye v Chubb & Sons Ltd* (1886) 5 RPC 641, HL; *White v Bertrams Ltd* (1897) 14 RPC 735, Ct of Sess ('in line with or parallel to'); *Patent Exploitation Ltd v Siemens Bros & Co Ltd* (1904) 21 RPC 541 at 547; *Patent Exploitation Ltd v American Electrical Novelty and Manufacturing Co Ltd* (1905) 22 RPC 316, CA ('semi-solid or plastic'); *Flour Oxidizing Co Ltd v Hutchinson* (1909) 26 RPC 597 ('conditioning or improving').

424. Effect of former decisions. A court is bound by a decision of a court of equal or superior status on the construction of a specification[1] and the breadth of the claims made in it[2] except, possibly, where that decision turns in a material respect on evidence which was either lacking in a previous case or which was materially different in the case before it[3]. It has also been held that such decisions are binding with respect to the question whether a specification is too vague or unintelligible to be construed by the court, but that they are not binding with respect to the question whether the proprietor of the patent has sufficiently described the nature of and the manner in which the invention is to be performed[4] or anticipation by specific documents not before the court when the earlier decision was given[5]. A decision of the comptroller[6] or on appeal from him[7] does not estop any party to civil proceedings in which infringement of a patent is in issue from alleging invalidity of the patent on any of the available grounds of revocation[8] whether or not any of the issues involved were decided in that decision[9].

1   As to the specification see PARA 318.
2   *Hills v Liverpool United Gaslight Co* (1862) 32 LJ Ch 28; *Otto v Steel* (1885) 3 RPC 109; *Edison and Swan United Electric Light Co Ltd v Holland* (1889) 41 ChD 28, 6 RPC 243, CA; *British Vacuum Co Ltd v Exton Hotels Co Ltd* (1908) 25 RPC 617.

3 *Novartis AG v Dexcel-Pharma Ltd* [2008] EWHC 1266 (Pat), [2008] FSR 773.
4 *Edison and Swan United Electric Light Co Ltd v Holland* (1889) 41 ChD 28, CA.
5 *Higginson and Arundel v Pyman* (1926) 43 RPC 291, CA. See also *Coflexip SA v Stolt Offshore MS Ltd (No 2)* [2004] EWCA Civ 213, [2004] FSR 708. As to judicial decisions as authorities generally see CIVIL PROCEDURE vol 11 (2009) PARA 91 et seq.
6 As to the comptroller see PARA 575.
7 As to appeals generally see PARA 570 et seq.
8 Ie under the Patents Act 1977 s 72 (see PARA 562).
9 Patents Act 1977 s 72(5).

7. VALIDITY

(1) INTRODUCTION

425. Validity of patents generally. The grounds on which patents may be revoked[1] are listed in the Patents Act 1977[2]. A patent may be revoked on the application of any person[3]. The Patents Act 1977 refers to patents as 'valid' or 'invalid', assuming, without so stating, that an 'invalid' patent is one that may be so revoked and a 'valid' patent is one that may not[4]. The grounds of invalidity of a patent are that the invention is not new[5], is obvious[6], is incapable of industrial application[7], is not an invention as defined by the Patents Act 1977[8], is socially objectionable[9], is a method of treatment or diagnosis[10], the specification is insufficient[11], the matter disclosed in the specification extends beyond that disclosed in the application for the patent as filed[12] or the protection conferred by the patent has been extended by an unallowable amendment[13].

1   As to proceedings for revocation see PARA 562 et seq.
2   See the Patents Act 1977 s 72(1); and PARA 429.
3   See the Patents Act 1977 s 72(1); and PARA 429. See *Oystertec's Patent* [2002] EWHC 2324 (Pat), [2003] RPC 559.
4   The additional ground of revocation open only to the comptroller under the Patents Act 1977 s 73(2) (see PARA 569) is not in general within the expression 'invalidity'. As to the comptroller see PARA 575. Further, by reason of s 74(4) (see PARA 519), a patent may be invalid only as against particular persons with a better title to it than its proprietor.
5   See PARA 434 et seq.
6   See PARA 451 et seq.
7   See PARA 487.
8   See PARA 301 et seq.
9   See PARA 430.
10 See PARA 432.
11 See PARA 489 et seq.
12 See PARA 497.
13 See PARA 498.

426. Partial invalidity. Most of the objections to the validity of patents are objections to particular claims of the specification[1]. A patent may thus be partially invalid because one or more claims are open to objection, although other claims are valid[2].

1   As to the specification generally see PARA 318. As to claims and their function see PARAS 323–324.
2   As to the consequences of invalidity of some claims see the Patents Act 1977 s 63 (see PARA 550) and s 72(4) (see PARA 562).

427. Curing invalidity. Invalidity of patents may be curable by amendment of the specification[1], either before, during or after proceedings for infringement, or for revocation of the patent[2].

1   As to the amendment of specifications see PARA 345 et seq.
2   As to the effect of amendment on the relief obtainable in proceedings for infringement see PARA 547. However, post-trial amendments by way of claim rewriting are not normally permitted as the validity of the new claims could be the subject of significant further debate which could necessitate a new trial: *Nikken Kosakusho Works v Pioneer Trading Co* [2005] EWCA Civ 906, [2006] FSR 41, [2005] All ER (D) 350 (Jun); *Vector Corpn v Glatt Air Techniques Inc* [2007] EWCA Civ 805, [2008] RPC 243, [2007] All ER (D) 297 (Oct).

428. Grant does not warrant validity. The examination of specifications[1] and investigation of the novelty[2] of the inventions claimed by them, and of the inventive step[3] claimed by the specification, carried out by the UK Intellectual Property Office[4] before granting a patent, do not warrant the validity of the patent, but a granted patent is prima facie valid[5].

1   As to the specification see PARA 318.
2   As to novelty see PARA 434 et seq.
3   As to the inventive step see PARA 451 et seq.
4   Ie under the Patents Act 1977 ss 17, 18 (see PARAS 327–328). As to the UK Intellectual Property Office see PARA 577.

5   *American Cyanamid Co v Ethicon Ltd* [1975] AC 396, [1975] 1 All ER 504, [1975] RPC 513, HL.

(2) VALIDITY AND INVALIDITY

(i) In general

429.   Grounds of invalidity. A patent may be revoked on any of the following grounds[1]:

(1)   that there is no patentable invention[2], that is say:
   (a)   that the invention was not new[3];
   (b)   that the invention did not involve an inventive step[4];
   (c)   that the invention was incapable of industrial application[5];
   (d)   that it was not an invention as defined by the Patents Act 1977[6];
   (e)   that it was contrary to public policy or morality[7];

(2)   that the patent specification is insufficient[8];

(3)   that the patent specification has been amended[9] so as to extend either the disclosure[10] in it or the protection conferred by it[11].

A patent may be revoked on the application of particular persons on the ground that the patent was granted to a person not entitled to be granted that patent[12]. These grounds of invalidity are exclusive[13].

Further, a patent may be liable to revocation by the comptroller[14] of his own motion on the ground that there is also a European patent (UK)[15] for the same invention[16].

1   Patents Act 1977 s 74(3).
2   See the Patents Act 1977 s 72(1)(a); and PARA 430. 'Patentable invention' means any invention in which the conditions specified in s 1(1)(a)–(d) are satisfied: s 1(1).
3   See the Patents Act 1977 ss 1(1)(a), 2; and PARA 434.
4   See the Patents Act 1977 ss 1(1)(b), 3; and PARA 451.
5   See the Patents Act 1977 ss 1(1)(c), 4; and PARA 487.
6   See the Patents Act 1977 s 1(1)(d), (2); and PARA 430.
7   See the Patents Act 1977 s 1(1)(d), (3), (4); and PARA 430.
8   See the Patents Act 1977 s 72(1)(c); and PARA 489.
9   As to the amendment of specifications see PARA 345 et seq.
10   See the Patents Act 1977 s 72(1)(d); and PARA 497.
11   See the Patents Act 1977 s 72(1)(e); and PARA 498.
12   See the Patents Act 1977 s 72(1)(b); and PARA 488.

13   Patents Act 1977 s 74(3). In particular a patent cannot be revoked on the ground that the claims are not supported by the description as required by s 14(5) (see PARA 318): *Genentech Inc's Patent* [1989] RPC 147 at 198, CA, per Purchas LJ, at 236 per Dillon LJ and at 260 per Mustill LJ.
14   As to the comptroller see PARA 575.
15   As to the meaning of 'European patent (UK)' see PARA 652 note 1.
16   See the Patents Act 1977 s 73(2); and PARA 569.

(ii) Patentable Subject Matter

430. Exclusions from patentability. A patent is invalid if the invention for which it has been granted[1] is not patentable[2]. Anything which consists of the following (among other things) is declared not to be an invention for the purposes of the Patents Act 1977[3]:

(1)   a discovery, scientific theory or mathematical method[4];

(2)   a literary, dramatic, musical or artistic work or any other aesthetic creation whatsoever[5];

(3)   a scheme, rule or method for performing a mental act[6], playing a game or doing business, or a program for a computer[7];

(4)   the presentation of information[8].

However, these exclusions prevent anything from being treated as an invention only to the extent that a patent or application for a patent relates to that thing as such[9].

When considering the question of patentability, the court has regard to the substance of what is being claimed and not to the form of the words used[10]. Thus, for example, claims to a conventional computer containing a novel computer program or to a process for programming such a computer with a novel program have been regarded as claims to a computer program as such and hence unpatentable[11]. Whether an alleged invention is patentable depends upon what technical contribution the invention as a whole makes to the known art[12]. There must be some technical advance on the prior art in the form of a new result[13]. Whilst a discovery as such cannot be patented[14], an inventor who on the basis of that discovery tells people how it can usefully be employed is entitled to a patent even though, once the discovery has been made, the way it can be so employed is obvious[15]. The ascription of a hitherto unknown property to a known substance is a discovery and as such unpatentable[16]. A claim to a method embracing a discovery which is speculative as to the method by which the discovery is to be embraced or which refers to developments in the art which are neither direct or immediate is a claim to a discovery as such[17].

In addition, a patent may not be granted for an invention the commercial exploitation of which would be contrary to public policy or morality[18] or for a method of treatment or diagnosis[19].

The Secretary of State[20] may by order vary the list of things excluded from patentability for the purpose of maintaining them in conformity with developments in science and technology[21].

1   For the purposes of the Patents Act 1977, an invention for a patent for which an application has been made or for which a patent has been granted is taken, unless the context otherwise requires, to be that specified in a claim of the specification of the application or patent, as the case may be, as interpreted by the description and any drawings contained in that specification; and the extent of the protection conferred by a patent or application for a patent is to be determined accordingly: s 125(1).

2   Patents Act 1977 ss 72(1)(a), 74(3).

3   This is not an exhaustive list: see the Patents Act 1977 s 1(2). A method of controlling traffic flow is not patentable: Case T-16/83 *Christian Franceries/Traffic regulation* [1988] EPOR 65, Technical Board of Appeal; *Lux Traffic Controls Ltd v Pike Signals Ltd, Lux Traffic Controls Ltd v Faronwise Ltd* [1993] RPC 107 at 138.

4   Patents Act 1977 s 1(2)(a). The following have been held unpatentable under s 1(2)(a): discovery of an amino acid sequence in human tissue plasminogen activator (t-PA) and claims based on t-PA per se, when not occurring naturally (*Genentech Inc's Patent* [1989] RPC 147, CA); method of calculating square roots with the aid of a computer and claims to a ROM characterised by the computer program stored in it (*Gale's Application* [1991] RPC 305 at 317, CA).

5   Patents Act 1977 s 1(2)(b). Original literary, dramatic, musical and artistic works and some
     other aesthetic creations are protected by copyright (see COPYRIGHT vol 23 (2013) PARA 653 et
     seq) or design right (see COPYRIGHT vol 23 (2013) PARA 1048 et seq). See also Case T-119/88
     Fuji/Coloured disk jacket [1990] EPOR 615, Technical Board of Appeal.

6   The correct interpretation of the mental act exclusion is that the exclusion applies to acts
     actually carried out mentally (*Re Halliburton Energy Services Inc's Patent Application* [2011]
     EWHC 2508 (Pat), [2012] RPC 297, [2012] Bus LR D65), and does not exclude claims limited
     to methods of the kind performed by the human mind even if carried out on the computer (see
     Kapur v Comptroller General of Patents, Designs and Trade Marks [2008] EWHC 649 (Pat),
     [2008] Bus LR D77, [2008] All ER (D) 142 (Apr)): on this basis, claims which specify that an
     invention is to be implemented using a computer are not to be considered to be excluded from
     patentability as a mental act: see *Practice Notice (Patents Act 1977: Patentability of Mental
     Acts)* [2012] Bus LR 1264. See further note 7.

7   Patents Act 1977 s 1(2)(c). Noting the cases cited in note 6, the following have been held to be
     unpatentable under the Patents Act 1977 s 1(2)(c): a data processing system for making a
     market in securities (*Merrill Lynch's Application* [1989] RPC 561, CA); a compiler which
     maximised the use of vector instructions (*Hitachi Ltd's Application* [1991] RPC 415); a
     computer so programmed that an expert could store his knowledge in a hierarchical form
     resulting in a system from which expert advice could be obtained (*Wang Laboratories Inc's
     Application* [1991] RPC 463); a method of matching silhouettes of unknown objects (e g ships)
     with those of known objects by digitally measuring the image of unknown object obtained by an
     imaging device and comparing it with the images of known objects stored in a computer
     memory (*Raytheon Co's Application* [1993] RPC 427); a computer program for modelling a
     synthetic crystal structure which allowed combined crystal structure to be portrayed more
     quickly than was otherwise possible (*Re Patent Application No 9204959.2 by Fujitsu Ltd*
     [1997] RPC 608, CA); a computer apparatus configured to provide a lottery playable via the
     internet (*Shopalotto.com Ltd v Comptroller General of Patents, Designs and Trade Marks*
     [2005] EWHC 2416 (Pat), [2006] IP & T 396); the coordination of transport processes
     (*Cappellini v Comptroller of Patents; Bloomberg LP v Comptroller of Patents* [2007] EWHC
     476 (Pat), [2007] FSR 663, [2007] All ER (D) 200 (Mar)). See also Case T-38/86 *IBM/Text
     clarity processing* [1990] EPOR 606, Technical Board of Appeal; Case T-65/86 *IBM/Text
     processing* [1990] EPOR 181, Technical Board of Appeal; *Aerotel Ltd v Telco Holdings Ltd; Re
     Macrossan's Application* [2006] EWCA Civ 1371, [2007] 1 All ER 225, [2007] RPC 117;
     Astron Clinica Ltd v Comptroller General of Patents, Designs and Trade Marks [2008] EWHC
     85 (Pat), [2008] 2 All ER 742, [2008] RPC 339; *Autonomy Corpn Ltd v Comptroller General
     of Patents Trade Marks and Designs* [2008] EWHC 146 (Pat), [2008] RPC 357, [2008] All ER
     (D) 81 (Feb); *Re Patent Application in the name of Protecting Kids The World Over
     (PKTWO) Ltd* [2011] EWHC 2720 (Pat), [2012] RPC 323, [2011] All ER (D) 31 (Nov); *HTC
     Europe Co Ltd v Apple Inc* [2013] EWCA Civ 451, [2013] RPC 776, [2013] All ER (D) 49
     (May); *Lantana Ltd v Comptroller General of Patents, Designs and Trade Marks* [2013] EWHC
     2673 (Pat), [2013] All ER (D) 37 (Sep). See also PARA 431.

8   Patents Act 1977 s 1(2)(d). See *Raytheon Co v Comptroller General of Patents, Designs and
     Trade Marks* [2007] EWHC 1230 (Pat), [2008] RPC 46, [2007] All ER (D) 360 (May).

9   Patents Act 1977 s 1(2).

10   *Lux Traffic Controls Ltd v Pike Signals Ltd, Lux Traffic Controls Ltd v Faronwise Ltd* [1993]
     RPC 107 at 139.

11   *Gale's Application* [1991] RPC 305 at 317, CA; *Wang Laboratories Inc's Application* [1991]
     RPC 463; *Raytheon Co's Application* [1993] RPC 427. But see *Astron Clinica Ltd v
     Comptroller General of Patents, Designs and Trade Marks* [2008] EWHC 85 (Pat), [2008]
     2 All ER 742, [2008] RPC 339; and UK IPO *Practice Note* [2008] RPC 356. The correct
     approach to patentability is set out in *Aerotel Ltd v Telco Holdings Ltd; Re Macrossan's
     Application* [2006] EWCA Civ 1371, [2007] 1 All ER 225, [2007] RPC 117 (see PARA 431).

12   Case T-204/84 *Vicom/Computer-related invention* [1987] EPOR 74, Technical Board of Appeal,
     cited with approval in *Genentech Inc's Patent* [1989] RPC 147 at 208, CA, per Purchas LJ;
     Merrill Lynch's Application [1989] RPC 561 at 569, CA; *Raytheon Co's Application* [1993]
     RPC 427 at 449. The correct approach to determining whether material is excluded is to take
     the claims of the patent, correctly construed, and consider what the claimed invention
     contributes to the art outside the excluded subject matter: *Research in Motion UK Ltd v Inpro
     Licensing SARL* [2006] EWHC 70 (Pat), [2006] RPC 517, [2006] All ER (D) 150 (Feb); affd
     [2007] EWCA Civ 51, [2007] All ER (D) 88 (Feb).

13   *Merrill Lynch's Application* [1989] RPC 561 at 569, CA (giving as an example a substantial increase in processing speed brought about by the use of a novel computer program). See also *Lux Traffic Controls Ltd v Pike Signals Ltd, Lux Traffic Controls Ltd v Faronwise Ltd* [1993] RPC 107 at 139.

14   This was also the case under the previous legislation: see eg *Hickton's Patent Syndicate v Patents and Machine Improvements Co* (1909) 26 RPC 339, CA.

15   *Genentech Inc's Patent* [1987] RPC 553 at 566, cited with approval in *Genentech Inc's Patent* [1989] RPC 147 at 208, CA, per Purchas LJ and at 240 per Dillon LJ; *Gale's Application* [1991] RPC 305 at 324, CA.

16   *Genentech Inc's Patent* [1989] RPC 147 at 248, CA, per Dillon LJ and at 263 per Mustill LJ (discovery of amino acid sequence of human tissue plasminogen activator (t-PA) leading to process for its production; claims to t-PA per se, other than naturally occurring t-PA, and to t-PA produced by recombinant DNA technology were claims to discoveries and as such not claims for the practical application of the discovery of the sequences).

17   *Genentech Inc's Patent* [1989] RPC 147 at 227, CA, per Purchas LJ.

18   Patents Act 1977 s 1(3) (substituted by SI 2000/2037). The corresponding provision of the Convention on the Grant of European Patents (Munich, 5 October 1973; TS 20 (1978); Cmnd 7090) (the European Patent Convention: see PARA 644) refers to inventions contrary to 'ordre public' or morality: art 53(a). Exploitation is not to be regarded as contrary to public policy or morality only because it is prohibited by any law in force in the United Kingdom or any part of it: Patents Act 1977 s 1(4) (substituted by SI 2000/2037). The purpose of the Patents Act 1977 s 1(4) is to enable eg the manufacture for export of devices which may offend against United Kingdom law, such as certain gaming machines, but which do not offend against the law of the country to which they are to be exported. As to the meaning of 'United Kingdom' see PARA 303 note 5. See eg *Harvard/Onco-mouse* [1991] EPOR 525, Examining Division. Plant varieties are protected under the Plant Varieties Act 1997: see AGRICULTURAL PRODUCTION AND MARKETING vol 1 (2008) PARA 1175 et seq. As to biotechnological inventions see PARA 433.

19   See the Patents Act 1977 s 4A; and PARA 432.

20   As to the Secretary of State see PARA 573.

21   Patents Act 1977 s 1(5). At the date at which this volume states the law no such order had been made.

431. Test for patentability. A four-step test to decide whether inventions are patentable subject matter has been suggested by the UK Intellectual Property Office[1] and approved by the Court of Appeal[2]. The following steps must be followed:

(1)   the claim must be properly construed[3];

(2)   the actual contribution must be identified[4];

(3)   the question whether the invention falls within the excluded subject matter[5] must be determined[6]; and

(4)   it must be decided if the actual or alleged contribution is technical in nature[7].

1   As to the UK Intellectual Property Office see PARA 577.

2   See *Aerotel Ltd v Telco Holdings Ltd; Re Macrossan's Application* [2006] EWCA Civ 1371 at [39]–[49], [2007] 1 All ER 225 at [39]–[49], [2007] RPC 117 at [39]–[49] per Jacob LJ, giving the judgment of the court. See also *Autonomy Corpn Ltd v Comptroller General of Patents Trade Marks and Designs* [2008] EWHC 146 (Pat), [2008] RPC 357, [2008] All ER (D) 81 (Feb). The UK Intellectual Property Office is of the view that this case provides a definitive statement of the law and it is now rarely necessary to refer back to previous case law: see UK IPO *Practice Notice* dated 2 November 2006 [2007] RPC 162, as modified by UK IPO *Practice Notice* dated 7 February 2008 [2008] RPC 356.

3   See *Aerotel Ltd v Telco Holdings Ltd; Re Macrossan's Application* [2006] EWCA Civ 1371 at [42], [2007] 1 All ER 225 at [42], [2007] RPC 117 at [42] per Jacob LJ, giving the judgment of the court.

4   This is an exercise in judgment probably involving the problem said to be solved, how the invention works, what its advantages are and looking at what the inventor has added to human knowledge; the formulation involves looking at substance not form: see *Aerotel Ltd v Telco Holdings Ltd; Re Macrossan's Application* [2006] EWCA Civ 1371 at [43], [2007] 1 All ER 225 at [43], [2007] RPC 117 at [43] per Jacob LJ, giving the judgment of the court.

5   As to excluded subject matter see PARA 430.

6 See *Aerotel Ltd v Telco Holdings Ltd; Re Macrossan's Application* [2006] EWCA Civ 1371 at [45], [2007] 1 All ER 225 at [45], [2007] RPC 117 at [45] per Jacob LJ, giving the judgment of the court.

7 See *Aerotel Ltd v Telco Holdings Ltd; Re Macrossan's Application* [2006] EWCA Civ 1371 at [46], [2007] 1 All ER 225 at [46], [2007] RPC 117 at [46] per Jacob LJ, giving the judgment of the court. Following the decision in *Aerotel Ltd v Telco Holdings Ltd; Re Macrossan's Application*, the UK Intellectual Property Office decided that computer programs or programs on a carrier were not patentable. The position was clarified in *Astron Clinica Ltd v Comptroller General of Patents, Designs and Trade Marks* [2008] EWHC 85 (Pat) at [51], [2008] 2 All ER 742 at [51], [2008] RPC 339 at [51] per Kitchen J (claims to computer programs are not necessarily excluded ... in a case where claims to a method performed by running a suitably programmed computer or to a computer programmed to carry out the method are allowable, then, in principle, a claim to the program itself should also be allowable). This ruling has been accepted by the UK Intellectual Property Office: see UK IPO *Practice Notice* dated 7 February 2008 [2008] RPC 356.

A claim to a computer program or computer based system which survived step three of the test in *Aerotel Ltd v Telco Holdings Ltd; Re Macrossan's Application* (see head (3) in the text) could never be rejected as excluded matter under step four (see head (4) in the text) on the basis that it did not involve a substantive technical contribution; they were, in reality, a single question: *Symbian Ltd v Comptroller General of Patents* [2008] EWCA Civ 1066, [2009] RPC 1, [2009] IP & T 214. See also *Autonomy Corpn Ltd v Comptroller General of Patents Trade Marks and Designs* [2008] EWHC 146 (Pat), [2008] RPC 357, [2008] All ER (D) 81 (Feb); *Blacklight Power Inc v Comptroller General of Patents* [2008] EWHC 2763 (Pat), [2009] RPC 173, [2009] Bus LR 748; *AT & T Knowledge Ventures LP's Patent Application* [2009] EWHC 343 (Pat), [2009] FSR 743, [2009] All ER (D) 27 (Mar); *HTC Europe Co Ltd v Apple Inc* [2013] EWCA Civ 451, [2013] RPC 776, [2013] All ER (D) 49 (May).

432. Methods of treatment or diagnosis. A patent may not be granted for the invention[1] of:

(1)   a method of treatment of the human or animal body by surgery or therapy[2]; or

(2)   a method of diagnosis practised on the human or animal body[3].

This exclusion does not apply to an invention consisting of a substance or composition for use in any such method[4]. In the case of an invention consisting of a substance or composition for use in any such method, the fact that the substance or composition forms part of the state of the art[5] does not prevent the invention from being taken to be new if the use of the substance or composition in any such method does not form part of the state of the art[6].

In the case of an invention consisting of a substance or composition for a specific use in any such method, the fact that the substance or composition forms part of the state of the art does not prevent the invention from being taken to be new if that specific use does not form part of the state of the art[7]. A new dosing regime may be enough to confer novelty[8].

1   As to the extent of an invention see PARA 430 note 1.

2   'Therapy' includes prophylactic as well as curative treatment: *Unilever Ltd (Davis's) Application* [1983] RPC 219. See also Case T-81/84 *Rorer/Dysmenorrhea* [1988] EPOR 297, Technical Board of Appeal; Case T-290/86 *ICI/Cleaning plaque* [1991] EPOR 157, Technical Board of Appeal. Cosmetic use is not a form of therapy: Case T-36/83 *Roussel Uclaf/Thenoyl peroxide* [1987] EPOR 1, Technical Board of Appeal. See also Case T-144/83 *Du Pont/Appetite suppressant* [1987] EPOR 6, Technical Board of Appeal. Dosing regimes are methods of treatment and are not patentable: *Bristol-Myers Squibb Co v Baker Norton Pharmaceuticals Inc* [2001] RPC 1, [2000] IP & T 908, CA; *Merck & Co Inc's Patents* [2003] EWCA Civ 1545, [2004] FSR 330.

3   Patents Act 1977 s 4A(1) (s 4A added by the Patents Act 2004 s 1). The exclusion does not prohibit other methods of treating animals, eg a method, which is industrially applicable, of preventing a sow from overlying her piglets: Case T-58/87 *Salminen/Pigs III* [1989] EPOR 125, Technical Board of Appeal.

4   Patents Act 1977 s 4A(2) (as added: see note 3).

5   See PARA 434.

6   Patents Act 1977 s 4A(3) (as added: see note 3). This allows claims of the type 'compound *x* for use in the treatment of diabetes' provided no prior use of or suggestion to use *x* as a pharmaceutical is known: *John Wyeth & Brother Ltd's Application, Schering AG's Application* [1985] RPC 545 at 558. Where a second medical use for a known compound has been discovered, a claim in the 'Swiss form' is allowable, that is a claim in the form 'the use of compound *x* or a pharmaceutically acceptable salt thereof in the preparation of a medicament for the therapeutic and/or prophylactic treatment of diabetes'. This type of claim was approved by the Patents Court sitting in banc in *John Wyeth & Brother Ltd's Application, Schering AG's Application* [1985] RPC 545. Such claims are also allowed by the European Patent Office (see PARA 644): see Case G-05/83 *Eisai/Second medical indication* [1979–1985] EPOR 241, Enlarged Board of Appeal. See *Bristol-Myers Squibb Co v Baker Norton Pharmaceuticals Inc* [2001] RPC 1, [2000] IP & T 908, CA. See also *Teva Pharmaceutical Industries Ltd v Merrell Pharmaceuticals Inc* [2007] EWHC 2276 (Ch), 102 BMLR 1, [2007] All ER (D) 170 (Oct). See also *Bristol-Myers Squibb Co v Baker Norton Pharmaceuticals Inc* [2001] RPC 1, [2000] IP & T 908, CA. See, however, note 7.

7   Patents Act 1977 s 4A(4) (as added: see note 3). This allows claims in the form 'compound X for use in the treatment of condition Y' and obviates the need for 'Swiss form' claims. See UK IPO *Practice Notice (Patents Act 1977: second medical use claims)* dated 26 May 2010 [2010] Bus LR 1242.

8   *Actavis UK Ltd v Merck & Co Inc* [2008] EWCA Civ 444, [2009] 1 All ER 196, [2008] RPC 631. In this case it was held that the Court of Appeal was free to depart from the ratio decidendi of its own earlier decision if it was satisfied that the European Patent Office Boards of Appeal had formed a settled view of European patent law which was inconsistent with that earlier decision. See also PARA 652.

433.   Biotechnological developments.   An invention[1] is not to be considered unpatentable solely on the ground that it concerns: (1) a product consisting of or containing biological material; or (2) a process by which biological material is produced, processed or used[2].

Biological material which is isolated from its natural environment or produced by means of a technical process may be the subject of an invention even if it previously occurred in nature[3].

The following are not patentable inventions:

(a)   the human body, at the various stages of its formation and development, and the simple discovery of one of its elements, including the sequence or partial sequence of a gene[4];

(b)   processes for cloning human beings[5];

(c)   processes for modifying the germ line genetic identity of human beings[6];

(d)   uses of human embryos for industrial or commercial purposes[7];

(e)   processes for modifying the genetic identity of animals which are likely to cause them suffering without any substantial medical benefit to man or animal, and also animals resulting from such processes[8];

(f)   any variety of animal or plant[9] or any essentially biological process[10] for the production of animals or plants, not being a micro-biological[11] or other technical process or the product of such a process[12].

The protection conferred by a patent on a biological material possessing specific characteristics as a result of the invention extends to any biological material derived from that biological material through propagation or multiplication in an identical or divergent form and possessing those same characteristics[13].

The protection conferred by a patent on a process that enables a biological material to be produced possessing specific characteristics as a result of the invention extends to biological material directly obtained through that process and to any other biological material derived from the directly obtained biological material through propagation or multiplication in an identical or divergent form and possessing those same characteristics[14].

The protection conferred by a patent on a product containing or consisting of genetic information extends to all material, save as provided for in head (c) above, in which the product is incorporated and in which the genetic information is contained and performs its function[15].

This protection[16] does not extend to biological material obtained from the propagation or multiplication of biological material placed on the market by the proprietor of the patent or with his consent, where the multiplication or propagation necessarily results from the application for which the biological material was marketed, provided that the material obtained is not subsequently used for other propagation or multiplication[17].

1　As to the meaning of 'invention' see PARA 301 note 2. Any provision of, or made under, the Patents Act 1977 is to have effect in relation to a patent or an application for a patent which concerns a biotechnological invention, subject to the provisions of s 76A, Sch A2: s 76A(1) (s 76A, Sch A2 added by SI 2000/2037). 'Biotechnological invention' means an invention which concerns a product consisting of or containing biological material or a process by means of which biological material is produced, processed or used; and 'biological material' means any material containing genetic information and capable of reproducing itself or being reproduced in a biological system: Patents Act 1977 s 130(1) (definitions added by SI 2000/2037). Nothing in the Patents Act 1977 s 76A or Sch A2 is to be read as affecting the application of any provision in relation to any other kind of patent or application for a patent: s 76A(2) (as so added).

2　Patents Act 1977 Sch A2 para 1 (as added: see note 1).

3　Patents Act 1977 Sch A2 para 2 (as added: see note 1).

4　Patents Act 1977 Sch A2 para 3(a) (as added: see note 1). An element isolated from the human body or otherwise produced by means of a technical process, including the sequence or partial sequence of a gene, may constitute a patentable invention, even if the structure of that element is identical to that of a natural element: Sch A2 para 5 (as so added). The industrial application of a sequence or partial sequence of a gene must be disclosed in the patent application as filed: Sch A2 para 6 (as so added). As to references to an application for a patent as filed see PARA 316 note 2.

5　Patents Act 1977 Sch A2 para 3(b) (as added: see note 1).

6　Patents Act 1977 Sch A2 para 3(c) (as added: see note 1).

7　Patents Act 1977 Sch A2 para 3(d) (as added: see note 1). 'Human embryo' includes any human ovum after fertilisation, any non-fertilised human ovum into which the cell nucleus from a mature human cell has been transplanted and any non-fertilised human ovum whose division and further development have been stimulated by parthenogenesis: see Case C-34/10 *Brüstle v Greenpeace eV* [2012] All ER (EC) 809, [2011] ECR I-9821, ECJ (invention enabling use of embryonic stem cells to produce more specialised precursor cells was not patentable).

8　Patents Act 1977 Sch A2 para 3(e) (as added: see note 1).

9　'Plant variety' means a plant grouping within a single botanical taxon of the lowest known rank, which grouping can be: (1) defined by the expression of the characteristics that results from a given genotype or combination of genotypes; (2) distinguished from any other plant grouping by the expression of at least one of the said characteristics; and (3) considered as a unit with regard to its suitability for being propagated unchanged: Patents Act 1977 Sch A2 para 11 (as added: see note 1).

10　'Essentially biological process' means a process for the production of animals and plants which consists entirely of natural phenomena such as crossing and selection: Patents Act 1977 Sch A2 para 11 (as added: see note 1).

11　'Microbiological process' means any process involving or performed upon or resulting in microbiological material: Patents Act 1977 Sch A2 para 11 (as added: see note 1).

12　Patents Act 1977 Sch A2 para 3(f) (as added: see note 1). Inventions which concern plants or animals may be patentable if the technical feasibility of the invention is not confined to a particular plant or animal variety: Sch A2 para 4 (as so added).

13　Patents Act 1977 Sch A2 para 7 (as added: see note 1).

14　Patents Act 1977 Sch A2 para 8 (as added: see note 1).

15 Patents Act 1977 Sch A2 para 9 (as added: see note 1). This protection does not extend to genetic information contained in dead material because that information no longer 'performs its function': see Case C-428/08 *Monsanto Technology LLC v Cefetra BV* [2011] All ER (EC) 209, [2010] ECR I-6765, ECJ.
16 Ie the protection referred to in the Patents Act 1977 Sch A2 paras 7–9 (see the text to notes 13–15).
17 Patents Act 1977 Sch A2 para 10 (as added: see note 1).

(iii) Lack of Novelty

434. Invention not new. A patent for an invention may be granted only if the invention is new[1]. An invention[2] is taken to be new if it does not form part of the state of the art[3]. The state of the art in the case of an invention is taken to comprise all matter (whether a product, a process, information about either, or anything else) which, at any time before the priority date[4] of that invention has been made available to the public[5], whether in the United Kingdom[6] or elsewhere, by written or oral description, by use or in any other way[7]. In addition, the state of the art in the case of an invention to which an application for a patent or a patent relates is taken to comprise matter contained in an application for another patent[8] which was published on or after the priority date of that invention, if the matter was contained in the application for that other patent both as filed and as published[9] and that the priority date of the matter is earlier than that of the invention[10]. Thus matter contained in a co-pending application is 'deemed' to be part of the prior art and can be used to attack the patent on the ground of lack of novelty[11].

For information to be 'made available to the public' the disclosure must be what has been called an 'enabling disclosure'[12], that is a disclosure which is sufficient to enable those skilled in the art to put the innovation into effect[13]. Disclosure and enablement are distinct concepts, each of which must be satisfied and each of which has different rules[14]. Thus, cases decided prior to the coming into force of the Patents Act 1977 where prior use alone could invalidate both product and process claims may no longer be good law[15]. In particular, prior secret use, whether by the patentee himself or by others, does not invalidate a patent[16].

1 Patents Act 1977 s 1(1)(a).
2 As to the extent of an invention see PARA 430 note 1.
3 Patents Act 1977 s 2(1).
4 As to the meaning of 'priority date' see PARA 310 note 6.
5 'Made available to the public' is accorded the same meaning as under the Patents Act 1949 (see the cases cited in PARA 445 et seq), namely that the requirement is satisfied if before its priority date the invention has been made known to at least one person other than its proprietor free in law and equity to deal with it as he pleases: see *Quantel Ltd v Spaceward Microsystems Ltd* [1990] RPC 83; *PLG Research Ltd v Ardon International Ltd* [1993] FSR 197 at 226; *Lux Traffic Controls Ltd v Pike Signals Ltd, Lux Traffic Controls Ltd v Faronwise Ltd* [1993] RPC 107. See also PARA 446.
6 As to the meaning of 'United Kingdom' see PARA 303 note 5.
7 Patents Act 1977 s 2(2).
8 This applies: (1) to an application for a patent under the Patents Act 1977 ss 14, 15 (see PARA 314 et seq) (see s 2(3); and PARA 434); (2) to an application for a European Patent (UK) (see s 78(1), (2); and PARA 653); and (3) to an international application for a patent (UK) (see s 89(1); and PARA 640). As to the meaning of 'European patent (UK)' see PARA 652 note 1; and as to the meaning of 'international application for a patent (UK)' see PARA 640 note 1.
    The occurrence of any of the events mentioned in the Patents Act 1977 s 78(5)(a) or (b) (see PARA 653) does not affect the continued operation of s 2(3) in relation to matter contained in an application for a European patent (UK) which by virtue of that provision has become part of the state of the art as regards other inventions; and the withdrawal of the designation of the United

Kingdom in the application does not prevent matter contained in an application for a European patent (UK) becoming part of the state of the art by virtue of s 2(3) as regards other inventions where the event occurs before the publication of that application: s 78(5A) (added by the Copyright, Designs and Patents Act 1988 Sch 5 para 22; and amended by the Patents Act 2004 Sch 1 paras 1, 3(1), (2)), reversing the effect of *L'Oreal's Application* [1986] RPC 19.

9   Patents Act 1977 s 2(3)(a). Any application made in relation to a patent in respect of which a prior application has been abandoned and published after it was abandoned is exempt from the state of art under s 2(3): *Woolard's Patent Application* [2002] EWHC 535 (Ch), [2002] RPC 767, overruling *Zbinden's Application* [2002] RPC 310.

10 Patents Act 1977 s 2(3)(b).

11 This is bare novelty only, not lack of inventive step: see PARA 451. The co-pending application must be construed as if it had been made available to the public just before the priority date of the patent in suit and in the light of the common general knowledge in the art at that time: *Genentech Inc's (Human Growth Hormone) Patent* [1989] RPC 613 at 644. The comptroller may of his own motion revoke a patent appearing to him to lack novelty only in this respect: see the Patents Act 1977 s 73(1); and PARA 569. As to the comptroller see PARA 575.

12 *Asahi Kasei Kogyo KK's Application* [1991] RPC 485 at 539, HL, per Lord Oliver of Aylmerton; *Quantel Ltd v Spaceward Microsystems Ltd* [1990] RPC 83 at 108.

13 Ie in the case of a claim to a product to enable the skilled man to make it (*Quantel Ltd v Spaceword Microsystems Ltd* [1990] RPC 83 at 108; *Genetech Inc's (Human Growth Hormone) Patent* [1989] RPC 613 at 634; Case T-206/83 *ICI/Pyridine herbicides* [1986] EPOR 232, Technical Board of Appeal (but see [1987] EPOR 112 (editors' note)), and in the case of a process to enable him to operate the process (*PLG Research Ltd v Ardon International Ltd* [1993] FSR 197 at 225; *Lux Traffic Controls Ltd v Pike Signals Ltd, Lux Traffic Controls Ltd v Faronwise Ltd* [1993] RPC 107 at 134). The standard of proof is that set out in *General Tire and Rubber Co v Firestone Tyre and Rubber Co Ltd* [1972] RPC 457 at 485, CA: *Lux Traffic Controls Ltd v Pike Signals Ltd, Lux Traffic Controls Ltd v Faronwise Ltd* at 129.

14 *Synthon BV v Smithkline Beecham* [2005] UKHL 59, [2006] 1 All ER 685, sub nom *Smithkline Beecham plc's (paroxetine methanesulfonate) patent* [2006] RPC 323. The matter relied upon as prior art must disclose subject matter which, if performed, would necessarily result in an infringement of the patent (see at [22] per Lord Hoffman); enablement means that the ordinary skilled person would have been able to perform the invention which satisfies the requirement of disclosure (see at [26] per Lord Hoffman).

15 In particular these cases where prior use of a product which did not reveal the nature or composition of a product nor the process by which it was made may not now be good law: see PARA 450. If, however, the prior art gives clear and unmistakable directions which enable a product to be made, that product forms part of the prior art even though nobody knew the product existed: *Merrell Dow Pharmaceuticals Ltd v NH Norton & Co Ltd* [1994] RPC 1 at 14 (metabolite produced in the human body as a result of taking a pharmaceutical as described in a prior patent). See also *Kavanagh Balloons Proprietary Ltd v Cameron Balloons Ltd* [2003] RPC 87 (revsd on other grounds [2003] EWCA Civ 1952, [2004] FSR 698, [2003] All ER (D) 212 (Dec)).

16 This follows from the phrase 'made available to the public'. The Patents Act 1977 s 64 provides a special defence to infringement for such third parties: see PARA 513.

435.   Non-prejudicial disclosures. The disclosure of matter constituting an invention[1] is to be disregarded in the case of a patent or an application for a patent if occurring later than six months immediately preceding the date of filing[2] the application for the patent and[3]:

   (1)   the disclosure was due to, or made in consequence of, the matter having been obtained unlawfully or in breach of confidence by any person:

      (a)   from the inventor[4] or from any other person to whom the matter was made available in confidence by the inventor or who obtained it from the inventor because he or the inventor believed he was entitled to obtain it; or

      (b)   from any other person to whom the matter was made available in confidence by any person mentioned in head (a) above or in this head or who obtained it from any such person because he or the person from whom he obtained it believed that he was entitled to obtain it[5];

(2) the disclosure was made in breach of confidence by any person who obtained the matter in confidence from the inventor or from any other person to whom it was made available, or who obtained it, from the inventor[6]; or

(3) the disclosure was due to, or made in consequence of[7], the inventor displaying the invention at an international exhibition[8] and the applicant states, on filing the application, that the invention has been so displayed and also, within the period of four months beginning immediately after the date of filing the application, files written evidence in support of the statement complying with any prescribed conditions[9].

1   As to the extent of an invention see PARA 430 note 1.
2   As to the meaning of 'date of filing' see PARA 315.
3   Patents Act 1977 s 2(4).
4   For these purposes, references to 'the inventor' include references to any proprietor of the invention for the time being: Patents Act 1977 s 2(5).
5   Patents Act 1977 s 2(4)(a).
6   Patents Act 1977 s 2(4)(b).
7   Publication before the exhibition, but in connection with it, is not 'in consequence' of display at the exhibition: *Re W Steel & Co Ltd's Application* [1958] RPC 411 (cited in PARA 730 note 7).
8   For these purposes, 'international exhibition' means an official or officially recognised international exhibition falling within the terms of the Convention relating to International Exhibitions (Paris, 22 November 1928; TS 9 (1931); Cmd 3776), as amended and supplemented by any Protocol to that Convention which is in force or falling within the terms of any subsequent treaty or convention replacing that convention: Patents Act 1977 s 130(1). The convention has been supplemented by Protocols, all signed at Paris, dated 10 May 1948 (TS 57 (1951); Cmd 8311), 16 November 1966 (TS 14 (1968); Cmnd 3557); 30 November 1972 (Misc 14 (1973); Cmnd 5317); 24 June 1982 (TS 82 (1983); Cmnd 9107); and 31 May 1988 (TS 4 (2003); Cm 5740). The convention applies to all international exhibitions (ie exhibitions where more than one state is invited to take part) except exhibitions lasting less than three weeks, fine arts exhibitions and exhibitions of an essentially commercial nature. Such official international exhibitions are rare. Rules may provide for stating in the Official Journal (Patents) (see PARA 578) that an exhibition is an international exhibition as defined by the Patents Act 1977 s 130(1); and any statement so published is conclusive evidence that the exhibition falls within the definition: s 130(2); Patents Rules 2007, SI 2007/3291, r 5(6).
9   Patents Act 1977 s 2(4)(c); Patents Rules 2007, SI 2007/3291, r 5(2) (amended by SI 2011/2052). The statement that an invention has been displayed at an international exhibition must be in writing: Patents Rules 2007, SI 2007/3291, r 5(1). However, where an applicant, on filing an international application for a patent (UK), states in writing to the receiving office that the invention has been displayed at an international exhibition then the prescribed period is two months beginning immediately after the date on which the national phase begins: rr 5(3), 67 (amended by SI 2011/2052). As to the meaning of 'international application for a patent (UK)' see PARA 640 note 1.
    The written evidence required by the Patents Act 1977 s 2(4)(c) must be in the form of: (1) a certificate issued by the authority responsible for the international exhibition; and (2) a statement, duly authenticated by that authority, identifying the invention as being the invention displayed at the exhibition: Patents Rules 2007, SI 2007/3291, r 5(4). The certificate must include the opening date of the exhibition (or if later, the date on which the invention was first displayed): r 5(5).

436.   Relevance of decided cases. Apart from the specific matters already noted[1], there is nothing to suggest that the Patents Act 1977 was intended to alter the concept of novelty in patent law, and reference may accordingly be made to earlier cases concerning novelty[2]. Cases decided by the European Patent Office[3] and the courts of member states of the European Patent Convention[4] are of persuasive authority[5].

1   See PARAS 430–435.
2   See PARA 437 et seq; and see in particular PARA 434 where 'enabling disclosure' and 'prior user' are discussed as to the differences over the cases decided before the Patents Act 1977.
3   See PARA 644.
4   Ie the Convention on the Grant of European Patents (Munich, 5 October 1973; TS 20 (1978); Cmnd 7090): see PARA 644 et seq.
5   See the Patents Act 1977 s 130(7) (amended by the Copyright, Designs and Patents Act 1988 Sch 8). The cases in the European Patent Office cited in PARAS 430–435, 451–498 have been referred to by the English courts.

437.   Test for novelty.   To anticipate a patent[1], a prior publication[2] or activity must contain the whole of the invention impugned[3], that is, all the features by which the particular claim attacked is limited. Thus, if a prior publication contains a clear description of, or clear instructions to do or make, something which would infringe the patentee's claim if carried out after the grant of the patentee's patent, the patentee's claim is bad for lack of novelty[4]. So also if, although it cannot be seen from a mere reading of a prior publication that a claim is anticipated, carrying out the directions contained in that prior publication will inevitably result in something being made or done which would infringe that claim[5]. The prior disclosure must be construed as it would have been understood by a person skilled in the art[6] at the date of the disclosure and not at the date of the subsequent patent[7].

Further, in order for the prior disclosure to constitute an anticipation, it must be an enabling disclosure in the sense that, if specific details are necessary for the practical working and real utility of the alleged invention, they must be found substantially in the prior publication[8]. Enablement means that the ordinary skilled person would have been able to perform the invention which satisfies the requirements of disclosure[9]. The concepts of disclosure and enablement are separate concepts and must be kept distinct[10]. If the prior disclosure is a written description, the skilled person is to be taken to be trying to understand what the author of the description meant, with his common general knowledge[11] forming the background to this exercise. Once the meaning of the prior disclosure has been ascertained, the disclosure is either of an invention which, if performed, would infringe the patent, or it is not. The person skilled in the art has no further part to play. For the purpose of enablement, the question is not what the skilled person would think the disclosure meant but whether he would be able to work the invention which the court has held it to disclose[12].

In particular, where what is claimed is a combination of integers so placed together that by their working interrelation they produce a new or improved result, the claim is not anticipated merely because the separate integers are old[13]. Thus a claim to such a combination cannot be shown to lack novelty by finding part of the combination in one prior document and part in another[14]. Equally, if any one or more of the features of the claim are new by themselves, or by themselves form a new combination, in the above sense, then the claim has novelty whatever other features may be present; it is no objection to the claim that it may be unnecessarily limited in scope[15].

1   'Anticipate' has come to mean specifically 'deprive of novelty' and it is used here in that sense. In older cases it often has the wider meaning of 'either deprive of novelty or render obvious'; it was so used in *British Thomson-Houston Co Ltd v Tungstalite Ltd* (1940) 57 RPC 271 at 289.
2   As to the meaning of 'publication' see PARA 445.
3   *Allmänna Svenska Elektriska AB v Burntisland Shipbuilding Co Ltd* (1952) 69 RPC 63 at 68, CA, citing *Otto v Linford* (1882) 46 LT 35, CA. As to sufficiency of prior publication see PARA 441.

4   *General Tire and Rubber Co v Firestone Tyre and Rubber Co Ltd* [1972] RPC 457 at 485, CA; *Letraset Ltd v Rexel Ltd* [1976] RPC 51, CA. See also *Molins v Industrial Machinery Co Ltd* [1937] 4 All ER 295 at 298, 55 RPC 31 at 40, CA.

5   *General Tire and Rubber Co v Firestone Tyre and Rubber Co Ltd* [1972] RPC 457 at 486, CA. The notional infringement must be necessarily entailed: *Synthon BV v Smithkline Beecham* [2005] UKHL 59 at [23], [2006] 1 All ER 685 at [23], sub nom *Smithkline Beecham plc's (paroxetine methanesulfonate) patent* [2006] RPC 323 at [23].

6   See PARA 441.

7   *Synthon BV v Smithkline Beecham* [2005] UKHL 59, [2006] 1 All ER 685, sub nom *Smithkline Beecham plc's (paroxetine methanesulfonate) patent* [2006] RPC 323.

8   *Asahi Kasei Kogyo KK's Application* [1991] RPC 485 at 538–539, HL.

9   *Synthon BV v Smithkline Beecham* [2005] UKHL 59 at [26], [2006] 1 All ER 685 at [26], sub nom *Smithkline Beecham plc's (paroxetine methanesulfonate) patent* [2006] RPC 323 at [26].

10 *Synthon BV v Smithkline Beecham* [2005] UKHL 59 at [28], [2006] 1 All ER 685 at [28], sub nom *Smithkline Beecham plc's (paroxetine methanesulfonate) patent* [2006] RPC 323 at [28].

11 See PARA 442.

12 *Synthon BV v Smithkline Beecham* [2005] UKHL 59 at [32], [2006] 1 All ER 685 at [32], sub nom *Smithkline Beecham plc's (paroxetine methanesulfonate) patent* [2006] RPC 323 at [32]. In testing the adequacy of the enablement, it may be assumed that the skilled man will have to use his skill and may have to learn by his mistakes: see *Synthon BV v Smithkline Beecham*, sub nom *Smithkline Beecham plc's (paroxetine methanesulfonate) patent* at [64]. It may be necessary to repeat any experiments or examples described in the prior document to demonstrate anticipation by actual result: see *Smithkline Beecham plc v Apotex Europe Ltd* [2004] EWCA Civ 1568, [2005] FSR 524; *Mayne Pharma Pty Ltd v Debiopharm SA* [2006] EWHC 164 (Pat), [2006] FSR 656; *Synthon BV v Smithkline Beecham*, sub nom *Smithkline Beecham plc's (paroxetine methanesulfonate) patent*.

13 *Martin and Biro Swan Ltd v H Millwood Ltd* [1956] RPC 125 at 132, HL, citing *British Celanese Ltd v Courtaulds Ltd* (1935) 52 RPC 171, HL; and *Clark v Adie* (1877) 2 App Cas 315 at 321, HL. If what is claimed is not a combination in this sense, but a 'mere collocation' of old integers without special working interrelation, the claim will be bad; but this objection is best put as 'not an invention within the meaning of the Act'.

14 Ie documents may not be 'mosaiced'. See *Allmänna Svenska Elektriska AB v Burntisland Shipbuilding Co Ltd* (1952) 69 RPC 63 at 68, CA; and *Martin and Biro Swan Ltd v H Millwood Ltd* [1956] RPC 125 at 138, HL.

15 *British United Shoe Machinery Co Ltd v A Fussell & Sons Ltd* (1908) 25 RPC 631 at 639, CA; *Molins v Industrial Machinery Co Ltd* [1937] 4 All ER 295 at 301, 55 RPC 31 at 43, CA.

438. Width of claim. A patent may be bad for want of novelty notwithstanding that something described in the specification, for example the embodiment of the invention described in detail and illustrated in the drawings, is new, for the claims will ordinarily be of such width as to cover other things besides a single embodiment, and a claim is bad if anything within it is old[1]. In particular, an anticipation[2] is nonetheless an anticipation because it fails to serve the purpose of the later invention[3], or is the work of an 'ignoramus'[4].

1   A clear example is *Molins v Industrial Machinery Co Ltd* [1937] 4 All ER 295, 55 RPC 31, CA.

2   As to the meaning of 'anticipate' see PARA 437 note 1.

3   *Molins v Industrial Machinery Co Ltd* [1937] 4 All ER 295, 55 RPC 31, CA. See also *Re Andrews' Patent* (1907) 24 RPC 349 at 371, CA, per Farwell LJ.

4   *Cleveland Graphite Bronze Co and Vandervell Products Ltd v Glacier Metal Co Ltd* (1949) 66 RPC 157 at 169, CA, per Greene MR.

439. Claim to method of use. There may be a valid patent for a new method of using an old machine or other article, or for an old article adjusted in a particular way[1]. Consequently, a claim to such a method of use[2] is not anticipated by a description of the article unless accompanied by clear and unmistakable instructions to use or adjust it in the manner claimed[3].

1   This proposition is clearly established by the cases cited in note 3 and in PARA 437 note 13, notwithstanding that the contrary proposition may be found in a number of decisions of inferior courts and tribunals.

2 Ie as distinct from a claim to the article itself, or to the article 'for' the new use: *Adhesive Dry Mounting Co Ltd v Trapp & Co* (1910) 27 RPC 341.
3 *Flour Oxidising Co Ltd v Carr & Co Ltd* (1908) 25 RPC 428, approved in *British Thomson-Houston Co Ltd v Metropolitan-Vickers Electrical Co Ltd* (1928) 45 RPC 1, HL; *Molins v Industrial Machinery Co Ltd* [1937] 4 All ER 295, 55 RPC 31, CA, explaining *British Thomson-Houston Co Ltd v Metropolitan-Vickers Electrical Co Ltd.*

440.   Selection patents. Since prima facie disclosure of a class involves disclosure of each of its members[1], a claim in the specification of a selection patent[2] to such a selected group prima facie lacks novelty[3], but such a claim may have not only novelty but also inventive subject matter if the members of the selected group have some special property not possessed by the class as a whole[4]. This property must be stated in the specification[5] as being a property in some sense peculiar to the selected class[6].

A mere statement of the properties which a substance must possess in order to serve the purpose for which the subjects of the later claim are required will not be regarded as a broad disclosure of the class of substances which possess those properties so as to make the claim a selection claim[7]. Beyond this, however, there is no reason to suppose that any special standard of disclosure is required[8]. The practice is to regard a general disclosure of substituted chemical compounds as disclosing only compounds having classes of substituents of which the specific examples given are fairly representative[9]. A document containing two lists of starting materials does not amount to a specific technical teaching of the combination of any two starting materials[10] and the disclosure of a racemate does not in itself amount to disclosure of each of its enantiomers[11].

A selection patent may be obtained even where the members of the selected class have been specifically disclosed and made provided that the alleged prior disclosure does not indicate that the selected class has the advantages predicted for the class[12]. Prior knowledge of the materials from which a substance may be synthesised, and of the method of synthesis, is not prior knowledge of the substance[13].

1 *Shell Refining and Marketing Co Ltd's Patent* [1959] RPC 154; on appeal [1960] RPC 35, CA.
2 As to the meaning of 'selection patent' see PARA 320.
3 As to the objection of lack of novelty generally, and as to the test to be applied, see PARA 437.
4 *Re IG Farbenindustrie AG's Patents* (1930) 47 RPC 289; *Re May and Baker Ltd and Ciba Ltd's Letters Patent* (1948) 65 RPC 255 at 281; *Shell Refining and Marketing Co Ltd's Patent* [1960] RPC 35 at 53–57, CA.
5 *Re IG Farbenindustrie AG's Patents* (1930) 47 RPC 289; *Hallen Co v Brabantia (UK) Ltd* [1991] RPC 195 at 218, CA.
6 *Shell Refining and Marketing Co Ltd's Patent* [1960] RPC 35 at 53, 57, CA, citing *Re IG Farbenindustrie AG's Patents* (1930) 47 RPC 289. In what sense the property must be peculiar to the class is not clear. For a chemical case in which the general class was too small to admit a valid selection see *Beecham Group Ltd's (Amoxycillin) Application* [1980] RPC 261, CA.
7 *Re Dreyfus, Moncrieff and Sammons' Application* (1945) 62 RPC 125.
8 *Shell Refining and Marketing Co Ltd's Patent* [1960] RPC 35 at 54, CA, doubting *Re Kendall and Fry's Applications* (1948) 65 RPC 323 on this point. In particular, the truth of the statements in the prior documents would seem to be immaterial.
9 *Re Kendall and Fry's Applications* (1948) 65 RPC 323.
10 *Decision T12/81 BAYER/Diastereomers* [1979–85] EPOR Vol B 308.
11 *Generics (UK) Ltd v H Lundbeck A/S* [2008] EWCA Civ 311, 101 BMLR 52, [2008] RPC 437 (affd [2009] UKHL 12, [2009] 2 All ER 955, 107 BMLR 121).
12 *EI du Pont de Nemours & Co (Witsiepe's) Application* [1982] FSR 303, HL (claim to polyesters based on 1,4-butane diol and having a specific property held valid over prior disclosure of a class of polyesters based on diols of which 1,4-butane diol was named as one of the diols suitable).
13 *Re May and Baker Ltd and Ciba Ltd's Letters Patent* (1948) 65 RPC 255 at 281.

441.   The skilled addressee. To anticipate a later invention, a publication must contain an enabling disclosure[1]. The notional 'person skilled in the art' to whom the prior publication and the specification are deemed to be addressed is the skilled man reasonably versed in the art in question and who has the common general knowledge in relation to that art[2]. He is assumed to be of standard competence, well acquainted with workshop technique, but without being of an imaginative or inventive turn of mind and who has carefully read the relevant literature[3]. It is well established that the skilled addressee may not be an individual but a team who combine a variety of skills[4]. In the case of inventions at the cutting edge of science and technology, the skilled person or team may, in fact, be very highly skilled indeed[5].

1   See PARA 437.
2   *General Tire and Rubber Co v Firestone Tyre and Rubber Co Ltd* [1972] RPC 457 at 482, CA; for examples of a 'person skilled in the art' see *Generics (UK) Ltd v Daiichi Pharmaceutical Co Ltd* [2009] EWCA Civ 646, 109 BMLR 78, [2009] RPC 828; *Unilever plc v SC Johnson & Son Ltd* [2012] EWPCC 19, [2012] All ER (D) 75 (Jun); *Mölnlycke Health Care AB v BSN Medical Ltd* [2012] EWHC 3157 (Pat), [2012] All ER (D) 141 (Nov). As to the attributes of the skilled person in relation to inventive step see PARA 455.
3   *General Tire and Rubber Co v Firestone Tyre and Rubber Co Ltd* [1972] RPC 457 at 504, CA, citing *Technograph Printed Circuits Ltd v Mills and Rockley (Electronics) Ltd* [1972] RPC 346, HL. See also *Windsurfing International Inc v Tabur Marine (Great Britain) Ltd* [1985] RPC 59 at 72, CA; *Pfizer's Patent* [2001] FSR 201 at 226–227; *Rockwater v Technip France SA* [2004] EWCA Civ 381, [2004] RPC 919, [2004] All ER (D) 63 (Apr); *Nichia Corpn v Argos Ltd* [2007] EWCA Civ 741 at [10], [2007] FSR 895 at [10].
4   *General Tire and Rubber Co v Firestone Tyre and Rubber Co Ltd* [1972] RPC 457 at 482, CA. See also *Genentech Inc's Patent* [1989] RPC 147 at 278, 280, CA. The notional skilled person is a legal construct and should not be equated to the lowest common denominator of all the persons skilled in the art at the time: *Halliburton Energy Services Inc v Smith International (North Sea) Ltd* [2005] EWHC 1623 (Pat) at [39], [2006] RPC 25 at [39]. Where the fictional skilled person is a team, consideration must be given to the reality of how teams operate in real research situations: see *Schlumberger Holdings Ltd v Electromagnetic Geoservices AS* [2010] EWCA Civ 819, [2010] RPC 851, [2011] IP & T 548 (notional skilled person might not be the same for every purpose: skilled addressee for purposes of obviousness may be different from skilled addressee for purposes of claim construction and legitimacy); *MedImmune Ltd v Novartis Pharmaceuticals UK Ltd* [2012] EWCA Civ 1234, [2013] RPC 659, [2013] IP & T 536.
5   See e g *Genentech Inc's (Human Growth Hormone) Patent* [1989] RPC 613 at 619–620 (skilled person a team of persons of PhD standard including microbiologists versed in recombinant DNA techniques and chemists skilled in the synthesis of biochemical compounds). See also *Genentech Inc's Patent* [1989] RPC 147 at 246, 278, CA.

442.   Common general knowledge. Common general knowledge is the sort of knowledge which would in fact be known by the appropriately skilled addressee[1]. It is the mental equipment that is necessary for competency in the field of endeavour in question and in that sense is knowledge over and above the general knowledge which an ordinary member of the public would possess[2]. It is different from 'public' knowledge which includes matter which has been publicly disclosed but which may be unknown to the skilled addressee[3]. Common general knowledge may include the contents of the standard textbooks that the skilled addressee would have[4] but a published patent specification would not usually be something which is common general knowledge although in a rapidly developing art the position may be different if it is proved that such specifications are commonly widely read[5].

1   For a recital of the law on common general knowledge see *Apimed Medical Honey Ltd v Brightwake Ltd (t/a Advancis medical)* [2012] EWCA Civ 5, [2012] RPC 373, [2012] All ER (D) 155 (Jan). As to the skilled addressee see PARA 441.

2   *Vector Corpn v Glatt Air Techniques Inc* [2007] EWCA Civ 805, [2008] RPC 243, [2007] All
     ER (D) 297 (Oct).
3   *General Tire and Rubber Co v Firestone Tyre and Rubber Co Ltd* [1972] RPC 457 at 482, CA;
     Beloit Technologies Inc v Valmet Paper Machinery Inc [1997] RPC 489, CA; *Re
     Richardson-Vicks Inc's Patent* [1997] RPC 888, CA; *Smithkline Beecham plc v Apotex
     Europe Ltd* [2004] EWCA Civ 1568, [2005] FSR 524 at 533; *Ivax Pharmaceuticals UK Ltd v
     Akzo Nobel NV* [2006] EWHC 1089 (Ch), [2007] RPC 45, [2006] All ER (D) 308 (May);
     Generics (UK) Ltd v Daiichi Pharmaceutical Co Ltd [2009] EWCA Civ 646, [2009] RPC 828,
     109 BMLR 78.
4   *Vector Corpn v Glatt Air Techniques Inc* [2007] EWCA Civ 805, [2008] RPC 243, [2007] All
     ER (D) 297 (Oct); *Unilever plc v SC Johnson & Son Ltd* [2012] EWPCC 19, [2012] All ER (D)
     75 (Jun). See also *Omnipharm Ltd v Merial* [2011] EWHC 3393 (Pat), [2012] All ER (D) 21
     (Jan) (it is not sufficient to prove common general knowledge that a particular disclosure is
     made in an article, or series of articles, in a scientific journal, no matter how wide the circulation
     of that journal might be, in the absence of any evidence that the disclosure is accepted generally
     by those who are engaged in the art to which the disclosure relates).
5   See *Bridgestone/Rubber Composition* [1990] EPOR 483.

443.   Drawings.   A drawing alone may constitute an anticipation[1] provided
that the whole invention is made clear by it. The question is what the skilled
addressee[2] would see in a technical drawing and this is a matter of evidence[3].

1   *Herrburger Schwander & Cie v Squire* (1889) 6 RPC 194, CA; *Electric Construction Co Ltd v
     Imperial Tramways Co Ltd* (1900) 17 RPC 537 at 550, CA. In many cases drawings with or
     without short descriptions have been held insufficient to amount to disclosure: see *Plimpton v
     Spiller* (1877) 6 ChD 412, CA; *Bray v Gardner* (1887) 4 RPC 400; *Watson, Laidlaw & Co Ltd
     v Pott, Cassels and Williamson* (1909) 26 RPC 349, Ct of Sess (on appeal (1911) 28 RPC
     565, HL). As to the meaning of 'anticipate' see PARA 437 note 1.
2   As to the skilled addressee see PARA 441.
3   *BSH Industries Ltd's Patent* [1995] RPC 183 at 190.

444.   Errors in publication.   Errors in a prior publication[1], or the drawings
attached to it, do not destroy its effect unless they would prevent the skilled
addressee[2] from grasping what it purports to disclose[3]. So, too, an error in
theory may not prevent a prior publication from being an anticipation[4] unless
the error conceals the meaning of the prior publication[5], even though the reader
can see it to be the work of an 'ignoramus'[6].

1   As to the meaning of 'publication' see PARA 445.
2   As to the skilled addressee see PARA 441.
3   *Barlow v Baylis* (1870) Griffin's Patent Cases (1884–1886) 44 at 45; *Amalgamated
     Carburetters Ltd v Bowden Wire Ltd* (1931) 48 RPC 105 at 119.
4   As to the meaning of 'anticipate' see PARA 437 note 1.
5   *Re Andrews' Patent* (1907) 24 RPC 349 at 366, CA; on appeal (1908) 25 RPC 477, HL. See
     also *Thomson v Macdonald & Co* (1891) 8 RPC 5.
6   *Cleveland Graphite Bronze Co and Vandervell Products Ltd v Glacier Metal Co Ltd* (1949)
     66 RPC 157 at 175, CA, per Greene MR; affd (1950) 67 RPC 149, HL (if, however, the
     question is one of obviousness, the weight to be given to such a publication will ordinarily be
     small).

445.   Meaning of 'published' and 'publication'.   In the Patents Act 1977,
'published' means made available to the public[1]. Publication of a document is
established by showing that it was exposed in such a way that the public in
general, or some section of it, had access to it, for example, in a bookshop[2], or a
room in a library to which the public had access[3]. Any document which can be
inspected as of right, at any place in the United Kingdom[4] by members of the
public, whether on payment of a fee or otherwise, is deemed to be published[5].
Alternatively, publication may be established by proving, either directly[6] or by
inference[7], that some member of the public saw and read it[8].

How soon after receipt a document may be presumed to have been published will normally be a question of fact[9]. A document in a foreign language is an effective publication[10].

1   See the Patents Act 1977 s 130(1); and PARA 326 note 7. 'Published' had the same meaning in the Patents Act 1949: see s 101 (repealed). See *Re Monsanto Co (Brignac's) Application* [1971] RPC 153, Patents Appeal Tribunal (where salesmen were given a limited number of copies of a bulletin and there was no fetter on them as regards information contained in it, there was held to be prior publication to the public).

2   *Lang v Gisborne* (1862) 31 Beav 133; *Pickard and Currey v Prescott* [1892] AC 263, 9 RPC 195, HL.

3   *United Telephone Co v Harrison, Cox-Walker & Co* (1882) 21 ChD 720; *Harris v Rothwell* (1887) 35 ChD 416 at 431, 4 RPC 225 at 232, CA; *Rucker v London Electric Supply Corpn Ltd* (1900) 17 RPC 279 at 295; *VD Ltd v Boston Deep Sea Fishing and Ice Co Ltd* (1935) 52 RPC 303.

4   As to the meaning of 'United Kingdom' see PARA 303 note 5.

5   Patents Act 1977 s 130(1). Identical provision was made in the Patents Act 1949: see s 101(1) (repealed). Documents in the library of the UK Intellectual Property Office, including in particular many foreign patent specifications and convention applications open to public inspection, fall into this category. As to the UK Intellectual Property Office see PARA 577.

6   *Re Crowther's Application for a Patent* (1933) 51 RPC 72.

7   *Pickard and Currey v Prescott* [1892] AC 263, 9 RPC 195, HL (where it was inferred that British subscribers to a foreign periodical would read it soon after receipt).

8   *Pickard and Currey v Prescott* [1892] AC 263, 9 RPC 195, HL; *Plimpton v Malcolmson* (1876) 3 ChD 531; *Humpherson v Syer* (1887) 4 RPC 407, CA. See also *Bristol-Myers Co's Application* [1969] RPC 146, DC.

9   *Harris v Rothwell* (1887) 35 ChD 416, 4 RPC 225, CA.

10 *Harris v Rothwell* (1887) 35 ChD 416, 4 RPC 225, CA. For all practical purposes, publication in any language counts.

446.   Confidential disclosure.   A document disclosed only to persons under a legal or moral obligation of confidence, so that they are not free to make use of the information acquired for their own purposes, is not published[1], for such persons are not members of the public[2]. A document sufficiently widely circulated may, however, be published, even though purporting to be confidential[3]. A document disclosed to persons under a public duty to publish the information acquired is published even though they agree to keep it confidential[4].

1   As to the meaning of 'published' see PARA 445.

2   *Humpherson v Syer* (1887) 4 RPC 407, CA; *Pilkington v Yeakley Vacuum Hammer Co* (1901) 18 RPC 459, CA; *Fomento Industrial SA, Biro Swan Ltd v Mentmore Manufacturing Co Ltd* [1956] RPC 87 at 89, CA; *Bristol-Myer Co's Application* [1969] RPC 146. See also *Re Underfeed Stoker Co Ltd and Robey's Application* (1924) 41 RPC 622; *Re G and J Weir Ltd's Application* (1925) 43 RPC 39; *Re Mooney's Application* (1927) 44 RPC 294; *Re Gallay's Application* [1959] RPC 141; *Re Monsanto Co (Brignac's) Application* [1971] RPC 153, Patents Appeal Tribunal; *PLG Research Ltd v Ardon International Ltd* [1993] FSR 197 at 225–226; *Kavanagh Balloons Propriety Ltd v Cameron Balloons Ltd* [2003] EWCA Civ 1952, [2004] RPC 87; *Visx Inc v Nidex Co* [1999] FSR 405 at 440.

3   *Re Williams' Application, Re Young's Application* (1943) 60 RPC 51; *Re Dalrymple's Application* [1957] RPC 449.

4   *Patterson v Gas Light and Coke Co* (1887) 3 App Cas 239, HL.

447.   Publication by sale, exhibition or samples.   Similar considerations as in the case of written publication[1] apply to publication by sale[2], exhibition or the use of samples of an article previously made. If the article relied on has been placed in the hands of the public and examination or analysis would afford sufficient information for its preparation[3], or if it has been exhibited or used in public so that its construction is apparent[4], the publication is effective so far as a later patent is concerned.

1   See PARAS 445–446. As to the meaning of 'publication' see PARA 445.

2   *Strachan and Henshaw Ltd v Pakcel Ltd* (1948) 66 RPC 49 at 68. See also *Re Wikmanshytte Bruks AB's Application* [1961] RPC 180 (sale for export and delivery fo b London held not to be prior use).

3   *Re Miller's Patent* (1898) 15 RPC 205, CA; *Re Stahlwerk Becker AG's Patent* (1918) 36 RPC 13, HL; *Re Monsanto Co (Brignac's) Application* [1971] RPC 153; *Bristol-Myers Co v Beecham Group Ltd* [1974] AC 646, [1974] 1 All ER 333, sub nom *Bristol-Myers Co (Johnson's) Application* [1975] RPC 127, HL.

4   *JD Insulating and Refrigerating Co Ltd v Thos Anderson Ltd* (1923) 41 RPC 1 at 31. See also *Carpenter v Smith* (1841) 1 Web Pat Cas 530; *Brereton v Richardson* (1883) 1 RPC 165; *Lifeboat Co Ltd v Chambers Bros & Co* (1891) 8 RPC 418; *Re Taylor's Patent* (1896) 13 RPC 482; *Stohwasser and Winter v Humphreys and Crook* (1900) 18 RPC 116; *Re Poulton's Patent* (1906) 23 RPC 506 at 508, CA; *Woodrow v Long, Humphreys & Co Ltd* (1933) 50 RPC 203 (affd 51 RPC 25, CA).

448.   Oral disclosure.   Prior oral disclosure of an invention is sufficient to invalidate a later patent for it[1]. The only question is whether any member of the public in the United Kingdom[2], not being one who himself invented it[3], has come into possession of it otherwise than in confidence[4].

1   *Humpherson v Syer* (1887) 4 RPC 407, CA.

2   As to the meaning of 'United Kingdom' see PARA 303 note 5.

3   *Dolland's Case* (1766) 1 Web Pat Cas 43.

4   See PARA 446.

449.   Publication by use.   An invention will be published[1], so as to invalidate a subsequent patent, even though there is no deliberate display of it and it never comes into the hands of the public, by its use in a public place, so as to enable members of the public to see and understand it[2]. Use on private premises, in a place where members of the public in fact penetrate so as to see the invention, will suffice[3]. The fact that the use excited no interest and created no public demand is immaterial[4].

1   As to the meaning of 'published' see PARA 445.

2   *Carpenter v Smith* (1841) 1 Web Pat Cas 530 at 534 per Lord Abinger CB; *Stead v Williams* (1843) 2 Web Pat Cas 126 at 136; *Croysdale v Fisher* (1884) 1 RPC 17; *Young and Neilson v Rosenthal & Co* (1884) 1 RPC 29; *Humpherson v Syer* (1887) 4 RPC 407, CA; *Lifeboat Co Ltd v Chambers Bros & Co* (1891) 8 RPC 418; *Re Taylor's Patent* (1896) 13 RPC 482; *Gramophone Co Ltd v Ruhl* (1910) 27 RPC 629 (on appeal (1911) 28 RPC 20, CA); *Woodrow v Long, Humphreys & Co Ltd* (1933) 50 RPC 203 at 207 (on appeal (1934) 51 RPC 25, CA); *Re Monsanto Co (Brignac's) Application* [1971] RPC 153, Patent Appeals Tribunal; *Windsurfing International Inc v Tabur Marine (Great Britain) Ltd* [1985] RPC 59, CA. See also *Lux Traffic Controls Ltd v Pike Signals Ltd, Lux Traffic Controls Ltd v Faronwise Ltd* [1993] RPC 107 at 134 (where it was said that what was made available was that which the skilled addressee would write down if asked to describe its construction and operation); *Kavanagh Balloons Propriety Ltd v Cameron Balloons Ltd* [2003] EWCA Civ 1952, [2004] RPC 87.

3   *Lewis v Marling* (1829) 1 Web Pat Cas 493; *Bentley v Fleming* (1844) 1 Car & Kir 587; *Moss v Malings* (1886) 33 ChD 603, 3 RPC 373; *Moseley v Victoria Rubber Co* (1887) 57 LT 142, 4 RPC 241; *Electrolytic Plating Apparatus Co Ltd v Holland* (1901) 18 RPC 521 at 527.

4   *Losh v Hague* (1837) 1 Web Pat Cas 200 at 205; *Windsurfing International Inc v Tabur Marine (Great Britain) Ltd* [1985] RPC 59, CA.

450.   Abandoned or accidental user.   The fact that the user has long been abandoned does not prevent invalidation unless the art is in fact lost[1].

It is probable that a user which was fortuitous, and from which the person using it gained no real knowledge of the invention, and would not have been led to adopt it, is insufficient to invalidate a subsequent patent[2].

1   In *Re Wright's Patent* (1843) 1 Web Pat Cas 736, PC, an extension of term was granted for a patent which admittedly was for the rediscovery of a process known in the Middle Ages but was since lost.
2   *Harwood v Great Northern Rly Co* (1860) 29 LJQB 193 at 202 per Blackburn J; on appeal (1862) 31 LJQB 198 at 200. Cf *Spilsbury and Abbott v Clough* (1842) 1 Web Pat Cas 255 at 259n and the cases there referred to; *Rockliffe v Priestman & Co* (1898) 15 RPC 155; *Boyce v Morris Motors Ltd* (1926) 44 RPC 105 at 134, CA; *John Wright and Eagle Range Ltd v General Gas Appliances Ltd* (1928) 46 RPC 169 at 176, 183, CA. A different view seems to have been taken in *British Thomson-Houston Co Ltd v Duram Ltd* (1917) 34 RPC 117 at 148 per Astbury J, although this point is not referred to in the judgments in the higher courts. See also *Technic Inc's Application* [1973] RPC 383, CA (user not fortuitous); *Windsurfing International Inc v Tabur Marine (Great Britain) Ltd* [1985] RPC 59 at 77, CA (user not trivial or fortuitous).

(iv) Obviousness

451.   Invention obvious.   An invention[1] is unpatentable, as involving no inventive step[2], if it is obvious to a person skilled in the art[3] having regard to any matter, whether a product, a process, information about either or anything else, which has at any time before the priority date[4] of the invention been made available to the public[5], whether in the United Kingdom or elsewhere[6], by written or oral description, by use or in any other way[7]. Unlike the scope of the prior art when considering the novelty of an invention[8], the prior art for testing obviousness does not include the contents of unpublished co-pending applications[9]. Apart from the lack of geographical and temporal limitations on the prior art there is no clear indication[10] that the Patents Act 1977 was intended to alter the accepted concept of obviousness. Reference may accordingly be made to earlier decided cases concerning obviousness[11].

1   As to the extent of an invention see PARA 430 note 1.
2   See the Patents Act 1977 s 1(1)(b); and PARA 429.
3   As to persons skilled in the art see PARAS 441, 455.
4   As to the meaning of 'priority date' see PARA 310 note 6.
5   As to the meaning of 'made available to the public' see PARA 434 notes 5, 12–16.
6   As to the meaning of 'United Kingdom' see PARA 303 note 5.
7   Patents Act 1977 ss 2(2), 3.
8   As to novelty see PARA 434 et seq.
9   For these purposes, the Patents Act 1977 s 2(3) is to be disregarded: s 3.
10 Whilst the test is a statutory test, the guidelines in *Windsurfing International Inc v Tabur Marine (Great Britain) Ltd* [1985] RPC 59, CA (see PARA 454) are widely regarded as useful: see *Pozzoli SPA v BDMO SA* [2007] EWCA Civ 588 at [14], [2007] FSR 872 at [14]; *Belvac Production Machinery Inc v Carnaudmetalbox Engineering Ltd* [2009] EWHC 292 (Ch), [2009] All ER (D) 266 (Feb). As to the effect of decisions of the European Patent Office and the courts of other countries which are parties to the Convention on the Grant of European Patents (Munich, 5 October 1973; TS 20 (1978); Cmnd 7090) (the European Patent Convention) see PARA 644.
11 See PARA 452 et seq.

452.   Relation to novelty.   Not everything that is new is inventive[1] and it is necessary to distinguish between the questions of obviousness and of lack of novelty[2].

1   See *Gadd and Mason v Manchester Corpn* (1892) 67 LT 576 at 578, 9 RPC 516 at 524, CA, and the cases there cited. See also *Harwood v Great Northern Rly Co* (1864) 11 HL Cas 654; *Riekmann v Thierry* (1897) 14 RPC 105, HL.

2   The approach of the appellate court to the issues of novelty and of obviousness may well be different as the former involves a precise legal standard whereas the latter does not: *Rockwater v Technip France SA* [2004] EWCA Civ 381 at [71]–[74], [2004] RPC 919 at [71]–[74].

453.   Relation to width of claim. Everything falling within the claim concerned must have inventive subject matter, or the claim will be invalid, even though it also covers things that are inventive[1]. One of the matters which it may be appropriate to take into account is whether it was obvious to try a particular route to an improved product or process[2].

1   *Woodrow v Long, Humphrey & Co Ltd* (1933) 51 RPC 25, CA. The typical case is that where what is described and illustrated in the specification is inventive, but most of the claims are wider than the invention: see e g *Raleigh Cycle Co Ltd v H Miller & Co Ltd* [1948] 1 All ER 308, 65 RPC 141, HL. See also *Halliburton Energy Service Inc v Smith International (North Sea) Ltd* [2005] EWHC 1623 (Pat) at [174], [2006] RPC 25 at [174].

2   See e g *Conor Medsystems Inc v Angiotech Pharmaceuticals Inc* [2007] EWCA Civ 5, [2007] RPC 487, 94 BMLR 122 (affd [2008] UKHL 49, [2008] 4 All ER 621, 103 BMLR 100); *Novartis AG v Generics (UK) Ltd* [2012] EWCA Civ 1623, [2012] All ER (D) 126 (Dec); *Smith & Nephew plc v Convatec Technologies Inc* [2012] EWCA Civ 1638, [2013] RPC 223, [2012] All ER (D) 147 (Dec); *MedImmune Ltd v Novartis Pharmaceuticals UK Ltd* [2012] EWCA Civ 1234 at [90]–[93], [2013] RPC 659 at [90]–[93], [2013] IP & T 536 at [90]–[93].

454.   Test of obviousness. The statutory question is whether the invention is obvious to the notional person skilled in the art. A four-stage test for obviousness has been established by the courts[1]:

(1)   identify the notional 'person skilled in the art'[2] and identify the relevant common general knowledge[3] of that person;

(2)   identify the inventive concept of the claim in question or if that cannot readily be done, construe it;

(3)   identify what, if any, differences exist between the matter cited as forming part of the 'state of the art' and the inventive concept of the claim or the claim as construed; and

(4)   decide whether, viewed without any knowledge of the alleged invention[4] as claimed, those differences constitute steps which would have been obvious to the person skilled in the art or whether they require any degree of invention[5].

The European Patent Office has adopted the so-called 'problem and solution' approach in order to assess inventive step. This approach requires: (a) determining the closest prior art; (b) establishing the objective technical problem to be solved; and (c) considering whether or not the claimed invention, starting from the closest prior art and the objective technical problem, would have been obvious to the skilled person. In most cases, this approach is unlikely to produce a different result from that produced by the adoption of the guidelines in heads (1) to (4) above, and where the results do differ this is likely to be due to the importance accorded by those guidelines to the common general knowledge of the skilled addressee[6].

1   See *Pozzoli SPA v BDMO SA* [2007] EWCA Civ 588, [2007] FSR 872, [2007] All ER (D) 275 (Jun), recasting the test established in *Windsurfing International Inc v Tabur Marine (Great Britain) Ltd* [1985] RPC 59 at 73, CA. 'The question of obviousness must be considered on the facts of each case. The court must consider the weight to be attached to any particular factor in the light of all the relevant circumstances. These may include such matters as the motive to find a solution to the problem the patent addresses, the number and extent of the possible avenues of research, the effort involved in pursuing them and the expectation of success' (*Generics (UK) Ltd v H Lundbeck A/S* [2007] EWHC 1040 (Pat) at [72], [2007] RPC 729 at [72], [2007] All ER (D) 87 (May), per Kitchin J (revsd on other grounds [2008] EWCA Civ 311, [2008] RPC 437, [2009] All ER (D) 152 (Apr); [2009] UKHL 12, [2009] 2 All ER 955, [2009] IP & T 496)).

The structured approach to deciding obviousness is useful, but not essential: *David J Instance Ltd v Denny Bros Printing Ltd* [2001] EWCA Civ 939, [2002] RPC 321, [2001] All ER (D) 201 (Jun). In connection with the application of the obviousness test see also *Haberman v Jackel International Ltd* [1999] FSR 683 (simplicity is not a bar to invention); *PLG Research Ltd v Ardon International Ltd* [1995] RPC 287, CA; *Reckitt & Colman Products Ltd v Richardson-Vicks Ltd; Smith Kline Beecham v Richardson-Vicks Inc* (1995) 25 BMLR 63; *Palmaz's European Patents (UK)* [2000] RPC 631, CA; *Minnesota Mining and Manufacturing Co v ATI Atlas Ltd* [2001] FSR 514; *Panduit Corpn v Band-It Co Ltd* [2002] EWCA Civ 465, [2003] FSR 127; *Smithkline Beecham plc v Apotex Europe Ltd* [2004] EWCA Civ 1568, [2005] FSR 524; *Novartis AG v Ivax Pharmaceuticals UK Ltd* [2006] EWHC 2506 (Pat), [2006] All ER (D) 172 (Oct); *Sabaf SpA v MFI Furniture Centres Ltd* [2004] UKHL 45, [2005] RPC 209; *Ultraframe (UK) Ltd v Eurocell Building Plastics Ltd* [2005] EWCA Civ 761, [2005] RPC 894, [2006] IP & T 222; *Ivax Pharmaceuticals UK Ltd v Akzo Nobel NV* [2006] EWHC 1089 (Ch), [2007] RPC 45; *Conor Medsystems Inc v Angiotech Pharmaceuticals Inc* [2008] UKHL 49, [2008] 4 All ER 621, [2008] RPC 716; *Schlumberger Holdings Ltd v Electromagnetic Geoservices AS* [2010] EWCA Civ 819, [2011] IP & T 548; *Hexal AG v AstraZeneca AB* [2013] EWCA Civ 454, [2013] All ER (D) 247 (Apr); *Regeneron Pharmaceuticals Inc v Genentech Inc* [2013] EWCA Civ 93, [2013] RPC 703, [2013] IP & T 619 (in considering obviousness it is not inappropriate for the court to consider the prospects for the invention's success).

2   As to who is the skilled addressee see PARA 455.

3   As to the extent of common general knowledge see PARA 456.

4   The courts have consistently warned against ex post facto analysis of the invention: *British Westinghouse Electric and Manufacturing Co v Braulik* (1910) 27 RPC 209 at 230, CA; *Samuel Parkes & Co Ltd v Cocker Bros Ltd* (1929) 46 RPC 241 at 249, CA; *Non-Drip Measure Co Ltd v Stranger's Ltd* (1943) 60 RPC 135 at 142, HL, per Lord Russell of Killowen; *Technograph Printed Circuits Ltd v Mills and Rockley (Electronics) Ltd* [1972] RPC 346 at 362, HL, per Lord Diplock; *Hickman v Andrews* [1983] RPC 147 at 193, CA; *Fichera v Flogates Ltd* [1984] RPC 257 at 274, CA; *C Van der Lely NV v Ruston's Engineering Co Ltd* [1985] RPC 461 at 498, CA; *Fairfax (Dental Equipment) Ltd v SJ Filhol Ltd* [1986] RPC 499 at 511, CA; *T Bonzel v Intervention Ltd (No 3)* [1991] RPC 553 at 579.

5   *Pozzoli SPA v BDMO SA* [2007] EWCA Civ 588 at [23], [2007] FSR 872 at [23], [2007] All ER (D) 275 (Jun) at [23] per Jacob LJ, giving the judgment of the court. See also *Windsurfing International Inc v Tabur Marine (Great Britain) Ltd* [1985] RPC 59, CA; *Fairfax (Dental Equipment) Ltd v SJ Filhol Ltd* [1986] RPC 499, CA; *Procter & Gamble Co v Peaudouce (UK) Ltd* [1989] FSR 180 at 189, CA; *Hallen Co v Brabantia (UK) Ltd* [1991] RPC 195 at 213, CA; *Helitune Ltd v Stewart Hughes Ltd* [1991] FSR 171 at 190; *Minnesota Mining & Manufacturing Co v Rennicks (UK) Ltd* [1992] RPC 331 at 350; *Shoketsu Kinzoku Kogyo KK's Patent* [1992] FSR 184 at 189; *PLG Research Ltd v Ardon International Ltd* [1993] FSR 197 at 231; *Mölnlycke AB v Procter & Gamble Ltd (No 5)* [1994] RPC 49 at 115, CA; *Ivax Pharmaceuticals UK Ltd v Akzo Nobel NV* [2006] EWHC 1089 (Ch), [2007] RPC 45; *Conor Medsystems Inc v Angiotech Pharmaceuticals Inc* [2008] UKHL 49, [2008] 4 All ER 621, [2008] RPC 716; *Generics (UK) Ltd v H Lundbeck A/S* [2009] UKHL 12, [2009] 2 All ER 955, [2009] IP & T 496; *Glenmark Generics (Europe) Ltd v Wellcome Foundation Ltd* [2013] EWHC 148 (Pat), 132 BMLR 105, [2013] All ER (D) 95 (Feb) (what matters is whether or not the invention is technically obvious, not whether it is commercially obvious).

6   *Ranbaxy UK Ltd v Warner-Lambert Co* [2005] EWHC 2142 (Pat) at [66]–[69], [2006] FSR 209 at [66]–[69].

455. The skilled addressee. The notional person against whom the obviousness of an invention must be tested is the uninventive person skilled in the art, capable of assimilating the contents of scores of specifications, but incapable of a scintilla of invention[1]. Where the relevant art is highly technical, the notional addressee may be a team as opposed to a single individual[2]; and, where the subject matter covers more than one discipline, the notional addressee may be expected to consult others or be a team[3].

1   *Technograph Printed Circuits Ltd v Mills and Rockley (Electronics) Ltd* [1972] RPC 346 at 355, HL, per Lord Reid. See also PARA 442 and the cases there cited.

2   *Osram-Robertson Lamp Works Ltd v Pope's Electric Lamp Co Ltd* (1917) 34 RPC 369, HL; *General Tire and Rubber Co v Firestone Tyre and Rubber Co Ltd* [1972] RPC 457 at 482,

485, CA; *Genentech Inc's (Human Growth Hormone) Patent* [1989] RPC 613 at 619. Where a notional addressee has to consult others, the test for obviousness must be based on the common knowledge of all and not on the narrow area of knowledge of each individual consulted: *Inhale Therapeutic Systems Inc v Quadrant Healthcare plc* [2002] RPC 419. See also *Halliburton Energy Services Inc v Smith International (North Sea) Ltd* [2005] EWHC 1623 (Pat) at [39], [2006] RPC 25 at [39]; *Hexal AG v AstraZeneca AB* [2013] EWCA Civ 454, [2013] All ER (D) 247 (Apr). Where the fictional skilled person is a team, consideration must be given to the reality of how teams operate in real research situations: see *Schlumberger Holdings Ltd v Electromagnetic Geoservices AS* [2010] EWCA Civ 819, [2010] RPC 851, [2011] IP & T 548; *MedImmune Ltd v Novartis Pharmaceuticals UK Ltd* [2012] EWCA Civ 1234, [2013] RPC 659, [2013] IP & T 536.

3   *Tetra Molectric Ltd v Japan Imports Ltd* [1976] RPC 547 at 583, CA; *Hickman v Andrews* [1983] RPC 147 at 189, CA.

456.   Common general knowledge.   The skilled addressee has the common general knowledge relevant to the art in question[1]. Common general knowledge includes not only the information that those engaged in the particular art concerned are likely to remember[2], but also the contents of those standard text books that those people would normally refer to on the particular topic concerned. In particular cases, a wider range of documents may form part of common general knowledge; thus patent specifications are not ordinarily common knowledge, but there are undoubtedly industries where specifications coming from leading research organisations are commonly read and referred to in the same way as a textbook[3].

Common general knowledge need not extend to all those engaged in the art concerned, but it certainly includes what is known to most of them[4]. However, not every widely circulated document becomes part of common general knowledge; to do so, it must also be generally accepted[5].

1   *General Tire and Rubber Co v Firestone Tyre and Rubber Co Ltd* [1972] RPC 457 at 482, CA; approving *British Acoustic Films Ltd v Nettlefold Productions Ltd* (1935) 53 RPC 221, CA. See also PARA 442 and the cases there cited.

2   Eg what is taught to students: *Automatic Coil Winder and Electrical Equipment Co Ltd v Taylor Electrical Instruments Ltd* (1943) 61 RPC 41 at 43, CA; *Allmänna Svenska Elektriska AB v Burntisland Shipbuilding Co Ltd* (1951) 68 RPC 227 (affd (1952) 69 RPC 63, CA).

3   This was said to be so in chemistry in *Vidal Dyes Syndicate Ltd v Levinstein Ltd* (1912) 29 RPC 245, CA. It appears still to be true over much of the chemical industry, and in other industries where practice is changing too fast for text books to keep up.

4   *British Celanese Ltd v Courtaulds Ltd* (1933) 50 RPC 259 at 280, CA; *British Acoustic Films Ltd v Nettlefold Productions Ltd* (1935) 53 RPC 221 at 250, CA.

5   *British Acoustic Films Ltd v Nettlefold Productions Ltd* (1935) 53 RPC 221, CA.

457.   Mindset of skilled person.   In addition to his common general knowledge[1], the skilled addressee will approach the prior art with the perspective and expectations of those in the relevant field as at the priority date of the invention: for example, there may be an established prejudice that something will not work or that something ought not to be done and the fact that the patentee has demonstrated that, contrary to the mistaken prejudice, something will work and is successful, points to there being an inventive step[2]. The prejudice must, however, be of a technical rather than a commercial nature[3].

1   See PARA 456.

2   *Union Carbide Corpn v BP Chemicals Ltd* [1998] RPC 1 at 13; *Pozzoli SPA v BDMO SA* [2007] EWCA Civ 588 at [25], [2007] FSR 872 at [25]. In such cases, the prior art can be said to comprise both the teaching of the prior document and the prejudice that it would not work or be impractical: see *Pozzoli SPA v BDMO SA* at [27]. See also *Angiotech's Patent* [2006] EWHC 260 (Pat) at [72], [2006] RPC 665 at [72] (whether safety concerns about a drug would lead to

it being rejected out of hand); *Vector Corpn v Glatt Air Techniques Inc* [2006] EWHC 1638 (Ch) at [134], [2007] RPC 255 at [134] (skilled addressee would be very wary of modifying fluidised bed designs on paper in the prior art).

3 *Hallen Co v Brabantia (UK) Ltd* [1991] RPC 195 at 213, CA; *Re Richardson-Vicks Inc's Patent* [1997] RPC 888 at 896 (difficulties of obtaining regulatory approval for a pharmaceutical).

458. Identification of the inventive concept. The inventive concept is not some generalised concept to be derived from the specification as a whole but the inventive concept of the claim in question[1]. The first stage is likely to be a question of construction to ascertain the meaning of the claim. The second stage is to identify the essence of the claim by distinguishing between the portions of the claim which matter and those portions which, although limitations on the ambit of the claim, do not[2]. The identification of the inventive concept requires a consideration of what the invention is[3]. The invention may be the idea of using established techniques to do something which no one had previously thought of doing, or it might be the way of achieving the goal or of how to overcome a problem which stands in the way of achieving the goal[4].

An invention may thus involve three stages:

(1) the definition of the problem to be solved or the difficulty to be overcome[5];

(2) the choice of the general principle to be applied in solving the problem or overcoming the difficulty[6]; and

(3) the choice of the particular means to be used[7].

Merit in any one of these stages, or in the whole combined, may support the invention.

1 *Brugger v Medic-Aid Ltd* [1996] RPC 635 at 656.
2 *Unilever plc v Chefaro Proprietaries Ltd* [1994] RPC 567 at 580; *Pozzoli SPA v BDMO SA* [2007] EWCA Civ 588, [2007] FSR 872. It is 'the subject matter of the claim, shorn of immaterial verbiage': *Halliburton Energy Services Inc v Smith International (North Sea) Ltd* [2005] EWHC 1623 (Pat), [2006] RPC 25. Appeals in obviousness cases frequently turn on whether the appellate court agrees or disagrees with the judge's assessment of what constituted the inventive step: see eg *Biogen Inc v Medeva plc* [1997] RPC 1 at 45, HL; *Technip France SA* [2004] EWCA Civ 381 at [125]–[130], [2004] RPC 919 at [125]–[130]; *Conor Medsystems Inc v Angiotech Pharmaceuticals Inc* [2007] EWCA Civ 5, [2007] RPC 487 (revsd [2008] UKHL 49, [2008] 4 All ER 621, [2008] RPC 716).
3 *Biogen Inc v Medeva plc* [1997] RPC 1 at 34; *Vector Corpn v Glatt Air Techniques Inc* [2006] EWHC 1638 (Ch), [2007] RPC 255.
4 *Biogen Inc v Medeva plc* [1997] RPC 1 at 34.
5 *Fawcett v Homan* (1896) 12 TLR 507, 13 RPC 398 at 405 per Lindley LJ. See also *Hickton's Patent Syndicate v Patents and Machine Improvements Co* (1909) 26 RPC 339, CA; *W and T Avery Ltd v H Pooley & Son Ltd* (1913) 30 RPC 160; *Teste v Coombes* (1924) 41 RPC 88 at 105, CA; *Benton and Stone Ltd v T Denston & Son* (1925) 42 RPC 284 at 297; *C Van der Lely NV v Ruston's Engineering Co Ltd* [1985] RPC 461 at 499, CA, per May LJ; *Vector Corpn v Glatt Air Techniques Inc* [2006] EWHC 1638 (Ch), [2007] RPC 255.
6 See *Hayward v Hamilton* (1881) Griffin's Patent Cases (1884–1886) 115, CA; *Hickton's Patent Syndicate v Patents and Machine Improvements Co Ltd* (1909) 26 RPC 339, CA.
7 All these stages need not exist separately. Sometimes the discovery of the result and the means is simultaneous (eg the discovery of water tabbies referred to in *Liardet v Johnson* (1778) 1 Web Pat Cas 53), or the choice of the principle renders the means obvious: see *Hickton's Patent Syndicate v Patents and Machine Improvements Co Ltd* (1909) 26 RPC 339, CA; *Benton and Stone Ltd v T Denston & Son* (1925) 42 RPC 284.

459. Prior art. The philosophy behind the doctrine of obviousness is that the public should not be prevented from doing anything which was merely an obvious extension or workshop variation of what was already known at the priority date. The skilled person is, therefore, treated as having access to every example of prior art and must be considered as sufficiently interested in the information, which he is deemed to have, to consider its practical application whether or not he would have done so in practice[1].

The fact that a document is old does not, per se, mean that it cannot be the basis of an obviousness attack[2]. Each pleaded piece of prior art has to be interpreted as at its date[3], but it has to be assessed for relevance as if it was being considered afresh at the priority date[4]. Nor can a piece of prior art be rejected simply because of its obscurity[5]. However, the significance to be accorded to different items of prior art may vary[6] and it must not be assumed that the significance of existing published material in relation to the problem the patentee seeks to solve will necessarily be apparent to the notional skilled person[7]. Less significance may be attached to documents which are in a technical field remote from that of the invention[8] or antiquarian interest only but the mere fact that the core pieces of prior art are old does not mean that the skilled addressee would have assumed that there were no valuable modifications worth trying out[9]. Where there is a vast literature of similar documents none of which points directly to the invention, a finding of obviousness is unlikely[10].

1   *PLG Research Ltd v Ardon International Ltd* [1995] RPC 287 at 313, CA. See also *Brugger v Medic-Aid Ltd* [1996] RPC 635 at 653.
2   *Brugger v Medic-Aid Ltd* [1996] RPC 635 at 653.
3   *Smithkline Beecham plc v Apotex Europe Ltd* [2004] EWCA Civ 1568 at [88], [2005] FSR 524 at [88].
4   *Smithkline Beecham plc v Apotex Europe Ltd* [2004] EWCA Civ 1568 at [88], [2005] FSR 524 at [88].
5   *PLG Research Ltd v Ardon International Ltd* [1995] RPC 287 at 313, CA, citing as an example *Windsurfing International Inc v Tabur Marine (Great Britain) Ltd* [1985] RPC 59, CA. See also PARA 456.
6   *Beloit Technologies Inc v Valmet Paper Machinery Inc* [1995] RPC 705 at 749 ('spectrum between documents mouldering on obscure shelves in a library and those to which ordinarily attention would be paid').
7   *Sandoz Ltd (Frei's Application)* [1976] RPC 449; *Windsurfing International Inc v Tabur Marine (Great Britain) Ltd* [1985] RPC 59, CA; *PLG Research Ltd v Ardon International Ltd* [1995] RPC 287 at 313, CA.
8   *Dow Chemical Co (Mildner's) Patent* [1975] RPC 165, CA (where there was an unsuccessful objection that the cited document was only in the packaging field and not in the cable field); *Imperial Chemical Industries Ltd (Pointer's) Application* [1977] FSR 434. In *Woven Plastic Products Ltd v British Ropes Ltd* [1970] FSR 47, CA, a Japanese utility model was not regarded as too obscure.
9   *Brugger v Medic-Aid Ltd* [1996] RPC 635 at 655.
10   *Olin Mathieson Chemical Corpn v Biorex Laboratories Ltd* [1970] RPC 157 at 184; *Hughes Tool Co v Ingersoll-Rand Co Ltd* [1977] FSR 406 at 409. A long list of prior art similar documents is sometimes referred to as a 'Simkins list' after Simkins who produced such a list in *Olin Mathieson Chemical Corpn v Biorex Laboratories Ltd*.

460.   Mosaic of publications. If, in order to arrive at the alleged invention, it is necessary to make a mosaic of extracts from documents published over a period of years[1], taking suggestions from one with suggestions from others independent of it[2], there can be little doubt that the claim has inventive subject matter[3]. This does not mean, however, that, in considering obviousness, prior documents must always be taken one at a time; the prior art must be considered as a whole[4] but any 'mosaic' of the relevant documents must be one which could be put together by the skilled man with no inventive capacity[5]. Nor can there be any objection to reading documents together where the later refers to the earlier[6]. Furthermore, where the claim is to a mere collocation, it is legitimate to cite separate documents against separate integers or steps of a process[7]. The sort of mosaic that can be put together by an unimaginative person with no inventive capacity will not found a valid patent[8].

1   *Von Heyden v Neustadt* (1880) as reported in 50 LJ Ch 126 at 128, CA. See also *Pfizer's Patent*
    [2001] FSR 201 at 228.
2   *Pope Appliance Corpn v Spanish River Pulp and Paper Mills Ltd* [1929] AC 269 at 278–279,
    46 RPC 23 at 54, PC, citing *British Ore Concentration Syndicate Ltd v Minerals Separation Ltd*
    (1908) 26 RPC 124 at 147, CA; on appeal (1909) 27 RPC 33, HL.
3   *Huddart v Grimshaw* (1803) Dav Pat Cas 265 at 278; *Lancashire Explosives Co Ltd v Roburite
    Explosives Co Ltd* (1895) 12 TLR 35 at 36, 12 RPC 470 at 483, CA; *Fawcett v Homan* (1896)
    12 TLR 507, 13 RPC 398 at 405; *British Thomson-Houston Co Ltd v Metropolitan-Vickers
    Electrical Co Ltd* (1928) 45 RPC 1, HL; *Lektophone Corpn v S G Brown Ltd* (1929) 46 RPC
    203 at 230; *Dow Chemical Co (Mildner's) Patent* [1975] RPC 165, CA. See, however, *Allmänna
    Svenska Electriska AB v Burntisland Shipbuilding Co Ltd* (1952) 69 RPC 63 at 68–70, CA
    (British and German specification of differing dates combined); *Smithkline Beecham plc v
    Apotex Europe Ltd* [2004] EWCA Civ 1568 at [96], [2005] FSR 524 at [96].
4   *Martin and Biro Swan Ltd v H Millwood Ltd* [1956] RPC 125 at 133, HL, affirming the law on
    this matter as stated by Jenkins LJ in *Allmänna Svenska Elektriska AB v Burntisland
    Shipbuilding Co Ltd* (1952) 69 RPC 63, CA.
5   *Technograph Printed Circuits Ltd v Mills and Rockley (Electronics) Ltd* [1972] RPC 346 at
    355, HL.
6   *Wilson v Wilson Bros Bobbin Co Ltd* (1911) 28 RPC 733 at 739, CA; *Sharpe and Dohme Inc
    v Boots Pure Drug Co Ltd* (1928) 45 RPC 153, CA.
7   *Sharpe and Dohme Inc v Boots Pure Drug Co Ltd* (1928) 45 RPC 153, CA, possibly exemplifies
    this: see generally PARA 482.
8   *Technograph Printed Circuits Ltd v Mills and Rockley (Electronics) Ltd* [1972] RPC 346 at
    355, HL, per Lord Reid. See also *Smithkline Beecham plc v Apotex Europe Ltd* [2004] EWCA
    Civ 1568 at [96], [2005] FSR 524 at [96].

461.   Effect of subsequent knowledge.   In interpreting a prior document it must be read as at the date of its publication[1]. Technical terms contained in an earlier publication must be given the meaning which they had at the date of that publication[2], and all knowledge, whether general, or as to the meaning of an earlier publication, acquired since the date of application for a later patent, must be excluded[3].

1   *Ore Concentration Co (1905) Ltd v Sulphide Corpn Ltd* (1914) 31 RPC 206 at 224, PC;
    General Tire and Rubber Co v Firestone Tyre and Rubber Co Ltd [1972] RPC 457 at 485, CA.
    The question whether the date should be that of publication or of writing of the document was
    not material to either of these cases.
2   *Betts v Menzies* (1862) 10 HL Cas 117; *General Tire and Rubber Co v Firestone Tyre and
    Rubber Co Ltd* [1972] RPC 457 at 485, CA. The publication must also be considered as
    directed to the problem at that date: *British Thomson-Houston Co Ltd v Metropolitan-Vickers
    Electrical Co Ltd* (1928) 45 RPC 1, HL.
3   *Bray v Gardner* (1887) 4 RPC 400 at 406, CA; *Ehrlich v Ihlee and Sankey* (1888) 5 RPC 437 at
    452, CA; *Re Lewis and Stirckler's Patent* (1896) 14 RPC 24; *Vidal Dyes Syndicate Ltd v
    Levinstein Ltd* (1912) 29 RPC 245 at 277, CA; *British Thomson-Houston Co Ltd v
    Metropolitan-Vickers Electrical Co Ltd* (1928) 45 RPC 1, HL; *Pope Appliance Corpn v Spanish
    River Pulp and Paper Mills Ltd* [1929] AC 269 at 272, 46 RPC 23 at 50, PC; *Stelos Re-Knit Ltd
    v Ladda-Mend Co Ltd* (1931) 48 RPC 435 at 444. See also *Unwin v Heath* (1855) 5 HL Cas
    505 at 523.

462.   Assessment of obviousness.   The modern practice in relation to the issue of inventive step is to identify a relatively small number of items of prior art and then to identify the differences between those core items of prior art and the alleged invention. The crucial question whether the difference between the inventive concept of the patent and the state of the art represents an obvious step is one on which expert evidence is essential[1]. The primary evidence is that of properly qualified expert witnesses[2] who will say whether or not in their opinions the relevant step would have been obvious to the skilled person having regard to the state of the art[3]. All other evidence is secondary to that primary evidence. Such secondary evidence may include what the inventor and others in the art actually thought and did[4], whether the invention satisfied a long-felt want[5] or whether the invention has been a commercial success[6].

It has been said that the question of whether an alleged invention is obvious or not cannot be further refined and that because it is a multi-factorial question it is impossible to devise a more detailed question which is suitable for all cases[7]. Nevertheless, courts have found it useful to pose the question in different ways: 'was it for practical purposes obvious to a skilled worker, in the field concerned, in the state of knowledge existing at the date of the patent to be found in the literature then available to him, that he would or should make the invention the subject of the claim concerned?'[8]; 'would the man skilled in the art be alerted to the possibilities?'[9]; 'so obvious that it would at once occur to anyone acquainted with the subject, and desirous of accomplishing the end?'[10]; 'would the person versed in the art assess the likelihood of success as sufficient to warrant actual trial?'[11]. It is possible to find the question posed as either 'was it obvious that a skilled man should' or 'was it obvious that a skilled man could' make the invention? and the correct question may depend upon whether the invention lies in ascertaining the problem to be solved or in the way in which the problem is solved[12].

1   *Molnlycke AB v Proctor & Gamble Ltd (No 5)* [1994] RPC 49 at 113, CA; *Angiotech's Patent* [2006] EWHC 260 (Pat) at [32], [2006] RPC 665 at [32]; *Nichia Corpn v Argos Ltd* [2007] EWCA Civ 741 at [31], [2007] FSR 895 at [31].

2   The expert witness should equate, as far as possible, to the skilled addressee (see PARA 491). A witness who lacks expertise in the particular area with which the patent is concerned may still be of assistance to the court even if he lacks contemporary experience because he may be able to read himself into the state of the art at the priority date and his general knowledge would provide a framework for his analysis: *Research in Motion UK Ltd v Inpro Licensing SARL* [2006] EWHC 70 (Pat) at [6], [2006] RPC 517 at [6].

3   See *Molnlycke AB v Proctor & Gamble Ltd (No 5)* [1994] RPC 49 at 113, CA; *Nichia Corpn v Argos Ltd* [2007] EWCA Civ 741 at [31], [2007] FSR 895 at [31]; *Actavis UK Ltd v Novartis AG* [2010] EWCA Civ 82, [2011] IP & T 30 (in particular at [36]–[37], per Jacob LJ, explaining the '5¼ inch plate' scenario).

4   *SKM SA v Wagner Spraytech (UK) Ltd* [1982] RPC 497 at 508, CA; *Pfizer's Patent* [2001] FSR 201 at 227. In *Nichia Corpn v Argos Ltd* [2007] EWCA Civ 741, [2007] FSR 895, the court considered the application of the rules of standard disclosure to such secondary evidence.

5   See e g *Pfizer's Patent* [2001] FSR 201 at 227. See also PARA 464.

6   *Pfizer's Patent* [2001] FSR 201 at 227; *Regeneron Pharmaceuticals Inc v Genentech Inc* [2013] EWCA Civ 93, [2013] RPC 703, [2013] IP & T 619 (in considering obviousness it is not inappropriate for the court to consider the prospects for the invention's success). See also PARA 464.

7   *Nichia Corpn v Argos Ltd* [2007] EWCA Civ 741 at [22], [2007] FSR 895 at [22]. See also the warning against over-elaboration in *Conor Medsystems Inc v Angiotech Pharmaceuticals Inc* [2007] EWCA Civ 5 at [44], [2007] RPC 487 at [44] (revsd [2008] UKHL 49, [2008] 4 All ER 621, [2008] RPC 716) approved in *Generics (UK) Ltd v H Lundbeck A/S* [2008] EWCA Civ 311, 101 BMLR 52, [2008] All ER (D) 152 (Apr) (affd [2009] UKHL 12, [2009] 2 All ER 955, 107 BMLR 121). It is not incumbent on a patentee to demonstrate in the specification that the invention will work or how it works, although he runs the risk of insufficiency if it does not work: *Conor Medsystems Inc v Angiotech Pharmaceuticals Inc* [2008] UKHL 49, [2008] 4 All ER 621, [2008] RPC 716.

8   *Killick v Pye Ltd* [1958] RPC 366 at 377, CA. The question was originally formulated by counsel (Sir Stafford Cripps) in *Sharpe and Dohme Inc v Boots Pure Drug Co Ltd* (1928) 45 RPC 153 at 163, CA.

9   *Johns-Manville Corpn's Patent* [1967] RPC 479 at 494, CA.

10 *Vickers, Sons & Co Ltd v Siddell* (1890) 15 App Cas 496, 7 RPC 292 at 304, HL, cited with approval in *PLG Research Ltd v Ardon International Ltd* [1995] RPC 287 at 314, CA.

11 *Johns-Manville Corpn's Patent* [1967] RPC 479 at 494, CA; *Technograph Printed Circuits Ltd v Mills and Rockley (Electronics) Ltd* [1972] RPC 346 at 355, HL; *Tetra Molectric Ltd v Japan Imports Ltd* [1976] RPC 547 at 581, CA. The skilled man is not, however, expected to try all

solutions unless he has a problem in mind and particular combinations might assist him in solving it: *Hallen Co v Brabantia (UK) Ltd* [1991] RPC 195 at 213, CA.

12 *Hallen Co v Brabantia (UK) Ltd* [1989] RPC 307 at 326; affd [1991] RPC 195 at 212, CA.

463.   Hindsight. When assessing obviousness it is always necessary to guard against an ex post facto analysis because once the invention has been established, it may be easy to show how it might be arrived at by starting from something known and taking a series of apparently easy steps[1]. Where the prior art offers many possible starting points for further development it may not be obvious, without hindsight, to choose the one which leads to the alleged invention[2].

1 *British Westinghouse Electric and Manufacturing Co v Braulik* (1910) 27 RPC 209 at 230, CA; *Non-Drip Measure Co Ltd v Stranger's Ltd* (1943) 60 RPC 135 at 142, HL; *Technograph Printed Circuits Ltd v Mills and Rockley (Electronics) Ltd* [1972] RPC 346, HL; *Van der Lely NV v Ruston's Engineering Co Ltd* [1985] RPC 461 at 498, CA; *T Bonzel v Intervention Ltd (No 3)* [1991] RPC 553 at 579; *Wheatley v Drillsafe Ltd* [2001] RPC 133 at 147, CA. See also *Generics (UK) Ltd v H Lundbeck A/S* [2007] EWHC 1040 (Pat) at [70], [2007] RPC 729 at [70], [2007] All ER (D) 87 (May), per Kitchin J (revsd on other grounds [2008] EWCA Civ 311, [2008] RPC 437, [2009] All ER (D) 152 (Apr); [2009] UKHL 12, [2009] 2 All ER 955, [2009] IP & T 496).

2 *PLG Research Ltd v Ardon International Ltd* [1995] RPC 287 at 313–314, CA.

464.   Whether the development required inventive skill. The question whether a development which in fact has been made required inventive skill or was the natural development of the particular art is one of considerable difficulty. Sometimes the intrinsic nature of the discovery itself may be sufficient to establish the inventive skill[1], but the general tendency of the human mind is to minimise a discovery after it has been made[2], and it is often necessary to have recourse to extrinsic evidence to show that what has been done by the patentee was not obvious[3].

If it can be shown that the particular development is one of great utility and has satisfied a long-felt want in the trade, the inference that it required inventive ingenuity is strong[4] and may be almost irresistible[5]. Commercial success is not in itself necessarily conclusive[6], and any inference from it may be displaced by evidence of material change in the conditions of the trade, creating a new demand[7]. In particular, commercial success not co-extensive with the claim[8], that is, due to matters or features other than the features to which the claim concerned is limited, such as superior workmanship or convenience[9], or features resulting from subsequent research work[10], tends to be of little weight. Invention may, however, be established by showing that the patented features played a part, in conjunction with other inventions, in enabling a long-felt want to be satisfied[11].

1 Ie the court may be impressed by the discovery as surprising and meritorious on its face, but there seems to be no modern instance of this. See, however, *Cleveland Graphite Bronze Co v Glacier Metal Co Ltd* (1950) 67 RPC 149 at 156, HL.

2 *Murray v Clayton* (1872) 7 Ch App 570 at 583 per James LJ; *Vickers, Sons & Co Ltd v Siddell* (1890) 15 App Cas 496 at 500, 7 RPC 292 at 304, HL, per Lord Herschell; *Incandescent Gas Light Co Ltd v De Mare Incandescent Gas Light System Ltd* (1896) 13 RPC 301 at 323 (affd 12 TLR 495, 13 RPC 559, CA); *Re Waterhouse's Patent* (1906) 23 RPC 470 at 476 per Romer LJ; *British Westinghouse Electric and Manufacturing Co v Braulik* (1910) 27 RPC 209 at 230, CA (approved in *Non-Drip Measure Co Ltd v Stranger's Ltd* (1943) 60 RPC 135 at 142, HL); *Pope Appliance Corpn v Spanish River Pulp and Paper Mills Ltd* [1929] AC 269 at 280, 46 RPC 23 at 55, PC; *Canadian General Electric Co Ltd v Fada Radio Ltd* [1930] AC 97 at 100, 47 RPC 69 at 88, PC.

3 See *Haberman v Jackel* [1999] FSR 683 at 697, per Laddie J ('the simpler a solution, the easier it is to explain and the easier it is to explain, the more obvious it can appear. This may be unfair to an inventor').

4   Murray v Clayton (1872) 7 Ch App 570; Von Heyden v Neustadt (1880) 14 ChD 230, CA;
     Haslam & Co Ltd v Hall (1887) 5 RPC 1 (on appeal (1888) 20 QBD 491, CA); American
     Braided Wire Co v Thomson (1888) 4 TLR 279, 5 RPC 113, CA (affd sub nom Thompson
     & Co v American Braided Wire Co (1889) 5 TLR 537, 6 RPC 518, HL); Boyd v Horrocks
     (1888) 5 RPC 557 at 576; Pirrie v York Street Flax Spinning Co Ltd (1894) 11 RPC 429, CA;
     Taylor and Scott v Annand and Northern Press and Engineering Co Ltd (1900) 18 RPC 53 at
     63, HL; British Vacuum Cleaner Co Ltd v Suction Cleaners Ltd (1904) 21 RPC 303 at 312; Van
     Berkel v RD Simpson Ltd 1907 SC 165, 24 RPC 117, Ct of Sess; Benton and Stone Ltd v
     T Denston & Son (1925) 42 RPC 284 at 297; British United Shoe Machinery Co Ltd v Lambert
     Howarth & Sons Ltd and Gimson Shoe Machinery Co Ltd (1927) 44 RPC 511 at 524; Pope
     Appliance Corpn v Spanish River Pulp and Paper Mills Ltd [1929] AC 269, 46 RPC 23, PC;
     Douglas Packing Co Inc, Douglas Pectin Corpn and Postum Co Inc v Evans & Co (Hereford
     and Devon) Ltd (1929) 46 RPC 493 at 508, CA; British United Shoe Machinery Co Ltd v
     Albert Pemberton & Co (1930) 47 RPC 134; Rheostatic Co Ltd v Robert Maclaren & Co Ltd
     (1935) 53 RPC 109 at 117, Ct of Sess; Sonotone Corpn v Multitone Electric Co Ltd (1955)
     72 RPC 131 at 145, CA; Re Kromschröder AG's Patent (Revocation) [1959] RPC 309 (revsd on
     another point [1960] RPC 75, CA). Cf C Van der Lely NV v Bamfords Ltd [1960] RPC 169 at
     193; affd [1961] RPC 296, CA. See also Re Inventa AG für Forschung und Patentverwertung's
     Application [1956] RPC 45 at 49; Tetra Molectric Ltd v Japan Imports Ltd [1976] RPC
     547, CA.
5   S Parkes & Co Ltd v Cocker Bros Ltd (1929) 46 RPC 241 at 248, CA, often approved: see
     eg Non-Drip Measure Co Ltd v Stranger's Ltd (1943) 60 RPC 135 at 143, HL; Cleveland
     Graphite Bronze Co v Glacier Metal Co Ltd (1950) 67 RPC 149 at 156, HL; Martin and Biro
     Swan Ltd v H Millwood Ltd [1956] RPC 125 at 139, HL; Raleigh Cycle Co Ltd v H Miller
     & Co Ltd (1946) 63 RPC 113 at 143, CA (affd [1948] 1 All ER 308, 65 RPC 141, HL).
6   Haberman v Jackel International Ltd [1999] FSR 683 at 699–701; Longbottom v Shaw (1891)
     8 RPC 333, HL. See also Riekmann v Thierry (1896) 14 RPC 105, HL; Cooper & Co
     (Birmingham) Ltd v Baedeker (1900) 17 RPC 209, CA; Thermos Ltd v Isola Ltd (1910)
     27 RPC 388; Wilson v Wilson Bros Bobbin Co Ltd (1911) 28 RPC 733, CA; Lang Wheels
     (Manufacturing) Ltd and Bland v Wilson (1938) 55 RPC 295 at 318; General Tire and
     Rubber Co v Firestone Tyre and Rubber Co Ltd [1972] RPC 457 at 503, CA; but see PARA 465.
     User by the defendant is often appealed to by the claimant as establishing inventive merit: see
     eg Vickers, Sons & Co Ltd v Siddell (1890) 15 App Cas 496, 7 RPC 292, HL; Deeley v Perkes
     [1896] AC 496 at 497, 13 RPC 581 at 589, HL; but as to this see Clark v Adie (1877) 2 App
     Cas 315 at 337, HL.
7   Re Gaulard and Gibbs' Patent (1890) 7 RPC 367 at 380, HL; Heginbotham Bros Ltd v Burne
     (1939) 56 RPC 399, CA. An example is a change of fashion: see Gosnell v Bishop (1888) 4 TLR
     397 at 398, 5 RPC 151 at 158, CA; Savage v DB Harris & Sons (1896) 12 TLR 332, 13 RPC
     364 at 374, CA; Bowen v EJ Pearson & Sons Ltd (1924) 42 RPC 101.
8   Colburn v FD Ward Ltd (1950) 67 RPC 73. See also eg Surface Silos Ltd v Beal [1960] RPC
     154 at 161, CA.
9   British United Shoe Machinery Co Ltd v EA Johnson & Co Ltd (1925) 42 RPC 243 at 254, CA;
     British Hartford-Fairmont Syndicate Ltd v Jackson Bros (Knottingley) Ltd (1932) 49 RPC 495
     at 552, CA; Paper Sacks Pty Ltd v Cowper (1935) 53 RPC 31, PC; Wildey and Whites
     Manufacturing Co Ltd v H Freeman and Letrik Ltd (1931) 48 RPC 405; Dow Chemical Co
     (Mildner's) Patent [1975] RPC 165, CA.
10   British Celanese Ltd v Courtaulds Ltd (1935) 152 LT 537 at 542, 52 RPC 171 at 194, HL. See
     also Tetra Molectric Ltd v Japan Imports Ltd [1976] RPC 547, CA (where commercial success
     was in part due to later inventions); and Rado v John Tye & Son Ltd [1967] RPC 297, CA (affd
     [1968] FSR 563, HL) (availability of new material).
11   Martin and Biro Swan Ltd v H Millwood Ltd [1956] RPC 125 at 139, HL. See also Haberman
     v Jackel International Ltd [1999] FSR 683 at 699–701.

465. Unfelt want. Where there was no felt want, but resigned acceptance of
the defects of what was made before, commercial success of the thing patented
may still create a prima facie case that it cannot have been obvious, or it would
have been done before[1].

1   Rosedale Associated Manufacturers Ltd v Carlton Tyre Saving Co Ltd [1959] RPC 189 at 213;
     on appeal [1960] RPC 59, CA. See also General Tire and Rubber Co v Firestone Tyre and

Rubber Co Ltd [1972] RPC 457 at 503, CA; *Beloit Technologies Inc v Valmet Paper Machinery Inc* [1995] RPC 705 at 754; *Dyson Appliances Ltd v Hoover Ltd* [2001] RPC 473 at 527.

466.   Invention the result of experiments. The fact that an alleged invention was arrived at only after a series of experiments may carry weight[1]. It is not necessary that an inventor should have laboured, for an invention may well be the result of a happy thought[2]; but, if the inventor, being equipped with the proper knowledge of his art[3], has been unable to arrive at the result claimed without a series of experiments, the inference is that the result was not obvious[4]. Such an inference is, however, easily displaced, for even a fully qualified person may be unaware of particular documents or practices, especially those not forming part of the common general knowledge of the art[5], or he may have been inhibited from carrying out experiments due to the existence of a competitor's patents[6]. Nevertheless evidence of what the inventor actually did[7] or what others in field were doing at the priority date may be relevant[8].

1   *Nichia Corpn v Argos Ltd* [2007] EWCA Civ 741, [2007] FSR 895.
2   *Re IG Farbenindustrie AG's Patents* (1930) 47 RPC 289 at 322; cf PARA 458.
3   *Allmänna Svenska Elektriska AB v Burntisland Shipbuilding Co Ltd* (1951) 68 RPC 227 at 241; on appeal (1952) 69 RPC 63 at 70, CA. See also *Riekmann v Thierry* (1896) 14 RPC 105 at 122, HL; *Beecham Group Ltd's (Amoxycillin) Application* [1980] RPC 261, CA.
4   See eg *Leo Pharma A/S v Sandoz Ltd* [2009] EWHC 996 (Pat), [2009] All ER (D) 140 (May) (affd [2009] EWCA Civ 1188, [2009] All ER (D) 230 (Nov)) (consideration of whether experimental repetition would lead to discovery of subject matter of patent claim).
5   See PARA 456.
6   See *Beecham Group Ltd's (Amoxycillin) Application* [1980] RPC 261, CA.
7   *SKM SA v Wagner Spraytech (UK) Ltd* [1982] RPC 497 at 505, CA; *Procter & Gamble Ltd v Peaudouce (UK) Ltd* [1989] FSR 180 at 190, CA.
8   See *Fichera v Flogates Ltd* [1984] RPC 257 at 277, CA; *Shoketsu Kinzoku Kogyo KK's Patent* [1992] FSR 184 at 190; *Chiron Corpn v Organon Technika Ltd (No 3), Chiron Corpn v Murex Diagnostics Ltd (No 3)* [1994] FSR 202 at 238. Such evidence is secondary in nature: see *Nichia Corpn v Argos Ltd* [2007] EWCA Civ 741, [2007] FSR 895; and PARA 462.

467.   Evidence as to the invention. Evidence that the opinion generally received before the alleged invention was made was that success could not be attained by the methods adopted by the inventor is permissible and is often relied on to establish inventiveness[1], as is evidence directed to explain the nature of the advance made, and the difference between the problem dealt with, the conditions obtaining, or the means employed, in the patentee's invention and in the alleged anticipations. Surprise among those in the industry concerned, either at the time the invention was made or subsequently, that the invention could achieve its purpose, is useful evidence[2].

1   See *British Liquid Air Co Ltd v British Oxygen Co Ltd* (1908) 25 RPC 577 at 601, CA; *Douglas Packing Co Inc, Douglas Pectin Corpn and Postum Co Inc v Evans & Co (Hereford and Devon) Ltd* (1929) 46 RPC 493 at 508, CA; cf *John Wright and Eagle Range Ltd v General Gas Appliances Ltd* (1928) 46 RPC 169 at 179, CA.
2   See eg *Mullard Radio Valve Co Ltd v Philco Radio and Television Corpn* [1936] 2 All ER 920, 53 RPC 323, HL; *Cleveland Graphite Bronze Co v Glacier Metal Co Ltd* (1950) 67 RPC 149, HL; *J Lucas (Batteries) Ltd v Gaedor Ltd* [1978] RPC 297 (affd [1978] RPC 389, CA).

468.   Relevance of decided cases. The approach to the assessment of inventive step has changed since the coming into force of the Patents Act 1977, with reliance being placed on the structured four-step test set out by the Court of Appeal[1]. However, many of the basic principles laid down by earlier cases have been retained and reference may accordingly be made to earlier case law[2]. Cases decided by the European Patent Office[3] and the courts of the member states of the European Patent Convention[4] are of persuasive authority[5].

1   See *Windsurfing International Inc v Tabur Marine (Great Britain) Ltd* [1985] RPC 59, CA; and PARA 454.
2   See PARAS 469–471.
3   See PARA 644. As to the approach to obviousness adopted by the European Patent Office see PARA 454.
4   Ie the Convention on the Grant of European Patents (Munich, 5 October 1973; TS 20 (1978); Cmnd 7090): see PARA 644 et seq.
5   See the Patents Act 1977 s 130(7) (amended by the Copyright, Designs and Patents Act 1988 Sch 8). See also PARA 436.

469.   Distinction between discovery and invention.   The difference between discovery and invention has been often emphasised[1], and it has been held that a patent cannot be obtained for a discovery in the strict sense[2]. If, however, the patented article or process has not actually been anticipated[3], so that the effect of the claims is not to prevent anything being done which has been done or proposed previously, the discovery which led to the patentee's devising a process or apparatus may supply the necessary element of invention required to support a patent[4]. This is certainly the case if it can be shown that, apart from the discovery, there would have been no apparent reason for making any variation in the former practice[5].

1   See eg *Reynolds v Herbert Smith & Co Ltd* (1903) 20 RPC 123 at 126.
2   *Lane Fox v Kensington and Knightsbridge Electric Lighting Co* [1892] 3 Ch 424, 9 RPC 413, CA. See also the Patents Act 1977 s 1(2)(a); and PARA 430.
3   As to the meaning of 'anticipate' see PARA 437 note 1.
4   *Hickton's Patent Syndicate v Patents and Machine Improvements Co Ltd* (1909) 26 RPC 339 at 347, CA; *Raleigh Cycle Co Ltd v H Miller & Co Ltd* (1946) 63 RPC 113 at 139, CA (affd [1948] 1 All ER 308, 65 RPC 141, HL); *Genentech Inc's Patent* [1989] RPC 147 at 239, CA, per Dillon LJ. A claim to a physical product, or process for making it, is not a claim to a discovery as such by reason only that the product is not defined by reference to its physical or chemical structure: *Chiron Corpn v Murex Diagnostics Ltd* [1996] RPC 535 at 605.
5   *Muntz v Foster* (1844) 2 Web Pat Cas 96 at 103 per Tindal CJ, discussed in *Pirrie v York Street Flax Spinning Co Ltd* (1894) 11 RPC 429 at 449, CA, and in *Dick v Ellam's Duplicator Co* (1900) 17 RPC 196, CA.

470.   Verification does not involve an inventive step.   Where the subject matter of an alleged invention has actually been proposed before, the verification of the fact that the earlier proposal works, or that it works commercially, will not be patentable[1], even if the claims can be so limited as not to lack novelty[2].

1   *Acetylene Illuminating Co Ltd v United Alkali Co Ltd* (1904) 22 RPC 145 at 155, HL; *Mouchel v Coignet* (1907) 24 RPC 229, CA (affd sub nom *Hennebique v W Cowlin & Sons* (1909) 26 RPC 280, HL); *Re Alsop's Patent* (1907) 24 RPC 733 at 759; *Sharpe and Dohme Inc v Boots Pure Drug Co Ltd* (1927) 44 RPC 367 (affd (1928) 45 RPC 153, CA); *Samuel Heap & Son Ltd v Bradford Dyers' Association Ltd* (1929) 46 RPC 254. Nor will the ascertainment of the properties of a known substance be patentable: *Re IG Farbenindustrie AG's Patents* (1930) 47 RPC 289 at 322. See also *Beecham Group Ltd's (Amoxycillin) Application* [1980] RPC 261 at 303, CA.
2   Any claim which actually covers the prior proposal is necessarily invalid for want of novelty: see PARA 434 et seq.

471.   Importance of new result.   In judging the presence of invention it may broadly be said that the result is more important than the means; sometimes the greatest inventive skill is shown by the smallest alteration[1]. Thus a machine which enables an important new result[2] to be obtained may be proper subject matter for a patent, although the difference between it and what went before is small, provided that the difference is such that without it the new result could not be obtained[3]. Similarly, a slight alteration or new direction in a process may lead to such important results as to constitute good subject matter for the grant of a patent[4]. An added benefit, however great, will not, however, found a valid patent if the claimed invention is obvious for another purpose[5].

1   *Electrolytic Plating Apparatus Co Ltd v Evans & Sons* (1900) 17 RPC 733 at 741. See also *Day v Davies* (1904) 22 RPC 34 at 42; *Giusti Patents and Engineering Works Ltd v Rees* (1923) 40 RPC 206 at 215.

2   As to the necessary amount of improvement see *Gramophone and Typewriter Ltd v Ullmann* (1906) 23 RPC 752 at 757, CA, approved in *Gramophone Co Ltd v Ruhl* (1910) 28 RPC 20 at 37, CA.

3   *Hinks & Son v Safety Lighting Co* (1876) 4 ChD 607; *Vickers, Sons & Co Ltd v Siddell* (1890) 15 App Cas 496, 7 RPC 292, HL; *Gammons v Battersby* (1904) 21 RPC 322, CA; *Re Brown's Patent* (1907) 25 RPC 86, CA. The improvement must be due to the change: see *R v Arkwright* (1785) 1 Web Pat Cas 64 at 72; *Pow v Taunton* (1845) 9 Jur 1056; *Edison and Swan United Electric Light Co Ltd v Holland* (1889) 5 TLR 294 at 298, 6 RPC 243 at 283, CA.

4   Among cases illustrating this point in which the patents have been upheld are *Re Hall's Patent* (1817) 1 Web Pat Cas 97; *Elliott v Aston* (1840) 1 Web Pat Cas 222; *Betts v Menzies* (1862) 10 HL Cas 117; *Betts v Neilson* (1868) 3 Ch App 429 (affd sub nom *Neilson v Betts* (1871) LR 5 HL 1); *Murray v Clayton* (1872) 7 Ch App 570; *Frearson v Loe* (1878) 9 ChD 48; *Hayward v Hamilton* (1881) Griffin's Patent Cases (1884–1886) 115, CA; *Edison and Swan Electric Light Co v Woodhouse and Rawson* (1887) 3 TLR 327, 4 RPC 79, CA; *Lyon v Goddard* (1893) 10 RPC 121 (affd sub nom *Goddard v Lyon* (1894) 11 RPC 354, HL); *English and American Machinery Co Ltd v Union Boot and Shoe Machine Co Ltd* (1894) 11 RPC 367, CA; *Edison-Bell Phonograph Corpn Ltd v Smith* (1894) 10 TLR 522, 11 RPC 389, CA; *Shrewsbury and Talbot Cab Co Ltd v Sterckx* (1895) 12 TLR 122, 13 RPC 44, CA; *Riekmann v Thierry* (1896) 14 RPC 105, HL; *Scott v Hamling & Co Ltd* (1896) 14 RPC 123; *Innes v Short and Beal* (1898) 15 RPC 449 at 451; *Day v Davies* (1904) 22 RPC 34; *Jandus Arc Lamp and Electric Co Ltd v Arc Lamps Ltd* (1905) 92 LT 447, 22 RPC 277; *Watson, Laidlaw & Co Ltd v Pott, Cassels and Williamson* (1911) 28 RPC 565, HL; *British Vacuum Cleaner Co Ltd v London and South Western Rly Co* (1912) 29 RPC 309, HL; *Simplex Concrete Piles Ltd v Stewart* (1913) 30 RPC 205; *Marine Torch Co v Holmes Marine Life Protection Association* (1913) 30 RPC 631 at 649, CA; *Roth v Cracknell* (1921) 38 RPC 120; *Re Merk-Wirz's Patent* (1923) 40 RPC 270; *Turner v Bowman* (1924) 42 RPC 29; *Boyce v Morris Motors Ltd* (1926) 44 RPC 105, CA; *Stelos Re-Knit Ltd v Ladda-Mend Co Ltd* (1931) 48 RPC 435. For chemical patents of this class see *Benno Jaffé and Darmstaedter Lanolin Fabrik v John Richardson & Co (Leicester) Ltd* (1894) 10 TLR 398, 11 RPC 261, CA; *Saccharin Corpn Ltd v Chemicals and Drugs Co Ltd* (1899) 17 RPC 28; *Re Max Müller's Patent* (1907) 24 RPC 465 at 469.

5   *Morgan & Co Ltd v Windover & Co* (1890) 7 RPC 131 at 134, HL; *Drysdale and Sidney Smith & Blyth Ltd (in liquidation) v Davey Paxman & Co (Colchester) Ltd* (1937) 55 RPC 95 at 113; *Parks-Cramer Co v G W Thornton & Sons Ltd* [1969] RPC 112 at 127, HL, per Lord Morris of Borth-y-Gest; *Hallen Co v Brabantia (UK) Ltd* [1991] RPC 195 at 216, CA.

472.   Possession of new functions. The presence of invention may often be established by showing that an article has unexpected and valuable uses, or that a process produces unexpected and valuable results; but in such a case, although a court will in general take into consideration all the advantages arising from the invention, and not merely those pointed out in the specification, it is necessary that the claim should be strictly limited to things or processes possessing the new functions[1].

1   *Raleigh Cycle Co Ltd v H Miller & Co Ltd* (1946) 63 RPC 113 at 136–137, CA, per Lord Greene MR; upheld [1948] 1 All ER 308, 65 RPC 141, HL. In the older cases, where the claims were limited (or deemed to be limited) to the invention 'as and for the purpose described', mention of the function in the specification was sufficient: see *Von der Linde v Brummerstaedt & Co* (1909) 26 RPC 289; *HE Curtis & Son Ltd v RH Heward & Co* (1923) 40 RPC 183, CA; *Sharpe and Dohme Inc v Boots Pure Drug Co Ltd* (1927) 44 RPC 367 (affd (1928) 45 RPC 153, CA); *British Celanese Ltd v Courtaulds Ltd* (1933) 50 RPC 259 at 271, CA (on appeal (1935) 152 LT 537, 52 RPC 171, HL). See also PARA 480 et seq.

473.   New chemical substance. In the case of a new chemical substance the question whether there is an inventive step generally depends on whether its production lay within the routine practice of some existing trade or manufacture[1], but, even if this is the case, there may yet be inventiveness if the new substance possesses valuable properties the existence of which was not obvious a priori, even though the method of synthesis is a known one, so long as it has not previously been applied to the particular starting materials concerned[2].

1   See *Sharpe and Dohme Inc v Boots Pure Drug Co Ltd* (1927) 44 RPC 367 (affd (1928) 45 RPC 153, CA); *Re IG Farbenindustrie AG's Patents* (1930) 47 RPC 289. Formerly the courts held the view that a new chemical substance was patentable even if the course of chemical development would have naturally led to it: see *Badische Anilin und Soda Fabrik v Levinstein* (1887) 12 App Cas 710 at 711–712, 4 RPC 449 at 462, HL (revsg (1885) 29 ChD 366, 2 RPC 73, CA, and restoring (1883) 24 ChD 156); *Badische Anilin und Soda Fabrik v Dawson* (1889) 6 RPC 387 at 393; *Acetylene Illuminating Co Ltd v United Alkali Co Ltd* (1904) 22 RPC 145 at 153, HL. The change of view does not mark any change in law but rather the appreciation that in certain branches of chemistry increased knowledge has rendered prediction as to modes of manufacture and properties of bodies in known series almost a matter of certainty. For other cases where articles or substances new in themselves were held not to be patentable see *Adamant Stone and Paving Co Ltd v Liverpool Corpn* (1896) 14 RPC 11 (on appeal (1897) 14 RPC 264, CA); *Dick v Ellam's Duplicator Co* (1900) 17 RPC 196, CA; *Hudson, Scott & Co Ltd v Barringer, Walls and Manners Ltd* (1906) 23 RPC 502, CA.

2   *Re May and Baker Ltd and Ciba Ltd's Letters Patent* (1948) 65 RPC 255 at 281 (affd (1950) 67 RPC 23, HL); *Beecham Group Ltd's (Amoxycillin) Application* [1980] RPC 261, CA. If the method of synthesis has previously been applied to the same starting materials, there may have been an inventive discovery of the properties of the product, but the product itself will lack novelty. Even so, the use of the product so as to reap the benefit of the newly discovered properties may be patentable if it is a 'manufacture': see PARA 474.

474.   Patent for analogous user. Many patents are for the user of old apparatus, integers or processes for a new purpose. Inventiveness in these cases has to be judged, in general, by considering whether the new user lies so far out of the track of the former use that it would not suggest itself naturally to a person reasonably skilled in the particular art but would require thought and study[1].

The inventive art necessary to support a patent for the new user may lie in the appreciation of the fact that the problem to be overcome may be solved by the use of old means[2], or in the adaptation of old means so as to overcome the special difficulties which occur in the particular problem[3]. In the first case it is usually necessary to establish that it was not known that the new and old problems were identical[4]. This may be expressed by saying that the new user must not be 'merely analogous' to the old user. The merit of an invention may lie in the determination of the real nature of the difficulties to be overcome[5], but, if these are known, then ingenuity must be shown either in the choice of a method for overcoming them or in the means for carrying out the method, although it is not necessary that the means should be new[6].

In considering whether user is analogous, attention must be paid not only to the means employed, but also the object for which they are employed. It is not sufficient to establish analogous user to show that the results sought to be attained by the new user, or some of them, were produced by the earlier user, fortuitously or to an unimportant extent[7].

Where the new user involves fresh difficulties for which the remedy is not obvious, the old user is not considered analogous[8]. Nor is an old user so considered where the new application makes use of properties or advantages not apparent or useful in the old[9].

The purpose of the rules relating to obviousness is to safeguard manufacturers from undue interference in the development of their methods, or in the use of the knowledge which has been accumulated in their own and other trades[10]. It is a question of fact whether a new use is to be regarded as an analogous user, and the formula 'analogous user' may merely beg the question which the court has to decide[11].

1   *Penn v Bibby* (1866) 2 Ch App 127 at 136. See also *Harwood v Great Northern Rly Co* (1864) 11 HL Cas 654 at 682; *Acetylene Illuminating Co Ltd v United Alkali Co Ltd* (1904) 22 RPC 145 at 155, HL. See also PARA 439. It has been said that the user may be analogous, though not obvious: *Bonnard v London General Omnibus Co Ltd* (1920) 38 RPC 1 at 11, HL.

2   See *No-Fume Ltd v Frank Pitchford & Co Ltd* (1935) 52 RPC 231, CA.

3   *Gadd and Mason v Manchester Corpn* (1892) 9 RPC 516 at 524, CA, approved in *Benmax v Austin Motor Co Ltd* as reported in (1955) 72 RPC 39 at 44–45, HL, and explained in *Lister & Co Ltd's Patent* [1966] RPC 30, DC. See also *Hayward v Hamilton* (1881) Griffin's Patent Cases (1884–1886) 115 at 116, CA; *British Liquid Air Co Ltd v British Oxygen Co Ltd* (1908) 25 RPC 577 at 601, CA (where the fact that scientific opinion thought the method impossible was held evidence against analogy); *Hickton's Patent Syndicate v Patents and Machine Improvements Co* (1909) 26 RPC 339 at 347, CA.

4   *Steiner v Heald* (1851) 20 LJ Ex 410, Ex Ch; *AG für Autogene Aluminium Schweissung v London Aluminium Co (No 2)* (1922) 39 RPC 296 at 308, HL.

5   See PARA 458.

6   *Dangerfield v Jones* (1865) 13 LT 142 (affd 14 WR 356); *Cannington v Nuttall* (1871) LR 5 HL 205; *Lawrence v Perry & Co Ltd* (1884) 2 RPC 179 at 188; *Reason Manufacturing Co Ltd v Ernest F Moy Ltd* (1902) 19 RPC 409 (on appeal (1903) 20 RPC 205, CA); *Kinmond v Keay* (1903) 20 RPC 497, Ct of Sess; *Hickton's Patents Syndicate v Patents and Machine Improvements Co* (1909) 26 RPC 339, CA. As to the application of old means to get over special defects in complicated machines see *Edison-Bell Phonograph Corpn Ltd v Smith* (1894) 11 RPC 389 at 398, CA, per Lord Esher MR; cf *British United Shoe Machinery Co Ltd v Hugh Claughton Ltd* (1906) 23 RPC 321 at 333.

7   *Flour Oxidizing Co Ltd v Carr & Co Ltd* (1908) 25 RPC 428; *Flour Oxidizing Co Ltd v Hutchinson* (1909) 26 RPC 597. See also *Harwood v Great Northern Rly Co* (1860) 29 LJQB 193 at 202; *Automatic Coal Gas Retort Co Ltd v Salford Corpn* (1897) 14 RPC 450; *Welsbach Incandescent Gas Light Co Ltd v John M'Grady & Co* (1901) 18 RPC 513; *Anti-Vibration Incandescent Lighting Co Ltd v Crossley* (1905) 22 RPC 441, CA; *J and J Evans, Taunton Ltd v Hoskins and Sewell Ltd* (1907) 24 RPC 517, CA.

8   *Penn v Bibby* (1866) 2 Ch App 127; *Cannington v Nuttall* (1871) LR 5 HL 205; *Gadd and Mason v Manchester Corpn* (1892) 9 RPC 516, CA; *British Liquid Air Co Ltd v British Oxygen Co Ltd* (1909) 26 RPC 509, HL (affg (1908) 25 RPC 577, CA); *Higginson and Arundel v Bentley and Bentley Ltd* (1922) 39 RPC 177, CA; *Hale v Coombes* (1924) 41 RPC 112 at 137, CA (on appeal (1925) 42 RPC 328, HL); *Higginson and Arundel v Pyman* (1926) 43 RPC 291, CA; *Mellor v William Beardmore & Co Ltd* (1926) 43 RPC 361 at 372.

9   *Neilson v Harford* (1841) 8 M & W 806; *Muntz v Foster* (1843) 2 Web Pat Cas 93; *Edison and Swan Electric Light Co v Woodhouse and Rawson* (1887) 3 TLR 327, 4 RPC 79, CA; *Moseley v Victoria Rubber Co* (1887) 57 LT 142, 4 RPC 241; *Hayward v Hamilton* (1881) Griffin's Patent Cases (1884–1886) 115, CA; *Hopkinson v St James's and Pall-Mall Electric Lighting Co* (1893) 10 RPC 46; *Pirrie v York Street Flax Spinning Co Ltd* (1894) 11 RPC 429, CA; *Cassel Gold Extracting Co Ltd v Cyanide Gold Recovery Syndicate* (1895) 12 RPC 232, CA; *Automatic Coal Gas Retort Co Ltd v Salford Corpn* (1897) 14 RPC 450; *Welsbach Incandescent Gas Lighting Co Ltd v John M'Grady & Co* (1901) 18 RPC 513; *Sandow Ltd v Szalay* (1905) 23 RPC 6, HL; *Hickton's Patent Syndicate v Patents and Machine Improvements Co* (1909) 26 RPC 339, CA; *Marconi and Marconi's Wireless Telegraph Co Ltd v British Radio-Telegraph and Telephone Co Ltd* (1911) 27 TLR 274, 28 RPC 181; *No-Fume Ltd v Frank Pitchford & Co Ltd* (1935) 52 RPC 231 at 256, CA.

10   *Gadd and Mason v Manchester Corpn* (1892) 67 LT 576, 9 RPC 516, CA; *Wood v Raphael* (1896) 13 RPC 730 at 735 (affd (1897) 14 RPC 496, CA); *Siddeley v London Hygienic Ice Co Ltd* (1897) 14 RPC 514; *Dredge v Parnell* (1899) 16 RPC 625, HL; *Donnersmarckhütte Oberschlesische Eisen und Kohlenwerke AG v Electric Construction Co Ltd* (1910) 27 RPC 774 at 779, 783, CA; *Gillies v Gane Milking Machine Co* (1916) 34 RPC 21 at 29, PC; *Simplex Lithograph Co v Sir Joseph Causton & Sons Ltd* (1921) 38 RPC 403, CA; *Wallace v Tullis, Russell & Co* (1921) 39 RPC 3 at 24, Ct of Sess; *JD Insulating and Refrigerating Co Ltd v Thos Anderson Ltd* (1923) 41 RPC 1 at 19; *Lister Bros v Thorp, Medley & Co* (1930) 47 RPC 99

(affd 47 RPC 526 at 535, CA); *VD Ltd v Boston Deep Sea Fishing and Ice Co Ltd* (1935) 52 RPC 303 at 327. The fact that workers in a particular trade are ignorant of devices used in other trades is not necessarily sufficient to make the use of such devices in that trade patentable: cf *Patent Bottle Envelope Co v Seymer* (1858) 28 LJCP 22; *Shaw v Barton and Loudon* (1895) 12 RPC 282 at 291; *Nadel v Martin* (1903) 20 RPC 721 at 743, CA.

11　*Benmax v Austin Motor Co Ltd* (1953) 70 RPC 284 at 289, CA. However, on appeal that formula was, in fact, used: see (1955) 72 RPC 39 at 45, HL.

475. When analogous user arises. A presumption of analogous user is strong where two methods have been employed in the manufacture of particular articles or in particular trades, and only one of those methods has been employed in the manufacture of different articles or in different trades, and an application is made for a patent for the use of the other method in the manufacture of the last-mentioned articles or in the last-mentioned trades[1]. The same applies where self-contained units of machinery, or processes fulfilling a function complete in itself, are sought to be transferred from one trade to another or to a different purpose in the same trade; if these units act in the old way, and achieve in their new environment a result not new in itself, there is, generally speaking, no sufficient subject matter to warrant the grant of a patent in respect of the new user[2].

A presumption of analogous user arises equally where there has been a duplication of an existing part of a patented apparatus without any alteration in its function or mode of action[3]. A similar presumption arises where the use of a mode of construction or action is extended without a new purpose being achieved[4]. Again, patents for making in one piece articles previously made in two or more pieces have generally been held to be invalid[5], and, similarly, division of itself does not in general involve an inventive step[6].

1　*Herrburger, Schwander & Cie v Squire* (1889) 6 RPC 194, CA; *Morgan & Co Ltd v Windover & Co* (1890) 7 RPC 131, HL; *Embossed Metal Plate Co Ltd v Saupe and Busch* (1891) 8 RPC 355; *Westley, Richards & Co v Perkes* (1893) 10 RPC 181; *Adamant Stone and Paving Co Ltd v Liverpool Corpn* (1896) 14 RPC 11 (on appeal (1897) 14 RPC 264, CA); *Wood v Raphael* (1897) 14 RPC 496, CA; *Rucker v London Electric Supply Corpn Ltd* (1900) 17 RPC 279; *Carter v Leyson (t/a Peckham Box Co)* (1902) 19 RPC 473, CA; *Baxter v Marsden* (1904) 22 RPC 18; *Northern Press and Engineering Co Ltd v Hoe & Co* (1906) 23 RPC 613, CA.

2　*Tatham v Dania* (1869) Griffin's Patent Cases (1884–1886) 213; *Bamlett v Picksley* (1875) Griffin's Patent Cases (1884–1886) 40; *Cropper v Smith* (1884) 1 RPC 81 at 88, 90, CA; *Britain v Hirsch* (1888) 5 RPC 226; *Leadbeater v Kitchin* (1890) 7 RPC 235; *Hazlehurst v Rylands* (1890) 9 RPC 1, CA; *Shaw v Barton and Loudon* (1895) 12 RPC 282; *Farbenfabriken vormals Friedrich Bayer & Co v Chemische Fabrik von Heydon* (1905) 22 RPC 501; *Nadel v Martin* (1905) 23 RPC 41, HL; *Von der Linde v Brummerstaedt & Co* (1909) 26 RPC 289; *Doulton & Co Ltd v Albion Clay Co Ltd* (1911) 28 RPC 638, CA; *British United Shoe Machinery Co Ltd v Standard Engineering Co Ltd* (1916) 33 RPC 245 at 268, CA; *Bonnard v London General Omnibus Co Ltd* (1920) 38 RPC 1, HL; *Clorius v Tonner* (1922) 39 RPC 242; *British Oxygen Co Ltd v Maine Lighting Co* (1924) 41 RPC 604 at 614, CA; *Bowen v EJ Pearson & Sons Ltd* (1924) 42 RPC 101; *Higginson and Arundel v Pyman* (1925) 43 RPC 113 at 136.

3　*Haslam & Co Ltd v Hall* (1887) 5 RPC 1 (on appeal (1888) 20 QBD 491, CA); *Deutsche Nahmaschinen Fabrik vormals Wertheim v Pfaff* (1890) 7 RPC 251, CA; *Elias v Grovesend Tinplate Co* (1890) 7 RPC 455, CA; *Fuller v Handy* (1903) 21 RPC 6; *Read v Stella Conduit Co* (1916) 33 RPC 191 at 199, CA; *SA Servo-Frein Dewandre v Citroen Cars Ltd* (1930) 47 RPC 221 at 273, CA; *Wildey and Whites Manufacturing Co Ltd v H Freeman and Letrik Ltd* (1931) 48 RPC 405.

4　*Nicoll v Swears and Wells* (1893) 69 LT 110, 10 RPC 240; *Allen v Horton* (1893) 10 RPC 412; *Siddall and Hilton Ltd v Wood* (1903) 21 RPC 230.

5　*Ormson v Clarke* (1863) 14 CBNS 475; *Blakey & Co v Latham & Co* (1888) 6 RPC 29 (on appeal (1889) 6 RPC 184, CA); *Longbottom v Shaw* (1891) 8 RPC 333 at 338, HL; *Woodrow v Long, Humphreys & Co Ltd* (1933) 51 RPC 25, CA.

6　*Macnamara v Hulse* (1842) 2 Web Pat Cas 128n.

476.   Analogous proposals. There can only be a question of analogous user where there has been actual use of the earlier matter and not merely a suggestion of such use, for example in a patent specification[1]. Analogous prior proposals may, however, in some cases invalidate a later claim[2].

1   *Pope Appliance Corpn v Spanish River Pulp and Paper Mills Ltd* [1929] AC 269 at 282, 46 RPC 23 at 56, PC; *No-Fume Ltd v Frank Pitchford & Co Ltd* (1935) 52 RPC 231 at 236, CA.
2   Such cases have been rare. An example, perhaps, is *Allmänna Svenska Elektriska AB v Burntisland Shipbuilding Co Ltd* (1952) 69 RPC 63, CA: see *Martin and Biro Swan Ltd v H Millwood Ltd* (1954) 71 RPC 458 at 459, CA, per Jenkins LJ, in argument. *Benmax v Austin Motor Co Ltd* (1953) 70 RPC 284 at 285, 293, CA, might have been an example, but on appeal a different view was taken on the prior document: see (1955) 72 RPC 39 at 46–47, HL. See also *Nadel v Martin* (1903) 20 RPC 721 at 741, 743, CA; *Gillette Safety Razor Co v Anglo-American Trading Co Ltd* (1913) 30 RPC 465 at 479, HL; *Servo-Frein Dewandre SA v Citroen Cars Ltd* (1930) 47 RPC 221 at 255, 278, CA.

477.   New use of old substance. A valid patent may be obtained for a new use of a known substance if the use is not obvious, or produces considerable advantages[1]; but the fact that the substance had been used for analogous purposes[2], or that analogous substances had been used for the new purpose[3], would invalidate the claim.

1   For examples of such patents see *Walton v Potter* (1841) 1 Web Pat Cas 585 (use of india rubber for holding teeth of cards); *Muntz v Foster* (1843) 2 Web Pat Cas 93 (use of special copper alloy for sheathing); *Innes v Short and Beal* (1898) 14 TLR 492, 15 RPC 449 (use of zinc powder to prevent furring in boilers). In *Re Martin and Hyam's Patent* (1855) 25 LTOS 170 it was suggested that the use of gutta percha for clogs would be patentable. In *United Telephone Co v Harrison, Cox-Walker & Co* (1882) 21 ChD 720, it was suggested that the use of mica in telephone tympana would not be in itself patentable. It was held that the use of block instead of sheet felt for bicycle handles was not subject matter sufficient for the grant of a patent in *Cooper & Co (Birmingham) Ltd v Baedeker* (1900) 17 RPC 209, CA. See also *Rushton v Crawley* (1870) LR 10 Eq 522; *United Telephone Co v Harrison, Cox-Walker & Co*; *McClay v Lawes & Co Ltd* (1905) 22 RPC 199 at 203.
2   *Riekmann v Thierry* (1896) 14 RPC 105, HL.
3   *Albo-Carbon Light Co v Kidd* (1887) 4 RPC 535 at 539 (use of solid instead of liquid naphtha to enrich gas). See also *Palmer Tyre Ltd v Pneumatic Tyre Co Ltd* (1899) 16 RPC 451 at 494.

478.   New use of old process. There may be invention in applying a process to a substance or use to which it has not previously been applied, if the application or its results are not obvious[1]. Most chemical patents fall within this category[2].

1   *Reitzman v Grahame-Chapman and Derustit Ltd* (1950) 68 RPC 25 at 38–39, CA, citing *Osram-Robertson Lamp Works Ltd v Pope's Electric Lamp Co Ltd* (1917) 34 RPC 369, HL; *Samuel Heap & Son Ltd v Bradford Dyers' Association Ltd* (1929) 46 RPC 254. Such new use was held to involve invention in *Crane v Price* (1842) 1 Web Pat Cas 393; *Steiner v Heald* (1851) 6 Exch 607, Ex Ch; *British Liquid Air Co Ltd v British Oxygen Co Ltd* (1908) 25 RPC 577 at 601, CA (affd (1909) 26 RPC 509, HL); *Osram Lamp Works Ltd v Z Electric Lamp Manufacturing Co Ltd* (1912) 29 RPC 401 at 421, 423; *Manbré and Garton Ltd v Albion Sugar Co Ltd* (1936) 53 RPC 281. Such new use was held not to involve invention in *British Thomson-Houston Co Ltd v Duram Ltd* (1918) 35 RPC 161, HL; *British Celanese Ltd v Courtaulds Ltd* (1933) 50 RPC 259 at 285, CA (affd (1935) 152 LT 537, 52 RPC 171, HL).
2   See e g *Re May and Baker Ltd and Ciba Ltd's Letters Patent* (1948) 65 RPC 255 at 281; and the other cases relating to selection patents cited in PARA 479.

479.   Selection patents. In the case of selection patents[1] the inventive step lies in the selection, from among a known class of bodies, apparatus or processes, of some which possess a special advantage. It is necessary for the validity of a selection patent that substantially the whole of the selected group should possess this advantage and that it must be peculiar to the group, or at least be possessed by only a limited class of things outside it[2]. Generally also, where there is no novelty in the method of preparation, the advantage should be of an unexpected character, or otherwise not obvious to persons skilled in the art[3].

The nature of the special characteristics on which the selection is based must, at least in chemical cases, be stated in the specification[4]. After-discovered advantages are highly unlikely to be capable of supporting inventiveness[5].

When the possible choice is limited to a small number of variants, selection can seldom afford matter for the grant of a patent[6].

1   As to the meaning of 'selection patent' see PARA 320. As to novelty of selection patents see PARA 440.
2   *Re May and Baker Ltd and Ciba Ltd's Letters Patent* (1948) 65 RPC 255 at 281, citing *Re IG Farbenindustrie AG's Patents* (1930) 47 RPC 289 at 322; *Shell Refining and Marketing Co Ltd's Patent* [1960] RPC 35 at 52, CA. For an example of a valid selection patent dealing with bacteriological processes see *Commercial Solvents Corpn v Synthetic Products Co Ltd* (1926) 43 RPC 185 at 225. See also *Farbwerke Hoechst AG v Unichem Laboratories* [1969] RPC 55.
3   *Re IG Farbenindustrie AG's Patents* (1930) 47 RPC 289 at 321, 323. On this point cf *Sharpe and Dohme Inc v Boots Pure Drug Co Ltd* (1927) 44 RPC 367; affd (1928) 45 RPC 153, CA.
4   *Re IG Farbenindustrie AG's Patents* (1930) 47 RPC 289 at 323. See also *Philips (Bosgra's) Application* [1974] RPC 241; *EI du Pont de Nemours & Co (Witsiepe's) Application* [1982] FSR 303, HL; *Hallen Co v Brabantia (UK) Ltd* [1991] RPC 195 at 218, CA.
5   *Re Richardson-Vicks Inc's Patent* [1995] RPC 568; *Ranbaxy UK Ltd v Warner-Lambert Co* [2005] EWHC 2142 (Pat), [2006] FSR 209.
6   *Simplex Lithograph Co v Sir Joseph Causton & Sons Ltd* (1921) 38 RPC 403, CA; *British Celanese Ltd v Courtaulds Ltd* (1933) 50 RPC 63 at 110, 114 (affd (1935) 152 LT 537, 52 RPC 171, HL). Except in chemical cases, the number of possible variants is usually too small for a selection of any one to be patentable. For a chemical case in which the general class was too small to admit a valid selection see *Beecham Group Ltd's (Amoxycillin) Application* [1980] RPC 261, CA. See, however, *EI du Pont de Nemours & Co (Witsiepe's) Application* [1982] FSR 303, HL (cited in PARA 440 note 12).

480.   Combination patents.   A combination or collocation of integers the production of which has required independent thought, ingenuity or skill may constitute good subject matter for the grant of a patent, provided that it enables a more efficient result to be obtained, even though all the integers are old[1]. This general statement covers two classes of invention:

(1)   combinations proper, in which the several integers are so placed together that by their working interrelation they produce a new or improved result[2], so that the combination is more than the mere sum of its integers[3]; and

(2)   combinations of a number of integers, mechanical or chemical, which produces a result superior to what was formerly achieved, even though each integer performs its old function[4].

Most claims appear at first sight to be combination claims, since they specify the use of a device either in particular machines or with other integers. It must, however, be borne in mind that claims are often so framed for the purpose of description or limitation, or in order to avoid questions of anticipation[5].

1   *Mercedes Daimler Motor Co Ltd v FIAT Motor Cab Co Ltd* (1915) 32 RPC 393 at 413, HL; *Canadian General Electric Co Ltd v Fada Radio Ltd* [1930] AC 97 at 101, 47 RPC 69 at 88, PC; *C Van der Lely NV v Bamfords Ltd* [1961] RPC 296 at 308, CA (affd [1963] RPC 61, HL).
2   *Martin and Biro Swan Ltd v H Millwood Ltd* [1956] RPC 125 at 132, HL, citing *British Celanese Ltd v Courtaulds Ltd* (1935) 52 RPC 171, HL; *Drysdale and Sidney Smith and Blyth Ltd v Davey Paxman & Co (Colchester) Ltd and Re Letters Patent No 274162* (1937) 55 RPC 95 at 114.
3   *Bamlett v Picksley* (1875) Griffin's Patent Cases (1884–1886) 40 at 44; *Allen v Oates and Green Ltd* (1898) 15 RPC 298 at 303 (affd 15 RPC 744); *Re Klaber's Patent* (1906) 23 RPC 461 at 469, HL; *British United Shoe Machinery Co Ltd v A Fussell & Sons Ltd* (1908) 25 RPC

631 at 657, CA. Examples illustrating forms of patentable combination will be found in *Cornish and Sievier v Keene and Nickels* (1835) 1 Web Pat Cas 512 at 517 (subsequent proceedings (1837) 3 Bing NC 570); *Spencer v Jack* (1864) 11 LT 242; *Cannington v Nuttall* (1871) LR 5 HL 205; *Murray v Clayton* (1872) 7 Ch App 570; *Harrison v Anderston Foundry Co* (1876) 1 App Cas 574, HL; *Vickers, Son & Co Ltd v Siddell* (1890) 15 App Cas 496, HL; *Nobel's Explosives Co Ltd v Anderson* (1894) 10 TLR 599, 11 RPC 519, CA; *Pneumatic Tyre Co Ltd v Caswell* (1896) 13 RPC 375, CA; *Fawcett v Homan* (1896) 12 TLR 507, 13 RPC 398; *Deeley v Perkes* [1896] AC 496 at 497, 13 RPC 581 at 589, HL; *Molassine Co Ltd v R Townsend & Co Ltd* (1905) 23 RPC 27; *Kelvin v Whyte, Thomson & Co* (1907) 25 RPC 177, Ct of Sess; *International Harvester Co of America v Peacock* (1908) 25 RPC 765, PC. In some of these cases the result was new in itself; in others the means for its production differed substantially from those formerly used for the same purpose. See also *Amp Inc v Hellermann Ltd* [1966] RPC 159 at 184, CA; *Rado v John Tye & Son Ltd* [1967] RPC 297 at 302, CA.

4 See PARA 482.

5 *Dredge v Parnell* (1898) 15 RPC 84 at 90, CA (affd (1899) 16 RPC 625, HL); *Pugh v Riley Cycle Co Ltd* (1914) 31 RPC 266 at 283, HL.

481.   Requisites of valid combination. The inventive step necessary to make a combination patentable may exist in all or any of the stages of invention[1]; and a patentable combination may be one producing a new result, or arriving at an old result in a better or cheaper way[2], or giving a useful choice of means[3]. Different considerations apply to each of these cases in order to arrive at a conclusion whether there is an inventive step in the particular combination. The fact that the result is new is itself cogent evidence of invention[4]; but, if the result is old, it is probably correct to regard the combination as being the result of intelligent choice rather than the result of an inventive step[5]. If it has been necessary to make modifications in the form or construction of all or any of the separate old integers included in the combination in order to ensure their more perfect interaction, there is a strong presumption that there has been invention[6]. In determining whether the combination of features of a claim is obvious, it is not legitimate to take the features one at a time[7].

1 As to the stages of invention see PARA 458.

2 *Cornish and Sievier v Keene and Nickels* (1835) 1 Web Pat Cas 512 at 517; *Crane v Price* (1842) 1 Web Pat Cas 393 at 409; *Spencer v Jack* (1864) 11 LT 242; *Cannington v Nuttall* (1871) LR 5 HL 205; *Murray v Clayton* (1872) 7 Ch App 570; *Harrison v Anderston Foundry Co* (1876) 1 App Cas 574, HL; *International Harvester Co of America v Peacock* (1908) 25 RPC 765, PC; *Mabuchi Motor KK's Patents* [1996] RPC 387 at 409. In some of these cases the result was new in itself; in others the means for its production differed substantially from those formerly used for the similar purpose.

3 *Scott v Hamling & Co Ltd* (1896) 14 RPC 123 at 140; *Assidoman Multipack Ltd v Mead Corpn* [1995] RPC 321 at 345–346.

4 *Crosthwaite Fire Bar Syndicate Ltd v Senior* (1909) 26 RPC 713 at 732.

5 *Donnersmarckhütte Oberschlesische Eisen und Kohlenwerke AG v Electric Construction Co Ltd* (1910) 27 RPC 774 at 783, CA.

6 *International Harvester Co of America v Peacock* (1908) 25 RPC 765 at 777, PC.

7 *Shoketsu Kinzoku Kogyo KK's Patent* [1992] FSR 184.

482.   Combination by selection. There can be a valid claim to a mere collocation of separate integers none of which interact[1], or of successive processes, or steps in a process, which are directed to different qualities of the article to be manufactured[2]. In such cases, however, it is prima facie sufficient to invalidate the claim that each integer, or part of the process, is old when taken by itself[3]; the claim can be valid only if invention was involved in selecting the best integers or process steps to put together[4], and only rarely (in the absence of interaction between the integers or steps) can the requirements for a valid selection patent be fulfilled[5]. It is relevant to the validity of such a claim whether the separate integers have been commonly used[6] or their use has been merely suggested in earlier specifications[7]. An important consideration is, however, whether the combination as a whole has resulted in a real advance in the art[8].

1   If some of the integers of the claim interact so as to constitute a true combination, it is no objection to the claim that it specifies other integers irrelevant to the combination, although these surplus integers will normally be disregarded in considering subject matter: *Edison-Bell Phonograph Corpn Ltd v Smith* (1894) 11 RPC 148 at 163 (affd 11 RPC 389, CA); *British Dynamite Co v Krebs* (1896) 13 RPC 190, HL; *British United Shoe Machinery Co Ltd v A Fussell & Sons Ltd* (1908) 25 RPC 631 at 649, CA.

2   An example perhaps is *Lightning Fastener Co Ltd v Colonial Fastener Co Ltd* (1934) 51 RPC 349, PC.

3   See *British Celanese Ltd v Courtaulds Ltd* (1933) 50 RPC 259 at 272, CA (on appeal (1935) 52 RPC 171, HL); and see *Williams v Nye* (1890) 7 RPC 62, CA; *Sharpe and Dohme Inc v Boots Pure Drug Co Ltd* (1927) 44 RPC 367 (affd (1928) 45 RPC 153, CA). See also *Saxby v Gloucester Waggon Co* (1881) 7 QBD 305 (affd (1883) Griffin's Patent Cases (1887) 56, HL); *Re Gaulard and Gibbs' Patent* (1890) 7 RPC 367, HL; *Northern Press and Engineering Co Ltd v Hoe & Co* (1906) 23 RPC 417 (on appeal 23 RPC 613, CA); *Thermos Ltd v Isola Ltd* (1910) 27 RPC 388; *Donnersmarckhütte Oberschlesische Eisen und Kohlenwerke AG v Electric Construction Co Ltd* (1910) 27 RPC 321 (on appeal 27 RPC 774, CA); *Hanks v Coombes* (1928) 45 RPC 237 at 256, CA.

4   *Saxby v Gloucester Waggon Co* (1881) 7 QBD 305 at 312; *Chadburn v Mechan & Sons* (1895) 12 RPC 120 at 154.

5   As to these requirements see PARA 479.

6   Ie so that their respective effects and limitations are known.

7   *Von Heyden v Neustadt* (1880) 50 LJ Ch 126 at 128. CA. See also PARA 479 et seq.

8   *Paterson Engineering Co Ltd v Candy Filter Co Ltd* (1932) 50 RPC 1 at 8, CA; *Shoketsu Kinzoku Kogyo KK's Patent* [1992] FSR 184.

483.   Omission.   There may be invention in the omission of a stage of a process[1], or of an unnecessary part of a machine[2], or of an unnecessary ingredient[3], or in appreciating that previous standards were unnecessarily high[4]. However, a patent of this sort presents great difficulty, and a claim based upon such an inventive step must be strictly limited to things making use of that step[5].

1   'It is just as much invention to reject the bad as to select the good': *British Westinghouse Electric and Manufacturing Co v Braulik* (1910) 27 RPC 209 at 224, CA, per Fletcher Moulton LJ. See also *Russell v Cowley* (1835) 1 Web Pat Cas 457, 465; *Booth v Kennard* (1857) 26 LJ Ex 305; *Leonhardt & Co v Kallé & Co* (1895) 12 RPC 103; *Badische Anilin und Soda Fabrik v Société Chimique des Usines du Rhône and Wilson* (1898) 14 RPC 875 (affd 15 RPC 359, CA).

2   *Minter v Mower* (1835) 1 Web Pat Cas 138. Cf *British Motor Syndicate Ltd v Universal Motor Carriage and Cycle Co Ltd* (1899) 16 RPC 113; *Beston v Watts* (1908) 25 RPC 19, CA.

3   *Cassel Gold Extracting Co Ltd v Cyanide Gold Recovery Syndicate* (1895) 11 TLR 345 at 348, 12 RPC 232 at 254, CA.

4   *Raleigh Cycle Co Ltd v H Miller & Co Ltd* (1946) 63 RPC 113 at 136–137, CA; affd [1948] 1 All ER 308, 65 RPC 141, HL.

5   *Raleigh Cycle Co Ltd v H Miller & Co Ltd* (1946) 63 RPC 113 at 137, CA, impliedly approved on appeal [1948] 1 All ER 308, 65 RPC 141, HL.

484.   Variation.   A variation in scale or degree in an article or process may form subject matter if it has brought about new and useful results[1].

Although it cannot be laid down as a rule of law that there is no patentable subject matter in printing or drawing on articles signs that facilitate their use, the courts have generally refused to recognise the validity of patents having such an object[2]. Similarly, variations in the shape of articles to adapt them for use on a particular machine do not generally form patentable subject matter, even though the machine itself is novel and constitutes a patentable invention[3].

In some cases, and particularly in the case of chemical patents, a variation of old methods has been held to constitute an inventive step because it is not possible to predict the new result from the results of the old methods without experiment and research[4].

1 *British Vacuum Cleaner Co Ltd v Suction Cleaners Ltd* (1904) 21 RPC 303; *British Vacuum Cleaner Co Ltd v London and South Western Rly Co* (1912) 29 RPC 309, HL. See also *Bovill v Cowan* [1867] WN 115; *Bovill v Crate* (1867) Griffin's Patent Cases (1887) 46 at 47; *Thompson v Moore* (1889) 23 LR Ir 599 at 657, 6 RPC 426 at 455; *Nobel's Explosives Co Ltd v Anderson* (1894) 10 TLR 599, 11 RPC 519, CA (affd (1895) 11 TLR 266, 12 RPC 164, HL); *Re Brown's Patent* (1907) 25 RPC 86 at 116, CA; *J Lucas (Batteries) Ltd v Gaedor Ltd* [1978] RPC 297. For the limitation of this principle see, however, *Donnersmarckhütte Oberschlesische Eisen und Kohlenwerke AG v Electric Construction Co Ltd* (1910) 27 RPC 774 at 783, CA. Many chemical process claims are of this nature.

2 *Philpott v Hanbury* (1885) 2 RPC 33; *James Duckett & Son Ltd and Duckett v Sankey & Son* (1899) 16 RPC 357 at 359; *Re Klaber's Patent* (1902) 19 RPC 174; cf *Johnson v Warner Bros Pictures Ltd* (1930) 48 RPC 343.

3 *Lamson Paragon Supply Co Ltd v Carter-Davis Ltd* (1930) 48 RPC 133.

4 *Electric Telegraph Co v Brett* (1851) 20 LJCP 123 at 131; *Moseley v Victoria Rubber Co* (1887) 57 LT 142 at 146, 4 RPC 241 at 252; *Nobel's Explosives Co Ltd v Anderson* (1894) 11 RPC 115 at 127; *Leonhardt & Co v Kallé & Co* (1895) 12 RPC 103; *Lancashire Explosives Co Ltd v Roburite Explosives Co Ltd* (1895) 12 TLR 35, 12 RPC 470, CA (affd (1897) 14 RPC 303, HL); *British Liquid Air Co Ltd v British Oxygen Co Ltd* (1908) 25 RPC 577 at 601, CA; *British United Shoe Machinery Co Ltd v A Fussell & Sons Ltd* (1908) 25 RPC 631 at 648, CA; *Osram Lamp Works Ltd v Z Electric Lamp Manufacturing Co Ltd* (1912) 29 RPC 401 at 421, 423; *Margreth v Acetylene Lamp Co* (1913) 30 RPC 184 at 192; *Ore Concentration Co* (1905) Ltd v Sulphide Corpn Ltd (1914) 31 RPC 206 at 226, PC; *Osram-Robertson Lamp Works Ltd v Pope's Electric Lamp Co Ltd* (1917) 34 RPC 369 at 396, HL. It is otherwise where existing knowledge pointed to the result as probable: see *Re Alsop's Patent* (1907) 24 RPC 733; *Sharpe and Dohme Inc v Boots Pure Drug Co Ltd* (1927) 44 RPC 367 (affd (1928) 45 RPC 153, CA).

485. Adjustments. The courts have generally held that there is no inventive step in a claim to working a machine, process or apparatus in a particular manner or for a particular object[1], or in adjustments to it or in it which are within the capacity of an expert workman[2], but there is no absolute rule; a new use of old apparatus may be validly patentable[3], and an adjustment may produce what is in effect a new article[4].

1 *Kay v Marshall* (1841) 8 Cl & Fin 245, 2 Web Pat Cas 79, HL; *Ralston v Smith* (1865) 11 HL Cas 223; *Bovill v Crate* (1867) Griffin's Patent Cases (1887) 46; *Pugh v Riley Cycle Co Ltd* (1914) 31 RPC 266 at 282, HL; *British United Shoe Machinery Co Ltd v Standard Rotary Machine Co Ltd* (1917) 35 RPC 33, HL; *British Thomson-Houston Co Ltd v Duram Ltd* (1918) 35 RPC 161, HL.

2 *Cincinnati Grinders Inc v BSA Tools Ltd* (1930) 48 RPC 33, CA.

3 *Flour Oxidizing Co Ltd v Carr & Co Ltd* (1908) 25 RPC 428 (a case often cited by higher courts).

4 *Molins v Industrial Machinery Co Ltd* [1937] 4 All ER 295, 55 RPC 31, CA, explaining *British Thomson-Houston Co Ltd v Metropolitan-Vickers Electrical Co Ltd* (1928) 45 RPC 1, HL; *Dyson Appliances Ltd v Hoover Ltd* [2001] RPC 473 at 529. Probably the real question is what adjustments an expert workman would have been likely to think of making: *Pugh v Riley Cycle Co Ltd* (1913) 30 RPC 514, CA; on appeal (1914) 31 RPC 266, HL.

486. Small results. Where a change has been made in a known article or process to effect a small result of trifling or dubious utility, or where it is not essential to the result obtained, the new variation thereby effected does not in general amount to an inventive step[1]. These so-called inventions generally consist in the choice of well-known variants to meet some special purpose often at the sacrifice of other advantages in the forms already in use, in circumstances which lend no weight to the argument that the novelty of the new variation implies that it was not obvious[2].

1   *Re Waterhouse's Patent* (1906) 23 RPC 470 at 477 per Romer LJ. See also *R v Arkwright* (1785) 1 Web Pat Cas 64; *Pow v Taunton* (1845) 9 Jur 1056; *Dangerfield v Jones* (1865) 13 LT 142. Use of the test stated in PARA 454 may, however, lead to such considerations as these being disregarded, as in *Killick v Pye Ltd* [1958] RPC 366, CA.
2   Examples of such patents are *Dobbs v Penn* (1849) 3 Exch 427; *Lawrence v Perry & Co Ltd* (1884) 2 RPC 179; *Re Haddan's Patent* (1885) 2 RPC 218; *Rowcliffe v Longford Wire, Iron and Steel Co Ltd* (1887) 4 RPC 281; *Fletcher v Arden, Hill & Co* (1887) 5 RPC 46; *Tucker v Kaye* (1891) 8 RPC 230, CA; *Wilson v Union Oil Mills Co Ltd* (1891) 9 RPC 57; *Murchland v Nicholson* (1893) 10 RPC 417, Ct of Sess; *Cera Light Co Ltd v Dobbie & Son* (1892) 11 RPC 10; *Montgomerie v Patterson* (1894) 11 RPC 633, Ct of Sess; *Sudbury v Lee and Glen* (1894) 11 RPC 58; *Savage v DB Harris & Sons* (1896) 12 TLR 332, 13 RPC 364, CA; *Beavis v Rylands Glass and Engineering Co Ltd* (1899) 17 RPC 93 (affd (1900) 17 RPC 704, CA); *Patent Exploitation Ltd v American Electrical Novelty and Manufacturing Co Ltd* (1905) 22 RPC 316, CA; *Nadel v Martin* (1905) 23 RPC 41, HL; *British United Shoe Machinery Co Ltd v Hugh Claughton Ltd* (1906) 23 RPC 321 (affd (1907) 24 RPC 33, CA); *Re Waterhouse's Patent* (1906) 23 RPC 470; *Stroud v Humber Ltd* (1906) 24 RPC 141; *Hill v Thomas & Sons* (1907) 24 RPC 415, CA; *Sirdar Rubber Co Ltd and Maclulieh v Wallington, Weston & Co* (1907) 97 LT 113, 24 RPC 539, HL; *Consolidated Pneumatic Tool Co Ltd v Clark* (1907) 24 RPC 593, CA; *Arnot v Dunlop Pneumatic Tyre Co Ltd* (1908) 25 RPC 309, HL; *Witham Bros Ltd and Lord v Catlow, Marsden and Dunn* (1908) 25 RPC 788; *Atkinson v Britton* (1910) 27 RPC 469, CA; *Pugh v Riley Cycle Co Ltd* (1914) 31 RPC 266 at 282, HL; *Mercedes Daimler Motor Co Ltd v FIAT Motor Cab Co Ltd* (1915) 32 RPC 393 at 414, HL; *Re Hancock's Patent* (1917) 34 RPC 283 at 288; *Bloxham v Kee-Less Clock Co* (1922) 39 RPC 195 at 211; *Rose v JW Pickavant & Co Ltd* (1923) 40 RPC 320; *Shaw v Burnet & Co* (1924) 41 RPC 432; *Thomas v South Wales Colliery Tramworks and Engineering Co Ltd* (1924) 42 RPC 22 at 28; *Tucker v Wandsworth Electrical Manufacturing Co Ltd* (1925) 42 RPC 480 at 491 (on appeal 42 RPC 531, CA); *White v Todd Oil Burners Ltd* (1929) 46 RPC 275 at 291.

(v) Industrial Application

487.   Capacity for industrial application.   An invention[1] is taken to be capable of industrial application if it can be made or used in any kind of industry, including agriculture[2].

1   As to the extent of an invention see PARA 430 note 1.
2   Patents Act 1977 s 4(1) (amended by the Patents Act 2004 Sch 2 paras 1(1), 4, Sch 3). The inclusion of agriculture is to remove any doubt that inventions such as new methods of treating crops are patentable.

(vi) Lack of Entitlement to Patent

488.   Patent granted to person not entitled.   A patent is invalid, as against a person with a good title, for a limited period after grant, if the grantee or one of the grantees was not a person entitled to be granted that patent[1]. The function of this provision is to enable cases of misappropriation of inventions or parts of inventions to be resolved; it is not appropriate to the resolution of mere disputes over ownership[2]. The issue of validity may be raised on the ground of disentitlement only by a person found by the court[3] or the comptroller[4] to be entitled to the grant of the patent or part of the patent concerned[5]. Either the proceedings in which the issue is raised, or the proceedings in which the rival title is established, must in general be commenced within two years beginning with the date of the grant[6] unless it is shown that some person registered[7] as a proprietor of the patent knew at the time of the grant or of the transfer of the patent to him that he was not entitled to the patent[8].

1   Patents Act 1977 s 72(1)(b) (substituted by the Copyright, Designs and Patents Act 1988 Sch 5 para 18); and see PARAS 429, 563–563. As to the persons entitled to a patent see the Patents Act 1977 s 7(2); and PARA 306.
2   The effect of a successful challenge to validity is to destroy the patent, which is rarely a practical way of resolving a dispute as to ownership. But see *Henry Bros (Magherafelt) Ltd v Ministry of Defence and Northern Ireland Office* [1997] RPC 693; affd [1999] RPC 442, [1998] All ER (D) 545, CA. As to disputes over ownership of patents see PARA 360 et seq.
3   Ie in an action for a declaration or on a reference under the Patents Act 1977 s 37: see PARA 365. As to the meaning of 'court' see PARA 619 note 1.
4   Ie on a reference under the Patents Act 1977 s 37. As to the comptroller see PARA 575.
5   Such a finding must precede an application to revoke on this ground (see the Patents Act 1977 s 72(2)(a); and see *Dolphin Showers Ltd and Brueton v Farmiloe* [1989] FSR 1 at 6), but it may be made in or concurrently with any other dispute over validity (see the Patents Act 1977 s 74(4), (5); and PARA 519). For example, it may be raised as a defence in infringement proceedings and the court can give directions as to how the issue should be determined: *Dolphin Showers Ltd and Brueton v Farmiloe*. A person to whom the right of a person entitled to be granted the patent has been assigned after the date of the grant of the patent cannot claim for revocation on this ground: *Dolphin Showers Ltd and Brueton v Farmiloe*.
6   See the Patents Act 1977 s 74(4)(b).
7   As to registration see PARA 583 et seq.
8   Patents Act 1977 s 74(4)(b). It appears, however, that, taking the provisions cited in notes 1–7 with s 37, a person who fails to act within the two-year period can thereafter apply to the comptroller (although he may not apply to the court: see s 37(9); and PARA 366) to determine title and can thereafter put validity in issue but not apply to revoke. This was probably not intended, and the effect on third persons of a resulting finding of invalidity is wholly obscure.

(vii) Insufficiency

489.   Patent specification insufficient. A patent is invalid if the specification[1] does not disclose[2] the invention clearly enough and completely enough to enable the invention to be performed by a person skilled in the art[3]. In an ordinary product claim, the product is the invention and it is sufficiently enabled if the specification and common general knowledge enables the skilled person to make it[4].

This objection corresponds closely to one branch of the objection to the validity of patents under the Patents Act 1949 known as 'insufficiency'[5], so the older cases are relevant[6]. Care must be taken, however, in applying the older authorities because of the differences in wording of the relevant provisions of the Patents Act 1949 and the Patents Act 1977 and because the question of sufficiency is one of fact[7].

1   As to the specification see PARA 318.
2   Matter is taken to have been disclosed in a specification if it was either claimed or disclosed, otherwise than by way of disclaimer or acknowledgment of prior art, in that specification: see the Patents Act 1977 s 130(3). The disclosure must be an enabling disclosure: *Biogen Inc v Medeva plc* [1997] RPC 1 at 47, HL; *Synthon BV v Smithkline Beecham* [2005] UKHL 59, [2006] 1 All ER 685, sub nom *Smithkline Beecham plc's (paroxetine methanesulfonate) patent* [2006] RPC 323. The test for enablement for insufficiency and for anticipation is the same: see *Synthon BV v Smithkline Beecham*, sub nom *Smithkline Beecham plc's (paroxetine methanesulfonate) patent*; and PARA 437.
3   Patents Act 1977 ss 72(1)(c), 74(3). As to persons skilled in the art see PARAS 455, 491. The test to be applied is whether the disclosure is sufficient to enable the whole width of the claimed invention to be performed, having regard to the nature and extent of the claim. Enablement of one embodiment of the patent will not always amount to sufficient disclosure: *Chiron Corpn v Murex Diagnostics Ltd (No 12); Chiron Corpn v Organon Teknika Ltd (No 12)* [1996] FSR 153, CA. See also *American Home Products Corpn v Novartis Pharmaceuticals UK Ltd* [2001] RPC 159, CA; *Pharmacia Corpn v Merck & Co, Inc* [2001] EWCA Civ 1610, [2002] RPC 775

at 834; *Norbrook Laboratories Ltd's Patent (Application for Revocation by Schering-Plough)* [2005] EWHC 2532 (Pat), [2006] FSR 302; *Halliburton Energy Services Inc v Smith International Inc* [2006] EWCA Civ 1715, [2006] All ER (D) 246 (Dec); *Kirin-Amgen Inc v Transkaryotic Therapies Inc* [2002] EWCA Civ 1096, [2003] RPC 31 at 71; *Kirin-Amgen Inc v Hoechst Marion Roussel Ltd* [2004] UKHL 46 at [103], [2005] 1 All ER 667 at [103], [2005] RPC 169 at [103] per Lord Hoffman (whether the specification is sufficient or not is highly sensitive to the nature of the invention. The first step is to identify the invention and decide what it claims to enable the skilled man to do. Then one can ask whether the specification enables him to do it); *Synthon BV v Smithkline Beecham* [2005] UKHL 59, [2006] 1 All ER 685, sub nom *Smithkline Beecham plc's (paroxetine methanesulfonate) patent* [2006] RPC 323; *Novartis AG v Johnson & Johnson Medical Ltd (t/a Johnson & Johnson Vision Care)* [2010] EWCA Civ 1039, 118 BMLR 15 (patent did not enable skilled person to predict whether particular product would satisfy requirement of claims without clinical testing); *Eli Lilly & Co v Human Genome Sciences Inc* [2008] EWHC 1903 (Pat) at [239]–[240], 105 BMLR 27 at [239]–[240], [2009] IP & T 306 at [239]–[240] (affd [2011] UKSC 51, [2012] 1 All ER 1154, [2012] RPC 102) (describing the key elements of the requirement that the specification disclose the invention clearly and completely enough for it to be performed by a person skilled in the art); *Corevalve Inc v Edwards Lifesciences AG* [2009] EWHC 6 (Pat), [2009] All ER (D) 66 (Jan) (affd [2010] EWCA Civ 704, [2010] FSR 821, [2010] All ER (D) 266 (Jun)) (there is a difference between the sufficiency of instructions for making a device and the sufficiency of instructions for telling a person how to use it). See also *Generics [UK] Ltd (t/a Mylan) v Yeda Research and Development Co Ltd* [2013] EWCA Civ 925, [2014] RPC 121, [2013] All ER (D) 370 (Jul); *Eli Lilly & Co v Janssen Alzheimer Immunotherapy* [2013] EWHC 1737 (Pat), [2014] RPC 1, [2013] All ER (D) 234 (Jun); *Eli Lilly & Co v Human Genome Sciences Inc* [2012] EWCA Civ 1185, [2012] All ER (D) 34 (Sep).

4   See *Generics (UK) Ltd v H Lundbeck A/S* [2008] EWCA Civ 311 at [27], 101 BMLR 52 at [27], [2008] RPC 437 at [27] per Lord Hoffman (affd [2009] UKHL 12, [2009] 2 All ER 955, [2009] RPC 407). In this case the Court of Appeal declined to find that the decision in *Biogen Inc v Medeva plc* [1997] RPC 1, 38 BMLR 149, HL, established a broad principle but was instead limited to 'product-by-process' claims.

5   Under the Patents Act 1949, it was an objection to the validity of a patent that the complete specification: (1) did not sufficiently and fairly describe the invention and the method by which it was to be performed; or (2) did not disclose the best method of performing it which was known to the applicant for the patent and for which he was entitled to claim protection: see s 32(1)(h) (repealed). Head (1) specified two distinct duties: *Vidal Dyes Syndicate Ltd v Levinstein Ltd* (1912) 29 RPC 245 at 265, CA. In connection with insufficienyl generally see *Regeneron Pharmaceuticals Inc v Genentech Inc* [2013] EWCA Civ 93 at [95]–[103], [2013] IP & T 619 at [95]–[103], [2013] All ER (D) 257 (Feb); *Hospira UK Ltd v Genentech Inc* [2014] EWHC 194 (Pat) at [119]–[143], [2014] All ER (D) 131 (Jun).

6   See PARA 491 et seq.

7   *Mentor Corpn v Hollister Inc* [1991] FSR 557 at 561; *Halliburton Energy Services Inc v Smith International Inc* [2006] EWCA Civ 1715 at [12], [2006] All ER (D) 246 (Dec) at [12]. The relevant statutory provisions are the Patents Act 1949 s 32(1)(h) (repealed) and the Patents Act 1977 s 72(1)(c). See also *Helitune Ltd v Stewart Hughes Ltd* [1991] FSR 171 at 201.

490.   Nature of objection to insufficiency of description. The specification must enable the invention to be performed to the full extent of the monopoly claimed[1]. In order to decide whether the specification is sufficient, the first step is to decide what the invention is and this is to be found by reading and construing the claims[2].

If the invention discloses a principle capable of general application, the claims may be in correspondingly general terms and the patentee does not need to show that he has proved its application in every general instance[3]. On the other hand, if the claims include a number of discrete methods or products, then the patentee has to enable the invention to be performed in respect of each of them[4]. The skilled man does not necessarily have to be put in the position of being able to perform all possible embodiments; it may sometimes be enough if he can make one embodiment using the information in the specification, his own common general knowledge and any reasonable trial and error[5]. The instructions must be such as to enable the skilled addressee to perform the invention using the common general knowledge, carrying out routine methods of trial and error, correcting obvious errors and omissions[6] but without undue effort[7] or prolonged research, inquiry or experiment[8].

1   *Biogen Inc v Medeva plc* [1997] RPC 1 at 48, HL. See also *Generics (UK) Ltd v H Lundbeck A/S* [2008] EWCA Civ 311, [2008] RPC 437, 101 BMLR 52 (affd [2009] UKHL 12, [2009] 2 All ER 955, [2009] RPC 407). The formulation in *Biogen Inc v Medeva plc* of what constituted insufficiency was initially regarded as extending the scope of the objection of insufficiency and a contrast was drawn between so-called 'Biogen' insufficiency and 'classical' insufficiency. There is, however, only one ground of insufficiency, namely that provided for in the Patents Act 1977 s 72(1)(c) (see PARA 489): *Kirin-Amgen Inc v Transkaryotic Therapies Inc* [2002] EWCA Civ 1096, [2003] RPC 31 at 65, CA.

2   *Synthon BV v Smithkline Beecham* [2005] UKHL 59, [2006] 1 All ER 685, sub nom *Smithkline Beecham plc's (paroxetine methanesulfonate) patent* [2006] RPC 323; *Generics (UK) Ltd v H Lundbeck A/S* [2008] EWCA Civ 311 at [29], [2008] RPC 437 at [29], 101 BMLR 52 at [29] (affd [2009] UKHL 12, [2009] 2 All ER 955, [2009] RPC 407).

3   *Biogen Inc v Medeva plc* [1997] RPC 1 at 48, HL. See also *Kirin-Amgen Inc v Hoechst Marion Roussel Ltd* [2004] UKHL 46, [2005] 1 All ER 667, [2005] RPC 169; *Norton's Patent* [2006] FSR 302.

4   *Biogen Inc v Medeva plc* [1997] RPC 1 at 48, HL. See also *Kirin-Amgen Inc v Hoechst Marion Roussel Ltd* [2004] UKHL 46, [2005] 1 All ER 667, [2005] RPC 169; *Norbrook Laboratories Ltd's Patent* [2006] FSR 302. See also *Genentech I/Polypeptide expression* (T 292/85) [1989] OJ EPO 275; *Exxon/Fuel Oils* (T 409/91) [1994] OJ EPO 653.

5   *Quantel Ltd v Spaceward Microsystems Ltd* [1990] RPC 83 at 136; *Mölnlycke AB v Procter & Gamble Ltd (No 5)* [1994] RPC 49 at 99, CA; *Chiron Corpn v Organon Technika Ltd (No 3)*, *Chiron Corpn v Murex Diagnostics Ltd (No 3)* [1994] FSR 202 at 240.

6   *Valensi v British Radio Corpn* [1973] RPC 337, CA (a case under the Patents Act 1949); *Helitune Ltd v Stewart Hughes Ltd* [1991] FSR 171 at 197.

7   *Halliburton Energy Services Inc v Smith International Inc* [2006] EWCA Civ 1715 at [19], [2006] All ER (D) 246 (Dec) at [19].

8   *Valensi v British Radio Corpn* [1973] RPC 337, CA (a case under the Patents Act 1949); *Helitune Ltd v Stewart Hughes Ltd* [1991] FSR 171; *Mentor Corpn v Hollister Inc* [1993] RPC 7.

491. The skilled addressee. The sufficiency of the directions depends on the presumed skill of the person to whom the specification is addressed[1], namely the person who is expected to carry the invention into practice[2], and he will be presumed to combine a reasonable amount of common sense with a knowledge of the technical area or areas to which the invention relates as they existed at the date of the patent[3].

The nature of the invention determines the level of sophistication required of the skilled addressee. For example, in the case of an elaborate scientific process the addressee may be presumed to be a competent scientist, such as would direct the operations of a factory[4], whereas in the case of a simple invention the directions should be sufficient to enable the ordinary workman to carry it out without further instructions[5]. In some cases the addressee, in order to be properly qualified, may need to possess more than one qualification, for example to be a chemist and also a mechanic[6]. Nowadays the addressee may be a graduate scientist or a research team[7].

1   Authorities on the nature of the skilled addressee in relation to novelty and to lack of inventive step are equally applicable in relation to insufficiency: *Synthon BV v Smithkline Beecham* [2005] UKHL 59, [2006] 1 All ER 685, sub nom *Smithkline Beecham plc's (paroxetine methanesulfonate) patent* [2006] RPC 323. As to such skilled addressees see PARA 455. However, it should be remembered that in relation to insufficiency the task of the skilled person is to attempt to perform the claimed invention and to have that goal in mind: *Synthon BV v Smithkline Beecham*, sub nom *Smithkline Beecham plc's (paroxetine methanesulfonate) patent*.

2   *Osram-Robertson Lamp Works Ltd v Pope's Electric Lamp Co Ltd* (1917) 34 RPC 369, HL.
For example, the lampmaker, and not the chemist, was held to be the addressee of a lamp patent
(*Z Electric Lamp Manufacturing Co Ltd v Marples, Leach & Co Ltd* (1910) 27 RPC 305 (on
appeal 27 RPC 737, CA); *Osram Lamp Works Ltd v Z Electric Lamp Manufacturing Co Ltd*
(1912) 29 RPC 401 at 424); and the skilled worker in gutta percha, and not the golf
professional, was held to be the addressee of a ball patent (*Haskell Golf Ball Co Ltd v
Hutchinson (No 2)* (1905) 22 RPC 478 at 493). Earlier cases tended to regard the specification
as being addressed in the first place to the factory manager, works chemist or metallurgist,
engineering draughtsman or the like (see e g *Leonhardt & Co v Kallé & Co* (1895) 12 RPC 103;
Knight v Argylls Ltd (1913) 30 RPC 321, CA; *Gold Ore Treatment Co of Western Australia Ltd
v Golden Horseshoe Estates Co Ltd* (1919) 36 RPC 95, PC). Nowadays, the courts are prepared
to accept that the specification may be addressed to persons with a high level of expertise:
Valensi v British Radio Corpn [1973] RPC 337, CA (addressees of a specification of a new
colour television system were held to be technicians, rather than the graduate scientists then
working in that field). See also *Standard Brands Inc's Patent (No 2)* [1981] RPC 499, CA;
Mentor Corpn v Hollister Inc [1991] FSR 557 at 562 (affd [1993] RPC 7 at 14, CA); *Chiron
Corpn v Organon Technika Ltd (No 3), Chiron Corpn v Murex Diagnostics Ltd (No 3)* [1994]
FSR 202 at 240; *Genentech Inc's Patent* [1989] RPC 147, CA; *Biogen Inc v Medeva plc* [1997]
RPC 1, HL; *Kirin-Amgen Inc v Hoechst Marion Roussel Ltd* [2004] UKHL 46, [2005] 1 All ER
667, [2005] RPC 169 (research team involved in recombinant DNA technology).

3   *Incandescent Gas Light Co Ltd v De Mare Incandescent Gas Light System Ltd* (1896) 13 RPC
301 at 320 (on appeal 12 TLR 495, 13 RPC 559, CA); *Re Tiemann's Patent* (1899) 16 RPC 561
at 575; *Z Electric Lamp Manufacturing Co Ltd v Marples, Leach & Co Ltd* (1910) 27 RPC 737
at 745, CA; *Submarine Signal Co v Henry Hughes & Son Ltd* (1931) 49 RPC 149. In
connection with the role of the skilled addressee in cases of claimed ambiguity see *Generics
[UK] Ltd (t/a Mylan) v Yeda Research and Development Co Ltd* [2013] EWCA Civ 925, [2014]
RPC 121, [2013] All ER (D) 370 (Jul).

4   *Badische Anilin und Soda Fabrik v Levinstein* (1887) 12 App Cas 710, 4 RPC 449, HL;
Incandescent Gas Light Co Ltd v De Mare Incandescent Gas Light System Ltd (1896) 13 RPC
301 at 327; *Re Tiemann's Patent* (1899) 16 RPC 561 at 574, 575. See also *Neilson v Harford*
(1841) 1 Web Pat Cas 295 at 331; *Edison and Swan United Electric Light Co Ltd v Holland*
(1889) 5 TLR 294 at 298, 6 RPC 243 at 280, CA.

5   *Plimpton v Malcolmson* (1876) 3 ChD 531 at 568; *Kraft, Kraft Cheese Co Inc and Kraft Walker
Cheese Co Pty Ltd v McAnulty* (1931) 48 RPC 536, PC.

6   *Osram-Robertson Lamp Works Ltd v Pope's Electric Lamp Co Ltd* (1917) 34 RPC 369 at
391, HL.

7   *American Cyanamid Co v Ethicon Ltd* [1979] RPC 215. See also *Helitune Ltd v Stewart
Hughes Ltd* [1991] FSR 171 at 197 (technician skilled in making radiation detectors). See also
the contemporary decisions cited in note 1.

492.   Subsequent knowledge.   The relevant date of compliance with the
requirement of sufficiency is the date of the application for the patent[1].
Subsequent knowledge may not be used either to supplement the disclosure or to
render a sufficient disclosure insufficient[2].

1   *Biogen Inc v Medeva plc* [1997] RPC 1 at 54, HL.
2   *Biogen Inc v Medeva plc* [1997] RPC 1 at 54, HL.

493.   Enablement.   Whether a specification is sufficient is a question of fact[1].
The requirements are that any directions given be both clear and complete[2]. It is
assumed that the skilled person is seeking success and not failure[3]. In some cases,
it may not be necessary to give detailed instructions as the skilled person might
naturally expect to determine such matters for himself provided he would have
no difficulty in so doing[4].

Directions must be sufficient for the due execution of the invention
throughout the range claimed[5], including special directions for special cases if the
competent workman is not likely to know these already[6]. In cases involving
patents for a class of processes, however, the patentee is not bound to give
exhaustive examples[7]. Although the directions must be sufficient for carrying out

the invention in all cases specifically described[8], it is not necessary that all possible ways in which the invention can be carried out should be described, since in many cases there may be alternatives involving invention which would come within the ambit of the claim. This is more particularly the case where the claim is of a functional nature[9]. The requirements for sufficiency are no stricter where the claim is of a functional nature[10]. A patentee need not deal with matters of scientific theory[11].

1   *Mentor Corpn v Hollister Inc* [1993] RPC 7; *Molnlycke AB v Procter & Gamble Ltd (No 5)* [1992] FSR 549, [1994] RPC 49; *Kirin-Amgen Inc v Transkaryotic Therapies Inc* [2002] RPC 1 at 117.

2   See the Patents Act 1977 s 72(1)(c); and PARAS 489–490.

3   *British Thomson-Houston Co Ltd v Corona Lamp Works Ltd* (1921) 39 RPC 49 at 92, HL; *Kirin-Amgen Inc v Transkaryotic Therapies Inc* [2002] EWCA Civ 1096 at [96], [2003] RPC 31 at [96], CA ('lawyers can often think up puzzles at the edge of a claim, but skilled persons are concerned with practicalities not puzzles').

4   *British Ore Concentration Syndicate Ltd v Minerals Separation Ltd* (1909) 26 RPC 124 at 139, CA.

5   *British Thomson-Houston Co Ltd v Corona Lamp Works Ltd* (1921) 39 RPC 49, HL; *Felton v Greaves* (1829) 3 C & P 611; *Vidal Dyes Syndicate Ltd v Levinstein Ltd* (1912) 29 RPC 245, CA. See also *Maxim-Nordenfelt Guns and Ammunition Co Ltd and Maxim v Anderson* (1897) 14 RPC 371, CA (on appeal (1898) 15 RPC 421, HL); *Re Tiemann's Patent* (1899) 16 RPC 561 at 575; *Kopp v Rosenwald Bros* (1902) 20 RPC 154, CA; *Carnegie Steel Co v Bell Bros Ltd* (1909) 26 RPC 265. Thus a patent for the production of dyes which named in the specification four bodies to be treated with sulphur was held to be bad because, although the directions for heating three of them were sufficient, they were insufficient as regards the fourth body: *Vidal Dyes Syndicate Ltd v Levinstein Ltd*.

6   The following are examples of insufficient directions: a patent for making belts from 'hard-woven' cotton canvas, of which only three out of ten known qualities were suitable for the invention, was held invalid in the absence of evidence that a workman would know which qualities to use: *Gandy v Reddaway* (1883) 2 RPC 49, CA. See also *Wegmann v Corcoran* (1879) 13 ChD 65, CA; *Badische Anilin und Soda Fabrik v Société Chimique des Usines du Rhône and Wilson* (1898) 14 RPC 875 (affd 15 RPC 359, CA); *Wilson Bros Bobbin Co Ltd v Wilson & Co (Barnsley) Ltd* (1902) 20 RPC 1 at 16, HL; *European Eibel Co Ltd v Edward Lloyd Ltd* (1911) 28 RPC 349; *Osram-Robertson Lamp Works Ltd v Pope's Electric Lamp Co Ltd* (1917) 34 TLR 24, 34 RPC 369 at 384, 394, HL; *Kraft, Kraft Cheese Co Inc and Kraft Walker Cheese Co Pty Ltd v McAnulty* (1931) 48 RPC 536, PC; *International de Lavaud Manufacturing Corpn Ltd, Stanton Ironworks Co Ltd and Cochrane (Middlesbro) Foundry Ltd v Clay Cross Co Ltd* (1941) 58 RPC 177 at 195; *Bristol-Myers Co (Johnson and Hardcastle's) Application* [1974] RPC 389 (where a salt was specified as a starting material but only the anhydrous form produced the invention claimed, and the directions were held to be insufficient). The case of *John Summers & Sons Ltd v Cold Metal Process Co* (1947) 65 RPC 75 at 110 possibly falls under this rule. The following are examples of sufficient directions: a patent which referred to the use of gunpowder or other proper combustible material was held sufficient on evidence that a competent workman would know what could be used (*Bickford v Skewes* (1841) 1 QB 938); flax and like yarns (*Pirrie v York Street Flax Spinning Co Ltd* (1894) 11 RPC 429, CA); where a patent for mattresses, after describing a particular mesh, stated that others could be used, it was held valid on evidence that a competent workman would know which meshes would produce the effect described (*J and J Evans, Taunton Ltd v Hoskins and Sewell Ltd* (1907) 24 RPC 517, CA).

7   *Re Gaulard and Gibbs' Patent* (1889) 6 RPC 215 at 224, CA (on appeal (1890) 7 RPC 367, HL); *Leonhardt & Co v Kallé & Co* (1895) 12 RPC 103; *British Dynamite Co v Krebs* (1896) 13 RPC 190, HL; *Thermit Ltd v Weldite Ltd* (1907) 24 RPC 441; *Minerals Separation Ltd v Ore Concentration Co (1905) Ltd* [1909] 1 Ch 744, 26 RPC 413, CA; *Flour Oxidizing Co Ltd v Hutchinson* (1909) 26 RPC 597.

8   *Amalgamated Carburetters Ltd v Bowden Wire Ltd* (1930) 48 RPC 105 at 122; *No-Fume Ltd v Frank-Pitchford & Co Ltd* (1935) 52 RPC 231 at 250, CA.

9   It is said that before the expiry of the original telephone patents there were 1,400 patents for improvements all of which fell within the main claims of the master patent.

10 See *International Business Machines Corpn's Application* [1970] RPC 533.

11 *Coles v Baylis, Lewis & Co* (1886) 3 RPC 178; *Leonhardt & Co v Kallé & Co* (1895) 12 RPC 103 at 116; *Atkins and Applegarth v Castner-Kellner Alkali Co Ltd* (1901) 18 RPC 281 at 295; *Re Andrews' Patent* (1907) 24 RPC 349 at 372, CA (on appeal (1908) 25 RPC 477, HL); *Re Le Rasoir Apollo, Letters Patent No 239,112* (1931) 49 RPC 1.

494. Exceptional cases. The courts are not anxious to find insufficiency, if the specification is fairly drawn[1], and will not do so merely because exceptional cases[2] or unlikely materials[3] might come within the words of the specification and will not work, or because the words do not exclude a mistake which a competent workman would not make[4]. The courts are also reluctant to find insufficiency on the ground that a claim purports to define its extent by reference to a qualitative rather than a quantitative requirement[5]. The question whether the directions contained in a specification are sufficient is generally one of fact depending on the evidence offered[6].

1 *Raleigh Cycle Co Ltd v H Miller & Co Ltd* [1948] 1 All ER 308 at 310, 65 RPC 141 at 147, HL.

2 *Morgan v Seaward* (1836) 1 Web Pat Cas 170 at 180.

3 A patentee gave directions to use carbon gas; carbon dioxide and carbon monoxide which were useless and which were covered by this description were excluded on the evidence that no competent workman would think of using them: *Edison and Swan Electric Lighting Co v Woodhouse and Rawson* (1887) 3 TLR 367, 4 RPC 99, CA; *Edison and Swan United Electric Light Co Ltd v Holland* (1889) 5 TLR 294, 6 RPC 243, CA. See also *Stevens v Keating* (1847) 2 Web Pat Cas 175 at 183; *Thermit Ltd v Weldite Ltd* (1907) 24 RPC 441; *Flour Oxidizing Co Ltd v Hutchinson* (1909) 26 RPC 597 at 626; *Osram-Robertson Lamp Works Ltd v Pope's Electric Lamp Co Ltd* (1917) 34 TLR 24, 34 RPC 369, HL.

4 *Osram-Robertson Lamp Works Ltd v Pope's Electric Lamp Co Ltd* (1917) 34 TLR 24, 34 RPC 369, HL; *Commercial Solvents Corpn v Synthetic Products Co Ltd* (1926) 43 RPC 185 at 222; *No-Fume Ltd v Frank Pitchford & Co Ltd* (1935) 52 RPC 231 at 243, CA. Errors in the drawings which would not mislead a workman will not invalidate a patent (*British United Shoe Machinery Co Ltd v A Fussell & Sons Ltd* (1908) 25 RPC 364 at 385; on appeal 25 RPC 631, CA), but such error must be an obvious one (*Knight v Argylls Ltd* (1913) 30 RPC 321, CA).

5 *Kirin-Amgen Inc v Transkaryotic Therapies Inc* [2002] RPC 1 at 116. See also *British Thomson-Houston Co Ltd v Corona Lamp Works Ltd* (1921) 39 RPC 49, HL; *Cleveland Graphite Bronze Co v Glacier Metal Co Ltd* (1950) 67 RPC 149, HL. See also PARA 493.

6 The burden of proof is on the person alleging that the patent is insufficient: *Kirin-Amgen Inc v Transkaryotic Therapies Inc* [2002] EWCA Civ 1096, [2003] RPC 31. It is often necessary for the allegation of insufficiency to be supported by the carrying out of experiments to show that the directions contained in the specification do not allow the invention to be performed. As to experiments see PARA 535; and see eg *Smithkline Beecham plc v Apotex Europe Ltd* [2004] EWCA Civ 1568, [2005] FSR 524; *Mayne Pharma Pty Ltd v Debiopharm SA* [2006] EWHC 164 (Pat), [2006] FSR 656.

495. Experiments. A description is insufficient if undue experimentation is requisite[1]. Trials to ascertain the best working conditions or to arrive at a successful result may be a necessity[2], but there must be sufficient directions for the competent reader of the specification to know what trials to make and how to perform them[3]. In particular, where the invention claimed is defined by words of degree, or in terms of the result to be achieved, the instructions must enable the reader, over the whole width of the claim, to obtain success with the aid of simple experiments only[4]. In a simple invention the description should make tests unnecessary[5]. Proportions may be given broadly, unless exactitude is of the essence of the invention or essential to success[6].

1 *No-Fume Ltd v Frank Pitchford & Co Ltd* (1935) 52 RPC 231, CA; *Valensi v British Radio Corpn* [1973] RPC 337, CA; *Standard Brands Inc's Patent (No 2)* [1981] RPC 499, CA; *Mentor Corpn v Hollister Inc* [1993] RPC 7 at 14, CA.

2 *Neilson v Harford* (1841) 1 Web Pat Cas 295 at 320; *Otto v Linford* (1882) 46 LT 35, CA;
   Edison and Swan United Electric Light Co Ltd v Holland (1889) 5 TLR 294, 6 RPC 243, CA;
   Leonhardt & Co v Kallé & Co (1895) 12 RPC 103 at 116; *British Dynamite Co v Krebs* (1896)
   13 RPC 190, HL; *Thermit Ltd v Weldite Ltd* (1907) 24 RPC 441 at 461; *Watson, Laidlaw
   & Co Ltd v Pott, Cassels and Williamson* (1911) 28 RPC 565, HL; *No-Fume Ltd v Frank
   Pitchford & Co Ltd* (1935) 52 RPC 231, CA.
3 *Fox v Astrachans Ltd* (1910) 27 RPC 377.
4 *British Thomson-Houston Co Ltd v Corona Lamp Works Ltd* (1921) 39 RPC 49, HL;
   No-Fume Ltd v Frank Pitchford & Co Ltd (1935) 52 RPC 231, CA.
5 *Hinks & Son v Safety Lighting Co* (1876) 4 ChD 607 at 617; *Fletcher v Arden, Hill & Co*
   (1887) 5 RPC 46; *Kinmond v Keay* (1903) 20 RPC 497, Ct of Sess.
6 Cases on this point were reviewed in *No-Fume Ltd v Frank Pitchford & Co Ltd* (1935) 52 RPC
   231, CA. Among the older cases where the directions as to proportions were found to be
   sufficient are *Muntz v Foster* (1843) 2 Web Pat Cas 93; *Patent Type Founding Co v Richard*
   (1859) John 381; *Betts v Menzies* (1862) 10 HL Cas 117; *Neilson v Betts* (1871) LR 5 HL 1;
   British Ore Concentration Syndicate Ltd v Minerals Separation Ltd (1909) 27 RPC 33, HL. For
   cases where the instructions were held to be insufficient see *Lane Fox v Kensington and
   Knightsbridge Electric Lighting Co* (1892) 9 RPC 413, CA; *Kinmond v Keay* (1903) 20 RPC
   497, Ct of Sess; *Nicholls v Kershaw* (1910) 27 RPC 237 at 250; *Vidal Dyes Syndicate Ltd v
   Levinstein Ltd* (1912) 29 RPC 245 at 260, CA. The danger of relying on indefinite adjectives
   such as 'deep' or 'shallow' was pointed out in *Re Taylor's Patent* (1916) 33 RPC 138, CA, but
   the specification may make it sufficiently clear what such terms mean: see *British
   Thomson-Houston Co Ltd v Corona Lamp Works Ltd* (1920) 37 RPC 277, CA; *British
   Thomson-Houston Co Ltd v Corona Lamp Works Ltd (No 2)* (1922) 39 RPC 212; *Re
   Lowndes' Patent* (1927) 45 RPC 48; *No-Fume Ltd v Frank Pitchford & Co Ltd* (1935) 52 RPC
   231, CA; *Dow Chemical AG v Spence Bryson & Co Ltd* [1984] RPC 359 at 391, CA.

496. Biological material and sequence listings. The specification of an
application for a patent, or of a patent, for an invention[1] which involves the use
of or concerns biological material is to be treated as disclosing the invention in a
manner which is clear enough and complete enough for the invention to be
performed by a person skilled in the art if it complies with the requirements for
depositing the biological material[2]. Where the specification of an application
discloses a sequence, it must include a sequence listing[3].

1 As to the meaning of 'invention' see PARA 301 note 2.
2 See the Patents Rules 2007, SI 2007/3291, r 13(1), Sch 1; and PARA 321.
3 See the Patents Rules 2007, SI 2007/3291, r 13(2), Sch 1; and PARA 322.

(viii) Extensions to Disclosure

497. Amendment extending disclosure. A patent is invalid if the matter
disclosed[1] in the specification of the patent extends beyond that disclosed in the
application for the patent as filed[2], because of amendments made to the
specification since the date of filing.

Similarly, a patent granted on a divisional application[3], or a new application
filed[4] following a dispute as to title, will be invalid if the matter disclosed in the
new specification extends beyond that disclosed in the patent application[5].

1 As to the meaning of 'disclosed' see PARA 489 note 3.
2 See the Patents Act 1977 ss 72(1)(d), 74(3). As to the meaning of 'application as filed' see PARA
   316 note 2. As to whether matter disclosed in the specification extends beyond that disclosed in
   the application as filed due to amendment see PARAS 351–352.
3 Ie under the Patents Act 1977 s 15(4): see PARA 315.
4 Ie under the Patents Act 1977 s 8(3) (see PARA 361), s 12 (see PARA 363) or s 37(4) (see PARA
   365). For limitations on such later applications disclosing matter extending beyond that
   disclosed in the patent application see s 76(1); and PARAS 351–352.
5 Patents Act 1977 ss 72(1)(d), 74(3).

(ix) Extensions to Protection

498. Amendment extending protection. A patent is invalid if the protection conferred by it is extended by amendment of the specification after grant[1]. The protection granted by a patent is that specified by the claims as interpreted by the description and drawings, if any[2].

1 See the Patents Act 1977 ss 72(1)(e), 74(3), 76(2); and PARA 351. Section 72(1)(e) relates only to post-grant amendments: *Liversedge v British Telecommunications plc (AC Egerton, third party)* [1991] RPC 229.
2 See the Patents Act 1977 s 125(1); and PARA 430 note 1.

8. INFRINGEMENT

(1) CAUSE OF ACTION FOR INFRINGEMENT

499. Questions arising on an alleged infringement. The question of infringement of a patent involves consideration of two matters. The first is whether the article or process alleged to infringe falls within the scope of the monopoly granted by the patent; and the second is whether the alleged infringer has done, in relation to that article or process, any act the monopoly in which is given by a patent to its proprietor[1].

1   See PARA 500 et seq.

500. The test of infringement. To determine whether a patent is infringed, the specification and, in particular, its claims must be construed, purposively and with due regard to the European Patent Convention[1], to determine its essential integers. If it then appears that the alleged infringement falls entirely within the words of some claim, no further question arises; the patent is infringed[2]. If, however, what is alleged to infringe is some variant of what is claimed, the question must be looked at more closely. The question in each case is whether persons with practical knowledge and experience of the kind of work in which the invention is intended to be used would understand that strict compliance with a particular descriptive word or phrase appearing in a claim was intended by the patentee to be an essential requirement of the invention so that any variant would fall outside the monopoly claimed, even though it could have no material effect on the way the invention worked[3]. In many cases, the following guidelines[4] have been found to be useful. There will still be infringement if, but only if:

(1) the variant has no material effect upon the way the invention works;

(2) it was obvious to a skilled reader, at the date of publication of the specification, that this was so; and

(3) it would be apparent to any skilled reader that the words of the claim from which the variant departs could not have been intended to exclude such minor variants[5].

It is not permissible to construe a claim by attempting to distil its principle in the light of an alleged infringement[6]. An integer may not be struck out from the claim merely because it does not appear to make any difference to the inventive concept[7]. Where a patent has multiple claims, it is reasonable to infer that an earlier claim will be read as wider than a later subsidiary claim[8].

1   See the Convention on the Grant of European Patents (Munich, 5 October 1973; TS 20 (1978); Cmnd 7090) (the European Patent Convention) art 69, Protocol; and PARA 644.

2   See eg *Société Nouvelle des Bennes Saphem v Edbro Ltd* [1983] RPC 345 at 359, CA; *Codex Corpn v Racal-Milgo Ltd* [1983] RPC 369, CA; *AC Edwards Ltd v Acme Signs & Displays Ltd* [1992] RPC 131, CA; *Minnesota Mining & Manufacturing Co v Rennicks (UK) Ltd* [1992] RPC 331; *Rediffusion Simulation Ltd v Link-Miles Ltd* [1993] FSR 369; *Scopema Sarl v Scot Seat Direct Ltd* [2013] EWPCC 32, [2013] All ER (D) 152 (Sep) (affd [2014] EWCA Civ 187, [2014] All ER (D) 269 (Feb)).

3   *Catnic Components Ltd v Hill & Smith Ltd* [1982] RPC 183 at 243, HL.

4   *Improver Corpn v Remington Consumer Products Ltd* [1990] FSR 181.

5   *Catnic Components Ltd v Hill & Smith Ltd* [1982] RPC 183 at 243, HL, where earlier cases are reviewed. This formulation has consistently been followed and reference back to earlier cases is unnecessary: *Codex Corpn v Racal-Milgo Ltd* [1983] RPC 369 at 380, CA. Whilst the formulation in *Improver Corpn v Remington Consumer Products Ltd* [1990] FSR 181 at 189, has been found useful by later courts, in *Wheatley v Drillsafe Ltd* [2001] RPC 133, CA, it was

stated that the issue of the construction of claims is a unitary one and the formulation in *Improver Corpn v Remington Consumer Products Ltd* simply aims to assist in arrival at the proper purposive and contextual interpretation. The formulation in *Improver Corpn v Remington Consumer Products Ltd* may be less useful in chemical cases: *Pharmacia Corpn v Merck & Co Inc* [2001] EWCA Civ 1610, [2002] RPC 775 at 796, [2001] All ER (D) 227 (Dec); *Kirin-Amgen Inc v Hoechst Marion Roussel Ltd* [2004] UKHL 46, [2005] 1 All ER 667, [2005] RPC 169. The formulation in *Catnic Components Ltd v Hill & Smith Ltd* was supported in *Kirin-Amgen Inc v Hoechst Marion Roussel Ltd* [2004] UKHL 46 at [45]–[48], [2005] 1 All ER 667 at [45]–[48], [2005] RPC 169 at [45]–[48] per Lord Hoffman, who emphasised that the *Improver* formulation forms guidelines and not formal rules (see at [52]). See also *Merck & Co Inc v Generics (UK) Ltd* [2003] EWHC 2842 (Pat), [2004] RPC 607 as to the permissibility of experiments directed to questions of construction of the type in *Catnic Components Ltd v Hill & Smith Ltd*.

6   *Nobel's Explosives Co Ltd v Anderson, Cordite Case* (1894) 11 RPC 519 at 523, CA (affd (1895) 12 RPC 164, HL); *Willemijn Houdstermaatschappij BV v Madge Networks Ltd* [1992] RPC 386, CA. But see *Rockwater v Technip France SA* [2004] EWCA Civ 381, [2004] RPC 919 at 952.

7   *Société Technique de Pulverisation STEP v Emson Europe Ltd* [1993] RPC 513 at 522; *Wesley Jessen Corpn v Coopervision Ltd* [2003] RPC 355 at 382; *Halliburton Energy Service Inc v Smith International (North Sea) Ltd* [2005] EWHC 1623 (Pat), [2006] RPC 25.

8   *Ultraframe (UK) Ltd v Eurocell Building Plastics Ltd* [2004] EWHC 1785 (Ch) at [77], [2005] RPC 111 at [77].

501.   Inessential integers.   It follows from the test of infringement[1] that infringement is not necessarily avoided by replacing an inessential integer by a variant, or omitting it altogether[2]. If, however, ingenuity or invention would be needed to appreciate that the integer concerned could be replaced in such a way, it is unlikely that it can be an inessential integer[3], or that the replacement could be obviously an immaterial variation.

1   See PARA 500.

2   *Catnic Components Ltd v Hill & Smith Ltd* [1982] RPC 183 at 237, HL; *Fairfax (Dental Equipment) Ltd v S J Filhol Ltd* [1986] RPC 499, CA; *Anchor Building Products Ltd v Redland Roof Tiles Ltd* [1990] RPC 283, CA; *T Bonzel v Intervention Ltd (No 3)* [1991] RPC 553; *Insituform Technical Services Ltd v Inliner UK plc* [1992] RPC 83; *Lux Traffic Controls Ltd v Pike Signals Ltd, Lux Traffic Controls Ltd v Faronwise Ltd* [1993] RPC 107; *PLG Research Ltd v Ardon International Ltd* [1993] FSR 197. See also *Kirin-Amgen Inc v Hoechst Marion Roussel Ltd* [2004] UKHL 46, [2005] 1 All ER 667, [2005] RPC 169.

3   See eg *Improver Corpn v Remington Consumer Products Ltd* [1990] FSR 181; *Southco Inc v Dzus Fastener Europe Ltd* [1992] RPC 299, CA.

502.   Colourable differences.   It also follows from the test of infringement[1] that infringement cannot be avoided by differences from what is claimed that are merely colourable, that is, by merely making the infringing manufacture appear to be different[2]. A difference or variant, although small, which results in something simpler than that patented[3], or leads to a new or significantly improved result[4], may very well be a material one. It depends on whether the skilled reader would not believe the patentee intended to exclude it from the claim and, if he would realise it, had no material effect on the way the inventive concept of the patent worked[5].

1   See PARAS 500–501.

2   See eg *Raleigh Cycle Co Ltd v H Miller & Co Ltd* [1948] 1 All ER 308, 65 RPC 141, HL (which contains instances of more than one difference held 'colourable'); *Beecham Group Ltd v Bristol Laboratories Ltd* [1978] RPC 153, HL (where one penicillin derivative was held to infringe a claim to another derivative as, chemically, it was equivalent to the claimed derivative 'temporarily masked'). See also the cases cited in PARA 501 note 2.

3   *Unwin v Heath* (1855) 5 HL Cas 505; *Plating Co Ltd v Farquharson* (1883) Griffin's Patent Cases (1884–1886) 187; *Nobel's Explosives Co Ltd v Anderson* (1895) 11 TLR 266, 12 RPC

164, HL; *Morris and Bastert v Young* (1895) 12 RPC 455 at 461, HL. These cases decided before *Catnic Components Ltd v Hill & Smith Ltd* [1982] RPC 183 at 237, HL should be regarded, however, as examples only.

4 *Vidal Dyes Syndicate Ltd v Levinstein Ltd* (1912) 29 RPC 245 at 275–276, CA; *RCA Photophone Ltd v Gaumont-British Picture Corpn Ltd and British Acoustic Films Ltd* (1936) 53 RPC 167 at 189, CA. These cases decided before *Catnic Components Ltd v Hill & Smith Ltd* [1982] RPC 183 at 237, HL (see PARA 500 note 5) should be regarded, however, as examples only.

5 *Insituform Technical Services Ltd v Inliner UK plc* [1992] RPC 83 at 92.

503. Ingenuity in infringement. Where the alleged infringing manufacture falls within the words of a claim, it is no defence to show that it involves ingenuity[1]. Only where it is not precisely within the words of any claim is the question whether it involved ingenuity relevant[2].

1 'The superadding of ingenuity to robbery does not make the operation justifiable': *Wenham Gas Co Ltd v Champion Gas Lamp Co* (1892) 9 RPC 49 at 56, CA, per Bowen LJ. See also *Proctor v Bennis* (1887) 36 ChD 740 at 756, 4 RPC 333 at 354, CA; *Haskell Golf Ball Co Ltd v Hutchinson (No 2)* (1908) 25 RPC 194, HL; *Marconi and Marconi's Wireless Telegraph Co Ltd v British Radio-Telegraph and Telephone Co Ltd* (1911) 28 RPC 181 at 218.

2 See PARA 500 et seq.

504. Time within which infringement may be committed. An actionable infringement may be committed from the date of publication of the application[1] until the expiration of the term of the patent[2], but no action for infringement may be commenced until the patent is granted[3]. An act done before the patent is granted[4] will infringe only if it infringes both within the scope of the monopoly of the patent as granted and also within the scope of the claims[5] contained in the application as first published[6].

1 Ie under the Patents Act 1977 s 16: see PARA 326.
2 As to the term of a patent see PARA 338.
3 See the Patents Act 1977 s 69(1), (2)(a).
4 As to grant see PARA 337.
5 Ie those claims as interpreted by the description and any drawings referred to in the description of claims.
6 See the Patents Act 1977 s 69(2)(b).

505. Articles sold by the proprietor of the patent. In the absence of special stipulations[1], articles manufactured or sold by the proprietor of the patent or his agents are licensed generally, and may be used or sold in any manner[2], and, if purchased abroad, may be imported into the United Kingdom[3]. Where a patented product[4] is disposed of by any of two or more proprietors to any person, that person and any other person claiming through him are entitled to deal with the product in the same way as if it had been disposed of by a sole registered proprietor[5]. Where the act complained of is manufacture or user, and is performed at the claimant's instigation, it is generally considered as licensed and does not constitute an infringement[6].

1 As to the effect of limiting conditions see PARA 379 et seq.
2 Where the patent contains claims for an integer per se, and also for its use in a specified combination, it seems that the sale of such an integer licenses its use in the combination: *Arnold v Bradbury* (1871) 6 Ch App 706. See also *Oxley v Holden* (1860) 8 CBNS 666.
3 *Betts v Willmott* (1871) 6 Ch App 239, CA. It is otherwise if the vendor is only a licensee under a foreign patent (*SA des Manufactures de Glaces v Tilghman's Patent Sand Blast Co* (1883) 25 ChD 1, CA); but, where manufacture took place in one of the EU member states either by the proprietor or with his consent (eg by a licensee), the articles purchased may be imported into the United Kingdom (Case 15/74 *Centrafarm BV v Sterling Drug Inc* [1974] ECR 1147, [1974]

2 CMLR 480, ECJ; Case 16/74 *Centrafarm BV v Winthrop BV* [1974] ECR 1183, [1974] 2 CMLR 480, ECJ). As to the meaning of 'United Kingdom' see PARA 303 note 5.

4　As to the meaning of 'patented product' see PARA 371 note 11.

5　Patents Act 1977 s 36(5). See PARA 371.

6　Eg where an agent of the claimant has given an order to the defendant to make an article in a way which infringed the patent (*Kelly v Batchelar* (1893) 10 RPC 289), or where the claimant was himself present on the occasion of user (*Henser and Guignard v Hardie* (1894) 11 RPC 421 at 427); but see to the contrary *Dunlop Pneumatic Tyre Co Ltd v Neal* [1899] 1 Ch 807, 16 RPC 247 (act of infringement held in such circumstances to have been established). This rule does not extend to a sale to an agent of the claimant made in the ordinary course of business (*Dunlop Rubber Co Ltd v Longlife Battery Depot* [1958] 3 All ER 197 at 201, [1958] 1 WLR 1033 at 1039, [1958] RPC 473 at 477), and such sales in response to test purchases are commonly relied on as instances of infringement.

506. Repairs.

506. Repairs. The owner of a patented article is entitled to make genuine repairs[1], or to replace parts of a combination which normally wear out more quickly than other parts[2], even if, in so doing, he would otherwise infringe any copyright belonging to the proprietor of the patent[3]. The implied licence to repair extends to the purchaser's agents and contractors[4].

1　These repairs must not, however, amount to making a substantially new article: *Dunlop Pneumatic Tyre Co Ltd v Neal* [1899] 1 Ch 807, 16 RPC 247; *Dunlop Pneumatic Tyre Co Ltd and Pneumatic Tyre Co Ltd v Excelsior Tyre, Cement and Rubber Co and Baker* (1901) 18 RPC 209; *Dunlop Pneumatic Tyre Co Ltd v Holborn Tyre Co Ltd* (1901) 18 RPC 222. In *Dunlop Pneumatic Tyre Co Ltd v David Moseley & Sons Ltd* (1904) as reported in 21 RPC 274 at 282, CA, Cozens-Hardy LJ expressed a doubt whether these decisions were not too favourable to the proprietor of the patent.

2　*Sirdar Rubber Co Ltd and Maclulieh Ltd v Wallington, Weston & Co* (1905) 22 RPC 257 (on appeal (1906) 23 RPC 132, CA; (1907) 24 RPC 539, HL); *Solar Thomson Engineering Co Ltd v Barton* [1977] RPC 537, CA; *Dellareed Ltd v Delkim Developments* [1988] FSR 329; *Schütz (UK) Ltd v Werit (UK) Ltd* [2011] EWCA Civ 303, [2011] IP & T 650.

3　*Solar Thomson Engineering Co Ltd v Barton* [1977] RPC 537, CA (implied licence under the copyright to give business efficacy to the right to repair a patented article). The owner's right to repair is not an independent right conferred upon him by licence, express or implied but is a residual right, forming part of the right to do whatever does not amount to making the product: *United Wire Ltd v Screen Repair Services (Scotland) Ltd* [2000] 4 All ER 353 at 358, [2001] RPC 439, HL, per Lord Hoffmann. As to copyright see COPYRIGHT vol 23 (2013) PARA 601 et seq.

4　*Solar Thomson Engineering Co Ltd v Barton* [1977] RPC 537, CA.

507. Agent's liability for infringement.

507. Agent's liability for infringement. The ordinary rules as to agency in tort[1] apply to infringement, so that in general both principals and agents are liable[2].

1　See AGENCY vol 1 (2008) PARA 164; TORT vol 97 (2010) PARA 431.

2　*Day v Davies* (1904) 22 RPC 34 at 42. See also *Sykes v Howarth* (1879) 48 LJ Ch 769; *Anderson v Patent Oxonite Co Ltd* (1886) 3 RPC 279; *Incandescent Gas Light Co Ltd v New Incandescent (Sunlight Patent) Gas Lighting Co Ltd* (1897) 76 LT 47, 15 RPC 81; *Incandescent Gas Light Co Ltd v Brogden* (1899) 16 RPC 179. An employee who has merely carried out his employer's orders should not, however, in general be joined as a defendant: *F Savage & Co Ltd v Brindle* (1896) 13 RPC 266. As to the distinction between agent and independent contractor see *Dixon v London Small Arms Co Ltd* (1876) 1 App Cas 632; *Howard and Bullough Ltd v Tweedales and Smalley* (1895) 12 RPC 519; *Henry Bros (Magherafelt) Ltd v Ministry of Defence and Northern Ireland Office* [1997] RPC 693; affd [1999] RPC 442, [1998] All ER (D) 545, CA.

508. Directors' liability for infringement.

508. Directors' liability for infringement. The directors of a company are not personally liable for infringements by the company, even if they are managing directors or the sole directors and shareholders, unless:

　(1)　they have formed the company for the purpose of infringing;

(2)   they have directly ordered or authorised the acts complained of; or

(3)   they have so authorised or ordered by implication[1].

A director may be liable for procuring infringement[2]. A knowing, deliberate, wilful participation in the alleged tort is not an essential pre-condition to personal liability[3]. The director's involvement must, however, be such as would render him liable as a joint tortfeasor if the company had not existed[4].

1   See *Belvedere Fish Guano Co Ltd v Rainham Chemical Works Ltd, Feldman and Partridge* [1920] 2 KB 487 at 521 et seq, CA, per Younger LJ (approved sub nom *Rainham Chemical Works Ltd v Belvedere Fish Guano Co* [1921] 2 AC 465, HL, where the subject is fully considered), from which it would appear that the judgment in *Betts v De Vitre* (1868) 3 Ch App 429 (affd sub nom *Neilson v Betts* (1871) LR 5 HL 1), which was followed in *Welsbach Incandescent Gas Light Co Ltd v Daylight Incandescent Mantle Co Ltd* (1899) 16 RPC 344 (on appeal (1900) 17 RPC 141, CA), must be taken as either overruled or only supportable by reason of the particular acts. See also *Performing Right Society Ltd v Ciryl Theatrical Syndicate Ltd* [1924] 1 KB 1 at 14, CA; *Wah Tat Bank Ltd v Chan Cheng Kum* [1975] AC 507 at 514, [1975] 2 All ER 257 at 259–260, PC; *CBS Songs Ltd v Amstrad Consumer Electronics plc* [1988] AC 1013, [1988] 2 All ER 484, [1988] RPC 567, HL (copyright). See also *British Thomson-Houston Co Ltd v Sterling Accessories Ltd* [1924] 2 Ch 33, 41 RPC 311 (where it was held that the signature by directors, as agents for the company, of a contract for the sale of infringing lamps would not make them liable for infringements); *Reitzman v Grahame-Chapman and Derustit Ltd* (1950) 67 RPC 178 at 185; on appeal 68 RPC 25, CA (director actively engaged in directing infringing activities), and *Leggatt v Hood's Original Licensees' Darts Accessories Ltd and Hood* (1950) 67 RPC 134 at 138; *Mentmore Manufacturing Co Ltd v National Merchandising Manufacturing Co Inc* (1978) 89 DLR (3d) 195 (Fed CA); *C Evans & Sons Ltd v Spriteband Ltd* [1985] 2 All ER 415, [1985] FSR 267, CA. See generally COMPANIES vol 14 (2009) PARA 585 et seq. As to the third ground of liability stated in the text, and as to the particulars necessary where directors are charged with infringement, see *British Thomson-Houston Co Ltd v Irradiant Lamp Works Ltd* (1924) 41 RPC 338; *C Evans & Sons Ltd v Spriteband Ltd*.

2   See PARA 509.

3   *C Evans & Sons Ltd v Spriteband Ltd* [1985] 2 All ER 415, [1985] FSR 267, CA; *MCA Records Inc v Charly Records Ltd* [2001] EWCA Civ 1441, [2002] FSR 401 (copyright).

4   *PLG Research Ltd v Ardon International Ltd* [1993] FSR 197 at 238.

509.   Procuring infringement.   The allegation of procuring infringement by others is probably a distinct tort based on the principle enunciated in *Lumley v Gye*[1] and must be separately pleaded with proper particularity[2]. There is, however, a difference between procuring an infringement and merely facilitating one[3]. The sale of a non-patented article to a person who, to the vendor's knowledge, intended to use it in a patented process does not amount to procuring infringement, nor does supply for that sole purpose[4].

1   See *Lumley v Gye* (1853) 2 E & B 216.

2   *Belegging-en Exploitatiemaatschapij Lavender BV v Witten Industrial Diamonds Ltd* [1979] FSR 59 at 64, CA.

3   *CBS Songs Ltd v Amstrad Consumer Electronics plc* [1988] RPC 567 at 609, HL, citing *Belegging-en Exploitatiemaatschappij Lavender BV v Witten Industrial Diamonds Ltd* [1979] FSR 59 at 65, CA; applied in *PLG Research Ltd v Ardon International Ltd* [1993] FSR 197 at 239; *Kalman v PCL Packaging (UK) Ltd* [1982] FSR 406.

4   *Townsend v Haworth* (1875) 12 ChD 831n, CA; *Dunlop Pneumatic Tyre Co Ltd v David Moseley & Sons Ltd* [1904] 1 Ch 612, 21 RPC 274, CA; *Belegging-en Exploitatiemaatschapij Lavender BV v Witten Industrial Diamonds Ltd* [1979] FSR 59, CA. See, however, PARA 512.

510.   Undertaking not to infringe.   The court will enforce a contractual undertaking given to the proprietor of a patent not to infringe the patent if the undertaking is limited to the term of the patent[1], even though the patent ceases to be in force before the end of that term[2]. If not so limited, the undertaking will normally be void as in unreasonable restraint of trade[3]. Prior specifications are not relevant to an action on such an undertaking[4]; nor is it open to the defendant to put validity in issue[5].

1   *Bescol (Electrics) Ltd v Merlin Mouldings Ltd* (1952) 69 RPC 297. As to the term of patents see PARA 338.

2   *Heginbotham Bros Ltd v Burne* (1939) 56 RPC 399, CA.

3   *Bescol (Electrics) Ltd v Merlin Mouldings Ltd* (1952) 69 RPC 297; *Dranez Anstalt v Hayek* [2002] EWCA Civ 1729, [2003] 1 BCLC 278, [2003] FSR 561 (terms of side-letter attached to agreement restraining inventor from competition with patent holder unenforceable). As to restraint of trade generally see COMPETITION vol 18 (2009) PARA 377 et seq.

4   *Heinemann Electric Co v Dorman and Smith Ltd* (1955) 72 RPC 162, CA. For cases of agreement not to put validity in issue or not to use a patented process see *Hills v Laming* (1853) 23 LJ Ex 60; *MacDougall Bros v Partington* (1890) 7 RPC 216; *Howard and Bullough Ltd v Tweedales and Smalley* (1896) 13 RPC 211; *Roberts v Graydon* (1904) 21 RPC 194; *Hay v Gonville* (1908) 25 RPC 161; *Watts v Everitt Press Manufacturing Co* (1910) 27 RPC 718, CA. For cases of estoppel by judgment see *Dudgeon v Thomson* (1877) 3 App Cas 34, HL; *Thompson v Moore* (1889) 23 LR Ir 599, 6 RPC 426; *Multiform Displays Ltd v Whitmarley Displays Ltd* [1956] RPC 143, CA (on appeal [1957] RPC 260, HL).

5   *C Van der Lely NV v Maulden Engineering Co (Beds) Ltd* [1984] FSR 157. This may, however, be incompatible with EU law: cf Case 65/86 *Bayer AG v Maschinenfabrik Hennocke GmbH v Süllhöfer* [1988] ECR 5249, [1990] 4 CMLR 182, [1990] FSR 300, ECJ (no-challenge clause in patent litigation settlement agreement).

(2)   ACTS OF INFRINGEMENT

511.   Direct infringement.   Subject to certain exceptions[1], a person infringes a patent[2] for an invention if, but only if, while the patent is in force[3], he does any of the following things in the United Kingdom[4] without the consent of the proprietor of the patent[5]:

(1)   where the invention is a product, he makes[6], disposes of[7], offers to dispose of[8], uses[9] or imports the product[10] or keeps it[11] whether for disposal or otherwise[12];

(2)   where the invention is a process, he uses the process or he offers it for use in the United Kingdom when he knows, or it is obvious to a reasonable person in the circumstances, that its use there without the consent of the proprietor would be an infringement of the patent[13];

(3)   where the invention is a process, he disposes of, offers to dispose of, uses or imports any product obtained directly[14] by means of that process or keeps any such product whether for disposal or otherwise[15].

In the case of goods manufactured abroad, no infringement is committed by a person whose possession has terminated before their introduction into the United Kingdom[16] unless there is a concerted design between the foreign supplier and the English importer to sell the goods in the United Kingdom[17]. Except where knowledge is an essential element of the tort, the knowledge of the infringer is immaterial[18] except on the question of damages[19].

1   Ie subject to the provisions of the Patents Act 1977 s 60: see PARAS 512–514.

2   As to infringement generally see PARA 499 et seq.

3   As to the term of patents see PARA 338.

4   As to the meaning of 'United Kingdom' see PARA 303 note 5.

5   Patents Act 1977 s 60(1). An act is not an infringement unless it falls within s 60(1), (2) or (3). In the application of s 60 to a patent of which there are two or more joint proprietors the reference to the proprietor is to be construed: (1) in relation to any act, as a reference to that proprietor or those proprietors who, by virtue of s 36 (see PARA 371) or any agreement referred to in s 36, is or are entitled to do that act without its amounting to an infringement; and (2) in

relation to any consent, as a reference to that proprietor or those proprietors who, by virtue of s 36 or any such agreement, is or are the proper person or persons to give the requisite consent: s 66(1).

6   For a detailed interpretation of the word 'makes', and a recital of the matters to be taken into account, see *Schutz (UK) Ltd v Werit (UK) Ltd* [2013] UKSC 16, [2013] 2 All ER 177, [2013] IP & T 321. See also *Goucher v Clayton* (1865) 11 Jur NS 462 at 465; *Lyon v Goddard* (1893) 11 RPC 113 ('makes' covers manufacture for sale in the United Kingdom or abroad).

7   'Disposal' includes selling: *Kalman v PCL Packaging (UK) Ltd* [1982] FSR 406. A sale abroad such that the vendor has no rights to dispose of in the United Kingdom is not an infringement: *Kalman v PCL Packaging (UK) Ltd*, applying *Badische Anilin und Soda Fabrik v Johnson & Co* (1897) 14 RPC 919, HL. See also *Sabaf SpA v MFI Furniture Centres Ltd* [2004] UKHL 45, [2005] RPC 10.

8   The offer must be made in the United Kingdom to dispose of the infringing articles within the jurisdiction: *Kalman v PCL Packaging (UK) Ltd* [1982] FSR 406. See also *Cincinnati Grinders Inc v BSA Tools Ltd* (1931) 48 RPC 33 at 51, CA.

9   Under the previous law the following constituted use: exhibition of an article for trade purposes (*Dunlop Pneumatic Tyre Co Ltd and Pneumatic Tyre Co Ltd v British and Colonial Motor Car Co Ltd* (1901) 18 RPC 313); use of articles as samples to procure orders to be executed abroad (*Badische Anilin und Soda Fabrik v Chemische Fabrik vormals Sandoz* (1903) 88 LT 490, 20 RPC 413, CA). This is probably still good law. See also *Smith Kline and French Laboratories Ltd v Douglas Pharmaceuticals Ltd* [1991] FSR 522, NZ CA (importation of sample for purposes of application for product licence).

10 Importation is the act of bringing the goods into the United Kingdom: see *Sabaf SpA v MFI Furniture Centres Ltd* [2004] UKHL 45, [2005] RPC 10.

11 The storage of goods by a carrier pending the settlement of a dispute between the proprietor and an alleged infringer has been held not to be 'keeping' for this purpose (*Smith Kline and French Laboratories Ltd v RD Harbottle Ltd* [1980] 1 CMLR 277, [1980] RPC 363) nor does delivering it to a third party amount to an infringing 'disposal' (*Kalman v PCL Packaging (UK) Ltd* [1982] FSR 406). Under the old law keeping a machine as a stand-by was an infringement (*British United Shoe Machinery Co Ltd v Simon Collier Ltd* (1909) 25 TLR 415, 26 RPC 534, CA; on appeal (1910) 27 RPC 567, HL) and so was possession for the purposes of infringement (*British United Shoes Machinery Co Ltd v Simon Collier Ltd*). Possession or the transport of an infringing article for the purpose of sale is infringement: *Betts v Neilson* (1868) 3 Ch App 429 (affd sub nom *Neilson v Betts* (1871) LR 5 HL 1); *Adair v Young* (1879) 12 ChD 13, CA; *United Telephone Co v London and Globe Telephone and Maintenance Co* (1884) 26 ChD 766, 1 RPC 117; *British Motor Syndicate Ltd v Taylor & Son Ltd* [1901] 1 Ch 122, (1900) 17 RPC 723, CA; *Saccharin Corpn Ltd v DTJ Lyle & Son Ltd* (1904) 21 RPC 604, CA; *Saccharin Corpn Ltd v Ross Bros* (1905) 22 RPC 246, Ct of Sess; *Morton-Norwich Products Inc v Intercen Ltd* [1978] RPC 501. A custom house agent who merely passes the goods through customs and delivers them to the consignee does not infringe: *Nobel's Explosives Co Ltd v Jones, Scott & Co* (1882) 8 App Cas 5, HL. As to the position of a warehousing and transporting agent see *Nobel's Explosives Co Ltd v Jones, Scott & Co*; *Washburn and Moen Manufacturing Co v Cunard Steamship Co and JC Parkes & Sons* (1889) 5 TLR 592, 6 RPC 398; *Badische Anilin und Soda Fabrik v Basle Chemical Works, Bindschedler* [1898] AC 200, HL. These cases are probably still good law.

12 Patents Act 1977 s 60(1)(a).

13 Patents Act 1977 s 60(1)(b). See, for example, *Tamglass Ltd OY v Luoyang Glass Technology Co Ltd* [2006] EWHC 65 (Ch), [2006] FSR 608, [2006] All ER (D) 207 (Jan).

14 See *Pioneer Electronics Capital Inc v Warner Music Manufacturing Europe GmbH* [1997] RPC 757, CA, where it was said that: (1) the product obtained directly by means of a patented process is the product with which the process ends; it does not cease to be the product so obtained if it is subjected to further processing which does not cause it to lose its identity, there being no such loss where it retains its essential characteristics; (2) it is a question of fact and degree whether a product with which the patented process ends retains its essential characteristics or not; (3) there is no free standing 'essential characteristics' test, such characteristics being relevant only to the question of loss of identity. See also *Monsanto Technology LLC v Cargill International SA* [2007] EWHC 2257 (Pat), [2008] FSR 153, [2007] All ER (D) 118 (Oct); *Halliburton Energy Services Inc v Smith International (North Sea) Ltd* [2005] EWHC 1623 (Pat), [2006] RPC 25 (affd [2006] EWCA Civ 1715, [2006] All ER (D) 246 (Dec)).

15 Patents Act 1977 s 60(1)(c). Cf the cases under the previous law: *United Horse-Shoe and Nail Co Ltd v Stewart* (1888) 13 App Cas 401, 5 RPC 260, HL (damages assessed on the basis that each sale in the United Kingdom of a nail made abroad on a patented machine was an

infringement, although the nails were not in themselves new). See also *Cartsburn Sugar Refining Co v Sharp* (1884) 1 RPC 181 at 186. The presence of a minor patented feature in a machine did not make articles made on it infringements; there was a question of degree: *Wilderman v FW Berk & Co Ltd* [1925] Ch 116, 42 RPC 79 at 87, where *United Horse-Shoe and Nail Co Ltd v Stewart* was not cited. In *VD Ltd v Boston Deep Sea Fishing and Ice Co Ltd* (1935) 52 RPC 303 at 322, Clauson J refused to hold that the sale of fish caught outside territorial limits with patented apparatus was an infringement of the patent.

16 *Kalman v PCL Packaging (UK) Ltd* [1982] FSR 406. This principle was established under previous law. Thus a foreigner posting such goods from abroad to a customer in the United Kingdom does not infringe since the post is the agent of the consignee: *Badische Anilin und Soda Fabrik v Johnson & Co* (1897) 14 RPC 919, HL. Nor does an agent in the United Kingdom who enters into a contract for delivery of such goods to a customer at a foreign port (*Saccharin Corpn Ltd v Reitmeyer & Co* [1900] 2 Ch 659, 17 RPC 606; *Badische Anilin und Soda Fabrik v Hickson* [1906] AC 419, 23 RPC 433, HL), but it is otherwise if goods are consigned to the defendant in the United Kingdom and then exported (*Betts v Neilson* (1868) 3 Ch App 429; affd sub nom *Neilson v Betts* (1871) LR 5 HL 1). The right to possession of the goods while in transit where the English buyer was not entitled to possession until the price was paid is sufficient possession: *Morton-Norwich Products Inc v Intercen Ltd* [1978] RPC 501. But where title to the goods passes abroad, arranging transportation to the United Kingdom at the purchaser's request is not an infringement: *Sabaf SpA v MFI Furniture Centres Ltd* [2004] UKHL 45, [2005] RPC 10.

17 *Morton-Norwich Products Inc v Intercen Ltd* [1978] RPC 501 at 512, 514. See also *Dow Chemical AG v Spence Bryson & Co Ltd* [1984] RPC 359 at 391, CA; *Puschner v Tom Palmer (Scotland) Ltd* [1989] RPC 430; *Unilever plc v Gillette (UK) Ltd* [1989] RPC 583 at 600, CA; *Intel Corpn v General Instrument Corpn (No 2)* [1991] RPC 235. See also *Mölnlycke AB v Procter & Gamble Ltd (No 4)* [1992] 4 All ER 47, [1992] RPC 21, CA and *Unilever plc v Chefaro Proprietaries Ltd* [1994] FSR 135, CA, where the circumstances which can give rise to joint tortfeasorship and common design are considered.

18 *Stead v Anderson* (1847) 2 Web Pat Cas 151 at 156; *Unwin v Heath* (1855) 5 HL Cas 505 at 537.

19 See the Patents Act 1977 s 62(1); and PARA 547.

512. Indirect infringement.   A person, other than the proprietor of the patent, infringes[1] a patent for an invention if, while the patent is in force[2] and without the proprietor's consent, he supplies or offers to supply in the United Kingdom[3] a person other than a licensee or other person entitled to work the invention[4] with any of the means, relating to an essential element of the invention, for putting the invention into effect when he knows, or it is obvious to a reasonable person in the circumstances, that those means are suitable for putting, and are intended to put, the invention into effect in the United Kingdom[5]. Where the means are a staple commercial product, the supply or offer to supply is not an infringement unless it was made for the purpose of inducing the person supplied, or, as the case may be, the person to whom the offer was made, to do an act which constitutes an infringement[6] of the patent[7].

1 Ie subject to the Patents Act 1977 s 60(3)–(7): see PARAS 511 note 5, 513–515.
2 As to the term of patents see PARA 338.
3 As to the meaning of 'United Kingdom' see PARA 303 note 5.

4 For these purposes, the reference to a person entitled to work an invention includes a reference to a person so entitled by virtue of the Patents Act 1977 s 55 (see PARA 404): s 60(6)(a). As to the position where a co-owner is working the invention for his own benefit see s 36(2)(a), (4); and PARA 371. A person who, by virtue of s 20B(4) or (5) (see PARA 333), s 28A(4) or (5) (see PARA 357), s 64 (see PARA 513) or s 117A(4) or (5) (see PARA 332), is entitled to do an act in relation to the invention without its constituting such an infringement is to be treated, so far as concerns that act, as a person entitled to work the invention: s 60(6)(b) (amended by the Copyright, Designs and Patents Act 1988 Sch 5 para 8(a); and SI 2004/2357). A person who does an act in relation to an invention which is prevented only by virtue of the Patents Act 1977 s 60(5)(a), (b) or (c) (see PARA 513) from constituting an infringement is not, however, to be so treated: s 60(6).

5 Patents Act 1977 s 60(2). An item can count as 'means ... relating to an essential element of the invention, for putting the invention into effect' if it plays a significant role in the working of the invention: see _Nestec SA v Dualit Ltd_ [2013] EWHC 923 (Pat), [2013] RPC 841, [2013] All ER (D) 207 (Apr); see also _Menashe Business Mercantile Ltd v William Hill Organisation Ltd_ [2002] EWCA Civ 1702, [2003] 1 All ER 279, [2003] RPC 575 (a supply of a program to customers in the United Kingdom which enabled them to access a host computer outside the United Kingdom was the supply of a means intended to put the invention into effect in the United Kingdom). The 'knowledge and intention' requirements of the Patents Act 1977 s 60(2) are satisfied if, at the time of supply or offer of supply, the supplier knows, or it is obvious in the circumstances, that ultimate users intend to put the invention into effect: see _Grimme Maschinenfabrik GmbH & Co KG v Derek Scott (t/a Scotts Potato Machinery)_ [2010] EWCA Civ 1110, [2011] FSR 193, [2010] All ER (D) 153 (Oct); _KCI Licensing Inc v Smith & Nephew plc_ [2010] EWCA Civ 1260, 117 BMLR 81. For a case involving indirect infringement see _Anchor Building Products Ltd v Redland Roof Tiles Ltd_ [1990] RPC 283, CA.

6 Ie by virtue of the Patents Act 1977 s 60(1): see PARA 511.

7 Patents Act 1977 s 60(3).

513. Excepted acts; right to continue prior use. An act which would otherwise constitute an act of infringement of a patent[1] does not do so[2] if:

(1) it is done privately and for purposes which are not commercial[3];

(2) it is done for experimental purposes relating to the subject matter of the invention[4];

(3) it consists of the extemporaneous preparation in a pharmacy of a medicine for an individual in accordance with a prescription given by a registered medical or dental practitioner or consists of dealing with a medicine so prepared[5];

(4) it consists of a specified use connected with ships, aircraft, hovercraft or vehicles[6];

(5) it consists of a specified use for plant propagation or animal reproduction by a farmer[7];

(6) it consists of an act done in conducting a study, test or trial which is necessary for and is conducted with a view to the application of the European directives governing veterinary medicinal products[8] or medicinal products for human use[9] or any other act which is required for the purpose of the application of those provisions[10].

Further, where a patent is granted for an invention, a person who in the United Kingdom[11] before the priority date[12] of the invention:

(a) does in good faith an act which would constitute an infringement of the patent if it were in force; or

(b) makes in good faith effective and serious preparations to do such an act,

has the right to continue to do the act or, as the case may be, to do the act, notwithstanding the grant of the patent; but this right does not extend to granting a licence to another person to do the act[13].

If the act was done, or the preparations were made, in the course of a business, the person entitled to the right so conferred may:

(i) authorise the doing of that act by any partners of his for the time being in that business; and

(ii) assign that right, or transmit it on death or, in the case of a body corporate on its dissolution, to any person who acquires that part of the business in the course of which the act was done or the preparations were made[14].

1 See PARAS 511–512.

2 Persons who carry out non-infringing acts within heads (1)–(3) in the text are not thereby persons entitled to use the invention for the purposes of the Patents Act 1977 s 60(2): see

s 60(6); and PARA 512 note 4. Further, the supply or the offer to supply such persons with essential means for putting the invention into effect amounts to infringement: see s 60(3); and PARA 512.

3   Patents Act 1977 s 60(5)(a).

4   Patents Act 1977 s 60(5)(b). For the purposes of s 60(5)(b), anything done in or for the purposes of a medicinal product assessment which would otherwise constitute an infringement of a patent for an invention is to be regarded as done for experimental purposes relating to the subject-matter of the invention: s 60(6D) (s 60(6D)–(6G) added by SI 2014/1997). In the Patents Act 1977 s 60(6D) 'medicinal product assessment' means any testing, course of testing or other activity undertaken with a view to providing data for any of the following purposes:

   (1)   obtaining or varying an authorisation to sell or supply, or offer to sell or supply, a medicinal product (whether in the United Kingdom or elsewhere) (s 60(6E)(a) (as so added));

   (2)   complying with any regulatory requirement imposed (whether in the United Kingdom or elsewhere) in relation to such an authorisation (s 60(6E)(b) (as so added));

   (3)   enabling a government or public authority (whether in the United Kingdom or elsewhere), or a person (whether in the United Kingdom or elsewhere) with functions of providing health care on behalf of such a government or public authority (s 60(6E)(c)(i)) (as so added)) or providing advice to, or on behalf of, such a government or public authority about the provision of health care (s 60(6E)(c)(ii) (as so added)), to carry out an assessment of suitability of a medicinal product for human use for the purpose of determining whether to use it, or recommend its use, in the provision of health care (s 60(6E)(c) (as so added)).

For these purposes 'medicinal product' means a medicinal product for human use or a veterinary medicinal product: s 60(6F) (as so added). As to the meaning of 'medicinal product for human use' see Council Directive (EC) 2001/83 (OJ L311, 28.11.2001, p 67) on the Community code relating to medicinal products for human use, art 1; and MEDICAL PRODUCTS AND DRUGS vol 75 (2013) PARA 25 (definition applied by the Patents Act 1977 s 60(6F) (as so added)). As to the meaning of 'veterinary medicinal product' see European Parliament and Council Directive (EC) 2001/82 (OJ L311, 28.11.2001, p 1) on the Community code relating to veterinary medicinal products, art 1; and MEDICAL PRODUCTS AND DRUGS vol 75 (2013) PARA 387 (definition applied by the Patents Act 1977 s 60(6F) (as so added)). Nothing in s 60(6D)–(6F) is to be read as affecting the application of s 60(5)(b) in relation to any act of a kind not falling within s 60(6D): s 60(6G) (as so added).

The difference in wording between s 60(5)(a) and s 60(5)(b) indicates that the 'experimental purposes' in s 60(5)(b) may have a commercial end in view (*Monsanto Co v Stauffer Chemical Co* [1985] RPC 515 at 538, CA) eg experiments carried out to see whether the experimenter could make a quality product commercially in accordance with the patent specification (*Micro Chemicals Ltd v Smith Kline & French Inter-American Corpn* (1971) 25 DLR (3d) 79 at 89, Can SC; *Monsanto Co v Stauffer Chemical Co* at 538). See also *Helitune Ltd v Stewart Hughes Ltd* [1991 RPC 78, [1991] FSR 171; *Lubrizol v Esso* [1998] RPC 727, CA. Trials carried out to discover something unknown or to test a hypothesis or to find out whether something which is known to work in specific conditions will work in other conditions can be regarded as experiments. Trials carried out to demonstrate to a third party that a product works or in order to amass information to satisfy a third party such as a customer or regulatory authority that the product works as its maker claims are, however, not acts done for experimental purposes: *Monsanto Co v Stauffer Chemical Co* at 542. It is not an infringement to carry out experiments for the purpose of challenging the validity of a patent or of an amendment or of establishing whether what the defendant is doing actually does infringe: see *Monsanto Co v Stauffer Chemical Co*; *Smith Kline & French Laboratories Ltd v Evans Medical Ltd* [1989] FSR 513. The experiments must relate to the subject matter of the invention the subject of the patent in respect of which infringement is alleged in the sense of having a real and direct connection with that subject matter: *Smith Kline & French Laboratories Ltd v Evans Medical Ltd* at 524. This can cause difficulties where a product is covered by both a master patent and a selection patent: see *Smith Kline & French Laboratories Ltd v Evans Medical Ltd* at 524.

5   Patents Act 1977 s 60(5)(c).

6   See the Patents Act 1977 s 60(5)(d)–(f); and PARA 514.

7   See the Patents Act 1977 s 60(5)(g), (h); and PARA 515.

8   Ie Parliament and Council Directive (EC) 2001/82 (OJ L311, 28.11.2001, p 1) on the Community code relating to veterinary medicinal products, art 13 paras 1–5: Patents Act 1977 s 60(7) (amended by SI 2005/2759).

9 Ie Parliament and Council Directive (EC) 2001/83 (OJ L311, 28.11.2001, p 67) on the Community code relating to medicinal products for human use, art 10 paras 1–4: Patents Act 1977 s 60(7) (amended by SI 2005/2759).
10 Patents Act 1977 s 60(5)(i) (added by SI 2005/2759).
11 As to the meaning of 'United Kingdom' see PARA 303 note 5.
12 As to the meaning of 'priority date' see PARA 310 note 6.
13 Patents Act 1977 s 64(1) (s 64 substituted by the Copyright, Designs and Patents Act 1988 Sch 5 para 17). Where a product is disposed of to another in exercise of the rights conferred by the Patents Act 1977 s 64(1) or (2), that other and any person claiming through him may deal with the product in the same way as if it had been disposed of by the registered proprietor of the patent: s 64(3) (as so substituted).
14 Patents Act 1977 s 64(2) (as substituted: see note 13).

514. Use of ships, aircraft, hovercraft and vehicles. An act which would otherwise infringe a patent[1] does not do so if it consists of:

(1) the use, exclusively for the needs of a ship registered in or belonging to a Convention country[2] (a 'relevant ship'), of a product or process in the body of such a ship[3] or in its machinery, tackle, apparatus or other accessories, where the ship has temporarily or accidentally entered the internal or territorial waters of the United Kingdom[4]; or

(2) the use of a product or process in the body or operation of an aircraft, hovercraft or vehicle so registered or belonging (a 'relevant aircraft, hovercraft or vehicle') which has temporarily or accidentally entered or is crossing the United Kingdom, including the air space above it and its territorial waters, or the use of accessories for such a relevant aircraft, hovercraft or vehicle[5]; or

(3) the use of an exempted aircraft[6] which has lawfully entered or is lawfully crossing the United Kingdom, including the air space above it and its territorial waters, or the importation into the United Kingdom, or the use or storage there, of any part or accessory for such an aircraft[7].

Furthermore, no lawful entry into the United Kingdom[8] or lawful transit across the United Kingdom, with or without landings, of an aircraft, other than an aircraft used in military, customs or police services, registered in any of certain countries or territories[9] may entail any seizure or detention[10] of the aircraft or any proceedings[11], or any other interference with the aircraft, on the ground that the construction, mechanism, parts, accessories or operation of the aircraft is or are an infringement of any patent, design or model[12]. Nor may the importation into, or storage in, the United Kingdom of spare parts and spare equipment for such an aircraft and their use and installation in the repair of such an aircraft entail any seizure or detention of the aircraft, parts or equipment or any proceedings, or any other interference with the aircraft, on the ground that the parts or equipment or their installation infringe any patent, design or model[13] unless the parts or equipment concerned are sold or distributed in the United Kingdom or exported from the United Kingdom for sale or distribution[14]. These provisions relate only to proceedings by or on behalf of persons in the United Kingdom[15], and to proceedings against the owner or operator of the aircraft[16], or, as the case may be, against the owner or operator of the aircraft or the owner of the parts or equipment[17].

Where these protective provisions do not apply, the use of patented articles on or over the territorial waters of the United Kingdom is an infringement of the patent[18]. Use outside territorial waters does not generally amount to an infringement[19] but acts done on the continental shelf or in connection with the exploration of the sea bed or subsoil or exploration of their natural resources constitute acts done in the United Kingdom[20] and so may infringe a patent.

1   See PARAS 511–512.

2   Ie a country, other than the United Kingdom, which is a party to the International Convention for the Protection of Industrial Property (Paris, 20 March 1883) (the 'Paris Convention'), as revised (Stockholm, 14 July 1967 to 13 January 1968; TS 61 (1970); Cmnd 4431), or which is a member of the World Trade Organisation. For these countries see PARA 628. As to the meaning of 'United Kingdom' see PARA 303 note 5. As to the World Trade Organisation see INTERNATIONAL RELATIONS LAW vol 61 (2010) PARA 461.

3   A claim to the whole ship (in casu a multi-hull vessel) so that the whole ship would be an infringement is also within the exclusion: *Stena Rederi AB v Irish Ferries Ltd* [2003] EWCA Civ 66, [2003] RPC 668.

4   Patents Act 1977 s 60(5)(d), (7) (s 60(7) amended by SI 1999/1899). As to the extent of the territorial waters (or sea) of the United Kingdom see the Territorial Sea Act 1987 and INTERNATIONAL RELATIONS LAW vol 61 (2010) PARA 124. For the purposes of the Patents Act 1977, the territorial waters of the United Kingdom are treated as part of the United Kingdom: see s 132(3); and PARA 305. 'Temporary' means transient or limited in time and does not depend on frequency: *Stena Rederi AB v Irish Ferries Ltd* [2003] EWCA Civ 66, [2003] RPC 668 (ferry crossing between Ireland and the United Kingdom was temporarily within the internal and territorial waters).

5   Patents Act 1977 s 60(5)(e), (7) (s 60(7) as amended: see note 4).

6   For these purposes, 'exempted aircraft' means an aircraft to which the Civil Aviation Act 1982 s 89 (aircraft exempted from seizure in respect of patent claims (see the text to notes 8–17)) applies: Patents Act 1977 s 60(7) (amended by the Civil Aviation Act 1982 Sch 15 para 19).

7   Patents Act 1977 s 60(5)(f).

8   The Civil Aviation Act 1982 s 89 is applied to Jersey by the Civil Aviation Act 1982 (Jersey) Order 1990, SI 1990/2145 (see art 2, Sch 1 Pt I, Sch 1 Pt II para 18) and to Guernsey by the Civil Aviation Act 1982 (Guernsey) Order 1992, SI 1992/230 (see art 2, Sch 1 Pt I, Sch 1 Pt II para 18) and is applied in adapted and modified form to certain overseas territories by the Civil Aviation Act 1949 (Overseas Territories) Order 1969, SI 1969/592 (see art 3, Sch 2 para 12, Sch 3).

9   Civil Aviation Act 1982 s 89(4)(a). As to the relevant countries and territories see the Aircraft (Exemption from Seizure on Patent Claims) Order 1977, SI 1977/829, art 4, Schedule. Her Majesty may by Order in Council exempt other aircraft: Civil Aviation Act 1982 s 89(4)(b). At the date at which this volume states the law no such Order in Council had been made.

10 Where it is alleged by any person interested that a foreign aircraft which is not an aircraft to which the Civil Aviation Act 1982 s 89 applies, and which is making a passage through or over the United Kingdom, infringes in itself or in any part of it any invention, design or model which is entitled to protection in the United Kingdom, it is lawful, subject to and in accordance with rules of court, to detain the aircraft until the owner thereof deposits or secures in respect of the alleged infringement a sum (the 'deposited sum') and thereupon the aircraft is not during the continuance or in the course of the passage subject to any lien, arrest, detention or prohibition, whether by order of a court or otherwise, in respect or on account of the alleged infringement: s 89(5), Sch 12 para 1. The deposited sum must be such sum as may be agreed between the parties interested or, in default of agreement, fixed by the Secretary of State or some person duly authorised on his behalf; and payment thereof must be made or secured to the Secretary of State in such manner as the Secretary of State approves: Sch 12 para 2. The deposited sum must be dealt with by such tribunal and in accordance with such procedure as may be specified by rules of court and any such rules may provide generally for carrying Sch 12 into effect: Sch 12 para 3. For these purposes, 'owner' includes the actual owner of an aircraft and any person claiming through or under him; and 'passage' includes all reasonable landings and stoppages in the course or for the purpose of the passage: Sch 12 para 4. At the date at which this volume states the law no such rules of court had been made. As to the Secretary of State see PARA 573.

11 As to the proceedings concerned see the text and notes 15–17.

12 Civil Aviation Act 1982 s 89(1). Section 89 gives effect to the Convention on International Civil Aviation (the 'Chicago Convention') (Chicago, 7 December 1944: TS 8 (1953); Cmd 8742) art 27: see AIR LAW vol 2 (2008) PARA 436. As to the Convention see AIR LAW vol 2 (2008) PARA 2 et seq.

13 Civil Aviation Act 1982 s 89(2).

14 Civil Aviation Act 1982 s 89(3).

15 See the Civil Aviation Act 1982 s 89(1), (2).

16 See the Civil Aviation Act 1982 s 89(1). See also note 17.

17 See the Civil Aviation Act 1982 s 89(2). So far as the aircraft itself is concerned, this is comprehensive except that it cannot prevent actions for damages by foreign patentees. So far as equipment or spares are concerned, the protection given seems to be comprehensive only on the assumption that the operator will import, store and fit his own equipment or spares.

18 See the Patents Act 1977 s 132(3), which provides that for the purposes of the Patents Act 1977 the territorial waters of the United Kingdom are to be treated as part of the United Kingdom.

19 *Newall v Elliott and Glass* (1864) 10 Jur NS 954; *Goucher v Clayton* (1865) 11 Jur NS 462 at 465; *VD Ltd v Boston Deep Sea Fishing and Ice Co Ltd* (1935) 52 RPC 303.

20 See the Patents Act 1977 s 132(4); and PARA 305.

515. Use of plant propagating material or animal reproductive material. An act which would otherwise infringe a patent[1] does not do so if it consists of:

(1)   the use by a farmer of the product of his harvest for propagation or multiplication by him on his own holding[2], where there has been a sale[3] of plant propagating material to the farmer by the proprietor of the patent or with his consent for agricultural use[4];

(2)   the use of an animal or animal reproductive material by a farmer for an agricultural purpose[5] following a sale to the farmer, by the proprietor of the patent or with his consent, of breeding stock or other animal reproductive material which constitutes or contains the patented invention[6].

1 See PARAS 511–512.

2 'Farmer's own holding' means any land which a farmer actually exploits for plant growing, whether as his property or otherwise managed under his own responsibility and on his own account: Patents Act 1977 s 60(6A), Sch A1 para 1 (s 60(6A), Sch A1 added by SI 2000/2037).

3 'Sale' includes any other form of commercialisation: Patents Act 1977 s 60(6C) (added by SI 2000/2037).

4 Patents Act 1977 s 60(5)(g) (added by SI 2000/2037). For the provisions restricting the circumstances in which the Patents Act 1977 s 60(5)(g) applies and for the provisions which apply where an act would constitute an infringement of the patent see s 60(6A), Sch A1 (as added: see note 2).

5 Use for an agricultural purpose: (1) includes making an animal or animal reproductive material available for the purposes of pursuing the farmer's agricultural activity; but (2) does not include sale within the framework, or for the purposes, of a commercial reproduction activity: Patents Act 1977 s 60(6B) (added by SI 2000/2037).

6 Patents Act 1977 s 60(5)(h) (added by SI 2000/2037).

9. PROCEEDINGS FOR INFRINGEMENT, THREATS AND REVOCATION

(1) INTRODUCTION

516. Nature of proceedings. The proceedings with which this part of the title is concerned[1] are proceedings for the infringement of a patent[2], proceedings for a declaration of non-infringement[3], proceedings to restrain groundless threats of infringement proceedings[4] and proceedings for the revocation of a patent[5]. All these proceedings may, in England and Wales, be brought in the Patents Court[6] or the Intellectual Property Enterprise Court[7] and proceedings to restrain threats must be so brought[8]; but proceedings for revocation or for a declaration of non-infringement of a patent may be brought before the comptroller[9], and the parties may by agreement refer a question of infringement to him[10]. Where certain proceedings[11] are pending before the court, proceedings[12] may not be instituted before the comptroller without the leave of the court[13].

The proprietor of a patent or any other person may request the comptroller to issue an opinion as to whether there has been an infringement of a patent or whether the invention in question is not patentable[14].

1 As to applications for prerogative orders see PARA 625.
2 As to proceedings for infringement see PARA 520 et seq.
3 As to proceedings for a declaration of non-infringement see PARA 554.
4 As to proceedings to restrain threats see PARA 555 et seq.
5 As to proceedings for revocation see PARA 562 et seq.
6 Patents Act 1977 ss 61(1), 70(1), 71(1), 72(1), 130(1). As to the Patents Court see PARA 619 et seq.
7 Patents Act 1977 ss 61(1), 70(1), 71(1), 72(1), 130(1). As to the Intellectual Property Enterprise Court see PARA 626 et seq.
8 Patents Act 1977 s 70(1).
9 Patents Act 1977 ss 71(1), 72(1). As to the comptroller see PARA 575.
10 See the Patents Act 1977 s 61(3); and PARA 553. Relief is limited to damages and a declaration (Patents Act 1977 s 61(1)(c), (e), (3)), with a certificate of contested validity (see s 65; and PARA 549). A declaration that a patent is valid is, however, not conclusive; the other party may challenge validity again in the event of High Court infringement proceedings: see s 72(5); and PARA 552. As an alternative, the parties may refer their dispute to arbitration, and there are provisions for sending a dispute referred to the comptroller to arbitration.
11 Ie any proceedings with respect to a patent such as are described in PARA 519.
12 Ie proceedings under the Patents Act 1977 s 61(3) (see PARA 553), s 69 (see PARA 546), s 71 (see PARA 554) or s 72 (see PARAS 562–563).
13 Patents Act 1977 s 74(7).
14 See the Patents Act 1977 ss 74A, 74B; and PARAS 517–518.

517. Opinions by the UK Intellectual Property Office. The proprietor of a patent or any other person may request the comptroller[1] to issue an opinion on a prescribed matter in relation to a patent[2]. An opinion can be requested even if the patent has expired or has been surrendered[3]. The comptroller must issue an opinion if requested to do so, but must not do so if:

(1)   the request appears to him to be frivolous or vexatious or the question upon which the opinion is sought appears to him to have been sufficiently considered in any relevant proceedings[4];

(2)   the requestor gives him notice in writing that the request is withdrawn[5]; or

(3)   for any reason he considers it inappropriate in all the circumstances to do so[6].

If the comptroller intends at any time to refuse the request under heads (1) to (3), he must notify the requester accordingly[7].

The comptroller must notify interested persons[8] of the request and must advertise it in such manner as he thinks fit[9].

If the request has not been refused or withdrawn, any person may, before the end of the relevant period, file observations on any issue raised by the request[10]. Such observations may include reasons why the comptroller should refuse the request[11].

An opinion under these provisions is not binding for any purposes[12].

An opinion must be prepared by an examiner[13].

In relation to a decision of the comptroller whether to issue an opinion under these provisions, for the purposes of the exercise of the comptroller's discretionary powers[14], only the person making the request for an opinion[15] is to be regarded as a party to a proceeding before the comptroller, and no appeal lies at the instance of any other person[16].

1　As to the comptroller see PARA 575. A request must be made on Patents Form 17 and must be accompanied by a copy and a statement setting out fully: (1) the question upon which an opinion is sought; (2) the requester's submissions on that question; and (3) any matters of fact which are requested to be taken into account: Patents Rules 2007, SI 2007/3291, r 93(1). The statement must be accompanied by: (a) the name and address of any persons, of whom the requester is aware, having an interest in that question; and (b) particulars of any relevant proceedings of which the requester is aware which relate to the patent in suit and which may be relevant to that question: r 93(2). 'Relevant proceedings' means proceedings (whether pending or concluded) before the comptroller, the court or the European Patent Office (see PARA 644): r 92. Where the requester is acting as an agent in making the request, the persons referred to in head (a) do not include the person for whom the requester is so acting: r 93(3). The statement must be accompanied by a copy of any evidence or other document (except a document which has been published by the comptroller or is kept at the UK Intellectual Property Office) which is referred to in the statement: r 93(4). Each such statement, evidence or other document must be provided in duplicate: r 93(5). As to the UK Intellectual Property Office see PARA 577.

2　Patents Act 1977 s 74A(1) (s 74A added by the Patents Act 2004 s 13(1); Patents Act 1977 s 73(1A)–(1C) added, s 74A(1) amended, by the Intellectual Property Act 2014 s 16(1), (4)). The prescribed matters are:

　(1)　whether a particular act constitutes, or (if done) would constitute, an infringement of the patent (Patents Rules 2007, SI 2007/3291, r 93(6)(a) (r 93(6) added by SI 2014/2401);

　(2)　whether, or to what extent, an invention for which the patent has been granted is not a patentable invention (Patents Rules 2007, SI 2007/3291, r 93(6)(b) (as so added));

　(3)　whether the specification of the patent discloses the invention clearly enough and completely enough for it to be performed by a person skilled in the art (r 93(6)(c) (as so added));

　(4)　whether the matter disclosed in the specification of the patent extends beyond that disclosed in the application for the patent as filed or, if the patent was granted on a new application, in the earlier application as filed (r 93(6)(d) (as so added));

　(5)　whether the protection conferred by the patent has been extended by an amendment which should not have been allowed (r 93(6)(e) (as so added));

　(6)　whether a supplementary protection certificate is invalid under Parliament and Council Regulation (EC) 469/2009 (OJ L152, 16.6.2009, p 1) concerning the creation of a supplementary protection certificate for medicinal products (the 'Medicinal Products Regulation': see PARAS 340–344) art 15 (Patents Rules 2007, SI 2007/3291, r 93(6)(f) (as so added)); and

　(7)　whether a supplementary protection certificate is invalid under Parliament and Council Regulation (EC) 1610/1996 (OJ L198, 8.8.96, p 30) concerning the creation of a supplementary protection certificate for plant protection products (the 'Plant Protection Products Regulation': see PARAS 340–344) art 15 (Patents Rules 2007, SI 2007/3291, r 93(6)(g) (as so added)).

　Where the comptroller issues an opinion under the Patents Act 1977 s 74A that an invention is not new or does not involve an inventive step (ie that s 1(1)(a) or (b) is not satisfied in relation to an invention for which there is a patent), the comptroller may revoke the patent: s 73(1A) (as so added). As to novelty see PARA 434 et seq; and as to lack of inventive step see PARA 451 et seq. The power under s 73(1A) may not be exercised before the end of the period in which the proprietor of the patent may apply under the rules (by virtue of s 74B: see PARA 518) for a review of the opinion or, if the proprietor applies for a review, the decision on the review is made (or, if there is an appeal against that decision, the appeal is determined): s 73(1B) (as so added). The comptroller may not exercise the power under s 73(1A) without giving the proprietor of the patent an opportunity to make any observations and to amend the specification of the patent without contravening s 76 (see PARA 351): s 73(1C) (as so added). See *Re DLP Ltd's Patent* [2007] EWHC 2669 (Pat), [2008] 1 All ER 839, [2008] RPC 257.

3   Patents Act 1977 s 74A(2) (as added: see note 2). As to the term of patents see PARA 338. As to surrender see PARA 358.
4   Patents Act 1977 s 74A(3)(a) (as added: see note 2); Patents Rules 2007, SI 2007/3291, r 94(1).
5   Patents Act 1977 s 74A(3)(a) (as added: see note 2); Patents Rules 2007, SI 2007/3291, r 94(2).
6   Patents Act 1977 s 74A(3)(b) (as added: see note 2).
7   Patents Rules 2007, SI 2007/3291, r 94(3).
8   The comptroller must notify each of the following persons of the request (except where the person concerned is the requester): (1) the patent holder; (2) any holder of a licence or sub-licence under the patent in suit (ie the patent to which that request relates) which has been registered under the Patents Rules 2007, SI 2007/3291, r 47 (see PARA 586); (3) any person who has made a request in respect of the patent in suit under r 54 (see PARA 579) regarding an opinion being requested under r 93; (4) any person who is specified under r 93(2)(a) (see note 1): r 95(1). In addition, the comptroller may notify of the request any persons who appear to him to be likely to have an interest in the question upon which the opinion is sought: r 95(2). The comptroller must send a copy of the form and statement filed under r 93(1) (see note 1) to each person so notified, together with a copy of such other documents filed under r 93 as he thinks fit: r 95(3).
9   Patents Rules 2007, SI 2007/3291, r 95(4). If the request is refused or withdrawn before a notification has been made under r 95(1), the patent holder alone must be notified of the request (and of the fact that it has been refused or withdrawn) and r 95(3), (4) do not apply: r 95(5).
10   Patents Rules 2007, SI 2007/3291, r 96(1). Any person who files observations must ensure that, before the end of four weeks beginning immediately after the date of advertisement under r 95(4), a copy of those observations is received: (1) where that person is not the patent holder, by the patent holder; and (2) by the requester: r 96(3), (7) (amended by SI 2011/2052). A person to whom observations are sent may, during the period of two weeks beginning immediately after the end of the four week period, file observations confined strictly to matters in reply: Patents Rules 2007, SI 2007/3291, r 96(4). Any person who files observations must ensure that, within that period of two weeks, a copy of those observations is received: (a) where that person is the requester, by the patent holder; and (b) where that person is the patent holder, by the requester: r 96(5). If it is reasonably possible, the observations filed under this rule and the copies of such observations are to be delivered only in electronic form or using electronic communications: r 96(6).
11   Patents Rules 2007, SI 2007/3291, r 96(2).
12   Patents Act 1977 s 74A(4) (as added: see note 2).
13   Patents Act 1977 s 74A(5) (as added: see note 2). After the end of the procedure under the Patents Rules 2007, SI 2007/3291, r 96, the comptroller must refer the request to an examiner for the preparation of the opinion: r 97(1). The comptroller must issue the opinion that has been prepared by sending a copy to: (1) the requester; (2) the patent holder; and (3) any other person who filed observations under r 96(1) (see the text to note 12): r 97(2).
14   Ie for the purposes of the Patents Act 1977 s 101: see PARA 591.
15   Ie under the Patents Act 1977 s 74A(1).
16   Patents Act 1977 s 74A(6) (as added: see note 2).

518. Review of opinion. Rules may make provision for a review before the comptroller[1], on an application by the proprietor or an exclusive licensee[2] of the patent in question, of an opinion[3] as to validity or infringement[4]. The rules may, in particular:

(1)   prescribe the circumstances in which, and the period within which, an application may be made[5];

(2)   provide that, in prescribed circumstances, proceedings for a review may not be brought or continued where other proceedings have been brought[6];

(3)   provide for there to be a right of appeal against a decision made on a review only in prescribed cases[7]; and

(4)   until a day to be appointed, make provision under which, in prescribed circumstances, proceedings on a review are to be treated for prescribed purposes as if they were proceedings for infringement of a patent[8], for declaration of non-infringement[9] or application for revocation[10] on the grounds that the invention is not a patentable invention[11].

The patent holder may, before the end of the period of three months beginning immediately after the date on which the opinion is issued, apply to the comptroller for a review of the opinion[12]. However, such proceedings for a review may not be brought (or if brought may not be continued) if the issue raised by the review has been decided in other relevant proceedings[13]. The application must be made on the prescribed form[14] and be accompanied by a copy and a statement in duplicate setting out the grounds on which the review is sought[15]. The statement must contain particulars of any relevant proceedings of which the applicant is aware which may be relevant to the question whether the proceedings for a review may be brought or continued[16].

The application may be made on the following grounds only:

(a)   that the opinion wrongly concluded that the patent in suit was invalid, or was invalid to a limited extent[17]; or

(b)   that, by reason of its interpretation of the specification of the patent in suit, the opinion wrongly concluded that a particular act did not or would not constitute an infringement of the patent[18].

On receipt of the application, the comptroller must send a copy of the form and statement filed to the requester (if different from the applicant) and any person who filed observations[19]. The comptroller must advertise the application in such manner as he thinks fit[20]. Before the end of the relevant period[21], any person may file a statement in support of the application or a counter-statement contesting it (which in either case must be in duplicate), and on so doing must become a party to the proceedings for a review[22].

On completion of the proceedings the comptroller must either set aside the opinion in whole or in part or decide that no reason has been shown for the opinion to be set aside[23]. The decision does not estop any party to any proceedings from raising any issue regarding the validity or the infringement of the patent[24]. No appeal[25] lies from a decision to set aside the opinion, except where the appeal relates to a part of the opinion that is not set aside[26].

1   As to the comptroller see PARA 575.

2   As to the meaning of 'exclusive licensee' see PARA 379 note 7.

3   Ie under the Patents Act 1977 s 74A: see PARA 517.

4   Patents Act 1977 s 74B(1) (s 74B added by the Patents Act 2004 s 13(1)). See the Patents Rules 2007, SI 2007/3291, rr 98–100; and the text and notes 12–26.

5   Patents Act 1977 s 74B(2)(a) (as added: see note 4).

6   Patents Act 1977 s 74B(2)(b) (as added: see note 4).

7   Patents Act 1977 s 74B(2)(d) (as added: see note 4).

8   Ie under the Patents Act 1977 s 61(1)(c) or (e): see PARA 516.

9   Ie under the Patents Act 1977 s 71(1): see PARA 554.

10   Ie under the Patents Act 1977 s 72(1)(a): see PARAS 429–430.

11   Patents Act 1977 s 74B(2)(c) (as added (see note 4); prospectively repealed by the Intellectual Property Act 2014 s 16(2)). At the date at which this volume states the law no day had been appointed for this purpose.

12   Patents Rules 2007, SI 2007/3291, r 98(1) (amended by SI 2011/2052).

13   Patents Rules 2007, SI 2007/3291, r 98(2). As to the meaning of 'relevant proceedings' see PARA 517 note 1.

14 The application must be made on Patents Form 2: see the Patents Rules 2007, SI 2007/3291, r 98(3).
15 Patents Rules 2007, SI 2007/3291, r 98(3).
16 Patents Rules 2007, SI 2007/3291, r 98(4).
17 Patents Rules 2007, SI 2007/3291, r 98(5)(a).
18 Patents Rules 2007, SI 2007/3291, r 98(5)(b).
19 Patents Rules 2007, SI 2007/3291, r 99(1). Observations are filed under r 96: see PARA 517.
20 Patents Rules 2007, SI 2007/3291, r 99(2).
21 The relevant period is: (1) four weeks beginning immediately after the date on which the application is advertised; or (2) if it expires later, the period of two months beginning immediately after the date on which the opinion is issued under the Patents Rules 2007, SI 2007/3291, r 97(2) (see PARA 517): r 99(4) (amended by SI 2011/2052).
22 Patents Rules 2007, SI 2007/3291, r 99(3). The comptroller must send to the other parties a copy of each statement or counter-statement filed under r 99(3): r 99(5). The following rules apply to the proceedings for a review: r 74 (overriding objective); r 79 (copies of documents); r 80(2)–(6) (evidence and the hearing); r 81 (alteration of time limits); r 82 (general powers of the comptroller in relation to proceedings before him); r 84 (hearings in public); r 87 (evidence in proceedings before the comptroller); r 83 (striking out a statement of case and summary judgment); r 85 (security for costs or expenses); r 86 (powers of comptroller to compel attendance of witness and production of documents): r 99(6), Sch 3 Pts 4, 5. For the purposes of r 83(3), a reference to 'the claimant' is a reference to the applicant for a review, and a reference to 'the defendant' is a reference to any other party: r 99(6).
23 Patents Rules 2007, SI 2007/3291, r 100(1). The hearing officer should only decide an opinion was wrong if the examiner had made an error of principle or reached a conclusion that was clearly wrong: *Re an appeal by DLP Ltd* [2007] EWHC 2669 (Pat), [2008] 1 All ER 839, [2008] RPC 257.
24 Patents Rules 2007, SI 2007/3291, r 100(2).
25 Ie under the Patents Act 1977 s 97: see PARA 571.
26 Patents Rules 2007, SI 2007/3291, r 100(3). An appeal did not involve an academic question and the Patents Court should not decline jurisdiction to hear such appeals. But the court should only reverse the decision of a hearing officer if he had failed to recognise an error of principle or clearly wrong conclusion in the opinion and so declined to set it aside: *Re an appeal by DLP Ltd* [2007] EWHC 2669 (Pat) at [22], [2008] 1 All ER 839 at [22], [2008] RPC 257 at [22].

519. Putting validity in issue. The validity of a patent[1] may only[2] be put in issue[3]:

(1)   by way of defence in infringement proceedings[4] or proceedings[5] for infringement of rights conferred by the publication of an application[6];

(2)   in proceedings[7] for threats[8];

(3)   in proceedings in which a declaration of non-infringement[9] is sought[10];

(4)   in revocation proceedings[11] before the court[12] or the comptroller[13];

(5)   in proceedings[14] on a dispute as to Crown use[15].

No determination may, however, be made in any such proceedings on the validity of a patent which any person puts in issue on the ground of lack of entitlement[16] unless:

(a)   it has been determined in entitlement proceedings[17] commenced by that person or in the proceedings in which the validity is in issue that the patent should have been granted to him and not some other person[18]; and

(b)   except where it has been so determined in entitlement proceedings, the proceedings in which the validity is in issue are commenced on or before the second anniversary of the grant of the patent or it is shown that any person registered as a proprietor of the patent knew at the time of the grant or of the transfer of the patent to him that he was not entitled to the patent[19].

1   As to validity see PARA 429 et seq.

2   Validity may not be put in issue in any other proceedings, and in particular no proceedings may be instituted, whether under the Patents Act 1977 or otherwise, seeking only a declaration as to the validity or invalidity of a patent: s 74(2). See *Arrow Generics Ltd v Merck & Co Inc* [2007] EWHC 1900 (Ch), [2007] FSR 920, [2007] All ER (D) 3 (Aug). As to opinions by the UK Intellectual Property Office as to validity or infringement see the Patents Act 1977 ss 74A, 74B; and PARAS 517–518. As to the UK Intellectual Property Office see PARA 577.

3   The only grounds on which validity may be put in issue, whether in proceedings for revocation under the Patents Act 1977 s 72 (see PARAS 562–563) or otherwise, are the grounds on which it may be revoked under s 72: s 74(3). For the purposes of the Patents Act 1977, the validity of a patent is not put in issue merely because the comptroller is considering its validity in order to decide whether to revoke it on his own initiative under s 73 (see PARA 569) or because its validity is being considered in connection with an opinion under s 74A or a review of such an opinion (see PARAS 517–518): s 74(8) (amended by the Patents Act 2004 s 13(2)). As to the comptroller see PARA 575.

4   Ie under the Patents Act 1977 s 61: see PARA 520 et seq.

5   Ie under the Patents Act 1977 s 69: see PARA 546.

6   Patents Act 1977 s 74(1)(a).

7   Ie under the Patents Act 1977 s 70: see PARA 555 et seq.

8   Patents Act 1977 s 74(1)(b).

9   Ie under the Patents Act 1977 s 71: see PARA 554.

10   Patents Act 1977 s 74(1)(c).

11   Ie under the Patents Act 1977 s 72: see PARA 562 et seq.

12   As to the meaning of 'court' see PARA 619 note 1.

13   Patents Act 1977 s 74(1)(d).

14   Ie under the Patents Act 1977 s 58: see PARA 409.

15   Patents Act 1977 s 74(1)(e).

16   Ie the ground mentioned in the Patents Act 1977 s 72(1)(b): see PARA 562.

17   For these purposes, 'entitlement proceedings', in relation to a patent, means a reference under the Patents Act 1977 s 37(1) (see PARA 365) on the ground that the patent was granted to a person not entitled to it or proceedings for a declaration that it was so granted: s 74(6) (amended by the Copyright, Designs and Patents Act 1988 Sch 5 para 10).

18   Patents Act 1977 s 74(4)(a). Where validity is put in issue by way of defence or counterclaim, the court or the comptroller, if it or he thinks it just to do so, must give the defendant an opportunity to comply with the condition in s 74(4)(a): s 74(5).

19   Patents Act 1977 s 74(4)(b) (amended by the Intellectual Property Act 2014 Schedule para 3(2)). As to registration see PARA 583 et seq.

(2) PROCEEDINGS FOR INFRINGEMENT

520. Claimants in proceedings for infringement. The right to bring a claim for infringement[1] belongs to the proprietor of the patent[2], to his exclusive licensees[3] and, in certain circumstances[4], to holders of compulsory licences[5] and licences of right[6]. The claimant probably need not first secure entry of his title on the register of patents[7], but failure to do so may limit his right to damages[8]. When a licensee sues alone, the proprietor must be made a defendant, although he is not liable for costs unless he acknowledges service of the claim form and takes part in the proceedings[9]. Where the proprietor sues, it is usual for exclusive licensees to be joined as claimants[10]. Previous proprietors may be joined where infringement took place before the change in ownership[11].

One of two or more joint proprietors may bring infringement proceedings without the concurrence of the others, provided that the others are made parties to the proceedings, although any joint proprietor who is made a defendant is not liable for any costs unless he acknowledges service of the claim form and takes part in the proceedings[12]. The right to sue survives to a personal representative[13]. Where the claimant is an equitable owner, he should join the registered proprietor as claimant or defendant[14]. The assignee of a distinct portion of a patent, or an assignee for a particular district, may sue alone for any infringement of his rights[15]. Compulsory licences and licences granted under patents in respect of which licences are available as of right give the licensee power to request the proprietor to take proceedings to prevent any infringement of the patent; and, if the proprietor refuses or neglects to do so within two months after being so requested, the licensee may institute proceedings for the infringement in his own name as if he were a proprietor, making the proprietor a defendant[16].

1　In the Patents Court proceedings in which the claimant makes a claim in respect of the infringement of a patent must be started by issuing a Part 7 claim form (see CIVIL PROCEDURE vol 11 (2009) PARA 116 et seq) or in existing proceedings under Part 20 (see CIVIL PROCEDURE vol 11 (2009) PARA 618 et seq): CPR 63.5. No proceedings for infringement may be instituted until the patent has been granted: Patents Act 1977 s 69(2)(a); and see *Therm-a-Stor Ltd v Weatherseal Windows Ltd* [1981] FSR 579, CA; and PARA 546.

2　Patents Act 1977 s 61(1). See *Xtralite (Rooflights) Ltd v Hartington Conway Ltd* [2003] EWHC 1872 (Ch), [2004] RPC 161, [2003] All ER (D) 555 (Jul) (estoppel preventing proprietor claiming ownership).

3　Patents Act 1977 s 67(1). The holder of an exclusive licence has the same right as the proprietor to bring proceedings in respect of any infringement committed after the date of the licence: s 67(1). As to the meanings of 'exclusive licence' and 'exclusive licensee' see PARA 379 note 7. As to the award of damages to an exclusive licensee see s 67(2); and PARA 544. See *SDL Hair Ltd v Next Row Ltd* [2013] EWPCC 31, [2013] All ER (D) 185 (Jun) (the fact that the patentee continued to deal in patented goods was not necessarily inconsistent with the existence of an exclusive licence).

4　See the text and note 14.

5　See the Patents Act 1977 s 49(4); and PARA 395.

6　See the Patents Act 1977 s 46(4); and PARA 391.

7　See PARA 583 et seq.

8　See the Patents Act 1977 s 68; and PARA 551. The advantage of securing a fresh assignment or grant of a different licence immediately before registration should be noted: see *Minnesota Mining & Manufacturing Co v Rennicks (UK) Ltd* [1992] FSR 118.

9　See the Patents Act 1977 s 46(4), (5) (licences of right: see PARA 391), s 49(4) (compulsory licences: see PARA 395), s 67(3) (exclusive licences).

10　This is done to enable them to claim damages: *Trico Products Corpn and Trico-Folberth Ltd v Romac Motor Accessories Ltd* (1933) 51 RPC 90.

11　The assignment of a patent or the grant of an exclusive licence under it may, however, confer on the assignee or licensee the right to bring proceedings under the Patents Act 1977 s 61 or s 69 (proceedings for infringements) or s 58 (disputes as to Crown use: see PARA 409): s 30(7).

12　Patents Act 1977 s 66(2).

13　See the Law Reform (Miscellaneous Provisions) Act 1934 s 1; and WILLS AND INTESTACY vol 103 (2010) PARA 1279.

14　*Spennymoor Foundry Ltd v Catherall and Geldard* (1909) 26 RPC 822; *Three Rivers District Council v Bank of England (Governor and Co)* [1996] QB 292, [1995] 4 All ER 312, CA. It is doubtful whether a mortgagor need join a mortgagee registered as such: *Van Gelder, Apsimon & Co v Sowerby Bridge United District Flour Society* (1890) 44 ChD 374, 7 RPC 208, CA. It would seem that a mortgagee cannot sue alone: *Van Gelder, Apsimon & Co v Sowerby Bridge United District Flour Society*.

15　*Dunnicliff and Bagley v Mallet* (1859) 7 CBNS 209; *Walton v Lavater* (1860) 8 CBNS 162; *Reitzman v Grahame-Chapman and Derustit Ltd* (1950) 67 RPC 178 (on appeal (1951) 68 RPC 25, CA).

16　See the Patents Act 1977 s 46(4) (licences of right: see PARA 391), s 49(4) (compulsory licences: see PARA 395). A proprietor-defendant who neither acknowledges service of the claim form nor takes part in the proceedings is not liable for costs: see ss 46(5), 49(4).

521.　Defendants in proceedings for infringement. The claimant to an infringement action may join as defendants all persons responsible for the breaches on which he sues, for example the manufacturer of or dealer in an infringing article, or a vendor and purchaser[1], or a principal and agent[2] or as joint tortfeasors being parties to a common design to infringe[3]. The directors of a company should not be joined as defendants unless they have done some act which makes them personally responsible[4]. Where the action is brought against a shipping company or railway in respect of goods carried by it, the consignee should also be joined[5]. In general the choice of defendants lies with the claimant, and other persons concerned will not be made defendants against the claimant's wish[6], although the defendants may apply to have them made defendants to a counterclaim or third parties in the normal way[7]. Where joinder of a defendant is otherwise proper, it is not improper to join him because the claimant's main motive is to obtain disclosure from him[8].

1   *Saccharin Corpn Ltd v DTJ Lyle & Son Ltd* (1904) 21 RPC 604, CA. Where both makers and users were sued, and only the makers delivered a defence, leave for judgment on motion against the users was refused: *Act für Cartonnagen Industrie v T Remus & Co and Burgon & Co* (1895) 12 RPC 94. A supplier may be liable for its customer's costs if it has funded the customer's defence: *Koninklijke Philips Electronics NV v Prico Digital Disc GmbH* [2003] EWHC 2589 (Ch), [2004] FSR 663, [2003] All ER (D) 51 (Sep). The liability to be sued survives against a personal representative: see the Law Reform (Miscellaneous Provisions) Act 1934 s 1; and WILLS AND INTESTACY vol 103 (2010) PARA 1279.
2   See PARA 507.
3   See PARA 508. An inference that a defendant has knowingly facilitated or assisted in infringement is an insufficient basis for joining him to the proceedings: *Sepracor Inc v Hoechst Marion Roussel Ltd* [1999] FSR 746, [1999] All ER (D) 80.
4   See PARA 508.
5   *Washburn and Moen Manufacturing Co v Cunard Steamship Co and JC Parkes & Sons* (1889) 5 TLR 592, 6 RPC 398.
6   *Moser v Marsden* [1892] 1 Ch 487, 9 RPC 214, CA; *Evans v Central Electric Supply Co Ltd* (1923) 40 RPC 357. In *Vavasseur v Krupp* (1878) 9 ChD 351, CA, one of the defendants was joined at his own request and obtained an order permitting him to remove the infringing articles. However, see *Tetra Molectric Ltd v Japan Imports Ltd (Win Lighter Corpn intervening)* [1976] RPC 541, CA, where a foreign manufacturer was added as a respondent to an appeal in an infringement action against an English distributor against the wishes of the proprietor of the patent.
7   As to joinder of parties see CIVIL PROCEDURE vol 11 (2009) PARA 210 et seq. Where there is no real dispute between the defendant and the party it seeks to join, joinder for the purposes of obtaining disclosure should be refused when there is no evidence that the disclosure will be of benefit: *Biogen Inc v Medeva plc* [1993] RPC 475.
8   *Mölnlycke AB v Procter & Gamble Ltd (No 4)* [1992] 4 All ER 47, [1992] 1 WLR 1112, [1992] RPC 21, CA, distinguished in *Biogen Inc v Medeva plc* [1993] RPC 475.

522.   Relief claimed.   The relief which may be claimed[1] in proceedings for infringement of a patent[2] is:

(1)   an injunction restraining the defendant from any apprehended act of infringement[3];

(2)   an order for him to deliver up or destroy any patented product[4] in relation to which the patent is infringed or any article in which that product is inextricably comprised[5];

(3)   damages in respect of the infringement[6];

(4)   an account of the profits derived by him from the infringement[7];

(5)   a declaration that the patent is valid and has been infringed by him[8]; and

(6)   further or other relief and costs[9].

The relief which may be claimed in infringement proceedings before the comptroller[10] is limited to relief under heads (3) and (5) above[11].

In determining whether to grant any relief and the extent of relief to be granted under the Patents Act 1977, the court[12] or the comptroller must apply the principles applied by the court in relation to that relief immediately before 1 June 1978[13].

1   In a claim for infringement the statement of case must contain particulars as specified in *Practice Direction — Intellectual Property Claims* PD 63 para 4: see PARA 526. A claim for unjust

enrichment is not permitted: *Union Carbide Corpn v BP Chemicals Ltd* [1998] FSR 1 (on appeal on a different point [1999] RPC 409, CA).

2   As to infringement see PARA 499 et seq.

3   Patents Act 1977 s 61(1)(a). See also PARA 520 note 1. As to injunctions see PARAS 536, 541–542.

4   As to the meaning of 'patented product' see PARA 371 note 11.

5   Patents Act 1977 s 61(1)(b). As to delivery up see PARA 548.

6   Patents Act 1977 s 61(1)(c). As to damages see PARA 543 et seq.

7   Patents Act 1977 s 61(1)(d). As to accounts of profits see PARA 543.

8   Patents Act 1977 s 61(1)(e). As to the validity of patents see PARA 429 et seq.

9   This is the usual additional relief claimed in the Chancery Division. As to costs see PARA 551.

10   Ie proceedings referred to under the Patents Act 1977 s 61(3): see PARA 553. As to the comptroller see PARA 575.

11   Patents Act 1977 s 61(3).

12   As to the meaning of 'court' see PARA 619 note 1.

13   Patents Act 1977 s 61(6). 1 June 1978 is the day on which s 61 was brought into force by the Patents Act 1977 (Commencement No 2) Order 1978, SI 1978/586, art 2.

523. Service out of the jurisdiction. In a claim brought upon an infringement committed within the jurisdiction, permission may be given to serve the claim form out of the jurisdiction either as a claim founded on a tort committed within the jurisdiction, or as a claim in which an injunction is sought ordering the defendant to do or refrain from doing something within the jurisdiction, or on the ground that the defendant out of the jurisdiction is a necessary or proper party to the claim properly brought against a person duly served within the jurisdiction[1]. No permission is, however, required[2] provided each claim is a claim which, by virtue of the Civil Jurisdiction and Judgments Act 1982, the court has power to hear and determine and provided certain conditions apply[3]. A prima facie case of infringement, or threatened infringement, within the jurisdiction must be shown[4], but the court will not decide doubtful questions of law or fact adversely to the claimant on an application for permission or on an application to discharge the order[5].

1   See CPR 6.36; *Practice Direction— Service out of the Jurisdiction* PD 6B para 3.1; and CIVIL PROCEDURE vol 11 (2009) PARA 170.

2   See CPR 6.33; and CIVIL PROCEDURE vol 11 (2009) PARAS 168–169.

3   As to these conditions see CPR 6.33; and CIVIL PROCEDURE vol 11 (2009) PARAS 168–169. The claimant must establish a 'good arguable case' that the court does so have jurisdiction: *Mölnlycke AB v Procter & Gamble Ltd (No 4)* [1992] 4 All ER 47, [1992] 1 WLR 1112, [1992] RPC 21, CA.

4   See *Badische Anilin und Soda Fabrik v Chemische Fabrik vormals Sandoz* (1903) 20 RPC 413, CA (on appeal (1904) 90 LT 733, 21 RPC 533, HL); *Electric Furnace Co v Selas Corpn of America* [1987] RPC 23, CA; *Raychem Corpn v Thermon (UK) Ltd* [1989] RPC 423; *Puschner v Tom Palmer (Scotland) Ltd* [1989] RPC 430.

5   *Badische Anilin und Soda Fabrik v Chemische Fabrik vormals Sandoz* (1903) 20 RPC 413, CA; on appeal (1904) 90 LT 733, 21 RPC 533, HL. The claimant must establish a 'good arguable case' ie a serious question which calls for a trial for its proper determination: *Unilever plc v Gillette (UK) Ltd* [1989] RPC 583 at 600, CA; *Mölnlycke AB v Procter & Gamble Ltd (No 4)* [1992] 4 All ER 47, [1992] RPC 21, CA. In the case of defendants in Scotland or Northern Ireland the question of forum conveniens will also be considered: *Lennon v Scottish Daily Record and Sunday Mail Ltd* [2004] EWHC 359 (QB), [2004] All ER (D) 34 (Mar); *Ivax Pharmaceuticals UK Ltd v Akzo Nobel NV* [2005] EWHC 2658 (Ch), [2006] FSR 888, [2005] All ER (D) 356 (Jul).

524. Claims against the Crown. Subject to certain statutory restrictions[1], civil proceedings lie against the Crown for an infringement committed by a servant or agent of the Crown[2], with the authority of the Crown, of a patent[3]. Save as so provided, no proceedings lie against the Crown by virtue of the Crown Proceedings Act 1947 in respect of the infringement of a patent[4]. Infringement by the Crown is, however, unlikely in view of its wide powers to make use of patented inventions for the services of the Crown[5].

1   Ie subject to the provisions of the Crown Proceedings Act 1947: see CROWN PROCEEDINGS AND CROWN PRACTICE vol 12(1) (Reissue) PARA 115 et seq. Thus an injunction may not be granted against the Crown: see s 21(1) proviso (a); and CROWN PROCEEDINGS AND CROWN PRACTICE vol 12(1) (Reissue) PARA 134.

2   As to the authority of agents generally see AGENCY vol 1 (2008) PARA 29 et seq.

3   Crown Proceedings Act 1947 s 3(1)(a) (s 3 substituted by the Copyright, Designs and Patents Act 1988 Sch 7 para 4(1)). The Patents Act 1977 does not affect the Queen in her private capacity but, subject to that, it binds the Crown: s 129.

4   Crown Proceedings Act 1947 s 3(1) (as substituted: see note 3). Nothing in the Crown Proceedings Act 1947 s 3 is to be construed as affecting the rights of a government department under the Patents Act 1977 s 55 (see PARAS 404–405) or the rights of the Secretary of State under s 22 (see PARAS 334–335): Crown Proceedings Act 1947 s 3(2) (as so substituted). As to the Secretary of State see PARA 573.

5   See the Patents Act 1977 ss 55–59; and PARA 403 et seq.

525.   Advertising proceedings.   It is not a contempt of court[1] for a claimant to advertise that he has brought a claim or that he will prosecute infringers[2], although he should not state that success is certain or that the defendant has infringed[3]. Similarly, the defendant must not state that the invention is old[4]. The publication of fair reports of proceedings in the court is permissible[5], but this may amount to contempt if the proceedings were collusive and another action is pending[6]. Statements about a pending action may amount to trade libel, if false and malicious[7].

1   As to contempt of court see CONTEMPT OF COURT.

2   *Fenner v Wilson* [1893] 2 Ch 656, 10 RPC 283; *Dunlop Pneumatic Tyre Co Ltd v Clifton Rubber Co Ltd* (1902) 19 RPC 527; *Haskell Golf Ball Co v Hutchinson and Main* (1904) 20 TLR 606, 21 RPC 497; *Mullard Radio Valve Co Ltd v Rothermel Corpn Ltd* (1933) 51 RPC 1; but see *Fusee Vesta Co v Bryant and May Ltd* (1887) 4 RPC 191 (threats after application to amend). See also *St Mungo Manufacturing Co v Hutchinson, Main & Co Ltd* (1908) 25 RPC 356, Ct of Sess. Cf *Carl-Zeiss-Stiftung v Rayner and Keeler Ltd* [1960] 3 All ER 289, [1960] 1 WLR 1145, [1961] RPC 1 (trade mark).

3   *Goulard and Gibbs v Lindsay & Co Ltd and Ferranti* (1887) 4 RPC 189; *Fenner v Wilson* [1893] 2 Ch 656, 10 RPC 283; and see *Mullard Radio Valve Co Ltd v Rothermel Corpn Ltd* (1933) 51 RPC 1.

4   *Daw v Eley* (1865) LR 1 Eq 38; *British Vacuum Cleaner Co Ltd v Suction Cleaners Ltd* (1904) 21 RPC 303; *St Mungo Manufacturing Co v Hutchinson, Main & Co Ltd* (1908) 25 RPC 356, Ct of Sess.

5   Misrepresentation may be treated as contempt: *Edlin v Pneumatic Tyre Co* (1893) 10 RPC 317; *Gillette Safety Razor Co v AW Gamage Ltd* (1906) 24 RPC 1. See also *Therm-a-Stor Ltd v Weatherseal Windows Ltd* [1981] FSR 579 at 582, CA.

6   *Roberts v Graydon* (1904) 21 RPC 194.

7   *Mentmore Manufacturing Co Ltd v Fomento (Sterling Area) Ltd* (1954) 72 RPC 12; on appeal (1955) 72 RPC 157, CA. As to trade libel or slander of goods generally see DEFAMATION vol 32 (2012) PARA 776 et seq.

526.   Statement of case.   In a claim for infringement of a patent the statement of case must show which of the claims in the specification of the patent are alleged to be infringed and give at least one example of each type of infringement alleged[1]. A copy of each document referred to in the statement of case, and where necessary a translation of the document, must be served with the statement of case[2].

Where the validity of a patent is challenged the statement of case must contain particulars of the remedy sought and the issues except those relating to validity of the patent[3]. The statement of case must have a separate document annexed to it headed 'Grounds of Invalidity' specifying the grounds on which validity of the patent is challenged and including particulars that will clearly define every issue (including any challenge to any claimed priority date) which it is intended to raise[4]. A copy of each document referred to in the Grounds of Invalidity, and where necessary a translation of the document, must be served with the Grounds of Invalidity[5].

An allegation that the patent is valid is often included[6]. If the specification has been amended[7], this may be stated and an allegation added that the original specification was framed in good faith and with reasonable skill and knowledge[8]. Where a certificate of contested validity[9] has been granted, the fact should be stated. Several patents may be sued on in one claim, provided that no inconvenience or oppression will arise from the plurality of issues[10].

1 *Practice Direction — Intellectual Property Claims* PD 63 para 4.1(1). As to these particulars see PARA 605; and as to allegations where directors are sued see *British Thomson-Houston Co Ltd v Irradiant Lamp Works Ltd* (1924) 41 RPC 338.
2 *Practice Direction — Intellectual Property Claims* PD 63 para 4.1(2).
3 *Practice Direction — Intellectual Property Claims* PD 63 para 4.2(1).
4 *Practice Direction — Intellectual Property Claims* PD 63 para 4.2(2). As to grounds of invalidity see PARA 429.
5 *Practice Direction — Intellectual Property Claims* PD 63 paras 4.1(2), 4.2(3).
6 It is, however, unnecessary: *Amory v Brown* (1869) LR 8 Eq 663. See also *Weber v Xetal Products Ltd* (1933) 50 RPC 211; *C Evans & Sons Ltd v Spritebrand Ltd* [1985] 2 All ER 415, [1985] FSR 267, CA; *PLG Research Ltd v Ardon International Ltd* [1993] FSR 197 at 238.
7 As to the amendment of specifications see PARA 345 et seq.
8 See the Patents Act 1977 s 62(3); and PARA 547. See also PARA 520 note 1.
9 As to certificates of contested validity see PARA 549.
10 In *Saccharin Corpn Ltd v Wild* [1903] 1 Ch 410, 20 RPC 243, CA, 23 patents were sued on, but an order was made limiting the number to three. In *Saccharin Corpn Ltd v R White & Sons Ltd* (1903) 88 LT 850, 20 RPC 454, CA, the number permitted was seven.

527. Particulars of infringement. In a claim for infringement of a patent the statement of case must be served[1]. General words are added reserving the right to claim damages for other similar breaches after disclosure[2]. 'Type of infringement' includes not only the quality of the act complained of, that is to say whether it is manufacture, assembly, offer for sale, sale, process etc, but also the nature of the act, namely that it took place within the appropriate time and constituted an infringement of the monopoly[3]. In the case of sale, the names of the customers may be required[4]. In the case of manufacture, place and time should normally be given[5]. The claimant need not construe his specification or indicate how he will argue that the act complained of constitutes an infringement of his patent[6].

1 See *Practice Direction —Intellectual Property Claims* PD 63 para 4.1(1), (2); and PARA 526. See also *Building Product Design Ltd v Sandtoft Roof Tiles Ltd* [2004] FSR 823 (inquiry as to damages limited to sole type of infringement pleaded). The alleged infringement might be based solely on proposed amendments to the patent: *Zipher Ltd v Markem Systems Ltd* [2007] EWHC 154 (Pat), [2007] FSR 481.
2 As to the effect of such general allegation see *AG für Autogene Aluminium Schweissung v London Aluminium Co Ltd* [1919] 2 Ch 67, 36 RPC 199, CA.
3 *Salopian Engineers Ltd v Salop Trailer Co Ltd* (1954) 71 RPC 223. See also *Sorata Ltd v Gardex Ltd* [1984] RPC 317 at 322, CA (where a patentee was not allowed to amend its particulars of infringement by alleging infringement by an article, having a different construction to the article already in issue, on the ground that this was a new cause of action which was statute-barred under the Limitation Act 1980 s 35(3)).
4 *Murray v Clayton* (1872) LR 15 Eq 115. In the case of sales of mass-produced articles identified by type, such particulars are seldom given. As to particulars to be given when a company and its directors are sued together see *British Thomson-Houston Co Ltd v Irradiant Lamp Works Ltd* (1924) 41 RPC 338.
5 The governing consideration is that the defendant should know the case which he has to meet (*Z Electric Lamp Manufacturing Co Ltd v Marples, Leach & Co Ltd* (1909) 26 RPC 762, CA),

and, therefore, certain of these details may be excused where this end can be attained otherwise, e g where the breach complained of is the manufacture of a specified article which is exhibited or otherwise identified, particulars of the date and place of manufacture might not be necessary. Greater particularity may be required where the defendant is only the user than where he is also the manufacturer: *Mandleberg v Morley* (1893) 10 RPC 256 at 260; cf *Mullard Radio Valve Co Ltd v Tungsram Electric Lamp Works (Great Britain) Ltd* (1932) 49 RPC 279. See also *Nolek Systems AB v Analytical Instruments Ltd* [1984] RPC 556; *Lubrizol Corpn v Esso Petroleum Co Ltd (No 3)* [1993] FSR 59.

6   *Wenham Co Ltd v Champion Gas Lamp Co Ltd and Todlenhaupt & Co* (1890) 63 LT 827, 8 RPC 22; *Marsden v Albrecht and Albrecht* (1910) 27 RPC 785, CA; *Lux Traffic Controls Ltd v Staffordshire Public Works Co Ltd* [1991] RPC 73.

528. Defence and admissions.

The defendant may by his defence[1]:

(1)   deny the claimant's title to the patent[2];

(2)   deny that he has infringed as alleged or at all[3];

(3)   plead leave and licence[4];

(4)   raise one or more objections to the validity of the patent[5];

(5)   assert that the action is somehow precluded by the Treaty on the Functioning of the European Union and, in particular, plead 'exhaustion of rights'[6] or that it offends against the EC Treaty[7];

(6)   allege that at the date of the infringement he was not aware, and had no reasonable grounds for supposing, that the patent existed[8];

(7)   deny, where the specification has been amended, that the original specification was drawn in good faith and with reasonable skill and knowledge[9].

These last two pleas relate only to claims for damages and an account of profits[10], and do not affect the question of an injunction. In some cases the defendant may also rely on an estoppel[11]. Where the defendant raises objections to validity, he may counterclaim for revocation[12], in which case the claimant must serve a defence to counterclaim[13].

The defendant may make an admission of the claim or part of the claim in accordance with the standard procedure[14].

1   In a claim for infringement, the period for service of the defence is 42 days after service of the claim form: CPR 63.7(a), 63.22(2). The claimant must file any reply to a defence and serve it on all other parties within 21 days of service of the defence: CPR 63.7(c). Apart from these two modifications, CPR Pt 15 applies to patent proceedings: CPR 63.7. As to CPR Pt 15 see CIVIL PROCEDURE vol 11 (2009) PARA 199 et seq.

2   The objection that the patent was granted to a person not entitled to it is a ground of invalidity: see the Patents Act 1977 s 72(1)(b), (2); and PARA 562.

3   The defendant may wish to raise the so-called 'Gillette' defence, namely that what he is doing differs from that which has been done of old only in non-patentable variations: *Gillette Safety Razor Co v Anglo-American Trading Co Ltd* (1913) 30 RPC 465 at 480, HL.

4   Where the licence relied on is that implied by purchase from the proprietor of the patent or his agent, the issue is raised by the plea of non-infringement (*Badische Anilin und Soda Fabrik v Dawson* (1889) 6 RPC 387; *Betts v Willmott* (1871) 6 Ch App 239, CA), but this does not apply where the purchase is from a licensee. A defendant who claims to have purchased from a licensee cannot compel the claimant to add the licensee as a defendant: *Evans v Central Electric Supply Co Ltd* (1923) 40 RPC 357. Where the alleged infringement is a breach of a limited licence (see PARA 384), the defendant may plead want of notice of the limiting conditions.

5   See the Patents Act 1977 s 74(1)(a); and PARA 519. The only grounds on which the validity of a patent may be put in issue are the grounds on which the patent may be revoked under s 72 (see PARAS 562–563): see s 74(3); and PARA 519.

6   Cf Case 15/74 *Centrafarm BV v Sterling Drug Inc* [1974] ECR 1147, [1974] 2 CMLR 480, ECJ.

7   Ie offends against the Treaty on the Functioning of the European Union (Rome, 25 March 1957; TS 1 (1973); Cmnd 5179) art 101 or art 102 (see EUROPEAN UNION vol 47A (2014) PARA 308): *Phillips Electronics NV v Ingman Ltd (t/a Diskxpress)* [1998] 2 CMLR 839, [1999] FSR 112; *Sandvik Aktiebolag v KR Pfiffner (UK) Ltd* [2000] FSR 17, [1999] All ER (D) 372; *Sandisk*

Corpn v Koninklijke Philips Electronics [2007] EWHC 332 (Ch), [2007] FSR 545, [2007] All ER (D) 357 (Feb); *Intel Corpn (a company incorporated in the state of Delaware USA) v VIA Technologies Inc* [2002] EWCA Civ 1905, [2003] FSR 574, [2002] All ER (D) 346 (Dec). As to the Treaty on the Functioning of the European Union in general see EUROPEAN UNION vol 47A (2014) PARA 6.

8   See the Patents Act 1977 s 62(1); and PARA 547. See also PARA 520 note 1.

9   See the Patents Act 1977 s 62(3); and PARA 547. Particulars are required of the respects in which the specification is defective, but not of what it ought to have said: *Crompton v Anglo-American Brush Electric Light Corpn* (1887) 35 ChD 283, 4 RPC 197, CA; *Z Electric Lamp Manufacturing Co Ltd v Marples, Leach & Co Ltd* (1910) 27 RPC 737, CA. See also *Unilin Beheer BV v Berry Floor NV* [2005] EWCA Civ 1292, [2006] FSR 495, [2005] All ER (D) 42 (Nov). The proprietor of the patent may be required to give particulars of the passages in the specification which he alleges contain sufficient directions: *Polaroid Corpn v Eastman Kodak Co* [1977] RPC 379, CA.

10 See PARA 543.

11 See PARA 552.

12 See the Patents Act 1977 s 74(1)(a); and PARA 519.

13 *Coventry Radiator Co Ltd v Coventry Motor Fittings Co Ltd* (1917) 34 RPC 239. The defence to counterclaim usually consists of a mere traverse. It is common to include with the defence to counterclaim a reply in the action, consisting of a simple joinder of issue: *Cincinnati Grinders Inc v BSA Tools Ltd* (1930) 48 RPC 33 at 43, CA. A reply may also be necessary in special cases where there is no counterclaim.

14 Ie in accordance with CPR Pt 14: see CIVIL PROCEDURE vol 11 (2009) PARA 187 et seq.

529.   Particulars of lack of novelty and obviousness.   No particulars are required of the respects in which the invention is alleged to be obvious or to lack novelty[1], but particulars are required of the prior publication and use relied upon[2]. Where common general knowledge is relied upon, it is sufficient to say so[3]; but, where it is intended to suggest that some specific document or prior use forms part of common general knowledge, this should be stated[4]. Further, if it is proposed to give evidence of some knowledge or practice outside the trade or art to which the patent appertains, this should be stated[5]. If any party wishes to rely upon the commercial success of a patent in answer to a plea of lack of inventive step, he must in his pleading set out the grounds on which he relies[6]. Commercial success abroad may be relevant[7].

1   *Morris and Bastert v Young* (1895) 12 RPC 455 at 460, HL.

2   See PARA 530.

3   *Holliday v Heppenstall Bros* (1889) 41 ChD 109, 6 RPC 320, CA.

4   *English and American Machinery Co Ltd v Union Boot and Shoe Machine Co Ltd* (1894) 11 RPC 367, CA. See also *Aluma Systems Inc v Hunnebeck GmbH* [1982] FSR 239 (discovery ordered of any specific documents relied upon). As to the meaning of 'common general knowledge' see PARAS 442, 456.

5   *Fox v Astrachans Ltd* (1910) 27 RPC 377 at 385. See also *British Thomson-Houston Co Ltd v Stonebridge Electrical Co Ltd* (1916) 33 RPC 166. In some of the older cases allegations of common general knowledge in a stated trade in a particular locality, eg London and Nottingham, were held sufficient: see *Jones v Berger* (1843) 1 Web Pat Cas 544; *Palmer v Wagstaffe* (1853) 22 LJ Ex 295; *Boyd v Horrocks* (1886) 3 RPC 285; but cf *Palmer v Cooper* (1853) 9 Exch 231 with *Palmer v Wagstaffe*. In *Fisher v Dewick* (1838) 1 Web Pat Cas 551n, *Holland v Fox* (1852) 1 WR 448, and *Morgan v Fuller (2)* (1866) LR 2 Eq 297, somewhat similar pleas were held too vague. Probably such a particular would be held sufficient if it made it clear that reliance was placed on general practice (within the specified limits) and not on individual practice.

6   The patentee must do more than merely cite sales figures of the particular products relied upon and must set out the defect, if there was one, in prior art products, how it was overcome and, if long felt want is to be established, the grounds on which the patentee relies: *John Deks Ltd v Aztec Washer Co* [1989] RPC 413.

7   *Unilever plc v Gillette (UK) Ltd* [1989] RPC 417.

530.   Particulars of lack of novelty, inventive step and of insufficiency. Where the Grounds of Invalidity[1] include an allegation:

(1)   that the invention is not a patentable invention because it is not new[2] or does not involve an inventive step[3], the particulars must specify details of the matter in the state of art relied on[4];

(2)   that the specification of the patent does not disclose the invention clearly enough and completely enough for it to be performed by a person skilled in the art[5], the particulars must state, if appropriate, which examples of the invention cannot be made to work and in which respects they do not work or do not work as described in the specification[6].

1   See PARA 526.
2   As to lack of novelty see PARA 434 et seq.
3   As to want of inventive step see PARA 437 et seq. In any proceedings in which the validity of a patent is challenged: (1) on the ground that the invention did not involve an inventive step, a party who wishes to rely on the commercial success of the patent must state the grounds on which he so relies in his statement of case; and (2) the court may order inspection of machinery or apparatus where a party alleges such machinery or apparatus was used before the priority date of the claim: *Practice Direction — Intellectual Property Claims* PD 63 paras 4.5, 4.6.
4   *Practice Direction — Intellectual Property Claims* PD 63 para 4.3(1). The details required are: (1) in the case of matter made available to the public by written description the date on which and the means by which it was so made available, unless this is clear from the face of the matter; and (2) in the case of matter made available to the public by use: (a) the date or dates of such use; (b) the name of all persons making such use; (c) the place of such use; (d) any written material which identifies such use; (e) the existence and location of any apparatus employed in such use; and (f) all facts and matters relied on to establish that such matter was made available to the public: PD 63 para 4.4(1), (2). In the case of books and other lengthy documents the passages relied on should be identified (*Harris v Rothwell* (1886) 3 RPC 243 at 246; affd (1887) 35 ChD 416, CA); and it is convenient to do this also in the case of lengthy specifications, or where only a part of a specification is relied on, but in other cases the defendant may simply state that he relies on the whole of a specification (*Edison-Bell Consolidated Phonograph Co Ltd v Columbia Phonograph Co* (1900) 18 RPC 4). As to the degree of particularity in describing prior users see *Avery Ltd v Ashworth, Son & Co Ltd* (1916) 33 RPC 235. Particular dates may be omitted where the user is alleged to have been regular and to have extended over a long period: *British Thomson-Houston Co Ltd v Crompton-Parkinson Ltd* (1935) 52 RPC 409, CA. Drawings were ordered in *Crosthwaite Fire Bar Syndicate v Senior* [1909] 1 Ch 801, 26 RPC 260. 'Apparatus' does not include ore or other substance worked on: *Minerals Separation Ltd v Ore Concentration Co (1905) Ltd* [1909] 1 Ch 744, 26 RPC 413, CA (inspection of samples produced by the process refused). Where samples are produced, the defendant need not say how they anticipate the claimant's patent: *Brown v WC Yuille & Co* (1915) 32 RPC 137, Ct of Sess.
        Where common general knowledge is relied upon, it is sufficient to say so (*Holliday v Heppenstall Bros* (1889) 41 ChD 109, 6 RPC 320, CA); but, where it is intended to suggest that some specific document or prior use forms part of common general knowledge, this should be stated (*English and American Machinery Co Ltd v Union Boot and Shoe Machine Co Ltd* (1894) 11 RPC 367, CA; *Aluma Systems Inc v Hunnebeck GmbH* [1982] FSR 239 (discovery ordered of any specific documents relied upon)). As to the meaning of 'common general knowledge' see PARAS 442, 456.
5   See PARA 489.
6   *Practice Direction —Intellectual Property Claims* PD 63 para 4.3(2).

531.   Amendment and further particulars. At any stage of the proceedings the court may order a party to serve further or better particulars of objections[1] or allow a party to amend particulars already served[2].

1   See *Godfrey L Cabot Inc v Philblack Ltd (No 2)* [1961] RPC 53, CA.
2   Permission to amend may be given at the trial itself (*Blakey & Co v Latham & Co* (1888) 6 RPC 29 at 36 (on appeal (1889) 5 TLR 301, CA); *Badische Anilin und Soda Fabrik v Société Chimique des Usines du Rhône and Wilson* (1898) 14 RPC 875 at 881 (affd 15 RPC 359, CA)),

but generally only where new matter has been recently discovered (*Moss v Malings* (1886) 33 ChD 603, 3 RPC 373 at 375; *Shrewsbury and Talbot Cab Co Ltd v Morgan* (1896) 13 RPC 75). In *Shoe Machinery Co Ltd v Cutlan* [1896] 1 Ch 108 at 115, 12 RPC 530 at 534, CA, leave was granted by the Court of Appeal after trial and while an appeal was pending but leave to amend to plead fresh prior art discovered pending appeal was refused in *Coflexip SA v Stolt Comex Seaway MS Ltd* [2001] 1 All ER 952, [2001] RPC 182, CA. Where a witness for the claimant disclosed an unpleaded prior user, the defendant was granted leave to amend without terms (*Franc-Strohmenger and Cowan Inc v Peter Robinson Ltd* (1930) 47 RPC 493 at 495); similarly where such a witness disclosed omission of essential directions from the specification (*Norton and Gregory Ltd v Jacobs* (1937) 54 RPC 58 at 68, 73).

532.   Case management. As soon as practicable the court must hold a case management conference[1]. Case management must be dealt with by a judge of the court or a master[2].

The claimant must apply for a case management conference within 14 days of the date when all defendants who intend to file and serve a defence have done so[3]. Where the claim has been transferred, the claimant must apply for a case management conference within 14 days of the date of the order transferring the claim, unless the court held or gave directions for a case management conference, when it made the order transferring the claim[4]. Any party may, at a time earlier than that provided above, apply in writing to the court to fix a case management conference[5]. If the claimant does not make an application as required, any other party may apply for a case management conference[6]. The court may fix a case management conference at any time on its own initiative[7].

Not less than four days before a case management conference, each party must file and serve an application notice for any order which that party intends to seek at the case management conference[8].

Unless the court orders otherwise, the claimant, or other party making the application, in consultation with the other parties, must prepare a case management bundle containing:

(1)   the claim form;
(2)   all statements of case (excluding schedules), except that, if a summary of a statement of case has been filed, the bundle should contain the summary, and not the full statement of case;
(3)   a pre-trial timetable, if one has been agreed or ordered;
(4)   the principal orders of the court; and
(5)   any agreement in writing made by the parties as to disclosure,

and must provide copies of the case management bundle for the court and the other parties at least four days before the first case management conference or any earlier hearing at which the court may give case management directions[9].

At the case management conference the court may direct that a scientific adviser be appointed[10] and a document setting out basic undisputed technology should be prepared[11].

Where a trial date has not been fixed by the court, a party may apply for a trial date by filing a certificate which must:

(a)   state the estimated length of the trial, agreed if possible by all parties;
(b)   detail the time required for the judge to consider the documents[12];
(c)   identify the area of technology; and
(d)   assess the complexity of the technical issues involved by indicating the complexity on a scale of one to five (with one being the least and five the most complex)[13].

1   CPR 63.8(3). The case management procedure under CPR Pt 26 (see CIVIL PROCEDURE vol 11 (2009) PARA 260 et seq) does not apply and CPR Pt 29 (see CIVIL PROCEDURE vol 11 (2009)

PARA 293 et seq) does not apply apart from CPR 29.3(2) (legal representatives to attend case management conferences), CPR 29.4 (the court's approval of agreed proposals for the management of proceedings) and CPR 29.5 (variation of case management timetable) (with the exception of CPR 29.5(1)(b), (c)): CPR 63.8(2). The provisions relating to case management conferences set out in *Practice Direction — The Multi-track* PD 29 para 5, excluding para 5.9 and modified so far as is made necessary and the provisions relating to failure to comply with case management directions in *Practice Direction — The Multi-track* PD 29 para 7 apply to patents cases (see CIVIL PROCEDURE vol 11 (2009) PARAS 295, 298): see *Practice Direction — Intellectual Property Claims* PD 63 para 5.1.

2   *Practice Direction — Intellectual Property Claims* PD 63 para 5.2.

3   *Practice Direction — Intellectual Property Claims* PD 63 para 5.3. As to the defence see PARA 528.

4   *Practice Direction — Intellectual Property Claims* PD 63 para 5.4.

5   *Practice Direction — Intellectual Property Claims* PD 63 para 5.5.

6   *Practice Direction — Intellectual Property Claims* PD 63 para 5.6.

7   *Practice Direction — Intellectual Property Claims* PD 63 para 5.7.

8   *Practice Direction — Intellectual Property Claims* PD 63 para 5.8.

9   *Practice Direction — Intellectual Property Claims* PD 63 para 5.9. The claimant, in consultation with the other parties, must revise and update the documents referred to in PD 63 para 5.9 appropriately as the case proceeds; this must include making all necessary revisions and additions at least seven days before any subsequent hearing at which the court may give case management directions: PD 63 para 5.12.

10   Ie under the Senior Courts Act 1981 s 70(3): see CIVIL PROCEDURE vol 12 (2009) PARA 1133. CPR 35.15 (see CIVIL PROCEDURE vol 11 (2009) PARA 863) applies to scientific advisers: see *Practice Direction —Intellectual Property Claims* PD 63 para 5.10.

11   *Practice Direction — Intellectual Property Claims* PD 63 para 5.10.

12   As to the status of documents pre-read by the judge prior to a hearing which in the event was not contested see *SmithKline Beecham Biologics SA v Connaught Laboratories Inc* [1999] 4 All ER 498, [2000] FSR 1.

13   *Practice Direction — Intellectual Property Claims* PD 63 para 5.11.

533.   Disclosure and inspection. The general rules relating to disclosure and inspection of documents[1] apply to patents claims with certain modifications[2].

Standard disclosure[3] does not require the disclosure of documents where the documents relate to:

(1)   the infringement of a patent by a product or process where, not less than 21 days before the date for service of a list of documents the defendant notifies the claimant and any other party of his intention to serve full particulars of the product or process alleged to infringe and any necessary drawings or other illustrations, and on or before the date for service the defendant serves those documents on the claimant and any other party[4];

(2)   any ground on which the validity of a patent is put in issue, except documents which came into existence within the period beginning two years before the earliest claimed priority date[5] and ending two years after that date[6]; and

(3)   the issue of commercial success[7].

Where the issue of commercial success arises and the commercial success relates to an article or product, the patentee must, within such time limit as the court may direct, serve a schedule containing:

(a)   an identification of the article or product (for example by product code number) which the patentee asserts has been made in accordance with the claims of the patent[8];

(b)   a summary by convenient periods of sales of any such article or product[9];

(c)　　a summary for the equivalent periods of sales, if any, of any equivalent prior article or product marketed before the article or product in head (a)[10]; and

(d)　　a summary by convenient periods of any expenditure on advertising and promotion which supported the marketing of the articles or products in heads (a) and (c)[11].

Where the commercial success relates to the use of a process a schedule must be served containing:

(i)　　an identification of the process which the patentee asserts has been used in accordance with the claims of the patent[12];

(ii)　　a summary by convenient periods of the revenue received from the use of such process[13];

(iii)　　a summary for the equivalent periods of the revenues, if any, received from the use of any equivalent prior art process[14]; and

(iv)　　a summary by convenient periods of any expenditure which supported the use of the process in heads (i) and (iii)[15].

Disclosure in patent actions is limited to the issues raised by the particulars[16]. Documents are relevant if they may fairly lead to a train of inquiry which would help to establish the case of the party seeking disclosure[17]. Where there is an inquiry as to damages or an account of profits is ordered[18], the defendants are not entitled to seal up the parts of their books containing the names of their customers[19]. In a proper case the court may order an innocent third person or an alleged tortfeasor to disclose information about infringement by others[20].

The court may allow disclosure even though it is alleged that, if given, a secret process[21] will be divulged, but in the exercise of its discretion it will, so far as possible, limit the order in such a way that the secret process is not compelled to be disclosed[22]. Disclosure has been ordered of the experimental work leading up to the making of the invention where an allegation of obviousness had been made[23].

1　Ie CPR Pt 31: see CIVIL PROCEDURE vol 11 (2009) PARA 538 et seq. In connection with disclosure see also the Justice and Security Act 2013 s 17; and CIVIL PROCEDURE.

2　CPR 63.9. See *Nichia Corpn v Argos Ltd* [2007] EWCA Civ 741, [2007] FSR 895 (it would be against the interests of justice if documents known to exist, or easily revealed, which would harm a party's own case or assist another party's case need not be disclosed because of a blanket prima facie rule against any standard disclosure in patent actions; standard disclosure should be carried out properly but the search should be tailor-made to the case).

3　See CPR Pt 31; and CIVIL PROCEDURE vol 11 (2009) PARA 542.

4　*Practice Direction — Intellectual Property Claims* PD 63 para 6.1(1). As to the adequacy of such process descriptions see *Taylor v Ishida (Europe) Ltd* [2000] FSR 224, [1999] All ER (D) 948; affd [2001] EWCA Civ 1092, [2001] IP & T 1209, [2001] All ER (D) 147 (Jul). The particulars so served must be accompanied by a signed written statement which must state that the person making the statement is personally acquainted with the facts to which the particulars relate, verifies that the particulars are a true and complete description of the product or process alleged to infringe, and understands that he or she may be required to attend court in order to be cross-examined on the contents of the particulars: PD 63 para 6.2.

5　As to the priority date see PARA 310 note 6.

6　*Practice Direction — Intellectual Property Claims* PD 63 para 6.1(2).

7　*Practice Direction — Intellectual Property Claims* PD 63 para 6.1(3).

8　*Practice Direction — Intellectual Property Claims* PD 63 para 6.3(1)(a).

9　*Practice Direction — Intellectual Property Claims* PD 63 para 6.3(1)(b).

10　*Practice Direction — Intellectual Property Claims* PD 63 para 6.3(1)(c).

11　*Practice Direction — Intellectual Property Claims* PD 63 para 6.3(1)(d).

12　*Practice Direction — Intellectual Property Claims* PD 63 para 6.3(2)(a).

13　*Practice Direction — Intellectual Property Claims* PD 63 para 6.3(2)(b).

14　*Practice Direction — Intellectual Property Claims* PD 63 para 6.3(2)(c).

15 *Practice Direction — Intellectual Property Claims* PD 63 para 6.3(2)(d).

16 *Avery Ltd v Ashworth, Son & Co Ltd* (1915) 32 RPC 560, CA; on appeal (1916) 33 RPC 235, HL. Neither party is bound to disclose documents unless they relate to the matters particularised: *Avery Ltd v Ashworth, Son & Co Ltd*. However, in appropriate circumstances the court may allow disclosure even though the mandatory requirements relating to the relevant particulars have not been complied with: *Visx Inc v Nidex Co* [1999] FSR 91; *Dendron GmbH v University of California* [2004] EWHC 1163 (Ch), [2004] FSR 475, [2004] All ER (D) 274 (May). If omitted particulars are within the knowledge of the other party it is generally proper to delay further particularisation until after disclosure: *Visx Inc v Nidex Co*. But a genuine case must be pleaded in sufficient detail to limit the area of disclosure and fishing amendments to pleadings are not permissible: *Visx Inc v Nidex Co*. Documents relating to an amendment of a patent or pleadings, affidavits or documents in another action need not be disclosed (*Avery Ltd v Ashworth, Son & Co Ltd*; *Intalite International NV v Cellular Ceilings Ltd* [1987] RPC 532), but documents relating to the same issues in former actions must be disclosed subject to the ordinary rules of privilege (*Haslam & Co Ltd v Hall* (1887) 5 RPC 1 (on appeal (1888) 20 QBD 491, 5 RPC 144, CA); *Bown v Sansom, Teale & Co* (1888) 5 RPC 510, CA; *Edison and Swan United Electric Light Co v Holland* (1888) 5 RPC 213, CA; *Thomson v Hughes* (1889) 7 RPC 187, CA). A general allegation of further breaches gives no right to extended disclosure: *Akt für Autogene Aluminium Schweissung v London Aluminium Co Ltd* [1919] 2 Ch 67 at 74, 36 RPC 199 at 207, CA. There may be some relaxation of these rules where the defendant alleges prior user by the claimant himself, in which case disclosure may be allowed before particulars are given: *Woolfe v Automatic Picture Gallery Ltd* (1901) 19 RPC 161, CA; *Re Martin's Patents* [1936] 1 All ER 711; *Visx Inc v Nidex Co* [1999] FSR 91. Disclosure will not be ordered where the allegation is lack of fair basis because this is entirely a matter of construction for the court: *Schering Agrochemicals Ltd v ABM Chemicals Ltd* [1987] RPC 185. If the defendant intends to rely on specific documents in support of an attack of lack of inventive step based on common general knowledge, he will be ordered to give disclosure of them: *Aluma Systems Inc v Hunnebeck GmbH* [1982] FSR 239.

17 *Compania Uruguaya de Fomento Industrial SA, Biro Swan Ltd v Mentmore Manufacturing Co Ltd* (1955) 72 RPC 287 at 302; affd [1956] RPC 87, CA. As to disclosure from non-parties see *American Home Products Corpn v Novartis Pharmaceuticals UK Ltd* [2001] EWCA Civ 165, [2001] RPC 159, [2001] FSR 784.

18 For inquiries as to damages and accounts of profits see PARA 543.

19 *Murray v Clayton* (1872) LR 15 Eq 115; *American Braided Wire Co v Thompson & Co* (1888) 5 RPC 375; *Saccharin Corpn Ltd v Chemicals and Drugs Co Ltd* [1900] 2 Ch 556, 17 RPC 612, CA. In such cases, where the court is dealing with a wrongdoer, the defendant will not be excused from giving full disclosure merely because of the consequences which may flow from that disclosure necessitated by his own wrongful act: *Murray v Clayton*, approved in *Saccharin Corpn Ltd v Chemicals and Drugs Co Ltd*.

20 *Norwich Pharmacal Co v Customs and Excise Comrs* [1974] AC 133, [1974] RPC 101, HL; *Smith Kline and French Laboratories Ltd v Global Pharmaceutics Ltd* [1986] RPC 394, CA.

21 As to inspection of processes alleged to be secret see PARA 534.

22 See *Warner-Lambert Co v Glaxo Laboratories Ltd* [1975] RPC 354, CA; *Roussel Uclaf v Imperial Chemical Industries plc* [1990] RPC 45 at 53, CA. As to the status of documents treated by the parties as confidential see *Lilly Icos Ltd v Pfizer Ltd* [2002] EWCA Civ 02, [2002] 1 All ER 842, [2002] FSR 809.

23 *Halcon International Inc v Shell Transport and Trading Co Ltd (Discovery No 2)* [1979] RPC 459; *SKM SA v Wagner Spraytech (UK) Ltd* [1982] RPC 497, CA; *Mölnlycke AB v Procter & Gamble Ltd (No 3)* [1990] RPC 498. Such disclosure should, however, be proportionate: *Nichia Corpn v Argos Ltd* [2007] EWCA Civ 741, [2007] FSR 895.

534. Inspection. The court has power to order inspection at the instance of either party[1], but it is careful to prevent such inspection being used as a means of discovering trade secrets. Where it appears that inspection by a claimant of an alleged infringing process will reveal such secrets, the order for inspection is made only where the claimant makes out a prima facie case of infringement, or where it appears that a real issue as to infringement can best be settled by inspection[2]; and in a proper case the inspection will be confined to experts and counsel, who will be pledged to secrecy as to any matters the disclosure of which is not necessary for the purposes of the case[3]. The court may appoint an independent expert to make the inspection. Where there is no question of trade secrets, inspection is freely granted[4].

1   The court may order the defendant to work his machinery for the purpose of inspection: *Germ Milling Co Ltd v Robinson* (1883) 1 RPC 11; *British Xylonite Co Ltd v Fibrenyle Ltd* [1959] RPC 252, CA, followed in *Unilever plc v Pearce* [1985] FSR 475. In many other cases such an order has been made by consent. In *Germ Milling Co Ltd v Robinson* an order was made for inspection on the premises of licensees of the claimant, but such an order does not compel a person not a party to the proceedings to permit inspection (see *Rylands v Ashley's Patent (Machine Made) Bottle Co* (1890) 7 RPC 175) and such inspection may be given by consent (see *Niche Generics v H Lundbeck A/S* [2003] EWHC 2590 (Pat), [2004] FSR 392). Orders may also be made enabling a party to take samples (see the Senior Courts Act 1981 s 33; CPR r 25.5; and CIVIL PROCEDURE vol 11 (2009) PARAS 114, 323), even samples to be tested to destruction (*Patent Type Founding Co v Walter* (1860) 8 WR 353). The court may give inspection of samples in its possession to parties in another action: *Smith v Lang* (1887) 7 RPC 148 at 150, CA. The court will not grant an order for inspection if the claimant's assertions as to infringement are speculative: *Wahl and Simon-Solitec Ltd v Buhler-Miag (England) Ltd* [1979] FSR 183.

2   *British Xylonite Co Ltd v Fibrenyle Ltd* [1959] RPC 252, CA and *Unilever plc v Pearce* [1985] FSR 475, where the earlier authorities are discussed.

3   For the terms of orders of this kind see *British Thomson-Houston Co Ltd v Duram Ltd (No 2)* (1920) 37 RPC 121; *Helps v Oldham Corpn* (1923) 40 RPC 68; *Sorbo Rubber Sponge Products Ltd v Defries* (1930) 47 RPC 454; *British Celanese Ltd v Courtaulds Ltd* (1933) 50 RPC 63 at 80 (on appeal 50 RPC 259, CA, (1935) 152 LT 537, 52 RPC 171, HL); *British Xylonite Co Ltd v Fibrenyle Ltd* [1959] RPC 90 (on appeal [1959] RPC 252, CA); *Warner-Lambert Co v Glaxo Laboratories Ltd* [1975] RPC 354, CA. The evidence as to the inspection may be taken in camera: *Badische Anilin und Soda Fabrik v Levinstein* (1885) 29 ChD 366, 2 RPC 73, CA.

4   The order may be made at any time. Thus in *Edler v Victoria Press Manufacturing Co* (1910) 27 RPC 114 and *Unilever plc v Pearce* [1985] FSR 475, inspection was ordered before the delivery of the statement of claim in order to allow the plaintiff to give proper particulars of breaches, whilst in *Badische Anilin und Soda Fabrik v Levinstein* (1885) 29 ChD 366, 2 RPC 73, CA and *McDougall Bros v Partington* (1890) 7 RPC 351, inspection was deferred until after the trial of a preliminary issue.

535.   Experiments, models and apparatus.   Where a party seeks to establish any fact by experimental proof conducted for the purpose of litigation, he must at least 21 days before service of the application notice for directions[1] or within such other time as the court may direct, serve on all parties a notice stating the facts which he seeks to establish and giving full particulars[2] of the experiments proposed to establish them[3]. A party upon whom a notice is so served must within 21 days after such service, serve on the other party a notice stating whether or not he admits each fact[4]. He may request the opportunity to inspect a repetition of all or a number of the experiments identified in the notice[5]. Where any fact which a party seeks to establish by experimental proof is not admitted, he must apply to the court for permission and directions by application notice[6].

Where a party intends to rely on any model or apparatus, he must apply to the court for directions at the first case management conference[7].

1   Ie under *Practice Direction — Intellectual Property Claims* PD 63 para 7.3: see the text to note 6.

2   Such particulars may have to include the numerical data generated as a result of carrying out the experiments: *Société Française Hoechst v Allied Colloids Ltd* [1991] RPC 245.

3   *Practice Direction — Intellectual Property Claims* PD 63 para 7.1. As to matters relating to repeat experiments, failure to give notice as to the experiments to be relied on in proceedings, and the effect of failure to disclose experiments, see *Electrolux Northern Ltd v Black & Decker* [1996] FSR 595. However, 'litigation chemistry' should be avoided: *SmithKline Beecham plc's Patent (No 2)* [2003] EWHC 2673 (Pat), [2003] RPC 607; *SmithKline Beecham plc v Apotex*

Europe Ltd [2004] EWCA Civ 1568, [2005] FSR 524; *Mayne Pharma Pty Ltd v Debiopharm SA* [2006] EWHC 164 (Pat), [2006] FSR 656, [2006] All ER (D) 137 (Feb).

4   *Practice Direction — Intellectual Property Claims* PD 63 para 7.2(1).

5   *Practice Direction — Intellectual Property Claims* PD 63 para 7.2(2).

6   *Practice Direction — Intellectual Property Claims* PD 63 para 7.3.

7   *Practice Direction — Intellectual Property Claims* PD 63 para 8.1. As to case management see PARA 532. As to the use of the streamlined procedure see *Research in Motion UK Ltd v Inpro Licensing SARL* [2007] EWCA Civ 51 at [4], [2007] All ER (D) 88 (Feb) at [4] per Jacob LJ. See also *Canady v Erbe Elektromedizin GmbH* [2005] EWHC 2946 (Pat), [2006] FSR 150, [2005] All ER (D) 327 (Dec), where the streamlined procedure was used for the infringement issue.

536. Interim injunctions. Infringement of a patent may be restrained by interim injunction[1] if the claimant can establish that he has an arguable case on the issues in the proceedings, normally validity and infringement, and that, if the injunction is refused, he will not be adequately compensated by an award of damages at the full trial[2]. If the defendant can establish that, if the injunction is granted and the claimant loses at the full trial, then he will not be adequately compensated by an award of damages, the court must then consider the balance of convenience[3]. In considering the balance of convenience, the court weighs the relative harm which will be caused to each party by the grant or refusal of the injunction and considers all facts put before it which suggest that one party or the other will be prejudiced. Relevant considerations include whether a party will be good for costs and damages[4], whether the patent is close to expiry so that the defendant is obtaining an unfair start over other competitors by infringing[5], whether one party is a manufacturer with an established business and the other is an importer[6], whether the grant of an injunction would deprive the public of a life-saving drug as distinct from a mere alternative medicine[7], whether the research investment of the proprietor of the patent for future projects would be jeopardised by the loss of revenue caused by the defendant's sales[8], whether the defendant started infringing with his eyes open[9], whether the defendant could have cleared the way by seeking revocation or a declaration of non-infringement[10] and whether the claimant delayed in seeking relief or acted promptly[11]. The claimant's fear that, unless the defendant is stopped by an injunction, others will be encouraged to infringe is not always a relevant consideration[12]. The fact that amendment proceedings are pending does not preclude the grant of an interim injunction[13].

A very common practice is for the defendant to undertake to keep an account until the trial of the action[14]. If an injunction is granted, the claimant must give a cross-undertaking as to any damages the defendant may suffer should it be held that there was no ground for granting it[15].

In a proper case an injunction may be granted without notice[16] and, where the claimant can establish that the defendant is likely to hide or destroy the evidence of infringement if notice were given, the court may grant an order without notice for inspection and removal of documents and infringing goods into the custody of the claimant's solicitor pending trial[17].

An interim injunction should not be granted to interfere with passage of a foreign aircraft over or through the United Kingdom[18].

1   As to interim injunctions generally see CIVIL PROCEDURE vol 11 (2009) PARAS 316, 383 et seq. In the case of certain infringements by civil aircraft covered by the Convention on International Civil Aviation (the 'Chicago Convention') (Chicago, 7 December 1944; TS 8 (1953); Cmd 8742) (see AIR LAW vol 2 (2008) PARA 2 et seq), such an injunction must not interfere with the aircraft: see PARA 514. As to detention on infringement by other civil aircraft see PARA 514 note 10.

2 A proprietor of a patent who grants licences but does not himself manufacture is unlikely to be able to establish that damages would not be an adequate remedy: see eg *Fleming Fabrications Ltd v Albion Cylinders Ltd* [1989] RPC 47, CA.

3 *American Cyanamid Co v Ethicon Ltd* [1975] AC 396, [1975] 1 All ER 504, [1975] RPC 513, HL. An injunction is likely to be granted if the defendant fails, on motion, to establish the elements of an arguable defence: *Quantel Ltd v Electronic Graphics Ltd* [1990] RPC 272. There must be a reasonably imminent commercial threat to the patent: see *Merck Sharp Dohme Corpn v Teva Pharma BV* [2012] EWHC 627 (Pat), [2012] FSR 693, [2012] All ER (D) 150 (Oct). See also *Merck Sharp Dohme Corpn v Teva Pharma BV* [2013] EWHC 1958 (Pat), 133 BMLR 177, [2013] All ER (D) 106 (Jul); *Novartis AG v Hospira UK Ltd* [2013] EWCA Civ 583, [2014] 1 WLR 1264, [2013] IP & T 810.

4 *Belfast Ropework Co Ltd v Pixdane Ltd* [1976] FSR 337 at 341–343, CA. The fact that a claimant would not be able to meet any liability on the cross-undertaking in damages is not the end of the matter; the court must adopt the course least likely to lead to ultimate injustice: *Fleming Fabrications Ltd v Albion Cylinders Ltd* [1989] RPC 47, CA.

5 *Corruplast Ltd v George Harrison (Agencies) Ltd* [1978] RPC 761, CA.

6 *Netlon Ltd v Bridport-Gundry Ltd* [1979] FSR 530, CA.

7 *Beecham Group Ltd v Bristol Laboratories Ltd* [1967] RPC 406, CA.

8 *Netlon Ltd v Bridport-Gundry Ltd* [1979] FSR 530, CA.

9 *Belfast Ropework Co Ltd v Pixdane Ltd* [1976] FSR 337, CA; *Improver Corpn v Remington Consumer Products Ltd* [1989] RPC 69, CA.

10 *SmithKline Beecham plc v Apotex Europe Ltd* [2004] EWCA Civ 1568, [2005] FSR 524.

11 See CIVIL PROCEDURE vol 11 (2009) PARA 374. Delay is generally reckoned from the time the claimant became aware of the actual infringement: *Osmond v Hirst* (1885) 2 RPC 265; *United Telephone Co v Equitable Telephone Association* (1888) 5 RPC 233. Laches as to one infringer may be no ground for refusing relief against another: *Pneumatic Tyre Co Ltd v Warrilow* (1896) 13 RPC 284; *Netlon Ltd v Bridport-Gundry Ltd* [1979] FSR 530, CA. Where there are several alleged infringers, the proper course is for the claimant to proceed promptly against one and ask the others to agree that the decision in the one action be accepted by them as binding: *Bovill v Crate* (1865) LR 1 Eq 388; and see *North British Rubber Co Ltd v Gormully and Jeffery Manufacturing Co* (1894) 12 RPC 17; *Act für Cartonnagen Industrie v Temler* (1899) 16 RPC 447.

12 *Conder International Ltd v Hibbing* [1984] FSR 312, CA.

13 *SmithKline Beecham plc v Apotex Europe Ltd* [2004] EWCA Civ 1568, [2005] FSR 524.

14 Terms as to the payment of profits etc into court are sometimes imposed: see *North British Rubber Co Ltd v Gormully and Jeffery Manufacturing Co* (1894) 12 RPC 17 at 21; *Pneumatic Tyre Co Ltd v Goodman & Son* (1896) 13 RPC 723; *Coco v AN Clark (Engineers) Ltd* [1969] RPC 41 (trade secrets); *Vernons & Co (Pulp Products) Ltd v Universal Pulp Containers Ltd* [1980] FSR 179 (trade secrets; copyright); *Brupat Ltd v Sandford Marine Products Ltd* [1983] RPC 61, CA (patent). In *Quantel Ltd v Shima Seiki Europe Ltd* [1990] RPC 436 an injunction was refused upon the defendant's providing a bank guarantee of £2 million, but the circumstances were unusual.

15 This is also required where the defendant undertakes not to infringe. Such an undertaking is automatically implied where it has not been expressly given. See also note 4. For a case of an inquiry as to such damages see *Smithkline Beecham plc v Apotex Europe Ltd* [2006] EWCA Civ 658, [2007] Ch 71, [2006] 4 All ER 1078, where the question of affected third parties is also considered. As to undertakings as to damages generally see CIVIL PROCEDURE vol 11 (2009) PARA 419 et seq.

16 The injunction in such a case will be limited to a short time, such as a week, so that the matter may then be heard inter partes.

17 *Anton Piller KG v Manufacturing Processes Ltd* [1976] Ch 55, [1976] 1 All ER 779, [1976] RPC 719, CA. Such relief is rare in patent cases, but is more frequently given in cases of copyright and trade mark infringements.

18 Nearly all such aircraft are absolutely protected by the Civil Aviation Act 1982 s 89. For those that are not, s 89(5), Sch 12 authorises 'seizure' of the aircraft only until security is given: see PARA 514 note 10.

537. Summary judgment and trial of preliminary issues.

Where a pure point of law is involved or the facts are not materially in dispute, a party is entitled to summary judgment on the claim or relevant issue[1]. However, it is generally difficult to identify and establish such clear cut issues in a patent action even though they might at first sight appear straightforward[2]. In particular, the construction of a claim[3] requires the court to adopt the mantle of the skilled addressee which requires the aid of expert evidence[4], and infringement often involves consideration of a purposive construction and whether any variant falls within the scope of the claim[5].

The court will sometimes order the trial of preliminary issues[6], but generally only in respect of issues relating to the right to sue[7]. It seldom permits the issues of validity and infringement to be separated but may do so in appropriate cases[8].

Applications to the court for leave to amend the patent in suit have often been tried separately before the hearing of the main proceedings[9].

1   See CPR Pt 24; and CIVIL PROCEDURE vol 11 (2009) PARA 524. See also *Anchor Building Products Ltd v Redland Roof Tiles Ltd* [1990] RPC 283, CA (no arguable case of infringement); *Dendron GmbH v University of California (No 3)* [2004] EWHC 589 (Pat), [2005] 1 WLR 200, [2004] FSR 861 (whether claimant an exclusive licensee).

2   *Strix Ltd v Otter Controls Ltd* [1991] FSR 354, CA (construction of claim and infringement); *Southco Inc v Dzus Fastener Europe Ltd* [1989] RPC 82 (construction of claim and infringement); *Monsanto & Co v Merck & Co Inc* [2000] RPC 77, CA (construction of claim).

3   As to the construction of claims see PARA 414.

4   *Southco Inc v Dzus Fastener Europe Ltd* [1989] RPC 82; *Monsanto & Co v Merck & Co Inc* [2000] RPC 77, CA.

5   *Strix Ltd v Otter Controls Ltd* [1991] FSR 354, CA. As to variants see PARA 414; and *Catnic Components Ltd v Hill & Smith Ltd* [1982] RPC 183, HL; *Improver Ltd v Remington Consumer Products Ltd* [1989] RPC 69, CA.

6   See PARA 532.

7   Eg whether the claimant's patent had been validly amended (*Woolfe v Automatic Picture Gallery Ltd* (1902) 19 RPC 425; affd [1903] 1 Ch 18, 20 RPC 177, CA); whether the terms of settlement in a former action debarred the claimant from suing (*Murex Welding Processes Ltd v Weldrics (1922) Ltd* (1933) 50 RPC 178); whether the defendant could avail himself of the defence that the claimant has inserted illegal restrictions in a contract with a third person (*Sarason v Fréney* [1914] 2 Ch 474, 31 RPC 252, 330, CA); whether the defendant enjoyed 'third party rights' (*AB Astra v Pharmaceutical Manufacturing Co* (1952) 69 RPC 252, CA); whether an undertaking unlimited in time was void as in unreasonable restraint of trade (*Bescol (Electrics) Ltd v Merlin Mouldings Ltd* (1952) 69 RPC 159); and whether the claimant held the patent in trust for the defendant (*Toogood and Jones Ltd v Soccerette Ltd* [1959] RPC 265). Cf *Dendron GmbH v University of California (No 3)* [2004] EWHC 589 (Pat), [2005] 1 WLR 200, [2004] FSR 861 (whether claimant an exclusive licensee). Preliminary trial has, however, been ordered of the issue whether the alleged infringing process was in use before the date of the patent: *Field v Daily Telegraph Ltd* (1950) 67 RPC 105, CA.

8   See *Canady v Erbe Elektromedizin GmbH* [2005] EWHC 2946 (Pat), [2006] FSR 150, [2005] All ER (D) 327 (Dec).

9   See PARA 346.

538. Burden of proof. The burden of proving title[1] and infringement[2] lies on the claimant. Probably the onus on all objections to validity lies on the defendant[3], but it is the practice for the claimant to lead evidence to establish validity, where appropriate[4]; and it has been usual to give formal evidence as to validity even if the defendant does not appear at the trial[5]. The onus on issues relating to prior user and publication lies on the defendant[6]. If the invention for which a patent has been granted is a process for obtaining a new product, the defendant must show that he obtained the product by a different process[7]. Where only validity is in issue in an infringement action, it is more appropriate for the defendant to open its case and call its witnesses first[8].

1   This is normally proved from the register, which is prima facie evidence of anything required or authorised to be registered: see the Patents Act 1977 s 32(9); and PARA 588. See *Virgin Atlantic Airways Ltd v Delta Air Lines Inc* [2011] EWCA Civ 162, [2011] RPC 551, [2012] IP & T 333 (arguable case for infringement on construction of 'for' claim); *Eli Lilly & Co Ltd v Neopharma Ltd* [2011] EWHC 1852 (Pat), [2011] FSR 991, [2011] All ER (D) 34 (Jul)

(claimant's application for summary judgment allowed in part, where no real arguable case with regard to one of three grounds of defence to patent claim; order made against defendant for security for costs).

2   If the point may be disputed, the claimant should give evidence that the articles complained of were not manufactured by him or his licensee: *Betts v Willmott* (1871) 6 Ch App 239, CA; and see PARA 384. The onus as to infringement may change during the course of the case: *Z Electric Lamp Manufacturing Co Ltd v Marples, Leach & Co Ltd* (1910) 27 RPC 737, CA. Where the claimant relies on statements by the defendant, they must be such as to negative the possibility of non-infringement: *Winby v Manchester etc Steam Tramways Co* (1889) 7 RPC 30, CA; *Wilson Bros Bobbin Co Ltd v Wilson & Co (Barnsley) Ltd* (1903) 20 RPC 1, HL. In *Parkinson v Simon* (1894) 11 RPC 238; affd 11 RPC 493, CA; (1895) 12 RPC 403, HL, it was held that, because the defendants called a part a 'deflector', it did not follow that it was a 'deflector' within the meaning of the specification.

3   See the Patents Act 1977 s 72; and PARA 562.

4   *Vidal Dyes Syndicate Ltd v Levinstein Ltd* (1912) 29 RPC 245 at 254, CA.

5   *Weber v Xetal Products Ltd* (1933) 50 RPC 211.

6   Rebutting evidence may be called on the issue of prior user: *Boyd v Horrocks* (1888) 5 RPC 557; affd (1892) 9 RPC 77, HL. Thus, where a description in a classical work was relied on as an anticipation, the claimant was allowed to read a passage from Ovid to show the true nature of the article there referred to: *Benno Jaffé and Darmstaedter Lanolin Fabrik v John Richardson & Co (Leicester) Ltd* (1894) 10 TLR 398, 11 RPC 261, CA. As to the burden of proof on issues of infringement and prior user generally see *Douglas Packing Co Inc, Douglas Pectin Corpn and Postum Co Inc v Evans & Co (Hereford and Devon) Ltd* (1929) 46 RPC 493, CA. As to the burden of proof where prior use by the patentee is alleged see *Memcor Australia Pty Ltd v Norit Membraan Technologie BV* [2003] FSR 779 at 792; *Kavanagh Balloons Propriety Ltd v Cameron Balloons Ltd* [2003] EWCA Civ 1952, [2004] RPC 87, [2003] All ER (D) 212 (Dec).

7   See the Patents Act 1977 s 100(1). In considering whether a party has discharged the burden imposed upon him by s 100, the court may not require him to disclose any manufacturing or commercial secret if it appears to the court that it would be unreasonable to do so: s 100(2). As to the meaning of 'court' see PARA 619 note 1.

8   *Boehringer Mannheim GmbH v Genzyme Ltd* [1993] FSR 716.

539.   Admissibility of evidence.   Whether validity is attacked or not, evidence of the state of common general knowledge, and of the meaning of technical terms, is always admissible for the purpose of enabling the court to construe the specification[1], but for this purpose the evidence must be strictly confined to what the skilled addressee[2] might be presumed to have known at the date of filing[3], and does not authorise a reference to patent specifications or little known scientific journals[4], unless they form part of the addressee's common general knowledge[5].

Oral evidence given for the claimant in a former action cannot be used against him in an action against another defendant[6], but the court will take note of the way the case was put in a previous action on the same patent[7]. It would seem that the court may allow production of the UK Intellectual Property Office file relating to an unpublished patent application if the interests of justice require it[8], notwithstanding that such files are not open to public inspection[9]. Where the claimant relies on intention to infringe as a threat entitling him to an injunction, evidence of the defendant's acts after action brought may be relevant[10].

Judicial notice must be taken of:

(1)   the European Patent Convention[11], the Community Patent Convention and the Patent Co-operation Treaty[12] (each of which is referred to as the 'relevant convention')[13];

(2)   any bulletin, journal or gazette published under the relevant convention and the register of European patents kept under the European Patent Convention[14]; and

(3)   any decision of, or expression of opinion by, the relevant convention court[15] on any question arising under or in connection with the relevant convention[16].

Any document mentioned in head (2) above is admissible as evidence of any instrument or other act thereby communicated of any convention institution[17].

Evidence of any instrument issued under the relevant convention by any convention institution, including any judgment or order of the relevant convention court, or of any document in the custody of any such institution or reproducing in legible form any information in such custody otherwise than in legible form, or any entry in or extract from such a document, may be given in any legal proceedings[18] by production of a copy certified as a true copy by an official of that institution; and any document purporting to be such a copy must be received in evidence without proof of the official position or handwriting of the person signing the certificate[19]. Evidence of any such instrument may also be given in any legal proceedings:

(a)   by production of a copy purporting to be printed by the Queen's Printer[20];

(b)   where the instrument is in the custody of a government department, by production of a copy certified on behalf of the department to be a true copy by an officer of the department generally or specially authorised to do so[21],

and any document purporting to be such a copy as is mentioned in head (b) above of an instrument in the custody of a department must be received in evidence without proof of the official position or handwriting of the person signing the certificate, or of his authority to do so, or of the document being in the custody of the department[22].

Provision is also made for evidence to be obtained in the United Kingdom for proceedings under the European Patent Convention[23].

1   As to construction of the specification see PARA 411 et seq.
2   As to the skilled addressee see PARA 441.
3   As to the meaning of 'date of filing' see PARA 315.
4   *Adie v Clark* (1876) 3 ChD 134, CA (on appeal sub nom *Clark v Adie (No 2)* (1877) 2 App Cas 423, HL); *Jandus Arc Lamp and Electric Light Co v Johnson* (1900) 17 RPC 361; *Roberts v Graydon* (1904) 21 RPC 194; *British Vacuum Co Ltd v Exton Hotels Co Ltd* (1908) 25 RPC 617; *British Ore Concentration Syndicate Ltd v Minerals Separation Ltd* (1908) 26 RPC 124 at 138, CA; *Campbell v G Hopkins & Sons (Clerkenwell) Ltd* (1933) 50 RPC 213, CA. The same rule applies to a prior user not sufficiently common to have become part of the ordinary trade knowledge: *Hay v Gonville* (1907) 25 RPC 161 at 168.
5   *Sutcliffe v Abbott* (1902) 20 RPC 50 at 55. As to the meaning of 'common general knowledge' see PARAS 443, 457.
6   *British Thomson-Houston Co Ltd v British Insulated and Helsby Cables Ltd* [1924] 2 Ch 160, 41 RPC 345, CA; on appeal (1925) 42 RPC 180, HL. An earlier judgment on an application to revoke is not relevant save on the question of construction of claims: *SmithKline Beecham plc v Apotex Europe Ltd* [2005] EWHC 1655 (Ch), [2006] 2 All ER 53, [2005] FSR 930.
7   *British Thomson-Houston Co Ltd v British Insulated and Helsby Cables Ltd* (1925) 42 RPC 180, HL.
8   *Pneumatic Tyre Co Ltd v English Cycle and Tyre Co* (1897) 14 RPC 851 (decided under the corresponding provisions of the Patents, Designs, and Trade Marks (Amendment) Act 1885 s 4). That case referred to an application of the opposite party, sought to be used in cross-examination. Disclosure of a third person's application would be another matter. But see *Bristol-Myers Squibb Co v Baker Norton Pharmaceuticals* [1999] RPC 253 at 274.
       As to the UK Intellectual Property Office see PARA 577.
9   See the Patents Act 1977 s 118(2); and PARA 579.
10   *Dowling v Billington* (1890) 7 RPC 191, CA; cf *Shoe Machinery Co Ltd v Cutlan* (1895) 12 RPC 342 (on appeal [1896] 1 Ch 108, 12 RPC 530, CA); *Welsbach Incandescent Gas Light Co Ltd v Dowle and London and Surburban Maintenance Co* (1899) 16 RPC 391.

11 As to this Convention see PARA 644 et seq.

12 As to the Patent Co-operation Treaty (ie the Patent Co-operation Treaty (Washington, 19 June 1970; TS 78 (1978); Cmnd 7340) see PARA 629 et seq.

13 Patents Act 1977 s 91(1)(a). As to judicial notice see CIVIL PROCEDURE vol 11 (2009) PARA 779 et seq.

14 Patents Act 1977 s 91(1)(b) (amended by the Patents Act 2004 Sch 2 paras 1(1), 20).

15 For these purposes, 'relevant convention court' does not include a court of the United Kingdom or of any other country which is a party to the relevant convention: Patents Act 1977 s 91(6). As to the meaning of 'relevant convention court' generally see PARA 363 note 6; and as to the meaning of 'United Kingdom' see PARA 303 note 5.

16 Patents Act 1977 s 91(1)(c).

17 Patents Act 1977 s 91(2). For these purposes, 'convention institution' means an institution established by or having functions under the relevant convention: s 91(6).

18 For these purposes, 'legal proceedings', in relation to the United Kingdom, includes proceedings before the comptroller: Patents Act 1977 s 91(6).

19 Patents Act 1977 s 91(3).

20 Patents Act 1977 s 91(4)(a).

21 Patents Act 1977 s 91(4)(b).

22 Patents Act 1977 s 91(4).

23 See the Patents Act 1977 s 92(1), (2), applying the Evidence (Proceedings in Other Jurisdictions) Act 1975 ss 1–3 (see CIVIL PROCEDURE vol 11 (2009) PARA 1055 et seq), for the purpose of proceedings before a relevant convention court under the European Patent Convention.

   An application to the comptroller for an order under the Evidence (Proceedings in Other Jurisdictions) Act 1975 as applied by the Patents Act 1977 s 92(1) must be: (1) made in writing; (2) supported by written evidence; (3) accompanied by the request as a result of which the application is made, and where appropriate, a translation of the request into English; and (4) accompanied by the prescribed fee: Patents Rules 2007, SI 2007/3291, r 62(1). The prescribed fee is nil: Patents (Fees) Rules 2007, SI 2007/3292, r 7(2). The application must be made without notice: Patents Rules 2007, SI 2007/3291, r 62(2). The comptroller may permit an officer of the European Patent Office to attend the hearing and either examine the witnesses or request the comptroller to put specified questions to the witnesses: r 62(3). Rule 62 is made under the Patents Act 1977 s 92(3), (4).

   The Perjury Act 1911 s 1(4) (see CIVIL PROCEDURE vol 11 (2009) PARA 1055), applies in relation to such proceedings under the European Patent Convention: Patents Act 1977 s 92(5).

540. **Expert evidence.** A large portion of the evidence in patent cases comprises expert evidence. The object of such evidence is mainly to instruct the court as to the state of knowledge, the meaning of terms of art or even of complete sentences or paragraphs of a technical character[1] and other surrounding circumstances so as to enable the court to read the specification with the understanding of the craftsman to whom it is addressed, and to form a true opinion on the various issues raised; but it is not the function of the witness to construe the specification or other documents[2]. In relation to inventive step, the primary evidence is that of the properly qualified experts who state whether or not in their opinions the relevant step would have been obvious to the skilled man having regard to the state of the art[3].

1 *American Cyanamid Co v Ethicon Ltd* [1979] RPC 215 at 251–253. See also *Molnlycke AB v Proctor & Gamble Ltd (No 5)* [1994] RPC 49, CA; *Rockwater v Technip France SA* [2004] EWCA Civ 381, [2004] RPC 919, [2004] All ER (D) 63 (Apr). As to the duties and responsibilities generally of expert witnesses see *The Ikarian Reefer* [1993] FSR 563.

2 What is important is the reasons put forward by the expert: *SmithKline Beecham plc v Apotex Europe Ltd* [2005] EWHC 1655 (Ch), [2006] 2 All ER 53, [2005] FSR 930.

3 *Molnlycke AB v Proctor & Gamble Ltd (No 5)* [1994] RPC 49 at 113, CA.

541. **Injunctions.** In a claim for infringement of a patent, an injunction for the remaining life of the patent will be granted after trial[1] against a defendant who has infringed or threatened to infringe a claim not found to be invalid[2], unless the circumstances negative the probability of infringement in the future[3] or the

grant of an injunction would be oppressive[4]. Normally[5] such an injunction would be against infringement of the patent generally[6]. Where an entry is made in the register that licences under a patent are available as of right[7], no injunction may be granted, unless the proceedings are for infringement by importation from a country which is not a member state of the European Union, if the defendant undertakes to take a licence[8].

An injunction cannot be granted in respect of a patent which has expired[9] and, when a claim is brought immediately before the expiration of a patent, an injunction may be refused[10]. If the defendant against whom an injunction has been granted has modified the infringing article in an attempt to avoid infringement, a claimant who alleges that the modified article infringes the patent should bring a second claim rather than proceed to enforce the injunction[11].

1   As to when an interim injunction may be granted see PARA 536; and as to injunctions generally see CIVIL PROCEDURE vol 11 (2009) PARA 331 et seq. In the case of certain aircraft covered by the Convention on International Civil Aviation (the 'Chicago Convention') (Chicago 7 December 1944; TS 8 (1953); Cmd 8742) an injunction must not interfere with the aircraft: see PARA 514.

2   *Killick v Pye Ltd* [1958] RPC 23 at 33; on appeal [1958] RPC 366 at 382, CA; *Chiron Corpn v Organon Teknika Ltd (No 10)* [1995] FSR 325. There is no modern case where a final injunction has been refused on the ground of delay. In *Gadd and Mason v Manchester Corpn* (1892) 9 RPC 516 at 528, CA, the defendants were permitted to continue to use a gas holder already erected, but restrained from building others, but see to the contrary *Automatic Coal Gas Retort Co Ltd v Salford Corpn* (1897) 14 RPC 450.

3   Eg where the defendant has before proceedings abandoned his business or the use of the infringing machine (*Caldwell v Vanvlissengen* (1851) 21 LJ Ch 97; *Kernot v Potter* (1862) 3 De GF & J 447; *Proctor v Bayley* (1889) 42 ChD 390, 6 RPC 538, CA; *Scott v Hull Steam Fishing and Ice Co Ltd* (1897) 14 RPC 143; *Hudson v Chatteris Engineering Works Co* (1898) 15 RPC 438; *Welsbach Incandescent Gas Light Co Ltd v New Incandescent (Sunlight Patent) Gas Lighting Co* [1900] 1 Ch 843, 17 RPC 237), or where the defendant has acted innocently and has promptly offered a proper undertaking (*Jenkins v Hope* [1896] 1 Ch 278, 13 RPC 57). Cf *Killick v Pye Ltd* [1958] RPC 23 at 33 (on appeal [1958] RPC 366 at 382, CA). Where an injunction is refused the patentee is usually given liberty to apply: e g *Raleigh Cycle Co Ltd v H Miller & Co Ltd* (1949) 66 RPC 23 at 43.

4   *Shelfer v City of London Electric Lighting Co* [1895] 1 Ch 287, 64 LJ Ch 216; *Ocular Sciences Ltd v Aspect Vision Care Ltd* [1997] RPC 289 (copyright); *Navitaire Inc v Easyjet Airline Co* [2004] EWHC 1725 (Ch), [2006] RPC 111.

5   As to the position where some claims are invalid see PARA 550.

6   *Mergenthaler Linotype Co v Intertype Co Ltd* (1926) 43 RPC 239 at 275, CA; *Coflexip SA v Stolt Comex Seaway MS Ltd* [2001] 1 All ER 952, [2001] RPC 182, CA. Sometimes the injunction is limited to specific claims (see *British United Shoe Machinery Co Ltd v Gimson Shoe Machinery Co Ltd (No 2)* (1929) 46 RPC 137 at 164), and sometimes to a special form (see *Dunlop Pneumatic Tyre Co Ltd v New Ixion Tyre and Cycle Co Ltd* (1898) 15 RPC 389; affd (1899) 16 RPC 16, CA). The injunction will, if necessary, be so limited as to permit the defendant to manufacture for the government: see *Commercial Solvents Corpn v Synthetic Products Co Ltd* (1926) 43 RPC 185. The fact that wide injunctions have been granted to stop flagrant infringers of intellectual property rights does not justify the supposition that all infringers of intellectual property rights have to be subject to the same orders: *Coflexip SA v Stolt Comex Seaway MS Ltd* [2001] 1 All ER 952, [2001] RPC 182, CA (which also provides guidance as to the form of injunction). See also *Kirin-Amgen Inc v Transkaryotic Therapies Inc (No 2)* [2002] RPC 187, [2001] All ER (D) 111 (May); *Kirin-Amgen Inc v Transkaryotic Therapies Inc (No 3)* [2005] FSR 875.

7   As to licences of right see PARA 391 et seq.

8   See the Patents Act 1977 s 46(3)(c); and PARA 391. See also *EI Du Pont de Nemours & Co v Enka BV (No 2)* [1988] RPC 497. As to settling terms of the licence see the Patents Act 1977 s 46(3)(a); and PARA 391.

9   *Saccharin Corpn Ltd v Quincey* [1900] 2 Ch 246 at 249, 17 RPC 337 at 339. It has been suggested, however, that an injunction may be granted after a patent has expired restraining the sale of infringing articles manufactured during its life (*Crossley v Derby Gas Light Co* (1834) 4 LJ Ch 25; *Price's Patent Candle Co Ltd v Bauwen's Patent Candle Co Ltd* (1858) 4 K & J

727) or to prevent the defendant from obtaining a springboard into the market after expiry of the patent (Case C-316/95 *Generics BV v Smith Kline & French Laboratories Ltd* [1997] RPC 801, 41 BMLR 116, ECJ). See also *Dyson Appliances Ltd v Hoover Ltd (No 2)* [2001] RPC 544 (injunction sought prior to expiry of patent was granted to extend beyond patent's expiry). See also note 10.

10 *Betts v Gallais* (1870) LR 10 Eq 392. See also *Welsbach Incandescent Gas Light Co Ltd v New Incandescent (Sunlight Patent) Gas Lighting Co* (1900) 17 RPC 237 at 254; but cf *Crossley v Beverley* (1829) 1 Russ & M 166n (where a defendant who had a large stock of pirated articles ready to be thrown on the market as soon as the patent expired was restrained); and *F Hoffmann-La Roche & Co AG v Inter-Continental Pharmaceuticals Ltd* [1965] Ch 795, [1965] 2 All ER 15, [1965] RPC 226, CA (where the defendants were entitled to have, but did not have, a compulsory licence, and an injunction was granted). See also *Dyson Appliances Ltd v Hoover Ltd (No 2)* [2001] RPC 544.

11 *Multiform Displays Ltd v Whitmarley Displays Ltd* [1957] RPC 260 at 262, HL.

542.   Stay of injunction.   The operation of an injunction may be stayed pending an appeal[1]. This is a matter entirely within the court's discretion but the court should seek so to arrange matters that, when the appeal comes on to be heard, the appellate court may be able to do justice between the parties, whatever the outcome of the appeal may be[2]. Where the injunction is stayed, the defendant may be required to keep an account[3], or give security for damages[4], or to pay damages into a secured account[5], and to enter the appeal within a specified time[6]. An undertaking as to damages may be required as a condition of refusing a stay[7].

1   *Kaye v Chubb & Sons Ltd* (1886) 4 RPC 23; *Ducketts Ltd v Whitehead* (1895) 12 RPC 187 at 191. See also *Minnesota Mining & Manufacturing Co v Johnson & Johnson Ltd* [1976] RPC 671, CA; *Strix Ltd v Otter Controls Ltd* [1991] FSR 354, CA; and *Novartis AG v Hospira UK Ltd* [2013] EWCA Civ 583, [2014] 1 WLR 1624, [2014] RPC 104 (interim injunction granted even though patent had been found invalid, pending appeal against finding of invalidity). A stay is usually granted if the claimant does not object.

2   *Minnesota Mining & Manufacturing Co v Johnson & Johnson Ltd* [1976] RPC 671 at 676, CA, where the earlier authorities were reviewed. See also *Quantel Ltd v Spaceward Microsystems Ltd (No 2)* [1990] RPC 147, CA; *Minnesota Mining & Manufacturing Co v Rennicks (UK) Ltd* [1992] RPC 331; *Mölnlycke AB v Procter & Gamble Ltd* [1992] FSR 549; *Optical Coating Laboratory Inc v Pilkington PE Ltd* [1993] FSR 310; *Kirin-Amgen Inc v Transkaryotic Therapies Inc (No 3)* [2005] FSR 875; *HTC Corpn v Nokia Corpn* [2013] EWCA Civ 1759, [2014] All ER (D) 233 (Jan) (grant of a stay pending an appeal is an exercise of discretion by the court intended, as far as possible, to minimise the loss and inconvenience to the ultimately successful party).

3   *Kaye v Chubb & Sons* (1886) 4 RPC 23, CA; *Bugges Insecticide Ltd v Herbon Ltd* [1972] RPC 197.

4   *National Opalite Glazed Brick and Tile Syndicate Ltd v Ceralite Syndicate Ltd* (1896) 13 RPC 649.

5   *Quantel Ltd v Spaceward Microsystems Ltd (No 2)* [1990] RPC 147, CA.

6   See *Rosedale Associated Manufacturers Ltd v Carlton Tyre Saving Co Ltd* [1959] RPC 189 at 219.

7   *Minnesota Mining and Manufacturing Co v Johnson and Johnson Ltd* [1976] RPC 671, CA; *Minnesota Mining & Manufacturing Co v Rennicks (UK) Ltd* [1992] RPC 331; *Kirin-Amgen Inc v Transkaryotic Therapies Inc (No 3)* [2005] FSR 875.

543.   Damages or profits.   A successful claimant in proceedings for infringement of a patent may claim damages in respect of the infringement[1] or an account of the profits derived by the defendant from the infringement[2], but the court may not, in respect of the same infringement, both award damages and order an account of profits[3].

An inquiry as to damages or account of profits is usually taken by a master, but, if difficult or complex questions are involved, may be taken by the patents judge in court[4]. The procedure is by way of written contentions supported by witness statements, supplemented by cross-examination of the deponents, if requested[5]. Both parties will normally be required to give disclosure[6]. The costs of the inquiry are always reserved. The inquiry extends to infringements not exemplified in the particulars of infringement, but merely covered by general words there[7]. The onus is on the claimant to establish the number of infringing articles sold[8]. Where judgment is signed on admissions, damages can only be claimed on admitted infringements[9]. The taking of an account or an inquiry as to damages will be stayed pending an appeal only in special circumstances[10].

The award of damages does not license the articles in respect of which they are paid, and the claimant can bring a further claim for damages against purchasers or users[11].

In taking an account of profits, it is the profit from the use of the invention that must be considered, not necessarily that from the entire infringing sale[12]. The taking of an account has the effect of condoning past infringements[13] but not those which may take place in the future[14]. Accordingly the claimant can bring a further claim for damages or an account against purchasers and users[15].

1   Patents Act 1977 s 61(1)(c). See also PARA 520 note 1. Where it is clear that nothing would be recovered on an inquiry as to damages, it may be refused (*United Telephone Co v Sharples* (1885) 29 ChD 164, 2 RPC 28; *Alfred Dunhill Ltd v Griffiths Bros* (1933) 51 RPC 93) but if the claim for damages is bona fide and arguable an inquiry will be ordered (*Kooltrade Ltd v XTS Ltd* [2001] FSR 158 at 167). As to the form of order directing an inquiry see *British Thomson-Houston Co Ltd v G and R Agency* (1925) 42 RPC 305; and as to damages generally see DAMAGES vol 12(1) (Reissue) PARA 801 et seq.

2   Patents Act 1977 s 61(1)(d). As to accounts of profit, which are rarely taken in practice, see EQUITABLE JURISDICTION vol 47 (2014) PARA 105.

3   Patents Act 1977 s 61(2). Before electing for an inquiry or an account, the claimant may be entitled to disclosure relating to the extent of the defendant's sales for the purpose of making the election: *Minnesota Mining & Manufacturing Co v C Jeffries Pty Ltd* [1993] FSR 189, Aust Fed Ct; *Island Records Ltd v Tring International plc* [1995] 3 All ER 444, [1996] 1 WLR 1256, [1995] FSR 560 (copyright); *Brugger v Medicaid* [1996] FSR 362 (copyright). As to electing between remedies see *Redrow Homes Ltd v Bett Bros plc* [1999] 1 AC 197, [1998] 1 All ER 385, [1998] RPC 793, HL (copyright case); *Spring Form Inc v Toy Brokers Ltd* [2002] FSR 276 at 288. See also *Celanese International Corpn v BP Chemicals Ltd* [1999] RPC 203.

4   *Cleveland Graphite Bronze Co Ltd v Glacier Metal Co Ltd* (1951) 68 RPC 181.

5   *General Tire and Rubber Co v Firestone Tyre and Rubber Co Ltd* [1975] RPC 203, CA.

6   *British United Shoe Machinery Co Ltd v Lambert Howarth & Sons Ltd* (1929) 46 RPC 315; *Rosedale Associated Manufacturers Ltd v Airfix Products Ltd* [1959] RPC 249. See also *Saccharin Corpn Ltd v Chemicals and Drugs Co Ltd* [1900] 2 Ch 556, 17 RPC 612, CA (disclosure of the names of the defendants' customers ordered on an account of profits); *British Thomson-Houston Co Ltd v Irradiant Lamp Works Ltd* (1923) 40 RPC 243; *Dyson Appliances Ltd v Hoover Ltd (No 3)* [2002] EWHC 500 (Pat), [2002] RPC 841. See, however, *Smith Kline & French Laboratories Ltd v Doncaster Pharmaceuticals Ltd* [1989] FSR 401 (disclosure of the defendant's customers' names refused where the judge assessed damages as a lump sum).

7   *Cleveland Graphite Bronze Co Ltd v Glacier Metal Co Ltd* (1951) 68 RPC 181; *Fichera v Flogates Ltd* [1984] RPC 257 at 292, CA.

8   *British Thomson-Houston Co Ltd v Goodman (Leeds) Ltd* (1925) 42 RPC 75; cf *Dunlop Pneumatic Tyre Co Ltd v Green* (1900) 17 RPC 234.

9   *United Telephone Co v Donohoe* (1886) 31 ChD 399, 3 RPC 45, CA.

10   See *J Lucas (Batteries) Ltd v Gaedor Ltd* [1978] RPC 389, CA (appeal on another patent which, if successful, would alter the basis of the account). See also *Minnesota Mining & Manufacturing Co v Rennicks (UK) Ltd* [1992] RPC 331 at 372 (stay refused); *Kirin-Amgen Inc v Transkaryotic Therapies Inc (No 3)* [2005] FSR 875 (stay refused); *Mölnlycke AB v Procter & Gamble Ltd* [1992] FSR 549 at 610 (stay refused). In practice some successful claimants do not proceed with the inquiry until after determination of the appeal.

11   *United Telephone Co Ltd v Walker and Oliver* (1886) 56 LT 508, 4 RPC 63; *Brockie Pell Arc Lamp Ltd v Johnson* (1900) 17 RPC 697; *Catnic Components Ltd v C Evans & Co (Builders*

Merchants) Ltd [1983] FSR 401 at 422. But the patentee cannot recover in total more than his loss: *Spring Form Inc v Toy Brokers Ltd* [2002] FSR 276.

12 *United Horse-Shoe and Nail Co Ltd v Stewart* (1888) 13 App Cas 401, 5 RPC 260, HL; *Celanese International Corpn v BP Chemicals Ltd* [1999] RPC 203; *Spring Form Inc v Toy Brokers Ltd* [2002] FSR 276. Cf PARA 544 text and note 6.

13 *Neilson v Betts* (1871) LR 5 HL 1; *De Vitre v Betts* (1872) LR 6 HL 319; *Watson v Holiday* (1882) 20 ChD 480; *Saccharin Corpn Ltd v Chemicals and Drugs Co* [1900] 2 Ch 556 at 558559, 17 RPC 612 at 615, CA.

14 *Codex Corpn v Racal-Milgo Ltd* [1984] FSR 87.

15 *Codex Corpn v Racal-Milgo Ltd* [1984] FSR 87. Where there are more than one claimant only one account will be ordered and an apportionment made: *Spring Form Inc v Toy Brokers Ltd* [2002] FSR 276. The account extends to all infringers sued: *Spring Form Inc v Toy Brokers Ltd*.

544. Measure of damages. Infringement of a patent is a statutory tort and accordingly damages recoverable are assessed in the same way as most other torts, following the elementary rules that the victim should be restored to the position he would have been in if no wrong had been done, and that the victim can recover loss which was foreseeable, caused by the wrong and not excluded from being recovered by public or social policy[1].

Where the claimant is a manufacturer, the ordinary measure of damages is prima facie the loss of the profit the claimant would have suffered had his sales not been diminished by the infringement[2], it being presumed, in the absence of evidence to the contrary, that sales by the infringer were taken from the claimant[3]. Where the claimant normally grants licences, even if he also manufactures, damages are usually assessed on a royalty basis, although the infringer cannot claim to be put on as favoured terms as a licensee[4]. To the extent that the infringements were not sold in competition with the patentee, he is entitled to a fair royalty on them, whether he grants licences or not[5]. Damages should be assessed on the basis of the amount which the defendant in reality has been obliged to pay, not the amount which he should or might have paid[6].

Where the subject of the patent forms an integral part of the article sold, or of the machinery used in making it, the claimant is entitled to the whole damage caused by the sale; but it may be relevant to what extent the damage is due to the use of the invention[7]. A patentee who has been compelled by infringement to reduce his own prices may claim the resulting loss of profit as damages[8]. Loss to a subsidiary company may be recoverable[9]. Loss of reputation due to infringements may be a head of damage[10] and so may the costs of disclosure proceedings against third parties to discover the identities of the defendants as infringers[11]. It is, however, unlikely that exemplary damages are available in a claim for patent infringement[12].

In awarding damages or granting any other relief in infringement proceedings brought by the holder of an exclusive licence[13], the court or the comptroller[14] must take into consideration any loss suffered or likely to be suffered by the exclusive licensee as such as a result of the infringement or, as the case may be, the profits derived from the infringement, so far as it constitutes an infringement of the rights of the exclusive licensee as such[15].

1 See *Gerber Garment Technology Inc v Lectra Systems Ltd* [1997] RPC 443 at 452, CA, per Staughton LJ. As to the assessment of damages for tort see DAMAGES vol 12(1) (Reissue) PARA 851 et seq; TORT vol 97 (2010) PARA 516.

2 The subject is discussed at length in *Meters Ltd v Metropolitan Gas Meters Ltd* (1911) 104 LT 113, 28 RPC 157, CA; *Watson, Laidlaw & Co Ltd v Pott, Cassels and Williamson* (1914) 31 RPC 104 at 152, HL; *British Thomson-Houston Co Ltd v Naamloos Vennootschap Pope's Metaaldraadlampenfabriek* (1923) 40 RPC 119, Ct of Sess; *General Tire and Rubber Co v Firestone Tyre and Rubber Co Ltd* [1975] 2 All ER 173, [1976] RPC 197, HL. Damages were given on the loss of profit basis in *Leeds Forge Co Ltd v Deighton's Patent Flue Co Ltd* (1908)

25 RPC 209, *Catnic Components Ltd v Hill & Smith Ltd* [1983] FSR 512 and *Gerber Garment Technology Inc v Lectra Systems Ltd* [1995] RPC 383 (affd in part [1997] RPC 443, CA). There is no rule of law restricting the scope of recovery to activities which themselves infringe the patent: *Gerber Garment Technology Inc v Lectra Systems Ltd* [1997] RPC 443 at 455, CA, per Staughton LJ.

3   *Leeds Forge Co Ltd v Deighton's Patent Flue Co Ltd* (1907) 25 RPC 209; *British United Shoe Machinery Co Ltd v A Fussell & Sons Ltd* (1910) 27 RPC 205; *Meters Ltd v Metropolitan Gas Meters Ltd* (1911) 104 LT 113, 28 RPC 157, CA. The burden of proof is on the defendant: see *Catnic Components Ltd v Hill & Smith Ltd* [1983] FSR 512.

4   *Boyd v Tootal, Broadhurst, Lee Co Ltd* (1894) 11 RPC 175; *Pneumatic Tyre Co Ltd v Puncture Proof Pneumatic Tyre Co Ltd* (1899) 16 RPC 209. See also *English and American Machinery Co Ltd v Union Boot and Shoe Machine Co* (1896) 13 RPC 64; *Automatic Coal Gas Retort Co Ltd v Salford Corpn* (1897) 14 RPC 450; *General Tire and Rubber Co v Firestone Tyre and Rubber Co* [1975] 2 All ER 173, [1976] RPC 197, HL. There seems no reason in principle why a claimant who can prove loss of sales should not claim damages for them, even though the defendant could have made those sales lawfully by taking a licence: cf the text and note 5; and the Patents Act 1977 s 46(3)(c) (see PARA 547).

5   *Watson, Laidlaw & Co Ltd v Pott, Cassels and Williamson* (1914) 31 RPC 104, HL; *Catnic Components Ltd v Hill & Smith Ltd* [1983] FSR 512.

6   *General Tire and Rubber Co v Firestone Tyre and Rubber Co Ltd* [1975] 2 All ER 173, [1976] RPC 197, HL.

7   *Meters Ltd v Metropolitan Gas Meters Ltd* (1911) 104 LT 113, 28 RPC 157, CA; *United Horse-Shoe and Nail Co Ltd v Stewart* (1888) 13 App Cas 401, 5 RPC 260, HL; *Coflexip SA v Stolt Comex Seaway MS Ltd* [2003] EWCA Civ 296, [2003] FSR 728 (where this issue is fully considered).

8   *United Horse-Shoe and Nail Co Ltd v Stewart* (1888) 13 App Cas 401, 5 RPC 260, HL (damages not given for a reduction in price due to lack of confidence in the patent); *American Braided Wire Co v Thomson* (1890) 44 ChD 274, 7 RPC 152, CA; *Meters Ltd v Metropolitan Gas Meters Ltd* (1911) 104 LT 113, 28 RPC 157, CA.

9   *Gerber Garment Technology Inc v Lectra Systems Ltd* [1997] RPC 443, CA.

10 *Pneumatic Tyre Co Ltd v Puncture Proof Pneumatic Tyre Co Ltd* (1899) 16 RPC 209.

11 *Morton-Norwich Products Inc v Intercen Ltd (No 2), Morton-Norwich Products Inc v United Chemicals (London) Ltd* [1981] FSR 337.

12 See *Morton-Norwich Products Inc v Intercen Ltd (No 2), Morton-Norwich Products Inc v United Chemicals (London) Ltd* [1981] FSR 337; *Catnic Components Ltd v Hill & Smith Ltd* [1983] FSR 512.

13 Ie proceedings brought under the Patents Act 1977 s 67(1): see PARA 520.

14 As to the comptroller see PARA 575.

15 Patents Act 1977 s 67(2). This right is concurrent with the patentee's right to relief: *Optical Coating Laboratory Inc v Pilkington PE Ltd* [1993] FSR 310. See also *Spring Form Inc v Toy Brokers Ltd* [2002] FSR 276.

545.   Period over which damages taken.   No damages may be awarded for acts of infringement before publication of the application for a patent[1] or more than six years before the proceedings were brought[2]. Damages run from the time when the claimants, or one of them, became the equitable owner of the patent, although the legal title must have been complete before action[3] and, in any event, a patent may be assigned or licensed together with the right to claim damages for previous infringements[4]. Damages are assessed on all acts of infringement down to the time of the assessment[5]. Possibly damages may be claimed in respect of sales after the expiration of the patent which were made in infringement during its life[6]. The court has a discretion to award interest on damages for all or part of the period between each act of infringement and the date of assessment[7]. The rate of interest is based on the cost of borrowing the money represented by the sum awarded as damages[8]. Compound interest is not, however, payable as a head of damages[9].

1   See the Patents Act 1977 s 69(1), (2); and PARA 546. As to publication of the application see PARA 326.

2   See the Limitation Act 1980 s 2; and LIMITATION PERIODS vol 68 (2008) PARA 979.

3   *United Horse-Shoe and Nail Co Ltd v Stewart* (1888) 13 App Cas 401 at 417, 5 RPC 260 at
     269, HL, per Lord Macnaghten, where he expressed the view that the claimants succeeded to
     the rights of their predecessors in title, and could claim damages for all infringements. See to the
     contrary *Wilderman v FW Berk & Co Ltd* [1925] Ch 116, 42 RPC 79, where the earlier
     decision was not cited. In *Ellwood v Christy* (1864) 34 LJCP 130, it was held that an account
     ran only from the completion of the legal title.
4   See the Patents Act 1977 s 30(7); and PARA 373.
5   Revocation of the patent after judgment does not affect the order for damages: *Poulton v
     Adjustable Cover and Boiler Block Co* [1908] 2 Ch 430, 25 RPC 661, CA.
6   See PARA 541.
7   See the Law Reform (Miscellaneous Provisions) Act 1934 s 3(1); and FINANCIAL SERVICES AND
     INSTITUTIONS vol 50 (2008) PARA 1915. Where there was infringement between the publication
     and the grant but commercial practice was to pay royalties only after the grant, the court
     awarded interest from the date of the grant only: *General Tire and Rubber Co v Firestone Tyre
     and Rubber Co Ltd* [1975] 2 All ER 173, [1976] RPC 197, HL. See also *Gerber Garment
     Technology Inc v Lectra Systems Ltd* [1997] RPC 443 at 487, CA.
8   *Tate & Lyle Food and Distribution Ltd v Greater London Council* [1981] 3 All ER 716; *Catnic
     Components Ltd v Hill & Smith Ltd* [1983] FSR 512 (where the appropriate rate was found to
     be the clearing bank base rate plus 2%).
9   *Catnic Components Ltd v Hill & Smith Ltd* [1983] FSR 512.

**546.   Damages for infringement of rights conferred by publication of
application for patent.**   An applicant for a patent has, as from the publication of
the application[1] for the patent until grant[2], the same right as he would have had,
if the patent had been granted on the date of publication, to bring proceedings
for damages for infringement[3]. The applicant is, however, entitled to bring
proceedings in respect of any act only:

(1)   after the patent has been granted[4]; and
(2)   if the act would, if the patent had been granted on the date of
       publication, have infringed not only the patent but also the claims as
       interpreted by the description and any drawings referred to in the
       description or claims in the form in which they were contained in the
       application immediately before the preparations for its publication were
       completed by the UK Intellectual Property Office[5].

1   Ie under the Patents Act 1977 s 16: see PARA 326.
2   As to grant see PARA 337.
3   Patents Act 1977 s 69(1). If the proceedings are before the comptroller, leave is required in
     certain cases: see PARA 519. As to the comptroller see PARA 575. Subject to s 69(2) and s 69(3)
     (see PARA 547), references in ss 60–62, 66–68 to a patent and its proprietor are to be respectively
     construed as including references to the application and the applicant; and references to a patent
     being in force, being granted, being valid or existing are to be construed accordingly: s 69(1).
4   Patents Act 1977 s 69(2)(a).
5   Patents Act 1977 s 69(2)(b). As to the UK Intellectual Property Office see PARA 577.

547.   Restrictions on the recovery of damages.   The right to recover damages
in proceedings for infringement of a patent is subject to the following statutory
restrictions:

(1)   in proceedings for the infringement of a patent, damages may not be
       awarded, and no order may be made for an account of profits, against a
       defendant who proves that at the date of the infringement he was not
       aware, and had no reasonable grounds for supposing, that the patent
       existed[1];
(2)   where an amendment of the specification of a patent[2] has been allowed,
       the court or the comptroller[3], when awarding damages or making an
       order for an account of profits in proceedings for an infringement of the
       patent committed before the decision to allow the amendment, must

take into account the following: (a) whether at the date of infringement the defendant knew, or had reasonable grounds to know, that he was infringing the patent; (b) whether the specification of the patent as published was framed in good faith and with reasonable skill and knowledge; (c) whether the proceedings are brought in good faith[4];

(3)   where one or more claims of the patent sued on are found to be invalid special provisions apply[5];

(4)   where an entry has been made in the register that licences under the patent are to be available as of right[6] and the claim is for infringement otherwise than by the importation of goods from a country which is not a member state of the European Union[7], and the defendant undertakes to take a licence, any amount recoverable by way of damages may not exceed double the amount which would have been payable by him as licensee if such a licence had been granted before the earliest infringement[8];

(5)   in respect of an infringement committed after a failure to pay a renewal fee and any additional fee within the prescribed period, and before any extension of that period[9], the court or the comptroller (in proceedings before him) may, if it or he thinks fit, refuse to award damages or order an account of profits[10].

1   Patents Act 1977 s 62(1). See also PARA 520 note 1. A person is not to be taken to have been aware, or to have had reasonable grounds for supposing, that the patent existed by reason only of the application to a product of the word 'patent' or 'patented', or any word or words expressing or implying that a patent has been obtained, unless the number of the patent or a relevant internal link accompanies the word or words: s 62(1) (s 62(1) amended, s 62(1A) added, by the Intellectual Property Act 2014 s 15). The reference to a 'relevant internal link' is a reference to an address of a posting on the internet which is accessible to the public free of charge and which clearly associates the product with the number of the patent: Patents Act 1977 s 62(1A) (as so added). The test is objective: *Lancer Boss Ltd v Henley Forklift Co Ltd and H and M Sideloaders Ltd* [1975] RPC 307 at 317. The current tendency is to hold that a prudent businessman should investigate the possibility of third party rights: see *Benmax v Austin Motor Co Ltd* (1953) 70 RPC 143 at 156 (on appeal, where this point did not arise, 70 RPC 284, CA); and [1955] AC 370, [1955] 1 All ER 326, 72 RPC 39, HL; *John Khalil Khawam & Co v K Chellaram & Sons (Nigeria) Ltd* [1964] 1 All ER 945, [1964] 1 WLR 711, [1964] RPC 337 at 344, PC. See also *Infabrics Ltd v Jaytex Ltd* [1980] Ch 282, [1980] 2 All ER 669, CA (copyright).

2   As to amendment of specifications see PARA 345 et seq.

3   As to the comptroller see PARA 575.

4   Patents Act 1977 s 62(3) (amended by SI 2006/1028). The Patents Act 1977 s 62(3) and s 62(2) do not apply to an infringement of the rights conferred by s 69 (see PARA 546), but, in considering the amount of damages for any such infringement, the court or the comptroller must consider whether or not it would have been reasonable to expect, from a consideration of the specification as published under s 16 (see PARA 326), that a patent would be granted conferring on the proprietor protection from an act of the same description as that found to infringe those rights, and, if the court or he finds that it would not have been reasonable, the court or he must reduce the damages to such an amount as the court or he thinks just: s 69(3).

     As to reasonable skill and knowledge see *General Tire and Rubber Co v Firestone Tyre and Rubber Co Ltd* [1975] 2 All ER 173, [1975] RPC 203, CA (failure to correct an obvious clerical error held not to show lack of reasonable skill); revsd on another ground [1976] RPC 197, HL; *Illinois Tool Works Inc v Autobars Co (Services) Ltd* [1974] RPC 337 at 373374 (specification involving more than one invention held to have been framed in good faith with reasonable skill and knowledge); *Hallen Co v Brabantia (UK) Ltd* [1990] FSR 134; *Rediffusion Simulation Ltd v Link-Miles Ltd* [1993] FSR 369 (where failure to delete a subsidiary claim and the corresponding description was held to show lack of reasonable skill); *Chiron Corpn v Organon Teknika Ltd (No 7)* [1994] FSR 458; *Kirin-Amgen Inc's Patent* [2002] EWHC 471 (Pat), [2002] RPC 43. The patentee should only be deprived of damages if the original passages in the specification were misleading: *Unilin Beheer BV v Berry Floor NV (No 2)* [2006] FSR 495 at 503, CA.

5　See the Patents Act 1977 s 63; and PARA 550. See also PARA 520 note 1.
6　As to licences of right see the Patents Act 1977 s 46; and PARA 391.
7　Probably this means that damages for infringement by importation of goods are not restricted. Any normal claim relating to imported goods would, however, involve acts of infringement apart from the importation itself.
8　Patents Act 1977 s 46(3)(c) (amended by the Copyright, Designs and Patents Act 1988 Sch 5 para 12(1), (2)).
9　As to renewal fees and extensions of the prescribed period see the Patents Act 1977 s 25(4); and PARA 339.
10　Patents Act 1977 s 62(2) (amended by the Patents Act 2004 Sch 2 paras 1(1), 15). See also s 69(3); and note 4.

548. Order for delivery up. An order may be made in infringement proceedings for the defendant to deliver up[1] or destroy any patented product[2] in relation to which the patent is infringed or any article in which that product is inextricably comprised[3]. Since, however, the object of such an order is to prevent further infringement, and not to punish the defendant, where possible the order will be restricted to removal and delivery up of infringing parts[4]. Delivery up may be refused of a machine that does not infringe until put into operation[5]. A stay of the operation of such an order will generally be granted pending an appeal where there is no risk of the articles being removed or sold[6].

1　This remedy is supplemental to the other reliefs, and the value of the articles delivered will not be deducted from the damages: *United Telephone Co Ltd v Walker and Oliver* (1886) 56 LT 508, 4 RPC 63. The defendant must pay the costs of complying with the order: *Practice Direction — Intellectual Property Claims* PD 63 para 26.1.
2　As to the meaning of 'patented product' see PARA 371 note 11.
3　Patents Act 1977 s 61(1)(b). See also PARA 520 note 1.
4　*Mergenthaler Linotype Co v Intertype Ltd* (1926) 43 RPC 381; *British United Shoe Machinery Co Ltd v Gimson Shoe Machinery Co Ltd* (1927) 45 RPC 85 (affd (1928) 45 RPC 290, CA). In *Morgan & Co Ltd v Windover & Co* (1890) 7 RPC 446, where the patent was for a combination of old parts, the defendant was allowed to keep the parts on removing them from the combination. Where, however, the full order for delivery up has been made, it will not, on an application to vary the minutes, be reduced to one for removal of infringing parts (*British Westinghouse Electric and Manufacturing Co Ltd v Electrical Co Ltd* (1911) 55 Sol Jo 689, 28 RPC 517 at 530), but a claimant who has omitted to ask for this order at the trial may obtain it by variation of the minutes (*Edison and Swan United Electric Light Co Ltd v Holland* (1888) 4 TLR 686, 5 RPC 459). See also *Walker v Wilson Dawes (Sales and Contracts) Ltd* [1964] RPC 246.
5　*Electric and Musical Industries Ltd v Lissen Ltd* (1936) 54 RPC 5 at 35.
6　*Lancashire Explosives Co Ltd v Roburite Explosives Co Ltd* (1895) 12 TLR 35, 12 RPC 470, CA (on appeal (1897) 14 RPC 303, HL); *S Parkes & Co Ltd v Cocker Bros Ltd* (1929) 46 RPC 241, CA. Sometimes the defendant's solicitor is required to give an undertaking: *Washburn and Moen Manufacturing Co v Patterson* (1883) 1 RPC 191; *Turner v Bowman* (1924) 42 RPC 29. In *British Thomson-Houston Co Ltd v Corona Lamp Works Ltd (No 2)* (1922) 39 RPC 212, a stay was refused on the claimant's undertaking to preserve the articles pending an appeal; and in *Mölnlycke AB v Procter & Gamble Ltd* [1992] FSR 549 delivery up to the claimant's solicitors pending appeal was ordered.

549. Certificate of contested validity. If in any proceedings before the court[1] or the comptroller[2] the validity of a patent[3] to any extent is contested, and that patent is found by the court or the comptroller to be wholly or partially valid[4], the court or the comptroller may certify the finding and the fact that the validity of the patent was so contested[5]. Where a certificate is so granted, then, if in any subsequent proceedings[6] before the court or the comptroller for infringement of or for revocation of the patent[7] a final order or judgment is made or given in favour of the party relying on the validity of the patent as found in the earlier proceedings, that party is entitled, unless the court or the comptroller otherwise directs, to his costs or expenses as between solicitor and own client[8], other than the costs or expenses of any appeal in the subsequent proceedings[9]. The grant of a certificate is discretionary[10]. It should not be granted unless the question of validity has been thoroughly canvassed[11], but it is not necessary that the court should have decided the issue of validity[12]. Nor is it necessary that the claimant should have succeeded on the issue of infringement[13].

A second certificate may be granted, and this is usually done where fresh objections are raised at a subsequent trial[14]. The certificate may be granted by any court[15]. It is doubtful whether the amendment of a patent after the grant of a certificate of validity affects a certificate[16]. A certificate may be granted for an expired patent[17].

1   As to the meaning of 'court' see PARA 619 note 1.
2   As to the comptroller see PARA 575.
3   As to validity see PARA 425 et seq.
4   As to where the subsequent dispute involves both a certified claim and an uncertified claim see *SmithKline Beecham plc v Apotex Europe Ltd (No 2)* [2005] FSR 559 at 566.
5   Patents Act 1977 s 65(1).
6   'Subsequent proceedings' means proceedings begun after the certificate has been granted: *Automatic Weighing Machine Co v Combined Weighing Machine Co* (1889) 6 RPC 120 at 126; *Automatic Weighing Machine Co v International Hygienic Society* (1889) 6 RPC 475; *Saccharin Corpn Ltd v Anglo-Continental Chemical Works* [1901] 1 Ch 414, 17 RPC 307; *SmithKline Beecham plc v Apotex Europe Ltd (No 2)* [2004] EWCA Civ 1703, [2005] FSR 559. It includes the continuation of proceedings in an existing action after a certificate of validity has been given in other proceedings: *Mölnlycke AB v Proctor & Gamble Ltd (No 5)* [1994] RPC 49 at 141, CA.
7   This does not apply in a threats claim, unless relief for infringement or revocation is asked for. As to proceedings for revocation see PARA 562 et seq.
8   'Solicitor and own client' costs no longer exist as a basic for taxation and the provision is taken to mean indemnity costs: *SmithKline Beecham plc v Apotex Europe Ltd (No 2)* [2005] FSR 559 at 564. As to costs see CPR Pts 4348; and CIVIL PROCEDURE.
9   Patents Act 1977 s 65(2).
10 *VD Ltd v Boston Deep Sea Fishing and Ice Co Ltd* (1934) 52 RPC 1 at 33, CA.
11 *Gillette Industries Ltd v Bernstein* [1942] Ch 45 at 49, [1941] 3 All ER 248 at 251, 58 RPC 271 at 285, CA; *Martin v CB Projection (Engineering) Ltd* (1948) 65 RPC 361.
12 *Re Volpertas' Patent* (1948) 65 RPC 355.
13 *Automatic Weighing Machine Co v Knight* (1889) 5 TLR 359, 6 RPC 297 at 307, CA; *Shoe Machinery Co Ltd v Cutlan* [1896] 1 Ch 667, 13 RPC 141; *Birch v Harrap & Co* (1896) 13 RPC 615, CA; *Pneumatic Rubber Stamp Co Ltd v Lindner* (1898) 15 RPC 525; *Morrison v Asplen* (1904) 21 RPC 557; *Hoffmann Manufacturing Co Ltd v Auto Machinery Co Ltd* (1911) 28 RPC 141 at 153, CA; *Vaisey, Bristol and Saxone Shoe Co Ltd v Toddlers Footwear (1954) Ltd* [1957] RPC 90 at 104. Where the Court of Appeal allows an appeal on the ground of non-infringement, it may allow the certificate to stand (*Hardmuth v Baker & Son* (1904) 22 RPC 66, CA), but this is not always done (see e g *Gillette Safety Razor Co v Anglo-American Trading Co Ltd* (1912) 29 RPC 341; *Submarine Signal Co v Henry Hughes & Son Ltd* (1931) 49 RPC 149).
14 *British Thomson-Houston Co Ltd v Corona Lamp Works Ltd* (1921) 39 RPC 49, HL. See also *Mölnlycke AB v Procter & Gamble Ltd* [1992] FSR 549.
15 In *British Thomson-Houston Co Ltd v Corona Lamp Works Ltd* (1921) 39 RPC 49, HL, the House of Lords remitted the case to the Chancery Division with directions to certify. In *Submarine Signal Co v Henry Hughes & Son Ltd* (1931) 49 RPC 149, the Court of Appeal discharged a certificate given by a lower court, although not finding the claim in question invalid.
16 In *Badische Anilin und Soda Fabrik v G Thompson & Co Ltd* (1904) 21 RPC 473 at 480 it was held that the certificate remained effective; but in *JB Brooks & Co Ltd v Rendall, Underwood & Co Ltd* (1906) 24 RPC 27 it was held that it did not.
17 *Kane and Pattison v J Boyle & Co* (1901) 18 RPC 325; *Leggatt v Hood's Original Darts Accessories Ltd and Hood* (1950) 68 RPC 3 at 22, CA.

550.   Partially valid patents.   If in proceedings for infringement in which validity is in issue it is found that the patent is only partially valid, the court[1] or the comptroller[2] may grant relief in respect of part of the patent found to be valid and infringed[3]. Where it is so found, the court or the comptroller, when awarding damages, costs or expenses or making an order for an account of profits, must take into account the following: (1) whether at the date of the infringement the defendant or defender knew, or had reasonable grounds to know, that he was infringing the patent; (2) whether the specification of the patent was framed in good faith and with reasonable skill and knowledge[4]; (3) whether the proceedings are brought in good faith; and any relief granted is subject to the discretion of the court or the comptroller as to costs or expenses and as to the date from which damages or an account should be reckoned[5]. The court or the comptroller may further direct, as a condition of any relief, that the specification of the patent be amended[6] to its or his satisfaction[7]. The court or the comptroller may also grant relief in the case of a European patent (UK)[8] on condition that the claims of the patent are limited to its or his satisfaction by the European Patent Office at the request of the proprietor[9].

Where at trial a patent had been valid and infringed but the patentee later sought to amend the claims, it was given the costs up to the date of judgment but no order for an injunction or delivery up[10]. To obtain such relief a patentee must start fresh proceedings[11].

1   As to the meaning of 'court' see PARA 619 note 1.
2   As to the comptroller see PARA 575.
3   Patents Act 1977 s 63(1). See also PARA 520 note 1.
4   As to good faith and reasonable skill and knowledge see *Page v Brent Toy Products Ltd* (1949) 67 RPC 4 at 20; *Ronson Products Ltd v A Lewis & Co (Westminster) Ltd* [1963] RPC 103; *General Tire and Rubber Co v Firestone Tyre and Rubber Co Ltd* [1973] FSR 79 at 120; *Hallen Co v Brabantia (UK) Ltd* [1990] FSR 134; *Rediffusion Simulation Ltd v Link-Miles Ltd* [1993] FSR 369; *Kirin-Amgen Inc's Patent* [2002] EWHC 471 (Pat), [2002] RPC 43; *Chiron Corpn v Organon Teknika Ltd (No 7)* [1994] FSR 458; *Kirin-Amgen Inc's Patent* [2002] EWHC 471 (Pat), [2002] RPC 43; *Unilin Beheer BV v Berry Floor NV (No 2)* [2005] EWCA Civ 1292, [2006] FSR 495.
5   Patents Act 1977 s 63(2) (amended by SI 2006/1028). The provision applies only where a finding has been made by the court or comptroller: *SmithKline Beecham plc v Apotex Europe Ltd (No 2)* [2004] EWCA Civ 1703, [2005] FSR 559. In recent practice relief is rarely, if ever, refused, and there is no instance of a special date for the reckoning of damages. As to the court's discretion and the relevance of the conduct of the proprietor of the patent see *VD Ltd v Boston Deep Sea Fishing and Ice Co Ltd* (1935) 52 RPC 303 at 331. See also *Auster Ltd v Perfecta Motor Equipments Ltd* (1924) 41 RPC 482; *Douglas Packing Co Inc, Douglas Pectin Corpn and Postum Co Inc v Evans & Co (Hereford and Devon) Ltd* (1929) 46 RPC 493, CA; *Hallen Co v Brabantia (UK) Ltd* [1990] FSR 134. As to damages see *Leggatt v Hood's Original Darts Accessories Ltd and Hood* (1950) 68 RPC 3 at 17, CA. See also *Gerber Garment Technology Inc v Lectra Systems Ltd* [1995] FSR 492, CA (presence of invalid claims in patent had no effect on defendant's conduct and therefore unjust to deprive claimant of any part of his damages).
6   Ie on an application for the purpose under the Patents Act 1977 s 75 (see PARAS 347–348), which may be made whether or not all other issues in the proceedings have been determined.
7   Patents Act 1977 s 63(3).
8   As to the meaning of 'European patent (UK)' see PARA 652 note 1.
9   Patents Act 1977 s 63(4) (added by the Patents Act 2004 s 3(1)). As to the European Patent Office see PARA 644.
10 *PLG Research Ltd v Ardon International Ltd (No 2)* [1993] FSR 698.
11 *Dudgeon v Thomson and Donaldson* (1877) 3 App Cas 34, HL; *Kenrick v Jefferson Ltd's Patent* (1911) 29 RPC 25; *PLG Research Ltd v Ardon International Ltd (No 2)* [1993] FSR 698.

551. Costs. Costs are allowed or disallowed in patent infringement actions on the same basis as in any other litigation[1] and normally costs follow the event[2]. Where, however, it is appropriate, the practice is to deal with costs on an issue basis so as to reflect the time and expense of the issues on which the parties succeeded[3]. However, that approach should not be applied automatically and it is always necessary to step back to see what is the overall effect of that approach[4]. The correct approach is to ask who is the overall winner in the litigation, whether he has lost on a suitably circumscribed issue and so should be deprived of his costs of that issue and whether it is an exceptional case such as to lead to an adverse costs order on an issue in favour of the overall loser[5]. Save in exceptional circumstances, the overall winner will be entitled to the general costs of the action, that is those costs which cannot be allocated to any particular issue[6]. In relation to costs which can be allocated to a particular issue but which the overall winner has lost he should be deprived of those costs only if it was unreasonable to have raised that issue[7]. The overall winner should only be ordered to pay the other party's costs of that issue if it is established that there is something more than conduct which justifies his being deprived of the costs of the issue in all the circumstances[8].

The estimation of costs in patent actions is not a precise science and most often the best that can be achieved is a result lacking mathematical precision[9]. Apportionment between issues may in practice be difficult and there may be a great deal of overlap, for example, where issues relating to obviousness, insufficiency and common general knowledge have been considered[10]. In some cases, the court has made an award giving the successful party or, sometimes each party, a percentage of their costs[11] rather than costs on an issue-by-issue basis and ordering a detailed assessment[12]. Where the costs are to be subject to a detailed assessment, it is common practice to make an interim order for costs[13].

Where one party has conducted the proceedings in an unreasonable manner it may be ordered to pay indemnity costs[14].

Where by virtue of any of certain transactions, instruments or events[15] a person becomes a proprietor of the patent or an exclusive licensee[16] and the patent is subsequently infringed before the transaction, instrument or event is registered, in proceedings for such an infringement, the court or comptroller must not award him costs or expenses unless it is registered within six months of its date or the court or the comptroller is satisfied that it was not practicable to register it before the end of that period and that it was registered as soon as practicable thereafter[17].

The court will not stay detailed assessment of costs pending an appeal unless the parties agree[18], subject, however, to the successful party's undertaking to repay if the appeal is successful[19].

1   As to the factors relevant to the court's discretion see CPR 44.3; *Westwood v Knight* [2011] EWPCC 11, [2011] FSR 847; and CIVIL PROCEDURE. See also *Monsanto Technology LLC v Cargill International SA* [2008] FSR 417 at 419. As to scale costs for claims in the Intellectual Property Enterprise Court see CPR 45.30–45.32; *Gimex International Group Import Export v Chill Bag Co Ltd* [2012] EWPCC 34, [2012] 6 Costs LR 1069, [2012] All ER (D) 117 (Sep).

2   See CPR 44.2(2)(a); and CIVIL PROCEDURE vol 12 (2009) PARA 1738. See e g *Tamglass Ltd OY v Luoyang Glass Technology Co Ltd* [2006] EWHC 445 (Ch), [2006] FSR 622, [2006] All ER (D) 201 (Feb).

3   *Stena Rederi AB v Irish ferries Ltd (No 2)* [2003] EWCA Civ 214, [2003] RPC 681 (order that claimant pay 20% of defendant's costs (defendant winning action on point of statutory construction) and that defendant pay 80% of claimant's costs (claimant winning on issues of validity and factual infringement) upheld). See also *Monsanto Technology LLC v Cargill International SA (No 2)* [2008] FSR 417 at 421; *Generics (UK) Ltd v H Lundbeck A/S* [2007] EWHC 1625 (Pat).

4   *Actavis Ltd v Merck & Co Inc* [2007] EWHC 1625 (Pat).

5   *Monsanto Technology LLC v Cargill International SA (No 2)* [2008] FSR 417 at 421. See also *Generics (UK) Ltd v H Lundbeck A/S* [2007] EWHC 1606 (Pat).

6 *Monsanto Technology LLC v Cargill International SA (No 2)* [2008] FSR 417 at 421.
7 *Monsanto Technology LLC v Cargill International SA (No 2)* [2008] FSR 417 at 421.
8 *Monsanto Technology LLC v Cargill International SA (No 2)* [2008] FSR 417 at 421.
9 *SmithKline Beecham plc v Apotex Europe Ltd (No 2)* [2004] EWCA Civ 1703, [2005] FSR 559.
10 See, for example, *Generics (UK) Ltd v H Lundbeck A/S* [2007] EWHC 1606 (Pat).
11 See, for example, *Stena Rederi AB v Irish ferries Ltd (No 2)* [2003] EWCA Civ 214, [2003] RPC 681; *Generics (UK) Ltd v H Lundbeck A/S* [2007] EWHC 1606 (Pat); *Monsanto Technology LLC v Cargill International SA (No 2)* [2008] FSR 417.
12 As to the approach of the court in relation to summary rather than detailed assessment see *Monsanto Technology LLC v Cargill International SA (No 2)* [2008] FSR 417 at 420; *Actavis UK Ltd v Novartis AG* [2009] EWHC 502 (Ch), [2009] All ER (D) 205 (Mar).
13 See, for example, *Marks (UK) Ltd v Teknowledge Ltd* [2000] FSR 138; *Rambus Inc v Hynix Semiconductor UK Ltd* [2004] EWHC 2313 (Pat), [2005] FSR 417.
14 *Marshalltown Trowel Co v Ceka Works Ltd* [2001] FSR 633 (claimant ordered to pay indemnity costs in respect of certain issues as it had unreasonably delayed in instructing an expert to advise on infringement and had unreasonably refused to admit proof of publication of certain documents). See also *Connaught Laboratories Inc's Patent* [1999] FSR 284 (indemnity costs against patentee who belatedly surrendered patent during revocation proceedings).
15 Ie any transaction, instrument or event to which the Patents Act 1977 s 33 applies: see PARAS 586–587. These include certain assignments, mortgages, grants, vestings and transfers.
16 As to the meaning of 'exclusive licence' see PARA 379.
17 Patents Act 1977 s 68 (amended by SI 2006/1028). See *Minnesota Mining & Manufacturing Co v Rennicks (UK) Ltd* [1992] RPC 331 at 366; *Insituform Technical Services Ltd v Inliner UK plc* [1992] RPC 83 at 105; *Bondax Carpets Ltd v Advance Carpet Tiles* [1993] FSR 162; *Mölnlycke AB v Procter & Gamble Ltd (No 5)* [1994] RPC 49 at 136, CA; *Schutz v Werit* [2013] UKSC 16, [2013] 2 All ER 177, [2013] IP & T 321. Where an exclusive licence replaces an earlier one, the later one must also be registered: *Spring Form Inc v Toy Brokers Ltd* [2002] FSR 276. See also *LG Electronics Inc v NCR Financial Solutions Group Ltd* [2003] FSR 428.
18 See e g *Quantel Ltd v Spaceward Microsystems Ltd (No 2)* [1990] RPC 147, CA (detailed assessment stayed on the defendant paying a very substantial sum into a joint account).
19 *British Thomson-Houston Co Ltd v Marconi's Wireless Telegraph Co Ltd, Electrics and Musical Instruments Ltd v Guildford Radio Stores and EK Cole Ltd* (1938) 55 RPC 71 at 94; *Heginbotham Bros Ltd v Burne* (1939) 56 RPC 87 at 96.

552. Estoppel and abuse of process. Where the issue of validity has been determined in the claimant's favour and a subsequent claim is brought against the same defendant, the defendant may be estopped, as a defence to the proceedings, from challenging validity even on new materials[1]. If the issue of validity has been determined in favour of the patentee but the patent is subsequently revoked at the instance of a third party, the defendant is estopped from challenging any order as to damages which has already been made[2]. Similarly, if the issue of validity has been decided against the claimant, he cannot bring a fresh claim against the defendant until the patent has been amended[3]. However, no decision of the comptroller (or on appeal from him)[4] estops any party to civil proceedings in which infringement of a patent is in issue from alleging[5] invalidity of that patent, whether or not any of the issues were decided in that decision[6].

A decision as to infringement only creates an estoppel[7] where the articles in question in the two claims are practically identical[8]; and the fact that the patent was broadly interpreted in the first proceedings does not prevent the defendant from contending in the second proceedings for a different construction[9]. However, it may be an abuse of process to bring a second action in respect of a different article which could have been the subject of the first action[10].

An assignor may not dispute validity against his assignee[11].

1 *Moore v Thomson* (1890) 7 RPC 325, HL; *Shoe Machinery Co Ltd v Cutlan* [1896] 1 Ch 667, 13 RPC 141; *Dunlop Pneumatic Tyre Co Ltd v Rimington Bros & Co Ltd* (1900) 17 RPC 665, CA; *Brown v Hastie & Co Ltd* (1906) 23 RPC 361, HL.

2 See PARA 568.
3 *Re Deeley's Patent* (1894) 11 RPC 72; *Horrocks v Stubbs* (1895) 12 RPC 540.
4 As to the comptroller see PARA 575; and as to appeals from him see PARA 571.
5 Ie on any of the grounds referred to in the Patents Act 1977 s 72(1): see PARA 562.
6 Patents Act 1977 s 72(5).
7 As to estoppel generally see ESTOPPEL.
8 *Thomson v Hughes* (1890) 7 RPC 71; *Moore v Thomson* (1890) 7 RPC 325, HL.
9 *Brown v Hastie & Co Ltd* (1906) 23 RPC 361, HL. See also *Dudgeon v Thomson* (1877) 3 App Cas 34, HL.
10 *Building Product Design Ltd v Sandtoft Roof Tiles Ltd (No 2)* [2004] FSR 834.
11 *Oldham v Langmead* (1789) Dav Pat Cas 157; *Walton v Lavater* (1860) 29 LJCP 275 at 279; *Chambers v Crichley* (1864) 33 Beav 374; *Franklin Hocking & Co Ltd v Hocking* (1887) 4 RPC 255 (affd 4 RPC 434, CA; revsd (1888) 6 RPC 69, HL); *Gonville v Hay* (1903) 21 RPC 49. Such estoppel does not apply to a partner of the assignor, at any rate, if not such at the time of assignment (*Axmann v Lund* (1874) 43 LJ Ch 655; *Heugh v Chamberlain* (1877) 25 WR 742; *Cropper v Smith* (1884) 26 ChD 700, 1 RPC 81 at 89, CA (on appeal (1885) 10 App Cas 249, HL)), nor where the assignment has been from the patentee's trustee in bankruptcy (*Cropper v Smith*).

553.   Infringement proceedings before the comptroller. The proprietor of a patent[1] and any other person may by agreement with each other refer to the comptroller[2] the question whether that other person has infringed the patent[3], although the only relief which may be claimed on the reference is damages[4] and a declaration[5] that the patent is valid and has been infringed by that person[6]. If the comptroller awards any sum by way of damages on a reference then the sum is recoverable under statute[7], if a county court so orders, or otherwise as if it were payable under an order of that court[8].

If it appears to the comptroller on a reference[9] that the question referred to him would more properly be determined by the court[10], he may decline to deal with it and the court has jurisdiction to determine the question as if the reference were proceedings brought in the court[11].

A decision of the comptroller in respect of a patent, or on appeal from the comptroller, does not estop any party to civil proceedings in which infringement of a patent is in issue from alleging invalidity on any ground on which a patent may be revoked[12], whether or not any of the issues involved were decided in the decision[13].

1 See PARA 306 et seq.
2 As to the comptroller see PARA 575. Leave is required in certain cases: see PARA 520. As to proceedings before the comptroller see the Patents Rules 2007, SI 2007/3291, Pt 7 (rr 73–91); and PARAS 598–606.
3 Patents Act 1977 s 61(3). Except so far as the context requires, in the Patents Act 1977 ss 62–132: (1) any reference to proceedings for infringement and the bringing of such proceedings includes a reference to a reference under s 61(3) and the making of such a reference; (2) any reference to a claimant or pursuer includes a reference to the proprietor of the patent; and (3) any reference to a defendant or defender includes a reference to any other party to the reference: s 61(4) (amended by the Patents Act 2004 Sch 2 paras 1(1), 14).
4 Ie under the Patents Act 1977 s 61(1)(c), (3): see PARA 522.
5 Ie under the Patents Act 1977 s 61(1)(e), (3): see PARA 522.
6 Patents Act 1977 s 61(3).
7 Ie under the County Courts Act 1984 s 85 (see CIVIL PROCEDURE vol 12 (2009) PARA 1283).
8 Patents Act 1977 s 61(7)(a) (added by the Patents Act 2004 s 11; amended by the Tribunals, Courts and Enforcement Act 2007 Sch 13 paras 39, 41; and by the Crime and Courts Act 2013 Sch 9 para 52(1)(b), (2) (but not so as to affect the wording of the text).
9 Ie a reference under the Patents Act 1977 s 61(3): see the text and notes 1–6.
10 As to the meaning of 'court' see PARA 619 note 1.
11 Patents Act 1977 s 61(5).
12 Ie any of the grounds referred to in the Patents Act 1977 s 72(1): see PARA 562.
13 Patents Act 1977 s 72(5).

(3) DECLARATION OF NON-INFRINGEMENT

554. Proceedings for declaration of non-infringement. Without prejudice to any other jurisdiction to make a declaration[1], the court[2] has power, in proceedings between any person and the proprietor of, or an exclusive licensee under[3], a patent, to make a declaration that an act does not or a proposed act would not constitute an infringement of the patent[4], and may do so notwithstanding that no assertion to the contrary has been made by the proprietor or licensee[5], if it is shown that:

(1) that person has applied in writing to the proprietor of the patent or licensee for a written acknowledgment to the effect of the declaration claimed, and has furnished him with full particulars in writing of the act in question[6]; and

(2) the proprietor or licensee has refused or failed to give any such acknowledgment[7].

Validity may be put in issue in the proceedings[8], which becomes in substance, apart from the special relief asked for, a claim for infringement in reverse.

The proceedings may in the alternative be brought before the comptroller[9].

1 See *SJ Filhol Ltd v Fairfax (Dental Equipment) Ltd* [1990] RPC 293; *Vax Appliances Ltd v Hoover plc* [1990] RPC 656. This is limited to acts within the United Kingdom: *Plastus Kreativ AB v Minnesota Mining and Manufacturing Co* [1995] RPC 438.

2 As to the meaning of 'court' see PARA 619 note 1.

3 See the Patents Act 1977 s 67(1); and PARA 520. As to the meaning of 'exclusive licensee' see PARA 379 note 7. See also PARA 520 note 1.

4 The burden of proof is on the person alleging non-infringement: *Mallory Mettalurgical Products Ltd v Black Sivalls and Bryson Inc* [1977] RPC 321 at 345; *Rohm & Haas Co v Collag Ltd* [2001] EWCA Civ 1589, [2002] FSR 445 at 454.

5 Patents Act 1977 s 71(1). See *Actavis UK Ltd v Eli Lilly & Company* [2014] EWHC 1511 (Pat), [2014] All ER (D) 21 (Jun) (in which the judge concluded that he could decide about infringement not only of the United Kingdom patent but also the same patent in several European jurisdictions). The court does not normally have jurisdiction to refuse a declaration: see *Henry Showell Ltd v Rodi and Wienenberger AG* (1966) 110 Sol Jo 286, [1966] RPC 441, CA. The consent of the patentee to proceedings under the Patents Act 1977 s 71 is not necessary: *Hawker Siddeley Dynamics Engineering Ltd v Real Time Developments Ltd* [1983] RPC 395 at 399 obiter per Whitford J. The court's general jurisdiction to make a declaration arises only in respect of an infringement which takes place within the United Kingdom, and only once the patent holder has claimed that an infringement has occurred: *Plastus Kreativ AB v Minnesota Mining and Manufacturing Co* [1995] RPC 438. The general jurisdiction cannot be invoked where the assertion of right is made in without-prejudice negotiations: *Unilever plc v Proctor & Gamble Co* [2001] 1 All ER 783, [2000] FSR 344, CA.

6 Patents Act 1977 s 71(1)(a). There is no obligation to furnish a specimen in addition to written particulars: *Plasticisers Ltd v Pixdane Ltd* [1979] RPC 327.

7 Patents Act 1977 s 71(1)(b).

8 Patents Act 1977 s 74(1)(c). The only grounds on which validity of a patent may be put in issue are the grounds on which the patent may be revoked under s 72 (see PARA 562): s 74(3). See further PARA 519.

9 Patents Act 1977 s 71(1). There is no appeal on fact from the comptroller's decision, beyond the Patents Court: see s 97(3); and PARA 571. As to the comptroller see PARA 575. A decision of the comptroller on validity in such proceedings is not fully conclusive (see s 72(5); and PARA 553) although he may grant a certificate of contested validity (see PARA 549). Subject to s 72(5), a declaration made by the comptroller under s 71(1) has the same effect as a declaration by the court: s 71(2). As to proceedings before the comptroller see the Patents Rules 2007, SI 2007/3291, Pt 7 (rr 73–91); and PARAS 598–606.

(4) PROCEEDINGS FOR THREATS

555. Proceedings for groundless threats. Where any person, whether or not the proprietor of or entitled to any right in a patent, by circulars, advertisements or otherwise[1] threatens[2] another person with proceedings for any infringement of a patent, a person aggrieved[3] by the threats[4], whether or not he is the person to whom they are made, may bring proceedings in the court[5] against him[6]. Such proceedings may not, however, be brought for: (1) a threat to bring proceedings for an infringement of a patent alleged to consist of making or importing a product for disposal or of using a process[7]; or (2) a threat, made to a person who has made or imported a product for disposal or used a process, to bring proceedings for an infringement alleged to consist of doing anything else in relation to that product or process[8].

In any such proceedings the claimant is entitled to the relief claimed, if he proves that the threats were so made and satisfies the court that he is a person aggrieved by them[9]. However, if the defendant proves that the acts in respect of which proceedings were threatened constitute or, if done, would constitute an infringement of a patent: (a) the claimant is entitled to the relief claimed only if he shows that the patent alleged to be infringed is invalid in a relevant respect; (b) even if the claimant does show that the patent is invalid in a relevant respect, he is not entitled to the relief claimed if the defendant proves that at the time of making the threats he did not know and had no reason to suspect that the patent was invalid in that respect[10]. The mere commencement by the defendant of infringement proceedings does not, however, bar the claimant's claim[11].

1   As to the meaning of this expression see PARA 558 note 4.

2   To circulate threats by others is not to threaten, but may nevertheless be restrained by injunction: see *Ellam v HF Martyn & Co* (1898) 68 LJ Ch 123, 16 RPC 28, CA.

3   As to who is aggrieved see PARA 558.

4   As to what constitutes a threat see PARA 557.

5   As to the meaning of 'court' see PARA 619 note 1.

6   Patents Act 1977 s 70(1). See also PARA 520 note 1. A party who has been threatened, whether directly or indirectly, does not need to prove damage in order to qualify to sue under s 70: *Brain v Ingledew Brown Bennison and Garrett (No 3)* [1997] FSR 511. As to the relief available see PARA 560. The validity of the patent may be put in issue in proceedings under s 70 (s 74(1)(b)), but only on one of the grounds on which the patent might be revoked under s 72 (see PARA 562) (s 74(3)). See further PARA 519.

7   Patents Act 1977 s 70(4)(a) (s 70(4) substituted by the Patents Act 2004 s 12(1), (3)); *Therm-a-Stor Ltd v Weatherseal Windows Ltd* [1981] FSR 579, CA. This exception extends to the making or importing of means essential for putting the invention into effect, thus making suppliers of components to a primary infringer susceptible to threats: *Therm-a-Stor Ltd v Weatherseal Windows Ltd*. The protection of the Patents Act 1977 s 70(4) may not be available, however, if the threats go wider than in respect of importation or manufacture for disposal and extend to articles already in existence: *Neild v Rockley* [1986] FSR 3; *Bowden Controls Ltd v Acco Cable Controls Ltd* [1990] RPC 427.

8   Patents Act 1977 s 70(4)(b) (as substituted: see note 7).

9   Patents Act 1977 s 70(2) (substituted by the Patents Act 2004 s 12(1), (2)). The patent infringed is not necessarily every patent mentioned in the threat: *Rosedale Associated Manufacturers Ltd v Carlton Tyre Saving Co Ltd* [1960] RPC 59 at 62, CA.

10   Patents Act 1977 s 70(2A) (added by the Patents Act 2004 s 12(1), (2)). The question whether the defence is available to the person making the threats is to be determined at trial and not at an interim stage: *Brain v Ingledew Brown Bennison and Garrett (No 2)* [1997] FSR 271.

11   *Cerosa Ltd v Poseidon Industrie AB* [1973] RPC 882. It is normal for a threats claim to be met by a counterclaim for relief for infringement, whether or not the making of the threat is admitted: see PARA 561.

556.   Remedy at common law. The making of false statements about existing proceedings or goods, whilst not in itself an actionable threat[1], may be actionable at common law if the statements are malicious[2].

1   *Surridge's Patents Ltd v Trico-Folberth Ltd* [1936] 3 All ER 26, 53 RPC 420.

2   See *Mentmore Manufacturing Co Ltd v Fomento (Sterling Area) Ltd* (1955) 72 RPC 157, CA; *Jaybeam Ltd v Abru Aluminium Ltd* [1976] RPC 308; and see DEFAMATION vol 32 (2012) PARA 776.

557.   What constitutes a threat. The question whether what was done was a threat is one of fact. The essential of a threat is an indication that the maker has rights, and intends to enforce them[1]. A person does not threaten another person with proceedings for infringement of a patent if he merely: (1) provides factual information about the patent; (2) makes inquiries of the other person for the sole purpose of discovering whether, or by whom, the patent has been infringed[2]; or (3) makes an assertion about the patent for the purpose of any inquiries so made[3]. It may be said generally that it is sufficient that the statement complained of would be reasonably believed by the person to whom it was addressed to be a threat of proceedings for infringement of a patent[4], even though no reference is in fact made to any such proceedings[5]. The nature of the interview at which statements are made is relevant in considering whether they amount to threats[6]. The alleged threat must in some way point to the articles or class of articles manufactured or used by the claimant. A general statement that the proprietor of the patent will protect his rights, or that action will be taken against infringers is not sufficient[7]; but the form is unimportant if the document read as a whole would be understood as a threat[8], and this may be so even if the document is in form a general warning[9]; and more especially is this the case if the document has been sent to customers of the claimant[10]. The state of the defendant's knowledge of the relations between the claimant and the person receiving the threats may be material[11]. A communication may threaten a person other than the person to whom it is made[12].

It is not necessary that the alleged threat should refer to what is actually happening; there may be a threat of proceedings in some future event. For example, a statement that, if a particular machine should be manufactured, it would infringe a particular patent might constitute a threat[13].

1   A threats action may not be brought in respect of threats made in genuine without-prejudice negotiations: *Schering Corpn v CIPLA Ltd* [2004] EWHC 2587 (Ch), [2005] FSR 575; *Kooltrade Ltd v XTS Ltd* [2001] FSR 158. See also *Rosedale Associated Manufacturers Ltd v Airfix Products Ltd* [1956] RPC 360 at 363 (on appeal [1957] RPC 239, CA, the point did not arise), a case decided under the corresponding provisions of the Registered Designs Act 1949 s 26 (see PARA 772); *Willis and Bates Ltd v Tilley Lamp Co* (1943) 61 RPC 8 at 11; *C and P Development Co (London) Ltd v Sisabro Novelty Co Ltd* (1953) 70 RPC 277 at 282, CA; *Unilever plc v Proctor & Gamble Co* [2001] 1 All ER 783, [2000] 1 WLR 2436, CA; *Kooltrade Ltd v XTS Ltd* [2001] FSR 158; *SDL Hair Ltd v Next Row Ltd* [2013] EWPCC 31, [2013] All ER (D) 185 (Jul).

2   Ie as mentioned in the Patents Act 1977 s 70(4)(a): see PARA 555.

3   Patents Act 1977 s 70(5) (substituted by the Patents Act 2004 s 12(1), (4)). See *Paul Trading Co Ltd v J Marksmith & Co Ltd* (1952) 69 RPC 301. See also PARA 520 note 1.

4   *C and P Development Co (London) Ltd v Sisabro Novelty Co Ltd* (1953) 70 RPC 277 at 280, 282, CA.

5   *Luna Advertising Co v Burnham & Co* (1928) 45 RPC 258.

6   *Paul Trading Co Ltd v J Marksmith & Co Ltd* (1952) 69 RPC 301 at 304, citing *Surridge's Patent's Ltd v Trico-Folberth Ltd* [1936] 3 All ER 26 at 2930, 53 RPC 420 at 423424.

7 *Brauer v Sharp* (1886) 3 RPC 193 at 197; *Dick v Haslam* (1891) 8 RPC 196; *Willoughby v Taylor* (1893) 11 RPC 45; *Crowther v United Flexible Metallic Tubing Co Ltd* (1905) 22 RPC 549; *WH Howson Ltd v Algraphy Ltd* [1965] RPC 183; *Speedcranes Ltd v Thomson* 1972 SC 324, [1978] RPC 221, Ct of Sess.

8 *Kurtz & Co v Spence & Sons* (1887) 57 LJ Ch 238 at 247, 5 RPC 161 at 173; *Johnson v Edge* [1892] 2 Ch 1, 9 RPC 142, CA; *Douglass v Pintsch's Patent Lighting Co* [1897] 1 Ch 176, 13 RPC 673; *Craig v Dowding* (1908) 98 LT 231, 25 RPC 259, CA; *Cars v Bland Light Syndicate Ltd* (1910) 28 RPC 33; *Luna Advertising Co v Burnham & Co* (1928) 45 RPC 258.

9 Eg if there are words in the warning which would point to the claimant's articles: see *Boneham and Hart v Hirst Bros & Co Ltd* (1917) 34 RPC 209.

10 *Johnson v Edge* [1892] 2 Ch 1, 9 RPC 142, CA.

11 *Weldrics Ltd v Quasi-Arc Co Ltd* (1922) 39 RPC 323. It has been said that it is for the defendant to show that the threats were not directed against the claimant: *Johnson v Edge* [1892] 2 Ch 1, 9 RPC 142, CA, per Lindley LJ.

12 *John Summers & Sons Ltd v Cold Metal Process Co* (1947) 65 RPC 75 at 9697. See also *Brain v Ingledew Brown Bennison and Garrett (No 3)* [1997] FSR 511.

13 *Kurtz v Spence* (1887) 36 ChD 770, 4 RPC 427, CA, explaining *Challender v Royle* (1887) 36 ChD 425 at 442, 4 RPC 363 at 375, CA; *Desiderio v Currus Ltd* (1935) 52 RPC 201. See also *Johnson v Edge* [1892] 2 Ch 1, 9 RPC 142, CA, per Lindley LJ; *Skinner & Co v Shew & Co* [1893] 1 Ch 413, sub nom *Skinner & Co v Perry* 10 RPC 1, CA. As to threats of proceedings if a patent should be granted see *Lebel Products Ltd v W Steel & Co Ltd* (1955) 72 RPC 115 (arguable question, whether justification possible).

558. To whom threats may be addressed. A threat may be either addressed to the claimant[1], or to his customers[2], or to manufacturers[3], or may be simply published to the world in general[4]. It may be contained in a solicitor's letter[5], or in a statement without prejudice[6], or in an answer to inquiries[7]. An ordinary solicitor's letter before action will usually constitute a threat, but, if a claim form follows within a reasonable time[8] and the recipient does not comply with the demands in the letter, the recipient is unlikely to be a person aggrieved by the threat[9]. A threat from solicitors comes with more force than a threat from a layman[10]. An oral threat is actionable[11], but a mere notification of the existence of a patent is not[12]. Where the threat is to some person other than the claimant, the claimant must show that his trade has been adversely affected[13].

1 *Driffield and East Riding Pure Linseed Cake Co v Waterloo Mills Cake and Warehousing Co* (1886) 31 ChD 638, 3 RPC 46; *Horne v Johnston Bros* (1921) 38 RPC 366.

2 *Burt v Morgan & Co Ltd* (1887) 3 TLR 666, 4 RPC 278; *Hoffnung & Co v Salsbury* (1899) 16 RPC 375; *Craig v Dowding* (1908) 25 RPC 1 (revsd 25 RPC 259, CA). See also *Speedcranes Ltd v Thomson* 1972 SC 324, [1978] RPC 221, Ct of Sess; *Bowden Controls Ltd v Acco Cable Controls Ltd* [1990] RPC 427.

3 *Willoughby v Taylor* (1893) 11 RPC 45; *Webb v Levinstein & Co Ltd* (1898) 15 RPC 78. See also *Bowden Controls Ltd v Acco Cable Controls Ltd* [1990] RPC 427.

4 *Johnson v Edge* [1892] 2 Ch 1, 9 RPC 142, CA. The Patents Act 1977 s 70(1) (see PARA 555) refers to threats by circulars, advertisements or otherwise, but the last word is not to be construed as ejusdem generis with the former: *Skinner & Co v Shew & Co* [1893] 1 Ch 413; sub nom *Skinner & Co v Perry* 10 RPC 1, CA, applied in *Speedcranes Ltd v Thomson* 1972 SC 324, [1978] RPC 221, Ct of Sess. Bringing proceedings against customers without joining the alleged primary infringer may be vexatious and an abuse of the process of the court: *Jacey (Printers) v Norton and Wright Group Ltd* [1977] FSR 475.

5 *Crampton v Patents Investment Co* (1888) 5 RPC 382 at 393 (affd (1889) 6 RPC 287, CA); *Combined Weighing and Advertising Co v Automatic Weighing Machine Co* (1889) 42 ChD 665, 6 RPC 502; *Engels v Hubert Unchangeable Eyelet Syndicate Ltd* (1902) 19 RPC 201, CA; but see *Day v Foster* (1890) 43 ChD 435, 7 RPC 54; *Earles Utilities Ltd v Harrison* (1934) 52 RPC 77. See also *Cerosa Ltd v Poseidon Industrie AB* [1973] RPC 882.

6 *Kurtz & Co v Spence & Sons* (1887) 57 LJ Ch 238 at 242, 5 RPC 161 at 173.

7 *Skinner & Co v Shew & Co* [1893] 1 Ch 413, sub nom *Skinner & Co v Perry* 10 RPC 1, CA.

8 If not, the threat is actionable: *Driffield and East Riding Pure Linseed Cake Co v Waterloo Mills Cake and Warehousing Co* (1886) 31 ChD 638, 3 RPC 46.

9   *Benmax v Austin Motor Co Ltd* (1953) 70 RPC 143 at 151, 157; on appeal 70 RPC 284 at 295, CA; although neither court had occasion actually to decide the point. If the recipient does comply with the demands in the letter, damages may be very heavy.

10 *HVE (Electric) Ltd v Cufflin Holdings Ltd* [1964] 1 All ER 674, [1964] 1 WLR 378, CA.

11 *Ellis & Sons v Pogson* (1922) 40 RPC 62 (affd [1923] 2 Ch 496, 40 RPC 179, CA); *Luna Advertising Co v Burnham & Co* (1928) 45 RPC 258.

12 See the Patents Act 1977 s 70(5); and PARA 557.

13 *Reymes-Cole v Elite Hosiery Co Ltd* [1965] RPC 102, CA.

559. Who may be liable. A claim lies against the person who makes the threat, whether or not he is a proprietor of a patent, for example a solicitor[1], but a mere statement by a solicitor that he would advise his client to bring infringement proceedings is not a threat[2].

In proceedings[3] for threats made by one person (A) to another (B) in respect of an alleged infringement of a patent for an invention, it is a defence for A to prove that he used his best endeavours, without success, to discover[4]:

(1)   where the invention is a product, the identity of any person who made or, in the case of an imported product, imported it for disposal[5];

(2)   where the invention is a process and the alleged infringement consists of offering it for use, the identity of a person who used the process[6];

(3)   where the invention is a process and the alleged infringement consists of disposing or offering to dispose of, use or import any product obtained directly by means of that process or keeping any such product[7], the identity of the person who used the process to produce the product in question[8],

and that he notified B accordingly, before or at the time of making the threats, identifying the endeavours used[9].

1   See eg *Brain v Ingledew Brown Bennison and Garrett* [1996] FSR 341, CA.

2   *Earles Utilities Ltd v Harrison* (1934) 52 RPC 77. See *Reckitt Benkiser UK v Home Pairfum Ltd* [2004] EWHC 302 (Pat), [2004] FSR 774 (defendants refused leave to join claimant's solicitors to the threats counterclaim).

3   Ie under the Patents Act 1977 s 70: see PARAS 555, 557.

4   Patents Act 1977 s 70(6) (added by the Patents Act 2004 s 12(1), (5)).

5   Patents Act 1977 s 70(6)(a) (as added: see note 4).

6   Patents Act 1977 s 70(6)(b) (as added: see note 4).

7   Ie an act falling within the Patents Act 1977 s 60(1)(c): see PARA 511.

8   Patents Act 1977 s 70(6)(c) (as added: see note 4).

9   Patents Act 1977 s 70(6) (as added: see note 4).

560. Relief for actionable threats. Unless the defendant proves the facts necessary to constitute a defence[1], the claimant in proceedings for groundless threats[2] is entitled, subject always to the court's discretion[3], to:

(1)   a declaration to the effect that the threats are unjustifiable[4];

(2)   an injunction against the continuance of the threats[5]; and

(3)   damages in respect of any loss which the claimant has sustained by the threats[6].

Such damages may include, for example, the loss of particular orders or of trade generally[7], loss of seasonal trade or delay in putting goods on the market[8], or the loss of an opportunity of disposing of a patent[9] or of making future sales[10], but not the cost of defending, or preparing to defend, a subsequent claim for infringement[11].

An interim injunction may be granted[12], but this will not usually be done where the defendant alleges infringement[13]. Where the threat was in wide terms, an injunction in wide terms will be granted[14].

1   Ie under the Patents Act 1977 s 70(2A) (see PARA 555) or s 70(6) (see PARA 559).

2   Ie under the Patents Act 1977 s 70(1): see PARA 555.

3   *Benmax v Austin Motor Co Ltd* (1953) 70 RPC 284 at 295296, CA (on appeal on other issues [1955] AC 370, [1955] 1 All ER 326, 72 RPC 39, HL); *Tudor Accessories Ltd v JN Somers Ltd* [1960] RPC 215; *HVE (Electric) Ltd v Cufflin Holdings Ltd* [1964] 1 All ER 674, [1964] 1 WLR 378, CA.

4   Patents Act 1977 s 70(3)(a). See also PARA 520 note 1.

5   Patents Act 1977 s 70(3)(b).

6   Patents Act 1977 s 70(3)(c) (amended by the Patents Act 2004 Sch 2 paras 1(1), 17). As to seeking to bring a new claim against new defendants where the original defendant went into liquidation leaving judgment for substantial damages unsatisfied see *Kooltrade Ltd v XTS Ltd* [2002] FSR 764.

7   *Ratcliffe v Evans* [1892] 2 QB 524, CA.

8   *Earles Utilities Ltd v Jacobs* (1934) 51 TLR 43, 52 RPC 72.

9   *Skinner & Co Ltd v Shew & Co* [1894] 2 Ch 581, sub nom *Skinner & Co v Perry* 11 RPC 406; *Solanite Signs Ltd v Wood* (1933) 50 RPC 315.

10   *Kooltrade Ltd v XTS Ltd* [2001] FSR 158 at 168.

11   *Benmax v Austin Motor Co Ltd* (1953) 70 RPC 143 at 157; on appeal 70 RPC 284 at 295, CA.

12   *Boneham and Hart v Hirst Bros & Co Ltd* (1917) 34 RPC 209; *Luna Advertising Co v Burnham & Co* (1928) 45 RPC 258; *HVE (Electric) Ltd v Cufflin Holdings Ltd* [1964] 1 All ER 674, [1964] 1 WLR 378, CA; *Bowden Controls Ltd v Acco Cable Controls Ltd* [1990] RPC 427.

13   *Stringer v Platnauer Ltd* (1932) 50 RPC 61; *Cabaret Electric Co Ltd v Marconi's Wireless Telegraph Co Ltd* (1934) 52 RPC 104. See to the contrary *International Sales Ltd v Trans-Continental Trading Co Ltd and Benno Maisel* (1934) 52 RPC 107; *Cerosa Ltd v Poseidon Industrie AB* [1973] RPC 882.

14   See *Mechanical Services (Trailer Engineering) Ltd v Avon Rubber Co Ltd* [1977] RPC 66.

561.   Procedure.   A defendant who seeks to justify the threats, and is interested in the patent said to be infringed, may counterclaim for relief for infringement, and the claimant may then counterclaim to the counterclaim for revocation of the patent[1]. If justification is pleaded, whether or not there are counterclaims, the procedure follows that of a normal infringement action[2]. In general a claimant has the right to begin; but, if the threats are admitted, the proprietor of the patent will begin, as in ordinary infringement proceedings[3].

1   *Lewis Falk Ltd v Jacobwitz* [1944] Ch 64, 61 RPC 116 (design); *John Summers & Sons Ltd v Cold Metal Process Co* (1947) 65 RPC 75.

2   For example, a defendant alleging that threats were justified must give particulars of acts of the claimant relied on as constituting an infringement: *Reymes-Cole v Elite Hosiery Co Ltd* [1961] RPC 277. Since a defendant usually justifies if the issue of threats is in doubt, a claim of this sort is often used to enable a possible infringer to bring questions of validity and infringement before the court.

3   *Crampton v Patents Investment Co* (1888) 5 RPC 382 (affd (1889) 6 RPC 287, CA); *Lewis Falk Ltd v Jacobwitz* [1944] Ch 64, 61 RPC 116; *W Lusty & Sons Ltd v Morris Wilkinson & Co (Nottingham) Ltd* [1954] 2 All ER 347, [1954] 1 WLR 911, 71 RPC 174 (registered design).

(5) PROCEEDINGS FOR REVOCATION

562.   Application to the court for revocation of patent.   The court[1] may revoke a patent on the application of any person[2] on, but only on, any of the following grounds[3]:

(1)   that the invention is not a patentable invention[4];

(2)   that the patent was granted to a person who was not entitled[5] to be granted that patent[6];

(3)   that the specification[7] does not disclose the invention clearly and completely enough for it to be performed by a person skilled in the art[8];

(4)   that the matter disclosed in the specification extends beyond that disclosed in the application for the patent, as filed[9], or, if the patent was granted on a new application[10], in the earlier application, as filed[11];

(5)   that the protection conferred by the patent has been extended by an amendment[12] which should not have been allowed[13].

Where the validity of a patent is challenged, the statement of case must contain particulars of the relief sought and the issues except those relating to validity[14]. The statement of case must have a separate document annexed to it headed 'Grounds of Invalidity' specifying the grounds on which validity of the patent is challenged[15].

The order made may be an order for the unconditional revocation of the patent or, where it is determined that one of the grounds mentioned above has been established, but only so as to invalidate the patent to a limited extent, an order that the patent be revoked unless within a specified time the specification is amended[16] to the court's satisfaction[17].

1   As to the meaning of 'court' see PARA 619 note 1.

2   See *Cairnstores Ltd v Aktiebolaget Hassle* [2002] FSR 564, [2001] All ER (D) 212 (Mar).

3   Patents Act 1977 s 72(1) (amended by the Patents Act 2004 Sch 2 paras 1(1), 18, Sch 3). These are the only grounds on which the validity of a patent may be put in issue, whether in revocation proceedings or otherwise: Patents Act 1977 s 74(3); and see PARA 519. As to validity generally see PARA 425 et seq.

4   Patents Act 1977 s 72(1)(a); and see PARA 430. As to the meaning of 'patentable invention' see PARA 429 note 2.

5   Ie under the Patents Act 1977 s 7(2): see PARA 306.

6   Patents Act 1977 s 72(1)(b) (substituted by the Copyright, Designs and Patents Act 1988 Sch 5 para 18); and see PARA 488. An application for revocation on this ground may only be made by a person found by the court in an action for a declaration, or found by the court or the comptroller on a reference under the Patents Act 1977 s 37 to determine entitlement after a grant (see PARA 365), to be entitled to be granted either that patent or a patent for part of the matter comprised in the specification of the patent sought to be revoked: s 72(2)(a). Such an application may not be made if that action was commenced or that reference was made after the second anniversary of the date of the grant of the patent sought to be revoked, unless it is shown that any person registered as its proprietor knew at the time of the grant or of the transfer of the patent to him that he was not entitled to the patent: s 72(2)(b) (amended by the Intellectual Property Act 2014 Schedule para 3(1)(b)).

7   As to specifications see PARA 318 et seq.

8   Patents Act 1977 s 72(1)(c); and see PARA 489.

9   As to the filing of the application see PARA 317.

10   Ie filed under the Patents Act 1977 s 8(3) (see PARA 361), s 12 (see PARA 363) or s 37(4) (see PARA 365) or as mentioned in s 15(9) (see PARA 316).

11   Patents Act 1977 s 72(1)(d) (amended by SI 2004/2357); and see PARA 497.

12   As to amendment see PARA 345 et seq.

13   Patents Act 1977 s 72(1)(e); and see PARA 498. See *Fosroc International Ltd v WR Grace & Co-Con* [2010] EWHC 1702 (Ch), [2010] All ER (D) 111 (Jul) (application for revocation was dismissed and defendant successfully applied to amend patent).

14   *Practice Direction — Intellectual Property Claims* PD 63 para 4.2(1).

15   *Practice Direction — Intellectual Property Claims* PD 63 para 4.2(2). As to grounds of invalidity see PARA 526.

16   The reference to the specification being amended is to its being amended under the Patents Act 1977 s 75 (see PARA 346) and also, in the case of a European patent (UK), to its being amended under any provision of the European Patent Convention under which the claims of the patent may be limited by amendment at the request of the proprietor: Patents Act 1977 s 72(4A) (added by the Patents Act 2004 s 4). As to the meaning of 'European patent (UK)' see PARA 652 note 1. As to the European Patent Convention see PARA 644 et seq.

17   Patents Act 1977 s 72(4) (amended by the Patents Act 2004 ss 4, 16(2), Sch 3).

563.   Application to the comptroller for revocation of patent. The comptroller[1] may revoke a patent on the application of any person on, but only on, any of the grounds[2] on which the court may revoke a patent[3].

On the application the comptroller may order the unconditional revocation of the patent, or its revocation unless the specification is amended to his satisfaction within a specified time[4]. Where the comptroller refuses to grant an application so made to him, no application, otherwise than by way of appeal[5] or by way of putting validity in issue in infringement proceedings, may be made to the court by the applicant in relation to the patent concerned without the leave of the court[6]. Where the comptroller has not disposed of such an application, the applicant may not apply to the court for revocation of the patent concerned unless the proprietor of the patent agrees that he may do so[7] or the comptroller certifies in writing that it appears to him that the question whether the patent should be revoked is one which would more properly be determined by the court[8]. A decision of the comptroller or on appeal from him does not estop any party to civil proceedings in which infringement is in issue from alleging invalidity of the patent on any of the grounds on which revocation may be ordered, whether or not any of the issues involved were decided in that decision[9].

1   As to the comptroller see PARA 575.
2   For these grounds see the Patents Act 1977 s 72(1); and PARA 562.
3   Patents Act 1977 s 72(1) (amended by the Patents Act 2004 Sch 2 paras 1(1), 18, Sch 3). As to proceedings before the comptroller see the Patents Rules 2007, SI 2007/3291, Pt 7 (rr 73–91); and PARAS 598–606.
4   See the Patents Act 1977 s 72(4); and PARA 562. Where, prior to the comptroller's deciding the matter, the applicant for revocation withdraws from the proceedings, the public interest requires that the comptroller should himself consider the matter: *Abbott Laboratories (Chu's) Patent* [1992] RPC 487.
5   As to appeals see PARA 570 et seq.
6   Patents Act 1977 s 72(6).
7   Patents Act 1977 s 72(7)(a).
8   Patents Act 1977 s 72(7)(b). Where the comptroller certifies that the court should determine the question whether a patent should be revoked, any person seeking the court's determination of that question must issue a claim form within 14 days of the comptroller's decision: CPR 63.11(2).
9   Patents Act 1977 s 72(5).

564.   Parties. All persons beneficially interested should be made parties to the application for revocation, and the court will insist on this being done if the interest appears on the register[1]. All parties having an interest will usually be allowed to appear[2], but it is unnecessary to join persons whose interest has ceased.

1   *Re Avery's Patent* (1887) 36 ChD 307, 4 RPC 322, CA; cf *Reitzman v Grahame-Chapman and Derustit Ltd* (1950) 67 RPC 178 at 189, 196 (where there was a counterclaim for revocation, and the proprietor of the patent, who was not a party to the proceedings, was made a defendant to the counterclaim to enable the patent to be revoked). As to the register see PARA 583 et seq.
2   *Re Miller's Patent* (1898) 15 RPC 205, CA. In *Re Haddan's Patent* (1885) 2 RPC 218, where the proprietor of the patent had assigned after presenting the petition, the new patentee was allowed to be substituted as respondent. Licensees, even if sole licensees, are not entitled to appear: *Re Stahlwerk Becker AG's Patent* (1917) 35 RPC 81; affd 35 RPC 210, CA; (1918) 36 RPC 13, HL. Where the patentee is subject to an administration order, the revocation proceedings may not be continued without the consent of the administrators or leave of the court: *Re Axis Genetics plc (in administration)* [2000] FSR 448.

565.   Procedure. Where the proprietor of the patent resides abroad, the claim form for revocation in certain circumstances may be served out of the jurisdiction without permission[1]. Security for costs can be directed to be given by an applicant for revocation, but not by a respondent[2]. A patent can only be revoked in open court[3], but it may be so revoked by consent or on affidavit evidence[4]. A proprietor may also surrender his patent[5]. The burden of proof in revocation proceedings is on the applicant for revocation[6], but the respondent is entitled to begin[7] and to give evidence in support of the patent and, if the applicant gives evidence impeaching the validity of the patent, the respondent is entitled to reply[8]. Apart from the above points, the procedure is the same as in a claim for infringement[9]. Normally any order for revocation is made with costs, even where there is no opposition[10].

As an applicant for revocation is considered to be acting in the public interest, neither he nor the proprietor of the patent is estopped by a decision in previous proceedings[11]. An expired patent may be revoked[12].

1   A claim form may be served on a defendant out of the jurisdiction where applicable conditions are satisfied: see CPR 6.33 (applied by CPR 63.14(1)); and CIVIL PROCEDURE vol 11 (2009) PARAS 168–169. A claim form relating to a registered right may be served: (1) on a party who has registered the right at the address for service given for that right in the UK Intellectual Property Office register, provided the address is within the jurisdiction; or (2) in accordance with CPR 6.33(1) or (2) (see CIVIL PROCEDURE) on a party who has registered the right at the address for service given for that right in the appropriate register at the UK Intellectual Property Office or the Office for Harmonisation in the Internal Market: CPR 63.14(2). As to the UK Intellectual Property Office see PARA 577.
2   See CPR 25.13; and CIVIL PROCEDURE vol 11 (2009) PARA 746.
3   *Re Clifton's Patent* [1904] 2 Ch 357, 21 RPC 515.
4   Revocation by consent was made on the application as to mode of trial in *Re Simmons' Patent* (1895) 12 RPC 446.
5   See the Patents Act 1977 s 29; and PARA 358. It seems that the proprietor may not surrender to avoid revocation: see *O and M Kleeman Ltd v Rosedale Associated Manufacturers Ltd* (1954) 71 RPC 271 (registered design); *Connaught Laboratories Inc's Patent* [1999] FSR 284. See also *Dyson Ltd's Patent* [2004] RPC 473; *Dyson Ltd's Patent (No 2)* [2003] RPC 848.
6   See e g *Re Jameson's Patent* (1902) 19 RPC 246.
7   This right may be waived: see *Re Edmond's Patent* (1888) 6 RPC 355 at 357.
8   Where, in a claim for threats (see PARA 557 et seq), a counterclaim in respect of infringement was withdrawn but the claimants sought revocation of the patent, the defendants were held to have the right to begin on the issue of validity: *John Summers & Sons Ltd v Cold Metal Process Co* (1948) 65 RPC 75 at 83. In *Boehringer Mannheim GmbH v Genzyme Ltd* [1993] FSR 716, however, it was stated that it was right for the defendant to open the case when, in infringement proceedings, only validity was in issue.
9   As to the procedure generally in an infringement claim see PARA 520 et seq.
10 *Re Scott's Patent* (1903) 20 RPC 604. Where two respondents are served and are separately represented, each is entitled to costs, even though one may have taken no part in the case: *Re Brown's Patent* (1907) 24 RPC 313.
11 *Re Lewis and Stirckler's Patent* (1897) 14 RPC 24.
12 *John Summers & Sons Ltd v Cold Metal Process Co* (1948) 65 RPC 75 at 121.

566. Stay of proceedings where concurrent proceedings in European Patent Office. A person contesting the validity of a European patent can bring both a claim for revocation in the English courts and opposition proceedings in the European Patent Office[1]. The approach to a stay of proceedings in such cases differs from ordinary commercial proceedings as the possibility of parallel proceedings in the European Patent Office and national courts is inherent in the legal arrangements in the European Patent Convention[2]. The discretion of the Patents Court to stay proceedings should be exercised to achieve a balance of justice in the particular case[3].

1   *Unilin Beheer BV v Berry Floor NV* [2007] EWCA Civ 364, [2008] 1 All ER 156, [2007] FSR 635. See PARA 644 et seq.

2   For the guidelines applicable when the Patents Court exercises its discretion to grant a stay on the ground that there are parallel proceedings pending in the European Patent Office see *Glaxo Group Ltd v Genentech Inc* [2008] EWCA Civ 23, [2008] All ER (D) 282 (Jan), [2008] FSR 459; *Virgin Atlantic Airways Ltd v Zodiac Seats UK Ltd (formerly Contour Aerospace Ltd)* [2013] UKSC 46, [2014] AC 160, [2013] 4 All ER 715; *Ipcom GmbH & Co KG v HTC Europe Co Ltd* [2013] EWCA Civ 1496, [2014] RPC 397, [2013] All ER (D) 234 (Nov) (summarising the guidance set out in *Glaxo Group Ltd v Genentech Inc*, as revised in the light of the decision in *Virgin Atlantic Airways Ltd v Zodiac Seats UK Ltd*); *Actavis Group PTC EHF v Pharmacia LLC* [2014] EWHC 2265 (Pat), [2014] All ER (D) 218 (Jul); *Actavis Group PTC EHF v Pharmacia LLC* [2014] EWHC 2611 (Pat), [2014] All ER (D) 274 (Jul). As to the European Patent Convention see PARA 644 et seq.

3   See note 2.

567.   Amendment of specification in revocation proceedings. There may be amendment of the specification of a patent in any proceedings in which validity may be put in issue[1]. If, in revocation proceedings, the court[2] decides that the patent is invalid, it may allow an application for leave to amend to be made to it, instead of revoking the patent[3].

1   See the Patents Act 1977 s 75; and PARAS 346–347.
2   As to the meaning of 'court' see PARA 619 note 1.
3   See the Patents Act 1977 s 75(1) (amended by the Patents Act 2004 Sch 2 paras 1(1), 19). In general a post-trial amendment where the patentee seeks to introduce a different claim from those under attack at the trial will not be allowed: *Nikken Kosakusho Works v Pioneer Trading Co* [2005] EWCA Civ 906, [2006] FSR 41. For a case where amendment was permitted see *Environmental Recycling Technologies plc v Upcycle Holdings Ltd* [2013] EWPCC 4, [2013] All ER (D) 365 (Feb).

568.   Effect of revocation. An order for revocation puts an end to an injunction, and the revocation may be relied upon in the inquiry as to damages[1]. Once an order for revocation issues, it must be lodged with the comptroller[2], and the patent then ceases to exist[3]. The practice is, however, to suspend the order for revocation pending appeal.

1   See *Virgin Atlantic Airways Ltd v Zodiac Seats UK Ltd (formerly Contour Aerospace Ltd)* [2013] UKSC 46, [2014] AC 160, [2013] 4 All ER 715.
2   As to the comptroller see PARA 575.
3   *Deeley v Perkes* [1896] AC 496, 13 RPC 581, HL. Even if the judgment is reversed and the order discharged, the proprietor of the patent may be unable to recover damages for acts committed between the time the order was made and its discharge: *Cincinnati Grinders Inc v BSA Tools Ltd* (1931) 48 RPC 33 at 59, 86, CA.

569.   Revocation of patent by the comptroller on his own initiative. If it appears to the comptroller[1] that an invention for which a patent has been granted formed part of the state of the art only by reason of its comprising matter contained in an application for another patent published on or after the priority date[2] of that invention[3], he may on his own initiative by order revoke the patent, but must first notify the proprietor of the patent that it appears to him that the patent ought to be revoked and must give the proprietor opportunity, within three months of the notification, of making observations and of amending the specification[4] of the patent[5] appropriately[6].

If it appears to the comptroller that a patent and a European patent (UK)[7] have been granted for the same invention[8] having the same priority date, and that the applications for the patents were filed by the same applicant or his successor in title, he must give the proprietor of the patent an opportunity of making observations and of amending the specification of the patent; and, if the proprietor fails to satisfy the comptroller that there are not two patents in respect of the same invention, or to amend the specification[9] so as to prevent there being two patents in respect of the same invention, the comptroller must revoke the patent[10]. The comptroller must not, however, take such action[11]:

(1)   before:

    (a)   the end of the period for filing an opposition[12] to the European patent (UK) under the European Patent Convention[13]; or

    (b)   if later, the date on which opposition proceedings are finally disposed of;

    and he must not then take any action if the decision is not to maintain the European patent or if it is amended so that there are not two patents in respect of the same invention[14];

(2)   if the European patent (UK) has been surrendered[15] before the date on which the patent is to be treated[16] as having been granted or, if proceedings for the surrender of the European patent (UK) have been begun before that date, until those proceedings are finally disposed of; and he must not then take any action if the decision is to accept the surrender of the European patent[17].

Where, however, the conditions set out above for the revocation of a patent are satisfied, the comptroller must revoke it even though the European patent (UK) has ceased to exist through failure to pay the renewal fees[18] or an offer to surrender it has been made[19]. The comptroller may maintain the patent only where the decision not to maintain the European patent is a decision of the European Patent Office[20] and not a voluntary decision of the proprietor[21].

1   As to the comptroller see PARA 575.
2   As to the meaning of 'priority date' see PARA 310 note 6.
3   Ie formed part of the state of the art only by virtue of the Patents Act 1977 s 2(3): see PARA 434.
4   As to the specification see PARA 318 et seq.
5   Ie so as to exclude any matter which formed part of the state of the art by virtue of the Patents Act 1977 s 2(3) without contravening s 76 (amendments not to include added matter: see PARA 351).
6   Patents Act 1977 s 73(1). The validity of a patent is not put in issue merely because the comptroller is considering its validity in order to decide whether to revoke it under s 73: see s 74(8); and PARA 519. In connection with revocations see also s 73(1A)–(1C); and see PARA 517.
7   As to the meaning of 'European patent (UK)' see PARA 652 note 1.
8   Ie if the claims of the United Kingdom patent and the European patent cover the same invention, whatever other linked inventions may be covered by the claims of either patent: *Marley Roof Tile Co Ltd's Patent* [1994] RPC 231 at 241, CA. Thus a claim to a product having a particular composition and particular qualities and a claim to that product made by a particular process are claims to the same invention: *Marley Roof Tile Co Ltd's Patent*. See also *Maag Gear Wheel and Machine Co Ltd's Patent* [1985] RPC 572.
9   See note 4.
10   Patents Act 1977 s 73(2) (substituted by the Copyright, Designs and Patents Act 1988 Sch 5 para 19).
11   Ie action under the Patents Act 1977 s 73(2).
12   As to such opposition proceedings see PARA 650.
13   As to the European Patent Convention see PARA 644 et seq.
14   Patents Act 1977 s 73(3) (substituted by the Copyright, Designs and Patents Act 1988 Sch 5 para 19).
15   Ie under the Patents Act 1977 s 29(1): see PARA 358.
16   Ie by virtue of the Patents Act 1977 s 25(1): see PARAS 337–338.
17   Patents Act 1977 s 73(4) (substituted by the Copyright, Designs and Patents Act 1988 Sch 5 para 19).
18   *Citizen Watch Co Ltd's Patent* [1993] RPC 1.
19   *Turner & Newall Ltd's Patent* [1984] RPC 49.
20   As to the meaning of 'European Patent Office' see PARA 644 note 1.
21   *Citizen Watch Co Ltd's Patent* [1993] RPC 1.

(6) APPEALS

570. Rights of appeal from the Patents Court and the Intellectual Property Enterprise Court. In all proceedings in the Patents Court[1] or the Intellectual Property Enterprise Court[2] relating to infringement[3], threats[4] or revocation[5], appeal lies, in the ordinary way, on a question of law or fact, to the Court of Appeal[6] and thence, with leave, to the Supreme Court[7]. In a proper case certified by the judge, appeal lies, with leave, direct from the Patents Court to the Supreme Court[8].

Subject to certain limitations appeal also lies to the Court of Appeal from a decision of the Patents Court on appeal from the comptroller[9].

1   As to the Patents Court see PARA 619 et seq.
2   As to the Intellectual Property Enterprise Court see PARA 626 et seq.
3   As to infringement proceedings see PARA 520 et seq.
4   As to proceedings for groundless threats see PARA 555 et seq.
5   As to revocation proceedings see PARA 562 et seq.
6   As to appeals from the Patents Court see PARA 624; and as to the Intellectual Property Enterprise Court see PARA 626. As to the hearing of appeals generally see CPR 52.11; and CIVIL PROCEDURE vol 12 (2009) PARA 1672 et seq.
7   See the Constitutional Reform Act 2005 s 40; and COURTS AND TRIBUNALS vol 24 (2010) PARA 657 et seq.
8   See the Administration of Justice Act 1969 ss 12, 13; and COURTS AND TRIBUNALS vol 24 (2010) PARA 659.
9   See PARA 571.

571. Rights of appeal from the comptroller. Appeal lies to the Patents Court[1] from any decision of the comptroller[2] under the Patents Act 1977 or the Patents Rules 2007 relating to infringement or revocation[3].

Appeal lies to the Court of Appeal from a decision of the Patents Court on such an appeal from the comptroller's decision only with the leave of the Patents Court or of the Court of Appeal[4], and only where either the ground of appeal is that the decision of the Patents Court is wrong in law[5] or the comptroller's decision was given under one of certain provisions[6].

1   As to appeals from the comptroller to the Patents Court, and as to the procedure, see PARAS 621–622; and as to the Patents Court see PARA 619 et seq.
2   As to the comptroller see PARA 575.
3   Patents Act 1977 s 97(1). There are exceptions in s 97(1)(a)–(d), but they do not concern infringement or revocation: see PARA 621. CPR Pt 52 applies to appeals from the comptroller: CPR 63.16(1). Patent appeals are made to the Patents Court: CPR 63.16(2). Where CPR Pt 52 requires a document to be served, it must also be served on the comptroller: CPR 63.16(3).
4   Patents Act 1977 s 97(3).
5   Patents Act 1977 s 97(3)(b).
6   Patents Act 1977 s 97(3)(a). The provisions relevant to infringement and revocation are s 61 (see PARA 553), s 72 (see PARA 563) and s 73 (see PARA 569). Decisions under s 71 (declaration of non-infringement: see PARA 554) are not included.

572. Nature of appeal and fresh evidence. Every appeal is limited to a review of the decision of the lower court unless the appellate court considers in any given case that it would be in the interests of justice to hold a re-hearing[1]. The appellate court is extremely reluctant to reverse the judge's evaluation of the facts[2] or in matters involving the exercise of a discretion[3]. It is also slow to interfere with the judge's evaluation of mixed questions of law and fact such as obviousness and insufficiency[4] which involve no question of principle but are simply a matter of degree[5]. Fresh points not involving new evidence may be taken provided that the other party is not thereby prejudiced[6]. Fresh evidence on appeal is only admitted on special grounds such as that the evidence could not have been discovered earlier and that it would probably have an important effect on the case[7].

1   See CPR 52.11; and CIVIL PROCEDURE vol 12 (2009) PARA 1672 et seq.

2   *Biogen Inc v Medeva plc* [1997] RPC 1 at 45, HL; *Designers Guild Ltd v Russell Williams (Textiles) Ltd* [2001] FSR 113 at 122, HL (copyright). But see *United Wire Ltd v Screen Repair Services (Scotland) Ltd* [2001] RPC 439 at 459, HL (identification of 'product' subject to repairs) and *Buchanan v Alba Diagnostics Ltd* [2004] UKHL 5, [2004] RPC 681 (whether invention an 'improvement' over an earlier one).

3   *Hadmor Productions Ltd v Hamilton* [1983] 1 AC 191 at 209, [1982] 1 All ER 1042, HL. But see *Yeda Research and Development Co Ltd v Rhone-Poulenc Rorer International Holdings Inc* [2007] UKHL 43, [2008] 1 All ER 425, [2008] RPC 1 (whether amendment pleaded new case of ownership in entitlement proceedings and whether amendment time-barred by statutory time limit).

4   *Synthon BV v Smithkline Beecham* [2005] UKHL 59, [2006] 1 All ER 685, sub nom *Smithkline Beecham plc's (paroxetine methanesulfonate) patent* [2006] RPC 323.

5   *Hadmor Productions Ltd v Hamilton* [1983] 1 AC 191 at 209, [1982] 1 All ER 1042, HL. See also *Wheatley v Drillsafe Ltd* [2001] RPC 133; *Pharmacia Corpn v Merck & Co Inc* [2001] EWCA Civ 1610, [2002] RPC 775; *Merck & Co Inc's Patents* [2004] FSR 330; *SmithKline Beecham plc v Apotex Europe Ltd (No 2)* [2004] EWCA Civ 1703, [2004] FSR 559. The court is less reluctant to interfere in matters not involving mixed questions of law and fact such as the interpretation of a patent and amendment (*Pharmacia Corpn v Merck & Co Inc* [2001] EWCA Civ 1610, [2002] RPC 775) or where the issue of novelty is what the prior art describes and whether it falls within the claim (*Technip France SA's Patent* [2004] EWCA Civ 381, [2004] RPC 919).

6   See eg *Cinpres Gas Injection Ltd v Melea Ltd* [2008] EWCA Civ 9, [2008] RPC 375.

7   For the general principles applicable to the admission of fresh evidence see *Ladd v Marshall* [1954] 3 All ER 745, [1975] 1 WLR 1489, CA. A defendant who found fresh prior art pending appeal was not entitled to amend its particulars to include the prior art nor to adduce fresh evidence concerning it on appeal it being held that the proper test was whether the defendant had done all that was necessary to locate the prior art and not whether what it had done by way of prior art searches was reasonable: *Coflexip SA v Stolt Comex Seaway MS Ltd* [2001] 1 All ER 952, [2001] RPC 182, CA. See also *MMI Research Ltd v Cellxion Ltd* [2012] EWCA Civ 7, [2012] All ER (D) 181 (Jan).

10. ADMINISTRATION; PATENT ATTORNEYS; THE COURTS

(1) ADMINISTRATION

(i) The Secretary of State, the Comptroller and the UK Intellectual Property Office

573. The Secretary of State. The Secretary of State[1] appoints the comptroller[2] and may authorise anyone to act for the comptroller[3]. The Secretary of State may appoint and remove examiners and other officers and clerks for the UK Intellectual Property Office[4], and as from a day to be appointed is required to report on the Office's activities and related matters[5].

The Secretary of State has particular functions relating to applications for patents where defence or public safety is involved[6] and in connection with Crown use of patents[7].

Neither the Secretary of State nor any officer of his is to be taken to warrant the validity of any patent granted under the Patents Act 1977 or any treaty or international convention[8] to which the United Kingdom is a party[9]. Nor does the Secretary of State or any such officer incur any liability by reason of or in connection with any examination or investigation required or authorised by that Act or any such treaty or convention, or any report or other proceedings consequent on any such examination or investigation[10].

1   In any enactment, 'Secretary of State' means one of Her Majesty's principal secretaries of state: see the Interpretation Act 1978 s 5, Sch 1; and STATUTES AND LEGISLATIVE PROCESS vol 96 (2012) PARA 1209. As to the office of Secretary of State see CONSTITUTIONAL AND ADMINISTRATIVE LAW vol 20 (2014) PARA 153. None of the functions of the Secretary of State relating to the administration of the patents system, so far as exercisable in relation to Wales, have been transferred to the Welsh Ministers pursuant to the Government of Wales Act 2006 s 58 or its predecessor legislation the Government of Wales Act 1998 s 22 (repealed): see STATUTES AND LEGISLATIVE PROCESS vol 96 (2012) PARAS 1033–1044.

2   See the Patents and Designs Act 1907 s 63(1) (amended by the Trade Marks Act 1994 Sch 4 para 2(1), (3)). As to the comptroller see PARA 575.

3   See the Patents and Designs Act 1907 s 62(3) (amended by the Trade Marks Act 1994 Sch 4 para 2(1), (2)); and PARA 575.

4   Patents and Designs Act 1907 s 63(1) (as amended: see note 2). The appointments are subject to the approval of the Treasury: Patents and Designs Act 1907 s 63(1) (as so amended). The salaries of those officers and clerks are determined by the Secretary of State with the concurrence of the Treasury: Patents and Designs Act 1907 s 63(2) (amended by the Trade Marks Act 1994 Sch 4 para 2(1), (3)). As to the UK Intellectual Property Office see PARA 577. As to the Treasury see CONSTITUTIONAL AND ADMINISTRATIVE LAW vol 20 (2014) PARAS 262–265.

5   As from a day to be appointed the Secretary of State must, before the end of the period of 6 months beginning with the end of each financial year (ie a period of 12 months ending with 31 March), lay before Parliament a report setting out: (1) his opinion of the extent to which during that year the activities of the UK Intellectual Property Office have contributed to the promotion of innovation and of economic growth in the United Kingdom, and legislation relating to intellectual property has been effective in facilitating innovation and economic growth in the United Kingdom; and (2) how the promotion of innovation and of economic growth in the United Kingdom was taken into account in the case of any legislation relating to intellectual property that was passed or made during that year: Intellectual Property Act 2014 s 21(1), (4). The reference to the activities of the UK Intellectual Property Office is a reference to the activities of the comptroller and the activities of the officers and clerks of the Office (s 21(2)); and the references to legislation relating to intellectual property do not include a reference to legislation relating to plant breeders' rights or rights under the Plant Varieties Act 1997 s 7 (see AGRICULTURAL PRODUCTION AND MARKETING vol 1 (2008) PARA 1175 et seq)

(Intellectual Property Act 2014 s 21(3)). 'Legislation' includes subordinate legislation within the meaning of the Interpretation Act 1978 (see STATUTES AND LEGISLATIVE PROCESS vol 96 (2012) PARA 608), and legislation of the European Union (see EUROPEAN UNION vol 47A (2014) PARA 92 et seq): Intellectual Property Act 2014 s 21(5). At the date at which this volume states the law the Intellectual Property Act 2014 s 21 had not been brought into force.

6   See the Patents Act 1977 s 22(1), (5), (6), (7)(b) (see PARA 334) and s 118(3) (see PARA 579).

7   See the Patents Act 1977 s 56(2)(c); and PARA 404.

8   As to treaties and conventions see PARA 628 et seq.

9   Patents Act 1977 s 116(a).

10 Patents Act 1977 s 116(b).

574. Secretary of State's power to make rules. The Secretary of State[1] may make such rules as he thinks expedient for regulating the business of the UK Intellectual Property Office[2] in relation to patents and applications for patents, including European patents[3], applications for European patents and international applications for patents[4], and for regulating all matters placed by the Patents Act 1977 under the direction or control of the comptroller[5].

Without prejudice to the generality of the above, rules may make provision:

(1) prescribing the form and contents of applications for patents and other documents which may be filed at the UK Intellectual Property Office and requiring copies to be furnished of any such documents[6];

(2) regulating the procedure to be followed in connection with any proceeding or other matter before the comptroller or the UK Intellectual Property Office and authorising the rectification of irregularities of procedure[7];

(3) requiring fees to be paid in connection with any such proceeding or matter or in connection with the provision of any service by the UK Intellectual Property Office and providing for the remission of fees in the prescribed circumstances[8];

(4) regulating the mode of giving evidence in any such proceeding and empowering the comptroller to compel the attendance of witnesses and the discovery of and production of documents[9];

(5) requiring the comptroller to advertise any proposed amendments of patents and any other prescribed matters, including any prescribed steps in any such proceeding[10];

(6) providing for the appointment of advisers to assist the comptroller in any proceeding before him[11];

(7) prescribing time limits for doing anything required to be done in connection with any such proceeding by the Patents Act 1977 or the rules and providing for the alteration of any period of time specified in the Patents Act 1977 or the rules[12];

(8) giving effect to an inventor's[13] right to be mentioned[14] and providing for an inventor's waiver of any such right to be subject to acceptance by the comptroller[15];

(9) without prejudice to any other provision of the Patents Act 1977, requiring and regulating the translation of documents in connection with an application for a patent or a European patent or an international application for a patent and the filing and authentication of any such translation[16];

(10) providing for the publication and sale of documents in the UK Intellectual Property Office and of information about such documents[17].

The comptroller may set out in directions any forms the use of which is required by rules; and any such directions must be published in the prescribed manner[18].

Rules may make different provision for different cases[19]; and rules authorising the rectification of irregularities of procedure or providing for the alteration of any period of time may authorise the comptroller to extend or further extend any period notwithstanding that the period has already expired[20]. Rules must:

(a)   provide for the publication by the comptroller of the Official Journal (Patents)[21];

(b)   require or authorise the comptroller to make arrangements for the publication of reports of cases relating to patents, trade marks, registered designs, copyright and design right[22].

Provision may also be made by rules prescribing the circumstances in which the specification of an application for a patent, or of a patent, for an invention which involves the use of or concerns biological material is to be treated as disclosing the invention in a manner which is clear enough and complete enough for the invention to be performed by a person skilled in the art[23]. The rules may in particular require the applicant or patentee to take such steps as may be prescribed for the purposes of making available to the public samples of the biological material and not to impose or maintain restrictions on the uses to which such samples may be put, except as may be prescribed[24]. The rules may provide that, in such cases as may be prescribed, samples need only be made available to such persons or descriptions of persons as may be prescribed; and the rules may identify a description of persons by reference to whether the comptroller has given his certificate as to any matter[25].

1   As to the Secretary of State see PARA 573.
2   As to the UK Intellectual Property Office see PARA 577.
3   As to the meaning of 'European patent' see PARA 644 note 5. There must be paid out of moneys provided by Parliament any sums required by any minister of the Crown or government department to meet any financial obligation of the United Kingdom under the European Patent Convention or the Patent Co-operation Treaty: Patents Act 1977 s 95(1) (amended by the Patents Act 2004 Sch 2 paras 1(1), 21(a), Sch 3). Any sums received by any minister of the Crown or government department in pursuance of that Convention or that Treaty must be paid into the Consolidated Fund; Patents Act 1977 s 95(2) (amended by the Patents Act 2004 Sch 2 paras 1(1), 21(b)). As to the meaning of 'United Kingdom' see PARA 303 note 5. As to the European Patent Convention see PARA 644 et seq; and as to the Patent Co-operation Treaty (ie the Patent Co-operation Treaty (Washington, 19 June 1970; TS 78 (1978); Cmnd 7340) see PARA 629 et seq. As to the Consolidated Fund see CONSTITUTIONAL AND ADMINISTRATIVE LAW vol 20 (2014) PARA 480.
4   As to the meaning of 'international application for a patent' see PARA 630 note 1.
5   Patents Act 1977 s 123(1). As to the comptroller see PARA 575. The power to make rules under s 123 includes power to make rules regulating the business of the UK Intellectual Property Office. As to current legislation see PARA 304.
6   Patents Act 1977 s 123(2)(a).
7   Patents Act 1977 s 123(2)(b).
8   Patents Act 1977 s 123(2)(c).
9   Patents Act 1977 s 123(2)(d).
10   Patents Act 1977 s 123(2)(e).
11   Patents Act 1977 s 123(2)(g).
12   Patents Act 1977 s 123(2)(h).
13   As to the meaning of 'inventor' see PARA 301 note 3.
14   Ie conferred by the Patents Act 1977 s 13: see PARA 307.
15   Patents Act 1977 s 123(2)(i) (substituted by the Patents Act 2004 Sch 2 paras 1(1), 26(1), (2)).
16   Patents Act 1977 s 123(2)(j).
17   Patents Act 1977 s 123(2)(l).

18 Patents Act 1977 s 123(2A) (added by the Patents Act 2004 Sch 2 paras 1(1), 26(1), (3)). The comptroller must publish any directions under the Patents Act 1977 s 123(2A) setting out forms in the Official Journal (Patents) (see PARA 578): Patents Rules 2007, SI 2007/3291, r 117(c).

19 Patents Act 1977 s 123(3).

20 Patents Act 1977 s 123(3A) (added by the Copyright, Designs and Patents Act 1988 Sch 5 para 29).

21 See the Patents Act 1977 s 123(6); and PARA 578.

22 See the Patents Act 1977 s 123(7); and PARA 578.

23 Patents Act 1977 s 125A(1) (added by the Copyright, Designs and Patents Act 1988 Sch 5 para 30; and amended by SI 2000/2037). An application for revocation of a patent under the Patents Act 1977 s 72(1)(c) (see PARA 562) may be made if any of the requirements of the rules cease to be complied with: s 125A(4) (added by the Copyright, Designs and Patents Act 1988 Sch 5 para 30). In exercise of the power so conferred the Secretary of State has made the Patents Rules 2007, SI 2007/3291, r 13(1), Sch 1: see PARAS 321, 496.

24 Patents Act 1977 s 125A(2) (added by the Copyright, Designs and Patents Act 1988 Sch 5 para 30; and amended by SI 2000/2037).

25 Patents Act 1977 s 125A(3) (added by the Copyright, Designs and Patents Act 1988 Sch 5 para 30).

575. The Comptroller General of Patents, Designs and Trade Marks. The Comptroller General of Patents, Designs and Trade Marks is appointed by the Secretary of State with the approval of the Treasury[1], and acts under the superintendence and direction of the Secretary of State[2].

The UK Intellectual Property Office is under the immediate control of the comptroller[3], who exercises a wide variety of statutory functions, both of an administrative and judicial nature[4]. Any act or thing directed to be done by or to the comptroller may be done by or to any officer authorised by the Secretary of State[5]. So far as judicial functions are concerned[6], the comptroller and any such officer are subject to the review of the Council on Tribunals[7].

A certificate purporting to be signed by the comptroller and certifying that any entry which he is authorised[8] to make has or has not been made, or that any other thing which he is so authorised to do has or has not been done, is prima facie evidence of the matters so certified[9].

The comptroller may appoint an adviser to assist him in any proceeding before him and must settle any question or instructions to be submitted or given to the adviser[10].

If the comptroller acts illegally the High Court may intervene by judicial review[11].

The Arbitration Act 1996[12] does not apply to any proceedings before the comptroller under the Patents Act 1977[13].

1 Patents and Designs Act 1907 s 63(1) (amended by the Trade Marks Act 1994 Sch 4 para 2(1), (3)(a)). As to the Secretary of State see PARA 573. As to the Treasury see CONSTITUTIONAL AND ADMINISTRATIVE LAW vol 20 (2014) PARAS 262–265.

2 Patents and Designs Act 1907 s 62(2) (amended by the Trade Marks Act 1994 Sch 4 para 2(1), (2)).

3 Patents and Designs Act 1907 s 62(2) (as amended: see note 2). As to the UK Intellectual Property Office see PARA 577.

4 As to appeals from the comptroller see PARA 621.

5 Patents and Designs Act 1907 s 62(3) (amended by the Trade Marks Act 1994 Sch 4 para 2(1), (2)).

6 See the Tribunals and Inquiries Act 1992 s 14(1) (which excludes executive functions from the control exercised by that Act); and JUDICIAL REVIEW vol 61 (2010) PARA 646.

7 See the Tribunals and Inquiries Act 1992 s 1(1), Sch 1 para 34. Procedural rules may be made only after consultation with the council: see s 8.

8 Ie under the Patents Act 1977 or the Patents Rules 2007, SI 2007/3291. As to current legislation see PARA 304.

9   Patents Act 1977 s 32(10) (substituted by the Patents, Designs and Marks Act 1986 Sch 1 para 4). As to the register as evidence see the Patents Act 1977 s 32(11); and PARA 588. A person may apply on Patents Form 23 for a certificate which certifies that an entry has or has not been made in the register or something which the comptroller is authorised to do has or has not been done: Patents Rules 2007, SI 2007/3291, r 46(3).

10   Patents Rules 2007, SI 2007/3291, r 102.

11   See PARA 625.

12   Ie the Arbitration Act 1996 Pt I (ss 184): see ARBITRATION vol 2 (2008) PARA 1209 et seq.

13   Patents Act 1977 s 130(8) (amended by the Arbitration Act 1996 Sch 3 para 33).

576. Annual report. The comptroller[1] must make an annual report and lay it before both Houses of Parliament[2] before 1 December in every financial year[3]. The report is made with respect to the execution of the Patents Act 1977 and the discharge of the comptroller's functions under the European Patent Convention[4] and the Patent Co-operation Treaty[5], and must include an account of all fees, salaries and allowances, and other money received and paid by him under that Act, that convention and that treaty during the previous financial year[6].

1   As to the comptroller see PARA 575.

2   As to the laying of documents before Parliament see STATUTES AND LEGISLATIVE PROCESS vol 96 (2012) PARA 1052.

3   Patents Act 1977 s 121 (amended by the Patents Act 2004 Sch 2 paras 1(1), 25, Sch 3).

4   As to this convention see PARA 644.

5   As to the Patent Co-operation Treaty (Washington, 19 June 1970; TS 78 (1978); Cmnd 7340) see PARA 629 et seq.

6   Patents Act 1977 s 121 (as amended: see note 3).

577. The UK Intellectual Property Office. The issuing of patents is the responsibility of the UK Intellectual Property Office (an operating name of the Patent Office), which is under the immediate control of the comptroller[1]. The UK Intellectual Property Office has a seal, impressions of which are judicially noticed and are to be admitted in evidence[2]. The comptroller may give directions specifying the hour at which the office is taken to be closed, and the days which are excluded days, for the purposes of the public transaction of business[3]. Any business done on any day after the hour so specified in relation to business of that class, or on a day which is an excluded day in relation to business of that class, is taken to have been done on the next following day which is not an excluded day; and, where the time for doing anything expires on an excluded day, that time is extended to the next following day which is not an excluded day[4]. The register of patents is kept at the UK Intellectual Property Office[5]. Unauthorised use of the words 'Patent Office' is an offence[6].

1   Patents and Designs Act 1907 s 62(2) (amended by the Trade Marks Act 1994 Sch 4 para 2(1), (2)). As to the comptroller see PARA 575.

2   Patents and Designs Act 1907 s 64.

3   Patents Act 1977 s 120(1) (amended by the Patents Act 2004 Sch 2 paras 1(1), 24(1), (2)(a), (b)). Directions under the Patents Act 1977 s 120 must be published in the prescribed manner: s 120(3) (added by the Patents Act 2004 Sch 2 paras 1(1), 24(1), (3)). The comptroller must publish any directions given under the Patents Act 1977 s 120(1) specifying hours of business or excluded days in the Official Journal (Patents) (see PARA 578): Patents Rules 2007, SI 2007/3291, r 117(b).

4   Patents Act 1977 s 120(2).

5   See the Patents Act 1977 s 32(1), (5); and PARA 583. As to the register generally see PARA 583 et seq.

6   See the Patents Act 1977 s 112; and PARA 610.

578. Publications and library. The comptroller[1] must publish 'The Official Journal (Patents)'[2], containing: (1) particulars of applications for and grants of patents and of other proceedings under the Patents Act 1977; (2) any directions specifying hours of business or excluded days[3]; (3) any directions setting out forms[4]; and (4) any other information that the comptroller considers to be generally useful or important[5]. The comptroller must make arrangements for the publication of reports of cases relating to patents, trade marks, registered designs and design right decided by him and of cases relating to patents, trade marks, registered designs, copyright and design right decided by any court or body, whether in the United Kingdom[6] or elsewhere[7]. The comptroller may also arrange for the publication and sale of copies of documents, in particular, specifications of patents and applications for patents in the UK Intellectual Property Office[8]. There is kept at the UK Intellectual Property Office an extensive library of United Kingdom and foreign patent specifications and of technical books and periodicals. The UK Intellectual Property Office publishes and sells copies of its Manual of Patent Practice[9].

1   As to the comptroller see PARA 575.
2   Patents Rules 2007, SI 2007/3291, r 117.
3   Ie under the Patents Act 1977 s 120(1): see PARA 577.
4   Ie under the Patents Act 1977 s 123(2A): see PARA 574.
5   Patents Act 1977 s 123(6); Patents Rules 2007, SI 2007/3291, r 117. The other proceedings referred to relate to patents other than proceedings for infringement and revocation (which are not under the Patents Act 1977) and any UK Intellectual Property Office proceedings or application requiring to be advertised. Among the matters required to be advertised in the Journal are notice of, and the comptroller's acceptance of, an offer to surrender a patent (see s 29(3); and PARA 358), the restoration of a lapsed patent (see r 40(9); and PARA 355), notice of an entry in the register that licences are to be available as of right (see r 43(2); and PARA 391) and proposed corrections of errors in patents or applications (see r 105(6); and PARA 353). As to the UK Intellectual Property Office see PARA 577.
6   As to the meaning of 'United Kingdom' see PARA 303 note 5.
7   Patents Act 1977 s 123(7) (amended by the Copyright, Designs and Patents Act 1988 Sch 7 para 22); Patents Rules 2007, SI 2007/3291, r 118.
8   Patents Act 1977 s 123(2)(l), (3); Patents Rules 2007, SI 2007/3291, r 119.
9   An updated Manual of Patent Practice was issued on 1 October 2014.

579.   Request for information as to patents and inspection of documents.
After publication of an application for a patent[1], the comptroller[2] must upon request and payment of the prescribed fee[3] give the person making the request such information, and permit him to inspect such documents, relating to the application as may be specified in the request, subject to any prescribed restrictions[4]. Until an application for a patent is published, documents or information constituting or relating to the application may not be published or communicated to any person by the comptroller without the applicant's consent[5].

The prescribed restrictions are as follows[6]. No document[7] may be inspected:
   (1)   where that document was prepared by the comptroller, an examiner or the UK Intellectual Property Office for internal use only[8];
   (2)   where the specified circumstances[9] exist, before the end of the period of 14 days beginning immediately after the date of the notification[10];
   (3)   where that document is a request or application for information[11]; or
   (4)   where that document includes matter which in the comptroller's opinion disparages any person in a way likely to damage him, or the inspection of which would in his opinion be generally expected to encourage offensive, immoral or anti-social behaviour[12].

Unless in a particular case the comptroller otherwise directs, no document may be inspected:

(a)   where that document was filed at the UK Intellectual Property Office in connection with an application for compensation of an employee[13];

(b)   where that document is treated as a confidential document[14];

(c)   where that document was prepared by the comptroller, an examiner or the UK Intellectual Property Office other than for internal use, and it contains information which the comptroller considers should remain confidential[15];

(d)   where that document relates to an international application for a patent and the International Bureau would not be permitted to allow access to that document under the Patent Co-operation Treaty[16]; or

(e)   where the comptroller has accepted a person's application to waive the right to be mentioned[17], and that person's name and address can be identified from that document as those of the inventor or of the person believed to be the inventor (or, as the case may be, his address can be so identified)[18].

Where a person is notified that an application for a patent has been made but not published[19], and that, if the patent is granted, the applicant will bring proceedings against that person in the event of his doing any act specified in the notification after the application is published, that person may make a request[20] for information and inspection of documents[21] even though the application has not been published[22]. Similarly, where an application for a patent is filed but not published, and a new application is filed in respect of any part of the subject matter of the earlier application, and is published, any person may make a request[23] for information and inspection of documents relating to the earlier application[24].

A person may request to be notified of any of the following events in relation to an application for a patent or in relation to a patent[25]:

(i)   an applicant requesting, or failing to request, a substantive examination before the end of the prescribed period[26];

(ii)   the application being published[27];

(iii)   the notice of grant of the patent being published[28];

(iv)   the application being terminated or withdrawn[29];

(v)   a request for an opinion as to validity or infringement[30];

(vi)   the patent ceasing to have effect[31];

(vii)   the renewal fee and any additional fee being paid during the specified period[32];

(viii)   an application being made for the restoration of the patent which has ceased to have effect[33];

(ix)   an entry being made in the register[34];

(x)   a document becoming available for inspection[35] (by reason of a prescribed restriction no longer applying to the document)[36];

(xi)   an application to register a transaction, instrument or event being made[37];

(xii)   a matter being published in the Official Journal (Patents)[38].

Where a person has made such a request, the comptroller must notify him that the relevant event has occurred as soon as practicable after the event[39]. However, the comptroller must not give him information or permit him to inspect a document unless he would be entitled to such information or to inspect such a document under the provisions set out above[40].

Rules of court must make provision empowering the court[41] in any proceedings before it under the Patents Act 1977, on or without the application of any party, to order the UK Intellectual Property Office to inquire into and report on any question of fact or opinion[42]. Where the court makes such an order on the application of a party, the fee payable to the UK Intellectual Property Office is at such rate as may be determined in accordance with rules of court and is a cost of the proceedings unless otherwise ordered by the court[43]. Where the court makes such an order of its own motion, the fee payable to the UK Intellectual Property Office is at such rate as may be determined by the Lord Chancellor with the approval of the Treasury and must be paid out of money provided by Parliament[44].

1	Ie under the Patents Act 1977 s 16: see PARA 326.
2	As to the comptroller see PARA 575.
3	A person may apply to the comptroller for a certified or uncertified copy of any relevant document and, on payment of a prescribed fee, he is entitled to such a copy: Patents Rules 2007, SI 2007/3291, r 48(1), (2). No fee is currently prescribed for these purposes. A person is not entitled to a copy of a relevant document where it is not available for inspection under the Patents Act 1977 s 118 or where making or providing such a copy would infringe copyright: Patents Rules 2007, SI 2007/3291, r 48(3). For these purposes, a relevant document is any of the following: (1) an application for a patent which has been published; (2) a specification of a patent; (3) any other document, or extract from any such document, kept at the UK Intellectual Property Office: r 48(4). An application under r 48(1) or (2) must be made on Patents Form 23: Patents Rules 2007, SI 2007/3291, r 48(5). As to the UK Intellectual Property Office see PARA 577.
4	Patents Act 1977 s 118(1). Section 118 does not entitle persons to demand the date of withdrawal of an unpublished application: see *Haberman v Comptroller-General of the Patent Office* [2003] EWHC 430 (Pat), [2004] RPC 414.
5	Patents Act 1977 s 118(2). Section 118(2) does not, however, prevent the comptroller from sending such information to the European Patent Office in accordance with any provision of the European Patent Convention (see PARA 644) (Patents Act 1977 s 118(3)(a)) or publishing or communicating to others any prescribed bibliographic information about an unpublished application for a patent (s 118(3)(b)). The bibliographic data so prescribed are: (1) the name of the applicant; (2) the title of the invention; (3) the number of the application; (4) the date of filing of the application; (5) where a declaration has been made for the purposes of s 5(2) (see PARA 310), the date of filing of each earlier relevant application specified in the declaration, its application number and the country it was filed in or in respect of; (6) where an application has been terminated or withdrawn, that information; and (7) where a transaction, instrument or event mentioned in s 32(2)(b) (see PARA 583) or s 33(3) (see PARA 586) is notified to the comptroller, that information: Patents Rules 2007, SI 2007/3291, r 55.
	The Patents Act 1977 s 118(2) does not prevent the Secretary of State from inspecting or authorising the inspection of an application for a patent or any connected documents under s 22(6) (see PARA 334): s 118(3) (amended by the Copyright, Designs and Patents Act 1988 Sch 5 para 28). As to the Secretary of State see PARA 573.
	The Patents Act 1977 s 118(2) also does not prevent the comptroller from sending any patent office outside the United Kingdom (ie an organisation which carries out, in relation to patents, functions of the kind carried out at the UK Intellectual Property Office) such information about unpublished applications for patents as that office requests: s 118(3)(aa), (3A)–(3C) (s 118(3)(aa), (3A)–(3C) added by the Intellectual Property Act 2014 s 18). Information may not be sent to a patent office in reliance on the Patents Act 1977 s 118(3)(aa) otherwise than in accordance with the working arrangements that the comptroller has made for that purpose with that office: s 118(3A) (as so added). Those arrangements must include provision for ensuring that the confidentiality of information of the kind referred to in s 118(3)(aa) sent by the comptroller to the patent office in question is protected: s 118(3B) (as so added).
6	Patents Rules 2007, SI 2007/3291, r 51(1). The prescribed restrictions for the purposes of the Patents Act 1977 s 118(1) are those set out in the Patents Rules 2007, SI 2007/3291, r 51(2), (3): r 51(1).
7	References to a document include part of a document: Patents Rules 2007, SI 2007/3291, r 51(4).
8	Patents Rules 2007, SI 2007/3291, r 51(2)(a).
9	Ie the circumstances specified in the Patents Act 1977 s 118(4).

10 Patents Rules 2007, SI 2007/3291, r 51(2)(b) (amended by SI 2011/2052). Notification is under the Patents Rules 2007, SI 2007/3291, r 52(2): see note 20.

11 Patents Rules 2007, SI 2007/3291, r 51(2)(c). The request or application is one made under the Patents Act 1977 s 118 or the Patents Rules 2007, SI 2007/3291, r 46(2) (see PARA 575), r 48(2) (see PARA 579) or r 54(1) (see note 25).

12 Patents Rules 2007, SI 2007/3291, r 51(2)(d).

13 Patents Rules 2007, SI 2007/3291, r 51(3)(a). Applications for compensation of an employee are made under the Patents Act 1977 s 40(1), (2) or s 41(8): see PARAS 369–370.

14 Patents Rules 2007, SI 2007/3291, r 51(3)(b). Documents are treated as confidential under r 53: see PARA 580.

15 Patents Rules 2007, SI 2007/3291, r 51(3)(c).

16 Patents Rules 2007, SI 2007/3291, r 51(3)(d). As to the Patent Co-operation Treaty (ie the Patent Co-operation Treaty (Washington, 19 June 1970; TS 78 (1978); Cmnd 7340) see PARA 629 et seq. As to the International Bureau see PARA 630.

17 Ie under the Patents Rules 2007, SI 2007/3291, r 11(1)(a), (b): see PARA 307.

18 Patents Rules 2007, SI 2007/3291, r 51(3)(e).

19 Ie under the Patents Act 1977 s 16: see PARA 326.

20 Where the circumstances specified in the Patents Act 1977 s 118(4) exist, a request under s 118(1) must be accompanied by evidence verifying their existence: Patents Rules 2007, SI 2007/3291, r 52(1). The comptroller must notify the applicant for the patent of any request: r 52(2). The notification must be accompanied by a copy of the request and the accompanying evidence: r 52(3). The applicant may, before the end of the period of 14 days beginning immediately after the date of the notification, inform the comptroller that the circumstances specified in the Patents Act 1977 s 118(4) do not exist; otherwise the comptroller may treat him as accepting that those circumstances exist: Patents Rules 2007, SI 2007/3291, r 52(4) (amended by SI 2011/2052). The comptroller does not have the power to impose confidentiality restrictions on the inspection: *Buralls of Wisbech Ltd's Application* [2004] RPC 285.

21 Ie under the Patents Act 1977 s 118(1).

22 Patents Act 1977 s 118(4).

23 See note 20.

24 Patents Act 1977 s 118(5).

25 Patents Rules 2007, SI 2007/3291, r 54(1). A request must be made on Patents Form 49: r 54(1). A request on Patents Form 49 must be for information regarding a single event only Patents Rules 2007, SI 2007/3291, r 54(4).

26 Patents Rules 2007, SI 2007/3291, r 54(5)(a). The period is that prescribed for the purposes of the Patents Act 1977 s 18(1): see PARA 328.

27 Patents Rules 2007, SI 2007/3291, r 54(5)(b).

28 Patents Rules 2007, SI 2007/3291, r 54(5)(c). Notice of grant of a patent is published under the Patents Act 1977 s 24: see PARA 337.

29 Patents Rules 2007, SI 2007/3291, r 54(5)(d).

30 Patents Rules 2007, SI 2007/3291, r 54(6)(a). A request for an opinion is made under the Patents Act 1977 s 74A: see PARA 517.

31 Patents Rules 2007, SI 2007/3291, r 54(6)(b). A patent ceases to have effect by reason of non-payment of renewal fees: see the Patents Act 1977 s 25(3); and PARA 339.

32 Patents Rules 2007, SI 2007/3291, r 54(6)(c). The period is that specified in the Patents Act 1977 s 25(4): see PARA 339.

33 Patents Rules 2007, SI 2007/3291, r 54(6)(d).

34 Patents Rules 2007, SI 2007/3291, r 54(7)(a). As to the register see PARA 583 et seq.

35 Ie available for inspection under the Patents Act 1977 s 118.

36 Patents Rules 2007, SI 2007/3291, r 54(7)(b).

37 Patents Rules 2007, SI 2007/3291, r 54(7)(c). An application to register is made under r 47: see PARA 586.

38 Patents Rules 2007, SI 2007/3291, r 54(7)(d). As to the Journal see PARA 578.

39 Patents Rules 2007, SI 2007/3291, r 54(2).

40 Patents Rules 2007, SI 2007/3291, r 54(3).

41 As to the meaning of 'court' see PARA 619 note 1.

42 Patents Act 1977 s 99A(1) (s 99A added by the Copyright, Designs and Patents Act 1988 Sch 5 para 26). At the date at which this volume states the law no rules of court had been so made.

43 Patents Act 1977 s 99A(2) (as added: see note 42).

44 Patents Act 1977 s 99A(3) (as added: see note 42). As to the Treasury see CONSTITUTIONAL AND ADMINISTRATIVE LAW vol 20 (2014) PARAS 262–265.

580.   Direction that document is confidential.   Where a person files a document[1] at the UK Intellectual Property Office[2] or sends it to an examiner or the comptroller[3], any person may request that the document be treated as a confidential document[4].

The comptroller must refuse any request where it relates to a Patents Form or any document filed in connection with a request for an opinion as to validity or infringement[5].

A request to treat a document as confidential must be made before the end of the period of 14 days beginning immediately after the date on which the document was filed at the UK Intellectual Property Office, or received by the comptroller, an examiner or the UK Intellectual Property Office[6]. Reasons for the request must be included[7].

If it appears to the comptroller that there is good reason for the document to remain confidential, he may direct that the document is to be treated as a confidential document; otherwise he must refuse the request[8]. Where a request has been made, the document must be treated as confidential until the comptroller refuses that request or gives such a direction[9]. Where the comptroller believes there is no longer a good reason for the direction to continue in force, he must revoke it[10].

1   References to a document include part of a document: Patents Rules 2007, SI 2007/3291, r 53(7).
2   As to the UK Intellectual Property Office see PARA 577.
3   As to the comptroller see PARA 575.
4   Patents Rules 2007, SI 2007/3291, r 53(1).
5   Patents Rules 2007, SI 2007/3291, r 53(2). A request for an opinion is made under the Patents Act 1977 s 74A: see PARA 517.
6   Patents Rules 2007, SI 2007/3291, r 53(3)(a) (amended by SI 2011/2052).
7   Patents Rules 2007, SI 2007/3291, r 53(3)(b).
8   Patents Rules 2007, SI 2007/3291, r 53(5).
9   Patents Rules 2007, SI 2007/3291, r 53(4).
10 Patents Rules 2007, SI 2007/3291, r 53(6).

581.   Fees, applications and notices.   The UK Intellectual Property Office[1] is required to charge fees in almost all cases in which an application is made to it or a notice given to it[2]. Applications are required to be made on forms provided for the purpose[3].

Any notice required or authorised to be given by or under the Patents Act 1977 or the Patents Rules 2007 and any application or other document so authorised or required to be made or filed, may be given, made or filed by post[4].

1   As to the UK Intellectual Property Office see PARA 577.
2   See the Patents (Fees) Rules 2007, SI 2007/3292. Except where otherwise specified, the fees to be paid in respect of any matters arising under the Patents Act 1977 are those specified in the Patents (Fees) Rules 2007, SI 2007/3292, r 2(1), Sch 1; and, in any case where a form is required by the Patents Rules 2007, SI 2007/3291, to be used and is specified in the Patents (Fees) Rules 2007, SI 2007/3292, Sch 1 as the corresponding form in relation to any matter, that form must be accompanied by the fee specified in respect of that matter: r 2(2). Where any provision of the Patents Rules 2007, SI 2007/3291, permits payment to be made before or after the form has been filed, the fee may be paid accordingly: Patents (Fees) Rules 2007, SI 2007/3292, r 2(3). Renewal fees and additional fees (see PARA 339) are specified in rr 4, 5, Sch 2.

A person may apply to the comptroller for the remission of a fee: Patents Rules 2007, SI 2007/3291, r 106(1). As to the comptroller see PARA 575. The comptroller may remit the whole or part of a search fee where: (1) in relation to an international application for a patent (UK) a copy of the International Search Report (see PARA 630) for that application is available to the comptroller; or (2) a new application for a patent is filed as mentioned in the Patents Act 1977 s 15(9) (see PARA 316) and, in connection with the earlier application, the applicant has already paid the search fee for the invention described in the new application: Patents Rules 2007, SI 2007/3291, r 106(2). As to the meaning of 'international application for a patent (UK)' see PARA 640 note 1. The comptroller may remit the whole or part of any fee where: (a) a person has requested the comptroller or an examiner to do something in accordance with the Patents Act 1977 or the Patents Rules 2007, SI 2007/3291; and (b) the request is withdrawn before it is carried out: r 106(3). The comptroller may remit the whole or part of the fee payable in respect of a request for an opinion under the Patents Act 1977 s 74A (see PARA 517) where he has refused the request: Patents Rules 2007, SI 2007/3291, r 106(4). Where a supplementary protection certificate lapses or is declared invalid (see PARA 340 et seq), the comptroller must remit any fee which has been paid in respect of the period beginning with the next anniversary of the start date following the date the certificate lapsed or was declared invalid and ending with the date the certificate would have expired but for its lapse or invalidity: r 106(5), (6). Any decision of the comptroller under r 106 is excepted from the right of appeal conferred by the Patents Act 1977 s 97 (see PARA 571): Patents Rules 2007, SI 2007/3291, r 106(7).

3   The forms of which the use is required by the Patents Rules 2007, SI 2007/3291, are those set out pursuant to directions under the Patents Act 1977 s 123(2A) (see PARA 574) and are referred to as Patents Forms: Patents Rules 2007, SI 2007/3291, r 4(1). Such a requirement to use a form is satisfied by the use of a form which is acceptable to the comptroller and contains the information required by the form as so set out: r 4(2). Such directions must be published in the Official Journal (Patents) in accordance with r 117(c) (see PARA 574): r 4(3). Unless the comptroller otherwise directs, to file any form or other document under the Patents Act 1977 or the Patents Rules 2007, SI 2007/3291, only one side of each sheet of paper must be used and the other side must remain blank: r 4(4). But where the information is delivered in electronic form or using electronic communications a requirement under the Patents Rules 2007, SI 2007/3291, to use a form, and the requirements in r 4(4), do not apply: r 4(5). Where any form or other document is delivered to the comptroller in electronic form or using electronic communications, any requirement in the Patents Rules 2007, SI 2007/3291, for multiple copies of that form or document to be filed does not apply: r 4(6).

The forms may not be modified in substance, and must be used for a purpose akin to that for which they are primarily intended: see *Re Salles' Application* (1927) 45 RPC 61.

4   Patents Act 1977 s 119.

582.   Use of electronic communications.

The comptroller[1] may give directions as to the form and manner in which documents to be delivered to the comptroller in electronic form or using electronic communications are to be delivered to him[2]. Such a direction may provide that in order for a document to be delivered in compliance with the direction it must be accompanied by one or more additional documents specified in the direction[3]. If a document to which such a direction applies is delivered to the comptroller in a form or manner which does not comply with the direction the comptroller may treat the document as not having been delivered[4].

Where a document is delivered using electronic communications, and there is a requirement for a fee to accompany the document, the comptroller may give directions specifying how the fee is to be paid and when the fee is deemed to have been paid[5]. The comptroller may also give directions specifying that a person who delivers a document to the comptroller in electronic form or using electronic communications cannot treat the document as having been delivered unless its delivery has been acknowledged[6]. The comptroller may give directions specifying how a time of delivery is to be accorded to a document delivered to him in electronic form or using electronic communications[7].

A direction under these provisions may be given: (1) generally; (2) in relation to a description of cases specified in the direction; (3) in relation to a particular person or persons[8]; and may be varied or revoked by a subsequent direction[9].

The delivery using electronic communications to any person by the comptroller of any document is deemed to be effected, unless the comptroller has otherwise specified, by transmitting an electronic communication containing the document to an address provided or made available to the comptroller by that person as an address of his for the receipt of electronic communications; and unless the contrary is proved such delivery is deemed to be effected immediately upon the transmission of the communication[10].

A requirement of the Patents Act 1977 that something must be done in the prescribed manner is satisfied in the case of something that is done using a document in electronic form, or using electronic communications, only if the directions that apply to the manner in which it is done are complied with[11].

The provisions set out above apply to delivery at, in, with or to the UK Intellectual Property Office[12] as they apply to delivery to the comptroller[13]. They also apply to delivery by the UK Intellectual Property Office as they apply to delivery by the comptroller[14].

1   As to the comptroller see PARA 575.
2   Patents Act 1977 s 124A(1) (added by SI 2003/512; and amended by SI 2006/1229).
3   Patents Act 1977 s 124A(2) (added by SI 2003/512).
4   Patents Act 1977 s 124A(3) (added by SI 2003/512; and amended by SI 2006/1229).
5   Patents Act 1977 s 124A(4), (5) (added by SI 2003/512; and amended by SI 2006/1229).
6   Patents Act 1977 s 124A(6) (added by SI 2003/512; and amended by SI 2006/1229).
7   Patents Act 1977 s 124A(7) (added by SI 2003/512; and amended by SI 2006/1229).
8   Patents Act 1977 s 124A(8) (added by SI 2003/512).
9   Patents Act 1977 s 124A(11) (added by SI 2003/512).
10 Patents Act 1977 s 124A(13) (added by SI 2003/512; and substituted by SI 2006/1229).
11 Patents Act 1977 s 124A(14) (added by SI 2003/512; and substituted by SI 2006/1229). In the case of an application made using a document in electronic form, or using electronic communications, a reference in the Patents Act 1977 to the application not having been made in compliance with rules or requirements of the Act includes a reference to its not having been made in compliance with any applicable directions under s 124A: s 124A(15) (added by SI 2003/512; and substituted by SI 2006/1229).
12 As to the UK Intellectual Property Office see PARA 577.
13 Patents Act 1977 s 124A(16) (added by SI 2006/1229).
14 Patents Act 1977 s 124A(16) (as added: see note 13).

(ii) The Register of Patents

583. The register. The comptroller[1] must maintain the register of patents which must comply with rules duly made[2] and must be kept in accordance with such rules[3]. The public has a right to inspect the register at the UK Intellectual Property Office at all convenient times[4]; but the register need not be kept in documentary form[5]. Any person who applies for a certified copy[6] of an entry in the register or a certified extract[7] from the register is entitled to obtain such a copy or extract on payment of a fee prescribed in relation to certified copies and extracts; and rules may provide that any person who applies for an uncertified copy or extract is to be entitled to such a copy or extract on payment of a fee prescribed in relation to uncertified copies and extracts[8].

The comptroller may publish or advertise such things done[9] in relation to the register as he thinks fit[10].

Falsification of the register is an offence[11].

1   As to the comptroller see PARA 575.
2   Ie rules made by virtue of the Patents Act 1977 s 32.
3   Patents Act 1977 s 32(1) (s 32 substituted by the Patents, Designs and Marks Act 1986 Sch 1 para 4). In the Patents Act 1977, except so far as the context otherwise requires, 'register', as a noun, means the register of patents; and 'register', as a verb, means, in relation to any thing, to register or register particulars, or enter notice, of that thing in the register and, in relation to a person, means to enter his name in the register; and cognate expressions are to be construed accordingly: s 32(14) (as so substituted). As to the application of s 32 to EU compulsory licences see PARA 401.

Without prejudice to any other provision of the Patents Act 1977 or rules, rules may make provision with respect to the following matters, including provision imposing requirements as to any of those matters: (1) the registration of patents and of published applications for patents; (2) the registration of transactions, instruments or events affecting rights in or under patents and applications; (3) the entering on the register of notices concerning opinions issued, or to be issued under s 74A (see PARA 517); (4) the furnishing to the comptroller of any prescribed documents or description of documents in connection with any matter which is required to be registered; (5) the correction of errors in the register and in any documents filed at the UK Intellectual Property Office in connection with registration; and (6) the publication and advertisement of anything done under the Patents Act 1977 or rules in relation to the register: s 32(2) (as so substituted; and amended by the Patents Act 2004 s 13(3)). As to the UK Intellectual Property Office see PARA 577.

4   Patents Act 1977 s 32(5) (as substituted: see note 3). In relation to any portion of the register kept otherwise than in documentary form, the right of inspection conferred by s 32(5) is a right to inspect the material on the register: s 32(8)(a) (as substituted: see note 3).

5   Patents Act 1977 s 32(4) (as substituted: see note 3).

6   For these purposes, 'certified copy' means a copy certified by the comptroller and sealed with the seal of the UK Intellectual Property Office: Patents Act 1977 s 32(13) (as substituted: see note 3).

7   For these purposes, 'certified extract' means an extract certified by the comptroller and sealed with the seal of the UK Intellectual Property Office: Patents Act 1977 s 32(13) (as substituted: see note 3).

8   Patents Act 1977 s 32(6) (as substituted: see note 3). In relation to any portion of the register kept otherwise than in documentary form, the right to a copy or extract conferred by s 32(6) or rules is a right to a copy or extract in a form in which it can be taken away and in which it is visible and legible: s 32(8)(b) (as so substituted). Applications under s 32(6) or rules made by virtue thereof must be made in such manner as may be prescribed: s 32(7) (as so substituted). An application under s 32(6) for a certified copy of an entry in the register, or a certified extract from the register, must be made on Patents Form 23: Patents Rules 2007, SI 2007/3291, r 46(1). A person may apply on Patents Form 23 for an uncertified copy of an entry in the register or an uncertified extract from the register and, on payment of the prescribed fee, he is entitled to such a copy or extract: Patents Rules 2007, SI 2007/3291, r 46(2).

The supply of copies by the comptroller is subject to the restrictions on the making of documents available in r 51: see PARA 579.

9   Ie under the Patents Act 1977 or the Patents Rules 2007, SI 2007/3291.

10   Patents Rules 2007, SI 2007/3291, r 45.

11   See the Patents Act 1977 s 109; and PARA 609.

584. Entries in the register. When an application for a patent is published[1], the comptroller[2] must enter each of the following matters in the register:

(1)   the name of the applicant;

(2)   the name and address of the person identified as the inventor[3];

(3)   the address of the applicant and his address for service[4];

(4)   the title of the invention;

(5)   the date of filing[5] of the application for a patent;

(6)   the application number;

(7)   where a declaration has been made as to an earlier application[6], the date of filing of each earlier relevant application specified in the declaration, its application number and the country it was filed in or in respect of; and

(8)   the date of the application's publication[7].

Where an application for a patent has been published, the comptroller must enter in the register as soon as practicable after the event to which they relate the date on which a request is made by an applicant for the substantive examination[8] of his application and the date on which an application is terminated or withdrawn[9].

When the patent is granted[10], the comptroller must enter in the register: (a) the date on which the comptroller granted the patent; (b) the name of the proprietor of the patent; (c) where the address of the proprietor or his address for service was not previously entered in the register[11], that address or address for service[12].

In relation to a request for an opinion as to validity or infringement[13], the comptroller must enter in the register as soon as practicable after the event occurs a notice that such a request has been received, a notice that such a request has been refused or withdrawn or a notice that an opinion has been issued[14].

A notice of any transaction, instrument or event affecting rights in or under a patent or application[15] must be entered in the register as soon as practicable after it occurs or, if later, when the application is published[16].

The comptroller may, at any time, enter in the register such other particulars as he thinks fit[17].

Where an application is made[18] to the comptroller for an entry in the register to the effect that licences under the patent are to be available as of right, the comptroller must, if satisfied that the proprietor of the patent is not precluded by contract from granting licences under the patent, make that entry[19].

1   As to publication see PARA 326.
2   As to the comptroller see PARA 575.
3   Where a person's application under the Patents Rules 2007, SI 2007/3291, r 11(1)(a) or (b) has been accepted by the comptroller (see PARA 307), the comptroller may omit from the register his name and address (or, as the case may be, his address) as that of the person believed to be the inventor: r 44(2).
4   As to the address for service see PARA 593.
5   As to the meaning of 'date of filing' see PARA 315.
6   Ie for the purposes of the Patents Act 1977 s 5(2): see PARA 310.
7   Patents Rules 2007, SI 2007/3291, r 44(1).
8   As to this request see PARA 328.
9   Patents Rules 2007, SI 2007/3291, r 44(3).
10 As to grant see PARA 337.
11 Ie under the Patents Rules 2007, SI 2007/3291, r 44(1).
12 Patents Rules 2007, SI 2007/3291, r 44(4).
13 Ie under the Patents Act 1977 s 74A: see PARA 517.
14 Patents Rules 2007, SI 2007/3291, r 44(5) (amended by SI 2014/2401).
15 Ie as mentioned in the Patents Act 1977 s 32(2)(b) (see PARA 583) or s 33(3) (see PARA 586).
16 Patents Rules 2007, SI 2007/3291, r 44(6).
17 Patents Rules 2007, SI 2007/3291, r 44(7).
18 Ie under the Patents Act 1977 s 46(1): see PARA 391.
19 Patents Act 1977 s 46(2).

585.   Trusts and equitable interests.   No notice of any trust, whether express, implied or constructive, may be entered in the register of patents[1]; and the comptroller[2] is not affected by any such notice[3]. Equities in respect of a patent are enforced in like manner as in respect of any other personal property[4], that is, against the legal owner of the property concerned[5].

1   As to the register see PARA 583.
2   As to the comptroller see PARA 575.
3   Patents Act 1977 s 32(3) (substituted by the Patents, Designs and Marks Act 1986 Sch 1 para 4). Notice of documents constituting equitable assignments must, however, be entered if priority of interest is to be preserved: see the Patents Act 1977 s 33; and PARA 586. The document must refer specifically to the patent in question and must be one on which specific performance could be ordered: *Re Parnell's Patent* (1888) 4 TLR 197, 5 RPC 126; *Re Fletcher's Patent* (1893) 62 LJ Ch 938, 10 RPC 252.
4   See the Patents Act 1977 s 30; and PARAS 372–373.
5   See PERSONAL PROPERTY vol 80 (2013) PARA 873. In practice it is more effective to secure registration of notice of a document disclosing the existence of the equity than to rely upon more ordinary methods of enforcing it.

586. Registration of certain transactions etc. A notice of any of the following transactions, instruments and events must be entered in the register of patents[1] as soon as practicable after it occurs or, if later, when the application is published[2]:

(1)   the assignment of a patent or application for a patent, or a right in it[3];

(2)   the mortgage of a patent or application or the granting of security over it[4];

(3)   the grant or assignment or mortgage of a licence or sub-licence under a patent or application[5];

(4)   the death of the proprietor or one of the proprietors of any such patent or application or any person having a right in or under a patent or application and the vesting by an assent of personal representatives of a patent, application or any such right[6]; and

(5)   any order or directions of a court or other competent authority either:

         (a)   transferring to any person a patent or application or any right in or under it; or

         (b)   that an application should proceed in the name of any person,

         and, in either case, the event by virtue of which the court or authority had power to make any such order or give any such directions[7].

An application to register or to give notice to the comptroller[8] of any such transaction, instrument or event must be made on the prescribed form[9]; and include evidence establishing the transaction, instrument or event[10]. The application may be made at any time[11] and, it appears, by any person.

1   There is no penalty for failure to register, but such failure may result in loss of rights: see PARA 587. As to the register see PARA 583 et seq.

2   See the Patents Rules 2007, SI 2007/3291, r 44(6). Provision is thus made for an interest not created by an instrument to be registered.

3   Patents Act 1977 s 33(3)(a). As to the application of the Patents Act 1977 s 32 to EU compulsory licences see PARA 401.

4   Patents Act 1977 s 33(3)(b). As to the entry of a mortgage interest see *Van Gelder, Apsimon & Co v Sowerby Bridge United District Flour Society* (1890) 44 ChD 374, CA.

5   Patents Act 1977 s 33(3)(c).

6   Patents Act 1977 s 33(3)(d).

7   Patents Act 1977 s 33(3)(e). See *Tamglass Ltd OY v Luoyang North Glass Technology Co Ltd (No 3)* [2006] EWHC 445 (Ch), [2006] FSR 622; *Siemens Schweiz AG v Thorn Security Ltd* [2007] EWHC 2242 (Ch), [2008] RPC 58.

8   As to the comptroller see PARA 575.

9   Patents Rules 2007, SI 2007/3291, r 47(1)(a). The application must be made on Patents Form 21: see the Patents Rules 2007, SI 2007/3291, r 47(1)(a).

10   Patents Rules 2007, SI 2007/3291, r 47(1)(b). The comptroller may direct that such evidence as he may require in connection with the application be sent to him within such period as he may specify: r 47(2).

11   If, however, the application is delayed, there may be possible loss of rights: see PARA 587.

587. Effect of registration of certain transactions etc. Any person who claims to have acquired the property in a patent or an application for a patent by virtue of any of certain transactions, instruments or events[1] is entitled as against any other person who claims to have acquired that property by virtue of an earlier transaction, instrument or event if at the time of the later transaction, instrument or event[2]:

(1)   the earlier transaction, instrument or event was not registered[3]; or

(2)   in the case of any application which has not been published, notice of the earlier transaction, instrument or event had not been given to the comptroller[4]; and

(3)   in any case, the person claiming under the later transaction, instrument or event did not know of the earlier transaction, instrument or event[5].

The above provisions apply equally to the case where any person claims to have acquired any right in or under a patent or application by virtue of such a transaction, instrument or event and that right is incompatible with any such right acquired by virtue of an earlier such transaction, instrument or event[6].

Where a person becomes the proprietor or one of the proprietors or an exclusive licensee[7] of a patent by virtue of any such transaction, instrument or event and the patent is subsequently infringed, before the transaction, instrument or event is registered in proceedings for such an infringement, the court or comptroller may not award him costs or expenses unless it was so registered within the period of six months beginning with its date or, if it was not practicable to register it within that period, it was registered as soon as practicable thereafter[8].

1   Ie a transaction, instrument or event to which the Patents Act 1977 s 33 applies: see s 33(3); and PARA 586.
2   Patents Act 1977 s 33(1).
3   Patents Act 1977 s 33(1)(a). As to registration see PARA 586. Where an application for the registration of a transaction, instrument or event has been made, but the transaction, instrument or event has not been registered, then, for the purposes of s 33(1)(a), registration of the application is treated as registration of the transaction, instrument or event: s 33(4).
4   Patents Act 1977 s 33(1)(b). As to the comptroller see PARA 575.
5   Patents Act 1977 s 33(1)(c).
6   Patents Act 1977 s 33(2).
7   As to the meaning of 'exclusive licensee' see PARA 379 note 7.
8   See the Patents Act 1977 s 68 (amended by SI 2996/1028); and PARA 551.

588.   The register as evidence.   The register of patents is prima facie evidence[1] of anything required or authorised[2] to be registered[3]. A certificate purporting to be signed by the comptroller[4] and certifying that any entry which he is authorised to make has or has not been made, or that any other thing which he is so authorised to do has or has not been done, is prima facie evidence of the matters so certified[5]. Each of the following, that is to say:

(1)   a copy of an entry in the register or an extract from the register which is supplied[6];

(2)   a copy of any document kept in the UK Intellectual Property Office[7] or an extract from any such document, any specification of a patent or any application for a patent which has been published[8],

which purports to be a certified copy[9] or a certified extract[10] must be admitted in evidence without further proof and without production of any original[11].

A person may apply to the comptroller, on the prescribed form[12] and on payment of the appropriate fee[13], for a certified or uncertified copy of an application for a patent which has been published, a specification of a patent or any other document or extract from any such document kept at the UK Intellectual Property Office[14].

1   A person who causes notice of a licence to be registered may be estopped from denying the existence of the licence: *Wilson v Fenton Bros (Glasgow) Ltd* 1957 SLT (Sh Ct) 3.
2   Ie by the Patents Act 1977 or the Patents Rules 2007, SI 2007/3291.
3   Patents Act 1977 s 32(9) (s 32 substituted by the Patents, Designs and Marks Act 1986 Sch 1 para 4; Patents Act 1977 s 32(9) amended by the Criminal Justice Act 2003 Sch 37 Pt 6).
4   As to the comptroller see PARA 575.
5   Patents Act 1977 s 32(10) (as substituted: see note 3).
6   Ie under the Patents Act 1977 s 32(6): see PARA 583.
7   As to the UK Intellectual Property Office see PARA 577.

8   As to the meaning of 'published' see PARA 326 note 7.
9   As to the meaning of 'certified copy' see PARA 583 note 6.
10 As to the meaning of 'certified extract' see PARA 583 note 7.
11 Patents Act 1977 s 32(11) (as substituted (see note 3); amended by the Criminal Justice Act 2003 Sch 37 Pt 6).
12 The application must be made on Patents Form 23: see the Patents Rules 2007, SI 2007/3291, r 48(5).
13 No fee is currently prescribed for these purposes. As to fees see PARA 581.
14 See the Patents Rules 2007, SI 2007/3291, r 48; and PARA 579. A person is not entitled to such a document where it is not available for inspection under the Patents Act 1977 s 118 (see PARA 579) or where making or providing such a copy would infringe copyright: Patents Rules 2007, SI 2007/3291, r 48(3).

589.   Correction and rectification of the register.   On the application of any person aggrieved[1], the court[2] may order the register of patents to be rectified by the making, variation or deletion of any entry in it[3]; and in such proceedings the court may determine any question which it may be necessary or expedient to decide in connection with the rectification of the register[4]. Where the court makes a vesting order[5] in respect of a patent, it may go on to order rectification accordingly[6].

Any person may request that a correction[7] be entered in the register or made to any application or other document filed at the UK Intellectual Property Office in respect of: (1) his name[8]; (2) his address; or (3) his address for service[9]. If the comptroller has reasonable doubts about whether he should make the correction he must inform the person making the request of the reason for his doubts and he may require that person to file evidence in support of the request[10]. If the comptroller has no doubts, or no longer has doubts, about whether he should make the correction, he must enter the correction in the register or make it to the application or document[11].

Any person may request the correction of an error in the register or in any document filed at the UK Intellectual Property Office in connection with registration[12]. The request must be made in writing and be accompanied by sufficient information to identify the nature of the error and the correction requested[13]. If the comptroller has reasonable doubts about whether there is an error he must inform the person making the request of the reason for his doubts and he may require that person to furnish a written explanation of the nature of the error or evidence in support of the request[14]. If the comptroller has no doubts, or no longer has doubts, about whether an error has been made he must make such correction as he may agree with the proprietor of the patent (or, as the case may be, the applicant)[15].

Where a body corporate has re-registered[16] with the same name as that with which it was registered immediately before the re-registration save for the substitution as, or the inclusion as, the last part of the name of the words 'public limited company' or their Welsh equivalent or the abbreviation 'plc' or its Welsh equivalent, then references to the name of the body corporate in any application to the comptroller, in the register and in any other record kept at, or any document issued by, the UK Intellectual Property Office and relating to patents are to be treated on and after the date of such re-registration as references to the name with which the body corporate is so re-registered[17].

1   As to the meaning of 'person aggrieved' cf JUDICIAL REVIEW vol 61 (2010) PARA 656.
2   As to the meaning of 'court' see PARA 619 note 1.
3   Patents Act 1977 s 34(1). For cases in which orders for rectification have been made see *Re Green's Patent* (1857) 24 Beav 145; *Re Morey's Patent* (1858) 25 Beav 581; *Re Horsley and Knighton's Patent* (1869) LR 8 Eq 475; *Re Hutchinson's Patent, Haslett v Hutchinson* (1891)

8 RPC 457, CA; *Re Fletcher's Patent* (1893) 62 LJ Ch 938, 10 RPC 252. No order for rectification will be made if, although incorrect when proceedings were begun, the entry is no longer incorrect at the date of the hearing: *Re Manning's Patent* (1902) 20 RPC 74. Applications for rectification were also refused in *Anderson v Patent Oxonite Co Ltd* (1886) 3 RPC 279; *Re Casey's Patent, Stewart v Casey* [1892] 1 Ch 104, 9 RPC 9, CA.

4 Patents Act 1977 s 34(2). Rules of court may provide for the notification of any application under s 34 to the comptroller and for giving effect to any order of the court on the application: s 34(3). As to the comptroller see PARA 575.

5 Ie under the Trustee Act 1925 s 51: see TRUSTS AND POWERS vol 98 (2013) PARA 324 et seq.

6 *Re IG Farbenindustrie AG's Agreement* [1941] Ch 147, [1940] 4 All ER 486, 58 RPC 31; revsd [1944] Ch 41, [1943] 2 All ER 525, 60 RPC 193, CA.

7 For these purposes, a request for a correction includes a correction made for the purposes of the Patents Act 1977 s 117 (see PARA 353): Patents Rules 2007, SI 2007/3291, r 49(6).

8 A request to correct a name must be made on Patents Form 20: Patents Rules 2007, SI 2007/3291, r 49(2). As to the UK Intellectual Property Office see PARA 577.

9 Patents Rules 2007, SI 2007/3291, r 49(1). A request for the correction of an address or an address for service must be made in writing: r 49(3).

10 Patents Rules 2007, SI 2007/3291, r 49(4).

11 Patents Rules 2007, SI 2007/3291, r 49(5).

12 Patents Rules 2007, SI 2007/3291, r 50(1), which is expressed to be subject to r 49 (see the text and notes 7–11).

13 Patents Rules 2007, SI 2007/3291, r 50(2).

14 Patents Rules 2007, SI 2007/3291, r 50(3).

15 Patents Rules 2007, SI 2007/3291, r 50(4).

16 As to re-registration see COMPANIES vol 14 (2009) PARA 167 et seq.

17 Patents (Companies Re-registration) Rules 1982, SI 1982/297, r 2.

(iii) Proceedings in the UK Intellectual Property Office

590. Discretionary powers. The comptroller[1] is given[2] wide discretionary powers in the conduct of proceedings. Thus he may, if he thinks fit, authorise the rectification of any irregularity of procedure connected with any proceeding or other matter before the comptroller, an examiner or the UK Intellectual Property Office[3], extend time limits except in specified cases[4], remit fees[5] and consent to the modification of prescribed forms[6].

The comptroller has a general discretion to refuse to take, or suspend the taking of, any proceedings on or in relation to an application of an enemy[7] for a patent[8]. Under the Patents Act 1977 the comptroller has some degree of discretion in respect of the determination of questions concerning entitlement to a patent[9], amendment to acknowledge a registered trade mark[10], the prohibition or restriction of publication of information prejudicial to defence or public safety[11], the amendment of a specification after grant[12], the award of compensation to an employee-inventor[13], matters relating to licences of right and compulsory licences[14], the revocation of a patent either on application[15] or on his own initiative[16] and the conversion of a European patent application[17].

1 As to the comptroller see PARA 575.

2 Ie by the Patents Rules 2007, SI 2007/3291.

3 Patents Rules 2007, SI 2007/3291, r 107(1). As to the UK Intellectual Property Office see PARA 577. Any rectification made under r 107(1) must be made: (1) after giving the parties such notice; and (2) subject to such conditions, as the comptroller may direct: r 107(2). A period of time specified in the Patents Act 1977 or listed in the Patents Rules 2007, SI 2007/3291, r 107, Sch 4 Pts 1–3 (whether it has already expired or not) may be extended under r 107(1) if, and only if: (a) the irregularity or prospective irregularity is attributable, wholly or in part, to a default, omission or other error by the comptroller, an examiner or the UK Intellectual Property Office; and (b) it appears to the comptroller that the irregularity should be rectified: r 107(3). See PARA 597.

4 See the Patents Rules 2007, SI 2007/3291, r 108; and PARA 597.

5 See the Patents Rules 2007, SI 2007/3291, r 106; and PARA 581.

6   See the Patents Rules 2007, SI 2007/3291, r 4; and PARA 581.
7   For these purposes, 'enemy' has the meaning assigned by the Trading with the Enemy Act 1939
    (see s 2; and ARMED CONFLICT AND EMERGENCY vol 3 (2011) PARA 198): Patents, Designs,
    Copyright and Trade Marks (Emergency) Act 1939 s 10(1).
8   Patents, Designs, Copyright and Trade Marks (Emergency) Act 1939 s 4(3).
9   See the Patents Act 1977 s 8 (determination before grant: see PARAS 360–361), s 9
    (determination after grant of questions referred before grant: see PARA 360) and s 37
    (determination of right to patent after grant: see PARA 365).
10 See the Patents Act 1977 s 19(2); and PARA 329.
11 See the Patents Act 1977 s 22; and PARA 334.
12 See the Patents Act 1977 s 27; and PARAS 346–347.
13 See the Patents Act 1977 s 40; and PARA 369.
14 See the Patents Act 1977 ss 46–49, s 51; and PARA 391 et seq.
15 See the Patents Act 1977 s 72; and PARAS 562–563.
16 See the Patents Act 1977 s 73; and PARA 569.
17 See the Patents Act 1977 s 81; and PARA 655.

591.   Hearing before exercise of discretionary powers.   Without prejudice to
any rule of law, the comptroller[1] must give to any party to a proceeding before
him an opportunity of being heard[2] before the comptroller exercises adversely to
that party any discretion vested in him by the Patents Act 1977 or the Patents
Rules 2007[3].

1   As to the comptroller see PARA 575.
2   Thus he must allow a formal hearing before a senior official, followed by a formal decision. In
    addition, it is the practice to permit informal discussion of objections between applicants and
    parties and the official making the objection. Objections by and discussions with officials other
    than the comptroller cannot, however, impose requirements under the Patents Act 1977. A letter
    from the comptroller raising objections is not a formal exercise of his discretion: see *Re S's
    Application* [1977] RPC 367, CA (a case relating to an application for a patent under the
    Patents Act 1949).
3   Patents Act 1977 s 101. As to proceedings before the comptroller see the Patents Rules 2007,
    SI 2007/3291, Pt 7 (rr 73–91); and PARA 598 et seq.

592.   Contested proceedings.   There is a standard procedure for contested
proceedings, which is used, with more or less variation, in proceedings of
different sorts[1].

The comptroller[2] may make an order for security for costs or expenses against
any party to proceedings before him under the Patents Act 1977 if the prescribed
conditions are met[3] and he is satisfied that it is just to make the order, having
regard to all the circumstances of the case; and in default of the required security
being given the comptroller may treat the reference, application or notice in
question as abandoned[4].

A party to proceedings before the comptroller[5] may appear before him in
person or be represented by any person whom he desires to represent him[6]. No
offence is committed under the enactments relating to the preparation of
documents by persons not legally qualified[7] by reason only of the preparation by
any person of a document, other than a deed, for use in such proceedings[8].

The rule of law which confers privilege from disclosure in legal proceedings[9]
in respect of communications made with a solicitor or a person acting on his
behalf, or in relation to information obtained or supplied for submission to a
solicitor or a person acting on his behalf, for the purpose of any pending or
contemplated proceedings before a court in the United Kingdom extends to such
communications so made for the purpose of any pending or contemplated
proceedings before the comptroller under the Patents Act 1977 or any of the
relevant conventions[10], or proceedings before the relevant convention court[11]
under any of those conventions[12].

In proceedings before him the comptroller may by order award to any party such costs as he considers reasonable and direct how and by what parties they are to be paid[13].

1 As to proceedings before the comptroller see the Patents Rules 2007, SI 2007/3291, Pt 7 (rr 73–91); and PARA 598 et seq.
2 As to the comptroller see PARA 575.
3 The conditions prescribed for the purposes of making an order for security for costs under the Patents Act 1977 s 107(4) are that the party against whom the order is made: (1) is resident outside the United Kingdom, but not resident in a Brussels Contracting State, a Lugano Contracting State, or a Regulation State, as defined in the Civil Jurisdiction and Judgments Act 1982 s 1(3) (see CONFLICT OF LAWS vol 19 (2011) PARA 366); (2) is a company or other body (whether incorporated inside or outside the United Kingdom) and there is reason to believe that it will be unable to pay another party's costs if ordered to do so; (3) has changed his address for service with a view to evading the consequences of the litigation; (4) has furnished an incorrect address for service; or (5) has taken steps in relation to his assets that would make it difficult to enforce an order for costs against him: Patents Rules 2007, SI 2007/3291, r 85(1). As to the meaning of 'United Kingdom' see PARA 303 note 5.
4 Patents Act 1977 s 107(4) (substituted by the Patents Act 2004 s 15).
5 Ie any proceedings under the Patents Act 1977 or any treaty or international convention to which the United Kingdom is a party: s 102(1) (s 102 substituted by the Copyright, Designs and Patents Act 1988 Sch 5 para 27). In its application to proceedings in relation to applications for, or otherwise in connection with, European patents, the Patents Act 1977 s 102 has effect subject to any restrictions imposed by or under the European Patent Convention: s 102(4) (as so substituted). As to the meaning of 'European patent' see PARA 644 note 5. As to the European Patent Convention see PARA 644 et seq.
6 Patents Act 1977 s 102(1) (as substituted: see note 5). Section 102(1) has effect subject to rules made under the Copyright, Designs and Patents Act 1988 s 281 (power of comptroller to refuse to recognise certain agents: see PARA 616): Patents Act 1977 s 102(3) (as so substituted).
7 For the purposes of the Patents Act 1977 s 102(2), as it has effect in relation to England and Wales, 'the enactment relating to the preparation of documents by persons not qualified' means the Legal Services Act 2007 s 14 (offence to carry on a reserved legal activity if not entitled: see LEGAL PROFESSIONS vol 65 (2008) PARA 586)) as it applies in relation to an activity which amounts to the carrying on of reserved instrument activities within the meaning of that Act: Patents Act 1977 s 102(2A) (as substituted (see note 5); added by the Legal Services Act 2007 Sch 21 para 40(a)).
8 Patents Act 1977 s 102(2) (as substituted: see note 5). Nothing in the Patents Act 1977 s 102 is to be taken to limit any entitlement to prepare deeds conferred on a registered patent attorney by virtue of the Legal Services Act 2007: Patents Act 1977 s 102(5) (as substituted (see note 5); further substituted by the Legal Services Act 2007 Sch 21 para 40(b)).
9 For these purposes, 'legal proceedings' includes proceedings before the comptroller; and the references to legal proceedings and pending or contemplated proceedings include references to applications for a patent or a European patent and to international applications for a patent: Patents Act 1977 s 103(2).
10 For these purposes, 'relevant conventions' means the European Patent Convention and the Patent Co-operation Treaty (ie the Patent Co-operation Treaty (Washington, 19 June 1970; TS 78 (1978); Cmnd 7340) see PARA 629 et seq): Patents Act 1977 s 103(2) (amended by the Patents Act 2004 Sch 2 paras 1(1), 22, Sch 3).
11 As to the meaning of 'relevant convention court' see PARA 363 note 6.
12 Patents Act 1977 s 103(1). As to patent agents' privilege see PARA 615.
13 Patents Act 1977 s 107(1). Any costs so awarded are, if the county court so orders, recoverable under the County Courts Act 1984 s 85 (see CIVIL PROCEDURE vol 12 (2009) PARA 1283) or otherwise as if they were payable under an order of that court: s 107(2) (amended by the Tribunals, Courts and Enforcement Act 2007 Sch 13 paras 39, 43; and by the Crime and Courts Act 2013 Sch 9 para 52(1)(b), (2) (but not so as to affect the wording of the text).

593.   Evidence before the comptroller. Where under the Patents Rules 2007[1] evidence may be filed, the evidence must be by witness statement, statement of case, affidavit, statutory declaration or in any other form which would be admissible as evidence in proceedings before the court[2]. A witness statement or a statement of case may only be given in evidence if it includes a statement of truth[3]. Evidence is to be by witness statement unless the comptroller directs or any enactment requires otherwise[4].

The comptroller has the powers of a judge of the High Court as regards the attendance of witnesses and the discovery and production of documents, but he has no power to punish summarily for contempt[5].

For the purposes of any proceeding under the Patents Act 1977 or the Patents Rules 2007, an address for service[6] must be furnished by: (1) an applicant for the grant of a patent; (2) a person who makes any other application, reference or request or gives any notice of opposition under the Patents Act 1977; and (3) any person opposing such an application, reference, request or notice[7]. The proprietor of a patent, or any person who has registered any right in or under a patent or application, may furnish an address for service by notifying the comptroller[8]. Where a person has furnished an address for service, he may substitute a new address for service by notifying the comptroller[9].

Where a person has failed to furnish an address for service[10] and the comptroller has sufficient information enabling him to contact that person, the comptroller must direct that person to furnish an address for service[11]. Where such a direction has been given, the person directed, before the end of the period of two months beginning immediately after the date of the direction, must furnish an address for service[12]. Where a direction was given and the period prescribed has expired, or the comptroller had insufficient information to give a such direction and the person has failed to furnish an address for service, then: (a) in the case of an applicant for the grant of a patent, the application is treated as withdrawn; (b) in the case of a person mentioned in head (2) above, his application, reference, request or notice of opposition is treated as withdrawn; and (c) in the case of a person mentioned in head (3) above, he is deemed to have withdrawn from the proceedings[13].

1 Ie the Patents Rules 2007, SI 2007/3291: see PARA 304.
2 Patents Rules 2007, SI 2007/3291, r 87(1). A witness statement, affidavit or statutory declaration must comply with the requirements of r 14, Sch 2 Pt 1 (see PARA 314) unless the comptroller otherwise directs: r 87(4). As to the comptroller see PARA 575.
3 Patents Rules 2007, SI 2007/3291, r 87(2). For the purposes of Pt 7 (rr 73–91) a statement of truth must be dated and signed by: (1) in the case of a witness statement, the person making the statement; and (2) in any other case, the party or his legal representative: r 87(5). As to statements of truth see CIVIL PROCEDURE vol 11 (2009) PARA 613.
4 Patents Rules 2007, SI 2007/3291, r 87(3).
5 Patents Rules 2007, SI 2007/3291, r 86.
6 An address for service must be an address in the United Kingdom, another EEA state or the Channel Islands: Patents Rules 2007, SI 2007/3291, r 103(4) (substituted by SI 2009/546). As to the meaning of 'United Kingdom' see PARA 303 note 5. As to the European Economic Area (EEA) Agreement see COMPETITION vol 18 (2009) PARA 36.
7 Patents Rules 2007, SI 2007/3291, r 103(1).
8 Patents Rules 2007, SI 2007/3291, r 103(2).
9 Patents Rules 2007, SI 2007/3291, r 103(3).
10 Ie under the Patents Rules 2007, SI 2007/3291, r 103(1). 'Address for service' means an address which complies with the requirements of r 103(4) (see note 6): r 104(5) (amended by SI 2009/546).
11 Patents Rules 2007, SI 2007/3291, r 104(1).
12 Patents Rules 2007, SI 2007/3291, r 104(2) (amended by SI 2011/2052). The prescribed time limit may not be extended: see PARA 597.
13 Patents Rules 2007, SI 2007/3291, r 104(3), (4).

594. Copies available to the comptroller. Where an applicant is not required to file a copy of an application at the UK Intellectual Property Office[1] because that application or a copy of that application is available to the comptroller[2], the comptroller must make a copy (or further copy) of that application and certify it accordingly[3].

1   As to the UK Intellectual Property Office see PARA 577.
2   As to the comptroller see PARA 575.
3   Patents Rules 2007, SI 2007/3291, r 112.

595.   Translations of documents.   Subject to certain exceptions[1], where any document[2] filed at the UK Intellectual Property Office[3], or sent to the comptroller[4], is in a language other than English or Welsh it must be accompanied by a translation into English of that document[5]. Where more than one copy of the document is filed or sent, a corresponding number of translations must accompany it[6]. Where a document is not accompanied by a translation, the comptroller may, if he thinks fit, take no further action in relation to that document[7].

In relation to an international application for a patent (UK)[8], where any document which is in a language other than English or Welsh is referred to in an International Search Report or International Preliminary Report on Patentability or cited in an International Preliminary Examination Report, and the relevant report is filed at the UK Intellectual Property Office, the comptroller may direct that a translation into English of that document be filed[9]. Where such a direction is given, a translation of that document must be filed before the end of the period of two months beginning immediately after the date on which the direction is given; otherwise the comptroller may, if he thinks fit, take no further action in relation to the application[10].

Subject to the power of the comptroller to require a translation[11], where a patent application or any document related to such application is filed at the UK Intellectual Property Office or sent to the comptroller in Welsh, and is not accompanied by a translation into English, the comptroller must obtain such a translation[12].

1   The requirement for translation does not apply to the following documents: (1) where the documents filed to initiate an application for a patent include something which is or appears to be a description of the invention, the document containing that thing; (2) a priority application; (3) a copy of an application provided under the Patents Act 1977 s 15(10)(b)(ii) (see PARA 315); (4) a copy of a specification of a European patent (UK) filed in connection with an application by the proprietor to amend the specification (see PARA 652); (5) a copy of an application for a European patent (UK) provided under s 81(2)(b)(ii) (see PARA 655); (6) an international application for a patent (UK), where a translation of the application or an amendment to it is a necessary translation (see PARA 642); (7) a document referred to in the Patents Rules 2007, SI 2007/3291, r 113(5) (see the text to note 9): r 113(2).
2   A reference to a document includes a reference to a part of a document: Patents Rules 2007, SI 2007/3291, r 113(8).
3   As to the UK Intellectual Property Office see PARA 577.
4   As to the comptroller see PARA 575.
5   Patents Rules 2007, SI 2007/3291, r 113(1). As to the consequences of not filing a translation of a priority document within the prescribed time see *Mitsui Engineering & Shipbuilding Co Ltd's Application* [1984] RPC 471. As to the difficulties with translated documents see *Siemens Schweiz AG v Thorne Security Ltd* [2007] EWHC 2242 (Ch), [2008] RPC 58.
6   Patents Rules 2007, SI 2007/3291, r 113(3).
7   Patents Rules 2007, SI 2007/3291, r 113(4).
8   As to the meaning of 'international application for a patent (UK)' see PARA 640 note 1.
9   Patents Rules 2007, SI 2007/3291, r 113(5). See PARA 630.
10 Patents Rules 2007, SI 2007/3291, r 113(6) (amended by SI 2011/2052).
11 Ie under the Patents Rules 2007, SI 2007/3291, r 82(1)(b): see PARA 604.
12 Patents Rules 2007, SI 2007/3291, r 113(7).

596. Certificates. A certificate purporting to be signed by the comptroller[1] and certifying that any entry which he is authorised to make[2] has or has not been made, or that any other thing which he is so authorised to do has or has not been done, is prima facie evidence of the matters so certified[3]. A person may apply on the prescribed form[4] and on payment of the appropriate fee[5], for a certificate which certifies that something which the comptroller is authorised to do has or has not been done[6].

1 As to the comptroller see PARA 575.

2 Ie by the Patents Act 1977 or the Patents Rules 2007, SI 2007/3291.

3 Patents Act 1977 s 32(10) (s 32 substituted by the Patents, Designs and Marks Act 1986 Sch 1 para 4). As to the register of patents as evidence see PARA 588.

4 An application must be made on Patent Form 23: see the Patents Rules 2007, SI 2007/3291, r 46(3).

5 No fee is currently prescribed for these purposes.

6 Patents Rules 2007, SI 2007/3291, r 46(3)(b).

597. Extension of time limits. Many of the time limits prescribed for the purposes of patents[1] may not be extended[2]. Other time limits[3] may be extended by the comptroller[4], if he thinks fit[5], for a period of two months where the request is made upon the prescribed form[6], no previous request has been made and the request is filed before the end of the period of two months beginning immediately after the date on which the relevant period of time expired[7]. The comptroller may, if he thinks fit, extend or further extend any such period of time[8] where a request is filed on the prescribed form[9] and the person making the request has furnished evidence supporting the grounds of the request, except where the comptroller otherwise directs[10]. Each request[11] for a period of time to be extended must be made on a separate form unless each of those requests relates to the same patent or application for a patent and the grant of each of those requests would result in the expiry of all the extended periods of time on the same date, in which case those requests may be combined and made on a single form[12]. Any extension[13] must be made after giving the parties such notice, and subject to such conditions, as the comptroller may direct[14]. An extension may be granted notwithstanding the period of time prescribed by the relevant rule has expired[15].

The comptroller must extend a period specified by the comptroller in connection with an application for a patent, or a patent if the applicant or the proprietor of the patent requests him to do so and the request complies with the prescribed requirements[16].

The comptroller may certify any day as an interrupted day where: (1) there is an event or circumstance causing an interruption in the normal operation of the UK Intellectual Property Office[17]; or (2) there is a general interruption or subsequent dislocation in the postal services of the United Kingdom[18]. Any such certificate of the comptroller must be displayed in the UK Intellectual Property Office and advertised in the Official Journal (Patents)[19]. The comptroller, where the time for doing anything under the Patents Act 1977 expires on an interrupted day, must extend that time to the next following day not being an interrupted day (or an excluded day)[20].

The comptroller must extend any period of time specified in the Patents Act 1977 or the Patents Rules 2007 where he is satisfied that the failure to do something under that Act or those Rules was wholly or mainly attributable to a delay in, or failure of, a communication service[21]. Any extension must be made after giving the parties such notice, and subject to such conditions, as the comptroller may direct[22].

1　Ie the time limits prescribed by the Patents Rules 2007, SI 2007/3291, r 6(2)(b) (declaration of priority for the purposes of the Patents Act 1977 s 5(2) made after the date of filing) (see PARA 310), the Patents Rules 2007, SI 2007/3291, r 7(1) (period for making a request to the comptroller for permission to make a late declaration of priority) (see PARA 310), r 32(1) (application to reinstate a terminated application) (see PARA 333), rr 37, 38 (renewal of patents) (see PARA 339), r 40(1) (application to restore a lapsed patent) (see PARA 355), r 41A (see PARA 652), r 43(4) (application to cancel entry that licence available as of right) (see PARA 392), r 58(3) (request for a direction under the Patents Act 1977 s 81) (see PARA 655), the Patents Rules 2007, SI 2007/3291, r 59(1) (request from a foreign industrial property office for a direction under the Patents Act 1977 s 81) (see PARA 655), the Patents Rules 2007, SI 2007/3291, r 66(3) (period for making a request to the comptroller for permission to make a late declaration of priority in respect of an international application for a patent (UK)) (see PARA 310), r 76(2) (notice of opposition), except in relation to an opposition under the Patents Act 1977 s 27(5) where there are pending before the court or the comptroller proceedings in which the validity of the patent is put in issue (see PARA 599), the Patents Rules 2007, SI 2007/3291, r 77(8), (10) (opposition periods) (see PARA 600), r 104(2) (period for filing an address for service), in relation to an application for a patent (see PARA 593), r 109 (extension of time limits specified by comptroller), r 116(2) (fee for supplementary protection certificate) (see PARA 341), Sch 1 para 8(5) (new deposits of biological material) (see PARA 321): Patents Rules 2007, SI 2007/3291, r 108(1), Sch 4 Pt 1 (amended by SI 2014/2401).
2　Patents Rules 2007, SI 2007/3291, r 108(1), Sch 4 Pt 1.
3　Ie any period of time prescribed by the following provisions: the Patents Rules 2007, SI 2007/3291, r 8(1), (2) (filing of information and priority documents) (see PARA 310), r 10(3) (filing of statement of inventorship and the right to be granted a patent) (see PARA 307), r 18(1) (missing parts) (see PARA 315), r 21 (extensions for new applications) (see PARA 307), r 22(1), (2), (5) (periods prescribed for the purposes of the Patents Act 1977 ss 15(10), 17(1)) (see PARAS 315, 327), the Patents Rules 2007, SI 2007/3291, r 28(2), (3), (5) (request for substantive examination) (see PARA 328), r 30 (period for putting an application in order) (see PARA 328), r 58(4) (request under the Patents Act 1977 s 81(2)(b)(i)) (see PARA 655), the Patents Rules 2007, SI 2007/3291, r 59(3) (request under the Patents Act 1977 s 81(2)(b)(ii)) (see PARA 655), the Patents Rules 2007, SI 2007/3291, r 60 (request for substantive examination following a direction under the Patents Act 1977 s 81) (see PARA 655), the Patents Rules 2007, SI 2007/3291, r 66(1), (2) (international applications for patents: entry into national phase) (see PARA 641), r 68 (international applications for patents: altered prescribed periods) (see PARA 307), Sch 1 para 3(2) (filing of information in relation to the deposit of biological matter) (see PARA 321): Sch 4 Pt 2.
4　As to the comptroller see PARA 575.
5　Patents Rules 2007, SI 2007/3291, r 108(1).
6　A request must be filed on Patents Form 52: Patents Rules 2007, SI 2007/3291, r 108(2)(a).
7　Patents Rules 2007, SI 2007/3291, r 108(2) (amended by SI 2011/2052).
8　Ie any period of time prescribed by the rules listed in the Patents Rules 2007, SI 2007/3291, Sch 4 Pt 2: see note 3.
9　Ie on Patents Form 52: see the Patents Rules 2007, SI 2007/3291, r 108(3).
10　Patents Rules 2007, SI 2007/3291, r 108(3).
11　Ie under the Patents Rules 2007, SI 2007/3291, r 108(2) or (3).
12　Patents Rules 2007, SI 2007/3291, r 108(4).
13　Ie under the Patents Rules 2007, SI 2007/3291, r 108(1) or (3).
14　Patents Rules 2007, SI 2007/3291, r 108(5). A period of time prescribed by the following rules listed in Sch 4 Pt 3 may be extended (or further extended) for a period of two months only: r 108(5). Those rules are: r 10(3) (filing of statement of inventorship and the right to be granted a patent) (see PARA 307), r 12(3), (9) (filing of name and address and translations) (see PARAS 314, 318), r 19 (new applications filed as mentioned in the Patents Act 1977 s 15(9)) (see PARA 315), the Patents Rules 2007, SI 2007/3291, r 21(1)(a), (2)(a) (extensions for new applications) (see PARA 307), r 22 (periods prescribed for the purposes of the Patents Act 1977 ss 15(10), 17(1)) (see PARAS 315, 327), the Patents Rules 2007, SI 2007/3291, r 28 (request for substantive examination) (see PARA 328), r 30 (period for putting application in order) (see PARA 328), r 58(4) (request under the Patents Act 1977 s 81(2)(b)(i)) (see PARA 655), the Patents Rules 2007, SI 2007/3291, r 59(3) (request under the Patents Act 1977 s 81(2)(b)(ii)) (see PARA

655), the Patents Rules 2007, SI 2007/3291, r 60 (request for substantive examination following a direction under the Patents Act 1977 s 81) (see PARA 655), the Patents Rules 2007, SI 2007/3291, r 66(1), (2) (international applications for patents: entry into national phase) (see PARA 641), r 68 (international applications for patents: altered prescribed periods) (see PARA 307): Sch 4 Pt 3.

15 Patents Rules 2007, SI 2007/3291, r 108(6). No extension may be granted in relation to the periods of time prescribed by the rules listed in Sch 4 Pt 3 (see note 14) after the end of the period of two months beginning immediately after the period of time as prescribed (or previously extended) has expired: r 108(7).

16 Patents Act 1977 s 117B(1), (2) (s 117B added by SI 2004/2357). A request under the Patents Act 1977 s 117B(2) must be: (1) made in writing; and (2) made before the end of the period prescribed by the Patents Rules 2007, SI 2007/3291, r 109(2): r 109(1). The period prescribed for the purposes of the Patents Act 1977 s 117B(3) is two months beginning immediately after the expiry of the period to which s 117B(2) applies: Patents Rules 2007, SI 2007/3291, r 109(2). An extension of a period under the Patents Act 1977 s 117B(2) expires at the end of the period prescribed for these purposes or, if sooner, at the end of the period prescribed for the purposes of s 20 (see PARA 331): s 117B(3) (as so added). If a period has already been extended under s 117B(2), that provision does not apply in relation to it again, and the comptroller may further extend the period subject to such conditions as he thinks fit: s 117B(4) (as so added). The provisions of s 117B(2) do not apply to a period specified in relation to proceedings before the comptroller: s 117B(5) (as so added).

17 Patents Rules 2007, SI 2007/3291, r 110(1)(a). As to the UK Intellectual Property Office see PARA 577.

18 Patents Rules 2007, SI 2007/3291, r 110(1)(b). As to the meaning of 'United Kingdom' see PARA 303 note 5.

19 Patents Rules 2007, SI 2007/3291, r 110(2). As to the Journal see PARA 578.

20 Patents Rules 2007, SI 2007/3291, r 110(3). This may be retrospective: see *Omron Tateisi Electronic Co's Application* [1981] RPC 125. See also *Armaturjonsson AB's Application* [1985] RPC 213.

21 Patents Rules 2007, SI 2007/3291, r 111(1). 'Communication service' means a service by which documents may be sent and delivered and includes post, electronic communications, and courier: Patents Rules 2007, SI 2007/3291, r 111(3).

22 Patents Rules 2007, SI 2007/3291, r 111(2).

(iv) Proceedings Heard before the Comptroller

598.   Application of procedural rules, overriding objective and publication of notices. Procedural rules govern certain proceedings before the comptroller[1] in relation to applications, references and requests[2] and oppositions[3]. Rules also apply to proceedings heard before the comptroller under the Patents Act 1977[4].

The procedural rules[5] set out a procedural code with the overriding objective of enabling the comptroller to deal with cases justly[6]. Dealing with a case justly includes, so far as is practicable:

(1)   ensuring that the parties are on an equal footing[7];

(2)   saving expense[8];

(3)   dealing with the case in ways which are proportionate to the amount of money involved, to the importance of the case, to the complexity of the issues and to the financial position of each party[9];

(4)   ensuring that it is dealt with expeditiously and fairly[10]; and

(5)   allotting to it an appropriate share of the resources available to the comptroller, while taking into account the need to allot resources to other cases[11].

The comptroller must seek to give effect to the overriding objective when he exercises any power given to him in relation to proceedings before him[12] or interprets any procedural rule[13]. The parties are required to help the comptroller to further the overriding objective[14].

The comptroller must advertise in the Official Journal (Patents)[15] any event to which it is possible to object under any of the oppositions which start proceedings[16] or the oppositions after proceedings have started[17].

1   As to the comptroller see PARA 575.

2   Ie proceedings under the provisions mentioned in the Patents Rules 2007, SI 2007/3291, r 73, Sch 3 Pt 1: r 73(1)(a). Those provisions are: the Patents Act 1977 s 8(1) (reference regarding entitlement in relation to a patent under the Patents Act 1977) (see PARA 361), s 10 (request for directions for handling a joint application) (see PARA 360), s 11(5) (reference regarding entitlement to a licence to continue working after transfer of application) (see PARA 362), s 12(1) (reference regarding entitlement in relation to a foreign or convention patent) (see PARA 363), s 12(4) (reference involving joint applications on entitlement in relation to a foreign or convention patent) (see PARA 363), s 13(3) (application to comptroller to remove person mentioned as inventor) (see PARA 307), s 37(1) (determination of right to patent after grant) (see PARA 365), s 38(5) (reference regarding entitlement to a licence to continue working after transfer of patent) (see PARA 367), s 40 (application for compensation by an employee) (see PARA 369), s 41(8) (application to vary order for compensation for certain inventions) (see PARA 370), s 46(3) (application to settle terms of licence available as of right) (see PARA 391), s 47(3) (application to cancel licence available as of right) (see PARA 392), s 48(1) (application for a compulsory licence) (see PARA 394), s 50A(2) (application following merger and market investigation) (see PARA 397), s 51(1) (application by minister following report of Competition Commission) (see PARA 398), s 52(2)(a) (application to cancel compulsory licence) (see PARA 399), s 61(3) (reference on question of infringement before the comptroller) (see PARA 522), s 71 (declaration of non-infringement) (see PARA 554), s 72 (application to revoke patent) (see PARA 562); the Patents Rules 2007, SI 2007/3291, r 10(2) (application to be mentioned as inventor) (see PARA 307), r 88(1) (application to hold proceedings in Scotland), Sch 1 para 7(4) (notice of objection to expert) (see PARA 321); specified provisions of Parliament and Council Regulation (EC) 816/2006 (OJ L157, 9.6.2006, p 1) on compulsory licensing of patents relating to the manufacture of pharmaceutical products for export to countries with public health problems (the 'Compulsory Licensing Regulation') relating to an application to terminate an EU compulsory licence, an application for an EU compulsory licence, an application to access books and records, an application for a review of an EU compulsory licence, or an application for the modification of an EU compulsory licence (see PARA 401); provisions of Parliament and Council Regulation (EC) 469/2009 (OJ L152, 16.6.2009, p 1) concerning the creation of a supplementary protection certificate for medicinal products (the 'Medicinal Products Regulation') relating to a request to review the lapse of supplementary protection certificate, an application for a declaration of invalidity of a supplementary protection certificate, or an application for the revocation of an extension of the duration of a supplementary protection certificate (see PARA 340); and specified provisions of Parliament and Council Regulation (EC) 1107/2009 (OJ L309, 24.11.2009, p 1) concerning the placing of plant protection products on the market (the 'Plant Protection Products Regulation').

3   Ie oppositions under the provisions mentioned in the Patents Rules 2007, SI 2007/3291, Sch 3 Pt 2: r 73(1)(b). Those provisions are: the Patents Act 1977 s 27(5) (opposition to amendment of specification after grant) (see PARA 347), s 29(2) (opposition to surrender of patent) (see PARA 358), s 47(6) (opposition to cancellation of licence available as of right), where the application was made by the proprietor of the patent (see PARA 392), s 75(2) (opposition to amendment during infringement or revocation proceedings) (see PARA 347), s 117(2) (opposition to correction of error in patents and applications) (see PARA 353).

4   Patents Rules 2007, SI 2007/3291, r 73(2). The rules listed in Sch 3 Pt 4 apply to such proceedings: r 73(2). The rules are: r 74 (overriding objective), r 79 (copies of documents) (see PARA 602), r 80(2)–(6) (evidence and the hearing) (see PARA 603), r 81 (alteration of time limits) (see PARA 604), r 82 (general powers of the comptroller in relation to proceedings before him) (see PARA 606), r 84 (hearings in public) (see PARA 606), r 87 (evidence in proceedings before the comptroller) (see PARA 593).

5   Ie the rules set out in the Patents Rules 2007, SI 2007/3291, Pt 7 (rr 73–91).

6   Patents Rules 2007, SI 2007/3291, r 74(1).

7   Patents Rules 2007, SI 2007/3291, r 74(2)(a).

8   Patents Rules 2007, SI 2007/3291, r 74(2)(b).

9   Patents Rules 2007, SI 2007/3291, r 74(2)(c). As to security for costs or expenses see r 85; and PARA 592.

10   Patents Rules 2007, SI 2007/3291, r 74(2)(d).

11   Patents Rules 2007, SI 2007/3291, r 74(2)(e).

12 Ie any power given to the comptroller by the Patents Rules 2007, SI 2007/3291, Pt 7.
13 Patents Rules 2007, SI 2007/3291, r 74(3).
14 Patents Rules 2007, SI 2007/3291, r 74(4).
15 Where the comptroller determines that no person could reasonably object to the correction, no advertisement need be published: Patents Rules 2007, SI 2007/3291, rr 75, 105(5).
16 Ie any of the provisions mentioned in the Patents Rules 2007, SI 2007/3291, Sch 3 Pt 2: see note 3.
17 Patents Rules 2007, SI 2007/3291, r 75. The oppositions after proceedings have started are under the Patents Act 1977 s 47(6) (opposition to cancellation of licence available as of right), where the application was made by a person other than the proprietor of the patent (see PARA 392), s 52(1) (opposition to an application for compulsory licence or under s 50A or s 51) (see PARAS 397–398), s 52(2)(b) (opposition to an application to cancel a compulsory licence) (see PARA 399): Patents Rules 2007, SI 2007/3291, Sch 3 Pt 3.

599. Starting proceedings. Proceedings are started when a person files in duplicate the relevant form[1] and his statement of grounds[2].

Any person may give notice of opposition to the amendment of a patent[3] before the end of the period of two weeks beginning immediately after the date of the advertisement of proposed amendment in the Official Journal (Patents)[4]. In the case of other oppositions[5], any person may give notice of opposition before the end of the period of four weeks beginning immediately after the date of the advertisement in the journal[6].

A statement of grounds must:

(1)   include a concise statement of the facts and grounds on which the claimant relies[7];

(2)   where applicable[8], include the grounds of objection to the draft licence[9];

(3)   where appropriate, include the period or terms of the licence which he believes are reasonable[10];

(4)   specify the remedy which he seeks[11];

(5)   where it accompanies an application under the Compulsory Licensing Regulation[12], include any information required by that Regulation[13];

(6)   be verified by a statement of truth[14]; and

(7)   comply with the statutory requirements for documents[15].

1 'Relevant form' means: (1) in relation to applications or requests under the provisions of Parliament and Council Regulation (EC) 469/2009 (OJ L152, 16.6.2009, p 1) concerning the creation of a supplementary protection certificate for medicinal products or Parliament and Council Regulation (EC) 1107/2009 (OJ L309, 24.11.2009, p 1) concerning the placing of plant protection products on the market, mentioned in the Patents Rules 2007, SI 2007/3291, Sch 3 Pt 1 (see PARA 598 note 2), Patents Form SP3; (2) in relation to applications, references or requests under any other provision mentioned in the Patents Rules 2007, SI 2007/3291, Sch 3 Pt 1, Patents Form 2; and (3) in relation to oppositions under the provisions mentioned in the Patents Rules 2007, SI 2007/3291, Sch 3 Pt 2 (see PARA 598 note 3), Patents Form 15: Patents Rules 2007, SI 2007/3291, r 76(3).
2 Patents Rules 2007, SI 2007/3291, r 76(1). 'Statement of grounds' means a statement filed by the claimant; and 'claimant' means a person who starts proceedings or is treated as starting proceedings under r 76(1): r 73(3).
3 Ie in the case of opposition under the Patents Act 1977 s 75(2): see PARA 347.
4 Patents Rules 2007, SI 2007/3291, r 76(2)(a) (amended by SI 2011/2052). As to the Journal see PARA 578.
5 Ie any of the other oppositions mentioned in the Patents Rules 2007, SI 2007/3291, Sch 3 Pt 2.
6 Patents Rules 2007, SI 2007/3291, r 76(2)(b) (amended by SI 2011/2052). The prescribed time limit may not be extended: see PARA 597.
7 Patents Rules 2007, SI 2007/3291, r 76(4)(a).
8 Ie in the case of the Patents Rules 2007, SI 2007/3291, r 89(5): see PARA 391.
9 Patents Rules 2007, SI 2007/3291, r 76(4)(b).
10 Patents Rules 2007, SI 2007/3291, r 76(4)(c).
11 Patents Rules 2007, SI 2007/3291, r 76(4)(d).

12 Ie Parliament and Council Regulation (EC) 816/2006 (OJ L157, 9.6.2006, p 1) on compulsory licensing of patents relating to the manufacture of pharmaceutical products for export to countries with public health problems (the 'Compulsory Licensing Regulation'): see PARA 401.
13 Patents Rules 2007, SI 2007/3291, r 76(4)(e).
14 Patents Rules 2007, SI 2007/3291, r 76(4)(f). 'Statement of truth' means a statement that the person making the statement believes that the facts stated in a particular document are true: r 73(3).
15 Patents Rules 2007, SI 2007/3291, r 76(4)(g). The statutory requirements for documents are those set out in Sch 2 Pt 1: see PARA 314.

600. Notification of the parties. The comptroller[1] must notify the applicant for, or proprietor of, the patent which is the subject matter of the case that proceedings have started[2]. In addition, the comptroller may notify any persons who appear to him to be likely to have an interest in the case that proceedings have started[3]. However, where such a person is the claimant[4], or has indicated in writing to the comptroller that he supports the claimant's case, the comptroller has no duty to notify him[5]. The comptroller must send the relevant form[6] and the statement of grounds[7] with the notification[8]. In that notification, the comptroller must specify a period within which the persons notified may file a counter-statement[9]; and any counter-statement must be filed in duplicate before the end of the period specified[10].

Where a person was notified that proceedings have started and that person fails to file a counter-statement[11], the comptroller must treat him as supporting the claimant's case[12].

1 As to the comptroller see PARA 575.
2 Patents Rules 2007, SI 2007/3291, r 77(1).
3 Patents Rules 2007, SI 2007/3291, r 77(2).
4 As to the meaning of 'claimant' see PARA 599 note 2.
5 Patents Rules 2007, SI 2007/3291, r 77(3).
6 As to the meaning of 'relevant form' see PARA 599 note 1.
7 As to the meaning of 'statement of grounds' see PARA 599 note 2.
8 Patents Rules 2007, SI 2007/3291, r 77(4).
9 Patents Rules 2007, SI 2007/3291, r 77(5). As to the counter-statement see PARA 601. Rule 77(5), (6) does not apply to an opposition under any of the provisions mentioned in Sch 3 Pt 3 (see PARA 598 note 17): r 77(7). In such oppositions, any counter-statement must be filed in duplicate before the end of the period of four weeks beginning immediately after the date of the advertisement in the Official Journal (Patents) (see PARA 578) mentioned in r 75 (see PARA 598): r 77(8) (amended by SI 2011/2052). The prescribed time limit may not be extended: see PARA 597.
10 Patents Rules 2007, SI 2007/3291, r 77(6). See note 9.
11 Ie under the Patents Rules 2007, SI 2007/3291, r 77(6) or (8).
12 Patents Rules 2007, SI 2007/3291, r 77(9).

601. The counter-statement. Any counter-statement filed by the defendant[1] must:

(1) state which of the allegations in the statement of grounds[2] he denies[3];
(2) state which of the allegations he is unable to admit or deny, but which he requires the claimant[4] to prove[5];
(3) state which of the allegations he admits[6];
(4) be verified by a statement of truth[7]; and
(5) comply with the formal requirements for documents[8].

Where the defendant denies an allegation he must state his reasons for doing so and, if he intends to put forward a different version of events from that given by the claimant, he must state his own version[9].

A defendant who fails to deal with an allegation in a counter-statement is taken to admit that allegation[10]. However, a defendant who fails to deal with an allegation but has set out in his counter-statement the nature of his case in relation to the issue to which the allegation is relevant, is taken to require the allegation to be proved[11].

1   'Defendant' means a person who files a counter-statement under the Patents Rules 2007, SI 2007/3291, r 77(6) or (8): r 73(3).
2   As to the meaning of 'statement of grounds' see PARA 599 note 2.
3   Patents Rules 2007, SI 2007/3291, r 78(1)(a).
4   As to the meaning of 'claimant' see PARA 599 note 2.
5   Patents Rules 2007, SI 2007/3291, r 78(1)(b).
6   Patents Rules 2007, SI 2007/3291, r 78(1)(c).
7   Patents Rules 2007, SI 2007/3291, r 78(1)(d). As to the meaning of 'statement of truth' see PARA 599 note 14.
8   Patents Rules 2007, SI 2007/3291, r 78(1)(e). The formal requirements are those set out in r 14, Sch 2 Pt 1: see PARA 314.
9   Patents Rules 2007, SI 2007/3291, r 78(2).
10   Patents Rules 2007, SI 2007/3291, r 78(3).
11   Patents Rules 2007, SI 2007/3291, r 78(4).

602. Copies of documents. Where a witness statement[1], statement of case[2], affidavit or statutory declaration (a 'relevant statement') refers to any other document, a copy of that document must accompany the relevant statement[3]. Where more than one copy of a relevant statement is filed, each copy of the statement must be accompanied by a copy of any document referred to in the statement[4]. These requirements do not apply where the relevant statement is sent to the comptroller[5] and the document referred to in the relevant statement was published by the comptroller or is kept at the UK Intellectual Property Office[6].

1   'Witness statement' means a written statement signed by a person that contains the evidence which that person would be allowed to give orally: Patents Rules 2007, SI 2007/3291, r 73(3).
2   'Statement of case' means the statement of grounds or the counter-statement and references to a statement of case include part of the statement of case: Patents Rules 2007, SI 2007/3291, r 73(3).
3   Patents Rules 2007, SI 2007/3291, r 79(1), (4).
4   Patents Rules 2007, SI 2007/3291, r 79(2).
5   As to the comptroller see PARA 575.
6   Patents Rules 2007, SI 2007/3291, r 79(3). As to the UK Intellectual Property Office see PARA 577.

603. Evidence rounds and the hearing. When the defendant[1] files a counter-statement[2], the comptroller[3] must as soon as practicable send the counter-statement to the claimant[4]. The comptroller must also specify the period within which the claimant must file the necessary form[5] and the periods within which evidence may be filed by the claimant and the defendant[6]. If the claimant wishes to continue the proceedings following receipt of the counter-statement, he must file the necessary form[7].

The comptroller may, at any time he thinks fit, give leave to either party to file evidence upon such terms as he thinks fit[8]. Under this provision, evidence is only to be considered to be filed when: (1) it has been received by the comptroller; and (2) it has been sent to all the other parties to the proceedings[9].

The comptroller must then give the parties an opportunity to be heard[10]. If any party requests to be heard, the comptroller must send to the parties notice of a date for the hearing[11].

When the comptroller has decided the matter he must notify all the parties of his decision, including his reasons for making the decision[12].

1   As to the meaning of 'defendant' see PARA 601 note 1.

2   As to the counter-statement see PARA 601.
3   As to the comptroller see PARA 575.
4   Patents Rules 2007, SI 2007/3291, r 80(1)(a). As to the meaning of 'claimant' see PARA 599 note 2.
5   Patents Rules 2007, SI 2007/3291, r 80(1)(aa) (added by SI 2010/33). The appropriate form in Patents Form 4: Patents Rules 2007, SI 2007/3291, r 80(1)(aa) (as so added). If the claimant fails to file Patents Form 4 within the period specified by the comptroller the claimant is deemed to have filed a request to withdraw from the proceedings: Patents Rules 2007, SI 2007/3291, r 81A (added by SI 2010/33).
6   Patents Rules 2007, SI 2007/3291, r 80(1)(b).
7   Patents Rules 2007, SI 2007/3291, r 80(1A) (added by SI 2010/33). The appropriate form in Patents Form 4: Patents Rules 2007, SI 2007/3291, r 80(1A) (as so added). See note 5. The fee payable on continuing proceedings following receipt of a counter-statement in accordance with r 80(1A) is £350: Patents (Fees) Rules 2007, SI 2007/3292, r 2, Sch 1 (amended by SI 2010/33).
8   Patents Rules 2007, SI 2007/3291, r 80(2). As to evidence in proceedings before the comptroller see PARA 593.
9   Patents Rules 2007, SI 2007/3291, r 80(3).
10   Patents Rules 2007, SI 2007/3291, r 80(4).
11   Patents Rules 2007, SI 2007/3291, r 80(5).
12   Patents Rules 2007, SI 2007/3291, r 80(6).

604.   General powers of the comptroller.   The comptroller[1] has a number of general procedural powers. The comptroller may extend or shorten (or further extend or shorten) any period of time which has been specified under any of the statutory provisions relating to proceedings[2].

Except where otherwise provided[3], the comptroller may give such directions as to the management of the proceedings as he thinks fit[4], and in particular he may:

(1)   require a document, information or evidence to be filed[5];
(2)   require a translation of a specification of a patent or application or any other document which is not in English[6];
(3)   require a party or a party's legal representative to attend a hearing[7];
(4)   hold a hearing and receive evidence by telephone or by using any other method of direct oral communication[8];
(5)   allow a statement of case[9] to be amended[10];
(6)   stay the whole, or any part, of the proceedings either generally or until a specified date or event[11];
(7)   consolidate proceedings[12];
(8)   direct that part of any proceedings be dealt with as separate proceedings[13]; and
(9)   direct that the parties attend a case management conference or pre-hearing review[14].

The comptroller may control the evidence by giving directions as to the issues on which he requires evidence, the nature of the evidence which he requires to decide those issues and the way in which the evidence is to be placed before him[15]. The comptroller may also use his power to exclude evidence which would otherwise be admissible[16].

When the comptroller gives directions[17], he may make them subject to conditions and may specify the consequence of failure to comply with the directions or a condition[18].

The comptroller has the powers of a judge of the High Court as regards the attendance of witnesses and the discovery and production of documents, but he has no power to punish summarily for contempt[19].

1   As to the comptroller see PARA 575.

2   Patents Rules 2007, SI 2007/3291, r 81(1). The statutory provisions relating to proceedings are those in Pt 7 (rr 73–91). An extension may be granted notwithstanding the period of time specified has expired: r 81(2).
3   Ie by the Patents Act 1977 or the Patents Rules 2007, SI 2007/3291.
4   Patents Rules 2007, SI 2007/3291, r 82(1).
5   Patents Rules 2007, SI 2007/3291, r 82(1)(a).
6   Patents Rules 2007, SI 2007/3291, r 82(1)(b).
7   Patents Rules 2007, SI 2007/3291, r 82(1)(c).
8   Patents Rules 2007, SI 2007/3291, r 82(1)(d). As to evidence rounds and the hearing see PARA 603.
9   As to the meaning of 'statement of case' see PARA 602 note 2.
10   Patents Rules 2007, SI 2007/3291, r 82(1)(e).
11   Patents Rules 2007, SI 2007/3291, r 82(1)(f).
12   Patents Rules 2007, SI 2007/3291, r 82(1)(g).
13   Patents Rules 2007, SI 2007/3291, r 82(1)(h).
14   Patents Rules 2007, SI 2007/3291, r 82(1)(i).
15   Patents Rules 2007, SI 2007/3291, r 82(2).
16   Patents Rules 2007, SI 2007/3291, r 82(2).
17   Ie under any provision of the Patents Rules 2007, SI 2007/3291, Pt 7 (rr 73–91).
18   Patents Rules 2007, SI 2007/3291, r 82(3).
19   Patents Rules 2007, SI 2007/3291, r 86. See also PARA 593.

605. Striking out a statement of case and summary judgment. A party may apply to the comptroller[1] for him to strike out a statement of case[2] or to give summary judgment[3].

The comptroller may strike out the statement of case if it appears to him that: (1) the statement of case discloses no reasonable grounds for bringing or defending the claim; (2) the statement of case is an abuse of process or is otherwise likely to obstruct the just disposal of the proceedings; or (3) there has been a failure to comply with a statutory provision[4] or a previous direction given by the comptroller[5].

The comptroller may give summary judgment against a claimant[6] or defendant[7] on the whole of a case or on a particular issue if: (a) he considers that that claimant has no real prospect of succeeding on the case or issue, or that defendant has no real prospect of successfully defending the case or issue; and (b) there is no other compelling reason why the case or issue should be disposed of at a hearing[8].

1   As to the comptroller see PARA 575.
2   As to the meaning of 'statement of case' see PARA 602 note 2.
3   Patents Rules 2007, SI 2007/3291, r 83(1).
4   Ie a provision of the Patents Act 1977 or the Patents Rules 2007, SI 2007/3291.
5   Patents Rules 2007, SI 2007/3291, r 83(2).
6   As to the meaning of 'claimant' see PARA 599 note 2.
7   As to the meaning of 'defendant' see PARA 601 note 1.
8   Patents Rules 2007, SI 2007/3291, r 83(3).

606. Hearings in public. Any hearing[1] before the comptroller[2] in proceedings relating to an application for a patent, or a patent, must be held in public[3]. However, any party to the proceedings may apply to the comptroller for a hearing to be held in private[4]. The comptroller may grant such an application where (1) he considers there is good reason for the hearing to be held in private; and (2) all the parties to the proceedings have had an opportunity to be heard on the matter, and where the application is granted the hearing must be held in private[5]. Any hearing of an application for a hearing to be held in private, or relating to an application for a patent which has not been published[6], must be held in private[7].

1　For these purposes, a reference to a hearing includes any part of a hearing: Patents Rules 2007, SI 2007/3291, r 84(5).
2　As to the comptroller see PARA 575.
3　Patents Rules 2007, SI 2007/3291, r 84(1).
4　Patents Rules 2007, SI 2007/3291, r 84(2).
5　Patents Rules 2007, SI 2007/3291, r 84(3).
6　As to publication see PARA 326.
7　Patents Rules 2007, SI 2007/3291, r 84(4).

(v)　Offences

607.　Unauthorised claim of patent rights. If a person falsely represents that anything disposed of by him for value is a patented product[1], he is liable on summary conviction to a fine[2]. For these purposes, a person who for value disposes of an article having stamped, engraved or impressed on it or otherwise applied to it the word 'patent' or 'patented' or anything expressing or implying that it is a patented product is taken to represent that the article is a patented product[3].

The above provisions[4] do not apply where the representation is made in respect of a product after the patent for that product or, as the case may be, the process in question has expired or been revoked and before the end of a period which is reasonably sufficient to enable the accused to take steps to ensure that the representation is not made, or does not continue to be made[5]. Where, however, the word 'patent' forms part of the accepted name of the article, its use will not be such a representation[6].

In proceedings for such an offence it is a defence for the accused to prove that he used due diligence to prevent the commission of the offence[7].

Even where a patent exists, to threaten to sue for infringement of it may be an actionable wrong[8].

1　As to the meaning of 'patented product' see PARA 371 note 11.
2　Patents Act 1977 s 110(1). The fine must not exceed level 3 on the standard scale: s 110(1) (amended by the Criminal Justice Act 1982 ss 39, 46). As to the standard scale see SENTENCING AND DISPOSITION OF OFFENDERS vol 92 (2010) PARA 142. As to offences by bodies corporate see PARA 611.
3　Patents Act 1977 s 110(2).
4　Ie the Patents Act 1977 s 110(1): see the text and notes 1–2.
5　Patents Act 1977 s 110(3).
6　*Sykes v Sykes* (1824) 3 B & C 541; *Cheavin v Walker* (1877) 5 ChD 850, CA; *Gridley v Swinborne* (1888) 52 JP 791, DC.
7　Patents Act 1977 s 110(4).
8　See PARA 555 et seq.

608.　Unauthorised claim that patent applied for. If a person represents that a patent has been applied for in respect of any article disposed of for value by him and:

　(1)　no such application has been made; or
　(2)　if made, has been refused or withdrawn,

he is liable on summary conviction to a fine[1]. For these purposes, a person who for value disposes of an article having stamped, engraved or impressed on it or otherwise applied to it the words 'patent applied for' or 'patent pending' or anything expressing or implying that a patent has been applied for in respect of the article is taken to represent that a patent has been applied for in respect of it[2]. Where, however, the word 'patent' forms part of the accepted name of the article, its use will not be such a representation[3].

Head (2) above does not, however, apply where the representation is made, or continues to be made, before the expiry of a period which commences with the refusal or withdrawal and which is reasonably sufficient to enable the accused to take steps to ensure that the representation is not made, or does not continue to be made[4].

In any proceedings for such an offence it is a defence for the accused to prove that he used due diligence to prevent the commission of such an offence[5].

1 Patents Act 1977 s 111(1). The fine must not exceed level 3 on the standard scale: s 111(1) (amended by the Criminal Justice Act 1982 ss 39, 46). As to the standard scale see SENTENCING AND DISPOSITION OF OFFENDERS vol 92 (2010) PARA 142. As to offences by bodies corporate see PARA 611.

2 Patents Act 1977 s 111(3).

3 *Sykes v Sykes* (1824) 3 B & C 541; *Cheavin v Walker* (1877) 5 ChD 850, CA; *Gridley v Swinborne* (1888) 52 JP 791, DC.

4 Patents Act 1977 s 111(2).

5 Patents Act 1977 s 111(4).

609.   Falsification of the register etc.   If a person makes or causes to be made a false entry in any register kept under the Patents Act 1977[1], or a writing falsely purporting to be a copy or reproduction of an entry in any such register, or produces or tenders or causes to be produced or tendered in evidence any such writing, knowing the entry or writing to be false, he is guilty of an offence[2].

1 As to the register of patents see PARA 583 et seq.

2 Patents Act 1977 s 109. A person guilty of such an offence is liable on conviction on indictment to imprisonment for a term not exceeding two years or a fine, or to both or on summary conviction to a fine not exceeding the prescribed sum: s 109 (amended by the Magistrates' Courts Act 1980 s 32(2)). As to the prescribed sum see SENTENCING AND DISPOSITION OF OFFENDERS vol 92 (2010) PARA 141. As to offences by bodies corporate see PARA 611.

610.   Use of the words 'Patent Office'.   If any person uses on his place of business, or on any document issued by him, or otherwise, the words 'Patent Office' or any other words suggesting that his place of business is, or is officially connected with, the UK Intellectual Property Office[1], he is liable on summary conviction to a fine[2].

1 As to the UK Intellectual Property Office see PARA 577.

2 Patents Act 1977 s 112. The fine must not exceed level 4 on the standard scale: s 112 (amended by the Criminal Justice Act 1982 ss 39, 46). As to the standard scale see SENTENCING AND DISPOSITION OF OFFENDERS vol 92 (2010) PARA 142. As to offences by bodies corporate see PARA 611.

611.   Offences by corporations.   Where an offence under the Patents Act 1977 which has been committed by a body corporate is proved to have been committed with the consent or connivance of, or to be attributable to any neglect on the part of, a director, manager, secretary or other similar officer of the body corporate, or any person who was purporting to act in any such capacity, he, as well as the body corporate, is guilty of that offence and is liable to be proceeded against and punished accordingly[1].

Where the affairs of a body corporate are managed by its members, the above provisions apply in relation to the acts and defaults of a member in connection with his functions of management as if he were a director of the body corporate[2].

1 Patents Act 1977 s 113(1).

2 Patents Act 1977 s 113(2).

(2) PATENT AGENTS AND PATENT ATTORNEYS

612. Meaning and function of 'patent agent'. Any individual, partnership or body corporate may carry on the business of acting as agent for others for the purpose of:

(1) applying for or obtaining patents, in the United Kingdom[1] or elsewhere; or

(2) conducting proceedings before the comptroller[2] relating to applications for, or otherwise in connection with, patents[3].

The above provisions do not, however, affect any restriction under the European Patent Convention[4] as to who may act on behalf of another for any purpose relating to European patents[5].

Most applications for patents are filed and prosecuted, and most UK Intellectual Property Office[6] proceedings are conducted, through patent agents[7]. A patent agent is expected to be familiar with the practice of obtaining patents, so that ignorance of decisions which have an important bearing on that practice would as a rule render him liable to a client injured in consequence[8].

1 As to the meaning of 'United Kingdom' see PARA 303 note 5.
2 As to the comptroller see PARA 575.
3 Copyright, Designs and Patents Act 1988 s 274(1). This provision is expressed to be subject to the Legal Services Act 2007: see the Copyright, Designs and Patents Act 1988 s 274(1) (amended by the Legal Services Act 2007 s 185(1), (2)).
4 As to the European Patent Convention see PARA 644 et seq.
5 Copyright, Designs and Patents Act 1988 s 274(2). As to the meaning of 'European patent' see PARA 644 note 5.
6 As to the UK Intellectual Property Office see PARA 577.
7 Any party to proceedings before the comptroller may, however, appear before the comptroller in person or be represented by any person whom he desires to represent him: see the Patents Act 1977 s 102(1); and PARA 592. Any act required or authorised by the Patents Act 1977 or the Patents Rules 2007, SI 2007/3291, to be done by or to any person in connection with an application for a patent, or any procedure relating to a patent, may be done by or to an agent authorised by that person orally or in writing: (1) where an agent is appointed when a person starts or joins any proceeding under the Patents Act 1977, once the comptroller has been notified of his appointment in writing; or (2) where an agent is appointed after a person has started or joined any proceeding under the Patents Act 1977, once Patents Form 51 has been filed in duplicate: Patents Rules 2007, SI 2007/3291, r 101(1). Where an agent has been authorised, the comptroller may, in any particular case, require the signature or presence of his principal: r 101(2). As to discovery of the patent agent's files in legal proceedings about the patent see PARA 615; and as to the appearance of patent agents on appeals to the Patents Court see PARA 622.
8 *Lee v Walker* (1872) LR 7 CP 121. As to the liability where an agent allows a patent to lapse see *Turnbull & Co v Cruikshank and Fairweather* (1905) 22 RPC 363 (on appeal 22 RPC 521, CA); as to the liability where an agent fails to put in order an application by the last possible date so that it becomes void see *Andrew Master Hones Ltd v Cruikshank and Fairweather* [1980] RPC 16; and as to liability for negligent statements apart from contract see *Hedley Byrne & Co Ltd v Heller & Partners Ltd* [1964] AC 465, [1963] 2 All ER 575, HL; *Caparo Industries plc v Dickman* [1990] 2 AC 605, [1990] 1 All ER 568, HL; and NEGLIGENCE vol 78 (2010) PARA 14. As to the steps a patent agent ought to take to verify the accuracy of data given to it by a specialist patent searching firm see *Arbiter Group plc v Gill Jennings & Every* [2001] RPC 67, CA; *Finecard International Ltd (t/a The Ninja Corpn) v Urquhart Dyke & Lord (a firm)* [2005] EWHC 2481 (Ch), [2006] FSR 505 (failure to record licence timeously).

613. Restrictions on practice. An individual who is not a registered patent attorney[1] must not:

(1) carry on a business, otherwise than in partnership, under any name or other description which contains the words 'patent agent' or 'patent attorney'; or

(2)   in the course of a business otherwise describe himself, or permit himself to be described, as a 'patent agent' or 'patent attorney'[2].

A partnership or other unincorporated body must not:

(a)   carry on a business under any name or other description which contains the words 'patent agent' or 'patent attorney'; or

(b)   in the course of a business otherwise describe itself, or permit itself to be described, as a firm of 'patent agents' or 'patent attorneys',

unless the partnership or other body is registered[3].

A body corporate must not:

(i)   carry on a business, otherwise than in partnership, under any name or other description which contains the words 'patent agent' or 'patent attorney'; or

(ii)   in the course of a business otherwise describe itself, or permit itself to be described, as a 'patent agent' or 'patent attorney',

unless the body corporate is registered[4].

Where the above provisions would be contravened by the use of the words 'patent agent' or 'patent attorney' in reference to an individual, partnership or body corporate, they are equally contravened by the use of other expressions in reference to that person, or his business or place of business, which are likely to be understood as indicating that he is entitled to be described as a 'patent agent' or 'patent attorney'[5].

A person who contravenes the above provisions commits an offence and is liable on summary conviction to a fine[6]; and proceedings for such an offence may be begun at any time within a year from the date of the offence[7].

The term 'patent attorney' may be used in reference to a solicitor, and a firm of solicitors may be described as a firm of 'patent attorneys', without any contravention of the above provisions[8]. No offence is committed under the England and Wales enactment[9] restricting the use of certain expressions in reference to persons not qualified to act as solicitors by the use of the term 'patent attorney' in reference to a registered patent agent or by the use of the term 'European patent attorney' in reference to a person on the European list[10].

1   For these purposes, 'registered patent attorney' means a person whose name is entered in the register kept under the Copyright, Designs and Patents Act 1988 s 275 (see PARA 617): s 275(2) (s 275 substituted, s 276(1)–(4) amended, by the Legal Services Act 2007 s 185(1), (3), (4), Sch 21 paras 75, 76).

2   Copyright, Designs and Patents Act 1988 s 276(1) (as amended: see note 1). Section 276 has effect subject to s 277 (persons entitled to describe themselves as European patent attorneys etc: see PARA 618) and s 278(1) (use of term 'patent attorney' in reference to solicitors): s 276(7).

3   Copyright, Designs and Patents Act 1988 s 276(2) (as amended: see note 1). The register in question is the register kept under s 275: see s 276(2) (as so amended); and PARA 617.

4   Copyright, Designs and Patents Act 1988 s 276(3) (as amended: see note 1). The register in question is the register kept under s 275: see s 276(3) (as so amended); and PARA 617. The Copyright, Designs and Patents Act 1988 s 276(3) does not, however, apply to a company which began to carry on business as a patent agent before 17 November 1917 if the name of a director or the manager of the company who is a registered patent attorney is mentioned as being so registered in all professional advertisements, circulars or letters issued by or with the company's consent on which its name appears: s 276(4) (as so amended). For these purposes, 'director', in relation to a body corporate whose affairs are managed by its members, means any member of the body corporate: Copyright, Designs and Patents Act 1988 s 286.

5   Copyright, Designs and Patents Act 1988 s 276(5).

6   The fine must not exceed level 5 on the standard scale: Copyright, Designs and Patents Act 1988 s 276(6). SENTENCING AND DISPOSITION OF OFFENDERS vol 92 (2010) PARA 142.

7   Copyright, Designs and Patents Act 1988 s 276(6). Proceedings for an offence under Pt V (ss 274–286) alleged to have been committed by a partnership must be brought in the name of the partnership and not in that of the partners; but without prejudice to any liability of theirs

under s 285(4): s 285(1). The following provisions apply for the purposes of such proceedings as in relation to a body corporate, namely any rules of court relating to the service of documents and the Magistrates' Courts Act 1980 s 46, Sch 3 (procedure on charge of offence by corporations: see MAGISTRATES vol 71 (2013) PARA 513): Copyright, Designs and Patents Act 1988 s 285(2). A fine imposed on a partnership on its conviction in such proceedings must be paid out of the partnership assets: s 285(3). Where a partnership is guilty of such an offence, every partner, other than the partner who is proved to have been ignorant of or to have attempted to prevent the commission of the offence, is also guilty of the offence and liable to be proceeded against and punished accordingly: s 285(4).

Where an offence under Pt V committed by a body corporate is proved to have been committed with the consent or connivance of a director, manager, secretary or other similar officer of the body, or a person purporting to act in any such capacity, he as well as the body corporate is guilty of the offence and liable to be proceeded against and punished accordingly: s 285(5).

8   Copyright, Designs and Patents Act 1988 s 278(1).
9   Ie the Solicitors Act 1974 s 21 (see LEGAL PROFESSIONS vol 65 (2008) PARA 591): Copyright, Designs and Patents Act 1988 s 278(3).
10 Copyright, Designs and Patents Act 1988 s 278(2). For these purposes, 'European list' means the list of professional representatives maintained by the European Patent Office (see PARA 644) in pursuance of the European Patent Convention: Copyright, Designs and Patents Act 1988 s 286. As to the European Patent Convention see PARA 644 et seq.

614.   Preparation of documents by patent agents.   No offence is committed under the enactments relating to the preparation of documents by persons not legally qualified[1] by reason only of the preparation by any person of a document, other than a deed, for use in proceedings before the comptroller[2].

1   As to the meaning of 'the enactment relating to the preparation of documents by persons not qualified' see PARA 592 note 7.
2   See the Patents Act 1977 s 102(2); and PARA 592 (s 102 substituted by the Copyright, Designs and Patents Act 1988 s 295, Sch 5 para 27).

615.   Privilege for communications with patent agents.   Where a patent attorney[1] acts for a client in relation to any communication as to any matter relating to the protection of any invention, design, technical information or trade mark, or as to any matter involving passing off[2], any applicable communication, document, material or other information is privileged from disclosure in like manner as if the patent attorney had at all material times been acting as the client's solicitor[3].

1   For these purposes, 'patent attorney' means: (1) a registered patent attorney or a person who is on the European list (Copyright, Designs and Patents Act 1988 s 280(3)(a) (s 280(1)(a), (3)(a)–(c) amended, s 280(1)(b), (3)(ba) added, s 280(2) substituted, by the Legal Services Act 2007 Sch 21 paras 75, 77, Sch 23); (2) a partnership entitled to describe itself as a firm of patent attorney or as a firm carrying on the business of a European patent attorney (Copyright, Designs and Patents Act 1988 s 280(3)(b) (as so amended)); (3) an unincorporated body (other than a partnership) entitled to describe itself as a patent attorney (s 280(3)(ba) (as so added)); or (4) a body corporate entitled to describe itself as a patent attorney or as a company carrying on the business of a European patent attorney (s 280(3)(c) (as so amended)). As to the meaning of 'registered patent attorney' see PARA 613 note 1; and as to the meaning of 'European list' see PARA 613 note 11.
2   Copyright, Designs and Patents Act 1988 s 280(1)(a) (as amended: see note 1). Documents, material or information relating to any such matter are also privileged under these provisions: s 280(1)(b) (as so added).
3   Copyright, Designs and Patents Act 1988 s 280(2) (as substituted: see note 1). As to the extension of privilege for communications with solicitors relating to patent proceedings see the Patents Act 1977 s 103; and PARA 592.

616.   Power of comptroller to refuse to deal with certain agents.   Any act required or authorised by the Patents Act 1977 or the Patents Rules 2007 to be done by or to any person in connection with an application for a patent, or any procedure relating to a patent, may be done by or to an agent authorised by that person orally or in writing[1]. Where an agent has been authorised, the comptroller may, in any particular case, require the signature or presence of his principal[2].

The comptroller is authorised to refuse to recognise as agent in respect of any business under the Patents Act 1977:

(1)   a person who has been convicted of a specified offence[3];

(2)   a person whose name has been erased from and not restored to the register of patent agents (or, as from a day to be appointed, the register of patent attorneys) on the ground of misconduct[4];

(3)   a person who is found by the Secretary of State to have been guilty of such conduct as would, in the case of a person registered in the register of patent agents (or, as from a day to be appointed, the register of patent attorneys), render the person liable to have the person's name erased from the register on the ground of misconduct[5];

(4)   a partnership or body corporate of which one of the partners or directors[6] is a person whom the comptroller could refuse to recognise under head (1), (2) or (3) above[7].

The comptroller must refuse to recognise as agent in respect of any business under the Patents Act 1977 a person who neither resides nor has a place of business in the United Kingdom[8], the Isle of Man or another member state of the European Union[9].

1   Patents Rules 2007, SI 2007/3291, r 101(1). Where an agent is appointed when a person starts or joins any proceeding under the Patents Act 1977, the comptroller must first be notified of his appointment in writing: Patents Rules 2007, SI 2007/3291, r 101(1)(a). Where an agent is appointed after a person has started or joined any proceeding under the Patents Act 1977, Patents Form 51 must first be filed in duplicate: Patents Rules 2007, SI 2007/3291, r 101(1)(b). As to the comptroller see PARA 575.

2   Patents Rules 2007, SI 2007/3291, r 101(2).

3   Copyright, Designs and Patents Act 1988 s 281(1), (2)(a); Patent Agents (Non-recognition of Certain Agents by Comptroller) Rules 1990, SI 1990/1454, r 3(a). The offence referred to is an offence under the Copyright, Designs and Patents Act 1988 s 276 (see PARA 613).

4   Copyright, Designs and Patents Act 1988 s 281(2)(b) (s 281(2)(b), (c) amended by SI 2009/3348; prospectively amended by the Legal Services Act 2007 Sch 21 paras 75, 78); Patent Agents (Non-recognition of Certain Agents by Comptroller) Rules 1990, SI 1990/1454, r 3(b) (r 3(b), (c) amended by SI 2009/3348). At the date at which this volume states the law no day had been appointed for the purposes of the amendments made by the Legal Services Act 2007. As to the register of patent attorneys see PARA 617 et seq. Rules may also authorise the comptroller to refuse to recognise a person who is suspended from the register (Copyright, Designs and Patents Act 1988 s 281(2)(b) (as so amended)), but at the date at which this volume states the law no such provision is made. Rules under these provisions may contain such incidental and supplementary provisions as appear to the Secretary of State to be appropriate and may in particular prescribe circumstances in which a person is or is not to be taken to have been guilty of misconduct: Copyright, Designs and Patents Act 1988 s 281(3). As to the Secretary of State see PARA 573.

5   Copyright, Designs and Patents Act 1988 s 281(2)(c) (as amended and prospectively amended: see note 4); Patent Agents (Non-recognition of Certain Agents by Comptroller) Rules 1990, SI 1990/1454, r 3(c) (as so amended).

6   As to the meaning of 'director' see PARA 613 note 4.

7   Copyright, Designs and Patents Act 1988 s 281(2)(d); Patent Agents (Non-recognition of Certain Agents by Comptroller) Rules 1990, SI 1990/1454, r 3(d).

8   As to the meaning of 'United Kingdom' see PARA 303 note 5.

9   Copyright, Designs and Patents Act 1988 s 281(5).

617. The register. There is a register of persons who act as agent for others for the purpose of applying for or obtaining patents[1]. The register is to be kept by the Chartered Institute of Patent Attorneys[2]. The person who keeps the register may make regulations which regulate the keeping of the register and the registration of persons and the carrying on of patent attorney work[3] by registered persons[4].

1 Copyright, Designs and Patents Act 1988 s 275(1) (s 275 substituted, s 275A added, by the Legal Services Act 2007 s 185(1), (3)).

2 Copyright, Designs and Patents Act 1988 s 275(3) (as substituted: see note 1). The Chartered Institute of Patent Attorneys was as founded in 1882 and was incorporated by Royal Charter in 1891. The Secretary of State may, by order, amend s 275(3) so as to require the register to be kept by the person specified in the order: s 275(4) (as so substituted). Before making an order under s 275(4), the Secretary of State must consult the Legal Services Board: s 275(5) (as so prospectively substituted). As to the Secretary of State see PARA 573. As to the Legal Services Board see LEGAL PROFESSIONS vol 65 (2008) PARA 303 et seq. At the date at which this volume states the law no such order had been made.

3 'Patent attorney work' means work done in the course of carrying on the business of acting as agent for others for the purpose of applying for or obtaining patents, in the United Kingdom or elsewhere, or conducting proceedings before the comptroller relating to applications for, or otherwise in connection with, patents: Copyright, Designs and Patents Act 1988 s 275A(7) (as added: see note 1).

4 Copyright, Designs and Patents Act 1988 s 275A(1) (as added: see note 1). 'Registered person' means a registered patent attorney, or a body (corporate or unincorporate) registered in the register kept under s 275: s 275A(7) (as so added). Those regulations may, amongst other things, make provision: (1) as to the educational and training qualifications, and other requirements, which must be satisfied before an individual may be registered or for an individual to remain registered; (2) as to the requirements which must be met by a body (corporate or unincorporate) before it may be registered, or for it to remain registered, including provision as to the management and control of the body; (3) as to the educational, training and other requirements to be met by regulated persons; (4) regulating the practice, conduct and discipline of registered persons or regulated persons; (5) authorising in such cases as may be specified in the regulations the erasure from the register of the name of any person registered in it, or the suspension of a person's registration; (6) requiring the payment of such fees as may be specified in or determined in accordance with the regulations; (7) about the provision to be made by registered persons in respect of complaints made against them; (8) about the keeping by registered persons or regulated persons of records and accounts; (9) for reviews of or appeals against decisions made under the regulations; and (10) as to the indemnification of registered persons or regulated persons against losses arising from claims in respect of civil liability incurred by them: s 275A(2) (as so added). 'Regulated person' means a person who is not a registered person but is a manager or employee of a body which is a registered person; and 'manager', in relation to a body, has the same meaning as in the Legal Services Act 2007 s 207 (see LEGAL PROFESSIONS vol 65 (2008) PARA 369): Copyright, Designs and Patents Act 1988 s 275A(7) (as so added). Regulations may make different provision for different purposes: s 275A(3) (as so added). Regulations under s 275A which are not regulatory arrangements within the meaning of the Legal Services Act 2007 (see s 21; and LEGAL PROFESSIONS vol 65 (2008) PARA 377) are to be treated as such arrangements for the purposes of that Act: Copyright, Designs and Patents Act 1988 s 275A(4) (as so added). The powers conferred to make regulations under s 275A are not to be taken to prejudice any other power which the person who keeps the register may have to make rules or regulations (however they may be described and whether they are made under an enactment or otherwise), or any rules or regulations made by that person under any such power: s 275A(6) (as so added). At the date at which this volume states the law no regulations had been made under s 275A.

618. European patent attorneys. The term 'European patent attorney' or 'European patent agent' may be used in the following cases without any contravention of the statutory provisions[1] relating to persons entitled to describe themselves as patent agents[2]:

(1)   an individual who is on the European list[3] may carry on business under a name or other description which contains the words 'European patent

attorney' or 'European patent agent' or otherwise describe himself, or permit himself to be described, as a 'European patent attorney' or 'European patent agent'[4];

(2) a partnership of which not less than the prescribed number or proportion of partners is on the European list may carry on a business under a name or other description which contains the words 'European patent attorneys' or 'European patent agents' or otherwise describe itself, or permit itself to be described, as a firm which carries on the business of 'European patent attorney' or 'European patent agent'[5];

(3) a body corporate of which not less than the prescribed number or proportion of directors[6] is on the European list may carry on business under a name or other description which contains the words 'European patent attorney' or 'European patent agent' or otherwise describe itself, or permit itself to be described, as a 'European patent attorney' or 'European patent agent'[7].

Where the term 'European patent attorney' or 'European patent agent' may, in accordance with the above provisions, be used in reference to an individual, partnership or body corporate, it is equally permissible to use other expressions in reference to that person, or to his business or place of business, which are likely to be understood as indicating that he is entitled to be described as a 'European patent attorney' or 'European patent agent'[8].

1   Ie the Copyright, Designs and Patents Act 1988 s 276: see PARA 613.
2   Copyright, Designs and Patents Act 1988 s 277(1).
3   As to the meaning of 'European list' see PARA 613 note 11.
4   Copyright, Designs and Patents Act 1988 s 277(2).
5   Copyright, Designs and Patents Act 1988 s 277(3).
6   As to the meaning of 'director' see PARA 613 note 4.
7   Copyright, Designs and Patents Act 1988 s 277(4).
8   Copyright, Designs and Patents Act 1988 s 277(5).

(3) THE PATENTS COURT

619. Constitution and jurisdiction of the Patents Court. All proceedings in the High Court[1] under the Registered Designs Act 1949[2], the Defence Contracts Act 1958[3] and the Patents Act 1977[4] must be started in the Patents Court, which is constituted as part of the Chancery Division[5], or in the Intellectual Property Enterprise Court[6]. The Patents Court also has an appellate jurisdiction[7]. For the purpose of determining any question in the exercise of its original or appellate jurisdiction under the Patents Act 1977, or under any treaty or international convention to which the United Kingdom[8] is a party, the Patents Court may make any order or exercise any other power which the comptroller[9] could have made or exercised for the purpose of determining that question[10].

An English court has jurisdiction to decide on matters of infringement or non-infringement of, not only European Patent (UK) patents, but also European Patent designations in other jurisdictions[11].

1   In the Patents Act 1977, 'court' means the High Court: Patents Act 1977 s 130(1) (definition amended by the Copyright, Designs and Patents Act 1988 Sch 7 para 23; and by the Crime and Courts Act 2013 Sch 9 para 27).
2   As to the Registered Designs Act 1949 see PARA 657 et seq.
3   As to the Defence Contracts Act 1958 see PARA 407; and ARMED CONFLICT AND EMERGENCY vol 3 (2011) PARAS 209–210.
4   As to current legislation see PARA 304.

5   See the Supreme Court Act 1981 s 6(1)(a); and COURTS AND TRIBUNALS vol 24 (2010) PARA 705. The judges of the Patents Court are such of the puisne judges of the High Court as the Lord Chief Justice may, after consulting the Lord Chancellor, from time to time nominate to be judges of the Patents Court: see s 6(2); and COURTS AND TRIBUNALS vol 24 (2010) PARA 705.

6   CPR 63.2. As to the Intellectual Property Enterprise Court see PARA 626. Claims in the Patents Court form a specialist list for the purpose of CPR 30.5: CPR 63.3. As to CPR 30.5 see CIVIL PROCEDURE vol 11 (2009) PARA 67.

7   See PARA 621. For the purpose of hearing appeals the Patents Court may consist of one or more judges of the court in accordance with directions given by the Lord Chief Justice of England and Wales after consulting the Lord Chancellor: Patents Act 1977 s 97(2) (amended by the Supreme Court Act 1981 Sch 7; and the Constitutional Reform Act 2005 Sch 4 paras 90, 91(1), (2)). See further PARA 622.

8   As to the meaning of 'United Kingdom' see PARA 303 note 5.

9   As to the comptroller see PARA 575.

10   Patents Act 1977 s 99.

11   See *Actavis Group HF v Eli Lilly & Co* [2012] EWHC 3316 (Pat), [2012] All ER (D) 347 (Nov) (affd [2013] EWCA Civ 517, [2013] RPC 985, [2013] All ER (D) 233 (May)). As to the meaning of 'European patent (UK)' see PARA 652 note 1.

620.   Scientific adviser.   At the case management conference[1] the Patents Court may direct that a scientific adviser be appointed[2] and that a document setting out basic undisputed technology should be prepared[3]. Where the court appoints one or more persons (an 'assessor'), the assessor must assist the court in dealing with a matter in which the assessor has skill and experience[4]. An assessor must take such part in the proceedings as the court may direct and in particular the court may: (1) direct the assessor to prepare a report for the court on any matter at issue in the proceedings; and (2) direct the assessor to attend the whole or any part of the trial to advise the court on any such matter[5]. If the assessor prepares a report for the court before the trial has begun, the court will send a copy to each of the parties and the parties may use it at trial[6]. Except where the remuneration of the assessor is to be paid out of money provided by Parliament[7], the remuneration to be paid to the assessor for his services is to be determined by the court and forms part of the costs of the proceedings[8] and the court may order any party to deposit in the court office a specified sum in respect of the assessor's fees and, where it does so, the assessor will not be asked to act until the sum has been deposited[9].

1   As to the case management conference see PARA 532.

2   Senior Courts Act 1981 s 70(3). Scientific advisors were appointed in e g *Valensi v British Radio Corpn* [1973] RPC 337, CA; *Re Genentec Inc's Patent, Genentech Inc v Wellcome Foundation Ltd* [1989] RPC 147; *Kirin-Amgen Inc v Hoechst Marion Rousel Ltd* [2004] UKHL 46, [2005] 1 All ER 667, [2005] RPC 169. Guidance as to the role of a scientific advisor was given in *Halliburton Energy Service Inc v Smith International (North Sea) Ltd* [2006] EWCA Civ 1599, [2007] RPC 428.

3   *Practice Direction — Intellectual Property Claims* PD 63 para 5.10.

4   See CPR 35.15(1), (2); and CIVIL PROCEDURE vol 11 (2009) PARA 863.

5   CPR 35.15(3); and CIVIL PROCEDURE vol 11 (2009) PARA 863.

6   CPR 35.15(4); and CIVIL PROCEDURE vol 11 (2009) PARA 863.

7   See CPR 35.15(7); and CIVIL PROCEDURE vol 11 (2009) PARA 863. The remuneration of any such assessor may be determined by the Lord Chancellor with the consent of the Treasury and must be defrayed out of money provided by Parliament: Senior Courts Act 1981 s 70(4). See note 2. As to the Treasury see CONSTITUTIONAL AND ADMINISTRATIVE LAW vol 20 (2014) PARAS 262–265.

8   CPR 35.15(5); and CIVIL PROCEDURE vol 11 (2009) PARA 863.

9   CPR 35.15(6); and CIVIL PROCEDURE vol 11 (2009) PARA 863.

621. Right of appeal to the Patents Court. Appeals from the comptroller lie to the Patents Court[1] from any decision of the comptroller under the Patents Act 1977 or under the Patents Rules 2007[2] except:

(1)   a decision whether an abstract adequately fulfils its purpose[3];

(2)   a decision to omit matter from a specification[4];

(3)   a decision to give directions prohibiting or restricting the publication or communication of information in the interests of defence or national security[5]; and

(4)   where a decision under the rules[6] provides for no right of appeal[7].

1   As to the constitution and jurisdiction of the Patents Court see PARA 619.
2   Patents Act 1977 s 97(1).
3   Ie a decision under the Patents Act 1977 s 14(7): see PARA 325.
4   Ie a decision under the Patents Act 1977 s 16(2): see PARA 326.
5   Ie a decision under the Patents Act 1977 s 22(1) or (2): see PARA 334.
6   Eg a decision made under the Patents Rules 2007, SI 2007/3291, r 106(1) or (2), whether to remit the whole or part of a search fee in certain cases: see r 106(7); and PARA 581.
7   Patents Act 1977 s 97(1).

622. Procedure on appeal to the Patents Court. For the purpose of hearing appeals from the comptroller[1], the Patents Court[2] consists of one or more judges of that court in accordance with directions given by the Lord Chief Justice of England and Wales after consulting the Lord Chancellor[3].

The provisions of the Civil Procedure Rules relating to appeals[4] apply to appeals from the comptroller[5]. Where those provisions require a document to be served, it must also be served on the comptroller[6].

An appeal from the comptroller to the Patents Court is by way of rehearing but with appropriate weight being given to the decision below[7]. Costs are in the discretion of the court[8].

1   Ie under the Patents Act 1977 s 97: see PARA 621. As to the comptroller see PARA 575.
2   As to the constitution and jurisdiction of the Patents Court see PARA 619.
3   Patents Act 1977 s 97(2) (amended by the Supreme Court Act 1981 Sch 7; and the Constitutional Reform Act 2005 Sch 4 paras 90, 91(1), (2)). The Lord Chief Justice may nominate a judicial office holder (as defined in the Constitutional Reform Act 2005 s 109(4): see COURTS AND TRIBUNALS vol 24 (2010) PARA 961) to exercise his functions under the Patents Act 1977 s 97(2): s 97(4) (added by the Constitutional Reform Act 2005 Sch 4 paras 90, 91(1), (3)).
4   Ie CPR Pt 52: see CIVIL PROCEDURE vol 12 (2009) PARA 1657 et seq.
5   CPR 63.16(1). Patent appeals are to be made to the Patents Court: CPR 63.16(2).
6   CPR 63.16(3).
7   See CPR 52.11; and CIVIL PROCEDURE vol 12 (2009) PARA 1672 et seq. See also *Thibierge & Comar SA v Rexam CFP Ltd* [2002] RPC 379.
8   See the Senior Courts Act 1981 s 51(1); and COURTS AND TRIBUNALS vol 24 (2010) PARA 693. The normal rule is that the party successful on the appeal is awarded taxed costs: *Ormron Tateisi Electronics Co's Patent* [1981] RPC 125; *Extrude Hone Corpn's Patent* [1982] RPC 361. This applies to appeals to which the comptroller is a party. See also *Reiss Engineering Co Ltd v Harris* [1987] RPC 171.

     In proceedings under the Patents Act 1977 s 40 (see PARA 369), s 70 (see PARA 555), s 71 (see PARA 554) or proceedings for infringement (see PARA 520 et seq), the court, in determining whether to award costs or expenses to any party and what costs or expenses to award, must have regard to all the relevant circumstances, including the financial position of the parties: s 106(1), (1A) (s 106(1) amended, and s 106(1A) added, by the Patents Act 2004 s 14(1)–(4)). If in any such proceedings the court directs that any costs of one party are to be paid by another party, the court may settle the amount of the costs by fixing a lump sum or may direct that the costs are to be taxed on a scale specified by the court, being a scale of costs prescribed by rules of court: Patents Act 1977 s 106(2) (amended by the Constitutional Reform Act 2005 Sch 11 para 23(1), (4)).

623. Appeals relating to unpublished applications. On an appeal from the UK Intellectual Property Office[1] relating to an unpublished application[2] the hearing will normally be in private: if it is of general importance, the decision may be published[3] after a suitable lapse of time[4].

1   As to the UK Intellectual Property Office see PARA 577.
2   As to publication see PARA 326.
3   Ie in the Reports of Patent Cases: see PARA 578.
4   As to early publication see PARA 578.

624. Appeals from the Patents Court. Appeal lies from a decision of the Patents Court in the exercise of its original jurisdiction, in the ordinary way, on a question of law or fact, to the Court of Appeal[1] and thence, with leave, to the Supreme Court[2].

Appeal lies to the Court of Appeal (and thence, with leave, to the Supreme Court) from a decision of the Patents Court on an appeal from a decision of the comptroller only with leave of the Patents Court or of the Court of Appeal[3], and only where either:

(1)   the ground of appeal is that the decision of the Patents Court is wrong in law[4]; or

(2)   the comptroller's decision was given under one of certain provisions of the Patents Act 1977[5].

Where an appeal lies to the Court of Appeal, the judge may, in a proper case, certify that the appeal may be made direct to the Supreme Court[6].

1   See the Senior Court Acts 1981 s 16(1); and COURTS AND TRIBUNALS vol 24 (2010) PARA 693. As to the procedure see CIVIL PROCEDURE vol 12 (2009) PARA 1657 et seq.
2   See the Constitutional Reform Act 2005 s 40; and COURTS AND TRIBUNALS vol 24 (2010) PARA 657 et seq.
3   Patents Act 1977 s 97(3). Where the appeal is from a decision of the Patents Court which was itself made on an appeal from a decision of the comptroller, the appellant must serve the appellant's notice on the comptroller in addition to the respondent: see *Practice Direction — Statutory Appeals and Appeals Subject to Special Provision* PD 52D para 13.1; and CIVIL PROCEDURE. The Patents Act 1977 s 97(3) is not impliedly repealed or amended by the Access to Justice Act 1999 s 55 (second appeals) (see CIVIL PROCEDURE vol 12 (2009) PARA 1682): *Smith International Inc v Specialised Petroleum Services Group Ltd* [2005] EWCA Civ 1357, [2006] 1 WLR 252, [2006] FSR 487.
4   Patents Act 1977 s 97(3)(b).
5   Patents Act 1977 s 97(3)(a). These provisions are ss 8, 12 and s 37 (entitlement questions: see PARAS 360, 361, 363, 365), s 18 (refusal of patent: see PARA 328), s 20 (failure of application: see PARA 331), s 27 (amendment of specification after grant: see PARA 346), s 40 (compensation to employee-inventor: see PARA 369), s 61 (infringement: see PARA 553), s 72 or s 73 (revocation: see PARAS 562–563) or s 75 (amendment in infringement or revocation proceedings: see PARA 562). Decisions under s 71 (declaration of non-infringement: see PARA 554) are not, however, included.
6   See the Administration of Justice Act 1969 ss 12, 13; and COURTS AND TRIBUNALS vol 24 (2010) PARA 659.

625. Prerogative orders. The High Court can intervene by prerogative order[1] if the comptroller[2] acts illegally and where the comptroller's decision is not subject to appeal[3].

1   As to prerogative orders see JUDICIAL REVIEW vol 61 (2010) PARA 687 et seq. Application for a prerogative order is by way of application for a judicial review under CPR Pt 54. See, however, the Patents Act 1977 s 116; and PARA 573. See eg *R (on the application of Penife International Ltd) v HM Comptroller-General of Patents, Trademarks and Designs* [2003] EWHC 3409 (Admin), [2004] RPC 737, [2004] All ER (D) 116 (Mar); *R (on the application of Ash & Lacy Building Products Ltd) v Comptroller General of Patents* [2002] EWHC 541 (Admin), [2002] RPC 939, [2002] All ER (D) 23 (Feb).

2   As to the comptroller see PARA 575.
3   As to the right of appeal from the comptroller see PARA 621.

(4) THE INTELLECTUAL PROPERTY ENTERPRISE COURT

626.   Procedure.   Proceedings may be brought in the Intellectual Property Enterprise Court[1] only where the amount or value of a claim is made for damages or an account of profits does not exceed £500,000[2], unless the parties agree that the Court has jurisdiction to award damages or profits in excess of that sum[3]. Proceedings before the Court are dealt with by an enterprise judge or a District Judge[4]. The provisions of the Civil Procedure Rules relating to the bringing of intellectual property claims[5] apply to claims started in or transferred to the Intellectual Property Enterprise Court, subject to specified modifications[6], and other provisions of the Civil Procedure Rules concerned with the transfer of proceedings[7], the contents of statements of case and statements of truth[8], the content and filing of defences and replies[9], disclosure and inspection[10], and the making of applications[11], are also applied in a modified form[12]. Provision is also made in connection with costs[13].

1   See PARAS 516, 619.
2   CPR 63.17A(1). Provision for determining the amount or value of a claim is made by CPR 63.17A(2).
3   CPR 63.17A(3).
4   See CPR 63.19.
5   Ie CPR Pt 63.
6   See CPR 63.17, 63.23, 63.27, 63.28. At the case management conference the Court may direct that a scientific adviser be appointed and that a document setting out basic undisputed technology should be prepared: see *Practice Direction — Intellectual Property Claims* PD 63 para 5.10; and PARA 620.
7   Ie CPR 30.5 (see CIVIL PROCEDURE vol 11 (2009) PARA 67) (applied with modifications by CPR 63.18).
8   Ie CPR Pt 16 (see CIVIL PROCEDURE vol 11 (2009) PARA 584 et seq) and CPR Pt 22 (see CIVIL PROCEDURE vol 11 (2009) PARA 613 et seq).
9   Ie CPR Pt 15 (see CIVIL PROCEDURE vol 11 (2009) PARA 199 et seq).
10 Ie CPR Pt 31 (see CIVIL PROCEDURE vol 11 (2009) PARA 538 et seq).
11 Ie CPR Pt 23 (see CIVIL PROCEDURE vol 11 (2009) PARA 303 et seq).
12 See CPR 63.18, 63.20, 63.21, 63.22, 63.24, 63.25.
13 See CPR 63.26.

(5) THE UNIFIED PATENT COURT

627.   Establishment.   The Unified Patent Court is a specialised court with exclusive jurisdiction for litigation relating to European patents[1] and European patents with unitary effect ('unitary patents')[2], established pursuant to the EU Agreement on a Unified Patent Court[3]. At the date at which this volume states the law the Agreement had yet to enter into force and the Court was accordingly not operational[4]. When operational, the Unified Patent Court will comprise a Court of First Instance[5], a Court of Appeal[6] and a Registry[7].

The Secretary of State[8] may by order make provision for giving effect in the United Kingdom to the provisions of the Agreement on a Unified Patent Court[9].

1   As to the meaning of 'European patent' see PARA 644 note 5.
2   As to European patents with unitary effect ('unitary patents') see PARA 645.
3   See the Agreement on a Unified Patent Court (Brussels, 19 February 2013) (OJ C175, 20.6.2013, p 1). The Unified Patent Court is to be treated for the purposes of the International Organisations Act 1968 s 1 (organisations of which the United Kingdom is a member: see

INTERNATIONAL RELATIONS LAW vol 61 (2010) PARA 309) as an organisation to which that section applies: Patents Act 1977 s 88B (ss 88A, 88B added by the Intellectual Property Act 2014 s 17).

4   The Agreement on a Unified Patent Court requires ratification by at least 13 member states, including France, Germany and the United Kingdom, in order to enter into force (see the Preamble): at the date at which this volume states the law the Agreement had been ratified only by Austria, Belgium, Denmark, France and Sweden.

5   See the Agreement on a Unified Patent Court arts 6–8.

6   See the Agreement on a Unified Patent Court art 9.

7   See the Agreement on a Unified Patent Court art 10.

8   As to the Secretary of State see PARA 573.

9   Patents Act 1977 s 88A(1) (as added: see note 3). Such an order may, in particular, make provision to confer jurisdiction on a court, remove jurisdiction from a court or vary the jurisdiction of a court and to require the payment of fees: s 88A(2) (as so added). An order may also make provision for varying the application of specified provisions of the Patents Act 1977 so that they correspond to provision made by the Agreement: Patents Act 1977 s 88A(3) (as so added). An order under s 88A may make provision which applies generally or in relation only to specified cases and make different provision for different cases, and may amend the Patents Act 1977 or any other enactment: s 88A(4), (5) (as so added). At the date at which this volume states the law no such order had been made.

11. INTERNATIONAL CONVENTIONS

(1) THE INTERNATIONAL CONVENTION FOR THE PROTECTION OF INDUSTRIAL PROPERTY

628. Convention countries. Nearly all countries with appreciable industry are parties to the International Convention for the Protection of Industrial Property (the 'Paris Convention')[1]. Such countries enjoy special protection for their vessels, aircraft and vehicles against claims for patent infringement[2]. In addition Her Majesty may by Order in Council[3] declare any country[4] to be a convention country for the purposes of establishing priority[5]. Thus, an application made in a declared convention country for protection of an invention[6] or an application which is treated, by law or treaty, by that country as equivalent to an application there, may be made the subject of a claim to priority in a United Kingdom application[7] in the same way as an earlier United Kingdom application[8].

1   Ie the International Convention for the Protection of Industrial Property (Paris, 20 March 1883) (the 'Paris Convention'), as revised (Stockholm, 14 July 1967 to 13 January 1968; TS 61 (1970); Cmnd 4431). For a list of members see note 5.

2   See the Patents Act 1977 s 60(5)(d), (e), (7); and PARA 514.

3   As to the making of such orders see PARA 574.

4   For these purposes, every colony, protectorate and territory subject to the authority or under the suzerainty of another country, and every territory administered by another country under the trusteeship system of the United Nations is taken to be a country in the case of which a declaration may be so made: Patents Act 1977 s 90(3).

5   Patents Act 1977 s 90(1). Her Majesty may by Order in Council direct that any of the Channel Islands or any colony is to be taken to be a convention country for those purposes: s 90(2) (amended by the Statute Law (Repeals) Act 1986).

     The following countries are declared to be convention countries by the Patents (Convention Countries) Order 2007, SI 2007/276, art 2, Schedule (amended by SI 2009/2746; SI 2013/538): Albania, Algeria, Andorra, Angola, Antigua and Barbuda, Argentina, Armenia, Australia, Austria, Azerbaijan, Bahamas, Bahrain, Bangladesh, Barbados, Belarus, Belgium, Belize, Benin, Bhutan, Bolivia, Bosnia and Herzegovina, Botswana, Brazil, Brunei Darussalam, Bulgaria, Burkina Faso, Burundi, Cambodia, Cameroon, Canada, Cape Verde, Central African Republic, Chad, Chile, China, Columbia, Comoros, Congo, Democratic Republic of the Congo, Costa Rica, Cote d'Ivoire, Croatia, Cuba, Cyprus, Czech Republic, Denmark, Djibouti, Dominica, Dominican Republic, Ecuador, Egypt, El Salvador, Equatorial Guinea, Estonia, Faeroe Islands, Fiji, Finland, France (including Overseas Departments and Territories), Gabon, Gambia, Georgia, Germany, Ghana, Greece, Grenada, Guatemala, Guinea, Guinea-Bissau, Guyana, Haiti, Holy See, Honduras, Hong Kong, Hungary, Iceland, India, Indonesia, Islamic Republic of Iran, Iraq, Ireland, Israel, Italy, Jamaica, Japan, Jordan, Kazakhstan, Kenya, Democratic People's Republic of Korea, Republic of Korea, Kuwait, Kyrgyzstan, Lao People's Democratic Republic, Latvia, Lebanon, Lesotho, Liberia, Libyan Arab Jamahiriya, Liechtenstein, Lithuania, Luxembourg, Macao, Former Yugoslav Republic of Macedonia, Madagascar, Malawi, Malaysia, Maldives, Mali, Malta, Mauritania, Mauritius, Mexico, Republic of Moldova, Monaco, Mongolia, Montenegro, Morocco, Mozambique, Myanmar, Namibia, Nepal, Netherlands, Netherlands Antilles and Aruba, New Zealand (including the Cook Islands, Niue and Tokelau), Nicaragua, Niger, Nigeria, Norway, Oman, Pakistan, Panama, Papua New Guinea, Paraguay, Peru, Philippines, Poland, Portugal, Qatar, Romania, Russian Federation, Rwanda, Saint Kitts and Nevis, Saint Lucia, Saint Vincent and the Grenadines, Samoa, San Marino, Sao Tome and Principe, Saudi Arabia, Senegal, Serbia, Seychelles, Sierra Leone, Singapore, Slovakia, Slovenia, Solomon Islands, South Africa, Spain, Sri Lanka, Sudan, Suriname, Swaziland, Sweden, Switzerland, Syrian Arab Republic, Taiwan, Tajikistan, United Republic of Tanzania, Thailand, Togo, Tonga, Trinidad and Tobago, Tunisia, Turkey, Turkmenistan, Uganda, Ukraine, United Arab Emirates, United States of America (including Puerto Rico and all territories and possessions), Uruguay, Uzbekistan, Vanuatu, Venezuela, Vietnam, Yemen, Zambia, Zimbabwe.

6   The application need not be for a patent; the convention expressly refers to an application for a patent or for the registration of a utility model (see the International Convention for the

Protection of Industrial Property art 4(A)(1)), and it is clear that an application for an 'inventor's certificate' would be sufficient: cf the Convention on the Grant of European Patents (the 'European Patent Convention') (Munich, 5 October 1973; TS 20 (1978); Cmnd 7090) art 87(1).

7   As to convention priority in respect of applications for European patents (UK) and international applications (UK) see PARAS 640–641.

8   See the Patents Act 1977 s 5; and PARA 310.

(2) THE PATENT CO-OPERATION TREATY

(i) The Treaty

629. International applications.   The Patent Co-operation Treaty[1] enables an applicant to file a single application for a patent, known as an 'international application'[2], which is then subject to a single international search[3] and, if desired, a single international preliminary examination[4], before being filed with whichever national patent offices the applicant specifies[5].

International applications may only be filed by residents or nationals of a contracting state[6].

1   Ie the Patent Co-operation Treaty (Washington, 19 June 1970; TS 78 (1978); Cmnd 7340). The United Kingdom ratified the treaty on 24 October 1977 and the treaty entered into force on 24 January 1978, except Chapter II (arts 31–42) which entered into force on 29 March 1978. The treaty is divided into five chapters of which only Chapter I (arts 3–30) (international applications and searches) and Chapter II (international preliminary examinations) are relevant. For the contracting states see note 6. There are also regulations governing applications under the Patent Co-operation Treaty ('the Patent Co-operation Treaty Regulations') which are periodically updated: the current regulations came into force on 1 July 2014.

 References in the Patents Act 1977 to the Patent Co-operation Treaty are references to that Treaty or any international convention or agreement replacing it, as amended or supplemented by any convention or international agreement, including in either case any protocol or annex, or in accordance with the terms of any such convention or agreement, and include references to any instrument made under any such convention or agreement: Patents Act 1977 s 130(6)(c).

2   As to filing an international application see PARA 630.

3   As to the international search see PARA 632.

4   As to the international preliminary examination see PARA 636.

5   As to the communication of international applications to national patent offices see PARA 634; as to the filing of an international application with the UK Intellectual Property Office see PARA 630. As to the UK Intellectual Property Office see PARA 577.

6   See the Patent Co-operation Treaty art 9(1). No provision of the Patent Co-operation Treaty is to be interpreted as diminishing the rights under the Paris Convention for the Protection of Industrial Property (see PARA 628) of any resident or national of any country party to that convention: Patent Co-operation Treaty art 1(2).

 The contracting states constitute the International Patent Co-operation Union (art 1(1)), of which the present members are Albania, Algeria, Angola, Antigua and Barbuda, Argentina, Armenia, Australia, Austria, Azerbaijan, Bahrain, Barbados, Belarus, Belgium, Belize, Benin, Bosnia and Herzegovina, Botswana, Brazil, Bulgaria, Burkina Faso, Cameroon, Canada, Central African Republic, Chad, China, Colombia, Comoros, Congo, Costa Rica, Côte d'Ivoire, Croatia, Cuba, Cyprus, Czech Republic, Democratic People's Republic of Korea, Denmark, Dominica, Dominican Republic, Ecuador, Egypt, El Salvador, Equatorial Guinea, Estonia, Finland, France, Gabon, Gambia, Georgia, Germany, Ghana, Greece, Grenada, Guatemala, Guinea, Guinea-Bissau, Holy See, Honduras, Hungary, Iceland, India, Indonesia, Islamic Republic of Iran, Ireland, Israel, Italy, Japan, Kazakhstan, Kenya, Kyrgyzstan, Lao People's Democratic Republic, Latvia, Lesotho, Liberia, Libyan Arab Jamahiriya, Liechtenstein, Lithuania, Luxembourg, Madagascar, Malawi, Malaysia, Mali, Malta, Mauritania, Mexico, Moldova, Monaco, Mongolia, Montenegro, Morocco, Mozambique, Namibia, Netherlands, New Zealand, Nicaragua, Niger, Nigeria, Norway, Oman, Papua New Guinea, Philippines, Poland, Portugal, Republic of Korea, Romania, Russian Federation, Saint Kitts and Nevis, Saint Lucia, Saint Vincent and the Grenadines, San Marino, Sao Tome and Principe, Senegal, Serbia, Seychelles, Sierra Leone, Singapore, Slovakia, Slovenia, South Africa, Spain, Sri Lanka, Sudan, Swaziland, Sweden, Switzerland, Syrian Arab Republic, Tajikistan, The former Yugoslav

Republic of Macedonia, Togo, Trinidad and Tobago, Tunisia, Turkey, Turkmenistan, Uganda, Ukraine, United Arab Emirates, United Kingdom, United Republic of Tanzania, United States of America, Uzbekistan, Vietnam, Zambia, Zimbabwe. The United Kingdom has extended the application of the Treaty to Hong Kong and to the Isle of Man.

630. Filing of international applications. An international application for a patent[1] must be filed with the prescribed receiving office[2], namely the national office of or acting for the contracting state of which the applicant is a resident, the national office of or acting for the contracting state of which the applicant is a national, or, irrespective of the contracting state of which the applicant is a resident or national, with the International Bureau of the World Intellectual Property Organisation in Geneva[3]. The receiving office must then transmit one copy of the application (the 'record copy'[4]) to the International Bureau, one copy (the 'search copy') to the appropriate international searching authority[5] and retains one copy (the 'home copy')[6].

United Kingdom[7] residents may not file international applications outside the United Kingdom without the written authority of the comptroller[8] if the application contains information relating to military technology or might be prejudicial to national security or to the safety of the public[9].

1 'International application for a patent' means an application made under the Patent Co-operation Treaty (Washington, 19 June to 31 December 1970; TS 78 (1978); Cmnd 7340): Patents Act 1977 s 130(1). In the Patent Co-operation Treaty and the Patent Co-operation Treaty Regulations (see PARA 629) 'application' means an application for the protection of an invention; and references to an 'application' are to be construed as references to applications for patents for inventions, inventors' certificates, utility certificates, utility models, patents or certificates of addition, inventors' certificates of addition, and utility certificates of addition: Patent Co-operation Treaty art 2(i). As to the form and contents of an international application see PARA 631.

2 Patent Co-operation Treaty art 10. 'Receiving office' means the national office or the intergovernmental organisation with which the application is filed: art 2(xv). As to the filing of applications see the Patents Rules 2007, SI 2007/3291, r 65. See also note 3.

3 Patent Co-operation Treaty Regulations r 19.1(a). Any contracting state may agree with another contracting state or any intergovernmental organisation that the national office of the latter state or the intergovernmental organisation may, for all or some purposes, act instead of the national office of the former state as receiving office for applicants who are residents or nationals of that former state: r 19.1(b). Notwithstanding such agreement, the national office of the former state is to be considered the competent receiving office: r 19.1(b). As to the World Intellectual Property Organisation see COPYRIGHT vol 23 (2013) PARA 999.

4 The record copy is considered the true copy of the application: Patent Co-operation Treaty art 12(2).

5 The international searching authority may be either a national office or an intergovernmental organisation, whose tasks include the establishing of documentary search reports on prior art with respect to inventions which are the subject of applications: Patent Co-operation Treaty art 16(1). The following national and regional offices have been appointed by the Assembly of the International Patent Co-operation Union (see PARA 629) under art 16(3) to act as international searching authorities: Australia, Austria, Canada, China, Finland, Japan, Republic of Korea, Nordic Patent Institute, the Russian Federation, Spain, Sweden, the United States of America, and the European Patent Organisation.

6 Patent Co-operation Treaty art 12(1). The fee to transmit an international application for a patent filed at the UK Intellectual Property Office to the International Bureau and the international searching authority is £75: Patents (Fees) Rules 2007, SI 2007/3292, r 7(3), (4) (r 7(3) amended by SI 2010/33). As to the UK Intellectual Property Office see PARA 577.

7 As to the meaning of 'United Kingdom' see PARA 303 note 5.

8 As to the comptroller see PARA 575.

9 See the Patents Act 1977 s 23(1), (1A); and PARA 336.

631. Form and contents of international applications. An international application[1] must contain a request, a description of the invention, one or more claims, one or more drawings where required, and an abstract[2]. The request must contain:

(1) a petition to the effect that the international application be processed according to the Patent Co-operation Treaty[3];

(2) the designation of the contracting state or states ('designated states') in which the applicant desires protection[4] and, if a regional patent[5] is available for any designated state, whether the applicant desires a regional patent[6];

(3) the name of and other prescribed data concerning the applicant and his agent, if any[7]; and

(4) the title of the invention[8] and the name of and other prescribed data concerning the inventor or inventors where the national law of at least one of the designated states requires this information to be filed at the time of filing a national application[9].

The description must disclose the invention in a manner sufficiently clear and complete for the invention to be carried out by a person skilled in the art[10]. The claim or claims must define the matter for which protection is sought, must be clear and concise and must be fully supported by the description[11]. The abstract merely serves the purpose of technical information and cannot be taken into account for any other purpose, particularly not for the purpose of interpreting the scope of the protection sought[12].

An international application may contain a declaration claiming priority from one or more earlier applications filed in or for any country party to the Paris Convention for the Protection of Industrial Property[13]. An international application must relate to only one invention or to a group of inventions linked by a single inventive concept[14].

There are specific regulations governing inventions relating to biological material[15] and nucleotide and amino acid sequence listings[16].

1 As to the meaning of 'international application' see PARA 630 note 1.

2 Patent Co-operation Treaty (Washington, 19 June to 31 December 1970; TS 78 (1978); Cmnd 7430) art 3(2). As to the language and form of an application see art 3(4); and the Patent Co-operation Treaty Regulations rr 3–12. As to the Patent Co-operation Treaty Regulations see PARA 629.

3 Patent Co-operation Treaty art 4(1)(i).

4 Unless the applicant asks for any other kind of protection as referred to in the Patent Co-operation Treaty art 43 (eg an inventor's certificate, a utility certificate or a utility model), the request is deemed to be a request for protection by the grant of a patent by or for the designated state: art 4(3).

5 Ie a patent granted by a national or intergovernmental authority having the power to grant patents effective in more than one state: Patent Co-operation Treaty art 2(iv). The European Patent (see PARA 644) is a regional patent which may be requested under art 4(1).

6 Patent Co-operation Treaty art 4(1)(ii).

7 Patent Co-operation Treaty art 4(1)(iii).

8 Patent Co-operation Treaty art 4(1)(iv).

9 See the Patent Co-operation Treaty art 4(1)(v). As to the filing of United Kingdom applications see PARA 314 et seq.

10 Patent Co-operation Treaty art 5.

11 Patent Co-operation Treaty art 6. In particular, wherever appropriate, claims must contain: (1) a statement indicating those technical features of the invention which are necessary for the definition of the claimed subject matter but which, in combination, are part of the prior art; and (2) a characterising portion, preceded by the words 'characterised by', 'characterised in that', 'wherein the improvement comprises' or any other words to the same effect, stating concisely

the technical features which, in combination with the prior art features, it is desired to protect: Patent Co-operation Treaty Regulations r 6.3(b).

12 Patent Co-operation Treaty art 3(3).
13 See the Patent Co-operation Treaty art 8. As to the Paris Convention for the Protection of Industrial Property see PARA 628.
14 See the Patent Co-operation Treaty Regulations r 13.
15 See the Patent Co-operation Treaty Regulations r 13 bis.
16 See the Patent Co-operation Treaty Regulations r 13 ter.

632.   The international search. On receipt of an international application[1] the international searching authority[2] carries out an international search[3], the purpose of which is to discover relevant prior art[4] to enable subsequent examination to assess novelty and inventive step. The international searching authority is not required to search subject matter which is not patentable under national laws[5]. After the search, the international searching authority draws up an international search report[6] which is sent to the International Bureau[7] and to the applicant[8].

1 As to the meaning of 'international application' see PARA 630 note 1.
2 As to the international searching authority see PARA 630 note 5.
3 Every international application is subject to an international search: Patent Co-operation Treaty (Washington, 19 June to 31 December 1970; TS 78 (1978); Cmnd 7340) art 15(1). As to the procedure before the international searching authority see art 17.
4 Patent Co-operation Treaty art 15(2). The search must be made on the basis of the claims, with due regard to the description and drawings, if any: art 15(3).
5 See the Patent Co-operation Treaty Regulations r 39, which lists the following exclusions: scientific and mathematical theories; plant or animal varieties or essentially biological processes for the production of plants and animals, other than microbiological processes and the products of such processes; schemes, rules or methods of doing business, performing purely mental acts or playing games; methods for treatment of the human or animal body by surgery or therapy, as well as diagnostic methods; mere presentations of information; computer programs to the extent that the international searching authority is not equipped to search prior art concerning such programs. Cf the exclusions from patentability under the United Kingdom law: see the Patents Act 1977 s 1(2); and PARA 430. As to the Patent Co-operation Treaty Regulations see PARA 629.
6 See the Patent Co-operation Treaty art 18.
7 See PARA 630.
8 Patent Co-operation Treaty art 18(2).

633.   Amendment of claims before the International Bureau. On receipt of the international search report[1] the applicant under an international application[2] is allowed to amend the claims once[3]. In addition, he may file a brief statement explaining the amendments[4]. The amendments must not go beyond the disclosure in the international application as filed[5].

1 As to the report see PARA 632.
2 As to the meaning of 'international application' see PARA 630 note 1.
3 See the Patent Co-operation Treaty (Washington, 19 June to 31 December 1970; TS 78 (1978); Cmnd 7340) art 19(1).
4 Patent Co-operation Treaty art 19(1).
5 See the Patent Co-operation Treaty art 19(2), (3). As to the filing of an international application see PARA 630. Amendment which goes beyond the original disclosure is not permitted under United Kingdom law: see the Patents Act 1977 s 76; and PARA 351.

634.   Communication of international applications to designated offices. An international application[1], together with the international search report[2], must be communicated to each designated office[3] by the International Bureau[4]. If the claims have been amended[5], the claims both as filed and as amended must be communicated[6].

Communication completes the international stage of an international application, the remaining procedures being governed solely by the national law of the designated state concerned. No designated office may process or examine an international application prior to the expiry of 30 months from its priority date[7].

1   As to the meaning of 'international application' see PARA 630 note 1.
2   As to the report see PARA 632.
3   'Designated office' means the national office of or acting for a designated state (see PARA 631): Patent Co-operation Treaty (Washington, 19 June to 31 December 1970; TS 78 (1978); Cmnd 7340) art 2(xiii).
4   Patent Co-operation Treaty art 20(1); Patent Co-operation Treaty Regulations r 47.1. A designated office may waive the requirement that the International Bureau transmit the application and report, in which case the applicant is responsible for transmission: Patent Co-operation Treaty arts 20(1), 22. As to the International Bureau see PARA 630. As to the Patent Co-operation Treaty Regulations see PARA 629.
5   As to the amendment of claims see PARA 633.
6   Patent Co-operation Treaty art 20(2).
7   Patent Co-operation Treaty arts 22, 23(1). As to the priority date of an international application see art 8. At the express request of the applicant any designated office may, however, process or examine an international application at any time: art 23(2).

635.   International publication.   An international application[1] must be published by the International Bureau[2] as promptly as possible after the expiry of 18 months from the priority date of the application[3], together with the international search report[4].

1   As to the meaning of 'international application' see PARA 630 note 1.
2   See PARA 630.
3   See the Patent Co-operation Treaty (Washington, 19 June to 31 December 1970; TS 78 (1978); Cmnd 7340) art 21(1), (2). As to the priority date of international applications see art 8; and as to the effects of publication see art 29.
4   See the Patent Co-operation Treaty art 21(3).

636.   International preliminary examination.   An applicant under an international application[1] who is either a resident or national[2] of a contracting state which has adhered to Chapter II[3] of the Patent Co-operation Treaty may request an international preliminary examination of his application provided that he has filed his application at the receiving office[4] of such a contracting state[5]. The international preliminary examination must be carried out by an international preliminary examining authority[6].

The demand for an international preliminary examination must be made separately from the international application itself[7], and must indicate the contracting state or states ('elected states') in which the applicant intends to use the results of the international preliminary examination[8]. Only designated states may be elected[9].

1   As to the meaning of 'international application' see PARA 630 note 1.
2   As to residence and nationality see PARA 629 note 6.
3   Ie the Patent Co-operation Treaty (Washington, 19 June to 31 December 1970, TS 78 (1978); Cmnd 7340) Chapter II (arts 31–42), dealing with international preliminary examinations.
4   As to the meaning of 'receiving office' see PARA 630 note 2.
5   See the Patent Co-operation Treaty art 31(2).
6   Patent Co-operation Treaty art 32(1).
7   Patent Co-operation Treaty art 31(3).
8   Patent Co-operation Treaty art 31(4)(a).
9   Patent Co-operation Treaty art 31(4)(a). As to designated states see PARA 631. The comptroller has power under the Patents Rules 2007, SI 2007/3291, r 107 (see PARA 590) to correct irregularities or errors in a demand filed at the UK Intellectual Property Office as the relevant

receiving office: *Prangley's Application* [1988] RPC 187, CA. See also *Vapocure Technologies Ltd's Application* [1990] RPC 1, CA. There is also power under the Patent Co-operation Treaty Regulations r 91.1 to correct obvious errors: see *Vapocure Technologies Ltd's Application*; *R v Comptroller-General of Patents, ex p Celltech Ltd* [1991] RPC 475; *Drazil's Application* [1992] RPC 479. As to the comptroller see PARA 575. As to the UK Intellectual Property Office see PARA 577. As to the Patent Co-operation Treaty Regulations see PARA 629.

637. Function and scope of international preliminary examinations. The purpose of an international preliminary examination[1] is to formulate a preliminary and non-binding opinion as to whether the invention claimed appears to be novel, to involve an inventive step, and to be industrially applicable[2]. For the purposes of the examination, a claimed invention is considered novel if it is not anticipated by the prior art[3], and it is considered to involve an inventive step if, having regard to the prior art, it is not at its priority date obvious to a person skilled in the art[4]. A claimed invention is considered to be industrially applicable if it can be made or used in any kind of industry[5]. Any contracting state[6] may, however, apply additional or different criteria for the purpose of deciding whether, in that state, the claimed invention is patentable[7]. The examination must take into consideration all the documents cited in the international search report[8] and may also consider any additional relevant documents[9], but the examining authority is not required to examine subject matter which is not patentable under national laws[10].

The international preliminary examination report must state in relation to each claim whether it appears to satisfy the criteria of novelty, inventive step and industrial applicability, but it must not contain any statement as to whether the claimed invention is or seems to be patentable under any national law[11]. The report is accompanied by the citation of documents believed to support the stated conclusion together with such further explanation as may be thought necessary[12]. The report is then sent to the applicant and to the International Bureau[13], and the report, together with any translations that may be required, are transmitted by the International Bureau to the national patent office of each elected state[14].

1 As to the examination generally see PARA 636.
2 Patent Co-operation Treaty (Washington, 19 June to 31 December 1970; TS 78 (1978); Cmnd 7340) art 33(1).
3 Patent Co-operation Treaty art 33(2). 'Prior art' is defined in the Patent Co-operation Treaty Regulations r 33, and essentially consists of every written disclosure made available to the public before the priority date of the application (see PARA 634). As to the Patent Co-operation Treaty Regulations see PARA 629.
4 Patent Co-operation Treaty art 33(3).
5 See the Patent Co-operation Treaty art 33(4).
6 As to contracting states see PARA 629 note 6.
7 Patent Co-operation Treaty art 33(5).
8 As to the report see PARA 632.
9 Patent Co-operation Treaty art 33(6).
10 See the Patent Co-operation Treaty Regulations r 67; which lists the following exclusions: scientific and mathematical theories; plant or animal varieties or essentially biological processes for the production of plants and animals, other than microbiological processes and the products of such processes; schemes, rules or methods of doing business, performing purely mental acts or playing games; methods for treatment of the human or animal body by surgery or therapy, as well as diagnostic methods; mere presentations of information; computer programs to the extent that the international searching authority is not equipped to search prior art concerning such programs. Cf the exclusions from patentability under the United Kingdom law: see the Patents Act 1977 s 1(2); and PARA 430. As to the Patent Co-operation Treaty Regulations see PARA 629.
11 See the Patent Co-operation Treaty art 35(2).

12 Patent Co-operation Treaty art 35(2).
13 Patent Co-operation Treaty art 36(1).
14 See the Patent Co-operation Treaty art 36(3). As to elected states see PARA 636.

638.   Amendment of claims before elected offices.   An applicant under an international application[1] may amend the claims, description and drawings once before each elected office[2] before the expiry of a specified period from the priority date[3]. The amendments must not go beyond the disclosure in the international application as filed unless permitted under the national law of the elected state[4], and must be in accordance with the national law of the elected state in all respects not provided for in the Patent Co-operation Treaty and the Implementing Regulations[5].

The international phase is then complete. Thereafter the application enters the national phase. No elected office may process the international application according to its own law before the expiry of 25 months from the priority date of the international application[6], unless the applicant requests an earlier processing[7].

1   As to the meaning of 'international application' see PARA 630 note 1.
2   'Elected office' means the national office of or acting for the elected state (see PARA 636): Patent Co-operation Treaty (Washington, 19 June to 31 December 1970; TS 78 (1978); Cmnd 7340) art 2(xiv).
3   Patent Co-operation Treaty art 41(1).
4   Patent Co-operation Treaty art 41(2).
5   Patent Co-operation Treaty art 41(3).
6   Patent Co-operation Treaty art 40(1). As to the priority date of an international application see PARA 634.
7   Patent Co-operation Treaty art 40(2).

639.   Patent agents and other representatives.   Any attorney, patent agent[1] or other person having the right to practise before the national office with which the international application[2] was filed[3] is entitled to practise before the International Bureau and the competent international searching and preliminary examination authorities[4] in respect of that application[5].

1   See PARA 612 et seq.
2   As to the meaning of 'international application' see PARA 630 note 1.
3   As to the filing of international applications see PARA 630.
4   As to these authorities see PARAS 632, 636.
5   Patent Co-operation Treaty (Washington, 19 June to 31 December 1970; TS 78 (1978); Cmnd 7340) art 49.

(ii) Incorporation of International Applications into the British Patent System

640.   Effect of international application for patent.   An international application for a patent (UK)[1] for which a date of filing has been accorded under the Patent Co-operation Treaty is treated[2] as an application for a patent under the Patents Act 1977[3].

If the application, or the designation of the United Kingdom in it, is withdrawn or deemed[4] to be withdrawn under the Treaty, it is treated as withdrawn under the Patents Act 1977[5].

An application is not, however, treated as withdrawn under the Patents Act 1977 if it, or the designation of the United Kingdom in it, is deemed to be withdrawn under the Treaty:

(1)   because of an error or omission in an institution having functions under the Treaty; or

(2)   because, owing to circumstances outside the applicant's control, the application was not received by the International Bureau[6] before the end of the time limited for that purpose under the Treaty,

or in such other circumstances as may be prescribed[7].

If an international application for a patent which designates the United Kingdom is refused a filing date under the Treaty and the comptroller determines that the refusal was caused by an error or omission in an institution having functions under the Treaty, he may direct that the application is to be treated as an application under the Patents Act 1977, having such date of filing as he may direct[8].

1   For these purposes, 'international application for a patent' means an application made under the Patent Co-operation Treaty (Washington, 19 June to 31 December 1970; TS 78 (1978); Cmnd 7340): Patents Act 1977 s 130(1). As to the Patent Co-operation Treaty see PARA 629 et seq. 'Designate' in relation to an application or a patent, means designate the country or countries (in pursuance of the European Patent Convention (see PARA 644 et seq) or the Patent Co-operation Treaty) in which protection is sought for the invention which is the subject of the application or patent and includes a reference to a country being treated as designated in pursuance of the convention or treaty: Patents Act 1977 s 130(1) (definition amended by the Patents Act 2004 Sch 1 paras 1, 9). An international application for a patent is not, by reason of being treated by virtue of the European Patent Convention as an application for a European patent (UK), to be treated also as an international application for a patent (UK): Patents Act 1977 s 130(4A) (added by the Patents Act 2004 Sch 1 paras 1, 9). As to the meaning of 'date of filing' see PARA 315; and as to the meaning of 'United Kingdom' see PARA 303 note 5.

2   Ie for the purposes of the Patents Act 1977 Pt I (ss 1–76A) and Pt III (ss 97–132) but subject to s 89A (international and national phases of applications: see PARA 641) and s 89B (adaptation of provisions in relation to international applications: see PARAS 641–643).

3   Patents Act 1977 s 89(1) (s 89 substituted by the Copyright, Designs and Patents Act 1988 Sch 5 para 25). As to international applications for patents under the Patents Act 1977 s 89 see the Patents Rules 2007, SI 2007/3291, Pt 6 (rr 64–72).

4   Ie except as mentioned in the Patents Act 1977 s 89(3): see the text and notes 6–7.

5   Patents Act 1977 s 89(2) (as substituted: see note 3).

6   See PARA 630.

7   Patents Act 1977 s 89(3) (as substituted: see note 3). See also note 8. See *Mitsubishi Jidosha Kogyo KK's Application* [1988] RPC 449 (where the application was saved under head (1) in the text). The other circumstance prescribed for the purposes of the Patents Act 1977 s 89(3) is where the comptroller determines that, in comparable circumstances in relation to an application under the Patents Act 1977 (other than an international application for a patent (UK)), he would have exercised his powers under the Patents Rules 2007, SI 2007/3291, r 107 (see PARA 590) or r 108 (see PARA 597) to prevent the application being treated as withdrawn: r 72. As to the comptroller see PARA 575.

8   Patents Act 1977 s 89(5) (as substituted: see note 3). The applicant may, before the end of the relevant period, make a written request to the comptroller to give a direction under s 89(5): Patents Rules 2007, SI 2007/3291, r 71(1). The relevant period is two months beginning immediately after the date on which the International Bureau, or the receiving office, notifies the applicant that his international application for a patent (UK) is refused a filing date under the Patent Co-operation Treaty: Patents Rules 2007, SI 2007/3291, r 71(4) (amended by SI 2011/2052). The applicant may notify the comptroller that the circumstances mentioned in the Patents Act 1977 s 89(3) (see the text and notes 6–7) or the Patents Rules 2007, SI 2007/3291, r 72 (see note 7) apply to his application: r 71(2). The request under r 71(1) must be accompanied by a statement of the reasons for the request and the fee prescribed for the purposes of the Patents Act 1977 s 89A(3) (see PARA 641): Patents Rules 2007, SI 2007/3291, r 71(3). Where the applicant has made a request to the comptroller under r 71(1), the comptroller may direct the applicant to furnish him with any document, information or evidence within such period as the comptroller may specify: r 71(5). Where the applicant fails, before the end of the period specified, to comply with such a direction, the comptroller may treat him as having withdrawn his request: r 71(6). Where the Patents Act 1977 s 89(3) applies or a direction has been given under s 89(5) the comptroller may: (1) alter any period of time (whether it has already expired or not) specified in the Act or listed in the Patents Rules 2007, SI 2007/3291, Sch 4 Pts 1–3 (see PARA 597); and (2) amend any document kept at the UK Intellectual Property

Office in relation to the application, subject to such conditions as the comptroller may direct: r 71(7). As to the UK Intellectual Property Office see PARA 577.

641. International and national phases of application. The provisions of the Patent Co-operation Treaty[1] relating to publication[2], search[3], examination[4] and amendment[5], and not those of the Patents Act 1977, apply to an international application for a patent (UK)[6] during the international phase of the application[7].

The international phase of the application means the period from the filing of the application in accordance with the Treaty until the national phase of the application begins[8]. The national phase of the application begins:

(1) when the prescribed period[9] expires, provided any necessary translation of the application into English has been filed at the UK Intellectual Property Office[10] and the prescribed fee[11] has been paid by the applicant[12]; or

(2) on the applicant expressly requesting the comptroller to proceed earlier with the national phase of the application, filing at the UK Intellectual Property Office:

    (a) a copy of the application[13], if none has yet been sent to the UK Intellectual Property Office in accordance with the Treaty; and

    (b) any necessary translation of the application into English[14],

and paying the prescribed fee[15].

Where, during the international phase the application is amended in accordance with the Treaty, the amendment is treated as made under the Patents Act 1977 if:

(i) when the prescribed period expires, any necessary translation of the amendment into English has been filed at the UK Intellectual Property Office; or

(ii) where the applicant expressly requests the comptroller to proceed earlier with the national phase of the application, there is then filed at the UK Intellectual Property Office a copy of the amendment, if none has yet been sent to the UK Intellectual Property Office in accordance with the Treaty and any necessary translation of the amendment into English;

otherwise the amendment must be disregarded[16].

During the international phase of the application the statutory provisions relating to the determination of questions of entitlement in relation to applications[17] do not apply and the statutory provisions relating to the determination of entitlement in relation to foreign and convention patents[18] apply notwithstanding the application; but after the end of the international phase the statutory provisions relating to the determination of questions of entitlement in relation to applications apply and the statutory provisions relating to the determination of entitlement in relation to foreign and convention patents do not[19].

When the national phase begins, the comptroller must refer the application for so much of the examination[20] and search[21] as he considers appropriate in view of any examination or search[22] carried out under the Treaty[23].

1 Ie the Patent Co-operation Treaty (Washington, 19 June to 31 December 1970; TS 78 (1978); Cmnd 7340): see PARA 629 et seq.
2 As to publication see PARA 635.
3 As to search see PARA 632.
4 As to examination see PARA 636.
5 As to amendment see PARA 633.
6 As to the meaning of 'international application for a patent' see PARA 640 note 1.

7   Patents Act 1977 s 89A(1) (s 89A added by the Copyright, Designs and Patents Act 1988 Sch 5 para 25).

8   Patents Act 1977 s 89A(2) (as added: see note 7).

9   The prescribed period for the purposes of the Patents Act 1977 s 89A(3)(a), (5)(a) is 31 months beginning immediately after: (1) where there is no declared priority date, the date of filing of the application; (2) where there is a declared priority date, that date: Patents Rules 2007, SI 2007/3291, r 66(1) (amended by SI 2011/2052). However, where the applicant has been notified under the Patents Rules 2007, SI 2007/3291, r 69(5) that a translation is missing (see note 10), the prescribed period is three months beginning immediately after the date of the notification: r 66(2) (amended by SI 2011/2052). As to the extension of time limits see PARA 597. If the prescribed period expires without the conditions mentioned in the Patents Act 1977 s 89A(3)(a) being satisfied, the application is taken to be withdrawn: s 89A(4) (as added: see note 7).

10 As to the UK Intellectual Property Office see PARA 577.

    A translation is necessary for the purposes of the Patents Act 1977 s 89A(3) where any of the following are not in English: (1) the international application for a patent (UK) as published in accordance with the Patent Co-operation Treaty; (2) where the information mentioned in the Patents Rules 2007, SI 2007/3291, r 13(1), Sch 1 para 3(2)(a), (b) (biological material) has been provided (see PARA 321), that information: r 69(1). Where the applicant expressly requests the comptroller to proceed with the national phase before the end of the period prescribed by r 66(1) (see note 9), the translation must include the request and abstract: r 69(2). But r 69(2) does not apply where a copy of the application, as published in accordance with the Patent Co-operation Treaty, is available to the comptroller: Patents Rules 2007, SI 2007/3291, r 69(3). A translation of an amendment is necessary for the purposes of the Patents Act 1977 s 89A(5) (see the text to note 16) where any amendment made to the application is not in English and has either been: (a) published under the Patent Co-operation Treaty; or (b) annexed to the International Preliminary Examination Report (see PARA 636): Patents Rules 2007, SI 2007/3291, r 69(4). At the end of the period prescribed by r 66(1) (see note 9), the comptroller must notify the applicant that a necessary translation is missing if: (i) a translation of the application has been filed, but a translation of the amendment has not been filed; or (ii) the information mentioned in Sch 1 para 3(2)(a), (b) (biological material) has been provided, but a translation of that information has not been filed, and the prescribed fee has been paid: r 69(5).

    Translations which are necessary for the purposes of the Patents Act 1977 s 89A(3) and (5) are necessary for only that part of the application which is in a language other than English: Patents Rules 2007, SI 2007/3291, r 70(1), (2). Where the application includes a drawing which is annotated, the translation must include either a copy of the original drawing where the original annotations have been replaced by annotations in English, or a new drawing with the annotations in English: r 70(3). Where a title has been established for the application by the international searching authority (see PARA 630 note 5), the translation must include that title (and not any title which was included in the application as it was originally filed): r 70(4). Where the description of the invention includes a sequence listing and the listing complies with the relevant requirements of the Patent Co-operation Treaty, the translation of the application may exclude a translation of the sequence listing: Patents Rules 2007, SI 2007/3291, r 70(5). These provisions apply to translations of amendments as they apply to translations of applications and accordingly references to 'application' are to be construed as references to 'amendment': r 70(6).

11 The prescribed fee to publish a translation filed at the UK Intellectual Property Office under the Patents Act 1977 s 89A(3) or (5) (international and national phases of application) is £12: Patents (Fees) Rules 2007, SI 2007/3292, r 7(1).

12 Patents Act 1977 s 89A(3)(a) (as added: see note 7). The comptroller must on payment of the prescribed fee publish any translation filed at the UK Intellectual Property Office under the Patents Act 1977 s 89A(3) or s 89A(5) (see the text to note 16): s 89A(6) (as so added).

13 For these purposes, a 'copy of the application' includes a copy published in accordance with the Treaty in a language other than that in which it was originally filed: Patents Act 1977 s 89A(3) (as added: see note 7).

14 Patents Act 1977 s 89A(3)(b) (as added: see note 7). See also note 12.

15 See the Patents Act 1977 s 89A(3) (as added: see note 7).

16 Patents Act 1977 s 89A(5) (as added: see note 7). See also notes 10, 12.

17 Ie the Patents Act 1977 s 8: see PARAS 360–361.

18 Ie the Patents Act 1977 s 12: see PARA 363.

19　Patents Act 1977 s 89B(4) (s 89B added by the Copyright, Designs and Patents Act 1988 Sch 5 para 25). See eg *Cannings' United States Application* [1992] RPC 459 (cited in PARA 364 note 4).
20　Ie under the Patents Act 1977 s 15A (see PARA 317), s 17 (see PARA 327).
21　Ie under the Patents Act 1977 ss 17, 18: see PARAS 327–328.
22　As to examination under the Treaty see PARA 636; and as to the search so carried out see PARA 632.
23　Patents Act 1977 s 89B(5) (as added: see note 19).

642.　International applications for patents (UK). Where an international application for a patent (UK)[1] is accorded a filing date[2] under the Patent Co-operation Treaty[3]:

(1)　that date or, if the application is redated under the Treaty[4] to a later date, that later date is treated as the date of filing[5] the application under the Patents Act 1977[6];

(2)　any declaration of priority made under the Treaty[7] is treated as made under the Patents Act 1977[8] and, where in accordance with the Treaty any extra days are allowed, the specified period of 12 months[9] is treated as altered accordingly[10]; and

(3)　any statement of the name of the inventor under the Treaty[11] is treated as a statement filed[12] under the Patents Act 1977[13].

If the application, not having been published under the Patents Act 1977, is published in accordance with the Treaty[14], it is treated[15] as published under the Patents Act 1977[16] when the national phase of the application begins or, if later, when published in accordance with the Treaty[17].

1　As to the meaning of 'international application for a patent ' see PARA 640 note 1.
2　The receiving office must accord as the international filing date the date of receipt of the international application, provided that that office has found that, at the time of receipt: (1) the applicant does not obviously lack, for reasons of residence or nationality, the right to file an international application with the receiving office; (2) the international application is in the prescribed language; (3) the international application contains at least the following elements: (a) an indication that it is intended as an international application; (b) the designation of at least one contracting state; (c) the name of the applicant, as prescribed; (d) a part which on the face of it appears to be a description; (e) a part which on the face of it appears to be a claim or claims: Patent Co-operation Treaty (Washington, 19 June to 31 December 1970; TS 78 (1978); Cmnd 7340) art 11(1). As to the receiving office see PARA 630.
3　As to the Patent Co-operation Treaty see PARA 629 et seq.
4　If the receiving office finds that the international application did not, at the time of receipt, fulfil the requirements listed in the Patent Co-operation Treaty art 11(1) (see note 2), it must invite the applicant to file the required correction: art 11(2).
5　As to the meaning of 'date of filing' see PARA 315.
6　Patents Act 1977 s 89B(1)(a) (s 89B added by the Copyright, Designs and Patents Act 1988 Sch 5 para 25).
7　Ie under the Patent Co-operation Treaty art 8.
8　Ie under the Patents Act 1977 s 5(2): see PARA 310.
9　Ie the period allowed under the Patents Act 1977 s 5(2)(a): see PARA 310.
10　Patents Act 1977 s 89B(1)(b) (as added (see note 6); and amended by SI 2004/2357).
11　Ie under the Patent Co-operation Treaty art 4(1)(v), (4).
12　Ie under the Patents Act 1977 s 13(2): see PARA 307.
13　Patents Act 1977 s 89B(1)(c) (as added: see note 6).
14　Ie under the Patent Co-operation Treaty art 21: see PARA 635.
15　Ie for purposes other than those mentioned in the Patents Act 1977 s 89B(3): see PARA 643.
16　Ie under the Patents Act 1977 s 16: see PARA 326.
17　Patents Act 1977 s 89B(2) (as added (see note 6); and amended by the Patents Act 2004 s 5, Sch 1 paras 1, 8).

643.　Effect of international applications for patents (UK). For the purposes of the statutory provisions relating to the use of an invention for the service of the

Crown[1] and the infringement of rights conferred by publication[2], the application, not having been published under the Patents Act 1977, is treated as duly published[3]:

(1)   if it is published in accordance with the Patent Co-operation Treaty[4] in English, on its being so published[5]; and

(2)   if it is so published in a language other than English on the due publication of a translation of the application[6] or on the service by the applicant of a translation into English of the specification of the application on the government department concerned or, as the case may be, on the person committing the infringing act[7].

1   Ie the Patents Act 1977 s 55: see PARAS 404–405.
2   Ie the Patents Act 1977 s 69: see PARAS 546–547.
3   Ie under the Patents Act 1977 s 16: see PARA 326.
4   Ie the Patent Co-operation Treaty (Washington, 19 June to 31 December 1970; TS 78 (1978); Cmnd 7340): see PARA 629 et seq.
5   Patents Act 1977 s 89B(3)(a) (s 89B added by the Copyright, Designs and Patents Act 1988 Sch 5 para 25). For these purposes, the reference to the service of a translation on a government department or other person is to its being sent by or delivered to that department or person: Patents Act 1977 s 89B(3) (as so added).
6   Ie in accordance with the Patents Act 1977 s 89A(6): see PARA 641.
7   Patents Act 1977 s 89B(3)(b) (as added: see note 5).

(3) THE EUROPEAN PATENT CONVENTION AND THE UNITARY PATENT

(i) The Convention

644. The European Patent Convention. Under the European Patent Convention[1] a person seeking protection for an invention may file a single application for a patent at the European Patent Office[2] specifying in which of the contracting states he desires to obtain protection[3]. After an examination for patentability[4] by the European Patent Office, a European patent[5] is granted. A European patent takes effect as a number of national patents operative in the states designated by the applicant[6]. A European patent may be opposed before the European Patent Office within the period of nine months after its grant[7]. If no opposition is entered or any such opposition is rejected, the validity of the European patent can thereafter be put in issue only in the national courts of the states designated by the applicant and is subject to the relevant national law[8]. Infringement of a European patent is governed solely by the national law of the state concerned[9]. After grant a European patent has the same territorial effect in the states for which it has been granted as does a national patent[10].

1   For these purposes, 'European Patent Convention' means the Convention on the Grant of European Patents (Munich, 5 October 1973; TS 20 (1978); Cmnd 7090): Patents Act 1977 s 130(1). The following states have acceded to the convention: Austria, Belgium, Bulgaria, Croatia, Cyprus, the Czech Republic, Denmark, Estonia, Finland, France, Germany, Greece, Hungary, Iceland, Ireland, Italy, Latvia, Liechtenstein, Lithuania, Luxembourg, Malta, Monaco, the Netherlands, Norway, Poland, Portugal, Romania, Slovakia, Slovenia, Spain, Sweden, Switzerland, Turkey and the United Kingdom.

     The European Patent Organisation has concluded 'extension agreements' with a number of states which are not parties to the European Patent Convention. Under these agreements, applicants for European patents may, on payment of an extension fee, obtain protection for their patents in the countries with which such agreements have been concluded. At the date at which this volume states the law, extension agreements are in force with the following states: Albania, Bosnia and Herzegovina, Macedonia, and Serbia: see EPO Official Journal 2006 p 325.

References in the Patents Act 1977 to the European Patent Convention are references to that Convention or any international convention or agreement replacing it, as amended or supplemented by any convention or international agreement, including in either case any protocol or annex, or in accordance with the terms of any such convention or agreement, and include references to any instrument made under any such convention or agreement: Patents Act 1977 s 130(6)(a).

2   For these purposes, 'European Patent Office' means the patent office established by the European Patent Convention: Patents Act 1977 s 130(1). As to the office generally see the European Patent Convention arts 4, 10–25; and as to the communication of information from the United Kingdom to the European Patent Office see the Patents Act 1977 s 94; and the Patents Rules 2007, SI 2007/3291, r 63. Any costs awarded by the European Patent Office are recoverable, if the county court so orders, the County Courts Act 1984 s 85 (see CIVIL PROCEDURE vol 12 (2009) PARA 1283) or otherwise as if they were payable under an order of that court: Patents Act 1977 s 93(a) (amended by the Tribunals, Courts and Enforcement Act 2007 Sch 13 paras 39, 42; and by the Crime and Courts Act 2013 Sch 9 para 52(1)(b), (2) (but not so as to affect the wording of the text).

3   See the European Patent Convention art 3.

4   As to the criteria of patentability see PARA 648.

5   'European patent' means a patent granted under the European Patent Convention: art 2(1); Patents Act 1977 s 130(1).

6   See the European Patent Convention art 2(2).

7   See the European Patent Convention arts 99–105.

8   See the European Patent Convention art 2(2).

9   European Patent Convention art 64(3).

10   European Patent Convention art 64(1). Where an undertaking has been given to prosecute an appeal with due diligence, resulting in a stay of revocation, that appeal may not be stayed pending the outcome of an European Patent Office decision on a related matter unless some other good grounds are shown to support such a stay: *Beloit Technologies Inc v Valmet Paper Machinery Inc* [1996] FSR 718, CA.

645.   The Unitary Patent.   A European patent with Unitary Effect (a 'unitary patent') is a European patent[1] granted under the terms of the European Patent Convention[2] to which unitary effect for the territory of all participating member states is given after grant[3]. At the date at which this volume states the law the unitary patent is yet to come into effect[4]. The European Patent Office[5] will be responsible for granting and administering requests for unitary patents[6].

1   As to the meaning of 'European patent' see PARA 644 note 5. As to the application see PARA 647.

2   As to the meaning of 'European Patent Convention' see PARA 644 note 1.

3   See Parliament and Council Regulation (EU) 1257/2012 (OJ L361, 31.12.2012, p 1) implementing enhanced cooperation in the area of the creation of unitary patent protection. The unitary patent was originally conceived in the Convention for the European Patent for the Common Market (Luxembourg, 15 December 1975; Cmnd 6553) (amended by the Agreement Relating to Community Patents (OJ L401, 30.12.89, p 1)).

4   Parliament and Council Regulation (EU) 1257/2012 (OJ L361, 31.12.2012, p 1) came into force on 20 January 2013 (see art 18), but will only apply from the date of entry into force of the Agreement on a Unified Patent Court (OJ C175, 20.6.2013, p 1), which at the date at which this volume states the law had yet to enter into force (see PARA 627).

5   As to the European Patent Office see PARA 644 note 2.

6   See Parliament and Council Regulation (EU) 1257/2012 (OJ L361, 31.12.2012, p 1) art 9.

646.   Filing an application for a European patent.   An applicant may file an application for a European patent[1] at the European Patent Office[2] or at the national patent office of a contracting state[3]. Persons resident in the United Kingdom[4] may, however, only file an application for a European patent at the UK Intellectual Property Office where the application could be prejudicial to national security or the safety of the public[5]. An application filed at a national patent office has the same effect as if it had been filed on the same day at the European Patent Office[6]. An application filed at a national patent office must be forwarded by that office within six weeks of filing to the European Patent Office unless the subject matter is obviously liable to secrecy[7].

1   As to the meaning of 'European patent' see PARA 644 note 5. As to the application see PARA 647.
2   As to the European Patent Office see PARA 644 note 2.
3   European Patent Convention art 75(1). As to the meaning of 'European Patent Convention' see PARA 644 note 1.
4   As to the meaning of 'United Kingdom' see PARA 303 note 5.
5   See the Patents Act 1977 s 23; and PARA 336. As to the UK Intellectual Property Office see PARA 577.
6   European Patent Convention art 75(1)(b).
7   See the European Patent Convention art 77. Failure by a national office to transmit the application within the prescribed period will result in loss of rights for which there is no restitution: see Case J-03/80 *Chubb/Failure to forward a European patent application* [1979–1985] EPOR 23, Legal Board of Appeal.

647. Form and contents of application for a European patent and date of filing. An application for a European patent[1] must contain a request for the grant of a European patent[2], a description of the invention[3], one or more claims[4], any drawings referred to in the description or the claims[5] and an abstract[6]. The application is subject to the payment of a filing fee and a search fee within one month of its filing[7], and must satisfy the conditions laid down in the Implementing Regulations[8].

All the contracting states[9] at the time of filing of the European patent application are deemed to be designated in the request for grant of a European patent[10]. Designation may be withdrawn at any time up to the grant of the European patent[11]. The application must designate the inventor[12]. If the applicant is not the inventor or the sole inventor, the designation must contain a statement indicating the origin of the right to the European patent[13]. The application must relate to one invention only or to a group of inventions so linked as to form a single general inventive concept[14], and must disclose the invention in a manner sufficiently clear and complete for it to be carried out by a person skilled in the art[15]. The claims must define the matter for which protection is sought, be clear and precise and be supported by the description[16]. Wherever appropriate, the claims must contain a statement of those technical features which are necessary for the definition of the claimed subject matter but which, in combination, are part of the prior art and a characterising portion, preceded by the expression 'characterised in that' or 'characterised by', stating the technical features which, in combination with the prior art features, it is desired to protect[17].

The date of filing of an application for a European patent is the date on which the documents filed by the applicant contain:

(1)   an indication that a European patent is sought;
(2)   information identifying the applicant or allowing the applicant to be contacted; and
(3)   a description or reference to a previously filed application[18].

Priority may be claimed from any convention application[19] filed during the period of 12 months preceding the date of filing of an application for a European patent[20].

1   As to the meaning of 'European patent' see PARA 644 note 5.
2   European Patent Convention art 78(1)(a). As to the meaning of 'European Patent Convention' see PARA 644 note 1.
3   European Patent Convention art 78(1)(b).
4   European Patent Convention art 78(1)(c).

5   European Patent Convention art 78(1)(d).
6   European Patent Convention art 78(1)(e).
7   European Patent Convention art 78(2).
8   European Patent Convention art 78(1). The Implementing Regulations are appended to the convention: see generally the Implementing Regulations rr 26–36. The Implementing Regulations have been amended from time to time.
9   For the contracting states see PARA 644 note 1.
10 European Patent Convention art 79(1). Designation may be subject to the payment of a designation fee: see art 79(2).
11 European Patent Convention art 79(3).
12 European Patent Convention art 81.
13 European Patent Convention art 81. The right to a European patent belongs to the inventor or his successors in title, except where the inventor is an employee, in which case the right to the patent is subject to the national law of the state in which he is mainly employed: see art 60.
14 European Patent Convention art 82. Plurality of invention is not, however, a ground of opposition: see PARA 650.
15 European Patent Convention art 83.
16 European Patent Convention art 84.
17 See the Implementing Regulations r 43(1).
18 European Patent Convention art 80; Implementing Regulations r 40(1).
19 As to convention applications see PARA 646.
20 See the European Patent Convention arts 87–89.

648.   Criteria of patentability.   A European patent[1] may be granted only in respect of an invention which is susceptible of industrial application[2], which is new and which involves an inventive step[3]. In particular the following are not regarded as patentable inventions:

(1)   discoveries, scientific theories and mathematical methods[4];

(2)   aesthetic creations[5];

(3)   schemes, rules and methods for performing mental acts, playing games or doing business, and programs for computers[6]; and

(4)   presentations of information[7].

European patents may not be granted in respect of methods for the treatment of the human or animal body by surgery or therapy and diagnostic methods practised on the human or animal body, but products, such as substances and compositions, for use in any such methods are patentable provided that the criteria of novelty and inventive step are satisfied[8].

A European patent may not be granted in respect of an invention the commercial exploitation of which would be contrary to 'ordre public' or morality[9], nor may it be granted in respect of plant or animal varieties or essentially biological processes for the production of plants or animals[10]. An invention is considered to be new if it does not form part of the state of the art[11]. The state of the art comprises everything that has been made available to the public by means of a written or oral description, by use, or in any other way before the date of filing of the European patent application[12]. In addition, the state of the art comprises for the purposes of assessing novelty, but not inventive step, the content of European patent applications as filed, the dates of filing of which are earlier than that of the application in suit but which were published on or after that date[13]. An invention involves an inventive step if, having regard to the state of the art, it is not obvious to a person skilled in the art[14].

1   As to the meaning of 'European patent' see PARA 644 note 5.
2   An invention is considered as susceptible of industrial application if it can be made or used in any kind of industry, including agriculture: European Patent Convention art 57. As to the meaning of 'European Patent Convention' see PARA 644 note 1. In connection with art 57 see *Eli Lilly & Co v Human Genome Sciences Inc* [2011] UKSC 51, [2012] 1 All ER 1154, [2012] RPC 102.

3   European Patent Convention art 52(1). Cf the Patents Act 1977 s 1(1); and PARA 429 et seq.
    Cases on patentability under the Patents Act 1977 are of persuasive authority. Likewise cases on
    patentability under the European Patent Convention are of persuasive authority in the English
    courts. See further PARAS 429–487 where both United Kingdom and European Patent Office
    cases are cited. The correct approach in determining whether an 'invention' was unpatentable
    within the terms of art 52(2), (3) was in four steps: (1) to properly construe the claim; (2) to
    identify the actual contribution; (3) to ask whether it fell solely within the excluded subject
    matter; and (4) to check whether the actual or alleged contribution was actually technical in
    nature: *Aerotel Ltd v Telco Holdings Ltd; Re Macrossan's Application* [2006] EWCA Civ 1371
    at [40]–[49], [2007] 1 All ER 225 at [40]–[49], [2007] RPC 117 at [40]–[49] per Jacob LJ,
    giving the judgment of the court.
4   European Patent Convention art 52(2)(a).
5   European Patent Convention art 52(2)(b).
6   European Patent Convention art 52(2)(c). A computer program product which comprises all the
    features enabling the implementation of a method and which, when loaded onto a computer, is
    capable of carrying out that method is patentable as a European patent: Case T-0935/97 *Re
    IBM's European Patent Application No 96 305 851.6* (1999) Times, 15 April.
7   European Patent Convention art 52(2)(d).
8   See the European Patent Convention art 53(c). See *Bristol-Myers Squibb Co v Baker Norton
    Pharmaceuticals Inc* [2001] RPC 1, [2000] IP & T 908, [2000] All ER (D) 713, CA.
9   European Patent Convention art 53(a). The exploitation is not deemed to be contrary to 'ordre
    public' or morality merely because it is prohibited by law or regulation in some or all of the
    contracting states: art 53(a). For the contracting states see PARA 644 note 1.
10 European Patent Convention art 53(b). Article 53(b) does not apply to microbiological processes
    or products of such processes: art 53(b).
11 European Patent Convention art 54(1). As to non-prejudicial disclosures see art 55.
12 European Patent Convention art 54(2). As to the date of filing of a European patent application
    see PARA 647.
13 European Patent Convention arts 54(3), 56.
14 European Patent Convention art 56. See *Armour Group plc v Leisuretech Electronics Pty Ltd*
    [2008] EWHC 2797 (Pat), [2008] All ER (D) 155 (Nov).

649.   Examination of an application for a European patent.   An application
for a European patent[1] is subject to a search to ascertain whether the criteria of
novelty and inventive step are satisfied[2] and is examined to ascertain whether it
meets the requirements of the European Patent Convention as to patentability[3].
The application must be published by the European Patent Office[4] as soon as
possible after the expiry of a period of 18 months from its priority date[5]. If the
application and the invention to which it relates meet the requirements of the
convention, the European Patent Office must grant the European patent[6]. As
soon as possible after it publishes the mention of the grant of a European patent,
the European Patent Office must publish the specification of the European
patent[7].

1   As to the meaning of 'European patent' see PARA 644 note 5.
2   See the European Patent Convention art 92. As to the meaning of 'European Patent Convention'
    see PARA 644 note 1.
3   See the European Patent Convention art 94. As to the criteria of patentability see PARA 648.
4   As to the European Patent Office see PARA 644 note 2.
5   See the European Patent Convention art 93. As to the priority date see PARA 647.
6   See the European Patent Convention art 97(1).
7   European Patent Convention art 98.

650.   Opposition.   Within nine months of the publication of the mention of the
grant of a European patent[1], any person may give notice to the European Patent
Office[2] of opposition to the European patent granted[3]. The opposition applies to
the European patent in all the contracting states[4] in which the patent has effect[5].
Opposition may be filed on the following grounds only:

(1) that the subject matter of the European patent is not patentable within the meaning of the European Patent Convention[6];

(2) that the European patent does not disclose the invention in a manner sufficiently clear and complete for it to be carried out by a person skilled in the art[7];

(3) that the subject matter of the European patent extends beyond the content of the application as filed or, if the patent was granted on a divisional application or on a new application filed by a person found to be entitled to the invention[8], that the subject matter extends beyond the content of the earlier applications as filed[9].

If the opposition is admissible, the Opposition Division of the European Patent Office must examine whether the grounds of opposition relied on prejudice the maintenance of the European patent[10]. If the Opposition Division is of the opinion that the grounds are so prejudicial, it must revoke the patent; otherwise, the opposition must be rejected[11]. Provision is made for amendment of the patent in opposition proceedings and the Opposition Division may decide to maintain the patent in its amended form[12].

1   As to the meaning of 'European patent' see PARA 644 note 5.
2   As to the European Patent Office see PARA 644 note 2.
3   European Patent Convention art 99(1). The notice of opposition will not be deemed to have been filed until the opposition fee has been paid: art 99(1). As to the meaning of 'European Patent Convention' see PARA 644 note 1. As to the procedure on opposition see art 99 and the Implementing Regulations rr 75–89.
4   For the contracting states see PARA 644 note 1.
5   European Patent Convention art 99(2). As to the effect of a European patent see PARA 651.
6   European Patent Convention art 100(a). As to the criteria of patentability see PARA 648.
7   European Patent Convention art 100(b).
8   Ie in accordance with the European Patent Convention art 61.
9   European Patent Convention art 100(c).
10 See the European Patent Convention art 101(1). Jurisdiction under the Patents Act 1977 s 72 (revocation proceedings: see PARA 562) exceeds that exercised by an Opposition Division under the European Patent Convention art 100; and a decision of an Opposition Division is not a final judicial determination of the validity of a patent: *Buehler AG v Chronos Richardson Ltd* [1998] 2 All ER 960, [1998] RPC 609, CA.
11 European Patent Convention art 101(2).
12 European Patent Convention art 101(3).

651. Effect of a European patent. A European patent[1] confers on the proprietor from the date of publication of the mention of its grant, in each contracting state[2] in respect of which it is granted, the same rights as would be conferred by a national patent granted in that state[3]. Any infringement of a European patent is dealt with by national law[4]. An application for a European patent which has been accorded a date of filing[5] is in each designated state[6] equivalent to a regular national filing where appropriate with the priority claimed for the European patent application[7]. A European patent application confers on the applicant, from the date of its publication[8], the same rights as would be conferred on him by a national patent application from the date of its publication[9]. The extent of protection conferred by a European patent or application for a European patent is determined by the terms of the claims, although the description and drawings must be used to interpret the claims[10]. In relation to infringement of a European patent and infringement of the rights conferred by publication, a European patent or application is regarded as void ab initio to the extent that the patent is revoked in opposition proceedings[11]. Any contracting state may provide that, if the text of the European patent is not in one of its official languages[12], a translation into one of its official languages must be filed and that on failure to file such a translation the European patent may be deemed void ab initio in that state[13].

1 As to the meaning of 'European patent' see PARA 644 note 5.
2 For the contracting states see PARA 644 note 1.
3 European Patent Convention art 64(1). Cf the Patents Act 1977 s 77; and PARA 652. As to the meaning of 'European Patent Convention' see PARA 644 note 1.
4 European Patent Convention art 64(3).
5 As to the date of filing of a European patent application see PARA 647.
6 As to the designation of states see PARA 647.
7 See the European Patent Convention art 66. Cf the Patents Act 1977 s 78(2), (3); and PARA 653.
8 As to publication of a European patent application see PARA 649.
9 See the European Patent Convention art 67(1), (2). Such rights are deemed never to have existed if the application is withdrawn, deemed to be withdrawn or refused or, in respect of a particular state, if the designation of that state is withdrawn or deemed to have been withdrawn: art 67(4). Cf the Patents Act 1977 ss 69, 78(7); and PARA 653.
10 European Patent Convention art 69(1). See also the Protocol on the interpretation of art 69.
11 See the European Patent Convention art 68. As to opposition see PARA 650.
12 The official languages of the European Patent Office are English, French and German: European Patent Convention art 14(1). All applications for European patents must be filed in one of these languages: art 14(2). As to the European Patent Office see PARA 644 note 2. See Case C-44/98 *BASF AG v Präsident des Deutschen Patentamts* [1999] ECR I-6269, [2001] 2 CMLR 435, (1999) Times, 12 October, ECJ.
13 See the European Patent Convention art 65.

(ii) Incorporation of the European Patent Convention into the British Patent System

652. Internal effect of a European patent (UK). A European patent (UK)[1] is treated[2], as from the date of publication of the mention of its grant in the European Patent Bulletin[3], as if it were a patent under the Patents Act 1977 granted in pursuance of an application made under that Act, and as if notice of the grant of the patent had, on the date of that publication, been published[4] in the Official Journal (Patents)[5].

Accordingly, the proprietor of a European patent (UK) then has, as respects the United Kingdom, the same rights and remedies, subject to the same conditions, as the proprietor of a patent under the Patents Act 1977[6]; and any statement made and any certificate filed under the European Patent Convention in respect of non-prejudicial disclosures[7] are respectively treated as a statement made and written evidence filed for the purposes of the corresponding provision[8] of the Patents Act 1977[9].

The above provisions[10] do not, however affect the operation in relation to a European patent (UK) of any provision of the European Patent Convention relating to the amendment or revocation of such a patent in proceedings before the European Patent Office[11].

Where in the case of a European patent (UK) proceedings for infringement[12] or under the Crown use provisions[13] have been commenced before the court[14] or the comptroller[15] and have not been finally disposed of and it is established in proceedings before the European Patent Office[16] that the patent is only partially valid, the provisions relating to the relief to be afforded in respect of partially valid patents[17] apply as they apply to proceedings in which the validity of a patent is put in issue and in which it is found that the patent is only partially valid[18].

Where a European patent (UK) has been amended in accordance with the European Patent Convention, the amendment has effect[19] as if the specification of the patent had been amended under the Patents Act 1977[20].

Where a European patent (UK) is revoked in accordance with the provisions of the European Patent Convention, it is treated[21] as having been revoked under the Patents Act 1977[22].

Where under the European Patent Convention a European patent (UK) is revoked for failure to observe a time limit and is subsequently restored or is revoked by the Board of Appeal and is subsequently restored by the Enlarged Board of Appeal, and between the revocation and publication of the fact that it has been restored a person begins in good faith to do an act which would constitute[23] an infringement of the patent or makes in good faith effective and serious preparations to do such an act, he has the right[24] to continue to do the act or, as the case may be, to do the act[25].

1   For these purposes, 'European patent (UK)' means a European patent designating the United Kingdom: Patents Act 1977 s 130(1). As to the meaning of 'European patent' see PARA 644 note 5. As to the meaning of 'United Kingdom' see PARA 303 note 5.
2   Ie for the purposes of the Patents Act 1977 Pt I (ss 1–76: new domestic law), and Pt III (ss 97–132: miscellaneous and general provisions).
3   Ie under the European Patent Convention art 97(3). As to the meaning of 'European Patent Convention' see PARA 644 note 1. 'European Patent Bulletin' means the bulletin of that name published under the European Patent Convention: Patents Act 1977 s 130(1).
4   Ie under the Patents Act 1977 s 24: see PARA 337.
5   Patents Act 1977 s 77(1). References in Pts I, III to a patent are to be construed accordingly: s 77(1)(b). As to the Journal see PARA 578. See *Actavis Group HF v Eli Lilly & Co* [2012] EWHC 3316 (Pat), [2012] All ER (D) 347 (Nov) (affd [2013] EWCA Civ 517, [2013] RPC 985, [2013] All ER (D) 233 (May)) (an English court has jurisdiction to decide on matters of infringement or non-infringement of, not only European Patent (UK) patents, but also European Patent designations in other jurisdictions). Recognition of the validity and effect of European patents under domestic law, recognised by the Patents Act 1977 s 77, is insufficient to create a jurisdictional link: see *Virgin Atlantic Airways Ltd v Jet Airways (India) Ltd* [2013] EWCA Civ 1713, [2014] RPC 516, [2014] All ER (D) 44 (Jan).
6   Patents Act 1977 s 77(1)(a).
7   Ie under the European Patent Convention art 55(1)(b), (2).
8   Ie the Patents Act 1977 s 2(4)(c): see PARA 435.
9   Patents Act 1977 s 77(1)(c).
10 Ie the Patents Act 1977 s 77(1): see the text to notes 1–9.
11 Patents Act 1977 s 77(2). As to the meaning of 'European Patent Office' see PARA 644 note 2. As to the application of the Patents Act 1997 s 77(2) to the situation where there are concurrent proceedings pending before the national court and the European Patent Office see *Beloit Technologies Inc v Valmet Paper Machinery Inc* [1997] RPC 489, CA.
12 Ie under the Patents Act 1977 ss 61–69: see PARA 499 et seq.
13 Ie under the Patents Act 1977 s 58: see PARA 409.
14 As to the meaning of 'court' see PARA 619 note 1. It is within the court's discretion to stay proceedings pending determination of validity by the European Patent Office: *Amersham International plc v Corning Ltd* [1987] RPC 53; *Pall Corpn v Commercial Hydraulics (Bedford) Ltd* [1989] RPC 703 at 709, CA; *Biogen Inc v Medeva plc* [1993] RPC 475; *Unilin Beheer BV v Berry Floor NV* [2007] EWCA Civ 364, [2008] 1 All ER 156, [2008] FSR 635; *Glaxo Group Ltd v Genentech Inc* [2008] EWCA Civ 23, [2008] FSR 459, [2008] All ER (D) 282 (Jan).
15 As to the comptroller see PARA 575.
16 Ie opposition proceedings under the European Patent Convention art 100: see PARA 650.
17 Ie the provisions of the Patents Act 1977 s 63 (see PARA 550) or, as the case may be, s 58(7)–(9) (see PARA 409).
18 Patents Act 1977 s 77(3) (substituted by the Copyright, Designs and Patents Act 1988 Sch 5 para 21(1), (2)).
19 See note 2.
20 Patents Act 1977 s 77(4) (substituted by the Copyright, Designs and Patents Act 1988 Sch 5 para 21(1), (3)).

21 See note 2.

22 Patents Act 1977 s 77(4A) (added by the Copyright, Designs and Patents Act 1988 Sch 5 para 21(1), (3)). The wording of the Patents Act 1977 s 77(4A) does not enable the court to question the propriety of the action of the European Patent Office Board of Appeal: *Lenzing AG's European Patent (UK)* [1997] RPC 245. See also *ITP SA v Coflexip Stena Offshore Ltd* 2004 SLT 1285, IH (domestic appeal proceedings would not be stayed pending outcome of appeal to European Court of Human Rights against decision of the European Patent Office Board of Appeal to revoke patent); *Unilin Beheer BV v Berry Floor NV* [2007] EWCA Civ 364, [2008] 1 All ER 156, [2007] FSR 635; *Glaxo Group Ltd v Genentech Inc* [2008] EWCA Civ 23, [2008] All ER (D) 282 (Jan), [2008] FSR 549. See *Actavis UK Ltd v Merck & Co Inc* [2008] EWCA Civ 444, [2009] 1 All ER 196, [2008] RPC 631 (Court of Appeal free to depart from the ratio decidendi of its own earlier decision if it was satisfied that the European Patent Office Boards of Appeal had formed a settled view of European patent law which was inconsistent with that earlier decision).

23 Ie apart from the Patents Act 1977 s 55: see PARAS 404–405.

24 Ie the rights conferred by the Patents Act 1977 s 28A(4), (5): see PARA 357.

25 Patents Act 1977 s 77(5) (amended by the Copyright, Designs and Patents Act 1988 Sch 5 para 8(b); and the Patents Act 2004 Sch 1 paras 1, 2). The Patents Act 1977 s 28A(6), (7) applies accordingly: s 77(5) (as so amended). Where, under the European Patent Convention, a European patent (UK) is revoked and subsequently restored (including where it is revoked by the Board of Appeal and subsequently restored by the Enlarged Board of Appeal), any fee that would have been imposed in relation to the patent after the revocation but before the restoration is payable within the prescribed period following the restoration: Patents Act 1977 s 77(5A) (added by the Intellectual Property Act 2014 Schedule para 6). The prescribed period for the purposes of the Patents Act 1977 s 77(5A) is two months: Patents Rules 2007, SI 2007/3291, r 41A (added by SI 2014/2401).

653. Internal effect of an application for a European patent (UK). An application for a European patent (UK)[1] having a date of filing under the European Patent Convention[2] is treated as an application for a patent under the Patents Act 1977, having that date as its date of filing, for the following purposes[3]:

    (1)   co-pending applications which may comprise part of the state of the art for the purposes of novelty[4];

    (2)   establishing priority[5];

    (3)   inventors' certificates[6];

    (4)   transactions in applications for patents[7];

    (5)   registration[8];

    (6)   co-ownership of applications[9];

    (7)   Crown use[10];

    (8)   infringement of rights conferred by publication[11];

    (9)   putting validity in issue[12];

    (10)   unauthorised claim of application for a patent[13]; and

    (11)   extent of protection conferred by an application[14].

An application for a European patent (UK) which is so treated as an application for a patent under the Patents Act 1977 has the following further incidents:

    (a)   any declaration of priority made in connection with an application under the European Patent Convention[15] is treated as a declaration made[16] under the Patents Act 1977[17];

    (b)   where a period of time relevant to priority is extended under the convention, the 12-month priority period specified in the Patents Act 1977[18] is treated as altered correspondingly[19];

    (c)   where the date of filing an application is redated under the Convention to a later date, that date is treated as the date of filing the application[20];

(d)   if the application is published in accordance with the Convention[21], it is treated[22] as having been published[23] under the Patents Act 1977[24];

(e)   any designation of the inventor under the convention[25] or any statement under the convention[26] indicating the origin of the right to a European patent is treated as having been filed under the corresponding provision[27] of the Patents Act 1977[28];

(f)   registration of the application in the register of European patents[29] is treated as registration under the Patents Act 1977[30].

The above provisions[31] cease to apply[32] to an application for a European patent (UK) if: (i) the application is refused, withdrawn or deemed to be withdrawn; or (ii) the designation of the United Kingdom in the application is withdrawn[33] or deemed to be withdrawn, but apply again if the rights of the applicant are re-established under the European Patent Convention as from their re-establishment[34]. Where between the above provisions ceasing to apply to any such application and the re-establishment[35] of the rights of the applicant a person begins in good faith to do an act which would constitute[36] an infringement of rights conferred by publication of the application if the above provisions then applied, or makes in good faith effective and serious preparations to do such an act, he has the right to continue to do the act or, as the case may be, to do the act, notwithstanding the above provisions applying again and notwithstanding the grant of the patent[37].

An application for a European patent (UK) published by the European Patent Office under the European Patent Convention in French or German is treated as published[38] for the purposes of the provisions of the Patents Act 1977 relating to Crown use[39] and infringement of rights conferred by an application[40] when a translation into English of the claims of the specification of the application has been filed and published by the UK Intellectual Property Office and the prescribed fee has been paid[41].

1   As to the meaning of 'European patent (UK)' see PARA 652 note 1.
2   Ie under the European Patent Convention art 80: see PARA 647. As to the meaning of 'European Patent Convention' see PARA 644 note 1.
3   Patents Act 1977 s 78(1), (2). Rules under s 32 (see PARA 583) may not impose any requirements as to the registration of applications for European patents (UK) but may provide for the registration of copies of entries relating to such applications in the European register of patents: s 78(4). As to the operation of the Patents Act 1977 s 78 in relation to international applications for a patent (UK) see s 79.
4   Ie the Patents Act 1977 s 2(3) (see PARA 434) and so much of s 14(7) (see PARA 325) as relates to s 2(3).
5   Ie the Patents Act 1977 ss 5, 6: see PARAS 310–312.
6   Ie so much of the Patents Act 1977 s 13(3) as relates to an application for an issue of a certificate under s 13(3): see PARA 307.
7   Ie the Patents Act 1977 s 30: see PARAS 372–373, 377.
8   Ie the Patents Act 1977 ss 32, 33: see PARA 583 et seq.
9   Ie the Patents Act 1977 s 36: see PARA 371.
10   Ie the Patents Act 1977 ss 55–59: see PARA 404 et seq.
11   Ie the Patents Act 1977 ss 60–69: see PARA 511 et seq.
12   Ie the Patents Act 1977 s 74: see PARA 519.
13   Ie the Patents Act 1977 s 111: see PARA 608.
14   Ie the Patents Act 1977 s 125: see PARA 301.
15   Ie under the European Patent Convention arts 87–89: see PARA 647.
16   Ie under the Patents Act 1977 s 5(2): see PARA 310.
17   Patents Act 1977 s 78(3)(a).
18   Ie the period allowed under the Patents Act 1977 s 5(2A)(a): see PARA 310.
19   Patents Act 1977 s 78(3)(b) (amended by SI 2004/2357).
20   Patents Act 1977 s 78(3)(c).
21   Ie in accordance with the European Patent Convention art 98: see PARA 649.

22 Ie subject to the Patents Act 1977 s 78(6) (see the text to notes 35–37) and s 79 (see note 3).

23 Ie under the Patents Act 1977 s 16: see PARA 326.

24 Patents Act 1977 s 78(3)(d).

25 Ie under the European Patent Convention art 62.

26 Ie under the European Patent Convention art 60.

27 Ie the Patents Act 1977 s 13(2): see PARA 307.

28 Patents Act 1977 s 78(3)(e).

29 See the European Patent Convention art 127.

30 Patents Act 1977 s 78(3)(f). As to registration see PARA 583 et seq.

31 Ie the Patents Act 1977 ss 78(1)–(3).

32 Ie subject to the Patents Act 1977 s 78(5A) (added by the Copyright, Designs and Patents Act 1988 s 295, Sch 5 para 22; and amended by the Patents Act 2004 s 5, Sch 1 paras 1, 3(1), (2)), which provides that the occurrence of any of the events mentioned in the Patents Act 1977 s 78(5)(a) or (b) does not affect the continued operation of s 2(3) (see PARA 434) in relation to matter contained in an application for a European patent (UK) which by virtue of s 2(3) has become part of the state of the art as regards other inventions; and the occurrence of any event mentioned in s 78(5)(b) (see head (ii) in the text) does not prevent matter contained in an application for a European patent (UK) becoming part of the state of the art by virtue of s 2(3) as regards other inventions where the event occurs before the publication of that application.

33 As to designation see PARA 647.

34 Patents Act 1977 s 78(5) (substituted by the Copyright, Designs and Patents Act 1988 Sch 5 para 22).

35 Ie under the European Patent Convention art 122.

36 The provisions of the Patents Act 1977 s 78(6)–(6B) apply in relation to the use of a patented invention for the services of the Crown (see PARAS 404–405) as they apply in relation to an infringement of the rights conferred by publication of the application (or, as the case may be, infringement of the patent): s 78(6C) (s 78(6) substituted, and s 78(6A)–(6C) added, by the Patents Act 2004 Sch 1 paras 1, 3(1), (3)). 'Patented invention' has the same meaning as in the Patents Act 1977 s 55 (see PARA 404).

37 Patents Act 1977 s 78(6) (as substituted: see note 36). The provisions of s 20B(5), (6) (see PARA 333) have effect for the purposes of s 78(6) as they have effect for the purposes of s 20B and as if the references to s 20B(4) were references to s 78(6): s 78(6A) (as so added). Subject to s 78(6A), the right conferred by s 78(6) does not extend to granting a licence to another person to do the act in question: s 78(6B) (as so added).

38 Ie under the Patents Act 1977 s 16: see PARA 326.

39 Ie the Patents Act 1977 s 55: see PARA 404.

40 Ie the Patents Act 1977 s 69: see PARAS 546–547.

41 Patents Act 1977 s 78(7), (8). An applicant may: (1) recover a payment by virtue of s 55(5) (see PARA 405) in respect of the use of the invention in question before publication of that translation; or (2) bring proceedings by virtue of s 69 in respect of an act mentioned in s 69 which is done before publication of that translation, if before that use or the doing of that act he has sent by or delivered to the government department which made use or authorised the use of the invention or, as the case may be, to the person alleged to have done the act, a translation into English of those claims: s 78(7). A translation into English of the claims of the specification of the application for a European patent (UK), which is filed under s 78(7) must be accompanied by Patents Form 54: Patents Rules 2007, SI 2007/3291, r 56(1)(b). The translation must comply with the formal requirements set out in Sch 2 Pts 1–3 (see PARAS 314, 319) except where a translation is delivered in electronic form or using electronic communications: r 56(2), (4). The translation and Patents Form 54 must be filed in duplicate: Patents Rules 2007, SI 2007/3291, r 56(3). As to the UK Intellectual Property Office see PARA 577.

654. Authentic text of European patents and applications.

The text of a European patent[1] or application for such a patent in the language of the proceedings, that is to say, the language in which proceedings relating to the patent or the application are to be conducted before the European Patent Office[2], is authentic text for the purposes of any domestic proceedings, that is to say, any proceedings relating to the patent or application before the comptroller[3] or the court[4].

Where the language of the proceedings is French or German, a translation into English of the claims of the application[5] is treated as the authentic text for the purpose of any domestic proceedings, other than proceedings for the revocation of the patent, if the patent or application as translated into English confers protection which is narrower than that conferred by it in French or German[6].

If any such translation results in a European patent or application conferring the narrower protection, the proprietor of or applicant for the patent may file a corrected translation with the UK Intellectual Property Office[7] and, if he pays the prescribed fee[8] within the period of 14 days beginning immediately after the day the corrected translation is filed, the UK Intellectual Property Office must publish it[9]. However:

(1)   any payment for any use of the invention which apart from the provisions relating to Crown use[10] would have infringed the patent as correctly translated, but not as originally translated, or in the case of an application would have so infringed it if the patent had been granted, is not recoverable under those provisions; and

(2)   the proprietor or applicant is not entitled to bring proceedings in respect of an act which infringed the patent as correctly translated, but not as originally translated, or in the case of an application would have so infringed it if the patent had been granted,

unless before that use or the doing of the act the corrected translation has been published by the UK Intellectual Property Office or the proprietor or applicant has sent the corrected translation by or delivered it to the government department which made use or authorised the use of the invention or, as the case may be, to the person alleged to have done that act[11].

Where a correction of a translation is published[12] and, before it is so published, a person begins in good faith to do an act which would not constitute an infringement of the patent as originally translated, or of the rights conferred by publication of the application as originally translated, but would do so under the amended translation, or makes in good faith effective and serious preparations to do such an act, he has the right to continue to do the act or, as the case may be, to do the act, notwithstanding the publication of the corrected translation and notwithstanding the grant of the patent[13].

1   As to the meaning of 'European patent' see PARA 644 note 5.
2   As to the European Patent Office see PARA 644 note 2.
3   As to the comptroller see PARA 575.
4   Patents Act 1977 s 80(1). As to the meaning of 'court' see PARA 619 note 1. See *Siemens Schweiz AG v Thorne Security Ltd* [2007] EWHC 2242 (Ch), [2008] RPC 58, [2007] All ER (D) 61 (Oct).
5   Ie under the Patents Act 1977 s 78: see PARA 653.
6   Patents Act 1977 s 80(2).
7   As to the UK Intellectual Property Office see PARA 577.
8   At the date at which this volume states the law, no fee is payable on filing a corrected translation under the Patents Act 1977 s 80(3): see the Patents (Fees) Rules 2007, SI 2007/3292, r 2, Sch 1.
9   Patents Act 1977 s 80(3); Patents Rules 2007, SI 2007/3291, r 57(6) (amended by SI 2011/2052). A corrected translation filed under the Patents Act 1977 s 80(3) must be accompanied by Patents Form 54: Patents Rules 2007, SI 2007/3291, r 57(1). The corrected translation must comply with the formal requirements set out in Sch 2 Pts 1–3 (see PARAS 314, 319): r 57(2). Where the corrected translation includes any drawings, all annotations in French or German must be replaced with annotations in English: r 57(3). The corrected translation and Patents Form 54 must be filed in duplicate except where a translation is delivered in electronic form or using electronic communications: Patents Rules 2007, SI 2007/3291, r 57(4), (5).
10   Ie the Patents Act 1977 s 55: see PARAS 404–405.
11   Patents Act 1977 s 80(3).
12   Ie under the Patents Act 1977 s 80(3): see the text and notes 8–12.
13   Patents Act 1977 s 80(4) (s 80(4) substituted, s 80(5)–(7) added, by the Patents Act 2004 Sch 1 paras 1, 4). The provisions of the Patents Act 1977 s 28A(5), (6) (see PARA 357) have effect for

the purposes of s 80(4) as they have effect for the purposes of s 28A and as if the references to s 28A(4) were references to s 80(4), and the reference to the registered proprietor of the patent included a reference to the applicant: s 80(5) (as so added). Subject to s 80(5), the right conferred by s 80(4) does not extend to granting a licence to another person to do the act in question: s 80(6) (as so added). The provisions of s 80(4)–(6) apply in relation to the use of a patented invention for the services of the Crown as they apply in relation to an infringement of the patent or of the rights conferred by the publication of the application; and 'patented invention' has the same meaning as in s 55 (see PARA 404): s 80(7) (as so added).

655. Conversion of European patent applications. The comptroller[1] may direct that, on compliance with the relevant conditions, an application for a European patent (UK)[2] is to be treated as an application under the Patents Act 1977 where the application is deemed to be withdrawn under the provisions of the European Patent Convention[3] relating to the time for forwarding applications to the European Patent Office[4].

The relevant conditions are:

(1)   that the applicant requests[5] the comptroller within the relevant prescribed period[6] (where the application was filed with the UK Intellectual Property Office[7]) to give a direction under these provisions[8], or the central industrial property office of a country which is party to the convention, other than the United Kingdom[9], with which the application was filed transmits within the relevant prescribed period[10] a request that the application should be converted into an application under the Patents Act 1977, together with a copy of the application[11]; and

(2)   that the applicant within the relevant prescribed period pays the application fee and, if the application is in a language other than English, files a translation into English of the application and of any amendments previously made in accordance with the convention[12].

Where an application for a European patent falls to be treated as an application for a patent under the Patents Act 1977 by virtue of a direction given by the comptroller under these provisions, then:

(a)   the date which is the date of filing the application under the European Patent Convention is treated as its date of filing for the purposes of the Patents Act 1977, but, if that date is redated under the Convention to a later date, that later date is to be treated for those purposes as the date of filing the application[13];

(b)   if the application satisfies a requirement of the convention corresponding to any of the requirements of the Patents Act 1977 or rules designated as formal requirements[14], it is to be treated as satisfying that formal requirement[15];

(c)   any document filed with the European Patent Office under any provision of the convention corresponding to certain provisions of the Patents Act 1977[16], or any rule made for the purposes of any of those provisions, is to be treated as filed with the UK Intellectual Property Office under that provision or rule[17]; and

(d)   the comptroller will refer the application for only so much of the examination[18] and search[19] required as he considers appropriate in view of any examination and search carried out under the convention[20].

1   As to the comptroller see PARA 575.
2   As to the meaning of 'European patent (UK)' see PARA 652 note 1.
3   As to the meaning of 'European Patent Convention' see PARA 644 note 1.

4 Patents Act 1977 s 81(1) (amended by the Patents Act 2004 Sch 1 paras 1, 5(1), (2)). See the European Patent Convention art 77.

5 A request under the Patents Act 1977 s 81(2)(b)(i) must be made in writing and accompanied by a copy of the notification by the European Patent Office that the application has been deemed to be withdrawn: Patents Rules 2007, SI 2007/3291, r 58(1). When making such a request, a person may also request the comptroller to send a copy of his application for a European patent (UK) and a copy of the request to the central industrial property office of any contracting state designated in the application: r 58(2). 'Contracting state' means a country which is a party to the European Patent Convention: Patents Rules 2007, SI 2007/3291, r 58(5). As to the parties to the convention see PARA 644 note 1. Where a request has been made under the Patents Act 1977 s 81(2)(b)(i), the period prescribed for the purposes of s 13(2) (see PARA 307), s 15(10)(d) (see PARA 315) and s 81(2)(c) is two months beginning immediately after the date on which the comptroller received that request: Patents Rules 2007, SI 2007/3291, r 58(4) (amended by SI 2011/2052).

6 The period prescribed for the purposes of the Patents Act 1977 s 81(2)(b)(i) is three months beginning immediately after the date of notification by the European Patent Office that the application has been deemed to be withdrawn: Patents Rules 2007, SI 2007/3291, r 58(3) (amended by SI 2011/2052). The prescribed time limit may not be extended: see PARA 597.

7 As to the UK Intellectual Property Office see PARA 577.

8 Patents Act 1977 s 81(2)(b)(i) (amended by the Patents Act 2004 Sch 1 paras 1, 5(1), (3)).

9 As to the meaning of 'United Kingdom' see PARA 303 note 5.

10 The period prescribed for the purposes of the Patents Act 1977 s 81(2)(b)(ii) is 20 months beginning immediately after: (1) where there is no declared priority date, the date of filing of the application; or (2) where there is a declared priority date, that date: Patents Rules 2007, SI 2007/3291, r 59(1) (amended by SI 2011/2052). The prescribed time limit may not be extended: see PARA 597. Where a request, transmitted under the Patents Act 1977 s 81(2)(b)(ii), has been received by the comptroller, he must notify the applicant accordingly: Patents Rules 2007, SI 2007/3291, r 59(2). Where a request has been transmitted under the Patents Act 1977 s 81(2)(b)(ii), the period prescribed for the purposes of s 13(2) (see PARA 307), s 15(10)(d) (see PARA 315) and s 81(2)(c) is four months beginning immediately after the date of that notification: Patents Rules 2007, SI 2007/3291, r 59(3) (amended by SI 2011/2052). As to the extension of time limits see PARA 599. As to priority dates and the date of filing under the European Patent Convention see PARA 647.

11 Patents Act 1977 s 81(2)(b)(ii).

12 Patents Act 1977 s 81(2)(c) (amended by the Patents Act 2004 Sch 1 paras 1, 5(1), (3)).

13 Patents Act 1977 s 81(3)(a). Where an application for a European patent (UK) falls to be treated as an application for a patent under the Patents Act 1977 by virtue of a direction under s 81, the period prescribed for the purposes of s 18(1) (see PARA 328) is two years beginning immediately after: (1) where there is no declared priority date, the date of filing of the application; or (2) where there is a declared priority date, that date: Patents Rules 2007, SI 2007/3291, r 60 (amended by SI 2011/2052). As to the extension of time limits see PARA 597.

14 As to the meaning of 'formal requirements' see PARA 327.

15 Patents Act 1977 s 81(3)(b).

16 Ie the Patents Act 1977 s 2(4)(c) (see PARA 435), s 5 (see PARA 310), s 13(2) (see PARA 307), s 14 (see PARA 314).

17 Patents Act 1977 s 81(3)(c).

18 Ie under the Patents Act 1977 s 15A (see PARA 317) and s 17 (see PARA 327).

19 Ie under the Patents Act 1977 s 18: see PARA 328.

20 Patents Act 1977 s 81(3)(d) (amended by SI 2004/2357). The Patents Act 1977 ss 15A, 17, 18 apply with any necessary modifications: s 81(3)(d).

(4) THE PATENT LAW TREATY

656. Requirements and procedures under the Patent Law Treaty. The Patent Law Treaty[1] was concluded on 1 June 2000 and has the aim of harmonising and streamlining patent law in respect of the administrative procedures associated with filing and prosecuting a patent application[2]. In particular, provision is made relating to:

(1)   the accordance of filing dates to applications[3];

(2)   the formal requirements for national and regional applications[4];

(3)   representation and communications[5];
(4)   validity of patents and revocation[6];
(5)   relief in respect of time limits[7];
(6)   the reinstatement of rights after a finding of due care or unintentionality by the patent authority[8]; and
(7)   the correction or addition of priority claims and the restoration of priority rights[9].

1   Ie the Patent Law Treaty (Geneva, 1 June 2000; TS 6 (2006); Cm 6779). The United Kingdom instrument of ratification was deposited on 22 December 2005 and the Treaty entered into force for the United Kingdom on 22 March 2006. The Patent Law Treaty is open to states members of the World Intellectual Property Organisation or states parties to the Paris Convention for the Protection of Industrial Property (see PARA 628). As to the World Intellectual Property Organisation see COPYRIGHT vol 23 (2013) PARA 999.
2   On 1 January 2005, United Kingdom patent law was significantly deregulated by the Regulatory Reform (Patents) Order 2004, SI 2004/2357 (which amended the Patents Act 1977), and the accompanying Patents (Amendment) Rules 2004, SI 2004/2358 (revoked). As a result, the law already met or exceeded the standards laid down in the Patent Law Treaty, so no further legislative changes arose from the ratification of the treaty.
3   See the Patent Law Treaty art 5.
4   See the Patent Law Treaty art 6.
5   See the Patent Law Treaty arts 7–9.
6   See the Patent Law Treaty art 10.
7   See the Patent Law Treaty art 11.
8   See the Patent Law Treaty art 12.
9   See the Patent Law Treaty art 13.

12. REGISTERED DESIGNS

(1) LEGISLATION AND ADMINISTRATION

(i) Legislation

657. Legislation relating to registered designs. The current legislation relating to registered designs[1] is contained in the Registered Designs Act 1949[2], which consolidated most of the previous registered designs legislation[3]. The 1949 Act was most recently amended in 2001 by the Registered Designs Regulations[4] which effected the changes necessary in order to comply with the European Directive on the legal protection of designs[5]. The treatment of current designs is therefore now covered by this legislation.

The term 'old design' is used in this title to denote designs granted pursuant to the Registered Designs Act 1949 as amended by the Copyright, Designs and Patents Act 1988[6]; whilst the term 'current design' is used to denote designs granted pursuant to the Registered Designs Act 1949 after its amendment by the Registered Designs Regulations 2001. Where the term 'design' is used simpliciter, the Registered Designs Act 1949 as amended applies equally to both old and current designs.

A unified system for obtaining a community design to which uniform protection is given with uniform effect throughout the entire territory of the Community was set up in 2002[7].

The UK Intellectual Property Office[8] procedure relating to registered designs is governed by rules made under the Registered Designs Act 1949[9]. Certain matters relating to registered designs are regulated by other statutes[10] and by rules of court[11]. The registered design legislation does not cover the parallel rights in artistic works[12].

1　As to the meaning of 'design' see PARA 711 (current designs) and PARA 717 (old designs). A product whose novelty resides in its design and not in its function may be protected as a registered design, as such a product is not patentable: see PARA 430.

2　The Registered Designs Act 1949 came into force on 1 January 1950: s 49(2).

3　Ie the Patents and Designs Act 1907 which replaced the Patents, Designs and Trade Marks Act 1883. Earlier statutes of importance in relation to designs included 5 & 6 Vict c 100 (Copyright of Designs) (1842); 6 & 7 Vict c 65 (Copyright of Designs) (1843); and the Copyright of Designs Act 1875 (all repealed).

4　Ie the Registered Designs Regulations 2001, SI 2001/3949. Further amendments were made by the Registered Designs Regulations 2003, SI 2003/550.

5　Ie Council Directive (EC) 98/71 (OJ L289, 28.10.1998, p 28) on the legal protection of designs, which provides for harmonisation in the European Community of the matters of registered design protection which most closely affect the functioning of the internal market. See *Oakley Inc v Animal Ltd* [2005] EWCA Civ 1191, [2006] Ch 337, [2006] RPC 301.

6　The Registered Designs Act 1949 was substantially amended by the Copyright, Designs and Patents Act 1988 Pt IV (ss 265–273), s 303(2), Schs 3, 8, with effect from 1 August 1989 (ie the commencement date of the Copyright, Designs and Patents Act 1988 Pt V). Some of the amendments affect only the registration of designs application for which was made on or after 1 August 1989. In respect of applications for registration made on or after that date the criteria for registrability are those contained in the substituted provisions of the Registered Designs Act 1949 s 1: see PARA 717. Applications for registration made before that date were required to satisfy the criteria for registrability contained in s 1 as originally enacted. All such applications which satisfied the old criteria have now matured into granted designs and therefore the regime for obtaining registration under the original Registered Designs Act 1949 is not set out in this work. The text of the Registered Designs Act 1949 in its amended form is set out in the Copyright, Designs and Patents Act 1988 Sch 4.

7　See Council Regulation (EC) 6/2002 (OJ L3, 5.1.2002, p 1) on Community Designs.

8 As to the UK Intellectual Property Office see PARA 577.

9 See the Registered Designs Act 1949 s 36; the Registered Designs Rules 2006, SI 2006/1975; and PARA 660.

10 Eg the Crown Proceedings Act 1947 s 3 (proceedings against the Crown for infringement: see PARA 748); and the Copyright, Designs and Patents Act 1988 Sch 1 paras 19, 20 (limitation of period of protection of artistic works which are registrable as designs: see COPYRIGHT vol 23 (2013) PARAS 924, 926).

11 See CPR Pt 63; *Practice Direction — Intellectual Property Claims* PD 63.

12 As to the concurrent existence of artistic copyright and design copyright see COPYRIGHT vol 23 (2013) PARA 673.

658. Legislation relating to old designs. The cancellation and invalidation of 'old designs', that is those designs resulting from an application made on or after 1 August 1989 and before 9 December 2001[1], remain governed by the Registered Designs Act 1949 as it had effect immediately before its amendment by the Registered Designs Regulations[2]. In relation to ownership, assignment, compulsory licensing and infringement, the amendments made by those Regulations apply with some modification to old designs as well as current designs[3].

Any licence granted before 9 December 2001 which permits anything which would otherwise be an infringement under the Registered Designs Act 1949 of the right in a registered design or the copyright in a registered design, continues in force, with necessary modifications, on or after that date[4].

1 See PARA 657.

2 Ie the Registered Designs Regulations 2001, SI 2001/3949. See reg 12(1)–(3). As to the validity of old designs see PARAS 717–733; and as to the validity of current designs see PARAS 711–716.

3 See the Registered Designs Regulations 2001, SI 2001/3949, reg 12(4)–(9). For further transitional provisions see reg 14(3)–(13).

4 Registered Designs Regulations 2001, SI 2001/3949, reg 14(1). As to licences see PARA 701. In determining the effect of any such licence, regard must be had to the purpose for which the licence was granted; and, in particular, a licence granted for the full term or extent of the right in a registered design or the copyright in a registered design is to be treated as applying, subject to its other terms and conditions, to the full term or extent of that right as extended by virtue of the Registered Designs Regulations 2001, SI 2001/3949: reg 14(2).

659. Territorial scope; convention countries. The Registered Designs Act 1949 has effect throughout the United Kingdom[1] and the Isle of Man, subject to modifications in its application to Northern Ireland[2] and the Isle of Man[3]. For the purposes of that Act, the territorial waters of the United Kingdom are treated as part of the United Kingdom[4]. The 1949 Act applies to things done in the United Kingdom sector of the continental shelf[5] on a structure or vessel which is present there for purposes directly connected with the exploration of the sea bed or subsoil or the exploration of their natural resources as it applies to things done in the United Kingdom[6].

With a view to the fulfilment of a treaty, convention[7], arrangement or engagement, Her Majesty may by Order in Council declare that any country, including a British overseas territory, specified in the Order is a convention country for the purposes either of all, or of some only, of the provisions of the Registered Designs Act 1949[8].

1 As to the meaning of 'United Kingdom' see PARA 303 note 5.

2 See the Registered Designs Act 1949 s 46 (amended by the Copyright, Designs and Patents Act 1988 Sch 3 para 33, Sch 8; SI 2006/1028).

3 See the Registered Designs Act 1949 s 47 (substituted by the Copyright, Designs and Patents Act 1988 Sch 3 para 24); and the Registered Designs (Isle of Man) Order 2001, SI 2001/3678.

4 Registered Designs Act 1949 s 47A(1) (s 47 added by the Copyright, Designs and Patents Act 1988 Sch 3 para 35).
5 For these purposes, 'United Kingdom sector of the continental shelf' means the areas designated by order under the Continental Shelf Act 1964 s 1(7) (see INTERNATIONAL RELATIONS LAW vol 61 (2010) PARA 172): Registered Designs Act 1949 s 47A(3) (as added: see note 4).
6 Registered Designs Act 1949 s 47A(2) (as added: see note 4).
7 See the International Convention further revising the Paris Convention for the Protection of Industrial Property (which includes industrial designs) of 20 March 1883 (Stockholm, 14 July 1967 to 13 January 1968; TS 61 (1970); Cmnd 4431); and PARA 628.
8 See the Registered Designs Act 1949 s 13; British Overseas Territories Act 2002 s 1(2). The convention countries so declared for all the purposes of the Act are listed in the Designs (Convention Countries) Order 2007, SI 2007/277 (amended by SI 2009/2747; SI 2013/539).

(ii) Administration

660. The Secretary of State and the registrar. The Secretary of State[1] may make such rules as he thinks expedient for regulating the business of the UK Intellectual Property Office[2] in relation to designs[3] and for regulating all matters placed by the Registered Designs Act 1949 under the direction or control of the registrar or the Secretary of State[4].

The Secretary of State appoints and supervises the Comptroller General of Patents, Designs and Trade Marks[5], who has immediate control of the UK Intellectual Property Office[6] and is the registrar for the purposes of the Registered Designs Act 1949[7]. In his annual report with respect to the execution of the Patents Act 1977[8] the comptroller must include a report with respect to the execution of the Registered Designs Act 1949 as if it formed part of or was included in the Patents Act 1977[9].

1 As to the Secretary of State see PARA 660.
2 As to the UK Intellectual Property Office see PARA 577.
3 As to the meaning of 'design' see PARA 711 (current designs) and PARA 717 (old designs).
4 Registered Designs Act 1949 s 36(1). In exercise of the power so conferred the Secretary of State has made the Registered Designs Rules 2006, SI 2006/1975. In connection with the scope of the Secretary of State's rule-making powers see the Registered Designs Act 1949 ss 36(1A), (1B), (2) (s 36(1A), (1B) added by the Copyright, Designs and Patents Act 1988 Sch 3 para 26(1), (3); Registered Designs Act 1949 s 36(1A) amended by the Intellectual Property Act 2014 s 12(3); and by SI 2001/3949).
5 See the Patents and Designs Act 1907 s 63(1); and PARA 575. The Secretary of State may authorise any officer to act for the comptroller: see s 62(3); and PARA 575.
6 See the Patents and Designs Act 1907 s 62(2); and PARA 573 et seq.
7 Registered Designs Act 1949 s 44(1).
8 As to the report see PARA 576.
9 Registered Designs Act 1949 s 42 (amended by the Patents Act 1977 Sch 5 para 3).

661. Requests to the registrar for opinions. The Secretary of State[1] may by regulations[2] make provision about the making of requests to the registrar[3] for an opinion on specified[4] matters relating to designs registered under the Registered Designs Act 1949[5] and designs of such other description as may be specified[6]. The regulations must require the registrar to give an opinion in response to a request made under the regulations, except in specified cases or circumstances[7], or where for any reason the registrar considers it inappropriate in all the circumstances to do so[8]. The regulations may confer discretion on the registrar[9]. An opinion given by the registrar under the regulations is not to be treated[10] as a decision of the registrar[11] but must provide for an appeal relating to an opinion given under the regulations to be made to an appointed person[12], and the regulations may make further provision in relation to such appeals[13]. The regulations must provide that an opinion given by the registrar under the regulations is not binding for any purposes[14], and must provide that neither the registrar nor any examiner or other officer of the UK Intellectual Property Office[15] is to incur any liability by reason of or in connection with any opinion given under the regulations or any examination or investigation undertaken for the purpose of giving such an opinion[16].

1   As to the Secretary of State see PARA 660.
2   The regulations may provide that a request made under the regulations must be accompanied by a fee of a specified amount and specified information: Registered Designs Act 1949 s 28A(3) (s 28A and the Copyrights, Designs and Patents Act 1988 s 249A (see the text and notes 2–16) added by the Intellectual Property Act 2014 s 11(1), (2)). Regulations under the Registered Designs Act 1949 s 28A may make different provision for different purposes and may include consequential, incidental, supplementary, transitional, transitory or saving provision: s 28A(9) (as so added). At the date at which this volume states the law no such regulations had been made.
3   As to the registrar see PARA 660.
4   In the Registered Designs Act 1949 s 28A 'specified' means specified in regulations thereunder: s 28A(10) (as added: see note 2).
5   Registered Designs Act 1949 s 28A(1)(a) (as added: see note 2).
6   Registered Designs Act 1949 s 28A(1)(b) (as added: see note 2). The descriptions of designs which may be specified in regulations under s 28A(1)(b) include, in particular designs in which design right subsists in accordance with the Copyright, Designs and Patents Act 1988 Pt 3 (ss 213–264: see COPYRIGHT vol 23 (2013) PARAS 1048–1150) and designs in relation to which there is a question whether design right so subsists: s 249A (as so added).
7   Registered Designs Act 1949 s 28A(2)(a) (as added: see note 2).
8   Registered Designs Act 1949 s 28A(2)(b) (as added: see note 2).
9   Registered Designs Act 1949 s 28A(8) (as added: see note 2).
10 Ie for the purposes of the Registered Designs Act 1949 s 27A (see PARA 669).
11 Registered Designs Act 1949 s 28A(6) (as added: see note 2).
12 Ie a person appointed under the Registered Designs Act 1949 s 27A.
13 Registered Designs Act 1949 s 28A(7) (as added: see note 2).
14 Registered Designs Act 1949 s 28A(4) (as added: see note 2).
15 As to the UK Intellectual Property Office see PARA 577.
16 Registered Designs Act 1949 s 28A(5) (as added: see note 2).

662. Proceedings before the registrar. The registrar[1] must give to any party to a proceeding before him an opportunity to be heard before exercising adversely to any party any discretion vested in him by or under the Registered Designs Act 1949[2].

The registrar may not give a person less than 14 days' notice of any hearing[3]. Hearings before the registrar of proceedings between two or more parties relating to an application for a registered design or a registered design, are held in public[4]. However, any party to the proceedings may apply to the registrar for the hearing to be held in private[5]. The registrar may only grant such an application if it is in the interests of justice for the hearing to be in held in private, and where all the parties to the proceedings have had an opportunity to be heard on the matter[6].

The registrar may give such directions as to the management of the proceedings as he thinks fit, and in particular he may (1) require a document, information or evidence to be filed; (2) require a translation of any document; (3) require a party or a party's legal representative to attend a hearing; (4) hold a hearing and receive evidence by telephone or by using any other method of direct oral communication; (5) allow a statement of case to be amended; (6) stay the whole, or any part, of the proceedings either generally or until a specified date or event; (7) consolidate proceedings; (8) direct that part of any proceedings be dealt with as separate proceedings[7]. At any stage of proceedings before him, the registrar may direct that the parties to the proceedings attend a case management conference or pre-hearing review[8]. The registrar may control the evidence by giving directions as to (a) the issues on which he requires evidence; (b) the nature of the evidence which he requires to decide those issues; and (c) the way in which the evidence is to be placed before him[9]. He may use his power to exclude evidence which would otherwise be admissible[10].

Evidence may be given by witness statement, statement of case, affidavit, statutory declaration, or in any other form which would be admissible as evidence in proceedings before the court[11]. The registrar has the powers of a judge of the Technology and Construction Court as regards the attendance of witnesses and their examination on oath, and as to the discovery and production of documents, but he has no power to punish summarily for contempt[12]. The rules applicable to the attendance of witnesses before such a referee apply in relation to the attendance of witnesses in proceedings before the registrar[13].

The registrar may appoint an adviser to assist him and must settle the question or instructions to be submitted or given to such adviser[14]. Where the registrar thinks fit, he may rectify any irregularity of procedure after giving the parties such notice, and subject to such conditions, as he may direct[15].

1 As to the registrar see PARA 660.
2 Registered Designs Act 1949 s 29 (amended by the Copyright, Designs and Patents Act 1988 Sch 3 para 18); Registered Designs Rules 2006, SI 2006/1975, r 18.
3 Registered Designs Rules 2006, SI 2006/1975, r 25.
4 Registered Designs Rules 2006, SI 2006/1975, r 20(1).
5 Registered Designs Rules 2006, SI 2006/1975, r 20(2). Any hearing or part of a hearing of an application under r 20(2) must be held in private: r 20(4), (5).
6 Registered Designs Rules 2006, SI 2006/1975, r 20(3).
7 Registered Designs Rules 2006, SI 2006/1975, r 19(3). The registrar may extend or shorten (or further extend or shorten) any period which has been specified: r 19(1).
8 Registered Designs Rules 2006, SI 2006/1975, r 19(2).
9 Registered Designs Rules 2006, SI 2006/1975, r 19(4). When the registrar gives directions he may make them subject to conditions and may specify the consequences of failure to comply with the directions or a condition: r 19(5).
10 Registered Designs Rules 2006, SI 2006/1975, r 19(4).
11 Registered Designs Act 1949 s 31(a) (substituted by the Copyright, Designs and Patents Act 1988 Sch 3 para 20); Registered Designs Rules 2006, SI 2006/1975, r 21(1). The general rule is that evidence at hearings is to be by witness statement unless the registrar or any enactment requires otherwise: r 21(3). A witness statement is a written statement signed by a person that contains the evidence which that person would be allowed to give orally: r 21(5). A witness statement or a statement of case may only be given in evidence if it includes a statement of truth: r 21(2). A statement of truth means a statement that the person making the statement believes that the facts stated in a particular document are true, and it must be dated and signed by (1) in the case of a witness statement, the maker of the statement; (2) in any other case, the party or his legal representative: r 21(4).
12 Registered Designs Act 1949 s 31(b) (substituted by the Copyright, Designs and Patents Act 1988 Sch 3 para 20); Registered Designs Rules 2006, SI 2006/1975, r 24. As to the Technology and Construction Court see COURTS AND TRIBUNALS vol 24 (2010) PARA 709.
13 Registered Designs Act 1949 s 31(c) (substituted by the Copyright, Designs and Patents Act 1988 Sch 3 para 20); Registered Designs Rules 2006, SI 2006/1975, r 21.
14 Registered Designs Rules 2006, SI 2006/1975, r 37.
15 Registered Designs Rules 2006, SI 2006/1975, r 38.

663. Fees, notices and communications. There must be paid in respect of the registration of designs and applications therefor, and in respect of other matters relating to designs arising under the Registered Designs Act 1949, such fees as may be prescribed by rules made by the Secretary of State with the consent of the Treasury[1]. Such fees must be collected in money[2].

Any notice required or authorised to be given by or under the Registered Designs Act 1949, and any application or other document so authorised or required to be made or filed, may be given, made or filed by post[3].

The registrar must extend any time or period where he is satisfied that the failure to do something was wholly or mainly attributed to a delay in, or failure of, a communication service (that is a service by which documents may be sent and delivered and includes post, electronic communications and courier)[4].

1   Registered Designs Act 1949 s 40 (amended by the Copyright, Designs and Patents Act 1988 Sch 3 para 30). In exercise of this power the Registered Designs Rules 2006, SI 2006/1975, were made. As to the Secretary of State see PARA 660.
2   See the Public Offices Fees (Patents, Designs and Trade Marks) Order 1964, SI 1964/45, art 1.
3   Registered Designs Act 1949 s 41.
4   Registered Designs Rules 2006, SI 2006/1975, r 41. As to the registrar see PARA 660. As to the use of electronic communications see PARA 665.

664.   Address for service.   For the purposes of any proceedings under the Registered Designs Act 1949, an address for service must be furnished by (1) an applicant for the registration of a design[1]; (2) a person who makes an application for a declaration of invalidity of a registered design[2]; (3) the registered proprietor of the design who opposes such an application[3]. The proprietor of a registered design, or any person who has registered any interest in a registered design, may furnish an address for service on the prescribed form[4]. Where a person has furnished an address for service he may substitute a new address for service by notifying the registrar[5].

Where a person has failed to furnish an address for service and the registrar has sufficient information enabling him to contact that person, the registrar must direct that person to furnish an address for service[6]. Where such a direction has been given, the person must furnish an address for service within two months beginning immediately after the date of the direction[7]. Where such a direction has been given and the two month period has expired (or where the registrar had insufficient information to give a direction) and the person has failed to furnish an address for service[8] then the person's application is treated as withdrawn[9].

1   An address for service furnished under head (1) in the text must be an address in the United Kingdom, another EEA State (ie a member state, Iceland, Liechtenstein or Norway) or the Channel Islands: Registered Designs Rules 2006, SI 2006/1975, r 42(4), (6) (r 42(4) substituted by SI 2009/546). As to registration of designs see PARA 684.
2   Ie under the Registered Designs Act 1949 s 11ZB: see PARA 734.
3   Registered Designs Rules 2006, SI 2006/1975, r 42(1). As to the proprietorship of registered designs see PARA 699.
4   Ie Form DF1A: Registered Designs Rules 2006, SI 2006/1975, r 42(2), Sch 1. An address for service furnished under this provision must be an address in the United Kingdom, another EEA State or the Channel Islands: r 42(4) (as substituted: see note 1).
5   Ie on Form DF1A in the Registered Designs Rules 2006, SI 2006/1975, Sch 1: r 42(3).
6   Registered Designs Rules 2006, SI 2006/1975, r 43(1), (5) (r 42(5) amended by SI 2009/546).
7   Registered Designs Rules 2006, SI 2006/1975, r 43(2) (amended by SI 2013/444).
8   Registered Designs Rules 2006, SI 2006/1975, r 43(3).
9   Ie (1) in the case of an applicant for the registration of a design, the application is treated as withdrawn; (2) in the case of a person applying under the Registered Designs Act 1949 s 11ZB for a declaration of invalidity, his application is treated as withdrawn; and (3) in the case of the proprietor who is opposing an application under s 11ZB, he is deemed to have withdrawn from the proceedings: Registered Designs Rules 2006, SI 2006/1975, r 43(4).

665.   Use of electronic communications.   The registrar[1] may give directions as to the form and manner in which documents to be delivered in electronic form or using electronic communications are to be delivered to him[2]. If a document to which a direction applies is delivered to the registrar in a form or manner which does not comply with the direction then the registrar may treat the document as not having been delivered[3].

The registrar may give directions specifying how and when the fee is to be paid where a document is delivered using electronic communications and there is a requirement for a fee to accompany the document[4]. The registrar may give directions specifying that a person who delivers a document to the registrar in electronic form or using electronic communications cannot treat the document as having been delivered unless its delivery has been acknowledged[5]. He may also give directions specifying how a time of delivery is to be accorded to a document delivered to him in electronic form or using electronic communications[6].

The delivery using electronic communications to any person by the registrar of any document is deemed to be effected, unless the registrar has otherwise specified, by transmitting an electronic communication containing the document to an address provided or made available to the registrar by that person as an address of his for the receipt of electronic communications; and unless the contrary is proved such delivery is deemed to be effected immediately upon the transmission of the communication[7].

A requirement of the Registered Designs Act 1949 that something must be done in the prescribed manner is satisfied in the case of something that is done using a document in electronic form, or using electronic communications, only if the directions made by the registrar are complied with[8].

A direction given by the registrar may be given generally, or in relation to a description of cases specified in the direction, or in relation to a particular person or persons; and it may be varied or revoked by a subsequent direction[9].

1 As to the registrar see PARA 660.
2 Registered Designs Act 1949 s 37A(1) (s 37A added by SI 2006/1229). Such a direction may provide that in order for a document to be delivered in compliance with the direction it must be accompanied by one or more additional documents specified in the direction: Registered Designs Act 1949 s 37A(2) (as so added). Section 37A applies to delivery at the UK Intellectual Property Office as it applies to delivery to the registrar, and it applies to delivery by the UK Intellectual Property Office as it applies to delivery by the registrar: Registered Designs Act 1949 s 37A(13) (as so added). As to the UK Intellectual Property Office see PARA 577.
3 Registered Designs Act 1949 s 37A(3) (as added: see note 2).
4 Registered Designs Act 1949 s 37A(4), (5) (as added: see note 2).
5 Registered Designs Act 1949 s 37A(6) (as added: see note 2).
6 Registered Designs Act 1949 s 37A(7) (as added: see note 2).
7 Registered Designs Act 1949 s 37A(10) (as added: see note 2).
8 Registered Designs Act 1949 s 37A(11) (as added: see note 2). A reference in the Registered Designs Act 1949 to the application not having been made in accordance with rules under the Act includes a reference to its not having been made in accordance with any applicable directions under s 37A: s 37A(12) (as so added).
9 Registered Designs Act 1949 s 37A(8), (9) (as added: see note 2).

666. Costs and security for costs. In any proceedings before him under the Registered Designs Act 1949 the registrar[1] may by order award to any party such costs as he may consider reasonable, and direct how and by what parties they are to be paid[2]. Any such order of the registrar may be enforced in the same way as an order of the High Court[3].

The registrar may require a person to give security for the costs of any application for invalidation of the registration of a design or appeal from any decision of the registrar under the Registered Designs Act 1949[4] if he is satisfied, having regard to all the circumstances of the case, that it is just to require such security, and that one or more of the following conditions applies[5]:

(1)   the person is resident outside the United Kingdom but is not resident in a Brussels Contracting State, or a Lugano Contracting State, or a Regulation State[6];

(2)   the person is a company or other body (whether incorporated inside or outside the United Kingdom) and there is reason to believe that it will be unable to pay the other person's costs if ordered to do so[7];

(3)   the person has changed his address since filing an address for service with a view to evading the consequences of the proceedings[8];

(4)   the person has furnished an incorrect address for service[9];

(5)   the person has taken steps in relation to his assets that would make it difficult to enforce an order for costs against him[10];

(6)   the person has failed to pay a costs order in relation to previous proceedings before the registrar or a court (whether or not the proceedings were between the same parties)[11].

In default of such security being given the registrar may treat the application or appeal as abandoned[12].

1   As to the registrar see PARA 660.
2   Registered Designs Act 1949 s 30(1) (s 30 substituted by the Copyright, Designs and Patents Act 1988 Sch 3 para 19); Registered Designs Rules 2006, SI 2006/1975, r 22.
3   Registered Designs Act 1949 s 30(2)(a) (as substituted: see note 2).
4   Registered Designs Act 1949 s 30(3) (as substituted (see note 2); amended by SI 2001/3949). As to invalidation of registration see PARA 734.
5   Registered Designs Rules 2006, SI 2006/1975, r 23(1).
6   Registered Designs Rules 2006, SI 2006/1975, r 23(2)(a) (amended by SI 2013/444); Civil Jurisdiction and Judgments Act 1982 s 1(3); and as to the Brussels and Lugano Contracting States and Regulation states see CONFLICT OF LAWS vol 19 (2011) PARA 366. As to the meaning of 'United Kingdom' see PARA 303 note 5.
7   Registered Designs Rules 2006, SI 2006/1975, r 23(2)(b).
8   Registered Designs Rules 2006, SI 2006/1975, r 23(2)(c).
9   Registered Designs Rules 2006, SI 2006/1975, r 23(2)(d).
10 Registered Designs Rules 2006, SI 2006/1975, r 23(2)(e).
11 Registered Designs Rules 2006, SI 2006/1975, r 23(2)(f).
12 Registered Designs Rules 2006, SI 2006/1975, r 23(3).

667. Agents. Any act required or authorised by the Registered Designs Act 1949 to be done by or to any person in connection with the registration of a design, or any procedure relating to a registered design, may be done by or to an agent authorised by that person orally or in writing[1]. An agent is only to be treated as authorised where he was nominated by the applicant at the time of making his application[2] and he has filed the relevant form[3]. Where an agent has been authorised, the registrar[4] may, if he thinks fit in any particular case, require the signature or presence of his principal[5].

The comptroller is authorised to refuse to recognise as agent in respect of any business under the Patents Act 1977:

(1)   a person who has been convicted of a specified offence[6];

(2)   a person whose name has been erased from and not restored to the register of patent agents (or, as from a day to be appointed, the register of patent attorneys) on the ground of misconduct[7];

(3)   a person who is found by the Secretary of State to have been guilty of such conduct as would, in the case of a person registered in the register of patent agents (or, as from a day to be appointed, the register of patent attorneys), render the person liable to have the person's name erased from the register on the ground of misconduct[8];

(4) a partnership or body corporate of which one of the partners or directors[9] is a person whom the comptroller could refuse to recognise under head (1), (2) or (3) above[10].

The comptroller must refuse to recognise as agent in respect of any business under the Patents Act 1977 a person who neither resides nor has a place of business in the United Kingdom[11], the Isle of Man or another member state of the European Union[12].

1　Registered Designs Rules 2006, SI 2006/1975, r 36(1).
2　Ie his application for registration, or his application for a declaration of invalidity under the Registered Designs Act 1949 s 11ZB (see PARA 734), or his application under s 19(1) or s 19(2) (see PARA 677).
3　Registered Designs Rules 2006, SI 2006/1975, r 36(2). The relevant form is Form DF1A: see Registered Designs Rules 2006, SI 2006/1975, r 36(2), Sch 1.
4　As to the registrar see PARA 660.
5　Registered Designs Rules 2006, SI 2006/1975, r 36(3).
6　Copyright, Designs and Patents Act 1988 s 281(1), (2)(a); Patent Agents (Non-recognition of Certain Agents by Comptroller) Rules 1990, SI 1990/1454, r 3(a). The offence referred to is an offence under the Copyright, Designs and Patents Act 1988 s 276 (see PARA 613).
7　Copyright, Designs and Patents Act 1988 s 281(2)(b) (s 281(2)(b), (c) amended by SI 2009/3348; prospectively amended by the Legal Services Act 2007 Sch 21 paras 75, 78); Patent Agents (Non-recognition of Certain Agents by Comptroller) Rules 1990, SI 1990/1454, r 3(b) (r 3(b), (c) amended by SI 2009/3348). At the date at which this volume states the law no day had been appointed for the purposes of the amendments made by the Legal Services Act 2007. As to the register of patent attorneys see PARA 617 et seq. Rules may also authorise the comptroller to refuse to recognise a person who is suspended from the register (Copyright, Designs and Patents Act 1988 s 281(2)(b) (as so amended)), but at the date at which this volume states the law no such provision is made. Rules under these provisions may contain such incidental and supplementary provisions as appear to the Secretary of State to be appropriate and may in particular prescribe circumstances in which a person is or is not to be taken to have been guilty of misconduct: Copyright, Designs and Patents Act 1988 s 281(3). As to the Secretary of State see PARA 660.
8　Copyright, Designs and Patents Act 1988 s 281(2)(c) (as amended and prospectively amended: see note 7); Patent Agents (Non-recognition of Certain Agents by Comptroller) Rules 1990, SI 1990/1454, r 3(c) (as so amended).
9　As to the meaning of 'director' see PARA 613 note 4.
10　Copyright, Designs and Patents Act 1988 s 281(2)(d); Patent Agents (Non-recognition of Certain Agents by Comptroller) Rules 1990, SI 1990/1454, r 3(d).
11　As to the meaning of 'United Kingdom' see PARA 303 note 5.
12　Copyright, Designs and Patents Act 1988 s 281(5).

(iii) The Court and Appeal Tribunal

668. The court. In the Registered Designs Act 1949, 'court' means the High Court[1], which means in practice that references and applications under the Act are heard by the Patents Court[2] or the Intellectual Property Enterprise Court[3]. A claim for infringement is not a reference or application for this purpose, but must also be heard by the Patents Court or the Intellectual Property Enterprise Court[4].

1　Registered Designs Act 1949 s 27(1)(a) (s 27 substituted by the Copyright, Designs and Patents Act 1988 Sch 3 para 16; Registered Designs Act 1949 s 27(1)(a) amended by the Crime and Courts Act 2013 Sch 9 para 21(1), (2)). As from a day to be appointed the Registered Designs Act 1949 s 27(1)(a) is subject to s 27A(6) (see PARA 669): s 27(1)(a) (prospectively amended by the Intellectual Property Act 2014 s 10(3)). At the date at which this volume states the law no day had been appointed for these purposes.
　　Provision may be made by rules of court with respect to proceedings in the High Court in England and Wales for references and applications under the Registered Designs Act 1949 to be dealt with by such judge of that court as the Lord Chief Justice, after consulting with the Lord Chancellor, may select for the purpose: s 27(2) (amended by the Constitutional Reform Act 2005 Sch 4 paras 35, 36(1), (2)). The Lord Chief Justice may nominate a judicial office

holder (as defined in s 109(4): see COURTS AND TRIBUNALS vol 24 (2010) PARA 961) to exercise his functions under the Registered Designs Act 1949 s 27(2): s 27(3) (added by the Constitutional Reform Act 2005 Sch 4 paras 35, 36(1), (3)).

2   As to the constitution and jurisdiction of the Patents Court see PARA 619.

3   See CPR 63.2. As to the Intellectual Property Enterprise Court see PARA 626.

4   See CPR Pt 63; and note 1.

669.   Appeals from decisions of the registrar. Until a day to be appointed[1], any appeal from the registrar[2] under the Registered Designs Act 1949 lies to the Registered Designs Appeal Tribunal[3]. The tribunal consists of one or more judges of the High Court nominated by the Lord Chief Justice after consulting the Lord Chancellor and one judge of the Court of Session nominated by the Lord President of the Court[4]. It is not part of the High Court, but is an inferior tribunal subject to control through the prerogative orders obtained on judicial review[5]. A party to an appeal before the tribunal may appear and be heard either in person or by a patent agent, a solicitor or counsel[6]. The tribunal may examine witnesses on oath and administer oaths for that purpose[7], although it normally acts on the evidence which was produced before the registrar[8]. Costs or expenses may be awarded by order[9] and the tribunal may direct how and by what parties the costs are to be paid[10], and may in prescribed circumstances require security for costs[11]. On an appeal any power which could have been exercised by the registrar in the proceedings from which the appeal is brought is exercisable by the tribunal[12]. Subject to these provisions, the tribunal may make its own rules for regulating all matters relating to proceedings before it under the Registered Designs Act 1949 including rights of audience[13]. There is an appeal to the tribunal only where one is provided by statute[14].

As from the appointed day[15] an appeal against a decision of the registrar under the Act may be made to a person appointed by the Lord Chancellor (an 'appointed person')[16], or the court[17]. On an appeal under these provisions to an appointed person, the appointed person may refer the appeal to the court if it appears to the appointed person that a point of general legal importance is involved, the registrar requests that the appeal be so referred, or such a request is made by any party to the proceedings before the registrar in which the decision appealed against was made[18]. Where the appointed person does not refer the appeal to the court he must hear and determine the appeal, and his decision is final[19]. The applicable provisions relating to costs[20] and evidence[21] apply to proceedings before an appointed person as they apply to proceedings before the registrar[22].

1   As from a day to be appointed, the Registered Designs Act 1949 ss 28, 44(1) (definition 'Appeal Tribunal') (see the text and notes 2–14) are repealed by the Intellectual Property Act 2014 s 10(4), and new provision governing appeals from decisions of the registrar is made by the Registered Designs Act 1949 ss 27A, 27B (prospectively added by the Intellectual Property Act 2014 s 10(2)) (see the text and notes 15–22). At the date at which this volume states the law no day had been appointed for the purpose of the repeal of the Registered Designs Act 1949 ss 28, 44(1) (definition 'Appeal Tribunal') effected by the Intellectual Property Act 2014 s 10(4) or for the purpose of the addition of the Registered Designs Act 1949 ss 27A, 27B by the Intellectual Property Act 2014 s 10(2), although 15 July 2014 has been appointed as the day on which s 10(2) comes into force for the purposes of appointing the appointed person under the Registered Designs Act 1949 ss 27A(1)(a), 27B (see the Intellectual Property Act 2014 (Commencement Order No 1) Order 2014, SI 2014/1715). The Registered Designs Act 1949 s 28 was formerly prospectively repealed, and a new s 27A making new provision governing appeals from decisions of the registrar was prospectively added, by the Tribunals, Courts and Enforcement Act 2007 s 143(1), (2), Sch 23 Pt 6, but these amendments were never brought into force and, in the light of the subsequent amendments effected by the Intellectual Property Act 2014, may be considered spent.

2   As to the registrar see PARA 660.
3   Registered Designs Act 1949 s 28(1) (prospectively repealed: see note 1).
4   Registered Designs Act 1949 s 28(2) (substituted by the Copyright, Designs and Patents
    Act 1988 Sch 3 para 17(1), (2); amended by the Constitutional Reform Act 2005 Sch 4
    paras 35, 37(1), (2); prospectively repealed (see note 1)). The Lord Chief Justice may nominate
    a judicial office holder (as defined in s 109(4): see COURTS AND TRIBUNALS vol 24 (2010) PARA
    961) to exercise his functions under the Registered Designs Act 1949 s 28(2): s 28(11) (added by
    the Constitutional Reform Act 2005 Sch 4 paras 35, 37(1), (3)).
        In the Registered Designs Act 1949, and the rules made under it, the Registered Designs
    Appeal Tribunal is referred to simply as the Appeal Tribunal: see s 44(1) (definition substituted
    by the Administration of Justice Act 1969 s 35(1), Sch 1; definition prospectively repealed (see
    note 1)). At any time when it consists of two or more judges, the jurisdiction of the Appeal
    Tribunal: (1) where in the case of any particular appeal the senior of those judges so directs, is to
    be exercised in relation to that appeal by both of the judges, or (if there are more than two) by
    two of them sitting together; and (2) in relation to any appeal in respect of which no such
    direction is given, may be exercised by any one of the judges; and, in the exercise of the
    jurisdiction, different appeals may be heard at the same time by different judges: Registered
    Designs Act 1949 s 28(2A) (added by the Administration of Justice Act 1969 s 24; as so
    prospectively repealed). The Lord Chancellor may appoint additional judges who are either
    judges of the Court of Appeal or persons who have held office as judges of the Court of Appeal
    or the High Court or one of Her Majesty's counsel: see the Administration of Justice Act 1970
    s 10(1), (1A) (s 10(1) amended, and s 10(1A) added, by the Constitutional Reform Act 2005
    Sch 4 para 66(1), (2); Administration of Justice Act 1970 s 10 prospectively repealed by the
    Tribunals, Courts and Enforcement Act 2007 Sch 23 Pt 6). The expenses of the Appeal Tribunal
    must be defrayed and the fees to be taken therein may be fixed as if the tribunal were a court of
    the High Court: Registered Designs Act 1949 s 28(3) (as so prospectively repealed).
5   An appeal to the Appeal Tribunal is not deemed to be a proceeding in the High Court:
    Registered Designs Act 1949 s 28(9) (prospectively repealed: see note 1). As to the prerogative
    orders generally see JUDICIAL REVIEW vol 61 (2010) PARA 602 et seq.
6   Registered Designs Appeal Tribunal Rules 1950, SI 1950/430, r 5A(1) (added by SI 1970/1075).
7   Registered Designs Act 1949 s 28(4) (prospectively repealed: see note 1).
8   See the Registered Designs Appeal Tribunal Rules 1950, SI 1950/430, r 6.
9   In awarding costs the Appeal Tribunal may either fix the amount or direct by whom and in what
    manner the amount is to be ascertained (Registered Designs Appeal Tribunal Rules 1950,
    SI 1950/430, r 10); and, if the costs are not paid within 14 days after the amount has been fixed
    or ascertained, or such shorter period as may be directed, the party to whom they are payable
    may apply to the tribunal for an order for payment (r 11). The practice is for the tribunal to
    award a fixed sum, not intended to amount to a full indemnity for the actual costs.
10 Registered Designs Act 1949 s 28(5) (amended by the Copyright, Designs and Patents Act 1988
    Sch 3 para 17(1), (3); and SI 2006/1028; prospectively repealed (see note 1)). Any such order
    may be enforced in England and Wales in the same way as an order of the High Court:
    Registered Designs Act 1949 s 28(5)(a) (as so amended).
11 See PARA 666.
12 Registered Designs Act 1949 s 28(7) (prospectively repealed: see note 1).
13 Registered Designs Act 1949 s 28(8) (amended by the Administration of Justice Act 1970
    s 10(5); prospectively repealed (see note 1)). Pursuant to this power it is provided that an appeal
    to the Registered Designs Appeal Tribunal must be lodged, by filing with the Registrar of the
    Appeal Tribunal at the Royal Courts of Justice, London, a notice of appeal in the form set out in
    the Registered Designs Appeal Tribunal Rules 1950, SI 1950/430, Schedule (amended by
    SI 1970/1075), on a matter of procedure, within 14 days, and in any other case within six
    weeks, after the date of the decision appealed from: Registered Designs Appeal Tribunal
    Rules 1950, SI 1950/430, r 1(1), (2) (r 1 substituted by SI 1970/1075)). The notice may be sent
    by post: Registered Designs Appeal Tribunal Rules 1950, SI 1950/430, r 12. Within two days of
    filing a notice of appeal the appellant must send a copy to the registrar and to any person who
    appeared, or gave notice of opposition, in the proceedings before the registrar: r 2 (amended by
    SI 1970/1075). A fee in cash or, if permitted by the registrar, by cheque must be taken on the
    filing of every notice of appeal: see the Registered Designs Appeal Tribunal (Fees) Order 1973,
    SI 1973/165, arts 2, 3. If, owing to exceptional circumstances, payment of the fee would cause
    undue hardship, it may be reduced or remitted by the Lord Chancellor in any particular case: see
    art 4. Where the registrar refuses to register a design included in an application, he must send to
    the applicant the written reasons for his decision; and the date on which the written reasons
    were sent to the applicant is deemed to be the date of the decision for the purposes of any
    appeal: Registered Designs Rules 2006, SI 2006/1975, r 8(5), (6).

The registrar may determine whether any decision is on a matter of procedure and any such determination is itself a decision on a matter of procedure: r 1(3) (as so substituted). The registrar may grant an extension on a request received before the expiration of the period specified, and the tribunal has power to grant such extensions as it may think fit on special application being made to it: see r 4 (substituted by SI 1970/1075). Not less than seven days' notice of the time and place appointed for the hearing of the appeal must be given by the Registrar of the Appeal Tribunal to the appellant and the registrar and to any opposing party, unless the tribunal expressly allows shorter notice: Registered Designs Rules 2006, SI 2006/1975, r 5. When a notice of appeal has been given, it is the duty of the registrar to transmit to the registrar of the tribunal all the papers relating to the matter: r 3. At the request of any party, any person who has made a declaration in the proceedings may be required to attend for cross-examination: r 8.

At any time when the Appeal Tribunal consists of two or more judges, the power to make rules is exercisable by the senior of those judges; but another of those judges may exercise that power if it appears to him that it is necessary for rules to be made and that judge or, if more than one, each of the judges, senior to him is for the time being prevented by illness, absence or otherwise from making them: Registered Designs Act 1949 s 28(8A) (added by the Administration of Justice Act 1969 s 24; as so prospectively repealed). The seniority of judges is to be reckoned by reference to the dates on which they were appointed judges of the High Court or the Court of Session: Registered Designs Act 1949 s 28(10) (added by the Administration of Justice Act 1969 s 24; substituted by the Copyright, Designs and Patents Act 1988 Sch 3 para 17(1), (4); as so prospectively repealed).

14   Cf *Re Monotype Corpn Ltd's Application* (1939) 56 RPC 243, Patents Appeal Tribunal.

15   See note 1.

16   Registered Designs Act 1949 s 27A(1)(a) (prospectively added: see note 1). A person is not eligible for appointment under s 27A(1)(a) unless he satisfies the judicial-appointment eligibility condition on a 5-year basis, is an advocate or solicitor in Scotland of at least 5 years' standing, is a member of the Bar of Northern Ireland or solicitor of the Court of Judicature of Northern Ireland of at least 5 years' standing, or has held judicial office: s 27B(1) (prospectively added: see note 1). An appointed person must hold and vacate office in accordance with his terms of appointment (s 27B(2) (as so prospectively added)), subject to the provisions that he is to be paid such remuneration (whether by way of salary or fees) and such allowances as the Secretary of State may with the approval of the Treasury decide (s 27B(3) (as so prospectively added)), he may resign office by notice in writing to the Lord Chancellor (s 27B(4) (as so prospectively added)), and the Lord Chancellor may by notice in writing remove him from office if he has become bankrupt or made an arrangement with his creditors, he is incapacitated by physical or mental illness, or he is, in the opinion of the Lord Chancellor, otherwise unable or unfit to perform his duties as an appointed person (s 27B(5) (as so prospectively added)). The Lord Chancellor may remove a person from office under s 27B(5) only with the concurrence of the appropriate senior judge: s 27B(7) (as so prospectively added). The appropriate senior judge is the Lord Chief Justice of England and Wales: s 27B(8) (as so prospectively added). As to the Treasury see CONSTITUTIONAL AND ADMINISTRATIVE LAW vol 20 (2014) PARAS 262–265.

     The day appointed for the coming into force of the Intellectual Property Act 2014 s 10(2) (see note 1) for the purposes of appointing the appointed person under the Registered Designs Act 1949 ss 27A(1)(a), 27B is 15 July 2014: Intellectual Property Act 2014 (Commencement Order No 1) Order 2014, SI 2014/1715. Before exercising a power under the Registered Designs Act 1949 s 27A or s 27B the Lord Chancellor must consult the Secretary of State: s 27B(6) (as so prospectively added).

17   Registered Designs Act 1949 s 27A(1)(b) (prospectively added: see note 1). 'The court' means the High Court (s 27A(6) (as so prospectively added); as to 'the court' see PARA 668.

18   Registered Designs Act 1949 s 27A(2) (prospectively added: see note 1). Before referring an appeal to the court under s 27A(2), the appointed person must give the appellant and any other party to the appeal an opportunity to make representations as to whether it should be so referred: s 27A(3) (as so prospectively added).

19   Registered Designs Act 1949 s 27A(4) (prospectively added: see note 1).

20   Ie the Registered Designs Act 1949 s 30: see PARA 666.

21   Ie the Registered Designs Act 1949 s 31: see PARA 662.

22   Registered Designs Act 1949 s 27A(5) (prospectively added: see note 1).

670. Appeal to the Court of Appeal. Permission to appeal must be obtained from the judge at first instance or, if he refuses, the Court of Appeal[1]. The appellate court acts by way of review of the decision rather than by way of a rehearing. Unless, therefore, the judge has misdirected himself there is no ground for interfering with his conclusion[2].

1	See CPR 52.3; and CIVIL PROCEDURE vol 12 (2009) PARA 1660.
2	See *Designers Guild Ltd v Russell Williams (Textiles) Ltd* [2001] 1 All ER 700 at 702, [2000] 1 WLR 2416, HL, per Lord Bingham of Cornhill. See also *Thermos Ltd v Aladdin Sales & Marketing Ltd* [2001] EWCA Civ 667, [2002] FSR 184; *Proctor & Gamble Co v Reckitt Benckiser (UK) Ltd* [2007] EWCA Civ 936, [2008] FSR 208.

(iv) Offences

671. Offences against secrecy provisions. If any person[1] fails to comply with a direction relating to the secrecy of a design[2], or makes or causes to be made an application for the registration of a design in contravention of the statutory provisions relating to secrecy[3], he is guilty of an offence and liable on conviction on indictment to imprisonment for a term not exceeding two years or a fine, or to both, or on summary conviction to imprisonment for a term not exceeding six months or a fine not exceeding the statutory maximum, or to both[4].

1	As to the meaning of 'person' see PARA 306 note 1. As to offences by bodies corporate see PARA 675.
2	Ie a direction given under the Registered Designs Act 1949 s 5: see PARA 687.
3	Ie in contravention of the Registered Designs Act 1949 s 5: see PARA 687.
4	Registered Designs Act 1949 s 33(1) (amended by the Copyright, Designs and Patents Act 1988 Sch 3 para 22(1), (2)). As to the statutory maximum see SENTENCING AND DISPOSITION OF OFFENDERS vol 92 (2010) PARA 140.

672. Falsification of the register. If any person[1] makes or causes to be made a false entry in the register of designs[2], or a writing falsely purporting to be a copy of an entry in that register, or produces or tenders or causes to be produced or tendered in evidence any such writing, knowing the entry or writing to be false, he is guilty of an offence and liable on conviction on indictment to imprisonment for a term not exceeding two years or a fine, or to both, or on summary conviction to imprisonment for a term not exceeding six months or a fine not exceeding the statutory maximum, or to both[3].

1	As to the meaning of 'person' see PARA 306 note 1. As to offences by bodies corporate see PARA 675.
2	As to the register of designs see PARA 676.
3	Registered Designs Act 1949 s 34 (amended by the Copyright, Designs and Patents Act 1988 Sch 3 para 23). As to the statutory maximum see SENTENCING AND DISPOSITION OF OFFENDERS vol 92 (2010) PARA 140.

673. Falsely representing a design as registered. If any person[1] falsely represents that a design applied to, or incorporated in, any product sold by him is registered, he is liable on summary conviction to a fine not exceeding level 3 on the standard scale[2].

If any person, after the right in a registered design has expired, marks any product to which the design has been applied or in which it has been incorporated with the word 'registered', or any word or words implying that there is a subsisting right in the design under the Registered Designs Act 1949, or causes any such product to be so marked, he is liable on summary conviction to a fine not exceeding level 1 on the standard scale[3].

1	As to the meaning of 'person' see PARA 306 note 1. As to offences by bodies corporate see PARA 675.

2   Registered Designs Act 1949 s 35(1) (amended by SI 2001/3949). As to the standard scale see SENTENCING AND DISPOSITION OF OFFENDERS vol 92 (2010) PARA 142. A person who sells a product having stamped, engraved or impressed on it or otherwise applied to it the word 'registered', or any other word expressing or implying that the design applied to, or incorporated in, the product is registered, is deemed to represent that the design applied to, or incorporated in, the product is registered: Registered Designs Act 1949 s 35(1) (amended by SI 2001/3949).

3   Registered Designs Act 1949 s 35(2) (amended by SI 2001/3949). For these purposes, the use in the United Kingdom in relation to a design of the word 'registered', or of any other word or symbol importing a reference (express or implied) to registration, is deemed to be a representation as to registration under the Registered Designs Act 1949 unless it is shown that the reference is to registration elsewhere than in the United Kingdom and that the design is in fact so registered: s 35(3) (added by SI 2005/2339). As to the meaning of 'United Kingdom' see PARA 303 note 5.

674.   Unauthorised copying in the course of a business. A person commits an offence[1] if, in the course of a business, he intentionally copies a registered design[2] so as to make a product exactly to that design or with features that differ only in immaterial details from that design[3]. The offence is committed if the person does these things knowing, or having reason to believe, that the design is a registered design and does them without the consent of the registered proprietor of the design[4].

A person commits an offence if in the course of a business he offers, puts on the market, imports, exports or uses, or stocks for one or more of those purposes, a product where a registered design has been intentionally copied so as to make the product exactly to the design or with features that differ only in immaterial details from the design[5]. The offence is committed if the person does these things without the consent of the registered proprietor of the design[6] and knowing, or having reason to believe, that a design has been intentionally copied without the consent of the registered proprietor so as to make the product exactly to the design or with features that differ only in immaterial details from the design, and the design is a registered design[7].

Statutory provisions relating to the enforcement of trades descriptions legislation are applicable to proceedings pursuant to these provisions[8]. Provision is also made for the forfeiture of infringing articles[9]. It is a defence for a person charged with an offence under these provisions to show that he reasonably believed that the registration of the design was invalid[10], or that he did not infringe the right in the design or reasonably believed that he did not do so[11].

1   A person guilty of an offence under the Registered Designs Act 1949 s 35ZA (see the text and notes 2–11) is liable on conviction on indictment to imprisonment for a term not exceeding ten years or to a fine or to both, and on summary conviction to imprisonment for a term not exceeding six months or to a fine not exceeding the statutory maximum or to both: s 35ZA(8)(a), (b) (ss 35ZA–36ZC added by the Intellectual Property Act 2014 s 13). As to the statutory maximum see SENTENCING AND DISPOSITION OF OFFENDERS vol 92 (2010) PARA 140.

2   In the Registered Designs Act 1949 s 35ZA 'registered design' includes a registered Community design: s 35ZA(7) (as added: see note 1). As to the meaning of 'design' see PARA 711 (current designs) and PARA 717 (old designs).

3   Registered Designs Act 1949 s 35ZA(1)(a) (as added: see note 1).

4   Registered Designs Act 1949 s 35ZA(1)(b) (as added: see note 1).

5   Registered Designs Act 1949 s 35ZA(2), (3)(a) (as added: see note 1). The reference in s 35ZA(3) to using a product in the course of a business does not include a reference to using it for a purpose which is merely incidental to the carrying on of the business: s 35ZA(6) (as so added).

6   Registered Designs Act 1949 s 35ZA(3)(b) (as added: see note 1). In s 35ZA a reference to the registered proprietor is, in the case of a registered Community design, to be read as a reference to the holder: s 35ZA(7) (as so added).

7   Registered Designs Act 1949 s 35ZA(3)(c) (as added: see note 1).

8   The Trade Descriptions Act 1968 s 27 (power to make test purchases: see CONSUMER PROTECTION vol 21 (2011) PARA 525), s 28 (power to enter premises and inspect and seize goods and documents: see CONSUMER PROTECTION vol 21 (2011) PARA 524), s 29 (obstruction of authorised officers: see CONSUMER PROTECTION vol 21 (2011) PARA 523) and s 33 (compensation for loss etc of seized goods: see CONSUMER PROTECTION vol 21 (2011) PARA 524) apply as if the Registered Designs Act 1949 s 35ZA were a provision of that Act: s 35ZB(1) (as added: see note 1). Any enactment which authorises the disclosure of information for the purpose of facilitating the enforcement of the Trade Descriptions Act 1968 applies as if the Registered Designs Act 1949 s 35ZA were a provision of that Act, and as if the functions of any person in relation to that section were functions under that Act: s 35ZB(2) (as so added). Nothing in s 35ZB is to be construed as authorising a local weights and measures authority to bring proceedings in Scotland: s 35ZB(3) (as so added).

9   A person who, in connection with the investigation or prosecution of an offence under the Registered Designs Act 1949 s 35ZA, has come into the possession of relevant products or articles may apply under s 35ZC for an order for the forfeiture of the products or articles: s 35ZC(1) (as added: see note 1). 'Relevant product' means a product which is made exactly to a registered design, or with features that differ only in immaterial details from a registered design, by copying that design intentionally (s 35ZC(2) (as so added)); and 'relevant article' means an article which is specifically designed or adapted for making copies of a registered design intentionally (s 35ZC(3) (as so added)). An application under s 35ZC may be made either to the court where proceedings have been brought for an offence under s 35ZA relating to some or all of the products or article or, where no such application for the forfeiture of the products or articles has been made, by way of complaint to a magistrates' court: s 35ZC(4) (as so added). On an application under s 35ZC, the court may make an order for the forfeiture of products or articles only if it is satisfied that an offence under s 35ZA has been committed in relation to the products or articles: s 35ZC(5) (as so added). A court may infer for the purposes of s 35ZC that such an offence has been committed in relation to any products or articles if it is satisfied that such an offence has been committed in relation to products or articles which are representations of them (whether by reason of being of the same design or part of the same consignment or batch or otherwise): s 35ZC(6) (as so added). Any person aggrieved by an order made under s 35ZC by a magistrates' court, or by a decision of such a court not to make such an order, may appeal against that order or decision to the Crown Court: s 35ZC(7)(a) (as so added). An order so made may contain such provision as appears to the court to be appropriate for delaying the coming into force of the order pending the making and determination of any appeal (including any application under the Magistrates' Courts Act 1980 s 111: see MAGISTRATES vol 71 (2013) PARA 703): Registered Designs Act 1949 s 35ZC(8) (as so added). Any products or articles forfeited under s 35ZC are to be destroyed in accordance with such directions as the court may give, although the court may, if it considers it appropriate to do so, direct that the products or articles to which the order relates must (instead of being destroyed) be released to such person and on such conditions as the court may specify: s 35ZC(9), (10) (as so added)

10 Registered Designs Act 1949 s 35ZA(4) (as added: see note 1).

11 Registered Designs Act 1949 s 35ZA(5) (as added: see note 1).

675. Offences by corporations and partnerships. Where an offence under the Registered Designs Act 1949 committed by a body corporate is proved to have been committed with the consent or connivance of a director[1], manager, secretary or other similar officer of the body, or a person purporting to act in any such capacity, he as well as the body corporate is guilty of the offence and liable to be proceeded against and punished accordingly[2].

Where a partnership (other than a Scottish partnership) is guilty of an offence under the Registered Designs Act 1949, every partner, other than a partner who is proved to have been ignorant of or to have attempted to prevent the commission of the offence, is also guilty of the offence and liable to be proceeded against and punished accordingly[3]; without prejudice to this, proceedings for an offence under the Act alleged to have been committed by a partnership are to be brought against the partnership in the name of the firm and not in that of the partners[4]. A fine imposed on a partnership (other than a Scottish partnership) on its conviction in such proceedings must be paid out of the partnership assets[5].

1   For these purposes, in relation to a body corporate whose affairs are managed by its members, 'director' means a member of the body corporate: Registered Designs Act 1949 s 35A(2) (s 35A added by the Copyright, Designs and Patents Act 1988 Sch 3 para 25).

2   Registered Designs Act 1949 s 35A(1) (as added: see note 1).

3   Registered Designs Act 1949 s 35A(6) (s 35A as added (see note 1); s 35A(3)–(6) added by the Intellectual Property Act 2014 s 14).

4   Registered Designs Act 1949 s 35A(3) (as added: see notes 1, 3). Rules of court relating to the service of documents, and the Magistrates' Courts Act 1980 Sch 3 (see CRIMINAL PROCEDURE vol 27 (2010) PARA 190) apply for the purposes of such proceedings as in relation to a body corporate: Registered Designs Act 1949 s 35A(4)(a), (b) (as so added).

5   Registered Designs Act 1949 s 35A(3) (as added: see notes 1, 3).

(2) THE REGISTER

676. Keeping of the register. The registrar[1] must maintain the register of designs, in which must be entered:

(1)   the names and addresses of proprietors[2] of registered designs;

(2)   notices of assignments[3] and of transmissions of registered designs; and

(3)   such other matters as may be prescribed or as the registrar may think fit[4].

The public has a right[5] to inspect the register at the UK Intellectual Property Office[6] at all convenient times[7], but the register need not be kept in documentary form[8].

The register is prima facie evidence of any matters required or authorised by the Registered Designs Act 1949 to be entered in it[9]; but no notice of any trust, whether express, implied or constructive, may be entered in the register, and the registrar is not affected by any such notice[10].

1   As to the registrar see PARA 660.

2   As to the proprietorship of registered designs see PARA 699.

3   As to assignment see PARA 700.

4   Registered Designs Act 1949 s 17(1) (substituted by the Patents, Designs and Marks Act 1986 Sch 1 para 3). The prescribed matters for the purposes of the Registered Designs Act 1949 s 17(1) are: (1) the registered proprietor's address for service; (2) the grant or cancellation of a licence under a registered design; (3) the granting or cancelling of a security interest (whether fixed or floating) over a registered design or any right in or under it; (4) an order of a court or other competent authority transferring a registered design or any right in or under it: Registered Designs Rules 2006, SI 2006/1975, r 27(1). An application to the registrar to enter any other matter in the register must be made in writing: r 27(2). Where the registrar has doubts about whether he should enter a matter in the register he must inform the person making the application of the reasons for his doubts, and he may require that person to furnish evidence in support of the application: r 27(4). As to rectification of the register see PARAS 696–697.

5   Ie subject to the provisions of the Registered Designs Act 1949 and to rules made by the Secretary of State.

6   As to the UK Intellectual Property Office see PARA 577. For the transaction of relevant business (ie the filing of any application or other document except an application for an extension under the Registered Designs Act 1949 s 8 or an application for the registration of a design or designs made by virtue of s 14 by the public) the UK Intellectual Property Office is open (1) on Monday to Friday between 9.00 am and midnight; and (2) on Saturday between 9.00 am and 1.00 pm: Registered Designs Rules 2006, SI 2006/1975, r 45(1), (3). For the transaction of all other business by the public under the Registered Designs Act 1949 the UK Intellectual Property Office is open between 9.00 am and 5.00 pm: Registered Designs Rules 2006, SI 2006/1975, r 45(2).

    The registrar may give directions specifying the hour at which the Patent Office is deemed to be closed on any day for the purposes of the transaction by the public of business under the Act or of any class of such business, and may specify days as excluded days for any such purposes: Registered Designs Act 1949 s 39(1) (amended by the Intellectual Property Act 2014 s 12(4)). For a saving for existing rules pending the appointed day see s 12(8), (9). Any business done under the Registered Designs Act 1949 on any day after the hours at which the UK Intellectual

Property Office is deemed to be closed, or on a day which is an excluded day, is deemed to have been done on the next following day not being an excluded day; and, where the time for doing anything expires on an excluded day, that time is extended to the next following day not being an excluded day: s 39(2). The following days are excluded days for the transaction by the public of business under the Registered Designs Act 1949: a Sunday, Good Friday, Christmas day or a day which is specified or proclaimed to be a bank holiday by or under the Banking and Financial Dealings Act 1971 s 1: Registered Designs Rules 2006, SI 2006/1975, r 46(1). A Saturday is an excluded day for the transaction by the public of business except relevant business (see r 45(1)): r 46(2).

The registrar may certify any day as an interrupted day where (1) there is an event or circumstance causing an interruption in the normal operation of the UK Intellectual Property Office; or (2) there is a general interruption or subsequent dislocation in the postal services of the United Kingdom: r 40(1). Any certificate of the registrar made under r 40(1) must be posted in the UK Intellectual Property Office and advertised in the journal: rr 40(2), 44. The registrar must, where the time for doing anything under the rules expires on an interrupted day, extend that time to the next following day not being an interrupted day (or an excluded day): r 40(3). 'Interrupted day' means a day which has been certified as such under r 40(1), and 'excluded day' means a day specified as such by r 46: r 40(4). As to the extension of time periods see r 39. As to delays in communication services see the Registered Designs Act 1949 s 41; and PARA 663.

The registrar may require the use of such forms as he may direct for representations or specimens of designs or other documents which may be filed at the UK Intellectual Property Office, and the forms, and any directions by the registrar about their use, are to be published in the prescribed manner (s 31A(1)(b), (2) (s 31A added by the Intellectual Property Act 2014 s 12(1))): for this purpose it is provided that any directions given by the registrar under the Registered Designs Act 1949 s 31A or s 39 must be published on such website as the registrar considers to be likely to bring them to the attention of those persons likely to be affected by them (Registered Designs Rules 2006, SI 2006/1975, r 2A (added by SI 2014/2405)).

7   Registered Designs Act 1949 s 17(4) (substituted by the Patents, Designs and Marks Act 1986 Sch 1 para 3). As to inspection of the register see PARA 678.

8   Registered Designs Act 1949 s 17(3) (substituted by the Patents, Designs and Marks Act 1986 Sch 1 para 3). In relation to any portion of the register kept otherwise than in documentary form: (1) the right of inspection conferred by the Registered Designs Act 1949 s 17(4) is a right to inspect the material on the register; and (2) the right to a copy or extract conferred by s 17(5) or rules is a right to a copy or extract in a form in which it can be taken away and in which it is visible and legible: s 17(7) (substituted by the Patents, Designs and Marks Act 1986 Sch 1 para 3).

9   Registered Designs Act 1949 s 17(8) (substituted by the Patents, Designs and Marks Act 1986 Sch 1 para 3). See PARA 683.

10 Registered Designs Act 1949 s 17(2) (substituted by the Patents, Designs and Marks Act 1986 Sch 1 para 3). See also PARA 585. The Registered Designs Act 1949 does not, however, contain a provision as to the effect of non-registration corresponding to the Patents Act 1977 s 33(1) (see PARA 587) but the Registered Designs Act 1949 s 19(5) (see PARA 677) provides a strong practical sanction against non-registration.

677.   Registration of assignments etc. Where any person becomes entitled by assignment, transmission or operation of law to a registered design or to a share in a registered design, or becomes entitled as mortgagee, licensee or otherwise to any other interest in a registered design, he must apply[1] to the registrar[2] in the prescribed manner for the registration of his title as proprietor[3] or co-proprietor or, as the case may be, of notice of his interest, in the register of designs[4].

Where application is so made for the registration of the title of any person, the registrar must, upon proof of title to his satisfaction:

(1)   where that person is entitled to a registered design or a share in a registered design, register him in the register of designs as proprietor or co-proprietor of the design and enter in that register particulars of the instrument or event by which he derives title; or

(2)   where that person is entitled to any other interest in the registered design, enter in that register notice of his interest, with particulars of the instrument, if any, creating it[5].

Where national unregistered design right[6] subsists in a registered design and the proprietor of the registered design is also the design right owner, an assignment of the national unregistered design right is to be taken to be also an assignment of the right in the registered design, unless a contrary intention appears[7].

An application for the registration of the title of any person becoming entitled by assignment to a registered design or a share in a registered design, or becoming entitled by virtue of a mortgage, licence or other instrument to any other interest in a registered design, may be made[8] in the prescribed manner by the assignor, mortgagor, licensor or other party to that instrument, as the case may be[9].

Where a body corporate has re-registered under the Companies Act 1985[10] with the same name as that with which it was registered immediately before the re-registration save for the substitution as, or the inclusion as, the last part of the name of the words 'public limited company' or their Welsh equivalent or the abbreviation 'plc' or its Welsh equivalent, then references to the name of the body corporate in any application to the registrar, in the register of designs and in any other record kept at, or any document issued by, the UK Intellectual Property Office and relating to designs are to be treated on and after the date of such re-registration as references to the name with which the body corporate is so re-registered[11].

Except for the purposes of an application to rectify the register[12], a document in respect of which no entry has been made in the register[13] may not be admitted in any court as evidence of the title of any person to a registered design or share of or interest in a registered design unless the court otherwise directs[14].

1 There is no penalty for failure to comply. 'Registered proprietor' means the person or persons for the time being entered in the register of designs as proprietor of the design: Registered Designs Act 1949 s 44(1). As to the proprietorship of registered designs see PARA 699.
2 As to the registrar see PARA 660.
3 See PARA 699.
4 Registered Designs Act 1949 s 19(1). An application under s 19(1) or s 19(2) must be made on Form DF12A: Registered Designs Rules 2006, SI 2006/1975, r 27(3), Sch 1. As to the register see PARA 676 et seq. As to rectification of the register see PARAS 696–697.
5 Registered Designs Act 1949 s 19(3).
6 As to national unregistered design right see COPYRIGHT vol 23 (2013) PARA 1048 et seq.
7 Registered Designs Act 1949 s 19(3B) (added by the Copyright, Designs and Patents Act 1988 Sch 3 para 10; and amended by SI 2001/3949).
8 Ie without prejudice to the Registered Designs Act 1949 s 19(1).
9 Registered Designs Act 1949 s 19(2). As to the prescribed manner for the making applications see note 4.
10 As to re-registration under the Companies Act 1985 see COMPANIES vol 14 (2009) PARA 167 et seq.
11 Designs (Companies Re-registration) Rules 1982, SI 1982/299, rr 1, 2. As to the UK Intellectual Property Office see PARA 577.
12 As to rectification by order of the court see PARA 697.
13 Ie under the Registered Designs Act 1949 s 19(3).
14 Registered Designs Act 1949 s 19(5).

678. Inspection of the register and supply of copies or extracts. The register of designs is in general[1] open to inspection by the public[2]. Any person who applies for a certified copy[3] of an entry in the register or a certified extract[4] from the register is entitled to obtain such a copy or extract on payment of a fee prescribed in relation to certified copies and extracts[5].

1 As to the secrecy of certain designs see PARA 687.

2　See the Registered Designs Act 1949 s 17(4); and PARA 676. The register and any representation or specimen of a registered design are open for inspection at the UK Intellectual Property Office during the hours the UK Intellectual Property Office is open for all classes of public business: Registered Designs Rules 2006, SI 2006/1975, r 28(1). As to the hours of business see PARA 676 note 6. However, whilst a direction under the Registered Designs Act 1949 s 5(1) (see PARA 687) in respect of a design remains in force, no representation or specimen of the design is open to inspection: Registered Designs Rules 2006, SI 2006/1975, r 28(2). As to the UK Intellectual Property Office see PARA 577.

3　For these purposes, 'certified copy' means a copy certified by the registrar and sealed with the seal of the UK Intellectual Property Office: Registered Designs Act 1949 s 17(12) (substituted by the Patents, Designs and Marks Act 1986 Sch 1 para 3).

4　For these purposes, 'certified extract' means an extract certified by the registrar and sealed with the seal of the UK Intellectual Property Office: Registered Designs Act 1949 s 17(12) (as substituted: see note 3).

5　Registered Designs Act 1949 s 17(5) (substituted by the Patents, Designs and Marks Act 1986 Sch 1 para 3). Applications under the Registered Designs Act 1949 s 17(5) or rules made by virtue thereof must be made in such manner as may be prescribed: s 17(6) (substituted by the Patents, Designs and Marks Act 1986 Sch 1 para 3). An application under the Registered Designs Act 1949 s 17(5) for a certified copy of an entry in the register or a certified extract from the register must be made on Form DF23 and be accompanied by the prescribed fee: Registered Designs Rules 2006, SI 2006/1975, r 32, Sch 1. A person may apply in writing accompanied by the prescribed fee to the registrar for a certified copy of any representation or specimen of a design, and that person is entitled to such a copy: r 33. As to fees see PARA 663.

　　As to the right to a copy or extract where the register is kept otherwise than in documentary form see the Registered Designs Act 1949 s 17(7)(b); and PARA 676. As to certified copies and certified extracts being admissible in evidence see s 17(10); and PARA 683.

679. Inspection of registered designs and associated documents.

Subject to special rules as to secrecy[1], where a design has been registered, the representation or specimen of the design is open to inspection at the UK Intellectual Property Office[2] on and after the day on which the certificate of registration[3] is granted[4]. As from a day to be appointed every document kept at the UK Intellectual Property Office in connection with the registered design must also be open to inspection on the same terms[5].

Where registration of a design has been refused or an application for registration has been abandoned in relation to any design, the application, so far as relating to that design, and any representation, specimen or other document which has been filed and relates to that design, are not at any time open to inspection at the UK Intellectual Property Office; nor are they published by the registrar[6].

1　See PARA 687.
2　As to the UK Intellectual Property Office see PARA 577.
3　As to the certificate of registration see PARA 692.

4　Registered Designs Act 1949 s 22(1)(a) (s 22 substituted by the Copyright, Designs and Patents Act 1988 Sch 3 para 12(1), (2); Registered Designs Act 1949 s 22(1) amended by SI 2006/1974). The Registered Designs Act 1949 s 22(1) has effect subject to s 22(4) (or, as from a day to be appointed, s 22(4)–(7)) and to any rules made under s 5(2) (see PARA 687): s 22(1) (as so substituted and amended; s 22(1) prospectively amended, s 22(1)(aa), (5)–(7) prospectively added, by the Intellectual Property Act 2014 s 9(2)–(5)). As to inspection by the public see PARAS 676, 678.

5　Registered Designs Act 1949 s 22(1)(aa) (as substituted and prospectively added: see note 4). As from a day to be appointed, for the purposes of s 22(1) a document is not to be regarded as open for inspection unless (in addition to being open for inspection in hard copy) it is made available by electronic transmission in such a way that members of the public may access it at a place and time individually chosen by them (s 22(5) (prospectively added: see note 4)) and the Secretary of State may by rules (which may confer a discretion on the registrar) specify cases or circumstances in which a document kept at the UK Intellectual Property Office in connection

with a registered design may not be inspected (s 22(6), (7) (as so prospectively added)). At the date at which this volume states the law no such rules had been made. As to the Secretary of State see PARA 573.
6   Registered Designs Act 1949 s 22(4) (substituted by SI 2006/1974). As to the registrar see PARA 660.

680. Information as to the existence of right in registered designs. On the request[1] of a person furnishing such information as may enable the registrar[2] to identify the design, and on payment of the prescribed fee[3], the registrar must inform him whether the design is registered, and whether any extension of the period of the right in the registered design has been granted, and must also state the date of registration and the name and address of the registered proprietor[4].

1   The request must be made on Form DF21 and be accompanied by the prescribed fee: Registered Designs Rules 2006, SI 2006/1975, r 31(1), Sch 1. Where the registration number is known by the person making the request, the request must include that number, and in any other case, it must be accompanied by a representation or specimen of the product in which the design has been incorporated or to which the design has been applied: r 31(2).
2   As to the registrar see PARA 660.
3   As to fees see PARA 663.
4   Registered Designs Act 1949 s 23 (substituted by the Copyright, Designs and Patents Act 1988 Sch 3 para 13; and amended by SI 2001/3949). As to the meaning of 'registered proprietor' see PARA 677 note 1. As to the proprietorship of registered designs see PARA 699.

681. Confidential information. Where a person files a document at the UK Intellectual Property Office[1] or sends it to the registrar[2] or the UK Intellectual Property Office, any person may request that the document be treated as a confidential document[3]. A request to treat a document as confidential must be made before the end of the period of 14 days beginning immediately after the date on which the document was filed at the UK Intellectual Property Office or received by the registrar or at the UK Intellectual Property Office, and must include reasons for the request[4].

Where such a request has been made, the document must be treated as confidential until the registrar refuses that request or makes a direction[5]. Where it appears that there is good reason for the document to remain confidential, the registrar may direct that the document is to be treated as a confidential document; otherwise he must refuse the request[6]. Where, however, the registrar believes there is no longer a good reason for the direction[7] to remain in force, he must revoke it[8].

1   As to the UK Intellectual Property Office see PARA 577.
2   As to the registrar see PARA 660.
3   Registered Designs Rules 2006, SI 2006/1975, r 30(1). References to a document include part of a document: r 29(4). As to the inspection of documents see PARA 682.
4   Registered Designs Rules 2006, SI 2006/1975, r 30(2) (amended by SI 2013/444).
5   Registered Designs Rules 2006, SI 2006/1975, r 30(3). The direction referred to in the text is one under r 30(4): see the text and note 6.
6   Registered Designs Rules 2006, SI 2006/1975, r 30(4).
7   Ie the direction under the Registered Designs Rules 2006, SI 2006/1975, r 30(4): see the text and note 6.
8   Registered Designs Rules 2006, SI 2006/1975, r 30(5).

682. Inspection of documents. Where a design[1] has been registered under the Registered Designs Act 1949, every document kept at the UK Intellectual Property Office[2] in connection with that design is open to inspection at the UK Intellectual Property Office on and after the date on which the certificate of registration is granted[3]. However, no document may be inspected before the end of the period of 14 days beginning immediately after the day it was filed at the UK Intellectual Property Office or received by the registrar or the UK Intellectual Property Office[4]. No document may be inspected where it was prepared by the registrar or the UK Intellectual Property Office for internal use only[5]. Nor may a document be inspected where it includes matter which in the registrar's opinion disparages any person in a way likely to damage him, or where its inspection would in his opinion be generally expected to encourage offensive, immoral or anti-social behaviour[6].

Unless, in a particular case, the registrar otherwise directs, no document may be inspected:

(1)   where (a) the document was prepared by the registrar or the UK Intellectual Property Office other than for internal use; and (b) it contains information which the registrar considers should remain confidential[7];

(2)   where it is treated as a confidential document[8].

1   As to the meaning of 'design' see PARA 711 (current designs) and PARA 717 (old designs).
2   References to a document include part of a document: Registered Designs Rules 2006, SI 2006/1975, r 29(4). As to the UK Intellectual Property Office see PARA 577.
3   Registered Designs Rules 2006, SI 2006/1975, r 29(1).
4   Registered Designs Rules 2006, SI 2006/1975, r 29(2)(a) (amended by SI 2013/444). As to the registrar see PARA 660.
5   Registered Designs Rules 2006, SI 2006/1975, r 29(2)(b).
6   Registered Designs Rules 2006, SI 2006/1975, r 29(2)(c).
7   Registered Designs Rules 2006, SI 2006/1975, r 29(3)(a).
8   Registered Designs Rules 2006, SI 2006/1975, r 29(3)(b). As to documents treated as confidential under r 30 see PARA 681.

683.   Evidence of entries, specimens and documents.   A certificate purporting to be signed by the registrar[1] and certifying that any entry which he is authorised by or under the Registered Designs Act 1949 to make has or has not been made, or that any other thing which he is authorised to do has or has not been done, is prima facie evidence of the matters so certified[2]. A copy of any entry in the register[3] or an extract from the register[4] or of any representation, specimen or document kept in the UK Intellectual Property Office[5] or an extract from any such document which purports to be a certified copy[6] or certified extract[7] must be admitted in evidence without further proof and without production of any original[8].

1   As to the registrar see PARA 660.
2   Registered Designs Act 1949 s 17(9) (substituted by the Patents, Designs and Marks Act 1986 Sch 1 para 3).
3   As to the register see PARA 676 et seq.
4   Ie a copy or extract supplied under the Registered Designs Act 1949 s 17(5): see PARA 678.
5   As to the UK Intellectual Property Office see PARA 577.
6   As to the meaning of 'certified copy' see PARA 678 note 3.
7   As to the meaning of 'certified extract' see PARA 678 note 4.
8   Registered Designs Act 1949 s 17(10) (substituted by the Patents, Designs and Marks Act 1986 Sch 1 para 3; and amended by the Criminal Justice Act 2003 Sch 37 Pt 6).

(3) PROCEDURE FOR REGISTRATION OF CURRENT DESIGNS

684.   Procedure for making application for registration.   An application for the registration of a design[1] (or designs) must be filed at the UK Intellectual Property Office[2] in the prescribed manner[3]. The registrar may require the use of such forms as he may direct for an application for the registration of a design[4]. An application for the registration of a design (or designs) in which national unregistered design right subsists must be made by the person claiming to be the design right owner[5]. An application for the registration of a design which, owing to any default or neglect on the part of the applicant, has not been completed so as to enable registration to be effected within such time as may be prescribed is deemed to be abandoned[6].

1   Ie any design application for registration of which is registered after 9 December 2001 (see the Registered Designs Regulations 2001, SI 2001/3949, reg 1): see PARA 657. As to the meaning of 'design' see PARA 711. A design may be cancelled if registered on the application of someone not entitled to apply: *Woodhouse UK plc v Architectural Lighting Systems* [2006] RPC 1, Patents County Court.
2   As to the UK Intellectual Property Office see PARA 577.
3   Registered Designs Act 1949 s 3(1) (s 3 substituted by SI 2001/3949; Registered Designs Act 1949 s 3(1)–(3) amended by SI 2006/1974; Registered Designs Act 1949 s 3(1) amended, s 31A added, by the Intellectual Property Act 2014 ss 6(2), 12(1), (2), (5)–(9))). Applications for the registration of a design or designs must include the identity of the person making the application, and in relation to each design, must either include a representation of the design, or be accompanied by a specimen of the design, and it must also be accompanied by the prescribed fee: Registered Designs Rules 2006, SI 2006/1975, r 4(1). As to fees see PARA 663. An application for the registration of a design or designs, which is a subsequent application for the purposes of the Registered Designs Act 1949 s 3B(3) (see PARA 686), must be made on Form DF2B and be accompanied by the prescribed fee: Registered Designs Rules 2006, SI 2006/1975, r 4(2), Sch 1. Where an application includes a representation of the design, the applicant may give his consent for its publication on Form DF2A or Form DF2B: Registered Designs Rules 2006, SI 2006/1975, r 4(3), Sch 1. A representation or specimen filed may be accompanied by a brief description of the design: r 4(5). A specimen may not be filed if it is hazardous or perishable; and where such a specimen is so filed it must be disregarded: r 4(6). An application for the registration of a design which is a repeating surface pattern is only treated as such if (1) the representation or specimen filed includes the complete pattern and a sufficient portion of the repeat in length and width to show how the pattern repeats; and (2) the application contains a statement that it relates to a repeating surface pattern: r 4(7).
        An application for the registration of a design must comply with the following requirements (r 5(1)):
        (1)   The first requirement is that the applicant has specified the product to which the design is intended to be applied or in which it is intended to be incorporated (r 5(2)).
        (2)   The second requirement is that the dimensions of any specimen of the design filed under r 4 must not exceed 29.7cm x 21cm x 1cm (r 5(3)).
    Nothing done to comply with the first requirement is to be taken to affect the scope of the protection conferred by the registration of a design: r 5(5).
4   Registered Designs Act 1949 s 31A(1)(a) (as added: see note 3). The forms, and any directions by the registrar about their use, are to be published in the prescribed manner (see note 3): s 31A(2) (as so added). Where a person purports to file something under s 3(1) and it is not in the prescribed form (see note 3) or it is not accompanied by the prescribed fee (see note 3), then the registrar must notify that person accordingly: Registered Designs Rules 2006, SI 2006/1975, r 4(4).
5   Registered Designs Act 1949 s 3(3) (as substituted and amended: see note 3).
6   Registered Designs Act 1949 s 3(5) (as substituted: see note 3). The time prescribed for the purposes of s 3(5) is 12 months beginning immediately after the date on which the application for registration of the design was made or treated as made (disregarding s 14): Registered Designs Rules 2006, SI 2006/1975, r 10(1) (amended by SI 2013/444).

685.   Determination of applications for registration. Subject to the design satisfying the requirements of registrability[1], the registrar[2] may not generally refuse to register a design[3] included in an application under the Registered Designs Act 1949[4]. However, he must refuse to register a design in the following circumstances. If it appears to the registrar that an application for the registration of a design (or designs) has not been made in accordance with the rules made under the Act, he may refuse to register any design included in it[5]. If it appears to the registrar that the applicant is not entitled[6] to apply for the registration of a design included in the application, he must refuse to register that design[7]. If it appears to the registrar that the application for registration includes something which does not fulfil the statutory requirements[8] or includes a design to which a ground of refusal[9] described below applies he must refuse to register that thing or that design[10].

A design must be refused registration if it involves the use of certain royal arms[11], national flags[12], insignias[13] or controlled Olympic representations[14]. A design must also be refused registration if it involves the use of emblems of Paris Convention countries[15], or the emblems of certain international organisations[16]. An appeal lies from any decision of the registrar under the provisions described above[17].

Where it appears to the registrar that he should refuse to register a design included in an application[18] he must notify the applicant accordingly[19]. The notification must include a 'statement of objections' setting out why it appears to the registrar that he should refuse to register the design[20]. The applicant may, before the end of the period of two months beginning immediately after the date of the notification, send his written observations on the statement of objections to the registrar[21]. The registrar must give the applicant an opportunity to be heard[22]. Where the registrar refuses to register a design included in an application, he must send to the applicant the written reasons for his decision[23].

Where the registrar decides that he should not refuse to register the design[24] and no representation of the design has been filed or a representation has been filed but it is not suitable for publication, then the registrar must direct the applicant to provide a suitable representation[25]. Where such a direction is given, the applicant must, before the end of the period of three months beginning immediately after the date of the direction, file a suitable representation (otherwise the registrar may refuse to register the design)[26].

1 Ie the requirements of the Registered Designs Act 1949 ss 1–1D: see PARAS 711–716.

2 As to the registrar see PARA 660.

3 As to the meaning of 'design' see PARA 711.

4 Registered Designs Act 1949 s 3A(1) (ss 3A, 3D, Sch A1 added by SI 2001/3949; Registered Designs Act 1949 s 3A(1)–(3) amended, s 3A(4) substituted, by SI 2006/1974).

5 Registered Designs Act 1949 s 3A(2) (as added and amended: see note 4).

6 Ie under the Registered Designs Act 1949 s 3(2) or s 3(3) (see PARA 684) or s 14 (see PARA 689). See also *Woodhouse UK plc v Architectural Lighting Systems* [2006] RPC 1, Patents County Court.

7 Registered Designs Act 1949 s 3A(3) (as added and amended: see note 4).

8 Ie (1) something which does not fulfil the requirements of the Registered Designs Act 1949 s 1(2) (see PARA 711); or (2) a design that does not fulfil the requirements of s 1C or s 1D (see PARAS 714–716).

9 Ie a design to which a ground of refusal mentioned in the Registered Designs Act 1949 Sch A1 applies: see the text and notes 11–17.

10 Registered Designs Act 1949 s 3A(4) (as added and substituted: see note 4).

11 A design must be refused registration if it involves the use of:
   (1) the Royal arms, or any of the principal armorial bearings of the Royal arms, or any insignia or device so nearly resembling the Royal arms or any such armorial bearing as to be likely to be mistaken for them or it;
   (2) a representation of the Royal crown or any of the Royal flags;
   (3) a representation of Her Majesty or any member of the Royal family, or any colourable imitation thereof; or
   (4) words, letters or devices likely to lead persons to think that the applicant either has or recently has had Royal patronage or authorisation;

unless it appears to the registrar that consent for such use has been given by or on behalf of Her Majesty or (as the case may be) the relevant member of the Royal family: Registered Designs Act 1949 Sch A1 para 1(1) (as added: see note 4).

12 A design must be refused registration if it involves the use of:
   (1)   the national flag of the United Kingdom (commonly known as the Union Jack); or
   (2)   the flag of England, Wales, Scotland, Northern Ireland or the Isle of Man,
and it appears to the registrar that the use would be misleading or grossly offensive: Registered Designs Act 1949 Sch A1 para 1(2) (as added: see note 4).

13 A design must be refused registration if it involves the use of:
   (1)   arms to which a person is entitled by virtue of a grant of arms by the Crown; or
   (2)   insignia so nearly resembling such arms as to be likely to be mistaken for them;
unless it appears to the registrar that consent for such use has been given by or on behalf of the person concerned and the use is not in any way contrary to the law of arms: Registered Designs Act 1949 Sch A1 para 1(3) (as added: see note 4).

14 A design must be refused registration if it involves the use of a controlled representation within the meaning of the Olympic Symbol etc (Protection) Act 1995 (see SPORTS LAW vol 96 (2012) PARA 160) unless it appears to the registrar that: (1) the application is made by the person for the time being appointed under the Olympic Symbol etc (Protection) Act 1995 s 1(2) (power of Secretary of State to appoint a person as the proprietor of the Olympics association right: see SPORTS LAW vol 96 (2012) PARA 159); or (2) consent for such use has been given by or on behalf of the person mentioned in head (1): Registered Designs Act 1949 Sch A1 para 1(4) (as added: see note 4).

15 A design must be refused registration if it involves the use of the flag of a Paris Convention country unless: (1) the authorisation of the competent authorities of that country has been given for the registration; or (2) it appears to the registrar that the use of the flag in the manner proposed is permitted without such authorisation: Registered Designs Act 1949 Sch A1 para 2(1) (as added: see note 4). For these purposes, 'Paris Convention country' means a country, other than the United Kingdom, which is a party to the Paris Convention for the Protection of Industrial Property (Paris, 20 March 1883), as revised (Stockholm, 14 July 1967 to 13 January 1968; TS 61 (1970); Cmnd 4431): Registered Designs Act 1949 Sch A1 para 5 (as so added).

A design must be refused registration if it involves the use of the armorial bearings or any other state emblem of a Paris Convention country which is protected under the Paris Convention unless the authorisation of the competent authorities of that country has been given for the registration: Registered Designs Act 1949 Sch A1 para 2(2) (as so added).

A design must be refused registration if:
   (a)   the design involves the use of an official sign or hallmark adopted by a Paris Convention country and indicating control and warranty;
   (b)   the sign or hallmark is protected under the Paris Convention; and
   (c)   the design could be applied to or incorporated in goods of the same, or a similar, kind as those in relation to which the sign or hallmark indicates control and warranty;
unless the authorisation of the competent authorities of that country has been given for the registration: Sch A1 para 2(3) (as so added).

The provisions Sch A1 para 2 as to national flags and other state emblems, and official signs or hallmarks, apply equally to anything which from a heraldic point of view imitates any such flag or other emblem, or sign or hallmark: Sch A1 para 2(4) (as so added). Nothing in Sch A1 para 2 prevents the registration of a design on the application of a national of a country who is authorised to make use of a state emblem, or official sign or hallmark, of that country, notwithstanding that it is similar to that of another country: Sch A1 para 2(5) (as so added).

State emblems of a Paris Convention country (other than the national flag), and official signs or hallmarks, are regarded as protected under the Paris Convention only if, or to the extent that: (i) the country in question has notified the United Kingdom that it desires to protect that emblem, sign or hallmark; (ii) the notification remains in force; and (iii) the United Kingdom has not objected to it or any such objection has been withdrawn: Registered Designs Act 1949 Sch A1 para 4(1), (3) (as so added).

16 A design must be refused registration if it involves the use of the armorial bearings, flags or other emblems or the abbreviations and names of international intergovernmental organisations of which one or more Paris Convention countries are members unless: (1) the authorisation of the international organisation concerned has been given for the registration; or (2) it appears to the registrar that the use of the emblem, abbreviation or name in the manner proposed is not such as to suggest to the public that a connection exists between the organisation and the design, or is not likely to mislead the public as to the existence of a connection between the user and the organisation: Registered Designs Act 1949 Sch A1 para 3(1), (2) (as added: see note 4).

The provisions of Sch A1 para 3 as to emblems of an international organisation apply equally to anything which from a heraldic point of view imitates any such emblem: Sch A1 para 3(3) (as so added). Nothing in Sch A1 para 3 affects the rights of a person whose bona fide use of the design in question began before 4 January 1962 (when the relevant provisions of the Paris Convention entered into force in relation to the United Kingdom): Registered Designs Act 1949 Sch A1 para 3(4) (as so added).

For these purposes the emblems, abbreviations and names of an international organisation are regarded as protected under the Paris Convention only if, or to the extent that: (1) the organisation in question has notified the United Kingdom that it desires to protect that emblem, abbreviation or name; (2) the notification remains in force; and (3) the United Kingdom has not objected to it or any such objection has been withdrawn: Registered Designs Act 1949 Sch A1 para 4(2), (3).

17 Registered Designs Act 1949 s 3D (as added: see note 4).

18 Ie (1) by reason of the application for the registration of that design not being made in accordance with the Registered Designs Rules 2006, SI 2006/1975, other than r 9(2) (see the Registered Designs Act 1949 s 3A(2)); or (2) by reason of s 3A(3) or s 3A(4) (see the text and notes 7–10): Registered Designs Rules 2006, SI 2006/1975, r 8(1)(a), (b).

19 Registered Designs Rules 2006, SI 2006/1975, r 8(1). Where the applicant files a representation of the design after being notified under r 8(1) that the application does not comply with the requirement that the dimensions of any specimen of the design filed under r 4(1)(b)(ii) must not exceed 29.7cm x 21cm x 1cm, then that representation is deemed to have been filed under r 4(1)(b)(i), and any specimen filed under r 4(1)(b)(ii) is treated as not having been filed (see PARA 684): r 5(4).

20 Registered Designs Rules 2006, SI 2006/1975, r 8(2).

21 Registered Designs Rules 2006, SI 2006/1975, r 8(3) (amended by SI 2013/444).

22 Registered Designs Rules 2006, SI 2006/1975, r 8(4).

23 Registered Designs Rules 2006, SI 2006/1975, r 8(5). The date on which the written reasons were sent to the applicant is deemed to be the date of the decision for the purposes of any appeal: r 8(6).

24 Ie for the reasons mentioned in the Registered Designs Rules 2006, SI 2006/1975, r 8(1)(a) or r 8(1)(b): see note 18.

25 Registered Designs Rules 2006, SI 2006/1975, r 9(1). 'Suitable representation' means a representation of the design which is suitable for publication: r 9(5).

26 Registered Designs Rules 2006, SI 2006/1975, r 9(2) (amended by SI 2013/444). See the Registered Designs Act 1949 s 3A(2); and the text and note 5. Where a suitable representation has been filed, the applicant must file his consent for its publication on Form DF2C (Registered Designs Rules 2006, SI 2006/1975, r 9(3), Sch 1), but this does not apply where the applicant consented to publication in accordance with r 4(3): r 9(4). See note 19.

686.   Modification of applications for registration. The registrar[1] may, at any time before an application for the registration of a design[2] (or designs) is determined, permit the applicant to make such modifications of the application as the registrar thinks fit[3].

Where, before it has been determined, an application for the registration of a design (or designs) has been modified in such a way that any design included in the application has been altered significantly, the registrar may, for the purpose of deciding whether and to what extent the design is new or has individual character[4], direct that the application so far as relating to that design is to be treated as having been made on the date on which it was so modified[5]. Where (1) an application for the registration of a design has disclosed more than one design and has been modified before it has been determined to exclude one or more designs from the application; and (2) a subsequent application for the registration of a design so excluded has, within such period (if any) as has been prescribed for such applications, been made by the person who made the earlier application or his successor in title, then the registrar may, for the purpose of deciding whether and to what extent the design is new or has individual character, direct that the subsequent application is to be treated as having been made on the date on which the earlier application was, or is treated as having been, made[6].

Where the registration of a design has been refused[7], the application for the design may be modified by the applicant if it appears to the registrar that the identity of the design is retained and that the modifications have been made in accordance with any rules made under the Registered Designs Act 1949[8].

Any such modification may, in particular, be effected by making a partial disclaimer in relation to the application[9].

An appeal lies from any decision of the registrar under the provisions described above[10].

1 As to the registrar see PARA 660.
2 As to the meaning of 'design' see PARA 711.
3 Registered Designs Act 1949 s 3B(1) (ss 3B, 3D added by SI 2001/3949; Registered Designs Act 1949 s 3B(1)–(4) amended by SI 2006/1974).
4 As to a design being new and having individual character see PARA 712.
5 Registered Designs Act 1949 s 3B(2) (as added and amended: see note 3).
6 Registered Designs Act 1949 s 3B(3) (as added and amended: see note 3). The period prescribed for the purposes of s 3B(3) is the period of two months beginning immediately after the date on which the earlier application was modified under s 3B(3): Registered Designs Rules 2006, SI 2006/1975, r 10(2) (amended by SI 2013/444).
7 Ie on the ground that the design does not fulfil the requirements of the Registered Designs Act 1949 s 1C or s 1D (see PARAS 714–716), or on the ground of refusal mentioned in Sch A1 (see PARA 685): see s 3A(4); and PARA 685.
8 Registered Designs Act 1949 s 3B(4) (as added and amended: see note 3). An application modified under s 3B(4) is to be treated as the original application and, in particular, as made on the date on which the original application was made or is treated as having been made: s 3B(5) (as so added).
9 Registered Designs Act 1949 s 3B(6) (as added and amended: see note 3). An application for the registration of a design may be accompanied by a disclaimer which (1) limits the scope or extent of protection being applied for in relation to the design; or (2) indicates that the application for registration relates to a design that forms only a part of the appearance of a product: Registered Designs Rules 2006, SI 2006/1975, r 6.
10 Registered Designs Act 1949 s 3D (as added: see note 3).

687. Secrecy of certain designs. Where an application for the registration of a design[1] has been made and it appears to the registrar[2] that the design is one of a class notified to him by the Secretary of State[3] as relevant for defence purposes, he may give directions for prohibiting or restricting the publication of information with respect to the design or the communication of such information to any person or class of persons specified in the directions[4]. The Secretary of State must by rules make provision for securing that, where such directions are given, the representation or specimen of the design is not open to public inspection at the UK Intellectual Property Office[5] during the continuance in force of the directions[6].

Where the registrar gives any such directions, he must give notice of the application and of the directions to the Secretary of State, and thereupon the following provisions have effect:

(1)   the Secretary of State must, upon receipt of such notice, consider whether the publication of the design would be prejudicial to the defence of the realm and, unless a notice under head (3) below has previously been given by that authority to the registrar, must reconsider that question before the expiration of nine months from the date of filing of the application for registration of the design and at least once in every subsequent year[7];

(2) for the above purpose, the Secretary of State may, at any time after the design has been registered or, with the consent of the applicant, at any time before the design has been registered, inspect the representation or specimen of the design filed in pursuance of the application[8];

(3) if upon consideration of the design at any time it appears to the Secretary of State that the publication of the design would not, or would no longer, be prejudicial to the defence of the realm, he must give notice to the registrar to that effect[9];

(4) on the receipt of any such notice the registrar must revoke the direction and may, subject to such conditions, if any, as he thinks fit, extend the time for doing anything required or authorised to be done by or under the Registered Designs Act 1949 in connection with the application or registration, whether or not that time has previously expired[10].

1 As to the meaning of 'design' see PARA 711.
2 As to the registrar see PARA 660.
3 As to the Secretary of State see PARA 660.
4 Registered Designs Act 1949 s 5(1) (amended by the Copyright, Designs and Patents Act 1988 Sch 3 para 3(1), (2)). Failure to comply with such directions is an offence: see PARA 671. These provisions have little or no application in practice.
5 As to the UK Intellectual Property Office see PARA 577.
6 Registered Designs Act 1949 s 5(2) (substituted by the Copyright, Designs and Patents Act 1988 Sch 3 para 3(1), (3); and amended by SI 2001/3949). Whilst a direction under the Registered Designs Act 1949 s 5(1) in respect of a design remains in force, no representation or specimen of the design is open to inspection: Registered Designs Rules 2006, SI 2006/1975, r 28.
7 Registered Designs Act 1949 s 5(3)(a).
8 Registered Designs Act 1949 s 5(3)(b) (amended by SI 2001/3949).
9 Registered Designs Act 1949 s 5(3)(c).
10 Registered Designs Act 1949 s 5(3)(d).

688. Filing abroad. Except under the authority of a written permit granted by or on behalf of the registrar[1], no person resident in the United Kingdom[2] may make or cause to be made any application outside the United Kingdom for registration of a design of any prescribed class[3] unless an application for the registration of the same design has been made in the United Kingdom not less than six weeks before the application outside the United Kingdom, and either no directions have been given[4] in relation to the application in the United Kingdom or all such directions have been revoked[5]. These provisions do not, however, apply in relation to a design for which an application for protection has first been filed in a country outside the United Kingdom by a person resident outside the United Kingdom[6].

1 As to the registrar see PARA 660.
2 As to the meaning of 'United Kingdom' see PARA 303 note 5. As to the territorial scope of the Registered Designs Act 1949 see PARA 659.
3 Ie any class which may be prescribed for the purposes of the Registered Designs Act 1949 s 5(4): see PARA 687. 'Prescribed' means prescribed by rules made by the Secretary of State: s 44(1). At the date at which this volume states the law no such rules had been made.
4 Ie directions of the registrar under the Registered Designs Act 1949 s 5(1): see PARA 687.
5 Registered Designs Act 1949 s 5(4).
6 Registered Designs Act 1949 s 5(4) proviso.

689. Applications under international convention. Certain countries which are parties to the International Convention for the Protection of Industrial Property[1] are declared to be convention countries for the purposes of the Registered Designs Act 1949[2]. An application for registration of a design (or designs)[3] in respect of which protection has been applied for in a convention country may be made by the person by whom the application for protection was made or his personal representative[4] or assignee[5]; but no application may be so made after the expiration of six months[6] from the date of the application for protection in a convention country or, where more than one such application for protection has been made, from the date of the first application[7].

Where an application for registration of a design or designs is made in this way, the application is to be treated, for the purpose of determining whether (and to what extent) that or any other design is new or has individual character, as made on the date of the application for protection in the convention country or, if more than one such application was made, on the date of the first such application[8].

Where a person has applied for protection for a design or designs by an application which:

(1)   in accordance with the terms of a treaty subsisting between two or more convention countries is equivalent to an application duly made in any one of those convention countries; or

(2)   in accordance with the law of any convention country is equivalent to an application duly made in that convention country,

he is deemed to have applied in that convention country[9].

1   Ie the International Convention further revising the Paris Convention for the Protection of Industrial Property of 20 March 1883 (Stockholm, 14 July 1967 to 13 January 1968; TS 61 (1970); Cmnd 4431).

2   See the Registered Designs Act 1949 s 13; and PARA 659.

3   As to the meaning of 'design' see PARA 711 (current designs) and PARA 717 (old designs).

4   For these purposes 'personal representative', in relation to a deceased person, includes the legal representative of the deceased appointed in any country outside the United Kingdom: Registered Designs Act 1949 s 44(4) (amended by SI 2001/3949). As to the meaning of 'United Kingdom' see PARA 303 note 5. As to the territorial scope of the Registered Designs Act 1949 see PARA 659.

5   For these purposes, 'assignee' includes the personal representative of a deceased assignee; and references to the assignee of any person include references to the assignee of the personal representative or assignee of that person: Registered Designs Act 1949 s 44(1).

6   There is no power to extend the time limit in individual cases, but rules may be made providing for extensions by reciprocal arrangement with other convention countries, in special circumstances: see the Registered Designs Act 1949 s 15 (amended by the Copyright, Designs and Patents Act 1988 Sch 3 para 8; and SI 2001/3949). At the date at which this volume states the law no such rules were in force.

7   Registered Designs Act 1949 s 14(1) (amended by SI 2006/1974). As to the date of registration, and as to protection from prior publication and registration, see PARA 691. As to the priority given to a convention application see *Deyhle's Design Applications* [1982] RPC 526, Registered Designs Appeal Tribunal; and PARA 690.

8   Registered Designs Act 1949 s 14(2) (substituted by the Copyright, Designs and Patents Act 1988 Sch 3 para 7; and amended by SI 2001/3949; SI 2006/1974). This is not to be construed as excluding the power to give directions under the Registered Designs Act 1949 s 3B(2) or s 3B(3) (see PARA 686) in relation to an application made by virtue of s 14: s 14(3) (amended by SI 2001/3949). As to the circumstances in which a design based on an application in a convention country can be registered under the Registered Designs Act 1949 s 14 with the priority date of the foreign application see *Deyhle's Design Applications* [1982] RPC 526, Registered Designs Appeal Tribunal. Patent priority may not, however, be claimed from a foreign design application: see *Agfa-Gevaert AG's Application* [1982] RPC 441. There is no power to postdate a convention application: *Allibert Exploitation's Application* [1978] RPC 261, Registered Designs Appeal Tribunal.

9   Registered Designs Act 1949 s 14(4).

690. Requisites for convention application. Where an application for the registration of a design or designs[1] is made[2] the applicant must comply with the following requirements[3]. The application must contain a declaration specifying both the date of making of each convention application and the country it was made in or in respect of[4]. The applicant must, before the end of the period of three months beginning immediately after the date on which the application was filed, file at the UK Intellectual Property Office[5] a copy of the representation of the design that was the subject of each convention application[6]. A copy of the representation must either be duly certified by the authority with which it was filed, or be verified to the satisfaction of the registrar[7]. Where any document relating to the convention application is in a language other than English or Welsh, the registrar may direct the applicant to provide a translation of the whole or any part of that document[8], and the translation must be filed before the end of the period of three months beginning immediately after the date of the direction[9].

1   As to the meaning of 'design' see PARA 711 (current designs) and PARA 717 (old designs).
2   Ie a convention application by virtue of the Registered Designs Act 1949 s 14: see PARA 689. A 'convention application' means an application for the protection of a design which has been made in a convention country: Registered Designs Rules 2006, SI 2006/1975, r 7(9).
3   Registered Designs Rules 2006, SI 2006/1975, r 7(1).
4   Registered Designs Rules 2006, SI 2006/1975, r 7(2).
5   As to the UK Intellectual Property Office see PARA 577.
6   Registered Designs Rules 2006, SI 2006/1975, r 7(3) (amended by SI 2013/444).
7   Registered Designs Rules 2006, SI 2006/1975, r 7(4). However, this does not apply where a copy of the convention application is kept at the UK Intellectual Property Office: r 7(5). Where the applicant fails to file a copy of the representation of the design which has been certified or verified in accordance with r 7(4), the convention application is to be disregarded for the purposes of the Registered Designs Act 1949 s 14(2) (see PARA 689): Registered Designs Rules 2006, SI 2006/1975, r 7(8).
8   Registered Designs Rules 2006, SI 2006/1975, r 7(6). Where the applicant fails to comply with a direction given under r 7(6), the convention application is to be disregarded for the purposes of the Registered Designs Act 1949 s 14(2) (see PARA 689): Registered Designs Rules 2006, SI 2006/1975, 7(8).
9   Registered Designs Rules 2006, SI 2006/1975, r 7(7) (amended by SI 2013/444).

(4) DURATION, RESTORATION AND SURRENDER

(i) Registration and its Duration

691. Date of registration. In general, a design[1], when registered, is registered as of the date on which the application was made or is treated as having been made[2]. However, this rule does not apply to registrations of designs where application for protection in a convention country has been made, or where an application for registration has been modified[3].

1   This provision applies both to current designs and old designs by virtue of the Registered Designs Regulations 2001, SI 2001/3949, reg 12(4), (6). As to the meaning of 'design' see PARA 711 (current designs) and PARA 717 (old designs).
2   Registered Designs Act 1949 s 3C(1) (s 3C added by SI 2001/3949). As to applications for registration see PARA 684.
3   The Registered Designs Act 1949 s 3C(1) does not apply to an application which is treated as having been made on a particular date by s 14(2) (see PARA 689) or by virtue of the operation of s 3B(3) or s 3B(5) (see PARA 686) by reference to s 14(2): s 3C(2) (as added: see note 2). A design, when registered, is registered as of:
    (1)   in the case of an application which is treated as having been made on a particular date by s 14(2), the date on which the application was made (s 3C(3)(a) as so added);
    (2)   in the case of an application which is treated as having been made on a particular date by virtue of the operation of s 3B(3) by reference to s 14(2), the date on which the earlier application was made (s 3C(3)(b) as so added);
    (3)   in the case of an application which is treated as having been made on a particular date

by virtue of the operation of s 3B(5) by reference to s 14(2), the date on which the original application was made (s 3C(3)(c) as so added).

692. Certificate of registration. The registrar[1] must grant a certificate of registration in the prescribed form to the registered proprietor[2] of a design[3] when the design is registered[4]. The certificate of registration of a design must include: (1) the name of the registered proprietor; (2) the date of registration; and (3) the registration number of the design[5].

When a design has been registered, the registrar must publish a representation of that design in the journal as soon as possible after the certificate of registration is granted[6].

In a case where he is satisfied that the certificate of registration has been lost or destroyed, or in any other case in which he thinks it expedient, the registrar may furnish one or more copies of the certificate[7]. Any request by the registered proprietor for a copy of the certificate of registration must be in writing and be accompanied by the prescribed fee[8]. Before considering the request, the registrar may require the person making the request to provide such information or evidence as the registrar thinks fit[9].

1   As to the registrar see PARA 660.
2   As to the proprietorship of registered designs see PARA 699.
3   This provision applies both to current designs and old designs by virtue of the Registered Designs Regulations 2001, SI 2001/3949, reg 12(4), (6). As to the meaning of 'design' see PARA 711 (current designs) and PARA 717 (old designs).
4   Registered Designs Act 1949 s 18(1).
5   Registered Designs Rules 2006, SI 2006/1975, r 26(1). Certificates of registration of old designs were governed by the corresponding provisions of the Registered Designs Rules 1995, SI 1995/2912 (revoked).
6   Registered Designs Rules 2006, SI 2006/1975, r 11(1), (3). When the registrar publishes the representation, he may also publish any other information he thinks is relevant to that design: r 11(2).
7   Registered Designs Act 1949 s 18(2).
8   Registered Designs Rules 2006, SI 2006/1975, r 26(2). As to fees see PARA 663.
9   Registered Designs Rules 2006, SI 2006/1975, r 26(3).

693. Duration of right in registered design. The right in a registered design subsists in the first instance for a period of five years from the date of the registration of the design[1]. The period for which the right subsists may be extended for a second, third, fourth and fifth period of five years, by applying to the registrar for an extension and paying the prescribed renewal fee[2]. If the first, second, third or fourth period expires without such application and payment being made, the right ceases to have effect; and the registrar must notify the proprietor[3] of that fact[4]. If during the period of six months immediately following the end of that period an application for extension is made and the prescribed renewal fee and any prescribed additional fee are paid, the right is treated as if it had never expired, with the result that:

(1)   anything done under or in relation to the right during that further period is treated as valid[5];

(2)   an act which would have constituted an infringement of the right if it had not expired is treated as an infringement[6]; and

(3)   an act which would have constituted use of the design for the services of the Crown[7] if it had not expired is treated as such use[8].

1   Registered Designs Act 1949 s 8(1) (s 8 substituted by the Copyright, Designs and Patents Act 1988 s 269(1)). As to the date of registration see PARA 692. As to the meaning of 'design' see PARA 711 (current designs) and PARA 717 (old designs).

In relation to old designs, the Registered Designs Act 1949 s 8 is subject to the proviso that the right in a design registered for further articles by virtue of the Registered Designs Act 1949 s 4 (now repealed) does not, however, extend beyond the end of the period, and any extended period, for which the right subsists in the original registered design: s 8(6) (as so substituted; repealed in relation to current designs); Registered Designs Regulations 2001, SI 2001/3949, reg 12(9).

2 Registered Designs Act 1949 s 8(2) (as substituted: see note 1). An application for an extension under s 8(2) or s 8(4) must be made on Form DF9A: Registered Designs Rules 2006, SI 2006/1975, r 12(1), Sch 1. An application under the Registered Designs Act 1949 s 8(2) may only be made during the period of six months ending with the date on which the relevant period of five years expires: Registered Designs Rules 2006, SI 2006/1975, r 12(2). On receipt of the prescribed renewal fee the registrar must notify the registered proprietor of the extension of the right in the registered design: r 12(3). As to fees see PARA 663. As to the registrar see PARA 660.

3 As to the proprietorship of registered designs see PARA 699.

4 Registered Designs Act 1949 s 8(3) (as substituted: see note 1). Where the right in a registered design has ceased to have effect by reason of s 8(3), the registrar must, before the end of the period of six weeks beginning immediately after the date on which the right ceased, send written notice to the registered proprietor of that fact: Registered Designs Rules 2006, SI 2006/1975, r 12(4) (amended by SI 2013/444). However, this does not apply where the renewal fee and the prescribed additional fee is paid before a notice is sent: Registered Designs Rules 2006, SI 2006/1975, r 12(5).

5 Registered Designs Act 1949 s 8(4)(a) (as substituted: see note 1).

6 Registered Designs Act 1949 s 8(4)(b) (as substituted: see note 1). As to infringement see PARA 738 et seq.

7 As to Crown use see PARA 705 et seq.

8 Registered Designs Act 1949 s 8(4)(c) (as substituted: see note 1).

(ii) Restoration of Lapsed Designs

694. Restoration of lapsed right in designs. Where the right in a registered design[1] has expired by reason of a failure to extend[2] the period for which the right subsists, an application for the restoration of the right in the design may be made to the registrar[3] within the period of 12 months beginning immediately after the date on which the right in the registered design expired[4]. The application may be made by the person who was the registered proprietor[5] of the design or by any other person who would have been entitled to the right in the design if it had not expired; and, where the design was held by two or more persons jointly, the application may, with the leave of the registrar, be made by one or more of them without joining the others[6]. The registrar must enter in the register[7] notice of the application and must publish such notice in the Official Journal (Patents)[8].

If the registrar is satisfied that failure of the proprietor to see that the period for which the right subsisted was extended was unintentional, he must, on payment of any unpaid renewal fee and any prescribed additional fee[9], order the restoration of the right in the design[10]. The order may be made subject to such conditions as the registrar thinks fit; and, if the proprietor of the design does not comply with any condition, the registrar may revoke the order and give such consequential directions as he thinks fit[11].

Where, however, upon consideration of that evidence, the registrar is not satisfied that a case for an order[12] has been made out, he must notify the applicant accordingly[13]. The applicant may, before the end of the period of one month beginning immediately after the date of that notification, request to be heard by the registrar[14]. Where the applicant requests such a hearing, the registrar must give him an opportunity to be heard; after which the registrar must determine whether the application is to be granted or refused[15]. Where the registrar decides not to make the order he must give the applicant written reasons for his refusal[16].

1   The provisions in the Registered Designs Act 1949 s 8A with regard to restoration of lapsed current designs apply equally to old designs: see the Registered Designs Regulations 2001, SI 2001/3949, reg 12(4). As to the meaning of 'design' see PARA 711 (current designs) and PARA 717 (old designs).
2   Ie in accordance with the Registered Designs Act 1949 s 8(2) or s 8(4): see PARA 693.
3   As to the registrar see PARA 660.
4   Registered Designs Act 1949 s 8A(1) (s 8A added by the Copyright, Designs and Patents Act 1988 s 269(1)); Registered Designs Rules 2006, SI 2006/1975, r 13(2) (amended by SI 2013/444). Rules altering the period for the purposes of the Registered Designs Act 1949 s 8A(1) may contain such transitional provisions and savings as appear to the Secretary of State to be necessary or expedient: s 8A(6). An application for the restoration of the right in a design under the Registered Designs Act 1949 s 8A must be made on Form DF29, and be supported by evidence of the statements made in the application: Registered Designs Rules 2006, SI 2006/1975, r 13(1), Sch 1.
5   As to the proprietorship of registered designs see PARA 699.
6   Registered Designs Act 1949 s 8A(2) (as added: see note 4).
7   As to the register see PARA 676 et seq.
8   Registered Designs Act 1949 s 8A(3) (as added: see note 4); Registered Designs Rules 2006, SI 2006/1975, r 13(3). As to the Journal see r 44; and PARA 578.
9   As to fees see PARA 663.
10   Registered Designs Act 1949 s 8A(4) (as added (see note 4); amended by SI 2006/1974). As to the effect of an order for restoration of the right in a registered design see PARA 695.
11   Registered Designs Act 1949 s 8A(5) (as added: see note 4).
12   Ie an order under the Registered Designs Act 1949 s 8A.
13   Registered Designs Rules 2006, SI 2006/1975, r 13(4).
14   Registered Designs Rules 2006, SI 2006/1975, r 13(5) (amended by SI 2013/444).
15   Registered Designs Rules 2006, SI 2006/1975, r 13(6).
16   Registered Designs Rules 2006, SI 2006/1975, r 13(7).

695. Effect of restoration of right order. Where an order for the restoration of the right in a registered design[1] is made[2], anything done under or in relation to the right during the period between expiry and restoration is treated as valid[3]; and anything done during that period which would have constituted an infringement if the right had not expired is treated as an infringement[4]:

(1)   if done at a time when it was possible for an application for an extension to be made[5]; or

(2)   if it was a continuation or repetition of an earlier infringing act[6].

If, after it was no longer possible for such an application for extension to be made and before publication of notice of the application for restoration[7], a person:

(a)   began in good faith to do an act which would have constituted an infringement of the right in the design if it had not expired; or

(b)   made in good faith effective and serious preparations to do such an act,

he has the right to continue to do the act or, as the case may be, to do the act, notwithstanding the restoration of the right in the design; but this does not extend to granting a licence to another person to do the act[8].

If, however, the act was done, or the preparations were made, in the course of a business, the person entitled to such right may:

(i)   authorise the doing of that act by any partners of his for the time being in that business; and

(ii)   assign that right, or transmit it on death (or in the case of a body corporate on its dissolution), to any person who acquires that part of the business in the course of which the act was done or the preparations were made[9].

The above provisions apply in relation to the use of a registered new design for the services of the Crown as they apply in relation to infringement of the right in the design[10].

1 The provisions in the Registered Designs Act 1949 s 8B apply to both current designs and old designs: see the Registered Designs Regulations 2001, SI 2001/3949, reg 12(4). As to the meaning of 'design' see PARA 711 (current designs) and PARA 717 (old designs).
2 Ie under the Registered Designs Act 1949 s 8A: see PARA 694.
3 Registered Designs Act 1949 s 8B(1), (2) (s 8B added by the Copyright, Designs and Patents Act 1988 s 269).
4 As to what constitutes infringement see PARA 738 et seq.
5 Ie under the Registered Designs Act 1949 s 8(4): see PARA 693.
6 Registered Designs Act 1949 s 8B(3) (as added: see note 3).
7 As to publication of the notice see PARA 694.
8 Registered Designs Act 1949 s 8B(4) (as added: see note 3). Where a product is disposed of to another in exercise of the rights conferred by the Registered Designs Act 1949 s 8B(4) or s 8B(5), that other and any other person claiming through him may deal with the product in the same way as if it had been disposed of by the registered proprietor of the design: s 8B(6) (as so added; and amended by SI 2001/3949). As to the meaning of 'product' see PARA 711 note 1. As to the proprietorship of registered designs see PARA 699.
9 Registered Designs Act 1949 s 8B(5) (as added: see note 3). See also note 8.
10 Registered Designs Act 1949 s 8B(7) (as added: see note 3). As to Crown use see PARA 705 et seq.

(iii) Correction; Rectification; Voluntary Cancellation

696. Corrections. The registrar[1] may correct any error in an application for the registration, or in the representation of a design[2], or any error in the register of designs[3]. A correction may be so made either upon a request in writing made by any person interested and accompanied by the prescribed fee[4], or without such a request[5]. Where, however, he proposes to make any such correction otherwise than in pursuance of a request, the registrar must give notice of the proposal to the registered proprietor[6] or the applicant for registration of the design, as the case may be, and to any other person who appears to him to be concerned, and must give them an opportunity to be heard before making the correction[7].

Any person may request[8] that an alteration to his name or address be entered in the register or be made to any application or other document filed at the UK Intellectual Property Office[9]. Where the registrar has doubts about whether he should make the alteration to a name or address he must inform the person making the request of the reason for his doubts, and he may require that person to furnish evidence in support of the request[10]. Where the registrar has no doubts (or no longer has doubts) about whether he should make the alteration, it must be entered in the register or made to the application or document[11].

1 As to the registrar see PARA 660.
2 As to the meaning of 'design' see PARA 711 (current designs) and PARA 717 (old designs).
3 Registered Designs Act 1949 s 21(1); applied to old designs by the Registered Designs Regulations 2001, SI 2001/3949, reg 12(4). As to the register of designs see PARA 676 et seq.
4 As to fees see PARA 663.
5 Registered Designs Act 1949 s 21(2).
6 As to the proprietorship of registered designs see PARA 699.
7 Registered Designs Act 1949 s 21(3).

8 The request in relation to an alteration to his name must be made on Form DF16A; and in relation to his address, must be made on Form DF16A or in writing: Registered Designs Rules 2006, SI 2006/1975, r 34(2), Sch 1.

9 Registered Designs Rules 2006, SI 2006/1975, r 34(1). As to the UK Intellectual Property Office see PARA 577.

10 Registered Designs Rules 2006, SI 2006/1975, r 34(3).

11 Registered Designs Rules 2006, SI 2006/1975, r 34(4).

697. Rectification by court order. On the application of the relevant person[1], the court[2] may order the register of designs[3] to be rectified by the making of an entry in it or the variation or deletion of any entry in it[4]. Applications fall into two classes: those affecting the proprietorship of the design[5]; and those affecting its validity. Orders which may be made by the court include, in particular, declarations of partial invalidity[6].

Notice of the application must be given in the prescribed form to the registrar[7], who is entitled to appear and be heard on the application and must appear if so directed by the court[8]. Any order so made by the court must direct that notice of the order be served on the registrar[9]; and, on receipt of the notice, the registrar must rectify the register accordingly[10].

A rectification of the register under the above provisions has effect as follows:

(1)   an entry made has effect from the date on which it should have been made;

(2)   an entry varied has effect as if it had originally been made in its varied form; and

(3)   an entry deleted is deemed never to have had effect,

unless, in any case, the court directs otherwise[11].

1   'Relevant person' means, in relation to current designs:
(1)   in the case of an application invoking any ground referred to in the Registered Designs Act 1949 s 11ZA(1)(c) (see PARA 734), any person concerned by the use in question (s 20(1A)(a) (added by SI 2001/3949; and amended by SI 2006/1974));
(2)   in the case of an application invoking the ground mentioned in the Registered Designs Act 1949 s 11ZA(1A) (see PARA 734), the appropriate person (s 20(1A)(b) (added by SI 2001/3949; and amended by SI 2006/1974));
(3)   in the case of an application invoking any ground mentioned in the Registered Designs Act 1949 s 11ZA(2), (3) or (4) (see PARA 734) the person able to make the objection (s 20(1A)(c) (added by SI 2001/3949)).

In relation to old designs and in relation to current designs in any case other than those mentioned in heads (1)–(3), 'relevant person' is any person aggrieved: Registered Designs Act 1949 s 20(1A)(d) (added by SI 2001/3949); applied to old designs by the Registered Designs Regulations 2001, SI 2001/3949, regs 1, 12(2), (4).

'Appropriate person' means, in relation to an earlier design protected by virtue of registration under the Registered Designs Act 1949 or Council Regulation (EC) 6/2002 (OJ L3, 5.1.2002, p 1) on Community Designs or an application for such registration, the registered proprietor of the design, the holder of the registered community design or (as the case may be) the applicant: Registered Designs Act 1949 s 20(1B) (added by SI 2001/3949; amended by SI 2003/550).

'Person aggrieved' is widely interpreted and generally includes any person who is, or probably might be, injured or affected by the error, entry or omission in question: see *Re Read and Greswell's Design* (1889) 42 Ch D 260, 6 RPC 471.

2   As to the meaning of 'court' see PARA 668.

3   As to the register of designs see PARA 676 et seq.

4   Registered Designs Act 1949 s 20(1) (amended by SI 2001/3949). See *Woodhouse UK plc v Architectural Lighting Systems* [2006] RPC 1, Patents County Court.

In proceedings under the Registered Designs Act 1949 s 20 the court may determine any question which it may be necessary or expedient to decide in connection with the rectification of the register: s 20(2). As to the procedure see CPR Pt 63; *Practice Direction — Intellectual Property Claims* PD 63. As to counterclaims for rectification in an infringement action see PARA 746.

5   Where an agent had by mistake registered a design under his own name, rectification was granted: see *Re Guiterman's Registered Designs* (1885) 55 LJ Ch 309; *Re Grocott's Design* (1899) 17 RPC 139. See also *Leara Trading Co Ltd's Designs* [1991] RPC 609.

6   Registered Designs Act 1949 s 20(6) (added by SI 2001/3949).

7   The prescribed manner of giving notice to the registrar for the purposes of the Registered Designs Act 1949 s 20(3) is by giving written notice: Registered Designs Rules 2006, SI 2006/1975, r 35(1). As to the registrar see PARA 660.

8   Registered Designs Act 1949 s 20(3).The registrar does not in general appear, but, if he does, the unsuccessful party will in general be ordered to pay his costs, and, even if he does not, a sum is ordered to be paid to cover his costs of considering the application: see *Re Saxton, Chatterton & Co's Design* (1914) 32 RPC 331; *Re Kestos Ltd Registered Design (No 725,716), Kestos Ltd v Kempat Ltd and Vivian Fitch Kemp* (1935) 53 RPC 139 at 158.

9   The prescribed manner of service on the registrar for the purposes of the Registered Designs Act 1949 s 20(4) is by filing a copy of the order at the UK Intellectual Property Office: Registered Designs Rules 2006, SI 2006/1975, r 35(2). As to the UK Intellectual Property Office see PARA 577.

10 Registered Designs Act 1949 s 20(4).

11 Registered Designs Act 1949 s 20(5) (added by the Copyright, Designs and Patents Act 1988 Sch 3 para 11).

698.   Voluntary cancellation.   The registrar[1] may, upon a request made in the prescribed manner[2] by the registered proprietor[3], cancel the registration of a design[4]. The registered proprietor may thus save costs by surrendering his design rather than become a party to legal proceedings[5]. A cancellation of registration takes effect from the date of the registrar's decision or from such other date as the registrar may direct[6].

1   As to the registrar see PARA 660.

2   A request to cancel the registration of a design must be made on Form DF19C: Registered Designs Rules 2006, SI 2006/1975, r 14, Sch 1.

3   As to the proprietorship of registered designs see PARA 699.

4   Registered Designs Act 1949 s 11 (substituted by SI 2001/3949). An appeal lies from any decision of the registrar under the Registered Designs Act 1949 s 11: s 11ZF (added by SI 2001/3949).

5   As to rectification by court order see PARA 720.

6   Registered Designs Act 1949 s 11ZE(1) (added by SI 2001/3949). An appeal lies from any decision of the registrar under the Registered Designs Act 1949 s 11ZE: s 11ZF (as added: see note 4).

(5) OWNERSHIP; ASSIGNMENT; LICENCES; CROWN USE

(i) Ownership

699.   Proprietorship of registered designs.   The author[1] of a design[2] is generally treated for the purposes of the Registered Designs Act 1949 as the original proprietor of the design[3], although where a design is created by an employee in the course of his employment, his employer is treated as the original proprietor of the design[4].

Where a design becomes vested, whether by assignment, transmission or operation of law, in any person other than the original proprietor, either alone or jointly with the original proprietor[5], that other person, or as the case may be the original proprietor and that other person, must be treated as the proprietor of the design[6].

1   'Author' of a design means the person who creates it: Registered Designs Act 1949 s 2(3) (s 2(1) substituted, s 2(1A), (1B), (3) added, by the Copyright Designs and Patents Act 1988 s 267). In the case of a design generated by computer in circumstances such that there is no human author,

the person by whom the arrangements necessary for the creation of the design are made is to be taken to be the author: Registered Designs Act 1949 s 2(4) (substituted by the Copyright Designs and Patents Act 1988 s 267).

2　As to the meaning of 'design' see PARA 711.

3　Registered Designs Act 1949 s 2(1) (as substituted: see note 1).

4　Registered Designs Act 1949 s 2(1B) (as added (see note 1); amended by the Intellectual Property Act 2014 s 6(1)). In these provisions 'employee', 'employment' and 'employer' refer to employment under a contract of service or of apprenticeship: Registered Designs Act 1949 s 44(1) (definition amended by the Copyright, Designs and Patents Act 1988 Sch 3 para 31(1), (8)).

5　This would appear to include a licensee: cf *Woolley v Broad* [1892] 1 QB 806, 9 RPC 208, DC.

6　Registered Designs Act 1949 s 2(2) (amended by SI 2001/3949). See also *Woodhouse UK plc v Architectural Lighting Systems* [2006] RPC 1, Patents County Court; *Ifejika v Ifejika* [2010] EWCA Civ 563, [2010] FSR 715, [2010] All ER (D) 258 (May).

(ii) Assignment and Devolution

700. Property in and dealing with registered designs and applications. A registered design[1] or an application for a registered design[2] is personal property[3] and is transmissible by assignment, testamentary disposition or operation of law in the same way as other personal property[4].

Any transmission of a registered design or an application for a registered design is subject to any rights vested in any other person of which notice is entered in the register of designs[5], or in the case of applications, notice is given to the registrar[6]. An assignment[7] of, or an assent relating to, a registered design or application for a registered design is not effective unless it is in writing signed by or on behalf of the assignor or, as the case may be, a personal representative[8].

A registered design or application for a registered design may be the subject of a charge in the same way as other personal property[9].

The proprietor of a registered design may grant a licence to use that registered design[10].

Any equities in respect of a registered design or an application for a registered design may be enforced in like manner as in respect of any other personal property[11].

1　As to the meaning of 'design' see PARA 711 (current designs) and PARA 717 (old designs).

2　As to applications see PARA 699 et seq.

3　Registered Designs Act 1949 s 15A (ss 15A–15C added by SI 2006/1028). See PERSONAL PROPERTY vol 80 (2013) PARA 805.

4　Registered Designs Act 1949 s 15B(1) (as added: see note 3). See PERSONAL PROPERTY vol 80 (2013) PARA 850 et seq.

5　As to the register of designs see PARA 676.

6　Registered Designs Act 1949 s 15B(2) (as added: see note 3). As to the registrar see PARA 660.

7　The Registered Designs Act 1949 s 15B(3), (4) (see the text and note 8) apply to assignment by way of security as in relation to any other assignment: s 15B(5) (as added: see note 3).

8　Registered Designs Act 1949 s 15B(3) (as added: see note 3). This requirement may be satisfied in a case where the assignor or personal representative is a body corporate by the affixing of its seal: s 15B(4) (as so added).

9　Registered Designs Act 1949 s 15B(6) (as added: see note 3). See CHOSES IN ACTION vol 13 (2009) PARA 26.

10　Registered Designs Act 1949 s 15B(7) (as added: see note 3).

11　Registered Designs Act 1949 s 15B(8) (as added: see note 3).

(iii) Licences

701. Licences. There are no special requirements relating to the grant of licences in respect of a registered design[1]. An 'exclusive licence' is a licence in writing signed by or on behalf of the proprietor of the registered design authorising the licensee to the exclusion of all other persons, including the person granting the licence to exercise a right which would otherwise be exercisable exclusively by the proprietor[2]. The licensee under an exclusive licence has the same rights against any successor in title who is bound by the licence as he has against the person granting the licence[3] and has, except as against the registered proprietor, the same rights and remedies in respect of matters occurring after the grant of the licence as if the licence had been an assignment[4].

1   In relation to old designs (see PARA 717), any licence which: (1) permits anything which would otherwise be an infringement under the Registered Designs Act 1949 of the right in a registered design or the copyright in a registered design; and (2) was granted by the registered proprietor of the design, or under s 10 or s 11A (see PARA 702), before 9 December 2001, continues in force, with necessary modifications, on or after that date: Registered Design Regulations 2001, SI 2001/3949, reg 14(1). In determining the effect of any such licence, regard must be had to the purpose for which the licence was granted; and, in particular, a licence granted for the full term or extent of the right in a registered design or the copyright in a registered design is to be treated as applying, subject to its other terms and conditions, to the full term or extent of that right as extended by virtue of the Registered Design Regulations 2001, SI 2001/3949: reg 14(2).
2   Registered Designs Act 1949 s 15C(1) (s 15C added by SI 2006/1028). See note 1. Cf an exclusive licensee under a patent: see PARA 379 note 7.
3   Registered Designs Act 1949 s 15C(2) (as added: see note 2). See note 1.
4   Registered Designs Act 1949 s 24F(1) (added by SI 2006/1028). See note 1. As to the rights and remedies of the exclusive licensee see PARA 745.

(iv) Compulsory Licences

702. Powers exercisable for the protection of the public interest.   Where a report of the Competition and Markets Authority[1] has been laid before Parliament containing conclusions to the effect:

(1)   on a competition reference, that a person was engaged in an anti-competitive practice which operated or may be expected to operate against the public interest; or

(2)   on a reference of public bodies and certain other persons[2], that a person is pursuing a course of conduct which operates against the public interest,

the appropriate minister or ministers[3] may apply to the registrar[4] to take action under these provisions[5].

Before making such an application, the appropriate minister or ministers must publish, in such manner as he or they think appropriate, a notice describing the nature of the proposed application and must consider any representations which may be made within 30 days of such publication by persons whose interests appear to him or them to be affected[6].

If on such an application it appears to the registrar that the matters specified in the Competition and Markets Authority's report as being those which in the opinion of the Competition and Markets Authority operate, or operated or may be expected to operate, against the public interest include conditions in licences granted in respect of a registered design by its proprietor[7] restricting the use of the design by the licensee or the right of the proprietor to grant other licences, he may by order cancel or modify any such condition[8].

An appeal lies from any order of the registrar[9].

1   As to the Competition and Markets Authority see PARA 397 note 1.
2   Ie a reference under the Competition Act 1980 s 11: see COMPETITION vol 18 (2009) PARA 10.
3   For these purposes 'appropriate minister or ministers' means the minister or ministers to whom the report of the Competition and Markets Authority was made: Registered Designs Act 1949

s 11A(7) (s 11A added by the Copyright, Designs and Patents Act 1988 s 270; Registered Designs Act 1949 s 11A(1), (3), (7) amended by SI 2014/892).
4   As to the registrar see PARA 660.
5   Registered Designs Act 1949 ss 11A(1) (as added and amended (see note 3); also amended by the Enterprise Act 2002 Sch 25 para 1(1), (2), Sch 26; and SI 1999/506).
6   Registered Designs Act 1949 ss 11A(2) (as added: see note 3).
7   As to the proprietorship of registered designs see PARA 699. As to the meaning of 'design' see PARA 711 (current designs) and PARA 717 (old designs).
8   Registered Designs Act 1949 s 11A(3) (as added and amended (see note 3); also amended by SI 2001/3949); Registered Designs Regulations 2001, SI 2001/3949, regs 1, 12(4).
9   Registered Designs Act 1949 s 11A(6) (as added: see note 3), s 28(1). See PARA 669.

703. Powers exercisable following merger and market investigations. The Competition and Markets Authority[1] or, as the case may be, the Secretary of State[2] may apply to the registrar[3] to take action[4] where:

(1)   the provisions of the Enterprise Act 2002 relating to powers to take remedial action following merger or market investigations[5] apply[6];

(2)   the Competition and Markets Authority or, as the case may be, the Secretary of State considers that it would be appropriate to make an application[7] for the purpose of remedying, mitigating or preventing a matter which cannot be dealt with under the enactment concerned[8]; and

(3)   the matter concerned involves conditions in licences granted in respect of a registered design by its proprietor[9] restricting the use of the design by the licensee or the right of the proprietor to grant other licences[10].

Before making an application the Competition and Markets Authority or, as the case may be, the Secretary of State must publish, in such manner as it or he thinks appropriate, a notice describing the nature of the proposed application and must consider any representations which may be made within 30 days of such publication by persons whose interests appear to it or him to be affected[11].

The registrar may, if it appears to him on an application that the application is made in accordance with the above provisions, by order cancel or modify any condition concerned of the kind mentioned in head (3) above[12]. An appeal lies from any order of the registrar[13].

1   As to the Competition and Markets Authority see PARA 397 note 1. References in the Registered Designs Act 1949 s 11AB (see the text and notes 2–13) to the Competition and Markets Authority are references to a CMA group except where the Enterprise Act 2002 s 75(2) applies or any other enactment mentioned in the Registered Designs Act 1949 s 11AB(1)(a) (see the text and note 6) applies and the functions of the Competition and Markets Authority under that enactment are being performed by the CMA Board by virtue of the Enterprise Act 2002 s 34C(3) or s 133A(2) (see COMPETITION): Registered Designs Act 1949 s 11AB(6) (s 11AB added by the Enterprise Act 2002 Sch 25 para 1(1), (3); Registered Designs Act 1949 s 11AB(1)(a), (b), (2), (3), (7) amended, s 11AB(6) substituted, s 11AB(9) added, by SI 2014/892). As to the meanings of 'CMA Board' and 'CMA Group' see the Enterprise and Regulatory Reform Act 2013 Sch 4; and COMPETITION (definition applied by the Registered Designs Act 1949 s 11AB(9) (as so added)).
2   As to the Secretary of State see PARA 660.
3   As to the registrar see PARA 660.
4   Registered Designs Act 1949 s 11AB(2) (as added and amended: see note 1). References in the Enterprise Act 2002 s 35, 36, 47, 63, 134, 141 or 141A (questions to be decided by the Competition and Markets Authority in its reports) to taking action under s 41(2), 55, 66, 138, 147 or 147A (see COMPETITION) include references to taking action under the Registered Designs Act 1949 s 11AB(2): s 11AB(7) (as so added and amended). See also the Enterprise Act 2002 (Protection of Legitimate Interests) Order 2003, SI 2003/1592, art 16, Sch 4 para 2.
5   Ie the Enterprise Act 2002 s 41(2), 55(2), 66(6), 75(2), 83(2), 138(2), 147(2), 147A(2) or s 160(2), or Sch 7 paras 5(2), 10(2): see COMPETITION.
6   Registered Designs Act 1949 s 11AB(1)(a) (as added and amended: see note 1). An order made by virtue of s 11AB in consequence of action under s 11AB(2) (see the text to notes 1–4) where

an enactment mentioned in s 11AB(1)(a) applies is to be treated, for the purposes of the Enterprise Act 2002 ss 91(3), 92(1)(a), 162(1) and 166(3) (duties to register and keep under review enforcement orders etc) (see COMPETITION), as if it were made under the relevant power in Pt 3 (ss 22–130) or (as the case may be) Pt 4 (ss 131–184) to make an enforcement order (within the meaning of the Part concerned): Registered Designs Act 1949 s 11AB(8) (as so added).

7   Ie under the Registered Designs Act 1949 s 11AB.
8   Registered Designs Act 1949 s 11AB(1)(b) (as added and amended: see note 1).
9   As to the proprietorship of registered designs see PARA 699. As to the meaning of 'registered design' see PARA 657.
10 Registered Designs Act 1949 s 11AB(1)(c) (as added: see note 1).
11 Registered Designs Act 1949 s 11AB(3) (as added and amended: see note 1).
12 Registered Designs Act 1949 s 11AB(4) (as added: see note 1).
13 Registered Designs Act 1949 s 11AB(5) (as added: see note 1). See PARA 693.

704.   War emergency licensing. Where an enemy or enemy subject is the proprietor of a registered design, the comptroller[1] may grant a licence in respect of the design to any person who is not an enemy or an enemy subject[2]. The comptroller must, however, be satisfied that the would-be licensee[3] desires to apply the design and is in a position to do so, and that the licence would be in the interest of all or any of Her Majesty's subjects[4]. Licences may be granted on any terms which the comptroller thinks fit, may be exclusive and may be made notwithstanding the existence of any other licence[5]. The comptroller has a general discretion to vary or revoke licences[6]. A licensee may sue for infringement[7].

1   Ie the registrar for the purposes of the Registered Designs Act 1949: see PARA 660.
2   See the Patents, Designs, Copyright and Trade Marks (Emergency) Act 1939 s 2(1). See further PARA 400 where this enactment, which extends similarly to patents and copyrights of enemies, is more fully discussed.
3   Application must be made by the would-be licensee and accompanied where necessary by evidence and a statement setting out the principal conditions of the proposed licence: see the Patents, Designs, Copyright and Trade Marks (Emergency) Act 1939 ss 2(1), 9; and PARA 400.
4   Patents, Designs, Copyright and Trade Marks (Emergency) Act 1939 s 2(1); and PARA 400.
5   See the Patents, Designs, Copyright and Trade Marks (Emergency) Act 1939 s 2(2)–(4), (6); and PARA 400.
6   See the Patents, Designs, Copyright and Trade Marks (Emergency) Act 1939 s 2(7), (8); and PARA 400.
7   See the Patents, Designs, Copyright and Trade Marks (Emergency) Act 1939 s 2(5); and PARA 400.

(v) Crown Use

705.   Crown rights of use. Any government department, and any person authorised in writing by a government department[1], may use any registered design for the services of the Crown[2]. For these purposes, the services of the Crown are deemed to include:

(1)   the supply to the government of any country outside the United Kingdom[3], in pursuance of an agreement or arrangement between Her Majesty's government in the United Kingdom and the government of that country, of products[4] required for the defence of that country or for the defence of any other country whose government is party to any agreement or arrangement with Her Majesty's government in respect of defence matters;

(2)   the supply to the United Nations, or to the government of any country belonging to that organisation, in pursuance of an agreement or arrangement between Her Majesty's government and that organisation

or government, of products required for any armed forces operating in pursuance of a resolution of that organisation or any organ of that organisation[5].

The power to use a registered design includes power to sell any such products to any such government or to that organisation and to sell to any person any products made in the exercise of these powers[6] which are no longer required for the purpose for which they were made[7].

During the period of any emergency[8] the above powers include power to use the registered design for any purpose which appears to the department necessary or expedient:

(a)   for the efficient prosecution of any war in which Her Majesty may be engaged;

(b)   for the maintenance of supplies and services essential to the life of the community;

(c)   for securing a sufficiency of supplies and services essential to the well-being of the community;

(d)   for promoting the productivity of industry, commerce and agriculture;

(e)   for fostering and directing exports and reducing imports, or imports of any classes, from all or any countries and for redressing the balance of trade;

(f)   generally for ensuring that the whole resources of the community are available for use, and are used, in a manner best calculated to serve the interests of the community; or

(g)   for assisting the relief of suffering and the restoration and distribution of essential supplies and services in any country or territory outside the United Kingdom which is in grave distress as the result of war;

and any references to the services of the Crown[9] are to be construed as including a reference to those purposes[10].

The purchaser of any products sold in the exercise of the Crown powers, and any person claiming through him, has power to deal with them in the same manner as if the rights in the registered design were held on behalf of the Crown[11].

1   The authority of a government department may be given either before or after the design is registered and either before or after the acts in respect of which the authority is given are done, and it may be given to any person whether or not he is authorised directly or indirectly by the registered proprietor to use the design: Registered Designs Act 1949 s 12, Sch 1 para 1(4). As to the meaning of 'design' see PARA 711 (current designs) and PARA 717 (old designs); and as to the meaning of 'registered proprietor' see PARA 677 note 1. In practice these provisions are not used.

2   Registered Designs Act 1949 Sch 1 para 1(1). For the corresponding provisions relating to patents see PARA 404 et seq.

     The power conferred by Sch 1 para 1(1) on a government department, or person authorised in writing by a government department, in relation to the use of registered designs for the services of the Crown is exercisable for the purposes of a visiting force or headquarters to the extent that it would be exercisable if the visiting force or headquarters were a part of any of the home forces: Visiting Forces and International Headquarters (Application of Law) Order 1999, SI 1999/1736, art 6, Sch 4 para 1(1). As to visiting forces see ARMED FORCES vol 3 (2011) PARA 405 et seq. This provision does not have effect to authorise the doing in relation to a registered design of anything falling within the Registered Designs Act 1949 Sch 1 para 1(6) (see the text to notes 3–5): Visiting Forces and International Headquarters (Application of Law) Order 1999, SI 1999/1736, art 6, Sch 4 para 1(2). In relation to the exercise of the powers conferred by Sch 4 para 1(1), the Registered Designs Act 1949 Sch 1 paras 1(2)–(5), (7), 2–3 has effect with any reference in those provisions to Crown use of a registered design being construed as a reference to the use of such a design for the purposes of a visiting force or headquarters: Visiting Forces and International Headquarters (Application of Law) Order 1999, SI 1999/1736, art 6, Sch 4 para 1(3).

3	As to the meaning of 'United Kingdom' see PARA 303 note 5; and as to the territorial scope of the Registered Designs Act 1949 see PARA 659.

4	As to the meaning of 'product' see PARA 711 note 1.

5	Registered Designs Act 1949 Sch 1 para 1(6) (substituted by the Defence Contracts Act 1958 s 1(1), (4); and amended by SI 2001/3949). As to the United Nations see INTERNATIONAL RELATIONS LAW vol 61 (2010) PARA 520 et seq. The amendment by SI 2001/3949 also applies to the registration of any design application for which was made before 9 December 2001: see the Registered Designs Regulations 2001, SI 2001/3949, regs 1, 12(4). As to the validity of old designs see PARA 717.

6	Ie the powers conferred by the Registered Designs Act 1949 Sch 1 para 1.

7	Registered Designs Act 1949 Sch 1 para 1(6) (as substituted and amended: see note 5).

8	For these purposes, 'period of emergency' means a period beginning on such date as may be declared by Order in Council to be the commencement, and ending on such date as may be so declared to be the termination, of a period of emergency for these purposes: Registered Designs Act 1949 Sch 1 para 4(2) (amended by the Copyright, Designs and Patents Act 1988 s 272, Sch 3 para 37). At the date at which this volume states the law no such order was in force.

9	Ie in the Registered Designs Act 1949 Sch 1: see the text and notes 1–8; and PARAS 706–710.

10	Registered Designs Act 1949 Sch 1 para 4(1).

11	Registered Designs Act 1949 Sch 1 para 1(7) (amended by SI 2001/3949). Nothing in the Registered Designs Act 1949 affects the right of the Crown or of any person deriving title directly or indirectly from the Crown to sell or use products forfeited under the laws relating to customs and excise: s 43(2) (amended by SI 2001/3949). As to the Crown's rights to dispose of or use articles so forfeited see the Customs and Excise Management Act 1979 s 139(4), (5), Sch 3 para 16; and CUSTOMS AND EXCISE vol 31 (2012) PARA 1152 et seq.

706. Compensation for Crown use. In so far as a design[1] has, before its date of registration, been duly recorded by or applied by or on behalf of a government department otherwise than in consequence of the communication of the design directly or indirectly by the registered proprietor[2] or any person from whom he derives title, any use of the design under Crown powers[3] may be made free of any royalty or other payment to the registered proprietor[4]. In so far as a design has not been so recorded or applied, however, any such use of the design made at any time after the date of its registration, or in consequence of any such communication, must, unless the design is invalid[5], be made on such terms as may be agreed on, either before or after use, between the government department and the registered proprietor with Treasury approval or as may, in default of agreement, be determined by the court[6], on a reference[7].

Where any use of a design is so made by or with the authority of a government department, then, unless it appears to the department that it would be contrary to the public interest to do so, the department must notify the registered proprietor as soon as practicable after the use is begun, and furnish him with such information as to the extent of the use as he may from time to time require[8].

1	As to the meaning of 'design' see PARA 711 (current designs) and PARA 717 (old designs).

2	As to the meaning of 'registered proprietor' see PARA 677 note 1.

3	Ie under the Registered Designs Act 1949 s 12, Sch 1 para 1: see PARA 705.

4	Registered Designs Act 1949 Sch 1 para 1(2).

5	See the Registered Designs Act 1949 Sch 1 para 3(2); and PARA 710.

6	Ie under the Registered Designs Act 1949 Sch 1 para 3: see PARA 710. As to the meaning of 'court' see PARA 668.

7	Registered Designs Act 1949 Sch 1 para 1(3). As to the Treasury see CONSTITUTIONAL AND ADMINISTRATIVE LAW vol 20 (2014) PARAS 262–265.

8	Registered Designs Act 1949 Sch 1 para 1(5).

707. Persons entitled to compensation. In general, compensation for the use of a design under Crown powers[1] is payable to the registered proprietor[2]. In certain circumstances, however, other persons may be entitled to compensation as follows:

(1) where an exclusive licence[3] granted otherwise than for royalties or other benefits determined by reference to the use of the design is in force under the design, then, in relation to any use of the design which would, but for the provisions as to Crown powers of use, be an infringement of the rights of the licensee, any compensation is payable to the licensee[4];

(2) where there is any other exclusive licence, the licensee is entitled to part of the compensation payable to the registered proprietor; and the apportionment must be such as, in default of agreement, may be determined by the court[5] as just, having regard to any expenditure incurred by the licensee in developing the design, or in making payments to the registered proprietor, other than royalties or other payments determined by reference to the use of the design, in consideration of the licence[6];

(3) subject to the entitlement under head (1) above, where the registered design, or the right to apply for or obtain registration of the design, has been assigned to the registered proprietor in consideration of royalties or other benefits determined by reference to the use of the design, the compensation must be divided between the registered proprietor and the assignor[7].

1 Ie under the Registered Designs Act 1949 s 12, Sch 1 para 1: see PARA 705.
2 See the Registered Designs Act 1949 Sch 1 para 1(3); and PARA 706. As to the meaning of 'registered proprietor' see PARA 677 note 1.
3 For these purposes, 'exclusive licence' means a licence from a registered proprietor which confers on the licensee, or on the licensee and persons authorised by him, to the exclusion of all other persons, including the registered proprietor, any right in respect of the registered design: Registered Designs Act 1949 Sch 1 para 2(5).
4 Registered Designs Act 1949 Sch 1 para 2(2)(a). There is then no right of compensation if the licensee uses the design under Crown authority: see Sch 1 para 2(2)(b).
5 As to the meaning of 'court' see PARA 668. As to the settlement of disputes see PARA 710.
6 Registered Designs Act 1949 Sch 1 para 2(4). If, before the amount of compensation has been agreed between the registered proprietor and the department, the licensee gives notice of his interest to the department, any agreement as to amount is of no effect unless made with the licensee's consent: Sch 1 para 2(4).
7 Registered Designs Act 1949 Sch 1 para 2(3)(a). Use by the registered proprietor, such as the Crown has power to authorise, to the order of a government department then attracts compensation as if made under Crown authority: Sch 1 para 2(3)(b).

708. Rights of third persons. Where any use of a registered design, or a design in respect of which an application for registration is pending, is made for the services of the Crown[1] either by a government department or a person authorised by a government department, or by the registered proprietor[2] or applicant for registration to the order of a government department, then the provisions of any licence, assignment or agreement made between the registered proprietor or applicant for registration or any person who derives title from him or from whom he derives title and any person other than a government department are of no effect so far as those provisions restrict or regulate the use of the design or any model, document or information relating to the design, or provide for the making of payments in respect of any such use or calculated by reference to such use[3]. In connection with such use of a design, the reproduction or publication of any model or document is not deemed to be an infringement of any copyright or national unregistered design right[4] subsisting in the model or document[5]. In such a case, the rules governing compensation for Crown use and the procedure for determination of disputes as to Crown use[6] apply as if the person entitled to the contractual provision or copyright or design right concerned was a registered proprietor[7].

1　Ie under the Registered Designs Act 1949 s 12, Sch 1 para 1: see PARA 705.
2　As to the meaning of 'registered proprietor' see PARA 677 note 1.
3　Registered Designs Act 1949 Sch 1 para 2(1). Nothing in the Registered Designs Act 1949 Sch 1 para 2 is, however, to be construed as authorising the disclosure to a government department or any other person of any model, document or information to the use of which that provision applies in contravention of any such licence, assignment or agreement: Defence Contracts Act 1958 s 1(3), (4). See COPYRIGHT vol 23 (2013) PARAS 653 et seq (copyright), 1048 et seq (design right).
4　'National unregistered design right' means design right within the meaning of the Copyright, Designs and Patents Act 1988 Pt III (see s 213; and COPYRIGHT vol 23 (2013) PARAS 610, 1048 et seq): Registered Designs Act 1949 s 44(1) (definition added by SI 2001/3949).
5　Registered Designs Act 1949 Sch 1 para 2(1) (amended by the Copyright, Designs and Patents Act 1988 Sch 3 para 37(1), (2); and by SI 2001/3949); Registered Designs Regulations 2001, SI 2001/3949, regs 1, 12(4).
6　Ie the Registered Designs Act 1949 Sch 1 para 1(3) (see PARA 705) and Sch 1 para 3 (see PARA 710).
7　See the Defence Contracts Act 1958 s 1(2), (4).

709. Compensation for loss of profit. Where Crown use[1] is made of a registered design, the government department concerned[2] must pay to the registered proprietor[3] or, if there is an exclusive licence[4] in force in respect of the design, to the exclusive licensee compensation for any loss resulting from his not being awarded a contract to supply the products[5] to which the design is applied or in which it is incorporated[6]. Compensation is payable only to the extent that such a contract could have been fulfilled from his existing manufacturing capacity; but it is payable notwithstanding the existence of circumstances rendering him ineligible for the award of such a contract[7]. In determining the loss, regard must be had to the profit which would have been made on such a contract and to the extent to which any manufacturing capacity was underused[8]. No compensation is, however, payable in respect of any failure to secure contracts for the supply of products to which the design is applied or in which it is incorporated otherwise than for the services of the Crown[9]. The amount so payable, if not agreed between the registered proprietor or licensee and the government department concerned with the approval of the Treasury, must be determined[10] by the court[11]; and it is in addition to any amount payable[12] in respect of Crown use[13].

1　For these purposes, 'Crown use', in relation to a design, means the doing of anything by virtue of the Registered Designs Act 1949 s 12, Sch 1 para 1 (see PARAS 705–706) which would otherwise be an infringement of the right in the design: Sch 1 para 2A(6) (Sch 1 para 2A added by the Copyright, Designs and Patents Act 1988 s 271(1), (2)). As to the meaning of 'design' see PARA 711 (current designs) and PARA 717 (old designs).
2　For these purposes, 'government department concerned', in relation to Crown use, means the government department by whom or on whose authority the act was done: Registered Designs Act 1949 Sch 1 para 2A(6) (as added: see note 1).
3　As to the meaning of 'registered proprietor' see PARA 677 note 1.
4　As to the meaning of 'exclusive licence' see PARA 707 note 3.
5　As to the meaning of 'product' see PARA 711 note 1.
6　Registered Designs Act 1949 Sch 1 para 2A(1) (as added (see note 1); and amended by SI 2001/3949); Registered Design Regulations 2001, SI 2001/3949, regs 1, 12(4). Cf the Patents Act 1977 s 57A; and PARA 408.
7　Registered Designs Act 1949 Sch 1 para 2A(2) (as added: see note 1).

8 Registered Designs Act 1949 Sch 1 para 2A(3) (as added: see note 1).
9 Registered Designs Act 1949 Sch 1 para 2A(4) (as added (see note 1); and amended by SI 2001/3949); Registered Design Regulations 2001, SI 2001/3949, regs 1, 12(4).
10 Ie on a reference under the Registered Designs Act 1949 Sch 1 para 3: see PARA 710.
11 As to the meaning of 'court' see PARA 668.
12 Ie in addition to any amount payable under the Registered Designs Act 1949 Sch 1 para 1 (see PARAS 705–706) or Sch 1 para 2 (see PARA 708).
13 Registered Designs Act 1949 Sch 1 para 2A(5) (as added: see note 1).

710. Settlement of disputes. Any dispute as to:

(1) the exercise by a government department or a person authorised by a government department of its powers to authorise use of designs[1]; or

(2) terms for the use of a design for the services of the Crown[2]; or

(3) the right of any person to receive any part of any compensation payable[3]; or

(4) the right of any person to receive compensation for loss of profit[4],

may be referred to the court[5] by either party to the dispute[6].

The court may at any time order the whole of any such proceedings, or any question or issue of fact arising in them, to be referred to a special or official referee or an arbitrator on such terms as the court may direct[7].

In any such proceedings to which a government department is a party, the department may:

(a) if the registered proprietor[8] is a party to the proceedings and the department is a relevant person[9], apply for invalidation of the registration of the design upon any ground upon which the registration of a design may be declared invalid on an application to the court[10];

(b) in any case and provided that the department would be the relevant person[11] if it had made an application on the grounds for invalidity being raised put in issue the validity of the registration of the design without applying for its invalidation[12].

In determining any dispute between a government department and any person as to terms for the use of a design for the services of the Crown, the court must have regard to any benefit or compensation which that person, or any person from whom he derives title, may have received, or may be entitled to receive, directly or indirectly from any government department in respect of the design in question[13]. If in such proceedings any question arises whether a design has been previously recorded or applied so as to exclude any right to compensation, and the disclosure of any document recording the design, or of any evidence of its application, would in the department's opinion be prejudicial to the public interest, the disclosure may be made confidentially to counsel for the other party or to an independent expert mutually agreed upon[14].

1 Ie the powers conferred by the Registered Designs Act 1949 s 12, Sch 1 para 1: see PARAS 705–706.
2 Ie under the Registered Designs Act 1949 Sch 1 para 1: see PARAS 705–706.
3 Ie under the Registered Designs Act 1949 Sch 1 para 1(3): see PARA 706.
4 Ie under the Registered Designs Act 1949 Sch 1 para 2A: see PARA 709.
5 As to the meaning of 'court' see PARA 668.
6 Registered Designs Act 1949 Sch 1 para 3(1) (substituted by the Copyright, Designs and Patents Act 1988 s 271(1), (3)).
7 Registered Designs Act 1949 Sch 1 para 3(5). References to the court in Sch 1 para 3(1)–(4) are to be construed accordingly: Sch 1 para 3(5). As to references to a special or official referee generally see ARBITRATION vol 2 (2008) PARA 1226; CIVIL PROCEDURE vol 12 (2009) PARA 1544.
8 As to the meaning of 'registered proprietor' see PARA 677 note 1.
9 Ie within the meaning of the Registered Designs Act 1949 s 20: see PARA 697.
10 Ie under the Registered Designs Act 1949 s 20: see PARA 697.

11 See note 9.
12 Registered Designs Act 1949 Sch 1 para 3(2) (amended by SI 2001/3949); Registered Design Regulations 2001, SI 2001/3949, regs 1, 12(4).
13 Registered Designs Act 1949 Sch 1 para 3(4).
14 Registered Designs Act 1949 Sch 1 para 3(3).

(6) VALIDITY

(i) Current Designs

711. Meaning of 'design'. 'Design' means the appearance of the whole or a part of a product[1] resulting from the features of, in particular, the lines, contours, colours, shape, texture or materials of the product or its ornamentation[2].

1 'Product' means any industrial or handicraft item other than a computer program; and, in particular, includes packaging, get-up, graphic symbols, typographic type-faces and parts intended to be assembled into a complex product: Registered Designs Act 1949 s 1(3) (s 1 substituted by SI 2001/3949). 'Complex product' means a product which is composed of at least two replaceable component parts permitting disassembly and reassembly of the product: Registered Designs Act 1949 s 1(3) (as so substituted).
2 Registered Designs Act 1949 s 1(2) (as substituted: see note 1).

712. Requirement of novelty and individual character. A design[1] is protected by a right in a registered design to the extent that the design is both new and has individual character[2]. For these purposes, a design is new if no identical design or no design whose features differ only in immaterial details has been made available to the public before the relevant date[3]. A design has individual character if the overall impression it produces on the informed user differs from the overall impression produced on such a user by any design which has been made available to the public before the relevant date[4].

In determining the extent to which a design has individual character, the degree of freedom of the author in creating the design is to be taken into consideration[5].

A design applied to or incorporated in a product which constitutes a component part of a complex product is only considered to be new and to have individual character (1) if the component part, once it has been incorporated into the complex product, remains visible during normal use of the complex product[6]; and (2) to the extent that those visible features of the component part are in themselves new and have individual character[7].

1 As to the meaning of 'design' see PARA 711.
2 Registered Designs Act 1949 s 1B(1) (s 1B added by SI 2001/3949). This legislation applies to the validity of any design application for which was made on or after 9 December 2001: see the Registered Designs Regulations 2001, SI 2001/3949, reg 1. As to the legislation relating to old designs see PARA 717. See *Bailey (t/a Elite Angling Products) v Haynes (t/a RAGS)* [2006] EWPCC 5, [2007] FSR 199, where this requirement is considered in the context of the Community unregistered design right.
3 Registered Designs Act 1949 s 1B(2) (as added: see note 2). 'Relevant date' means the date on which the application for the registration of the design was made or is treated by virtue of s 3B(2), (3) or (5) (see PARA 686) or s 14(2) (see PARA 689) as having been made: s 1B(7) (as so added). The 'sector concerned' is that corresponding to the prior art: *Green Lane Products Ltd v PMS International Group Ltd* [2007] EWHC 1712 (Pat), [2008] FSR 1, [2007] All ER (D) 305 (Jul); affd [2008] EWCA Civ 358, [2009] IP & T 233, [2008] All ER (D) 313 (Apr). As to when a design is made available to the public see PARA 713.
4 Registered Designs Act 1949 s 1B(3) (as added: see note 2). See note 3. See *Bailey (t/a Elite Angling Products) v Haynes (t/a RAGS)* [2006] EWPCC 5, [2007] FSR 199; Case C-345/13 *Karen Millen Fashions Ltd v Dunnes Stores* [2014] All ER (D) 156 (Jun), ECJ; *Samsung Electronics (UK) Ltd v Apple Inc* [2012] EWHC 1882 (Pat), [2012] All ER (D) 139 (Jul) (affd

[2012] EWCA Civ 1339, [2013] IP & T 15) (in forming his 'overall impression' the informed user can disregard 'totally banal' elements common to all examples of the type of product in issue and concentrate on features that are 'arbitrary or different from the norm'). As to the interpretation of 'informed user' in the context of Council Regulation (EC) 6/2002 (OJ L3, 5.1.2002, p 1) on Community Designs art 10 see *Proctor & Gamble Co v Reckitt Benckiser (UK) Ltd* [2007] EWCA Civ 936, [2008] FSR 208; Case C-281/10 *PepsiCo Inc v Grupo Promer Mon Graphic SA* [2011] ECR I-10153, [2012] FSR 183 ('informed user' is somewhere between the 'average consumer' and a sectoral expert). See also *Woodhouse UK plc v Architectural Lighting Systems* [2006] RPC 1; *J Choo (Jersey) Ltd v Towerstone Ltd* [2008] EWHC 346 (Ch), [2008] FSR 485, [2008] All ER (D) 35 (Jan); *Rolawn Ltd v Turfmech Machinery Ltd* [2008] EWHC 989 (Pat) at [110], [2008] RPC 663 at [110], [2008] All ER (D) 77 (May).

5   Registered Designs Act 1949 s 1B(4) (as added: see note 2). See *Proctor & Gamble Co v Reckitt Benckiser (UK) Ltd* [2007] FSR 290; affd [2007] EWCA Civ 936, [2008] FSR 208. For a case involving a limited degree of design freedom see *Utopia Tableware Ltd v BBP Marketing Ltd* [2013] EWHC 3483 (IPEC), [2013] All ER (D) 162 (Nov).

6   Registered Designs Act 1949 s 1B(8)(a) (as added: see note 2). 'Normal use' means use by the end user; but does not include any maintenance, servicing or repair work in relation to the product: s 1B(9) (as so added). As to the meanings of 'product' and 'complex product' see PARA 711 note 1.

7   Registered Designs Act 1949 s 1B(8)(b) (as added: see note 2).

713. Made available to the public. A design[1] has been made available[2] to the public before the relevant date[3] if:

(1)   it has been published (whether following registration or otherwise), exhibited, used in trade or otherwise disclosed before that date[4]; and

(2)   the disclosure does not fall within any of the following categories[5]:

    (a)   it could not reasonably have become known before the relevant date in the normal course of business to persons carrying on business in the European Economic Area and specialising in the sector concerned[6];

    (b)   it was made to a person other than the designer, or any successor in title of his, under conditions of confidentiality (whether express or implied)[7];

    (c)   it was made by the designer, or any successor in title of his, during the period of 12 months immediately preceding the relevant date[8];

    (d)   it was made by a person other than the designer, or any successor in title of his, during the period of 12 months immediately preceding the relevant date in consequence of information provided or other action taken by the designer or any successor in title of his[9]; or

    (e)   it was made during the period of 12 months immediately preceding the relevant date as a consequence of an abuse in relation to the designer or any successor in title of his[10].

1   As to the meaning of 'design' see PARA 711.

2   As to the meaning of 'made available' see *Dyson Ltd v Qualtex (UK) Ltd* [2004] EWHC 2981 (Ch), [2005] RPC 395; affd [2006] EWCA Civ 166, [2006] RPC 769 (taking orders for articles not yet in existence does not make the design available).

3   As to the relevant date see PARA 712 note 3.

4   Registered Designs Act 1949 s 1B(5)(a) (s 1B added by SI 2001/3949). The concept is similar but not identical to that of prior publication in relation to old designs: see PARA 728.

5   Registered Designs Act 1949 s 1B(5)(b) (as added: see note 4).

6   Registered Designs Act 1949 s 1B(6)(a) (as added: see note 4). As to the European Economic Area Agreement see COMPETITION vol 18 (2009) PARA 36.

7   Registered Designs Act 1949 s 1B(6)(b) (as added: see note 4).

8   Registered Designs Act 1949 s 1B(6)(c) (as added: see note 4).

9   Registered Designs Act 1949 s 1B(6)(d) (as added: see note 4).

10   Registered Designs Act 1949 s 1B(6)(e) (as added: see note 4).

714.   Designs dictated by their technical function.   A right in a registered design[1] does not subsist in features of appearance of a product[2] which are solely dictated by the product's technical function[3].

1   As to the meaning of 'design' see PARA 711.
2   As to the meaning of 'product' see PARA 711 note 1.
3   Registered Designs Act 1949 s 1C(1) (s 1C added by SI 2001/3949). See *Landor & Hawa International Ltd v Azure Designs Ltd* [2006] EWCA Civ 1285, [2007] FSR 181, [2006] All ER (D) 17 (Aug), [2007] FSR 181 at 194. See also *Bailey (t/a Elite Angling Products) v Haynes (t/a RAGS)* [2006] EWPCC 5, [2007] FSR 199, where it was held that a design is only excluded from registration if it is the only design by which the product can perform its function. Cf the position in relation to old designs: see PARA 723. This legislation applies to the registration of any design application for which was made on or after 9 December 2001: see the Registered Designs Regulations 2001, SI 2001/3949, reg 1. As to the validity of old designs see PARA 717.

715.   The 'must fit' exclusion.   A right in a registered design[1] does not subsist in features of appearance of a product[2] which must necessarily be reproduced in their exact form and dimensions so as to permit the product in which the design is incorporated or to which it is applied to be mechanically connected to, or placed in, around or against, another product so that either product may perform its function[3]. However, this does not prevent a right in a registered design subsisting in a design serving the purpose of allowing multiple assembly or connection of mutually interchangeable products within a modular system[4].

1   As to the meaning of 'design' see PARA 711.
2   As to the meaning of 'product' see PARA 711 note 1.
3   Registered Designs Act 1949 s 1C(2) (s 1C added by SI 2001/3949). This legislation applies to the registration of any design application for which was made on or after 9 December 2001: see the Registered Designs Regulations 2001, SI 2001/3949, reg 1. As to the validity of old designs see PARA 717.
4   Registered Designs Act 1949 s 1C(3) (as added: see note 3).

716.   Designs contrary to public policy or morality.   A right in a registered design[1] does not subsist in a design which is contrary to public policy or to accepted principles of morality[2].

1   As to the meaning of 'design' see PARA 711.
2   Registered Designs Act 1949 s 1D (added by SI 2001/3949). This legislation applies to the registration of any design application for which was made on or after 9 December 2001: see the Registered Designs Regulations 2001, SI 2001/3949, reg 1. As to the validity of old designs see PARA 717. See *Masterman's Design* [1991] RPC 89, Registered Design Appeal Tribunal (considering the Registered Designs Act 1949 s 43(1) (now repealed), which provided that nothing in the Registered Designs Act 1949 was to be construed as authorising or requiring the registrar to register a design the use of which would, in his opinion, be contrary to law or morality).

(ii) Old Designs

717.   Meaning of 'design'.   In relation to old designs[1], 'design' means features of shape, configuration, pattern or ornament[2] applied to an article[3] by any industrial process, being features which in the finished article appeal to and are judged by the eye[4], but does not include:

(1)   a method or principle of construction; or
(2)   features of shape or configuration of an article which:
    (a)   are dictated solely by the function[5] which the article has to perform; or

(b) are dependent upon the appearance of another article of which the article is intended by the author[6] of the design to form an integral part[7].

An old design is not validly registered unless it complies with this statutory definition[8]. In addition, no design in respect of any article or set of articles is validly registered unless it was new at the date of application[9]; but a design is not to be regarded as new if it is the same as a design registered in respect of the same or any other article in pursuance of a prior application or published in the United Kingdom[10] in respect of the same or any other article before the date of the application, or if it differs from such a design only in immaterial details or in features which were variants commonly used in the trade[11].

An old design is not validly registered in respect of an article if the appearance of the article is not material, that is, if aesthetic considerations are not normally taken into account to a material extent by persons acquiring or using articles of that description, and would not be so taken into account if the design were to be applied to the article[12]. The Secretary of State[13] has made rules providing for excluding from registration designs for certain articles of a primarily literary or artistic character[14].

1 Ie designs applications for registration of which were registered before 9 December 2001 (see the Registered Designs Regulations 2001, SI 2001/3949, regs 1, 12(2), (3)): see PARA 657. The Registered Designs Act 1949, so far as it applies in relation to any registration made before 9 December 2001 which is in respect of any features of shape, configuration, pattern or ornament which do not fall within the new definition of 'design' in that Act (see PARA 711), applies as if the features concerned were included within the new definition of 'design': Registered Designs Regulations 2001, SI 2001/3949, reg 14(12), (13).

2 See PARA 719. Dimensions may form part of a 'design': *A Fulton Co Ltd v Totes Isotoner (UK) Ltd* [2003] RPC 499; affd [2003] EWCA Civ 1514, [2004] RPC 301.

3 As to the meaning of 'article' see PARA 720.

4 As to the eye as judge see PARA 721.

5 See PARA 723.

6 As to the meaning of 'author' see PARA 699.

7 Registered Designs Act 1949 s 1(1) (substituted by the Copyright, Designs and Patents Act 1988 s 265(1)). See further PARA 724. This legislation applies to the registration of any design application for which was made before 9 December 2001: see the Registered Designs Regulations 2001, SI 2001/3949, regs 1, 12(2). As to the validity of current designs see PARA 711.

8 See eg *Amp Inc v Utilux Pty Ltd* [1972] RPC 103, HL; and PARA 721.

9 Registered Designs Act 1949 s 1(2) (substituted by the Copyright, Designs and Patents Act 1988 s 265(1)).

10 As to the meaning of 'United Kingdom' see PARA 303 note 5.

11 Registered Designs Act 1949 s 1(4) (substituted by the Copyright, Designs and Patents Act 1988 s 265(1)). The Registered Designs Act 1949 s 1(4) has effect subject to s 4 (see PARA 733), s 6 (see PARAS 729–732) and s 16 (protection of designs communicated under international agreements): s 1(4) (as so substituted). As to novelty see PARA 727.

12 Registered Designs Act 1949 s 1(3) (substituted by the Copyright, Designs and Patents Act 1988 s 265(1)). As to material appearance see PARA 721.

13 As to the Secretary of State see PARA 660.

14 Registered Designs Act 1949 s 1(5) (substituted by the Copyright, Designs and Patents Act 1988 s 265(1)). In exercise of the power so conferred the Secretary of State made the Registered Designs Rules 1995, SI 1995/2912, r 26.

718. Capability of something being applied to an article. In relation to old designs[1], a design is not for the article itself but for something capable of being applied to the article[2]. In the case of a design for shape this distinction is chiefly a matter of words[3], but in other cases it may be of importance, as questions of novelty and infringement have to be determined not merely by looking at the design as shown in the drawing lodged with the application, but also by considering how its appearance would be affected by alterations in the shape of the article to which it is applied[4].

1 Ie designs applications for registration of which were registered before 9 December 2001 (see the Registered Designs Regulations 2001, SI 2001/3949, regs 1, 12(2), (3)): see PARA 657. As to the meaning of 'design' see PARA 717.

2 *Dover Ltd v Nürnberger Celluloidwaren Fabrik Gebrüder Wolff* [1910] 2 Ch 25 at 28, 27 RPC 498 at 503, CA. See also *Re Clarke's Registered Design, Clarke v Sax & Co Ltd* [1896] 2 Ch 38 at 43, 13 RPC 351 at 359, CA; *Re Bayer's Design, Bayer v Symington* (1907) 25 RPC 56, HL; *Deyhle's Design Applications* [1982] RPC 526, Registered Designs Appeal Tribunal; *Ford Motor Co Ltd's Design Applications* [1995] RPC 167 at 178, HL.

3 *Re Clarke's Registered Design, Clarke v Sax & Co Ltd* [1896] 2 Ch 38 at 43, 13 RPC 351 at 359, CA.

4 *Re Bayer's Design, Bayer v Symington* (1907) 25 RPC 56, HL. As to flexible articles see *Schmittzehe v Roberts* (1955) 72 RPC 122. Cf *Bailey (t/a Elite Angling Products) v Haynes (t/a RAGS)* [2006] EWPCC 5, [2007] FSR 199 at 213.

719.   Shape, configuration, pattern or ornament. In relation to old designs[1] there is no statutory definition of 'shape', 'configuration', 'pattern' or 'ornament', but it has been said that shape and configuration apply to three dimensions, and pattern or ornament to two[2]. Two identical designs may be validly registered, one for pattern and one for shape[3]. Where a design is registered for pattern and for shape, all that is protected is the combination[4]. Although there was a distinction between registering a design for a shape and registering for a pattern, one cannot, in a pattern design, ignore earlier shape designs when considering novelty[5]. It is not necessary that a design should be apparent upon an external examination of the article; it is sufficient that it will in practice have customer eye appeal[6].

1 Ie designs applications for registration of which were registered before 9 December 2001 (see the Registered Designs Regulations 2001, SI 2001/3949, regs 1, 12(2), (3)): see PARA 657. As to the meaning of 'design' see PARA 717.

2 *Re Kestos Ltd Registered Design (No 725,716), Kestos Ltd v Kempat Ltd and Vivian Fitch Kemp* (1935) 53 RPC 139 at 152; and see *Sommer Allibert (UK) Ltd v Flair Plastics Ltd* [1987] RPC 599, CA. It was not necessary, however, for the applicant to elect between them: *Heath & Sons Ltd v Rollason* [1898] AC 499, 15 RPC 441, HL.

3 *Pearson v Morris Wilkinson & Co* (1906) 23 RPC 738. There cannot, however, be two registrations of the design of a single article differing only in statements claiming novelty for the shape of different parts of the article: *Evered & Co Ltd's Applications (Design)* [1961] RPC 105, Patents Appeal Tribunal.

4 *John Harper & Co Ltd v Wright and Butler Lamp Manufacturing Co Ltd* [1896] 1 Ch 142, 12 RPC 483, CA; *Re Manchester's Designs, Manchester v Umfreville & Son* (1907) 24 RPC 782.

5 *Dymo Industries Inc's Application* [1982] RPC 437, Registered Designs Appeal Tribunal.

6 *P Ferrero and CSpA's Application* [1978] RPC 473, Registered Designs Appeal Tribunal (multi-layered chocolate egg); *KK Suwa Seikosha's Design Application* [1982] RPC 166, Registered Designs Appeal Tribunal (display panel for digital watch visible only when battery connected); *Apple Computer Inc's Design Applications* [2002] FSR 602, [2001] All ER (D) 336 (Oct) (computer icons only visible after computer switched on). As to eye appeal see further PARA 721.

720.   Article. In relation to old designs[1], a design could be registered in respect of any article, or set of articles[2]. 'Article' means any article of manufacture and includes any part of an article if that part is made and sold separately[3]. An article must, however, perform some function other than merely carrying the design[4], and a building is not an article within this definition[5]. Moreover, there were excluded from registration designs to be applied to any of the following articles, namely:

(1)   works of sculpture, other than casts or models used or intended to be used as models or patterns to be multiplied by any industrial process[6];

(2)   wall plaques, medals and medallions[7];

(3)   printed matter primarily of a literary or artistic character, including book jackets, calendars, certificates, coupons, dress-making patterns, greetings cards, labels, leaflets, maps, plans, playing cards, postcards, stamps, trade advertisements, trade forms and cards, transfers and similar articles[8].

1   Ie designs applications for registration of which were registered before 9 December 2001 (see the Registered Designs Regulations 2001, SI 2001/3949, reg 1): see PARA 657. As to the meaning of 'design' see PARA 717.

2   For these purposes, 'set of articles' means a number of articles of the same general character ordinarily on sale or intended to be used together, to each of which the same design, or the same design with modifications or variations not sufficient to alter the character or substantially to affect the identity thereof, is applied: Registered Designs Act 1949 s 44(1). Any reference to an article in respect of which a design is registered is to be construed, in the case of a design registered in respect of a set of articles, as a reference to any article of that set: s 44(2). Any question whether a number of articles constitute a set is to be determined by the registrar; and notwithstanding anything in the Registered Designs Act 1949 any such determination of the registrar is final: s 44(3). See *Apple Computer Inc's Design Applications* [2002] FSR 602, [2001] All ER (D) 336 (Oct) (consideration of 'article'). This legislation applies to the registration of any design application for which was made before 9 December 2001: see the Registered Designs Regulations 2001, SI 2001/3949, regs 1, 12(2). As to the validity of current designs see PARA 711.

3   Registered Designs Act 1949 s 44(1). The meaning of the protection afforded by a registration is not ambiguous merely because the design is intended to be applied only to part of the article which is not sold separately: see *Portable Concrete Buildings Ltd v Bathcrete Ltd* [1962] RPC 49. Parts of articles which are not, in themselves, intended by the proprietor to be made and sold separately are not 'articles' within the definition: *Sifam Electrical Instrument Co Ltd v Sangamo Weston Ltd* [1971] 2 All ER 1074, [1973] RPC 899 (fronts of electrical meters held not to be 'articles'); *Ford Motor Co Ltd and Iveco Fiat SpA's Design Applications* [1993] RPC 399, Registered Designs Appeal Tribunal, affd sub nom *R v Registered Designs Appeal Tribunal, ex p Ford Motor Co Ltd* [1995] 1 WLR 18, [2005] RPC 167, HL (vehicle component parts such as main body panels, doors, bonnet lids, boot lids and windscreens for motor cars); *A Fulton Co Ltd v Totes Isotoner (UK) Ltd* [2003] RPC 499 (an umbrella case held to be 'an article').

4   *Re Littlewoods Pools Ltd's Application* (1949) 66 RPC 309, Patents Appeal Tribunal (decided under the Patents and Designs Act 1907 (repealed), but there seems no reason why a similar principle should not apply).

5   *Re Collier & Co Ltd's Application* (1937) 54 RPC 253, Assistant Comptroller. A design for a portable building is registrable: see *Portable Concrete Buildings Ltd v Bathcrete Ltd* [1962] RPC 49.

6   Registered Designs Rules 1995, SI 1995/2912, r 26(1). As to the Secretary of State's power to make rules providing for the exclusion from registration of designs see PARA 717. As to the preservation of the Registered Designs Rules 1995, SI 1995/2912, in relation to old designs see the Registered Designs (Amendment) Rules 2001, SI 2001/3950, rr 27–30 (revoked). As to the rules governing current designs see the Registered Designs Rules 2006, SI 2006/1975; and PARA 711 et seq.

7   Registered Designs Rules 1995, SI 1995/2912, r 26(2); and see *Reliance (Nameplates) Ltd v Art Jewels Ltd* [1953] 1 All ER 759, [1953] 1 WLR 530, 70 RPC 86 (coronation medallion).

8   Registered Designs Rules 1995, SI 1995/2912, r 26(3). A pre-printed web for a computer was held not to be printed matter of a primarily artistic character: see *Lamson Industries Ltd's Application* [1978] RPC 1, Registered Designs Appeal Tribunal.

721.   Eye the judge. Old designs[1] are validly registered only in respect of features of shape, configuration, pattern or ornament[2] which in the finished article appeal to and are judged by the eye[3]. It is necessary that a design should show some new effect clearly distinguishable by the eye from what has gone before[4] and that the change should be such that some degree of real mental activity has been needed for its production[5]. The criteria on which the court acts differ according to whether the improvement has or lacks artistic merit. A new and agreeable artistic effect often defies analysis of its causes, and the eye rightly appreciates it as something really different from what has gone before, without considering in what the distinction consists[6]. The eye is the judge of the existence of a difference between a design and what has gone before[7], but in judging the importance of that difference it would seem that other factors may properly be taken into account. Although increased utility is not a necessary ingredient of a novel design[8], it may assist in showing that the design is really new and distinct from what has gone before, for, had such variation in fact been obvious and needed no mental activity, the probability is that it would have been made before, and on account of its increased utility would have persisted[9].

Those designs which appeal to the eye might nevertheless be invalid if the appearance of the article is not material, that is, if aesthetic considerations are not normally taken into account to a material extent by persons acquiring or using articles of that description, and would not be so taken into account if the design were to be applied to the article[10].

1   Ie designs applications for registration of which were registered before 9 December 2001 (see the Registered Designs Regulations 2001, SI 2001/3949, regs 1, 12(2), (3)): see PARA 657. As to the meaning of 'design' see PARA 717.

2   See PARA 719.

3   See the Registered Designs Act 1949 s 1(1); and PARA 717. This legislation applies to the registration of any design application for which was made before 9 December 2001: see the Registered Designs Regulations 2001, SI 2001/3949, regs 1, 12(2). As to the validity of current designs see PARA 711. 'Judged by the eye' means the eye using normal vision: *Amp Inc v Utilux Pty Ltd* [1970] RPC 397, CA; revsd [1972] RPC 103, HL, without affecting this point. It is the eye of the customer not the court which is relevant: see *Amp Inc v Utilux Pty Ltd* [1972] RPC 103, HL; *Kevi A/S v Suspa-Verein UK Ltd* [1982] RPC 173; *A Fulton Co Ltd v Totes Isotoner (UK) Ltd* [2003] RPC 499; affd [2003] EWCA Civ 1514, [2004] RPC 301.

4   *Re Le May's Registered Design, Le May v Welch* (1884) 28 ChD 24, CA. See also *Lazarus v Charles* (1873) LR 16 Eq 117; *Re Smith's Registered Design, Smith v Hope Bros* (1889) 6 RPC 200; *Re Kestos Ltd Registered Design (No 725,716), Kestos Ltd v Kempat Ltd and Vivian Fitch Kemp* (1935) 53 RPC 139 at 153. For examples of decisions where variations have been considered too small to support novelty see *Negretti and Zambra v WF Stanley & Co Ltd* (1925) 42 RPC 358; *Re Wingate's Registered Design (No 768,611)* (1934) 52 RPC 126; *Re Associated Colour Printers Ltd's Application (No 814,271)* (1937) 54 RPC 203, Patents Appeal Tribunal. For small improvements held registrable see *Jackson v Testar* (1919) 36 RPC 289; *Rose v JW Pickavant & Co Ltd* (1923) 40 RPC 320; *Cartwright v Coventry Radiator Co* (1925) 42 RPC 351; *Wells v Attaché Case Manufacturing Co Ltd* (1931) 49 RPC 113; *Re Kestos Ltd Registered Design (No 725,716), Kestos Ltd v Kempat Ltd and Vivian Fitch Kemp*. In most of these latter cases, although the design was upheld, it was held not to be infringed.

5   *Dover Ltd v Nürnberger Celluloidwaren Fabrik Gebrüder Wolff* [1910] 2 Ch 25 at 28, 27 RPC 498 at 503, CA.

6   Cf *Heath & Sons Ltd v Rollason* [1898] AC 499 at 502, 503, 15 RPC 441 at 447, HL, per Lord Herschell; *Wallpaper Manufacturers Ltd v Derby Paper Staining Co* (1925) 42 RPC 443.

7   *Re Morton's Design* (1899) 17 RPC 117; *Gillard v Worrall* (1904) 22 RPC 76; *Re Bayer's Design, Bayer v Symington* (1907) 25 RPC 56, HL. See also *Harrison v Taylor* (1859) 4 H & N 815, Ex Ch.

8   *Hecla Foundry Co v Walker, Hunter & Co* (1889) 14 App Cas 550 at 556, 6 RPC 554 at 559, HL. See also *Re Clarke's Registered Design, Clarke v Sax & Co Ltd* [1896] 2 Ch 38 at 43, 13 RPC 351 at 358, CA; *Re Morton's Design* (1899) 17 RPC 117. As to shapes dictated purely by function see PARA 723.

9   *Tyler & Sons v Sharpe Bros & Co* (1893) 11 RPC 35 (where a large sale was considered some evidence of substantial novelty); *Gillard v Worrall* (1904) 22 RPC 76. There are dicta opposed to this view (see the cases cited in note 8), but, with the possible exception of *Re Clarke's Registered Design, Clarke v Sax & Co Ltd* [1896] 2 Ch 38 at 43, 13 RPC 351 at 358, CA, the remarks were directed to the non-essentiality of utility, or to the point that the protection accorded to the design did not cover other designs attaining the same end, rather than to the

exclusion of the consideration of utility on the question of substantial novelty: *Walker, Hunter & Co v Falkirk Iron Co* (1887) 4 RPC 390, Ct of Sess; *Hecla Foundry Co v Walker, Hunter & Co* (1889) 14 App Cas 550, 6 RPC 554, HL; *Heinrichs v Bastendorff* (1893) 10 RPC 160; *Infields v Rosen Ltd* [1939] 1 All ER 121, 56 RPC 163.

10 Registered Designs Act 1949 s 1(3) (substituted by the Copyright, Designs and Patents Act 1988 s 265(1)). The purpose of this provision was to exclude from registration articles which have some appeal to the eye but which are purchased or acquired primarily for their function and where little or no attention is paid to the look of the article.

722. Method or principle of construction.

In relation to old designs[1], although a design might in some cases incidentally protect a mode of manufacture[2], a registration would not be valid if it was for a method or principle of construction in itself[3]; and the registration of a design in order to cover all alternatives is invalid, as it would give the same result[4]. If what is registered, however, has the requisites of a novel and original design, it is no objection that it could also have been protected by letters patent[5], or that it is in fact protected by letters patent granted to the proprietor, so long as there has been no prior publication[6]. A design cannot be considered as protecting a combination of movements of machinery used in its manufacture[7].

1 Ie designs applications for registration of which were registered before 9 December 2001 (see the Registered Designs Regulations 2001, SI 2001/3949, regs 1, 12(2), (3)): see PARA 657. As to the meaning of 'design' see PARA 717.

2 *Re Bayer's Design, Bayer v Symington* (1907) 25 RPC 56 at 60, HL, per Lord Macnaghten.

3 See the Registered Designs Act 1949 s 1(1)(a); and PARA 717. This legislation applies to the registration of any design application for which was made before 9 December 2001: see the Registered Designs Regulations 2001, SI 2001/3949, regs 1, 12(2). As to the validity of current designs see PARA 711.

  See *Moody v Tree* (1892) 9 RPC 333 (basket made by osiers being worked in singly with the butt ends outwards); *Cooper v Symington* (1893) 10 RPC 264 (method of fixing corset bucks); *Re Bayer's Design, Bayer v Symington* (1907) 25 RPC 56, HL (corset with seams cut horizontally); *Pugh v Riley Cycle Co Ltd* [1912] 1 Ch 613, 29 RPC 196; *EJ Pearson & Sons v DB Harris & Sons Ltd* (1912) 29 RPC 632; *Phillips v Harbro Rubber Co* (1920) 37 RPC 233, HL; *Re Kestos Ltd Registered Design (No 725,716), Kestos Ltd v Kempat Ltd and Vivian Fitch Kemp* (1935) 53 RPC 139. For examples of unsuccessful attempts to invalidate design as covering a method or principle of construction see *Rosedale Associated Manufacturers Ltd v Airfix Products Ltd* [1956] RPC 360 (on appeal [1957] RPC 239, CA); *Gardex Ltd v Sorata Ltd* [1986] RPC 623. See also *A Fulton Co Ltd v Grant Barnett & Co* [2001] RPC 257, [2000] All ER (D) 1270; *Oren v Red Box Toy Factory Ltd* [1999] FSR 785, [1999] All ER (D) 98; *Landor & Hawa International Ltd v Azure Designs Ltd* [2006] EWCA Civ 1285, [2007] FSR 181, [2006] All ER (D) 17 (Aug); *Bailey (t/a Elite Angling Products) v Haynes (t/a RAGS)* [2006] EWPCC 5, [2007] FSR 199.

4 *Phillips v Harbro Rubber Co* (1920) 37 RPC 233, HL; *Re Kestos Ltd Registered Design (No 725,716), Kestos Ltd v Kempat Ltd and Vivian Fitch Kemp* (1935) 53 RPC 139; *Wilson v Chalco Ltd* (1922) 39 RPC 252.

5 *Walker, Hunter & Co v Falkirk Iron Co* (1887) 4 RPC 390. Ct of Sess; *Rogers v Driver* (1850) 16 QB 102. In practice, since the decision in *Amp Inc v Utilux Pty Ltd* [1972] RPC 103, HL, it is unlikely that a registered design could validly co-exist with a patent for the same article; but see *Gardex Ltd v Sorata Ltd* [1986] RPC 623.

6 *Werner Motors Ltd v AW Gamage Ltd* [1904] 2 Ch 580, 21 RPC 621, CA. As to prior publication see PARA 728.

7 *Re Plackett's Registered Design* (1892) 9 RPC 436 at 438.

723. Function of article.

An old design[1] is invalid if it is registered in respect of features of shape or configuration which are dictated solely by the function which the article[2] to be made in that shape or configuration has to perform[3]; nor can valid protection be acquired for a mere mechanical device[4]. Where an article is purely functional, so that its shape has no customer or consumer[5] eye appeal, that shape is not a design and therefore any registration for the same is invalid[6].

A particular shape or configuration is dictated solely by function if its relevant features are brought about by, or are attributable only to, the function which the article in that shape or configuration is to perform, even if the same function could equally well be performed by an article of a different shape[7]. The exclusion of features dictated by function must be construed as treating the whole shape or configuration as registrable, assuming that it had eye appeal, unless every feature was dictated solely by functional considerations, in which case the exclusion operates even though the article might also have eye appeal; but any feature which went beyond those dictated solely by function would entitle the shape or configuration as a whole to protection[8] unless the appearance of the article is not material[9].

1   Ie a design application for registration of which was registered before 9 December 2001 (see the Registered Designs Regulations 2001, SI 2001/3949, regs 1, 12(2), (3)): see PARA 657. As to the meaning of 'design' see PARA 717.

2   As to the meaning of 'article' see PARA 720.

3   See the Registered Designs Act 1949 s 1(1)(b)(i); and PARA 717. This legislation applies to the registration of any design application for which was made before 9 December 2001: see the Registered Designs Regulations 2001, SI 2001/3949, regs 1, 12(2). As to the validity of current designs see PARA 711.
     See *Stenor Ltd v Whitesides (Clitheroe) Ltd* [1948] AC 107, [1947] 2 All ER 241, 65 RPC 1, HL; *Rosedale Associated Manufacturers Ltd v Airfix Products Ltd* [1957] RPC 239, CA; *P B Cow & Co Ltd v Cannon Rubber Manufacturers Ltd* [1959] RPC 240 (on appeal [1959] RPC 347, CA); *Scripto Inc v Tallon Ltd* [1960] RPC 262.

4   *Tecalemit Ltd v Ewarts Ltd (No 2)* (1927) 44 RPC 503; *Re Kestos Ltd Registered Design (No 725,716), Kestos Ltd v Kempat Ltd and Vivian Fitch Kemp* (1935) 53 RPC 139 at 151.

5   See *Kevi A/S v Suspa Verein UK Ltd* [1982] RPC 173, expressly extending the decision in *Amp Inc v Utilux Pty Ltd* [1972] RPC 103, HL, to ultimate consumers as well as immediate customers.

6   *Amp Inc v Utilux Pty Ltd* [1972] RPC 103, HL, where electrical connectors were held not to be designs within the meaning of the Registered Designs Act 1949, notwithstanding the fact that they might, in order to perform their function, have been differently shaped. See *Lamson Industries Ltd's Application* [1978] RPC 1, Registered Designs Appeal Tribunal (pre-printed web for a computer held not to be a design because it had no customer eye appeal).

7   *Interlego AG v Tyco Industries Inc* [1988] RPC 343 at 355, PC.

8   *Interlego AG v Tyco Industries Inc* [1988] RPC 343 at 353–355, PC.

9   See the Registered Designs Act 1949 s 1(3); and PARA 717. As to the appearance of an article being material see PARA 721.

724. Features dependent upon appearance of another article (the 'must match' exclusion). An old design[1] is invalid if it is registered in respect of features of shape or configuration which are dependent upon the appearance of another article[2] of which the article is intended by the author of the design to form an integral part[3]. The word 'integral' is present so as not to exclude from valid registration items which do not stand alone but which nevertheless do not form part of a whole article such as cups and saucers, knives and forks[4]. Items such as vehicle main body panels, doors, bonnet lids, boot lids and windscreens have been held not to be validly registrable whilst items such as wing mirrors, wheels, seats and steering wheels have been held not to be so excluded from registrability on the basis that the first category of articles do form an integral part of a vehicle and, on replacement, must be replaced by another article of the same shape or configuration[5].

1   Ie a design application for registration of which was registered before 9 December 2001 (see the Registered Designs Regulations 2001, SI 2001/3949, regs 1, 12(2), (3)): see PARA 657. As to the meaning of 'design' see PARA 717.

2   As to the meaning of 'article' see PARA 720.

3 See the Registered Designs Act 1949 s 1(1)(b)(ii); and PARA 717. This provision is often referred to as the 'must match' exclusion. This legislation applies to the registration of any design application for which was made before 9 December 2001: see the Registered Designs Regulations 2001, SI 2001/3949, regs 1, 12(2). As to the validity of current designs see PARA 711.

4 *Ford Motor Co Ltd and Iveco Fiat SpA's Design Applications* [1993] RPC 399, Registered Designs Appeal Tribunal; affd sub nom *R v Registered Designs Appeal Tribunal, ex p Ford Motor Co Ltd* [1995] 1 WLR 18, HL. Cf, in relation to unregistered design right, *Dyson Ltd v Qualtex (UK) Ltd* [2006] EWCA Civ 166, [2006] RPC 769.

5 *Ford Motor Co Ltd and Iveco Fiat SpA's Design Applications* [1993] RPC 399 at 420, Registered Designs Appeal Tribunal; affd sub nom *R v Registered Designs Appeal Tribunal, ex p Ford Motor Co Ltd* [1994] RPC 545 (affd, on a different point, [1995] RPC 167). Items in the first category were also held unregistrable as not being 'articles' within the meaning of the Registered Designs Act 1949 s 44(1): see PARA 720.

725. Novelty. In order to be validly registered, an old design[1] had to be 'new'[2]. There was no requirement for originality[3]. There is no statutory definition of 'new' but a design is not to be regarded as 'new' if it is the same as a design registered in respect of the same or any other article in pursuance of a prior application or published in the United Kingdom in respect of the same or any other article before the date of the application, or if it differs from such a design only in immaterial details or in features which are variants commonly used in the trade[4].

A design must be considered as applied to the article for which it was to be registered, and valid registration could be obtained for the application of a design such as a picture to a particular article, even though the picture itself was old[5].

1 Ie a design application for registration of which was registered before 9 December 2001 (see the Registered Designs Regulations 2001, SI 2001/3949, regs 1, 12(2), (3)): see PARA 681. As to the meaning of 'design' see PARA 717. See also *Oakley Inc v Animal Ltd* [2005] EWCA Civ 1191, [2006] Ch 337, [2006] RPC 301.

2 See the Registered Designs Act 1949 s 1(2); and PARA 717. This legislation applies to the registration of any design application for which was made before 9 December 2001: see the Registered Designs Regulations 2001, SI 2001/3949, regs 1, 12(2). As to the validity of current designs see PARA 711. As to the requirement of novelty in current designs see PARA 712.

3 Cf the Registered Designs Act 1949 s 1 (as originally enacted).

4 See the Registered Designs Act 1949 s 1(4); and PARA 717. See *Household Articles Ltd's Registered Design* [1998] FSR 676, Patents Court; *A Fulton Co Ltd v Totes Isotoner (UK) Ltd* [2003] RPC 499 (affd [2003] EWCA Civ 1514, [2004] RPC 301). As to the meaning of 'United Kingdom' see PARA 303 note 5.

5 *Saunders v Wiel* [1893] 1 QB 470, 10 RPC 29, CA, overruling *Adams v Clementson* (1879) 12 ChD 714. See also *Dover Ltd v Nürnberger Celluloidwaren Fabrik Gebrüder Wolff* [1910] 2 Ch 25 at 29, 27 RPC 498 at 504. The novelty of the design may consist in contriving a copy or imitation of a figure, which may itself be common to the world, in such a manner as to render it applicable to an article of manufacture: see *Saunders v Wiel* [1893] 1 QB 470 at 476, 10 RPC 29 at 33, CA. See also *Dean's Rag Book Co Ltd v Pomerantz & Sons and Re Dean's Rag Book Co Ltd and Patents and Designs Acts 1907 to 1928* (1930) 47 RPC 485 (figure of Mickey Mouse); *Re Gutta Percha and Rubber (London) Ltd (No 789,574)* (1935) 52 RPC 383, Patents Appeal Tribunal (embossing to imitate coconut matting). As to the meaning of 'article' see PARA 720.

726. Combinations, improvements and trade variants. In relation to old designs[1], a design might be new even if the parts of which it was composed were old[2], but two matters could not be combined together and validly registered as a new design. Although the requirements for a valid combination are not as strict as in the case of patents[3], as a general rule there has to be some artistic or other advantage from the combination besides that possessed by the parts separately[4], or at least the combination must have involved some artistic or mental effort[5]. In particular, the choice of variants commonly used in the trade[6], or of the leading features of well-known articles, do not in general constitute a valid combination[7]. The omission of certain parts might also constitute novelty, but not where that omission is a mere result of a new use of the article[8]. Similarly, purely functional features must be ignored when considering novelty[9].

While the court bears in mind that the law of designs exists for the purpose of protecting innovations which do not involve such invention as is necessary for the subject matter of a patent[10], it rightly considers that there must be some check on the hampering of industries which would result if every unimportant alteration of shape or pattern could become the subject of a monopoly[11].

1   Ie a design application for registration of which was registered before 9 December 2001 (see the Registered Designs Regulations 2001, SI 2001/3949, regs 1, 12(2), (3)): see PARA 657. As to the meaning of 'design' see PARA 717.
2   *Sherwood and Cotton v Decorative Art Tile Co* (1887) 4 RPC 207; *Heinrichs v Bastendorff* (1893) 10 RPC 160; *Re Rollason's Registered Design* [1897] 1 Ch 237, 14 RPC 909, CA (affd sub nom *Heath & Sons Ltd v Rollason* [1898] AC 499, 15 RPC 441, HL).
3   In the following cases combinations were held registrable: *Heinrichs v Bastendorff* (1893) 10 RPC 160 (writing table, the various parts of which were old); *S Knowles & Co Ltd v Bennett & Sons and Bigio* (1895) 12 RPC 137; *Nevill v John Bennett & Sons* (1898) 15 RPC 412; *Wallpaper Manufacturers Ltd v Derby Paper Staining Co* (1925) 42 RPC 443 (combination of old floral designs in a wallpaper).
4   In the following cases combinations were held not registrable: *Hothersall v Moore* (1891) 9 RPC 27 (combination of old red border with yellow chamois leather centre); *Lazarus v Charles* (1873) LR 16 Eq 117 (combination of two old baskets to form double basket); *Mulloney v Stevens* (1864) 10 LT 190 (three ribbons and a button all considered old, combined into a badge; this, however, is a very doubtful case, and is overruled in part by *Saunders v Wiel* [1893] 1 QB 470, 10 RPC 29, CA; *Repetition Woodwork Co Ltd and Hilton v Briggs (t/a Lifford Office Equipment Manufacturing Co)* (1924) 41 RPC 449). See also *Gramophone Co Ltd v Magazine Holder Co* (1911) 28 RPC 221, HL; *Re Universal Plastics Ltd's Application* [1958] RPC 439; *Sebel & Co Ltd's Application* [1959] RPC 12; *Sebel & Co Ltd's Application (No 2)* [1959] RPC 19; *Vlisco BV's Application* [1980] RPC 509, Designs Registry.
5   *Phillips v Harbro Rubber Co* (1919) 36 RPC 79 at 85, CA. See also *Re Britvic's Application* [1960] RPC 201, Patents Appeal Tribunal; note 4; and PARA 721. See also *Household Articles Ltd's Registered Design* [1998] FSR 676, Patent Court.
6   See PARA 725.
7   *Pugh v Riley Cycle Co Ltd* (1914) 31 RPC 266 at 283, HL; *Phillips v Harbro Rubber Co* (1920) 37 RPC 233, HL; *Re Universal Plastics Ltd Application (No 884,686)* [1958] RPC 439.
8   *Re Clarke's Registered Design, Clarke v Sax & Co Ltd* [1896] 2 Ch 38 at 47, 13 RPC 351 at 360, CA.
9   *Re Carr's Application* [1973] RPC 689, Registered Designs Appeal Tribunal.
10 *Harrison v Taylor* (1859) 4 H & N 815, Ex Ch.
11 See the cases cited in PARA 721 note 4.

727.   Scope of designs; statement of novelty.   In relation to old designs[1], except in the case of a registration for the pattern or ornament of a design to be applied to a textile article, to wallpaper or similar wall covering or to lace or to sets of textile articles or lace, a statement satisfactory to the registrar[2] of the features of the design for which novelty[3] was claimed has to appear on each representation or specimen of the design[4]. Such a statement is often of great value, as on the one hand it may prevent the registration being interpreted as made for some feature which is old, and on the other it may prevent the registration being confined to non-essential details only put in to show the real design properly[5]. The purpose of a statement of novelty is to direct attention to the part or parts of the illustrated design which are claimed to introduce into it the alleged novel contribution[6].

In interpreting a design the court will look at it with the eye of a craftsman[7]. In the absence of a specific statement to the contrary, the statement of novelty is not assumed to claim as an essential detail something which is notoriously old[8], nor, except in the case of some purely decorative designs[9], is it assumed, unless stated, that the design is intended to be confined to the particular shape or kind of common article on which the design is shown, where the shape of such article has to be continually varied in common use[10]. A design is always to be considered as capable of being applied on a larger or smaller scale, if the proportions are kept the same[11]. A design which is broadly new will be given a wider interpretation when testing infringement than a design which is a mere detailed modification of some older well-known design[12]. Where a feature is only shown in minute form or indistinctly, the court is unwilling to presume that it is intended as a distinctive feature[13]. Subject to these rules, the registration is presumed to be for the design as a whole and not for any special feature[14]. Colour can be an element of the design, although normally differences in colour are unlikely to be important[15].

In a claim of infringement the same construction must be put on the design for the purpose of determining the issues of novelty and of infringement, and, by analogy, in rectification proceedings, evidence of what the proprietor has claimed to cover by the registration has been admitted against him[16].

1   Ie designs application for registration of which were registered before 9 December 2001 (see the Registered Designs Regulations 2001, SI 2001/3949, regs 1, 12(2), (3)): see PARA 657. As to the meaning of 'design' see PARA 717.
2   As to the registrar see PARA 660.
3   As to novelty see PARA 725.
4   See the Registered Designs Rules 1995, SI 1995/2912, r 15 (now revoked). In *Thomas N Nutbrown Ltd v Taylor, Law & Co Ltd* [1957] RPC 36, a certificate of validity was refused because no statement of the novelty claimed had been filed.
5   See *Walker, Hunter & Co v Falkirk Iron Co* (1887) 14 R 1072, Ct of Sess, at 1082–1083, 4 RPC 390 at 395; *Phillips v Harbro Rubber Co* (1920) 37 RPC 233, HL. The statement may refer to a specimen: see *Re Gutta Percha and Rubber (London) Ltd (No 789,574) Application* (1935) 52 RPC 383, Patents Appeal Tribunal.
6   *Kent and Thanet Casinos Ltd v Bailey's School of Dancing Ltd* [1965] RPC 482 (where the statement of novelty related only to a specific illustration and did not define a general class of pattern). See also *Gaskell & Chambers Ltd v Measure Master Ltd* [1993] RPC 76 (where the statement of novelty was confined to shape and configuration, it was held that ornament was of no concern). See also *Woodhouse UK plc v Architectural Lighting Systems* [2006] RPC 1, Patents County Court.
7   *Varley v Keighley Ironworks Society Ltd* (1896) 14 RPC 169; *Heath & Sons Ltd v Rollason* [1898] AC 499, 15 RPC 441, HL; *Phillips v Harbro Rubber Co* (1920) 37 RPC 233, HL.
8   This applies whether novelty is disputed or not: *Gramophone Co Ltd v Magazine Holder Co* (1911) 28 RPC 221, HL. See also *Walker & Co v A G Scott & Co Ltd* (1892) 9 RPC 482; *Staples v Warwick* (1906) 23 RPC 609, CA. The court is not bound by an admission as to the novelty and originality of the design: *Gramophone Co Ltd v Magazine Holder Co*.
9   See *Rollason's Registered Design* [1898] 1 Ch 237 at 244–245, 14 RPC 909 at 912, CA (where the design was for a coffin plate and Lindley MR expressed the view that, although the claim was for pattern only, the outline could not be left out of account as it really formed part of the pattern).
10 *Re Bayer's Design, Bayer v Symington* (1906) 24 RPC 65, CA; affd (1907) 25 RPC 56, HL. In *Stephenson, Blake & Co v Grant, Legros & Co* (1917) 34 RPC 192, CA, it was held that a design for a fount of type only protected the letters in the order shown. The order in this case was set aside as premature without consideration of the point. Sec also *Re Associated Colour Printers Ltd's Application (No 814,271)* (1937) 54 RPC 203, Patents Appeal Tribunal. As to designs for flexible articles see *Schmittzehe v Roberts* (1955) 72 RPC 122.
11 *Re Bayer's Design, Bayer v Symington* (1906) 24 RPC 65 at 72, CA; affd (1907) 25 RPC 56, HL.
12 *Simmons v Mathieson & Co Ltd* (1911) 28 RPC 486, CA. See also *Re Plackett's Registered Design* (1892) 9 RPC 436. Cf *John Harper & Co Ltd v Wright and Butler Lamp Manufacturing Co Ltd* [1896] 1 Ch 142, 12 RPC 483, CA; *Jackson v Testar* (1919) 36 RPC 289; *Repetition Woodwork Co Ltd and Hilton v Briggs (t/a Lifford Office Equipment*

Manufacturing Co) (1924) 41 RPC 449; *Negretti and Zambra v WF Stanley & Co Ltd* (1925) 42 RPC 358; *Gaskell & Chambers Ltd v Measure Master Ltd* [1993] RPC 76. Cf *Bailey (t/a Elite Angling Products) v Haynes (t/a RAGS)* [2006] EWPCC 5, [2007] FSR 199.

13 *Pilkington Bros Ltd v Abrahams & Son* (1914) 32 RPC 61. In *Vandervell & Co v Lundberg & Sons* (1915) 33 RPC 60, where a design was registered for a switch box, the court refused to consider as a distinctive feature the special switch shown in the representation.

14 *Holdsworth v M'Crea* (1867) LR 2 HL 380; *Thom v Syddall* (1872) 26 LT 15; *Dover Ltd v Nürnberger Celluloidwaren Fabrick Gebrüder Wolff* [1910] 2 Ch 25, 27 RPC 498, CA; *Sackett and Barnes v Clozenberg* (1909) 27 RPC 104; *Pugh v Riley Cycle Co Ltd* [1912] 1 Ch 613 at 618, 29 RPC 196 at 202; *Pilkington Bros Ltd v Abrahams & Sons* (1914) 32 RPC 61. This rule that the design was primarily to be considered for the combination, and not for the separate parts, was not formerly clearly understood and adopted: see e g *Norton v Nicholls* (1859) 1 E & E 761. A design to be applied to both ends of an article has been held not to be infringed by an article having the design applied to one end only: see *Portable Concrete Buildings Ltd v Bathcrete Ltd* [1962] RPC 49.

15 *Smith, Kline and French Laboratories Ltd's Design Application* [1974] RPC 253, Registered Designs Appeal Tribunal; *Cook and Hurst's Design Application* [1979] RPC 197, Registered Designs Appeal Tribunal, where colours applied in particular locations were sufficient to permit the registration of a design of England football shirt. In *Re Associated Colour Printers Ltd's Application (No 814,271)* (1937) 54 RPC 203, Patents Appeal Tribunal, it was said that colour formed no part of a design, but in *Gottschalck & Co v Velez & Co* (1936) 53 RPC 403, colour was clearly taken into account as a distinguishing feature. See also *Norton v Nicholls* (1859) 1 E & E 761; *Nevill v John Bennett & Sons* (1898) 15 RPC 412. In *Re Calder Vale Manufacturing Co Ltd Registered Design, Re Lappett Manufacturing Co Ltd* (1934) 52 RPC 117 at 125, it was said that colour was of secondary importance.

16 *Benchairs Ltd v Chair Centre Ltd* [1974] RPC 429, CA. See also *Re Plackett's Registered Design* (1892) 9 RPC 436; *Re Bayer's Design, Bayer v Symington* (1906) 24 RPC 65, CA (affd (1907) 25 RPC 56, HL). It seems difficult to justify the admission of such evidence, as construction is a matter of law. In *Vandervell & Co v Lundberg & Sons* (1915) 33 RPC 60, the plaintiff's advertisements were used against them on the question of construction.

728.   Prior publication.   In general, the registration of an old design[1] in respect of any article[2] is invalid if it is the same as a design which before the date of the application for registration was registered or published in the United Kingdom in respect of the same or any other article, or which differs from such a design only in immaterial details or in features which are variants commonly used in the trade[3]. The general rules as to what constitutes publication of a design resemble those respecting publication in relation to a patent[4].

1   Ie a design application for registration of which was registered before 9 December 2001 (see the Registered Designs Regulations 2001, SI 2001/3949, regs 1, 12(2), (3)): see PARA 657. As to the meaning of 'design' see PARA 717.

2   As to the meaning of 'article' see PARA 720.

3   See the Registered Designs Act 1949 s 1(4) (substituted by the Copyright, Designs and Patents Act 1988 s 265(1)). There are exceptions in relation to confidential disclosures (see PARA 729), disclosures at certified exhibitions (see PARA 730), artistic works (see PARA 731), disclosures to government departments (see PARA 732), and registration of the same design for other articles (see PARA 733).

4   See PARAS 445–450. If even a single article has passed into public use, it voids a subsequent registration: *Leatheries Ltd v Lycett Saddle and Motor Accessories Co Ltd* (1909) 26 RPC 166. Exposure in a room to which any members of the public have access is in general publication: *Barker v Associated Manufacturers (Gowns and Mantles) Ltd* (1933) 50 RPC 332; *Re Pressler & Co Ltd Registered Design (No 272,672), A Pressler & Co Ltd v Gartside & Co (of Manchester) Ltd and Widd and Owen Ltd* (1933) 50 RPC 240; *Re Vredenburg's Registered Design No 788,451* (1934) 52 RPC 7; *Kangol (Manufacturing) Ltd v Centrokomise (London) Ltd* [1937] 3 All ER 179, 54 RPC 211.

729.   Confidential disclosures.   The registration of an old design[1] is not invalidated, by reason only of:

(1)   the disclosure of the design by the proprietor[2] to any other person in

such circumstances as would make it contrary to good faith for that
other person to use or publish the design[3];

(2)   the disclosure of the design in breach of good faith by any person other
       than the proprietor of the design[4]; or

(3)   in the case of a new or original textile design intended for registration,
       the acceptance of a first and confidential order for goods bearing the
       design[5].

It would seem that discussion with a view to an order is not publication if the
circumstances are such that it would be contrary to good faith to disclose the
design[6].

1   Ie a design application for registration of which was registered before 9 December 2001 (see the
     Registered Designs Regulations 2001, SI 2001/3949, regs 1, 12(2), (3)): see PARA 657. As to the
     meaning of 'design' see PARA 717.
2   As to the proprietorship of current registered designs see PARA 699.
3   Registered Designs Act 1949 s 6(1)(a); cf PARA 446.
4   Registered Designs Act 1949 s 6(1)(b). See *Chudzikowski v Sowak* [1956] RPC 332; on appeal
     [1957] RPC 111, CA.
5   Registered Designs Act 1949 s 6(1)(c). Before the Patents and Designs Act 1907 (repealed) it was
     held that mere discussion with a probable customer did not invalidate registration (*Heinrichs v
     Bastendoff* (1893) 10 RPC 160), but that, where a traveller showed the design to customers and
     accepted an order, that invalidated subsequent registration (*Winfeld & Son v Snow Bros* (1890)
     8 RPC 15; *Blank v Footman, Pretty & Co* (1888) 39 ChD 678, 5 RPC 653).
6   *Gunston v Winox Ltd* [1921] 1 Ch 664, 38 RPC 40, CA. See also *British Insulated and Helsby
     Cables Ltd v London Electric Wire Co and Smith's Ltd* (1913) 30 RPC 620; *Re Registered
     Design No 742,187 of Mallards Ltd v Gibbons Bros Rotary Co Ltd* (1931) 48 RPC 315. For
     another case where communication was held not to be confidential see *Kangol
     (Manufacturing) Ltd v Centrokomise (London) Ltd* [1937] 3 All ER 179, 54 RPC 211.

730.   Exhibitions.   The registration of an old design[1] is not invalidated, by
reason only:

(1)   that a representation of the design, or any article[2] to which the design
       had been applied, had been displayed, with the consent of the
       proprietor[3] of the design, at an exhibition certified by the Secretary of
       State[4] for this purpose[5];

(2)   that after any such display and during the period of the exhibition a
       representation of the design or any such article had been displayed by
       any person without the consent of the proprietor[6]; or

(3)   that a representation of the design had been published in consequence of
       any such display as is mentioned in head (1) above[7],

if the application for registration of the design was made not later than six
months after the opening of the exhibition[8].

1   Ie a design application for registration of which was registered before 9 December 2001 (see the
     Registered Designs Regulations 2001, SI 2001/3949, regs 1, 12(2), (3)): see PARA 657. As to the
     meaning of 'design' see PARA 717.
2   As to the meaning of 'article' see PARA 720.
3   As to the proprietorship of current registered designs see PARA 699.
4   As to the Secretary of State see PARA 660. A certificate issued by the Secretary of State will be
     valid only if issued not later than the date on which the exhibition opened: *Mod-Tap Corpn v
     BI Communications plc* [1999] RPC 333.
5   Registered Designs Act 1949 s 6(2)(a) (amended by the Copyright, Designs and Patents
     Act 1988 Sch 3 para 4).
6   Registered Designs Act 1949 s 6(2)(b).
7   Registered Designs Act 1949 s 6(2)(c). Publication in a journal prior to display at a certified
     exhibition is not in consequence of that display and is not protected: *Re W Steel & Co Ltd's
     Application* [1958] RPC 411.
8   Registered Designs Act 1949 s 6(2).

731. Artistic works. In relation to old designs[1], where an application had been made by or with the consent of the owner of copyright[2] in an artistic work[3] for the registration of a corresponding design[4], the design is not to be treated as being other than new by reason only of any use made of the artistic work[5], save where the previous use consisted of or included the sale, letting for hire or offer or exposure for sale or hire of articles[6] to which had been applied industrially[7] the design in question or a design differing from it only in immaterial details or in features which are variants commonly used in the trade, and that previous use was made by or with the consent of the copyright owner[8]. The burden of proof under these provisions lies on the proprietor[9].

1   Ie designs application for registration of which were registered before 9 December 2001 (see the Registered Designs Regulations 2001, SI 2001/3949, regs 1, 12(2), (3)): see PARA 657. As to the meaning of 'design' see PARA 717.
2   Ie under the Copyright, Designs and Patents Act 1988 Pt I (ss 1–179): see COPYRIGHT vol 23 (2013) PARAS 656 et seq, 716 et seq.
3   For these purposes, 'artistic work' has the same meaning as in the Copyright, Designs and Patents Act 1988 Pt I (see COPYRIGHT vol 23 (2013) PARA 674): Registered Designs Act 1949 s 44(1) (definition added by the Copyright Act 1956 s 44(5); and amended by the Copyright, Designs and Patents Act 1988 Sch 3 para 31(1), (2)).
4   For these purposes, 'corresponding design', in relation to an artistic work, means a design which, if applied to an article, would produce something which would be treated for the purposes of the Copyright, Designs and Patents Act 1988 Pt I as a copy of that work: Registered Designs Act 1949 s 44(1) (definition added by the Copyright Act 1956 s 44(5); and amended by the Copyright, Designs and Patents Act 1988 Sch 3 para 31(1), (5)). As to such copies see COPYRIGHT vol 23 (2013) PARA 861 et seq.
5   Registered Designs Act 1949 s 6(4) (added by the Copyright Act 1956 s 44(1); substituted by the Copyright, Designs and Patents Act 1988 Sch 3 para 4).
6   Ie other than articles specified in rules made in pursuance of the Registered Designs Act 1949 s 1(5): see PARA 720. The benefit is not lost if the sale or hire, or offer for sale or hire, took place outside the United Kingdom: *Bissell AG's Design* [1964] RPC 125.
7   The Secretary of State may make provision by rules as to the circumstances in which a design is to be regarded for these purposes as 'applied industrially' to articles, or any description of articles: Registered Designs Act 1949 s 6(6) (added by the Copyright Act 1956 s 44(1); substituted by the Copyright, Designs and Patents Act 1988 Sch 3 para 4). A design is regarded as 'applied industrially' if it is applied to more than 50 articles which do not all together constitute a single set of articles as defined in the Registered Designs Act 1949 s 44(1) (see PARA 720) or to goods manufactured in lengths or pieces, not being hand-made goods: Registered Designs Rules 1995, SI 1995/2912, r 35 (now revoked). Whether sales have taken place is irrelevant to the question of whether a design has been applied industrially, as it is sufficient that the articles have been produced: *Bampal Materials Handling Ltd's Design* [1981] RPC 44, Design Registry.
8   Registered Designs Act 1949 s 6(5) (added by the Copyright Act 1956 s 44(1); substituted by the Copyright, Designs and Patents Act 1988 Sch 3 para 4).
9   *Bampal Materials Handling Ltd's Design* [1981] RPC 44, Design Registry.

732. Government departments. The registration of an old design[1] is not invalidated, by reason only of the communication of the design by the proprietor[2] to a government department or to a person authorised by it to consider the merits of the design, or of anything done in consequence of such a communication[3].

1   Ie designs application for registration of which were registered before 9 December 2001 (see the Registered Designs Regulations 2001, SI 2001/3949, regs 1, 12(2), (3)): see PARA 657. As to the meaning of 'design' see PARA 717.
2   As to the proprietorship of current registered designs see PARA 699.
3   Registered Designs Act 1949 s 6(3).

733. Registration of design for further articles. Where the registered proprietor[1] of an old design[2] registered in respect of any article[3] made an application:

(1) for registration in respect of one or more other articles, of that design[4]; or

(2) for registration in respect of the same or one or more other articles, of a design consisting of the registered design with modifications or variations not sufficient to alter the character or substantially to affect the identity thereof[5],

the registration made on that application is not invalidated by reason only of the previous registration or publication of the design[6].

The right in a design registered by virtue of these provisions does not, however, extend beyond the end of the period, and any extended period, for which the right subsists in the original registered design[7].

Where any person made an application for the registration of an old design in respect of any article and either:

(a) that design had been previously registered by another person in respect of some other article[8]; or

(b) the design to which the application related consisted of a design previously registered by another person in respect of the same or some other article with modifications or variations not sufficient to alter the character or substantially to affect the identity thereof[9],

then, if, at any time while the application was pending, the applicant became the registered proprietor of the design previously registered, the above provisions applied as if at the time of making the application the applicant had been the registered proprietor of that design[10].

1 As to the meaning of 'registered proprietor' see PARA 677 note 1.
2 Ie a design application for registration of which was registered before 9 December 2001 (see the Registered Designs Regulations 2001, SI 2001/3949, regs 1, 12(2), (3)): see PARA 657. As to the meaning of 'design' see PARA 717.
3 As to the meaning of 'article' see PARA 720.
4 Registered Designs Act 1949 s 4(1)(a). As to the effect of prior publication generally see PARA 728.
5 Registered Designs Act 1949 s 4(1)(b); and see *Sebel & Co Ltd's Application* [1959] RPC 12; *Sebel & Co Ltd's Application (No 2)* [1959] RPC 19.
6 Registered Designs Act 1949 s 4(1).
7 Registered Designs Act 1949 s 4(1) proviso (substituted by the Copyright, Designs and Patents Act 1988 Sch 3 para 2). As to the duration of the right in a registered design see PARA 693.
8 Registered Designs Act 1949 s 4(2)(a).
9 Registered Designs Act 1949 s 4(2)(b).
10 Registered Designs Act 1949 s 4(2).

(7) DECLARATION OF INVALIDITY

734. Grounds for invalidity of registration of a current design. The registration of a current design[1] may be declared invalid:

(1) on the ground that it does not fulfil the requirements of the definition of 'design' in the Registered Designs Act 1949[2];

(2) on the ground that it does not fulfil the requirements of the statutory provisions relating to novelty, technical function and public policy[3]; or

(3) where any statutory ground of refusal applies[4].

The registration of a design (the 'later design') may be declared invalid if it is not new or does not have individual character when compared to a design which:

(a)   has been made available to the public on or after the relevant date[5]; but

(b)   is protected as from a date prior to the relevant date by virtue of (i) registration under the Registered Designs Act 1949 or the Community Design Regulation or an application for such registration; or (ii) an international registration designating the Community[6].

The registration of a design may be declared invalid on the ground of the registered proprietor not being the proprietor of the design and the proprietor of the design objecting[7]. The registration of a design involving the use of an earlier distinctive sign may be declared invalid on the ground of an objection by the holder of rights to the sign which include the right to prohibit in the United Kingdom such use of the sign[8]. The registration of a design constituting an unauthorised use of a work protected by the law of copyright in the United Kingdom may be declared invalid on the ground of an objection by the owner of the copyright[9].

An appeal lies from any decision of the registrar under these provisions[10].

1   As to the meaning of 'design' see PARA 711. For the purposes of the Registered Designs Act 1949 ss 11ZA, 11ZB, 11ZC, 11ZE (other than s 11ZE(1): see PARA 698) references to the registration of a design include references to the former registration of a design; and those sections apply, with necessary modifications, in relation to such former registrations: s 11ZA(5) (ss 11ZA, 11ZB, 11ZF added by SI 2001/3949). As to registrations under the Registered Designs Act 1949 which have resulted from applications made on or after 1 August 1989 and before 9 December 2001 see the Registered Designs Regulations 2001, SI 2001/3949, reg 12. The Registered Designs Act 1949 as it had effect immediately before the coming into force of the Registered Design Regulations 2001, SI 2001/3949, continues to apply in relation to post-1989 registrations so far as the Registered Designs Act 1949 relates to the cancellation or invalidation of such registrations (other than cancellation by virtue of s 11(3) and by reference to an expiry of copyright occurring on or after 9 December 2001 (ie the date on which the Regulations came into force)): see reg 12(2). Accordingly, the amendments and repeals made by the Registered Design Regulations 2001, SI 2001/3949, do not, so far as they relate to the cancellation or invalidation of registrations, apply in relation to post-1989 registrations: reg 12(3).

2   Registered Designs Act 1949 s 11ZA(1)(a) (as added (see note 1); s 11ZA(1)(a)–(c) substituted, s 11ZA(1A), (1B) added, s 11ZB(1)–(3), (5) amended, by SI 2006/1974). As to the requirements of the definition of 'design' in the Registered Designs Act 1949 s 1(2) see PARA 711. Any person interested may make an application to the registrar for a declaration of invalidity under the Registered Designs Act 1949 s 11ZA(1)(a): s 11ZB(1) (as so added and amended). As to applications for invalidity see PARA 735.

3   Registered Designs Act 1949 s 11ZA(1)(b) (as added and substituted: see notes 1, 2). The statutory provisions referred to in the text are s 1B (novelty and individual character: see PARA 712), s 1C (designs dictated by their technical function: see PARAS 714–715), s 1D (designs contrary to public policy or morality: see PARA 716). Any person interested may make an application to the registrar for a declaration of invalidity under the Registered Designs Act 1949 s 11ZA(1)(b): s 11ZB(1) (as so added and amended).

4   Registered Designs Act 1949 s 11ZA(1)(c) (as added and substituted: see notes 1, 2). As to the statutory grounds of refusal see Sch A1; and PARA 685. Any person concerned by the use in question may make an application to the registrar for a declaration of invalidity under s 11ZA(1)(c): s 11ZB(2) (as so added and amended).

5   Registered Designs Act 1949 s 11ZA(1A)(a) (as added: see notes 1, 2). 'Relevant date' means the date on which the application for the registration of the later design was made or is treated by virtue of s 3B(2), (3) or (5) (see PARA 686) or s 14(2) (see PARA 689) as having been made: s 11ZA(1B) (as so added). The relevant person may make an application to the registrar for a declaration of invalidity under s 11ZA(1A): s 11ZB(3) (as so added and amended). 'Relevant person' means, in relation to an earlier design protected by virtue of registration under the Registered Designs Act 1949 or Council Regulation (EC) 6/2002 (OJ L3, 5.1.2002, p 1) on Community Designs ('the Community Design Regulation') or an application for such registration, the registered proprietor of the design, the holder of the registered community design or (as the case may be) the applicant: Registered Designs Act 1949 s 11ZB(4) (as so added; amended by SI 2003/550).

6   Registered Designs Act 1949 s 11ZA(1A)(b) (as added (see notes 1, 2); substituted by SI 2007/3378).

7   Registered Designs Act 1949 s 11ZA(2) (as added: see notes 1, 2). As to the proprietorship of
    registered designs see PARA 699. The person able to make an objection under s 11ZA(2) may
    make an application to the registrar for a declaration of invalidity: s 11ZB(5) (as so added and
    amended).
8   Registered Designs Act 1949 s 11ZA(3) (as added: see note 1). As to the meaning of 'United
    Kingdom' see PARA 303 note 5. The person able to make an objection under s 11ZA(3) may
    make an application to the registrar for a declaration of invalidity: s 11ZB(5) (as added and
    amended: see notes 1, 2).
9   Registered Designs Act 1949 s 11ZA(4) (as added: see note 1). See further COPYRIGHT vol 23
    (2013) PARAS 656 et seq, 716 et seq. The person able to make an objection under s 11ZA(4) may
    make an application to the registrar for a declaration of invalidity: s 11ZB(5) (as added and
    amended: see notes 1, 2).
10 Registered Designs Act 1949 s 11ZF (as added: see note 1). As to the registrar see PARA 660.

735.   Application for declaration of invalidity.   An application for a
declaration of invalidity may be made to the registrar in relation to a design at
any time after the design has been registered[1]. An application for a declaration of
invalidity must be in the prescribed form and include a statement of the grounds
on which the application is made[2]. The statement of grounds must include a
concise statement of the facts and grounds on which the applicant relies and be
verified by a statement of truth[3]. The registrar[4] must send a copy of the form and
the statement of case to the registered proprietor[5]. The registrar must specify a
period within which the registered proprietor must file a counter-statement[6]. The
registered proprietor must file his counter-statement on the prescribed form[7] and
send a copy of it to the applicant within that period, otherwise the registrar may
treat him as not opposing the application[8]. In his counter-statement the
registered proprietor must include a concise statement of the facts on which he
relies[9]. He must also state which of the allegations in the statement of grounds he
denies, which of the allegations he is unable to admit or deny, but which he
requires the applicant to prove, and also which allegations he admits[10]. The
counter-statement must be verified by a statement of truth[11].

When the period specified for filing the counter-statement has expired, the
registrar must specify the periods within which evidence may be filed by the
parties[12]. Where the applicant for a declaration of invalidity files no evidence
(other than his statement of grounds) in support of his application, the registrar
may treat him as having withdrawn his application[13]. The registrar may, at any
time if he thinks fit, give leave to either party to file evidence upon such terms as
he thinks fit[14]. Evidence may only be considered to be filed when it has been
received by the registrar and it has been sent to all other parties to the
proceedings[15].

The registrar must give the parties an opportunity to be heard[16], and where
any party requests to be heard, the registrar must send to the parties notice of a
date for the hearing[17].

1   Registered Designs Act 1949 s 11ZB(6) (s 11ZB added by SI 2001/3949). As to who may make
    applications for invalidity under the Registered Designs Act 1949 s 11ZA see s 11ZB; and PARA
    734 note 4. As to applications in relation to old designs see the Registered Designs Act 1949
    s 11(2) (amended by the Copyright, Designs and Patents Act 1988 ss 272, 303(2), Sch 3
    para 6(1), (2), Sch 8).
2   Registered Designs Rules 2006, SI 2006/1975, r 15(1). The application must be made on Form
    DF19A: see the Registered Designs Rules 2006, SI 2006/1975, r 15(1).
3   Registered Designs Rules 2006, SI 2006/1975, r 15(2).
4   As to the registrar see PARA 660.
5   Registered Designs Rules 2006, SI 2006/1975, r 15(3). As to the proprietorship of registered
    designs see PARA 699. 'Statement of case' means the statement of grounds filed by the applicant
    or the counter-statement filed by the registered proprietor; and references to the statement of
    case include part of the statement of case: r 15(7).

6 Registered Designs Rules 2006, SI 2006/1975, r 15(4).
7 Ie on Form DF19B: see the Registered Designs Rules 2006, SI 2006/1975, r 15(5).
8 Registered Designs Rules 2006, SI 2006/1975, r 15(5).
9 Registered Designs Rules 2006, SI 2006/1975, r 15(6)(a).
10 Registered Designs Rules 2006, SI 2006/1975, r 15(6)(b)–(d).
11 Registered Designs Rules 2006, SI 2006/1975, r 15(6).
12 Registered Designs Rules 2006, SI 2006/1975, r 16(1).
13 Registered Designs Rules 2006, SI 2006/1975, r 16(2).
14 Registered Designs Rules 2006, SI 2006/1975, r 16(3).
15 Registered Designs Rules 2006, SI 2006/1975, r 16(4).
16 Registered Designs Rules 2006, SI 2006/1975, r 16(5).
17 Registered Designs Rules 2006, SI 2006/1975, r 16(6).

736. Determination of application for declaration of invalidity. Where an application has been made to the registrar[1] for a declaration of invalidity in relation to a registration of a current design[2] and it appears to the registrar that the application has not been made in accordance with any rules made under the Registered Designs Act 1949, he may refuse the application[3]. If it appears to the registrar that the application has not been made in accordance with the statutory provisions[4], he must refuse the application[5]. Subject to this, the registrar must make a declaration of invalidity if it appears to him that the ground of invalidity specified in the application has been established in relation to the registration[6]. Otherwise the registrar must refuse the application[7].

When the registrar has made a decision on the application for a declaration of invalidity, he must send the parties written notice of it, stating the reasons for his decision[8]. The date on which the decision was sent to the applicant is deemed to be the date of the decision for the purposes of any appeal[9].

A declaration of invalidity in relation to a current design may be a declaration of partial invalidity[10]. Where the registrar declares the registration of a design invalid to any extent, the registration is, to that extent, treated as having been invalid from the date of registration or from such other date as the registrar may direct[11].

An appeal lies from any decision of the registrar under these provisions[12].

1 As to the registrar see PARA 660.
2 Registered Designs Act 1949 s 11ZC(1) (ss 11ZC, 11ZE, 11ZF added by SI 2001/3949). As to applications for declarations of invalidity see PARA 735.
3 Registered Designs Act 1949 s 11ZC(2) (as added: see note 2).
4 Ie the Registered Designs Act 1949 s 11ZB: see PARA 757.
5 Registered Designs Act 1949 s 11ZC(3) (as added: see note 2).
6 Registered Designs Act 1949 s 11ZC(4) (as added: see note 2). As to the grounds of invalidity see PARA 734.
7 Registered Designs Act 1949 s 11ZC(5) (as added: see note 2).
8 Registered Designs Rules 2006, SI 2006/1975, r 17(1).
9 Registered Designs Rules 2006, SI 2006/1975, r 17(2).
10 Registered Designs Act 1949 s 11ZC(6) (as added: see note 2).
11 Registered Designs Act 1949 s 11ZE(2) (as added: see note 2).
12 Registered Designs Act 1949 s 11ZF (as added: see note 2).

737. Modification of registration. Where the registrar[1] intends to declare the registration of a current design invalid[2], he must inform the registered proprietor of that fact[3]. The registered proprietor may make an application to the registrar for the registrar to make such modifications to the registration of the design as the registered proprietor specifies in his application[4]. Such modifications may, in particular, include the inclusion on the register of a partial disclaimer by the registered proprietor[5]. If it appears to the registrar that the application has not been made in accordance with the rules made under the Registered Designs

Act 1949, the registrar may refuse the application[6]. If it appears to the registrar that the identity of the design is not retained or the modified registration would be invalid[7], the registrar must refuse the application[8]. Otherwise the registrar must make the specified modifications[9]. An appeal lies from any decision of the registrar under these provisions[10].

A modification of a registration has effect, and is to be treated always to have had effect, from the grant of registration[11].

1   As to the registrar see PARA 660.
2   Ie under the Registered Designs Act 1949 s 11ZA(1)(b) or (c), (1A), (3) or (4): see PARA 734.
3   Registered Designs Act 1949 s 11ZD(1), (2) (ss 11ZD, 11ZF added by SI 2001/3949; the Registered Designs Act 1949 s 11ZD(1) amended by SI 2006/1974). As to the proprietorship of registered designs see PARA 699.
4   Registered Designs Act 1949 s 11ZD(3) (as added: see note 3).
5   Registered Designs Act 1949 s 11ZD(4) (as added: see note 3).
6   Registered Designs Act 1949 s 11ZD(5) (as added: see note 3).
7   Ie by virtue of the Registered Designs Act 1949 s 11ZA: see PARA 734.
8   Registered Designs Act 1949 s 11ZD(6) (as added: see note 3).
9   Registered Designs Act 1949 s 11ZD(7) (as added: see note 3).
10 Registered Designs Act 1949 s 11ZF (as added: see note 3).
11 Registered Designs Act 1949 s 11ZD(8) (as added: see note 3).

(8) RIGHTS ON REGISTRATION; INFRINGEMENT AND THREATS

738.   Right given by registration of a design. The registration of a design[1] under the Registered Designs Act 1949 gives the registered proprietor[2] the exclusive right to use the design and any design which does not produce on the informed user a different overall impression[3].

Any reference[4] to the use of a design includes a reference to:

(1)   the making, offering, putting on the market, importing, exporting or using of a product in which the design is incorporated or to which it is applied; or

(2)   stocking such a product for those purposes[5].

In determining whether a design produces a different overall impression on the informed user, the degree of freedom of the author in creating his design is to be taken into consideration[6].

The right conferred is subject to any limitation attaching to the registration in question, including, in particular, any partial disclaimer or any declaration by the registrar or a court of partial invalidity[7].

The right in a registered design is infringed by a person who, without the consent of the registered proprietor, does anything which is the exclusive right[8] of the registered proprietor[9].

1   As to the meaning of 'design' see PARA 711 (current designs) and PARA 717 (old designs). In relation to old designs, the registered proprietor is not entitled to prevent any person from continuing to carry out acts begun by him before 9 December 2001 and which, at that time, the registered proprietor would have been unable to prevent: see the Registered Designs Regulations 2001, SI 2001/3949, reg 14(3).
2   As to the meaning of 'registered proprietor' see PARA 677 note 1.
3   Registered Designs Act 1949 s 7(1) (s 7 substituted, s 7A added, by SI 2001/3949). See PARA 739. This legislation also applies to the registration of any design application for which was made before 9 December 2001: see the Registered Designs Regulations 2001, SI 2001/3949, regs 1, 12(4). The fact that post-1989 registrations are in respect of any articles, or sets of articles, is to be disregarded: reg 12(5). As to the validity of old designs see PARA 717.
4   Ie for the purposes of the Registered Designs Act 1949 s 7(1) and s 7A (see PARA 740).

5 Registered Designs Act 1949 s 7(2) (as substituted: see note 3).
6 Registered Designs Act 1949 s 7(3) (as substituted: see note 3). See PARA 739. For a case involving a limited degree of design freedom see *Utopia Tableware Ltd v BBP Marketing Ltd* [2013] EWHC 3483 (IPEC), [2013] All ER (D) 162 (Nov).
7 Registered Designs Act 1949 s 7(4) (as substituted: see note 3). See PARA 686.
8 Ie by virtue of the Registered Designs Act 1949 s 7.
9 Registered Designs Act 1949 s 7A(1) (as added: see note 3). This legislation also applies to the registration of any design application for which was made before 9 December 2001: see the Registered Designs Regulations 2001, SI 2001/3949, regs 1, 12(4).

739. Test for infringement. A design infringes the right given by registration if it does not produce on the informed user a different overall impression[1]. An informed user is not the same as a person 'skilled in the art' of patent law[2] nor the average consumer of trade mark law[3]. The informed user is a user who has experience of other similar articles and who will be reasonably discriminatory; he is able to appreciate enough detail to decide whether a design creates an overall impression which has individual character and whether an alleged infringement produces a different overall impression[4]. The test of different overall impression is imprecise as it is necessarily subjective[5]. It is sufficient to avoid infringement if the accused product is of a design which produces a 'different overall impression'; there is no policy requirement that the difference be 'clear'[6]. The overall impression is what strikes the mind of the informed user when it is carefully viewed, not what he may recollect afterwards[7].

1 See the Registered Designs Act 1949 s 7(1); and PARA 738.
2 *Procter & Gamble Co v Reckitt Benckiser (UK) Ltd* [2007] EWCA Civ 936 at [16], [2007] IP & T 464 at [16], [2008] FSR 208 at [16] per Jacob LJ. As to persons skilled in the art in relation to patent law see PARA 455.
3 *Procter & Gamble Co v Reckitt Benckiser (UK) Ltd* [2007] EWCA Civ 936 at [24], [2007] IP & T 464 at [24], [2008] FSR 208 at [24] per Jacob LJ.
4 *Procter & Gamble Co v Reckitt Benckiser (UK) Ltd* [2007] EWCA Civ 936 at [23], [2007] IP & T 464 at [23], [2008] FSR 208 at [23] per Jacob LJ. See also *Woodhouse UK plc v Architectural Lighting Systems* [2006] RPC 1; *Samsung Electronics (UK) Ltd v Apple Inc* [2012] EWHC 1882 (Pat), [2012] All ER (D) 139 (Jul) (affd [2012] EWCA Civ 1339, [2013] IP & T 15) (in forming his 'overall impression' the informed user can disregard 'totally banal' elements common to all examples of the type of product in issue and concentrate on features that are 'arbitrary or different from the norm'). Note that in *Samsung Electronics (UK) Ltd v Apple Inc*, in which the product (a tablet computer) was clearly desirable but not essential, it made sense for the 'informed user' to be characterised as being a person particularly attentive to details and sensitive to aesthetics.
5 *Procter & Gamble Co v Reckitt Benckiser (UK) Ltd* [2007] EWCA Civ 936 at [34], [2007] IP & T 464 at [34], [2008] FSR 208 at [34] per Jacob LJ. See also *J Choo (Jersey) Ltd v Towerstone Ltd* [2008] EWHC 346 (Ch), [2008] All ER (D) 35 (Jan), [2008] FSR 485. As to the level of detail applied by the 'informed user' see *Samsung Electronics (UK) Ltd v Apple Inc* [2012] EWHC 1882 (Pat), [2012] All ER (D) 139 (Jul) (affd [2012] EWCA Civ 1339, [2013] IP & T 15); Case C-281/10 *PepsiCo Inc v Grupo Promer Mon Graphic SA* [2011] ECR I-10153, [2012] FSR 183 ('informed user' is somewhere between the 'average consumer' and a sectoral expert).
6 *Procter & Gamble Co v Reckitt Benckiser (UK) Ltd* [2007] EWCA Civ 936 at [19], [2007] IP & T 464 at [19], [2008] FSR 208 at [19] per Jacob LJ.
7 *Procter & Gamble Co v Reckitt Benckiser (UK) Ltd* [2007] EWCA Civ 936 at [25], [2007] IP & T 464 at [25], [2008] FSR 208 at [25] per Jacob LJ.

740. Exceptions to infringement. The right in a registered design[1] is not infringed by:
(1) an act which is done privately and for purposes which are not commercial[2];
(2) an act which is done for experimental purposes[3];
(3) an act of reproduction for teaching purposes or for the purpose of

making citations provided that the act of reproduction is compatible with fair trade practice and does not unduly prejudice the normal exploitation of the design and mention is made of the source[4];

(4)   the use of equipment on ships or aircraft which are registered in another country but which are temporarily in the United Kingdom[5];

(5)   the importation into the United Kingdom of spare parts or accessories for the purpose of repairing such ships or aircraft[6]; or

(6)   the carrying out of repairs on such ships or aircraft[7].

The right in a registered design is not infringed by an act which relates to a product in which any design protected by the registration is incorporated or to which it is applied if the product has been put on the market in the European Economic Area by the registered proprietor or with his consent[8].

The right in a registered design of a component part which may be used for the purpose of the repair of a complex product so as to restore its original appearance is not infringed by the use for that purpose of any design protected by the registration[9].

No proceedings may be taken in respect of an infringement of the right in a registered design committed before the date on which the certificate of registration[10] of the design under the Registered Designs Act 1949 is granted[11].

1   As to the meaning of 'design' see PARA 711 (current designs) and PARA 717 (old designs).
2   Registered Designs Act 1949 s 7A(2)(a) (s 7A added by SI 2001/3949). This legislation also applies to the registration of any design application for which was made before 9 December 2001: see the Registered Designs Regulations 2001, SI 2001/3949, regs 1, 12(4). As to the validity of old designs see PARA 717.
3   Registered Designs Act 1949 s 7A(2)(b) (as added: see note 2).
4   Registered Designs Act 1949 s 7A(2)(c), (3) (as added: see note 2).
5   Registered Designs Act 1949 s 7A(2)(d) (as added: see note 2). As to the meaning of 'United Kingdom' see PARA 303 note 5.
6   Registered Designs Act 1949 s 7A(2)(e) (as added: see note 2).
7   Registered Designs Act 1949 s 7A(2)(f) (as added: see note 2).
8   Registered Designs Act 1949 s 7A(4) (as added: see note 2). As to the meaning of 'registered proprietor' see PARA 677 note 1. As to the European Economic Area Agreement see COMPETITION vol 18 (2009) PARA 36.
9   Registered Designs Act 1949 s 7A(5) (as added: see note 2).
10 As to the certificate of registration see PARA 692.
11 Registered Designs Act 1949 s 7A(6) (as added: see note 2). In relation to old designs, the registered proprietor is not entitled to prevent any person from continuing to carry out acts begun by him before 9 December 2001 and which, at that time, the registered proprietor would have been unable to prevent: see the Registered Design Regulations 2001, SI 2001/3949, reg 14(3).

741.   Right of prior use.   A person who, before the application date[1], used a registered design[2] in good faith or made serious and effective preparations to do so may continue to use the design for the purposes for which, before that date, the person had used it or made the preparations to use it[3]. This does not apply if the design which the person used, or made preparations to use, was copied from the design which was subsequently registered[4]. The right so conferred on a person does not include a right to licence another person to use the design[5], and the person on whom the right is so conferred also may not assign the right, or transmit it on death (or in the case of a body corporate on its dissolution), unless the design was used, or the preparations for its use were made, in the course of a business, and the right is assigned or transmitted with the part of the business in which the design was used or the preparations for its use were made[6].

1   For these purposes the 'application date', in relation to a registered design, means the date on which an application for the registration was made under the Registered Designs Act 1949 s 3

(see PARA 684) or, where an application for the registration was treated as having been made by virtue of s 14(2) (see PARA 689), the date on which it was treated as having been so made: s 7B(2) (s 7B added by the Intellectual Property Act 2014 s 7(1)).

2   As to the meaning of 'design' see PARA 711 (current designs) and PARA 717 (old designs).

3   Registered Designs Act 1949 s 7B(1) (as added: see note 1).

4   Registered Designs Act 1949 s 7B(3) (as added: see note 1).

5   Registered Designs Act 1949 s 7B(4) (as added: see note 1).

6   Registered Designs Act 1949 s 7B(5) (as added: see note 1).

742.   Claims for infringement.   An infringement of the right in a registered design[1] is actionable by the registered proprietor[2]. In an action for infringement all such relief by way of damages[3], injunctions[4], accounts or otherwise is available to him as is available in respect of the infringement of any other property right[5].

If in any proceedings before the court the validity of the registration of a design is contested, and it is found by the court that the design is, to any extent, validly registered, the court may certify that the validity of the registration of the design was contested in those proceedings[6]. Where any such certificate has been granted, then if in any subsequent proceedings before the court for infringement of the right in the registered design or for invalidation of the registration of the design, a final order or judgment is made or given in favour of the registered proprietor, unless the court otherwise directs, he is entitled to his costs as between solicitor and client[7]. This does not apply to the costs of any appeal in any such proceedings[8].

1   As to the meaning of 'design' see PARA 711 (current designs) and PARA 717 (old designs). As to the right given by registration see the Registered Designs Act 1949 s 7; and PARA 738.

2   Registered Designs Act 1949 s 24A(1) (s 24A added by SI 2006/1028). As to the meaning of 'registered proprietor' see PARA 677 note 1. The Registered Designs Act 1949 s 24A has effect subject to s 24B (exemption of innocent infringer from liability: see PARA 743): s 24A(3) (as so added). As to the concurrent right of an exclusive licensee see PARA 745.

3   The court will readily infer that a proportion of the infringing sales would have benefited the registered proprietor, even where the design is not licensed to others, but the burden of proof of loss lies on the claimant. Damages may be awarded as a reasonable royalty on infringing sales: *P B Cow Ltd v Cannon Rubber Manufacturers Ltd* [1961] RPC 236. As to damages generally see PARA 544 et seq; and DAMAGES vol 12(1) (Reissue) PARA 801 et seq. See also *Rosedale Associated Manufacturers v Airfix Products Ltd* [1959] RPC 249 (inquiry as to damages). An account of profits may also be granted: see EQUITABLE JURISDICTION vol 47 (2014) PARA 105. Accounts are rarely taken.

4   The proper form of injunction is against 'infringing the design', not 'the design or any part of it', since the registration only protects the whole: *John Harper & Co Ltd v Wright and Butler Lamp Manufacturing Co Ltd* [1896] 1 Ch 142 at 158, 12 RPC 483 at 496, CA. Where, in the case of an old design, the registration is for shape only or pattern only, the injunction may be limited accordingly (*Re Manchester's Design, Manchester v Umfreville & Son* (1907) 24 RPC 782), although this would seem to be unnecessary. In *JT Smith and JE Jones Ltd v Service, Reeve & Co Ltd* [1914] 2 Ch 576, 31 RPC 319, Sargant J held that, where there had been infringement, the claimant was entitled to the publicity of an injunction; but in *Winkle & Co Ltd v Cent & Son* (1914) 31 RPC 473, CA, the court held that, where the defendant had offered an undertaking, this would in general be sufficient. As to injunctions generally see CIVIL PROCEDURE vol 11 (2009) PARA 331 et seq.

5   Registered Designs Act 1949 s 24A(2) (as added: see note 2). As to the reliefs available see PARA 536; and CIVIL PROCEDURE vol 11 (2009) PARA 315 et seq.

6   Registered Designs Act 1949 s 25(1) (amended by SI 2001/3949); Registered Designs Regulations 2001, SI 2001/3949, regs 1, 12(4). As to such certificates see PARA 549.

7   Registered Designs Act 1949 s 25(2) (amended by the Copyright, Designs and Patents Act 1988 s 272, Sch 3 para 14; and by SI 2001/3949); Registered Designs Regulations 2001, SI 2001/3949, regs 1, 12(4).

8   Registered Designs Act 1949 s 25(2) proviso.

743.   Exemption of innocent infringer from liability.   In proceedings for the infringement of the right in a registered design[1] damages may not be awarded against a defendant who proves that at the date of the infringement he was not aware, and had no reasonable ground for supposing, that the design was registered[2].

For these purposes, a person is not deemed to have been aware or to have had reasonable grounds for supposing that the design was registered by reason only of the marking of a product[3] with: (1) the word 'registered' or any abbreviation thereof; or (2) any word or words expressing or implying that the design applied to, or incorporated in, the product has been registered, unless the number of the design accompanied the word or words or the abbreviation in question[4]. Nothing in the above provisions affects the power of the court[5] to grant an injunction in any proceedings for infringement of the right in a registered design[6].

1   As to the meaning of 'design' see PARA 711 (current designs) and PARA 717 (old designs). As to the right given by registration see the Registered Designs Act 1949 s 7; and PARA 738.
2   Registered Designs Act 1949 s 24B(1) (s 24B added by SI 1006/1028; Registered Designs Act 1949 s 24B(1) amended by the Intellectual Property Act 2014 s 10(1)). This defence is not available in respect of Community designs: *J Choo (Jersey) Ltd v Towerstone Ltd* [2008] EWHC 346 (Ch), [2008] All ER (D) 35 (Jan), [2008] FSR 485.
3   As to the meaning of 'product' see PARA 711 note 1.
4   Registered Designs Act 1949 s 24B(2) (as added: see note 2).
5   As to the meaning of 'court' see PARA 668.
6   Registered Designs Act 1949 s 24B(3) (as added: see note 2).

744.   Order for delivery up and disposal.   Where a person:

(1)   has in his possession, custody or control for commercial purposes[1] an infringing article[2]; or

(2)   has in his possession, custody or control anything specifically designed or adapted for making articles to a particular design which is a registered design, knowing or having reason to believe that it has been or is to be used to make an infringing article,

the registered proprietor[3] in question may apply to the court[4] for an order that the infringing article or other thing be delivered up to him or to such other person as the court may direct[5].

An application may not be made after the end of the period of six years from the date on which the article or thing in question was made, unless the registered proprietor is under a disability[6] or is prevented by fraud or concealment from discovering the facts entitling him to apply for an order, in which case an application may be made at any time before the end of the period of six years from the date on which he ceased to be under a disability or, as the case may be, could with reasonable diligence have discovered those facts[7].

No order may be made unless the court also makes, or it appears to the court that there are grounds for making, an order as to the disposal of infringing articles[8]. A person to whom an infringing article or other thing is delivered up in pursuance of an order for delivery up, if an order as to disposal is not made, must retain it pending the making of such an order, or the decision not to make such an order[9].

An application may be made to the court for an order that an infringing article or other thing delivered up in pursuance of an order[10] must be: (a) forfeited to the registered proprietor; or (b) destroyed or otherwise dealt with as the court may think fit, or for a decision that no such order should be made[11]. In considering what order, if any, should be made, the court must consider whether other remedies available in an action for infringement of the right in a registered design would be adequate to compensate the registered proprietor and to protect his interests[12]. Where there is more than one person interested[13] in an article or other thing, the court must make such order as it thinks just and may, in particular, direct that the thing be sold, or otherwise dealt with, and the proceeds divided[14]. If the court decides that no order should be made, the person in whose possession, custody or control the article or other thing was before being delivered up is entitled to its return[15].

1   The reference to an act being done in relation to an article for 'commercial purposes' is to its being done with a view to the article in question being sold or hired in the course of a business: Registered Designs Act 1949 s 24C(7) (ss 24C, 24D, 24E, 24G added by SI 2006/1028).

2   In the Registered Designs Act 1949, 'infringing article', in relation to a design, is to be construed in accordance with s 24G, which states that an article is an infringing article if its making to that design was an infringement of the right in a registered design: Registered Designs Act 1949 s 24G(1), (2) (as added: see note 1). As to the meaning of 'design' see PARA 711 (current designs) and PARA 717 (old designs). As to the right given by registration see PARA 738. An article is also an infringing article if: (1) it has been or is proposed to be imported into the United Kingdom; and (2) its making to that design in the United Kingdom would have been an infringement of the right in a registered design or a breach of an exclusive licensing agreement relating to that registered design: s 24G(3) (as so added). As to the meaning of 'United Kingdom' see PARA 303 note 5. As to exclusive licensing agreements see PARA 701. Nothing in s 24G(3) is to be construed as applying to an article which may be lawfully imported into the United Kingdom by virtue of an enforceable EU right within the meaning of the European Communities Act 1972 s 2(1) (see CONSTITUTIONAL AND ADMINISTRATIVE LAW vol 20 (2014) PARA 28): Registered Designs Act 1949 s 24G(5) (as so added; amended by SI 2011/1043). Where it is shown that an article is made to a design which is or has been a registered design, it is to be presumed until the contrary is proved that the article was made at a time when the right in the registered design subsisted: Registered Designs Act 1949 s 24G(4) (as so added).

3   As to the meaning of 'registered proprietor' see PARA 677 note 1.

4   As to the meaning of 'court' see PARA 668.

5   Registered Designs Act 1949 s 24C(1) (as added: see note 1). Nothing in s 24C affects any other power of the court: s 24C(8) (as so added). As to the jurisdiction of the county court in Northern Ireland see s 24E (as so added).

6   For this purpose, 'disability', in England and Wales, has the same meaning as in the Limitation Act 1980 (see LIMITATION PERIODS vol 68 (2008) PARA 1170): Registered Designs Act 1949 s 24C(5) (as added: see note 1).

7   Registered Designs Act 1949 s 24C(2)–(4) (as added: see note 1).

8   Registered Designs Act 1949 s 24C(2) (as added: see note 1). An order as to the disposal of infringing articles is made under s 24D: see the text and notes 10–15.

9   Registered Designs Act 1949 s 24C(6) (as added: see note 1).

10   Ie an order under the Registered Designs Act 1949 s 24C: see the text and notes 1–9.

11   Registered Designs Act 1949 s 24D(1) (as added: see note 1).

12   Registered Designs Act 1949 s 24D(2) (as added: see note 1).

13   References to a person having an interest in an article or other thing include any person in whose favour an order could be made in respect of it under the Registered Designs Act 1949 s 24D, under the Trade Marks Act 1994 s 19 (including that provision as applied by the Community Trade Mark Regulations 2006, SI 2006/1027, reg 4 (see TRADE MARKS AND TRADE NAMES vol 97A (2014) PARA 446)), under the Copyright, Designs and Patents Act 1988 ss 114, 204, 231 (see COPYRIGHT vol 23 (2013) PARAS 969, 1082. 1259); or under the Community Design Regulations 2005, SI 2005/2339, reg 1C (see PARA 756): Registered Designs Act 1949 s 24D(5) (as added: see note 1).

14   Registered Designs Act 1949 s 24D(3) (as added: see note 1).

15   Registered Designs Act 1949 s 24D(4) (as added: see note 1).

745. Rights and remedies of exclusive licensee. In relation to a registered design[1], an exclusive licensee[2] has, except against the registered proprietor[3], the same rights and remedies in respect of matters occurring after the grant of the licence as if the licence had been an assignment[4]. His rights and remedies are concurrent with those of the registered proprietor[5].

In an action brought by an exclusive licensee by virtue of these provisions, a defendant may avail himself of any defence which would have been available to him if the action had been brought by the registered proprietor[6]. Where an action for infringement of the right in a registered design brought by the registered proprietor or an exclusive licensee relates (wholly or partly) to an infringement in respect of which they have concurrent rights of action, the proprietor or, as the case may be, the exclusive licensee may not, without the leave of the court[7], proceed with the action unless the other is either joined as a claimant or added as a defendant[8].

Where an action for infringement of the right in a registered design is brought which relates (wholly or partly) to an infringement in respect of which the registered proprietor and an exclusive licensee have concurrent rights of action, the court, in assessing damages, must take into account: (1) the terms of the licence; and (2) any pecuniary remedy already awarded or available to either of them in respect of the infringement[9]. No account of profits may be directed if an award of damages has been made, or an account of profits has been directed, in favour of the other of them in respect of the infringement[10]. If an account of profits is directed, the court may apportion the profits between the registered proprietor and the exclusive licensee as the court considers just, subject to any agreement between them[11]. These provisions apply whether or not the proprietor and the exclusive licensee are both parties to the action[12].

The registered proprietor must notify any exclusive licensee having concurrent rights before applying for an order for delivery up of an infringing article[13]; and the court may on the application of the licensee make such order[14] as it thinks fit having regard to the terms of the licence[15].

1   As to the meaning of 'design' see PARA 711 (current designs) and PARA 717 (old designs).
2   As to exclusive licensees see PARA 701.
3   As to the meaning of 'registered proprietor' see PARA 677 note 1.
4   Registered Designs Act 1949 s 24F(1) (s 24F added by SI 2006/1028). As to assignment see PARA 700.
5   Registered Designs Act 1949 s 24F(2) (as added: see note 4). References to the registered proprietor in the provisions of the Registered Designs Act 1949 relating to infringement are to be construed accordingly: s 24F(2) (as so added).
6   Registered Designs Act 1949 s 24F(3) (as added: see note 4).
7   As to the meaning of 'court' see PARA 668.
8   Registered Designs Act 1949 s 24F(4) (as added: see note 4). A registered proprietor or exclusive licensee who is added as a defendant in pursuance of s 24F(4) is not liable for any costs in the action unless he takes part in the proceedings: s 24F(5) (as so added). The provisions of s 24F(4) and (5) do not affect the granting of interlocutory relief on the application of the registered proprietor or an exclusive licensee: s 24F(6) (as so added).
9   Registered Designs Act 1949 s 24F(7)(a) (as added: see note 4).
10 Registered Designs Act 1949 s 24F(7)(b) (as added: see note 4).
11 Registered Designs Act 1949 s 24F(7)(c) (as added: see note 4).
12 Registered Designs Act 1949 s 24F(7) (as added: see note 4).
13 Ie an order under the Registered Designs Act 1949 s 24C: see PARA 744.
14 Ie under the Registered Designs Act 1949 s 24C: see PARA 744.
15 Registered Designs Act 1949 s 24F(8) (as added: see note 4).

746.   Defences.   The ordinary defences in an action for infringement are a denial of the infringement, a plea of leave and licence, or an attack on the validity of the registration[1].

1   Such attacks are generally on the ground of default of title, or lack of novelty or subject matter, or that the applicant was not the author. As to validity see PARA 711 et seq. Where, in an action to restrain the infringement of a registered design, the defendant has admitted the novelty and originality of the claimant's design, the court is not precluded from inquiring whether the design

is in fact novel and original, and, if it is of opinion that it is not so, giving judgment for the defendant on that ground: see *Gramophone Co Ltd v Magazine Holder Co* (1911) 28 RPC 221, HL, and cf *Re Schwerin's Patent* (1914) 31 RPC 229; *Vandervell & Co v Lundberg & Sons* (1915) 33 RPC 60. Defences based on EU law may be pleaded: see eg Case 187/80 *Merck & Co Inc v Stephar BV and Petrus Stephanus Exler* [1981] ECR 2063, [1981] 3 CMLR 463, ECJ (free movement of goods); Case 144/81 *Keurkoop BV v Nancy Kean Gifts BV* [1982] ECR 2853, [1983] 2 CMLR 47, ECJ (no EU bar to infringement claim where claimant obtained design from abroad); Case C-267/95 *Merck & Co Inc v Primecrown Ltd* [1996] ECR I-6285, [1997] FSR 237, ECJ. As to a 'Gillette' defence where a defendant establishes either that a registered design did not cover the product in question or that it was invalid because of prior publication see *Carflow Products (UK) Ltd v Linwood Securities (Birmingham) Ltd* [1996] FSR 424 (no breach of registered design, as defendant's design had been registered and disclosed in circumstances of non-confidentiality prior to registration of claimant's design).

747. Expert evidence. The place for evidence in registered design cases is very limited[1]. Generally speaking 'expert' evidence as to what the ordinary consumer would see in cases involving registered designs for consumer products is unlikely ever to be useful. Litigants should not feel that their case might be disadvantaged by not having an expert in an area when expert evidence is unnecessary. Evidence of technical or factual matters, as opposed to consumer 'eye appeal' can on the other hand, sometimes have a part to play, that would be to give the court information or understanding which it could otherwise not provide itself[2].

1 See *Procter & Gamble Co v Reckitt Benckiser (UK) Ltd* [2007] EWCA Civ 936 at [4], [2008] FSR 208 at [4] per Jacob LJ.

2 *Oren v Red Box Toy Factory Ltd* [1999] FSR 785 at [11], [1999] All ER (D) 98 at [11] per Jacob J. See also *Thermos Ltd v Aladdin Sales and Marketing Ltd* [2000] FSR 402, [1999] All ER (D) 1160 per Jacob J at first instance ('in future in registered design actions, I think the court should take care before allowing any expert evidence'); affd [2001] EWCA Civ 667, [2002] FSR 184, [2001] All ER (D) 129 (May).

748. Claims against the Crown. Subject to certain statutory restrictions[1], civil proceedings lie against the Crown for an infringement committed by a servant or agent of the Crown[2], with the authority of the Crown, of the right in a registered design[3]. Save as so provided, no proceedings lie against the Crown by virtue of the Crown Proceedings Act 1947 in respect of the infringement of the right in a registered design[4].

1 Ie subject to the provisions of the Crown Proceedings Act 1947: see CROWN PROCEEDINGS AND CROWN PRACTICE vol 12(1) (Reissue) PARA 102 et seq. Thus an injunction may not be granted against the Crown: see s 21(1) proviso (a); and CROWN PROCEEDINGS AND CROWN PRACTICE vol 12(1) (Reissue) PARA 134.

2 As to the authority of agents generally see AGENCY vol 1 (2008) PARA 29 et seq.

3 Crown Proceedings Act 1947 s 3(1)(c) (s 3 substituted by the Copyright, Designs and Patents Act 1988 Sch 7 para 4(1)).

4 Crown Proceedings Act 1947 s 3(1) (as substituted: see note 3). Nothing in the Crown Proceedings Act 1947 s 3 is to be construed as affecting the rights of a government department under the Registered Designs Act 1949 s 12, Sch 1 (see PARA 705 et seq) or the rights of the Secretary of State under s 5 (see PARA 687): Crown Proceedings Act 1947 s 3(2) (as so substituted).

749. Proceedings for threats. Where by circulars, advertisements or otherwise any person, whether entitled to or interested in a registered design, threatens[1] any other person with proceedings for infringement of the right in a registered design[2], any person aggrieved[3] thereby may bring a claim[4] against him for relief[5]. Unless in any such claim the defendant proves that the acts in respect of which proceedings were threatened constitute or, if done, would constitute, an infringement of the right in a registered design the registration of which is not shown by the claimant to be invalid, the claimant is entitled to the following relief:

(1)   a declaration to the effect that the threats are unjustifiable;

(2)   an injunction[6] against the continuance of the threats; and

(3)   such damages, if any, as he has sustained thereby[7].

Proceedings may not, however, be brought in respect of a threat to bring proceedings for infringement alleged to consist of the making or importing of anything[8].

There is also a common law right of action for malicious falsehood, which may be applicable if the threats have been made in bad faith and, subject to the statutory provision[9] under which special damage need not be proved, if damage has resulted[10].

1   The essence of a threat (see generally PARA 555 et seq) is an indication that the maker has rights and intends to enforce them: *Rosedale Associated Manufacturers Ltd v Airfix Products Ltd* [1956] RPC 360 (on appeal [1957] RPC 239, CA, the point did not arise). The nature of the interview at which statements are made is relevant in considering whether they amount to threats: see *Paul Trading Co Ltd v J Marksmith & Co Ltd* (1952) 69 RPC 301 at 304. See also *Finkelstein v Billig* (1930) 47 RPC 516 (threats not found).

2   A mere notification that a design is registered does not constitute a threat of proceedings: Registered Designs Act 1949 s 26(3). As to the meaning of 'design' see PARA 711 (current designs) and PARA 717 (old designs). Little more is, however, needed to constitute a threat: see eg *Jaybeam Ltd v Abru Aluminium Ltd* [1976] RPC 308.

3   As to the meaning of 'person aggrieved' cf JUDICIAL REVIEW vol 61 (2010) PARA 656. As to the person to whom the threats may be addressed see PARA 558.

4   If he is the registered proprietor of the design, the defendant may counterclaim for infringement and it is then open to the claimant to counterclaim further for rectification of the register: see *Lewis Falk Ltd v Jacobwitz* [1944] Ch 64, 61 RPC 116. As to claims for infringement see PARA 742; and as to counterclaims for rectification see PARA 746.

5   Registered Designs Act 1949 s 26(1) (amended by the Copyright, Designs and Patents Act 1988 Sch 3 para 15(1), (2)). The Registered Designs Act 1949 s 26 corresponds to the Patents Act 1977 s 70: see PARA 555 et seq.
     Where at the trial the defendant admits the threats but counterclaims for relief for infringement, he may have the right to open the case on the questions relating to infringement: see *W Lusty & Sons Ltd v Morris Wilkinson & Co (Nottingham) Ltd* [1954] 2 All ER 347, [1954] 1 WLR 911, 71 RPC 174. The duty falling on the court is to consider what is the fair mode of trying that which is shown to be the substantial matter: see *Pearson v Holden* (1948) 65 RPC 424 at 426.

6   An interim injunction may be granted: see eg *Boneham and Hart v Hirst Bros & Co Ltd* (1917) 34 RPC 209; *International Sales Ltd v TransContinental Trading Co Ltd and Benno Maisel* (1934) 52 RPC 107; *Jaybeam Ltd v Abru Aluminium Ltd* [1976] RPC 308. In *Selsdon Fountain Pen Co Ltd v British Joint Association of Goldsmiths, Silversmiths, Horological and Kindred Trades* (1950) 67 RPC 108, interlocutory relief was refused on the ground of delay in seeking it.

7   Registered Designs Act 1949 s 26(2) (amended by the Copyright, Designs and Patents Act 1988 Sch 3 para 15(1), (2); and SI 2006/1028).

8   Registered Designs Act 1949 s 26(2A) (added by the Copyright, Designs and Patents Act 1988 Sch 3 para 15(1), (3)). See also *Bowden Controls Ltd v Acco Cable Controls Ltd* [1990] RPC 427.

9   Ie the Defamation Act 1952 s 3(1): see DEFAMATION vol 32 (2012) PARA 785.

10   See *Barley v Walford* (1846) 9 QB 197; *Jaybeam Ltd v Abru Aluminium Ltd* [1976] RPC 308; cf DEFAMATION vol 32 (2012) PARAS 776, 785.

(9) COMMUNITY DESIGNS

750.   Community designs in general.   In December 2001, the EU Member States agreed on a regulation creating a community design[1]. The regulation creates a system in which a single design application can give protection throughout the EU. There are two types of Community design right: (1) a registered right, which gives monopoly protection to original designs for up to 25 years[2]; and (2) an unregistered right, which gives protection against deliberate copying of designs for up to three years[3].

The unregistered design right has been available since 6 March 2002, and the registered design right since 1 April 2003. Applicants for registered community designs must apply to the Office for Harmonisation in the Internal Market (OHIM)[4].

1   Ie Council Regulation (EC) 6/2002 (OJ L3, 5.1.2002, p 1) on Community Designs (the 'Community Design Regulation'). The Community Design Regulation has been implemented by the Community Design Regulations 2005, SI 2005/2339. A 'community design' is a design which complies with the conditions contained in the Community Design Regulation: art 1.1; Community Design Regulations 2005, SI 2005/2339, reg 1(2). The provisions governing community designs mirror the provisions of the Registered Designs Act 1949 ss 1–1D (which partly implement Council Directive (EC) 98/71 (OJ L289, 28.10.1998, p 28) on the legal protection of designs). See PARAS 711–716.

2   See PARA 751 et seq.

3   See the Community Design Regulation art 1.2. The protection of unregistered community designs is covered elsewhere in this work: see COPYRIGHT.

4   As to the right to a community design see the Community Design Regulation arts 14–18; as to the effects of a community design see arts 19–26; as to community designs as objects of property see arts 27–34; as to applications for a registered community design see arts 35–44; as to the registration procedure see arts 45–50; as to surrender and invalidity see arts 51–54; as to appeals see arts 55–61; as to procedure before the office see arts 62–78; as to jurisdiction and procedure in legal actions relating to community designs see arts 79–94; as to the effects on member states see arts 95–96. As to the Office for Harmonisation in the Internal Market see TRADE MARKS AND TRADE NAMES vol 97A (2014) PARA 163 et seq. As to the operation of the Community design system see e g Case C-32/08 *Fundacion Espanola para la Innovaction de la Artesania (FEIA) v Cul de Sac Espacio Creativo* [2009] ECR I-5611, [2010] Bus LR 466, ECJ; *Samsung Electronics (UK) Ltd v Apple Inc* [2012] EWCA Civ 729, [2013] IP & T 1. As to the fee payable in respect of an application for a registered community see the Community Design (Fees) Regulations 2002, SI 2002/2942. As to the implementation of the Community Design Regulation and the fees payable to OHIM see Commission Regulation (EC) 2245/2002 (OJ L341, 17.12.2002, p 28) and Commission Regulation (EC) 2246/2002 (OJ L341, 17.12.2002, p 54).

751.   Registrability of community designs.   A design is protected by a registered community design[1], if registered in the required manner[2]. 'Design' means the appearance of the whole or a part of a product[3] resulting from the features of, in particular, the lines, contours, colours, shape, texture or materials of the product itself or its ornamentation[4].

1   See PARA 750. As to the meaning of 'community design' see PARA 750 note 1.

2   Council Regulation (EC) 6/2002 (OJ L3, 5.1.2002, p 1) on Community Designs (the 'Community Design Regulation') art 1.2(b). The design must be registered in the manner provided for in the Community Design Regulation: see art 1.2(b).

3   'Product' means any industrial or handicraft item, including inter alia parts intended to be assembled into a complex product, packaging, get-up, graphic symbols and typographic typefaces, but excluding computer programs: Community Design Regulation art 3(b). 'Complex product' means a product which is composed of multiple components which can be replaced permitting disassembly and re-assembly of the product: art 3(c).

4   Community Design Regulation art 3(a). Cf the Registered Designs Act 1949 s 1(2): see PARA 711.

752.   Requirement of novelty and individual character.   A registered community design[1] is protected to the extent that it is new and has individual character[2]. For these purposes, a design is new if no identical design or no design whose features differ only in immaterial details has been made available to the public before the date of filing of the application for registration of the design for which protection is claimed, or, if priority is claimed, the date of priority[3]. A design has individual character if the overall impression it produces on the informed user differs from the overall impression produced on such a user by any design which has been made available to the public before the date of filing the application for registration or, if a priority is claimed, the date of priority[4].

In assessing individual character, the degree of freedom of the designer in developing the design is to be taken into consideration[5].

A design applied to or incorporated in a product which constitutes a component part of a complex product is only considered to be new and to have individual character (1) if the component part, once it has been incorporated into the complex product, remains visible during normal use of the complex product; and (2) to the extent that those visible features of the component part are in themselves new and have individual character[6].

1   As to the meaning of 'community design' see PARA 750 note 1.
2   Council Regulation (EC) 6/2002 (OJ L3, 5.1.2002, p 1) on Community Designs (the 'Community Design Regulation') art 4.1. See also PARA 712.
3   Community Design Regulation art 5.1, 5.2.
        For the purpose of applying the Community Design Regulation art 5 (novelty) and art 6 (individual character), a design is deemed to have been made available to the public if it has been published following registration or otherwise, or exhibited, used in trade or otherwise disclosed, before the date of filing of the application for the Community registered design except where these events could not reasonably have become known in the normal course of business to the circles specialised in the sector concerned, operating within the Community: art 7.1. The 'sector concerned' is that corresponding to the prior art: *Green Lane Products Ltd v PMS International Group Ltd* [2007] EWHC 1712 (Pat), [2008] FSR 1, [2007] All ER (D) 305 (Jul); affd [2008] EWCA Civ 358, [2009] IP & T 233, [2008] All ER (D) 313 (Apr). See also Cases C-101/11P and C-102/11P *Newman v Jose Manuel Baena Grupo, SA* [2013] All ER (D) 190 (Jan), ECJ; Case 180/11 *Bericap Zarodastechnikai Bt v Plastinova 2000 Kft* [2013] All ER (D) 264 (Feb), ECJ; *Magmatic Ltd v PMS International Ltd* [2013] EWHC 1925 (Pat), [2013] All ER (D) 164 (Jul); Case C-479/12 *H Gautzsch Großhandel GmbH & Co KG v Münchener Boulevard Möbel Joseph Duna GmbH* [2014] Bus LR 391, [2014] All ER (D) 223 (Feb) (concerning an unregistered design).
        A disclosure is not to be taken into consideration for the purpose of applying the Community Design Regulation arts 5 and 6 and if a design for which protection is claimed under a registered community design has been made available to the public: (1) by the designer, his successor in title, or a third person as a result of information provided or action taken by the designer or his successor in title; and (2) during the 12-month period preceding the date of filing of the application or, if a priority is claimed, the date of priority: art 7.2. Article 7.2 also applies if the design has been made available to the public as a consequence of an abuse in relation to the designer or his successor in title: art 7.3.
4   Community Design Regulation art 6.1. As to the interpretation of 'informed user' see *Proctor & Gamble Co v Reckitt Benckiser (UK) Ltd* [2007] EWCA Civ 936, [2008] RPC 1; *Magmatic Ltd v PMS International Ltd* [2014] EWCA Civ 181, [2014] IP & T 588; Case C-345/13 *Karen Millen Fashions Ltd v Dunnes Stores* [2014] Bus LR 756, [2014] All ER (D) 156 (Jun).
5   Community Design Regulation art 6.2. A product with a high technical specification is likely to impose greater technical constraints, and leave the designer a lesser degree of freedom, than one with a low technical specification: see *Dyson Ltd v Vax Ltd* [2010] EWHC 1923 (Pat), [2011] Bus LR 232, [2010] All ER (D) 319 (Jul) (affd [2011] EWCA Civ 1206, [2013] Bus LR 328, [2011] All ER (D) 220 (Oct)). See also Case T-337/12 *El Hogar Perfecto del Siglo XXI, SL v Office for Harmonisation in the Internal Market (Trade Marks and Designs)* [2014] IP & T 114, [2013] All ER (D) 249 (Nov), EGC. For a case involving a limited degree of design freedom see *Utopia Tableware Ltd v BBP Marketing Ltd* [2013] EWHC 3483 (IPEC), [2013] All ER (D) 162 (Nov).
6   Community Design Regulation art 4.2. 'Normal use' means use by the end user; but does not include any maintenance, servicing or repair work: art 4.3. As to the meanings of 'product' and 'complex product' see PARA 751 note 3.

753. Designs dictated by their technical function. A registered community design[1] does not subsist in features of appearance of a product[2] which are solely dictated by the product's technical function[3].

1   As to the meaning of 'community design' see PARA 750 note 1.
2   As to the meaning of 'product' see PARA 751 note 3.
3   Council Regulation (EC) 6/2002 (OJ L3, 5.1.2002, p 1) on Community Designs (the 'Community Design Regulation') art 8.1. See also PARA 714. Article 8.1 denies protection to those features of a product's appearance that are chosen exclusively for the purpose of designing a product that performs its function, as opposed to features that are chosen for the purpose of enhancing the product's visual appearance: see *Dyson Ltd v Vax Ltd* [2010] EWHC 1923 (Pat), [2011] Bus LR 232, [2010] All ER (D) 319 (Jul) (affd [2011] EWCA Civ 1206, [2013] Bus LR 328, [2011] All ER (D) 220 (Oct)).

754. The 'must fit' exclusion. A right in a registered community design[1] does not subsist in features of appearance of a product[2] which must necessarily be reproduced in their exact form and dimensions so as to permit the product in which the design is incorporated or to which it is applied to be mechanically connected to, or placed in, around or against, another product so that either product may perform its function[3]. However, this does not prevent a community design subsisting in a design serving the purpose of allowing multiple assembly or connection of mutually interchangeable products within a modular system[4].

1   As to the meaning of 'community design' see PARA 750 note 1.
2   As to the meaning of 'product' see PARA 751 note 3.
3   Council Regulation (EC) 6/2002 (OJ L3, 5.1.2002, p 1) on Community Designs (the 'Community Design Regulation') art 8.1. See also PARA 714.
4   Community Design Regulation art 8.4.

755. Designs contrary to public policy or morality. A registered community design[1] does not subsist in a design which is contrary to public policy or to accepted principles of morality[2].

1   As to the meaning of 'community design' see PARA 750 note 1.
2   Council Regulation (EC) 6/2002 (OJ L3, 5.1.2002, p 1) on Community Designs (the 'Community Design Regulation') art 9.

756. Infringement proceedings. In an action for infringement of a community design[1] all such relief by way of damages, injunctions, accounts or otherwise is available to the holder of the community design as is available in respect of the infringement of any other property right[2]. This is subject, however, to the proviso that in an action for the infringement of the right in a registered Community design damages may not be awarded against a person who proves that at the date of the infringement they were not aware, and had no reasonable ground for supposing, that the design was registered[3]; and that in an action for the infringement of an unregistered Community design, damages may not be awarded against a person who proves that at the date of the infringement that they were not aware, and had no reason to believe, that the design to which the action relates was protected as an unregistered Community design[4].

Where a person: (1) has in his possession, custody or control for commercial purposes[5] an infringing article[6]; or (2) has in his possession, custody or control anything specifically designed or adapted for making articles to a particular design which is a community design, knowing or having reason to believe that it has been or is to be used to make an infringing article, the holder of the community design in question may apply to the community design court for an order that the infringing article or other thing be delivered up to him or to such other person as the court may direct[7]. An application may not be made after the end of the period of six years from the date on which the article or thing in question was made, unless during the whole or any part of that period the holder of the community design is under a disability[8], or is prevented by fraud or concealment from discovering the facts entitling him to apply for an order, in which case an application may be made at any time before the end of the period of six years from the date on which he ceased to be under a disability or, as the case may be, could with reasonable diligence have discovered those facts[9].

No order may be made unless the court also makes, or it appears to the court that there are grounds for making, an order as to disposal of infringing articles[10]. A person to whom an infringing article or other thing is delivered up in pursuance of an order for delivery up, if an order as to disposal is not made, must retain it pending the making of an order, or the decision not to make such an order[11].

An application may be made to the community design court for an order that an infringing article or other thing delivered up in pursuance of an order[12] must be: (a) forfeited to the holder of the community design; or (b) destroyed or otherwise dealt with as the court may think fit, or for a decision that no such order should be made[13]. In considering what order, if any, should be made, the court must consider whether other remedies available in an action for infringement of the right in a community design would be adequate to compensate the holder and to protect his interests[14]. Where there is more than one person interested[15] in an article or other thing, the court must make such order as it thinks just and may, in particular, direct that the thing be sold, or otherwise dealt with, and the proceeds divided[16]. If the court decides that no order should be made, the person in whose possession, custody or control the article or other thing was before being delivered up is entitled to its return[17].

1   As to the meaning of 'community design' see PARA 750 note 1. As to the test for infringement see *Procter & Gamble Co v Reckitt Benckiser (UK) Ltd* [2007] EWCA Civ 936, [2008] IP & T 704, [2008] FSR 208; *Woodhouse UK plc v Architectural Lighting Systems* [2006] RPC 1; and PARA 739. See also *Green Lane Products Ltd v PMS International Group Ltd* [2007] EWHC 1712 (Pat), [2008] FSR 1, [2007] All ER (D) 305 (Jul); affd [2008] EWCA Civ 358, [2009] IP & T 233, [2008] All ER (D) 313 (Apr). For the mirror provisions in relation to registered designs protected under the Registered Designs Act 1949 see PARA 744. The defence of innocent infringement is not available in respect of infringement of a community design: *J Choo (Jersey) Ltd v Towerstone Ltd* [2008] EWHC 346 (Ch), [2008] FSR 485, [2008] All ER (D) 35 (Jan).

2   Community Design Regulations 2005, SI 2005/2339, reg 1A(2) (regs 1A–1D added by SI 2006/1028; Community Design Regulations 2005, SI 2005/2339, reg 1A(2) amended, reg 1A(3)–(5) added, by SI 2014/2400). The Community Design Regulations 2005, SI 2005/2339, regs 1A–1D are without prejudice to the duties of the community design court under the provisions of Council Regulation (EC) 6/2002 (OJ L3, 5.1.2002, p 1) on Community Designs (the 'Community Design Regulation') art 89(1)(a)–(c): Community Design Regulations 2005, SI 2005/2339, reg 1A(1) (as so added). Where in an action for infringement or for threatened infringement a community design court finds that the defendant has infringed or threatened to infringe a community design, it must, unless there are special reasons for not doing so, order the following measures: (1) an order prohibiting the defendant from proceeding with the acts which have infringed or would infringe the community design; (2) an order to seize the infringing products; (3) an order to seize materials and implements predominantly used in order to manufacture the infringing goods, if their owner knew the effect for which such use was intended or if such effect would have been obvious in the circumstances: Community Design Regulation art 89(1)(a)–(c).
     For the purposes of the Community Design Regulation the High Court and the Intellectual Property Enterprise Court (see PARA 626) are designated as community design courts in England and Wales: Community Designs (Designation of Community Design Courts) Regulations 2005, SI 2005/696, reg 2(1); Community Design Regulations 2005, SI 2005/2339, reg 1(2). For the

purpose of hearing appeals from judgments of those courts, the Court of Appeal is designated as community design court: Community Designs (Designation of Community Design Courts) Regulations 2005, SI 2005/696, reg 2(2); Community Design Regulations 2005, SI 2005/2339, reg 1(2).

3   Community Design Regulations 2005, SI 2005/2339, reg 1A(3) (as added: see note 2). For the purpose of reg 1A(3), a person is not deemed to have been aware or to have had reasonable grounds for supposing that the design was registered by reason only of the marking of a product with the word 'registered' or any abbreviation of that word, or any word or words expressing or implying that the design applied to, or incorporated in, the product has been registered, unless the number of the design accompanied the word or words or the abbreviation in question: reg 1A(4) (as so added).

4   Community Design Regulations 2005, SI 2005/2339, reg 1A(5) (as added: see note 2).

5   The reference to an act being done in relation to an article for 'commercial purposes' are to its being done with a view to the article in question being sold or hired in the course of a business: Community Design Regulations 2005, SI 2005/2339, reg 1B(7) (as added: see note 2).

6   An article is an infringing article if its making to that design was an infringement of a community design: Community Design Regulations 2005, SI 2005/2339, reg 1D(1), (2) (as added: see note 2). An article is also an infringing article if: (1) it has been or is proposed to be imported into the United Kingdom; and (2) its making to that design in the United Kingdom would have been an infringement of a community design or a breach of an exclusive licensing agreement relating to that community design: reg 1D(3) (as so added). As to the meaning of 'United Kingdom' see PARA 303 note 5. Where it is shown that an article is made to a design which is or has been a community design, it is presumed until the contrary is proved that the article was made at a time when the right in the community design subsisted: reg 1D(4) (as so added). Nothing in reg 1D(3) is to be construed as applying to an article which may be lawfully imported into the United Kingdom by virtue of an enforceable EU right within the meaning of the European Communities Act 1972 s 2(1) (see CONSTITUTIONAL AND ADMINISTRATIVE LAW vol 20 (2014) PARA 28): Community Design Regulations 2005, SI 2005/2339, reg 1D(5) (as so added; amended by SI 2011/1043).

7   Community Design Regulations 2005, SI 2005/2339, reg 1B(1) (as added: see note 2). Nothing in reg 1B affects any other power of the court: reg 1B(8) (as added: see note 2). As to the community design court see note 2.

8   For this purpose, 'disability', in England and Wales, has the same meaning as in the Limitation Act 1980 (see LIMITATION PERIODS vol 68 (2008) PARA 1170): Community Design Regulations 2005, SI 2005/2339, reg 1B(5) (as added: see note 2).

9   Community Design Regulations 2005, SI 2005/2339, reg 1B(2), (3), (4) (as added: see note 2).

10   Community Design Regulations 2005, SI 2005/2339, reg 1B(2) (as added: see note 2). An order as to disposal of infringing articles is made under reg 1C: see the text and notes 12–17.

11   Community Design Regulations 2005, SI 2005/2339, reg 1B(6) (as added: see note 2).

12   Ie an order under the Community Design Regulations 2005, SI 2005/2339, reg 1B: see the text and notes 1–11.

13   Community Design Regulations 2005, SI 2005/2339, reg 1C(1) (as added: see note 2).

14   Community Design Regulations 2005, SI 2005/2339, reg 1C(2) (as added: see note 2).

15   References to a person having an interest in an article or other thing include any person in whose favour an order could be made in respect of it under the Community Design Regulations 2005, SI 2005/2339, reg 1C, under the Registered Designs Act 1949 s 24D (see PARA 744), under the Copyright, Designs and Patents Act 1988 ss 114, 204, 231 (see COPYRIGHT vol 23 (2013) PARAS 969, 1082. 1259, under the Trade Marks Act 1994 s 19 (including that provision as applied by the Community Trade Mark Regulations 2006, SI 2006/1027, reg 4 (see TRADE MARKS AND TRADE NAMES vol 97A (2014) PARA 446)): Community Design Regulations 2005, SI 2005/2339, reg 1C(5) (as added: see note 2).

16   Community Design Regulations 2005, SI 2005/2339, reg 1C(3) (as added: see note 2).

17   Community Design Regulations 2005, SI 2005/2339, reg 1C(4) (as added: see note 2).

757. Remedy for groundless threats of infringement proceedings. Where any person (whether entitled to or interested in a community design[1] or not) by circulars, advertisements or otherwise threatens any other person with proceedings for infringement of a community design[2], any person aggrieved thereby may bring an action against him for relief[3]. The claimant is entitled to the following relief: (1) a declaration to the effect that the threats are unjustifiable; (2) an injunction against the continuance of the threats; and

(3) such damages, if any, as he has sustained by reason of the threats[4]. However, if the defendant proves that the acts in respect of which proceedings were threatened constitute or, if done, would constitute an infringement of a registered community design the claimant is entitled to the relief claimed only if he shows that the registration is invalid[5].

Proceedings may not be brought in respect of a threat to bring proceedings for an infringement alleged to consist of the making or importing of anything[6].

1 As to the meaning of 'community design' see PARA 750 note 1.
2 Mere notification that a design is a registered community design does not constitute a threat of proceedings for these purposes: Community Design Regulations 2005, SI 2005/2339, reg 2(6).
3 Community Design Regulations 2005, SI 2005/2339, reg 2(1). For the mirror provisions in relation to registered designs protected under the Registered Designs Act 1949 see PARA 749.
4 Community Design Regulations 2005, SI 2005/2339, reg 2(2).
5 Community Design Regulations 2005, SI 2005/2339, reg 2(3). In relation to a design protected by virtue of an international registration designating the Community, the reference to a registration being invalid includes a reference to the effects of the international registration being declared invalid: Community Design Regulations 2005, SI 2005/2339, reg 2(6A) (added by SI 2007/3378).
6 Community Design Regulations 2005, SI 2005/2339, reg 2(5).

758. Falsely representing a design as a registered community design. It is an offence for a person falsely to represent that a design applied to, or incorporated in, any product sold by him is a registered community design[1]. It is also an offence for a person, after a registered community design has expired, to represent, expressly or by implication, that a design applied to, or incorporated in, any product sold is still registered as a community design[2].

1 Community Design Regulations 2005, SI 2005/2339, reg 3(1). As to the meaning of 'community design' see PARA 750 note 1. A person guilty of such an offence is liable on summary conviction to a fine not exceeding level 3 on the standard scale: reg 3(3). As to the standard scale see SENTENCING AND DISPOSITION OF OFFENDERS vol 92 (2010) PARA 142.
2 Community Design Regulations 2005, SI 2005/2339, reg 3(2). A person guilty of such an offence is liable on summary conviction to a fine not exceeding level 1 on the standard scale: reg 3(4).

759. Privileged communications. Any communication as to any matter relating to the protection of any design between a person and his professional designs representative[1], or for the purposes of obtaining, or in response to a request for, information which a person is seeking for the purpose of instructing his professional designs representative, is privileged from disclosure in legal proceedings in the same way as a communication between a person and his solicitor or, as the case may be, a communication for the purpose of obtaining, or in response to a request for, information which a person is seeking for the purpose of instructing his solicitor[2].

1 'Professional designs representative' means a person who is on the special list of professional representatives for design matters referred to in Council Regulation (EC) 6/2002 (OJ L3, 5.1.2002, p 1) on Community Designs ('the Community Design Regulation') art 78: Community Design Regulations 2005, SI 2005/2339, reg 4(3).
2 Community Design Regulations 2005, SI 2005/2339, reg 4(1), (2). As to privileged communications between a person and his solicitor see CONFIDENCE AND INFORMATIONAL PRIVACY vol 19 (2011) PARA 36; LEGAL PROFESSIONS vol 65 (2008) PARAS 740–741.

760. Use of community designs for services of the Crown. A government department, or a person authorised in writing by a government department, may without the consent of the holder of a community design[1]: (1) do anything for the purpose of supplying products for the services of the Crown[2]; or (2) dispose of products no longer required for the services of the Crown; and nothing done by virtue of these provisions infringes the community design[3].

The authority of a government department in respect of Crown use[4] of a community design may be given to a person either before or after the use and whether or not he is authorised, directly or indirectly, by the holder of the community design to do anything in relation to the design[5]. A person acquiring anything sold in the exercise of such powers, and any person claiming under him, may deal with it in the same manner as if the Crown was the holder of the community design[6].

Provision is made as to the settlement of terms for Crown use[7], the rights of third parties in case of Crown use[8], compensation for loss of profit[9] and the reference of disputes relating to Crown use[10].

1   As to the meaning of 'community design' see PARA 750 note 1.
2   References for this purpose to 'services of the Crown' are limited to those which are necessary for essential defence or security needs: Community Design Regulations 2005, SI 2005/2339, reg 5, Schedule para 1(2).
3   Community Design Regulations 2005, SI 2005/2339, Schedule para 1(1).
4   'Crown use', in relation to a community design, means the doing of anything by virtue of the provisions set out in the text which would otherwise be an infringement of the community design: Community Design Regulations 2005, SI 2005/2339, Schedule para 1(3).
5   Community Design Regulations 2005, SI 2005/2339, Schedule para 1(4).
6   Community Design Regulations 2005, SI 2005/2339, Schedule para 1(5).
7   See the Community Design Regulations 2005, SI 2005/2339, Schedule para 2.
8   See the Community Design Regulations 2005, SI 2005/2339, Schedule para 3.
9   See the Community Design Regulations 2005, SI 2005/2339, Schedule para 4.
10 See the Community Design Regulations 2005, SI 2005/2339, Schedule para 5.

(10) INTERNATIONAL REGISTRATION

761–800.   International registration.   The Hague System of international registrations of industrial designs is applicable among the countries party to the Hague Agreement[1]. It is administered by the International Bureau of the World Intellectual Property Organisation (WIPO) located in Geneva, Switzerland[2]. The Hague system allows the owner of an industrial design to have his design protected in several countries by filing a single application with the International Bureau of WIPO, in one language, with one set of fees in one currency[3]. An international registration produces the same effects in each of the designated countries as if the design had been registered there directly unless protection is refused by the competent office of that country[4]. The Hague System also simplifies the subsequent management of the industrial design, since it is possible to record subsequent changes or to renew the registration through a simple single procedural step with the International Bureau of WIPO[5].

The Secretary of State[6] may by order make provision for giving effect in the United Kingdom to the provisions of the Hague Agreement[7].

1   Ie the Geneva Act of the Hague Agreement Concerning the International Registration of Industrial Designs (2 July 1999). The EU acceded to the Geneva Act on 1 January 2008: see Council Decision (EC) 954/2006 (OJ L386, 29.12.2006, p 28).
2   See the Geneva Act art 22. As to the World Intellectual Property Organisation see COPYRIGHT vol 23 (2013) PARA 999.
3   See the Geneva Act Chapter I (arts 3–18).
4   See the Geneva Act art 14.
5   See the Geneva Act art 16.
6   As to the Secretary of State see PARA 660.

7 Registered Designs Act 1949 s 15ZA(1) (s 15ZA added by the Intellectual Property Act 2014 s 8(1)). At the date at which this volume states the law no such order had been made. Such an order may, in particular, make provision about the making of applications for international registrations at the UK Intellectual Property Office, the procedures to be followed where an international registration designates the United Kingdom, the effect of an international registration which designates the United Kingdom, the communication of information to the International Bureau, and the payment of fees: Registered Designs Act 1949 s 15ZA(2) (as so added). An expression used in s 15ZA(2) and in the Hague Agreement has the same meaning in the Registered Designs Act 1949 s 15ZA(2) as it has in the Agreement: s 15ZA(4) (as so added) An order under s 15ZA may amend the Registered Designs Act 1949 and apply specified provisions of the Act with such modifications as may be specified: s 15ZA(3) (as so added). As to the UK Intellectual Property Office see PARA 577.

PEERAGES AND DIGNITIES

1. THE GRANTING OF HONOURS AND DIGNITIES; IN GENERAL

801.   Source of peerages and dignities.   The Crown is the fountain of all honour and dignity[1]. The powers of the Crown in this respect are unlimited, so that heritable dignities of a kind not used before may be created[2]. The dignities now usually created are peerages and knighthoods[3]. The power to grant armorial bearings is delegated by the Crown to the Kings of Arms, and the right to bear arms must be regarded as a dignity[4]. The Crown may also grant warrants of precedence[5].

1   *Prince's Case* (1606) 8 Co Rep 1 at 18b; and see CONSTITUTIONAL AND ADMINISTRATIVE LAW vol 20 (2014) PARA 567 et seq.
2   Report on the Dignity of a Peer of the Realm (1829 reprint) vol II p 37. This report was first printed in 1822 and reprinted in 1826 and 1829 with different paginations. The pagination used in this title is that of the 1829 reprint.
3   As to peerages see PARA 803 et seq. As to knighthoods see PARAS 865–867.
4   *Manchester Corpn v Manchester Palace of Varieties Ltd* [1955] P 133 at 147, [1955] 1 All ER 387 at 392, Court of Chivalry, per Lord Goddard (Surrogate). As to the law of arms see PARA 870 et seq.
5   Warrants of precedence are normally issued in order to grant to widows or children the precedence which they would have enjoyed if their husbands or fathers had lived to inherit a peerage: see e g *Strange of Knokin and Stanley Baronies Case* (1920) Minutes of Evidence, App 243.

802.   Abuses in connection with the grant of honours.   If any person:

(1)   accepts or obtains or agrees to accept or attempts to obtain from any person, for himself or for any other person, for any purpose; or

(2)   gives, or agrees or proposes to give, or offers to any person,

any gift, money or valuable consideration, as an inducement or reward for procuring or assisting or endeavouring to procure the grant of a dignity or title of honour to any person, or otherwise in connection with such a grant, he is guilty of an offence[1]; and he is also liable to forfeit any such gift, money or consideration which he received and which is capable of forfeiture[2].

A contract for the purchase of a title is contrary to public policy and void[3].

1   See the Honours (Prevention of Abuses) Act 1925 s 1(1), (2); and CRIMINAL LAW vol 26 (2010) PARA 463. A person guilty of this offence is liable: (1) on conviction on indictment to imprisonment for a term not exceeding two years or to a fine of any amount, or to both; or (2) on summary conviction to imprisonment for a term not exceeding three months or to a fine not exceeding the prescribed sum, or to both: s 1(3) (amended by virtue of the Criminal Law Act 1977 s 32(1); and by virtue of the Magistrates' Courts Act 1980 s 32(2)); and see the Criminal Law Act 1967 s 1. As to the prescribed sum see SENTENCING AND DISPOSITION OF OFFENDERS vol 92 (2010) PARA 141.
2   See the Honours (Prevention of Abuses) Act 1925 s 1(3); and CRIMINAL LAW vol 26 (2010) PARA 463.
3   *Parkinson v College of Ambulance Ltd and Harrison* [1925] 2 KB 1; and see CONTRACT vol 22 (2012) PARA 434.

2. THE PEERAGE

(1) THE PEERAGE GENERALLY

803. Meaning of 'peerage'. Before the House of Lords Act 1999, 'peerage'[1] was defined as a dignity to which attached the right to a summons by name to sit and vote in Parliament[2]. However, in 1999 the automatic right of hereditary peers to membership of the House of Lords was ended[3]. Whilst peerage remains the means of summoning persons to the House of Lords not all peers are members of the House. There are peers who are not lords of Parliament, and there are lords of Parliament who are entitled to be summoned and to sit and vote in Parliament but who are not peers, namely the lords spiritual[4].

1 The word 'peerage' is used in several senses. Probably its most usual meaning in common parlance is any dignity of nobility, such as an earldom or a barony (see PARA 804), but a second meaning can be each of two or more dignities of nobility vested in the same peer with different lines of succession, and there is a third sense in which a peerage is used as comprehending all the dignities of nobility held by a peer, and constituting the status of an individual peer: see the *Fermoy Peerage Case* (1856) 5 HL Cas 716 at 741 per Crowder J.

2 *Norfolk Earldom Case* [1907] AC 10 at 17, HL, per Lord Davey. The right was, however, modified by the Acts of Union so that peers of Scotland and peers of Ireland sat in the Parliament of the United Kingdom by representative peers only: see the Union with Scotland Act 1706; the Union with Ireland Act 1800; and PARA 825 note 1.

3 Unless excepted from the operation of the House of Lords Act 1999 s 1, no-one may be a member of the House of Lords by virtue of a hereditary peerage: see the House of Lords Act 1999 ss 1, 2; and PARA 825. As to life peers and hereditary peers see PARA 807.

4 Bishops to whom a writ of summons has been issued are not peers but are lords of Parliament: HL Standing Orders (2013) (Public Business) no 6. See also ECCLESIASTICAL LAW vol 34 (2011) PARA 201.

804. Degrees of peerage. The right to a peerage is distinct from a title of honour conferring a particular rank in the peerage, which is merely a collateral matter[1]. There are five degrees of peerage[2], namely:

(1)   duke[3];
(2)   marquess[4];
(3)   earl[5];
(4)   viscount[6]; and
(5)   baron[7].

Life peers are entitled to rank as barons for life[8].

1 *Norfolk Earldom Case* [1907] AC 10 at 17, HL, per Lord Davey.

2 The ancient degrees are earl and baron. The others have been added in the exercise of the Crown's prerogative: Report on the Dignity of a Peer of the Realm (1829 reprint) vol II p 37.

3 Duke is the highest degree of peerage, although third in order of antiquity. The title was first created in 1337 for Edward, eldest son of Edward III, as Duke of Cornwall: 2 Co Inst 5; 9 Co Rep 49a; Charter Roll, 11 Edw III. The title of Duke of Cornwall belongs to the Heir Apparent by inheritance: see further CROWN AND ROYAL FAMILY vol 12(1) (Reissue) PARAS 30–31.

4 Marquess is the second degree of peerage in precedence, but fourth in antiquity. It was first introduced into England as a title or dignity in 1385 when Robert de Vere, Earl of Oxford, was created Marquess of Dublin: Selden's Titles of Honor (3rd Edn) 38, 693; 2 Co Inst 5. The creation was by charter and for life only, precedence being given between the dukes and the earls: 3 Rotuli Parliamentorum 209.

5 Earl is the third degree of peerage in order of precedence, but the first in antiquity: Cruise on Dignities (2nd Edn) c 1 s 55; Co Rep 49a. In Norman times an earldom was something of an office as well as a dignity: *Norfolk Earldom Case* [1907] AC 10, HL. Earls and barons are the only dignities known to have existed before the constitution of Parliament.

6 Viscount is the most recent degree of peerage and ranks after earl but above baron: Selden's *Titles of Honor* (3rd Edn) 630. The first introduction of the title into England was in 1440, when, by letters patent and investiture, John Lord Beaumont was created Viscount of Beaumont: 2 Co Inst 5.

7 Baron is the fifth degree of peerage and ranks after viscount. At the time of the Norman conquest and even as late as Magna Carta there were greater and lesser barons (Cruise on Dignities (2nd Edn) c 1 ss 50–54), but the greater barons were the only persons who seem to have enjoyed what afterwards came to be known as the dignity of peerage. As to the term 'baron' in the sense of nobility see Pike's *Constitutional History of the House of Lords* 6, 7.

8 See the Life Peerages Act 1958 s 1(1), (2)(a) (s 1(1) amended by the Constitutional Reform Act 2005 Sch 17 Pt 2 para 15, Sch 18 Pt 5).

805. Classification of peers. The following are the five classes of peers[1]: (1) peers of England[2]; (2) peers of Scotland[3]; (3) peers of Great Britain (that is, those peers created between the dates of the Union with Scotland and the Union with Ireland[4]); (4) peers of Ireland[5]; and (5) peers of the United Kingdom (that is those peers created since the Union with Ireland[6]).

1 As to the creation of peers see PARA 813 et seq. As to the degrees of peerage see PARA 804. As to the privileges of peers see PARA 823 et seq.
2 See PARA 813.
3 See PARA 813.
4 Ie between 1707 and 1801: see the Union with Scotland Act 1706; and the Union with Ireland Act 1800. See PARA 813. As to the Union with Scotland and the Union with Ireland see CONSTITUTIONAL AND ADMINISTRATIVE LAW vol 20 (2014) PARAS 62 et seq, 83.
5 Ie a peer of that part of the United Kingdom called Ireland. See PARA 813.
6 Ie 1801: see the Union with Ireland Act 1800. See PARA 813.

806. Peeresses. In addition to peers there are peeresses in their own right of England, of Scotland and of the United Kingdom. Most of them have inherited their peerages, although hereditary peerages have occasionally been conferred upon women[1]. Peeresses in their own right possess all the privileges of peerage[2]. A life peerage may be conferred on a woman, who thereby becomes entitled to writs of summons to attend and to sit and vote in the House of Lords[3].

1 Eg Viscountess Daventry in 1943. As to hereditary peers see PARA 807.
2 See the Peerage Act 1963 s 6. As to the privileges of peerage generally see PARA 823 et seq; and as to the rights and privileges of peeresses see PARA 827.
3 See the Life Peerages Act 1958 s 1(1), (2)(b), (3) (s 1(1) amended by the Constitutional Reform Act 2005 Sch 17 Pt 2 para 15, Sch 18 Pt 5). As to life peers sitting in the House of Lords see PARA 824.

807. Hereditary peers and life peers. The Crown has historically had power to create hereditary peerages under the prerogative and may also create peerages for life pursuant to statute[1]. Whilst hereditary peerages pass to successive generations[2], life peerages confer the title only for the duration of the peer's life[3]. Under the Life Peerages Act 1958, Her Majesty has power by letters patent to confer on any person a peerage for life entitling him to rank as a baron[4] under such style as may be appointed by the letters patent[5].

1 As to the Crown as the source of peerages PARA 801. As to the royal prerogative generally see CONSTITUTIONAL AND ADMINISTRATIVE LAW vol 20 (2014) PARA 166; CROWN AND ROYAL FAMILY vol 12(1) (Reissue) PARA 46 et seq. As to the creation of peers see PARA 813 et seq. As to the classification of peers see PARA 805.
2 As to the estate in and descent of dignities see PARA 808.
3 See PARAS 808, 830. See also PARA 815.
4 As to barons and the other degrees of peerage see PARA 804.
5 See the Life Peerages Act 1958 s 1(1), (2)(a) (s 1(1) amended by the Constitutional Reform Act 2005 Sch 17 Pt 2 para 15, Sch 18 Pt 5).

808. Estate in and descent of dignities. The dignity of a life peer does not descend to his heirs; he is entitled to rank as a baron only during his life[1].

In contrast, a hereditary peerage is an incorporeal and impartible hereditament, inalienable and descendible according to the words of limitation contained in the grant[2]. A baronetcy is not one of the degrees of peerage[3], but it is nevertheless an incorporeal hereditament descendible in accordance with the grant[4]. Each successive heir to a hereditary peerage takes under the original grant. A declaration of legitimacy obtained pursuant to the provisions of the Legitimacy Declaration Act 1858 (now repealed) is binding for all purposes and extends to dignities[5]. A limitation to a man 'and his heirs' will not carry it to collateral heirs[6]. Baronies by writ are presumed to be limited to heirs of the body[7]. The origin of the early Irish baronies is prescriptive and their descent has always been to the heirs male of the body lawfully begotten or to be begotten of the presumed grantee[8].

A dignity which is descendible is within the Statute of Westminster the Second[9] and is descendible as an estate tail and not as a fee simple conditional, although no place is named in its creation[10].

1 See the Life Peerages Act 1958 s 1(2); and see PARAS 807, 830. See also PARA 815. As to life peers see PARA 807.

2 *Nevil's Case* (1604) 7 Co Rep 33a; *R v Viscount Purbeck* (1678) Show Parl Cas 1 at 5, HL; *Norfolk Earldom Case* [1907] AC 10, HL. For a general discussion of this point see also *Viscountess Rhondda's Case* [1922] 2 AC 339, HL. A peerage cannot, therefore, be the subject of a trust or pass to a trustee in bankruptcy: *Buckhurst Peerage Case* (1876) 2 App Cas 1, HL. See also *Re Earl of Aylesford's Settled Estates* (1886) 32 ChD 162; *Earl Cowley v Countess Cowley* [1901] AC 450, HL. As to grant by letters patent see PARA 815. As to hereditary peers see PARA 807.

3 See PARAS 804, 861–864.

4 *Re Rivett-Carnac's Will* (1885) 30 ChD 136.

5 *Ampthill Peerage Case* [1977] AC 547, [1976] 2 All ER 411, HL.

6 *Wiltes Peerage Case* (1869) LR 4 HL 126, not following the *Devon Peerage Case* (1831) 2 Dow & Cl 200, HL.

7 *Vaux Peerage Case* (1837) 5 Cl & Fin 526, HL; *Braye Peerage Case* (1839) 6 Cl & Fin 757, HL; *Hastings Peerage Case* (1841) 8 Cl & Fin 144, HL. As to the creation of baronies by writ see PARA 822.

8 See PARAS 805, 822.

9 Ie 13 Edw 1 (Statute of Westminster the Second) (1285) c 1 (De Donis Conditionalibus): see REAL PROPERTY AND REGISTRATION vol 87 (2012) PARA 112.

10 *Re Rivett-Carnac's Will* (1885) 30 ChD 136. See REAL PROPERTY AND REGISTRATION vol 87 (2012) PARA 3. The provision of the Settled Land Act 1925 that, where personal chattels are settled to devolve with settled land, they may be sold by the tenant for life applies where such chattels are settled to devolve with a dignity, the dignity as an incorporeal hereditament being 'land' for this purpose: see ss 67, 117(1)(ix) (amended by the Trusts of Land and Appointment of Trustees Act 1996 Sch 3 para 2(13)); and SETTLEMENTS vol 91 (2012) PARAS 842–844.

809. Effect of legitimation and adoption. The statutory provisions relating to legitimation by extraneous law[1] and legitimation by subsequent marriage[2] do not affect the succession to any hereditary dignity or title of honour or render any person capable of succeeding to or transmitting a right to succeed to any dignity or title[3]. Legitimation of the child of a void marriage[4], so far as it affects the succession to a dignity or title of honour, or the devolution of property settled with it, applies only to children born after 28 October 1959[5].

An adoption does not affect the descent of any peerage or dignity or title of honour[6]. Children adopted by peers of the realm are accorded styles and courtesy titles appropriate to the younger children of peers[7].

1 See the Legitimacy Act 1976 s 3; and CHILDREN AND YOUNG PERSONS vol 9 (2012) PARA 145. As to peers in Scotland see the *Strathmore Peerage Case* (1821) 6 Bli NS 487, HL, and Minutes of Evidence (where the father was newly domiciled in England at the time of marriage, and it was held that there was no legitimation); *Lauderdale Peerage Case* (1885) 10 App Cas 692, HL (where the father was domiciled in Scotland and the children, although described in the will as illegitimate, were legitimated by a death-bed marriage). As to legitimation by extraneous law see also CONFLICT OF LAWS vol 19 (2011) PARAS 618–619; and as to domicile see CONFLICT OF LAWS vol 19 (2011) PARA 336 et seq.

2 See the Legitimacy Act 1976 s 2; and CHILDREN AND YOUNG PERSONS vol 9 (2012) PARA 145.

3 Legitimacy Act 1976 Sch 1 para 4(2). Apart from s 1 (see CHILDREN AND YOUNG PERSONS vol 9 (2012) PARA 144), nothing in the Legitimacy Act 1976 affects the devolution of any property limited, expressly or not, to devolve (as nearly as the law permits) along with any dignity or title of honour: Sch 1 para 4(3). As to evidence in relation to legitimacy see PARA 860.

The position in Scotland is different in the case of succession to a pre-Union hereditary title: see the unreported judgment of Lord Lyon King of Arms dated 28 February 2008.

4 Ie under the Legitimacy Act 1976 s 1: see CHILDREN AND YOUNG PERSONS vol 9 (2012) PARA 144.

5 Legitimacy Act 1976 Sch 1 para 4(1). Section 1 does not, however, affect the operation or construction of any disposition coming into operation before 29 October 1959 except so far as may be necessary to avoid the severance from a dignity or title of honour of property limited, expressly or not, to devolve (as nearly as the law permits) along with the dignity or title of honour: Sch 1 para 3(b).

6 Adoption Act 1976 s 44(1); Adoption and Children Act 2002 s 71(1). Nor does it affect the devolution of any property limited, expressly or not, to devolve (as nearly as the law permits) with a peerage or dignity or title of honour (Adoption Act 1976 s 44(2); Adoption and Children Act 2002 s 71(2)); however, this applies only if and so far as a contrary intention is not expressed in the instrument, and has effect subject to the terms of the instrument (Adoption Act 1976 s 44(3); Adoption and Children Act 2002 s 71(3)). See also CHILDREN AND YOUNG PERSONS vol 9 (2012) PARA 416.

7 See the Royal Warrant dated 30 April 2004. The Scottish titles of 'Master of' and 'Mistress of' are specifically excepted: see the Royal Warrant dated 30 April 2004.

810. Effect of artificial insemination or surrogacy. Prior to 4 April 1988, a child born as a result of artificial insemination by a third party donor was considered illegitimate and the donor, not the mother's husband, was the legal father of the child[1].

Where a child was born in England and Wales between 4 April 1988 and 1 August 1991 as the result of the artificial insemination of a woman who: (1) was at the time of the insemination a party to a marriage (being a marriage which had not at that time been dissolved or annulled); and (2) was artificially inseminated with the semen of some person other than the other party to that marriage, then, unless it is proved to the satisfaction of the court that the other party to that marriage did not consent to the insemination, the child is to be treated in law as the child of the parties to that marriage and is not to be treated as the child of any person other than the parties to that marriage[2]. This does not affect the succession to any dignity or title of honour or render any person capable of succeeding to or transmitting a right to succeed to any such dignity or title[3].

In relation to children carried by women as a result of the placing in them of embryos or of sperm and eggs, or of their artificial insemination (as the case may be), between 1 August 1991 and 6 April 2009[4], the provisions of the Human Fertilisation and Embryology Act 1990 relating to assisted reproduction[5] define the mother and the father of the child in question; however, nothing in those provisions[6] affects the succession to any dignity or title of honour or renders any person capable of succeeding to or transmitting a right to succeed to any such dignity or title, or the devolution of any property limited, expressly or not, to devolve (as nearly as the law permits) along with any dignity or title of honour[7].

In relation to children carried by women as a result of the placing in them of embryos or of sperm and eggs, or their artificial insemination (as the case may be), after 6 April 2009[8], the provisions of the Human Fertilisation and Embryology Act 2008 relating to assisted reproduction[9] define the mother, father or other parent of the child in question; however, nothing in those provisions[10] affects the succession to any dignity or title of honour or renders any person capable of succeeding to or transmitting a right to succeed to any such dignity or title, or the devolution of any property limited, expressly or not, to devolve (as nearly as the law permits) along with any dignity or title of honour[11].

1 See the Family Law Reform Act 1987 (Commencement No 1) Order 1988, SI 1988/425; *Re M (Child Support Act: parentage)* [1997] 3 FCR 383, [1997] 2 FLR 90; and CHILDREN AND YOUNG PERSONS vol 9 (2012) PARA 113.

2 See the Family Law Reform Act 1987 s 27(1); the Human Fertilisation and Embryology Act 1990 s 49(4); and CHILDREN AND YOUNG PERSONS vol 9 (2012) PARAS 6, 113.

3 See the Family Law Reform Act 1987 s 27(3); and CHILDREN AND YOUNG PERSONS vol 9 (2012) PARAS 6, 113.

4 See the Human Fertilisation and Embryology Act 1990 s 49(3); the Human Fertilisation and Embryology Act 2008 s 57(2); and CHILDREN AND YOUNG PERSONS vol 9 (2012) PARAS 114–116.

5 See the Human Fertilisation and Embryology Act 1990 ss 27–29; and CHILDREN AND YOUNG PERSONS vol 9 (2012) PARAS 115–117.

6 Ie specifically the Human Fertilisation and Embryology Act 1990 ss 27(1), 28(2)–(4), (5A)–(5I), read with s 29: see s 29(4) (amended by the Human Fertilisation and Embryology (Deceased Fathers) Act 2003 s 2(1), Schedule para 16).

7 See the Human Fertilisation and Embryology Act 1990 s 29(4) (as amended: see note 6); and CHILDREN AND YOUNG PERSONS vol 9 (2012) PARA 118.

8 See the Human Fertilisation and Embryology Act 2008 s 57(1); and CHILDREN AND YOUNG PERSONS vol 9 (2012) PARA 120.

9 See the Human Fertilisation and Embryology Act 2008 ss 33–48; and CHILDREN AND YOUNG PERSONS vol 9 (2012) PARAS 121–127.

10 Ie specifically the Human Fertilisation and Embryology Act 2008 ss 33(1), 35–47, read with s 48: see s 48(7).

11 See the Human Fertilisation and Embryology Act 2008 s 48(7); and CHILDREN AND YOUNG PERSONS vol 9 (2012) PARA 128.

811. Effect of a potentially polygamous marriage. The succession to any dignity or title of honour is not affected by the operation of the statutory provision which confirms that a marriage entered into outside England and Wales before 8 January 1996 between parties neither of whom is already married is not void under the law of England and Wales on the ground that it is entered into under a law which permits polygamy and that either party is domiciled in England and Wales[1].

1 See the Private International Law (Miscellaneous Provisions) Act 1995 ss 5, 6(6)(d); and CONFLICT OF LAWS vol 19 (2011) PARA 523.

812. Consequences of issue of gender recognition certificate. A person of either gender who is aged at least 18 may make an application for a gender recognition certificate on the basis of either living in the other gender, or having changed gender under the law of a country or territory outside the United Kingdom[1]. The fact that a person's gender has become the acquired gender does not affect the descent of any peerage or dignity or title of honour, and does not affect the devolution of any property limited, expressly or not, by a will or other instrument to devolve (as nearly as the law permits) along with any peerage or dignity or title of honour unless an intention that it should do so is expressed in the will or other instrument[2].

1   See the Gender Recognition Act 2004 s 1(1); and REGISTRATION CONCERNING THE INDIVIDUAL vol 88 (2012) PARA 267.
2   Gender Recognition Act 2004 s 16.

(2) CREATION OF PEERS

(i) Limitations on Creation

813.   Limitations on creation. The Crown has power to create any number of peerages of the United Kingdom[1]. Since the Act of Union with Scotland[2] no new peer of England or Scotland can be created[3]; and since the Act of Union with Ireland[4] no new peer of Great Britain can be created[5]. The power to create new peers in the peerage of Ireland[6] is not now exercised[7].

1   See CONSTITUTIONAL AND ADMINISTRATIVE LAW vol 20 (2014) PARA 569. As to the classification of peers see PARA 805.
2   Ie the Union with Scotland Act 1706.
3   See the Union with Scotland Act 1706 preamble art XXII (repealed).
4   Ie the Union with Ireland Act 1800.
5   See the Union with Ireland Act 1800 art 4.
6   Ie under the Union with Ireland Act 1800 art 4, which entitled the Crown to create a limited number of new Irish peers in 'that part of the United Kingdom called Ireland', as the peerages existing at the time of the Union of Great Britain and Ireland became extinct: see art 4; *Bloomfield Peerage Case* (1831) 2 Dow & Cl 344, HL; *Fermoy Peerage Case* (1856) 5 HL Cas 716.
7   The power was last exercised in 1898, and it now appears to be obsolete as the only part of Ireland within the United Kingdom and forming part of Her Majesty's dominions is Northern Ireland. See the Northern Ireland Constitution Act 1973 s 1 (repealed); and CONSTITUTIONAL AND ADMINISTRATIVE LAW vol 20 (2014) PARAS 3, 569. As to the peerage of Ireland see PARA 805.

(ii) Current Methods of Creating New Peers

814.   Creation of peerage by letters patent. Hereditary peerages may be conferred on men and women alike[1], as may life peerages[2]. Today a peerage is created by the Sovereign by letters patent under the Great Seal[3]. The letters patent are enrolled on the patent rolls[4].

1   The power to create hereditary peerages is now rarely exercised: see PARA 821 note 5. As to hereditary peers see PARA 807. As to peeresses in their own right see PARA 806.
2   See the Life Peerages Act 1958 s 1(3). As to life peers see PARA 807.
3   See the Life Peerages Act 1958 s 1(1) (amended by the Constitutional Reform Act 2005 Sch 17 Pt 2 para 15, Sch 18 Pt 5); and CONSTITUTIONAL AND ADMINISTRATIVE LAW vol 20 (2014) PARA 569. As to the form of grant by letters patent see PARA 815; and as to letters patent generally see CONSTITUTIONAL AND ADMINISTRATIVE LAW vol 20 (2014) PARA 594. As to the use of the Great Seal see CONSTITUTIONAL AND ADMINISTRATIVE LAW vol 20 (2014) PARA 583; and as to a warrant under the sign manual as authority for passing the seal see CONSTITUTIONAL AND ADMINISTRATIVE LAW vol 20 (2014) PARA 586. As to historical methods of creation see PARAS 821–822.
4   As to enrolment on the patent rolls see CONSTITUTIONAL AND ADMINISTRATIVE LAW vol 20 (2014) PARA 593 note 3.

815.   Form of grant by letters patent. The Life Peerages Act 1958 provides that the Sovereign has power by letters patent to confer on any person a peerage for life[1]. Except to the extent authorised by these provisions, a limitation by letters patent of the dignity for the life of the patentee is invalid[2].

Letters patent creating a hereditary peerage must specify the patentee, the name of the dignity and its limitation to future heirs of the patentee[3]. The limitation must be one known to the law[4]. The rule in England is a limitation to heirs male of the body lawfully begotten or to be begotten with an occasional addition of special remainders to bring in the daughters and their issue, brothers, nephews and collaterals, but ultimately the descent is always fixed in an heir male line. A limitation to heirs male as distinct from heirs male of the body is void in England[5], but not in Scotland. The presumption of law now in the case of a Scottish peerage, where the original grant has been lost or cannot be found, is that the limitation was to the heirs male generally[6], but this presumption is rebuttable[7].

1   See the Life Peerages Act 1958 s 1(1) (amended by the Constitutional Reform Act 2005 Sch 17 Pt 2 para 15, Sch 18 Pt 5). As to life peers see PARA 807.

2   *Wensleydale Peerage Case* (1856) 5 HL Cas 958.

3   For forms of letters patent to be used see the Crown Office (Forms and Proclamations Rules) Order 1992, SI 1992/1730, art 2(1), Schedule Pt III (amended by SI 2000/3064). As to hereditary peers see PARA 807.

4   *Wiltes Peerage Case* (1869) LR 4 HL 126 at 153, 162 per Lord Chelmsford LC; *Cope v Earl De la Warr* (1873) 8 Ch App 982; *Buckhurst Peerage Case* (1876) 2 App Cas 1 at 20, HL, per Lord Cairns LC; Cruise on Dignities (2nd Edn) c 3 s 76. A grant without words of limitation is bad in England. In Scotland a grant in fee would be presumed.

5   *Devon Peerage Case* (1831) 2 Dow & Cl 200, HL; *Wiltes Peerage Case* (1869) LR 4 HL 126. See Nicolas's Report on Proceedings on Claim to the Earldom of Devon (1832), with appendices of the Nevill, Purbeck, Lovell and Oxford Cases; Finlason's History of Hereditary Dignities 98 et seq, with special reference to the Earldom of Wiltes (1869).

6   *Perth Earldom Case* (1848) 2 HL Cas 865; *Herries Peerage Case* (1858) LR 2 Sc & Div 258, HL; *Mar Peerage Case* (1875) 1 App Cas 1 at 24, 36, HL (and see the cases there cited). As to remainders generally see Palmer's Peerage Law in England 64 et seq.

7   *Herries Peerage Case* (1858) LR 2 Sc & Div 258, HL; *Mar Peerage Case* (1876) 1 App Cas 1, HL.

816. Effect of shifting clause in letters patent. A shifting clause in letters patent directing that a dignity should pass from the holder of the dignity to another person by special remainder upon the holder's succession to an older or greater dignity is bad; but this does not render the letters patent themselves invalid; nor are they by reason of any limitation becoming incapable of taking effect[1]. A special remainder after the exhaustion of the original limitation is good, the remainder taking effect as a new grant[2].

1   *Buckhurst Peerage Case* (1876) 2 App Cas 1, HL; cf the *Wiltes Peerage Case* (1869) LR 4 HL 126. A shifting clause may, however, be valid to impede succession: *Cope v Earl De la Warr* (1873) 8 Ch App 982. An example of a shifting clause may be found in the very elaborate letters patent creating the earldom of Cromartie, printed in Sir William Fraser's 'Cromartie Book'. At the date at which this volume states the law there had been no occasion for an examination of the validity of the patent by the House of Lords.

2   *Purbeck's Case* (1678) Collins's Baronies by Writ (1734 Edn) 293; Report on the Dignity of a Peer of the Realm (1829 reprint) vol II p 58. This view is disputed in Palmer's Peerage Law in England 83–85.

817. Creation of peerage by Act of Parliament. In order to create a peerage when the desired limitations of the dignity are such as cannot validly be granted by letters patent[1], recourse must be had to an Act of Parliament[2].

1   As to creation of peerages by letters patent see PARA 814; and as to limitations see PARA 815.

2   For the need see the *Lucas Peerage Case* (1907).

818. Territorial designation to title. The naming of a place is not essential to the creation of a peerage[1]. It is customary, however, to include a territorial designation on the creation of a viscount or baron[2]. If there is more than one peerage having the same personal name, a place name will form part of the name of the second or any subsequent peerage[3].

1   *R v Knollys* (1694) 1 Ld Raym 10; *Re Rivett-Carnac's Will* (1885) 30 ChD 136.
2   See the Crown Office (Forms and Proclamations Rules) Order 1992, SI 1992/1730, art 2(1), Schedule Pt III, Forms D, E (amended by SI 2000/3064).
3   Eg Simon, created in 1940, Simon of Wythenshawe, created in 1947, and Simon of Glaisdale, appointed a Lord of Appeal in Ordinary in 1971. In such circumstances a subsequent peerage is sometimes created with a double territorial designation in the form Somervell of Harrow, of Ewelme, co Oxford. Where a barony was created by writ of summons and sitting (see PARA 822), there was no territorial addition unless at some time two or more persons of the same name were summoned to the same Parliament. Then the territorial addition forms part of the name of the peerage (eg Strange of Knokin).

819. Oath of allegiance. The oath of allegiance[1] or solemn affirmation is to be taken by all members on their introduction to the House of Lords[2].

1   See the Promissory Oaths Act 1868 s 14(5). See also CONSTITUTIONAL AND ADMINISTRATIVE LAW vol 20 (2014) PARA 599. For the form of oath see s 2.
2   Since 1999 the creation of a hereditary peerage does not entitle the peer to sit in the House of Lords (see PARA 825). As regards a peer who is not a member of the House of Lords, it is not clear when, if at all, the occasion for taking the oath of allegiance would now arise.

820. Refusal of peerage. A person cannot refuse to accept a peerage[1], even if conferred upon him in his infancy[2], but the usual custom is for the Prime Minister to make a preliminary inquiry whether the proposed grantee would welcome the grant.

1   *Egerton v Earl Brownlow* (1853) 4 HL Cas 1. See CONSTITUTIONAL AND ADMINISTRATIVE LAW vol 20 (2014) PARA 572. Refusal of a peerage is to be distinguished from disclaimer: see PARAS 836–837.
2   *Mortimer Sackville's Case* (1719), cited in 2 App Cas 6n, HL; *Duke of Queensberry's Case* (1719) 1 P Wms 582, HL.

(iii) Historical Methods of Creation

821. Modes of creation. Peers of the various classes and degrees[1] have been created by Act of Parliament[2], by charter[3] and by letters patent[4]. Almost all peerages created today are created by letters patent pursuant to the Life Peerages Act 1958[5]. Baronies were originally created by writ of summons to Parliament followed by a sitting and this appears to have been the method usually followed down to the middle of the reign of Henry VIII[6]. A writ by the name of any rank in the peerage other than that of baron does not create a peerage of that rank[7]. The first creation of a baron by letters patent appears to have been in 1388, when John de Beauchamp of Holt was created Lord de Beauchamp and Baron of Kidderminster, the grant being to him and the heirs male of his body[8].

In the time of Henry VI the opinion was held that peerages by tenure existed[9], and this opinion persisted in some degree until 1861[10].

1   See PARAS 804–805.
2   See *Prince's Case* (1606) 8 Co Rep 1 at 13b. As to creation by Act of Parliament see PARA 817. It is sometimes difficult to decide whether a particular instrument is an Act of Parliament or a charter granted in Parliament, but the distinguishing feature seems to be the assent of the Commons in full Parliament. The validity of the instrument may depend on this distinction. As to such Acts see Palmer's Peerage Law in England 46 et seq. The early view was that higher dignities, such as dukedoms, marquisates and earldoms, which entitled the holders to attend the King's Councils and Parliaments, were created by public investiture by the Sovereign himself, generally in Parliament, and that written documents were evidence of creation rather than creation itself. Any special course of succession and special money or land grants to support the

dignity would, of necessity, be indicated in an Act of Parliament, a charter or letters patent. Viscounts and barons seem never to have been invested. Subtle changes of wording seem to indicate that by the middle of the fifteenth century the view was that earldoms and higher dignities were created by charter or patent and that investiture was the outward sign of creation. Modern patents contain a clause dispensing with investiture.

3   See notes 2, 4.

4   As to creation of peerages by letters patent see PARA 814. In the Report on the Dignity of a Peer of the Realm (1829 reprint) vol V, a number of charters and letters patent creating dignities are printed of which a few relate to baronies. These creations are by letters patent of Henry VI and Edward IV. The earlier creations contained no clear limitation, but some make provision for the sustentation of the dignity which is limited to heirs or heirs male of the body. Stamp duty, formerly exigible on the grant of letters patent of peerages and other honours, dignities and promotions, was abolished by the Finance Act 1937 s 30 (repealed) and the Finance Act 1938 ss 51, 55(7), Sch 5 (repealed).

5   See PARA 814. The power to create hereditary peerages is now rarely exercised. At the date at which this volume states the law, the most recent occasion was in 2011 when HRH Prince William was created Duke of Cambridge, Earl of Strathearn and Baron Carrickfergus. The most recent non-royal hereditary peerage was created in 1984, when Harold Macmillan was created the Earl of Stockton and Viscount Macmillan of Ovenden. As to life peers and hereditary peers see PARA 807.

6   As to the creation of baronies by writ see PARA 822.

7   *Norfolk Earldom Case* [1907] AC 10, HL.

8   Report on the Dignity of a Peer of the Realm (1829 reprint) vol V p 81; Palmer's Peerage Law in England 263.

9   See the *Arundel Case* (1433) 4 Rot Parl 441, cited in Palmer's Peerage Law in England 179. Coke, Selden, Madox and Blackstone were of opinion that there was a sound historical foundation for this view.

10 See the *Berkeley Peerage Case* (1861) 8 HL Cas 21. The whole topic is reviewed in Palmer's Peerage Law in England 178 et seq.

822.   Creation of barony by writ. Formerly, a writ of summons to Parliament addressed to a person, followed by the sitting of that person in Parliament, created in him a barony by writ descendible to the heirs general of his body, unless the person summoned was an official or his presence in Parliament was accounted for by some other reason[1]. There must be definite proof that the person summoned actually sat in Parliament[2]. Proof that a person received a writ of summons to Parliament raises no presumption that the person actually sat[3]; nor is it sufficient to prove that a person received a writ of summons and account for his failure to attend, as where he was serving abroad in the wars when the Parliament was held[4]. Proof that a person sat in Parliament raises a presumption that he sat in response to a writ of summons[5]. The sitting must have been during the Parliament to which the person was summoned. His presence during the preliminary proceedings, for example prior to the arrival of one of the estates, or during the subsequent proceedings, for example after the departure of one of the estates, is not sufficient[6].

A writ of summons known as a 'writ of acceleration' was formerly a device to enable the heir apparent to a peer possessing more than one peerage entitled to a writ of summons to the House of Lords to be summoned to the House of Lords in the place of the most junior title, thus enabling the heir to take up a seat in the House of Lords before his father's death but avoiding the creation of a further peerage[7]. Writs of acceleration have not been possible since the House of Lords Act 1999 changed the law so that a hereditary peerage no longer confers the right to sit in the House of Lords[8] unless the individual is specifically excepted[9].

A barony created by writ is also known as a barony in fee. There is only one Irish barony in fee, that of le Poer, in virtue of a writ of summons and sitting in the Irish House of Lords in 1375[10].

1   This doctrine is historically unsound, but it is now well entrenched in the law: see the *Clifton Barony Case* (1673) Collins's Baronies by Writ (1734 Edn) 291, HL; Co Litt 16b; Com Dig, Dignity (C 3). See also the *Vaux Peerage Case* (1837) 5 Cl & Fin 526, HL; *Braye Peerage Case* (1839) 6 Cl & Fin 757, HL; *Hastings Peerage Case* (1841) 8 Cl & Fin 144 at 157, HL; and the *Wharton Peerage Case* (1845) 12 Cl & Fin 295, HL. Grant of a hereditary peerage by letters patent requires words of inheritance, whereas a writ of summons to the House of Lords, followed by taking a seat, enured to the heirs of the grantee's body without express words. In the latter case the writ had to be followed by taking a seat in Parliament, whereas in the former the title enured and descended in accordance with the grant, whether the grantee took his seat or not: 1 Bl Com (14th Edn) 400.

2   For this purpose Parliament means a Parliament consisting of lords spiritual and temporal and the elected representatives of counties, cities and boroughs: see PARLIAMENT vol 78 (2010) PARA 801. The earliest Parliament recognised to fall within this description is the Model Parliament of 1295, and at least one subsequent so-called Parliament, the Parliament of Lincoln held in 1300, has not been regarded as falling within this description: *St John Peerage Case* [1915] AC 282, HL (where the phrase 'plenum parlementum' is discussed); *Beauchamp Barony Case* [1925] AC 153, HL.

3   *Beauchamp Barony Case* [1925] AC 153, HL; *St John Peerage Case* [1915] AC 282, HL (and the cases there cited). As to evidence of creation of peerage see also PARA 856.

4   *De Wahull Peerage Case* (1892) cited in [1915] AC at 291.

5   *St John Peerage Case* [1915] AC 282 at 305, HL, per Lord Parker of Waddington; approved in the *Beauchamp Barony Case* [1925] AC 153, HL.

6   *Beauchamp Barony Case* [1925] AC 153, HL. As to evidence of sitting generally see PARA 856.

7   See Palmer's Peerage Law in England 129–132; Pike's Constitutional History of the House of Lords 273. In one case a son was summoned in respect of his mother's barony: *Montacute and Monthermer Peerages Case* (1874) LR 7 HL 305; *Pole of Montague Peerage Case* (1929). In former times, but not since the reign of Henry VIII, writs were also issued in right of the wife: see Palmer's Peerage Law in England 133–136. A writ of acceleration was last used in 1992 when Viscount Cranbourne was issued with a writ of summons in acceleration to a minor barony held by his father, the Marquis of Salisbury.

8   See the House of Lords Act 1999 s 1; and PARA 825.

9   See the House of Lords Act 1999 s 2; and PARA 825. Any writ of summons issued for the Parliament in session when the House of Lords Act 1999 was passed in right of a hereditary peerage had no effect after that session unless it was issued to a person who, at the end of the session, was specifically excepted: s 5(2). As to hereditary peers see PARA 807.

10 This barony is referred to in the *Le Power and Coroghmore Barony Case* (1921) Report of Attorney General 5, 6.

(3) PRIVILEGES AND PRECEDENCE

(i) Privileges

823. Privilege of sitting and voting in Parliament. The most important privilege of a peer is to sit and vote in Parliament[1]. However, whilst it is a privilege, membership of the House of Lords is not an automatic or universal right for all peers[2]. For those who are entitled, though, it is not only a privilege, but a duty, for members of the House of Lords must attend the sittings of the House or, if they cannot do so, must obtain leave of absence[3].

However, a member of the House of Lords is, while he holds any disqualifying judicial office, disqualified for sitting or voting in the House[4] (but is not disqualified for receiving a writ of summons to attend)[5].

1   *Norfolk Earldom Case* [1907] AC 10 at 17, HL.

2   The privilege extends to life peers, and to elected hereditary peers (of any class of peerage save those who are only peers of Ireland: see PARA 825 note 1): see PARLIAMENT vol 78 (2010) PARA 834. As to the privilege, and as to restrictions on sitting in the House of Lords, see PARAS 824–825. As to the classification of peers see PARA 805. As to life peers and hereditary peers see PARA 807.

3   HL Standing Orders (2013) (Public Business) no 22(1). A member who is unable to attend regularly need not apply for leave of absence if he proposes to attend as often as he reasonably can: HL Standing Orders (2013) (Public Business) no 22(1).
4   Constitutional Reform Act 2005 s 137(3). As to disqualifying judicial office see s 137(4) (which refers to the offices specified in the House of Commons Disqualification Act 1975 Sch 1 Pt 1; and the Northern Ireland Assembly Disqualification Act 1975 Sch 1 Pt 1); and PARLIAMENT vol 78 (2010) PARA 908.
5   Constitutional Reform Act 2005 s 137(5).

824. Entitlement of life peers to sit and vote in the House of Lords.

Life peers are entitled to receive writs of summons to attend the House of Lords and sit and vote accordingly[1]. This does not, however, entitle a person to receive a writ of summons to attend the House of Lords, or to sit and vote in that House, at any time when disqualified by law[2].

1   See the Life Peerages Act 1958 s 1(2)(b). See also PARLIAMENT vol 78 (2010) PARA 843. As to the disqualification of members of the House of Lords for sitting or voting while holding judicial office see the Constitutional Reform Act 2005 s 137; and PARA 823 text and note 4.
2   See the Life Peerages Act 1958 s 1(4). The disqualifications apply to:
    (1)   persons under the age of 21 years (see HL Standing Orders (2013) (Public Business) no 2; and PARLIAMENT vol 78 (2010) PARA 840);
    (2)   aliens (see the Act of Settlement (1700 or 1701) s 3; and BRITISH NATIONALITY vol 4 (2011) PARA 411; PARLIAMENT vol 78 (2010) PARA 840);
    (3)   bankrupts (see the Insolvency Act 1986 ss 426A(1)(b), (4), 427(1)(a), (3); and BANKRUPTCY AND INDIVIDUAL INSOLVENCY vol 5 (2013) PARA 722; PARLIAMENT vol 78 (2010) PARA 840);
    (4)   persons being convicted of treason or certain other offences, until pardoned, or until completion of sentence (see the Forfeiture Act 1870 s 2; and CRIMINAL PROCEDURE vol 27 (2010) PARA 64; PARLIAMENT vol 78 (2010) PARA 840);
    (5)   holders of disqualifying judicial office (see note 1; and PARA 823 text and note 4).

825. Eligibility of certain hereditary peers to sit and vote in the House of Lords.

Until 1999 holders of hereditary peerages were automatically entitled to a seat in the House of Lords[1]. The House of Lords Act 1999 introduced the rule that no-one is to be a member of the House of Lords by virtue of a hereditary peerage[2]; however, at any one time 90 hereditary peers are excepted from the rule[3] and, once excepted, a hereditary peer continues to be so throughout his life (until an Act of Parliament provides to the contrary)[4].

The excepted hereditary peers consist of the following categories:

(1)   two peers elected[5] by the Labour hereditary peers; 42 peers elected by the Conservative hereditary peers; three peers elected by the Liberal Democrat hereditary peers; 28 peers elected by the cross-bench hereditary peers;

(2)   15 peers, elected by the whole House, from among those ready to serve as Deputy Speakers or in any other office as the House may require; and

(3)   any peer holding the office of Earl Marshal or performing the office of Lord Great Chamberlain[6].

Standing Orders make the following provision for filling vacancies among the people excepted from the rule[7]. In the event of the death of a hereditary peer excepted under category (1) only the excepted hereditary peers in the group in which the vacancy has occurred are entitled to vote[8]. In the event of the death of a hereditary peer excepted under category (2) the whole House is entitled to vote[9]. The Clerk of the Parliaments must maintain, and publish annually, a register of hereditary peers (other than peers of Ireland) who wish to stand in any by-election[10]. By-elections are conducted in accordance with arrangements made by the Clerk of the Parliaments and must generally take place within three months of a vacancy occurring[11]. In the event of a tie between two or more candidates the matter (if not resolved by the electoral arrangements adopted by the House) is decided by the drawing of lots[12]. The Clerk of the Parliaments may refer any question concerning the propriety of the electoral process to the Committee for Privileges[13].

Any question whether a person is excepted from the rule is decided by the Clerk of the Parliaments, whose certificate is conclusive[14].

Hereditary peers elected under the procedure described above are entitled to sit and vote in the House of Lords provided they are not disqualified for membership of the House[15].

1   This applied to peers of England, Great Britain and the United Kingdom. As to the classification of peers see PARA 805. As to hereditary peers see PARA 807.

    Peers of Scotland were also entitled to sit in the House of Lords: see the Peerage Act 1963 s 4. Prior to the Peerage Act 1963, Scottish peers elected representatives to sit in the House of Lords. See further PARLIAMENT vol 78 (2010) PARA 834 note 4.

    Peers of Ireland were excluded (see the Union with Ireland Act 1800; *Robinson v Lord Rokeby* (1803) 8 Ves 601; *Irish Peer Case* (1806) Russ & Ry 117), but the Union with Ireland Act 1800 provided for their representation in the Parliament of the United Kingdom by 28 elected representative peers of Ireland (see art 4 (as originally enacted)). However, the right to elect representative peers ceased to be effective on the passing of the Irish Free State (Agreement) Act 1922: see *Petition of the Earl of Antrim* [1967] 1 AC 691, [1966] 3 WLR 1141, HL. No election was held after that, and the last representative peer of Ireland died in 1961. See further PARLIAMENT vol 78 (2010) PARA 834 note 4.

2   House of Lords Act 1999 s 1. See also *Baron Mereworth v Ministry of Justice* [2011] EWHC 1589 (Ch), [2012] Ch 325 (the House of Lords Act 1999 s 1 removes the right to receive a writ of summons entitling a hereditary peer to be a member of the House of Lords).

    The House of Lords Act 1999 s 1 does not apply in relation to anyone excepted from it by or in accordance with Standing Orders of the House: House of Lords Act 1999 s 2(1).

3   House of Lords Act 1999 s 2(2), (5). Anyone excepted as holder of the office of Earl Marshal, or as performing the office of Lord Great Chamberlain, does not count towards that limit: s 2(2).

4   House of Lords Act 1999 s 2(3).

5   Elections are conducted in accordance with arrangements made by the Clerk of the Parliaments: see HL Standing Orders (2013) (Public Business) no 9(3). As to the requirements of registration see HL Standing Orders (2013) (Public Business) no 9(4).

6   HL Standing Orders (2013) (Public Business) no 9(1), (2). See note 3.

7   House of Lords Act 1999 s 2(4); HL Standing Orders (2013) (Public Business) nos 9(7), (8), 10(1), (4).

8   HL Standing Orders (2013) (Public Business) no 10(2), (4).

9   HL Standing Orders (2013) (Public Business) no 10(3), (4).

10 HL Standing Orders (2013) (Public Business) no 10(5). Any hereditary peer (not previously in receipt of a writ of summons) who wishes to be included in this register maintained by the Clerk of the Parliaments must petition the House and any such petition is referred to the Lord Chancellor to consider and report upon whether such peer has established his right to be included in the register: see HL Standing Orders (2013) (Public Business) no 11; and PARA 845.

11 HL Standing Orders (2013) (Public Business) no 10(6). The time limit was extended in order to allow the by-election following the death of Lord Methuen to take place on 21 October 2014, after the summer recess: see 755 HL Official Report (5th series), 30 July 2014, col 1593.

12 HL Standing Orders (2013) (Public Business) nos 9(5), 10(7).

13 HL Standing Orders (2007) (Public Business) nos 9(6), 10(7).

14 House of Lords Act 1999 s 2(6).

15 As to disqualification see PARA 824 note 2.

826.   Non-excepted hereditary peers entitled to vote and sit in the House of Commons.   The holder of a hereditary peerage is not disqualified by virtue of that peerage for voting at elections to the House of Commons or being, or being elected as, a member of that House[1]. This does not apply to any peer who is a member of the House of Lords[2].

1   House of Lords Act 1999 s 3(1). Peers of Ireland were qualified to be or be elected as a member
     of the House of Commons: see the Union with Ireland Act 1800 art 4. As to the classification of
     peers see PARA 805. As to hereditary peers see PARA 807.

2   Ie any hereditary peer who is excepted from the operation of the House of Lords Act 1999 s 1
     by virtue of s 2 (see PARA 825): see s 3(2).

827.   Peeresses.   Peeresses in their own right and peeresses by marriage
generally have the same rights and privileges as peers[1]. Although a peeress by
marriage loses the rights and privileges if she marries a commoner, a peeress in
her own right in the same event retains them[2]. A woman on whom a life peerage
has been conferred has the right to sit and vote in Parliament[3].

1   See PARA 806. The Peerage Act 1963 provides that a woman who is the holder of a hereditary
     peerage (whatever the terms of the letters patent or other instrument, if any, creating that
     peerage) has the same right to receive writs of summons to attend the House of Lords, and to sit
     and vote in that House, and is subject to the same disqualifications in respect of membership of
     the House of Commons and elections to that House, as a man holding that peerage (see s 6);
     however, in 1999 the automatic right of hereditary peers to membership of the House of Lords
     was ended (see PARAS 803, 825). Peeresses by marriage have never been entitled to sit and vote
     in the House of Lords.
          Although the privilege of peerage (as opposed to Parliamentary privilege) extends to a
     peeress by marriage, the provisions which provide for equality of marriage (see the Marriage
     (Same Sex Couples) Act 2013 s 11(1), (2); and MATRIMONIAL AND CIVIL PARTNERSHIP LAW) do
     not apply to the common law concerning the acquisition of a right to, or interest in, a peerage,
     and all titles, rights, offices, privileges and precedence attaching to it, by a person who marries
     or who is married to a peer holding that peerage: Marriage (Same Sex Couples) Act 2013
     (Consequential and Contrary Provisions and Scotland) Order 2014, SI 2014/560, Sch 2 para 2.

2   *Acton's Case* (1603) 4 Co Rep 117a; *Countess of Rutland's Case* (1606) 6 Co Rep 52b; Co Litt
     16b; *Countess Rivers' Case* (1650) Sty 252; *Anon* (1676) 1 Vent 298; cf *Earl Cowley v Countess
     Cowley* [1901] AC 450, HL; 1 Bl Com (14th Edn) 401; HL Standing Orders (2013) (Public
     Business) no 83.

3   See the Life Peerages Act 1958 s 1(1), (2)(b), (3) (s 1(1) amended by the Constitutional Reform
     Act 2005 Sch 17 Pt 2 para 15, Sch 18 Pt 5); and PARA 806.

828.   Privileges as regards legal proceedings.   A peer is at all times free from
arrest in civil cases[1]. The distinction between civil and criminal process depends
upon whether the arrest is to punish a breach of the law or merely to compel
performance of a civil obligation[2]. Process for contempt of court may be served
against him only if the contempt is by its nature or by its incidents criminal[3].
Since the ordinary remedies against a receiver are not available against him, a
peer ought not to be appointed as a receiver[4]. A court order may, however, be
enforced against a peer by sequestration[5].

Where a party to legal proceedings desires to plead privilege of Parliament on
account of peerage, he must assert that he is a peer and a member of the House
of Lords; if he merely alleges facts on which the jury may find that he is a peer,
he will be treated as being a commoner and will be estopped by judgment against
him from setting up his peerage[6]. It has been held that, if the peerage is denied by
the other side, the party pleading peerage must state in his reply how he claims
the dignity[7].

In legal proceedings a peer of Ireland should be described by his proper name
with the addition of his title and degree, but without the expression 'commonly
called', which is used only with courtesy titles of children of dukes, marquesses,
earls, viscounts or barons[8].

The former privilege of a peer to be tried by his peers in cases of treason,
felony or misprision of either has been abolished[9]; and criminal proceedings
against peers now follow the same course as for any other person[10].

A peer who is a claimant and out of the jurisdiction must give the usual security for costs[11].

A peer may provide professional legal services as an advocate in civil and criminal causes (including claims of peerage brought before the Committee for Privileges and Conduct), and in proceedings of private bill committees of either House of Parliament[12].

1   *Countess of Shrewsbury's Case* (1612) 12 Co Rep 94, PC; *Foster v Jackson* (1615) Hob 52 at 61; *Couche v Lord Arundel* (1802) 3 East 127. See also PARLIAMENT vol 78 (2010) PARA 1085. This privilege extends to Scottish and Irish peers: *Davis v Lord Rendlesham* (1817) 7 Taunt 679; *Storey v Birmingham* (1823) 3 Dow & Ry KB 488; *Coates v Lord Hawarden* (1827) 7 B & C 388; *Digby v Lord Stirling* (1831) 8 Bing 55.
2   *Stourton v Stourton* [1963] P 302, [1963] 1 All ER 606 (attachment).
3   *Wellesley v Duke of Beaufort, Long Wellesley's Case* (1831) 2 Russ & M 639 at 665; *Stourton v Stourton* [1963] P 302, [1963] 1 All ER 606. See also CONTEMPT OF COURT vol 22 (2012) PARA 125.
4   *A-G v Gee* (1813) 2 Ves & B 208. See also RECEIVERS vol 88 (2012) PARA 50.
5   *Pheasant v Pheasant* (1670) 2 Vent 340n; *Eyre v Countess of Shaftsbury* (1722) 2 P Wms 103 at 110. As to sequestration see CIVIL PROCEDURE vol 12 (2009) PARA 1380 et seq.
6   *Digby v Alexander* (1832) 9 Bing 412 at 414. Note that a hereditary peerage no longer confers an automatic right to sit in the House of Lords: see PARA 825.
7   *Earl of Stirling v Clayton* (1832) 1 Cr & M 241.
8   *R v Graham* (1791) 2 Leach 547. In general, a peer should be described by his first name and his title in documents; neither his family name nor his residence should be stated.
9   The Criminal Justice Act 1948 s 30(1) has been repealed: see the Criminal Law Act 1967 s 10(2), Sch 3 Pt I; and the Statute Law (Repeals) Act 1977 s 1(1), Sch 1 Pt IV.
10 See CRIMINAL PROCEDURE.
11 *Lord Aldborough v Burton* (1834) 2 My & K 401. As to security for costs generally see CIVIL PROCEDURE vol 11 (2009) PARA 745 et seq.
12 See also LEGAL PROFESSIONS vol 66 (2009) PARA 1113; STATUTES AND LEGISLATIVE PROCESS vol 96 (2012) PARA 943.

(ii) Precedence

829.   Precedence of peers.   The House of Lords Precedence Act 1539 regulates the precedence of peers and certain office holders in Parliament[1], but in practice peers today arrange themselves in the Chamber of the House by party or group rather than degree of peerage and rank. Outside Parliament, precedence is determined by royal warrant[2], building on statute and letters patent of earlier ages. The Lord Chamberlain no longer publishes consolidated scales of precedence[3], but various texts replicate the tables[4].

1   See the House of Lords Precedence Act 1539 ss 1–8 (s 2 amended by the Statute Law Revision Act 1948; and the House of Lords Precedence Act 1539 ss 3, 5–8 amended by the Statute Law Revision Act 1888).
2   See eg Royal Warrant dated 4 July 2006 (which established the rank and precedence of the Lord Speaker of the House of Lords as being immediately after that of the Speaker of the House of Commons).
3   Such scales are different in England and Wales and in Scotland, and for men and women.
4   See eg D G Squibb *Order of Precedence in England and Wales* (1981).

(4) EXTINCTION OR SUSPENSION OF A PEERAGE

(i) Extinction of a Life Peerage

830.   Extinction of life peerage.   Life peerages become extinct on the death of the holder[1].

1   Life Peerages Act 1958 s 1(2). See also PARAS 807, 808.

(ii) Extinction or Suspension of a Hereditary Peerage

831. Extinction of hereditary peerage by failure of issue. On failure of the heirs indicated at the creation of a hereditary peerage the peerage becomes extinct[1].

1 *Knollys' Case* (1694) Marcham's Report 464, sub nom *R v Earl of Banbury* Skin 517 (where the House of Lords held that the first Earl of Banbury left no sons, and consequently that the earldom became extinct by failure of issue). As to hereditary peers see PARA 807.

832. Abeyance. The doctrine of abeyance relates not to the extinction of a peerage[1], but to the state of suspense into which a hereditary peerage falls when co-heirship occurs in the succession. Hitherto the doctrine of abeyance has been accepted by the House of Lords only in respect of baronies in fee, that is, baronies created by writ of summons and sitting[2]. Two claims have been made in respect of earldoms in fee, but no direct decision was given on the point of abeyance[3]. Abeyance does not apply to Scottish peerages[4]; it is not known before the seventeenth century, and it was not fully developed until the nineteenth century[5].

When the owner of a fief died leaving no male issue but more than one daughter, his land fell to his daughters in equal shares, although for a landed barony it was held that the eldest daughter must have the chief residence where seisin was taken for the whole[6].

A dignity being impartible and all the daughters having equal rights in it, the peerage right is held to be latent in all the co-heirs[7].

1 See PARA 831.
2 See PARA 822.
3 The point was expressly left open in the *Norfolk Earldom Case* [1907] AC 10, HL, and in the *Oxford Earldom Case* (1912). See also the Complete Peerage by GEC (1910 Edn) vol IV App H 708 et seq. The earldoms of Arlington (1672) and Cromartie (1861) were both created by letters patent limiting them to the grantee and the heirs of his body. Neither has yet come before the House of Lords for decision. An abeyance in the earldom of Cromartie was terminated by the Crown solely on the report of the Attorney General, by letters patent dated 25 February 1895 granting the title to a woman who held it, as the Countess of Cromartie, until her death in 1962, when she was succeeded by the 4th Earl of Cromartie. Both the Arlington and Cromartie patents contain viscounties with a similar limitation to heirs of the body of the grantee.

   As to the procedure for a petition to claim a peerage in abeyance see PARA 848.
4 *Herries Peerage Case* (1858) LR 2 Sc & Div 258, HL.
5 The law of abeyance, as distinguished from co-heirship, first enunciated in the seventeenth century, is set forth in the letters patent dated 7 May 1663, and in the Act of Parliament confirming the same, creating Mary, Countess of Kent, to be Baroness Lucas of Crudwell, which provided that, if at any time after the death of the said Mary, and in default of heirs male of her body, begotten by the Earl of Kent, there should be more persons than one who should be co-heirs of her body, so that the King or his heirs might declare which of them should have the dignity or otherwise, the dignity should be suspended or extinguished, then, nevertheless, the dignity should not be suspended or extinguished, but should go and be held and enjoyed from time to time by such of the said co-heirs as by course of descent and the common law of the realm should be inheritable in other entire and indivisible inheritances as, namely, an office of honour and public trust, or a castle for the necessary defence of the realm, and the like in case such inheritance had been given and limited to the said countess and the heirs of her body by the said earl begotten: *Lucas Peerage Case* (1907). See also the Report on Peerages in Abeyance (1927) Evidence 48 et seq, and the documents accompanying it.
6 2 Pollock and Maitland's History of English Law (2nd Edn) 274, 275, citing Bracton.
7 It was formerly held to revert or be escheated to the fountain of honour, ie the Crown, but the law was subsequently ascertained to be that a peerage in co-heirs was not extinguished, and that the Sovereign possessed it only so long as co-heirship existed; so that, if at any future time there should be but one heir, the right revived and the dignity was said to have been in abeyance:

Willoughby de Broke Barony Case (1695) Cruise on Dignities (2nd Edn) c 5 s 62, Collins's Baronies by Writ (1734 Edn) 321, sub nom *Verney's Case* Skin 432, HL. See also the *Lucas Peerage Case* (1907).

833. Termination of abeyance. The Crown is not obliged to terminate an abeyance[1]. The Crown can terminate an abeyance in favour of any co-heir[2], but may not grant the dignity to anyone but a co-heir[3]. Certain limitations on the power to call peerages out of abeyance have been accepted by the Crown. The most important of these limitations are:

(1) that no abeyance is to be terminated after the lapse of a century; and

(2) that no petition is to proceed where the petitioner represents less than one-third of the entire dignity unless he is a child of the last holder[4].

In the case of a commoner, the termination of an abeyance in a barony is effected by writ of summons[5]. Formerly, before women could receive a writ of summons, this was done by letters patent if the petitioner was a woman[6].

In the case of a person already holding a higher dignity, the lesser is, it seems, confirmed to him by the Sovereign's declaration under the Great Seal[7].

The Sovereign cannot extinguish the title when in abeyance or dispose of it to a stranger[8]; and, when only one of the co-heirs remains, that heir is entitled to the dignity[9].

1 As to abeyance see PARA 832. As to the procedure for a petition to claim a peerage in abeyance see PARA 848.
2 Com Dig, Dignity (C 3); and see CONSTITUTIONAL AND ADMINISTRATIVE LAW vol 20 (2014) PARA 573. A claim to a peerage in abeyance is made by petitioning the Crown: see PARA 848.
3 See the declaration in the *Lucas Peerage Case* (1907).
4 See the Report on Peerages in Abeyance (1927) 11.
5 As to barons and the other degrees of peerage see PARA 804. As to baronies by writ see PARA 822.
6 For an example of letters patent determining an abeyance in favour of a woman see the *Strange of Knokin and Stanley Baronies Case* (1920) Minutes of Evidence, App 128. As to peeresses in their own right see PARA 806.
7 Cruise on Dignities (2nd Edn) c 5 s 43. As to the use of the Great Seal see CONSTITUTIONAL AND ADMINISTRATIVE LAW vol 20 (2014) PARA 583.
8 Cruise on Dignities (2nd Edn) c 5 s 37.
9 Cruise on Dignities (2nd Edn) c 5 s 56; *Lord Willoughby de Broke Barony Case* (1695) Cruise on Dignities (2nd Edn) c 5 s 62, Collins's Baronies by Writ (1734 Edn) 321, sub nom *Verney's Case* Skin 432, HL.

834. Merger. If the holder of a peerage succeeds to the Crown, the dignity merges in the Crown and can only be revived or recreated by a new grant[1].

A previous title does not merge in a new grant. Thus, a barony by writ does not merge in a new grant by letters patent[2], and a lesser title does not merge in a greater one subsequently united in the same person by grant or otherwise[3], since, even if the greater title becomes extinct through failure of inheritable blood under the particular limitations of the grant, the lesser may continue as originally limited and is not necessarily extinguished with the greater[4].

1 See *Lord Oranmore's Case* (1848) 2 HL Cas 910; cf the *Buckhurst Peerage Case* (1876) 2 App Cas 1 at 28, HL, per Lord Cairns LC. The effect of the Sovereign becoming co-heir to a barony by writ in abeyance has never been argued, but it would be within the Crown's right to terminate the abeyance in its own favour; merger might then arise. As to the titles of the Crown see CROWN AND ROYAL FAMILY vol 12(1) (Reissue) PARA 39. As to abeyance see PARAS 832–833, 848.
2 *Lord De la Warre's Case* (1597) 11 Co Rep 1a at 1b; *Willoughby de Broke Barony Case* (1695) Collins's Baronies by Writ (1734 Edn) 321 at 325. As to barons and the other degrees of peerage see PARA 804. As to the creation of baronies by writ see PARA 822. As to creation of peerages by letters patent see PARA 814.

3   See the *Grey de Ruthyn Case* (1640) Collins's Baronies by Writ (1734 Edn) 195, HL; Cruise on Dignities (2nd Edn) c 4 s 58; *Roos Barony Case* (1666) Collins's Baronies by Writ (1734 Edn) 261, HL; *Fitzwalter's Case* (1669) Collins's Baronies by Writ (1734 Edn) 268 at 286.

4   See note 3.

835.   Resignation and surrender.   A peer of England, Ireland, Great Britain or the United Kingdom[1] cannot surrender, resign[2] or extinguish his dignity by fine, grant or any other conveyance to the Crown. A Scottish peer could resign his dignity into the hands of the Crown in order to extinguish it, or, which was usual, resign for a charter of novodamus altering the course of descent[3].

1   See PARA 805.

2   *Norfolk Earldom Case* [1907] AC 10, HL; *Re Parliamentary Election for Bristol South East* [1964] 2 QB 257, [1961] 3 All ER 354, Election Ct. Before the seventeenth century it was supposed that a peer had power to surrender or resign, and some earls did in fact surrender their earldoms. At the time the validity of these surrenders was never questioned. In 1626 the then claim to the earldom of Oxford was submitted for the opinion of the judges. In giving his opinion, Dodridge J said in reference to a peerage, 'he cannot alien or give away this interest because it is a personal dignity annexed to the posterity and fixed in the blood': *Willoughby of Eresby and Oxford Case* (1626) W Jo 96 at 123, HL. In the *Grey de Ruthyn Case* (1640) Collins's Baronies by Writ (1734 Edn) 195 at 256, the House of Lords resolved 'That no person that hath any Honour in him, and a Peer of this Realm, may alien or transfer the Honour to any other person' and 'That no Peer of this Realm can drown, or extinguish his honour (but that it descend to his descendants) neither by surrender, grant, fine, nor any other conveyance to the King'. A similar declaration was made in *R v Viscount Purbeck* (1678) Show Parl Cas 1 HL; and see the Report on the Dignity of a Peer of the Realm (1829 reprint) vol II pp 25, 26. These authorities were reviewed in the *Norfolk Earldom Case* [1907] AC 10, HL, and strictly followed, a surrender in 1302 of an earldom by its then holder being declared invalid. The same earldom had been re-granted in 1312 and from this root the 1907 claimant derived his title, but it was held that the re-grant was invalid since the surrender in 1302 was illegal. A peer cannot 'oust and kill the rights of those entitled in remainder': *Norfolk Earldom Case* at 14 per Lord Ashbourne.

3   The power seems to have been abolished by the Union with Scotland Act 1706.

836.   Disclaimer.   Any person who succeeds to a hereditary peerage of England, Scotland, Great Britain or the United Kingdom[1] on or after 31 July 1963[2] may, by an instrument of disclaimer delivered to the Lord Chancellor, disclaim that peerage for his life[3]. Any such instrument of disclaimer must be delivered within the period of 12 months beginning with the day on which the person succeeds to that peerage[4]. An instrument of disclaimer may not be delivered by a person who is an excepted hereditary peer entitled to sit in the House of Lords[5].

1   As to the classification of peers see PARA 805. As to hereditary peers see PARA 807.

2   Ie the commencement date of the Peerage Act 1963. Section 1 also applies to a person who succeeded to a peerage before 31 July 1963, but in that case the period within which an instrument of disclaimer could be delivered was 12 months beginning with that date or, if the person was under 21 years of age, 12 months beginning with the day on which he attained that age: s 1(3)(a).

The first hereditary peer to disclaim his title in this way was Anthony Wedgwood Benn (formerly Viscount Stansgate).

3   Peerage Act 1963 s 1(1). As to the form, delivery, certification and registration of instruments see s 1(5), Sch 1.

4   Peerage Act 1963 s 1(2). If the person is under the age of 21 years when he succeeds, the period of 12 months begins with the day on which he attains that age: s 1(2).

In reckoning the period for the delivery of an instrument of disclaimer by any person, no account is to be taken of any time during which that person is shown to the satisfaction of the Lord Chancellor to have been subject to any infirmity of body or mind rendering him incapable of exercising or determining whether to exercise his rights under s 1: s 1(4).

5   See the Peerage Act 1963 s 1(2) (amended by the House of Lords Act 1999 s 4(1), Sch 1 para 1). The reference in the text to an excepted hereditary peer is a reference to a person who is excepted from the House of Lords Act 1999 s 1 by virtue of s 2: see PARA 825.

837. Effects of disclaimer. The disclaimer of a peerage by any person under the Peerage Act 1963 is irrevocable[1]. From the date on which the instrument of disclaimer is delivered the disclaimer operates to divest that person (and, if he is married, his wife) of all right or interest to or in the peerage, and all attached titles, rights, offices, privileges and precedence[2]. The disclaimer also operates to relieve the person of all obligations and disabilities of the peerage[3]. The disclaimer does not, however, accelerate the succession to that peerage nor does it affect its devolution on his death[4].

Where a peerage is disclaimed under the Peerage Act 1963, no other hereditary peerage may be conferred upon the person by whom it is disclaimed[5]. The disclaimer of a peerage does not affect any right, interest or power (whether arising before or after the disclaimer) of the person by whom the peerage is disclaimed, or of any other person, to, in or over any estates or other property limited or settled to devolve with that peerage[6].

1   Peerage Act 1963 s 3(1). As to disclaimer of a peerage see PARA 836.
2   Peerage Act 1963 s 3(1)(a).
3   Peerage Act 1963 s 3(1)(b) (amended by the House of Lords Act 1999 s 4(2), Sch 2).
4   Peerage Act 1963 s 3(1).
5   Peerage Act 1963 s 3(2) (amended by the House of Lords Act 1999 Sch 2).
6   Peerage Act 1963 s 3(3).

838. Forfeiture. Forfeiture of all civil rights follows upon attainder[1]. Dignities held by the attainted person, or to which any person claiming through him becomes heir, escheat to the Crown and the blood of the attainted person is 'corrupted', so that he cannot subsequently inherit, nor transmit to his heirs the capacity to inherit, any such dignity[2].

The barony of an attainted person was not preserved by his son's having been summoned to Parliament in his father's barony prior to the attainder[3].

If, however, an attainted person dies without issue before becoming heir to a dignity, the succession to the dignity is not affected[4], nor is the inheritance of a dignity under a special remainder barred by the attainder of an heir under the prior limitation[5].

On the attainder of one co-heir to a barony in abeyance, the dignity does not escheat to the Crown; the title of the other co-heir or co-heirs is not affected[6].

Forfeiture without attainder has been imposed by Act of Parliament[7].

1   Attainder was the extinction of civil rights and powers which formerly resulted from a judgment of death or outlawry against a person convicted of treason or felony. Persons can even be attainted by Act of Parliament after death: 4 Bl Com (14th Edn) 380; Co Litt 390b; 1 Chitty's Criminal Law (2nd Edn) 723. A judgment of outlawry standing in the way of a claim to a dormant barony, although clearly erroneous, cannot be overlooked, but must be reversed: *Wharton Peerage Case* (1845) 12 Cl & Fin 295, HL. As to bills of attainder see COURTS AND TRIBUNALS vol 24 (2010) PARA 643.
2   2 Bl Com (14th Edn) 253; 4 Bl Com (14th Edn) 380; Chitty's Criminal Law (2nd Edn) 727 et seq.
3   *Montacute and Monthermer Peerages Case* (1874) LR 7 HL 305 at 315 per Lord Cairns LC, and at 316 per Lord Hatherley.
4   *Perth Earldom Case* (1848) 2 HL Cas 865. See also the *Southesk Earldom Case* (1848) 2 HL Cas 908. For example, if A has three sons, B, C and D, the line of B remains pure, the line of C becomes corrupt through attainder of a descendant, and the line of D remains pure. The issue of B and C becomes extinct, and the descendant of D becomes heir of the person ennobled. If in

fact any descendant of C became heir, all the descendants of D are barred. The chief authority for this statement of the law is the *Airlie Earldom Case* (1813) Cruise on Dignities (2nd Edn) c 4 s 86.

5 By the terms of the grant, enjoyment by the second grantee is made to depend upon a future event. Both creations are emanations of the same royal prerogative, perfectly distinct and independent of each other; therefore the forfeiture of the first by treason does not prevent the second from arising and taking effect at the time appointed: *Somerset Dukedom Case* (1750) 2 Eden 379; Report on the Dignity of a Peer of the Realm (1829 reprint) vol II p 57. See also the *Somerset Dukedom Case* (1926) Minutes of Proceedings 218.

6 *Braye Peerage Case* (1839) 6 Cl & Fin 757, HL; *Camoys Peerage Case* (1839) 6 Cl & Fin 789, HL; *Beaumont Peerage Case* (1840) 6 Cl & Fin 868, HL. As to abeyance see PARAS 832–833, 848.

7 26 Hen 8 c 13 (High Treason) (1534) (repealed).

839. Restitution of blood. The effect of an attainder[1] can only be removed by statute. In the case of attainder by statute, this takes the form of a repealing Act. Restitution of blood does not revive a forfeited dignity. It does, however, enable the attainted person or his heirs subsequently to inherit a dignity other than the one which has been forfeited[2].

1 As to attainder see PARA 838 note 1.
2 *Montacute and Monthermer Peerages Case* (1874) LR 7 HL 305.

(iii) Deprivation of Peerage

840. Deprivation of peerage. No peer can be deprived of peerage except by or under the authority of an Act of Parliament[1].

1 Com Dig, Dignity (E); *Earl of Waterford's Case* (1832) 6 Cl & Fin 133, HL; *Earl of Shrewsbury's Case* (1612) 12 Co Rep 106, PC; *R v Knowles* (1694) 12 Mod Rep 55. In the reign of Edward IV, George Nevill, Duke of Bedford, was degraded by Act of Parliament on account of poverty: 4 Co Inst 355; 1 Bl Com (14th Edn) 402. See also the *Earl of Shrewsbury's Case* at 108; *Viscount Purbeck's Case* (1678) Collins's Baronies by Writ (1734 Edn) 293 at 306. In such a case it seems that the title would be extinguished. There is an old authority to the effect that a peer may be degraded by the Sovereign if he wastes his estate, but this is no longer recognised as the law: see 1 Bl Com (14th Edn) 402.

By the Titles Deprivation Act 1917 any peers who during the 1914–18 war bore arms against the Crown or adhered to the enemy had their actions subjected to inquiry by a committee of the Privy Council appointed under the Act: see s 1. The committee's report was then referred to both Houses of Parliament and the Crown: see s 1(3). The Dukes of Albany, Cumberland and Brunswick and Viscount Taaffe were so dealt with and, by Order in Council dated 28 March 1919, SR & O 1919/475 (spent), their names were struck off the Roll of the House of Lords and they were deprived of their titles. Deprivation is absolute for the individual concerned (see s 1(4)), but his successor may petition the Crown for restoration of the peerage (see s 2). The petition may be referred to the committee under the Titles Deprivation Act 1917; and, if the committee is satisfied that no disability under the Act has been incurred by the petitioner and that he is well affected to the Crown, the Crown may direct a restoration of the peerage: see s 2.

(5) CLAIMS TO HEREDITARY PEERAGES

(i) The Roll of the Peerage

841. The Roll of the Peerage; list of complete peerage and evidence of dignity and rank. The Roll of the Peerage is maintained by the Lord Chancellor[1], in consultation with Garter Principal King of Arms and Lord Lyon King of Arms[2], as the official register in which those inheriting peerages seek inclusion as evidence of their dignity and rank[3]. The Roll has a broader scope than its predecessor, the parliamentary Roll of the Lords[4], in that it records peers of

Ireland as well as those of England, Scotland, Great Britain and the United Kingdom[5]. The Roll is the authoritative list of the complete peerage[6], and is evidence in cases of dispute. Proof of succession is not required for any purpose of inheritance, but a peer who does not prove his succession is not entered on the Roll or entitled to be included on the Clerk of the Parliaments' register of candidates to stand in any by-election to fill a vacancy occurring by death among the 90 elected hereditary peers[7], nor is he entitled to any precedence attaching to his peerage or to be addressed or referred to by any title attaching to that peerage in any civil or military commission, letters patent or other official document[8]. Whether or not a person succeeding to a peerage intends to stand in a by-election for the House of Lords, he should apply for entry on the Roll; inclusion is not automatic[9].

1 The Royal Warrant dated 1 June 2004 refers to the Secretary of State for Constitutional Affairs but, at the date at which this volume states the law, responsibility for the Roll of the Peerage lies with the Lord Chancellor and Secretary of State for Justice.
2 As to Kings of Arms see PARA 879.
3 The Royal Warrant dated 1 June 2004 required that a roll, to be called the Roll of the Peerage, should be prepared and then maintained. As to hereditary peers see PARA 807.
4 This was maintained by the Clerk of the Parliaments until the enactment of the House of Lords Act 1999 as a list of lords entitled to a writ of summons in order of precedence.
5 See the Royal Warrant dated 1 June 2004 para 9. As to the classification of peers see PARA 805.
6 See the Royal Warrant dated 1 June 2004 para 1.
7 See HL Standing Orders (2013) (Public Business) no 11. As to inclusion in the Clerk of the Parliaments' register see PARA 845. As to the eligibility of elected hereditary peers to sit and vote in the House of Lords see PARA 825.
8 Royal Warrant dated 1 June 2004 para 3.
9 Application should be made through the Crown Office. The Crown Office is a department of the Ministry of Justice, located in the House of Lords; its address is Crown Office, House of Lords, London, SW1A 0PW. As to applications to be entered on the Roll of the Peerage see further PARA 846.
   A person succeeding to a hereditary peerage should apply for inclusion on the Roll of the Peerage at the time of succession as, if a claim is not made on the death of the late peer, it becomes progressively more difficult and expensive for each succeeding generation to produce the required evidence to support a peerage claim. As to such evidence see PARA 855 et seq.

(ii) Jurisdiction

842. Jurisdiction of the Crown. Jurisdiction to determine a claim to a dignity exists only in the Sovereign. The Sovereign has in fact at various periods referred claims to different authorities, such as the Lord Treasurer of England and the Earl Marshal[1]. A question of dignity or honour cannot be tried by a court of law[2]. In practice all claims of any difficulty are now referred to the House of Lords[3]; the House then refers them to the Committee for Privileges[4].

1 See Squibb's High Court of Chivalry 159, 160. As to the Earl Marshal see PARA 878 note 5.
2 *Earl Cowley v Countess Cowley* [1901] AC 450, HL. See also *Re Parliamentary Election for Bristol South East* [1964] 2 QB 257, [1961] 3 All ER 354, Election Ct, where the matter in issue was not whether the respondent had succeeded to a peerage, but whether he was thereby disqualified from sitting in the House of Commons, notwithstanding that he had not applied for or received a writ of summons to attend the House of Lords. As to peers sitting in the House of Commons see PARA 826.
3 As to the role of the House of Lords in determining peerage claims see Erskine May's Parliamentary Practice (24th Edn, 2011) p 182. As to the jurisdiction of the House of Lords see PARA 843.
4 As to the Committee for Privileges see PARA 853.

843. Jurisdiction of the House of Lords. Whilst a hereditary peerage no longer confers on the holder an automatic right to sit in the House of Lords[1], the

House of Lords still has inherent jurisdiction over claims to the right to sit and vote in the House[2]. The House of Lords claims to have an inherent right to decide claims to Irish peerages[3]. In practice all peerage claims of any difficulty are now referred to the House of Lords[4].

1   As to hereditary peers see PARA 807. As to the removal of the automatic right to sit in the House of Lords see PARA 825.
2   See COURTS AND TRIBUNALS vol 24 (2010) PARA 642.
3   See the *Earl of Waterford's Case* (1832) 6 Cl & Fin 133, HL. In 1922, J W de la Poer petitioned the Crown claiming to be Baron of le Power and Coroghmore in the Peerage of Ireland, and asking that the outlawry of a predecessor in title might be removed; on reference by the Crown, the House resolved that the barony was created by letters patent of Henry VIII in 1535, and, but for the outlawry of a predecessor in title, that the barony would now be vested in the petitioner: *Le Power and Coroghmore Barony Case* (1921). Claims to Irish peerages are now made by petition to the House of Lords: see PARA 847.
4   See PARA 842.

(iii) Procedure

844. Methods of claiming a peerage. Claims to peerages arise either by immediate succession or to terminate an abeyance[1]. Peerage claims by immediate succession may be to determine: (1) whether a peer is eligible to stand in a by-election to the House of Lords[2]; or (2) a claim to an Irish peerage[3].

1   As to abeyance see PARA 832; as to termination of abeyance see PARA 833; and as to the procedure for a petition to claim a peerage in abeyance see PARA 848.
2   See PARA 845.
3   See PARA 847.

845. Petition to determine whether a peer is eligible to stand in a by-election to the House of Lords. If a person who succeeds to an eligible peerage[1] wishes to stand in a by-election for membership of the House of Lords as an elected hereditary peer[2] he must petition the House of Lords to prove his succession and right to be included in the Clerk of the Parliaments' register of hereditary peers[3]. Such petitions are referred to the Lord Chancellor to consider and report whether the petitioner has established his right to be included in the register[4]. The Crown Office examines the claim on behalf of the Lord Chancellor[5]. If the Lord Chancellor is satisfied that the claim has been made out he reports this to the House of Lords, the succession is recorded in the minutes of proceedings of the House and the peer is entered on the Clerk of the Parliaments' register and on the Roll of the Peerage[6]. If the Lord Chancellor is not satisfied that the petitioner has established his right to be included in the register, he reports that the claim is proper to be considered by the Committee for Privileges[7]. The House of Lords then refers the petition to the Committee which examines the claim as if it were a reference by the Crown[8].

1   Ie a peerage in the peerage of England, Scotland, Great Britain or the United Kingdom: see PARA 825. As to the classification of peers see PARA 805.
2   As to by-elections see PARA 825. As to hereditary peers see PARA 807.
3   HL Standing Orders (2013) (Public Business) no 11. As to the Clerk of the Parliaments' register of hereditary peers see HL Standing Orders (2013) (Public Business) no 10(5); and PARA 825.
4   HL Standing Orders (2013) (Public Business) no 11.
5   The Crown Office is a department of the Ministry of Justice, located in the House of Lords; its address is Crown Office, House of Lords, London, SW1A 0PW.
6   As to the Roll of the Peerage see PARA 841.
7   As to the Committee for Privileges see PARA 853.
8   As to reference by the Crown see PARA 850.

846. Application to be entered on the Roll of the Peerage. Where membership of the House of Lords is not at issue (that is, where the claimant has no interest in standing for election to the House of Lords under the by-election procedure[1]), the procedure on a claim by right to a peerage of England, Scotland, Great Britain or the United Kingdom[2] is begun by application to the Lord Chancellor[3] for entry on the Roll of the Peerage[4]. The application is made in a similar manner to those applications made before the passing of the House of Lords Act 1999 when applying for a writ of summons to Parliament[5]. The Crown Office administers the procedure[6]. A claim is made initially by letter with proof[7], but no petition is required[8]. If the claim is straightforward, the Lord Chancellor admits it and enters the claimant on the Roll. If the claim is complex or is opposed, the Lord Chancellor refuses to enter the claimant on the Roll. It is only when the Lord Chancellor refuses the application for entry on the Roll of the Peerage that a petition to the Crown becomes necessary[9].

1   As to standing for election to the House of Lords under the by-election procedure see PARA 825.
2   As to the classification of peers see PARA 805.
3   See PARA 841 note 1.
4   As to the Roll of the Peerage see PARA 841.
5   As to the effect of the House of Lords Act 1999 see PARA 825. As to baronies by writ see PARA 822.
6   The Crown Office is a department of the Ministry of Justice, located in the House of Lords; its address is Crown Office, House of Lords, London, SW1A 0PW.
7   As to evidence see PARA 855 et seq.
8   See the text and note 9.
9   As to petition to the Crown see PARA 850.

847. Claim to a peerage in the peerage of Ireland. The procedure on a claim to an Irish peerage[1] is by petition direct to the House of Lords[2]. The petition is referred by the House to the Lord Chancellor for his report, and if he is satisfied that the claim has been made out, he reports this to the House. The succession is recorded in the minutes of proceedings of the House and the peer is entered on the Roll of the Peerage[3]. If the Lord Chancellor is not satisfied that the claim to the peerage has been established, he reports that the claim is proper to be considered by the Committee for Privileges[4]. The House of Lords refers the petition to the Committee which examines the claim as if it were a reference by the Crown[5].

1   See PARAS 805, 813.
2   HL Standing Orders (2013) (Public Business) no 79.
3   As to the Roll of the Peerage see PARA 841.
4   As to the Committee for Privileges see PARA 853.
5   As to reference by the Crown see PARA 850. At the date at which this volume states the law, no such petition has yet been considered by the Committee for Privileges. The petition of Viscount Mountgarret claiming the Earldoms of Ormond and Ossory in the Peerage of Ireland was referred to the Committee on 30 November 2000, the Lord Chancellor having reported that 'the petition was proper to be considered by the Committee for Privileges'. The petition was withdrawn on 24 January 2001.

848. Petition to claim peerage in abeyance. A claim to a peerage in abeyance[1] is made by petitioning the Crown through the Lord Chancellor that the petitioner may be declared a co-heir and that the abeyance may be terminated in his favour[2]. Since 1927 the Crown has indicated that no claim for a peerage in abeyance will be received in cases where the abeyance lasted for more than one hundred years. This decision followed a recommendation of the Select Committee on Peerages in Abeyance 1927[3].

Claims to Irish peerages in abeyance must be notified to the Crown[4]; then the claimant must petition the House of Lords, and the claim is referred to the Committee for Privileges[5].

1   As to abeyance see PARA 832.
2   As to termination of abeyance see PARA 833.

3   The Select Committee on Peerages in Abeyance 1927 (referred to as the Sumner Committee, after the name of the Chairman, Lord Sumner) also recommended that an exception should be made in favour of petitions which had already been presented at the time when the Committee was appointed. The case of the Barony of Grey of Codnor was held to benefit from this exception, and the claim was successful: see the Report of the Committee of Privileges on the Barony of Grey of Codnor, June 1989 (HL Paper (1988–89) no 59–1).

4   HL Standing Orders (2013) (Public Business) no 80.
5   HL Standing Orders (2013) (Public Business) no 80. As to the Committee for Privileges see PARA 853.

849.   Petition to remove attainder or other disqualification.   Where a peerage is affected by attainder[1] or other disqualification, a petition to the Crown claiming the peerage, or praying for the termination of an abeyance[2] in the peerage, should refer to the disqualification and contain a prayer that, if it appears that such a disqualification exists, Her Majesty will be pleased to order that a Bill be introduced into Parliament for removal of the disqualification[3]. On the House resolving that but for the disqualification the petitioner would be entitled to a peerage, or that but for the disqualification the peerage would be in abeyance and the petitioner would be a co-heir, a Bill may be introduced, signed by the Crown[4], for removing the disqualification. When this Bill has received royal assent, the claimant or co-heir may again petition the Crown, and the Crown refers the petition to the House of Lords. The same procedure is then followed as in an ordinary petition to terminate an abeyance[5].

Claims for restoration of peerage under the Titles Deprivation Act 1917[6] are made by petition to the Crown but are referred to a committee of the Privy Council and not to the House of Lords[7].

1   As to attainder see PARA 838 note 1.
2   As to abeyance see PARA 832; as to termination of abeyance see PARA 833; and as to the procedure for a petition to claim a peerage in abeyance see PARA 848.
3   As to personal Bills see STATUTES AND LEGISLATIVE PROCESS vol 96 (2012) PARA 953 et seq. See also Erskine May's Parliamentary Practice (24th Edn, 2011) p 936.
4   As to the Crown's consent see Erskine May's Parliamentary Practice (24th Edn, 2011) pp 661, 1012.
5   As to a petition to terminate an abeyance see PARA 848.
6   See PARA 840 note 1.
7   See the Titles Deprivation Act 1917 s 2; and PARA 840 note 1.

850.   Claims in cases of dispute or doubt: petition to the Crown.   Any person pursuing a claim to a peerage after the Lord Chancellor has refused entry on the Roll of the Peerage[1] or praying for the termination of an abeyance[2] must proceed by petition to the Crown. The petition is presented through the Crown Office[3], which refers it to the Attorney General to report on the claim[4]. Petitions relating to pre-Union Scottish peerages are referred to the Lord Advocate[5], as are post-Union peerages with a strong Scottish connection[6].

In a claim by right the law officer usually advises the Crown to refer the claim to the House of Lords[7].

In the case of petitions to terminate an abeyance[8] it may be said generally that if:

(1)   the Attorney General is satisfied that no improper arrangement has been entered into between the petitioner and co-heirs, or any of them;

(2)   the petitioner does not come within the exceptions laid down by the House of Lords; and

(3)   on the hearing before the Attorney General no question of law or pedigree is at issue,

the Attorney General recommends the exercise of royal discretion to grant or refuse the petition without reference to the House of Lords. However, if the Attorney General is of the opinion that there may be grounds for doubting the propriety of any arrangement between co-heirs, he must recommend a reference to the House of Lords, since it is for the House, and not the Attorney General, to decide whether any impropriety exists in the agreement[9].

When a petition is referred to the Attorney General he requires the petitioner to attend before him with written and oral evidence in order to establish a prima facie case[10].

Persons wishing to make a claim to a peerage in respect of which a petition by another claimant is already before the House of Lords must proceed by petition to the Crown presented through the Crown Office, even when such persons have obtained the permission of the House to be heard in opposition to the other petition[11].

Where a petitioner desires only to obtain permission to be heard in opposition to a claim of peerage, or to claim a peerage of Ireland[12], or where his claim relates to an incidental matter such as precedence, place in the House or some similar question, the petition should be addressed and presented to the House of Lords. Although there is no standing order which lays down the time limits within which such petitions should be lodged, it is recommended that a petition should be presented at least two weeks before the date on which the Committee for Privileges[13] is expected to sit.

Any petition in pursuance of a claim for a peerage must set out in detail the facts which prove that the peerage has descended to the claimant or the facts which prove that the peerage is in abeyance and that the claimant is one of the co-heirs, stating also who are the other co-heirs[14].

1   See PARA 846. As to the Roll of the Peerage see PARA 841.

2   See PARA 848. As to abeyance see PARA 832; and as to termination of abeyance see PARA 833.

3   The Crown Office is a department of the Ministry of Justice, located in the House of Lords; its address is Crown Office, House of Lords, London, SW1A 0PW.

4   As to preliminary examination by the Attorney General see PARA 852.

5   As to Scottish peerages, and the classification of peers generally, see PARA 805.

6   See the Minutes of Evidence of the Committee for Privileges in the Viscountcy of Oxfuird Peerage Claim, 1977. The procedure was first followed in the Earldom of Annandale and Hartfell Peerage Claim, 1985: see the Report from the Committee for Privileges, together with the proceedings of the Committee and speeches of counsel (HL Paper (1984–85) no 228–1).

7   See PARA 842. The House of Lords will then refer the claim to the Committee for Privileges: see PARA 853.

8   See note 2.

9   As to how arrangements between co-heirs are to be dealt with see the Special Report of the Committee for Privileges on Peerages in Abeyance (the 'Strange case') (HL Paper (1985–86) no 176) and the Lords Journals 16 and 18 December 1986. For an earlier case see the Minutes of Evidence taken before the Committee for Privileges in the Barony of Vaux Peerage Claim, 1938.

10 See eg the Report of the House of Lords Select Committee on Peerages in Abeyance (1927) pp 37–40 (where the nature of this investigation is clearly examined); and see also the Lords Journals 31 May, 6, 7, and 11 July 1927 (which record the checks placed on the termination in abeyance). As to making out a prima facie case see further PARA 852; and as to evidence see further PARA 855 et seq.

11 In the case of the Barony of Moynihan a petition opposing the claim was presented by Daniel Moynihan. The petition was deposited the day before the Committee was to meet; the Committee made it clear that they only exceptionally agreed to consider the petition: see Proceedings for the Committee for Privileges on the Barony of Moynihan (HL Paper (1996–97) no 53–1, pp 5, 6).

12 See PARA 847.

13 As to the Committee for Privileges see PARA 853.

14 See PARA 855 et seq.

851.   Lapse of time.   Lapse of time, if satisfactorily explained, is no bar to a claim to a peerage[1], but, if unexplained, may give rise to a presumption against the right of the claimant[2].

1   Com Dig, Dignity (E); *Hastings Peerage Case* (1841) 8 Cl & Fin 144 at 163–165, HL; *Fitzwalter Peerage Case* (1844) 10 Cl & Fin 946 at 957, HL.

2   *De Wahull Peerage Case* (1892) Minutes of Evidence 88.

852.   Preliminary examination.   The petition[1] for a claim to a peerage is in the first instance lodged with the Crown Office[2]. If the petition is found to be genuine, the Lord Chancellor takes the pleasure of the Crown upon it. The Crown usually orders the petition to be referred to the Attorney General for examination and report. The Attorney General then requires the petitioner to make out a prima facie case by the lodgment of a pedigree and proofs properly prepared, and, if dissatisfied with the measure of proof, requires further evidence. The petitioner is then instructed to appear before the Attorney General on a fixed date; he may appear in person or by agent or counsel. The Attorney General puts such questions as he deems fit in relation to the pedigree and the evidence produced. Subsequently his report to the Crown is prepared. The Attorney General may report:

(1)   that the petition and evidence is not such as to justify any step being taken; or

(2)   that the petition should be referred to the House of Lords[3]; or

(3)   exceptionally, that the evidence is such as to justify an immediate exercise of the royal favour to grant the prayer of the petitioner if the Crown be so pleased.

The report is sent to the Lord Chancellor, who takes the Crown's pleasure upon it. This is expressed either by no action being taken or by adopting the recommendation of the Attorney General[4].

Petitions in respect of Scottish peerages[5] or those with a sufficient Scottish connection are reported on by the Lord Advocate[6].

1   As to claims by petition see PARA 850.

2   The Crown Office is a department of the Ministry of Justice, located in the House of Lords; its address is Crown Office, House of Lords, London, SW1A 0PW.

3   As to referral to the House of Lords, and thence to the Committee for Privileges, see PARA 853.

4   In the preliminary proceedings the Attorney General is solely the servant of the Crown and owes no duty to the House of Lords: see the Report on Peerages in Abeyance (1927) Minutes of Evidence 38.

5   As to Scottish peerages, and the classification of peers generally, see PARA 805.

6   *Viscountcy of Oxfuird Case* (1977) 1986 SLT (Lyon Ct) 8, HL.

853.   Reference of claim to the Committee for Privileges.   If a petition on a peerage claim is referred to the House of Lords, the House refers it to the Committee for Privileges[1] which hears the claim in accordance with the Standing Orders of the House[2]. The Committee may examine witnesses on oath, order the production of documents and hear counsel[3]. When the claim comes before the

Committee, the Attorney General represents the Crown's interest and takes up a position of nominal opposition, but is present more especially to advise the Committee when requested to do so[4]. If the petition is in respect of a pre-Union Scottish peerage, or a post-Union peerage deemed to have a sufficient Scottish connection, the Lord Advocate has charge of the Crown's interest. In a proper case the Committee may assign counsel to take up a case where the claimant is prevented by lack of means[5]. The Committee may in proper cases hear persons who are not claimants, but appear to be concerned[6]. An objector may himself claim the peerage, or he may object on other grounds[7].

It is the duty of the Committee to consider the effect of any clause in a patent in the case referred to it[8].

1   A Committee for Privileges and Conduct is appointed at the beginning of every session; it consists of 16 peers, of whom two must be former holders of high judicial office: HL Standing Orders (2013) (Public Business) no 77. In any claim of peerage, the Committee must sit with three holders of high judicial office, who have the same speaking and voting rights as the members of the Committee: HL Standing Orders (2013) (Public Business) no 77. As to the Committee for Privileges see further PARLIAMENT vol 78 (2010) PARA 886.

2   See HL Standing Orders (2013) (Public Business) no 78; and see also PARLIAMENT vol 78 (2010) PARA 838. The requirements vary from time to time and must be ascertained; but generally the claimant is required to hand in his case, stating precisely the creation and limitation of the dignity and the steps by which the right has descended, with the relative documents in an appendix to the case. See further note 3.

    An objector, or a person who is otherwise concerned, also proceeds by way of petition to the House of Lords.

3   A petitioner must, within six weeks from the date of the presentation of his petition to the House of Lords, lodge his case, pedigree and proofs with the Clerk of the Parliaments: HL Standing Orders (2013) (Public Business) no 78(1).

    The House has laid down directions with regard to documents delivered in at the Bar in evidence in peerage claims, and the examination of those documents when printed by order of the House. Records and documents in public custody may be proved before the Committee by copies officially certified as in ordinary legal proceedings; the production of originals of such documents is not required except on an order of the Lord Speaker or Chairman of Committees: HL Standing Orders (2013) (Public Business) no 78(2). Originals of records and documents in private custody, together with copies of them, must be produced and proved before the Committee: HL Standing Orders (2013) (Public Business) no 78(2).

    In unopposed claims the record of the documentary evidence given before the Committee is examined by an examiner appointed by the Crown Agent; and the Crown Agent may, if he think fit, similarly appoint an examiner in opposed claims: HL Standing Orders (2013) (Public Business) no 78(3). The cost of the examination is borne by the claimant: HL Standing Orders (2013) (Public Business) no 78(3).

    The fees to be charged are such as are authorised from time to time by the House of Lords: HL Standing Orders (2013) (Public Business) no 78(4).

4   If the Attorney General is unable to be present at the hearing of the claim, the Solicitor General takes his place. In cases of great importance both law officers appear. A difficulty arises when counsel for the claimant becomes a law officer of the Crown during the hearing of the claim. In the *Tracy Peerage Case* (1843) 10 Cl & Fin 154 at 160n, HL, counsel for the claimant became Attorney General and subsequently appeared for the Crown, the Solicitor General appearing for the claimant. In the *Wharton Peerage Case* (1845) 12 Cl & Fin 295 at 299, HL, the Solicitor General had appeared for the claimant; on his appointment to be Attorney General, he did not appear and the new Solicitor General appeared for the Crown (*Wharton Peerage Case* at 301n, 302n). In the *Shrewsbury Peerage Case* (1858) 7 HL Cas 1, counsel for the claimant appeared for the claimant after becoming Attorney General; the Solicitor General appeared for the Crown. In the *Somerset Dukedom Case* (1926) the Attorney General had previously appeared for one of the parties before succeeding to office and the Solicitor General appeared for the Crown.

5   *Earl Roscommon's Case* (1828) 6 Cl & Fin 97, HL. This has not been done for more than a century. If the case is genuine and well founded, the petitioner finds few practical difficulties before the Committee for Privileges.

6   See note 2.

7 *Slane Peerage Case* (1835) 5 Cl & Fin 23, HL; *Braye Peerage Case* (1839) 6 Cl & Fin 757, HL; *Shrewsbury Peerage Case* (1858) 7 HL Cas 1. Cf *Berkeley Peerage Case* (1861) 8 HL Cas 21; *Norfolk Earldom Case* [1907] AC 10, HL (where the holder of an earldom of Norfolk other than that in question was allowed to oppose); and the preliminary proceedings in the claims to the earldoms of Warwick and Salisbury which were alleged to be in fee, where the Earls of Warwick and of Salisbury, holding earldoms of later creation, were allowed to appear in opposition.

8 *Buckhurst Peerage Case* (1876) 2 App Cas 1, HL.

854. Report of the Committee for Privileges.

854. Report of the Committee for Privileges. Where a peerage claim is referred to the Committee for Privileges[1], the Committee resolves on the claim and reports to the House of Lords. If the Committee is satisfied on a claim for the determination of an abeyance that any arrangement entered into between the petitioner and any co-heir is tainted with any impropriety, the Committee must make no report to the House except that the arrangement is not shown to have been a proper one[2]. The House usually resolves in the terms of the Committee's decision and the resolutions are reported to the Crown[3]. Exceptionally, the House refers back the report to the Committee for Privileges for reconsideration[4].

1 See PARA 853.
2 HL Standing Orders (2013) (Public Business) no 81. As to abeyance see PARAS 832–833, 848.
3 See the Report on Peerages in Abeyance (1927) Minutes of Evidence 41, 47.
4 Such a reference back was made in 1922 in *Viscountess Rhondda's Case* [1922] 2 AC 339, HL, and as a result the Committee resolved in a sense contrary to the original report.

(iv) Evidence

855. Admissibility of evidence. The admissibility of evidence in a peerage claim is entirely within the jurisdiction of the committee hearing the claim[1], but ordinarily the rules of evidence prevailing in the civil courts are followed[2]. The committee will usually accept evidence admitted and recorded in previous claims, especially in relation to pedigrees, with all just exceptions, to the date of admission, but application for permission to use the evidence must be obtained before it will be admitted[3].

1 The following have been tendered in evidence in various cases, and have been received or rejected according to the circumstances: private Acts of Parliament (*Wharton Peerage Case* (1845) 12 Cl & Fin 295, HL; *Shrewsbury Peerage Case* (1858) 7 HL Cas 1); copies of inscriptions no longer legible (*Shrewsbury Peerage Case*); inscriptions on tombs in churches (*Shrewsbury Peerage Case*); statements in wills as to pedigree (*Shrewsbury Peerage Case*); incomplete documents and records (*Slane Peerage Case* (1835) 5 Cl & Fin 23, HL; *Crawford and Lindsay Peerages Case* (1848) 2 HL Cas 534; *Shrewsbury Peerage Case*; cf the *Vaux Peerage Case* (1837) 5 Cl & Fin 526, HL); coat of arms in St George's Chapel, Windsor (*Shrewsbury Peerage Case*; *Berkeley Peerage Case* (1861) 8 HL Cas 21 at 37); records from the Heralds' College (*Vaux Peerage Case* at 541, 544; *Tracy Peerage Case* (1843) 10 Cl & Fin 154 at 157, HL; *Shrewsbury Peerage Case* at 24, 31, 33). As to proof of handwriting see the *Fitzwalter Peerage Case* (1844) 10 Cl & Fin 193, 946, HL; the *Shrewsbury Peerage Case*; and CIVIL PROCEDURE vol 11 (2009) PARAS 832–834. Blood test evidence to determine paternity is admissible in peerage claims: *Re Moynihan* [2000] 1 FLR 113, HL. As to the measure of value for pedigree purposes to be attached to funeral certificates and visitations from the College of Arms see the *Strange of Knokin and Stanley Baronies Case* (1920) Minutes of Evidence xvi, xxii–xxxvi. In the *Fairfax Peerage Case* [1908] WN 226, HL, a predecessor of the claimant having made out his claim in 1800, the claimant produced in evidence the testimony of relatives, an old family Bible, and monumental inscriptions (there being no early record of births, deaths and marriages in Virginia, USA, where the family had settled since 1750, and most of the records having been destroyed by the Northern Army during the American Civil War), and the committee accepted secondary evidence in support of the claim to the barony. As to the admissibility of reputation and family tradition see CIVIL PROCEDURE vol 11 (2009) PARA 830.

2   For a summary of the evidence admissible in a peerage claim see Palmer's Peerage Law in England 235–240.

3   Eg in the *Latymer Peerage Case* (1912) the evidence of pedigree in the de Scales claim of 1856 was admitted so far as collaterals were concerned, but counsel said he considered that the direct line should be proved strictly. In the *Oxford Earldom Case* (1912) the pedigree material used in the Latymer claim was freely admitted. Both petitioners were co-heirs to the barony as well as to the earldom. The present practice is for a petitioner to lodge an incidental petition asking for permission to use pedigree or other evidence admitted in previous claims. See also the *Strange of Knokin and Stanley Baronies Case* (1920) Documents accompanying the Joint Case 9. If satisfied that there is no question at issue, the officers of the House of Lords then arrange for formal permission from the House. The record reads that the petition has been read and ordered as prayed subject to all just exceptions, with a liberty to all concerned to take objections hereafter. This practice is intended to save time, trouble and expense in the presentation of evidence already on record and to which no person interested objects. See the records in the *St John Peerage Case* [1915] AC 282, HL, and the *Fitzwalter Peerage Case* (1925) 157 Lords Journals 8. Copies of charters illustrating the descents in offices of honour produced in the *Lord Great Chamberlain's Case* (1902) were allowed to be reprinted and used without further proof in the *Lucas Peerage Case* (1907): see speeches of counsel. See also the *Beauchamp and Mordaunt Baronies Case* (1928) Proceedings and Evidence lxiii.

856.   Evidence of creation. In all peerage claims evidence of creation, descent and extinction of nearer heirs[1] must be proved. In addition, in a claim to be declared co-heir to a barony in abeyance[2], the persons who are the other co-heirs must, so far as it is known, be stated, and their pedigree proved[3], and it must be proved that they have all been served with notice of the claim[4]. It is necessary to ascertain, so far as is possible, the fractional part ascribed to each co-heir in the co-heirship[5].

To prove the creation of the dignity the claimant must produce the instrument of creation or, if it cannot be found, the enrolment[6], or give such evidence as the House of Lords requires[7].

In the case of baronies by writ[8], the claimant must produce from the Close Rolls[9] the record of the writ of summons and proof of sitting from the Journals of the House of Lords[10]. In cases before the dates of existing Journals[11], he must prove by record that the ancestor took part in some proceeding which necessitated his presence as a peer[12]. This is sufficiently proved by evidence that a particular peer was appointed to do some act, hear some appeal or be a member of some commission[13].

1   Proof of extinction is always difficult. It is not so strictly required for co-heirships in abeyance claims as for definite claims to a peerage as of right. Generally, a skilled searcher of records should be employed and searches made in the period in question for certificates of birth, marriage and death, wills, legal proceedings, monumental inscriptions, public notices etc. The searcher is required to give oral evidence of the nature of searches made and to produce the results. For this kind of material see *Le Power and Coroghmore Barony Case* (1921) Minutes of Evidence xxviii–xxxi. On negative results see the *Beauchamp and Mordaunt Baronies Case* (1928) Proceedings and Evidence xvii–xx.

2   As to abeyance see PARAS 832–833, 848.

3   *Braye Peerage Case* (1839) 6 Cl & Fin 757 at 766. Strict proof of the pedigree of co-heirs is not insisted on where conclusive proof is impossible: see the *Braye Peerage Case*; and the *Fitzwalter Peerage Case* (1844) 10 Cl & Fin 946, HL.

4   *Vaux Peerage Case* (1837) 5 Cl & Fin 526, HL; *Braye Peerage Case* (1839) 6 Cl & Fin 757 at 789. Notice by post has been held insufficient: *Camoys Peerage Case* (1839) 6 Cl & Fin 789 at 794, HL. See also the *Latymer Peerage Case* (1912) Minutes of Evidence 3, 4.

5   See the Report on Peerages in Abeyance (1927) 6. This requirement means a more exact searching for co-heirs and therefore reasonable searches must be prosecuted: Report on Peerages in Abeyance (1927) 7, 11. The thoroughness of search required may be gathered from the *Strange of Knokin and Stanley Baronies Case* (1920) Minutes of Evidence xlv et seq.   '

6   *Tracy Peerage Case* (1843) 10 Cl & Fin 154 at 156, 157, HL; and see PARA 814.

7	The instrument of creation of ancient dignities is usually lost, but some act may be on record which implies creation: see the *Crawford and Lindsay Peerages Case* (1848) 2 HL Cas 534, where the proof accepted in the claim to the earldom of Crawford was an entry in the Lord Treasurer's accounts of the expense of creating that dignity and two royal dukedoms in Parliament. Creation of the barony by letters patent was proved by producing from State Papers, Ireland, Henry VIII vol II No 68, a bill indented that the Master of the Rolls in Ireland had received from Cromwell, Secretary of State, two creations (one for Sir Richard Power) as Barons of Parliament in Ireland, together with a copy of a letter from the Lord Chancellor to Cromwell from the British Museum Cotton MSS asking Cromwell to have these two patents which 'I have made' dealt with: see the *Le Power and Coroghmore Barony Case* (1921) Minutes of Evidence, App I. As to proof by circumstantial evidence see also the *Mar Peerage Case* (1875) 1 App Cas 1, HL. Statements by chroniclers and contemporary historians are not admissible as evidence of creation: *Vaux Peerage Case* (1837) 5 Cl & Fin 526, HL. In all such cases the existence of the dignity is abundantly proved by records, and it is merely its origin which is required to be established. Cf also the *Perth Earldom Case* (1848) 2 HL Cas 865. In the absence of the original letters patent the committee may accept an examined copy coming from proper custody: *Earl of Lanesborough's Case* (1848) 1 HL Cas 510n; *Saye and Sele Barony Case* (1848) 1 HL Cas 507; cf the *Huntly Peerage Case* (1838) 5 Cl & Fin 349, HL. The limitations of the peerage may be proved from the Journals of the House of Lords: *Saye and Sele Barony Case*; *Lord Dufferin and Claneboye's Case* (1837) 4 Cl & Fin 568, HL. See also the *Dudhope Peerage Case* (1952) Proceedings and Judgment 127 (where the destination of the peerage was proved by the index to the Great Seal Register of Scotland, the relevant leaves of the Register being missing, and a certified extract from the Privy Council minutes); and the *Dundee Earldom Case* (1953) Proceedings and Judgment 46 (where the passing of the patent was proved by an entry in the records of the Scottish Parliament and the terms of the limitation by copies in the British Museum and the Advocates' Library of Signatures ordaining a patent to be made under the Great Seal of Scotland). As to the presumption in the case of a Scottish peerage where no evidence of the limitations is to be found see PARA 815.

8	As to baronies by writ see PARA 822.

9	Palgrave's Parliamentary Writs is a useful guide. If the Close Roll is lost, the writ may be presumed from an otherwise unexplained sitting: *Hastings Peerage Case* (1841) 8 Cl & Fin 144, HL.

10	As to the Journals as evidence see PARLIAMENT vol 78 (2010) PARA 868.

11	The published Journals of the House of Lords date from 1510: see the *Vaux Peerage Case* (1837) 5 Cl & Fin 526, HL.

12	What constitutes a proceeding in Parliament may be a matter of argument: see the *Hastings Peerage Case* (1841) 8 Cl & Fin 144 at 150, 151, 160–162, HL; Cruise on Dignities (2nd Edn) c 5 s 71. In the *Cromwell Peerage Case* (1920) proof of evidence of sitting was given that the ancestor acted as a witness in Parliament of two patents for the settlement of the Crown (Document No 7), and was appointed as a trier of petitions (Document No 10). See also the *Strange of Knokin and Stanley Baronies Case* (1920) (Documents Nos 32, 41, 42, 49, 50). See also generally the *Strabolgi Peerage Case* (1914) Minutes of Evidence; and Lord Atkinson's speech in the *Beauchamp Barony Case* [1925] AC 153, HL. The name of a man summoned may appear as a witness to a charter mentioned in the Rolls of Parliament, but it is also necessary to show that the charter was actually made in Parliament: *Montacute and Monthermer Peerages Case* (1928) Proceedings and Evidence xxv. A writ of summons to an individual, and a Parliament Roll which records that the individual attended, and had been made an earl by investiture in Parliament, is sufficient evidence that he was present in Parliament as a baron before his investiture as an earl (Minutes of Evidence xxxiii), but a Parliament Roll which records the appointment of several persons to act as an Embassy to France is not evidence that one of them, who also received a summons to that Parliament, received an appointment which could have been made only in his capacity as a peer (Minutes of Evidence xxvi–xxxiii).

13	*Botetourt Peerage Case* (1764) Palmer's Peerage Law in England 46 (where the roll of 50 Edw III, showing John, Lord Botetourt, to have been a mainpernor of Parliament, was allowed as proof of sitting); *Cromwell Peerage Case* (1920) Document No 2. The mainperning must, however, have taken place in full Parliament and not have been completed elsewhere; otherwise it is insufficient to prove physical presence: see the *Montacute and Monthermer Peerages Case* (1928) Proceedings and Evidence xx, xxv and App 4 p 2. In the *Mowbray and Segrave Peerage Case* (1877) Minutes of Evidence, a statement or recital in letters patent describing the patentee as Baron Mowbray was admitted to prove termination of an abeyance.

857.   Evidence of descent. The claimant must prove descent from the original grantee within the original limitation[1], except in proving a claim to a barony which, having been revived after being previously in abeyance, is again in abeyance, where it is sufficient to prove descent from the holder in whose favour it was last revived[2].

If the peerage, validly created, has ceased to exist or its extinction in law can be argued, the Committee for Privileges may hear the argument and decide the question whether there is a dignity capable of being claimed before allowing any evidence of pedigree to be adduced[3].

1   *Grey de Ruthyn Case* (1640) Collins's Baronies by Writ (1734 Edn) 256, HL.
2   *Fitzwalter Peerage Case* (1844) 10 Cl & Fin 946, HL. The complete descent should, however, be set out in the petition and leave obtained to refer to the evidence given in the proceedings on the previous abeyance. As to such leave see PARA 855 note 3. As to abeyance see PARAS 832–833, 848.
3   This may happen in cases of attainder: see the *Southesk Earldom Case* (1848) 2 HL Cas 908. As to attainder see PARA 838 note 1. The power was also exercised in the *Duke of Montrose's Case* (1853) 1 Macq 57, 401, Lord Lindsay's Report 3, HL. See also the *Le Power and Coroghmore Barony Case* (1921) Minutes of Evidence, in which the point of validity of letters patent of creation was first settled before proceeding to pedigree evidence. The procedure of allowing a claimant to prove his right subject to attainder or other obstacle has, however, been more often adopted.

858.   Declarations as to pedigree. Declarations by living persons[1] as to pedigree are admissible in peerage claims, whatever the weight attached to them may be. When made by near relations, they are always admitted[2]. Any declaration made after litigation is contemplated may, however, be rejected[3].

A peer may give evidence and subsequently participate in the judgment in the same case[4].

Formerly, resort might be had to an action to perpetuate testimony, but this procedure has fallen into disuse[5].

1   As to declarations as to pedigree by deceased persons see CIVIL PROCEDURE vol 11 (2009) PARA 830. A written declaration by a deceased person is not always admissible: *Berkeley Peerage Case* (1811) 4 Camp 401, HL; cf the *Shrewsbury Peerage Case* (1858) 7 HL Cas 1. Probably the Volumes of Sheets of Peers Pedigrees, signed and certified on their honour and handed in during the period 1767–1802 by virtue of a standing order of the House, remitted to the Committee for Privileges for examination and filed by the officers of the House, are admissible to prove the items of pedigree. There are four such volumes in the library of the House, which undoubtedly are records of the House in the custody of its officers. The pedigrees are records to the date of the peer's introduction and are valuable as a record of his family for several generations before his birth, and for the then condition of his descendants and some collaterals. Before its extinction under the Union with Ireland Act 1800, the House of Peers (Ireland) passed a similar order; a pedigree duly recorded under the order was accepted as evidence in the *Westmeath Earldom Case* (1871). As to the value generally to be attached to signed pedigrees not in official custody, and as to the weight certification by the College of Arms may have, see the *Montacute and Monthermer Peerages Case* (1928) Proceedings and Evidence xlix–li.
2   As to statements by remote relations see the *Lindsay Peerage Case* (1877) Minutes of Evidence.
3   See CIVIL PROCEDURE vol 11 (2009) PARA 830. In the *Annandale Peerage Case* (1878) Minutes of Evidence, a printed case was admitted to prove that a pedigree alleged to come from the charter chest was in reality prepared after litigation had been contemplated. See also the *Berkeley Peerage Case* (1811) 4 Camp 401, HL; and the *Slane Peerage Case* (1835) 5 Cl & Fin 23, HL.
4   *R v Five Popish Lords* (1685) 7 State Tr 1217, 1458, HL; *R v Earl of Macclesfield* (1725) 16 State Tr 767, HL.
5   Actions to perpetuate testimony were governed by RSC Ord 39 r 15, but there is no equivalent provision in the CPR: see EQUITABLE JURISDICTION vol 47 (2014) PARA 73. Such actions were not appropriate where the real question in dispute could be determined at once by other proceedings (eg proceedings to obtain a declaration of legitimacy): see *West v Lord Sackville* [1903] 2 Ch 378, CA.

859. Documentary evidence. Where there are no letters patent creating a barony and no enrolment can be found[1], the creation of a peerage may be proved by proof of writ of summons and sitting in the House of Lords[2].

Documents in public custody may be proved by copies officially certified as in ordinary legal proceedings[3]; but documents in private custody must be proved by production of the original[4].

1 As to creation of peerages by letters patent see PARA 814; and as to enrolment on the patent rolls see CONSTITUTIONAL AND ADMINISTRATIVE LAW vol 20 (2014) PARA 593 note 3.
2 *Hastings Peerage Case* (1841) 8 Cl & Fin 144 at 150, 151, HL. As to the creation of baronies by writ see PARA 822. As to the abolition of the automatic right of all hereditary peers to sit in the House of Lords see PARA 825.
3 HL Standing Orders (2013) (Public Business) no 78(2); 84 Lords Journals 96; and see PARA 853 note 3. As to the proof of wills prior to 1700 see the *Fitzwalter Peerage Case* (1844) 10 Cl & Fin 946 at 952, HL. See also the *Shrewsbury Peerage Case* (1858) 7 HL Cas 1. As to the French marriage registers see the *Perth Earldom Case* (1848) 2 HL Cas 865; and as to the general rules for proof of records see CIVIL PROCEDURE vol 11 (2009) PARAS 884–888.
4 HL Standing Orders (2013) (Public Business) no 78(2); and see PARA 853 note 3.

860. Legitimacy. Questions as to legitimacy frequently arise in connection with claims to peerages[1]. The status of a legitimate or lawful heir may be questioned in respect of an ancestor, but has usually arisen in respect of the claimant himself at the instance of a counterclaimant or the Crown[2]. In such cases the physical fact of impotency or of non-access[3] or of non-generating access, as the case may be, may always be lawfully proved by means of such legal evidence as is strictly admissible in every other case in which it is necessary that a physical fact be proved[4].

A declaration of legitimacy[5] binds the Crown and extends to peerage claims[6]. There are only two exceptions to the binding effect of such a declaration:

(1)   it must not prejudice any person not cited or made a party, unless that person claims through a person cited or made a party; and

(2)   it must not prejudice any person if obtained by fraud or collusion[7].

1 The ordinary law as to legitimacy in relation to succession to land and the effect of domicile applies: see CHILDREN AND YOUNG PERSONS vol 9 (2012) PARA 94 et seq; CONFLICT OF LAWS vol 19 (2011) PARAS 336 et seq, 618 et seq. As to legitimation see PARA 809. The liability of a peer to attend in Parliament when his presence is required does not prevent him from acquiring a foreign domicile: *Hamilton v Dallas* (1875) 1 ChD 257.
2 *Banbury Peerage Case* (1811) 1 Sim & St 153, fully reported in Nicolas's Treatise on Adulterine Bastardy (1836 Edn) 182–187. For a case where a claimant brought a petition in the Probate Division of the High Court of Justice under the Legitimacy Declaration Act 1858 ss 4, 11 (repealed) see *Sackville-West v A-G* [1910] P 143. See also *Sussex Peerage Case* (1844) 11 Cl & Fin 85, HL, where the Duke of Sussex was married to Lady Augusta Murray validly by the law of Rome, although the parties were not domiciled in Rome, but the marriage was invalid under the Royal Marriages Act 1772 s 1 (see CROWN AND ROYAL FAMILY vol 12(1) (Reissue) PARA 36).
3 *Saye and Sele Barony Case* (1848) 1 HL Cas 507.
4 *Banbury Peerage Case* (1811) 1 Sim & St 153, Minutes of Evidence 269. Impotency and impossibility of access were formerly the only allegations which could rebut the presumption that the mother's husband is the father. As to the presumption of legitimacy see CHILDREN AND YOUNG PERSONS vol 9 (2012) PARA 94 et seq; and see also MATRIMONIAL AND CIVIL PARTNERSHIP LAW vol 72 (2009) PARA 355. As to access see also the *Gardner Peerage Case* (1826) Le Marchant's Report, Petition, Case and Minutes of Evidence; *The Poulett Peerage* [1903] AC 395, HL. As to admissible evidence to prove non-access see the Matrimonial Causes Act 1973 s 48(1), abrogating the rule in *Russell v Russell* [1924] AC 687, HL (where the cases are reviewed). As to a declaration by either spouse as to non-access before marriage see *The Poulett Peerage* at 398 per Lord Halsbury LC. See further the *Saye and Sele Barony Case* (1848) 1 HL Cas 507; and *The Aylesford Peerage* (1885) 11 App Cas 1, HL. As to impotency and incapacity to consummate marriage see MATRIMONIAL AND CIVIL PARTNERSHIP LAW vol 72 (2009) PARA 336 et seq.

5   As to such declarations see the Family Law Act 1986 s 56; and CHILDREN AND YOUNG PERSONS vol 9 (2012) PARA 110. On a petition for such a declaration the court has no power to declare that the petitioner is entitled to succeed to a peerage: see *Frederick v A-G* (1874) LR 3 P & D 196.

6   *Ampthill Peerage Case* [1977] AC 547, [1976] 2 All ER 411, HL (referring to the Legitimacy Declaration Act 1858 (repealed), which corresponded to the Matrimonial Causes Act 1973 s 45 (repealed)).

7   See the *Ampthill Peerage Case* [1977] AC 547, [1976] 2 All ER 411, HL.

3. OTHER DIGNITIES

(1) THE BARONETAGE

861. Baronetcy. The hereditary dignity of baronet was first instituted by James I in 1611, to be granted to those persons who should contribute to the expenses of the Plantation of Ulster[1]. In 1625 it was decided to encourage the Plantation of Nova Scotia in the same manner. There are now five classes of baronets, namely:

(1) baronets of England, created between 1611 and 1707;

(2) baronets of Ireland, created between 1618 and 1801;

(3) baronets of Nova Scotia, created between 1625 and 1707;

(4) baronets of Great Britain, created between 1707 and 1801; and

(5) baronets of the United Kingdom, created since 1801.

A baronetcy is created by letters patent under the Great Seal[2], but the dignity is not one of the five degrees of peerage[3], nor is it part of the knighthood[4]. A baronetcy is an incorporeal hereditament, and is descendible as an estate tail[5]. The oath of allegiance must be taken by all baronets on their creation[6].

1 See 1 Bl Com (14th Edn) 403.

2 For the form of letters patent to be used in the creation of a baronet see the Crown Office (Forms and Proclamations Rules) Order 1992, SI 1992/1730, art 2(1), Schedule Pt III, Form I. There is now no limit to the number of baronetcies which the Crown may create. It had been originally promised that the number of baronets of England should not exceed 200, and that vacancies by extinction of issue should not be filled up. However, up to the Union with Scotland in 1707, 697 baronetcies of England, 58 baronetcies of Ireland and 166 baronetcies of Nova Scotia had been created. After the promulgation of the Union with Scotland Act 1706, England and Scotland ceased to exist in contemplation of law, and it is conceived that no new baronetcy of either kingdom could be created; but, whereas the question of the peerage of each kingdom was carefully dealt with in the Act, no reference to the baronetage appears in it. As to the use of the Great Seal see CONSTITUTIONAL AND ADMINISTRATIVE LAW vol 20 (2014) PARA 583.

3 As to the degrees of peerage see PARA 804.

4 As to the knighthood see PARA 865 et seq.

5 A baronetcy is an incorporeal hereditament, and, being limited to the heirs of the body, is within 13 Edw 1 (Statute of Westminster the Second) (1285) c 1 (De Donis Conditionalibus), (see REAL PROPERTY AND REGISTRATION vol 87 (2012) PARA 112), and is descendible as an estate tail and not a fee simple conditional, although no place is named in its creation: *Re Rivett-Carnac's Will* (1885) 30 ChD 136. See further PARA 808.

Under the Settled Land Act 1925 s 67 (replacing the Settled Land Act 1882 s 37), where personal chattels are settled to devolve with settled land, they may be sold by the tenant for life. It has been held that this provision applies where personal chattels are settled to devolve with a dignity such as a baronetcy; the dignity as an incorporeal hereditament is land within the above provision: *Re Rivett-Carnac's Will*. See also SETTLEMENTS vol 91 (2012) PARAS 842–844.

6 See the Promissory Oaths Act 1868 s 14(5); PARA 819; and CONSTITUTIONAL AND ADMINISTRATIVE LAW vol 20 (2014) PARA 599. For the form of oath see s 2.

862. Privileges of baronets. The letters patent creating a baronetcy set out the privileges, rights, precedences and advantages which attach to the baronetcy[1]; a baronet has no privileges except those stated in his patent.

Baronets have the right to the title or prefix 'Sir' and may use the post-nominal abbreviation of 'Bt' or 'Bart'. A baronetess in her own right has the prefix 'Dame' and may use the abbreviation 'Btess'. The wife of a baronet is entitled to the prefix 'Dame' although socially is always styled 'Lady', but the husband of a baronetess has no special form of address.

Baronets are entitled to certain armorial differences and the right to wear a distinctive badge in accordance with the Royal Warrants dated 17 November

1629 (baronets of Nova Scotia) and 13 April 1929 (all other baronets). A baronet ranks above all knights[2] except Knights of the Garter[3], and takes precedence among other baronets according to priority in date of creation[4].

1 See the Crown Office (Forms and Proclamations Rules) Order 1992, SI 1992/1730, art 2(1), Schedule Pt III, Form I. See also PARA 861.
2 As to the degrees of peerage see PARA 804. The King originally covenanted that he and his successors would never create any new dignity having precedence between barons, lords of Parliament, and baronets, and it has been contended that a warrant granting precedence to the children of life peers is a breach of this covenant. It is thought, however, that a distinct hereditary dignity was meant.
   Some of the first created baronets claimed to be knighted, and as the result of a controversy respecting their precedence, the King covenanted that all the then baronets, and the eldest sons or heirs apparent of baronets, should be knighted at their request on reaching the age of 21. This right was abolished by Royal Warrant dated 19 December 1827.
3 As to Knights of the Garter see PARA 866.
4 All the evidence relating to the status of a baronet which can be collected from the public records purports to be printed in: (1) The Herald and Genealogist vol III p 193 et seq; (2) Pixley's History of the Baronetage (1900); (3) Cockayne's Baronetage vol I Preface v et seq; and (4) The Baronetage (Anon 1911). See also Selden's Titles of Honor (3rd Edn) 679. Careful study of such evidence raises doubt whether the King intended to create a degree of nobility, or whether he merely intended to grant a hereditary pre-eminence among esquires similar to the distinction of knights banneret and ordinary knights, for the persons whom it was proposed to dignify with the prefix 'Sir' and the suffix 'Baronet' were those who would in the ordinary course of military tenure be called upon to accept knighthood.

863. Claim to baronetcy. A claim to a baronetcy should in the first instance be made to the Crown Office[1] on behalf of the Lord Chancellor[2] and, if not allowed, should be made by petition to the Queen in Council and determined by a committee of the Privy Council[3].

1 The Crown Office is a department of the Ministry of Justice, located in the House of Lords; its address is Crown Office, House of Lords, London, SW1A 0PW.
2 The Royal Warrants (see note 3) refer to the Secretary of State for the Home Department but, at the date at which this volume states the law, responsibility for the official roll of the baronetcy lies with the Lord Chancellor and Secretary of State for Justice. As to the official roll see PARA 864.
3 Royal Warrant dated 8 February 1910, London Gazette, 15 February 1910; Royal Warrant dated 10 March 1922, London Gazette, 17 March 1922, p 2234.
   It was the practice of James I to refer claims to dignities to the commissioners for exercising the office of Earl Marshal, when during his reign that office was in commission and there was no Earl Marshal, and it was promised that baronetcies should be subject to the jurisdiction of the Earl Marshal or the commissioners, as the case might be. No commissioners or other functionaries for exercising the office of Earl Marshal have existed for the last two centuries as there has always been an Earl Marshal. The rights of the Earl Marshal are expressly saved by the Royal Warrant dated 8 February 1910, except in so far as they are contained in the cancelled warrants dated 3 December 1783, 24 February 1785 and 30 September 1789: Royal Warrant dated 8 February 1910 arts 12, 13. As to the Earl Marshal see PARA 878 note 5.
   The current practice is that, if the Lord Chancellor, after obtaining a report from the Garter King of Arms (see PARA 879), finds any difficulty in advising the Sovereign as to the validity of any claim to be placed on the roll, the claim will be referred to the Attorney General for England or the Lord Advocate for Scotland, as the case may be, for opinion, and ultimately to the Privy Council: Royal Warrant dated 10 March 1922 arts 2, 3. Claims to baronetcies of Ireland would now probably be referred to the Attorney General for England: cf CONSTITUTIONAL AND ADMINISTRATIVE LAW vol 20 (2014) PARAS 274, 276. See also PARA 813.
   A committee of the Privy Council appointed by Orders in Council dated 5 March 1910 and 22 March 1928 sits as a judicial body to hear claims which may be referred. Several claims have been heard. The committee follows the rules of evidence in force in the ordinary courts of law, and probably would also have regard to the practice followed in peerage cases as to proofs of pedigree. The hearing is public, and, as a rule, reported in the press.
   The Family Law Act 1986 s 56 (declarations of parentage, legitimacy and legitimation: see CHILDREN AND YOUNG PERSONS vol 9 (2012) PARA 110) gives no jurisdiction to investigate or

decide a claim to a baronetcy: see *Frederick v A-G* (1874) LR 3 P & D 196 (concerning an equivalent provision in the Legitimacy Declaration Act 1858 (repealed)).

864. Official roll. No person may be officially styled a baronet unless his name appears on the official roll[1] which is maintained by the Crown Office[2], and is published from time to time[3]. A registrar has been appointed[4] and his duties are defined by royal warrant[5].

1 Royal Warrant dated 8 February 1910 art 2.
2 The Royal Warrant dated 8 February 1910 refers to the Secretary of State for the Home Department but, at the date at which this volume states the law, responsibility for the official roll of the baronetcy lies with the Lord Chancellor and Secretary of State for Justice: see the Transfer of Functions (Miscellaneous) Order 2001, SI 2001/3500, art 3, Sch 1 para 2. The Crown Office is a department of the Ministry of Justice, located in the House of Lords; its address is Crown Office, House of Lords, London, SW1A 0PW.
3 Royal Warrant dated 8 February 1910 arts 1, 3, 5, 6, 11.
4 Royal Warrant dated 8 February 1910 art 7. The first registrar and assistant registrar were appointed by Order in Council dated 5 March 1910.
5 Royal Warrant dated 8 February 1910 arts 8, 9; Royal Warrant dated 10 March 1922 art 4.

(2) KNIGHTHOOD, ORDERS AND DECORATIONS

865. In general. Knighthood[1] is a personal dignity conferred for life. It is not of a particular kingdom, like a peerage or a baronetcy, but is a dignity recognised in every part of the Sovereign's dominions[2].

An individual of the male sex[3] is now legally entitled to use the prefix 'Sir' and to rank before untitled persons once the Sovereign's intention to confer the honour of knighthood has been officially published[4]. The individual is formally created a knight when the Sovereign or an appointed lieutenant[5] (usually a knight[6]) directs the individual to kneel and strikes the individual's shoulder with a naked sword[7]. A knight can also be created by letters patent[8]. The oath of allegiance must be taken by all knights on their creation[9].

1 For the history of knighthood out of England and the early history in England see Selden's Titles of Honor (3rd Edn) 361 et seq, 451 et seq, 636 et seq; Nicolas's History of the Orders of Knighthood of the British Empire. The most authentic list of English knights is in Shaw's Knights of England (1906).
2 See *Lord Advocate v Walker Trustees* [1912] AC 95 at 104, HL.
3 As to the eligibility of women for knighthoods see PARA 866.
4 As to the degrees of peerage see PARA 804.
5 By virtue of his office, the Lord Lieutenant of Ireland had authority to confer knighthood: unanimous opinion of the judges summoned by the King in Council 1823; and see 1 Nicolas's History of the Orders of Knighthood of the British Empire, Introduction, xiii.
6 See 1 Nicolas's History of the Orders of Knighthood of the British Empire, Introduction, xv.
7 If a Sovereign knights a Sovereign, he also passes his arm around the shoulders. Knighthood was formerly conferred by ceremonial investiture, which is now represented by the accolade. Much of the ceremonial of the investiture still survives in the ceremony of the coronation, eg in the vesting of the Sovereign in garments of a sacerdotal character and presenting him with the sword and spurs: see CROWN AND ROYAL FAMILY vol 12(1) (Reissue) PARA 20.
8 Knights have also been created by letters patent since 1777: 1 Nicolas's History of the Orders of Knighthood of the British Empire, Introduction, xv.
9 See the Promissory Oaths Act 1868 s 14(5); PARA 819; and CONSTITUTIONAL AND ADMINISTRATIVE LAW vol 20 (2014) PARA 599. For the form of oath see s 2.

866. Orders of knighthood. The age of chivalry engendered societies whose membership was restricted to knights. Of these the earliest in England was a society known as the Order of the Garter[1], founded by Edward III in or about 1348[2]. It is limited to 24 knights in addition to the Sovereign (who is head of the order) and the Prince of Wales, but the Sovereign has the power to create additional royal knights and may appoint foreign Sovereigns as extra knights. Provision was made for the appointment of foreign knights in 1954. Historically the Garter was not normally bestowed on peers, particularly prior to the reign of Edward IV. Knights of the Garter take precedence in England before Privy Councillors and baronets[3].

Another society of knights in England, the precise origin of which is not clear, is the Order of the Bath[4]. The order was originally civil in nature but was converted into a military order during the reign of George III as a consequence of the Napoleonic War. George III also divided the Order into different grades of companionship. Because of such changes the Order has lost the medieval character preserved by the Garter. The Order of the Bath is now divided into two branches, military and civil[5].

Other orders of knighthood are:

(1)   Knights of St Andrew or the Thistle, founded or revived in Scotland by James II in 1687[6], and re-established on 31 December 1703;

(2)   Knights of St Patrick, founded in Ireland by George III on 5 February 1783[7], and revived in 1833;

(3)   Knights of the Order of the Star of India, founded in 1861, and used to reward service in connection with India[8];

(4)   Knights of St Michael and St George, founded in 1818[9] to reward service in the Mediterranean, chiefly Maltese and Ionic, but now used to reward any colonial or diplomatic service;

(5)   Knights of the Order of the Indian Empire, founded to commemorate the title of Emperor or Empress of India in 1878[10];

(6)   Knights of the Royal Victorian Order, founded in 1896[11];

(7)   Knights of the Order of the British Empire, founded in 1917[12].

1   See Statutes of the Order of the Garter.
2   The year 1344 was given by Selden: see Selden's Titles of Honor (3rd Edn) 657; 1 Bl Com (14th Edn) 403. The first 25 knights, called Knights Founders, the first being Edward, Prince of Wales, had been created before or on St George's Day 1348: see 1 Shaw's Knights of England (1906) 1. For a history of the Order of the Garter see Nicolas's History of the Orders of Knighthood of the British Empire vols 1, 2.
3   1 Bl Com (14th Edn) 403; and see PARA 862. As to the baronetage see PARAS 861–864.
4   The bath was the first part of the ceremonial for creating a knight (see Anstis's Knighthood of the Bath 5), but to call knights of the twelfth century Knights of the Bath (see 1 Shaw's Knights of England (1906) 109) seems somewhat strange. It is considered that knighthood by baptism existed side by side with knighthood by accolade. The antiquity of the bath is illustrated by the coronation ceremony. The ancient practice was for the King to bathe at the palace of Westminster the day before he proceeded to the Abbey, with a number of youthful aspirants who were knighted by the King when crowned, after investiture as a knight by the Church: see 1 Bl Com (14th Edn) 404. For a history of the Knights of the Bath see 3 Nicolas's History of the Orders of Knighthood of the British Empire 3 et seq.
5   The Order is also divided into three classes, namely Knights Grand Cross, Knights Commanders (both of which are entitled to be called 'knight') and Companions, who take precedence of esquires but are not entitled to be called 'knight'. Each class is restricted in point of numbers. The Order is now open to women, with the substitution of 'Dame' for 'Knight'.
6   3 Nicolas's History of the Orders of Knighthood of the British Empire 3 et seq.
7   4 Nicolas's History of the Orders of Knighthood of the British Empire 3 et seq. No appointment has been made since 1936 when the honour was conferred upon the Duke of York (later George VI).
8   London Gazette dated 25 June 1861 p 2621. It consists of the Sovereign, the Grand Master, and a fixed number of Companions divided into three classes, namely Knights Grand Commanders, Knights Commanders and Companions. No appointment has been made since India became independent in 1947.

9   Letters Patent dated 27 April 1818. Both sexes are eligible. The Order comprises a fixed number of Knights Grand Cross and Dames Grand Cross, Knights Commanders and Dames Commanders, and Companions. Each class ranks next after the corresponding class of the Order of the Star of India. For a history of the Knights of St Michael and St George see 4 Nicolas's History of the Orders of Knighthood of the British Empire 3.

10 The Order consists of the Sovereign, the Grand Master, and three classes, namely Knights Grand Commanders, Knights Commanders, and Companions. Each class ranks next after the corresponding class of the Order of St Michael and St George. No appointment has been made since India became independent in 1947.

11 London Gazette dated 24 April 1896 p 2455. Both sexes are eligible. The Order consists of the Sovereign, the Grand Master and ordinary members. It is divided into five classes, namely Knights Grand Cross and Dames Grand Cross, Knights Commanders and Dames Commanders, Commanders, and Members of the Fourth and Fifth Classes. Knights Grand Cross and Knights Commanders rank after the corresponding classes of the Order of the Indian Empire. Commanders and members of the Fourth Class, known as Lieutenants, rank after Companions of the Indian Empire. Members of the Fifth Class rank after the eldest sons of knights bachelors. The Order is given to reward those who have rendered extraordinary, important or personal services to the Sovereign; foreigners may be appointed honorary members. The number of members is unlimited.

   There is also a decoration, known as the Royal Victorian Chain, which is not part of the Order.

12 London Gazette dated 24 August 1917 p 8791. Both sexes are eligible. The Order consists of the Sovereign, the Grand Master and five classes, namely, Knights Grand Cross and Dames Grand Cross, Knights Commanders and Dames Commanders, Commanders, Officers and Members. In 1918 it was divided into two sections, civil and military. It is bestowed for service in civil life and as a recognition for military service in peace and war.

867.   Knights bachelor and miscellaneous orders.

867.   Knights bachelor and miscellaneous orders.   Knights bachelor, or ordinary knights, are those who are merely created knights but belong to no particular Order[1].

There are numerous orders and decorations which do not confer any title or right of precedence[2].

1   Originally there were no orders of knights, all knights being either knights banneret or knights bachelor. The distinction between the two, which is no longer of significance, was purely military; knights banneret were entitled to a banner in time of war and to have command over knights bachelor, who were only entitled to a pennon. See 1 Bl Com (14th Edn) 404, 405. As to the orders of knighthood see PARA 866.

2   Examples are the Victoria Cross, instituted by Royal Warrant dated 29 January 1856 for conspicuous bravery in the field; the Order of Victoria and Albert, instituted in 1862 and confined to women, the last surviving member being Princess Alice, Countess of Athlone, who died in 1981; the Albert Medal, founded by Royal Warrant dated 7 March 1866 for gallantry in saving life at sea or on land (and exchanged in 1971 for the George Cross); the Imperial Order of the Crown of India, instituted on 31 December 1877 and confined to women; the Royal Red Cross, founded by Royal Warrant dated 23 April 1883 and confined to women; the Distinguished Service Order, instituted in 1886 for commissioned officers; the Order of Merit, founded on 23 June 1902 as a special distinction for eminent persons and limited to 24 members; the Imperial Service Order, instituted in 1902 for members of the Civil Service and limited to 850 home and 575 overseas companions; the Edward Medal, founded by Royal Warrant dated 13 July 1907 for heroism in mines and quarries (and exchanged in 1971 for the George Cross); the Territorial Decoration, founded in 1908; the Order of the Companions of Honour, founded on 4 June 1917 and limited to 65 companions; and the George Cross, instituted by Royal Warrant dated 24 September 1940 (amended 8 May 1941 and 3 November 1942) for gallantry, normally limited to civilians.

(3) FOREIGN DIGNITIES, ORDERS AND DECORATIONS

868.   Foreign dignities.   Dignities created by foreign Sovereigns are not recognised by law in the United Kingdom, but licences to accept and enjoy them have been granted by the Sovereign by warrant addressed to the Earl Marshal[1].

A petition stating good reason for leave to bear such a title in England was formerly addressed to the Sovereign and sent to the Secretary of State for the Home Department in the same manner as other petitions for warrants of precedency, change of name and similar matters[2]. However, the availability of this procedure was terminated by royal warrant in 1932, and there is now no procedure for recognising foreign titles. A foreign title lawfully used in England gives no precedence in law[3], but it is usually recognised in courtesy.

1 For an example of a licence see the *De Scales Peerage Case* (1857) Minutes of Evidence 71. As to the Earl Marshal see PARA 878 note 5.
2 As to petitions for warrants of precedency, change of name etc see PARAS 829, 875.
3 As to the degrees of peerage see PARA 804; and as to precedence see PARA 829.

869. Foreign orders and decorations. Orders and decorations granted by a foreign Sovereign are not recognised in law in the United Kingdom[1].

Rules concerning the wearing of foreign orders and medals by British citizens are administered in accordance with Her Majesty's wishes by the Secretary of State for Foreign and Commonwealth Affairs, to whom all applications for Her Majesty's permission to make use of such distinctions should be addressed[2]. These rules on the acceptance and wearing of foreign awards preclude the acceptance of medals for events in the distant past or more than five years previously[3].

1 See the ruling in the case of the Knights of the Guelphic Order of Hanover (which was founded in 1815 by George IV whilst Prince Regent, and not conferred since the death of William IV in 1837).
2 See the UK Rules on the Acceptance of Foreign Awards (published 15 June 2012).
3 See the UK Rules on the Acceptance of Foreign Awards (published 15 June 2012). See also HL Official Report (5th Series), 11 January 2005, written answers col 34.

4. ARMORIAL BEARINGS

(1) THE LAW OF ARMS

870. The law of arms. The use of arms, crests, supporters and other armorial insignia is governed by the law of arms. The law of arms is not part of the common law, although it is part of the law of England and is noticed as such by the common law courts[1]. The substance of the law of arms is to be found in the customs and usages of the Court of Chivalry[2].

1 *Paston v Ledham* (1459) YB 37 Hen VI, Pasch, pl 8; *R v Parker* (1668) 1 Sid 353.
2 4 Co Inst 125; *Puryman v Cavendish* (1397) Close Roll 21 Ric II, p 1 m 5. As to the Court of Chivalry see PARA 884.

871. Descent of armorial bearings. Arms are usually granted to the grantee and his descendants with due and proper differences according to the laws of arms[1]. Sometimes arms are granted with an extended limitation embracing all the descendants of the father or some more remote ancestor of the grantee[2]. Arms descend to males in the first instance[3], but on the failure of male descendants they may be transmitted through females as quarterings.

1 A grant of arms is a document in which every member of the family is interested, and whichever of them has possession of it is entitled to keep it, but may be called upon by the others to produce it: *Stubs v Stubs* (1862) 1 H & C 257. See PARA 870.
2 For a copy of a grant with an extended limitation see *Stubs v Stubs* (1862) 1 H & C 257.
3 *Wiltes Peerage Case* (1869) LR 4 HL 126 at 153 per Lord Chelmsford.

872. Right to bear arms. Arms may only be borne by virtue of ancestral right or of a grant made under lawful authority[1]. Ancestral right is normally proved from the records of the College of Arms[2], especially those relating to the heralds' visitations[3].

1 See Squibb's High Court of Chivalry 184, 185.
2 As to the College of Arms see PARA 881.
3 As to visitations see PARA 883. As to the heralds and other officers of the College of Arms see PARA 878 et seq. As to the descent of armorial bearings see PARA 871.

873. Grants of arms. The right to grant and regulate armorial bearings has from earliest times been inherent in the office of a King of Arms[1] within his province, as representative of the Sovereign, and since the sixteenth century express words delegating this royal prerogative have been inserted in the letters patent of their appointments[2]. Since the seventeenth century the right of the English Kings of Arms has, however, been subject to regulation by the Earl Marshal, whose warrant is necessary in every case to enable them to assign new arms[3]. The Earl Marshal's warrant is issued in response to a memorial signed by or on behalf of the proposed grantee[4]. The modern practice is for grants of arms to bodies corporate to be made by all three Kings of Arms. A grant to a natural person is made by Garter and the King of Arms of the province in which the grantee resides[5].

1 As to Kings of Arms see PARA 879.
2 As to the appointment of Kings of Arms see PARA 878. As to the royal prerogative generally see CONSTITUTIONAL AND ADMINISTRATIVE LAW vol 20 (2014) PARA 166; CROWN AND ROYAL FAMILY vol 12(1) (Reissue) PARA 46 et seq.
3 As to the Earl Marshal see PARA 878 note 5.
4 The memorial is usually prepared by one of the officers of arms (see PARA 878 et seq). It should be carefully drafted since, if approved, the allegations contained in it will be repeated in the

warrant and ultimately in the grant. Stamp duty formerly exigible on the grant of arms or armorial ensigns only was abolished by the Finance Act 1949 ss 35, 52(10), Sch 8 Pt I para 16, Sch 11 Pt V (all now repealed or spent).

5   As to the provinces of the Kings of Arms see PARA 879 note 1.

874.   Jurisdiction over arms.   Complaints relating to the usurpation of armorial bearings are dealt with by the Court of Chivalry[1]. The common law courts have no jurisdiction in those matters[2]. The Court of Chivalry is the only surviving civil law court, and its procedure is in accordance with the forms of the civil law[3].

Appeals from the Court of Chivalry to the Judicial Committee of the Privy Council, to which the jurisdiction of the Court of Delegates was transferred in 1832, have been abolished[4].

1   See eg *Manchester Corpn v Manchester Palace of Varieties Ltd* [1955] P 133 at 149, [1955] 1 All ER 387 at 393, Court of Chivalry, per Lord Goddard (Surrogate). As to the Court of Chivalry see PARA 884.
2   *Duke of Buckingham's Case* (1514) Keil 170; *R v Parker* (1668) 1 Sid 353.
3   See *A Verbatim Report of the Case in the High Court of Chivalry of The Lord Mayor, Aldermen and Citizens of the City of Manchester versus The Manchester Palace of Varieties Limited* published by the Heraldry Society (1955).
4   *Blount's Case* (1737) 1 Atk 295; Privy Council Appeals Act 1832 s 3 (repealed); Judicial Committee Act 1833 s 3; Judicial Committee Act 1844 s 11; Ecclesiastical Jurisdiction Measure 1963 s 87, Sch 5 (repealed).

875.   Grant of arms and procedure to obtain royal licence for change of surname and bearing of arms.   The granting of arms is part of the prerogative of the Sovereign[1], which is delegated, by letters patent under the Great Seal, to the Kings of Arms[2], to exercise in accordance with the law of arms[3].

In order to obtain a royal licence authorising a change of surname and the bearing of the arms of another family[4], an application must be made to the College of Arms[5] for a petition in proper form, stating the reasons for the application and other necessary matters, to be drawn up by one of the officers of arms[6], to be signed by the applicant, and submitted to the Crown Office[7] and through the Lord Chancellor to the Sovereign. The granting of a licence is a matter of discretion in which the Sovereign is advised by the Lord Chancellor, subject to an assurance by Garter King of Arms on behalf of the Earl Marshal that he has no objection to the granting of a licence[8].

1   As to the royal prerogative generally see CONSTITUTIONAL AND ADMINISTRATIVE LAW vol 20 (2014) PARA 166; CROWN AND ROYAL FAMILY vol 12(1) (Reissue) PARA 46 et seq. To use arms, other than the royal arms (see CROWN AND ROYAL FAMILY vol 12(1) (Reissue) PARAS 43–44), without a grant or other title is not unlawful in the sense that any penalty is attached. Arms, being in the nature of dignities and governed by similar rules both in origin and enjoyment, are not within the jurisdiction of the ordinary courts of law but are within the jurisdiction of the Court of Chivalry: see *Earl Cowley v Countess Cowley* [1901] AC 450 at 456, HL; *Manchester Corpn v Manchester Palace of Varieties Ltd* [1955] P 133, [1955] 1 All ER 387, Court of Chivalry; and PARA 874. As to the Court of Chivalry see PARA 884.
2   As to Kings of Arms see PARA 879. As to their appointment see PARA 878. As to the use of the Great Seal see CONSTITUTIONAL AND ADMINISTRATIVE LAW vol 20 (2014) PARA 583.
3   As to the law of arms see PARA 870.
4   As to name and arms clauses see SETTLEMENTS vol 91 (2012) PARAS 646, 649–650. A royal licence is not necessary merely to effect a change of surname, although it is a method by which such a change can be authenticated: see PERSONAL PROPERTY vol 80 (2013) PARA 802; REGISTRATION CONCERNING THE INDIVIDUAL vol 88 (2012) PARAS 326, 328, 330 et seq.
5   As to the College of Arms see PARA 881.
6   As to the officers of arms see PARA 878 et seq.
7   The Crown Office is a department of the Ministry of Justice, located in the House of Lords; its address is Crown Office, House of Lords, London, SW1A 0PW.

8   For the purposes of obtaining advice, the Lord Chancellor consults Garter King of Arms on behalf of the Earl Marshal on the terms of the petition and the genealogical and heraldic aspects of the case. As to the Earl Marshal see PARA 878 note 5.

    No precise rules are laid down as to the exercise of the discretion, and probably no such rules could well be formulated. It may be broadly stated, however, that, while an application for a royal licence for change of surname only may be rejected on the ground that a royal licence is not necessary for this purpose, an application to transfer arms, in compliance with a request contained in a will or in consideration of some pecuniary or other benefit, or based on representation in blood traced to some maternal ancestor, will be favourably considered; whereas an application made in pursuance of a direction which is coupled with a forfeiture clause is invariably granted. An application for which no reasonable ground is alleged, or which is made from mere caprice, is, however, likely to be rejected. As to change of name see PERSONAL PROPERTY vol 80 (2013) PARA 802; REGISTRATION CONCERNING THE INDIVIDUAL vol 88 (2012) PARA 326 et seq.

876. Issue of royal warrant licensing change of surname and bearing of arms.

When the prayer of a petition[1] is granted, a warrant addressed to the Earl Marshal[2] following in its terms the allegations of the petition is issued under the royal sign manual[3]. The royal warrant so issued is duly recorded in the College of Arms[4] by warrant of the Earl Marshal and is usually notified in the London Gazette. In its terms the licence is permissive; it does not purport to confer a new name or to grant new arms[5].

1   As to the procedure to obtain a royal licence for the change of surname by petition see PARA 875.
2   As to the Earl Marshal see PARA 878 note 5.
3   As to the royal sign manual see CONSTITUTIONAL AND ADMINISTRATIVE LAW vol 20 (2014) PARA 582.
4   As to the College of Arms see PARA 881.
5   Fees are payable (eg for preparing and presenting the petition, for reporting and recording the royal licence, and for granting or exemplifying the arms), but stamp duty on exemplifications and on grants to use a surname and arms was abolished by the Finance Act 1949 ss 35, 52(10), Sch 8 Pt I para 16, Sch 11 Pt V (all now repealed or spent).

877. Exemplification and record of arms.

As regards armorial bearings the royal licence[1] contains a proviso that the arms are to be exemplified according to the law of arms and recorded in the College of Arms[2], and that otherwise the licence and permission are void and of no effect[3].

    It is the duty of the Kings of Arms[4], as the delegated representatives of the Sovereign, to determine the arms of the testator or settlor, and to exemplify these to the person authorised by the royal licence to bear them. Should the testator or settlor have had no valid claim to arms, the Kings of Arms grant arms to be borne by the applicant in compliance with the terms of the royal licence[5].

1   See PARA 876.
2   As to the law of arms see PARA 870. As to the College of Arms see PARA 881.

3   For an example of a royal licence see the *Cromwell Peerage Claim* (1922), App 177; and see the London Gazette dated 28 October 1960 p 7285.
4   As to Kings of Arms see PARA 879.

5   *Austen v Collins* (1886) 54 LT 903. An obligation to assume arms cannot be satisfied by a mere de facto user; the authority of a royal licence through the College of Arms is required: *Re Berens, Re Dowdeswell, Berens-Dowdeswell v Holland-Martin* [1926] Ch 596 at 605; and see SETTLEMENTS vol 91 (2012) PARAS 646, 650.

(2) THE OFFICERS OF ARMS AND THE HIGH COURT OF CHIVALRY

878. Officers of arms and their appointment. There are three ranks of officers of arms, namely: (1) Kings of Arms[1]; (2) Heralds[2]; and (3) Pursuivants[3]. The officers are often referred to indifferently as 'heralds'. There are three Kings of Arms, six Heralds and four Pursuivants. They are members of the royal household and are appointed by the Sovereign by letters patent under the Great Seal[4], and are under the jurisdiction of the Earl Marshal[5].

1   As to Kings of Arms see PARA 879.
2   As to Heralds see PARA 880.
3   As to Pursuivants see PARA 880.
4   As to the royal household see CONSTITUTIONAL AND ADMINISTRATIVE LAW vol 20 (2014) PARAS 283–284. As to the use of the Great Seal see CONSTITUTIONAL AND ADMINISTRATIVE LAW vol 20 (2014) PARA 583.
5   The office of Earl Marshal is hereditary in the family of the Duke of Norfolk. As to offices connected with the royal household that descend by inheritance see CONSTITUTIONAL AND ADMINISTRATIVE LAW vol 20 (2014) PARA 283. As to his duties at coronations see CROWN AND ROYAL FAMILY vol 12(1) (Reissue) PARA 20. See further PARAS 884–885.

879. Kings of Arms. The English Kings of Arms are: (1) Garter; (2) Clarenceux; and (3) Norroy and Ulster[1]. The senior of these is the Garter King of Arms, the office of which was constituted at a chapter of the Order of the Garter held in 1415, at which he was declared to be an officer of the Order and sovereign within the office of arms over all other officers of arms of the kingdom of England.

1   The provinces and jurisdictions of Clarenceux and of Norroy and Ulster in England are south and north of the river Trent respectively. The jurisdiction of Garter in England is not restricted, and he has also an imperial jurisdiction over persons not domiciled in the United Kingdom. Lyon King of Arms has jurisdiction in Scotland, and Norroy and Ulster King of Arms in Northern Ireland. There are also kings of arms of the Orders of the Bath, St Michael and St George, and the British Empire, but these are only titular kings of arms and have no armorial functions, and they are not members of the College of Arms. As to the College of Arms see PARA 881.

880. Heralds and Pursuivants. There are six Heralds, and they are known as Windsor, Chester, Lancaster, Somerset, York and Richmond[1]. There are four Pursuivants, known as Rouge Croix, Rouge Dragon, Bluemantle and Portcullis. It is not the function of Heralds or Pursuivants to grant arms, although they act as agents for applicants for grants of arms[2].

1   The number of Heralds has varied from time to time. Heralds were originally, as their name suggests, ambassadors or messengers, the bearers of compliment or defiance from one prince to another, habited for the purpose with the armorial insignia of their masters. The habit still survives in the Herald's tabard.
2   As to grants of arms see PARA 873.

881. The College of Arms. The College of Arms consists of the Kings of Arms[1], Heralds[2] and Pursuivants[3]. They were incorporated in 1556[4] by King Philip and Queen Mary, who gave them a mansion called Derby House, which stood (until it was destroyed by the Great Fire of London in 1666) on the site of the present building known as the College of Arms or Heralds' College[5].

1   As to Kings of Arms see PARA 879.
2   As to Heralds see PARA 880.
3   As to Pursuivants see PARA 880.

4   The officers of arms had earlier been incorporated as the College of Heralds by letters patent of
     Richard III in 1484, but on the King's death his acts were declared void.

5   Both this charter and the earlier one of 1484 (see note 4) are printed in *Noble's History of the
     College of Arms*. The College of Arms is situated at 130 Queen Victoria Street, London, EC4V
     4BT.

882.   Heralds and Pursuivants Extraordinary.   Heralds Extraordinary and
Pursuivants Extraordinary are occasionally appointed[1]. They are nominated by
the Earl Marshal and appointed by royal warrant addressed to the Earl
Marshal[2]. They are not members of the College of Arms and have only
ceremonial duties[3].

1   The present extraordinary officers of arms are the New Zealand Herald Extraordinary, the
     Maltravers Herald Extraordinary, the Wales Herald Extraordinary, the Norfolk Herald
     Extraordinary, the Arundel Herald Extraordinary, and the Fitzalan Pursuivant Extraordinary.
2   As to the Earl Marshal see PARA 878 note 5.
3   The uniform and insignia of an extraordinary officer of arms are identical with those of an
     officer in ordinary of the same rank, save for a slight difference in the design of the sceptre. As
     to the College of Arms and the officers of arms see PARA 878 et seq.

883.   Visitations.   It was the duty of the provincial Kings of Arms, as ministers
responsible for the true bearing of arms, to visit their provinces[1]. In the sixteenth
and seventeenth centuries special royal commissions were issued to the Kings of
Arms to visit the different counties in England and Wales and record the arms
and pedigrees of all who could establish a right to the title of esquire or
gentleman[2]. The visitations were carried out county by county. The gentry in the
respective counties were directed to attend the visiting King of Arms or his
deputy at such place as he should direct, and to make proof of their arms, or
disclaim a right to arms. The sheriffs were ordered to assist in securing
attendance and generally to aid the King of Arms in the effective performance of
his duty. Most of the counties were thus visited two or three times in the 150
years covered by the visitations, either by the Kings of Arms themselves or by
Heralds[3] appointed by them as their deputies, and the census of arms thus taken
may be considered to be practically exhaustive of those then capable of proof.

The official returns to these royal commissions, called visitations, are kept in
the College of Arms[4] and are evidence in the courts of law[5]. The proper witness
to produce them is an officer of arms[6].

1   As to Kings of Arms and their provinces see PARA 879.
2   The practice began in 1530: see Wagner *Heralds and Heraldry in the Middle Ages* 9 et seq. As to
     visitations before 1530 see Wagner 106 et seq. The last visitation was held in 1687. The royal
     commissions were addressed to the Kings of Arms in their respective provinces. The
     commissions also gave authority to destroy all representations of coat armour the right to which
     was not proved.
3   As to Heralds see PARA 880.
4   As to the College of Arms see PARA 881.
5   The visitations have often been received in evidence in peerage claims. For example, the
     deputation of visitation in 1681 was put in evidence in the *Shrewsbury Peerage Case* (1854)
     Minutes of Evidence 663, 664. On some occasions, however, the commission to hold a visitation
     has also been required: see *Palmer's Peerage Law in England* 236.
        The 'Visitations' in the Harleian collection and other manuscripts in the British Museum and
     other libraries, many of which have been printed, are at best only copies of the official
     visitations. Some are merely notes taken by the Heralds who acted as deputies to the Kings of
     Arms, from which, after examination and collation in London with other records in the College
     of Arms, the official visitations were compiled. These manuscripts cannot be relied on to
     correspond with the official visitations, and many of them bear very little relation to their
     alleged originals.

6   As to the officers of arms see PARA 878. As to the admissibility and production of public
    documents see CIVIL PROCEDURE vol 11 (2009) PARAS 821, 884, 902 et seq; and as to ancient
    documents generally see CIVIL PROCEDURE vol 11 (2009) PARAS 869–875.

884.   The High Court of Chivalry.   The Lord High Constable and the Earl
Marshal are two great officers of state whose duties in the Middle Ages were
largely connected with the army in the field[1]. From about 1348 onwards they
jointly held a court, known as the High Court of Chivalry or Curia Militaris, in
which offences committed out of the realm and matters relating to arms not
triable under the common law were tried[2]. Since the beginning of the sixteenth
century appointments to the office of Lord High Constable have been made only
on special occasions, mostly coronations[3], but the Court of Chivalry has
continued to be held before the Earl Marshal alone and in consequence it has
often been known as the Earl Marshal's Court[4]. Questions of right to arms,
precedence, descent and other kindred matters of honour which are not within
the jurisdiction of the ordinary courts of law are decided there[5]; a declaration by
Charles II in 1672 defined the Earl Marshal as next and immediate officer under
the Sovereign for determining and ordering all matters concerning arms, ensigns
of nobility, honour and chivalry. The court last sat in 1954[6], but until then had
not sat for over 200 years[7].

1   As to the Earl Marshal see PARA 878 note 5.
2   The powers and jurisdiction of the court were defined by 8 Ric 2 c 5 (Jurisdiction of Constable
    and Marshal) (1384), and 13 Ric 2 stat 1 c 2 (Jurisdiction of Constable and Marshal) (1389),
    both repealed by the Statute Law Revision and Civil Procedure Act 1881 s 3.
3   As to coronations see CROWN AND ROYAL FAMILY vol 12(1) (Reissue) PARAS 18–26.
4   In practice the Earl Marshal may delegate his role to a surrogate who is a professional lawyer:
    see note 6.
5   As to the High Court of Chivalry see also COURTS AND TRIBUNALS vol 24 (2010) PARA 822.
6   *Manchester Corpn v Manchester Palace of Varieties Ltd* [1955] P 133, [1955] 1 All ER 387,
    Court of Chivalry (this case was heard before the Duke of Norfolk (Earl Marshal) and
    Lord Goddard CJ (Surrogate)). For the practice and procedure of the court see Squibb's High
    Court of Chivalry 191 et seq.
7   Squibb's High Court of Chivalry 117.

885.   Powers of officers of arms.   The jurisdiction of the Earl Marshal[1],
coupled with the inherent right of the Kings of Arms[2] to regulate arms, and the
power expressly delegated to them by the Sovereign to grant arms, constitute the
authority of the officers of arms over all matters of arms and descent and
kindred subjects[3]. As officers of the Earl Marshal their acts in matters armorial
cannot be questioned in any court of law[4]. The records of their official acts are
preserved in the College of Arms[5].

1   As to the Earl Marshal and his jurisdiction see PARAS 878 note 5, 884.
2   As to Kings of Arms see PARA 879.
3   As to the officers of arms see PARA 878.
4   *Austen v Collins* (1886) 54 LT 903.
5   As to the College of Arms see PARA 881.

886.   Privileges of officers of arms.   The officers of arms[1], whether in ordinary
or extraordinary[2], are exempt from election or appointment as mayor, sheriff or
churchwarden or to any other public office in a city, town or village and from
tolls in markets and other places[3].

1   As to the officers of arms see PARA 878.
2   See PARA 878 et seq.

3   It is recited in a charter of confirmation dated 4 June 1549, printed in Anstis's Register of the
     Most Noble Order of the Garter (1724), Preface xxiv et seq, that these privileges have been
     enjoyed for 'time out of man's memory'. The charter also confirms an exemption from all taxes,
     but this has not been claimed for many years. Being a common law exemption, it appears,
     however, not to have been excluded by the Income Tax Act 1842 s 187 (repealed), which was in
     similar terms to the Income and Corporation Taxes Act 1988 s 829(4) (repealed). See now the
     Income Tax Act 2007, which provides that no provision in letters patent granted by the Crown
     is to be construed as conferring exemption from income tax (see s 844(1), (2)) and that any
     provision of the letters patent purporting to override the effect of this provision is void (see
     s 844(3)); and see INCOME TAXATION vol 58A (2014) PARA 1760.

INDEX

Partnership

References are to paragraph numbers; superior figures refer to notes

References are to paragraph numbers; superior figures refer to notes

References are to paragraph numbers; superior figures refer to notes

Patents and Registered Designs

References are to paragraph numbers; superior figures refer to notes

References are to paragraph numbers; superior figures refer to notes

References are to paragraph numbers; superior figures refer to notes

PATENT CO-OPERATION
   TREATY—*continued*
  international applications
    under—*continued*
    British patent system, incorporation
     into—
      effect of application, 640, 643
      filing date, 642
      generally, 640
      international and national phases,
       641
      publication, 642, 643
      refusal of filing date, 640
      translated application, filing,
       641n[10]
   content, 631
   designate: meaning, 640n[1]
   designated offices, communication
    to, 634
   effect, 640
   filing—
    generally, 630
    persons eligible to file, 629
    procedure, 630
   form and content of, 631
   international application: meaning,
    629
   international application for a patent:
    meaning, 630n[1], 640n[1]
   International Bureau—
    amendment of claims before, 633
    filing with, 630
    practice before, 639
    publication by, 635
   international preliminary
    examination—
    function of, 637
    report, 637
    request for, 636
    scope of, 637
   international search, 632
   patent agents, practice of, 639
   patent attorney, practice of, 639
   publication, 635
   single preliminary examination,
    subject to, 629
   single search, subject to, 629
   withdrawal, 640

PATENT LAW TREATY
  requirements and procedures under,
   656

PATENT LEGISLATION
  current, 304
  functions, 304
  territorial scope, 305

PATENT LICENCE
  agreement to grant, 378, 383
  assignment—
   distinguished, 380
   power to assign, 381
  binding nature of, 377
  chemical compound invented at date
   of, 383
  compulsory—
   abuse of monopoly, in case of—
    appeals, 399
    arbitration, 399
    Competition and Markets
     Authority report, powers
     following, 398
    exercise of power, 396
    grounds for, 394
    market investigation, powers
     following, 397
    merger, powers following, 397
    opposition, 399
    purposes to be secured, 396
    relevant considerations, 396
    relief for, 395
   enemy patents in time of war, 400
   EU licences, 401
   infringement of patent, proceedings
    for, 520
   pharmaceutical products, EU
    procedures for, 401
   provisions applying, 393
   types of, 393
  construction, 383
  covenants—
   generally, 386
   not to dispute validity of patent, 387
   quiet enjoyment, 386
  exclusive licence—
   meaning, 379
   infringement of patent proceedings,
    520n[3]
  extent of licence, between different
   countries, 384
  form, 378
  implied licence, 383, 384
  implied terms, 385
  improvement made by licensee—
   assignment of patent for, 376
   improvement: meaning, 376n[3]
  limited licence, 384
  limits, 379
  parol licence, enforceability, 378
  personal nature of, 379n[2], 383
  power to license, 377
  quiet enjoyment, 386
  registration, 377

References are to paragraph numbers; superior figures refer to notes

PATENT LICENCE—*continued*
restraint of trade, terms in, 402
restrictions on use—
    EU law, whether contravening, 384
    generally, 384
right, of—
    entry in register—
        application for, 391
        cancellation of, 392
        generally, 391
        proceedings to prevent infringement,
            licensee requiring, 391
royalties under—
    generally, 388
    interest on, 388
    payment of, 388
    recovery action, plea of invalidity no
        defence to, 387
    suing for, 388
sole licence: meaning, 379
sub-licence under—
    assignment or mortgage, 377
    grant, 377
termination, 389
use and exercise, licence to, 383
validity of patent, licensee challenging,
    387
war, effect of, 390

PATENT OFFICE. *See* intellectual
    property office

PATENT SPECIFICATION
admissions in, 417
amendment. *See* PATENT APPLICATION
    (amendment)
amino acid sequence, disclosing, 322
biological material, for, 321
body, 323
claims—
    advantage of invention, statement as
        to, 414
    arrangement of, 324
    careful preparation, need for, 323
    construction of—
        different language in, 420
        former decisions, effect of, 424
        generally, 414
        'or', interpretation of, 423
        particular use or purpose, effect of
            claims for, 419
        Protocol as guideline, 414
        single, 422
        'substantially as described', use of
            phrase, 421
    requirements, 318
    unworkable embodiments, 415
consistory clause in, 323

PATENT SPECIFICATION—*continued*
construction—
    admissions, effect of, 417
    advantage of invention, statement as
        to, 414
    approach to, 412
    claims. *See* claims *above*
    common general knowledge of art,
        414
    court's need for instruction, 411
    dictionary, specification supplying
        own, 416
    former decisions, effect of, 424
    general rule, 411
    'or', interpretation of, 423
    original specification, reference to,
        418
    Protocol as guideline, 414
    purposive, 414
    reading of specification as a whole,
        413, 414
contents, 318
dictionary, internal, 416
disclosure of matter in, 489n^2
drawings in, 318, 319
format, 323
insufficiency of, leading to invalidity.
    See INVALIDITY OF PATENT
    (insufficiency of specification)
nucleotide sequence, disclosing, 322
omission of matters from, on
    publication, 326
order of, 318n^3
original specification, reference to, 418
preamble, 323
publication by European Patent Office,
    649
selection patent in, 320
sequence listing in, 322
two or more inventions, 318n^9

PATENT SYSTEM
historical development, 302
purpose, 301
rationale, 301

PATENTABILITY
European Patent Convention, under,
    644, 648, 649
observations on, dealing with, 330

PATENTS COURT
appeals from—
    Court of Appeal, to, 570, 624
    fresh evidence on, 572
    generally, 570
    nature of, 572
    right of, 570
    Supreme Court, to, 570, 624

References are to paragraph numbers; superior figures refer to notes

VALIDITY OF PATENT—*continued*
  revocation, proceedings for. *See under*
    REVOCATION OF PATENT
  specification—
    amendments to. *See* amendments to
      specification *above*
    insufficiency of. *See* insufficiency of
      specification *above*

VEHICLE
  infringement of patent, exclusions, 515

WAR
  enemy patents in time of, compulsory
    licensing, 400
  patent licence, effect, 390
WORLD INTELLECTUAL PROPERTY
  ORGANISATION
  International Bureau—
    amendment of claims before, 633
    filing with, 630
    practice before, 639
    publication by, 635

Peerages and Dignities

ABEYANCE
  doctrine of, 832
  peerage in, claim to, 848

ADOPTION
  dignity or title of honour, effect on, 809
  peerage, dignity or title of honour, effect
    on, 809

ARMORIAL BEARINGS
  arms—
    exemplification and record of, 877
    grant of, 873, 875
    jurisdiction over, 874
    law of, 870
    right to bear, 872
  change of surname, royal licence for,
    875
  College of Arms, 881
  descent of, 871
  dignity, right to bear arms as, 801
  Earl Marshal, warrant of, 873
  Garter King of Arms, 879
  grant of, 873
  Heralds, 878, 880
  Heralds Extraordinary, 882
  High Court of Chivalry, 884
  Kings of Arms, 879
  officers of arms—
    Garter King of Arms, 879
    Heralds, 878, 880
    Heralds Extraordinary, 882
    Kings of Arms, 879
    powers of, 885
    power to grant, 801
    privileges, 886
    Pursuivants, 880
    Pursuivants Extraordinary, 882

ARMORIAL BEARINGS—*continued*
  officers of arms—*continued*
    ranks, 878
    visitations, 883
    Pursuivants, 880
    Pursuivants Extraordinary, 882
    regulation of, 873
    royal commissions, 883
    royal warrant, issue of, 876

ARREST
  civil cases, in, privileges of peers, 828

ARTIFICIAL INSEMINATION
  dignity or title of honour, effect on, 810

ATTAINDER
  meaning, 838n[1]
  co-heir, of, 838
  effects, removal by statute, 839
  forfeiture of rights on, 838
  petition to remove, 849

BARONET
  classes of, 861
  oath of allegiance, 861
  official roll, 864
  privileges, 862

BARONETAGE
  institution of, 861

BARONETCY
  claims to, 863
  creation of, 861
  descent of, 808
  incorporeal hereditament, as, 808

BARONY BY WRIT
  creation, 822

BARONY IN FEE
  Irish barony in fee, 822

References are to paragraph numbers; superior figures refer to notes

References are to paragraph numbers; superior figures refer to notes

PEERAGE—*continued*
  hereditary—*continued*
    creation, 807
    descent of, 808
    extinction of peerage, 831
    failure of issue, 831
    generally, 806
    House of Lords, sitting and voting
      in, 824
  legitimation, effect, 808
  life. *See under* PEER
  merger of, 834
  potentially polygamous marriage,
    effect, 811
  precedence, warrant of, 801n[5]
  preliminary inquiry prior to grant, 820
  refusal, impossibility of, 820
  resignation, 835
  Roll of—
    application to be entered on, 846
    maintenance of, 841
  source of, 801

PEERAGE—*continued*
  surrender, 835
  surrogacy, effect, 810
  tenure, by, 821
  territorial designation, 818
  uses of term, 803n[1]
PEERESS
  generally, 806
  life peerage, 806
  privileges attaching to, 806
SURROGACY
  dignity or title of honour, effect on, 810
TITLE
  contract for purchase of, void nature
    of, 802
WARRANT OF PRECEDENCE
  grant of, 801
WRIT OF ACCELERATION
  purpose, 822
WRIT OF SUMMONS
  abeyance, termination of, 833
  Parliament, to, 822

Words and Phrases

Words in parentheses indicate the context in which the word or phrase is used

---

References are to paragraph numbers; superior figures refer to notes